The Wordsworth
*Dictionary of English
Usage*

Wordsworth Reference

Previously published as *The Wordsworth Concise English Dictionary* by Wordsworth Editions Ltd, Cumberland House, Crib Street, Ware, Hertfordshire SG12 9ET.

Reissued 1995 as *The Wordsworth Dictionary of English Usage.*

ISBN 1-85326-335-4

Printed and bound in Denmark by Nørhaven.

The paper in this book is produced from pure wood
pulp, without the use of chlorine or any other substance
harmful to the environment. The energy used in its
production consists almost entirely of hydroelectricity
and heat generated from waste materials, thereby
conserving fossil fuels and contributing little to the
greenhouse effect.

Preface

This dictionary has been designed to meet the basic needs of English learners the world over. It is easy to use. The vocabulary has been deliberately restricted to a fairly simple level and the grammatical information is uncomplicated. Clear and abundant guidance is given towards the achieving of lively, effective and idiomatic English speech.

This help is provided in various ways: some notorious and commonly-encountered difficulties of English grammar, spelling and usage are dealt with by means of 'reminders' printed in grey-tinted boxes at the appropriate word; there is generous coverage of phrases and idioms; plentiful examples are given of words as they are typically used in everyday speech; finally, a number of full-page illustrations are supplied showing 'families' of things — tools, vegetables, vehicles, for instance — which help the user to identify some of the objects defined in the dictionary. The following guide shows how an entry in the dictionary is arranged:

Different spellings	**jail, gaol** [dʒeil] *n* (a) prison: *You ought to be sent to jail for doing that.*	*If a word can be spelt in a different way, this other spelling is given.*
	'emphasize, -ise *v* to lay or put emphasis on	
Sound and stress	**adept** [ə'dept] *adj* highly skilled: *He's very adept at keeping his balance.*– ['adept] *n* an expert.	*Next comes the pronunciation (see the Pronunciation Guide). The mark is placed before the syllable that is stressed.*
	ˌacro'batics *n pl* acrobatic performances	*Sometimes another syllable is also stressed, but not so strongly. The mark ˌ is placed before it.*
Differences between American and British English	**defence**, (*Amer*) **defense** [di'fens] *n* 1 the act or action of defending against attack: *the defence of Rome; He spoke in defence of the plans.*	*You will often find American variations given, in spelling,*
	debris ['deibri:, (*Amer*) də'bri:] *n* 1 the remains of something broken, destroyed *etc*:	*in pronunciation*
	bonnet ['bonit] *n* 1 (*usu* baby's or (old) woman's) head-dress fastened under the chin *eg* by strings. 2 (*Amer* **hood**) the cover of a motor-car engine.	*and in vocabulary.*

Plurals	**jetty** [ˈdʒeti] – *pl* **jetties** – *n* a small pier for use as a landing-place.	*Plurals are given where there may be difficulty— for instance with words ending in -y,*
	potato [pəˈteitou] – *pl* **po'tatoes** – *n* **1** a type of plant with round underground stems (called **tubers**) which are used as a vegetable.	*and words ending in -o.*
Difficult or irregular verbs	**stink** [stiŋk] – *pt* **stank** [staŋk] : *ptp* **stunk** [stʌŋk] – *v* to have a very bad smell: *That fish stinks; The house stinks of cats.*	*The past tense and past participle are given for irregular verbs*
	sip [sip] – *pt, ptp* **sipped** – *v* to drink in very small mouthfuls.— *n* a very small mouthful: *She took a sip of the medicine.*	*and for verbs that double their last letter in the past tense and past participle (it is also doubled in the present participle).*
Feminine forms	**heir** [eə] – *fem* **heiress** – *n* a person who by law receives wealth, property *etc* when the owner dies.	*The feminine form is given if there is one.*
Parts of speech	**name** [neim] *n* **1** a word by which a person, place or thing is called: *My name is Rachel; She knows all the flowers by name.* **2** reputation; fame: *He has a name for honesty.* – *v* **1** to give a name to: *They named the child Thomas.*	*Next comes an abbreviation showing the part of speech (see the List of Abbreviations). Here, **name** is shown as a noun, and as a verb,*
	liquid [ˈlikwid] *adj* able to flow; not solid, but not a gas: *liquid nitrogen; The ice-cream has become liquid.*—*n* a substance which flows, like water: *a clear liquid.*	¹ *liquid is shown as an adjective and noun,*
	lemon [ˈlemən] *n, adj* **1** (of) a type of oval, juicy, citrus fruit with pale yellow skin and very sour juice: *She added the juice of a lemon to the pudding; a lemon drink.*	*and **lemon** is shown as both noun and adjective.*

Negative forms	**intelligible** [in'telidʒəbl] *adj* (*neg* **un-**) able to be understood.	(*neg* **un-** means that you can just add **un-** to form the negative. So the negative of **intelligible** *is* **unintelligible**.
Definition (meaning)	**coma** ['koumə] *n* a long-continuing unconscious state: *He was in a coma for several days after the accident.*	Next, the meaning of the word is explained.
Different meanings	**hostile** ['hostail] *adj* **1** unfriendly; warlike: *hostile tribesmen.* **2** belonging to an enemy: *a hostile army.* **3** showing dislike or opposition to something: *a hostile attitude.*	If the word has several meanings, they are separately numbered.
Examples	**complain** [kəm'plein] *v* **1** to state one's displeasure, dissatisfaction *etc*: *I'm going to complain to the police about the noise.* **2** (with **of**) to state that one has (pain, discomfort *etc*): *He's complaining of difficulty in breathing.*	To make the meaning clearer, there is often an example showing the word being used.
Words used in grammar	**conjunction** [kən'dʒʌŋkʃən] *n* a word that connects sentences, clauses or words: *John sang <u>and</u> Mary danced*; *I'll do it <u>if</u> you want.*	A word used in grammar is often explained by an underlined example of it. Here 'and' and 'if' are underlined to show that they are conjunctions.

This example shows the arrangement of a whole entry:

main word	**creep** [kri:p] — *pt*, *ptp* **crept** [krept] — *v* **1** to move slowly, quietly or secretly: *He crept into the bedroom.* **2** to move on hands or knees or with the body close to the ground: *The cat crept towards the bird.* **3** (of plants) to grow along the ground, up a wall *etc*.
derivatives (words formed from the main word)	'**creeper** *n* a creeping plant. '**creepy** *adj* causing feelings of fear *etc*: *The house is rather creepy at night.* '**creepily** *adv*. '**creepiness** *n*.
compounds (two-word expressions)	,**creepy-'crawly** — *pl* ,**creepy-'crawlies** — *n* a small creeping insect.
phrases and idioms	**creep up on** to approach slowly and stealthily: *Old age creeps up on us all.* **make someone's flesh creep** to scare or horrify someone.

Help with certain difficulties in English is given in grey 'boxes' placed at the end of some entries—for instance:

at **comprise**	The team **comprises** (not **comprises of**) five members	*a reminder that 'comprise' does not need the preposition 'of'*
at **fulfil**	**fulfil** begins with **ful-** (not **full-**) and ends with **-fil** (not **-fill**); the past tense is **fulfilled** and present participle **fulfilling**.	*help with spelling the parts of this verb*
at **it**	**its** is an adjective or pronoun expressing possession: *a cat and its kittens.* **it's** is short for **it is** or **it has**: *It's raining heavily.*	*a guide to show the difference between 'its' and 'it's'*

Illustrations: the sign * (placed next to a word) means that there is an illustration for this word on one of the pages of illustrations. You will find a note at the bottom of the page telling you where to find the illustration.

Grammar: the sign † directs you to the Grammatical Notes at the end of the book.

When a double hyphen (=) is used to divide a word at the end of a line (see **razor= blade**), this means that the word is always spelt with a hyphen.

List of Illustrations

Pronunciation Guide

symbol	example	
a	[bag]	bag
a:	[ba:θ]	bath
e	[hed]	head
i	[milk]	milk
i:	[fi:l]	feel
o	[boks]	box
o:	[ho:l]	hall
u	[fut]	foot
u:	[blu:]	blue
ʌ	[lʌv]	love
ə	['ribən]	ribbon
ə:	[fə:st]	first
ai	[fain]	fine
au	[laud]	loud
ei	[pein]	pain
eə	[heə]	hair
iə	[hiə]	here
oi	[dʒoin]	join
ou	[gou]	go
uə	[puə]	poor
p	[peidʒ]	page
b	[bo:l]	ball
t	['teibl]	table
d	[dog]	dog
k	[kik]	kick
g	[get]	get
m	[mad]	mad
n	[neim]	name
ŋ	[baŋ]	bang

Pronunciation Guide

symbol	example	
l	[leik]	lake
r	[reis]	race
f	[fi:t]	feet
v	[vois]	voice
θ	[θiŋ]	thing
ð	[ðou]	though
s	[seif]	safe
z	[zu:]	zoo
ʃ	[ʃip]	ship
ʒ	['meʒə]	measure
h	[ha:f]	half
w	[weit]	wait
j	[jʌŋ]	young
tʃ	[tʃi:z]	cheese
dʒ	['dʒakit]	jacket

List of Abbreviations

abbrev	abbreviation, abbreviated;	*pers*	person;
adj	adjective;	*pfx*	prefix;
adv	adverb;	*pl*	plural;
Amer	American;	*pls*	plurals;
cap	capital;	*pp.*	pages;
compar	comparative;	*prep*	preposition;
conj	conjunction;	*pron*	pronoun;
E	East;	*prp*	present participle;
eg	for example;	*prt*	present tense;
esp	especially;	*pt*	past tense;
etc	et cetera, and so on;	*ptp*	past participle;
fem	feminine;	*ptps*	past participles;
ie	that is;	*pts*	past tense;
interj	interjection;	®	registered trademark;
masc	masculine;	*S*	South;
n	noun;	*sing*	singular;
N	North;	*TV*	television;
neg	negative;	*UK*	United Kingdom;
n pl	noun plural;	*US*	United States
ns	nouns;		(of America);
n sing	noun singular;	*usu*	usually;
orig	originally;	*v*	verb;
p.	page;	*W*	West.

a, an [ə(n)] *adj* (**a** is used before words beginning with a consonant *eg a boy*, or consonant sound *eg a union*; **an** is used before words beginning with a vowel *eg an owl*, or vowel sound *eg an honour*.) **1** one: *There is a boy in the garden.* **2** any; every: *An owl can see in the dark.* **3** for each; per: *We earn $6 an hour.*

> a before hotel, historian.
> an before heir, honest, honour, hour.

A–Z/A to Z [eitə'zed] *n* a small book of information in alphabetical order, *esp* a guide to the streets of a town or city.

aback [ə'bak]: **taken aback** surprised and *usu* rather upset: *She was taken aback by his rudeness.*

abandon [ə'bandən] *v* **1** to leave, not intending to return to: *They abandoned the stolen car.* **2** to give (oneself) completely to: *He abandoned himself to despair.*
a'bandoned *adj* **1** shameless: *an abandoned young woman.* **2** having been left without any intention of returning to or reclaiming: *The police found the abandoned car.*
a'bandonment *n*: *Lack of money led to the abandonment of this plan.*

abashed [ə'baʃt] *adj* (*neg* **un-**) embarrassed: *He was abashed at the compliments he received.*

abate [ə'beit] *v* to become less: *The storm abated.*
a'batement *n*.

abattoir ['abətwa:, (*Amer*) abə'twa:r] *n* a place where animals are killed for food; a slaughterhouse.

abbess *see* **abbot**.

abbey ['abi] *n* **1** the building(s) in which a Christian (*usu* Roman Catholic) group of monks or nuns lives. **2** the church now or formerly belonging to it: *Westminster Abbey.*

abbot ['abət] – *fem* **abbess** ['abes] – *n* the male head of an abbey.

abbreviate [ə'bri:vieit] *v* to shorten (a word, phrase *etc*): *Frederick is often abbreviated to Fred.*
ab,brevi'ation *n* a shortened form of a word *etc*: *Maths is an abbreviation of mathematics.*

ABC [eibi:'si:] *n* **1** the alphabet: *The child has not learnt his ABC.* **2** the simplest and most basic knowledge: *the ABC of engineering.*

abdicate ['abdikeit] *v* **1** to leave or give up the position and authority of a king or queen: *The king abdicated (the throne) in favour of his son.* **2** to leave or give up (responsibility, power *etc*): *He abdicated all responsibility for the work to his elder son.* ,**abdi'cation** *n*.

abdomen ['abdəmən] *n* the part of the body between the hips and the lower ribs.
ab'dominal [-'do-] *adj*.

abduct [əb'dʌkt] *v* to take (someone) away against his will *usu* by trickery or violence; to kidnap: *The president has been abducted.*
ab'duction [-ʃən] *n*.

abet [ə'bet] – *pt, ptp* **a'betted** – *v* to help or encourage to do something wrong: *He abetted his cousin in robbing the bank.*

abeyance [ə'beiəns]: **in abeyance** left undecided *usu* for a short time: *The matter was left in abeyance.*

abhor [əb'ho:] – *pt, ptp* **ab'horred** – *v* to hate very much: *The headmaster abhors violence.*
ab'horrence [-'ho-] *n*.
ab'horrent [-'ho-] *adj* (*with* **to**) hateful: *Fighting was abhorrent to him.*

abide [ə'baid] *v* to put up with; to tolerate: *I can't abide noisy people.*
a'bide by – *pt, ptp* **a'bided** – to act according to; to be faithful to: *They must abide by the rules of the game.*

ability [ə'biləti] – *pl* **a'bilities** – *n* **1** the power, knowledge *etc* to do something: *I shall do the job to the best of my ability.* **2** a skill: *a man of many abilities.*

abject ['abdʒekt] *adj* miserable; wretched: *abject poverty.* '**abjectly** *adv*.

ablaze [ə'bleiz] *adj* **1** burning strongly: *The building was ablaze when the fire brigade arrived.* **2** very bright: *The street was ablaze with lights.*

able ['eibl] *adj* **1** having enough strength, knowledge *etc* to do something: *He was able to open the door; He will come if he is able.* **2** clever and skilful; capable: *a very able nurse.* '**ably** *adv*.

abnormal [ab'no:məl] *adj* not normal: *His behaviour is abnormal for a child of his age.*
abnor'mality [-'ma-] *n*. **ab'normally** *adv*.

aboard [ə'bo:d] *adv, prep* on (to) or in(to) (a means of transport): *We were aboard for several hours; He went aboard the ship/train/aircraft.*

abolish [ə'boliʃ] *v* to put an end to (a custom, law *etc*): *We must abolish the death penalty.* ,**abo'lition** [-] *n*.

A-bomb ['eibom] *n* an atomic bomb.

abominable [ə'bominəbl] *adj* very bad; terrible: *What abominable weather!* **a'bominably** *adv*.

abominate [ə'bomineit] *v* to detest: *He abominates cruelty.* **a,bomi'nation** *n*.

aborigine [abə'ridʒini] *n* an original inhabitant of a country, *esp* Australia. ,**abo'riginal** *adj*.

abort [ə'bo:t] *v* **1** to lose or bring about the loss of (an unborn child) from the womb. **2** (of a plan *etc*) to (cause to) come to nothing. **3** to stop or abandon (a space mission, *eg* the firing of a rocket) before it is completed. **a'bortion** [-ʃən] *n*.

a'bortive [-tiv] *adj* unsuccessful: *an abortive attempt to climb the mountain.*

abound [ə'baund] *v* **1** (*with* **in** or **with**) to have plenty of: *The east coast abounds in good farming land.* **2** to be very plentiful: *Fish abound in these waters.*

about [ə'baut] *prep* on the subject of: *We talked about our plans; What's the book about? – prep, adv* **1** (*sometimes* **round about**) near (in place, time, size *etc*): *about five miles away;* (*round*) *about six o'clock; just about big enough.* **2** in different directions; here and there: *The children ran about (the garden).* **3** in or on some part (of a place *etc*): *You'll find him somewhere about (the office).* **4** around or surrounding: *She wore a coat about her shoulders; He lay with his clothes scattered about. – adv* (in military commands *etc*) in the opposite direction: *About turn!*

be about to to be going to (perform an action): *I am about to leave the office.*

above [ə'bʌv] *prep* **1** in a higher position than: *a picture above the fireplace.* **2** greater than: *The child's intelligence is above average.* **3** too good for: *The police must be above suspicion. – adv* **1** higher up: *seen from above.* **2** (in a book *etc*) earlier or higher up on the page: *See above.*

a,bove-'board *adj* open and honourable; not secret: *His dealings are all above-board.*

above all most importantly: *He is strong, brave and, above all, honest.*

abrasion [ə'breiʒən] *n* an injury caused by scraping or grazing the skin: *minor abrasions.*

a'brasive [-siv] *adj* tending to make surfaces rough when rubbed on to them: *An abrasive material is unsuitable for cleaning baths. – n* something used for scraping or rubbing a surface: *Sandpaper is an abrasive.*

abreast [ə'brest] *adv* side by side: *They walked along the road three abreast.*

keep abreast of to remain up to date with: *keeping abreast of recent scientific developments.*

abridge [ə'bridʒ] *v* to make (*esp* a book) shorter. **a'bridged** *adj*. **a'bridg(e)ment** *n*.

abroad [ə'brɔːd] *adv* **1** in or to another country: *He lived abroad for many years.* **2** current; going around: *There's a rumour abroad that she is leaving.*

abrupt [ə'brʌpt] *adj* **1** sudden; unexpected: *The car came to an abrupt halt.* **2** (of a person's manner of speaking *etc*) rude or sharp. **a'bruptly** *adv*. **a'bruptness** *n*.

abscess ['abses] *n* a painful swelling, containing pus: *He has a bad abscess under that tooth.*

absent ['absənt] *adj* not present: *Johnny was absent from school with a cold. –* [əb'sent] *v* to keep (oneself) away: *He absented himself from the meeting.*

'absence *n* **1** the condition of not being present: *His absence was noticed.* **2** a time during which a person *etc* is not present: *After an absence of five years he returned home.*

,absen'tee *n* a person who is not present, *esp* frequently (*eg* at work, school *etc*).

,absen'teeism *n* being often absent from work *etc* without good reason: *Absenteeism is a problem in some industries.*

,absent-'minded *adj* not noticing what is going on around one because one is thinking deeply: *an absent-minded professor.* **,absent='mindedly** *adv*. **,absent-'mindedness** *n*.

absolute ['absəluːt] *adj* complete: *absolute honesty.*

,abso'lutely *adv* completely: *It is absolutely impossible for me to go.*

absolution *see* **absolve.**

absolve [əb'zolv] *v* to make free or release (from a promise, duty or blame): *He was absolved of all blame.*

absolution [absə'luːʃən] *n* forgiveness, *esp* of sins: *The priest granted the man absolution.*

absorb [əb'zoːb] *v* **1** to soak up: *The cloth absorbed the ink I had spilled.* **2** to take up the whole attention of (a person): *He was completely absorbed in his book.*

ab'sorbent *adj* able to soak up: *absorbent paper.*

ab'sorption [-'zoːp-] *n*.

abstain [əb'stein] *v* (*often with* **from**) not to do, take *etc*: *He abstained (from voting in the election); He abstained from alcohol.*

ab'stention [-'sten-] *n* the act of abstaining: *At the election of the new chairman the voting was six for, three against, and two abstentions.*

abstemious [əb'stiːmiəs] *adj* taking little food, drink *etc*: *She was being very abstemious as she was trying to lose weight; an abstemious young man.* **ab'stemiously** *adv*. **ab'stemiousness** *n*.

abstention *see* **abstain.**

abstinence ['abstinəns] *n* the act or habit of abstaining, *esp* from alcohol.

abstract ['abstrakt] *adj* **1** (of a noun) referring to something which exists as an idea and which is not physically real: *Truth, poverty and bravery are abstract nouns.* **2** (of painting, sculpture *etc*) concerned with colour, shape, texture *etc* rather than showing things as they really appear: *an abstract sketch of a vase of flowers. – n* a summary (of a book, article *etc*).

abstruse [əb'struːs] *adj* difficult to understand: *abstruse reasoning.* **ab'struseness** *n*.

absurd [əb'səːd] *adj* unreasonable or ridicu-

lous: *These demands are absolutely absurd.*
ab'surdly *adv.* **ab'surdity** (*pl* **ab'surdities**),
ab'surdness *ns.*
abundance [ə'bʌndəns] *n* a large amount: *an
abundance of food*; *There was food in abundance.*
a'bundant *adj* plentiful: *abundant proof.*
a'bundantly *adv.*
abuse [ə'bju:z] *v* **1** to use wrongly, *usu* with
harmful results: *She abused her privileges by
taking too long a holiday.* **2** to insult or
speak roughly to: *She abused the servants.* –
[ə'bju:s] *n* **1** insulting language: *He shouted
abuse at her.* **2** the wrong use of something:
This toy has been subjected to a lot of abuse.
a'busive [-siv] *adj* using insulting language:
He wrote an abusive letter to the manager.
a'busively *adv.* **a'busiveness** *n.*
abysmal [ə'bizməl] *adj* very great (in a bad
sense); very bad: *abysmal ignorance*; *The
weather is abysmal.* **a'bysmally** *adv.*
abyss [ə'bis] *n* a very deep or bottomless hole
or chasm.
academy [ə'kadəmi] – *pl* **a'cademies** – *n* **1** a
higher school for special study: *Academy of
Music.* **2** a society to encourage science, art
etc: *The Royal Academy.* **3** a type of senior
school.
academic [akə'demik] *adj* of or concerning
study *esp* in schools, colleges *etc*: *an academic career.* – *n* a university or college
teacher. **aca'demically** [akə'de-] *adv.*
accede [ək'si:d] : **accede to** to agree to : *He
acceded to my request.*
accelerate [ək'seləreit] *v* **1** to increase speed:
The driver accelerated to pass the other car.
2 to make (something) happen sooner:
Worry accelerated his death. **ac,cele'ration** *n.*
ac'celerator *n* a pedal, lever *etc* that controls
the speed or acceleration of a machine.
accent ['aksənt] *n* **1** (a mark used to show)
the stress on a syllable: *The accent is on the
second syllable.* **2** a mark used to show the
pronunciation of a letter in certain languages: *Put an accent on the e in début.*
3 emphasis: *The accent must be on hard
work.* **4** a special way of pronouncing
words in a particular area *etc*: *an American
accent.* – [ək'sent] *v* to pronounce with
stress or emphasis: *The second syllable is
accented.*
accept [ək'sept] *v* **1** to take (something offered): *He accepted the gift.* **2** to believe in,
agree to or acknowledge: *We accept your
account of what happened*; *Their proposal
was accepted*; *He accepted responsibility for
the accident.*
ac'ceptable *adj* **1** satisfactory: *The decision
should be acceptable to most people.* **2** pleasing: *a very acceptable gift.* **ac'ceptably** *adv.*
ac'ceptance *n* *We have had few acceptances
to our invitation.*

ac'cepted *adj* generally recognized: *It is an
accepted fact that the world is round.*
access ['akses] *n* **1** way or right of approach
or entry: *We gained access to the house
through a window.* **2** way or right to meet
(someone) or use (something): *Senior students have access to the library at weekends.*
ac'cessible *adj* (of a person or place) able to
be reached or approached easily: *His house
is not accessible by car.* **ac,cessi'bility** *n.*
accession [ək'seʃən] *n* **1** a coming to the position of king or queen: *in the year of the
Queen's accession (to the throne).* **2** an addition: *There are several new accessions to
the library.*
accessory [ək'sesəri] – *pl* **ac'cessories** – *n*
1 something additional (*eg* a handbag,
scarf, shoes *etc*) to the main part of a
woman's clothing, or a radio, seat-covers
etc to a car): *She wore matching accessories.*
2 (*legal*) a person who helps somebody, *esp*
a criminal.
accident ['aksidənt] *n* **1** an unexpected happening, often harmful, causing injury *etc*:
There has been a road accident. **2** chance: *I
met her by accident.*
,acci'dental [-'den-] *adj* happening by
chance or accident: *an accidental discovery.*
,acci'dentally [-'den-] *adv.*
acclaim [ə'kleim] *v* **1** to applaud or welcome
enthusiastically: *The footballer was acclaimed by the fans.* **2** to declare (someone)
ruler, winner *etc* by enthusiastic approval:
They acclaimed him king. – *n* enthusiastic
approval.
acclamation [aklə'meiʃən] *n* a noisy
demonstration of applause, agreement, approval *etc.*
acclimatize, -ise [ə'klaimətaiz] *v* to make or
become accustomed to a new climate, new
surroundings *etc*: *It took them several
months to become acclimatized to the heat.*
ac,climati'zation, -s- *n.*
accommodate [ə'komədeit] *v* **1** to find or be a
place for: *The house could accommodate two
families.* **2** to oblige: *They did their best to
accommodate him by carrying out his wishes.*
ac'commodating *adj* obliging; helpful.
ac,commo'dation *n* **1** room(s) in a house or
hotel in which to live, *esp* for a short time:
*It is difficult to find accommodation in
London in August.* **2** space for something:
*There is accommodation for your car behind
the hotel.*

accommodate has two **c**s and two **m**s.

accompany [ə'kʌmpəni] *v* **1** to go with (someone or something): *He accompanied her to
the door.* **2** to play a musical instrument to
go along with (a singer *etc*): *He accompanied her on the piano.*
ac'companiment *n* something that accom-

panies: *I'll play the piano accompaniment while you sing.*

ac'companist *n* a person who plays a musical accompaniment.

accomplice [əˈkʌmplis, (*Amer*) -ˈkom-] *n* a person who helps another, *esp* in crime: *The thief's accomplice warned him that the police were coming.*

accomplish [əˈkʌmpliʃ, (*Amer*) -ˈkom-] *v* to complete (something) successfully: *Have you accomplished your task?*

ac'complished *adj* skilled: *an accomplished singer.*

ac'complishment *n* **1** completion. **2** a special skill: *She has many different accomplishments.*

accord [əˈkoːd] *v* **1** (*with* with) to agree with: *His story accords with what I saw happen.* **2** to grant or give to (a person): *They accorded the president great respect.* – *n* agreement: *That is not in accord with your original statement.*

ac'cordance: in accordance with in agreement with: *The money will be given out in accordance with his instructions.*

ac'cordingly *adv* **1** in agreement (with the circumstances *etc*): *Find out what has happened and act accordingly.* **2** therefore: *He was very worried about the future of the firm and accordingly he did what he could to help.*

according to **1** as said or told by: *According to John, the bank closes at 3 p.m.* **2** in agreement with: *He acted according to his promise.* **3** in the order of: *books arranged according to their subjects.* **4** in proportion to: *You will be paid according to the amount of work you have done.*

of one's own accord of one's own free will: *He did it of his own accord, without being forced to.*

with one accord (everybody) in agreement: *With one accord they stood up to cheer him.*

accordion [əˈkoːdiən] *n* a musical instrument with bellows and a keyboard.

accost [əˈkost] *v* to approach and speak to, *esp* in an unfriendly way: *I was accosted in the street by four men with guns.*

account [əˈkaunt] *n* **1** a statement of money owing: *Send me an account.* **2** (*usu in pl*) a record of money received and spent: *You must keep your accounts in order;* (*also adj*) *an account book.* **3** an arrangement by which a person keeps his money in a bank: *I have (opened) an account with the local bank.* **4** an arrangement by which a person makes a regular (*eg* monthly) payment instead of paying at the time of buying: *I have an account at Smiths.* **5** a description or explanation (of something that has happened): *a full account of his holiday.*

ac'countancy *n* the work of an accountant: *He is studying accountancy.*

ac'countant *n* a keeper or inspector of (money) accounts: *He employs an accountant to deal with his income tax.*

account for to give a reason for; to explain: *I can account for the mistake.*

on account of because of: *She stayed indoors on account of the bad weather.*

on my, his *etc* **account** because of me, him *etc* or for my, his *etc* sake: *You don't have to leave early on my account.*

on no account not for any reason: *On no account must you open that door.*

take (something) into account, take account of (something) to consider (something which is part of the problem *etc*): *We must take his illness into account when assessing his work.*

accredited [əˈkreditid] *adj* officially recognized: *the Queen's accredited representative.*

accumulate [əˈkjuːmjuleit] *v* (*usu* of things) to gather or be gathered together in a large quantity: *Rubbish accumulates very quickly in our house.*

ac'cumulation *n.*

ac'cumulator *n* a type of electric battery.

accurate [ˈakjurət] *adj* **1** exactly right: *an accurate drawing.* **2** making no mistakes: *an accurate memory.* **'accurately** *adv.* **accuracy** *n.*

accursed [əˈkəːsid] *adj* **1** under a curse. **2** hateful.

accuse [əˈkjuːz] *v* (*with* of) to charge (someone) with having done something wrong: *They accused him of stealing the car.* **,accu'sation** [a-] *n.*

the accused the person(s) accused in a court of law: *The accused was found not guilty.*

accustom [əˈkʌstəm] *v* to make (*esp* oneself) familiar with or used to: *He soon accustomed himself to the idea.*

ac'customed *adj* usual: *his accustomed seat.*

accustomed to familiar with or used to: *I am not accustomed to being treated like this.*

ace [eis] *n* **1** the one in playing-cards: *the ace of spades.* **2** a person who is expert at anything: *He's an ace with a rifle.* **3** a serve in tennis in which the ball is not touched by the opposing player.

ache [eik] *n* a continuous pain: *I have an ache in my stomach.* – *v* **1** to be in continuous pain: *My tooth aches.* **2** to have a great desire: *I was aching to tell him the news.*

achieve [əˈtʃiːv] *v* to gain or reach successfully: *He has achieved his ambition,* **a'chievement** *n*: *his academic achievements; the achievement of his ambition.*

acid [ˈasid] *adj* **1** (of taste) sharp or sour: *Lemons and limes are acid fruits.* **2** sarcastic: *acid humour.* – *n* a substance, containing hydrogen, which will dissolve metals *etc*: *She spilled some acid which burned a hole in her dress.*

a'cidity *n* the quality of containing acid or too much acid.

acknowledge [ək'nolidʒ] *v* **1** to admit as being fact: *He acknowledged defeat*; *He acknowledged that I was right.* **2** to say (*usu* in writing) that one has received (something): *He acknowledged the letter.* **3** to give thanks for: *He acknowledged their help.* **4** to greet someone: *He acknowledged her by waving.* **acknowledg(e)ment** *n*.

acme ['akmi] *n* the highest point: *the acme of perfection.*

acne ['akni] *n* a common skin disease with pimples: *Acne is common among young people.*

acoustic [ə'ku:stik] *adj* having to do with hearing or with sound: *This hall has acoustic problems.*

a'coustics 1 *n pl* the characteristics (*eg* of a room or hall) which make hearing in it good or bad. **2** *n sing* the science of sound.

acquaint [ə'kweint] *v* **1** to make (*usu* oneself) familiar (with): *You must acquaint yourself with the routine of the office.* **2** to inform (a person) of: *Have you acquainted her with your plans?*

acquaintance *n* **1** a person whom one knows slightly. **2** (with **with**) knowledge: *My acquaintance with the works of Shakespeare is slight.*

be acquainted with to know or be familiar with: *I'm not acquainted with her father.*

make someone's acquaintance to get to know someone: *I made her acquaintance when on holiday in France.*

acquiesce [akwi'es] *v* to agree: *After a lot of persuasion, he finally acquiesced.* **acqui'escence** *n*. **acqui'escent** *adj*.

acquire [ə'kwaiə] *v* to get: *He acquired a knowledge of English.*

acquisition [akwi'ziʃən] *n* **1** the act of acquiring: *the acquisition of more land.* **2** something acquired: *Her recent acquisitions included a piano.*

acquisitive [ə'kwizətiv] *adj* eager to get possessions: *an acquisitive child.* **ac'quisitiveness** *n*.

acquit [ə'kwit] – *pt, ptp* **ac'quitted** – *v* to declare (an accused person) to be innocent: *The judge acquitted her of murder.* **ac'quittal** *n*: *He was released from prison following his acquittal.*

acrid ['akrid] *adj* harsh in smell or taste: *The acrid smell of smoke filled the room.*

acrobat ['akrəbat] *n* a person in a circus *etc* who performs gymnastics. **,acro'batic** *adj*. **,acro'batics** *n pl* acrobatic performances.

across [ə'kros] *prep* **1** to the other side (of); from one side to the other side of: *He took her across the road.* **2** at the other side (of):

The butcher's shop is across the street. – *adv* to the other side or to the speaker's side: *He dived in off the river-bank and swam across.*

act [akt] *v* **1** to do something: *It's time the government acted to lower taxes.* **2** to behave: *He acted foolishly at the meeting.* **3** to perform (a part) in a play: *He has acted (the part of Romeo) in many theatres*; *I thought he was dying, but he was only acting* (=pretending). – *n* **1** something done: *Running away is an act of cowardice*; *He committed many cruel acts.* **2** (*often* with *cap*) a law: *Acts of Parliament.* **3** a section of a play: *'Hamlet' has five acts.* **4** an entertainment: *an act called 'The Smith Family'.*

acting *adj* temporarily carrying out the duties of: *He is acting president of the society.*

'actor – *fem also* **'actress** – *n* a performer in a play.

act as to do the work or duties of: *He acts as head of department when his boss is away.*

act on 1 to do something following the advice *etc* of someone: *I am acting on the advice of my lawyer.* **2** to have an effect on: *Certain acids act on metal.*

act on behalf of/act for to do something for (someone else); to act as the representative of (someone): *My lawyer is acting on my behalf*; *He is also acting on behalf of my mother*; *She is acting for the headmaster in his absence.*

in the act (of) at the exact moment (of doing something): *He was caught in the act (of stealing my car).*

put on an act to pretend: *I thought she had hurt herself but she was only putting on an act.*

action ['akʃən] *n* **1** something done: *Action, not talking, is necessary if we are to defeat the enemy*; *Take action immediately*; *The firemen are ready to go into action.* **2** movement: *Tennis needs a good wrist action.* **3** a legal case: *He brought an action for divorce against his wife.* **4** the events (of a play, film *etc*): *The action of the play takes place on an island.* **5** a battle; fighting: *He was killed in action*; *Our troops fought an action against the enemy.*

in action working: *Is your machine still in action?*

out of action not working: *My car's out of action this week.*

activate ['aktiveit] *v* to put into force or operation: *The smoke activated the fire alarms.*

active ['aktiv] *adj* **1** energetic or lively; able to work *etc*: *At seventy, he's no longer very active.* **2** (busily) involved: *She is an active supporter of women's rights.* **3** causing an effect or effects: *Yeast is an active ingredient in bread-making.* **4** in force: *The rule is still active.* **5** (of volcanoes) still likely to erupt. **6** of the form of a verb in which the subject performs the action of the verb: *The dog bit the man.* **'activeness** *n.*

'actively *adv*: *actively engaged in politics.*

ac'tivity – *pl* **ac'tivities** – *n* **1** the state of being active or lively: *The streets are full of activity this morning.* **2** something which one does as a pastime, as part of one's job, *etc*: *His activities include fishing and golf.*

actor, actress *see* **act.**

actual ['aktʃuəl] *adj* real; existing; not imaginary: *In actual fact he is not as stupid as you think he is.*

‚actu'ality [-'a-] *n* (a) reality: *the actuality of the situation.*

'actually *adv* **1** really: *She actually saw the accident happen.* **2** in fact: *Actually, I'm doing something else this evening.*

acupuncture ['akjupʌktʃə] *n* a method of treating illness *etc* by sticking needles into the patient's skin at certain points.

acute [ə'kjuːt] *adj* **1** (of a disease *etc*) severe but not lasting very long: *They think his illness is acute rather than chronic.* **2** very great: *There is an acute shortage of teachers.* **3** quick-witted: *As a businessman, he's very acute.* **4** (of the senses) keen: *acute hearing.* **a'cutely** *adv.* **a'cuteness** *n.*

acute angle an angle of less than ninety degrees.

ad [ad] short for **advertisement**: *I'll put an ad in the newspaper.*

adamant ['adəmənt] *adj* determined or insistent: *an adamant refusal.*

adapt [ə'dapt] *v* to change or alter (so as to fit a different situation, *etc*): *She always adapted easily to new circumstances; He has adapted the play for television.* **‚adap'tation** [a-] *n.*

a'daptable *adj* willing or able to change to fit in with different circumstances: *Children are usually very adaptable.* **a‚dapta'bility** *n.*

a'daptor *n* a device which enables an electrical plug of one type to be used in a socket of another type, or several plugs to be used in the same socket at the same time.

add [ad] *v* **1** (*often with* **to**) to put (one thing) to or with (another): *He added water to his whisky.* **2** (*often with* **to, together, up**) to find the total of (various numbers): *Add these figures together; Add 124 to 356; He added up the figures.* **3** to say something extra: *He explained, and added that he was sorry.* **4** (*with* **to**) to increase: *His illness had added to their difficulties.*

ad'dition *n* **1** the act of adding: *The child is not good at addition.* **2** something added: *They've had an addition to the family.*

ad'ditional *adj*: *This has meant additional work for me.*

addict ['adikt] *n* a person who has become dependent on something, *esp* drugs: *a drug addict; a television addict.*

ad'dicted *adj* (*often with* **to**) dependent on (*esp* a drug): *He is addicted to alcohol.* **ad'diction** [-ʃən] *n.*

addition *see* **add.**

address [ə'dres] *v* **1** to put a name and address on (an envelope *etc*): *Address the parcel clearly.* **2** to speak or write to: *I shall address my remarks to you only.* – [(*Amer*) 'adres] *n* **1** the name of the house, street, town *etc* where a person lives: *His address is 30 Main St, Edinburgh.* **2** a speech: *He made a long and boring address.*

‚addres'see [ad-] *n* the person to whom a letter *etc* is addressed.

adept [ə'dept] *adj* highly skilled: *He's very adept at keeping his balance.* – ['adept] *n* an expert.

adequate ['adikwət] *adj* sufficient; enough: *He does not earn a large salary but it is adequate for his needs.* **'adequately** *adv.* **'adequacy** *n.*

adhere [əd'hiə] *v* **1** (*often with* **to**) to stick (to): *This tape doesn't adhere (to the floor) very well.* **2** (*with* **to**) to remain loyal (to): *I'm adhering to my principles.* **ad'herence** *n.* **ad'herent** *n* a follower; supporter: *an adherent of Marx.*

adhesion [əd'hiːʒən] *n* the act or quality of adhering (to).

ad'hesive [-siv] *adj* able to adhere; sticky: *adhesive tape.* – *n* a substance which makes things stick: *The tiles would not stick as he was using the wrong adhesive.*

adjacent [ə'dʒeisənt] *adj* (*often with* **to**) lying next (to): *We had adjacent rooms in the hotel; They have bought the house adjacent to mine.*

†**adjective** ['adʒiktiv] *n* a word which describes a noun: *a red flower; air which is cool.* **‚adjec'tival** [-'tai-] *adj.*

adjoin [ə'dʒoin] *v* to be next to or joined to: *His house adjoins the hotel.*

adjourn [ə'dʒəːn] *v* to stop (a meeting *etc*), intending to continue it at another time or place: *We shall adjourn (the meeting) until Wednesday.* **a'djournment** *n.*

adjudicate [ə'dʒuːdikeit] *v* to act as a judge (in an artistic competition *etc*). **a‚djudi'cation, a'djudicator** *ns.*

adjust [ə'dʒʌst] *v* **1** (*often with* **to**) to change so as to make or be better suited: *He soon adjusted to his new way of life.* **2** to change (the position of, setting of): *Adjust the setting of the alarm clock.*

a'djustable *adj* able to be adjusted: *This car has adjustable seats.*

a'djustment *n.*

† see Grammatical Notes on pp. 627–632

administer [əd'ministə] *v* **1** to govern or manage: *He administers the finances of the company.* **2** to carry out (the law *etc*). **3** to give (medicine, help *etc*): *The doctor administered drugs to the patient.*

ad'ministrate [-streit] *v* to govern or manage.

ad‚mini'stration *n* **1** management: *He's in charge of administration at the hospital.* **2** (the people who carry on) the government of a country *etc*.

administrative [-strətiv, (*Amer*) -streitiv] *adj*: *an administrative post*; *administrative ability.*

ad'ministrator [-strei-] *n*.

admirable *see* **admire**.

admiral ['admərəl] *n* (*with cap in titles*) the commander of a navy.

admire [əd'maiə] *v* **1** to look at with great pleasure and often to express this pleasure: *I've just been admiring your new car.* **2** to have a very high opinion of (something or someone): *I admire John's courage.*

'admirable ['admə-] *adj* extremely good: *His behaviour during the riot was admirable.*

'admirably ['admə-] *adv* extremely well: *He's admirably suited to the job.*

admiration [admi'reiʃən] *n*: *They were filled with admiration at the team's performance.*

ad'mirer *n* **1** one who admires (someone or something): *He is an admirer of Mozart.* **2** a man who is attracted by a particular woman: *She has many admirers.*

ad'miring *adj*: *an admiring glance.*
ad'miringly *adv.*

admission *see* **admit**.

admit [əd'mit] – *pt*, *ptp* **ad'mitted** – *v* **1** to allow to enter: *This ticket admits one person.* **2** to say that one accepts as true: *He admitted (that) he was wrong.*

ad'missible [-səbl] *adj* allowable: *admissible evidence.*

ad'mission [-ʃən] *n* **1** being allowed to enter; entry: *They charge a high price for admission.* **2** (an) act of accepting the truth of (something): *an admission of guilt.*

ad'mittance *n* the right or permission to enter: *The notice said 'No admittance'.*

ad'mittedly *adv* as is generally accepted: *Admittedly, she is not well.*

admonish [əd'moniʃ] *v* to scold or rebuke: *The judge admonished the young man for fighting in the street.* ‚**admo'nition** [ad-] *n.*

adolescent [adə'lesnt] *adj* in the stage between childhood and adulthood. – *n* a person at this stage of life: *Adolescents often quarrel with their parents.*
‚**ado'lescence** *n.*

adopt [ə'dopt] *v* **1** to take (a child of other parents) as one's own: *Since they had no children of their own they decided to adopt a little girl.* **2** to take (something) as one's

own: *After going to France he adopted the French way of life.* **a'doption** [-ʃən] *n.*

a'doptive [-tiv] *adj*: *his adoptive father.*

adore [ə'do:] *v* **1** to love or like very much: *He adores his children.* **2** to worship.

a'dorable *adj*; *an adorable little baby.*
a'dorably *adv.*

‚**ado'ration** [adə-] *n* worship or great love.

a'doring *adj*: *adoring parents.* **a'doringly** *adv.*

adorn [ə'do:n] *v* to make beautiful, with decorations *etc*: *Their house is adorned with beautiful antique ornaments.* **a'dornment** *n.*

adrift [ə'drift] *adj*, *adv* drifting: *adrift on the open sea.*

adroit [ə'droit] *adj* skilful: *his adroit handling of the boat.* **a'droitly** *adv.* **a'droitness** *n.*

adulation [adju'leiʃən] *n* foolishly excessive praise: *The teenager's adulation of the pop-group worried her parents.* **'adulatory** *adj.*

adult ['adʌlt, (*esp Amer*) ə'dʌlt] *adj* **1** fully grown: *an adult gorilla.* **2** mature: *adult behaviour.* – *n* a fully grown human being: *That film is suitable only for adults.*

adultery [ə'dʌltəri] *n* sexual intercourse between a husband and a woman who is not his wife or between a wife and a man who is not her husband.

advance [əd'va:ns] *v* **1** to move forward: *The army advanced towards the town*; *Our plans are advancing well*; *He married the boss's daughter to advance* (=improve) *his chances of promotion.* **2** to supply (someone) with (money) on credit: *The bank will advance you $500.* – *n* **1** moving forward or progressing: *We've halted the enemy's advance*; *Great advances in medicine have been made in this century.* **2** a payment made before the normal time: *Can I have an advance on my salary?* **3** (*usu in pl*) an attempt at (*esp* sexual) seduction. – *adj* **1** made *etc* before the necessary or agreed time: *an advance payment.* **2** made beforehand: *an advance booking.* **3** sent ahead of the main group or force: *the advance guard.*

advanced *adj* having made a lot of progress; at a high level: *an advanced computer course*; *in the advanced stages of the illness.*

in advance **1** before(hand): *Can you pay me in advance?* **2** in front: *I've been sent on in advance* (*of the main force*).

advantage [əd'va:ntidʒ] *n* **1** (a) gain or benefit: *There are several advantages in being self-employed.* **2** in tennis, the first point gained after deuce.

advantageous [advən'teidʒəs] *adj* having or giving an advantage: *Because of his experience he was in an advantageous position for promotion.* ‚**advan'tageously** *adv.*

have an/the advantage (over) to be in a better or more advantageous position (than): *As she already knew French, she had an advantage over the rest of the class.*

take advantage of to make use of (a situation, person *etc*) in such a way as to benefit oneself: *He took full advantage of all his business opportunities.*

advent ['advent] *n* coming or arrival: *the advent of space travel.*

adventure [əd'ventʃə] *n* a bold or exciting undertaking or experience: *He wrote a book about his adventures in the Antarctic.*

ad'venturer *n* a person who seeks adventure or fortune.

ad'venturous *adj* liking or eager for adventure(s). **ad'venturously** *adv*.

†**adverb** ['advə:b] *n* a word used before or after a verb, before an adjective or preposition, or with another adverb to show time, manner, place, degree *etc*: *Yesterday he looked more carefully in the box, and there he found a very small key with a hole right through it.* **ad'verbial** *adj*. **ad'verbially** *adv*.

adversary ['advəsəri] – *pl* **'adversaries** – *n* an opponent; an enemy: *his adversary in the chess match.*

adverse ['advə:s] *adj* unfavourable: *adverse criticism.* **'adversely** *adv*.

ad'versity *n* misfortune or hardship.

advert ['advə:t] short for **advertisement**: *I saw your advert in yesterday's newspaper.*

advertise ['advətaiz] *v* to make (something) known to the public by any of various methods: *I've advertised (my house) in the newspaper; They advertised on TV for volunteers.*

advertisement [əd'və:tismənt, (*Amer*) advər'taizmənt] *n* (*also* **ad** [ad], **advert** ['advə:t]) a film, newspaper announcement, poster *etc* making something known, *esp* in order to persuade people to buy it: *an advertisement for toothpaste on television; She replied to my advertisement for a secretary.*

'advertiser *n* a person who advertises.

advice [əd'vais] *n* suggestions to a person about what he should do: *You must seek legal advice if you want a divorce; Let me give you a piece of advice.*

advise [əd'vaiz] *v* **1** to give advice to; to recommend: *My lawyer advises me to buy the house.* **2** (*with* **of**) to inform: *This letter is to advise you of our interest in your proposal.*

ad'visable *adj* (of actions) wise: *The doctor does not think it advisable for you to drink alcohol.* **ad,visa'bility** *n*.

ad'viser, ad'visor *n* a person who advises.

ad'visory *adj* giving advice: *an advisory leaflet; He acted in an advisory capacity.*

> **advice** is a noun and never used in the plural: *to give advice/a piece of advice/some advice.*
> **advise** is a verb: *He advises us not to go.*

advocate ['advəkət] *n* a supporter, a person who is in favour (of): *an advocate of reform.* – [-keit] *v* to recommend: *He advocated increasing the charges.*

aerial ['eəriəl] *n* (*Amer* **an'tenna**) a wire or rod (or a set of these) able to send or receive radio waves *etc*: *a television aerial.* – *adj* in or from the air: *aerial photography.*

aerobatics [eərə'batiks] *n pl* acrobatics performed by an aircraft or high in the air.

aerodrome ['eərədroum] *n* a place (*usu* private or military) where aircraft are kept and from which they fly.

aeronautics [eərə'no:tiks] *n sing* the science or practice of flying: *Aeronautics is a popular science.* **,aero'nautical** *adj*.

aeroplane ['eərəplein] *n* (*often abbrev* **plane**: *Amer* **'airplane**) a machine for flying which is heavier than air and has wings.

aerosol ['eərəsol] *n* a mixture of liquid or solid particles and gas under pressure which is released from a container in the form of a mist: *Many deodorants come in the form of aerosols;* (*also adj*) *an aerosol spray.*

afar [ə'fa:] *adv* from, at or to a distance: *The three wise men came from afar.*

affable ['afəbl] *adj* pleasant and easy to talk to: *an affable young man.* **'affably** *adv*. **,affa'bility** *n*.

affair [ə'feə] *n* **1** happenings *etc* which are connected with a particular person or thing: *the Suez affair.* **2** a thing: *The new machine is a weird-looking affair.* **3** (*often in pl*) business; concern(s): *financial affairs; Where I go is entirely my own affair.* **4** a love relationship: *His wife found out about his affair with another woman.*

affect [ə'fekt] *v* **1** to act or have an effect on: *Rain affects the grass; His kidneys have been affected by the disease.* **2** to move the feelings of: *She was deeply affected by the news of his death.*

affection [ə'fekʃən] *n* liking or fondness: *I have great affection for her, but she never shows any affection towards me.*

af'fectionate [-nət] *adj* having or showing affection: *an affectionate child; She is very affectionate towards her mother.* **af'fectionately** *adv*.

affiliated [ə'filieitid] *adj* connected with or joined to (a larger group *etc*) as a member: *an affiliated branch of the union.*

af,fili'ation *n* a connection with (an organization *etc*): *What are his political affiliations?*

affirm [ə'fə:m] *v* to state something positively and firmly: *Despite all the policeman's questions the lady continued to affirm that she was innocent.* **,affir'mation** [a-] *n*.

af'firmative [-tiv] *adj, n* saying or indicating yes to a question, suggestion *etc*: *He gave an affirmative nod; a reply in the affirmative.*

affix [əˈfiks] *v* to attach (something) to an object *etc*: *Affix the stamp to the envelope.*

afflict [əˈflikt] *v* to give pain or distress to (a person *etc*): *She is continually afflicted by/ with headaches.*

afˈfliction [-ʃən] *n*: *Her deafness is a great affliction to her.*

affluent [ˈafluənt] *adj* wealthy: *He is becoming more and more affluent.*

ˈaffluence *n* wealth.

afford [əˈfoːd] *v* **1** (*usu with* **can, could**) to be able to spend money, time *etc* on or for something: *I can't afford (to buy) a new car.* **2** (*usu with* **can, could**) to be able to do (something) without causing oneself trouble, difficulty *etc*: *She can't afford to be rude to her employer no matter how rude he is to her.*

affront [əˈfrʌnt] *n* an insult, *usu* one made in public: *His remarks were obviously intended as an affront to her.* – *v* to insult or offend: *We were affronted by the offhand way in which they treated us.*

afloat [əˈflout] *adj* floating: *We've got the boat afloat at last.*

afoot [əˈfut] *adj* in progress or happening: *There is a scheme afoot to improve recreational facilities in the area.*

aforesaid [əˈfoːsed] *adj* said, named *etc* before (*usu* in an earlier part of a document).

afraid [əˈfreid] *adj* **1** feeling fear or being frightened (of a person, thing *etc*): *The child is not afraid of the dark; She was afraid to go.* **2** sorry (to have to say that): *I'm afraid I don't agree with you.*

Afro- [afrou] (*as part of a word*) African: *ˌAfro-Aˈmerican.*

after [ˈaːftə] *prep* **1** later in time or place than: *After the car came a bus.* **2** following (*often indicating repetition*): *one thing after another; night after night.* **3** behind: *Shut the door after you!* **4** in search or pursuit of: *He ran after the bus.* **5** considering: *After all I've done you'd think he'd thank me; It's sad to fail after all that work.* **6** (*Amer*: in telling the time*) past: *It's a quarter after ten.* – *adv* later in time or place: *They arrived soon after.* – *conj* later than the time when: *After she died we moved house twice.*

ˈaftermath [-maθ] *n* the situation *etc* resulting from an important, *esp* unpleasant, event: *The country is still suffering from the aftermath of the war.*

ˈafterthought *n* a later thought.

ˈafterwards *adv* later or after something else has happened or happens: *He told me afterwards that he had not enjoyed the film.*

after all 1 (used when giving a reason for doing something *etc*) taking everything into consideration: *I won't invite him. After all, I don't really know him.* **2·**in spite of every-

thing that has/had happened, been said *etc*: *It turns out he went by plane after all.*

be after to be looking for something: *What are you after?*; *The police are after him.*

afternoon [aːftəˈnuːn] *n* the time between morning and evening: *tomorrow afternoon; He works for us three afternoons a week; Tuesday afternoon; (also adj*) *afternoon tea.*

again [əˈgen] *adv* once more or another time: *He never saw her again; He hit the child again and again; Don't do that again!*; *He has been abroad but he is home again now.*

against [əˈgenst] *prep* **1** in opposition to: *They fought against the enemy; Dropping litter is against the law* (=illegal). **2** in contrast to: *The trees were black against the evening sky.* **3** touching or in contact with: *He stood with his·back against the wall; The rain beat against the window.* **4** in order to protect against: *vaccination against tuberculosis.*

agar-agar [ˈaːgaːrˈaːgaːr] *n* (a jelly made from) seaweed, used in medicine, cooking *etc*.

age [eidʒ] *n* **1** the amount of time during which a person or thing has existed : *He went to school at the age of six (years); What age is she?* **2** (*often with cap*) a particular period of time: *This machine was the wonder of the age; the Middle Ages.* **3** the quality of being old: *This wine will improve with age; With the wisdom of age he regretted the mistakes he had made in his youth.* **4** (*usu in pl*) a very long time: *We've been waiting (for) ages for a bus.* – *v* – *prp* **ˈag(e)ing** – to (cause to) grow old or look old: *He has aged a lot since I last saw him; His troubles have aged him.*

aged *adj* **1** [ˈeidʒid] old: *an aged man.* **2** [eidʒd] of the age of : *a child aged five.*

ˈageless *adj* never growing old or never looking older: *ageless beauty.*

ˈage-old *adj* done, known *etc* for a very long time: *an age-old custom.*

the aged [ˈeidʒid] old people: *care for the aged.*

(come) of age (to become) old enough to be considered legally an adult (*eg* in Britain aged eighteen or over).

agency *see* **agent.**

agenda [əˈdʒendə] *n* a list of things to be done, *esp* at a meeting: *What's on the agenda this morning?*

agent [ˈeidʒənt] *n* **1** a person or thing that acts: *detergents and other cleaning agents.* **2** a person who acts for someone in business *etc*: *our agent in London; a theatrical agent.* **3** (*esp* **secret agent**) a spy: *an agent for the Russians.*

ˈagency – *pl* **ˈagencies** – *n* the office or business of an agent: *an advertising agency.*

by/through the agency of by the action of:

The meeting was arranged through the agency of a friend.

aggravate ['agrəveit] *v* **1** to make worse: *His bad temper aggravated the situation.* **2** to make (someone) angry or impatient: *She was aggravated by the constant questions.* ,aggra'vation *n.*

aggregate ['agrigət] *n* a total: *What is the aggregate of goals from the two football matches?*

aggresive [ə'gresiv] *adj* ready to attack or oppose; quarrelsome: *He's a most aggressive boy – he is always fighting at school.* ag'gressively *adv.* ag'gressiveness *n.* ag'gression [-ʃən] *n* (a feeling of) hostility. ag'gressor *n* (in a war *etc*) the party which attacks first.

aggrieved [ə'gri:vd] *adj* unhappy or hurt because of unjust treatment: *He felt aggrieved at his friend's distrust.*

aghast [ə'ga:st] *adj* struck with horror: *She was aghast at the mess.*

agile ['adʒail] *adj* able to move quickly and easily: *The antelope is very agile.* a'gility [-'dʒi-] *n.*

agitate ['adʒiteit] *v* **1** to make (someone) excited and anxious: *The news agitated her.* **2** to try to arouse public feeling and action: *That group is agitating for prison reform.* **3** to shake: *The tree was agitated by the wind.* 'agitated *adj.* ,agi'tation *n.* 'agitator *n* a person who tries constantly to stir up public feeling: *a political agitator.*

ago [ə'gou] *adv* at a certain time in the past: *two years ago; Long ago, men lived in caves; How long ago did he leave?*

agog [ə'gog] *adj* eager and excited: *We were all agog at the news.*

agony ['agəni] – *pl* 'agonies – *n* great pain or suffering: *The dying man was in agony; agonies of regret.* 'agonized, -s- *adj* showing agony: *He had an agonized expression on his face as he lost the match.* 'agonizing, -s- *adj* causing agony: *an agonizing pain.* agonizingly, -s- *adv.*

agree [ə'gri:] – *pt, ptp* a'greed – *v* **1** (*often with* with) to think or say the same (as): *I agreed with them that we should try again; The newspaper report does not agree with what he told us.* **2** to say that one will do or allow something: *He agreed to go; He agreed to our request.* **3** (*with* with) to be good for (*usu* one's health): *Cheese does not agree with me.* **4** to be happy and friendly together: *John and his wife don't agree.* a'greeable *adj* pleasant: *She is a most agreeable person.* a'greeably *adv.* a'greement *n* **1** the state of agreeing: *We are all in agreement.* **2** a business, political *etc* arrangement, spoken or written: *You have*

broken our agreement; We have signed an agreement.

agriculture ['agrikʌltʃə] *n* (the science of) the cultivation of land: *He is studying agriculture.* ,agri'cultural *adj.*

aground [ə'graund] *adj, adv* (of ships) (stuck) on the bed of the sea *etc* in shallow water: *Our boat ran aground.*

ahead [ə'hed] *adv* (*often with* of) in front; in advance: *He went on ahead of me; We are well ahead (of our rivals).*

aid [eid] *n* help: *Rich countries give aid to developing countries; The teacher uses visual aids; He came to my aid when my car broke down.* – *v* to help: *I was aided in my search by the library staff.* in aid of as a financial help to (a charity *etc*): *The collection is in aid of the blind.*

ail [eil] *v* **1** to be ill: *The old lady has been ailing for some time.* **2** to trouble: *What ails you?* 'ailment *n* an illness, *usu* not serious or dangerous: *Children often have minor ailments.*

aim [eim] *v* **1** (*usu with* at, for) to point or direct something at; to try to hit or reach *etc*: *He picked up the rifle and aimed it at the target.* **2** (*with* to, at) to plan, intend or to have as one's purpose: *He aims at finishing tomorrow; We aim to please our customers.* – *n* **1** the act of or skill at aiming: *His aim is excellent.* **2** what a person intends to do: *My aim is to become prime minister.* 'aimless *adj* without purpose: *an aimless life.* 'aimlessly *adv.* 'aimlessness *n.* take aim to aim: *He took aim at the target.*

air [eə] *n* **1** the mixture of gases we breathe; the atmosphere: *Mountain air is pure.* **2** the space above the ground; the sky: *Birds fly through the air.* **3** appearance: *The house had an air of neglect.* **4** a tune: *She played a simple air on the piano.* – *v* **1** to expose to the air in order to dry or make more fresh *etc*: *to air linen.* **2** to make known: *He loved to air his opinions.* 'airily *adv* in a light-hearted manner: *She airily dismissed all objections.* 'airiness *n.* 'airing *n* a short walk *etc* in the open air: *She took the baby for an airing.* 'airless *adj* **1** (of weather) still and windless: *It was a hot, airless night.* **2** (of a room *etc*) stuffy and without fresh air. 'airy *adj* **1** with plenty of (fresh) air: *an airy room.* **2** light-hearted and not serious: *an airy disregard for authority.* 'airborne *adj* in the air or flying: *We were airborne five minutes after boarding the plane; airborne germs.* ,air-con'ditioned *adj* having air-conditioning: *an air-conditioned building.*

,air-con'ditioner *n* an apparatus providing air-conditioning.

,air-con'ditioning *n* a method of providing a room, building *etc* with air of a controlled temperature and humidity.

'aircraft – *pl* 'aircraft – *n* any of several types of machine for flying in the air: *Enemy aircraft have been sighted.*

aircraft carrier a ship which carries aircraft and which aircraft can use for landing and taking off.

'airfield *n* an area of ground (with buildings *etc*) where (*usu* military) aircraft are kept and from which they fly.

air force the part of the armed services which uses aircraft: *the army, navy and air force.*

'air-gun *n* a gun that is worked by air under pressure.

air hostess a young woman who looks after passengers in an aircraft.

air letter a letter sent by airmail.

'airlift *n* an operation to move cargo or people, carried out by air.

'airline *n* (a company that owns) a regular air transport service: *Which airline are you travelling by?*

'airliner *n* a (*usu* large) aircraft for carrying passengers.

'air-lock *n* a bubble in a pipe which prevents liquid from flowing along it.

'airmail *n* a system of carrying mail by air: *Send this parcel by airmail*; (*also adj*) *an airmail letter.*

'airman *n* a member of an air force.

'airplane *n* (*Amer*) an aeroplane.

'airport *n* a place where passenger aircraft arrive and depart, with buildings for customs, waiting-rooms *etc.*

'air-pump *n* a pump for forcing air in or out of something.

'air-raid *n* an attack by aircraft.

'airship *n* an aircraft that is lighter than air and can be steered *etc.*

'airtight *adj* (of a container *etc*) into or through which air cannot pass: *an airtight seal on a bottle.*

'airway *n* a regular course followed by aircraft.

on the air broadcasting (regularly) on radio or television.

put on airs/give oneself airs to behave as if one is better or more important than others: *She gives herself such airs that everyone dislikes her.*

aisle [ail] *n* a passage between rows of seats *etc* in a church, cinema *etc.*

ajar [ə'dʒɑː] *adj* partly open: *The door was ajar when I returned.*

akin [ə'kin] *adj* (*often with* to) similar in nature: *This problem is akin to the one we had last year.*

alacrity [ə'lakrəti] *n* quick and cheerful willingness: *He obeyed with alacrity.*

alarm [ə'lɑːm] *n* 1 sudden fear: *We did not share her alarm at the suggestion.* 2 something that gives warning of danger, attracts attention *etc*: *Sound the alarm!*; *a fire-alarm*; (*also adj*) *an alarm clock.* – *v* to make (someone) afraid: *The least sound alarms the old lady.*

a'larming *adj* disturbing or causing fear: *alarming news.* a'larmingly *adv.*

alas! [ə'las] *interj* used to express grief: *Alas, he died young!*

album ['albəm] *n* 1 a book with blank pages for holding photographs, stamps *etc.* 2 a long-playing gramophone record: *I haven't got the group's latest album.*

alcohol ['alkəhol] *n* liquid made by the fermentation or distillation of sugar, present in intoxicating drinks, used also as a fuel, and in thermometers: *I never drink alcohol – I drink orange juice.*

,alco'holic *adj* 1 of or containing alcohol: *Is cider alcoholic?* 2 caused by alcohol: *an alcoholic stupor.* – *n* a person who suffers from a dependence on alcohol.

'alcoholism *n* the condition suffered by an alcoholic.

alcove ['alkouv] *n* a small section of a room *etc* formed by part of the wall being set back.

ale [eil] *n* the name given to certain kinds of beer: *two pints of ale.*

alert [ə'ləːt] *adj* 1 quick-thinking: *She's very old but still very alert.* 2 (*with* to) watchful and aware: *You must be alert to danger.* – *n* a signal to be ready for action. – *v* to make (someone) alert; to warn: *The sound of gunfire alerted us to our danger.* a'lertly *adv.* a'lertness *n.*

on the alert on the watch (for): *We were on the alert for any sound that might tell us where he was.*

algae ['aldʒiː] *n pl* a group of simple plants which includes seaweed.

algebra ['aldʒibrə] *n* a method of calculating using letters and signs to represent numbers. ,alge'braic [-breiik] *adj.*

alias ['eiliəs] *n* a false name: *What alias did the crook use this time?* – *adv* otherwise known as: *John Smith, alias Peter Jones.*

alibi ['alibai] *n* the fact or a statement that a person accused of a crime was somewhere else when it was committed: *Has he an alibi for the night of the murder?*

alien ['eiliən] *adj* foreign: *alien customs.* – *n* a foreigner: *Aliens are not welcome there.*

'alienate [-neit] *v* to make someone feel unfriendly to one: *He alienated his wife by his cruelty to her.* ,alie'nation *n.*

alight[1] [ə'lait] – *pt, ptp* a'lighted – *v* 1 to get down from or out of: *to alight from a bus.*

2 (*with* **on**) to settle or land on: *The bird alighted on the fence.*

alight[2] [ə'lait] *adj* burning; very bright: *The bonfire was still alight*; *His eyes were alight with joy.*

align [ə'lain] *v* 1 to put in a straight line or in parallel lines. 2 to attach (oneself) to one side in an argument, politics *etc*: *He aligned himself with the rebels.*

alike [ə'laik] *adj* like one another; similar: *Twins are often very alike.* – *adv* in the same way: *He treated all his children alike.*

alimentary [ali'mentəri] : **alimentary canal** the passage for the digestion of food in animals, including the gullet, stomach and intestines.

alive [ə'laiv] *adj* 1 living and not dead: *Queen Victoria was still alive in 1900.* 2 full of activity: *The town was alive with policemen on the day of the march.*

alive to aware of: *He was alive to the dangers of the situation.*

alkali ['alkəlai] *n* a substance, the opposite of acid, such as soda. **'alkaline** [-lain] *adj.*

all [o:l] *adj*, *pron* 1 the whole (of): *He ate all the cake*; *He has spent all of his money.* 2 every one (of a group) when taken together: *They were all present*; *All men are equal.* – *adv* entirely: *all alone*; *dressed all in white.* 2 (*with* **the**) much; even: *Your low pay is all the more reason to find a new job*; *I feel all the better for a shower.*

,all-'clear *n* (*usu with* **the**) a signal or formal statement that a time of danger *etc* is over: *They sounded the all-clear after the air-raid.*

'all-out *adj* using the greatest effort possible: *an all-out attempt.*

'all-round *adj* 1 including or applying to every part, person, thing *etc*: *an all-round pay rise.* 2 good at all parts of a subject *etc*: *an all-round sportsman.*

,all-'rounder *n* a person who is good at many kinds of work, sport *etc*.

all along the whole time (that something was happening): *I knew the answer all along.*

all at once 1 all at the same time: *Don't eat those cakes all at once!* 2 suddenly: *All at once the light went out.*

all in with everything included: *Is that the price all in?*

all in all considering everything: *We haven't done badly, all in all.*

all over 1 over the whole of (a person, thing *etc*): *My car is dirty all over.* 2 finished: *The excitement's all over now.* 3 everywhere: *We've been looking all over for you!*

all right 1 unhurt; not ill or in difficulties *etc*: *You look ill. Are you all right?* 2 an expression of agreement to do something: *'Will you come?' 'Oh, all right.'*

in all in total, when everything is added up: *I spent three hours in all waiting for buses last week.*

Write **all right** (not **alright**).

allay [ə'lei] *v* to make less: *He allayed her fears.*

allege [ə'ledʒ] *v* to say, *esp* in making a legal statement, without giving proof: *He alleged that I had been with the accused on the night of the murder.* **allegation** [ali'geiʃən] *n*.

allegiance [ə'li:dʒəns] *n* loyalty to a person, group, idea *etc*: *I have no allegiance to any political party.*

allergy ['alədʒi] – *pl* **'allergies** – *n* an unusual sensitiveness of the body which causes certain people to be affected in a bad way by something *usu* harmless: *The rash on her face is caused by an allergy to grass.*

allergic [-'lə:-] *adj* (*with* **to**) affected in a bad way by (certain) things: *He is allergic to certain flowers.*

alleviate [ə'li:vieit] *v* to make an improvement by lessening (pain *etc*): *The drugs will alleviate the pain.* **al,levi'ation** *n*.

alley ['ali] *n* 1 (*often* **'alleyway**) a narrow street in a city *etc* (*usu* not wide enough for vehicles). 2 a long narrow area used for the games of bowling or skittles: *a bowling alley.*

alliance, allied *see* **ally.**

alligator ['aligeitə] *n* a kind of large reptile closely related to the crocodile, found mainly in the rivers of the warmer parts of America.

allocate ['aləkeit] *v* 1 to give (to someone) for his own use: *He allocated a room to each student.* 2 to set apart (for a particular purpose): *They allocated $500 to the project.* **,allo'cation** *n*.

allot [ə'lot] – *pt*, *ptp* **al'lotted** – *v* to give (each person) a fixed share of or place in (something): *They have allotted all the money to the various people who applied.*

al'lotment *n* a small part of a larger piece of public ground rented to a person to grow vegetables *etc*.

allow [ə'lau] *v* 1 not to forbid or prevent: *He allowed me to enter*; *Playing football in the street is not allowed.* 2 (*with* **for**) to take into consideration when judging or deciding: *These figures allow for price rises.* 3 to give, *esp* for a particular purpose or regularly: *His father allows him too much money.*

al'lowance *n* 1 a fixed sum or quantity given regularly: *His father made him an allowance of $20 a month.* 2 something (*usu* a quantity) allowed: *This dress pattern has a seam allowance of 1 cm.*

make allowance for to take into consideration when deciding *etc*: *We've made allowance for the fact that everyone has different tastes.*

alloy ['aloi] *n* a mixture of two or more metals.

allude [ə'lu:d] *v* (*with* **to**) to mention: *He did not allude to the remarks made by the previous speaker.*

al'lusion [-ʒən] *n* (the act of making) a mention or reference: *The prime minister made no allusion to the war in his speech.*

alluring [ə'ljuəriŋ] *adj* attractive, tempting.

allusion *see* **allude**.

ally [ə'lai] *v* to join by political agreement, marriage, friendship *etc*: *Small countries must ally themselves with larger countries in order to survive.* − ['alai] *n* a state, person *etc* allied with another: *The two countries were allies at that time.*

al'liance *n*: *the alliance between Britain and France; The three countries entered into an alliance.*

'allied ['a-] *adj* **1** joined by political agreement or treaty: *The allied forces entered the country.* **2** (*with* **with**) together with; joined to: *Her beauty allied with her intelligence made her a successful model.* **3** (*with* **to**) related to; resembling: *The ape is closely allied to man.*

almanac ['o:lmənak] *n* a calendar *usu* with information about the phases of the moon *etc*.

almighty [o:l'maiti] *adj* having complete power; very great: *almighty God.*

almond ['a:mənd] *n* **1** (*also* **almond tree**) a kind of tree related to the peach. **2** the kernel of its fruit: *The cake had raisins and almonds in it.*

almost ['o:lmoust] *adv* nearly but not quite: *She is almost five years old; She almost fell under a moving car.*

alms [a:mz] *n pl* money *etc* given to the poor.

aloft [ə'loft] *adv* high up; overhead: *He held the banner aloft.*

alone [ə'loun] *adv* **1** with no-one else; by oneself: *He lived alone; She is alone in believing that he is innocent.* **2** only: *He alone can remember.*

all alone completely by oneself: *He has been all alone since the death of his wife.*

along [ə'loŋ] *prep* **1** from one end to the other: *He walked along several streets; The wall runs along the river.* **2** at a point at the end or on the length of: *There's a post-box somewhere along this street.* − *adv* **1** onwards or forward: *He ran along beside me; Come along, please!* **2** to the place mentioned: *I'll come along in five minutes.* **3** in company, together: *I took a friend along with me.*

a,long'side *prep, adv* beside or close to (the side of a ship, a pier *etc*): *He berthed alongside his friend's boat.*

aloof [ə'lu:f] *adv* apart or at a distance from other people: *I kept aloof from the whole*

business. − *adj* not sociable and friendly: *People find the new teacher rather aloof.*

a'loofness *n*.

aloud [ə'laud] *adv* so as can be heard: *He read the letter aloud.*

alphabet ['alfəbit] *n* the letters of a written language arranged in order: *I have learned all the letters of the Greek alphabet.*

,alpha'betical [-'be-] *adj*: *in alphabetical order.* **,alpha'betically** *adv*.

alpine ['alpain] *adj* of the Alps or other high mountains: *alpine flowers.*

already [o:l'redi] *adv* **1** before a particular time; previously: *I had already gone when Tom arrived; I don't want that book − I've read it already.* **2** before the expected time: *Are you leaving already?; He hasn't gone already, has he?*

also ['o:lsou] *adv* in addition or besides; too: *He is studying German but he is also studying French; They know him and I know him also.*

altar ['o:ltə] *n* **1** in some Christian churches the table on which the bread and wine are consecrated during the celebration of communion: *The bride and groom stood before the priest at the altar.* **2** a table *etc* on which offerings are made to a god.

alter ['o:ltə] *v* to make or become different; to change: *Will you alter this dress (to fit me)?; The town has altered a lot in the last two years.*

,alte'ration *n*: *The alterations he has made to the play have not improved it.*

alternate ['o:ltəneit] *v* to use, do *etc* by turns, repeatedly, one after the other: *John alternates between teaching and studying*; *He tried to alternate red and yellow tulips along the path as he planted them.* − [o:l'tə:nət] *adj* **1** coming, happening *etc* in turns, one after the other: *The water came in alternate bursts of hot and cold.* **2** every second (day, week *etc*): *My friend and I take the children to school on alternate days.*

al'ternately [-'tə:nət-] *adv*: *She felt alternately hot and cold.* **alter'nation** *n*.

alternative [o:l'tə:nətiv] *adj* offering a choice of a second possibility: *An alternative arrangement can be made if my plans don't suit you.* − *n* a choice between two (or sometimes more) things or possibilities: *You leave me no alternative but to dismiss you; I don't like fish. Is there an alternative on the menu?* **al'ternatively** *adv*.

although [o:l'ðou] *conj* in spite of the fact that: *Although he hurried, the shop was closed when he got there.*

although should not be followed by **but**: *Although he is poor, he is honest* (not *Although he is poor but he is honest*).

altitude ['altitju:d] *n* height above sea-level: *What is the altitude of the town?*

alto ['altou] – *pl* **'altos** – *n* (a singer having) a singing voice of the lowest pitch for a woman.

altogether [o:ltə'geðə] *adv* **1** completely: *I'm not altogether satisfied.* **2** on the whole and considering everything: *I'm wet, I'm tired and I'm cold. Altogether I'm not feeling very cheerful.*

aluminium [alju'miniəm], (*Amer*) **aluminum** [ə'lu:minəm] *n, adj* (of) an element, a light, silver-coloured metal used in making saucepans *etc*: *pans made of aluminium*; *aluminium foil, rivet, tray.*

always ['o:lweiz] *adv* **1** at all times: *I always work hard*; *I'll always remember her.* **2** continually or repeatedly: *He is always making mistakes.*

am *see* **be.**

amah ['a:mə] *n* **1** in Eastern Countries, a native female servant. **2** a baby's nurse, *esp* a wet-nurse.

amass [ə'mas] *v* to gather or collect in a large quantity: *He amassed an enormous quantity of information.*

amateur ['amətə, (*Amer*) -tʃər] *n* **1** a person who takes part in a sport *etc* without being paid for it: *The tennis tournament was open only to amateurs.* **2** someone who does something for the love of it and not for good money: *For an amateur, he was quite a good photographer..* – *adj*: *an amateur golfer*; *amateur photography.*

ama'teurish [-'tə:-] *adj* not very skilful: *an amateurish drawing.*

amaze [ə'meiz] *v* to surprise greatly: *I was amazed at his stupidity.*

a'mazement *n* great surprise: *To my amazement, he had never heard of her.*

a'mazing *adj*: *an amazing sight.* **a'mazingly** *adv.*

ambassador [am'basədə] – *fem* **am'bassadress** – *n* the government minister appointed to act for his government in another country: *the British Ambassador to Italy.* **am‚bassa'dorial** [-'do:-] *adj.*

amber ['ambə] *n, adj* (of) a hard yellow or brownish substance, formed from resin, used in making jewellery *etc*: *made of amber*; *an amber brooch.*

ambiguous [am'bigjuəs] *adj* having more than one possible meaning: *After the cat caught the mouse, it died is an ambiguous statement* (*ie* it is not clear whether *it* = the cat or = the mouse). **am'biguously** *adv.* **‚ambi'guity** [-'gju:-] *n.*

ambition [am'biʃən] *n* **1** the desire for success, fame, power *etc*: *He is full of ambition and energy.* **2** the desire eventually to become or do something special: *His ambition is to be Prime Minister.*

am'bitious *adj*: *He is very ambitious*; *That plan is too ambitious.* **am'bitiously** *adv.* **am'bitiousness** *n.*

amble ['ambl] *v* to walk without hurrying: *We were ambling along enjoying the scenery.*

ambulance ['ambjuləns] *n* a vehicle for carrying the sick and injured to hospital *etc*: *Call an ambulance – this man is very ill!*

ambulance ends in **-ance** (not **-ence**).

ambush ['ambuʃ] *v* to wait in hiding for and make a surprise attack on: *They planned to ambush the enemy as they marched towards the captial.* – *n* **1** an attack made in this way. **2** the group of people making the attack.

amend [ə'mend] *v* to correct or improve: *We shall amend the error as soon as possible.*

make amends to do something to improve the situation after doing something wrong, stupid *etc*: *He gave her a present to make amends for his rudeness.*

amenity [ə'mi:nəti] – *pl* **a'menities** – *n* something that makes life more pleasant or convenient: *This part of town has a lot of amenities – good shops, parks etc.*

amiable ['eimiəbl] *adj* likeable; pleasant and good-tempered. **‚amia'bility** *n.* **'amiably** *adv.*

amicable ['amikəbl] *adj* friendly: *The dispute was finally settled in a very amicable manner.* **'amicably** *adv.*

amid, amidst [ə'mid(st)] *preps* in the middle of; among: *Amid all the confusion, the real point of the meeting was lost; amidst the shadows.*

amiss [ə'mis] *adj* wrong: *Their plans went amiss.*

ammo ['amou] *short for* **ammunition.**

ammonia [ə'mouniə] *n* **1** a strong-smelling gas made of hydrogen and nitrogen. **2** a solution of this gas in water, used for cleaning *etc.*

ammunition [amju'niʃən] *n* things used in the firing of a gun *etc* (*eg* bullets, gunpowder, shells): *How long will the soldiers' ammunition last?*

amnesia [am'ni:ziə] *n* loss of memory: *After falling on his head he suffered from amnesia.*

amnesty ['amnəsti] – *pl* **'amnesties** – *n* a general pardon given to people who have done wrong *esp* against the government: *The murderer was released under the amnesty declared by the new president.*

amok [ə'mok], **amuck** [ə'mʌk]: **run amok/amuck** to rush about madly, attacking everybody and everything: *The prisoner ran amok and killed two prison officers.*

among, amongst [ə'mʌŋ(st)] *prep* **1** in the middle of: *a house among the trees.* **2** in shares or parts to each person (in a group *etc*): *Divide the chocolate amongst you.*

see also **between.**

amount [ə'maunt] v (with to) **1** to add up to: *The bill amounted to $15.* **2** to be equal to: *Borrowing money and not returning it amounts to stealing.* – n a quantity, *esp* of money: *a large amount of money in the bank.*

ampère ['ampeə] n (*also* **amp** [amp]) (*often abbrev* **A** *when written*) the unit by which an electric current is measured.

amphibian [am'fibiən] n **1** a creature that spends part of its life on land and part in water: *Frogs are amphibians.* **2** a vehicle designed to move on land or in the water. **3** an aircraft designed to fly from land or water. **am'phibious** adj.

amphitheatre, (*Amer*) **amphitheater** ['amfiθiətə] n an oval or circular building with rows of seats surrounding a central space, used as a theatre or arena.

ample ['ampl] adj (more than) enough: *There is ample space for four people.* '**amply** adv.

amplify ['amplifai] v **1** to make larger, *esp* by adding details to. **2** to make (the sound from a radio, record-player *etc*) louder by using an amplifier. ,**ampli'fication** [-fi-] n. '**amplifier** n a piece of equipment for increasing the strength or power-level of electric currents *esp* so as to increase loudness: *You need a new amplifier for your stereo equipment.*

amputate ['ampjuteit] v (of a surgeon *etc*) to cut off (an arm or leg *etc*): *They are going to have to amputate (his left leg).* ,**ampu'tation** n.

amuse [ə'mju:z] v **1** to make (someone) laugh: *I was amused at the monkey's antics.* **2** to interest or give pleasure to (for a time): *They amused themselves playing cards.*
a'musement n **1** the state of being amused or of finding something funny: *a smile of amusement.* **2** an entertainment or interest: *surfing and other holiday amusements.*
a'musing adj rather funny or humorous: *an amusing story.* **a'musingly** adv.

an see **a**.

anaemia, (*Amer*) **anemia** [ə'ni:miə] n a medical condition caused by not having enough red cells in the blood.
a'naemic adj suffering from anaemia.

anaesthetic, (*Amer*) **anesthetic** [anəs'θetik] n a substance, used in surgery *etc*, that causes lack of feeling in a part of the body or unconsciousness.
,**anaes'thesia** [-'θi:ziə, (*Amer*) -ʒə] n loss of consciousness or of feeling caused by an anaesthetic.
anaesthetist [ə'ni:sθətist, (*Amer*) ə'nes-] n the doctor responsible for giving an anaesthetic to the patient during a surgical operation.
anaesthetize, -ise [ə'ni:sθətaiz, (*Amer*)

ə'nes-] v to make (someone) unable to feel pain *etc* (by giving an anaesthetic to).

analysis [ə'naləsis] – pl **a'nalyses** [-si:z] – n **1** (a) detailed examination of something (a sentence, a chemical compound *etc*) *esp* by breaking it up into the parts of which it is made up: *The chemist is making an analysis of the poison; close analysis of the situation.* **2** (*esp Amer*) psycho-analysis: *He is undergoing analysis for his emotional problems.*
analyse, (*Amer*) **analyze** ['anəlaiz] v **1** to examine the nature of (something) *esp* by breaking up (a whole) into parts: *The doctor analysed the blood sample.*
analyst ['anəlist] n **1** a person who analyses: *a chemical analyst.* **2** (*esp Amer*) a psychiatrist.
analytical [anə'litikl] adj.

anarchy ['anəki] n **1** the absence or failure of government: *Total anarchy followed the defeat of the government.* **2** disorder and confusion.
'**anarchist** n **1** a person who believes that governments are unneccessary or undesirable. **2** a person who tries to overturn the government by violence. '**anarchism** n.

anatomy [ə'natəmi] n the science of the structure of the (*usu* human) body, *esp* the study of the body by cutting up dead animal and human bodies. **anatomical** [anə'tomikl] adj. ,**ana'tomically** adv.
a'natomist n a person who specializes in anatomy.

ancestor ['ansistə, (*Amer*) -ses-] – fem '**ancestress** – n a person who was a member of one's family a long time ago and from whom one is descended. **an'cestral** [-'ses-] adj.
'**ancestry** – pl '**ancestries** – n a line of ancestors coming down to one's parents: *He is of noble ancestry.*

anchor ['aŋkə] n **1** something, *usu* a heavy piece of metal with points which dig into the sea-bed, used to hold a boat in one position. **2** something that holds someone or something steady. – v to hold (a boat *etc*) steady (with an anchor): *They have anchored (the boat) near the shore; He used a stone to anchor his papers.*
'**anchorage** [-ridʒ] n a place which is safe, or used, for anchoring boats: *a sheltered anchorage.*
at anchor (of a ship) anchored: *The ship lay at anchor in the bay.*

ancient ['einʃənt] adj **1** relating to times long ago, *esp* before the collapse of Rome: *ancient history.* **2** very old: *an ancient sweater.*

and [ənd, and] conj **1** joining two statements, pieces of information *etc*: *I opened the door and went inside; The hat was blue and red; a mother and child.* **2** in addition to: *2 and*

2 makes 4. **3** as a result of which: *Try hard and you will succeed.* **4** used instead of 'to' with a verb: *Do try and come!*

anecdote ['anikdout] *n* a short amusing story, *esp* a true one: *He told us anecdotes about politicians that he knew.*

anesthetic *see* **anaesthetic**.

angel ['eindʒəl] *n* **1** a messenger or attendant of God: *The angels announced the birth of Christ to the shepherds.* **2** a very good or beautiful person: *She's an absolute angel about helping us.*
angelic [an'dʒelik] *adj* like an · angel. **an'gelically** *adv.*
'angel-fish *n* a brightly-coloured tropical fish with spiny fins.

anger ['angə] *n* a violent, bitter feeling (against someone or something): *He was filled with anger about the way he had been treated.* – *v* to make someone angry: *His words angered her very much.*
'angry *adj* **1** feeling or showing anger: *He was so angry that he was unable to speak*; *angry words*; *She is angry with him*; *The sky looks angry – it is going to rain.* **2** red and sore-looking: *He has an angry cut over his left eye.* **'angrily** *adv.*

angry at something: *We were angry at the delay.*
angry with someone: *He is angry with his sister.*

angle[1] ['angl] *n* **1** the (amount of) space between two straight lines or surfaces that meet: *an angle of 90°.* **2** a point of view: *from a journalist's angle.* **3** a corner.
angular ['angjulə] *adj* **1** having (sharp) angles: *an angular building.* **2** (of a person) thin and bony: *She is tall and angular.* **angularity** [-'la-] *n.*
angle[2] ['angl] *v* to use a rod and line to try to catch fish: *angling for trout.*
'angler *n* a person who fishes with a rod and line. **'angling** *n.*

Anglican ['anglikən] *n, adj* (a member) of the Church of England.

anglicize, -ise ['anglisaiz] *v* to make English or more like English: *After living in England for ten years, he had become very anglicized.*

Anglo- [anglou] (*as part of a word*) English: *Anglo-American.*

angry *see* **anger**.

angsana [aŋ'saːnə] *n* a large tropical tree with sweet-smelling yellow flowers.

anguish ['angwiʃ] *n* very great pain of body or mind; agony: *The woman suffered terrible anguish when her child died.*

angular, angularity *see* **angle**[1].

animal ['animəl] *n* **1** a living being which can feel things and move freely: *man and other animals.* **2** an animal other than man: *a*

book on man's attitude to animals; (*also adj*) *animal behaviour.*
animal eater an animal that eats only other animals: *Tigers and lions are animal eaters.*

animate ['animeit] *v* to make lively: *Joy animated his face.* – [-mət] *adj* living.
'animated [-mei-] *adj* **1** lively: *An animated discussion.* **2** made to move as if alive: *animated dolls/cartoons.* **,ani'mation** *n.*

animosity [ani'mosəti] *n* (a) strong dislike or hatred: *The rivals regarded one another with animosity.*

ankle ['aŋkl] *n* the (area around the) joint connecting the foot and leg: *She has broken her ankle.*

annals ['anlz] *n pl* yearly historical accounts of events: *This king is mentioned several times in annals of the period.*

annex [ə'neks] *v* to take possession of (*eg* a country). – ['aneks] (*also* **'annexe**) *n* a building added to, or used as an addition to, another building: *a hotel annexe.* **,annex'ation** [a-] *n.*

annihilate [ə'naiəleit] *v* to destroy completely: *The epidemic annihilated the population of the town.* **an,nihi'lation** *n.*

anniversary [anə'vəːsəri] – *pl* **anni'versaries** – *n* the day of the year on which something once happened and is remembered: *We celebrated our fifth wedding anniversary.*

announce [ə'nauns] *v* **1** to make known publicly: *Mary and John have announced their engagement.* **2** to make known the arrival or entrance of: *He announced the next singer.*
an'nouncement *n*: *an important announcement.*
an'nouncer *n* a person who introduces programmes or reads the news on radio or television.

annoy [ə'nɔi] *v* to make (someone) rather angry or impatient: *Please go away and stop annoying me!*
an'noyance *n* **1** something which annoys: *That noise has been an annoyance to me for weeks!* **2** the state of being annoyed: *He was red in the face with annoyance.*
an'noyed *adj* made angry: *My mother is annoyed with me*; *He was annoyed at her remarks.*
an'noying *adj*: *annoying habits.* **an'noyingly** *adv.*

annual ['anjuəl] *adj* **1** happening every year: *an annual event.* **2** of one year: *What is his annual salary?* – *n* **1** a book of which a new edition is published every year: *children's annuals.* **2** a plant that lives for only one year.
'annually *adv*: *His salary is increased annually.*

annul [ə'nʌl] – *pt, ptp* **an'nulled** – *v* to declare (that something is) not valid and cancel

Animals

Key

1	Cheetah	6	Porcupine
2	Otter	7	Rhinoceros
3	Deer	8	Ant-eater
4	(Water) buffalo	9	Gibbon
5	Jaguar	10	Orang-utan

(*esp* a marriage or legal contract). **an'nulment** *n*.

anoint [ə'noint] *v* to smear or cover with ointment or oil *esp* in a religious ceremony: *anointed by a priest*.

anon [ə'non] short for **anonymous**, when used instead of the name of the author of a poem *etc*.

anonymous [ə'nonəməs] *adj* without the name of the author, giver *etc* being known or given: *The donor wished to remain anonymous*; *an anonymous poem*. **a'nonymously** *adv*. **anonymity** [anə'niməti] *n*.

another [ə'nʌðə] *adj, pron* **1** a different (thing or person): *This letter isn't from Tom – it's from another friend of mine*; *The coat I bought was dirty, so the shop gave me another*. **2** (one) more of the same kind: *Have another biscuit!*; *You didn't tell me you wanted another of those!*

answer ['a:nsə] *n* **1** something said, written or done that is caused by a question *etc* from another person: *She refused to give an answer to his questions*. **2** the solution to a problem: *The answer to your transport difficulties is to buy a car*. – *v* **1** to make an answer to a question, problem, action *etc*: *Answer my questions, please*; *Why don't you answer the letter?* **2** to open (the door), pick up (the telephone) *etc* in reponse to a knock, ring *etc*: *He answered the telephone as soon as it rang*; *Could you answer the door, please?* **3** to be suitable or all that is necessary (for): *This will answer my requirements*. **4** (*often with* to) to be the same as or correspond to (a description *etc*): *The police have found a man answering (to) that description*.

'answerable *adj* (*usu with* to, for) to have the responsibility: *I will be answerable to you for his good behaviour*; *She is answerable for the whole project*.

answer for 1 (*often with* to) to bear the responsibility or be responsible for (something): *I'll answer to your mother for your safety*. **2** to suffer or be punished (for something): *You'll answer for your rudeness one day!*

ant [ant] *n* a type of small insect, related to bees, wasps *etc*, thought of as hardworking.

** **'ant-eater** *n* any of several toothless animals with long snouts, that feed on ants.

'ant-hill *n* a mound of earth built as a nest by ants.

antagonist [an'tagənist] *n* an opponent or enemy.

an'tagonism *n* unfriendliness, hostility. **an͵tago'nistic** *adj*. **an͵tago'nistically** *adv*.

an'tagonize, -ise *v* to make an enemy of (someone): *You are antagonizing her by your rudeness*.

Antarctic [ant'a:ktik] *adj, n* (with **the**) (of) the area round the South Pole.

antelope ['antəloup] – *pls* **'antelopes, 'antelope** – *n* any of several types of quick-moving, graceful, horned animal related to the goat and cow: *a herd of antelope*.

antenna [an'tenə] *n* **1** (*pl* **an'tennae** [-ni:]) a feeler of an insect. **2** (*pl* **an'tennas**) (*Amer*) an aerial (for a radio *etc*).

anthem ['anθəm] *n* **1** a piece of music for a church choir *usu* with words from the Bible. **2** a song of praise: *a national anthem*.

anthology [an'θolədʒi] – *pl* **an'thologies** – *n* a collection of pieces of poetry or prose: *an anthology of love poems*.

anthracite ['anθrəsait] *n* a kind of very hard coal that burns almost without any smoke or flames.

anthropology [anθrə'polədʒi] *n* the study of human society, customs, beliefs *etc*. **anthropo'logical** [-'lo-] *adj*. **͵anthro'pologist** *n*.

anti- [anti] (*as part of a word*) **1** against, as in **anti-aircraft**. **2** the opposite of, as in **anti-clockwise**.

anti-aircraft [anti'eəkra:ft] *adj* used against enemy aircraft: *anti-aircraft defences*.

antibiotic ['antibai'otik] *n* a medicine which is used to kill the bacteria that cause disease.

anticipate [an'tisəpeit] *v* **1** to expect (something): *I'm not anticipating any trouble*. **2** to see what is going to be wanted, required *etc* in the future and do what is necessary: *A businessman must try to anticipate what his customers will want*.

an͵tici'pation *n*: *I'm looking forward to the concert with anticipation* (= expectancy, excitement).

anticlimax [anti'klaimaks] *n* a dull or disappointing ending to a play, activity *etc* after increasing excitement: *After the weeks of preparation, the concert itself was a bit of an anticlimax*.

anticlockwise [anti'klokwaiz] *adv, adj* moving in the opposite direction to that in which the hands of a clock move: *The wheels turn anticlockwise*; *in an anticlockwise direction*.

antics ['antiks] *n pl* odd or amusing behaviour: *The children laughed at the monkey's antics*.

antidote ['antidout] *n* a medicine *etc* which is given to prevent a poison acting on a person *etc*: *If you are bitten by a poisonous snake, you have to be given an antidote*.

antifreeze ['antifri:z] *n* a substance which is added to a liquid, *usu* water (*eg* in the radiator of a car engine), to prevent it from freezing.

antique [an'ti:k] *adj* **1** old and *usu* valuable: *an antique chair*. **2** old or old-fashioned: *That car is positively antique*. **3** (of a shop *etc*) dealing in antiques: *an antique business*. – *n* something made long ago (*usu* more

than a hundred years ago) which is valuable or interesting: *He collects antiques.*

antiquated ['antikweitid] *adj* old or out of
fashion: *an antiquated car.*

antiquity [an'tikwəti] *n* **1** ancient times, *esp*
those of the ancient Greeks and Romans:
the gods and heroes of antiquity. **2** great
age: *a statue of great antiquity.* **3** (*pl*
an'tiquities) something remaining from
ancient times (*eg* a statue, a vase): *Roman
antiquities.*

antiseptic [anti'septik] *n, adj* (of) a substance
that destroys bacteria (*eg* in a wound): *You
ought to put some antiseptic on that cut; an
antiseptic cream.*

antisocial [anti'souʃəl] *adj* **1** against the welfare of the community *etc*: *It is antisocial to
drop rubbish in the street.* **2** not wanting the
company of others: *Since his wife died, he
has become more and more antisocial.*

antler ['antlə] *n* a deer's horn.

antonym ['antənim] *n* a word opposite in
meaning to another word. *Big and small are
antonyms.*

anvil ['anvil] *n* a block, *usu* of iron, on which
metal objects (*eg* horse-shoes) are hammered into shape: *the blacksmith's anvil.*

anxiety *see* **anxious.**

anxious ['aŋkʃəs] *adj* **1** worried about what
may happen or have happened: *She is
anxious about her father's health.* **2** causing
worry, fear or uncertainty: *an anxious moment.* **3** wanting very much (to do *etc* something): *He's very anxious to please.*
'anxiously *adv.*
anxiety [aŋ'zaiəti] *n*: *His health is a great
anxiety to me; filled with anxiety about her
child's health.*

any ['eni] *pron, adj* **1** one, some, no matter
which: *'Which dress shall I wear?' 'Wear
any (dress)'; 'Which dresses shall I pack?'
'Pack any (dresses)'.* **2** (in questions and
negative sentences *etc*) one, some: *John has
been to some interesting places but I've never
been to any; Have you been to any interesting places?; We have hardly any coffee left.* –
adj every: *Any schoolboy could tell you the
answer.* – *adv* at all; (even) by a small
amount: *Is this book any better than the last
one?; His writing hasn't improved any.*

'anybody, 'anyone *pron* **1** (in questions, and
negative sentences *etc*) some person: *Is
anybody there?* **2** any person, no matter
which: *Get someone to help* – *anyone will
do.* **3** everyone: *Anyone could tell you the
answer to that.*

'anyhow *adv* **1** anyway: *Anyhow, even if the
problem does arise, it won't affect us.* **2** in a
careless, untidy way: *Books piled anyhow on
shelves.*

'anything *pron* **1** (in questions, and negative
sentences *etc*) some thing: *Can you see

anything?; I can't see anything.* **2** a thing of
any kind: *You can buy anything you like;
'What would you like for your birthday?'
'Anything will do.'*

'anyway *adv* nevertheless; in spite of what
has been or might be said, done *etc*: *My
mother says I mustn't go but I'm going
anyway; Anyway, she can't stop you.*

'anywhere *adv* in any place at all: *Have you
seen my gloves anywhere?; I can't find them
anywhere; 'Where will I put these?' 'Anywhere will do.'*

at any rate at least: *It's a pity it has started
to rain, but at any rate we can still enjoy
ourselves at the cinema; The Queen is coming to see us – at any rate, that's what John
says.*

in any case nevertheless: *I don't believe the
story but I'll check it in any case.*

apart [ə'paːt] *adv* separated by a certain distance: *The trees were planted three metres
apart; with his feet apart; Their policies are
far apart; She sat apart from the other
people.*

apart from except for: *I can't think of
anything I need, apart from a car.*

come apart to break into pieces: *The book
came apart in my hands.*

take apart to separate (something) into the
pieces from which it is made: *He took the
engine apart.*

tell apart (*usu with* **can, cannot** *etc*) to
recognize the difference between; to distinguish: *I cannot tell the twins apart.*

apartment [ə'paːtmənt] *n* **1** a room, *usu*
rented, in a private house. **2** a flat. **3** a single
room in a house: *a five-apartment house.*

apathy ['apəθi] *n* a lack of interest or enthusiasm: *his apathy towards his work.*
,apa'thetic [-'θe-] *adj.* **,apa'thetically** *adv.*

ape [eip] *n* a large monkey with little or no
tail.

aperture ['apətjuə] *n* **1** an opening or hole.
2 (the size of) the opening (*eg* in a camera)
through which light passes.

apex ['eipeks] *n* the highest point or tip (of
something): *the apex of a triangle; the apex
of a person's career.*

aphid ['eifid] *n* a very small insect that lives on
plants, *esp* a greenfly.

apiary ['eipiəri] – *pl* **'apiaries** – *n* a place
(containing several hives) where bees are
kept.

apiece [ə'piːs] *adv* to, for, by *etc* each one of a
group: *They got two chocolates apiece.*

apologetic *see* **apologize.**

apologize, -ise [ə'polədʒaiz] *v* to say that one
is sorry, for having done something wrong,
for a fault *etc*: *I must apologize to her for
my rudeness.*
a,polo'getic [-'dʒetik] *adj* showing regret or
saying one is sorry for having done some-

thing wrong *etc*: *an apologetic letter*.
a,polo'getically *adv*.
a'pology – *pl* a'pologies – *n*: *Please accept my apology for not arriving on time*; *He made his apologies for not attending the meeting*.
apostle [ə'posl] *n* (*often with cap*) a man sent out to preach the gospel in the early Christian church, *esp* one of the twelve disciples of Christ: *Matthew and Mark were apostles*. **apostolic** [apə'stolik] *adj*.
apostrophe [ə'postrəfi] *n* a mark (') which is used to show that a letter or letters has/have been omitted from a word, and which is also used in possessive phrases and in the plurals of letters: *the boy's coat*; *the boys' coats*; *There are two n's in 'cannot' but only one in 'can't'*.
appal, (*Amer*) **appall** [ə'po:l] – *pt, ptp* ap'palled – *v* to horrify or shock: *We were appalled by the bomb damage*. ap'palling *adj*. ap'pallingly *adv*.
apparatus [apə'reitəs] – *pls* ,appa'ratus, ,appa'ratuses – *n* machinery, tools or equipment: *chemical apparatus*; *gymnastic apparatus*.
apparent [ə'parənt] *adj* 1 easy to see; evident: *It is quite apparent to all of us that you haven't done your work properly*. 2 seeming but perhaps not real: *his apparent unwillingness*.
ap'parently *adv* it seems that; I hear that: *Apparently he is not feeling well*.
appeal [ə:pi:l] *v* 1 (*often with* to) to ask earnestly for something: *She appealed (to him) for help*. 2 to take a case one has lost to a higher court *etc*; to ask (a referee, judge *etc*) for a new decision: *He appealed against a three-year sentence*. 3 (*with* to) to be pleasing: *This place appeals to me*. – *n* 1 (the act of making) a request (for help, a decision *etc*): *The appeal raised $500 for charity*; *a last appeal for help*; *The judge rejected his appeal*. 2 attraction: *Music holds little appeal for me*.
ap'pealing *adj* 1 pleasing: *an appealing little girl*. 2 showing that a person wishes help *etc*: *an appealing glance*.
appear [ə'piə] *v* 1 to come into view: *A man suddenly appeared round the corner*. 2 to arrive (at a place *etc*): *He appeared in time for dinner*. 3 to come before or present oneself/itself before the public or a judge *etc*: *He is appearing on television today*; *He appeared before Judge Scott*. 4 to look or seem as if (something is the case): *It appears that he is wrong*; *He appears to be wrong*.
ap'pearance *n* 1 what can be seen (of a person, thing *etc*): *From his appearance he seemed very wealthy*. 2 the act of coming into view or coming into a place: *The*

thieves ran off at the sudden appearance of two policemen. 3 the act of coming before or presenting oneself/itself before the public or a judge *etc*: *his first appearance on the stage*.
appease [ə'pi:z] *v* to calm or satisfy (a person, desire *etc*) *usu* by giving what was asked for or is needed: *She appeased his curiosity by explaining the situation to him*. ap'peasement *n*.
appendicitis [əpendi'saitis] *n* the inflammation of the appendix in the body which *usu* causes pain and often requires the removal of the appendix by surgery.
appendix [ə'pendiks] *n* 1 (*pl* sometimes ap'pendices [-si:z]) a section, *usu* containing extra information, added at the end of a book, document *etc*. 2 a narrow tube leading from the large intestine: *She's had her appendix removed*.
appetite ['apitait] *n* a desire for food: *Exercise gives you a good appetite*.
'appetizer, -s- *n* (*esp Amer*) something eaten or drunk before or at the beginning of a meal in order to increase the appetite: *They ate smoked salmon as an appetizer*.
'appetizing, -s- *adj* which increases the appetite: *an appetizing smell*.
applaud [ə'plo:d] *v* to praise or show approval, by clapping the hands: *to applaud a speech/a singer*.
ap'plause [-z] *n* praise or approval, expressed by clapping: *The President received great applause at the end of his speech*.
apple ['apl] *n* a round fruit (*usu* with a green or red skin) which can be eaten: *an apple tree*; *a slice of apple*.
the apple of someone's eye a person or thing which is greatly loved: *She is the apple of her father's eye*.
upset the apple cart to bring into disorder: *The football team were doing very well when their best player upset the apple cart by breaking his leg*.
apply [ə'plai] *v* 1 (*with* to) to put (something) on or against something else: *to apply ointment to a cut*. 2 (*with* to) to use (something) for some purpose: *He applied his wits to planning their escape*. 3 (*with* for) to ask for (something) formally: *You could apply (to the manager) for a job*. 4 (*with* to) to concern: *This rule does not apply to him*. 5 to be in force: *The rule doesn't apply at weekends*.
ap'pliance [ə'plai-] *n* an instrument or tool used for a particular job: *washing-machines and other electrical appliances*.
'applicable ['apli-] *adj*: *This rule is not applicable (to me) any longer*. ,applica'bility *n*.
'applicant ['apli-] *n* a person who applies

(for a job *etc*): *There were two hundred applicants for the job.*

,appli'cation [apli-] *n* **1** a formal request; an act of applying: *several applications for the new job; The syllabus can be obtained on application to the headmaster.* **2** hard work: *He has got a good job through sheer application.* **3** an ointment *etc* applied to a cut, wound *etc*.

apply oneself, one's mind (*with* to) to give one's full attention or energy (to a task *etc*): *If he would apply himself he could pass his exams.*

appoint [ə'point] *v* **1** to give (a person) a job or position: *They appointed him manager; They have appointed a new manager.* **2** to fix or agree on (a time for something): *to appoint a time for a meeting.*

ap'pointed *adj*: *He arrived before the appointed time.*

ap'pointment *n* **1** (an) arrangement to meet someone; *I made an appointment to see him.* **2** the job or position to which a person is appointed: *His appointment was for one year only.*

appreciate [ə'pri:ʃieit] *v* **1** to be grateful for (something): *I appreciate all your hard work.* **2** to value (someone or something) highly: *Mothers are very often not appreciated.* **3** understand; to be aware of: *I appreciate your difficulties but I cannot help.* **4** to increase in value: *My house has appreciated (in value) considerably over the last ten years.*

ap'preciable [-ʃəbl] *adj* noticeable; considerable: *an appreciable increase.* **ap'preciably** [-ʃəbli] *adv.*

ap,preci'ation *n* **1** gratefulness: *I wish to show my appreciation for what you have done.* **2** the state of valuing or understanding something: *a deep appreciation of poetry.* **3** the state of being aware of something: *He has no appreciation of our difficulties.* **4** an increase in value. **5** a written article *etc* which describes the qualities of something: *an appreciation of the new book.*

ap'preciative [-ʃətiv] *adj* giving due thanks or praise; grateful: *an appreciative audience.* **ap'preciatively** *adv.*

apprehend [apri'hend] *v* **1** to arrest: *The police apprehended the thief.* **2** to understand.

,appre'hension [-ʃən] *n* **1** fear. **2** understanding.

,appre'hensive [-siv] *adj* anxious; worried: *an apprehensive expression.* **,appre'hensively** *adv.* **,appre'hensiveness** *n.*

apprentice [ə'prentis] *n* a (*usu* young) person who is leaning a trade. – *v* to make (someone) an apprentice: *His father apprenticed him to an engineer.*

ap'prenticeship *n* the state of being, or the

time during which a person is, an apprentice: *He is serving his apprenticeship as a mechanic.*

approach [ə'proutʃ] *v* to come near (to): *The car approached (the traffic lights) at top speed; Christmas is approaching.* – *n* **1** the act of coming near: *The boys ran off at the approach of a policeman.* **2** a road, path *etc* leading to a place: *All the approaches to the village were blocked by fallen rock.* **3** an attempt to obtain or attract a person's help, interest etc: *They have made an approach to the government for help; That fellow makes approaches to (* = he tries to become friendly with) *every woman he meets.*

ap'proachable *adj* **1** friendly. **2** that can be reached: *The village is not approachable by road.*

ap'proaching *adj*: *the approaching dawn.*

approbation [aprə'beiʃən] *n* approval: *His bravery received the approbation of the whole town.*

appropriate [ə'proupriət] *adj* suitable; proper: *Her clothes were appropriate to the occasion; Complain to the appropriate authority.* **ap'propriateness** *n.*

ap'propriately *adv* suitably: *appropriately dressed for the occasion.*

approve [ə'pru:v] *v* **1** (often *with* of) to be pleased with or think well of (a person, thing *etc*): *I approve of your decision.* **2** to agree to (something): *The committee approved the plan.*

ap'proval *n* the act or state of agreeing to or being pleased with (a person, thing *etc*): *This proposal meets with my approval.*

on approval to be sent or given back to a shop *etc* if not satisfactory: *She bought two dresses on approval.*

approximate [ə'proksimət] *adj* very nearly correct or accurate; not intended to be absolutely correct: *Give me an approximate answer!; Can you give me an approximate price for the job?*

ap'proximately *adv* nearly; more or less: *There will be approximately five hundred people present.*

ap,proxim'ation *n* **1** a figure, answer *etc* which is not (intended to be) exact: *This figure is just an approximation.* **2** the process of estimating a figure *etc*: *We decided on a price by a process of approximation.*

apricot ['eiprikɔt] *n* an orange-coloured fruit like a small peach.

April ['eiprəl] *n* the fourth month of the year, the month following March.

apron ['eiprən] *n* **1** a piece of cloth, plastic *etc* worn over the front of the clothes for protection against dirt *etc*: *She tied on her apron before preparing the dinner.* **2** something like an apron in shape, *eg* a hard surface for aircraft on an airfield. **3** (also 'apron-stage) the part of the stage in a theatre which is in front of the curtain.

apt [apt] adj 1 (with to) likely: He is apt to get angry if you ask a lot of questions. 2 suitable: an apt remark. 3 clever; quick to learn: an apt student. 'aptly adv. 'aptness n.

aptitude ['aptitju:d] n (sometimes with for) (a) talent or ability: an aptitude for mathematics.

aqualung ['akwəlʌŋ] n an apparatus worn by divers on their backs which supplies them with oxygen to breathe.

aquarium [ə'kweəriəm] – pls a'quariums, a'quaria – n a glass tank, or a building containing tanks, for keeping fish and other water animals.

aquatic [ə'kwatik] adj living, growing, or taking place in water: aquatic plants/sports.

Arabic ['arəbik] : Arabic numerals 1, 2 etc, as opposed to Roman numerals, I, II etc.

arable ['arəbl] adj on which crops are grown: arable land.

arbitrary ['a:bitrəri] adj not decided by rules or laws but by a person's own opinion: He made a rather arbitrary decision to close the local cinema without consulting other people. 'arbitrarily adv.

arbitrate ['a:bitreit] v to act as an arbitrator in a dispute etc: He has been asked to arbitrate in the dispute between the workers and management.
,arbi'tration n the making of a decision by an arbitrator: The dispute has gone/was taken to arbitration.
'arbitrator n a person who makes a judgement in a dispute etc.

arc [a:k] n a part of the line which forms a circle or other curve.

arcade [a:'keid] n a covered passage or area usu with shops, stalls etc: a shopping arcade; an amusement arcade.

arch [a:tʃ] n 1 the top part of a door etc or a support for a roof etc which is built in the shape of a curve. 2 a monument which is shaped like an arch: the Marble Arch in London. 3 anything that is like an arch in shape: The rainbow formed an arch in the sky. 4 the raised part of the sole of the foot.
– v to (cause to) be in the shape of an arch: The cat arched its back.
arched adj: an arched doorway.
'archway n an arched passage, door or entrance.

archaeology [a:ki'olədʒi] n the study of objects belonging to ancient times (eg buildings, tools etc found in the earth).
archae'ologist n.
,archaeo'logical [-'lo-] adj: archaeological research/remains.

archangel [a:keindʒel] n a chief angel.

archbishop [a:tʃ'biʃəp] n a chief bishop.

archer ['a:tʃə] n a person who shoots with a bow and arrows.
'archery n the art or sport of shooting with a bow.

archipelago [a:ki'peləgou] – pl ,archi'-pelago(e)s – n a group of islands.

architect ['a:kitekt] n a person who designs buildings etc.
'architecture [-tʃə] n the art of designing buildings: He's studying architecture; modern architecture. ,archi'tectural adj.

archives ['a:kaivz] n pl (a place for keeping) old documents, historical records etc.
'archivist [-ki-] n a person who looks after archives.

archway see arch.

Arctic ['a:ktik] adj 1 of the area round the North Pole: the Arctic wilderness. 2 (no cap) very cold: arctic conditions.
the Arctic the area round the North Pole.

ardent ['a:dənt] adj enthusiastic; passionate: an ardent supporter of a political party.
'ardently adv.

ardour, (Amer) ardor ['a:də] n enthusiasm; passion.

arduous ['a:djuəs, (Amer) -dʒu-] adj difficult; needing hard work: an arduous task.
'arduously adv. 'arduousness n.

are see be.

area ['eəriə] n 1 the extent or size of a flat surface: This garden is twelve square metres in area. 2 a place; part (of a town etc): Do you live in this area?

arena [ə'ri:nə] n any place for a public show contest etc: a sports arena.

aren't see be.

argue ['a:gju:] v (with with someone, about something) to quarrel with (a person) or discuss (something) with a person in a not very friendly way: I'm not going to argue; Will you children stop arguing with each other about whose toy that is! 2 (with for, against) to suggest reasons for or for not doing something: I argued for/against accepting the plan. 3 (with into, out of) to persuade (a person) (not) to do something: I'll try to argue him into going; He argued her out of buying the dress. 4 to discuss, giving one's reasoning: She argued the point very cleverly.
'arguable adj able to be put forward in argument: It is arguable that he would have been better to go.
'argument n 1 a quarrel or unfriendly discussion: They are having an argument about/over whose turn it is. 2 a set of reasons; a piece of reasoning: The argument for/against going; a philosophical argument.
,argu'mentative [-'mentətiv] adj fond of arguing.

arid ['arid] adj dry: The soil is rather arid.
a'ridity, 'aridness ns.

arise [ə'raiz] – pt arose [ə'rouz] : ptp arisen [ə'rizn] – v 1 to come into being: *These problems have arisen as a result of your carelessness*; *Are there any matters arising from our earlier discussion?* 2 to get up or stand up.

aristocracy [arə'stokrəsi] n in some countries, the nobility and others of the highest social class, who *usu* own land.
  'aristocrat [-krat, (*Amer*) ə'ristəkrat] n a member of the aristocracy.
  ,aristo'cratic [-'kra-, (*Amer*) ə,ristə'kratik] adj (of people, behaviour *etc*) proud and noble-looking: *an aristocratic manner*.
  ,aristo'cratically adv.

arithmetic [ə'riθmətik] n the art of counting by numbers. arithmetical [ariθ'metikl] adj.

arm¹ [a:m] n 1 the part of the body between the shoulder and the hand: *He has broken both his arms*. 2 anything shaped like or similar to this: *She sat on the arm of the chair*.
  'armful n as much as a person can hold in one arm or in both arms: *an armful of flowers/clothes*.
  'armband n a strip of cloth *etc* worn round the arm: *The people all wore black armbands as a sign of mourning*.
  'armchair n a chair with arms at each side.
  'armpit n the hollow under the arm at the shoulder.
  ,arm-in-'arm adv (of two or more people) with arms linked together: *They walked along arm-in-arm*.
  keep at arm's length to avoid becoming too friendly with someone: *She keeps her new neighbours at arm's length*.
  with open arms with a very friendly welcome: *He greeted them with open arms*.

arm² [a:m] v 1 to give weapons to (a person *etc*): *to arm the police*. 2 to prepare for battle, war *etc*: *They armed for battle*.
  armed adj having a weapon or weapons: *An armed man robbed the bank*; *Armed forces entered the country*.
  arms n pl 1 weapons: *Does the police force carry arms?* 2 a design *etc* which is used as the symbol of the town, family *etc* (*see also* coat of arms).
  be up in arms to be very angry and make a great protest (about something): *He is up in arms about the decision to close the road*.
  take up arms (*often with* against) to begin fighting: *The peasants took up arms against the dictator*.

armament ['a:məmənt] n (*usu in pl*) equipment for war, *eg* the guns *etc* of a ship, tank *etc*.

armistice ['a:mistis] n (an agreement) stopping fighting (in a war, battle *etc*): *An armistice was declared*.

armour, (*Amer*) armor ['a:mə] n 1 formerly, a metal suit worn by knights *etc* as a protection while fighting: *a suit of armour*. 2 a metal covering to protect ships, tanks *etc* against damage from weapons.
  'armoured adj 1 (of vehicles *etc*) protected by armour: *an armoured car*. 2 made up of armoured vehicles: *an armoured division of an army*.
  'armoury – pl 'armouries – n the place where weapons are made or kept.

army ['a:mi] – pl 'armies – n 1 a large number of men armed and organized for war: *The two armies met at dawn*. 2 a large number (of people *etc*): *an army of tourists*.

aroma [ə'roumə] n the (*usu* pleasant) smell that a substance has or gives off: *the aroma of coffee*.
  aromatic [arə'matik] adj: *aromatic herbs*.

arose see arise.

around [ə'raund] prep, adv 1 on all sides of or in a circle about (a person, thing *etc*): *Flowers grew around the tree*; *They danced around the fire*; *There were flowers all around*. 2 here and there (in a house, room *etc*): *Clothes had been left lying around (the house)*; *I wandered around*. – prep near to (a time, place *etc*): *around three o'clock*. – adv 1 in the opposite direction: *Turn around!* 2 near-by: *If you need me, I'll be somewhere around*.

arouse [ə'rauz] v to cause or give rise to (something): *His actions aroused my suspicions*.

arrange [ə'reindʒ] v 1 to put in some sort of order: *Arrange these books in alphabetical order*; *She arranged the flowers in a vase*. 2 to plan or make decisions (about future events): *We have arranged a meeting for next week*; *I have arranged to meet him tomorrow*. 3 to make (a piece of music) suitable for particular voices or instruments: *music arranged for choir and orchestra*.
  ar'rangement n: *I like the arrangement of the furniture*; *flower-arrangements*; *They've finally come to some sort of arrangement about sharing expenses*; *a new arrangement for guitar and orchestra*.
  ar'rangements n pl plans; preparations: *Have you made any arrangments for a meeting with him?*; *funeral arrangements*.

array [ə'rei] 1 things, people *etc* arranged in some order: *an impressive array of fabrics*. 2 clothes: *in fine array*. – v 1 to put (things, people *etc*) in some order for show *etc*: *goods arrayed on the counter*. 2 to dress (oneself) *eg* in fine clothes.

arrears [ə'riəz] n pl money which should have been paid because it is owed but which has not been paid: *rent arrears*.
  in arrears not up to date (*eg* in payments): *He is in arrears with his rent*.

arrest [ə'rest] *v* **1** to capture or take hold of (a person) because he or she has broken the law: *The police arrested the thief.* **2** to stop: *Economic difficulties arrested the growth of industry.* – **1** the act of arresting; being arrested: *The police made several arrests*; *He was questioned after his arrest.* **2** a stopping of action: *Cardiac arrest is another term for heart failure.*

under arrest in the position of having been arrested: *The thief was placed under arrest.*

arrive [ə'raiv] *v* to reach (a place, the end of a journey *etc*): *They arrived home last night*; *The parcel arrived yesterday.*

ar'rival *n* **1** the act of arriving: *I was greeted by my sister on my arrival.* **2** a person, thing *etc* that has arrived: *I wish he would stop calling our baby the new arrival.*

arrive at to reach: *The committee failed to arrive at a decision.*

arrogant ['arəgənt] *adj* extremely proud; thinking that one is much more important than other people. **'arrogantly** *adv.* **'arrogance** *n.*

arrow ['arou] *n* **1** a thin, straight stick with a point, which is fired from a bow. **2** a sign shaped like an arrow *eg* to show which way to go: *You can't get lost – just follow the arrows.*

arrowhead *n* **1** a water plant with leaves shaped like an arrowhead. **2** the tip of an arrow, shaped to a point.

arsenal ['a:sənl] *n* a factory or store for weapons, ammunition *etc.*

arsenic [a:snik] *n* **1** an element used to make certain poisons. **2** a poison made with arsenic.

arson ['a:sn] *n* the crime of setting fire to (a building *etc*) on purpose.

art [a:t] *n* **1** painting and sculpture: *I'm studying art at school*; *Do you like modern art?*; (*also adj*) *an art gallery, an art college.* **2** any of various creative forms of expression: *painting, music, dancing, writing and the other arts.* **3** an ability or skill; the (best) way of doing something: *the art of conversation/war.*

'artful *adj* clever; having a lot of skill (*usu* in a bad sense): *an artful thief.* **'artfully** *adv.* **'artfulness** *n.*

arts *n pl* (*often with cap*) languages, literature, history, as opposed to scientific subjects.

artery ['a:təri] – *pl* **'arteries** – *n* **1** a blood-vessel that carries the blood from the heart through the body. **2** a main route of travel and transport.

arterial [a:'tiəriəl] *adj*: *arterial disease*; *arterial roads.*

artful *see* art.

arthritis [a:'θraitis] *n* pain and swelling in the joints of the body. **ar'thritic** [-'θri-] *adj.*

article ['a:tikl] *n* **1** a thing or an object: *This shop sells articles of all kinds*; *articles of clothing.* **2** a piece of writing in a newspaper or magazine: *He has written an article on the new sports centre for a local magazine.* **3 the** (the definite article) or **a/an** (the indefinite article).

articulate [a:'tikjuleit] *v* to speak or pronounce: *The teacher articulated (his words) very carefully.* – [-lət] *adj* able to express one's thoughts clearly: *He's unusually articulate for a three-year-old child.* **ar'ticulately** [-lət-] *adv.* **ar'ticulateness** [-lət-] *n.* **ar,ticu'lation** *n.*

artificial [a:ti'fiʃəl] *adj* made by man; not natural; not real: *artificial flowers*; *Did you look at the colour in artificial light or in daylight?* **art'ficially** *adv.* **,artifici'ality** [-ʃi'a-] *n.*

artificial respiration the process of forcing air into and out of the lungs *eg* of a person who has almost drowned.

artillery [a:'tiləri] *n* **1** large guns. **2** (*often with cap*) the part of an army which looks after and fires such guns.

artisan ['a:tizan, (*Amer*) -zn] *n* a skilled workman.

artist ['a:tist] *n* **1** a person who paints pictures or is a sculptor or is skilled at one of the other arts. **2** a singer, dancer, actor *etc*; an artiste: *He announced the names of the artists who were taking part in the show.*

ar'tistic *adj* **1** liking or skilled in painting, music *etc*: *She draws and paints – she's very artistic.* **2** created or done with skill and good taste: *That flower-arrangement looks very artistic.* **ar'tistically** *adv.*

'artistry *n* artistic skill: *the musician's artistry.*

artiste [a:'ti:st] *n* a person who performs in a theatre, circus *etc*: *a troupe of circus artistes.*

as [az] *conj* **1** when; while: *I met John as I was coming home*; *We'll be able to talk as we go.* **2** because: *As I am leaving tomorrow, I've bought you a present.* **3** in the same way that: *If you are not sure how to behave, do as I do.* **4** used to introduce a statement of what the speaker knows or believes to be the case: *As you know, I'll be leaving tomorrow.* **5** though: *Old as I am, I can still fight*; *Much as I want to, I cannot go.* **6** used to refer to something which has already been stated and apply it to another person: *Tom is English, as are Dick and Harry.* – *adv* used in comparisons, *eg* the first *as* in the following example: *The bread was as hard as a brick.* – *prep* **1** used in comparisons, *eg* the second *as* in the following example: *The bread was as hard as a brick.* **2** like: *He was dressed as a woman.* **3** with certain verbs *eg* regard, treat, describe, ac-

cept: *I am regarded by some people as a bit of a fool*; *He treats the children as adults.* **4** in the position of: *He is greatly respected both as a person and as a politician.*

as for with regard to; concerning: *The thief was caught by the police almost immediately. As for the stolen jewels, they were found in a dustbin.*

as if/as though in the way one would expect if: *He acted as if he were mad*; *He spoke as though he knew all about our plans*; *He opened his mouth as if to speak*; *You look as if you are going to faint.*

as to as far as (something) is concerned; with regard to: *I'm willing to read his book, but as to publishing it, that's a different matter.*

asbestos [az'bestɔs] *n*, *adj* (of) a mineral that will not burn which can protect against fire: *an asbestos suit.*

ascend [ə'send] *v* to climb, go, or rise up: *The smoke ascended into the air.*

a'scendancy/a'scendency *n* control or power (over): *They have the ascendancy over the other political groups.*

a'scent [-t] *n* **1** the act of climbing or going up: *The ascent of Mount Everest.* **2** a slope upwards: *a steep ascent.*

ascend the throne to be crowned king or queen.

ascertain [asə'tein] *v* to find out: *We shall never ascertain the truth.* ,ascer'tainable *adj.*

ascetic [ə'setik] *adj* avoiding pleasure and comfort, *esp* for religious reasons: *Monks lead ascetic lives.* – *n* an ascetic person. **a'scetically** *adv.* **a'sceticism** [-sizəm] *n.*

ascribe [ə'skraib] *v* to think of as done or caused by someone or something: *He ascribed his success to the help of his friends.*

ash [aʃ] *n* the dust *etc* that remains after anything is burnt: *cigarette ash*; *the ashes of the bonfire.*

'ashen *adj* (of someone's face *etc*) very pale with shock *etc.*

'ashes *n pl* the remains of a human body after cremation: *Her ashes were scattered at sea.*

'ashtray *n* a dish or other container for cigarette ash.

ashamed [ə'ʃeimd] *adj* feeling shame: *He was ashamed of his bad work, ashamed to admit his mistake, ashamed of himself.*

ashore [ə'ʃoː] *adv* on or on to the shore: *The sailor went ashore.*

aside [ə'said] *adv* on or to one side: *They stood aside to let her pass*; *I've put aside two tickets for you to collect.* – *n* words spoken (*esp* by an actor) which other people (on the stage) are not supposed to hear: *She whispered an aside to him.*

put aside (*often with* **for**) to keep (something) for a particular person or occasion: *Would you put this book aside for me and I'll* collect it later; *We have put aside the dress you ordered.*

ask [aːsk] *v* **1** to put a question: *He asked me what the time was*; *Ask the price of that scarf*; *Ask her where to go*; *Ask him about it*; *If you don't know, ask.* **2** to express a wish to someone for something: *I asked her to help me*; *I asked (him) for a day off*; *He rang and asked for you*; *Can I ask a favour of you?* **3** to invite: *He asked her to his house for lunch.*

ask after to make inquiries about the health *etc* of: *She asked after his father.*

ask for 1 to express a wish to see or speak to (someone): *When he telephoned he asked for you*; *He is very ill and keeps asking for his daughter.* **2** to behave as if inviting (something unpleasant): *Going for a swim when you have a cold is just as asking for trouble.*

for the asking you may have (something) simply by asking for it; *This table is yours for the asking.*

asleep [ə'sliːp] *adj* **1** sleeping: *The baby is asleep.* **2** of arms and legs *etc*, numb: *My foot's asleep.*

fall asleep: *He fell asleep eventually.*

aspect ['aspekt] *n* **1** a part of something to be thought about: *We must consider every aspect of the problem.* **2** a side of a building *etc* or the direction it faces in. **3** look or appearance: *His face had a frightening aspect.*

asphalt ['asfalt, (*Amer*) -foːlt] *n*, *adj* (of) a mixture containing tar, used to make roads, pavements *etc*: *The workmen are laying asphalt*; *an asphalt playground.*

aspire [ə'spaiə] *v* (*usu with* **to**) to try very hard to reach (something difficult, ambitious *etc*): *He aspired to the position of president.* ,aspi'ration [aspi-] *n* (*often in pl*) an ambition: *aspirations to become a writer.*

aspirin ['aspərin] *n* a (tablet of a) kind of pain-killing drug: *The child has a fever – give her some/an aspirin.*

ass [as] *n* **1** a donkey. **2** a stupid person.

assail [ə'seil] *v* to attack, torment: *He was assailed with questions*; *assailed by doubts.* **as'sailant** *n* a person who attacks: *His assailant came up behind him in the dark.*

assassinate [ə'sasineit] *v* to murder, *esp* for political reasons: *The president was assassinated by terrorists.* **as,sassi'nation** *n.* **as'sassin** *n* a person who assassinates.

assault [ə'soːlt] *v* **1** to attack, *esp* suddenly: *The youths assaulted the night watchman.* **2** to attack sexually; to rape. – *n* **1** a (sudden) attack: *a night assault on the fortress*; *His speech was a vicious assault on his opponent.* **2** a sexual attack; a rape.

assemble [ə'sembl] *v* **1** (of people) to come together: *The crowd assembled in the hall.*

2 to call or bring together: *He assembled his family and told them of his plan.* **3** to put together (a machine *etc*): *He assembled the model aeroplane.*

as'sembly *n* **1** a collection of people (*usu* for a particular purpose): *a legislative assembly*; *The school meets for morning assembly at 8.30.* **2** the act of assembling or putting together.

assent [ə'sent] *n* agreement: *The Queen gave the royal assent to the bill.* – *v* (*with* **to**) to agree: *They assented to the proposal.*

assert [ə'sɔːt] *v* **1** to say definitely: *She asserted that she had not borrowed his book.* **2** to insist on: *He should assert his independence.* **as'sertion** [-ʃən] *n*.

as'sertive [-tiv] *adj* (too) inclined to assert oneself.

assert oneself to state one's opinions confidently and act in a way that will make people take notice of one: *You must assert yourself more if you want promotion.*

assess [ə'ses] *v* **1** to estimate or judge the quality or quantity of: *Can you assess my chances of winning?* **2** to estimate in order to calculate tax due on: *My income has been assessed wrongly.* **as'sessment** *n*. **as'sessor** *n*.

asset ['aset] *n* anything useful or valuable; an advantage: *He is a great asset to the school.* **'assets** *n pl* the total property, money *etc* of a person, company *etc*.

assign [ə'sain] *v* **1** to give to someone as his share or duty: *They assigned the task to us.* **2** to order or appoint: *He assigned three men to the job.*

as'signment *n* a duty assigned to someone: *You must complete this assignment by tomorrow.*

assimilate [ə'siməleit] *v* to take in and digest: *Plants assimilate food from the earth*; *I can't assimilate all these facts at once.* **as,simi'lation** *n*.

assist [ə'sist] *v* to help: *The junior doctor assisted the surgeon at the operation.*

as'sistance *n* help: *Do you need assistance?* **as'sistant** *n* **1** a person who assists; a helper: *a laboratory assistant*; (*also adj*) *an assistant headmaster.* **2** a person who serves in a shop.

associate [ə'sousieit] *v* **1** to connect in the mind: *He always associated the smell of tobacco with his father.* **2** (*usu with* **with**) to join (with someone) in friendship or work: *They don't usually associate (with each other) after office hours.* – [-et] *adj* **1** having a lower position or rank: *an associate professor.* **2** joined or connected: *associate organizations.* – *n* a colleague or partner; a companion.

association *n* **1** a club, society *etc*. **2** a friendship or partnership. **3** a connection in the mind: *The house had associations with her dead husband.*

in association with together with: *We are acting in association with the London branch of our firm.*

assorted [ə'sɔːtid] *adj* mixed; of or containing various different kinds: *assorted colours*; *assorted sweets.*

as'sortment *n* a mixture or variety: *an assortment of garments.*

assume [ə'sjuːm] *v* **1** to take or accept as true: *I assume (that) you'd like time to decide.* **2** to take upon oneself or accept (authority, responsibility *etc*): *He assumed the rôle of leader in the emergency.* **3** to put on (a particular appearance *etc*): *He assumed a look of horror.*

as'sumed *adj* pretended; not genuine: *assumed astonishment*; *He wrote under an assumed name* (= not using his real name). **as'sumption** [-'sʌmp-] *n* something assumed: *On the assumption that we can produce four pages an hour, the work will be finished tomorrow.*

assure [ə'ʃuə] *v* **1** to tell positively: *I assured him (that) the house was empty.* **2** to make (someone) sure: *You may be assured that we shall do all we can to help.*

as'surance *n* **1** confidence: *an air of assurance.* **2** a promise: *He gave me his assurance that he would help.* **3** insurance: *life assurance.*

as'sured *adj* certain and confident: *an assured young woman.*

asterisk ['astərisk] *n* a star-shaped mark (*) used in printing to draw attention to a note *etc*.

asthma ['asmə, (*Amer*) 'azmə] *n* an illness which causes difficulty in breathing out, resulting from an allergy *etc*. **asthmatic** [as'matik, (*Amer*) az-] *adj*.

astonish [ə'stoniʃ] *v* to surprise greatly: *I was astonished by his ignorance.* **a'stonishing** *adj*: *an astonishing sight.* **a'stonishment** *n*: *To my astonishment she burst into tears.*

astound ['əstaund] *v* to make (someone) very surprised: *I was astounded to hear of his imprisonment.* **a'stounding** *adj*: *an astounding piece of news.*

astray [ə'strei] away from the right direction; missing, lost: *The letter has gone astray*; *We were led astray by the inaccurate map.*

astride [ə'straid] *prep* with legs on each side of: *She sat astride the horse.* – *adv* (with legs) apart: *He stood with legs astride.*

astrology [ə'strolədʒi] *n* the study of the stars and their influence on people's lives: *I don't have faith in astrology.* **a'strologer** *n*. **astrological** [astrə'lodʒikl] *adj*.

***astronaut** ['astrənoːt] *n* a person who travels

in space: *Who was the first astronaut to land on the moon?*

astronomy [ə'stronəmi] *n* the study of the stars and their movements: *He is studying astronomy.* **a'stronomer** *n.*

astronomic(al) [astrə'nomik(l)] *adj* **1** (of numbers or amounts very large: *The cost of the new building was astronomical.* **2** of astronomy: *astronomical observations.*

astute [ə'stju:t] *adj* clever: *an astute businessman.* **a'stuteness** *n.*

asylum [ə'sailəm] *n* **1** safety; protection: *He was granted political asylum.* **2** an old name for a home for people who are mentally ill.

at [at] *prep* showing **1** position: *They are not at home; She lives at 33 Forest Road.* **2** direction: *He looked at her; She shouted at the boys.* **3** time: *He arrived at ten o'clock; The children came at the sound of the bell.* **4** state or occupation: *The countries are at war; She is at work.* **5** pace or speed: *He drove at 120 kilometres per hour.* **6** cost: *bread at $1.20 a loaf.*

at all in any way: *I don't like it at all.*

atap *see* **attap.**

ate *see* **eat.**

atheism ['eiθiizəm] *n* the belief that there is no God.

'atheist *n* a person who does not believe in God.

,athe'istic *adj.*

athlete ['aθli:t] *n* a person who is good at sport, *esp* running, jumping *etc*: *Hundreds of athletes took part in the games.*

ath'letic [-'le-] *adj* **1** of athletics: *He is taking part in the athletic events.* **2** good at athletics; strong and able to move easily and quickly: *He looks very athletic.*

ath'letics [-'le-] *n sing* the sports of running, jumping *etc* or competitions in these: *Athletics was my favourite activity at school.*

atlas ['atləs] *n* a book of maps: *My atlas is out of date.*

atmosphere ['atməsfiə] *n* **1** the air surrounding the earth: *The atmosphere is polluted.* **2** any surrounding feeling: *There was a friendly atmosphere in the village.*

,atmos'pheric [-'fe-] *adj*: *atmospheric disturbances.*

atom ['atəm] *n* **1** the smallest part of an element. **2** anything very small: *There's not an atom of truth in what she says.*

a'tomic [-'to-] *adj.*

atom(ic) bomb a bomb using atomic energy.

atomic energy very great energy obtained by breaking up the atoms of some substances.

atomic power power (for making electricity *etc*) obtained from atomic energy.

atrocious [ə'trouʃəs] *adj* **1** very bad: *Your handwriting is atrocious.* **2** extremely cruel: *an atrocious crime.* **a'trociousness** *n.*

atrocity [ə'trosəti] *n* an extremely cruel and

wicked act: *The invading army committed many atrocities.*

attach [ə'tatʃ] *v* to fasten or join: *I attached a label to my bag.*

at'tached *adj* (*with* **to**) fond of: *I'm very attached to my brother.*

at'tachment *n* **1** something extra attached: *There are several attachments for this food-mixer.* **2** (*with* **for/to**) liking or affection: *I feel attachment for this town.*

attack [ə'tak] *v* **1** to make a sudden, violent attempt to hurt or damage: *He attacked me with a knife; The village was attacked from the air.* **2** to speak or write against: *The Prime Minister's policy was attacked in the newspapers.* **3** (in games) to attempt to score a goal. **4** to make a vigorous start on: *It's time we attacked that pile of work.* – *n* **1** an act or the action of attacking: *The brutal attack killed the old man; They made an air attack on the town.* **2** a sudden bout of illness: *heart attack; an attack of 'flu.*

attain [ə'tein] *v* to gain; to achieve: *He attained all his ambitions.*

attap, atap ['atap] *n* the nipah palm, whose leaves are used for thatching.

attempt [ə'tempt] *v* to try: *He attempted to reach the dying man, but did not succeed; He did not attempt the last question in the exam.* – *n* **1** a try: *They failed in their attempt to climb Everest; She made no attempt to run away.* **2** an attack: *They made an attempt on his life but he survived.*

attend [ə'tend] *v* **1** to go to or be present at: *He attended the meeting; He will attend school till he is sixteen.* **2** (*with* **to**) to listen or give attention to: *Attend carefully to what the teacher is saying!* **3** to deal with: *I'll attend to that problem tomorrow.* **4** to look after; to help or serve: *Two doctors attended her all through her illness; The queen was attended by four ladies.*

at'tendance *n*: *His attendance* (= the number of times he attends) *at school is poor; Attendances* (= the number of people attending) *at the concerts went down after the price of tickets increased.*

at'tendant *n* a person employed to look after someone or something: *a car-park attendant.*

in attendance in the position of helping or serving: *There was no doctor in attendance at the road accident.*

attendance ends in **-ance** (not **-ence**).

attention [ə'tenʃən] *n* **1** notice: *He tried to attract my attention; Pay attention to your teacher!* **2** care: *That broken leg needs urgent attention.* **3** concentration of the mind: *His attention wanders.* **4** (in the army *etc*) a position in which one stands very straight with hands by the sides and feet together: *He stood to attention.*

at'tentive [-tiv] *adj* giving attention: *The children were very attentive when the teacher was speaking; attentive to her needs.*
at'tentively [-tiv-] *adv*: *They listened attentively.* **at'tentiveness** *n.*

attic ['atik] *n* a room at the top of a house under the roof: *They store old furniture in the attic.*

attire [ə'taiə] *n* clothing: *in formal attire.* – *v* to dress: *attired in silk.*

attitude ['atitju:d] *n* **1** a way of thinking or acting *etc*: *What is your attitude to politics?* **2** a position of the body: *The artist painted the model in various attitudes.*

attorney [ə'tə:ni] *n* **1** a person who has the legal power to act for another person. **2** (*Amer*) a lawyer.

attract [ə'trakt] *v* **1** to cause (someone or something) to come towards: *A magnet attracts iron; I tried to attract her attention.* **2** to arouse (someone's) liking or interest: *She attracted all the young men in the neighbourhood.*
at'traction [-ʃən] *n* **1** the act or power of attracting: *magnetic attraction.* **2** something that attracts: *The attractions of the hotel include a golf-course.*
at'tractive [-tiv] *adj* **1** pleasant and good-looking: *an attractive girl; young and attractive.* **2** likeable; tempting: *an attractive personality; He found the proposition attractive.* **at'tractively** *adv.* **at'tractiveness** *n.*

attribute [ə'tribjut] *v* **1** to think of as being written, made *etc* by: *The play is attributed to Shakespeare.* **2** to think of as being caused by: *He attributed his illness to the cold weather.* – ['atribju:t] *n* a quality that is a particular part of a person or thing: *Intelligence is not one of his attributes.*

auction ['o:kʃən] *n* a public sale in which each thing is sold to the person who offers the highest price: *They held an auction; He sold the house by auction.* – *v* to sell something in this way: *He auctioned all his furniture before emigrating.*
,auctio'neer *n* a person who is in charge of selling things at an auction.

audacious [o:'deiʃəs] *adj* bold and daring: *an audacious plan.* **au'dacity** [-'dasə-] *n.*

audible ['o:dəbl] *adj* able to be heard: *When the microphone broke her voice was barely audible.* **,audi'bility** *n.*

audience ['o:diəns] *n* **1** a group of people watching or listening to a performance *etc*: *The audience at the concert; a television audience.* **2** a formal interview with someone important *eg* a king: *an audience with the Pope.*

audience ends in -ence (not -ance).

audio- [o:diou] (*as part of a word*) of sound or hearing.

audio-typist ['o:dioutaipist] *n* a typist who types from a recording on a tape-recorder *etc*.

audio-visual [o:diou'viʒuəl] : **audio-visual aids** *n pl* films, recordings *etc* used in teaching.

audit ['o:dit] *n* an official examination of financial accounts. – *v* to examine financial accounts officially.
'auditor *n* a person who audits accounts.

audition [o:'diʃən] *n* a trial performance for an actor, singer, musician *etc*: *She had an audition for a part in the television play.*

auditorium [o:di'to:riəm] *n* the part of a theatre, *etc* where the audience sits.

augment [o:g'ment] *v* to increase in amount or make bigger in size or number. **,augmen'tation** *n.*

August ['o:gəst] *n* the eighth month of the year.

august [o:'gʌst] *adj* full of nobility and dignity.

aunt [a:nt] *n* the sister of one's father or mother, or the wife of one's uncle: *My Aunt Anne died last week; The child went to the circus with her favourite aunt.*
'auntie, 'aunty ['a:nti] *n* an aunt: *Auntie Jean; Where's your auntie?*

aura ['o:rə] *n* a particular feeling or atmosphere: *An aura of mystery surrounded her.*

aural ['o:rəl] *adj* of the ear or hearing: *an aural test.*

auspices ['o:spisiz]: **under the auspices of** arranged or encouraged by (a society *etc*): *This exhibition is being held under the auspices of the Arts Council.*
au'spicious [-ʃəs] *adj* giving hope of success: *You haven't made a very auspicious start to your new job.*

austere [o:'stiə] *adj* severely simple and plain; without luxuries or unnecessary expenditure: *an austere way of life.* **au'sterity** [-'ste-] *n.*

authentic [o:'θentik] *adj* true, real or genuine: *an authentic signature.* **,authen'ticity** [-sə-] *n.*

author ['o:θə] – *fem sometimes* **'authoress** – *n* the writer of a book, article, play *etc*: *He used to be a well-known author but his books are out of print now.*
'authorship *n* the state or fact of being an author.

authority [o:'θorəti] – *pl* **au'thorities** – *n* **1** the power or right to do something: *He gave me authority to act on his behalf.* **2** a person who is an expert, or a book that can be referred to, on a particular subject: *He is an authority on Roman history.* **3** (*usu in pl*) the person or people who have power in an administration *etc*: *The authorities would not allow public meetings.* **4** a natural quality in a person which makes him able to control and influence people: *a man of authority.*

au,thori'tarian adj considering obedience to authority more important than personal freedom: an 'authoritarian government.

au'thoritative [-tətiv, (Amer) -teitiv] adj said or written by an expert or a person in authority: an authoritative opinion.

authorize, -ise ['o:θəraiz] v 1 to give the power or right to do something: I authorized him to sign the documents; I authorized the payment of $100 to John Smith. ,authori'zation, -s- n.

auto- [o:tou] (as part of a word) 1 for or by oneself or itself. 2 Same as auto.

auto ['o:tou] short for **automobile** or **automatic**.

autobiography [o:təbai'ogrəfi] n the story of a person's life written by himself. ,autobio'-graphic(al) [-'gra-] adj.

autocrat ['o:təkrat] n a ruler who has total control: The Tsars of Russia were autocrats.

autocracy [o:'tokrəsi] n government by an autocrat.
,auto'cratic adj 1 having absolute power: an autocratic government. 2 expecting complete obedience: a very autocratic father.

autograph ['o:təgra:f] n a person's signature, esp as a souvenir: She collected autographs of film stars. – v to write one's name on (esp for a souvenir): The actor autographed her programme.

automatic [o:tə'matik] adj 1 (of a machine etc) working by itself: an automatic washing-machine. 2 (of an action) without thinking: an automatic response. – n a self-loading gun: He has two automatics and a rifle.
'automated [-mei-] adj working by automation.
,auto'matically adv: This machine works automatically; He answered automatically.
,auto'mation n (in factories etc) the use of machines, esp to work other machines: Automation has resulted in people losing their jobs.

automaton [o:'tomətən] – pls **au'tomata** [-tə], **au'tomatons** – n a human-shaped machine that can be operated to move by itself.

automobile ['o:təmobi:l, (Amer) o:təmə'bi:l] n (Amer: abbrev 'auto ['o:tou] – pl 'autos) a motor-car.

autonomy [o:'tonəmi] n the power or right of a country etc to govern itself.
au'tonomous adj self-governing.

autopsy ['o:topsi] – pl 'autopsies – n a medical examination of a body after death.

autumn ['o:təm] n (Amer **fall**) the season of the year when leaves change colour and fall and fruits ripen, September to October or November in cooler northern regions.
autumnal [o:'tʌmnəl] adj.

auxiliary [o:g'ziljəri] adj helping; additional:

auxiliary forces; an auxiliary nurse. – n – pl au'xiliaries – 1 an additional helper. 2 a soldier serving with another nation.

avail [ə'veil]: **of no avail, to no avail** of no use or effect: He tried to revive her but to no avail; His efforts were of no avail.

available [ə'veiləbl] adj able or ready to be used: The hall is available on Saturday night; All the available money has been used. a,vaila'bility n.

avalanche ['avəla:nʃ] n a fall of snow and ice down a mountain: Two skiers were buried by the avalanche.

avarice ['avəris] n strong desire for money etc; greed. ,ava'ricious [-ʃəs] adj.

avenge [ə'vendʒ] v to take revenge for a wrong on behalf of someone else: He avenged his brother/his brother's death. a'venger n.

avenue ['avinju:] n 1 a road, often with trees along either side. 2 (often abbrev **Ave.** when written) a word used in the names of certain roads or streets: His address is 14 Swan Avenue.

average ['avəridʒ] n the result of adding several amounts together and dividing the total by the number of amounts: The average of 3, 7, 9 and 13 is 8 (=32÷4). – adj 1 obtained by finding the average of amounts etc: average price; the average temperature for the week. 2 ordinary; not exceptional: The average person is not wealthy; His work is average. – v to form an average: His expenses averaged (out at) 15 dollars a day.

averse [ə'və:s] adj (with **to**) having a dislike for: averse to hard work.
a'version [-ʃən, (Amer) -ʒən] n a feeling of dislike.

avert [ə'və:t] v 1 to turn away, esp one's eyes: She averted her eyes from the dead animal. 2 to prevent: to avert disaster.

aviary ['eiviəri] – pl 'aviaries – n a place in which birds are kept.

aviation [eivi'eiʃən] n 1 (the science or practice of) flying in aircraft. 2 the industry concerned with aircraft manufacture, design etc.

avid ['avid] adj eager: avid for information; an avid reader. 'avidly adv. a'vidity n.

*****avocado** [avə'ka:dou] – pl ,avo'cados – n (also **avocado pear**) a kind of pear-shaped tropical fruit.

avoid [ə'void] v to keep away from (a place, person or thing): He drove carefully to avoid the holes in the road; Avoid the subject of money. a'voidance n.

await [ə'weit] v to wait for: We await your arrival with expectation.

awake [ə'weik] – pt **awoke** [ə'wouk]: ptps a'waked, a'woken – v to wake from sleep:

* see illustration on p. 201

He was awoken by a noise; He awoke suddenly. – adj not asleep: Is he awake?

a'waken v 1 to awake: I was awakened by the song of the birds. 2 to start (a feeling of interest, guilt etc): His interest was awakened by the lecture.

award [ə'wo:d] v 1 to give (someone something that he has won or deserved): They awarded her first prize. 2 to give: He was awarded damages of $5000. – n a prize etc awarded: The film awards were presented annually.

aware [ə'weə] adj knowing; informed; conscious (of): Is he aware of the problem?; Are they aware that I'm coming? **a'wareness** n.

away [ə'wei] adv 1 to or at a distance from the person speaking or the person or thing spoken about: He lives three miles away (from the town); Go away!; Take it away! 2 in the opposite direction: She turned away so that he would not see her tears. 3 (gradually) into nothing: The noise died away. 4 continuously: They worked away until dark. 5 (of a football match etc) not on the home ground: The team is playing away this weekend; (also adj) an away match.

awe [o:] n wonder and fear: The child looked in awe at the king. – v to fill with awe: He was awed by his new school.

'awe-inspiring, **'awesome** adjs causing awe: The waterfall was awe-inspiring; an awesome sight.

'awestruck adj filled with awe: awestruck by the mountains.

awful ['o:ful] adj 1 very great: an awful rush. 2 very bad: This book is awful; an awful experience. 3 severe: an awful headache. **'awfully** adv very: awfully silly. **'awfulness** n.

awhile [ə'wail] adv for a short time: Wait awhile.

awkward ['o:kwəd] adj 1 not graceful or elegant: an awkward movement. 2 difficult or causing difficulty, embarrassment etc: an awkward question; an awkward silence; His cut is in an awkward place. **'awkwardly** adv. **'awkwardness** n.

awoke(n) see awake.

axe, (Amer) **ax** [aks] n a tool with a (long) handle and a metal blade for cutting down trees and cutting wood etc into pieces. – v 1 to get rid of; to dismiss: They've axed 50% of their staff. 2 to reduce (costs, services etc): Government spending in education has been axed.

axiom ['aksiəm] n a fact or statement which is definitely true and accepted as a principle or rule.

axis ['aksis] – pl **axes** ['aksi:z] – n 1 the real or imaginary line on which a thing turns (as the axis of the earth, from North Pole to South Pole, around which the earth turns). 2 a fixed line used as a reference, as in a graph: He plotted the temperatures on the horizontal axis.

axle ['aksl] n the rod on which a wheel turns: the back axle of the car.

Bb

babble ['babl] v 1 to talk indistinctly or foolishly: What are you babbling about now? 2 to make a continuous and indistinct noise: The stream babbled over the pebbles. – n such talk or noises.

babe [beib] n 1 a baby: a babe in arms (= a small baby not yet able to walk). 2 see baby.

baboon [bə'bu:n, (Amer) ba-] n a kind of large monkey with a dog-like face.

baby ['beibi] – pl **'babies** – n 1 a very young child: Some babies cry during the night; (also adj) a baby boy. 2 (esp Amer, often **babe**) a girl or young woman.

'babyish adj like a baby; not mature: a babyish child that cries every day at school.

baby buggy/carriage (Amer) a pram.

baby grand a small grand piano.

'baby-sit v to remain in a house to look after a child while its parents are out: She baby-

sits for her friends every Saturday. **'baby-sitter**, **'baby-sitting** ns.

bachelor ['batʃələ] n an unmarried man: He's a confirmed bachelor (= he has no intention of ever marrying); (also adj) a bachelor flat (= a flat suitable for one person).

back [bak] n 1 in man, the part of the body from the neck to the bottom of the spine: She lay on her back. 2 in animals, the upper part of the body: She put the saddle on the horse's back. 3 that part of anything opposite to or furthest from the front: the back of the house; She sat at the back of the hall. 4 in football, hockey etc a player who plays behind the forwards. – adj of or at the back: the back door. – adv 1 to, or at, the place or person from which a person or thing came: I went back to the shop; He gave the car back to its owner. 2 away (from something); not near (something): Move *back! Let the ambulance get to the injured man*; *Keep back from me or I'll hit you!* **3** towards the back (of something): *Sit back in your chair.* **4** in return; in response to: *When the teacher is scolding you, don't answer back.* **5** to, or in, the past: *Think back to your childhood.* – *v* **1** to (cause to) move backwards: *He backed (his car) out of the garage.* **2** to help or support: *Will you back me against the others?* **3** to bet or gamble on: *I backed your horse to win.*

'**backer** *n* a person who supports someone or something, *esp* with money: *the backer of the new theatre.*

'**backbite** *v* to criticize a person when he is not present.

'**backbiting** *n*: *Constant backbiting by her colleagues led to her resignation.*

'**backbone** *n* **1** the spine: *the backbone of a fish.* **2** the chief support: *The older employees are the backbone of the industry.*

'**backbreaking** *adj* (of a task *etc*) very difficult or requiring very hard work: *Digging the garden is a backbreaking job.*

'**back'date** *v* **1** to put an earlier date on (a cheque *etc*): *He should have paid his bill last month and so he has backdated the cheque.* **2** to make payable from a date in the past: *Our rise in pay was backdated to April.*

'**back'fire** *v* **1** (of a motor-car *etc*) to make a loud bang because of unburnt gases in the exhaust system: *The car backfired.* **2** (of a plan *etc*) to have unexpected results, often opposite to the intended results: *His scheme backfired (on him), and he lost money.*

'**background** *n* **1** the space behind the principal or most important figures or objects of a picture *etc*: *He always paints ships against a background of stormy skies*; *trees in the background of the picture.* **2** happenings that go before, and help to explain, an event *etc*: *the background to a situation.* **3** a person's origins, education *etc*: *She was ashamed of her humble background.*

'**backhand** *n* **1** in tennis *etc*, a stroke or shot with the back of one's hand turned towards the ball: *a clever backhand*; *His backhand is very strong.* **2** writing with the letters sloping backwards: *I can always recognize her backhand.* – *adv* using backhand: *She played the stroke backhand*; *She writes backhand.*

'**backlog** *n* a pile of uncompleted work *etc* which has collected: *a backlog of orders because of the strike.*

'**back-'number** *n* an out-of-date copy or issue of a magazine *etc*: *He collects back-numbers of comic magazines.*

'**backside** *n* the bottom or buttocks: *He sits on his backside all day long and does no work.*

'**backstroke** *n* in swimming, a stroke made

when lying on one's back in the water: *The child is good at backstroke.*

'**backwash** *n* **1** a backward current *eg* that following a ship's passage through the water: *the backwash of the steamer.* **2** the unintentional results of an action, situation *etc*: *The backwash of that firm's financial troubles affected several other firms.*

'**backwater** *n* **1** a stretch of river not in the main stream. **2** a place not affected by what is happening in the world outside. *That village is rather a backwater.*

'**back'yard** *n* (*esp Amer*) a garden at the back of a house *etc*: *He grows vegetables in his backyard.*

back down to give up one's opinion, claim *etc*: *She backed down in the face of strong opposition.*

back of (*Amer*) behind: *He parked back of the store.*

back on to (of a building *etc*) to have its back next to (something): *My house backs on to the racecourse.*

back out 1 to move out backwards: *He opened the garage door and backed (his car) out.* **2** to withdraw from a promise *etc*: *You promised to help – you mustn't back out now!*

back up to support or encourage: *The new evidence backed up my arguments.*

have one's back to the wall to be in a very difficult or desperate situation: *He certainly has his back to the wall as he has lost his job and cannot find another one.*

put someone's back up to anger someone: *He put my back up with his boasting.*

take a back seat to take an unimportant position: *At these discussions he always takes a back seat and listens to others talking.*

backward ['bakwəd] *adj* **1** aimed or directed backwards: *He left without a backward glance.* **2** less advanced in mind or body than is normal for one's age: *a backward child.* **3** late in developing a modern culture, mechanization *etc*: *That part of Britain is still very backward*; *the backward peoples of the world.* '**backwardness** *n*.

'**backwards** *adv* **1** towards the back: *He glanced backwards.* **2** with one's back facing the direction one is going in: *The child walked backwards into a lamp-post.* **3** in the opposite way to that which is usual: *Can you count from 1 to 10 backwards?* (= starting at 10 and counting to 1).

backwards and forwards in one direction and then in the opposite direction: *The dog ran backwards and forwards across the grass.*

bend/fall over backwards to try very hard: *He bent over backwards to get us tickets for the concert.*

bacon ['beikən] *n* the flesh of the back and sides of a pig, salted and dried, used as food.

bacteria [bak'tiəriə] – *sing* **bac'terium** [-əm] – *n pl* organisms not able to be seen except under a microscope, found in rotting matter, in air, in soil and in living bodies, some being the germs of disease: *a throat infection caused by bacteria.*

bac‚teri'ology [-'olədʒi] *n* the study of bacteria.

bac‚terio'logical [-'lo-] *adj.* **bac‚teri'ologist** *n.*

bactrian *see* **camel.**

bad [bad] – *compar* **worse** [wəːs]: *superl* **worst** [wəːst] – *adj* **1** not good; not efficient: *He is a bad driver; His eyesight is bad; They are bad at tennis* (= they play tennis badly). **2** wicked; immoral: *a bad man; He has done some bad things.* **3** unpleasant: *bad news.* **4** rotten: *This meat is bad.* **5** causing harm or injury: *Smoking is bad for your health.* **6** (of a part of the body) painful, or in a weak state: *She has a bad heart; I have a bad head* (= headache) *today.* **7** unwell: *I am feeling quite bad today.* **8** serious or severe: *a bad accident; a bad mistake.* **9** (of a debt) not likely to be paid: *The firm loses money every year from bad debts.*

'badly – *compar* **worse**: *superl* **worst** – *adv* **1** not well, efficiently or satisfactorily: *He plays tennis very badly.* **2** to a serious or severe extent: *He badly needs a haircut; The dress is badly stained.*

'badness *n.*

badly off not having much *esp* money: *We can't go on holiday – we are too badly off.*

feel bad (about something) to feel upset or ashamed about something: *I feel bad about forgetting to telephone you.*

go from bad to worse to get into an even worse condition *etc* than before: *Things are going from bad to worse for the firm – not only are we losing money but there's going to be a strike as well.*

not bad quite good: *'Is she a good swimmer?' 'She's not bad.'*

too bad unfortunate: *It's too bad that he has left.*

bade *see* **bid.**

badge [badʒ] *n* a mark, emblem or ornament showing rank, occupation, or membership of a society, team *etc*: *a school badge on a blazer.*

badger ['badʒə] *n* a burrowing animal of the weasel family. – *v* to annoy or worry: *He badgered the authorities until they gave him a new passport.*

badminton ['badmintən] *n* a game played on a court with a shuttlecock and rackets. – *Also adj*: *a badminton match; a badminton court.*

baffle ['bafl] *v* to puzzle (a person): *I was baffled by her attitude towards her husband.*

baffling *adj*: *a baffling crime.*

bag [bag] *n* **1** a container made of soft material (*eg* cloth, animal skin, plastic *etc*): *She carried a small bag.* **2** a quantity of fish or game caught: *Did you get a good bag today?* – *v* – *pt, ptp* **bagged** – **1** to put into a bag. **2** to kill (game).

'baggy *adj* loose, like an empty bag: *He wears baggy trousers.*

bags of a large amount of: *He's got bags of money.*

in the bag as good as done or complete (in the desired way): *Your appointment is in the bag.*

baggage ['bagidʒ] *n* luggage: *He sent his baggage on in advance.*

bagpipes ['bagpaips] *n pl* a wind instrument consisting of a bag fitted with pipes, played in Scotland *etc*: *He wants to learn to play the bagpipes.*

bail[1] [beil] *n* a sum of money which is given to a court of law to get an untried prisoner out of prison until the time of his trial, and which acts as security for his return: *bail of $500.*

bail out to set (a person) free by giving such money to a court of law: *He was bailed out by his father. – See also* **bale out** *under* **bale**[2].

bail[2] [beil] *n* one of the cross-pieces laid on the top of the wicket in cricket.

bail[3] *see* **bale**[2].

bait [beit] *n* food used to attract fish, animals *etc* which one wishes to catch, kill *etc*: *Before he went fishing he dug up some worms for bait.* – *v* to put bait on or in (a hook, trap *etc*): *He baited the mousetrap with cheese.*

baize [beiz] *n* a type of coarse woollen cloth, often green, *usu* used for covering card-tables *etc.*

bake [beik] *v* **1** to cook in an oven: *I'm going to bake* (*bread*) *today; She baked the ham.* **2** to dry or harden by heat: *The sun is baking the ground dry.*

baked *adj*: *baked ham; freshly baked bread.*

'baker *n* **1** a person who bakes: *He is a qualified baker; She is a good baker.* **2** a baker's shop.

'bakery – *pl* **'bakeries** – *n* a place where baking is done and/or where bread, cakes *etc* are sold: *I bought some cakes at the bakery.*

'baking *n* the act or art of cooking bread, cakes *etc.*

baking powder a powder used to make cakes *etc* rise: *This sponge cake is very flat – you can't have used enough baking powder.*

a baker's dozen thirteen.

balance ['baləns] *n* **1** a weighing instrument. **2** a state of physical steadiness: *The child was walking along the wall when he lost his balance and fell.* **3** state of mental or emotional steadiness: *The balance of her mind was disturbed.* **4** the amount by which the two sides of a financial account (money spent and money received) differ: *I have a balance* (= amount remaining) *of $100 in my bank account*; *a large bank balance.* – *v* **1** (of two sides of a financial account) to make or be equal: *I can't get these accounts to balance.* **2** to make or keep steady: *She balanced the jug of water on her head*; *The girl balanced on her toes.*

balance sheet a paper showing a summary and balance of financial accounts.

in the balance in an undecided or uncertain state: *Her fate is (hanging) in the balance.*

off balance not steady: *He hit me while I was off balance.*

on balance having taken everything into consideration: *On balance I think Miss Smith is a better tennis player than my sister.*

balcony ['balkəni] – *pl* **balconies** – *n* **1** a platform built out from the wall of a building: *Many hotel rooms have balconies.* **2** in theatres *etc*, an upper floor: *We sat in the balcony of the cinema*; *(also adj)* balcony seats.

bald [bo:ld] *adj* **1** (of people) with little or no hair on the head: *a bald head*; *He is going bald* (= becoming bald). **2** (of birds, animals) without feathers, fur *etc*: *a bald patch on the dog's back.* **3** bare or plain: *a bald statement of the facts.* **'baldness** *n*.

'balding *adj* becoming bald.

'baldly *adv* in a plain or bare way: *He answered her questions baldly.*

bale[1] [beil] *n* a large bundle of goods or material (cloth, hay *etc*) tied together: *a bale of cotton.*

bale[2] [beil] *v* (*also* **bail**) to clear (water out of a boat with buckets *etc*): *Several gallons of water were baled out of the boat.*

bale out to parachute from a plane in an emergency. – *See also* **bail out** *under* **bail**[1].

baleful ['beilful] *adj* evil or harmful: *a baleful influence.* **'balefully** *adv*.

ball[1] [bo:l] *n* **1** anything roughly round in shape: *a ball of wool.* **2** a round object used in games: *a tennis ball.*

ball-'bearings *n pl* in machinery *etc*, small steel balls that help the revolving of one part over another.

'ballcock *n* a valve in a cistern.

'ballpoint *n* a pen having a tiny ball as the writing point. – *Also adj*: *a ballpoint pen.*

on the ball quick, alert and up-to-date: *The new manager is really on the ball.*

start/set, keep the ball rolling to start or keep something going, *esp* a conversation: *He can be relied on to start the ball rolling at parties.*

ball[2] [bo:l] *n* a formal dance: *a ball at the palace.*

'ballroom *n* a large room for a formal dance. – *Also adj*: *ballroom dancing.*

ballad ['baləd] *n* a simple, often sentimental, song: *Older people prefer ballads to pop music.*

ballerina [balə'ri:nə] *n* a female (often principal) ballet-dancer: *Pavlova was a famous ballerina.*

ballet ['balei, (*Amer*) ba'lei] *n* **1** a theatrical performance of dancing with set steps and mime, often telling a story: *Swan Lake is my favourite ballet.* **2** the art of dancing in this way: *She is taking lessons in ballet*; *(also adj)* a ballet class.

'ballet-dancer *n*.

ballistic missile [ba'listik 'misail] a missile guided for part of its course but falling like an ordinary bomb.

balloon [bə'lu:n] *n* a large bag, made of light material and filled with a gas lighter than air: *They decorated the dance-hall with balloons.*

ballot ['balət] *n* a method of voting in secret by marking a paper and putting it into a box: *They held a ballot to choose a new chairman*; *The question was decided by ballot.*

ballyhoo [bali'hu:, (*Amer*) 'balihu:] *n* noisy or sensational advertising or publicity: *a lot of ballyhoo about the filmstar's visit.*

balm [ba:m] *n* something that soothes: *The music was balm to my ears.* **'balmy** *adj*. **'balminess** *n*.

balsa ['bo:lsə] *n* **1** (*also* **balsa tree**) a tropical American tree. **2** (*often* **'balsa-wood**) its very lightweight wood: *His model aeroplane is made of balsa.*

balsam ['bo:lsəm] *n* a pleasant-smelling substance obtained from certain trees: *He inhaled balsam when he had a bad cold.*

bamboo [bam'bu:] *n, adj* (of) a type of gigantic grass with hollow, jointed, woody stems: *furniture made of bamboo*; *bamboo furniture.*

ban [ban] *n* an order that a certain thing may not be done: *a ban on smoking.* – *v* – *pt, ptp* **banned** – to forbid: *The government banned publication of his book.*

banana [bə'na:nə] *n* the long curved fruit, yellow-skinned when ripe, of a type of very large tropical tree.

band[1] [band] *n* **1** a strip of material to put round something: *a rubber band.* **2** a stripe of a colour *etc*: *a skirt with a band of red in it.* **3** in radio *etc*, a group of frequencies or wavelengths: *the medium waveband.*

band[2] [band] *n* **1** a number of persons forming a group: *a band of robbers.* **2** a body of musicians: *a brass band*; *a dance band.* – *v* to unite or gather together for a purpose: *They banded together to oppose the building of the garage.*

bandage ['bandidʒ] *n* (a piece of) cloth for binding up a wound, or a broken bone: *She had a bandage on her injured finger. – v* to cover with a bandage: *The doctor bandaged the boy's foot.*

bandit ['bandit] *n* an outlaw or robber, *esp* as a member of a gang: *They were attacked by bandits in the mountains.*

bandy ['bandi] *adj* (of legs) bent outwards at the knee: *She wears long skirts to hide her bandy legs.* **bandy-'legged** [-legid] *adj.*

bang [baŋ] *n* **1** a sudden loud noise: *The door shut with a bang.* **2** a blow or knock: *a bang on the head from a falling branch. – v* **1** to close with a sudden loud noise: *He banged the door.* **2** to hit or strike violently, often making a loud noise: *The child banged his drum; He banged the book down angrily on the table.* **3** to make a sudden loud noise: *We could hear the fireworks banging in the distance.*

'banger *n* an explosive firework: *The child was frightened by the bangers at the firework display.*

bangle ['baŋgl] *n* a bracelet worn on the arm or leg: *gold bangles.*

banish ['baniʃ] *v* to send away (*usu* from a country), *esp* as a punishment: *He was banished (from the country) for treason.* **'banishment** *n.*

banister ['banistə] *n* **1** (*often pl*) the handrail of a staircase and the posts supporting it. **2** one of the posts supporting the handrail.

banjo ['bandʒou] – *pl* **'banjo(e)s** – *n* a stringed musical instrument similar to the guitar: *He plays the banjo; Play me a tune on the banjo.*

bank[1] [baŋk] *n* **1** a mound or ridge (of earth *etc*): *The child climbed the bank to pick flowers.* **2** the ground at the edge of a river, lake *etc*: *The river overflowed its banks.* **3** a raised area of sand under the sea: *a sand-bank. – v* **1** (*often with* **up**) to form into a bank or banks: *The earth was banked up against the wall of the house.* **2** to tilt (an aircraft *etc*) while turning: *The plane banked steeply.*

bank[2] [baŋk] *n* **1** a place where money is lent or exchanged, or put for safety and/or to acquire interest: *He has plenty of money in the bank; I must go to the bank today.* **2** a place for storing other valuable material: *A blood bank. – v* to put into a bank: *He banks his wages every week.*

'banker *n* a person who owns or manages a bank.

bank book a book recording money deposited in, or withdrawn from, a bank.

banker's card (*also* **cheque card**) a card issued by a bank guaranteeing payment of the holder's cheques.

bank holiday a day on which banks are closed (and which is often also a public holiday).

'bank-note *n* a piece of paper issued by a bank, used as money.

bank on to rely on: *Don't bank on me – I'll probably be late.*

bank[3] [baŋk] *n* a collection of rows (of instruments *etc*): *The modern pilot has banks of instruments.*

bankrupt ['baŋkrʌpt] *adj* unable to pay one's debts: *He has been declared bankrupt. – n* a person who is unable to pay his debts. – *v* to make bankrupt: *His wife's extravagance soon bankrupted him.* **'bankruptcy** *n.*

banner ['banə] *n* **1** a military flag. **2** a large strip of cloth bearing a slogan *etc*: *Many of the demonstrators were carrying banners.*

banquet ['baŋkwit] *n* a feast or ceremonial dinner at which speeches are often made.

bantam ['bantəm] *n* a small variety of domestic fowl: *She keeps bantams*; (*also ·adj*) *a bantam cock.*

banter ['bantə] *n* friendly teasing: *The sick boy was cheered up by the noisy banter of his friends.*

banyan ['banjən] *n* a tree that grows on wet land. Its branches have hanging roots that grow down and start new trunks.

baptize, -ise [bap'taiz] *v* to dip (a person) in water, or sprinkle (someone) with water, as a symbol of acceptance into the Christian church, *usu* also giving him a name: *She was baptized Mary but calls herself Jane.*

'baptism [-tizəm] *n* (an act of) baptizing: *the baptism of the baby.* **bap'tismal** *adj.*

bar [ba:] *n* **1** a rod or oblong piece (*esp* of a solid substance): *a gold bar; a bar of chocolate; iron bars on the windows.* **2** a broad line or band: *The blue material had bars of red running through it.* **3** a bolt: *a bar on the door.* **4** a counter at which or across which articles of a particular kind are sold: *a snack bar; Your whisky is on the bar.* **5** a public house. **6** a measured division in music: *Sing the first ten bars.* **7** something which prevents (something): *His carelessness is a bar to his promotion.* **8** the rail at which the prisoner stands in court: *The prisoner at the bar collapsed when he was sentenced to ten years' imprisonment. – v – pt, ptp* **barred** – **1** to fasten with a bar: *Bar the door.* **2** to prevent from entering: *He's been barred from the club.* **3** to prevent (from doing something): *My lack of money bars me from going on holiday. – prep* except: *All bar one of the family had measles.*

'barmaid, 'barman, (*mainly Amer*) **'bartender** [-tendə] *n* a person who serves at the bar of a public-house or hotel.

barb [ba:b] *n* **1** a backward-facing point on

an arrowhead, fishing-hook *etc.* **2** a hurtful remark.

barbed *adj*: *a barbed arrow/remark.*

barbed wire wire with sharp points at intervals: *I tore my skirt on that barbed wire*; (*also adj with hyphen*) *a barbed-wire fence.*

barbarous ['ba:bərəs] *adj* **1** uncultured and uncivilized: *barbarous habits.* **2** brutal: *a barbarous assault.* '**barbarousness** *n.*

bar'barian [-'beəriən] *n* an uncultured and uncivilized person. – *adj*: *barbarian customs.*

barbecue ['ba:bikju:] *n* **1** a framework for grilling meat *etc* over a charcoal fire: *We cooked the steak on a barbecue.* **2** a party in the open air, at which food is barbecued. – *v* to cook on a barbecue: *He barbecued a chicken.*

barber ['ba:bə] *n* a person who cuts men's hair, shaves their beards *etc.*

bare [beə] *adj* **1** uncovered or naked: *bare skin*; *bare floors.* **2** empty: *bare shelves.* **3** of trees *etc*, without leaves. **4** worn thin; *The carpet is a bit bare.* **5** basic; essential: *the bare necessities of life.* – *v* to uncover: *The dog bared its teeth in anger.*

'**barely** *adv* scarcely or only just: *We have barely enough food.*

'**bareness** *n.*

'**bareback** *adv, adj* without a saddle: *I enjoy riding bareback.*

'**barefaced** *adj* openly impudent: *a bare-faced lie.*

'**barefoot(ed)** *adj, adv* not wearing shoes or socks *etc*: *The children go barefoot on the beach.*

,**bare'headed** *adj, adv* not wearing a hat *etc.*

bargain ['ba:gin] *n* **1** something bought cheaply and giving good value for money: *This carpet was a real bargain.* **2** an agreement made between people: *I'll make a bargain with you.* – *v* to argue about or discuss a price *etc*: *I bargained with him and finally got the price down.*

bargain for to expect or take into consideration: *I didn't bargain for everyone arriving at once.*

***barge** [ba:dʒ] *n* **1** a flat-bottomed boat for carrying goods *etc.* **2** a large power-driven boat. – *v* **1** to move (about) clumsily: *He barged about the room.* **2** to bump (into): *He barged into me.* **3** (*with* in(to)) to push one's way (into) rudely: *She barged in without knocking.*

baritone ['baritoun] *n* (a singer with) a deep male voice between bass and tenor.

bark[1] [ba:k] *n* the short, sharp cry of a dog, fox *etc.* – *v* **1** to make this sound: *The dog barked at the stranger.* **2** to utter abruptly: *She barked a reply.*

bark[2] [ba:k] *n* the covering of the trunk and branches of a tree: *He stripped the bark off*

the branch. – *v* to take the skin off (part of the body) by accident: *I barked my shin on the table.*

barley ['ba:li] *n* a type of grain used for food and for making beer and whisky: *The farmer has harvested his barley.*

barley sugar a kind of hard sweet made by melting and cooling sugar.

barmaid, barman *see* **bar**.

barn [ba:n] *n* a building in which grain, hay *etc* are stored: *The farmer keeps his tractor in the barn.*

barnacle ['ba:nəkl] *n* a kind of small shellfish that sticks to rocks and the bottoms of ships.

barometer [bə'romitə] *n* an instrument which indicates changes of weather: *The barometer is falling – it is going to rain.*

barometric [barə'metrik] *adj*: *barometric pressure.*

baron ['barən] – *fem* '**baroness** – *n* **1** a nobleman: *He was made a baron*; *Baron Rothschild.* **2** an important, powerful person: *a newspaper baron.*

barracks ['barəks] *n sing or pl* a building or buildings for housing soldiers: *confined to barracks* (=not allowed to leave the barracks).

barrage ['bara:ʒ, (*Amer*) bə'ra:ʒ] *n* **1** something that keeps back an enemy: *a barrage of gunfire.* **2** an overwhelming number: *a barrage of questions.* **3** a man-made barrier across a river.

barrel ['barəl] *n* **1** a container of curved pieces of wood or of metal: *The barrels contain beer.* **2** a long, hollow, cylindrical shape, *esp* the tube-shaped part of a gun: *The bullet jammed in the barrel of the gun.*

barren ['barən] *adj* not able to produce crops, fruit, young *etc*: *barren soil*; *a barren fruit-tree*; *a barren woman.* '**barrenness** *n.*

barricade [bari'keid] *n* a barrier put up to block a street *etc*: *There were barricades keeping back the crowds.* – *v* to block something (*eg* a street) with a barricade.

barrier ['bariə] *n* **1** something put up as a defence or protection: *a barrier between the playground and the busy road.* **2** something that causes difficulty: *His deafness was a barrier to promotion.*

barrister ['baristə] *n* a lawyer qualified to present cases in court.

barrow ['barou] *n* **1** a wheelbarrow. **2** a small (*usu* two-wheeled) cart.

bartender *see* **bar**.

barter ['ba:tə] *v* to trade by giving (one thing) in exchange (for another): *The bandits bartered gold for guns.* – *n* goods used in bartering: *Some tribes use sea-shells as barter.*

basalt ['baso:lt] *n* any of certain types of dark-coloured rock.

base[1] [beis] *n* **1** the foundation, support, or

lowest part (of something), or the surface on which something is standing: *the base of the statue*; *the base of the triangle*; *the base of the tree.* **2** the main ingredient of a mixture: *This paint has oil as a base.* **3** a headquarters, starting-point *etc*: *an army base.* – *v* (*often with* **on**) to use as a foundation, starting-point *etc*: *I base my opinion on evidence*; *Our group was based in Paris.*
'**baseless** *adj* without foundation or reason: *a baseless claim.*

base² [beis] *adj* wicked or worthless: *base desires.* '**basely** *adv*. '**baseness** *n*.

*****baseball** ['beisbɔːl] *n* an American game played with bat and ball.

basement ['beismənt] *n* the lowest floor of a building, *usu* below ground level: *She lives in a basement*; (*also adj*) *a basement flat.*

bash [baʃ] *v* (*sometimes with* **in**) to beat or smash (in): *The soldiers bashed in the door.* – *n* **1** a heavy blow: *a bash with his foot.* **2** a dent: *a bash on the car's nearside door.*
bash on/ahead (with) to go on doing something *esp* in a careless or inattentive way: *In spite of his father's advice he bashed on with the painting.*
have a bash at to make an attempt at: *Although he was not a handyman, he had a bash at mending the lock.*

bashful ['baʃful] *adj* shy: *a bashful girl*; *a bashful smile.* '**bashfully** *adv*. '**bashfulness** *n*.

basic ['beisik] *adj* **1** of, or forming, the main part or foundation of something: *Your basic theory is wrong.* **2** restricted to a fundamental level, elementary: *a basic knowledge of French.*
'**basically** *adv* fundamentally: *She seems strict, but basically* (= in reality) *she's very nice*; *Her job, basically, is to deal with foreign customers.*

basin ['beisn] *n* **1** a bowl for washing oneself in: *a wash-hand basin.* **2** a wide, open dish for preparing food in: *a pudding-basin.* **3** the area drained by a river: *the basin of the Nile.* **4** the deep part of a harbour: *There were four yachts anchored in the harbour basin.*

basis ['beisis] – *pl* '**bases** [-siːz] *n* that on which a thing rests or is founded: *This idea is the basis of my argument.*

bask [baːsk] *v* to lie (*esp* in warmth or sunshine): *The seals basked in the warm sun.*

basket ['baːskit] *n* **1** a container made of strips of wood, rushes *etc* woven together: *She carried a large basket.*
'**basketball** *n* a game in which goals are scored by throwing a ball into a net on a high post. – *Also adj*: *a basketball court.*
'**basketry** *n* basketwork.
'**basketwork** *n* articles made of plaited rushes *etc*. – *Also adj*: *a basketwork chair.*

bass¹ [beis] – *pl* '**basses** – *n* (a singer having) a male voice of the lowest pitch.

bass² [bas] – *pl* **bass**, (*rare*) '**basses** – *n* a type of fish of the perch family.

bassoon [bə'suːn, (*Amer*) ba-] *n* a woodwind musical instrument which gives a very low sound.

bastard ['baːstəd] *n* a child born of parents not married to each other. – *Also adj*: *a bastard son.*

bastion ['bastjən, (*Amer*) 'bastʃən] *n* a person, place or thing which acts as a defence: *He's one of the last bastions of the old leisurely way of life.*

.bat¹ [bat] *n* a shaped piece of wood *etc* for striking the ball in cricket, baseball, table-tennis *etc*. – *v* – *pt*, *ptp* **batted** – **1** to use a bat: *He bats with his left hand.* **2** to strike (the ball) with a bat: *He batted the ball.*
'**batsman** ['bats-] *n* a person who bats in cricket.
off one's own bat completely by oneself (without help): *He wrote the letter to the newspaper off his own bat.*

bat² [bat] *n* a mouse-like animal which flies, *usu* at night.
'**batty** *adj* crazy: *a batty old man.*

batch [batʃ] *n* a number of things made, delivered *etc*, all at one time: *a batch of bread*; *The letters were sent out in batches.*

bated ['beitid]: **with bated breath** breathing only slightly, due to anxiety, excitement *etc*: *The crowd watched the rescue of the child with bated breath.*

bath [baːθ] – *pl* **baths** [baːðz] – *n* **1** a large container for holding water in which to wash the whole body: *I'll fill the bath with water for you.* **2** an act of washing in a bath: *I had a bath last night.* **3** a container of liquid *etc* in which something is immersed: *a bird bath.* – *v* to wash in a bath: *I'll bath the baby.*
.**bath'chair** *n* a kind of wheeled chair for an invalid.
'**bathroom** *n* **1** a room in a house *etc* which contains a bath. **2** (*esp Amer*) a lavatory.
'**bathtub** *n* a bath (for washing in).

bathe [beið] *v* **1** to put into water: *He bathed his feet*; *I'll bathe your wounds.* **2** to go swimming: *She bathes in the sea every day.* – *n* an act of swimming: *a midnight bathe.*
'**bather** *n*. '**bathing** *ns*.

batik ['batik] *n* a method of dyeing patterns on cloth by waxing certain areas so that they remain uncoloured.

baton ['batn, (*Amer*) ba'ton] *n* **1** a short, heavy stick, carried by a policeman as a weapon. **2** a light, slender stick used when conducting an orchestra or choir: *The conductor raised his baton.*

batsman *see* **bat¹**.

***** see illustration on p. 206

battalion [bə'taljən] *n* a large body of foot soldiers forming part of a brigade.

batten ['batn] *n* a piece of wood used for keeping other pieces in place: *These strips are all fastened together with a batten.*

batter ['batə] *v* to beat with blow after blow: *He was battered to death with a large stick.*

battery ['batəri] – *pl* **'batteries** – *n* **1** a series of two or more electric cells arranged to produce, or store, a current: *a torch battery.* **2** an arrangement of cages in which laying hens *etc* are kept. **3** a group of large guns (and the people manning them). **4** a long series: *a battery of questions.*

battle ['batl] *n* a fight between opposing armies or individuals: *the last battle of the war.* – *v* to fight.

'battlefield *n* the place where a battle is, or was, fought: *dead bodies covered the battlefield.*

'battleship *n* a heavily armed and armoured warship.

batty *see* **bat**².

bawdy ['bɔːdi] *adj* vulgar and coarse: *bawdy jokes.*

bawl [bɔːl] *v* to shout or cry loudly: *He bawled something rude; The baby has bawled all night.*

bay¹ [bei] *n* a wide inward bend of a coastline: *anchored in the bay; Botany Bay.*

bay² [bei] *n* a separate compartment, area or room *etc* (*usu* one of several) set aside for a special purpose: *a bay in a library.*

bay window a window jutting out from a room.

bay³ [bei] *adj* (of horses) reddish-brown in colour.

bay⁴ [bei] *n* (*also* **bay tree**) the laurel tree, the leaves of which are used for seasoning and in victory wreaths.

bay⁵ [bei] *v* (*esp* of large dogs) to bark: *The hounds bayed at the fox.*

bayonet ['beiənit] *n* a knife-like instrument of steel fixed to the end of a rifle barrel.

bazaar [bə'zɑː] *n* **1** an Eastern market place. **2** a sale of goods of various kinds, *esp* home-made or second-hand.

be [biː] – *prt* **am** [am], **are** [ɑː], **is** [iz]: *pt* **was** [wɒz], **were** [wə:]; *prp* **'being**: *ptp* **been** [biːn, (*Amer*) bin]: *subjunctive* **were** [wə:]: *short forms* **I'm** [aim] (**I am**), **you're** [juə] (**you are**), **he's** [hiːz] (**he is**), **she's** [ʃiːz] (**she is**), **it's** [its] (**it is**), **we're** [wiə] (**we are**), **they're** [ðeə] (**they are**): *neg short forms* **isn't** ['iznt] (**is not**), **aren't** [ɑːnt] (**are not**), **wasn't** ['wɒznt] (**was not**), **weren't** [wə:nt] (**were not**) – *v* **1** used with a present participle to form the progressive or continuous tenses: *I'm reading; I am being followed; What were you saying?* **2** used with a present participle to form a type of future tense: *I'm going to London.* **3** used with a past participle to form the passive voice: *He was shot.* **4** used with an infinitive to express several ideas, *eg* necessity (*When am I to leave?*), purpose (*The letter is to tell us he's coming*), a possible future happening (*If he were to lose, I'd win*) *etc.* **5** used in giving or asking for information about something or someone: *I am Mr Smith; Is he alive?; She wants to be an actress; The money will be ours; They are being silly.*

'being *n* **1** existence: *When did the Roman Empire come into being?* **2** any living person or thing: *beings from outer space.*

the be-all and end-all the final aim apart from which nothing is of any real importance: *This job isn't the be-all and end-all of existence.*

beach [biːtʃ] *n* the sandy or stony shore of a sea or lake: *Children love playing on the beach.* – *v* to drive or pull (a boat *etc*) up on to a beach: *We'll beach the boat here and continue on foot.*

beacon ['biːkən] *n* **1** a type of light, fire *etc* that warns of danger, *eg* the light in a lighthouse. **2** a radio station or transmitter that sends out signals to guide shipping or aircraft.

bead [biːd] *n* a little ball of glass *etc* strung with others in a necklace *etc*: *She's wearing two strings of wooden beads.*

'beady *adj* (of eyes) small and bright: *the beady eyes of the bird.*

beak [biːk] *n* the hard, horny (*usu* pointed) part of a bird's mouth: *The bird had a worm in its beak.*

beaker ['biːkə] *n* **1** a large drinking-glass or mug: *a beaker of hot milk.* **2** a deep glass container used in chemistry.

beam [biːm] *n* **1** a long straight piece of wood, often used in ceilings. **2** a ray of light *etc*: *a beam of sunlight.* **3** the greatest width of a ship or boat. – *v* **1** to smile broadly: *She beamed with delight.* **2** to send out (rays of light, radio waves *etc*): *This transmitter beams radio waves all over the country.*

bean [biːn] *n* **1** any one of several kinds of pod-bearing plant or its seed: *black beans; green beans; red beans.* **2** the bean-like seed of other plants: *coffee beans.*

bear¹ [beə] – *pt* **bore** [bɔː] : *ptp* **borne** [bɔːn] – *v* **1** (*usu with* **cannot**, **could not** *etc*) to put up with or endure: *I couldn't bear it if he left.* **2** to be able to support: *Will the table bear my weight?* **3** (*ptp in passive* **born** [bɔːn]) to produce (children): *She has borne* (*him*) *several children; She was born on July 7.* **4** to carry: *He was borne shoulder-high after his victory.* **5** to have: *The cheque bore his signature.* **6** to turn or fork: *The road bears left here.*

'bearable *adj* able to be endured.

'bearer *n* a person or thing that bears: *the bearer of bad news.*

'bearing *n* **1** manner, way of standing *etc*: *a military bearing.* **2** (*usu in pl*: sometimes short for **ball-'bearings**) a part of a machine that has another part moving in or on it.

'bearings *n pl* location, place on a map *etc*; *The island's bearings are 10° North, 24° West.*

bear down on 1 to approach quickly and often threateningly: *The angry teacher bore down on the child.* **2** to exert pressure on: *The weight is bearing down on my chest.*

bear fruit to produce fruit.

bear out to support or confirm: *This bears out what you said.*

bear up to keep up courage, strength *etc* (under strain): *She's bearing up well after her shock.*

bear with to be patient with (someone): *Bear with me for a minute, and you'll see what I mean.*

find/get one's bearings to find one's position with reference to *eg* a known landmark: *If we can find this hill, I'll be able to get my bearings.*

lose one's bearings to become uncertain of one's position: *He's confused me so much that I've lost my bearings completely.*

bear[2] [beə] *n* a large heavy animal with thick fur and hooked claws.

'bearskin *n, adj* (of) the skin of a bear.

beard [biəd] *n* **1** the hair that grows on the chin: *a man's beard; a goat's beard.* **2** a group of hair-like tufts on an ear of corn: *the beard on barley.*

'bearded *adj*: *bearded men.*

beast [bi:st] **1** a four-footed (*esp* large) animal: *beasts of the jungle.* **2** a cruel, brutal person. **3** an unpleasant person: *Arthur is a beast for refusing to come!*

'beastly *adj* **1** like a beast. **2** disagreeable: *What a beastly thing to do!* **'beastliness** *n*.

beat [bi:t] – *pt* **beat**: *ptp* **'beaten** – *v* **1** to strike or hit repeatedly: *Beat the drum.* **2** to win against: *She beat me in a contest.* **3** to mix thoroughly: *to beat an egg.* **4** to move in a regular rhythm: *My heart is beating faster than usual.* **5** to mark or indicate (musical time) with a baton *etc*: *A conductor beats time for an orchestra.* – *n* **1** a regular stroke or its sound: *I like the beat of that song.* **2** a regular or usual course: *a policeman's beat.* **'beater, 'beating** *ns*.

'beaten *adj* **1** overcome; defeated: *the beaten team; He looked tired and beaten.* **2** mixed thoroughly: *beaten egg.*

beat about the bush to approach a subject in an indirect way, without coming to the point or making any decision.

beat down 1 (of the sun) to give out great

heat: *The sun's rays beat down on us.* **2** to (force to) lower a price by bargaining: *We beat the price down; We beat him down to a good price.*

beat it to go away: *Beat it, or I'll hit you!; She told her little brother to beat it.*

beat off to succeed in overcoming or preventing: *The old man beat off the youths who attacked him; He beat the attack off easily.*

beat a (hasty) retreat to go away in a hurry: *The children beat a hasty retreat when he appeared.*

beat up to punch, kick or hit (a person) severely and repeatedly: *He beat up an old lady.*

off the beaten track away from main roads, centres of population *etc*.

beauty ['bju:ti] – *pl* **'beauties** – *n* **1** a quality very pleasing to the eye, ear *etc*: *Her beauty is undeniable.* **2** a woman or girl having such a quality: *She was a great beauty in her youth.* **3** something or someone remarkable: *His new car is a beauty!*

'beautiful *adj*: *a beautiful woman; Those roses are beautiful.* **'beautifully** *adv*.

'beautify [-fai] *v* to make beautiful: *She beautified the room with flowers.*

beauty queen a girl or woman who is voted the most beautiful in a contest.

beauty spot 1 a place of great natural beauty: *a famous beauty spot.* **2** a mark (often artificial) on the face, intended to emphasize beauty.

beaver ['bi:və] *n* **1** an animal with strong front teeth, noted for its skill in damming streams. **2** its fur.

became *see* **become.**

because [bi'koz] *conj* for the reason that: *I can't go because I am ill.*

because of on account of: *I can't walk because of my broken leg.*

beck [bek]: **at someone's beck and call** always ready to carry out someone's wishes: *He has servants at his beck and call.*

beckon ['bekən] *v* to summon (someone) by making a sign with the fingers.

become [bi'kʌm] – *pt* **became** [bi'keim]: *ptp* **be'come** – *v* **1** to come or grow to be: *Her coat has become badly torn; She has become even more beautiful.* **2** to qualify or take a job as: *She became a doctor.* **3** (*with* of) to happen to: *What became of her son?* **4** to suit: *That dress really becomes her.*

be'coming *adj* attractive: *a very becoming dress.* **be'comingly** *adv*.

bed [bed] *n* **1** a piece of furniture, or a place, to sleep on: *The child sleeps in a small bed; a bed of straw.* **2** the channel (of a river) or floor (of a sea) *etc*. **3** a plot in a garden: *a bed of flowers.* **4** layer: *a bed of chalk below the surface.*

-bedded (*as part of a word*) having (a certain

number or type of) bed(s): *a double-bedded room*.

'bedding *n* mattress, bedclothes *etc.*

'bedbug *n* a small blood-sucking insect that lives in houses, especially beds.

'bedclothes [-klouðz, (*Amer*) -klouz] *n pl* sheets, blankets *etc.*

'bedcover *n* a top cover for a bed.

'bedridden *adj* in bed for a long period because of age or sickness: *She has been bedridden since the car accident.*

'bedroom *n* a room for sleeping in.

'bedside *n* the place or position next to a person's bed: *He was at her bedside when she died*; (*also adj*) *a bedside table.*

'bedspread *n* a top cover for a bed: *Please remove the bedspread before you get into bed.*

'bedtime *n* the time at which one normally goes to bed: *Seven o'clock is the children's bedtime*; (*also adj*) *a bedtime story.*

bed and breakfast lodging for the night, and breakfast only (not lunch or dinner).

bed of roses an easy or comfortable place, job *etc*; *Life is not a bed of roses.*

go to bed 1 to get into bed: *I'm sleepy – I think I'll go to bed now*; *What time do you usually go to bed?* **2** (*often with* **with**) to have sexual intercourse with; to have a love affair with.

bedlam ['bedləm] *n* (a place of) noise, confusion or uproar: *Their house is bedlam.*

bee [bi:] *n* **1** a four-winged insect that makes honey. **2** (*esp Amer*) a meeting for combined work and enjoyment: *a knitting bee.*

'beehive *n* a box in which bees are kept, and where they store their honey.

'beeswax ['bi:zwaks] *n* the yellowish solid substance produced by bees for making their cells, and used in polishing wood.

a bee in one's bonnet an idea which has become fixed in one's mind: *She has a bee in her bonnet about going to America.*

make a bee-line for to take the most direct way to; to go immediately to: *Fred always makes a bee-line for the prettiest girl at a party.*

beech [bi:tʃ] *n* **1** (*also* **beech tree**) a kind of forest tree with smooth silvery bark and small nuts: *That tree is a beech*; (*also adj*) *a beech forest.* **2** its wood.

beef [bi:f] *n* the flesh of a bull, cow or ox, used as food.

beefy *adj* **1** of or like beef: *a beefy taste.* **2** having a lot of fat or muscle: *a beefy man.*

beehive *see* bee.

been *see* be.

beer [biə] *n* a type of alcoholic drink made from malted barley flavoured with hops.

small beer something unimportant: *This is small beer compared with his usual work.*

beeswax *see* bee.

beetle ['bi:tl] *n* an insect with four wings.

befall [bi'fo:l] – *pt* **befell** [bi'fel] : *ptp* **be'fallen** – *v* to happen to (a person or thing): *A disaster has befallen her.*

before [bi'fo:] *prep* **1** earlier than: *before the war*; *He'll come before very long.* **2** in front of: *She was before me in the queue.* **3** rather than: *Honour before wealth.* – *adv* earlier: *I've seen you before.* – *conj* earlier than the time when: *Before I go, I must phone my parents.*

be'forehand [-hand] *adv* before the time when something else is done: *If you're coming, let me know beforehand.*

befriend [bi'frend] *v* to take as a friend: *The old man befriended her when she was lonely.*

beg [beg] – *pt, ptp* **begged** – *v* **1** to ask (someone) for (money, food *etc*): *The old man was so poor that he had to beg in the street*; *He begged (me) for money.* **2** to ask (someone) desperately or earnestly: *I beg you not to do it.*

'beggar *n* a person who lives by begging: *The beggar asked for money for food.* – *v* to make very poor: *He was beggared by the collapse of his firm.*

beggar description to be so great in some way that it cannot be described: *Her beauty beggars description.*

beg to differ to disagree: *You may think that he should get the job but I beg to differ.*

began *see* begin.

beggar *see* beg.

begin [bi'gin] – *prp* **be'ginning**: *pt* **began** [bi'gan]: *ptp* **begun** [bi'gʌn] – *v* to come, or bring, into being, to start: *He began to talk*; *The meeting began early.* **be'ginning** *n.*

be'ginner *n* someone who is just learning how to do something: *'Does he paint well?' 'He's not bad for a beginner'.*

to begin with 1 at first: *I didn't like him to begin with, but now he's one of my best friends.* **2** firstly: *There are many reasons why I don't like her – to begin with, she doesn't tell the truth.*

begonia [bi'gouniə] *n* a tropical plant with pink flowers and often coloured leaves.

begrudge [bi'grʌdʒ] *v* to envy (someone something): *I begrudge him his success.*

beguile [bi'gail] *v* **1** to occupy (time) pleasantly: *He beguiled the time with gardening.* **2** to charm or amuse (a person): *She beguiled the children with stories.*

be'guiling *adj* charming: *a beguiling smile.*

be'guilingly *adv.*

begun *see* begin.

behalf [bi'ha:f]: **on behalf of (someone)** for, or in the interests of: *on behalf of all our members*; *I'm collecting on behalf of the blind.*

behave [bi'heiv] *v* **1** to act in a suitable way, to conduct oneself (well): *If you come, you* must behave (*yourself*); *The child always behaves* (*himself*) *at his grandmother's.* **2** to act or react: *He always behaves like a gentleman*; *Metals behave in different ways when heated.*

be'haviour, (*Amer*) **be'havior** [-jə] *n* **1** way of behaving: *the behaviour of the pupils.* **2** actions or reactions: *the behaviour of rats*; *the behaviour of metals in acids.*

,well-, ,badly- *etc* **be'haved** *adj* good (bad *etc*) in manners or conduct: *badly-behaved children.*

beheld *see* **behold.**

behind [bi'haind] *prep* **1** at or towards the back of: *behind the door.* **2** remaining after: *The tourists left their litter behind them.* **3** in support: *We're right behind him on this point.* – *adv* **1** at the back: *following behind.* **2** (*also* **be'hindhand** [-hand]) not up to date: *behind with his work.* **3** remaining: *He left his book behind*; *We stayed behind after the party.* – *n* the buttocks: *a smack on the behind.*

behind someone's back without someone's knowledge or permission: *He sometimes bullies his sister behind his mother's back.*

behold [bi'hould] – *pt, ptp* **beheld** [bi'held] – *v* to see: *What a sight to behold!*

beige [beiʒ] *n* a pale pinkish-yellow colour. – *Also adj*: *a beige hat.*

being *see* **be.**

belated [bi'leitid] *adj* happening *etc*, late or too late: *a belated birthday card*; *belated thanks.*

be'latedly *adv.*

belch [beltʃ] *v* **1** to give out air noisily from the stomach through the mouth: *He belched after eating too much.* **2** (*often with* **out**) (of a chimney, *etc*) to throw (out) violently: *factory chimneys belching* (*out*) *smoke.* – *n* an act of belching.

beleaguered [bi'li:gəd] *adj* under attack: *a beleaguered castle*; *The city was beleaguered.*

belfry ['belfri] – *pl* **'belfries** – *n* the part of a (church) tower in which bells are hung.

belie [bi'lai] – *prp* **be'lying**: *ptp* **be'lied** – *v* to give a false idea or impression of (something): *His innocent face belies his cunning.*

belief *see* **believe.**

believe [bi'li:v] *v* **1** to regard (something) as true: *I believe his story.* **2** to trust (a person), accepting what he says as true: *I believe you.* **3** to think (that): *I believe he's ill.* **be'lievable** *adj.*

be'lief [-f] *n* **1** faith or trust: *I have no belief in his ability.* **2** (*often in pl*) something believed: *Christian beliefs.*

be'liever *n* a person who has (*esp* religious) beliefs: *a true believer.*

believe in to accept the existence or recognize the value of (something): *Do you*

believe in ghosts?; *He believes in capital punishment.*

belittle [bi'litl] *v* to make to seem unimportant (*usu* by harsh criticism): *She belittled his achievements.*

bell [bel] *n* **1** a hollow object, *usu* of metal, which gives a ringing sound when struck by the clapper inside: *church bells.* **2** any other mechanism for giving a ringing sound: *Our doorbell is broken.*

bellicose ['belikous] *adj* warlike or quarrelsome: *a bellicose nation.*

belligerent [bi'lidʒərənt] *adj* **1** unfriendly; hostile: *a belligerent stare*; *She is very belligerent and quarrelsome.* **2** waging war: *belligerent nations.*

bel'ligerence *n.* **bel'ligerently** *adv.*

bellow ['belou] *v* to roar like a bull: *The headmaster bellowed at the children.* – *n* an act of roaring.

bellows ['belouz] *n pl* an instrument for making a current of air.

belly ['beli] – *pl* **'bellies** – *n* the part of the body between the breast and the thighs, containing the bowels: *the horse's belly*; *I've a pain in my belly.*

'belly-laugh *n* a loud, deep laugh: *the belly-laughs of the rugby players in the bar.*

belong [bi'loŋ] *v* **1** (*with* **to**) to be the property of: *This book belongs to me.* **2** (*with* **to**) to be a native, member *etc* of: *I belong to the sailing club.* **3** (*with* **with**) to go together with: *This shoe belongs with that shoe.*

be'longings *n pl* personal possessions: *She can't have gone away – all her belongings are still here.*

beloved [bi'lʌvid] *adj* much loved: *my beloved country.* – *n* a person very dear to one: *My beloved left me for another.*

below [bə'lou] *prep* lower in position, rank, standard *etc* than: *She hurt her leg below the knee*; *His work is below standard.* – *adv* in a lower place: *We looked at the houses* (*down*) *below.*

belt [belt] *n* **1** a long (narrow) piece of leather, cloth *etc* worn round the waist: *a trouser-belt*; *He tightened his belt.* **2** a similar object used to set wheels in motion: *the belt of a vacuum-cleaner.* **3** a zone of country *etc*: *a belt of trees*; *an industrial belt.* – *v* **1** to fasten with a belt: *He belted his trousers on.* **2** to strike (with or without a belt): *He belted the disobedient dog.*

'belted *adj.*

bemused [bi'mju:zd] *adj* bewildered or greatly puzzled: *a bemused look.*

bench [bentʃ] *n* **1** a long (*usu* wooden) seat: *a park bench.* **2** a work-table for a carpenter *etc*: *tools on the workbench.*

bend [bend] – *pt, ptp* **bent** [bent] – *v* **1** to make, become, or be, angled or curved: *Bend your arm*; *She bent down to pick up the* *coin*; *The road bends to the right*; *He could bend an iron bar*. **2** to force (someone) to do what one wants: *He bent me to his will*. – *n* a curve or angle: *a bend in the road*.

the bends agonizing pains, *esp* in the joints, affecting divers when they surface too quickly.

bent on determined on: *bent on winning*.

beneath [bi'ni:θ] *prep* **1** in a lower position than; under; below: *beneath the floorboards*; *beneath her coat*. **2** not worthy of: *It is beneath my dignity to do that*. – *adv* below or underneath: *They watched the boat breaking up on the rocks beneath*.

benediction [benə'dikʃən] *n* a prayer giving blessing.

benefactor ['benəfaktə] *n* a person who gives friendly help, often in the form of money: *the benefactor of the school*.

beneficial [benə'fiʃəl] *adj* having good effects: *Fresh air is beneficial to your health*.

bene'ficiary [-ʃəri, (*Amer*) -ʃieri] – *pl* **bene'ficiaries** – *n* a person who receives a gift *etc* (*usu* in a will).

benefit ['benəflit] *n* something good to receive, an advantage: *the benefit of experience*; *the benefits of fresh air and exercise*. – *v* – *pt*, *ptp* **'benefited** – **1** (*usu* with **from** or **by**) to gain advantage: *He benefited from the advice*. **2** to do good to: *The long rest benefited her*.

give (someone) the benefit of the doubt to assume that someone is telling the truth because one cannot be sure that he is not doing so.

benevolence [bi'nevələns] *n* generosity and desire to do good.
be'nevolent *adj*: *a benevolent father*.
be'nevolently *adv*.

benign [bi'nain] *adj* **1** kind, well-wishing: *a benign smile*. **2** not fatal: *a benign tumour*.
be'nignly *adv*: *smiling benignly*.

bent[1] *see* **bend**.

bent[2] [bent] *n* a natural inclination: *a bent for mathematics*.

bequeath [bi'kwi:ð] *v* to leave (personal belongings) by will: *She bequeathed her art collection to the town*.
bequest [bi'kwest] *n* something bequeathed in a will: *I received a bequest in my uncle's will*.

bereaved [bi'ri:vd] *adj* having lost, through death, someone dear: *a bereaved mother*.
be'reavement *n*: *The family has suffered two bereavements recently*.

bereft [bi'reft] *adj* (with **of**) having had something taken away: *bereft of speech*.

berry ['beri] – *pl* **'berries** – *n* a kind of small (often juicy) fruit: *holly berry*; *ripe strawberries*; *Those berries are poisonous*.

berth [bə:θ] *n* **1** a sleeping-place in a ship *etc*. **2** a place in a port *etc* where a ship can be moored. – *v* to moor (a ship): *The ship berthed last night*.

beseech [bi'si:tʃ] – *pts*, *ptps* **besought** [bi'sɔ:t], **be'seeched** – *v* to beg: *Don't kill him* – *I beseech you!*

beset [bi'set] – *pt*, *ptp* **be'set** – *v* to attack on all sides: *beset by thieves*.

beside [bi'said] *prep* **1** by the side of or near: *beside the window*; *She sat beside her sister*. **2** compared with: *She looks ugly beside her sister*.

be'sides *prep* in addition to: *Is anyone coming besides John?* – *adv* also: *These shoes are expensive* – *besides, they're too small*; *She has three sons and an adopted one besides*.

be beside oneself (with) to be in a state of very great, uncontrolled emotion: *She was beside herself with excitement as her holiday approached*.

be beside the point to be irrelevant: *You will have to go. Whether you want to go is beside the point*.

besiege [bi'si:dʒ] *v* **1** to surround (*eg* a town) with an army. **2** (with **with**) to overwhelm with: *The reporters besieged me with questions about the plane crash*.

besought *see* **beseech**.

best [best] *adj*, *pron* (something which is) good to the greatest extent: *the best book on the subject*; *the best (that) I can do*; *She is my best friend*; *Which method is (the) best?*; *The flowers are at their best just now*. – *adv* in the best manner: *She sings best (of all)*. – *v* to defeat: *He was bested in the argument*.

best man the bridegroom's attendant at a wedding.

best'seller *n* something (*usu* a book) which sells very many copies: *Ernest Hemingway wrote several bestsellers*.

the best part of most of; nearly (all of): *I've read the best part of two hundred books on the subject*.

do one's best to try as hard as possible: *He'll do his best to be here on time*.

for the best intended to have the best results possible: *We don't want to send the child away to school but we're doing it for the best*.

get the best of to win, or get some advantage from, (a fight, argument *etc*): *He was shouting a lot, but I think I got the best of the argument*.

make the best of it to do all one can to turn a failure *etc* into something successful: *She is disappointed at not getting into university but she'll just have to make the best of it and find a job*.

bestow [bi'stou] *v* (with **on**) to give (*esp* a title, award *etc*) to someone: *The Queen bestowed a knighthood on him.* **be'stowal** *n*.

bet [bet] – *pts, ptps* **bet, 'betted** – *v* (*often with* **on**) to gamble (*usu* with money) *eg* on a racehorse: *I'm betting on that horse.* – *n* **1** an act of betting: *I won my bet.* **2** a sum of money betted: *Place your bets.*

an even bet an equal chance.

take a bet (*often with* **on**) to bet: *Are you willing to take a bet on whether he'll come or not?*

you bet certainly; of course.

betray [bi'trei] *v* **1** to act disloyally or treacherously towards (*esp* a person who trusts one): *He betrayed his own brother (to the enemy).* **2** to give away (a secret *etc*): *Never betray a confidence!* **3** to show (signs of): *Her pale face betrayed her fear.* **be'trayal** *n*. **be'trayer** *n*.

betroth [bi'trouð, (*Amer*) bi'tro:θ] *v* to promise in marriage: *She was betrothed to her husband at the age of twenty.*
be'trothal *n*.
be'trothed *n* the person to whom one is betrothed: *May I introduce you to my betrothed?*

better ['betə] *adj* **1** good to a greater extent: *His new car is better than his old one.* **2** stronger in health; recovered (from an illness): *I feel better today; She's better now.* **3** preferable: *Better to do it now than later.* – *adv* well to a greater extent: *He sings better now than he did before.* – *pron* someone or something which is good to a greater extent than the other (of two people or things): *He's the better of the two.* – *v* to improve (on): *He's bettered all previous records; The situation has bettered a little.*
better off richer; happier in some way: *He'd be better off working as a miner; You'd be better off without him.*
the better part of most of: *He talked for the better part of an hour.*
get the better of to overcome; to win (against): *He got the better of his opponent/the argument.*

> *He is better today* (not *He is more better*). *He is much better* is correct.

> *You had better come/You'd better come* (not *You better come*).

between [bi'twi:n] *prep* **1** in, to, through or across the space dividing two people, places, times *etc*: *between the car and the pavement; between 2 o'clock and 2.30; between meals.* **2** concerning the relationship of two things or people: *the difference between right and wrong.* **3** by the combined action of; working together: *They managed it between them.* **4** part to one (person or

thing), part to (the other): *Divide the chocolate between you.*
between you and me/between ourselves in confidence: *Between you and me, I think he's rather nice.*

> **between** is usually used for two.
> **among** is usually used for more than two.

bevel ['bevəl] *n* a slanting edge (rather than a sharp corner): *A chisel has a bevel on its cutting edge.*
'bevelled *adj*: *bevelled glass.*

beverage ['bevəridʒ] *n* a drink, *esp* tea, coffee, or other non-alcoholic drink.

beware [bi'weə] – used mostly in the imperative and the infinitive – *v* **1** (*usu with* **of**) to be careful (of): *Beware of the dog.* **2** to be careful: *He told them to beware.*

bewilder [bi'wildə] *v* to amaze or puzzle: *She was bewildered when her husband suddenly left her; bewildered by the instructions.*
be'wilderment *n*.

bewitch [bi'witʃ] *v* to cast a spell on, to charm: *She bewitched us with her smile.*
be'witching *adj*.

beyond [bi'jond] *prep* **1** on the farther side of: *My house is just beyond those trees.* **2** farther on than (something) in time or place: *I cannot plan beyond tomorrow.* **3** out of the range, power *etc* of: *beyond help.* **4** other than: *What is there to say beyond what's already been said?*
beyond compare having no equal: *His achievements are beyond compare.*
beyond one's means too expensive(ly): *A painting by Picasso is beyond my means; He lives well beyond his means* (= he spends more money than he earns).

bi-annual [bai'anjuəl] *adj* happening twice a year: *a bi-annual event; The dinner is bi-annual, not annual.* ˌbi-'annually *adj*.

bias ['baiəs] *n* **1** favouring of one or other (side in an argument *etc*) rather than remaining neutral: *a bias against people of other religions.* **2** a weight on or in an object (*eg* a bowl for playing bowls) making it move in a particular direction. – *v* – *pt, ptp* **'bias(s)ed** – to influence (*usu* unfairly): *He was biased by the report in the newspapers.* **'bias(s)ed** *adj* (*neg* **un-**) favouring one side rather than another: *a biased judgement.*

bib [bib] *n* **1** a cloth *etc* tied under a child's chin to catch spilt food *etc*. **2** the top part of an apron or overalls, covering the chest.

Bible ['baibl] *n* (*with* **the**) the sacred writings of the Christian Church, consisting of the Old and New Testaments.
biblical ['biblikəl] *adj* (*often with* cap) of or like the Bible: *biblical references.*

bibliography [bibli'ogrəfi] – *pl* **bibli'ographies** – *n* a list of books.

bicentenary [baisen'ti:nəri, (*Amer*) bai'sentəneri] (*pl* **bicen'tenaries**), **bicentennial** [baisen'teniəl] *n* a two-hundredth anniversary: *the bicentenary of American independence.*

biceps ['baiseps] *n pl* the large muscles in the front of the upper arm: *The boxer has enormous biceps.*

*bicycle ['baisikl] *n* (*often abbrev* **bike** [baik], **cycle** ['saikl]) a pedal-driven vehicle with two wheels and a seat. – *v* (*usu abbrev* **'cycle**) to ride a bicycle: *He bicycled slowly up the hill.*

bid [bid] *v* 1 – *pt, ptp* **bid** – to offer (an amount of money) at an auction: *John bid ($1000) for the painting.* 2 (*with* **for**) – *pt, ptp* **bid** – to state a price (for a contract): *My firm is bidding for the contract for the new road.* 3 – *pt* **bade** [bad], *ptp* **'bidden** – to tell (someone) to (do something): *He bade me enter.* 4 – *pt* **bade** [bad], *ptp* **'bidden** – to express a greeting *etc* (to someone): *He bade me farewell.* – *n* 1 an offer of a price: *a bid of $20.* 2 an attempt (to obtain): *a bid for freedom.* **'bidder** *n.* **'bidding** *n.*

'biddable *adj* obedient: *a biddable child.*

bide [baid] : **bide one's time** to wait for a good opportunity: *I'm just biding my time until he makes a mistake.*

biennial [bai'eniəl] *adj* (of plants *etc*) lasting for two years: *Wallflowers are biennial; a biennial plant.*

bifocal [bai'foukəl] *adj* (of lenses) having two points of focus, which help people to see things close at hand and things far away.

big [big] *adj* 1 large in size: *a big car.* 2 important: *a big event.*

big game large animals (*usu* lions, tigers *etc*) that are hunted: *He hunts big game in Africa; a big game hunter.*

bigamy ['bigəmi] *n* marriage to two wives or two husbands at once (a crime in some countries): *He's been charged with committing bigamy.* **'bigamist** *n.* **'bigamous** *adj.*

bigot ['bigət] *n* a person who constantly and stubbornly holds a particular point of view *etc*: *a religious bigot.* **'bigoted** *adj.*

'bigotry *n* bigoted attitude or behaviour.

bike *see* **bicycle**.

bikini [bi'ki:ni] *n* a brief two-piece swimming costume for women.

bilateral [bai'latərəl] *adj* affecting, signed, or agreed, by two sides, countries *etc*: *a bilateral agreement.*

bile [bail] *n* 1 a yellowish thick bitter fluid in the liver. 2 anger or irritability.

bilious ['biljəs] *adj* 1 of, or affected by, too much bile: *a bilious attack.* **'biliousness** *n.*

bilingual [bai'liŋgwəl] *adj* 1 written or spoken in two languages: *a bilingual dictionary.* 2 speaking two languages equally well: *a bilingual waiter.*

bill[1] [bil] *n* a bird's beak: *a bird with a yellow bill.*

bill[2] [bil] *n* 1 an account of money owed for goods *etc*: *an electricity bill.* 2 (*Amer*) a banknote: *a five-dollar bill.* 3 a poster used for advertising. – *v* to send an account (to someone): *We'll bill you next month for your purchases.*

'billboard *n* a large board on which advertising posters are displayed: *He stuck posters on the billboard.*

'billfold *n* (*Amer*) a wallet: *a billfold full of dollars.*

fill the bill to be suitable; to be exactly what is required: *We are looking for a new car and this will fill the bill.*

billet ['bilit] *n* a private house *etc* where soldiers are given food and lodging. – *v* – *pt, ptp* **'billeted** – to give lodging to (*eg* soldiers): *The men are billeted in the church hall.*

billiards ['biljədz] *n sing* a game played with long thin sticks (**cues**) and balls, on a table.

billion ['biljən] – *pls* **'billion** (1, 3), **'billions** (2, 3) – *n* 1 often in the UK, the number 1 000 000 000 000; in the US and often in the UK, the number 1 000 000 000: *a billion; several billion.* 2 often in the UK, the figure 1 000 000 000 000; in the US and often in the UK, the figure 1 000 000 000. 3 a billion pounds or dollars: *The sum involved amounts to several billion(s).* – *adj* often in the UK, 1 000 000 000 000 in number; in the US and often in the UK, 1 000 000 000 in number: *a few billion stars.*

'billionth *n* one of a billion equal parts.

billow ['bilou] *n* a large wave. **'billowy** *adj.*

billow out to move in a way similar to large waves: *The sails billowed out in the strong wind; Her skirt billowed out in the breeze.*

billy-goat ['biligout] *n* a male (*usu* adult) goat.

bi-monthly [bai'mʌnθli] *adj, adv* 1 (happening) once in every two months. 2 (happening) twice a month.

bin [bin] *n* a container (*usu* metal or plastic, often large) in which corn *etc* is stored or rubbish is collected: *a waste-paper bin; a dustbin.*

binary ['bainəri]: **the binary system** the system of writing and calculating with numbers which uses only two digits (0 and 1) and has 2 as a base (101 = 1 four, 0 twos, 1 unit = 5).

bind [baind] – *pt, ptp* **bound** [baund] – *v* 1 to tie up: *The doctor bound up the patient's leg with a bandage; The robbers bound up the bank manager with rope.* 2 to fasten together and put a cover on the pages of (a book): *Bind this book in leather.*

'binding *n* the covering in which the leaves of a book are fixed: *leather binding.*

* see illustration on p. 595

-bound (as part of a word) prevented from making progress by a particular thing: *The ship was fogbound.*

bingo ['biŋgou] *n* a gambling game using cards with numbered squares.

binoculars [bi'nokjuləz] *n pl* an instrument for making distant objects look nearer, with separate eyepieces for each eye: *He looked at the ship on the horizon through his binoculars.*

biochemistry [baiə'kemistri] *n* the chemistry of living things: *He is studying the biochemistry of the blood*; (also *adj*) *a biochemistry lecture.* ,bio'chemical [-mikəl] *adj.* ,bio'chemist *n.*

biography [bai'ogrəfi] – *pl* bi'ographies – *n* a written account by someone of another person's life: *a biography of Nelson.* bi'ographer *n.* ,bio'graphic(al) [-'gra-] *adj.*

biology [bai'olədʒi] *n* the science of living things: *human biology*; (also *adj*) *a biology lesson.* bio'logical [-'lo-] *adj.* bio'logically [-'lo-] *adv.* bi'ologist *n.*

biological warfare the use of germs as a weapon.

bionics [bai'oniks] *n sing* the use of biological principles in the design of computers *etc.* bi'onic *adj* of or using bionics.

biped ['baiped] *n* an animal with two feet (*eg* man).

birch [bə:tʃ] *n* 1 (*also* birch tree) a kind of small tree with pointed leaves valued for its wood: *That tree is a birch*; (also *adj*) *birch leaves.* 2 its wood: *a desk made of birch*; (also *adj*) *a birch desk.*

bird [bə:d] *n* a two-legged feathered creature, with a beak and two wings, with which most can fly: *Kiwis and ostriches are birds which cannot fly.*

bird's-eye view a general view from above: *a bird's-eye view of the town from an aeroplane.*

bird's nest fern a large fern with long and wide fronds and hairy roots.

birth [bə:θ] *n* 1 (an) act of coming into the world, being born: *the birth of her son*; *deaf since birth.* 2 the beginning: *the birth of civilization.*

birth control prevention of the conception of children.

'birthday *n* the anniversary of the day on which a person was born: *Today is his birthday*; (also *adj*) *a birthday party.*

'birthmark *n* a permanent mark on the skin at or from birth: *She has a red birthmark on her face.*

'birthplace *n* the place where a person *etc* was born: *Shakespeare's birthplace.*

'birthrate *n* the number of births per head of population over a given period.

give birth (to) (of a mother) to produce (a

baby) from the womb: *She has given birth to two sets of twins.*

biscuit ['biskit] *n* 1 (*Amer* 'cookie) a crisp, sweet piece of dough baked in small flat cakes. 2 a similar savoury flat cake. 3 (*Amer*) a small soft round cake.

bisect [bai'sekt] *v* to cut into two equal parts: *A diagonal line across a square bisects it.*

bishop ['biʃəp] *n* 1 a Christian clergyman in charge of a group of churches, *usu* in a large city or area: *the Bishop of Lincoln*; *He was made a bishop two years ago.* 2 one of the pieces in chess.

bison ['baisn] – *pls* 'bison, (*rare*) 'bisons – *n* 1 the American buffalo: *a herd of bison.* 2 the large European wild ox.

bit¹ [bit] *n* 1 a small piece: *a bit of bread.* 2 a piece of any size: *a bit of advice.* 3 a short time: *Wait a bit longer.*

bit by bit gradually: *Move the pile of rocks bit by bit.*

do one's bit to take one's share in a task: *Each of us will have to do his bit if we are to finish the job soon.*

in, to bits in(to) *usu* small pieces: *The broken mirror lay in bits on the floor*; *He loves taking his car to bits.*

bit² *see* bite.

bit³ [bit] *n* the part of a bridle which a horse holds in its mouth.

bitch [bitʃ] *n* 1 the female of the dog, wolf or fox. 2 a (bad-tempered or unpleasant) woman.

'bitchy *adj* (*usu* of women) fond of making unpleasant comments about people: *She is sometimes very bitchy about her colleagues.*

bite [bait] – *pt* bit [bit] : *ptp* bitten ['bitn] – *v* to seize, grasp or tear (something) with the teeth or jaws: *The dog bit his leg*; *He was bitten by a mosquito.* – *n* 1 an act of biting or the piece or place bitten: *a bite from the apple*; *a mosquito bite.* 2 the nibble of a fish on the end of one's line: *I've been fishing for hours without a bite.*

'biting *adj* 1 very cold and causing discomfort: *a biting wind.* 2 wounding or hurtful: *a biting remark.*

bite the dust to fail; to be unsuccessful: *That's another scheme that's bitten the dust.*

bitter ['bitə] *adj* 1 having a sharp, acid taste like lemons *etc*, and sometimes unpleasant: *a bitter orange.* 2 full of pain or sorrow: *She learned from bitter experience*; *bitter disappointment.* 3 hostile: full of hatred or opposition: *bitter enemies.* 4 very cold: *a bitter wind.* 'bitterness *n.*

'bitterly *adv*: *bitterly disappointed*; *bitterly cold.*

*'bittergourd *n* a long, fleshy, bitter-tasting fruit usually used as a vegetable.

bitumen ['bitjumin] *n* a black, sticky substance obtained from petroleum. **bi'tuminous** [-'tju:mi-] *adj.*

bi-weekly [bai'wi:kli] *adj, adv* **1** (happening *etc*) once every two weeks. **2** (happening *etc*) twice each week.

bizarre [bi'za:] *adj* odd or very strange: *a bizarre turn of events.*

black [blak] *adj* **1** of the colour in which these words are printed: *black paint.* **2** without light: *a black night*; *The night was black and starless.* **3** dirty: *Your hands are black!*; *black hands from lifting coal.* **4** without milk: *black coffee.* **5** evil: *black magic.* **6** (*often offensive: currently acceptable in the US, S Africa etc*) Negro, of African, West Indian descent. **7** (*esp S Africa*) coloured; of mixed descent (increasingly used by people of mixed descent to refer to themselves). – *n* **1** the colour in which these words are printed: *Black and white are opposites.* **2** something (*eg* paint) black in colour: *I've used up all the black.* **3** *n* (*often with cap: often offensive: currently acceptable in the US, S Africa etc*) a Negro; a person of African, West Indian *etc* descent. – *v* to make black. **'blackness** *n.*

'blacken *v* **1** to make or become black: *The sky blackened before the storm.* **2** to make to seem bad: *She blackened his character.* **3** to clean with black polish: *He blackened his boots.*

black art/magic magic performed for evil reasons: *He tries to practise black magic.*

'blackbird *n* a dark-coloured bird of the thrush family.

'blackboard *n* a dark-coloured board for writing on in chalk (used *esp* in schools).

black box a built-in machine for automatic recording of the details of a plane's flight: *They found the black box two miles away from the wreckage of the crashed plane.*

black eye an eye with bad bruising around it (*eg* from a punch): *George gave me a black eye.*

'blackhead *n* a small black-topped lump in a pore of the skin, *esp* of the face.

'blacklist *n* a list of people who are out of favour *etc*. – *v* to put (a person *etc*) on such a list.

'blackmail *v* to obtain money illegally from (a person), *usu* by threatening to make known something which the victim wants to keep secret. – *n* the act of blackmailing: *money got by blackmail.* **'blackmailer** *n.*

Black Maria [mə'raiə] a prison van: *The policeman took the three suspects to the police station in a Black Maria.*

black market (a place for) the illegal buying and selling, at high prices, of goods that are scarce, rationed *etc*: *coffee on the black market.*

black marketeer a person who sells goods on the black market.

'blackout *n* **1** a period of darkness produced by putting out all lights: *Accidents increase during a blackout.* **2** a ban (on news *etc*): *a blackout of news about the coup.* **3** a period of unconsciousness: *He has had several blackouts during his illness.*

black sheep a member of a family or group who is unsatisfactory in some way: *My brother is the black sheep of the family.*

'blacksmith *n* a person who makes and repairs by hand things made of iron: *The blacksmith made a new shoe for the horse.*

black and blue badly bruised: *After the fight the boy was all black and blue.*

black out to lose consciousness: *He blacked out for almost a minute.*

in black and white in writing or print: *Would you put that down in black and white?*

bladder ['bladə] *n* the bag-like part of the body in which the urine collects.

blade [bleid] *n* **1** the cutting part of a knife *etc*: *His penknife has several different blades.* **2** the flat part of a leaf *etc*: *a blade of grass.* **3** the flat part of an oar.

blame [bleim] *v* **1** to consider someone or something responsible for something bad: *I blame the wet road for the accident.* **2** to find fault with (a person): *I don't blame you for wanting to leave.* – *n* the responsibility (for something bad): *He takes the blame for everything that goes wrong.* **'blameless** *adj* innocent: *a blameless life.*

bland [bland] *adj* **1** (of food *etc*) mild, tasteless: *That soup is very bland.* **2** (of people, their actions *etc*) showing no emotion: *a bland smile.* **'blandly** *adv.* **'blandness** *n.*

blank [blaŋk] *adj* **1** (of paper) without writing or marks: *a blank sheet of paper.* **2** expressionless: *a blank look.* **3** (of a wall) having no door, window *etc.* – *n* **1** (in forms *etc*) a space left to be filled (with a signature *etc*): *Fill in all the blanks!* **2** a blank cartridge: *The soldier fired a blank.* **'blankly** *adv* with a blank expression: *He looked at me blankly.* **'blankness** *n.*

blank cartridge a cartridge without a bullet.

blank cheque a signed cheque on which the sum to be paid has not been entered.

go blank to become empty: *My mind went blank when the police questioned me.*

blanket ['blaŋkit] *n* **1** a warm covering made of wool *etc*: *a blanket on the bed* **2** something which covers like a blanket: *a blanket of mist.* – *adj* covering all of a group of things: *a blanket instruction.* – *v pt, ptp* **'blanketed** – to cover, as if with a blanket: *The hills were blanketed in mist.*

blare [bleə] *v* (*often with* **out**) to make a loud, harsh sound: *The radio blared (out music).* – *n*: *the blare of trumpets.*

blasphemous ['blasfəməs] *adj* (of speech or writing about God, religion *etc*) irreverent and without respect.

blast [bla:st] *n* 1 a strong, sudden stream (of air): *a blast of cold air*. 2 a loud sound: *a blast on the horn*. 3 an explosion: *the blast from a bomb*. – *v* 1 to tear (apart *etc*) by an explosion: *The door was blasted off its hinges*. 2 (*often with* **out**) to come or be sent out, very loudly: *Music (was being) blasted out from the radio*.

'**blasting** *n* in mining *etc*, the breaking up of rock *etc* by explosives.

blast furnace *n* a furnace for melting iron ore using blasts of hot air.

at full blast at full power, speed *etc*. *He had the radio going at full blast* (= as loud as possible).

blast off (of rockets, spacecraft *etc*) to take off and start to rise (*n* '**blast-off**).

blatant ['bleitənt] *adj* very obvious; shameless: *a blatant lie*; *blatant disrespect*. '**blatantly** *adv*.

blaze[1] [bleiz] *n* 1 a bright light or fire: *A neighbour rescued her from the blaze*. 2 an outburst (of anger, emotion *etc*): *a blaze of fury*. 3 a bright display: *a blaze of colour*. – *v* (of a fire, the sun) to burn, shine brightly. '**blazing** *adj* 1 burning brightly: *a blazing fire*. 2 extremely angry: *a blazing row*.

blaze[2] [bleiz]: **blaze a trail** to lead or show the way towards something new: *He blazed a trail in the field of nuclear power*.

blazer ['bleizə] *n* a type of jacket, often part of a school·uniform.

bleach [bli:tʃ] *n* liquid *etc* used for whitening clothes *etc*. – *v* to lose colour; to whiten: *The sun has bleached his red shirt*; *His hair bleached in the sun*.

bleak [bli:k] *adj* 1 cold and unsheltered: *a bleak landscape*. 2 not hopeful: *a bleak outlook for the future*.

bleat [bli:t] *v* to make the noise of a sheep, lamb or goat: *The lamb bleated for its mother*.

bleed [bli:d] – *pt, ptp* **bled** [bled] – *v* to lose blood: *Her nose was bleeding badly*.

'**bleeding** *adj* losing blood: *a bleeding wound*.

bleep [bli:p] *n* 1 a short, high-pitched burst of sound. 2 (*also* '**bleeper**) a small instrument for making this sound: *Call Dr Smith on his bleep!* – *v* to make a short, high-pitched sound, *usu* by electronic means: *Satellites bleep as they circle the earth*.

blemish ['blemiʃ] *n* a stain, mark or fault: *a blemish on an apple*. – *v* to spoil.

blend [blend] *v* to mix together: *Blend the eggs and milk together*; *These two colours blend well*. – *n* a mixture.

'**blender** *n* a machine for mixing things together, *esp* in cooking.

bless [bles] – *pt* **blessed**: *ptps* **blessed, blest** – to ask God to show favour to: *Bless this ship*.

blessed ['blesid] *adj* holy: *the Blessed Virgin*. '**blessedly** [-sid-] *adv*. '**blessedness** [-sid-] *n*.

'**blessing** *n* 1 a wish or prayer for happiness or success: *The priest gave them his blessing*. 2 any cause of happiness: *Her son was great blessing to her*.

a blessing in disguise something that has proved to be fortunate after seeming unfortunate.

blew *see* **blow**[2].

blight [blait] *n* a disease in plants that withers them: *potato blight*.

blind [blaind] *adj* 1 not able to see: *a blind man*. 2 (*with* **to**) unable to notice: *She is blind to his faults*. 3 hiding what is beyond: *a blind corner*. 4 of or for blind people: *a blind school*. – *n* 1 (*often in pl*) a screen to prevent light coming through a window *etc*: *The sunlight is too bright – pull down the blinds!* 2 something intended to mislead or deceive: *He did that as a blind*. – *v* to make blind: *He was blinded in the war*.

'**blinding** *adj* 1 tending to make blind: *a blinding light*. 2 sudden: *He realized, in a blinding flash that she was the murderer*.

'**blindly** *adv*. '**blindness** *n*.

blind alley a situation without any way out: *This is a blind alley of a job*.

'**blindfold** *n* a piece of cloth *etc* put over the eyes to prevent someone from seeing: *The kidnappers put a blindfold over the child's eyes*. – *v* to put a blindfold on (some person or animal). – *adj, adv* with the eyes covered by a cloth *etc*: *She came blindfold into the room*.

blind spot 1 any matter about which one always shows lack of understanding: *She seems to have a blind spot about physics*. 2 an area which is impossible or difficult to see due to an obstruction.

the blind leading the blind one inexperienced or incompetent person telling another about something: *My teaching you about politics will be a case of the blind leading the blind*.

blink [bliŋk] *v* to move (the eyelids) rapidly up and down: *It is impossible to stare for a long time without blinking*. – *n* a rapid movement of the eyelids.

bliss [blis] *n* very great happiness: *the bliss of a young married couple*. '**blissful** *adj*. '**blissfully** *adv*.

blister ['blistə] *n* 1 a thin bubble on the skin, containing liquid: *My feet have blisters after walking so far*. 2 a similar spot on any surface: *blisters on paintwork*. – *v* to (cause to) rise in a blister or blisters.

blithe [blaið] *adj* happy and light-hearted: *She is merry and blithe*. '**blithely** *adv*.

blitz [blits] *n* a sudden, vigorous attack, *orig* in war. – *v* to make an attack on (*usu* in war): *They blitzed London during the war.*

blizzard ['blizəd] *n* a blinding storm of wind and snow: *Two climbers are missing after yesterday's blizzard.*

blob [blob] *n* a (*usu* small) shapeless mass of liquid *etc*: *a blob of paint; a blob of wax.*

bloc [blok] *n* a group of nations *etc* who have an interest or purpose in common: *the European trade bloc.*

block [blok] *n* **1** a flat-sided mass of wood or stone *etc*: *blocks of stone.* **2** a piece of wood used for certain purposes: *a chopping-block.* **3** a connected group of houses, offices *etc*: *a block of flats; an office block.* **4** a barrier: *a road block.* **5** (*esp Amer*) a group of buildings bounded by four streets: *a walk round the block.* – *v* to make (progress) difficult or impossible: *The crashed cars blocked the road.*

bloc'kade [-'keid] *n* something which blocks every approach to a place by land or sea. – *v*: *The ships blockaded the town.*

'blockage [-kidʒ] **1** *n* something causing a pipe *etc* to be blocked: *a blockage in the pipe.*

blocked *adj* obstructed: *I have a bad cold – my nose is blocked.*

block capital/letter a capital letter written in imitation of printed type, *eg* the letters in NAME.

'blockhead *n* a stupid person.

blond [blond] – *fem* **blonde** – *adj* having light-coloured hair: *a blond child.*

blonde *n* a woman with light-coloured hair.

blood [blʌd] *n* **1** the red fluid pumped through the body by the heart: *Blood poured from the wound in his side.* **2** descent or ancestors: *He is of royal blood.*

'bloodless *adj* **1** without the shedding of blood: *a bloodless victory.* **2** anaemic: *She is definitely bloodless.*

'bloody *adj* **1** stained with blood: *a bloody shirt; His clothes were torn and bloody.* **2** bleeding: *a bloody nose.* **3** murderous and cruel: *a bloody battle.* **4** used vulgarly for emphasis: *That bloody car ran over my foot!*

'bloodcurdling *adj* terrifying and horrible: *a blood-curdling scream.*

blood donor a person who gives blood for use by another person in transfusion *etc*.

blood group/type any one of the types into which human blood is classified: *Her blood group is O.*

'blood-poisoning *n* an infection of the blood: *He is suffering from blood-poisoning.*

blood pressure the (amount of) pressure of the blood on the walls of the blood-vessels: *The excitement will raise his blood pressure.*

'bloodshed *n* deaths or shedding of blood: *There was much bloodshed in the battle.*

'bloodshot *adj* (of eyes) full of red lines and inflamed with blood.

'bloodstained *adj* stained with blood: *a bloodstained bandage.*

'bloodstream *n* the blood flowing through the body: *The poison entered her blood-stream.*

'bloodthirsty *adj* **1** eager to kill people: *a bloodthirsty warrior.* **2** (of a film *etc*) full of scenes in which there is much killing. **'bloodthirstiness** *n*.

'blood-vessel *n* any of the tubes in the body through which the blood flows: *He has burst a blood-vessel.*

in cold blood while free from excitement or passion: *He killed his son in cold blood.*

bloom [blu:m] *n* **1** a flower: *These blooms are withering now.* **2** the state of flowering: *The flowers are in bloom.* **3** freshness: *in the bloom of youth.* – *v* to flower or flourish: *Daffodils bloom in the spring.*

blossom ['blosəm] *n* flowers, *esp* of a fruit tree: *beautiful blossom; apple blossom.* – *v* **1** to develop flowers: *My plant has blos-somed.* **2** to flourish: *She blossomed into a beautiful woman.* **'blossoming** *adj*.

blot [blot] *n* **1** a spot or stain (often of ink): *an exercise book full of blots.* **2** something ugly: *a blot on the landscape.* – *v* – *pt, ptp* **'blotted** – **1** to spot or stain, *esp* with ink: *I blotted this sheet of paper in three places when my nib broke.* **2** to dry with blotting-paper: *Blot your signature before you fold the paper.*

'blotter *n* a pad or sheet of blotting-paper.

'blotting-paper *n* soft paper used for drying up ink.

blot one's copybook to make a bad mistake: *He has really blotted his copybook by being late for the interview.*

blot out to hide from sight: *The rain blotted out the view.*

blotch [blotʃ] *n* a discoloured mark: *Those red blotches on her face are very ugly.*

blouse [blauz] *n* a woman's (often loose) garment for the upper half of the body: *a skirt and blouse.*

blow[1] [blou] *n* **1** a stroke or knock: *a blow on the head.* **2** a sudden misfortune: *Her hus-band's death was a real blow.*

blow[2] [blou] – *pt* **blew** [blu:]: *ptp* **blown** – *v* **1** (of a current of air) to be moving: *The wind blew more strongly.* **2** (of *eg* wind) to cause (something) to move in a given way: *The explosion blew off the lid;* **3** to be moved by the wind *etc*: *The door must have blown shut.* **4** to drive air (upon or into): *Please blow into this tube!* **5** to make a sound by means of (a musical instrument *etc*): *He blew the horn loudly.*

'blowhole *n* a breathing-hole (through the

ice for seals *etc*) or a nostril (*esp* on the head of a whale *etc*).

'**blow-lamp**, '**blow-torch** *n* a lamp for aiming a very hot flame at a particular spot: *The painter burned off the old paint with a blow-lamp.*

'**blowout** *n* **1** the bursting of a car tyre: *That's the second blowout I've had with this car.* **2** (on *eg* an oil rig) a violent escape of gas *etc*.

'**blowpipe** *n* a tube from which a dart (often poisonous) is blown.

blow one's top to become very angry: *She blew her top when he arrived home late.*

blow out to extinguish or put out (a flame *etc*) by blowing: *The wind blew out the candle*; *The child blew out the match.*

blow over to pass and become forgotten: *The trouble will soon blow over.*

blow up 1 to break into pieces, or be broken into pieces, by an explosion: *The bridge blew up/was blown up.* **2** to fill with air or a gas: *He blew up the balloon.* **3** to lose one's temper: *If he says that again I'll blow up.*

blubber ['blʌbə] *n* the fat of whales and other sea animals.

blue [blu:] *adj* **1** of the colour of a cloudless sky: *blue paint*; *Her eyes are blue.* **2** sad or depressed: *I'm feeling blue today.* – *n* **1** the colour of a cloudless sky: *That is a beautiful blue.* **2** a blue paint, material *etc*: *We'll have to get some more blue.* **3** the sky or the sea: *The balloon floated off into the blue.*

'**blueness** *n*.

'**bluish** *adj* quite blue; close to blue: *a bluish green.*

'**bluebottle** *n* a kind of large house-fly with a blue abdomen.

'**bluecollar** *adj* (of workers) wearing overalls and working in factories *etc*: *Bluecollar workers are demanding the same pay as office staff.*

'**blueprint** *n* a detailed photographic plan of work to be carried out: *the blueprints for a new airport.*

once in a blue moon very seldom: *He visits his mother once in a blue moon.*

out of the blue without warning: *He arrived out of the blue, without phoning first.*

the blues low spirits; depression: *He's got the blues today but he's usually cheerful.*

bluff¹ [blʌf] *adj* rough, hearty and frank: *a bluff and friendly manner.*

bluff² [blʌf] *v* to try to deceive by pretending to have something that one does not have: *He bluffed his way through the exam without actually knowing anything.* – *n* an act of bluffing.

blunder ['blʌndə] *v* **1** to stumble (about or into something): *He blundered into the door.* **2** to make a (bad) mistake: *He really blundered when he insulted the boss's wife.* – *n* a (bad) mistake.

blunt [blʌnt] *adj* **1** (of objects) having no point or sharp edge: *a blunt knife.* **2** (of people) (sometimes unpleasantly) straightforward or frank in speech: *She was very blunt, and said that she did not like him.* – *v* to make less sharp: *This knife has been blunted by years of use.*

'**bluntly** *adv*. '**bluntness** *n*.

blur [blə:] *n* something not clearly seen: *Everything is just a blur when I take my spectacles off.* – *v* – *pt, ptp* **blurred** – to make or become unclear: *The rain blurred my vision.*

blurt [blə:t]: **blurt out** to say (something) suddenly: *He blurted out the whole story.*

blush [blʌʃ] *n* a red glow on the skin caused by shame, embarrassment *etc*. – *v* to show shame, embarrassment *etc* by growing red in the face: *That girl blushes easily.*

boa ['bouə] *n* (*usu* **boa constrictor**) a large snake that kills by winding itself round its prey.

boar [bo:] *n* **1** a male pig (*esp* the wild variety).

board [bo:d] *n* **1** a strip of timber: *The floorboards of the old house were rotten.* **2** a flat piece of wood for a special purpose: *notice-board*; *chessboard.* **3** meals: *board and lodging.* **4** an official group of persons administering an organization *etc*: *the board of directors.* – *v* **1** to enter, or get on to (a vehicle, ship, plane *etc*): *This is where we board the bus.* **2** to live temporarily and take meals (in someone else's house): *He boards at Mrs Smith's during the week.*

'**boarder** *n* a person who temporarily lives, and takes his meals, in someone else's house.

'**boarding-house** *n* a house where people live and take meals as paying guests.

'**boarding-school** *n* a school which provides accommodation and food as well as instruction.

across the board applying in all cases: *They were awarded wage increases across the board*; (*also adj*) *an across-the-board increase.*

go by the board to be abandoned: *All my plans went by the board when I lost my job.*

boast [boust] *v* to talk with too much pride: *He was always boasting about how clever his son was.* – *n* the words used in talking proudly about something: *His boast is that he has never yet lost a match.* '**boastful** *adj*. '**boastfully** *adv*. '**boastfulness**, '**boasting** *ns*.

boat [bout] *n* **1** a small vessel for travelling over water: *We'll cross the stream by boat.* **2** a larger vessel for the same purpose; a ship: *to cross the Atlantic in a passenger boat.* **3** a serving-dish shaped like a boat: *a*

gravy-boat. – *v* to sail about in a small boat for pleasure: *They are boating on the river*.
'boatman *n* a man in charge of a small boat in which fare-paying passengers are carried.
in the same boat in the same, *usu* difficult, position or circumstances: *We're all in the same boat as far as low wages are concerned.*
boatswain, bosun ['bousn] *n* an officer who looks after a ship's boats, ropes, sails *etc*.
bob [bob] – *pt, ptp* **bobbed** – *v* to move (up and down): *The cork was bobbing about in the water.*
bobsleigh ['bobslei], **bobsled** ['bobsled] *ns* a vehicle on metal runners used in crossing (and sometimes racing on) snow and ice.
bodice ['bodis] *n* the upper part of a woman's or child's dress: *The dress had an embroidered bodice.*
bodily *see* **body**.
body ['bodi] – *pl* **'bodies** – *n* **1** the whole frame of a man or animal including the bones and flesh: *Athletes have to look after their bodies.* **2** a dead person: *The battlefield was covered with bodies.* **3** the main part of anything: *the body of the hall.* **4** a mass: *a huge body of evidence.* **5** a group of persons acting as one: *professional bodies.*
'bodily *adj* of the body: *bodily needs.* – *adv* by the entire (physical) body: *They lifted him bodily and carried him off.*
'bodyguard *n* a guard or guards to protect (*esp* an important person): *the president's bodyguard.*
'bodywork *n* the outer casing of a car *etc*: *The bodywork of his new car has rusted already.*
bog [bog] *n* very wet ground; marsh.
'boggy *adj*: *boggy ground.*
be bogged down to be hindered in movement; to be prevented from making progress: *The tractor is bogged down in the mud.*
bogie, bogey ['bougi] *n* a four- or six-wheeled frame, supporting part of a long vehicle, *eg* a railway carriage.
bogus ['bougəs] *adj* false; not genuine: *She was fooled by his bogus identity card.*
boil[1] [boil] *v* **1** to turn rapidly from liquid to vapour when heated: *I'm boiling the water; The water's boiling.* **2** to cook by boiling in water *etc*: *I've boiled the potatoes.*
'boiler *n* a vessel in which water is heated or steam is produced.
'boiling-point *n* the temperature at which something boils.
boil over to boil and overflow: *The pan of water boiled over and spilt on the floor.*
boil[2] [boil] *n* an inflamed swelling on the skin: *His neck is covered with boils.*
boisterous ['boistərəs] *adj* wild and noisy: *a boisterous child.*
bold [bould] *adj* **1** daring or fearless: *a bold plan of attack.* **2** striking and well-marked:

a dress with bold stripes. **3** (of type) thick and clear, **like this**. **'boldly** *adv*. **'boldness** *n*.
bold as brass very cheeky: *She walked in late as bold as brass.*
bolero ['bolərou] – *pl* **'boleros** – *n* a short jacket with no fastening.
bollard ['bola:d] *n* **1** a post for controlling traffic: *The pedestrian shopping area has been closed off with bollards.* **2** a short post on a wharf or ship round which ropes are fastened.
bolster ['boulstə] *n* a long, often round pillow. – *v* – *pt, ptp* **'bolstered** – (*often with* **up**) to prop up: *We're getting a loan to bolster (up) the economy.*
bolt [boult] *n* **1** a bar to fasten a door *etc*: *We have a bolt as well as a lock on the door.* **2** a round bar of metal, often with a screw thread for a nut: *nuts and bolts.* **3** a flash of lightning. **4** a roll (of cloth): *a bolt of silk.* – *v* **1** to fasten with a bolt: *He bolted the door.* **2** to swallow hastily: *The child bolted her food.* **3** to go away very fast: *The horse bolted in terror.*
,bolt(-)'upright *adv* absolutely upright: *She sat bolt upright in the chair with her back very straight.*
a bolt from the blue a sudden, unexpected happening: *His resignation was a bolt from the blue.*
bomb [bom] *n* a hollow case containing explosives *etc*: *The enemy dropped a bomb on the factory and blew it up.* – *v* **1** to drop bombs on: *London was bombed several times.* **2** to fail miserably: *The play bombed on the first night.*
'bomber *n* **1** an aeroplane built for bombing. **2** a person who bombs: *Bombers have caused many deaths in Northern Ireland.*
'bombshell *n* a piece of startling news: *His resignation was a real bombshell.*
bombard [bəm'ba:d] *v* **1** to attack with artillery: *They bombarded the town.* **2** to direct questions *etc* at: *The reporters bombarded the film star with questions.* **bom'bardment** *n*.
bonanza [bə'nanzə] *n* a sudden increase (in profits *etc*): *Shopkeepers in seaside towns enjoy a bonanza in hot summers.*
bond [bond] *n* **1** something used for tying (*esp* a person): *They released the prisoner from his bonds.* **2** something that unites or joins people together: *a bond of friendship.*
bonded store/warehouse a warehouse where goods are kept until customs or other duty on them is paid.
bondage ['bondidʒ] *n* slavery.
bone [boun] *n* **1** the hard substance forming the skeleton of man, animals *etc*: *Bone decays far more slowly than flesh.* **2** a piece of this substance: *She broke two of the bones in her foot.* – *v* to take the bones out of (fish *etc*).

'**bony** *adj* **1** like bone: *a bony substance.* **2** full of bones: *This fish is very bony.* **3** thin: *bony fingers.*

bone china china in whose manufacture the ashes of burnt bones are used.

bone idle very lazy: *He could find a job but he's bone idle.*

a bone of contention a cause of argument or quarrelling: *Ownership of the boat was a bone of contention between the two men for many years.*

have a bone to pick with (someone) to have something to argue about with (a person).

to the bone 1 thoroughly and completely: *I was chilled to the bone.* **2** to the minimum: *I've cut my expenses to the bone.*

bonfire ['bonfaiə] *n* a large fire in the open air, often built to celebrate something.

bonnet ['bonit] *n* **1** (*usu* baby's or (old) woman's) head-dress fastened under the chin *eg* by strings. **2** (*Amer* **hood**) the cover of a motor-car engine.

bonsai ['bonsai] *n* a small decorative evergreen shrub or tree grown in a pot, which has been prevented from growing to its usual size by various methods.

bonus ['bounəs] *n* **1** an addition to the sum due as interest, dividend, or wages. **2** something unexpected or extra: *The extra two days holiday was a real bonus.*

bony *see* **bone**.

boo [bu:] – *pl* **boos** – *n* a derisive shout, made *eg* by a disapproving crowd: *the boos of the disappointed football supporters.* – *v* – *pt, ptp* **booed** – to make such a sound at a person *etc*: *The crowd booed* (*him*).

boob [bu:b] *n* a mistake: *Forgetting to invite her to the party was a real boob.* – *v* to make a mistake.

booby ['bu:bi] – *pl* '**boobies** – *n* a stupid person.

booby prize a prize for the lowest score *etc*: *John came last and got the booby prize.*

book [buk] *n* **1** a number of sheets of paper (*esp* printed) bound together: *an exercise book.* **2** a piece of writing, bound and covered: *I've written a book on Shakespeare.* **3** a record of bets. – *v* **1** to buy or reserve (a ticket, seat *etc*) for a play *etc*: *I've booked four seats for Friday's concert.* **2** to hire in advance: *We've booked the hall for Saturday.*

'**bookable** *adj* able to be reserved in advance: *Are these seats bookable?*

'**booking** *n* a reservation.

'**booklet** [-lit] *n* a small, thin book: *a booklet about the history of the town.*

'**bookbinding** *n* putting the covers on books. '**bookbinder** *n*.

'**bookcase** *n* a set of shelves for books.

'**booking-office** *n* an office where travel tickets *etc* are sold: *a queue at the station booking-office.*

'**bookmaker** *n* a professional betting man who takes bets and pays winnings.

'**bookmark** *n* something put in a book to mark a particular page.

'**bookshelf** *n* a shelf on which books are kept.

'**bookworm** *n* a person who reads a lot.

booked up having every ticket sold: *The theatre is booked up for the season.*

book in to sign one's name on the list of guests at an hotel *etc*: *We have booked in at the Royal Hotel.*

by the book strictly according to the rules: *She always does things by the book.*

boom[1] [bu:m] *n* a sudden increase in a business *etc*: *a boom in the sales of TV sets.* – *v* to increase suddenly (and profitably): *Business is booming this week.*

boom[2] [bu:m] *v* (*often with* **out**) to make a hollow sound, like a large drum or gun: *His voice boomed out over the loudspeaker.* – *n* such a sound.

boomerang ['bu:məraŋ] *n* a curved piece of wood used by Australian aborigines which, when thrown, returns to the thrower.

boon [bu:n] *n* a blessing: *It's been a real boon to have a car this week.*

boor [buə] *n* a coarse, ill-mannered person. '**boorish** *adj*.

boost [bu:st] *v* to expand; to make greater; to improve: *We've boosted the sales figures*; *It's boosted his reputation.* – *n* a piece of help, encouragement *etc*: *This publicity will give our sales a real boost.*

'**booster** *n* **1** a person or thing that boosts: *That was a real morale booster for me* (= That made me feel more cheerful and optimistic). **2** a device for increasing power, force *etc*: *I've fixed a booster on the TV aerial to improve the signal.* **3** the first stage of a rocket that works by several stages.

boot [bu:t] *n* **1** a covering for the foot and lower part of the leg, *usu* made of leather *etc*: *a pair of suede boots.* **2** (*Amer* **trunk**) a place for luggage in a motor-car *etc*. – *v* to kick: *He booted the ball out of the goal.*

give, get the boot to dismiss (someone) or to be dismissed (*usu* from a job): *He got the boot for always being late.*

bootee [bu:'ti:] *n* a (*usu* knitted woollen) boot for a baby.

booth [bu:ð, (*Amer*) -θ] *n* **1** a tent or stall, *esp* at a fair: *the fortuneteller's booth.* **2** a small compartment for a given purpose: *a phone booth*; *a polling-booth.*

booty ['bu:ti] *n* goods taken from *eg* an enemy by force (*esp* in wartime): *The soldiers shared the booty among themselves*; *the burglars' booty.*

booze [bu:z] *n* alcoholic drink: *Have you got*

enough booze for the party? – *v* to drink alcoholic drinks.

border ['bɔːdə] *n* **1** the edge of a particular thing: *the border of a picture/handkerchief.* **2** the boundary of a country: *They'll ask for your passport at the border.* **3** a flower bed round the edge of a lawn *etc*: *a flower border.* – *v* (*with* **on**) to come near to or lie on the border of: *Germany borders on France.*

'**borderline** *adj* doubtful; on the border between one thing and another: *He was a borderline case, so we gave him an additional exam to see if he would pass it.* – *n* the border between one thing and another: *He was on the borderline between passing and failing.*

bore[1] [bɔː] *v* to make (a hole *etc* in something): *They bored a tunnel under the sea.* – *n* the size of the hollow barrel of a gun.
'**borehole** *n* a hole made by boring, *esp* to find oil *etc*.

bore[2] [bɔː] *v* to make (someone) feel tired and uninterested, by being dull *etc*: *He bores everyone with stories about his travels.* – *n* a dull, boring person or thing.
'**boredom** *n* the state of being bored.
'**boring** *adj*: *a boring job*; *This book is boring.*

bore[3] **born, borne** *see* **bear**[1].

borough ['bʌrə, (*Amer*) 'bɔːrou] *n* in Britain, a town or area with certain rights.

borrow ['borou] *v* to take (something, often money) temporarily with the intention of returning it: *He borrowed a book from the library.* '**borrower, 'borrowing** *ns*.

borrow from: *I borrow money from a friend.*
lend to: *My friend lends money to me | My friend lends me money.*

bosom ['buzəm] *n* **1** a woman's breasts: *She has a large bosom.* **2** the chest: *She held him tenderly to her bosom.* **3** the innermost part: *in the bosom of his family.* – *adj* intimate; close: *a bosom friend.*

boss [bos] *n* the master or manager: *the boss of the factory.* – *v* (*usu with* **about/around**) to order: *Stop bossing everyone about!*
'**bossy** *adj* liking to order others about.
'**bossily** *adv*. '**bossiness** *n*.

bosun *see* **boatswain**.

botany ['botəni] *n* the scientific study of plants. **bo'tanic(al)** [-'ta-] *adj*.
'**botanist** *n* a person who studies botany.
botanic(al) gardens *n sing or pl* a public park for the growing of native and foreign plants.

both [bouθ] *adj, pron* the two; the one and the other: *We both went; Both* (*the*) *men are dead; The men are both dead; Both are dead.*

bother ['boðə] *v* **1** to annoy or worry: *The*

noise bothered the old man. **2** to take the trouble: *Don't bother to write – it isn't necessary.* – *n* **1** trouble, nuisance or worry. **2** something or someone that causes bother: *What a bother all this is!*
'**bothersome** *adj* causing bother or annoyance: *a bothersome cough.*

bottle ['botl] *n* a hollow narrow-necked container for holding liquids *etc*: *a lemonade bottle.* – *v* to put into bottles.
'**bottleneck** *n* a place where slowing down or stopping of traffic, progress *etc* occurs: *a bottleneck caused by roadworks.*
bottle up to prevent (*eg* one's feelings) from becoming obvious: *Don't bottle up your anger.*

bottom ['botəm] *n* **1** the lowest part of anything: *the bottom of the sea.* **2** the part of the body on which a person sits.
'**bottomless** *adj* very deep: *a bottomless pit.*
be at the bottom of to be the cause of (*usu* something bad): *Who's at the bottom of these rumours?*
get to the bottom of to discover the explanation or the real facts of (a mystery *etc*).

bougainvillaea [buːgən'viliə] *n* a vine with small flowers and purple or red leaves.

bough [bau] *n* a branch of a tree: *the bough of an apple tree.*

bought *see* **buy**.

boulder ['bouldə] *n* a large rock or stone: *a boulder on the hillside.*

bounce [bauns] *v* **1** to (cause to) spring or jump back from a solid surface. **2** (of a cheque) to be sent back unpaid, because of lack of money in a bank account. – *n* **1** (of a ball *etc*) an act of springing back: *With one bounce the ball went over the net.* **2** energy: *She has a lot of bounce.*
'**bouncing** *adj* strong and lively: *a bouncing baby.*

bound[1] *see* **bind**.

bound[2] [baund]: **-bound** (*as part of a word*) going in a particular direction: *westbound traffic.*
bound for on the way to: *bound for Africa.*
bound to 1 certain to: *He's bound to notice your mistake.* **2** obliged to: *I felt bound to mention it.*
See also **-bound** *under* **bind**.

bound[3] [baund] *n* (*usu in pl*) limits of some kind: *beyond the bounds of coincidence.*
'**boundless** *adj* having no limit: *boundless energy.*
out of bounds outside the permitted area or limits: *The cinema was out of bounds for the boys from the local boarding-school.*

bound[4] [baund] *n* a spring; a leap: *He reached me in one bound.* – *v* to move in this way: *The dog bounded over eagerly to where I was sitting.*

boundary ['baundəri] – *pl* '**boundaries** – *n*

1 an often imaginary line separating one thing from another: *the boundary between two towns.* **2** (in cricket) a hit which crosses the boundary line round the field, scoring four runs or six runs.

boundless *see* **bound**³.

bounty ['baunti] *n* **1** generosity in giving. **2** (*pl* **'bounties**) something given out of generosity.

bouquet [bu'kei] *n* **1** a bunch of flowers: *The bride carried a bouquet of roses.* **2** the perfume of wine.

bout [baut] *n* **1** a period (of): *a bout of coughing.* **2** a (*usu* boxing) contest: *a bout of fifteen five-minute rounds.*

boutique [bu:'ti:k] *n* a fashionable, *usu* small shop, *esp* one selling clothes: *She prefers small boutiques to large stores.*

bow¹ [bau] *v* **1** to bend (the head and often also the upper part of the body) forwards in greeting a person *etc*: *He bowed to the ladies; They bowed their heads in prayer.* **2** (*with* **to**) to accept: *I bow to your superior knowledge.* – *n* a bowing movement: *He made a bow to the ladies.*
bowed *adj* (often with **down**) bent downwards, *eg* by the weight of something: *The trees were bowed down with fruit.*

bow² [bou] *n* **1** a springy curved rod bent by a string, by which arrows are shot. **2** a rod with horsehair stretched along it, by which the strings of a violin *etc* are sounded. **3** a looped knot of material: *Her dress is decorated with bows.*

bow³ [bau] *n* (*often in pl*) the front of a ship or boat: *The waves broke over the bows.*

bowel ['bauəl] *n* **1** (*usu in pl*) the part of the digestive system below the stomach; the intestines: *The surgeon removed part of her bowel.* **2** (*in pl*) the inside of something, *esp* when deep: *the bowels of the earth.*

bowl¹ [boul] *n* a wooden ball rolled along the ground in playing bowls. – *See also* **bowls** *below.* – *v* **1** to play bowls. **2** to deliver or send (a ball) towards the batsman in cricket. **3** to put (a batsman) out by hitting the wicket with the ball: *Smith was bowled for eighty-five* (= Smith was put out after making eighty-five runs). – *n* **'bowler.**
'bowling *n* the game of skittles, bowls or something similar.
bowls *n sing* a game played on a smooth green with bowls having a bias: *a game of bowls.*
'bowling-alley *n* **1** a long narrow set of wooden boards along which one bowls at skittles. **2** a building which contains several of these.
'bowling-green *n* a smooth piece of grass for playing bowls on.
bowl over to knock down: *I was bowled over*

in the rush for the door; His generosity bowled me over.

bowl² [boul] *n* **1** a round, deep dish *eg* for mixing or serving food *etc*: *a baking-bowl; a soup bowl.* **2** a round hollow part, *esp* of a tobacco pipe, a spoon *etc*: *The bowl of this spoon is dirty.*

bowler¹ *see* **bowl**¹.

bowler² ['boulə] *n* (*also* **bowler hat**) a type of hard, round felt hat.

box¹ [boks] *n* **1** a case for holding something: *a wooden box; a matchbox.* **2** in a theatre *etc*, a group of seats separated from the rest of the audience. – *v* to put (something) into boxes: *Will you box these apples?*
Boxing day December 26, the day after Christmas day.
box number a number used *eg* in a newspaper advertisement instead of a full address.
box office a ticket office in a theatre, concert-hall *etc*: *There's a queue at the box office for tonight's show.*

box² [boks] *v* to fight (someone) with the fists: *Years ago, fighters used to box without wearing padded gloves.* – *n* a blow on the ear with the hand.
'boxer *n*: *He's a champion boxer.*
'boxing *n* the sport of fighting with the fists.
'boxing-glove *n* a boxer's padded glove.
'boxing-match *n*.

boy [boi] *n* **1** a male child: *She has three girls and one boy.* **2** (*as part of another word*) a male (often adult) who does a certain job: *a cowboy; a paper-boy.*
'boyhood *n* the time of being a boy: *a happy boyhood;* (*also adj*) *boyhood memories.*
'boyfriend *n* a girl's favourite male friend.

boycott ['boikot] *v* to refuse to have any dealings with (a firm, country *etc*). – *n* a refusal to deal with a firm *etc*.

bra [bra:] short for **brassière**.

brace [breis] *n* **1** something that draws together and holds tightly: *a brace to straighten teeth.* **2** a pair *usu* of game-birds: *a brace of pheasants.* – *v* to make (often oneself) firm or steady: *He braced himself for the struggle.*
'braces *n pl* (*Amer* **su'spenders**) straps over the shoulders for holding up the trousers.
'bracing *adj* healthy: *bracing sea air.*

bracelet ['breislit] *n* an ornament worn round the wrist or arm: *a gold bracelet.*

bracket ['brakit] *n* **1** (*usu in pl*) marks (*eg* ( ), [ ], { }, ⟨ ⟩ *etc*) used to group together one or more words *etc*. **2** a support for a shelf *etc*: *The shelf fell down because the brackets were not strong enough.* – *v* – *pt, ptp* **'bracketed** – **1** to enclose (words *etc*) by brackets. **2** (*sometimes with* **together**) to group together (similar or equal people or things).
bracket fungus a round, flat fungus that

grows out horizontally on the trunks of trees.

brackish ['brakiʃ] *adj* (of water) tasting slightly of salt, often unpleasantly.

brag [brag] – *pt, ptp* **bragged** – *v* to boast.

braid [breid] *v* to wind together (*esp* strands of hair). – *n* threads twisted together and used as decoration on uniforms *etc*: *gold braid on the admiral's uniform.*

braille [breil] *n* a system of printing for the blind, using raised dots.

brain [brein] *n* **1** the centre of the nervous system : *an injury to the brain*; (*also adj*) *brain surgery, brain damage*. **2** (*often in pl*) cleverness: *a good brain*; *You've plenty of brains*. **3** a clever person: *He's one of the best brains in the country.*
'**brainless** *adj* stupid: *a brainless idiot.*
'**brainy** *adj* clever: *She's a brainy child.*
'**brainchild** *n* a favourite theory, invention, *etc* thought up by a particular person: *This entire process is Dr Smith's brainchild.*
brain drain the loss of experts to another country (*usu* in search of better salaries *etc*): *As a result of the brain drain Britain does not have enough doctors.*
'**brainwash** *v* to force (a person) to confess *etc* by putting great (psychological) pressure on him: *The terrorists brainwashed him into believing in their ideals.*
'**brainwave** *n* a sudden bright idea.

braise [breiz] *v* to stew (meat *etc*) slowly in a closed dish.

brake [breik] *v* to slow down or stop: *He braked (the car) suddenly.* – *n* (*often in pl*) a device for doing this: *He put on the brake(s).*

branch [braːntʃ] *n* **1** an arm-like part of a tree: *He cut some branches off the oak tree.* **2** an offshoot from the main part (of a business, railway *etc*): *There isn't a branch of that store in this town*; (*also adj*) *That train runs on the branch line.* – *v* (*usu* with **out/off**) to spread out like, or into, a branch or branches: *The road to the coast branches off here.*

brand [brand] *n* **1** a maker's name or trademark: *a new brand*; (*also adj*) *a brand name.* **2** a variety: *He has his own brand of humour.* **3** a mark on cattle *etc* to show who owns them, made with a hot iron. – *v* **1** to mark cattle *etc* with a hot iron. **2** to make a permanent impression on: *His name is branded on my memory.* **3** to attach (permanent) disgrace to: *branded for life as a thief.*
,**brand-'new** *adj* completely new: *a brand-new dress.*

brandish ['brandiʃ] *v* to wave (*esp* a weapon) about: *He brandished the stick above his head.*

brandy ['brandi] – *pl* '**brandies** – *n* a type of

strong alcoholic spirit made from wine: *Brandy is usually drunk after dinner.*

brash [braʃ] *adj* cheekily self-confident and impolite: *a brash young man.*

brass [braːs] *n* **1** an alloy of copper and zinc: *This plate is made of brass*; (*also adj*) *a brass door-knocker.* **2** wind musical instruments which are made of brass or other metal. '**brassy** *adj*.
brass band a band of players of (mainly) brass wind instruments.
get down to brass tacks to deal with basic principles or matters: *Let's stop arguing about nothing and get down to brass tacks.*

brassière ['brasiə, (*Amer*) brə'ziər] (*usu abbrev* **bra** [braː]) *n* a woman's undergarment supporting the breasts.

bravado [brə'vaːdou] *n* (a show of) daring: *He's full of bravado, but really he's a coward.*

brave [breiv] *adj* without fear of danger, pain *etc*: *a brave soldier*; *a brave deed*; *You're very brave*; *It was brave of him to fight such an enemy.* – *v* to meet or face boldly: *They braved the cold weather.* – *n* a Red Indian warrior.
'**bravely** *adv*: *He met his death bravely.*
'**bravery** *n*.

bravo [braː'vou, (*Amer*) 'braː'vou] *interj* (when applauding a performer *etc*) well done!

brawl [broːl] *n* a noisy quarrel or physical fight: *The police were called out to a brawl in the street.* – *v* to fight noisily.

brawn [broːn] *n* muscle or physical strength. '**brawny** *adj*.

bray [brei] *n* the cry of an ass. – *v* to make such a cry.

brazen ['breizn] *adj* impudent or shameless: *a brazen young woman.*
brazen it out to face a situation with impudent boldness: *She knew her deception had been discovered but decided to brazen it out.*

breach [briːtʃ] *n* **1** a breaking (of a promise *etc*). **2** a gap, break or hole: *a breach in the castle wall*; *a breach in security.* – *v* to make an opening in or break (someone's defence).
breach of the peace a riot, disturbance or public fight: *guilty of breach of the peace.*

bread [bred] *n* **1** a type of food made of flour or meal baked: *bread and butter.* **2** one's living: *This is how I earn my daily bread.*
'**breadcrumbs** *n pl* very tiny pieces of bread: *Dip the fish in egg and breadcrumbs.*
'**breadwinner** *n* a person who earns money to keep a family: *When her husband died she had to become the breadwinner.*
bread and butter (a way of earning) one's living: *Writing novels is my bread and butter.*
on the breadline with barely enough to live

on: *The widow and her children are on the breadline.*

bread and butter *takes a singular verb.*

breadth [bredθ] *n* **1** width; size from side to side: *the breadth of a table.* **2** scope or extent: *breadth of outlook.* **3** a distance equal to the width (of a swimming-pool *etc*).

break [breik] – *pt* **broke** [brouk]: *ptp* **broken** ['broukən] – *v* **1** to divide into two or more parts (by force). **2** (*usu with* **off/away**) to separate (a part) from the whole (by force). **3** to make or become unusable. **4** to go against, or not act according to (the law *etc*): *He broke his appointment at the last minute.* **5** to do better than (a sporting *etc* record). **6** to interrupt: *She broke her journey in London.* **7** to put an end to: *He broke the silence.* **8** to make or become known: *They gently broke the news of his death to his wife.* **9** (of a boy's voice) to fall in pitch. **10** to soften the effect of (a fall, the force of the wind *etc*). **11** to begin: *The storm broke before they reached shelter.* – *n* **1** a pause: *a break in the conversation.* **2** a change: *a break in the weather.* **3** an opening. **4** a chance or piece of (good or bad) luck: *This is your big break.*

'**breakable** *adj* (*neg* **un-**) likely to break: *breakable toys.* – *n* (*usu in pl*) something likely to break.

'**breakage** [-kidʒ] *n* the act of breaking, or its result(s).

'**breaker** *n* a (large) wave which breaks on rocks or the beach.

'**breakdown** *n* **1** (*often* **nervous breakdown**) a mental collapse. **2** a mechanical failure causing a stop: *The car has had another breakdown.* – *See also* **break down**.

break-in *see* **break in(to)**.

'**breakneck** *adj* (*usu* of speed) dangerous: *He drove at breakneck speed.*

breakout *see* **break out**.

'**breakthrough** *n* a sudden solution of a problem leading to further advances, *esp* in science.

'**breakwater** *n* a barrier to break the force of the waves.

break away to escape from control: *The dog broke away from its owner.*

break down 1 to use force on (a door *etc*) to cause it to open. **2** to stop working properly: *My car has broken down.* **3** to fail: *The talks have broken down.* **4** to be overcome with emotion: *She broke down and wept.*

break in(to) 1 to enter (a house *etc*) by force or unexpectedly (*n* '**break-in**: *The Smiths have had two break-ins recently*). **2** to interrupt (someone's conversation *etc*).

break loose to escape from control: *The dog has broken loose.*

break off to stop: *She broke off in the middle of a sentence.*

break out 1 to appear or happen suddenly: *War has broken out.* **2** to escape (from prison, restrictions *etc*): *A prisoner has broken out* (*n* '**breakout**).

break the ice to overcome the first shyness *etc*: *Let's break the ice by inviting our new neighbours for a meal.*

break up 1 to divide, separate or break into pieces: *He broke up the old furniture and burnt it*; *John and Mary broke up* (= separated from each other) *last week*; **2** to finish or end: *The meeting broke up at 4.40.*

make a break for it to make an (attempt to) escape: *When the guard is not looking, make a break for it.*

breakfast ['brekfəst] *n* the first meal of the day: *What time do you serve breakfast?*; *I have coffee and toast at breakfast*; *I never eat breakfast.* – *v* to have breakfast: *They breakfasted on the train.*

'**breakfast-time** *n*: *I'll deal with that at breakfast-time.*

breast [brest] *n* **1** either of a woman's two milk-producing glands on the front of the upper body. **2** the front of a body between the neck and belly: *He clutched the child to his breast*; *This recipe needs three chicken breasts.* – *v* **1** to face or oppose: *breast the waves.* **2** to come to the top of: *As we breasted the hill we saw the enemy in the distance.*

'**breastfeed** *v* to feed (a baby) with milk from the breast. '**breastfed** *adj*.

'**breaststroke** *n* a style of swimming in which the arms are pushed out in front and then sweep backwards.

breath [breθ] *n* **1** the air drawn into, and then sent out from, the lungs: *My dog's breath smells terrible.* **2** an act of breathing: *Take a deep breath.*

'**breathless** *adj* having difficulty in breathing normally: *His asthma makes him breathless*; *He was breathless after climbing the hill.* '**breathlessly** *adv*. '**breathlessness** *n*.

hold one's breath to stop breathing (often because of anxiety or to avoid being heard): *He held his breath as he watched the daring acrobat.*

out of breath breathless (through running *etc*): *I'm out of breath after climbing all these stairs.*

under one's breath in a whisper: *He swore under his breath.*

breath *is a noun: He held his breath.* breathe *is a verb: He found it difficult to breathe.*

breathe [briːð] *v* **1** to draw in and let out (air

etc) from the lungs: *He was unable to breathe because of the smoke*; *She breathed a sigh of relief.* **2** to tell (a secret): *Don't breathe a word of this to anyone.*
'**breather** *n* a short rest or break from work *etc*: *I must have a breather before I do any more.*

bred *see* **breed**.

breech [briːtʃ] *n* the back part of a gun, where it is loaded.

breeches ['britʃiz, (*Amer*) 'briː-] *n pl* trousers, *esp* ones coming just below the knee: *riding breeches.*

breed [briːd] – *pt, ptp* **bred** [bred] – *v* **1** to produce young: *Rabbits breed often.* **2** to keep animals for the purpose of breeding young: *I breed dogs and sell them as pets.* – *n* a type, variety or species (of animal): *a breed of dog.*
bred [bred] *adj* (*often as part of a word*) **1** (of people) brought up in a certain way or place: *a well-bred young lady*; *American born and bred.* **2** (of animals) brought up or reared in a certain way: *a pure-bred dog.*
'**breeding** *n* education and training; good manners: *a man of good breeding.*

breeze [briːz] *n* a gentle wind: *There's a lovely cool breeze today.*
'**breezy** *adj* **1** windy: *a breezy day.* **2** (of people *etc*) bright, lively: *She's always so bright and breezy*; *a breezy young man.*

brethren *see* **brother**.

brevity *see* **brief**.

brew [bruː] *v* **1** to make (beer, ale *etc*): *He brews beer at home.* **2** to make (tea *etc*): *She brewed another pot of tea.* **3** to prepare: *There's a storm brewing.* '**brewer** *n*.
'**brewery** – *pl* '**breweries** – *n* a place for brewing beer *etc*.

bribe [braib] *n* a gift offered to persuade a person to do something, *usu* dishonest: *Policemen are not allowed to accept bribes.* – *v* to give (someone) a bribe: *He bribed the guards to let him out of prison.*
'**bribery** *n*.

brick [brik] *n* (a block of) baked clay used for building: *a pile of bricks*; (*also adj*) *a brick wall.*
'**brickbat** *n* an insult: *They hurled brickbats at the politician throughout his speech.*
'**bricklayer** *n* a person who builds (houses *etc*) with bricks.

bride [braid] *n* a woman about to be married, or newly married: *The bride wore a white dress.*
'**bridal** *adj* **1** of a wedding: *the bridal feast.* **2** of a bride: *bridal finery.*
'**bridegroom** *n* a man about to be married, or newly married.
'**bridesmaid** ['braidzmeid] *n* an unmarried woman attending the bride at a wedding.

bridge [bridʒ] *n* **1** a structure carrying a road

or railway over a river *etc*. **2** the narrow raised platform for the captain of a ship. **3** the bony part (of the nose). **4** the support of the strings of a violin *etc*. – *v* **1** to build a bridge over: *They bridged the stream.* **2** to close a gap, pause *etc*: *He bridged the awkward silence with a funny remark.*

bridle ['braidl] *n* the harness on a horse's head to which the reins are attached.

brief [briːf] *adj* not long; short: *a brief visit*; *a brief account.* – *n* a short statement of facts (*esp* in a lawsuit, of a client's case): *a lawyer's brief.* – *v* to give detailed instructions to (*esp* a barrister, group of soldiers *etc*): *The astronauts were briefed before the space mission.*
'**briefing** *n* instructions and information: *The pilots were given a briefing before they left.*
'**briefly** *adv*: *He told me briefly what he knew.*
briefs *n pl* (used *esp* in shops) women's pants or men's underpants: *a pair of briefs.*
brevity ['brevəti] *n* shortness (of speech, writing, time *etc*): *He is well known for the brevity of his speeches.*
'**briefcase** *n* a light case for papers, made of leather *etc*: *a businessman's briefcase.*
in brief in a few words: *In brief, we have been successful.*

brigade [bri'geid] *n* **1** a body of troops. **2** a uniformed group of people organized for a particular purpose: *Call the fire brigade!*
brigadier [brigə'diə] *n* in the army, the commander of a brigade.

bright [brait] *adj* **1** shining with much light: *bright sunshine.* **2** (of a colour) strong and bold: *a bright red car.* **3** cheerful: *a bright smile.* **4** clever: *bright children.* '**brightly** *adv*. '**brightness** *n*.
'**brighten** *v* (*often with* **up**) to make or become bright or brighter: *The new wallpaper brightens up the room.*

brilliant ['briljənt] *adj* **1** very bright: *the bird's brilliant feathers.* **2** very clever: *a brilliant scholar.* '**brilliantly** *adv*.
'**brilliance** *n* **1** brightness: *the brilliance of the moon.* **2** cleverness: *his brilliance as a surgeon.*

brim [brim] *n* **1** the top edge of a cup, glass *etc*: *The jug was filled to the brim.* **2** the edge of a hat: *She pulled the brim of her hat down over her eyes.* – *v* – *pt, ptp* **brimmed** – to be, or become, full to the brim: *Her eyes were brimming with tears.*

brine [brain] *n* **1** very salty water: *a jar of olives in brine.*
'**briny** *adj* (of water) very salty.

bring [briŋ] – *pt, ptp* **brought** [brɔːt] – *v* **1** to make (something or someone) come (to or towards a place): *I'll bring plenty of food* with me; *Bring him to me!* **2** to result in: *This medicine will bring you relief.*

bring about to cause: *His disregard for danger brought about his death.*

bring back to (cause to) return: *She brought back the umbrella she borrowed; Her singing brings back memories of my mother.*

bring down to cause to fall: *The storm brought all the trees down.*

bring home to to prove or show (something) clearly to (someone): *His illness brought home to her how much she depended on him.*

bring off to achieve (something attempted): *They brought off an unexpected victory.*

bring round to bring back from unconsciousness: *Fresh air brought him round.*

bring up to rear or educate: *Her parents brought her up to be polite.* **2** to introduce (a matter) for discussion: *Bring the matter up at the next meeting.*

bring towards the speaker: *Mary, bring me some coffee.*

take away from the speaker: *Take these cups away.*

fetch from somewhere else and bring to speaker: *Fetch me my book from the bedroom.*

*brinjal ['brinja:l] *n* the green or purple fruit of the egg plant used as a vegetable.

brink [briŋk] *n* the edge or border of a steep, dangerous place or of a river.

brisk [brisk] *adj* active or fast moving: *a brisk walk; Business was brisk today.* '**briskly** *adv*.

bristle ['brisl] *n* a short, stiff hair on an animal or brush: *The dog's bristles rose when it was angry.*

'**bristly** *adj* **1** having bristles; rough: *a bristly moustache.*

brittle ['britl] *adj* hard but easily broken: *brittle materials.* '**brit·leness** *n*.

broad [bro:d] *adj* **1** wide; great in size from side to side: *a broad street.* **2** from side to side: *two metres broad.* **3** general; not detailed: *We discussed the plans in broad outline.*

'**broaden** *v* to make or become broad or broader.

'**broadly** *adv* generally: *Broadly speaking, I'd say your chances are poor.*

broad daylight full daylight: *The child was attacked in broad daylight.*

,**broad-'minded** *adj* ready to allow others to think or act as they choose without criticizing them: *a broad-minded headmaster.*

broadcast ['bro:dka:st] – *pt, ptp* '**broadcast** – *v* **1** to send out (radio and TV programmes *etc*): *He broadcasts regularly.* **2** to make (something) widely known. – *n* a television or radio programme: *I heard his broadcast last night.* '**broadcaster** *n*. '**broadcasting** *n*.

brocade [brə'keid, (*Amer*) brou-] *n, adj* (of)

a (*usu* silk) material having a raised design on it: *curtains made of blue brocade; brocade curtains.*

brochure ['brouʃuə] *n* a short booklet giving information about holidays, products *etc*: *Get some brochures from the travel agent.*

broil [broil] *v* (*Amer*) to grill (food): *She broiled the chicken.*

broke [brouk] *v see* **break**. – *adj* completely without money: *I'm broke till pay day.*

broken ['broukən] *adj* **1** *see* **break**: *a broken window; My watch is broken.* **2** interrupted: *broken sleep.* **3** uneven: *broken ground.* **4** (of language) not fluent: *He speaks broken English.* **5** ruined: *The children come from a broken home* (= their parents are no longer living together).

,**broken-'hearted** *adj* overcome by grief.

broker ['broukə] *n* a person employed to buy and sell (*esp* shares *etc*) for others: *an insurance broker; a stockbroker.*

bronchitis [broŋ'kaitis] *n* inflammation of the air passages in the lungs, causing difficulty in breathing: *Wet weather makes his bronchitis worse.* **bron'chitic** *adj*.

bronze [bronz] *n, adj* **1** (of) an alloy of copper and tin: *The medal is (made of) bronze.* **2** (of) its reddish brown colour. **3** (a work of art) made of bronze: *an exhibition of bronzes.*

'**bronzed** *adj* suntanned: *a bronzed face.*

bronze medal in athletics competitions, the medal awarded as third prize.

brooch [broutʃ] *n* a decoration, *esp* for a woman's dress, fastened by a pin: *She wore a brooch on the collar of her dress.*

brood [bru:d] *v* **1** (of birds) to sit on eggs. **2** to think (about something) anxiously for some time: *There's no point in brooding about what happened.* – *n* **1** the number of young hatched at one time.

brook[1] [bruk] *n* a small stream.

brook[2] [bruk] *v* to put up with: *He will not brook any interference.*

broom [bru:m] *n* **1** a wild shrub of the pea family with (*usu* yellow) flowers: *The hillside was covered in broom.* **2** a long-handled sweeping brush.

brother ['brʌðə] *n* **1** the title given to a male child to describe his relationship to the other children of his parents: *I have two brothers.* **2** a fellow member of any group (*also adj*: *brother officers*). **3** (*pl also* **brethren** ['breðrən]) a member of a religious group: *The brothers of the order prayed together; The brethren met daily.*

'**brotherhood** *n* **1** the state of being a brother; *the ties of brotherhood.* **2** an association of men for a certain purpose.

'**brother-in-law** – *pl* '**brothers-in-law** – *n* **1** the brother of one's husband or wife. **2** the husband of one's sister.

brought see **bring**.

brow [brau] n 1 the eyebrow: *huge, bushy brows.* 2 the forehead. 3 the top (of a hill): *over the brow of the hill.*

brown [braun] adj 1 of a dark colour between red and yellow: *brown paint*; *Her eyes are brown.* 2 suntanned: *She was very brown after her holiday in Greece.* – n 1 (any shade of) a colour similar to toasted bread, tanned skin, coffee *etc.* 2 something (*eg* paint, polish *etc*) brown in colour: *I prefer the brown to the green.* – v to make or become brown.

brownie ['brauni] n 1 (*with cap*: short for **Brownie Guide**) a junior Girl Guide. 2 (*Amer*) a sweet chocolate and nut cake.

browse [brauz] v 1 (of people) to glance through a book *etc* casually: *I don't want to buy a book – I'm just browsing.* 2 (of animals) to feed (on shoots or leaves of plants). – n an act of browsing.

bruise [bru:z] n an injury caused by a blow to a person or a fruit, turning the skin a dark colour: *bruises all over his legs*; *apples covered in bruises.* – v to cause or develop such a mark on the skin: *She bruised her forehead*; *She bruises easily.*

brunette [bru:'net] n a woman with brown or dark hair: *He prefers blondes to brunettes.*

brunt [brʌnt] : **bear the brunt of** to bear the wost of the effect of (a blow, attack *etc*): *I bore the brunt of his abuse/the storm.*

brush [brʌʃ] n 1 an instrument with bristles, wire, hair *etc* for cleaning, scrubbing *etc*: *a toothbrush*; *He sells brushes.* 2 an act of brushing. 3 a bushy tail of a fox. 4 a disagreement: *a slight brush with the law.* – v 1 to rub with a brush: *He brushed his jacket.* 2 to remove (dust *etc*) by sweeping with a brush: *brush the floor.* 3 to make tidy by using a brush: *Brush your hair!* 4 to touch lightly in passing: *The leaves brushed her face.*

brush aside to pay no attention to: *She brushed aside my objections.*

brush away to wipe off: *She brushed away a tear*; *She brushed it away.*

brush up (*with* **on**) to refresh one's knowledge of (*eg* a language): *He brushed up his Spanish before he went on holiday.*

give, get the brush-off to reject or be rejected abruptly.

brusque [brusk, (*Amer*) brʌsk] adj blunt and abrupt in manner: *a brusque reply.* '**brusquely** adv. '**brusqueness** n.

brute [bru:t] n 1 an animal other than man: *My dog died yesterday, the poor brute*; (*also adj*) *brute force.* 2 a cruel person. '**brutal** adj very cruel or severe: *a brutal beating.* **bru'tality** [-'ta-] n. '**brutish** adj of, or like, a brute: *brutish manners.*

bubble ['bʌbl] n a floating ball of air or gas: *bubbles in lemonade.* – v to form or rise in bubbles: *The champagne bubbled in the glass.* '**bubbly** adj having bubbles. **bubble over** 1 to be full (with happiness *etc*): *bubbling over with excitement.*

buccaneer [bʌkə'niə] n a type of pirate.

buck [bʌk] n the male of the deer, hare, rabbit *etc*: *a buck and a doe.* – v (of a horse or mule) to make a series of rapid jumps into the air. '**buckskin** n, adj (of) a soft leather made of deerskin or sheepskin. **buck up** 1 to hurry: *You'd better buck up if you want to catch the bus.* 2 to cheer up: *She bucked up when she heard the news.* **pass the buck** to pass on responsibility (to someone else): *Whenever he is blamed for anything, he tries to pass the buck.*

bucket ['bʌkit] n a container for holding water, milk *etc*: *We carried water in buckets to the burning house.*

buckle ['bʌkl] n a fastening for a strap or band: *a belt with a silver buckle.* – v 1 to fasten with a buckle: *He buckled on his sword.* 2 (*usu* of something metal) to make or become bent or crushed: *The metal buckled in the great heat.*

bud [bʌd] n a shoot of a tree or plant, containing undeveloped leaves or flower(s) or both: *Are there buds on the trees yet?*; *a rosebud.* – v – pt, ptp **'budded** – to begin to grow: *The trees are budding.* '**budding** adj just beginning to develop: *a budding poet.* **in bud** producing buds: *The flowers are in bud.*

Buddhism ['budizəm, (*Amer*) 'bu:-] n the religion founded by Gautama or Buddha. '**Buddhist** n a believer in Buddhism. – adj: *a Buddhist monk.*

buddy ['bʌdi] – pl **'buddies** – n (*esp Amer*) a friend.

budge [bʌdʒ] v to (cause to) move, even slightly: *I can't budge it*; *It won't budge!*

budgerigar ['bʌdʒəriga:] (*abbrev* '**budgie** ['bʌdʒi]) n a type of small (*orig* Australian) brightly-coloured bird, often kept as a pet.

budget ['bʌdʒit] n any plan showing how money is to be spent: *my budget for the month.* – v – pt, ptp **'budgeted** – 1 to make a plan showing this: *We must try to budget or we shall be in debt.* 2 (*with* **for**) to allow for (something) in a budget: *I hadn't budgeted for a new car.*

budgie see **budgerigar**.

buff [bʌf] n a dull yellow colour. – adj: *a buff envelope.*

***buffalo** ['bʌfəlou] – pls **'buffalo**, **'buffalo(e)s** – n 1 a large kind of ox, *esp* the Asian and

African varieties. **2** the American variety of ox; the bison.

buffer ['bʌfə] *n* an apparatus for lessening the force with which a moving object strikes something.

buffet¹ ['bʌfit] *n* a blow with the hand or fist: *a buffet on the side of the head.* – *v* – *pt, ptp* '**buffeted** – **1** to strike with the fist. **2** to knock about: *The boat was buffeted by the waves.*

buffet² ['bufei, (*Amer*) bə'fei] *n* **1** a refreshment bar, *esp* in a railway station or on a train *etc*: *We'll get some coffee at the buffet.* **2** a (*usu* cold) meal set out on tables from which people help themselves. – *Also adj*: *a buffet supper.*

bug [bʌg] *n* **1** an insect that lives in dirty houses and beds: *a bedbug.* **2** an insect: *There's a bug crawling up your arm.* **3** a germ or infection: *a stomach bug.* **4** a small hidden microphone. – *v* – *pt, ptp* **bugged** – **1** to place small hidden microphones in (a room *etc*): *The spy's bedroom was bugged.* **2** to annoy: *What's bugging him?*

buggy ['bʌgi] – *pl* '**buggies** – *n* a light, open, one-horse vehicle.

bugle ['bju:gl] *n* a musical wind instrument *usu* made of brass, used chiefly for military signals: *He plays the bugle.* '**bugler** *n*.

build [bild] – *pt, ptp* **built** [-t] – *v* to form or construct from parts: *build a house/railway/bookcase.* – *n* physical form: *a man of heavy build.*

'**builder** *n* a person who builds houses *etc*: *The builder who built our house has gone bankrupt.*

'**building** *n* **1** the art or business of putting up (houses *etc*) (*also adj*: *a building contractor*). **2** anything built: *The new supermarket is a very ugly building.*

,**built-'in** *adj* forming a permanent part of the building *etc*: *Built-in cupboards save space.*

,**built-'up** *adj* covered with houses *etc*: *a built-up area.*

build up 1 to increase (the size or extent of): *The traffic begins to build up around five o'clock.* **2** to strengthen gradually (a business, one's health, reputation *etc*): *His father built up that grocery business from nothing.*

bulb [bʌlb] *n* **1** the ball-shaped part of the stem of certain plants, *eg* onions, tulips *etc*, from which their roots grow. **2** (*also* '**light=bulb**) a pear-shaped glass globe surrounding the element of an electric light. **3** the pear-shaped end of a thermometer.

'**bulbous** *adj* like a bulb, *esp* in shape: *a bulbous nose.*

bulbul ['bulbul] *n* a songbird of Asia or Arica.

bulge [bʌldʒ] *n* a swelling: *the bulge of her hips.* – *v* to swell out: *His muscles bulged.*

bulk [bʌlk] *n* **1** the greater part: *The bulk of his money was spent on food.* **2** (great) size or mass: *the bulk of a parcel*; *His huge bulk appeared round the corner.* – *adj* in bulk: *bulk buying.*

'**bulky** *adj* large in size, awkward to carry *etc*: *a bulky parcel*; *This is too bulky to send by post.*

in bulk in large quantities: *Huge tankers now carry oil in bulk*; *They like to buy goods in bulk.*

bull [bul] *n* **1** the male of the ox family and of the whale, walrus, elephant *etc*. **2** a bull's-eye.

'**bullock** [-lək] *n* **1** a young bull. **2** a castrated bull, an ox, often used to pull **bullock carts**.

'**bullfight** *n* in Spain *etc* a fight between a bull and men on horseback and on foot. '**bullfighter** *n*.

'**bullring** *n* the enclosed area where a bullfight takes place.

'**bull's-eye** *n* the centre of a target, *esp* in archery, darts *etc*.

bulldozer ['buldouzə] *n* a (*usu* large) tractor for clearing obstacles and levelling ground. '**bulldoze** *v* to use a bulldozer on: *They bulldozed the building site.*

bullet ['bulit] *n* a piece of metal *etc* fired from certain hand guns: *He was killed by machine-gun bullets.*

bulletin ['bulətin] *n* **1** an official (verbal) report of news: *a bulletin about the Queen's illness.* **2** a printed information-sheet: *a monthly bulletin of local news.*

bullfight *see* bull.

bullion ['buliən] *n* gold or silver in bulk, not made into coins.

bullock *see* bull.

bully ['buli] – *pl* '**bullies** – *n* a person who hurts or frightens other, weaker people: *The fat boy was a bully at school.* – *v* to act like a bully towards.

bulrush ['bulrʌʃ] *n* a tall strong water plant.

bulwark ['bulwək] *n* a wall built as a defence, often made of earth.

bum¹ [bʌm] *n* the buttocks.

bum² [bʌm] *n* (*esp Amer*) a tramp or worthless person: *He doesn't work – he's just a bum.* – *adj* worthless: *a bum job.*

bumble-bee ['bʌmblbi:] *n* a kind of large bee with a hairy body.

bump [bʌmp] *v* to knock or strike (something): *She bumped into me*; *I bumped my head against the ceiling.* – *n* **1** (the sound of) a blow or knock: *We heard a loud bump.* **2** a swelling or raised part: *a bump on the head*; *This road is full of bumps.*

'**bumper** *n* (*Amer* '**fender**) a bar on a motor vehicle to lessen damage when it collides with anything. – *adj* excellent in some way, *esp* by being large: *a bumper crop.*

'**bumpy** *adj* uneven: *a bumpy road.*

bump into to meet (someone) by accident: *I bumped into him in the street.*

bumpkin ['bʌmpkin] *n* a clumsy or stupid country person: *a country bumpkin.*

bun [bʌn] *n* a kind of sweet cake: *a currant bun.*

bunch [bʌntʃ] *n* a number of things fastened or growing together: *a bunch of bananas.* – *v* (*often with* **up** *or* **together**) to come or put together in bunches, groups *etc*: *Traffic often bunches on a motorway.*

bundle ['bʌndl] *n* a number of things bound together: *a bundle of rags.* – *v* 1 (*often with* **up** *or* **together**) to make into bundles: *Bundle up all your things and bring them with you.* 2 to go, put or send (away) in a hurried or disorderly way: *They bundled him out of the room.*

bung [bʌŋ] *n* the stopper of the hole in a barrel, a small boat *etc.* – *v* 1 to block with such a stopper. 2 to throw: *Bung it over here.*

bungalow ['bʌŋgəlou] *n* a (*usu* small) house of one storey: *They live in a small bungalow.*

bungle ['bʌŋgl] *v* to do (something) clumsily or badly: *Someone has bungled.*

bunk [bʌŋk] *n* a sleeping-berth in a ship's cabin.

bunker ['bʌŋkə] *n* 1 a hollow containing sand on a golf course. 2 an underground shelter against bombs *etc.*

bunsen ['bʌnsn] : **bunsen** (**burner**) *n* a gas burner which produces a smokeless flame of great heating power: *Several of the bunsens in the chemistry laboratory are out of order.*

bunting ['bʌntiŋ] *n* flags for use in celebrations.

buoy [boi, (*Amer*) 'buːi] *n* a floating anchored mark, acting as a guide, warning or mooring point for boats. – *See also* **lifebuoy.**

'**buoyancy** *n* the ability to float on water or in the air: *the buoyancy of a balloon.*

'**buoyant** *adj.*

burden ['bəːdn] *n* 1 something to be carried: *He carried a heavy burden up the hill; The ox is sometimes a beast of burden* (= an animal that carries things). 2 something difficult to carry or withstand: *the burden of taxation.* – *v* to put a responsibility *etc* on (someone): *burdened with cares.*

bureau ['bjuərou] – *pls* '**bureaux** [-z], '**bureaus** – *n* 1 a writing-desk with drawers. 2 (*Amer*) a chest of drawers. 3 an office for collecting and supplying information *etc*: *a travel bureau.*

bureaucracy [bju'rokrəsi] *n* 1 a system of government by officials working for a government. 2 a country having such a

government which uses such officials. ,**bureau'cratic** *adj.*

burglar ['bəːglə] *n* a person who enters a house *etc* illegally to steal: *The burglar stole her jewellery.*

'**burglary** – *pl* '**burglaries** – *n* (an act of) illegally entering a house *etc* to steal: *He has been charged with burglary.*

'**burgle** *v*: *Our house has been burgled.*

burial *see* **bury.**

burly ['bəːli] *adj* (of a person) big, strong and heavy: *a big burly farmer.*

burn [bəːn] – *pts, ptps* **burned, burnt** [-t] – *v* 1 to destroy, damage or injure by fire, heat, acid *etc*: *The fire burned all my papers; I've burnt the meat.* 2 to use as fuel. 3 to make (a hole *etc*) by fire, heat, acid *etc*: *The acid burned a hole in my dress.* 4 to catch fire: *Paper burns easily.* – *n* an injury or mark caused by fire *etc*: *His burns will take a long time to heal: a burn in the carpet.*

'**burner** *n* any device producing a flame: *I'll have to use a burner to get this paint off.*

burnish ['bəːniʃ] *v* to make (metal) bright by polishing: *They burnished the silver.*

burnt *see* **burn.**

burrow ['bʌrou, (*Amer*) 'bəː-] *n* a hole dug for shelter: *a rabbit burrow.* – *v* 1 to make holes underground or in a similar place for shelter *etc*: *The mole burrows underground; He burrowed under the bedclothes.*

burst [bəːst] – *pt, ptp* **burst** – *v* 1 to break open or in pieces suddenly: *The bag/balloon burst.* 2 (*with* **in, into, through** *etc*) to come or go suddenly or violently: *He burst in without knocking; He burst into the room; She burst into tears.* 3 (of rivers) to overflow or flood (the banks): *The river has burst its banks.* – *n* 1 a break or explosion: *a burst in the pipes.* 2 an (*often* sudden and short) outbreak: *a burst of applause.*

burst open to open suddenly or violently: *The door burst open and she rushed in.*

bury ['beri] *v* 1 to place (a dead body) in a grave, the sea *etc.* 2 to hide (under the ground *etc*): *My socks are buried somewhere in this drawer.*

'**burial** *n* (an instance of) burying (a dead body) in a grave *etc*: *my grandfather's burial:* (*also adj*) *a burial service.*

bury the hatchet to stop quarrelling: *Let's bury the hatchet and be friends.*

bus [bʌs] *n* a large road vehicle for carrying passengers: *He came by bus.* – *v* – *prp* '**bus(s)ing** – *pt, ptp* **bus(s)ed** – to carry by bus.

bus stop a place where buses stop to let passengers on or off.

bush [buʃ] *n* 1 a growing thing between a tree and a plant in size: *a rose bush.* 2 (in Australia, Africa *etc*) wild uncultivated country.

'bushy *adj* thick and spreading: *bushy eyebrows*; *a bushy tail*.

business ['biznis] **1** *n* occupation; buying and selling: *Selling china is my business*; *The shop does more business at Christmas than at any other time*. **2** *n* a shop, a firm: *He owns his own business*. **3** concern: *Make it your business to help him*; *Let's get down to business* (= Let's start the work *etc* that must be done).

'businesslike *adj* practical; alert and prompt: *a businesslike approach to the problem*; *She is very businesslike*.

'businessman – *fem* **'businesswoman** – *n* a person who makes a living from some form of trade or commerce, not from one of the professions.

on business in the process of doing business or something official.

bust [bʌst] *n* **1** a woman's chest: *She has a very small bust*. **2** a sculpture of a person's head and shoulders: *a bust of Julius Caesar*.

bustle ['bʌsl] *v* (*often with* **about**) to busy oneself (often noisily or fussily): *She bustled about doing things all day*. – *n* hurry, fuss or activity.

busy ['bizi] *adj* **1** having a lot (of work *etc*) to do: *I am very busy*. **2** full of traffic, people, activity *etc*: *The roads are busy*, *a busy time of year*. **3** (*esp Amer*) (of a telephone line) engaged: *All the lines to New York are busy*. – *v* (*sometimes with* **with**) to occupy (oneself) with: *She busied herself preparing the meal*.

'busily *adv*.

but [bʌt] *conj* used to show a contrast between two or more things: *John was there but Peter was not*. – *prep* except (for): *no-one but me*; *the next road but one*.

butcher ['butʃə] *n* a person whose business is to kill cattle *etc* for food and/or sell their flesh. – *v* **1** to kill for food. **2** to kill cruelly: *All the prisoners were butchered by the dictator*.

butt[1] [bʌt] *v* to strike (someone or something) with the head: *He fell over when the goat butted him*.

butt in to interrupt or interfere: *Don't butt in while I'm speaking!*

butt[2] [bʌt] *n* someone whom others criticize or tell jokes about: *She's the butt of all his jokes*.

butt[3] [bʌt] *n* **1** the thick and heavy end (*esp* of a rifle). **2** the end of a finished cigar, cigarette *etc*: *His cigarette butt was the cause of the fire*.

butter ['bʌtə] *n* a fatty substance made from cream by churning. – *v* to spread with butter: *She buttered the bread*.

'buttery *adj*: *a buttery knife*.

'butterfingers *n* a person who is likely to drop things which he or she is carrying.

'butterscotch [-skotʃ] *n* a kind of hard toffee made with butter.

butter up to flatter (someone) *usu* because one wants him to do something for one.

butterfly ['bʌtəflai] – *pl* **'butterflies** – *n* a type of insect with large (often coloured) wings.

buttock ['bʌtək] *n* (*usu in pl*) either half of the part of the body on which one sits: *She smacked the child on the buttocks*.

button ['bʌtn] *n* **1** a knob or disc used as a fastening: *I lost a button off my coat*. **2** a small knob pressed to operate something: *This button turns the radio on*. – *v* (often with **up**) to fasten by means of buttons.

'buttonhole *n* the hole or slit into which a button is put. – *v* to catch someone's attention and hold him in conversation: *He buttonholed me and began telling me the story of his life*.

buttress ['bʌtris] *n* a support built on to the outside of a wall.

buxom ['bʌksəm] *adj* (of a woman) plump and *usu* attractive: *a buxom blonde*.

buy [bai] – *prp* **'buying**: *pt, ptp* **bought** [bɔːt] – *v* to get (something) by exchanging it for money: *He has bought a car*.

buzz [bʌz] *v* **1** (of an insect) to make a noise by beating its wings *eg* when flying: *The bees buzzed angrily*. **2** to be filled with or make a similar noise: *My ears are buzzing*; *The crowd was buzzing with excitement*. – *n* (*sometimes with* **a**) a buzzing sound: *a buzz of conversation*.

'buzzer *n* an electrical or other apparatus producing a buzzing sound.

by [bai] *prep* **1** next to; near; at the side of: *by the door*; *He sat by his sister*. **2** past: *going by the house*. **3** through; along; across: *We came by the main road*. **4** used (in the passive voice) to show the person or thing which performs an action: *struck by a stone*. **5** using: *He's going to contact us by letter*; *We travelled by train*. **6** from; through the means of: *I met her by chance*; *by post*. **7** (of time) not later than: *by 6 o'clock*. **8** during the time of. **9** to the extent of: *taller by ten centimetres*. **10** used to give measurements *etc*: *4 metres by 2 metres*. **11** in quantities of: *fruit sold by the kilo*. **12** in respect of: *a teacher by profession*. – *adv* **1** near: *They stood by and watched*. **2** past: *A dog ran by*. **3** aside; away: *money put by for an emergency*.

'bygones: let bygones be bygones to forgive and forget past causes of ill-feeling.

'bypass *n* a road which avoids an obstruction or a busy area: *Take the bypass round the city*. – *v* to avoid (a place) by taking such a road.

'by-product *n* something obtained or formed during the making of something

else: *Coal tar is a by-product of the process of obtaining gas from coal.*
'bystander *n* a person who watches but does not take part.
by and by after a short time: *By and by, everyone went home.*
by and large mostly; all things considered: *Things are going quite well, by and large.*

by oneself 1 alone: *He was standing by himself at the bus-stop.* **2** without anyone else's help: *He did the job (all) by himself.*
by the way incidentally: *By the way, have you a moment to spare?*

> **by** is used for forms of transport: *by train*; *by aeroplane*; *by land*; *by sea.*

Cc

cab [kab] *n* **1** (*esp Amer*) a taxi: *Could you call a cab for me?* **2** the driver's compartment of a railway engine, lorry *etc*.
cabaret ['kabərei̯] *n* an entertainment given in a restaurant *etc*: *a singer in a cabaret*.
*****cabbage** ['kabidʒ] *n* a type of vegetable with edible (*usu* green) leaves: *He bought a cabbage*.
cabin ['kabin] *n* **1** a small house or hut (made *eg* of logs): *a lóg cabin*. **2** a (small) room in a ship for sleeping in: *We've a four-berth cabin*. **3** the part of an aircraft containing seating for passengers.
cabinet ['kabinit] *n* **1** a piece of furniture with shelves and doors or drawers: *a filing cabinet*. **2** in Britain and some other countries the group of chief ministers who govern a country: *The Prime Minister has chosen a new Cabinet*.
cable ['keibl] *n* **1** (a) strong rope or chain for hauling or tying anything, *esp* a ship. **2** (a set of) wires for carrying electric current or signals: *They are laying (a) new cable*. **3** (a rope made of) strands of metal wound together for supporting a bridge *etc*. **4** (*also* **'cablegram**) a telegram sent by cable. – *v* to telegraph by cable: *I cabled news of my mother's death to our relations in Canada*.
cabomba [kə'bombə] *n* an aquatic plant with feathery leaves.
cacao [kə'ka:ou, (*Amer*) kə'keiou] *n* the tropical tree from whose seeds cocoa and chocolate are made.
cackle ['kakl] *n* **1** the sound made by a hen or goose. **2** a laugh which sounds like this: *an evil cackle*. – *v* to make such a sound.
cactus ['kaktəs] – *pls* **'cacti** [-tai], **'cactuses** – *n* a prickly plant whose stem stores water.
caddie, caddy[1] ['kadi] *n* a person who carries clùbs for a golfer.
caddy[2] ['kadi] – *pl* **'caddies** – *n* a small box for keeping tea-leaves in.
cadet [kə'det] *n* **1** a student in a military, naval or police school: *an army cadet*; *a police cadet*. **2** a schoolboy taking military training. – *Also adj*: *a school cadet force*.

café ['kafei, (*Amer*) ka'fei] *n* a (*usu* small) shop where meals and (non-alcoholic) drinks are served.
cafeteria [kafə'tiəriə] *n* a self-service restaurant: *This department store has a cafeteria*.
caffeine ['kafi:n, (*Amer*) ka'fi:n] *n* a drug found in coffee and tea.
caftan, kaftan ['kaftan] *n* a type of long flowing dress or robe sometimes brightly-coloured.
cage [keidʒ] *n* **1** a box of wood, wire *etc* for holding birds or animals: *The lion has escaped from its cage*; *a bird-cage*. **2** a lift in a mine. – *v* to put in a cage: *Some people think that it is cruel to cage wild animals*.
'cagebird *n* a bird, *eg* a canary, suitable for keeping in a cage.
cagey ['keidʒi] *adj* secretive: *He's very cagey about his plans*. **'caginess** *n*.
cajole [kə'dʒoul] *v* to coax (someone into doing something), often by flattery: *The little girl cajoled her father into buying her a new dress*.
cake [keik] *n* **1** a food made by baking a mixture of flour, fat, eggs, sugar *etc*: *a piece of cake*; *a plate of cream cakes*; *a Christmas cake*. **2** a piece of other food pressed into shape: *fishcakes*; *oatcakes*. **3** a flattened hard mass: *a cake of soap*. – *v* to cover in the form of a dried mass: *His shoes were caked with mud*.
calamity [kə'laməti] – *pl* **ca'lamities** – *n* a great misfortune: *It will be a calamity if he fails his exam*. **ca'lamitous** *adj*.
calcium ['kalsiəm] *n* an element of which one compound (**calcium carbonate**) forms limestone, chalk *etc*.
calculate ['kalkjuleit] *v* to count or estimate, using numbers: *Calculate the number of days in a century*. **'calculable** *adj*. **ˌcalcu'lation**.
'calculator *n* a machine for calculating: *Use a calculator for adding all those numbers*.
calendar ['kaləndə] *n* **1** a table showing the months and days of the year: *Look at the calendar and tell me which day of the week*

November 22nd is. **2** a list of important dates or events: *The football team's calendar is complete now.*

calendar ends in **-ar** (not **-er**).

calf[1] [ka:f] – *pl* **calves** [ka:vz] – *n* **1** the young of a cow, elephant, whale *etc*. **2** (*also* **'calfskin**) leather made from the skin of the young of a cow.
calve [ka:v] *v* to give birth to a calf: *The cow calved last night.*
calf[2] [ka:f] – *pl* **calves** [ka:vz] – *n* the thick fleshy back part of the leg below the knee: *She has slim ankles but fat calves.*
caliber *see* **calibre.**
calibrate ['kalibreit] *v* **1** to mark out the scale on (a measuring instrument). **2** to correct or adjust (the scale or instrument): *He calibrated the weighing machine.*
calibre, (*Amer*) **caliber** ['kalibə] *n* **1** the inner diameter of a gun barrel *etc*. **2** (of a person) quality of character; ability: *a salesman of extremely high calibre.*
call [ko:l] *v* **1** to give a name to: *My name is Alexander but I'm called Sandy by my friends.* **2** to regard (something) as: *I saw you turn that card over – I call that cheating.* **3** to speak loudly (to someone) to attract attention *etc*: *Call everyone over here*; *She called louder so as to get his attention.* **4** to summon; to ask (someone) to come (by letter, telephone *etc*): *They called him for an interview for the job*; *He called a doctor.* **5** to make a visit: *I shall call at your house this evening*; *You were out when I called.* **6** to telephone: *I'll call you at 6 p.m.* **7** (in card games) to bid. – *n* **1** an exclamation or shout: *a call for help.* **2** the song of a bird: *the call of a blackbird.* **3** a (*usu* short) visit: *The teacher made a call on the boy's parents.* **4** the act of calling on the telephone: *I've just had a call from the police.* **5** (*usu with* **the**) attraction: *the call of the sea.* **6** a demand: *There's less call for coachmen nowadays.* **7** a need or reason: *You've no call to say such things!*
'caller *n*.
'calling *n* a trade or profession: *Teaching is a worthwhile calling.*
'call-box *n* a public telephone box.
call for 1 to demand or require: *This calls for quick action.* **2** to collect: *I'll call for you at eight o'clock.*
call off to cancel: *The party's been called off.*
call on to visit: *I'll call on him tomorrow.*
call up to telephone (someone): *He called me up from the airport.*
give (someone) a call to telephone (someone): *I'll give you a call tomorrow.*
on call keeping (oneself) ready to come out to an emergency: *Which of the doctors is on call tonight?*

calligraphy [kə'ligrəfi] *n* (the art of) beautiful, decorative handwriting.
callous ['kaləs] *adj* unfeeling; cruel: *a callous person/attack.* **'callously** *adv*. **'callousness** *n*.
calm [ka:m] *adj* **1** still or quiet: *a calm sea*; *The weather was calm.* **2** not anxious or excited: *a calm person/expression*; *Please keep calm!* – *n* **1** (a period of) absence of wind and large waves. **2** peace and quiet: *He enjoyed the calm of the library.* – *v* to make calm: *Calm yourself!* **'calmly** *adv*. **'calmness** *n*.
calm down to make or become calm: *He tried to calm her down by giving her some brandy: Calm down!*
calorie ['kaləri] *n* (*abbrev* **cal** *when written*) **1** a unit of heat. **2** a unit of energy given by food: *My diet allows me 1200 calories per day.* ˌcalo'rific *adj*.
calve, calves *see* **calf**[1], **calf**[2].
calypso [kə'lipsou] – *pl* **ca'lypsos** – *n* a West Indian folk-song, telling of a current event and sometimes made up as the singer goes along.
came *see* **come.**
camel ['kaməl] *n* a desert animal with one (**dromedary** ['dromədəri]) or two (**bactrian (camel)** ['baktriən]) humps on its back, used for carrying goods and/or people.
camellia [kə'mi:liə] *n* (the red or white flower of) an evergreen shrub from eastern Asia.
cameo ['kamiou] – *pl* **'cameos** – *n* an engraved stone with a raised design, used as jewellery.
camera ['kamərə] *n* **1** an apparatus for taking still or (**'movie-camera**) moving photographs. **2** in television, an apparatus which receives a picture and turns it into electrical impulses for transmitting.
camouflage ['kaməfla:ʒ] *n* something, *eg* protective colouring, that makes an animal, person, building *etc* difficult for enemies to see against the background: *The tiger's stripes are an effective camouflage in the jungle*; *The soldiers wound leaves and twigs round their helmets as camouflage.* – *v* to conceal with camouflage.
camp [kamp] *n* **1** a piece of ground with tents pitched on it. **2** a collection of buildings, huts or tents in which people stay temporarily for a certain purpose: *a holiday camp.* **3** a military station, barracks *etc*. **4** a party or side: *They belong to different political camps.* – *v* (*also* **go camping**) to set up, and live in, a tent/tents: *We camped on the beach*; *We go camping every year.*
'camper *n* **1** a person who goes camping. **2** (*esp Amer*) a motor-caravan.
'camping *n*.
camp bed (*Amer* **cot**) a light folding bed (not only for camping): *The visitor will have to sleep on a camp bed.*

camp-fire *n* the fire on which campers cook, and round which they sit in the evening *etc.*

'campsite *n* a piece of land on which tents may be pitched.

campaign [kam'pein] *n* **1** the operations of an army while fighting in one area or for one purpose: *the Burma campaign in the Second World War.* **2** a series of organized actions in support of a cause: *a campaign against smoking.* – *v* to take part in a campaign: *He has campaigned against smoking for years.* **cam'paigner** *n.*

camphor ['kamfə] *n* a strongly scented whitish substance, used for various medical and industrial purposes: *Mothballs contain camphor.*

campus ['kampəs] *n* college or university grounds: *The new library was built in the centre of the campus.*

can¹ [kan] – *neg* **can't** [ka:nt], **cannot** ['kanət] – *v* **1** to be able to: *You can do it if you try hard.* **2** to know how to: *Can you drive a car?* **3** (*usu* **may**) to have permission to: *You can go if you behave yourself.* **4** used in questions to indicate surprise, disbelief *etc*: *What can he be doing all this time?*

can² [kan] *n* a metal container for liquids and many types of food: *oil-can; beer-can; six cans of beer.* – *v* – *pt, ptp* **canned** – to put (*esp* food) into cans, *usu* to preserve it: *a factory for canning raspberries.* **canned** *adj* put in cans: *canned peas.* **'cannery** – *pl* **'canneries** – *n* a factory where goods are canned.

canal [kə'nal] *n* **1** a (*usu* narrow) man-made waterway: *barges on the canal; the Panama Canal.* **2** a passage in the body carrying fluids, food *etc.*

canary [kə'neəri] – *pl* **ca'naries** – *n* a type of small, yellow, singing bird, kept as a pet.

can-can ['kankan]: **the can-can** a type of high-kicking dance.

cancel ['kansəl] – *pt, ptp* **'cancelled**, (*Amer*) **'canceled** – *v* **1** to decide or announce that (something already arranged *etc*) will not be done *etc*: *He cancelled his appointment.* **2** to mark (stamps) with a postmark. **3** to stop payment of (a cheque, subscription *etc*). **,cancel'lation** *n.*

cancel out to undo the effect of: *We don't want our profits to be cancelled out by extra expenses.*

cancer ['kansə] *n* **1** a diseased growth in the body, often fatal: *The cancer has spread to her stomach.* **2** the (often fatal) condition caused by such diseased growth(s): *He is dying of cancer.* **'cancerous** *adj.*

candid ['kandid] *adj* saying just what one thinks, without hiding anything: *Do you like my hairstyle? – Be candid.* **'candidly** *adv.* **'candour** [-də], **'candidness** *ns.*

candidate ['kandidət, (*Amer*) -deit] *n* a person who enters for a competition or examination (for a job, prize *etc*): *a candidate for the job of manager; a parliamentary candidate.* **'candidacy** [-dəsi], **'candidature** [-dətʃə] *ns* being a candidate.

candied *see* **candy.**

candle ['kandl] *n* a moulded piece of wax with a wick in the centre, for giving light: *We had to use candles when the electric lights went out.* **'candle-light** *n* the light from a candle: *We had dinner by candle-light.* **'candlestick** *n* a holder for a candle.

candour *see* **candid.**

candy ['kandi] – *pl* **'candies** – *n* **1** sugar formed into a solid mass by boiling. **2** (*Amer*) a sweet or sweets; (a piece of) confectionery: *That child eats too much candy; Have a candy!* **'candied** *adj* covered with sugar: *candied fruits.* **candy floss** (*Amer* **cotton candy**) flavoured sugar spun into a fluffy ball on the end of a stick.

cane [kein] *n* **1** the stem of certain types of plant (*eg* sugar plant, bamboo *etc*). **2** a stick used as an aid to walking or as an instrument of punishment: *He beat the child with a cane.* – *v* to beat with a cane: *The schoolmaster caned the boy.* **cane sugar** sugar obtained from the sugar cane.

canine ['keinain] *adj* like, or of, a dog or dogs: *canine characteristics.* **canine teeth** in man, the four sharp-pointed teeth.

canister ['kanistə] *n* a box or case *usu* of metal.

cannabis ['kanəbis] *n* a drug made from Indian hemp, whose use is illegal in many countries: *He is hooked on* (= addicted to) *cannabis.*

cannibal ['kanibəl] *n* **1** a person who eats human flesh. **2** an animal *etc* which eats others of its own species. **'cannibalism** *n.* **,canniba'listic** *adj.*

cannon ['kanən] – *pls* **'cannons, 'cannon** – *n* a type of large gun used formerly, mounted on a carriage. – *v* (*with* **into**) to hit or collide with: *He came rushing round the corner and cannoned into me.* **'cannonball** *n* a ball of iron, shot from a cannon.

cannot *see* **can¹.**

canoe [kə'nu:] *n* a light narrow boat driven by a paddle or paddles. – *v* to travel by canoe: *He canoed over the rapids.* **ca'noeist** *n.*

canon ['kanən] *n* **1** a rule (*esp* of the church). **2** a clergyman belonging to a cathedral. **3** a list of saints. **4** a musical composition in which one part enters after another in imitation. **ca'nonical** [-'no-] *adj.*

'canonize, -ise *v* to place in the list of saints: *Joan of Arc was canonized in 1920.* **,canoni'zation, -s-** *n.*

canopy ['kanəpi] – *pl* **'canopies** – *n* a covering hung over a throne, bed *etc* or (on poles) as a shelter.

cant [kant] *n* **1** insincere talk: *politicians' cant.* **2** the special slang of a particular group of people: *thieves' cant.*

can't *see* **can**[1].

cantankerous [kan'taŋkərəs] *adj* quarrelsome: *a cantankerous old man.*

canteen [kan'ti:n] *n* **1** a place where meals are sold in a factory, barracks *etc*. **2** a case for, or of, cutlery. **3** a small container used by soldiers for holding water *etc*.

canter ['kantə] *n* (of a horse) an easy gallop: *He went off at a canter.* – *v* to gallop easily: *The horse cantered over the meadow.*

canvas ['kanvəs] – *pl* **'canvases** – *n* **1** (*also adj*) (of) a coarse cloth made of hemp or flax *etc*, used for sails, tents *etc*, and for painting on: *canvas sails.* **2** (a piece of canvas for) a painting: *He painted twenty canvases.*

under canvas in tents: *living under canvas.*

canvass ['kanvəs] *v* to go round (an area) asking (people) for (support, votes, custom *etc*): *We're canvassing for the Conservative Party candidate.* **'canvasser** *n.*

canyon ['kanjən] *n* a deep valley between high steep banks, *usu* containing a river: *the Grand Canyon.*

cap [kap] *n* **1** a hat with a peak: *a chauffeur's cap.* **2** a covering for the head, not with a peak: *a swimming cap; a nurse's cap.* **3** a cover or top (of a bottle, pen *etc*): *Replace the cap after you've finished with the pen.*

capped *adj* having a cap or covering: *snow-capped mountains.*

capable ['keipəbl] *adj* **1** clever *esp* in practical ways: *She'll manage somehow – she's so capable!* **2** (*with* **of**) clever enough to; likely to; able to: *He is capable of doing better; He is quite capable of cheating us.* **'capably** *adv.* **,capa'bility** *n.*

capacious [kə'peiʃəs] *adj* roomy, holding a lot: *a capacious handbag.*

capacity [kə'pasəti] – *pl* **ca'pacities** – *n* **1** ability to hold, contain *etc*: *This tank has a capacity of 300 gallons.* **2** ability: *his capacity for remembering facts.* **3** position: *in his capacity as a leader.*

cape[1] [keip] *n* a long, loose, sleeveless outer garment hanging from the shoulders and fastening at the neck: *a waterproof cycling cape.*

cape[2] [keip] *n* a headland sticking out into the sea: *The fishing-boat rounded the cape; Cape Breton.*

caper ['keipə] *v* to leap or jump about: *The*

child was capering about. – *n* **1** a frisky jump. **2** a piece of playful behaviour.

capillary [kə'piləri, (*Amer*) 'kapileri] – *pl* **capillaries** – *n* a tube with a very small diameter, *esp* (*in pl*) the tiny vessels that join veins to arteries.

capital[1] ['kapitl] *n* **1** the chief town or seat of government: *Paris is the capital of France.* **2** (*also* **capital letter**) any letter of the type found at the beginning of sentences, proper names *etc*: *THESE ARE CAPITAL LETTERS/CAPITALS.* **3** money (for investment *etc*): *You need capital to start a new business.* – *adj* **1** involving punishment by death: *a capital offence.* **2** excellent: *a capital idea.* **3** (of a city) being a capital: *Paris and other capital cities.*

'capitalism *n* a system of economics in which money and business are controlled by capitalists.

'capitalist *n* a person who has much money in business concerns. **'capitalist, ,capita'listic** *adjs.*

capital[2] ['kapitl] *n* in architecture, the top part of a column of a building *etc*.

capitulate [kə'pitjuleit] *v* to surrender *usu* on agreed conditions: *We capitulated to the enemy.* **ca,pitu'lation** *n.*

caprice [kə'pri:s] *n* **1** an *esp* unreasonable sudden change of mind *etc*; a whim: *I'm tired of the old man and his caprices.* **2** a fanciful and lively piece of music *etc*.

capricious [kə'priʃəs] *adj* changeable: *She may change her mind – she's very capricious.* **ca'priciously** *adv.* **ca'priciousness** *n.*

capsize [kap'saiz] *v* (of a boat) to overturn, often sinking afterwards.

capstan ['kapstən] *n* a drum-shaped machine, used for winding *eg* a ship's anchor-cable.

capsule ['kapsju:l, (*Amer*) -sl] *n* **1** a small gelatine case containing a dose of medicine *etc*. **2** a closed metal container: *a space capsule.*

captain ['kaptən] *n* **1** the commander of a ship, an aircraft, or a group of soldiers. **2** (*abbrev* **Capt.**, *when written in titles*) the leader of a team or club. – *v* to be captain of (something non-military): *John captained the football team last year.*

'captaincy *n* the job of captain: *the captaincy of the team.*

caption ['kapʃən] *n* a title or short note written on or beneath an illustration, cartoon, cinema or TV film *etc*: *a witty caption.*

captivate ['kaptiveit] *v* to charm, fascinate, or hold the attention of: *He was captivated by her beauty.*

captive ['kaptiv] *n* a prisoner: *Two of the captives escaped.* – *adj* kept prisoner: *captive soldiers; The children were taken/held captive.*

cap'tivity *n* a state of being a prisoner, caged *etc*: *animals in captivity in a zoo.*

'captor *n* a person who captures someone: *He managed to escape from his captors.*

'capture [-tʃə] *v* 1 to take by force, skill *etc*: *The soldiers captured the castle*; *Several animals were captured.* 2 to take possession of (a person's attention *etc*): *The story captured his imagination.* – *n* 1 the act of capturing. 2 something caught: *A kangaroo was his most recent capture.*

car [ka:] *n* 1 (*Amer* ,automo'bile) a (*usu* privately-owned) motor vehicle on wheels for carrying people: *What kind of car do you have?*; *'Did you go by car?'* 2 a section for passengers in a train *etc*: *a dining-car.* 3 (*Amer*) a railway carriage for goods or people: *a freight car.*

car park (*Amer* **parking lot**) a piece of land or a building where cars may be parked.

carafe [kə'raf] *n* a glass bottle for serving water, wine *etc.*

caramel ['karəmel] *n* 1 sugar melted and browned, used for flavouring: *This sauce is flavoured with caramel.* 2 a sweet made with sugar, butter *etc*, a toffee.

carat ['karət] *n* 1 a measure of weight for precious stones. 2 a unit for stating the purity of gold: *an eighteen-carat gold ring.*

caravan ['karəvan] *n* 1 a vehicle on wheels for living in, now pulled by car *etc*, formerly by horse: *a holiday caravan*; *a gypsy caravan.* 2 a group of people travelling together for safety *esp* across a desert on camels: *a caravan of merchants.*

carbohydrate [ka:bə'haidreit] *n* (any of a group of) substances containing carbon, hydrogen and oxygen, *esp* the sugars and starches found in food: *Potatoes are full of carbohydrate.*

carbon ['ka:bən] *n* an element occurring as diamond and graphite and also in coal *etc.*

carbon copy a copy of writing or typing made by means of carbon paper.

carbon dioxide [dai'oksaid] a gas present in the air, breathed out by man and other animals.

carbon monoxide [mə'noksaid] a colourless, very poisonous gas which has no smell: *Carbon monoxide is given off by car engines.*

carbon paper a type of paper coated with carbon *etc* which makes a copy when placed between the sheets being written or typed.

carburettor, (*Amer*) **carburetor** ['ka:bjuretə, (*Amer*) -bərei-] *n* a part of an internal-combustion engine in which air is mixed with fuel.

carcase, (*esp Amer*) **carcass** ['ka:kəs] *n* a dead body, *usu* animal, not human: *The carcases of various animals hung in the butcher's shop.*

card [ka:d] *n* 1 thick paper or thin board: *shapes cut out from card.* 2 (*also* **'playing= card**) a small piece of such paper *etc* with designs, used in playing certain games: *a pack of cards.* 3 a similar object used for *eg* sending greetings, showing membership of an organization, storing information *etc*: *a birthday card*; *a membership card*; *a business card.*

cards *n sing* the game(s) played with playing-cards: *He cheats at cards.*

'cardboard *n*, *adj* (of) a stiff kind of paper often made up of several layers: *a cardboard box.*

cardiac ['ka:diak] *adj* of the heart: *This patient has a cardiac complaint*; *cardiac failure.*

cardigan ['ka:digən] *n* a knitted jacket which buttons up the front.

cardinal ['ka:dənl] *adj* chief; principal: *cardinal sins.* – *n* (the status of) one of the men next in rank to the Pope in the Roman Catholic Church.

cardinal numbers numbers expressing quantity (1, 2, 3 *etc*). – *See also* **ordinal numbers**.

care [keə] *n* 1 close attention: *Do it with care.* 2 keeping; protection: *Your belongings will be safe in my care.* 3 (a cause for) worry: *free from care*; *all the cares of the world.* – *v* 1 to be anxious or concerned: *Don't you care if you fail?*; *I couldn't care less* (= It's of no importance to me); *She really cares about her career.* 2 to be willing (to): *Would you care to have dinner with me?*

'careful *adj* 1 taking care; being cautious: *Be careful when you cross the street*; *a careful driver.* 2 thorough: *a careful search.*

'carefully *adv.* **'carefulness** *n.*

'careless *adj* not careful (enough): *This work is careless*; *a careless worker.*

'carelessly *adv.* **'carelessness** *n.*

'carefree *adj* light-hearted: *a carefree attitude.*

'caretaker *n* a person who looks after a building *etc.*

'careworn *adj* worn out by worry: *a careworn face.*

'care for 1 to look after (someone): *The nurse will care for you.* 2 to be fond of: *I don't care for him enough to marry him.*

care of (*usu written* **c/o**) at the house or address of.

take care to be cautious, watchful, thorough *etc*: *Take care or you will fall!*

take care of to look after: *Their aunt took care of them when their parents died.*

career [kə'riə] *n* 1 a way of making a living (*usu* professional): *a career in publishing.* 2 course; progress (through life): *The present government is nearly at the end of its*

career. – *v* to move rapidly and dangerously: *The brakes failed and the car careered
down the hill.*

caress [kə'res] *v* to touch gently and lovingly:
She caressed the horse's neck. – *n* an act of
touching in this way: *a loving caress.*

cargo ['ka:gou] – *pl* 'cargoes – *n* a load of
goods carried by a ship *etc*: *a cargo of
cotton.*

caricature ['karikətjuə] *n* a drawing or imitation (of someone or something) which is so
exaggerated as to appear ridiculous: *Cari-
catures of politicians appear in the newspapers every day.*
'**caricaturist** *n* a person who makes carica-
tures.

caries ['keərii:z] *n* decay or rottenness of the
teeth.

carnage ['ka:nidʒ] *n* the slaughter of great
numbers of people: *the carnage of war.*

carnival ['ka:nivəl] *n* a public entertainment,
often involving processions of people in
fancy dress *etc*: *a winter carnival.*

carnivore ['ka:nivo:] *n* a flesh-eating animal:
The lion is a carnivore. **car'nivorous** *adj.*

carol ['karəl] *n* a song of joy or praise, *esp* for
Christmas.

carouse [kə'rauz] *v* to take part in a noisy
drinking session. **ca'rousal** *n.*

carousel [karə'sel] *n* (*Amer*) a merry-go-
round.

carp [ka:p] *pl* **carp** – *n* a freshwater fish found
in ponds and rivers.

carpenter ['ka:pəntə] *n* a craftsman in wood.
'**carpentry** *n* the work of a carpenter.

carpet ['ka:pit] *n* a woven covering for floors
etc. – *v* to cover with a carpet: *They haven't
carpeted the floor yet.*

carriage ['karidʒ] *n* **1** the act or cost of conveying and delivering goods: *Does that
price include carriage?* **2** a vehicle for carrying (*esp* in Britain, railway passengers): *the
carriage nearest the engine*; *a railway carriage.* **3** *esp* formerly, a horse-drawn passenger vehicle. **4** the part of a typewriter
which moves back and forwards, carrying
the paper. **5** posture; way of walking.
'**carriageway** *n esp* in Britain, the part of a
road used by cars *etc*: *The overturned bus
blocked the whole carriageway.*

carrion ['kariən] *n* dead animal flesh, eaten by
other animals: *Vultures feed on carrion.*

carrot ['karət] **1** *n* (a vegetable with) an
edible, orange, pointed root.

carry ['kari] *v* **1** to take from one place *etc* to
another: *She carried the child over the river*;
Flies carry disease. **2** to go from one place
to another: *Sound carries better over water.*
3 to support: *These stone columns carry the
weight of the whole building.* **4** to have or
hold: *This job carries great responsibility.*
5 to approve (a bill, *etc*) by a majority of

votes: *The parliamentary bill was carried by
forty-two votes.* **6** to hold (oneself) in a
certain way: *He carries himself like a soldier.*
be/get carried away to be overcome by one's
feelings: *She was/got carried away by the
excitement.*
carry forward to add on (a number from
one column of figures to the next): *I forgot
to carry the 2 forward.*
carry off to take away by carrying: *She
carried off the screaming child.*
carry on 1 to continue: *You must carry on
working*; *Carry on with your work.* **2** to
manage (a business *etc*): *He carries on a
business as a grocer.*
carry out to accomplish: *He carried out the
plan.*
carry weight to have influence: *His opinion
carries a lot of weight around here.*

cart [ka:t] *n* **1** a two-wheeled (*usu* horse-
drawn) vehicle for carrying loads: *a farm
cart.* **2** (*Amer*) a small wheeled vehicle
pushed by hand, for carrying groceries, golf
clubs *etc.* – *v* **1** to carry (in a cart): *He
carted the manure into the field.* – **2** to
carry: *I don't want to cart this luggage
around all day.*
'**cartwheel** *n* **1** a wheel of a cart. **2** a sideways somersault.

cartilage ['ka:təlidʒ] *n* a firm elastic substance
found in the bodies of men and animals.

cartography [ka:'togrəfi] *n* map-making.
car'tographer *n.* ,**carto'graphic** [-'gra-] *adj.*

carton ['ka:tən] *n* a cardboard or plastic
container: *orange juice sold in cartons.*

cartoon [ka:'tu:n] *n* **1** a drawing making fun
of someone or something: *a cartoon of the
Prime Minister in the newspaper.* **2** a film
consisting of a series of drawings in which
the people and animals give the impression
of movement: *a Walt Disney cartoon.*
car'toonist *n* a person who draws cartoons.

cartridge ['ka:tridʒ] *n* **1** a case containing the
explosive charge (and *usu* a bullet) for a
gun. **2** a stylus of a record-player and its
holder. **3** a plastic container of photographic film or recording tape. **4** a tube
containing ink for loading a fountain pen.

carve [ka:v] *v* **1** to make designs, shapes *etc*
by cutting a piece of wood *etc*: *A figure
carved out of wood.* **2** to cut up (meat) into
slices: *Father carved the joint.*
'**carving** *n* a design, ornament *etc* carved
from wood, stone *etc.*
carve out to achieve or gain (something):
He carved out a career for himself.

cascade [kas'keid] *n* a waterfall: *a magnificent
cascade.* – *v* to fall in or like a waterfall:
Water cascaded over the rock; *Dishes cascaded off the table.*

case[1] [keis] *n* **1** an instance or example:

another case of child-beating; a bad case of measles. **2** a particular situation: It's different in my case. **3** a legal trial: The judge in this case is very fair. **4** an argument or reason: There's a good case for thinking he's wrong. **5** (usu with the) a fact: I don't think that's really the case. **6** a form of a pronoun (eg **he** or **him**), noun or adjective showing its relation to other words in the sentence.
in case in order to guard against a possibility: I'll take an umbrella in case (it rains).
in case of if (a particular thing) happens: In case of fire, telephone the fire brigade.
in that case if that should happen or should have happened: You're leaving? In that case, I'm leaving too.

case² [keis] n **1** a container or outer covering: a case of medical instruments; a suitcase. **2** a crate or box: six cases of whisky. **3** a piece of furniture for displaying or containing things: a glass case full of china; a bookcase.

cash [kaʃ] n **1** coins or paper money, not cheques, credit cards etc: Do you wish to pay cash? **2** payment by money or cheque as opposed to payment by account: Cash or account, madam? **3** money in any form: He has plenty of cash. – v to turn into, or exchange for, money: You may cash a traveller's cheque here; Can you cash a cheque for me?
cashier [ka'ʃiə] n a person who receives and pays out money (eg in a bank), works at a cash register etc: a bank cashier; a cashier in a supermarket.
,cash-and-'carry n a store where goods are sold more cheaply for cash and taken away by the buyer.
cash register a machine for holding money, which records the amount put in.
cash in to exchange for money: I've cashed in all my shares.
cash in on to take financial or other advantage of (a situation etc): He is the sort of person who cashes in on other people's misfortunes.

cashew ['kaʃu:] n a type of small nut: Is that a cashew? – adj: a cashew nut.

cashier¹ see **cash**.

cashier² [ka'ʃiə] v to dismiss (a military officer) from a post in disgrace.

cashmere [kaʃ'miə, (Amer) 'kaʒmiər] n, adj (of) a type of material made from fine goats' hair: a cashmere sweater.

casino [kə'si:nou] – pl ca'sinos – n a building with gambling tables etc.

cask [ka:sk] n a barrel for holding liquids, usu wine: three casks of sherry.

casket ['ka:skit] n **1** a small case for holding jewels etc. **2** (esp Amer) a coffin.

cassava [kə'sa:və] n (also **tapioca plant**) a tropical plant, whose roots yield tapioca.

casserole ['kasəroul] n **1** a covered dish in which food is both cooked and served: an earthenware casserole. **2** the food cooked in a casserole: I've made a casserole for dinner.

cassette [kə'set] n a plastic container holding photographic film or magnetic tape: I've put a new cassette in my camera; I bought a cassette of Scottish music; (also adj) a cassette recorder.

cassia ['kasiə, 'kaʃə] n any of several types of tropical tree or shrub of the pea family with small yellow or pink flowers.

cassock ['kasək] n a long robe worn by clergymen and church choir-singers.

cast [ka:st] – pt, ptp **cast** – v **1** to throw: The angler cast his line into the river; These facts cast new light on the matter; She cast him a look of hatred. **2** to get rid of; to take off: Some snakes cast their skins. **3** to shape (metal etc) by pouring into a mould: Metal is melted before it is cast. **4** to give a part in a play etc to: She was cast as Lady Macbeth. **5** to select the actors for (a film etc): The director is casting (the film) tomorrow. **6** to give (a vote): I cast my vote for the younger candidate. – n **1** a throw: At his third cast he caught a fish. **2** something made by moulding: The doctor put a plaster cast on his broken leg. **3** a mould: The hot metal is poured into a cast. **4** the complete set of actors in a play, opera etc: the whole cast of the play. **5** something that is ejected by certain animals, eg the earthworm: worm casts all over the grass.

'castaway n a shipwrecked person.

casting vote the deciding vote of the chairman of a meeting when the other votes are equally divided.

cast iron unpurified iron melted and shaped in a mould.

'cast-iron adj **1** made of cast iron: a cast-iron frying-pan. **2** very strong: cast-iron muscles.

'cast-off n, adj (a piece of clothing etc) no longer needed: cast-off clothes; I don't want my sister's cast-offs.

cast off 1 to untie (the mooring lines of a boat). **2** (also **cast aside**) to reject as unwanted. **3** in knitting, to finish (the final row of stitches).

cast on in knitting, to make the first row of stitches.

castanets [kastə'nets] n pl two hollow pieces of ivory or hard wood struck together as a rhythm for (esp Spanish) dances.

caste [ka:st] n a social class esp in India: the lowest caste; (also adj) the caste system.

caster¹ ['ka:stə]: **caster sugar** fine sugar used in baking etc.

caster² see **castor**.

castle ['ka:sl] n **1** a large building strengthened against attack: the Norman castles of

England and Wales; *Windsor Castle*. **2** (*also* **rook**) a piece in chess.

castor, caster ['ka:stə] *n* a small wheel on the legs of furniture to make it easier to move.

castor oil [ka:stər'oil, (*Amer*) 'kastəroil] an oil from a tropical plant, used in medicine *etc*.

castrate [kə'streit, (*Amer*) 'kastreit] *v* to remove the sexual organs of (a male animal): *The bull has been castrated.* **ca'stration** *n*.

casual ['kaʒuəl] *adj* **1** not careful: *I took a casual glance at the book.* **2** informal: *casual clothes.* **3** happening by chance: *a casual remark.* **4** not regular or permanent: *casual labour.* **'casually** *adv.* **'casualness** *n*.

casualty ['kaʒuəlti] – *pl* **'casualties** – *n* a person who is wounded or killed in a battle, accident *etc*: *There were hundreds of casualties when the factory went on fire.*
casualty department a hospital department for treating accidental injuries.

*casuarina [kaʒuə'ri:nə] *n* a tall, feathery tree with drooping, jointed, green branches and scale-like leaves.

cat [kat] *n* **1** a small, four-legged, fur-covered animal often kept as a pet: *a Siamese cat.* **2** a large wild animal of the same family (*eg* tiger, lion *etc*): *the big cats.*
'catty *adj* **1** spiteful, malicious: *She's catty even about her best friend; catty remarks.*
'catcall *n* a shrill whistle showing disagreement or disapproval: *the catcalls of the audience.*
'catfish *n* any of a family of scaleless fish with long feelers round the mouth.
'catgut *n* a kind of cord made from the intestines of sheep *etc*, used for violin strings *etc*.
.cat's-'eye® *n* a small, thick piece of glass fixed in the surface of a road to reflect light and guide drivers at night.
'catsuit *n* a woman's close-fitting one-piece trouser suit.
'cattail *n* a tall plant that grows in wet places, with flowers shaped like a cat's tail.
let the cat out of the bag to let a secret become known unintentionally.

cataclysm ['katəklizəm] *n* a violent disaster or upheaval; disaster. **.cata'clysmic** *adj*.

catalogue, (*Amer*) **catalog** ['katəlog] *n* (a book containing) an ordered list of names, goods, books *etc*: *a library catalogue.* – *v* to put in an ordered list: *She catalogued the books in alphabetical order of author's name.*

catalyst [katəlist] *n* **1** a substance which causes or assists a chemical change in another substance without itself undergoing any permanent chemical change. **2** someone or something that helps bring about a change. **.cata'lytic** *adj*.

catamaran [katəmə'ran] *n* a sailing-boat with two parallel hulls.

catapult ['katəpʌlt] *n* (*Amer* **'slingshot**) a small forkèd stick with an elastic string fixed to the two prongs for firing small stones *etc, usu* used by children. – *v* to throw violently: *The driver was catapulted through the windscreen when his car hit the wall.*

cataract ['katərakt] *n* a clouding of the lens of the eye causing difficulty in seeing.

catarrh [kə'ta:] *n* inflammation of the lining of the nose and throat causing a discharge of thick fluid.

catastrophe [kə'tastrəfi] *n* a sudden great disaster: *earthquakes and other natural catastrophes; Her brother's death was a catastrophe for the family.* **catastrophic** [katə'strofik] *adj.* **.cata'strophically** *adv*.

catcall *see* **cat**.

catch [katʃ] – *pt, ptp* **caught** [ko:t] – *v* **1** to stop and hold (something which is moving); to capture: *He caught the cricket ball; The cat caught a mouse; Did you catch any fish?; I tried to catch his attention.* **2** to be in time for, or get on (a train, bus *etc*): *I'll have to catch the 9.45 (train) to London.* **3** to surprise (someone) in the act of: *I caught him stealing (my vegetables).* **4** to become infected with (a disease or illness): *He caught flu.* **5** to (cause to) become accidentally attached or held: *The child caught her fingers in the car door.* **6** to hit: *The punch caught him on the chin.* **7** to manage to hear: *Did you catch what she said?* **8** to start burning: *I dropped a match on the pile of wood and it caught (fire) immediately.* – *n* **1** an act of catching: *He took a fine catch behind the wicket.* **2** a small device for holding (a door *etc*) in place: *The catch on my suitcase is broken.* **3** the total amount (of *eg* fish) caught: *the largest catch of mackerel this year.* **4** a trick or problem: *There's a catch in this question.*
'catching *adj* infectious: *Is chicken-pox catching?*
'catchy *adj* (of a tune) attractive and easily remembered.
'catch-phrase, 'catch-word *ns* a phrase or word in popular use for a time.
catch someone's eye to attract someone's attention: *The advertisement caught my eye; I couldn't catch the waiter's eye and so we were last to be served.*
catch on 1 to become popular: *The fashion caught on.* **2** to understand: *He's a bit slow to catch on.*
catch out 1 to put out (a batsman) at cricket by catching the ball after it has been hit and before it touches the ground. **2** to cause (someone) to fail by means of a trick,

a difficult question *etc*: *The last question in the exam caught them all out.*

catch up to come level (with): *We caught him up at the corner*; *Ask the taxi-driver if he can catch up with that lorry*; *We waited for him to catch up*; *She had a lot of schoolwork to catch up on after her illness.*

catechism ['katikizəm] *n* **1** a book (*esp* religious) of instructions by means of question and answer. **2** a series of searching questions on any subject.

category ['katəgəri] – *pl* '**categories** – *n* a class or division of things (or people): *various categories of goods on sale.*
'**categorize, -ise** *v* to put (things or people) into a category.

cater ['keitə] *v* **1** to provide food *etc*: *We cater for all types of functions.* **2** to supply what is needed: *We cater for all educational needs.* '**caterer**, '**catering** *ns*.

caterpillar ['katəpilə] *n* the larva of a butterfly or moth that feeds upon the leaves of plants: *There's a caterpillar on this lettuce.* – *adj* moving on endless belts: *a caterpillar tractor.*

catfish, catgut *see* **cat**.

cathedral [kə'θi:drəl] *n* the principal church of a district under a bishop.

catholic ['kaθəlik] *adj* **1** wide-ranging in one's taste *etc*: *a catholic taste in books.* **2** (*with cap*) Roman Catholic. – *n* (*with cap*) a Roman Catholic.
Catholicism [kə'θolisizəm] *n* Roman Catholicism.

catsuit, cattail *see* **cat**.

cattle ['katl] *n pl* grass-eating animals, *esp* cows, bulls and oxen: *That farmer does not keep sheep but he keeps several breeds of cattle.*

caught *see* **catch**.

cauldron ['ko:ldrən] *n* a large deep pot (used *esp* by witches) for boiling things in.

cauliflower ['koliflauə] *n* a vegetable of the cabbage family whose white flower-head is used as food.

cause [ko:z] *n* **1** something or someone that produces an effect or result: *Having no money is the cause of all my misery.* **2** a reason for an action; a motive: *You had no cause to treat your wife so badly.* **3** an aim or concern for which an individual or group works: *cancer research and other deserving causes*; *in the cause of peace.* – *v* to make (something) happen; to bring about; to be the means of: *What caused the accident?*; *He caused me to drop my suitcase.*

causeway ['ko:zwei] *n* a raised pathway, road *etc* over wet ground or shallow water.

caustic ['ko:stik] *adj* **1** burning by chemical action: *caustic soda.* **2** (of remarks) bitter or sarcastic: *caustic comments.* '**caustically** *adv.*

cauterize, -ise ['ko:təraiz] *v* to burn (a wound) with a caustic substance or a hot iron (to destroy infection).

caution ['ko:ʃən] *n* **1** carefulness (because of possible danger *etc*): *Exercise caution when crossing this road.* **2** in law, a warning: *The policeman gave him a caution for speeding.* – *v* to give a warning to: *He was cautioned for drunken driving.* '**cautionary** *adj.*
'**cautious** *adj* having or showing caution; careful: *She used to trust everyone but she's more cautious now*; *a cautious driver.* '**cautiously** *adv.*

cavalcade [kavəl'keid] *n* a ceremonial procession.

cavalier [kavə'liə] *n* in former times, a horseman or knight.

cavalry ['kavəlri] *n or n pl* (the part of an army consisting of) horse-soldiers: *The cavalry were/was ordered to advance.*

cave [keiv] *n* a large natural hollow in rock or in the earth: *The children explored the caves.*
'**caveman** [-man] *n* in prehistoric times, a person who lived in a cave: *Cavemen dressed in the skins of animals.*
cave in (of walls *etc*) to collapse.

cavern ['kavən] *n* a large cave.
'**cavernous** *adj* huge and hollow: *a cavernous hole.*

caviar(e) ['kavia:, (*Amer*) kavi'a:] *n* the pickled eggs (roe) of a certain large fish, used as food.

cavity ['kavəti] – *pl* '**cavities** – *n* a hollow place; a hole: *The dentist said she had three cavities in her teeth*; *The thief hid the necklace in a cavity in the wall.*

cease [si:s] *v* to stop or (bring to an) end: *They were ordered to cease firing*; *That department has ceased to exist*; *This foolishness must cease!*; *Cease this noise!*
'**ceaseless** *adj* continuous; never ceasing: *ceaseless noise.* '**ceaselessly** *adv.*

cedar ['si:də] *n* **1** a cone-bearing evergreen tree. **2** (*also* '**cedarwood**) its hard, sweet-smelling wood.

ceiling ['si:liŋ] *n* the inner roof (of a room *etc*): *Paint the ceiling before you paint the walls.*

celebrate ['seləbreit] *v* to mark by giving a party *etc* in honour of (a happy or important event): *I'm celebrating (my birthday) today.*
'**celebrated** *adj* famous: *a celebrated actress.*
,**cele'bration** *n*: *birthday celebrations.*
ce'lebrity [-'le-] – *pl* **ce'lebrities** – *n* a well-known person: *celebrities from the world of entertainment.*

celery ['seləri] *n* the long juicy edible stalks of a type of vegetable, used in salads *etc*.

celestial [sə'lestiəl, (*Amer*) sə'lestʃəl] *adj* of

heaven or the skies: *Stars are celestial bodies*.

celibacy ['selibəsi] *n* the state of being unmarried or of refraining from sexual intercourse, *esp* in obedience to religious vows. **'celibate** [-bət] *adj*.

cell [sel] *n* 1 a small room (*esp* in a prison or monastery). 2 a very small piece of the substance of which all living things are made; the smallest unit of living matter: *The human body is made up of cells*. 3 (the part containing the electrodes in) an electrical battery. 4 one of many small compartments making up a structure: *the cells of a honeycomb*.

cellular ['seljulə] *adj* consisting of cells: *cellular tissue*. 2 containing tiny hollow spaces: *Foam rubber is a cellular substance*.

cellar ['selə] *n* a room, *esp* underground, *esp* for stores of coal or wine.

cello, 'cello ['tʃelou] *n* (short for **'violoncello**) a stringed musical instrument similar to, but much larger than, a violin.
'cellist, 'cellist *n* a person who plays the cello.

cellophane (® in the UK) ['seləfein] *n* a type of clear wrapping material: *flowers wrapped in cellophane*; (*also adj*) *cellophane wrapping*.

cellular *see* **cell**.

cellulose ['seljulous] *n* the chief substance in the cell walls of plants, also found in woods, used in the making of plastic, paper *etc*.

Celsius ['selsiəs] *adj* (*often abbrev* **C** *when written*) centigrade: *twenty degrees Celsius; 20° C*.

Celsius ends in -sius (not -cius)

cement [sə'ment] *n* 1 a mixture of clay and lime (*usu* with sand and water added) used for sticking things (*eg* bricks) together in building and to make concrete for making very hard surfaces. 2 any of several types of glue. 3 a substance used to fill cavities in teeth. – *v* to join firmly with cement.

cemetery ['semətri, (*Amer*) -teri] – *pl* **'cemeteries** – *n* a piece of ground, *usu* not round a church, where people are buried.

cenotaph ['senɑtɑːf] *n* a monument to a person or people buried elsewhere, *esp* a monument built in memory of soldiers *etc* killed in war.

censor ['sensə] *n* an official who examines films *etc* and has the power to remove any of the contents which might offend people: *Part of his film has been banned by the censor*. 2 an official (*eg* in the army) who examines letters *etc* and removes information which the authorities do not wish to be made public for political reasons *etc*. – *v*:

This film has been censored; *The soldiers' letters are censored*.

cen'sorious [-'soː-] *adj* very critical: *She is censorious about the behaviour of young people*.
'censorship *n* the policy of censoring: *Some people disapprove of censorship*.

censure ['senʃə] *v* to criticize or blame: *He was censured for staying away from work*. – *n* criticism or blame.

census ['sensəs] – *pl* **'censuses** – *n* an official counting *esp* of a country's inhabitants: *When was the last census in Britain?*

cent [sent] *n* a coin equal to the hundredth part of a dollar, rupee, rand *etc*.

centenary [sen'tiːnəri, (*Amer*) 'sentəneri] (*pl* **cen'tenaries**), **centennial** [sen'teniəl] *ns* a hundredth anniversary: *The firm is celebrating its centenary this year*.
centenarian [sentə'neəriən] *n* a person who is a hundred or more years old.

centigrade ['sentigreid] *adj* (*often abbrev* **C** *when written*) as measured on a centigrade thermometer: *twenty degrees centigrade; 20° C*.
centigrade thermometer a thermometer which shows the temperature at which water freezes as 0°, and that at which it boils as 100°.

centimetre ['sentimiːtə] *n* a unit of length equal ot one-hundredth of a metre.

centipede ['sentipiːd] *n* a type of very small worm-like animal with many legs.

central ['sentrəl] *adj* 1 belonging to or near the centre (*eg* of a town): *His flat is very central*. 2 principal or most important: *the central point of his argument*.
'centralize, -ise *v* to bring under one control. **centrali'zation, -s-** *n*.
'centrally *adv*: *centrally situated*.
central heating heating of a building by water, steam or air through pipes from one central boiler *etc*.

centre, (*Amer*) center ['sentə] *n* 1 the middle point, or middle of anything; the point or area farthest from the edge: *the centre of a circle; the city centre*. 2 a place having, or designed for, a particular activity, interest *etc*: *a centre of industry; a shopping-centre; a sports-centre*. 3 the main point (of interest *etc*): *the centre of attention*. – *v* 1 to place, or to be, at the centre. 2 (*with* **on**) to concentrate round: *Her plans always centre on her child*.

centrifugal [sen'trifjugəl] *adj* tending to move away from a centre: *centrifugal force*.

century ['sentʃuri] *n* – *pl* **'centuries** – 1 a (period of a) hundred years: *the 19th century; for more than a century*. 2 in cricket, a hundred runs: *He has just made his second century this year*.

ceramic [sə'ramik] *adj* (of the art) of pottery.

– *n* something made of pottery: *She sells ceramics, but they are very expensive.*
ce'ramics *n sing* the art of pottery.
cereal ['siəriəl] *n* **1** a kind of grain used as food: *Wheat and barley are cereals*; (*also adj*) *cereal crops.* **2** a type of breakfast food prepared from such grain.
cerebral ['serəbrəl, (*Amer*) sə'ri:brəl] *adj* of the brain.
ceremony ['serəmǝni, (*Amer*) -mouni] – *pl* **'ceremonies** – *n* **1** a sacred or formal act, *eg* a wedding, funeral *etc*: *a marriage ceremony.* **2** solemn display and formality: *pomp and ceremony.*
,cere'monial [-'mou-] *adj* formal or official: *a ceremonial occasion such as the opening of parliament.* **,cere'monially** *adv.*
,cere'monious [-'mou-] *adj* (*neg* **un-**) carefully formal or polite. **,cere'moniously** *adv.*
certain ['sə:tn] *adj* **1** true or without doubt: *It's certain that the world is round.* **2** sure: *I'm certain he'll come*; *He is certain to forget*; *Being late is a certain way of losing one's job.* **3** one or some, not definitely named: *certain doctors*; *a certain Mrs Smith*; (*also pron*) *certain of his friends.* **5** slight; some: *a certain hostility in his manner*; *a certain amount.*
'certainly *adv* **1** definitely: *I can't come today, but I'll certainly come tomorrow.* **2** of course: *You may certainly have a chocolate.* – *interj* of course: *'May I borrow your typewriter?' 'Certainly!'*; *'Certainly not!'*
'certainty – *pl* **'certainties** – *n* **1** something which cannot be doubted: *It's a certainty that he will win.* **2** freedom from doubt: *Is there any certainty of success?*
for certain definitely: *She may come but she can't say for certain.*
make certain to act so that, or check that, something is sure: *Make certain you arrive early*; *I think he's dead but you'd better make certain.*
certificate [sə'tifikət] *n* a written official declaration of some fact: *a marriage certificate.*
certify ['sə:tifai] *v* **1** to declare formally (*eg* that something is true): *I certify that I witnessed the signing of his will.* **2** to declare officially that (someone) is insane. **cer,tifi-'cation** *n.*
cessation [se'seiʃən] *n* stopping or ceasing: *the cessation of activities.*
chafe [tʃeif] *v* **1** to make warm by rubbing with the hands. **2** to make or become sore by rubbing: *These tight shoes chafe my feet.* **3** to become impatient: *Everyone's chafing at the delay.*
chagrin ['ʃagrin, (*Amer*) ʃə'grin] *n* disappointment and annoyance.
chain [tʃein] *n* **1** a series of (*esp* metal) links or rings passing through one another: *The dog was fastened by a chain*; *She wore a silver*

chain round her neck. **2** a series: *a chain of events.* – *v* to fasten or bind with chains: *The prisoner was chained to the wall.*
chain mail armour made of iron links.
chain store one of a series of shops (often department stores) under the same ownership.
chair [tʃeə] *n* **1** a movable seat for one person, with a back to it: *a table and four chairs.* **2** the position of a person who is chairman at a meeting *etc*: *Who is in the chair?* **3** the office of a university professor: *He holds the chair of History at this university.* – *v* to be chairman at (a meeting *etc*): *He chaired the meeting last night.*
'chairlift *n* a set of seats hanging from a cable, used to take skiers *etc* up a mountain.
'chairman, -person, -woman *ns* a person who takes charge of or directs a meeting.
'chairmanship *n.*

Address a male chairman as **Mr Chairman**, and a female chairman as **Madam Chairman**.

chalet ['ʃalei, (*Amer*) ʃa'lei] *n* **1** in Switzerland, a summer hut in the mountains for shepherds *etc*. **2** a small (wooden) house used by holidaymakers *etc*.
chalice ['tʃalis] *n* a wine-cup, *esp* one used in religious services.
chalk [tʃɔ:k] *n* **1** a white rock; a type of limestone. **2** (a piece of) a chalk-like substance used for writing (*esp* on blackboards): *a box of chalks.*
'chalky *adj* **1** of or like chalk: *a chalky substance.* **2** white or pale: *Her face looked chalky.*
'chalkboard *n* a smooth board, *usu* green, for writing or drawing on with crayon or chalk.
challenge ['tʃalindʒ] *v* **1** to ask (someone) to take part in a contest: *He challenged his brother to a round of golf.* **2** to question (someone's authority or right, the truth of a statement *etc*). – *n* **1** an invitation to a contest: *He accepted his brother's challenge to a fight.* **2** the act of questioning someone's right, a statement *etc*.
'challenger *n.*
'challenging *adj* demanding effort; difficult: *a challenging job/idea.*
chamber ['tʃeimbə] *n* **1** a room. **2** the place where an assembly (*eg* Parliament) meets: *There were few members left in the chamber.* **3** such an assembly: *the Upper and Lower Chambers.* **4** an enclosed space or cavity *eg* the part of a gun which holds the bullets: *Many pistols have chambers for six bullets.*
'chambermaid *n* a female servant or hotel worker in charge of bedrooms.
chamber music music for a small group of

players, suitable for a room rather than a large hall.

chameleon [kə'mi:liən] *n* a small lizard which is able to change colour.

chamois ['ʃamwa:, (*Amer*) 'ʃami] – *pl* 'chamois – *n* **1** a small antelope living in mountainous country. **2** (*also* shammy ['ʃami] – *pl* 'shammies) (a piece of) soft washing leather *orig* made from its skin.

champ [tʃamp] *v* (*esp* of horses) to chew noisily.
champing at the bit impatient.

champagne [ʃam'pein] *n* a type of white sparkling wine, *esp* from Champagne in France, often drunk at celebrations *etc*.

champion ['tʃampiən] *n* **1** in games, competitions *etc*, a competitor who has defeated all others: *this year's golf champion*; (*also adj*) *a champion boxer*. **2** a person who defends a cause: *a champion of human rights*. – *v* to defend or support: *He championed the cause of human rights for many years*.
'championship **1** a contest held to decide who is the champion; *The tennis championship will be decided this afternoon*. **2** the act of defending or supporting: *his championship of civil rights*.

chance [tʃa:ns] *n* **1** luck or fortune: *It was by chance that I found out the truth*. **2** an opportunity: *Now you have a chance to do well*. **3** a possibility: *He has no chance of winning*. **4** (a) risk: *There's an element of chance in this business deal*. – **1** to risk: *I may be too late but I'll just have to chance it*. **2** to happen accidentally or unexpectedly: *I chanced to see him last week*. – *adj* happening unexpectedly: *a chance meeting*.
'chancy *adj* risky or uncertain: *a chancy arrangement*.
chance on, upon 1 to meet by accident: *I chanced on a friend of yours*. **2** to discover by accident: *I chanced upon some information*.
by any chance used in enquiring about the possibility of something: *Are you by any chance free tonight?*
by chance by luck; without planning: *They met by chance*.
an even chance equal probability for and against: *We have an even chance of success*.
the chances are it is likely (that): *The chances are he can't come tomorrow*.

chancellor ['tʃa:nsələ] *n* **1** a state or legal official of various kinds: *The Lord Chancellor is the head of the English legal system*. **2** the head of a university.

chandelier [ʃandə'liə] *n* a frame with many holders for lights, which hangs from the ceiling.

change [tʃeindʒ] *v* **1** to make or become different: *They have changed the time of the train*; *He has changed since I saw him last*.

2 to give or leave (one thing *etc* for another): *She changed my library books for me*. **3** (*sometimes with* into) to remove (clothes *etc*) and replace them by clean or different ones: *I'm just going to change (my shirt)*; *I'll change into an old pair of trousers*. **4** (*with* into) to make into or become (something different): *The prince was changed into a frog*. **5** to give or receive (one kind of money for another): *Could you change this bank-note for cash?* – *n* **1** the process of becoming or making different: *The town is undergoing change*. **2** an instance of this: *a change in the programme*. **3** a substitution of one thing for another: *a change of clothes*. **4** coins rather than paper money: *I'll have to give you a note – I have no change*. **5** money left over or given back from the amount given in payment: *He paid with a dollar and got 20 cents change*. **6** a holiday, rest *etc*: *He has been ill – the change will do him good*.
'changeable *adj* changing often; liable to change often: *changeable moods*.
change hands to pass into different ownership: *This car has changed hands three times*.
a change of heart a change in attitude.
change one's mind to alter one's intention or opinion (about something): *He was going to go to France but he changed his mind*.
for a change to be different; for variety: *We're tired of the car, so we'll walk for a change*.

changeling ['tʃeindʒliŋ] *n* a child secretly left in place of another by the fairies *etc*.

channel ['tʃanl] *n* **1** the bed of a stream or other way through which liquid can flow: *a sewage channel*. **2** a passage of deeper water in a river, through which ships can sail. **3** a narrow stretch of water joining two seas: *the English Channel*. **4** a means of sending or receiving information *etc*: *We got the information through the usual channels*. **5** (in television, radio *etc*) a band of frequencies for sending or receiving signals: *BBC Television now has two channels*. – *v* – *pt, ptp* 'channelled, (*Amer*) 'channeled – **1** to make a channel in. **2** to direct into a particular course: *He channelled all his energies into the project*.

chant [tʃa:nt] *v* **1** to recite in a singing manner: *The monks were chanting their prayers*. **2** to repeat (a phrase, slogan *etc*) over and over out loud: *The crowd was chanting 'We want more!'* – *n* **1** a kind of sacred song. **2** a phrase or slogan constantly repeated: *'Stop the cuts!' was the chant*.

chaos ['keios] *n* complete disorder or confusion: *The place was in utter chaos after the burglary*. cha'otic [-tik] *adj*. cha'otically *adv*.

chap [tʃap] *n* a man: *He's a nice chap*.

chapel ['tʃapəl] *n* **1** a place of Christian worship *eg* attached to an institution: *a college chapel.* **2** a part of a larger church, with its own altar.

chaperone ['ʃapəroun] *n* someone, *esp* an older lady, who accompanies a girl in public. – *v: Their aunt chaperoned the two girls at the ball.*

chaplain ['tʃaplin] *n* a clergyman attached to a ship, regiment *etc.*

chapped [tʃapt] *adj* (of skin) cracked and rough: *chapped lips.*

chapter ['tʃaptə] *n* a main division of a book: *There are fifteen chapters in his new book.*
a chapter of accidents a whole series of disasters.

char [tʃa:] – *pt, ptp* **charred** – *v* to burn or turn black by fire or heat: *The wood was charred by the intense heat.*

character ['karəktə] *n* **1** the set of qualities that make someone or something different from others; type: *You can tell a man's character from his handwriting*; *Publicity of this character is not good for the firm.* **2** a set of qualities that are considered admirable in some way: *He showed great character in dealing with the danger.* **3** reputation: *They tried to damage his character.* **4** a person in a play, novel *etc: Rosencrantz is a minor character in Shakespeare's 'Hamlet'.* **5** an odd or amusing person: *This fellow's quite a character!* **6** a letter used in typing *etc: Some characters on this typewriter are broken.*
,character'istic *adj* (*neg* **un-**) typical (of a person *etc*): *He spoke with characteristic shyness; That kind of behaviour is characteristic of him.* – *n* a typical quality: *It is one of his characteristics to be obstinate.*
,characte'ristically *adv.*
'characterize, -ise *v* **1** to be the obvious feature of: *The giraffe is characterized by its long neck.* **2** to describe (as): *She characterized him as weak and indecisive.*
,characteri'zation, -s- *n.*

charade [ʃə'ra:d, (*Amer*) ʃə'reid] *n* a piece of ridiculous pretence which is so obvious that it does not deceive anyone.
cha'rades *n sing* a game in which each syllable of a word, and then the whole word, is acted and the audience has to guess the word.

charcoal ['tʃa:koul] *n* the black part of partly burned wood *etc*, used as fuel and for drawing.

charge [tʃa:dʒ] *v* **1** to ask as the price (for something): *They charge 50 cents for a pint of milk, but they don't charge for delivery.* **2** to make a note of (a sum of money) as being owed: *Charge the bill to my account.* **3** (*with* **with**) to accuse (of something illegal): *He was charged with theft.* **4** to attack by moving quickly (towards): *We charged (towards) the enemy on horseback.* **5** to rush: *The children charged down the hill.* **6** to make or become filled with electricity: *Please charge my car battery.* **7** to load (a gun *etc*). **8** to make (a person) responsible for (a task *etc*): *He was charged with seeing that everything went well.* – *n* **1** a price or fee: *What is the charge for a telephone call?* **2** something with which a person is accused: *He faces three charges of murder.* **3** an attack made by moving quickly: *the charge of the Light Brigade.* **4** the electricity in something: *a positive or negative charge.* **5** someone one takes care of: *These children are my charges.* **6** a quantity of gunpowder: *Put the charge in place and light the fuse.*
'charger *n* formerly, a horse used in battle.
in charge of responsible for: *I'm in charge of thirty men.*
in someone's charge in the care of someone: *You can leave the children in his charge.*
take charge 1 (*with* **of**) to begin to control, organize *etc: The department was in chaos until he took charge (of it).* **2** (*with* **of**) to take into one's care: *The policeman took charge of the gun.*

chariot ['tʃariət] *n* a two-wheeled vehicle used in ancient warfare or racing.
chario'teer *n* a chariot driver.

charity ['tʃarəti] – *pl* **'charities** – *n* **1** kindness (*esp* in giving money to poor people): *She gave clothes to the gypsies out of charity.* **2** an organization set up to collect money for the needy, for medical research *etc: Many charities sent money to help the victims of the disaster.*
'charitable *adj* **1** (*neg* **un-**) kind. **2** of a charity: *a charitable organization.*
'charitably *adv.*

charm [tʃa:m] *n* **1** (a) pleasant quality or attraction: *Her charm made up for her lack of beauty.* **2** a magical spell: *The witch recited a charm.* **3** something believed to have the power of magic or good luck: *She wore a lucky charm.* – *v* **1** to attract and delight: *He can charm any woman.* **2** to influence by magic: *He charmed the snake from its basket.*
'charming *adj* very attractive: *a charming smile.* **'charmingly** *adv.*

chart [tʃa:t] *n* **1** a map of part of the sea. **2** a table or diagram giving information: *a weather chart.* – *v* **1** to make a chart of: *He charted the Black Sea.* **2** to make a table of information about: *I'm charting our progress.*

charter ['tʃa:tə] *n* a formal document giving rights or privileges. – *v* to let or hire (a ship, aircraft *etc*) on contract: *The travel company had chartered three aircraft for their* *holiday flights. – adj: a charter plane; a charter flight.*

chary ['tʃeəri] *adj* (with **of**) cautious: *Be chary of lending money to someone you don't know very well.*

chase [tʃeis] *v* **1** to run after; to pursue: *He chased after them but did not catch them; We chased them by car.* **2** (*with* **away, off** *etc*) to cause to run away: *I often have to chase the boys away from my fruit trees. – n* **1** an act of chasing: *We caught him after a 120 kph chase.* **2** hunting (of animals): *the pleasures of the chase.*

give chase to chase: *The thieves ran off and the policeman gave chase.*

chasm ['kazəm] *n* a deep opening between high rocks *etc*: *The climber could not cross the chasm.*

chassis ['ʃasi] *– pl* 'chassis [-z] *– n* the frame of a motor car *etc.*

chaste [tʃeist] *adj* pure and virtuous.
chastity ['tʃastəti], 'chasteness *ns.*

chasten ['tʃeisn] *v* to humble by punishment, suffering *etc.*

chastise [tʃas'taiz] *v* to punish by beating *etc.*
chastisement ['tʃastizmənt] *n.*

chastity *see* **chaste.**

chat [tʃat] *– pt, ptp* 'chatted *– v* to talk in a friendly and informal way: *They chatted about the weather. – n* (a) friendly and informal talk: *a chat over coffee; women's chat.*
'chatty *adj* **1** fond of chatting: *a chatty old lady.* **2** having a friendly style: *a chatty letter.*

chatter ['tʃatə] *v* **1** to talk quickly and noisily about unimportant things: *The children chattered among themselves.* **2** (of teeth) to knock together with the cold *etc*: *teeth chattering with terror. – n* rapid, noisy talk: *childish chatter.*
'chatterbox *n* a talkative person.

chauffeur ['ʃoufə, (*Amer*) ʃou'fə:r] *n* a person employed as a car-driver for a rich or important person.

chauvinism ['ʃouvinizəm] *n* unthinking enthusiasm for a particular country, cause *etc.*
'chauvinist *n.* ,chauvi'nistic *adj.*
male chauvinist a man who believes that women are inferior to men.

cheap [tʃi:p] *adj* **1** low in price: *Eggs are cheap just now.* **2** of poor quality; vulgar; contemptible: *cheap jewellery; a cheap trick.*
'cheaply *adv.* **'cheapness** *n.*

cheat [tʃi:t] *v* to act dishonestly to gain an advantage: *He cheats at cards; He was cheated (out of ten dollars). – n* **1** a person who cheats: *He only wins because he is a cheat.* **2** a dishonest trick.

check [tʃek] *v* **1** to see if something (*eg* a sum) is correct or accurate: *Will you check my addition?* **2** to see if something (*eg* a ma-

chine) is in good condition or working properly: *Have you checked the engine (over)?* **3** to hold back; to stop: *We've checked the flow of water from the burst pipe. –* **1** an act of testing or checking. **2** something which prevents or holds back: *a check on imports.* **3** in chess, a position in which the king is attacked: *He put his opponent's king in check.* **4** a pattern of squares: *I like the red check on that material.* **5** a ticket received in return for handing in baggage *etc.* **6** (*esp Amer*) a bill: *The check please, waiter!* **7** (*Amer*) a cheque.
checked *adj* having a pattern of check: *She wore a checked skirt; Is the material checked or striped?*
'checkbook *n* (*Amer*) a chequebook.
'checkmate *n* in chess, a position from which the king cannot escape. *– v* to put (an opponent's king) in this position.
'checkout *n* a place where payment is máde for goods bought in a supermarket.
'checkpoint *n* a barrier where cars, passports *etc* are inspected, or a point that contestants in a race must pass.
'check-up *n* a medical examination to discover the state of a person's health: *my annual check-up.*
check in to arrive (at a hotel) and sign the register: *We checked in last night.*
check out 1 to leave (a hotel), paying one's bill *etc*: *You must check out before 12 o'clock.* **2** (*esp Amer*) to test: *I'll check out your story.*
check up (on) to investigate to see if (someone or something) is reliable, honest, true *etc*: *Have you been checking up on me?*
checkers *see* **chequers.**

cheek [tʃi:k] *n* **1** the side of the face below the eye: *pink cheeks.* **2** impudence or disrespectful behaviour: *He had the cheek to refuse me entrance.*
'cheeky *adj* impudent: *a cheeky remark.*
'cheekiness *n.*

cheep [tʃi:p] *v* to make the shrill sound of a young bird. *– n* **1** such a sound. **2** a single sound or word: *I have not heard a cheep from the baby since he went to bed.*

cheer [tʃiə] *n* **1** a shout of approval, encouragement or welcome: *Three cheers for the Queen!* **2** mood: *Be of good cheer. – v* to give a shout of approval *etc* (to): *The crowd cheered the new champion.*
'cheerful *adj* full of, or causing, happiness: *a cheerful smile; cheerful news.* **'cheerfully** *adv.* **'cheerfulness** *n.*
'cheerless *adj* gloomy: *a cheerless room.*
cheers! *interj* **1** used as a toast when drinking. **2** cheerio! **3** thanks!
'cheery *adj* lively and happy. **'cheerily** *adv.* **'cheeriness** *n.*
cheer up to make or become (more cheer-

ful): *He cheered up when he saw her; The flowers will cheer her up.*

cheerio! [tʃəri'ou] *interj* used when leaving someone.

cheese [tʃiːz] *n* (any type of) a food prepared from the curd of milk and *usu* pressed into a mass or shape: *Cheese is full of protein.*
'**cheesecake** *n* a type of sweet food made with cheese *etc.*
cheesed off bored.

*****cheetah** ['tʃiːtə] *n* a very swift-running animal of the cat family.

chef [ʃef] *n* a head cook, *esp* a man, in a hotel *etc.*

chemical, chemist *see* **chemistry.**

chemistry ['kemistri] *n* (the science that deals with) the nature of substances and the ways in which they act on, or combine with, each other: *Chemistry was his favourite subject; the chemistry of the blood.*
'**chemical** *adj* of chemistry: *a chemical reaction.* – *n* a substance used in or obtained by a chemical process: *Some chemicals give off harmful fumes.*
'**chemist** *n* 1 a scientist who studies or works in chemistry: *an industrial chemist.* 2 (*Amer* '**druggist**) a person who makes up and sells medicines and *usu* also soap, make-up *etc.* 3 a chemist's shop: *Where is the nearest chemist?*

cheongsam [tʃi'oŋ'sam] *n* a close-fitting garment with a high, round collar and slits on the skirt, worn by women in China.

cheque, (*Amer*) **check** [tʃek] *n* a written order on a printed form telling a bank to pay money to the person named: *to pay by cheque.*
'**cheque-book** *n* a book of cheque forms.
cheque card *see* **banker's card.**

chequers, (*Amer*) **checkers** ['tʃekəz] *n* 1 *sing* the game of draughts. 2 *pl* the pieces used in this game.

cherish ['tʃeriʃ] *v* 1 to protect and love (a person): *She cherishes that child.* 2 to keep (a hope, idea *etc*) in the mind: *She cherishes the hope that he will return.*

cherry ['tʃeri] – *pl* '**cherries** – *n* 1 a type of small *usu* red fruit with a stone.

cherub ['tʃerəb] *n* an angel with wings and the plump face and body of a child. **che'rubic** [-'ruː-] *adj.*

chess [tʃes] *n* a game for two played with thirty-two (*usu* black and white) pieces ('**chessmen**) on a board ('**chessboard**) with sixty-four (*usu* black and white) squares.

chest[1] [tʃest] *n* the part of the body between the neck and waist, containing the heart and the lungs: *a severe pain in his chest.*
get something off one's chest to tell the truth about something that is worrying one.

chest[2] [tʃest] *n* a large, strong wooden or metal box: *The sheets were kept in a wooden chest.*
chest of drawers a piece of furniture fitted with several drawers.

chestnut ['tʃesnʌt] 1 a reddish-brown nut (one type being edible). 2 a reddish-brown horse. 3 a boring old joke or story. – *adj* of the colour of ripe chestnuts: *chestnut hair.*

chew [tʃuː] *v* to break (food *etc*) with the teeth before swallowing: *If you chew your food properly it is easier to digest.*
'**chewing-gum** *n* a type of sweet made from sweetened and flavoured gum.

chic [ʃiːk] *adj* stylish: *She looks very chic.*

chick [tʃik] *n* a baby bird: *One of the chicks fell out of the blackbird's nest.*

chicken ['tʃikin] *n* 1 a young bird, *esp* a young hen: *She keeps chickens.* 2 its flesh used as food: *a plate of fried chicken.*
,**chicken-'hearted** *adj* cowardly.
'**chicken-pox** *n* an infectious disease with fever and red itchy spots.
chicken out to avoid doing something because of cowardice: *He chickened out at the last minute.*

chicory ['tʃikəri] *n* a plant whose leaves are used in salads and whose root is ground and mixed with coffee.

chide [tʃaid] *v* to scold.

chief [tʃiːf] *adj* greatest in importance *etc*: *the chief cause of disease.* – *n* the head of a clan or tribe, or a department, business *etc.*
'**chiefly** *adv* mainly: *She became ill chiefly because she did not eat enough.*
'**chieftain** [-tən] *n* the head of a clan, tribe *etc.*

chiffon ['ʃifon, (*Amer*) ʃi'fon] *n, adj* (of) a thin, light material made from silk *etc*: *a chiffon dress.*

chiku, ciku ['tʃiːkuː] *n* a sweet tropical fruit with a thin brown skin.

child [tʃaild] – *pl* **children** ['tʃildrən] – *n* 1 a young human being of either sex. 2 a son or daughter: *Her youngest child is five years old.*
'**childhood** *n* the state or time of being a child: *Her childhood was a time of happiness.*
'**childish** *adj* like a child; silly: *a childish remark.* '**childishly** *adv.* '**childishness** *n.*
'**childless** *adj* having no children: *the childless couple.*
'**childlike** *adj* innocent; like a child: *childlike faith; trustful and childlike.*
'**childbirth** *n* the act of giving birth to a child: *She died in childbirth.*
child's play something very easy: *Climbing that hill will be child's play.*

chili *see* **chilli.**

chill [tʃil] *n* 1 coldness: *There's a chill in the air.* 2 an illness which causes shivering: *I think I've caught a chill.* – *adj* cold: *a chill*

* see illustration on p. 17

wind. – v to make cold (without freezing): *Have you chilled the wine?*
'chilly *adj* cold: *a chilly day.*
'chilliness *n.*

chilli, chili ['tʃili] – *pls* 'chilli(e)s, 'chili(e)s – *n* the hot-tasting pod of a type of pepper, often dried, powdered and used in sauces *etc.*

chime [tʃaim] *n* (the ringing of) a set of tuned bells: *the chime of the clock. – v* 1 to (cause to) ring: *The church bells chimed.* 2 (of a clock) to indicate the time by chiming: *The clock chimed 9 o'clock.*

chimney ['tʃimni] *n* a passage for the escape of smoke *etc* from a fireplace or furnace: *a factory chimney.*

chimpanzee [tʃimpən'zi:] *n* a type of small African ape.

chin [tʃin] *n* the part of the face below the mouth: *His beard completely covers his chin.*

china ['tʃainə] *n* a fine kind of baked and glazed clay; porcelain: *a plate made of china*; (*also adj*) *a china vase.*

chink [tʃiŋk] *n* a narrow opening: *a chink in the curtains*; *There was no chink of light in the room.*

chip [tʃip] – *pt, ptp* chipped – *v* to knock or strike small pieces off: *This glass (was) chipped when I knocked it over. – n* 1 a place from which a small piece is broken: *There's a chip in the edge of this saucer.* 2 (*Amer* french fry) (*usu in pl*) a cut piece of potato (fried): *steak and chips.* 3 a counter representing a certain value, used in gambling.
chip in 1 to interrupt: *He chipped in with a remark.* 2 to give (money): *He'll chip in with a dollar.*

chipmunk [tʃipmʌŋk] *n* a type of N. American squirrel with a bushy tail and black-and-white-striped back.

chiropodist [ki'ropədist] *n* a person who treats minor disorders of the feet.
chi'ropody *n* the work of a chiropodist.

chirp [tʃə:p], chirrup ['tʃirəp] *ns* the sharp, shrill sound of certain birds and insects. – *v* to make such a sound.

chirpy ['tʃə:pi] *adj* lively and happy: *a chirpy tune*; *I'm feeling chirpy today.*

*chisel ['tʃizl] *n* a tool with a cutting edge at the end. –*v* – *pt, ptp* 'chiselled, (*Amer*) 'chiseled – to cut or carve (wood *etc*) with a chisel.

chit [tʃit] *n* a brief note: *You must hand in a chit stating your expenses before you receive any money.*

chivalry ['ʃivəlri] *n* 1 kindness and courteousness *esp* towards women or the weak. 2 the principles of behaviour of medieval knights. 'chivalrous *adj* (*neg* un-).

chlorine ['klo:ri:n] *n* an element, a yellowish-green gas with a suffocating smell, used as a disinfectant *etc*: *They put too much chlorine in the swimming-pool.*

chloroform ['klorəfo:m] *n* a liquid, the vapour of which, when breathed in, causes unconsciousness.

chlorophyll ['klorəfil] *n* the colouring matter of the green parts of plants.

chocolate ['tʃokələt] *n* 1 a paste made from the seeds of the cacao tree. 2 a sweet or drink made from it: *Have a chocolate*; *a cup of chocolate. – adj* of, made from, covered with, chocolate: *chocolate ice-cream*; *chocolate biscuits.*

choice [tʃois] *n* 1 an act or the power of choosing: *You have no choice – you must do it.* 2 a thing chosen: *Which car was your original choice?*

choir ['kwaiə] *n* a group of singers: *He used to sing in the church choir.*

choke [tʃouk] *v* 1 to (cause to) stop, or partly stop, breathing: *The gas choked him*; *He choked to death.* 2 to block: *This pipe was choked with dirt. – n* an apparatus in a car engine *etc* to prevent the passage of too much air when starting the engine.

cholera ['kolərə] *n* a highly infectious, often fatal disease occurring in hot countries.

choose [tʃu:z] – *pt* chose [tʃouz]: *ptp* chosen ['tʃouzn] – *v* 1 to take (one thing rather than another from a number of things) according to what one wants: *Always choose (a book) carefully.* 2 to decide (on one course of action rather than another): *If he chooses to resign, let him do so.*
nothing/not much to choose between hardly any difference between: *There's not much to choose between the two methods.*

chop[1] [tʃop] – *pt, ptp* chopped – *v* (*sometimes with* up) to cut (into small pieces): *He chopped up the vegetables. – n* a slice of mutton, pork *etc* containing a rib.
'chopper *n* 1 an instrument for chopping. 2 a helicopter.
'choppy *adj* (of the sea) rough. 'choppiness *n.*
chop and change to keep changing (*esp* one's mind).
chop down to cause (*esp* a tree) to fall by cutting it with an axe: *He chopped down the fir tree.*

chop[2] [tʃop] *n* (*in pl*) the jaws or mouth, *esp* of an animal: *the wolf's chops.*

chopper, choppy *see* chop[1].

chopsticks ['tʃopstiks] *n pl* two small sticks of wood, ivory *etc* used by the Chinese *etc* to eat with.

choral ['ko:rəl] *adj* of, for, or to be sung by, a choir: *choral music.*

chord [ko:d] *n* in music, a number of notes played together.

chore [tʃo:] *n* a piece of housework or other hard or dull job.

chorister ['koristə] *n* a member of a (church) choir, a boy.

chorus ['kɔːrəs] – *pl* '**choruses** – *n* **1** a group of singers: *the festival chorus.* **2** a group of singers and dancers in a musical show. **3** part of a song repeated after each verse: *The audience joined in the chorus.* **4** something said or shouted by a number of people together: *He was greeted by a chorus of cheers.* – *v* to sing or say together: *The children chorused 'Goodbye, Miss Smith'.*

chose, chosen *see* **choose.**

Christ [kraist] *n* Jesus.

christen ['krisn] *v* **1** to baptize into the Christian church: *The priest christened three babies today.* **2** to give (a name) to: *She was christened Joanna.*

Christian ['kristʃən] *n* a follower of or a believer in Christ. – *adj*: *He had a Christian upbringing.*

,**Christi'anity** [-'anəti] *n* the religion of Christ.

christian name (*Amer* **given name**) the personal name given in addition to the surname: *Peter is his christian name.*

Christmas ['krisməs] *n* an annual festival in memory of the birth of Christ, held on December 25, Christmas Day.

Christmas Eve December 24.

'**Christmas-tree** *n* a (*usu* fir) tree on which decorations and Christmas gifts are hung.

chromatic [krə'matik, (*Amer*) krou-]: **chromatic scale** a series of musical notes, each separated from the next by a semitone.

chrome [kroum] *n* an alloy of chromium and steel used for car-fittings *etc.*

chromium ['kroumiəm] *n* a metallic element used in various metal alloys.

chronic ['kronik] *adj* (*esp* of a disease) lasting a long time: *a chronic illness.* '**chronically** *adv.*

chronicle ['kronikl] *n* a record of (*esp* historical) events in order of time. – *v* to make such a record of. '**chronicler** *n.*

chronology [krə'nolədʒi] *n* (a list illustrating) the order of events in time. **chronological** [kronə'lodʒikəl] *adj.* ,**chrono'logically** *adv.*

chrysalis ['krisəlis] *n* the form taken by some insects (*eg* butterflies) at an early stage in their development.

chrysanthemum [kri'sanθəməm] *n* a type of garden flower with a large, bushy head.

chubby ['tʃʌbi] *adj* plump: *a baby's chubby face.*

chuck [tʃʌk] *v* to throw: *Chuck this rubbish in the dustbin.*

chuckle ['tʃʌkl] *v* to laugh quietly: *He sat chuckling over a funny book.* – *n* such a laugh.

chum [tʃʌm] *n* a close friend: *a school chum.*

chunk [tʃʌŋk] *n* a thick piece of anything, as wood, bread *etc*: *chunks of meat.*

'**chunky** *adj* **1** solid and strong: *a chunky body.* **2** containing chunks.

church [tʃəːtʃ] *n* **1** a building for public Christian worship. **2** a group of Christians considered as a whole: *the Catholic Church.*

'**churchyard** *n* the burial ground round a church.

churn [tʃəːn] *n* **1** a machine for making butter. **2** a large milk can.

chute [ʃuːt] *n* **1** a sloping channel for sending down water, rubbish *etc.* **2** a similar structure in a playground, for children to slide down. **3** a parachute.

chutney ['tʃʌtni] *n* a sauce made from fruit, vegetables and spices: *tomato chutney.*

cicada [si'kaːdə] *n* an insect that makes a loud chirping noise.

cider ['saidə] *n* an alcoholic drink made from apples.

cigar [si'gaː] *n* a roll of tobacco leaves for smoking.

cigarette [sigə'ret, (*Amer*) 'sigəret] *n* a tube of finely cut tobacco rolled in thin paper.

ciku *see* **chiku.**

cinch [sintʃ] *n* **1** a certainty: *It's a cinch!* **2** something easy.

cinder ['sində] *n* a piece of burnt coal, wood *etc*: *the cinders in the fireplace.*

cine-camera ['sinikamərə] *n* a camera for taking moving pictures.

cinema ['sinəmə] *n* a building in which films are shown: *He enjoys going to the cinema but he prefers the theatre.*

cinnamon ['sinəmən] *n* the bark of a tree of the laurel family, used as a spice.

cipher ['saifə] *n* secret writing; a code: *The message was written in cipher.*

*****circle** ['səːkl] *n* **1** a figure (○) bounded by one line, every point on which is equally distant from the centre. **2** something in the form of a circle: *She was surrounded by a circle of admirers.* **3** a group of people: *a circle of close friends*; *wealthy circles.* **4** a balcony in a theatre *etc*: *We sat in the circle at the opera.* – **1** to move in a circle round something: *The cows circled round the farmer who was bringing their food.* **2** to draw a circle round: *Please circle the word you think is wrong.*

circuit ['səːkit] *n* **1** a journey or course round something: *the earth's circuit round the sun*; *three circuits of the race-track.* **2** a race-track, running-track *etc.* **3** the path of an electric current and the parts through which it passes. **4** a journey or tour made regularly and repeatedly *eg* by salesmen, sportsmen *etc.*

circuitous [sə'kjuitəs] *adj* round-about; not direct: *a circuitous route.*

circular ['səːkjulə] *adj* **1** having the form of a circle: *a circular piece of paper.* **2** leading back to the point from which it started: *a circular road.* – *n* a notice *etc, esp* advertis-

ing something, sent to a number of persons:
We often get circulars advertising holidays.
circu'larity [-'la-] *n.*

circulate ['sə:kjuleit] *v* **1** to (cause to) go
round in a fixed path coming back to a
starting-point: *Blood circulates through the
body.* **2** to (cause to) spread or pass around
(news *etc*): *There's a rumour circulating that
she is getting married.*
,circu'lation *n.* **'circulatory** [-lə-] *adj.*

circumcise ['sə:kəmsaiz] *v* to remove the foreskin of (a man). **,circum'cision** [-'siʒən] *n.*

circumference [sə'kʌmfərəns] *n* (the length
of) the boundary line of a circle or anything
circular in shape: *the circumference of a
circle/wheel.*

circumnavigate [sə:kəm'navigeit] *v* to sail
round (*esp* the world).
'circum,navi'gation *n.*

circumstance ['sə:kəmstans] *n* **1** a condition
(time, place *etc*) connected with an event:
*In the circumstances, I don't see what else I
could have done.*

circus ['sə:kəs] – *pl* **'circuses** – *n* **1** a travelling
show with performances by horsemen,
acrobats, animals *etc*: *The children went to
the circus.* **2** an open space in a town *etc*
where several roads meet: *Piccadilly Circus.*

cistern ['sistən] *n* a tank *etc* for storing water
(*esp* for a lavatory).

citadel ['sitədl] *n* a fortress, *esp* in or near a
city.

citizen ['sitizn] *n* **1** an inhabitant of a city or
town: *a citizen of London.* **2** a member of a
state or country: *a British citizen; a citizen
of the USA.*
'citizenship *n* the status, rights and duties of
a citizen, *esp* of a particular country *etc*: *He
has applied for British citizenship.*

citric ['sitrik]: **citric acid** the acid which gives
lemons and certain other fruits their sour-
ness.
citrus fruit ['sitrəs] a type of fruit including
the lemon, orange, lime *etc.*

city ['siti] – *pl* **'cities** – *n* **1** a very large town.
2 a town, *usu* with a cathedral, granted
special rights.

civic ['sivik] *adj* of or belonging to a city or
citizen: *Our offices are in the new civic
centre; civic duties.*

civil ['sivl] *adj* **1** polite, courteous. **2** of the
state or community: *civil rights.* **3** ordinary; not military or religious: *civil life.*
4 concerned with law cases which are not
criminal.
civilian [si'viljən] *n* a person who has a civil
job, not in the armed forces.
civility [si'viləti] *n* politeness: *Treat
strangers with civility.*
'civilly *adv* politely.
civil engineer *see* **engineer.**

civil liberties/rights the rights of a citizen
according to the law of the country.
civil servant a member of the civil service.
civil service the organization which runs the
administration of a state.
civil war (a) war between citizens of the
same state: *the American Civil War.*

civilize, -ise ['sivilaiz] *v* to change the ways of
(a primitive people) to those found in a
more advanced type of society: *The
Romans tried to civilize the ancient Britons.*
,civili'zation, -s- *n* **1** the act of civilizing, or
process or state of being civilized. **2** a civilized people and their way of life: *the
ancient civilizations of Egypt and Greece.*

clad [klad] *adj* **1** clothed: *clad in silk; leather-
clad motor-cyclists.* **2** covered: *iron-clad
warships.*

claim [kleim] *v* **1** to say that something is a
fact: *He claims to be the best runner in the
class.* **2** to demand as a right: *You must
claim your money back if the goods are
damaged.* **3** to state that one is the owner
of: *Does anyone claim this book?* – *n* **1** a
statement (that something is a fact): *Her
claim that she was the millionaire's daughter
was disproved.* **2** (a demand for) a payment
of compensation *etc*: *a claim for damages
against her employer.* **3** a demand for something which (one says) one owns or has a
right to: *a rightful claim to the money.*
'claimant *n* a person who makes a claim: *a
claimant to the throne.*

clair'voyance [kleə'voiəns] *n* the power of
seeing things not able to be perceived by the
normal senses (*eg* details about life after
death). **clair'voyant** *n, adj.*

clam [klam] *n* a shellfish with two shells joined
together, used as food.

clamber ['klambə] *v* to climb by holding on
with hands and feet: *clambering over the
rocks.*

clammy ['klami] *adj* damp and sticky:
clammy hands.

clamour, (*Amer*) **clamor** ['klamə] *n* (a) loud
uproar. – *v* (*esp* of a crowd demanding
something) to make such an uproar *etc*:
*They're all clamouring to get their money
back.*
'clamorous *adj.*

clamp [klamp] *n* a piece of wood, iron *etc*
used to fasten things together or to
strengthen them. – *v* to bind together with a
clamp: *They clamped the iron rods together.*
clamp down (*with* **on**) to check or control
strictly.

clan [klan] *n* a tribe or group of families (*esp*
Scottish) under a single chief, *usu* all having
one surname.

clandestine [klan'destin] *adj* secret or hidden.

clang [klaŋ] *v* to produce a loud ringing

clank 79 **clean**

sound: *The heavy gate clanged shut.* – *n* such a sound: *a loud clang.*

clank [klaŋk] *v* to produce a sound like that made by heavy pieces of metal striking each other: *The chains clanked.* – *n* such a noise: *the clank of pans in the kitchen.*

clap [klap] – *pt, ptp* **clapped** – *v* **1** to strike the palms of the hands together *eg* to show approval, to mark a rhythm, or to gain attention *etc*: *When the singer appeared, the audience started to clap loudly; They clapped the speech enthusiastically; Clap your hands in time to the music.* **2** to strike (someone) with the palm of the hand, often in a friendly way: *He clapped him on the back and congratulated him.* **3** to put suddenly (into prison, chains *etc*): *They clapped him in jail.* – *n* **1** a sudden noise (of thunder). **2** an act of clapping: *They gave the performer a clap; He gave me a clap on the back.*

clarify ['klarəfai] *v* to make or become clear (in meaning *etc*): *Would you please clarify your last statement?* ˌclarifiˈcation [-fi] *n*.

clarinet [klarə'net] *n* a type of musical wind instrument, *usu* made of wood, and played by means of keys and fingers covering combinations of holes. ˌclariˈnettist (*Amer usu* ˌclariˈnetist) *n*.

clarity ['klarəti] *n* **1** the state of being clear or easy to see through: *water remarkable for its clarity.* **2** the state of being easy to see, hear or understand: *She spoke with great clarity.*

clash [klaʃ] *n* **1** a loud noise, like *eg* swords striking together: *the clash of metal on metal.* **2** a serious disagreement or difference: *a clash of personalities.* **3** a battle: *a clash between opposing armies.* **4** (of two or more things) an act of interfering with each other because of happening at the same time: *a clash between classes.* – *v* **1** to strike together noisily: *The cymbals clashed.* **2** to fight (in battle): *The two armies clashed at the mouth of the valley.* **3** to disagree violently: *They clashed over wages.* **4** to interfere (with something or each other) because of happening at the same time: *The two lectures clash.* **5** (of colours) to appear unpleasant when placed together: *The (colour of the) jacket clashes with the (colour of the) skirt.*

clasp [klɑːsp] *n* a fastening made of two parts which link together (*eg* on a necklace). – *v* to grasp, hold tightly. *She clasped the money in her hand.*

class [klɑːs] – *pl* **'classes** – *n* **1** a group of people or things that are alike in some way: *The dog won first prize in its class in the dog show.* **2** (the system according to which people belong to) one of a number of social groups: *the upper class; the middle class; the*

working class; (*also adj*) *the class system.* **3** a grade or rank (of merit): *musicians of a high class.* **4** a number of students or scholars taught together: *John and I are in the same class.* **5** a school lesson or college lecture *etc*: *a French class.* – *v* to regard as being of a certain type: *He classes all women as stupid.*

'classmate *n* a pupil in the same school class.

'class-room *n* a room in a school where a class is taught.

classical ['klasikəl] *adj* **1** (*esp* of literature, art *etc*) of ancient Greece and Rome: *classical studies.* **2** (of music) having the traditional, established harmony and/or form: *He prefers classical music to popular music.* **3** (of literature) considered to be of the highest class.

'classic *adj* **1** standard or best: *the classic example.* **2** (of literature, art *etc*) of the highest quality. **3** (of dress *etc*) simple, elegant and traditional. – *n* **1** an established work of literature of high quality: *I have read all the classics.* **2** (*in pl*) the language and literature of Greece and Rome: *He is studying classics.*

classify ['klasifai] *v* to put into, or be in, a particular class or group: *How are the books in the library classified?* ˌclassifiˈcation [-fi-] *n*.

clatter ['klatə] *n* a loud noise like hard objects falling, striking against each other *etc*: *the clatter of children climbing the stairs.* – *v* to (cause to) make such a noise: *She clattered the dishes in the sink.*

clause [klɔːz] *n* **1** a part of a sentence having its own subject and predicate, *eg* either of the two parts of this sentence: *John has a friend/who is rich.* **2** a paragraph in a contract, will, or act of parliament.

claustrophobia [klɔːstrə'foubiə] *n* fear of narrow, small or enclosed places. ˌclaustro'phobic *adj*.

claw [klɔː] *n* **1** one of the hooked nails of an animal or bird: *The cat sharpened its claws on the tree-trunk.* **2** the foot of an animal or bird with hooked nails: *The owl held the mouse in its claw.* **3** (the pointed end of) the leg of a crab *etc*. – *v* to scratch or tear (at something) with claws or nails: *The two cats clawed at each other.*

clay [klei] *n* a soft, sticky type of earth which is often baked into pottery, china, bricks *etc*.

clean [kliːn] *adj* **1** free from dirt, smoke *etc*: *a clean window; a clean dress.* **2** neat and tidy in one's habits: *Cats are very clean animals.* **3** unused: *a clean sheet of paper.* **4** free from evil or indecency: *a clean life; keep you language clean!* **5** neat and even: *a clean cut.* – *adv* completely: *He got clean*

away. – *v* to (cause to) become free from dirt *etc*: *Will you clean the windows?*
'**cleaner** *n.*
'**cleanly**[1] *adv*: *The knife cut cleanly through the cheese.*
cleanly[2] ['klenli] *adj* clean in personal habits. '**cleanliness** ['klen-] *n.*
clean up to clean (a place) thoroughly: *She cleaned (the room) up after they went home.*
a clean bill of health a certificate saying that a person, the crew of a ship *etc* is entirely healthy (*esp* after being ill): *I've been off work but I've got a clean bill of health now.*
a clean slate a fresh start: *After being in prison he started his new job with a clean slate.*
come clean to tell the truth about something, often about something about which one has previously lied.
make a clean sweep to get rid of everything unnecessary or unwanted: *The new manager made a clean sweep of all the lazy people in the department.*
cleanse [klenz] *v* to make clean: *This cream will cleanse your skin; cleansed of guilt.*
'**cleanser** *n* something which cleans, *esp* a cosmetic used to clean the face.
clear [kliə] *adj* 1 easy to see through; transparent: *clear glass.* 2 free from mist or cloud: *Isn't the sky clear!* 3 easy to see, hear or understand: *a clear explanation; The details on that photograph are very clear.* 4 free from difficulty or obstacles: *a clear road ahead.* 5 free from guilt *etc*: *a clear conscience.* 6 free from doubt *etc*: *Are you quite clear about what I mean?* 7 (*often with* **of**) without (risk of) being touched, caught *etc*: *Is the ship clear of the rocks? clear of danger.* 8 (*often with* **of**) free: *clear of debt; clear of all infection.* – *v* 1 to make or become free from obstacles *etc*: *He cleared the table; I cleared my throat; He cleared the path of debris.* 2 (*often with* **of**) to prove the innocence of; to declare to be innocent: *He was cleared of all charges.* 3 (of the sky *etc*) to become bright, free from cloud *etc.* 4 to get over or past something without touching it: *He cleared the jump easily.*
'**clearance** 1 the act of clearing or removing: *The clearance of these trees from the front of the window will give you more light.* 2 the clear area between two objects: *You can drive the lorry under the bridge – there's a clearance of half a metre.* 3 (a certificate) giving permission for something to be done.
'**clearing** *n* a piece of land cleared of wood *etc* for cultivation: *a clearing in the forest.*
'**clearly** *adv.* '**clearness** *n.*
,**clear-**'**cut** *adj* having a clear outline; plain and definite: *clear-cut features.*
'**clearway** *n* a stretch of road on which motorists are forbidden to stop.

clear off to go away: *He cleared off without saying a word.*
clear out 1 to get rid of: *He cleared the rubbish out of the attic.* 2 to make tidy by emptying *etc*: *He has cleared out the attic.*
clear up 1 to make clear, tidy *etc*: *Clear up this mess!* 2 to become better *etc*: *If the weather clears up, we'll go for a picnic.*
in the clear no longer under suspicion, in danger *etc.*
cleave[1] [kliːv] – *pts* **cleft** [kleft], **cleaved, clove** [klouv]: *ptps* **cleft, cloven** ['klouvn] – *v* to split or divide.
'**cleavage** [-vidʒ] *n* the act of splitting; a split.
'**cleaver** *n* a butcher's knife.
cloven hoof a hoof, like those of cows, sheep *etc*, which has a split up the centre.
cleave[2] [kliːv] – *pt, ptp* **cleaved**: **cleave to** to stick to.
clef [klef] *n* in music, a sign (*eg* 𝄢 *or* 𝄞) on the stave fixing the pitch of the notes.
cleft [kleft] *n* an opening made by splitting: *a cleft in the rocks.*
clement ['klemənt] *adj* 1 (of weather *etc*) mild. 2 merciful. '**clemency** *n.*
clench [klentʃ] *v* to close tightly together: *He clenched his teeth/fist.*
clergy ['kləːdʒi] *n* the ministers, priests *etc* of the Christian religion: *the clergy of the Church of England.*
'**clergyman** *n* one of the clergy; a priest, minister *etc.*
clerical[1] *adj* ['klerikəl] of the clergy: *He is wearing a clerical collar.*
clerical[2] ['klerikəl] *adj* of a clerk or of his work: *a clerical error.*
clerk [klaːk, (*Amer*) kləːk] *n* 1 a person who deals with letters, accounts *etc* in an office. 2 a public official in charge of the business affairs of the town council *etc*: *the town clerk.* 3 (*Amer*) a shop-assistant.
clever ['klevə] *adj* 1 quick to learn and understand: *a clever child.* 2 skilful: *a clever carpenter.* 3 (of things) showing cleverness: *a clever idea.* '**cleverly** *adv.* '**cleverness** *n.*
cliché ['kliːʃei, (*Amer*) kliːʃei] *n* a phrase which has been used too often, and has become meaningless.
click [klik] *n* a short, sharp sound, like that of a light-switch being turned on: *the click of the camera.* – *v* to (cause to) make such a sound: *The soldier clicked his heels together; The gate clicked.*
client ['klaiənt] *n* 1 a person who receives professional advice from a lawyer, accountant *etc.* 2 a customer: *That hairdresser is very popular with his clients.*
clientèle [kliːonˈtel] *n* a group or type of clients: *a bank's clientèle.*
cliff [klif] *n* a high steep rock, *esp* one facing the sea.

climate ['klaimət] *n* **1** the weather conditions of a region (temperature, moisture *etc*): *Britain has a temperate climate.* **2** the conditions in a country *etc*: *the economic/moral climate.* **cli'matic** [-'ma-] *adj.*

climax ['klaimaks] – *pl* **'climaxes** – *n* the highest point; the most dramatic moment: *the climax of the novel.*

climb [klaim] *v* **1** (of a person *etc*) to go up or towards the top of (a mountain, wall, ladder *etc*): *He climbed up the ladder; The child climbed the tree.* **2** to rise or ascend. – *n* **1** an act of going up: *a rapid climb to the top of his profession.* **2** a route or place to be climbed: *The guide showed us the best climb.* **'climber** *n.*

clinch [klintʃ] *v* to settle or come to an agreement about (an argument or a bargain): *The businessmen clinched the deal.*

cling [kliŋ] – *pt, ptp* **clung** [klʌŋ] – *v* (*usu with* **to**) to stick (to); to grip tightly: *The mud clung to her shoes; She clung to her husband as he said goodbye; He clings to an impossible hope; The boat clung to* (= stayed close to) *the coastline.*

clinic ['klinik] *n* a place or part of a hospital where a particular kind of medical treatment or advice is given: *He is attending the skin clinic.* **'clinical** *adj* **1** of a clinic. **2** based on observation of the patient.

clink [kliŋk] *n* a ringing sound: *the clink of coins.* – *v* to (cause to) make such a sound: *They clinked their glasses together.*

clip¹ [klip] – *pt, ptp* **clipped** – *v* **1** to cut (foliage, an animal's hair *etc*) with scissors or shears: *The shepherd clipped the sheep; The hedge was clipped.* **2** to strike sharply: *She clipped him over the ear.* – *n* **1** an act of clipping. **2** a sharp blow: *a clip on the ear.* **'clipper** *n* **1** (*in pl*) a tool for clipping: *hedge-clippers; nail-clippers.* **2** a type of fast sailing-ship. **'clipping** *n* a thing clipped off or out of something, *esp* a newspaper: *She collects clippings about the royal family.*

clip² [klip] – *pt, ptp* **clipped** – *v* to fasten with a clip: *Clip these papers together.* – *n* something for holding things together or in position: *a paper-clip; a hair-clip; bicycle-clips* (= round pieces of metal *etc* for holding the bottom of trouser legs close to the leg).

clique [kli:k] *n* a group of people who are friendly with each other but exclude others: *the golf-club clique.* **'cliqu(e)y, 'cliquish** *adjs.*

cloak [klouk] *n* a loose outer garment without sleeves, covering most of the body; something that conceals: *a woollen cloak; They arrived under cloak of darkness.* – *v* to cover

or hide: *He used a false name to cloak his activities.*

'cloakroom *n* **1** a room for coats, hats *etc.* **2** a lavatory: *the ladies' cloakroom.*

clock [klok] *n* **1** an instrument for measuring time, but not worn on the wrist like a watch: *We have five clocks in our house; an alarm clock* (= a clock with a ringing device for waking one up in the morning). **2** an instrument for measuring speed of a vehicle or distance travelled by a vehicle: *My car has 120 000 miles on the clock.* – *v* to register (a time) on a stopwatch *etc.*

'clockwise *adv* in the direction of the movement of the hands of a clock: *The children moved clockwise round the room, then anti-clockwise.*

'clockwork *n* machinery similar to that of a clock: *a toy which works by clockwork.*

clock in, out/on, off to register or record time of arriving at or leaving work.

like clockwork very smoothly and without faults: *Everything went like clockwork.*

round the clock the whole day and the whole night: *to work round the clock.*

clod [klod] *n* a thick lump, *esp* of earth.

clog¹ [klog] *n* **1** a shoe made entirely of wood: *Dutch clogs.* **2** a shoe with a wooden sole.

clog² [klog] – *pt, ptp* **clogged** – (*often with* **up**) to make or become blocked: *The drain is clogged* (up) *with hair.*

cloister ['kloistə] *n* a covered walk forming part of a monastery, church or college.

close¹ [klous] *adv* **1** near in time, place *etc*: *He stood close to his mother; Follow close behind.* **2** tightly; neatly: *a close-fitting dress.* – *adj* **1** near in relationship: *a close friend.* **2** having a narrow difference between winner and loser: *a close contest; The result was close.* **3** thorough: *a close examination of the facts; Keep a close watch on him.* **4** tight: *a close fit.* **5** without fresh air: *a close atmosphere; The weather was close and thundery.* **6** mean: *He's very close* (*with his money*). **7** secretive: *They're keeping very close about the business.*

'closely *adv*: *Look closely at him; She resembles her father closely.*

'closeness *n.*

close call/shave a narrow (often lucky) escape: *That was a close shave – that car nearly ran you over.*

,close-'set *adj* (of eyes *etc*) positioned very near each other.

'close-up *n* a photograph or film taken near the subject and thus big in scale: *The close-up of the model showed her beautiful skin.*

close at hand nearby; not far off: *My mother lives close at hand.*

close on almost; nearly: *She's close on sixty.*

close to 1 near in time, place, relationship

etc: close to 3 o'clock; close to the hospital; close to his mother. **2** almost; nearly: *close to fifty years of age.*

close² [klouz] *v* **1** to make or become shut, often by bringing together two parts so as to cover an opening: *The baby closed his eyes; Close the door; The shops close on Sundays.* **2** to finish; to come or bring to an end: *The meeting closed with everyone in agreement.* **3** to complete or settle (a business deal). *– n* a stop, end or finish: *the close of day; towards the close of the nineteenth century.*

close down 1 (of a business) to close permanently: *High levels of taxation have caused many firms to close down.* **2** (of a TV or radio station *etc*) to stop broadcasting for the day (*n* **'closedown**).

close up 1 to come or bring closer together: *He closed up the space between the lines of print.* **2** to shut completely: *He closed up the house when he went on holiday.*

closet ['klozit] *n* (*Amer*) a cupboard: *a clothes closet.*

'closeted *adj* engaged in a private conversation in a separate room from other people: *They're closeted in his office.*

closure ['klouʒə] *n* an act of closing: *the closure of a factory.*

clot [klot] *n* **1** soft or fluid matter (*esp* blood) formed into a solid mass: *a clot of blood.* **2** a fool or an idiot. *– v – pt, ptp* **'clotted** – to form into clots: *Most people's blood clots easily.*

cloth [kloθ] *– pl* **cloths** [kloθs, (*Amer*) klo:ðz] *– n* (a piece of) woven material from which clothes and many other items are made: *a tablecloth; a face-cloth; a floor-cloth; Woollen cloth is often more expensive than other cloths.*

clothe [klouð] *– pt, ptp* **clothed** *– v* **1** to provide with clothes: *The widow did not have enough money to clothe her children.* **2** to put clothes on: *She was clothed in silk; She clothed herself in the most expensive materials.*

clothes [klouðz, (*Amer*) klouz] *n pl* **1** things worn as coverings for various parts of the body: *She wears beautiful clothes.* **2** bedclothes: *The child pulled the clothes up tightly.*

'clothing *n* clothes: *warm clothing.*

there is no singular form for **clothes**.

cloud [klaud] **1** a mass of tiny drops of water floating in the sky: *white clouds in a blue sky; The hills were hidden in cloud.* **2** a great number or quantity of anything small moving together: *a cloud of flies.* **3** something causing fear, depression *etc: a cloud of sadness. – v* **1** (*often with* **over**) to become cloudy: *The sky clouded over and it began to*

rain. **2** to (cause to) become blurred or not clear: *Her eyes were clouded with tears.* **3** to (cause to) become gloomy or troubled: *His face clouded at the unhappy news.*

'cloudless *adj* free from clouds: *a cloudless sky.*

'cloudy *adj* **1** full of, having, or covered with clouds: *It is a bit cloudy today.* **2** not clear: *a cloudy photograph/memory.*

'cloudburst *n* a sudden heavy shower of rain.

under a cloud in trouble or disgrace.

clove¹ [klouv] *n* the flower bud of a tropical tree dried for use as a spice.

clove² [klouv] *n* a section of a bulb: *a clove of garlic.*

clove³, cloven *see* **cleave¹**.

clover ['klouvə] *n* a plant with leaves in three parts, used as food for cattle *etc*.

clown [klaun] *n* **1** a person who works in a circus, performing funny acts (*usu* ridiculously dressed). **2** any person who behaves ridiculously. *– v* to behave ridiculously: *Stop clowning.*

'clownish *adj*.

club [klʌb] *n* **1** a heavy stick *etc* used as a weapon. **2** a bat or stick used in certain games (*esp* golf): *Which club will you use?* **3** a number of people meeting for study, pleasure, games *etc: the local tennis club.* **4** the place where these people meet: *He goes to the club every Friday.* **5** one of the playing-cards of the suit clubs. *– v – pt, ptp* **clubbed** – to beat or strike with a club: *They clubbed him to death.*

clubs *n pl* (sometimes treated as *n sing*) one of the four card suits: *the six of clubs.*

cluck [klʌk] *n* (a sound like) the call of a hen. *– v* to make such a sound.

clue [klu:] *n* anything that helps to solve a mystery, puzzle *etc: The car number was a clue to the identity of the murderer; I can't answer the second clue in this crossword.*

'clueless *adj* (of a person) stupid: *He's quite clueless about art.*

not to have a clue to be ignorant: *'How does that work?' 'I haven't a clue.'*

clump¹ [klʌmp] *n* a group (*eg* of trees or bushes).

clump² [klʌmp] *v* to walk heavily and noisily.

clumsy ['klʌmzi] *adj* awkward in movement *etc: He's very clumsy – he's always dropping things.*

'clumsily *adv*. **'clumsiness** *n*.

clung *see* **cling**.

cluster ['klʌstə] *n* a closely-packed group (of people or things): *a cluster of berries; They stood in a cluster. – v* (*often with* **round**) to group together in clusters: *They clustered round the door.*

clutch [klʌtʃ] *v* **1** (*with* **at**) to try to take hold of: *I clutched at a floating piece of wood to* *save myself from drowning.* **2** to hold tightly (in the hands): *She was clutching a 50-cent piece.* – *n* control or power: *He fell into the clutches of the enemy.* **2** (the pedal operating) a device by means of which two moving parts of an engine may be connected or disconnected: *He released the clutch and the car started to move.*

clutch at straws to hope that something may help one in a hopeless situation.

clutter ['klʌtə] *n* state of untidiness: *The house is in a clutter.*

'cluttered *adj* untidy; too full of furniture *etc*: *Some people think it's a beautiful room but it's too cluttered for my taste.*

co- [kou] (*as part of a word*) **1** joint or working *etc* together, as in **co-author**. **2** with or together, as in **co-exist**.

coach [koutʃ] *n* **1** a railway carriage: *The last two coaches of the train were derailed.* **2*** a bus for tourists *etc*. **3** a trainer in athletics, sport *etc*: *the tennis coach.* **4** a private teacher: *They employed a coach to help their son with his mathematics.* **5** a four-wheeled horsedrawn vehicle. – *v* to prepare (a person) for an examination, contest *etc*: *He coached his friend for the Latin exam.*

'coachbuilder *n* a person or business concerned with building the bodies for modern vehicles.

'coachman *n* the driver of a horsedrawn carriage.

coal [koul] *n* a black mineral burned for fuel, heat *etc*.

'coalfield *n* an area where there is coal to be mined.

'coalmine *n* a mine from which coal is dug.

haul (someone) over the coals to scold.

coalition [kouə'liʃən] *n* a *usu* temporary union or alliance, *esp* of states or political parties.

coarse [kɔːs] *adj* **1** rough in texture or to touch; not fine: *This coat is made of coarse material.* **2** rude, vulgar or unrefined: *coarse jokes.* **'coarsely** *adv.* **'coarseness** *n.*

'coarsen *v* (to cause to) become coarse: *The laundry-work coarsened her hands.*

coast [koust] *n* the side or border of land next to the sea: *The coast was very rocky.* – *v* to travel downhill (in a vehicle, on a bicycle *etc*) without the use of any power such as the engine or pedalling: *He coasted for two miles after the car ran out of petrol.*

'coastal *adj* of or near the coast: *a coastal town.*

'coaster *n* **1** a vessel that sails along near the coast. **2** a small mat for putting under a drinking-glass *etc*.

'coastguard *n* a person or group of people, employed to watch the coast for smugglers, ships in distress *etc*.

coat [kout] *n* **1** an item of outdoor clothing, with sleeves, that covers from the shoulders *usu* to the knees: *a coat and hat.* **2** a jacket: *a man's coat and trousers.* **3** the hair or wool of an animal: *Some dogs have smooth coats.* **4** a covering (eg of paint): *This wall will need two coats of paint.* – *v* to cover: *She coated the biscuits with chocolate.*

'coating *n* (a) covering: *chocolate coating.*

coat of arms a family badge or crest.

coax [kouks] *v* to persuade by flattery, by patient and gentle treatment *etc*: *He coaxed her into going to the dance by saying she was the best dancer he knew; He coaxed some money out of his mother.*

cobalt ['koubɔːlt] *n* a silver-white metal element with compounds that give a blue colouring.

cobble[1] ['kobl] *n* a rounded stone formerly used in paving streets.

cobble[2] ['kobl] *v* **1** to mend (shoes). **2** to make or repair badly or roughly.

'cobbler *n* a person who mends shoes.

cobra ['koubrə] *n* a poisonous snake found in India and Africa.

cobweb ['kobweb] *n* a spider's web: *You can't have cleaned this room – there are cobwebs in the corner.*

cocaine [kə'kein] *n* an addictive drug formerly used to deaden pain.

cock [kok] *n* **1** the male of birds, *esp* of the domestic fowl: *a cock and three hens;* (*also adj*) *a cock sparrow.* **2** a kind of tap for controlling the flow of liquid, gas *etc*. **3** a slang word for the penis. – *v* **1** to cause to stand upright or to lift: *The dog cocked its ears.* **2** to draw back the hammer of (a gun). **3** to tilt up or sideways (*esp* a hat).

cockerel ['kokərəl] *n* a young farmyard cock.

'cocky *adj* conceited; over-confident: *a cocky attitude.*

cock-and-bull story an absurd, unbelievable story.

'cock-crow *n* early morning: *He gets up at cock-crow.*

'cock-eyed *adj* ridiculous: *a cock-eyed idea.*

,cock'sure *adj* very or too confident: *He was cocksure about passing the exam.*

cockade [kə'keid] *n* formerly, a knot of ribbon worn as a hat-badge.

cockatoo [kokə'tuː] – *pl* **cocka'toos** – *n* a parrot with a large crest.

cockerel *see* **cock.**

cockney ['kokni] *n* **1** a native of the City of London. **2** his speech: *He spoke cockney;* (*also adj*) *a cockney accent.*

cockpit ['kokpit] *n* a compartment in which the pilot of an aeroplane, driver of a racing-car *etc* sits: *He climbed into the cockpit and drove off.*

cockroach ['kokroutʃ] – *n* a beetle-like insect which is a household pest.

cocksure *see* **cock.**

* see illustration on p. 595

cocktail ['kokteil] **1** an alcoholic drink mixed from various spirits *etc*. **2** a mixed dish of a number of things: *a fruit cocktail.*

cocky *see* **cock.**

cocoa ['koukou] *n* **1** (a powder made from) the crushed seeds of the cacao tree, used in making chocolate. **2** a drink made from the powder: *a cup of cocoa.*

coconut ['koukənʌt] *n* **1** a large nut containing a white solid lining and a clear liquid. **2** its lining, used as food.

cocoon [kə'ku:n] *n* a silk covering spun by many insect larvae, and in which they live while turning into butterflies.

cod [kod] – *pl* **cod** – a type of edible fish found in northern seas.

cod-liver oil an oil obtained from cod's liver, rich in vitamins A and D.

coddle ['kodl] *v* to treat with great care like an invalid; to pamper: *She tended to coddle her youngest child.*

code [koud] *n* **1** a collection of laws or rules: *a code of behaviour.* **2** a (secret) system of words, letters, or symbols: *the Morse Code*; *The message was in code*; *We have deciphered the enemy's code.* **3** a system of symbols *etc* for translating one type of language into another: *There are a number of codes for putting English into a form usable by a computer.* – *v* to put into (secret, computer *etc*) code: *Have you coded the material for the computer?*

co-educational [kouedju'keiʃənl] (*abbrev* **co-ed** ['koued]) *adj* of the education of pupils or students of both sexes in the same school or college: *a co-educational school.*

coerce [kou'ə:s] *v* to force (a person into doing something). **co'ercion** [-ʃən] *n.*

co-exist [kouig'zist] *v* (*esp* of nations, races *etc*) to exist side by side (*esp* peacefully). **co-ex'istence** *n.*

coffee ['kofi] *n* (a drink made from) the ground beans of a shrub grown in *eg* Brazil. – *adj* the colour of the drink when mixed with milk.

'coffee-pot *n* a container from which to serve coffee.

'coffee-shop *n* a café serving coffee *etc.*

coffin ['kofin] *n* (*Amer* **'casket**) a box for a dead body to be buried or cremated in: *The coffin was placed in the grave.*

cog [kog] *n* one of a series of teeth around the edge of a wheel which fits into one of a similar series in a similar wheel (or into a chain as in a bicycle) causing motion: *The cogs in the gear-wheels of a car get worn down.*

cogitate ['kodʒiteit] *v* to think carefully. **,cogi'tation** *n.*

cognac ['konjak] a kind of high-quality French brandy.

coherent [kə'hiərənt] *adj* clear and logical: *He was able to give a coherent account of what had happened.* **co'herently** *adv.* **co'herence** *n.*

cohort ['kouho:t] *n* a group of people: *His supporters followed him in cohorts.*

coiffure [kwa'fjuə] *n* a hairstyle: *an elaborate coiffure.*

coil [koil] *v* to wind into loops: *The snake coiled (itself) round the tree.* – *n* **1** a length of something wound into a loop or loops: *a coil of rope*; *a coil of hair.* **2** a wound length of wire for conducting electricity: *the coil in an electric fire.*

coin [koin] *n* a piece of metal used as money: *a handful of coins.* – *v* **1** to make metal into (money): *When was that dollar coined?* **2** to invent (a word, phrase *etc*): *The scientist coined a word for the new process.*

'coinage [-nidʒ] *n* **1** the process of coining. **2** the money (system) used in a country: *Britain now uses decimal coinage.*

coincide [kouin'said] *v* **1** to occupy (often by accident) the same space or time: *Her arrival coincided with his departure.* **2** to agree: *This coincides with what he told us*; *Their tastes in music coincide.*

coincidence [kou'insidəns] *n* (an) accidental happening of one event at the same time as another: *By a strange coincidence we were both on the same train.* **co,inci'dental** [-'den-] *adj.*

coke [kouk] *n* a type of fuel obtained from coal.

colander ['kʌləndə] *n* a bowl with small holes in it for draining water off vegetables.

cold [kould] *adj* **1** low in temperature: *cold water*; *cold meat and salad.* **2** lower in temperature than is comfortable: *I feel cold.* **3** unfriendly: *His manner was cold.* – *n* **1** the state of being cold or of feeling the coldness of one's surroundings: *She has gone to live in the South of France because she cannot bear the cold in Britain*; *He was blue with cold.* **2** an illness with running nose, coughing *etc*: *He has a bad cold*; *She has caught a cold*; *You might catch cold.*

'coldly *adv* in an unfriendly way: *She looked at me coldly.*

'coldness *n.*

,cold-'blooded *adj* **1** having blood (like that of a fish) which takes the same temperature as the surroundings of the body: *cold-blooded creatures.* **2** cruel and unfeeling: *cold-blooded murder.*

cold war a major, *esp* political, struggle between nations which involves military threats but not fighting.

get cold feet to lose courage: *I was going to apply for the job but I got cold feet.*

give (someone) the cold shoulder (*also* **,cold-'shoulder** *v*) to show that one is unwilling to be friendly with (a person): *All the neigh-*

bours gave her the cold shoulder; *He cold-shouldered all his sister's friends.*

in cold blood deliberately and unemotion-ally: *He killed them in cold blood.*

cole-slaw ['koulslo:] a salad made with finely-cut raw cabbage.

coleus ['kouliəs] *n* a type of plant with varie-gated leaves.

colic ['kolik] *n* severe pain in the abdomen.

collaborate [kə'labəreit] *v* **1** to work together (with someone) on a piece of work: *He and his brother collaborated on a book about aeroplanes.* **2** to work along (with some-one) to betray secrets *etc*: *He was known to have collaborated with the enemy.* **col,labo'ration** *n*. **col'laborator** *n*.

collage [ko'la:ʒ] *n* a design made by pasting pieces of paper, cloth, photographs *etc* on to a surface.

collapse [kə'laps] *v* **1** to fall down and break into pieces: *The bridge collapsed under the weight of the traffic.* **2** (of a person) to fall down *esp* unconscious, because of illness, shock *etc*: *She collapsed with a heart attack.* **3** to break down, fail: *The talks between the two countries have collapsed.* **4** to fold up or to (cause to) come to pieces (intentionally): *Do these chairs collapse?* **col'lapsible** *adj* able to be folded up *etc*: *These chairs are collapsible.*

collar ['kolə] *n* **1** the part of a garment at the neck *esp* of a shirt, jacket *etc*: *This collar is too tight.* **2** something worn round the neck: *The dog's name was on its collar.* – *v* to seize, get hold of: *He collared the speaker as he left the room.*

'collar-bone *n* either of two bones joining breast-bone and shoulder-blade.

colleague ['koli:g] *n* a person with whom one is associated in a profession or occupation: *He gets on well with his colleagues.*

collect [kə'lekt] *v* **1** to bring or come together; to gather: *People are collecting in front of the house*; *I collect stamps*; *I'm collecting (money) for cancer research*; *He's trying to collect his thoughts.* **2** to call for and take away: *She collects the children from school each day.*

col'lected *adj* **1** gathered together in one book *etc*: *the collected poems of Robert Burns.* **2** composed; cool: *She appeared quite calm and collected.*

col'lection [-ʃən] *n* **1** (an) act of collecting: *Your letter won't get to London tomorrow – you've missed the last collection* (= of mail from a postbox) *for today.* **2** a set of objects *etc* collected: *a stamp collection.*

col'lective [-tiv] *adj* **1** of a number of people *etc* combined into one group: *This success was the result of a collective effort.* **2** of a noun, taking a singular verb but standing for many things taken as a whole: *'Cattle' is*

a collective noun. – *n* a farm or organization run by a group of workers for the good of all of them.

col'lectively *adv*: *They were collectively re-sponsible for the man's death.*

col'lector *n* a person who collects, as a job or as a hobby: *a ticket-collector/stamp-collector.*

college ['kolidʒ] *n* (any or all of the buildings housing) a higher-education institution: *He is at agricultural college.*

collide [kə'laid] *v* to strike together (*usu* acci-dentally) with great force: *The cars collided in the fog*; *The van collided with a lorry.*

collision [kə'liʒən] *n* a crash; a violent striking together (of *eg* two vehicles): *Ten people were injured in the collision between the bus and the car.*

collier ['koliə] *n* a person who works in a coalmine: *Collier is another word for a coalminer.*

'colliery – *pl* **'collieries** – *n* a coalmine.

collision *see* **collide**.

colloquial [kə'loukwiəl] *adj* of or used in everyday informal, *esp* spoken, language: *a colloquial expression.* **col'loquially** *adv*.

col'loquialism *n* an expression used in collo-quial language.

cologne *see* **eau-de-cologne**.

colon[1] ['koulən] *n* the punctuation mark (:), used *eg* to separate sentence-like units within a sentence, or to introduce a list *etc*.

colon[2] ['koulon] *n* a part of the large intes-tine.

colonel ['kə:nl] *n* (*often abbrev* **Col.** *when written*) an army officer in charge of a regiment.

colonial *etc see* **colony**.

colonnade [kolə'neid] *n* a row of pillars.

colony ['koləni] – *pl* **'colonies** – *n* **1** (a group of people who form) a settlement in one country *etc* which is under the rule of another country: *France used to have many colonies in Africa.* **2** a group of people having the same interests, living close to-gether: *a colony of artists.* **3** a collection of animals, birds *etc*, of one type, living to-gether: *a colony of gulls.*

co'lonial [-'lou-] *adj*: *Britain was formerly a colonial power.* – *n* **co'lonialism.** – *n* and *adj* **co'lonialist.**

'colonize, -ise *v* to establish a colony in (a place): *The English colonized New England in 1620.*

'colonist *n*. **,coloni'zation, -s-** *n*.

colossal [kə'losəl] *adj* very big; enormous: *a colossal increase in the price of books.*

colour, (*Amer*) **color** ['kʌlə] *n* **1** a quality which objects have, and which can be seen, only when light falls on them: *What colour is her dress?*; *Red, blue and yellow are colours.* **2** paint(s): *That artist uses water-*

colours. **3** (a) skin-colour varying with race: *people of all colours.* **4** vividness; interest: *There's plenty of colour in his stories.* – *adj* (of photographs *etc*) in colour, not black and white: *colour film*; *colour television.* – *v* **1** to put colour on; to paint: *They coloured the walls yellow.*

'**coloured** *adj* **1** having colour: *She prefers white baths to coloured baths.* **2** belonging to a dark-skinned race: *There are only two white families living in this street – the rest are coloured.* – *n* (sometimes used impolitely) a dark-skinned person *esp* of Negro origin.

'**colourful** *adj* **1** full of colour: *a colourful pattern.* **2** vivid and interesting: *a colourful account of his experiences.*

'**colouring** *n* **1** something used to give colour: *She put pink colouring in the icing.* **2** complexion: *She had very high colouring* (= a very pink complexion).

'**colourless** *adj* **1** without colour: *Water is colourless.* **2** not lively or interesting: *a colourless young woman.*

'**colours** *n pl* **1** the distinction of winning a place in the team in some sports: *He won his cricket colours last season.* **2** a flag: *Army regiments salute the colours when on parade.* **3** a tunic of certain colours worn by a jockey to show that his race-horse belongs to a certain person.

'**colour-blind** *adj* unable to tell the difference between certain colours: *As he was colourblind he could not distinguish between red and green.*

'**colour-scheme** *n* an arrangement or choice of colours in decorating a house *etc*.

,**off-'colour** *adj* not feeling well: *He was a bit off-colour the morning after the party.*

colour in to put colour into (drawings *etc*): *He coloured in all the oblong shapes on the page.*

show oneself in one's true colours to show or express one's real character, opinion *etc*: *He pretends to be very generous but he showed himself in his true colours when he refused to give money to charity.*

with flying colours with great success: *He passed his exam with flying colours.*

colt [koult] *n* a young horse.

column ['koləm] *n* **1** a stone or wooden pillar used to support or adorn a building: *the carved columns in the temple.* **2** something similar in shape: *a column of smoke.* **3** a vertical row (of numbers): *He added up the column* (*of figures*) *to find the answer.* **4** a vertical section of a page of print: *a newspaper column.* **5** a section in a newspaper, often written regularly by a particular person: *He writes a daily column about sport.* **6** a long file of soldiers marching in short rows: *a column of infantry.* **7** a long line of vehicles *etc*, one behind the other.

columnist ['koləmnist] *n* a person who writes regular articles for a newspaper.

coma ['koumə] *n* a long-continuing unconscious state: *He was in a coma for several days after the accident.*

comb [koum] *n* **1** a toothed instrument for separating or smoothing hair *etc*. **2** an object (often decorative) of similar appearance worn by some women to keep a hairstyle in place. **3** the honey cells made by bees: *a honeycomb.* **4** the crest of some birds. – *v* **1** to arrange and smooth with a comb: *Comb your hair!* **2** to search (a place) thoroughly (for something): *They combed the hills for the missing climber.*

combat ['kombat, (*Amer*) kəm'bat] *n* (an act of) fighting: *The two knights met each other in single combat.* – *v* to fight against; to oppose: *The residents of the town tried to combat the government's plans to build a motorway.*

combatant ['kombətənt, (*Amer*) kəm'batənt] *n* a person who is fighting: *They eventually separated the combatants.*

combine [kəm'bain] *v* to join together in one whole; to unite: *They combined* (*forces*) *to fight the enemy; The chemist combined calcium and carbon.* – ['kombain] *n* an association of trading companies: *a large manufacturing combine.*

,**combi'nation** [-bi-] *n* **1** (the result of) combining or being combined: *The town was a combination of old and new architecture.* **2** a set of numbers used to open certain types of lock: *He couldn't open the safe as he had forgotten the combination;* (*also adj*) *a combination lock.*

combine harvester a machine that both harvests and threshes crops.

combustible [kəm'bʌstəbl] *adj* liable to catch fire and burn: *combustible materials.*

combustion [kəm'bʌstʃən] *n* burning: *the combustion of gases.*

come [kʌm] – *pt* **came** [keim], *ptp* **come** – *v* **1** to move *etc* towards the person speaking or writing, or towards the place being referred to by him: *Come here!; Are you coming to the dance?; John has come to see me; Have any letters come for me?* **2** to become near or close to something in time or space: *Christmas is coming soon.* **3** to happen or be situated: *The letter 'd' comes between 'c' and 'e' in the alphabet.* **4** (*often with* **to**) to happen (by accident): *How did you come to break your leg?* **5** to arrive at (a certain state *etc*): *What are things coming to? We have come to an agreement.* **6** (*with* **to**) (of numbers, prices *etc*) to amount (to): *The total comes to 51.* – *interj* expressing disapproval, drawing attention *etc*: *Come, come! That was very rude of you!*

'comer *n*: *late-comers will not be admitted*; *We welcome all comers.*

'coming *n*: *the comings and goings of the people in the street.*

'comeback *n* a return (*esp* to show business): *The actress made a comeback years after retiring.*

'comedown *n* a fall in dignity *etc*: *The smaller car was a bit of a comedown after the Rolls Royce.*

come about to happen: *How did that come about?*

come across to meet or find by chance: *He came across some old friends.*

come along 1 to come with or accompany the person speaking *etc*: *Come along with me!* 2 to progress: *How are things coming along?*

come by to get: *How did you come by that black eye?*

come down to decrease; to become less: *Tea has come down in price.*

come into one's own to have the opportunity of showing what one can do *etc*: *He has at last come into his own as a pop-singer.*

come off 1 to fall off: *Her shoe came off.* 2 to turn out (well); to succeed: *The gamble didn't come off.*

come on 1 to appear on stage or the screen: *They waited for the comedian to come on.* 2 hurry up!: *Come on – we'll be late for the party!* 3 don't be ridiculous!: *Come on, you don't really expect me to believe that!*

come out 1 to become known: *The truth finally came out.* 2 to be published: *This newspaper comes out once a week.* 3 to strike: *The men have come out (on strike).* 4 (of a photograph) to be developed: *This photograph has come out very well.* 5 to be removed: *This dirty mark won't come out.*

come round 1 (also come around) to visit: *Come round and see us soon.* 2 to regain consciousness: *He won't come round for twenty minutes at least.*

come to to regain consciousness: *When will he come to after the operation?*

come to light to be discovered: *The theft only came to light when the owners returned from holiday.*

come upon to meet, find or discover by chance: *She came upon a solution to the problem.*

come up with to think of; to produce: *He's come up with a great idea.*

come what may whatever happens: *I'll give you my support, come what may!*

to come (in the) future: *in the days to come.*

comedy ['komədi] – *pl* 'comedies – *n* 1 a play of a pleasant or amusing kind: *We went to see a comedy last night.* 2 humour: *They all saw the comedy of the situation.*

comedian [kə'mi:diən] – *fem* comedienne [kəmi:di'en, (*Amer*) kə'mi:diən] – *n* a performer who tells jokes or acts in comedies.

comely ['kʌmli] *adj* (*usu* of women) pleasant to look at. 'comeliness *n*.

comet ['komit] *n* a type of heavenly body which leaves a trail of light behind it as it moves.

comfort ['kʌmfət] *n* 1 a pleasant condition of being physically or mentally relaxed, happy, warm *etc*: *They now live in comfort.* 2 anything that provides a little luxury, or makes one feel happier, or better able to bear misfortune: *He enjoyed the comforts of the hotel*; *Her presence was a comfort to him in his grief*; *words of comfort.*

'comfortable *adj* in comfort; pleasantly relaxed: *He looked very comfortable in his chair.* 2 producing a good physical feeling: *a comfortable chair.* 3 financially secure without being rich: *a comfortable standard of living.* 'comfortably *adv*.

'comforting *adj* producing a pleasant or relaxed feeling: *a comforting thought.*

be comfortably off to have enough money to live in comfort.

comic ['komik] *adj* 1 of comedy: *a comic actor*; *comic opera.* 2 causing amusement: *comic remarks.* – *n* 1 an amusing person, *esp* a professional comedian. 2 a children's periodical containing funny stories, adventures *etc* in the form of comic strips.

'comical *adj* funny: *It was comical to see the chimpanzee pouring out a cup of tea.*

comic strip a series of small pictures showing stages in an adventure.

comma ['komə] *n* the punctuation mark (,) used to show a slight pause *etc*.

command [kə'ma:nd] *v* 1 to order: *I command you to leave the room immediately!* 2 to have authority over: *He commanded a regiment of soldiers.* 3 to have by right: *He commands great respect.* – *n* 1 an order: *They obeyed his commands.* 2 control: *He was in command of the operation.*

commandant [komən'dant, (*Amer*) 'koməndant] *n* an officer who has the command of a place or a body of troops.

com'mander *n* 1 a person who commands: *He was the commander of the expedition.* 2 in the British navy, an officer of the rank next below the captain.

com'manding *adj* 1 impressive: *He has a commanding appearance.* 2 with a wide view: *The house had a commanding position on the hill.*

com'mandment *n* a command given by God, *esp* one of the ten given to Moses.

com,mander-in-'chief *n* the officer in supreme command of an army, or of the entire forces of the state.

commandeer [kəmən'diə] *v* to seize (private property) for use by the army *etc* during wartime: *They commandeered the castle.*

commando [kə'ma:ndou] – *pl* com'mandos – *n* (a member of) a unit of troops specially trained for tasks requiring special courage and skill.

commemorate [kə'meməreit] *v* **1** (of people) to honour the memory of (someone) by a solemn celebration: *We always commemorate his birthday.* **2** (of things) to serve as a memorial to (someone or something): *This inscription commemorates those who died.* **com'memorative** [-tiv] *adj.* **com,memor'ation** *n.*

commence [kə'mens] *v* to begin: *the church service commenced with a hymn.* **com'mencement** *n.*

commend [kə'mend] *v* **1** to praise: *His ability was commended.* **2** to give (someone or something) to be looked after: *I commend him to your care.* **com'mendable** *adj* praiseworthy: *His courage during the storm was commendable.* **,commen'dation** [ko-] *n* praise.

comment ['koment] *n* (a) spoken or written remark: *He made several comments about her untidy appearance.* – *v* (*with* **on**) to make such a remark: *He commented on her appearance.* **'commentary** – *pl* **'commentaries** – *n* (*also* **running commentary**) a series of broadcast comments by a reporter at a ceremony, sports event *etc.* **'commentate** [-teit] *v* to give a commentary: *Who is commentating on the football match?* **'commentator** *n.*

commerce ['komə:s] *n* the exchange of goods between nations or people; trade on a large scale: *He is engaged in commerce.* **commercial** [kə'mə:ʃəl] *adj* **1** connected with commerce: *Private cars are allowed to use this road but not commercial vehicles.* **2** (likely to be) profitable: *a commercial proposition.* **3** paid for by advertisements: *commercial television.* – *n* a TV or radio advertisement: *I enjoyed the play but the commercials irritated me.* **commercialize, -ise** [kə'mə:ʃəlaiz] *v* to try to make (something) a source of profit: *Christmas has become commercialized.* **commercialism** [kə'mə:ʃəlizəm] *n.* **commercial traveller** a travelling representative of a business firm.

commiserate [kə'mizəreit] *v* to express sympathy (with). **com,mise'ration** *n.*

commission [kə'miʃən] **1** money earned by a person who sells things for someone else. **2** an order for a work of art: *a commission to paint the president's portrait.* **3** an official

paper giving authority, *esp* to an army officer *etc*: *My son got his commission last year.* **4** an official group appointed to report on a specific matter: *the Royal Commission on Education.* – *v* **1** to give an order (*esp* for a work of art) to: *He was commissioned to paint the Lord Mayor's portrait.* **2** to give a military commission to.

com,missio'naire [-'neə] *n* a doorkeeper in uniform: *the commissionaire at the cinema.* **com'missioner** *n* a representative of the government in a district or department.

in/out of commission in, or not in, a usable, working condition.

commit [kə'mit] – *pt, ptp* com'mitted – *v* **1** to perform; to do (*esp* something illegal): *He committed the murder when he was drunk.* **2** to hand over (a person) to an institution *etc* for treatment, safekeeping *etc*: *committed to prison.* **3** to put (oneself) under a particular obligation: *She has committed herself to finishing the book this year.* **com'mitment** *n* obligation: *She could not take the job because of family commitments.* **com'mittal** *n* the act of committing (to an institution). **com'mitted** *adj* pledged to do, or to support, something: *He was committed to looking after his uncle; He is a committed socialist.*

committee [kə'miti] *n or n pl* a number of persons, selected from a larger body, to deal with some special business, *eg* the running of the larger body's affairs: *The committee meet(s) today;* (*also adj*) *a committee meeting.*

committee is spelt with **-mm-, -tt-, -ee-**.

commodious [kə'moudiəs] *adj* spacious.

commodity [kə'modəti] – *pl* com'modities – *n* an article which is bought or sold: *soap, toothpaste and other household commodities.*

commodore ['komədo:] *n* **1** in the British navy, (of) the rank next above captain.

common ['komən] *adj* **1** seen or happening often; quite normal or usual: *a common occurrence; These birds are not so common nowadays.* **2** belonging equally to, or shared by, more than one: *This knowledge is common to all of us; We share a common language.* **3** publicly owned: *common property.* **4** coarse or impolite: *She uses some very common expressions.* **5** of ordinary, not high, social rank: *the common people.* **6** of a noun, not beginning with a capital letter (except at the beginning of a sentence): *The house is empty.* – *n* (a piece of) public land for everyone to use, with few or no buildings: *the village common.* **'commoner** *n* a person who is not of high rank: *The royal princess married a commoner.*

common knowledge something known to

everyone or to most people: *Surely you know that already – it's common knowledge.*

'commonplace *adj* very ordinary and uninteresting: *commonplace remarks.*

'common-room *n* in a college, school *etc* a sitting-room for the use of a group.

common sense practical good sense: *If he has any common sense he'll change jobs.*

the Common Market an association of certain European countries to establish free trade (without duty, tariffs *etc*) among them.

the (House of) Commons the lower house of the British parliament.

in common (of interests, attitudes, characteristics *etc*) shared or alike: *They have nothing in common – I don't know why they're getting married.*

commonwealth ['kɔmənwelθ] *n* an association of states who have joined together for their common good: *the Commonwealth of Australia.*

commotion [kə'mouʃən] *n* (a) confused, noisy uproar: *He was woken by a commotion in the street.*

communal *see* **commune.**

commune ['kɔmjuːn] *n* a group of people living together and sharing everything they own.

'communal *adj* **1** of a community: *The communal life suited them.* **2** shared: *a communal television aerial.*

communicate [kə'mjuːnikeit] *v* **1** to tell (information *etc*): *She communicated the facts to him.* **2** to get in touch (with): *It's difficult to communicate with her now that she has left the country.*

com,muni'cation *n* **1** (an act, or means, of) conveying information: *Communication is difficult in some remote parts of the country.* **2** a piece of information given, a letter *etc*: *I received your communication in this morning's post.*

com,muni'cations *n . pl* means of sending messages or of transporting (*eg* troops and supplies).

com'municative [-tiv] *adj* (*neg* **un-**) talkative; sociable: *She's not very communicative this morning.*

communication cord a chain *etc* in a railway carriage, to be pulled in an emergency.

communion [kə'mjuːnjən] *n* the sharing of thoughts and feelings; fellowship.

(Holy) Communion in the Christian Church, the service which commemorates the meal taken by Christ with His disciples before His crucifixion.

communiqué [kə'mjuːnikei] *n* an official announcement.

communism ['kɔmjunizəm] *n* (*often with cap*) a system of government under which there is no private industry and (in some forms)

no private property, most things being state-owned.

'communist *n* (*often with cap*) a person who believes in communism: *He is a Communist;* (*also adj*) *a Communist leader.*

community [kə'mjuːnəti] – *pl* **com'munities** – *n* **1** a group of people *esp* having the same religion or nationality and living in the same general area: *the West Indian community in London.* **2** the public in general: *He did it for the good of the community;* (*also adj*) *a community worker, a community centre.*

commute [kə'mjuːt] *v* **1** to travel regularly between two places, *esp* between home in the suburbs and work in the city. **2** to change (a criminal sentence) for one less severe: *His death sentence was commuted to life imprisonment.*

com'muter *n* a person who travels to work daily.

compact¹ [kəm'pakt] *adj* fitted neatly together in a small space: *Our new house is very compact.* –['kɔmpakt] *n* a small container for women's face-powder: *a powder-compact with a mirror.*

compact² ['kɔmpakt] *n* an agreement: *The management and trade union leaders finally signed a compact.*

companion [kəm'panjən] *n* **1** a person *etc* who accompanies another person as a friend *etc*: *She was his constant companion in his childhood.* **2** a helpful handbook on a particular subject: *The Gardening Companion.*

com'panionable *adj* pleasantly friendly.

com'panionship *n* state of being or of having companion(s): *She enjoys the companionship of young people.*

company ['kʌmpəni] – *pl* **'companies** – *n* **1** a number of people joined together for a (commercial) purpose: *a glass-manufacturing company.* **2** guests: *I'm expecting company tonight.* **3** companionship: *I was grateful for her company; She's always good company.* **4** a group of companions: *He got into bad company.* **5** a large group of soldiers, *esp* part of an infantry battalion.

keep (someone) company to go, stay *etc* with (someone): *I'll come too, and keep you company.*

part company (with) to leave or separate: *They parted company (with each other) at the bus stop.*

comparable, comparative *see* **compare.**

compare [kəm'peə] *v* **1** to put (things *etc*) side by side in order to see to what extent they are the same or different: *If you compare his work with hers you will find hers more accurate; This is a good essay compared with your last one.* **2** to describe as being similar to: *She compared him to a monkey.* **3** to be near in standard or quality: *He just can't compare with Mozart.*

comparable ['kompərəbl] *adj* of the same kind, on the same scale *etc*: *The houses were not at all comparable in size.*

comparative [kəm'parətiv] *adj* **1** judged by comparing with something else: *the comparative quiet of the suburbs.* **2** (of an adjective or adverb used in comparisons) between positive and superlative, as the following underlined words: *a bigger book*; *a better man*; *Blacker is a comparative adjective*; *(also n) What is the comparative of 'bad'?*

com'paratively *adv*: *This house was comparatively cheap.*

comparison [kəm'parisn] *n* (an act of) comparing: *There's no comparison between Beethoven and pop music; Living here is cheap in comparison with London.*

compare with is used to bring out similarities and differences between two things of the same type: *He compared his pen with mine and decided mine was better.* **compare to** is used when pointing out a similarity between two different things: *Stars are often compared to diamonds.*

compartment [kəm'pa:tmənt] *n* a separate part or division *eg* of a railway carriage: *We couldn't find an empty compartment in the train; The drawer was divided into compartments.*

compass ['kampəs] *n* **1** an instrument with a magnetized needle, used to find directions: *If he had carried a compass he would not have lost his way on the hills.* **2** (*in pl*) an instrument with two movable legs, for drawing circles *etc.* **3** scope or range.

compass rose the circular drawing showing directions on a plan or map.

compassion [kəm'paʃən] *n* sorrow or pity for the sufferings of another person. **com'passionate** [-nət] *adj.*

compatible [kəm'patəbl] *adj* able to agree or exist successfully side by side. **com,pati'bility** *n.* **com'patibly** *adv.*

compatriot [kəm'patriət, (*Amer*) -'pei-] *n* a fellow-countryman: *Many of his compatriots were killed in the war.*

compel [kəm'pel] – *pt, ptp* **com'pelled** – *v* to force: *They compelled me to betray my country.*

compensate ['kompənseit] *v* **1** to give money to (someone) or to do something else to make up for loss or wrong they have experienced: *This payment will compensate (her) for the loss of her job.* **2** to undo the effect of a disadvantage *etc: The love the child received from his grandmother compensated for the cruelty of his parents.* **compensatory** [kəm'pensətəri] *adj.*

,**compen'sation** *n* payment *etc* given for loss or injury: *He received a large sum of money as compensation when he was injured at work.*

compère ['kompɛ:] *n* a person who introduces the different acts and items of an entertainment.

compete [kəm'pi:t] *v* to try to beat others in a contest, fight *etc: We are competing against them in the next round; Are you competing with her for the job?*

competition [kompə'tiʃən] *n* **1** the act of competing; rivalry: *Competition makes children try harder.* **2** people competing for a prize *etc: There's a lot of competition for this job.* **3** a contest for a prize: *Have you entered the tennis competition?*

competitive [kəm'petətiv] *adj* **1** (of a person) enjoying competition: *a competitive child.* **2** (of a price, *etc*) not expensive, therefore able to compete successfully with the prices *etc* of rivals. **3** (of sport *etc*) organised in such a way as to produce a winner: *I prefer hill-climbing to competitive sports.*

competitor [kəm'petitə] *n* a person *etc* who takes part in a competition; a rival: *All the competitors finished the race.*

competent ['kompətənt] *adj* capable; skilled: *a competent pianist; competent to drive a car.* '**competence** *n.* '**competently** *adv.*

competition, competitive, competitor *see* **compete.**

compile [kəm'pail] *v* to make (a book, table *etc*) from information collected from other books *etc: He compiled a French dictionary.* **compilation** [kompi'leiʃən] *n.* **com'piler** *n.*

complacent [kəm'pleisnt] *adj* showing satisfaction with one's own situation: *a complacent attitude.* **com'placence, com'placency** *ns.* **com'placently** *adv.*

complain [kəm'plein] *v* **1** to state one's displeasure, dissatisfaction *etc: I'm going to complain to the police about the noise.* **2** (*with of*) to state that one has (pain, discomfort *etc*): *He's complaining of difficulty in breathing.*

com'plaint *n* **1** (a statement of one's) dissatisfaction: *The customer made a complaint about the lack of hygiene in the food shop.* **2** a sickness, disease, disorder *etc: He's always suffering from some complaint or other.*

complement ['kompləmənt] *n* **1** in a sentence, the words of the predicate, not including the verb. **2** (something added to make) a complete number or amount. – *v* to complete, fill up. *adj* **comple'mentary**.

the **complement** (not **compliment**) of a verb.

complete [kəm'pli:t] *adj* **1** whole; with nothing missing: *a complete set of Shakespeare's plays.* **2** thorough: *My car needs a complete overhaul*; *a complete surprise.* **3** finished: *My picture will soon be complete.* − *v* to finish; to make complete: *When will he complete the job?*; *This stamp completes my collection.*

com'pletely *adv*: *I am not completely satisfied.*

com'pleteness *n*.

com'pletion [-ʃən] *n* finishing or state of being finished: *You will be paid on completion of the work.*

complex ['kompleks, (*Amer*) kəm'pleks] *adj* **1** composed of many parts: *a complex piece of machinery.* **2** complicated or difficult: *a complex problem.* − ['kompleks] *n* **1** something made up of many different pieces: *The leisure complex will include a swimming-pool, tennis courts, a library etc.* **2** (*often used loosely*) an abnormal mental state caused by experiences in one's past which affect one's behaviour: *She has a complex about her weight*; *inferiority complex.*

complexity [kəm'pleksəti] − *pl* **com'plexities** − *n* **1** the quality of being complex. **2** something complex.

complexion [kəm'plekʃən] *n* the colour or appearance of the skin *esp* of the face: *a beautiful complexion.*

complexity *see* **complex**.

compliance, compliant *see* **comply**.

complicate ['komplikeit] *v* to make difficult: *His illness will complicate matters.*

'complicated *adj* (*neg* **un-**) difficult to understand: *complicated instructions.*

,compli'cation *n* **1** something making a situation *etc* more difficult: *Taking the dog with us on holiday will be an added complication.* **2** a development (in an illness *etc*) which makes things worse.

compliment ['kompləmənt] *n* an expression of praise or flattery: *He's always paying her compliments.* − [kompli'ment] *v* to praise or flatter: *He complimented her on her cooking.*

,compli'mentary [-'men-] *adj* (*neg* **un-**) **1** flattering or praising: *complimentary remarks.* **2** given free: *a complimentary ticket.*

with compliments used when sending a gift *etc*: *'With compliments from a secret admirer'.*

to pay a **compliment** (not **complement**).

comply [kəm'plai] *v* to act in the way that someone else has commanded or wished: *You must comply (with her wishes).* **com'pliance** *n*.

com'pliant *adj* willing to comply.

component [kəm'pounənt] *n* a part of a machine (*eg* a car), instrument (*eg* a radio)

etc: *He bought components for the television set he was repairing.*

compose [kəm'pouz] *v* **1** to form by putting parts together: *A word is composed of several letters.* **2** to write (*eg* music, poetry *etc*): *Mozart began to compose when he was six years old.* **3** to control (oneself) after being upset.

com'posed *adj* (of people) quiet and calm: *She looked quite composed.*

com'poser *n* a writer, *esp* of a piece of music.

composition [kompə'ziʃən] *n* **1** something composed, *eg* music: *his latest composition.* **2** the act of composing: *the difficulties of composition.* **3** an essay written as a school exercise: *The children had to write a composition about their holiday.* **4** the parts of which a thing is made: *Have you studied the composition of the chemical?*

com'posure [-ʒə] *n* calmness: *I admired her composure.*

composition *see* **compose**.

compost ['kompost, (*Amer*) -poust] *n* rotting vegetable matter *etc* used as fertilizer.

composure *see* **compose**.

compound[1] ['kompaund] *adj* composed of a number of parts: *a compound substance.* − *n* a substance, word *etc* formed from two or more elements: *The word racetrack is a compound*; *chemical compounds.*

compound[2] ['kompaund] *n* a fenced or walled-in area, *eg* round a factory, school *etc*.

comprehend [kompri'hend] *v* **1** to understand. **2** to include.

,compre'hensible *adj* capable of being understood.

,compre'hension [-ʃən] *n* the act or power of understanding: *After reading the passage the teacher asked questions to test the children's comprehension.*

'compre'hensive [-siv] *adj* **1** including many things: *The school curriculum is very comprehensive.*

,compre'hensively *adv*.

,compre'hensiveness *n*.

comprehensive school one that provides education for children of all abilities.

compress [kəm'pres] *v* to press together; to force into a narrower space: *All his belongings were compressed into a very small suitcase.*

com'pressible *adj*. **com'pression** [-ʃən] *n*.

compressed air air which is at a pressure higher than atmospheric pressure: *Deep sea divers breathe compressed air.*

comprise [kəm'praiz] *v* to contain or consist of: *Her family comprises two sons and a daughter.*

The team **comprises** (not **comprises of**) five members.

compromise ['komprəmaiz] *n* (a) settlement of differences in which each side gives up something it has previously demanded: *We argued for a long time but finally arrived at a compromise.*

compulsion [kəm'pʌlʃən] *n* compelling or being compelled: *You are under no compulsion to go.*
com'pulsory *adj* which must be done or carried out: *Is it compulsory for me to attend the class?; a compulsory examination.*
com'pulsorily *adv.*

compute [kəm'pju:t] *v* to calculate or estimate. **,compu'tation** [kom-].

computer [kəm'pju:tə] *n* a *usu* large electronic machine capable of storing and processing large amounts of information and of performing calculations.
com'puterize, -ise *v* to put (information *etc*) into a form suitable for use by a computer: *Are you intending to computerize your book-ordering system?*

comrade ['komrid, (*Amer*) -rad] *n* a close companion: *his comrades in battle.*
'comradeship *n*: *the comradeship of the office.*

con [kon] – *pt, ptp* **conned** – *v* to trick or persuade dishonestly: *He conned her into giving him money.* – *n* a dishonest trick.
'con-man *n* someone who cons people.

concave [kon'keiv] *adj* (of an object or surface) curved inwards: *Spoons are concave.*
con'cavity [-'ka-] *n.*

conceal [kən'si:l] *v* to hide or keep secret: *He concealed his disappointment from his friends.* **con'cealment** *n.*

concede [kən'si:d] *v* to admit: *He conceded that he had been wrong.* **2** to grant (*eg* a right).

conceit [kən'si:t] too much pride in oneself: *He's full of conceit about his good looks.*
con'ceited *adj* having too much pride in oneself: *She's conceited about her artistic ability.*

conceit is spelt with -ei-.

conceive [kən'si:v] *v* **1** to form (an idea *etc*) in the mind. **2** to imagine: *I can't conceive why you did that.* **3** (of a woman) to become pregnant.
con'ceivable *adj* able to be imagined or thought of. **con'ceivably** *adv.*

conceive is spelt with -ei-.

concentrate ['konsəntreit] *v* **1** to give all one's energies, attention *etc* to one thing: *I wish you'd concentrate (on what I'm saying).* **2** to bring together in one place: *He concentrated his soldiers at the gateway.* **3** to make (a liquid) stronger by boiling to reduce its volume.
'concentrated *adj* (of a liquid *etc*) made stronger; not diluted: *concentrated orange juice.*
,concen'tration *n*: *She lacks concentration – she will never pass the exam.*

concentric [kən'sentrik] *adj* (of circles) having a common centre.

concept ['konsept] *n* an idea or theory: *His design was a new concept in town-planning.*
conception [kən'sepʃən] *n* **1** the act of conceiving. **2** an idea grasped or understood: *We can have no conception of the size of the universe.*

concern [kən'sə:n] *v* **1** to have to do with: *This order doesn't concern us; So far as I'm concerned, you can do what you like.* **2** (*with* for *or* about) to make (*usu* oneself) uneasy: *Don't concern youself about her.* **3** (*with* with *or* in) to interest (oneself) in: *He doesn't concern himself with unimportant details.* – *n* **1** something that concerns or belongs to one: *His problems are not my concern.* **2** anxiety: *The condition of the patient is giving rise to concern.* **3** a business: *a shoe-manufacturing concern.*
con'cerning *prep* about: *He wrote to me concerning a business arrangement.*

concert ['konsət] *n* a musical entertainment: *an orchestral concert.*
in concert together: *to act in concert.*

concerted [kən'sə:tid] *adj* carried out by people acting together: *a concerted effort.*

concertina [konsə'ti:nə] *n* a portable musical wind instrument with bellows and a keyboard.

concerto [kən'tʃə:tou] – *pl* **con'certos** – *n* a piece of music written for one or more solo instruments and orchestra: *a piano concerto.*

concession [kən'seʃən] *n* **1** something granted: *As a concession we were given a day off work to go to the wedding.*

conciliate [kən'silieit] *v* to win over or regain the support, friendship *etc* of. **con,cili'ation** *n.* **con'ciliatory** *adj.*

concise [kən'sais] *adj* brief but comprehensive: *a clear concise statement.* **con'cisely** *adv.* **con'ciseness** *n.*

conclave ['konkleiv] *n* a private, secret meeting.

conclude [kən'klu:d] *v* **1** to come or bring to an end: *to conclude a meeting; He concluded by thanking everyone.* **2** to come to believe: *We concluded that you weren't coming.*
con'clusion [-ʒən] *n* **1** an end: *the conclusion of his speech.* **2** a judgement: *I came to the conclusion that the house was empty.*
con'clusive [-siv] *adj* convincing: *conclusive proof.* **con'clusively** *adv.* **con'clusiveness** *n.*

concoct [kən'kokt, (*Amer*) kon-] *v* to put together, make up or invent: *I've concocted a new drink for you to try; The child concocted a story about having been attacked.*
con'coction [-ʃən] *n.*

concord ['koŋko:d] *n* agreement; state of peace.

concrete ['koŋkr:t] *adj* **1** made of concrete: *concrete slabs*. **2** able to be seen and felt; real or definite: *A wooden table is a concrete object*. – *n* a mixture of cement with sand *etc* used in building. – *v* to spread with concrete: *We'll have to concrete the garden path*.
'concreteness *n*.

concubine ['koŋkjubain] *n* an old word for a woman who lives with a man as his lover but is not his wife.

concur [kən'kə:] – *pt, ptp* **con'curred** – *v* to agree; to come together, or coincide.
con'currence [-'kʌ-, (*Amer*) -'kə:-] *n*.
concurrent [kən'kʌrənt, (*Amer*) -'kə:-] *adj*.
con'currently *adv*.

concussed [kən'kʌst] *adj* suffering from concussion: *He was concussed for several hours*.
con'cussion [-ʃən] *n* temporary harm to the brain caused by a heavy blow on the head: *suffering from concussion*.

condemn [kən'dem] *v* **1** to criticize as morally wrong or evil: *Everyone condemned her for being cruel to her child*. **2** to sentence to (a punishment): *She was condemned to death*. **3** to declare (a building) to be unfit to use: *These houses have been condemned*. **condemnation** [kondem'neiʃən] *n*.
condemned cell a cell for a prisoner under sentence of death.

condense [kən'dens] *v* **1** to make smaller: *They have produced a condensed version of the book for children*. **2** to make (a liquid) thicker, stronger or more concentrated: *condensed milk*. **3** (of vapour) to turn to liquid: *Steam condensed on the kitchen windows*.
‚conden'sation [konden-] *n* **1** the act of condensing. **2** liquid formed from vapour: *I can't see out because of the condensation on the window*.

condescend [kondi'send] *v* to agree graciously (to do something).
‚conde'scending *adj* giving the impression that one is superior: *a condescending manner*. **‚conde'scendingly** *adv*.
‚conde'scension [-ʃən] *n*.

condiment ['kondimənt] *n* a seasoning (*esp* salt or pepper).

condition [kən'diʃən] **1** state or circumstances in which a person or thing is: *The house is not in good condition*; *He is in no condition to leave hospital*; *under ideal conditions*; *living conditions*; *variable conditions*. **2** something that must happen or be done before some other thing happens or is done; a term or requirement in an agreement: *It was a condition of his going that he should pay his own expenses*; *That is one of the conditions in the agreement*. – *v* **1** to affect or control: *behaviour conditioned by circumstances*. **2** to put into the required state: *air-conditioned buildings*; *Well-conditioned hair*.
con'ditional *adj* depending on certain conditions: *This offer of a university place is conditional on your being able to pass your final school exams*; *a conditional offer*. **con'ditionally** *adv*.
con'ditioner *n* something which helps in conditioning: *hair-conditioner*.
on condition that if, and only if (something is done): *You will be paid tomorrow on condition that the work is finished*.

condolence [kən'doulɔns] *n* sympathy: *a letter of condolence*.

condone [kən'doun] *v* to excuse or forgive: *He could not condone lying*.

conduct [kən'dʌkt] *v* **1** to lead or guide: *We were conducted down a narrow path by the guide*; *a conducted tour*. **2** to carry or allow to flow: *Most metals conduct electricity*. **3** to direct (an orchestra, choir *etc*). **4** to behave (oneself): *He conducted himself well at the reception*. **5** to manage or carry on (a business). – ['kondʌkt] *n* **1** behaviour: *His conduct at school was disgraceful*. **2** the way in which something is managed, done *etc*: *the conduct of the affair*.
con'duction [-ʃən] *n* transmission of heat *etc* by a conductor.
con'ductor *n* **1** a thing that conducts heat or electricity: *Copper is a good conductor of heat*. **2** a director of an orchestra, choir *etc*. **3** (*fem* **con'ductress**) a person who collects fares on a bus *etc*: *a bus conductor*. **4** (*Amer*) a guard on a train.

*__cone__ [koun] *n* **1** a solid figure with a point and a base in the shape of a circle or oval. **2** the fruit of the pine, fir *etc*: *fir-cones*. **3** a pointed holder for ice cream; *an ice-cream cone*. **4** a warning sign placed next to roadworks *etc* or where parking is not allowed.
conical ['konikəl] *adj* cone-shaped.

confectioner [kən'fekʃɔnə] *n* a person who makes or sells sweets or cakes.
con'fectionery *n* **1** sweets, chocolates *etc*. **2** the shop or business of a confectioner.

confederate [kən'fedərət] *n* a person who has agreed to work with others (*eg* on something dishonest): *He and his confederates were found with stolen money in their possession*.
con'federacy [-rəsi] – *pl* **con'federacies** – *n* a league or alliance (of states *etc*).
con‚fede'ration *n* (the forming of) a league or alliance, *esp* of states *etc*.

confer [kən'fə:] – *pt, ptp* **con'ferred** – *v* **1** (*often with* **with**) to consult each other: *The staff conferred (with the headmaster)* *about the new timetable.* **2** (*with* **on**) to give (an honour) to someone: *The university conferred degrees on two famous scientists.*

conference ['konfərəns] *n* a meeting for discussion: *The conference of heart specialists was held in New York.*

confess [kən'fes] *v* to make known that one is guilty, wrong *etc*; to admit: *He confessed* (*to the crime*); *He confessed that he had broken the vase*; *It was stupid of me, I confess.*

con'fession [-ʃən] *n* **1** acknowledgment of a crime or fault: *The youth made a confession to the police officer.* **2** (an) act of confessing one's sins to a priest: *She went to confession every Friday.*

con'fessional [-ʃə-] *n* the seat *etc* where a priest sits when hearing confessions.

con'fessor *n* a priest who hears confessions.

confetti [kən'feti] *n* small pieces of coloured paper thrown in celebration at weddings.

confide [kən'faid] *v* to tell one's private thoughts to someone: *He confided in his brother*; *He confided his fears to his brother.*

confidence ['konfidəns] *n* **1** trust or belief in someone's ability: *I have great confidence in you.* **2** belief and faith in one's own ability: *She shows a great deal of confidence for her age.*

confident ['konfidənt] *adj* having a great deal of trust (*esp* in oneself): *She is confident that she will win*; *a confident boy.*

confidential [konfi'denʃəl] *adj* **1** secret; not to be told to others: *confidential information.* **2** trusted to keep secrets: *a confidential secretary.*

confidentiality ['konfidenʃi'aləti] *n.*

,confi'dentially *adv* secretly; not wishing to have the information passed on to anyone else: *She could not tell me what he said – he was speaking confidentially.*

con'fiding *adj* trustful. **con'fidingly** *adv.*

in confidence as a secret; confidentially: *He told me the story in* (*strictest*) *confidence.*

confine [kən'fain] *v* **1** to keep within limits; to stop from spreading: *They succeeded in confining the fire to a small area.* **2** to shut up or imprison: *The prince was confined in the castle for three years.*

con'fined *adj* **1** (*with* **to**) kept in or shut up in: *confined to bed with a cold.* **2** narrow, small: *a confined space.*

con'finement *n* **1** state of being shut up or imprisoned: *solitary confinement.* **2** (the time of) the birth of a child: *her third confinement.*

'confines ['kon-] *n pl* limits or boundaries: *within the confines of the city.*

confirm [kən'fɔːm] *v* **1** to establish or make quite certain: *They confirmed their hotel booking by letter.* **2** to admit to full mem-

bership of certain Christian churches. **,confir'mation** [kon-] *n.*

con'firmed *adj* settled in a habit or way of life: *a confirmed bachelor/drunkard.*

confiscate ['konfiskeit] *v* to seize or take (something) away, *usu* as a penalty: *The teacher confiscated the boy's comic which he was reading in class.* **,confi'scation** *n.*

conflagration [konflə'greiʃən] *n* a great fire: *Ten people perished in the conflagration.*

conflict ['konflikt] *n* **1** (a) disagreement: *There was considerable conflict about which plan should be accepted.* **2** a fight or battle. – [kən'flikt] *v* to contradict each other; to disagree: *The two accounts of what had happened conflicted* (*with each other*).

confluence ['konfluəns] *n* a flowing together of two rivers.

conform [kən'fɔːm] *v* **1** to behave, dress *etc* in the way that most other people do. **2** (*with* **to**) to act according to; to be in agreement with: *Your clothes must conform to the regulation school pattern.* **con'formity** *n.*

confound [kən'faund] *v* to puzzle and surprise greatly.

confront [kən'frʌnt] *v* **1** to bring face to face with: *He was confronted with the evidence of his crime.* **2** to face in a hostile manner; to oppose: *They confronted the enemy at dawn.* **,confron'tation** [kon-] *n.*

confuse [kən'fjuːz] *v* **1** to put in disorder: *He confused the arrangements by arriving late.* **2** to mix up in one's mind: *I always confuse John and his twin brother.* **3** to make puzzled: *He completely confused me by his questions.*

con'fused *adj* **1** mixed up: *The message I received was rather confused.* **2** mixed up in the mind: *in a confused state of mind.* **con'fusedly** [-zidli] *adv.*

con'fusion [-ʒən] *n.*

congeal [kən'dʒiːl] *v* (*esp* of blood, grease *etc*) to solidify when cooled.

congenial [kən'dʒiːniəl] *adj* agreeable; pleasant.

congenital [kən'dʒenitl] *adj* (of diseases or deformities) existing at or before birth. **con'genitally** *adv.*

congested [kən'dʒestid] *adj* over-crowded; over-full. **con'gestion** [-tʃən] *n.*

con,glome'ration [kənglomə'reiʃən] *n* a mixed heap or collection: *a conglomeration of old clothes.*

congratulate [kən'gratjuleit] *v* (*often with* **on**) to express pleasure and joy to (a person) at a happy event, a success *etc*: *She congratulated him on passing his driving test.* **con'gratulatory** [-lə-] *adj.*

con,gratu'lation *n* (*usu in pl*): *Warmest congratulations on the birth of your baby*; *a message of congratulation.*

congregate ['kɔŋgrigeit] v to come or bring together: *A large crowd congregated in the street.*

,congre'gation n a group gathered together, *esp* people in a church for a service, or belonging to a church: *The minister visited all the members of his congregation.*

congress ['kɔŋgres, (*Amer*) -gris] n 1 a formal meeting, *esp* an assembly of delegates *etc*. 2 a law-making body or parliament, *esp* that of the United States: *He has been elected to Congress.* **con'gressional** [-ʃənl] *adj*.

'**congressman,** '**congresswoman** *ns*.

congruent ['kɔŋgruənt] *adj* of two or more geometrical figures, touching at all points when one is fitted on top of the other: *congruent triangles.*

con'gruity [-'gru:-] n.

conical *see* **cone**.

conifer ['kɔnifə, (*Amer*) 'kou-] n a cone-bearing tree, *eg* the fir: *The larch tree is a conifer.*

co'niferous *adj* cone-bearing.

conjecture [kən'dʒektʃə] n (an) opinion formed on slight evidence; a guess: *He made several conjectures about where his son might be.* – v to guess. **con'jectural** *adj*.

conjugal ['kɔndʒugəl] *adj* of marriage.

conjugate ['kɔndʒugeit] v to give the different parts of (a verb). ,**conju'gation** n.

conjunction [kən'dʒʌŋkʃən] n a word that connects sentences, clauses or words: *John sang and Mary danced; I'll do it if you want.* **in conjunction (with)** (acting) together (with).

conjure ['kʌndʒə, (*Amer*) 'kɔn-] v to perform tricks (**conjuring tricks**) that seem magical, as an entertainment. '**conjuror,** '**conjurer** n.

connect [kə'nekt] v 1 to join or be joined in some way; to tie or fasten or link together: *He connected the radio to the mains; This road connects the two farms; a connecting link; This telephone line connects with the President.* 2 to associate in the mind: *People tend to connect money with happiness.*

con'nection [-ʃən] n 1 something that connects or is connected: *a faulty electrical connection.* 2 (a) state of being connected or related: *My connection with their family is very slight; I wish to talk to you in connection with my daughter's career.* 3 a useful person whom one can contact, *esp* in business: *his connections in the clothing trade.* 4 a train, bus *etc* to which one changes from another in the course of a journey: *As the local train was late, I missed the connection to London.*

connive [kə'naiv] v (*with* **at**) to make no attempt to hinder (something wrong or illegal): *Her mother connived at the child's truancy.* **con'nivance** n.

connoisseur [kɔnə'sə:] n an expert judge of *eg* art, music, wine *etc*: *Let him choose the wine – he's the connoisseur.*

conquer ['kɔŋkə] v to overcome or defeat: *The Normans conquered England in the eleventh century; You must conquer your fear of the dark.* '**conqueror** n.

conquest ['kɔŋkwest] n (an) act of conquering: *The Norman Conquest; He's impressed with you – you've made a conquest.*

conscience ['kɔnʃəns] n (that part of one's mind which holds one's) knowledge or sense of right and wrong: *The injured man was on her conscience because she was responsible for the accident; She had a bad conscience about the injured man; He had no conscience about dismissing the men.*

conscientious [kɔnʃi'enʃəs] *adj* careful and hard-working: *a conscientious pupil.* ,**consci'entiously** *adv.* ,**consci'entiousness** n.

conscious ['kɔnʃəs] *adj* 1 aware of oneself and one's surroundings; not asleep or in a coma or anaesthetized *etc*: *The patient was conscious.* 2 (*sometimes with* **of**) aware or having knowledge (of): *They were conscious of his disapproval.* '**consciously** *adv.*

'**consciousness** n: *The patient soon regained consciousness.*

conscript ['kɔnskript] n a person legally ordered by the state to serve in the armed forces *etc*. – [kən'skript] v legally to order (someone) to serve in the armed forces *etc*: *He was conscripted into the army.* **con'scription** [-ʃən] n.

consecrate ['kɔnsikreit] v to set apart for a holy use; to dedicate to God: *The bishop consecrated the new church.* ,**conse'cration** n.

consecutive [kən'sekjutiv] *adj* following one after the other in regular order: *He visited us on two consecutive days, Thursday and Friday.* **con'secutively** *adv.*

consensus [kən'sensəs] n the feeling of most people: *The consensus of opinion is that we should do this.*

consent [kən'sent] v to give permission or agree (to): *I consent to that plan.* – n agreement; permission: *You have my consent to leave.*

consequence ['kɔnsikwəns, (*Amer*) -kwens] n 1 a result: *This decision will have important consequences.* 2 importance: *A small error is of no consequence.*

'**consequently** *adv* therefore: *She didn't explain it clearly – consequently, he didn't understand.*

conservation, conservatism *etc see* **conserve**.

conservatory [kən'sə:vətri, (*Amer*) -to:ri] – *pl* **con'servatories** – n 1 a kind of greenhouse, or a glass-walled part of a building, in which plants are grown. **2** a school of music, art *etc*.

conserve [kən'sɔːv] *v* to keep from changing, being damaged or lost: *We must conserve the country's natural resources*; *This old building should be conserved.* – *n* something preserved, *eg* fruits in sugar, jam *etc*.

‚conser'vation [kon-] *n* the act of conserving *esp* wildlife, the countryside, old buildings *etc*.

‚conser'vationist [kon-] *n* a person who is interested in conservation.

con'servatism [-vətizəm] *n* dislike of change.

con'servative [-tiv] *adj* **1** disliking change: *Older people tend to be conservative in their attitudes*; *conservative opinions*. **2** in politics, wanting to avoid major changes and to keep business and industry in private hands.

consider [kən'sidə] *v* **1** to think about (carefully): *He considered their comments.* **2** to feel inclined towards: *I'm considering leaving this job.* **3** to take into account: *You must consider other people's feelings.* **4** to regard as being: *They consider him unfit for that job.*

con'siderable *adj* great: *considerable wealth*; *a considerable number of people*.

con'siderably *adv*: *Considerably fewer people came than I expected*.

considerate [kən'sidərət] *adj* thoughtful about others: *He is always considerate to elderly people*.

con‚side'ration *n* **1** (the act of) thinking about something, *esp* the needs or feelings of other people: *He stayed at home out of consideration for his mother.* **2** a fact to be taken into account in making a decision *etc*: *The cost of the journey is our main consideration*.

con'sidering *prep* taking into account; despite: *Considering his deafness he manages to understand very well*.

take into consideration to allow for (in considering a situation or problem): *You must take his illness into consideration before dismissing him.*

consign [kən'sain] *v* to put into or deliver to: *The body was consigned with reverence to the grave.*

con'signment *n* a load (of goods): *the latest consignment of books.*

consist [kən'sist] *v* (*with* **of**) to be composed or made up: *The house consists of six rooms.*

con'sistency¹ *n* the degree of thickness or firmness: *of the consistency of dough.*

consistent [kən'sistənt] *adj* **1** (*often with* **with**) in agreement (with): *The two statements are not consistent*; *The second statement is not consistent with the first.* **2** always (acting, thinking or happening) according to the

same rules or principles; the same or regular: *He was consistent in his attitude*; *a consistent style of writing.*

con'sistency² *n*: *the consistency of his work.*

con'sistently *adv*: *His work is consistently good.*

console [kən'soul] *v* to comfort: *She could not console the weeping child.*

‚conso'lation [kon-] *n* **1** the act of consoling. **2** something that consoles: *His great wealth was no consolation for the loss of his reputation*; (*also adj*) *a consolation prize* (for someone who just failed to win).

consolidate [kən'solideit] *v* to make or become solid; to strengthen. **con‚soli'dation** *n*.

consonant ['konsənənt] *n* any letter of the alphabet except *a, e, i, o, u*.

consort ['konsɔːt] *n* a (*esp* royal) wife or husband: *prince consort* (= the husband of a reigning queen). – [kən'sɔːt] *v* (*with* **with**) to have dealings or associations (with, *usu* in a bad sense): *He's been consorting with drug-addicts.*

consortium [kən'sɔːtiəm, (*Amer*) -ʃiəm] *n* an association, union, *esp* of bankers or businessmen.

conspicuous [kən'spikjuəs] *adj* very noticeable: *Her blond hair made her conspicuous in the crowd.*

con'spicuously *adv*. **con'spicuousness** *n*.

conspire [kən'spaiə] *v* to plot or secretly make plans together: *They conspired with the terrorists to overthrow the government.*

con'spiracy [-'spi-] – *pl* **con'spiracies** – *n* (a plan made by) conspiring: *The government discovered the conspiracy in time.*

con'spirator [-'spi-] *n* a person who conspires.

constable ['kʌnstəbl, (*Amer*) 'kon-] *n* a policeman, *esp* one not of high rank.

con'stabulary [-'stabju-] – *pl* **con'stabularies** – *n* a police force.

constant ['konstənt] *adj* **1** never stopping: *a constant noise.* **2** unchanging: *It must be kept at a constant temperature.* **3** faithful: *He remained constant.* **'constantly** *adv*. **'constancy** *n*.

constellation [konstə'leiʃən] *n* a named group of stars: *The Plough and Orion are constellations.*

consternation [konstə'neiʃən] *n* astonishment or dismay: *To my consternation, when I reached home I found I had lost the key of the house.*

constipated ['konstipeitid] *adj* having difficulty in passing waste matter (as regularly as normal) from the bowels.

‚consti'pation *n*.

constituent [kən'stitjuənt] *n* **1** a necessary part: *Hydrogen is a constituent of water.* **2** a voter from a particular member of parliament's constituency: *He deals with all his* *constituents' problems. – adj: He broke it down into its constituent parts.*

con'stituency – *pl* **con'stituencies** – *n* the group of voters, or the area in which they live, represented by a member of parliament.

constitute ['konstitjuːt] *v* to form; to make up; to be: *Nuclear waste constitutes a serious danger.*

,**consti'tution** *n* **1** a set of rules governing an organization; the supreme laws and rights of a country's people *etc*: *the constitution of the country.* **2** physical characteristics, health *etc*: *He has a strong constitution.* ,**consti'tutional** *adj* legal according to a given constitution: *The proposed change would not be constitutional.* ,**consti'tutionally** *adv.*

constrict [kən'strikt] *v* to press tightly; to cramp: *The tight collar was constricting his neck.*

construct [kən'strʌkt] *v* to build; to put together: *They are planning to construct a new supermarket near our house*; *Construct a sentence containing 'although'.* **con'struction** [-ʃən] *n* **1** (a way of) constructing or putting together: *The bridge is still under construction.* **2** something built: *That construction won't last long.* '**con'structive** [-tiv] *adj* helpful; having to do with making, not with destroying: *Constructive criticism tells you both what is wrong and also what to do about it.* **con'structively** *adv.* **con'structor** *n* a person who constructs: *a constructor of bridges.*

construction site a building site.

construction worker a builder.

consul ['konsəl] *n* an agent who looks after his country's residents in (part of) a foreign country: *the British Consul in Berlin.* **2** either of the two chief magistrates in ancient Rome. '**consular** [-sju-] *adj.* **consulate** ['konsjulət, (*Amer*) -sələt] *n* the office or residence of a consul.

consult [kən'sʌlt] *v* **1** to seek advice or information from: *Consult your doctor*; *He consulted his watch*; *He consulted with me about what we should do next.* **2** (of a doctor *etc*) to give professional advice: *He consults on Mondays and Fridays.* **con'sultant** *n* **1** a person who gives professional advice: *He is consultant to a firm of engineers*; (*also adj*) *a consultant engineer.* **2** a senior hospital doctor specializing in a particular branch of medicine: *His condition is so serious that they have sent for the consultant*; (*also adj*) *a consultant physician.* ,**consul'tation** [kon-] *n*: *How much does he charge for a consultation?*

consume [kən'sjuːm] *v* **1** to eat or drink: *He consumes a huge amount of food.* **2** to use:

How much electricity do you consume per month? **3** to destroy, *eg* by fire: *The entire building was consumed by fire.*

con'sumer *n* a person who eats, uses, buys things *etc*: *The average consumer spends 12 dollars per year on toothpaste.*

consumption [kən'sʌmpʃən] *n* the act of consuming: *The consumption of coffee has increased.*

consumer goods goods which can be used immediately to satisfy human needs, *eg* clothing, food, TV sets *etc.*

consummate ['konsəmeit] *v* to complete or fulfil. – [-mət] *adj* complete; perfect. ,**consum'mation** *n.*

consumption *see* **consume.**

contact ['kontakt] *n* **1** physical touch or nearness: *Her hands came into contact with acid*; *Has she been in contact with measles?* **2** communication: *I've lost contact with all my old friends*; *We have succeeded in making (radio) contact with the ship*; *How can I get in contact with him?* **3** a person with influence, knowledge *etc* which might be useful: *I made several good contacts in London.* **4** (a place where) a wire *etc* carrying electric current (may be attached): *the contacts on the battery.* **5** a person who has been near someone with an infectious disease: *We must trace all known contacts of the cholera victim.* **6** a person or thing that provides a means of communicating with someone: *His radio is his only contact with the outside world.* – *v* to get in touch with in order to give or share information *etc*: *I'll contact you by telephone.*

contact lens a small plastic lens on the eyeball worn, instead of spectacles, to improve sight.

contagious [kən'teidʒəs] *adj* spreading from one person to another by physical contact: *Is this skin disease contagious?* **con'tagion** *n* an infection.

contain [kən'tein] *v* **1** to keep or have inside: *This box contains a pair of shoes*; *How much milk does this jug contain?* **2** to control: *He could hardly contain his excitement.* **con'tainer** *n* **1** something made to contain things: *He brought his lunch in a plastic container.* **2** a very large sealed metal box for carrying goods on a lorry, ship *etc*: *The ship carried twenty containers*; (*also adj*) *a container ship*, a container lorry.*

contaminate [kən'tamineit] *v* to make impure: *The town's water-supply has been contaminated by chemicals from the factory.* **con,tami'nation** *n.*

contemplate ['kontəmpleit] *v* **1** to think seriously (about): *I was contemplating (= feeling inclined towards) having a holiday*; *She contemplated her future gloomily.* **2** to look thoughtfully at: *He was contemplating the* ceiling. **,contem'plation** n. **contemplative** [kən'templətiv, (*Amer*) 'kɔntəmpleitiv] *adj*. **con'templatively** *adv*.

contemporary [kən'tempərəri] *adj* 1 living at, happening at or belonging to the same period: *That chair and the painting are contemporary – they both date from the seventeenth century.* 2 of the present time; modern: *contemporary art.* – *n* – *pl* **con'temporaries** – a person living at the same time: *She was one of my contemporaries at university.*

contempt [kən'tempt] n 1 very low opinion; scorn: *She spoke with utter contempt of her husband's behaviour.* 2 disregard for the law.

con'temptible *adj* deserving contempt: *His behaviour was contemptible.* **con'temptibly** *adv*.

con'temptuous [-tʃuəs] *adj* showing contempt: *a contemptuous sneer.* **con'temptuously** *adv*.

contend [kən'tend] v 1 (*usu with* **with**) to struggle against. 2 (*with* **that**) to say or maintain (that).

con'tender n a person who has entered a competition (for a title *etc*).

con'tention n 1 an opinion put forward. 2 argument; disagreement.

con'tentious [-ʃəs] *adj* quarrelsome.

content[1] [kən'tent] *adj* satisfied; quietly happy: *He doesn't want more money – he's content with what he has.* – n the state of being satisfied or quietly happy: *You're on holiday – you can lie in the sun to your heart's content.* – v to satisfy: *As the TV's broken, you'll have to content yourself with listening to the radio.*

con'tented *adj* satisfied; quietly happy: *a contented sigh.*

con'tentedly *adv*. **con'tentment** n.

content[2] ['kɔntent] n 1 the subject matter (of a book, speech etc): *the content of his speech.* 2 the amount of something contained: *Oranges have a high vitamin C content.*

'contents n pl 1 the things contained in something: *He drank the contents of the bottle.* 2 a list of the things contained *esp* in a book: *Look up the contents at the beginning of the book.*

contention, contentious *see* **contend**.

contest ['kɔntest] n a struggle, competition *etc* to gain an advantage or victory: *a sporting contest.*

con'testant n a person who takes part in a contest: *He is the youngest contestant in the swimming competition.*

context ['kɔntekst] n the parts directly before or after a word or phrase (written or spoken) which affect its meaning: *This statement, taken out of its context, gives a wrong impression of the speaker's opinions.*

continence *see* **continent**[2].

continent[1] ['kɔntinənt] n 1 one of the great divisions of the land surface of the world – Europe, America, Australia, Asia or Africa. 2 Europe excluding Britain: *We are going to the continent for our holidays.* **,conti'nental** [-'nen-] *adj*.

continental breakfast a light breakfast of rolls and coffee.

continent[2] ['kɔntinənt] *adj* able to control *esp* the bladder and/or bowel. **'continence** n.

contingent [kən'tindʒənt] n a number or group, *esp* of soldiers.

con'tingency – *pl* **con'tingencies** – n a chance happening: *We're prepared for all contingencies.*

continue [kən'tinju:] v 1 to go on being, doing *etc*; to last or keep on: *She continued to run*; *They continued running*; *He will continue in his present job*; *The noise continued for several hours*; *The road continues for 150 kilometres.* 2 to go on (with) often after a break or pause: *He continued his talk after the interval*; *This story is continued on p. 53.*

con'tinual *adj* very frequent; repeated many times: *continual interruptions.* **con'tinually** *adv*.

con,tinu'ation n 1 the act of continuing, often after a break or pause: *the continuation of his studies.* 2 something which carries on, *esp* a further part of a story *etc*: *This is a continuation of what he said last week.*

,conti'nuity [kɔn-] n 1 the state of being continuous or logically related: *It is important to children to have some continuity in their education.* 2 the detailed arrangement of the parts of a story *etc* for a film script *etc*. – *adj*: *a continuity girl.*

con'tinuous *adj* joined together, or going on, without interruption: *a continuous series*; *continuous rain*; *continuous movement.* **con'tinuously** *adv*: *It rained continuously all day.*

continual means frequent, again and again.
continuous means non-stop, without interruption.

contort [kən'tɔːt] v to twist or turn violently: *His face was contorted with pain.* **con'tortion** [-ʃən] n.

con'tortionist n an entertainer who contorts his body.

contour ['kɔntuə] n 1 an outline: *the contours of the coastline.* 2 (*also* **contour line**) on a map, a line joining points at the same height or depth.

contraband ['kɔntrəband] n goods which are

legally forbidden to be brought into a country. – *adj*: *contraband cigarettes*.

contraception [kontrə'sepʃən] *n* the prevention of conceiving children; birth-control. **,contra'ceptive** [-tiv] *n* (a pill *etc*) preventing pregnancy.

contract [kən'trakt] *v* **1** to make or become smaller, less, shorter, tighter *etc*: *Metals expand when heated and contract when cooled*; *'I am' is often contracted to 'I'm'*; *Muscles contract*. **2** [*Amer* 'kontrakt] to promise legally in writing: *They contracted to supply us with cable*. **3** to become infected with (a disease): *He contracted malaria*. **4** to promise (in marriage). – ['kontrakt] *n* a legal written agreement: *He has a four-year contract* (*of employment*) *with us*; *The firm won a contract for three new aircraft*. **con'traction** [-ʃən] *n* **1** an act of contracting: *contraction of metals*; *contraction of muscles*. **2** a word shortened in speech or spelling: *'I'm' is a contraction of 'I am'*. **con'tractor** *n* a person or firm that promises to do work or supply goods at a fixed rate: *a building contractor*.

contradict [kontrə'dikt] *v* to say the opposite of; to argue or disagree with: *It's unwise to contradict your boss*. **,contra'diction** [-ʃən] *n*. **,contra'dictory** *adj*.

contraption [kən'trapʃən] *n* a strange machine or apparatus: *He tried to fly over the Atlantic in a home-made contraption*.

contrary¹ ['kontrəri] *adj* (*often with* **to**) opposite (to) or in disagreement (with): *That decision was contrary to my wishes*; *Contrary to popular belief he is an able politician*. – *n* (*with* **the**) the opposite.
on the contrary the very opposite (is true): *'Are you busy?' 'No, on the contrary, I'm out of work.'*

contrary² [kən'treəri] *adj* obstinate; unreasonable. **con'trariness** *n*.

contrast [kən'tra:st] *v* **1** to show marked difference from: *His words contrast with his actions*. **2** to compare so as to show differences: *Contrast fresh and frozen vegetables and you'll find the fresh ones taste better*. – ['kontra:st] *n* **1** difference(s) in things or people that are compared: *The contrast between their attitudes is very marked*. **2** a thing or person that shows a marked difference (to another): *She's a complete contrast to her sister*.

contravene [kontrə'vi:n] *v* to go against or break (a law, principle *etc*). **,contra'vention** [-'venʃən] *n*.

contribute [kən'tribjut] *v* **1** to give (money, help *etc*) along with others: *Have you contributed* (*any money*) *to this charity?*; *I've been contributing* (*articles*) *to this paper for many years*. **2** (*with* **to**) to help to cause to

happen: *His gambling contributed to his downfall*.
,contri'bution [kon-] *n* **1** the act of contributing. **2** something contributed, *esp* money: *Would you like to make a contribution to this charity?*
con'tributor *n*.

contrite ['kontrait] *adj* deeply sorry for something one has done. **'contriteness, contrition** [kən'triʃən] *n*.

contrive [kən'traiv] *v* **1** to manage (to do something): *He contrived to remove the money from her bag*. **2** to make in a clever way: *He contrived a tent from an old sack*. **con'trivance** *n* **1** the act of contriving. **2** something contrived (*esp* something mechanical): *a contrivance for making the door open automatically*.

control [kən'troul] *n* **1** the right of directing or of giving orders; power or authority: *She has control over all the decisions in that department*; *She has no control over that dog*. **2** the act of holding back or restraining: *control of prices*; *I know you're angry but you must not lose control* (*of yourself*). **3** (*often in pl*) a lever, button *etc* which operates (a machine *etc*): *The clutch and accelerator are foot controls*. **4** a point or place at which an inspection takes place: *passport control*. – *v* – *pt*, *ptp* **con'trolled** – **1** to direct or guide; to have power or authority over: *The captain controls the whole ship*; *Control your dog!* **2** to hold back; to restrain (oneself or one's emotions *etc*): *Control yourself!* **3** to keep to a fixed standard: *The government is controlling prices*.
con'troller *n* a person or thing that controls: *an air-traffic controller*.
con'trol-tower *n* a building at an airport from which take-off and landing instructions are given.
in control (**of**) in charge (of): *She is very much in control* (*of the situation*).
out of control not under the authority or power of someone: *The brakes failed and the car went out of control*; *Those children are completely out of control* (= wild and disobedient).
under control: *Keep your dog under control!*; *Everything's under control now*.

controversy [kən'trovəsi, 'kontrəvə:si] – *pl* **controversies** – *n* (an) argument between opposing points of view: *the controversy over the appointment of the new chairman*.
controversial [kontrə'və:ʃəl] *adj* causing controversy: *His new book is very controversial*. **,contro'versially** *adv*.

convalesce [konvə'les] *v* to recover health and strength after an illness: *He is convalescing in the country*.
,conva'lescent *n* a person who is recovering

from an illness: *Convalescents often need a special diet.* – *adj* **1** recovering health and strength after illness. **2** for convalescents: *a convalescent home.*
,conva'lescence *n.*

convection [kən'vekʃən] *n* the passing of heat through liquids or gases by means of currents.

convene [kən'viːn] *v* to (cause to) assemble or come together: *to convene a meeting.* con'vener.

convenient [kən'viːnjənt] *adj* **1** suitable; not causing trouble or difficulty: *When would it be convenient for me to come?* **2** easy to use, run *etc*: *a convenient size of house.* **3** easy to reach *etc*; accessible: *Keep this in a convenient place.* con'veniently *adv.*
con'venience *n* **1** the state or quality of being convenient; freedom from trouble or difficulty: *the convenience of living near the office.* **2** any means of giving ease or comfort: *the conveniences of modern life.* **3** (*also* public convenience) a public lavatory.

convent ['konvənt, (*Amer*) -vent] *n* a building in which nuns live.
convent school one run by nuns.

convention [kən'venʃən] *n* **1** a way of behaving that has become usual; (an) established custom: *Shaking hands when meeting people is a normal convention in many countries*; *He does not care about convention.* **2** in the US, a meeting of delegates from a political party for nominating a presidential candidate. **3** an assembly of people of a particular profession *etc*.
con'ventional *adj* (*neg* un-) according to the accepted standards *etc*; not outrageous or eccentric: *conventional dress*; *the more conventional forms of art.* con,ventio'nality [-'na-] *n.*

converge [kən'vɜːdʒ] *v* to (cause to) move towards or meet at one point: *The roads converge in the centre of town.* con'vergence *n.* con'vergent *adj.*

conversation [konvə'seiʃən] *n* talk between people: *to carry on a conversation .*
,conver'sational *adj* **1** informal or colloquial: *conversational English.* **2** fond of talking: *He's in a conversational mood.*

converse[1] [kən'vɜːs] *v* to talk: *It is difficult to converse with people who do not speak your language.*

converse[2] ['konvɜːs] *n* the opposite; the contrary.
conversely [kon'vɜːsli] *adv.*

conversion [kən'vɜːʃən, (*Amer*) -ʒən] *n* the act of converting: *his conversion to Christianity*; *the conversion of the house into a hotel.*

convert [kən'vɜːt] *v* **1** to change from one thing into another: *He has converted his house into four separate flats*; *This sofa converts into a bed.* **2** to change from one

religion *etc* to another: *He was converted to Christianity.* – ['konvɜːt] *n* a person who has been converted to a particular religion *etc*: *a convert to Buddhism.*

con'vertible *adj* that may or can be converted: *a convertible sofa.* – *n* a car with a folding or detachable top. con,verti'bility *n.*

convex ['konveks] *adj* (of an object or surface) curved outwards, like the surface of the eye: *a convex lens.* con'vexity *n.*

convey [kən'vei] *v* **1** to carry: *Huge ships convey oil from the Middle East.* **2** to transfer the ownership of (property by legal means).
con'veyance *n* **1** the act of conveying: *the conveyance of goods.* **2** a vehicle of any kind: *A bus is a public conveyance.*
con'veyancing *n* the branch of the law dealing with transfer of property.
con'veyor *n* a person or thing that conveys.
conveyor belt an endless, moving belt carrying articles from one place to another in a factory *etc*: *She put nuts on the chocolates as they went down the conveyor belt.*

convict [kən'vikt] *v* to prove or declare (someone) guilty: *She was convicted of theft.* – ['konvikt] *n* a person serving a sentence for a crime: *Two of the convicts have escaped from prison.*
con'viction [-ʃən] *n* **1** the passing of a sentence on a guilty person: *She has had two convictions for drunken driving.* **2** (a) strong belief: *It's my conviction that he's right.*

convince [kən'vins] *v* to persuade (a person) that something is true: *Her smile convinced me that she was happy*; *She is convinced of his innocence.*
con'vincing *adj* (*neg* un-) having the power to convince: *a convincing argument.*

convivial [kən'viviəl] *adj* pleasantly sociable and friendly. con'vivially *adv.* con,vivi'ality [-'a-] *n.*

convoy ['konvoi] *n* **1** a group of ships, lorries, cars *etc* travelling together: *an army convoy.* **2** a fleet of merchant ships escorted for safety by warships.

convulse [kən'vʌls] *v* to shake violently: *convulsed with laughter.* con'vulsive [-siv] *adj.* con'vulsively *adv.*
con'vulsion [-ʃən] *n* (*often in pl*) a sudden stiffening or jerking of the muscles of the body.

cook [kuk] *v* to prepare (food) or become ready by heating: *She cooked the chicken*; *The chicken is cooking in the oven.* – *n* a person who cooks, *esp* for a living: *She was employed as a cook at the embassy.*
'cooker *n* **1** an apparatus on which food is cooked: *She has an electric cooker.* **2** an apple *etc* used in cooking, not for eating raw.
'cookery *n* the art or practice of cooking

food: *She was taught cookery at school*; (*also adj*) *cookery classes*.
'**cookery-book** *n* (*Amer* '**cook-book**) a book of instructions on how to prepare and cook various dishes.
cook up to invent or make up a false story *etc*: *He cooked up a story about his car having broken down*.
cookie ['kuki] *n* (*Amer*) a biscuit.
cool [ku:l] *adj* **1** slightly cold: *cool weather*. **2** calm or not excitable: *He's very cool in a crisis*. **3** not very friendly: *He was very cool towards me*. – *v* **1** to make or become less warm: *The jelly will cool better in the refrigerator*; *She cooled her hands in the stream*. **2** to become less strong: *His affection for her has cooled*; *Her anger cooled*. – *n* cool air or atmosphere: *the cool of the evening*.
'**coolly** *adv*. '**coolness** *n*.
cool-'headed *adj* able to act calmly.
cool down 1 to make or become less warm: *Let your food cool down a bit!* **2** to make or become less excited or less emotional: *He was very angry but he's cooled down now*.
keep one's cool not to become over-excited or confused: *If you keep your cool you won't fail*.
lose one's cool not to keep one's cool.
coolie ['ku:li] *n* an Indian or Chinese labourer.
coop [ku:p] *n* a box or cage for keeping fowls or small animals in: *a chicken-coop*.
coop up to shut into a small place: *We've been cooped up in this tiny room for hours*.
co-operate [kou'opəreit] *v* to work together: *They have promised to co-operate* (*with us*) *in the planning of the exhibition*.
co-ope'ration *n* **1** the act of working together. **2** willingness to act or work together: *I would be grateful for your co-operation*.
co-'operative [-tiv] *adj*: *a helpful and co-operative pupil*.
co-ordinate [kou'o:dineit] *v* to adjust (a movement or action) so that it fits in or works smoothly (with other movements or actions): *In swimming the movement of one's arms and legs must be co-ordinated*.
co-ordi'nation *n*.
cop [kop] *n* a slang abbreviation of **copper²**.
cope [koup] *v* to manage; to deal with successfully: *I can't cope with all this work*.
copious ['koupiəs] *adj* plentiful: *a copious supply*. '**copiously** *adv*. '**copiousness** *n*.
copper¹ ['kopə] *n* **1** an element, a metal of a brownish-red colour: *This pipe is made of copper*. **2** (a piece of) money made of copper or a substitute: *Have you any coppers in your change?* – *adj* **1** made of copper: *a copper pipe*. **2** (*also* '**copper-coloured**) of the colour of copper.
copper² ['kopə] *n* a British nickname for a policeman: *Run – there's a copper after you!*

copra ['koprə, (*Amer*) 'kou-] *n* the dried kernel of the coconut which gives coconut oil.
copy ['kopi] – *pl* '**copies** – *n* **1** an imitation or reproduction of: *That dress is a copy of one I saw at a Paris fashion show*; *He made eight copies of the pamphlet on the photocopier*. **2** a single book, newspaper *etc*: *Can I have six copies of this dictionary, please?* **3** written or typed material for publishing: *He writes copy for advertisements*. – *v* to make an imitation or reproduction of (something): *Copy the way I speak*; *Copy this passage into your notebook*.
'**copier** *n* a photocopier.
'**copyright** *n* (*usu abbrev* ©) the sole right to reproduce a literary, dramatic, musical or artistic work, and also to perform, translate, film, or record such a work.
coral ['korəl] *n, adj* **1** (of) a hard substance of various colours, made up of skeletons of a kind of tiny animal: *a necklace made of coral*; *a coral reef*. **2** (of) an orange-pink colour.
cord [ko:d] *n* **1** (a piece of) thin rope or thick string: *The burglars tied up the nightwatchman with thick cord*. **2** a string-like part of the body: *the spinal cord*; *the vocal cords*. **3** a length of electric cable or flex attached to an electrical appliance: *the cord of his electric razor*. **4** a kind of velvet fabric with a ribbed appearance; (*in pl*) trousers made of this: *a pair of cords*.
cordial ['ko:diəl, (*Amer*) 'ko:rdʒl] *adj* (of greetings *etc*) warm and affectionate: *a cordial welcome*. – *n* a refreshing drink: *lime juice cordial*.
,**cordi'ality** [-'a-] *n*. '**cordially** *adv*.
cordon ['ko:dn] *n* a line of sentries or policemen to prevent people from entering an area: *They've put a cordon round the house where the bomb is planted*.
cordon off to enclose with a cordon: *The police cordoned off the area where the gunman was*.
core [ko:] *n* the innermost part of something, *esp* fruit: *an apple-core*; *the core of the earth*. – *v* to take out the core of (fruit): *Core the apples*.
cork [ko:k] *n* **1** the outer bark of the cork tree (an oak of S Europe, N Africa *etc*): *Cork floats well*; (*also adj*) *cork floor-tiles*. **2** a stopper for a bottle *etc* made of cork: *Put the cork back in the wine-bottle*. – *v* to put a cork or stopper in: *He corked the bottle*.
'**corkscrew** *n* a tool with a screw-like spike, used for drawing corks from bottles.
corn¹ [ko:n] *n* **1** the seeds of cereal plants, *esp* (in Britain) wheat, or (in N America) maize. **2** (*Amer* **grain**) the plants themselves: *a field of corn*.

corned beef salted beef (*usu* cooked and canned).

'cornflour *n* finely ground (*esp* maize) flour.

'cornflower *n* a blue-flowered plant.

corn² [ko:n] *n* a little bump of hard skin found on the foot: *I have a corn on my little toe.*

cornea ['ko:niə] *n* the transparent covering of the eyeball.

corner ['ko:nə] *n* **1** a point where two lines, walls, roads *etc* meet: *the corners of a cube*; *the corner of the street.* **2** a place, *usu* a small quiet place: *a secluded corner.* **3** in football, a free kick from the corner of the field: *We've been awarded a corner.* – *v* **1** to force (a person or animal) into a place from which it is difficult to escape: *The thief was cornered in an alley.* **2** to turn a corner: *He cornered on only three wheels*; *This car corners very well.*

'cornered *adj* **1** having (a given number of) corners: *a three-cornered hat.* **2** forced into a position from which it is difficult to escape: *A cornered animal can be very dangerous.*

cut corners to use less money, effort, time *etc* when doing something than was thought necessary, often giving a poorer result.

turn the corner 1 to go round a corner. **2** to get past a difficulty or danger: *He was very ill but he's turned the corner now.*

cornet ['ko:nit, (*Amer*) ko:r'net] *n* **1** a brass musical instrument similar to the trumpet. **2** a cone-shaped wafer biscuit for holding ice-cream: *an ice-cream cornet.*

cornflour, cornflower *see* corn¹.

corny ['ko:ni] *adj* not original or interesting: *a corny joke.*

coronary ['korənəri] *adj* (of arteries) supplying blood to the heart. – *n* – *pl* **'coronaries** – an attack of coronary thrombosis.

coronary thrombosis a heart disease caused by blockage of one of the coronary arteries.

coronation [korə'neiʃən] *n* the act or ceremony of crowning a king or queen.

coroner ['korənə] *n* an official who inquires into the causes of accidental or sudden, unexpected deaths.

coronet ['korənit] *n* **1** a small crown. **2** an ornamental headdress: *a coronet of flowers.*

corporal¹ ['ko:pərəl] *n* (often abbrev **Corp.** when written) (a person of) the rank below sergeant.

corporal² ['ko:pərəl] *adj* of the body: *The headmaster disapproves of caning and all other forms of corporal punishment.*

corporate ['ko:pərət] *adj* united: *corporate effort.*

,corpo'ration *n* a body of people acting as one individual *eg* for administration or business purposes: *the British Broadcasting Corporation.*

corps [ko:] – *pl* **corps** [ko:z] *n* **1** a division of an army: *The Royal Armoured Corps.* **2** a group or company: *the diplomatic corps.*

corpse [ko:ps] *n* a dead body, *esp* of a human being: *Don't move the corpse before you send for the police.*

corpulent ['ko:pjulənt] *adj* fat: *a corpulent old man.* **'corpulence** *n.*

corpuscle ['ko:pʌsl] *n* one of the red or white cells in the blood.

correct [kə'rekt] *v* **1** to remove faults and errors from: *These spectacles will correct his eye defect.* **2** (of a teacher *etc*) to mark errors in: *I have fourteen exercise books to correct.* – *adj* **1** free from faults or errors: *This sum is correct.* **2** right; not wrong: *Did I get the correct idea from what you said?*; *You are quite correct.* **cor'rection** [-ʃən] *n.*

cor'rective [-tiv] *adj* setting right: *corrective treatment.*

cor'rectly *adv.*

cor'rectness *n.*

correspond [korə'spond] *v* **1** (*with* **to**) to be similar; to match: *A bird's wing corresponds to the arm and hand in humans.* **2** (*with* **with**) to be in agreement with; to match. **3** to communicate by letter (with): *Do they often correspond (with each other)?*

,corre'spondence *n* **1** agreement; similarity or likeness. **2** (communication by) letters: *I must deal with that (big pile of) correspondence.*

,corre'spondent *n* **1** a person with whom one exchanges letters: *He has correspondents all over the world.* **2** a person who contributes news to a newspaper *etc*: *He's foreign correspondent for 'The Times'.*

,corre'sponding *adj* similar, matching: *The rainfall this month is not as high as for the corresponding month last year.*

correspondence course a course of lessons by post: *a correspondence course in accountancy.*

corridor ['korido:] *n* a passageway, *esp* one off which rooms open: *Go along the corridor and up the stairs.*

corroborate [kə'robəreit] *v* to support or confirm (evidence *etc* already given): *She corroborated her sister's story.* **cor,robo'ration** *n.* **cor'roborative** [-rətiv] *adj.*

corrode [kə'roud] *v* to destroy or eat away (as rust, chemicals *etc* do). **cor'rosion** [-ʒən] *n.* **cor'rosive** [-siv] *adj* tending to corrode.

corrugated ['korəgeitid] *adj* shaped into ridges: *corrugated iron.*

corrupt [kə'rʌpt] *v* to make or become evil or bad: *He was corrupted by the bad influence of two friends.* – *adj* **1** bad or evil: *The*

government is corrupt. **2** impure: *a corrupt form of English.*
cor'ruptible *adj.* **cor,rupti'bility** *n.*
cor'ruption [-ʃən] *n* **1** the act of corrupting. **2** a word that has changed considerably from its original form: *Caterpillar is probably a corruption of the Old French word 'chatepelose' meaning 'hairy cat'.*
corset ['kɔːsit] *n* a close-fitting stiff undergarment to support the body.
cortège [kɔː'teʒ] *n* a procession, *esp* at a funeral.
cosily, cosiness *see* **cosy.**
cosmetic [koz'metik] *adj* designed to increase the beauty and hide the defects of something, *esp* the face: *She had cosmetic surgery to improve the shape of her nose.* – *n* a preparation for this purpose: *She's quite pretty – she does not need to wear so many cosmetics* (= lipstick, eye-shadow *etc*).
cosmic ['kozmik] *adj* having to do with the universe or outer space: *cosmic rays.*
'cosmonaut [-nɔːt] *n* a person who travels in space; an astronaut.
the cosmos ['kozmos, (*Amer*) -məs] *n* the universe.
cosmopolitan [kozmə'politən] *adj* belonging to all parts of the world: *The population of London is very cosmopolitan.*
cosmos *see* **cosmic.**
cosset ['kosit] – *pt, ptp* **'cosseted** – *v* to treat with too much kindness; to pamper.
cost [kost] – *pt, ptp* **cost** – *v* **1** to be obtainable at a certain price: *This jacket costs 75 dollars; The victory cost two thousand lives.* **2** (*pt, ptp* **'costed**) to estimate the cost of (a future project). – *n* the price to be paid (for something): *What is the cost of this coat?*
'costly *adj* costing much: *a costly wedding-dress.* **'costliness** *n.*
costs *n pl* the expenses of a legal case: *He won his case and was awarded costs of $500.*
at all costs no matter what the cost or outcome may be: *We must prevent disaster at all costs.*
costume ['kostjuːm] *n* **1** an outfit, *esp* for a particular purpose: *swimming-costume.* **2** dress, clothes: *eighteenth-century costume.*
cosy, (*Amer*) cozy ['kouzi] *adj* warm and comfortable: *a cosy chat; a cosy armchair.* – *n* a covering for a teapot (**'tea-cosy**) or for an egg (**'egg-cosy**), to keep it warm.
'cosily *adv.* **'cosiness** *n.*
cot [kot] *n* **1** (*Amer* **crib**) a small bed with high sides for a child *etc*: *One of the wooden rails of the cot is broken.* **2** (*Amer*) a camp bed.
cottage ['kotidʒ] *n* a small house, *esp* in the country or in a village: *a holiday cottage in Devon.*
cotton¹ ['kotn] *n* **1** a soft substance got from

the seeds of the cotton plant, used in making thread or cloth. **2** the yarn or cloth made from this: *a reel of cotton; This shirt is made of cotton;* (*also adj*) *a cotton shirt.*
cotton candy (*Amer*) candy floss.
,cotton'wool *n* (*Amer* **absorbent cotton**) loose cotton pressed into a mass, for absorbing liquids, wiping or protecting an injury *etc*: *She bathed the wound with cotton wool.*
cotton² ['kotn] : **cotton on** *v* to understand: *He'll soon cotton on* (*to what you mean*).
couch¹ [kautʃ] *n* a type of sofa for sitting or lying on: *The doctor asked him to lie on the couch.*
couch² [kautʃ] *v* to express (in words): *He couched his reply in vague terms.*
cougar ['kuːgə] *n* (*esp Amer*) a puma.
cough [kof] *v* to make a harsh sound when bringing air or harmful matter form the lungs or throat: *He's coughing badly because he has a cold.* – *n* **1** an act of coughing: *He gave a cough.* **2** an illness causing coughing: *a smoker's cough.*
'cough-mixture *n* a medicine used for relieving coughing.
cough up a slang expression for to pay: *It's time you coughed up* (*the money I lent you*).
could [kud] – *neg short form* **couldn't** ['kudnt] – *v* **1** *pt of* **can**: *They asked if I could drive a car; I said I couldn't; She asked if she could go.* **2** used to express a possibility: *I could go but I'm not going to; I could do it next week if you helped me.*
could have used to express a possibility in the past: *We could have gone, but we didn't.*
council ['kaunsəl] *n* **1** a group of people formed in order to advise *etc*: *The King formed a council of wise men; the Council for Recreation.* **2** in the UK, a body of people elected to control the workings of local government in a county, region, district *etc.*
'councillor *n* a person who is elected to serve on a council.
counsel ['kaunsəl] *n* **1** advice: *He'll give you good counsel on your problems.* **2** a barrister or advocate: *counsel for the defence.* – *v* – *pt, ptp* – **'counselled, (*Amer*) 'counseled** – to advise; to recommend.
'counsellor, (*Amer*) counselor *n* a person who gives advice.
count¹ [kaunt] *n* nobleman in certain countries, equal in rank to a British earl.
'countess *n* **1** the wife or widow of an earl or count. **2** a woman of the same rank as an earl or count in her own right.
count² [kaunt] *v* **1** to name the numbers up to: *Count* (*up to*) *ten.* **2** to calculate using numbers: *Count* (*up*) *the number of pages; Count how many people there are; There were six people present, not counting the chairman.* **3** to be important or have an

effect or value: *What he says doesn't count*; *All these essays count towards my final mark.* **4** to consider: *Count yourself lucky to be here.* – *n* **1** an act of numbering: *They took a count of how many people attended.* **2** a charge brought against a prisoner *etc*: *She faces three counts of theft.* – *adj see* **countable**.

'countable *adj* **1** capable of being numbered: *Millionths of a second are countable only on very complicated instruments.* **2** (*neg* **un-**: *also* **count**) (of a noun) capable of forming a plural and using the definite or indefinite article: *Table is a count(able) noun, but milk is an uncountable noun.*

'counter¹ *n* a token used in numbering or playing certain games; *counters for playing ludo etc.*

'countless *adj* very many: *Countless pebbles.*

'countdown *n* (used *orig* of a rocket) a counting backwards to check the time remaining until the beginning of an event, regarded as zero: *It's five minutes to countdown.*

count on to rely on (a person or happening): *I'm counting on you to persuade her.*

out for the count 1 (of a boxer) still not standing after the count of ten. **2** exhausted; asleep: *He was out for the count for several hours after his long walk.*

countenance ['kauntinəns] *n* the face. – *v* to encourage or accept: *We can't possibly countenance the spending of so much money.*

counter¹ *see* **count²**.

counter² ['kauntə] *adv* (with **to**) in the opposite direction or manner to: *The election is running counter to the forecasts.* – *v* to meet or answer (a stroke or move *etc* by another): *He successfully countered all criticisms.*

counter- against or opposite: *counterclockwise.*

counter³ ['kauntə] *n* a kind of table or surface on which goods are laid: *Can you get me some sweets from the confectionery counter?*

counteract [kauntər'akt] *v* to undo or prevent the effect of: *the government's efforts to counteract inflation.* **,counter'action** *n*.

counter-attack ['kauntərətak] *n* an attack in reply to an attack: *The enemy made a counter-attack.* – *v* to make such an attack (on): *Our troops counter-attacked.*

counterfeit ['kauntəfit] *adj* **1** copied or made in imitation *esp* with a dishonest purpose: *counterfeit money.* **2** not genuine or not real. – *v* **1** to make a copy of for dishonest purposes: *to counterfeit banknotes.* **2** to pretend: *She counterfeited friendship.*

counterfoil ['kauntəfoil] *n* a section able to be detached or removed from a cheque *etc* and kept by the giver as a receipt.

counterpane ['kauntəpein] *n* a top cover for a bed.

counterpart ['kauntəpa:t] *n* a person or thing equivalent to another in position *etc*: *American teenagers and their British counterparts.*

countess *see* **count¹**.

country ['kʌntri] – *pl* **'countries** – *n* **1** any of the nations of the world; the land occupied by a nation: *Canada is a larger country than Spain.* **2** the people of a country: *The whole country is in agreement with your views.* **3** (*usu with* **the**) districts where there are fields, moors *etc* as opposed to towns and areas with many buildings: *a quiet holiday in the country*; (*also adj*) *country districts.* **4** an area or stretch of land: *hilly country.*

country dance a (style of) dance in which partners are arranged in parallel lines.

'countryman – *fem* **'countrywoman** – *n* a person born in the same country as another: *Churchill and Chamberlain were fellow countrymen.*

'countryside *n* country areas: *the English countryside.*

county ['kaunti] – *pl* **'counties** – *n* a large administrative unit of local government in England and Wales and in the US.

coup [ku:] *n* **1** a sudden successful action: *He achieved a real coup by completing this deal.* **2** a coup d'état: *There's been a coup in one of the African republics.*

coup d'état [ku:dei'ta:] – *pl* **coups d'état** [ku:dei-] – a sudden and violent change in government: *The president was killed during the coup d'état.*

coupé ['ku:pei, (*Amer*) ku:'pei] *n* a two-door car with a fixed roof.

couple ['kʌpl] *n* **1** two; a few: *Can I borrow a couple of chairs?*; *I knew a couple of people at the party, but not many.* **2** a man and wife, or a boyfriend and girlfriend: *a married couple*; *The young couple have a child.* – *v* to join together: *The coaches were coupled (together), and the train set off.*

'couplet [-lit] *n* two lines of verse, one following the other, which rhyme with each other.

'coupling *n* a link for joining things together: *The railway carriage was damaged when the coupling broke.*

coupon ['ku:pon] *n* **1** a piece of paper *etc* giving one the right to something, *eg* a gift or discount price: *This coupon gives 50 cents off your next purchase.* **2** a betting form for the football pools.

courage ['kʌridʒ, (*Amer*) 'kɔ:-] *n* the quality that makes a person able to meet dangers without fear; bravery: *It took courage to sail the Atlantic singlehanded.*

courageous [kə'reidʒəs] *adj* having courage: *a courageous soldier.* **cou'rageously** *adv*.

courier ['kuriə] *n* 1 a guide who travels with, and looks after, parties of tourists: *a courier on a coach trip.* 2 a messenger.

course [kɔːs] *n* 1 a series (of lectures, medicines *etc*): *I'm taking a course (of lectures) in sociology*; *He's having a course of treatment for his leg.* 2 a division or part of a meal: *Now we've had the soup, what's (for) the next course?* 3 the ground over which a race is run or a game (*esp* golf) is played: *a racecourse*; *a golf-course.* 4 the path or direction in which something moves: *the course of the Nile.* 5 the progress or development of events: *Things will run their normal course despite the strike.* 6 a way (of action): *What's the best course of action in the circumstances?*
in the course of during: *In the course of our talk, he told me about the accident.*
in due course at the appropriate or normal time: *In due course, this seed will grow into a tree.*
of course naturally or obviously: *Of course, he didn't tell me any secrets*; *Of course I can swim.*
off, on course (not) heading in the right direction: *to drift off course*; *We're back on course.*

court [kɔːt] *n* 1 a place where legal cases are heard: *a magistrates' court*; *the High Court.* 2 the judges and officials of a legal court: *The accused is to appear before the court on Friday.* 3 a marked-out space for certain games: *a tennis-court*; *a squash court.* 4 the officials, councillors *etc* of a king or queen: *the court of King James.* 5 the palace of a king or queen: *Hampton Court.* 6 an open space surrounded by houses or by the parts of one house. – *v* 1 to try to win the love of; to woo. 2 to try to gain (admiration *etc*). 3 to seem to be deliberately risking (disaster *etc*).
'**courtier** [-tiə] *n* a member of the court of a king or queen: *He was one of King James' courtiers.*
'**courtly** *adj* having fine manners. '**courtliness** *n*.
'**courtship** *n* courting or wooing.
'**courthouse** *n* a building where legal cases are held.
,**court-'martial** – *pl* ,**courts-'martial** – *n* a court held by officers of the armed forces to try offences against discipline.
'**courtyard** *n* a court or enclosed ground beside, or surrounded by, a building: *the courtyard of the castle.*

courteous ['kɔːtiəs] *adj* polite; considerate and respectful: *It was courteous of him to write a letter of thanks.* '**courteously** *adv*.
'**courteousness** *n*.

courtesy ['kɔːtəsi] *n* 1 politeness; considerate and respectful behaviour: *Everyone appreciates courtesy.*

courtier *see* **court.**

cousin ['kʌzn] *n* a son or daughter of one's uncle or aunt.
first/full cousin a son or daughter of one's uncle or aunt.
second cousin a child of one's parent's first cousin.

cove [kouv] *n* a small bay or inlet of the sea: *They bathed in a quiet cove.*

covenant ['kʌvənənt] *n* an agreement between two people or two parties to do, or not to do, something: *She signed a covenant to give money to the school fund.*

cover ['kʌvə] *v* 1 to put or spread something on, over or in front of: *They covered (up) the body with a sheet*; *My shoes are covered in paint.* 2 to be enough to pay for: *Will 10 dollars cover your expenses?* 3 to travel: *We covered forty miles in one day.* 4 to stretch over a length of time *etc*: *His diary covered three years.* 5 to protect: *Are we covered by your car insurance?* 6 to report on: *I'm covering the race for the local newspaper.* 7 to point a gun at: *I had him covered.* – *n* 1 something which covers, *esp* a cloth over a table, bed *etc*: *a table-cover*; *a bed-cover*; *They replaced the cover on the manhole.* 2 something that gives protection or shelter: *The soldiers took cover from the enemy gunfire*; *insurance cover.* 3 something that hides: *He escaped under cover of darkness.*
'**coverage** [-ridʒ] *n* 1 the amount of protection given by insurance: *insurance coverage.* 2 the extent of the inclusion of items in a news report *etc*: *The TV coverage of the Olympic Games was extensive.*
'**covering** *n*: *My car has a covering of dirt.*
'**cover-girl** *n* a girl pictured on a magazine cover.
'**cover-up** *n* an attempt to hide or conceal (something illegal or dishonest).

coverlet ['kʌvəlit] *n* a top cover for a bed.

covet ['kʌvit] – *pt, ptp* '**coveted** – *v* to desire or wish for eagerly (*esp* something belonging to someone else): *I coveted her fur coat.*
'**covetous** *adj*. '**covetously** *adv*.
'**covetousness** *n*.

cow[1] [kau] *n* 1 the female of cattle used for giving milk: *He has ten cows and a bull.* 2 the female of certain other animals *eg* the elephant, whale.
'**cowboy** *n* in the US, a man who looks after cattle on a ranch.
'**cowherd** *n* a person who looks after cows.
'**cowhide** *n, adj* (of) the skin of a cow made into leather: *a bag made of cowhide*; *a cowhide bag.*

cow[2] [kau] *v* to subdue or frighten: *She looked slightly cowed after her interview with the headmaster.*

coward ['kauəd] *n* a person who shows fear easily or is easily frightened: *I am such a coward — I hate going to the dentist.* '**cowardly** *adj*. '**cowardice** [-dis], '**cowardliness** *ns*.

cower ['kauə] *v* to draw back and crouch in fear: *He was cowering away from the fierce dog.*

cowl [kaul] *n* (a cap or hood like) a monk's hood.

coxswain ['koksn] *n* **1** (*often abbrev* **cox** [koks]) a person who steers a (small, *usu* racing) boat. **2** a petty officer in charge of a boat and crew.

coy [koi] *adj* (pretending to be) shy: *She gave her brother's friend a coy smile.* '**coyly** *adv*. '**coyness** n.

cozy *see* **cosy.**

crab [krab] *n* an edible sea animal with a shell and five pairs of legs, the first pair having claws.

crack [krak] *v* **1** to (cause to) break partly without falling to pieces: *The window cracked down the middle.* **2** to break (open): *He cracked the peanuts between his finger and thumb.* **3** to make a sudden sharp sound of breaking: *The twig cracked as I stood on it.* **4** to make (a joke): *He's always cracking jokes.* **5** to open (a safe) by illegal means. **6** to solve (a code). **7** to give in to torture or similar pressures: *The spy finally cracked under their questioning and told them everything he knew.* – *n* **1** a split or break: *There's a crack in this cup.* **2** a narrow opening: *The door opened a crack.* **3** a sudden sharp sound: *the crack of whip.* **4** a blow: *a crack on the jaw.* **5** a joke: *He made a crack about my big feet.* – *adj* expert: *a crack racing-driver.*

cracked *adj* **1** damaged by cracks: *a cracked cup.* **2** crazy: *She must be cracked!*

'**cracker** *n* **1** a thin crisp biscuit. **2** a small exploding firework: *fire crackers.* **3** a decorated paper tube, containing paper hats *etc*, which gives a loud crack when pulled apart. '**crackers** *adj* crazy: *You must be crackers to believe that!*

get cracking to get moving quickly.

have a crack (at) to have a try at.

crackle ['krakl] *v* to make a continuous cracking noise: *The dry branches crackled under my feet.* – *n*: *the crackle of burning wood.* '**crackling** *n* the crisp rind of roast pork. '**crackly** *adj*: *The radio reception is very crackly here.*

cradle ['kreidl] *n* **1** a child's bed *esp* one in which it can be rocked. **2** a frame of similar shape, *eg* one under a ship that is being built or repaired. – *v* to hold or rock as if in a cradle: *She cradled the child in her arms.*

craft [kra:ft] *n* **1** an art or skill: *the craft of wood-carving.* **2** (*pl* **craft**) a boat or ship:

sailing craft. **3** cunning or trickery: *craft and deceit.*

'**crafty** *adj* cunning and sly. '**craftily** *adv*. '**craftiness** *n*.

'**craftsman** ['kra:ftsmən] *n* a person who is skilled at making things (*esp* by hand). '**craftsmanship** ['kra:fts-] *n*.

crag [krag] *n* a rough, steep mountain or rock.

'**craggy** *adj* rocky; rugged, irregular.

cram [kram] – *pt, ptp* **crammed** – *v* **1** to fill very full: *The drawer was crammed with papers.* **2** to push or force: *He crammed food into his mouth.* **3** to prepare (someone) in a short time for an examination: *He is being crammed for his university entrance exam.*

cramp [kramp] *n* (a) painful stiffening of the muscles: *The swimmer got cramp and drowned.* – *v* **1** to put into too small a space: *We were all cramped together in a tiny room.* **2** to restrict; *Lack of money cramped our efforts.*

crane [krein] *n* a machine with a long arm and a chain, for raising heavy weights. – *v* to stretch out (the neck, to see round or over something): *He craned his neck in order to see round the corner.*

'**crane-driver** *n* a person operating a crane.

crank [kraŋk] *n* a person with strange or odd ideas. '**cranky** *adj*. '**crankiness** *n*.

cranny *see* **nook.**

crash [kraʃ] *n* **1** a noise as of heavy things breaking or falling on something hard: *I heard a crash, and looked round to see that he'd dropped all the plates.* **2** a collision: *There was a crash involving three cars.* **3** a failure of a business *etc*: *the Wall Street crash.* – *v* **1** to (cause to) fall with a loud noise: *The glass crashed to the floor.* **2** to drive or be driven violently (against, into): *He crashed (his car); His car crashed into a wall.* **3** (of aircraft) to land or be landed in such a way as to be damaged or destroyed: *His plane crashed in the mountains.* **4** (of a business) to fail. **5** to force one's way noisily (through, into): *He crashed through the undergrowth.* – *adj* rapid and concentrated: *a crash course in computer technology.*

'**crash-helmet** *n* a covering for the head, worn for protection by racing-motorists, motor cyclists *etc*.

,**crash-'land** *v* to land (an aircraft), *usu* in an emergency, with the undercarriage up.

crass [kras] *adj* **1** very obvious or very great: *a crass mistake.* **2** stupid. **3** insensitive.

crate [kreit] *n* a container *usu* made of wooden slats, for carrying goods, fruit *etc*: *three crates of bananas.*

crater ['kreitə] *n* **1** the bowl-shaped mouth of

a volcano. **2** a hollow made in the ground by a bomb *etc*.

cravat [krə'vat] *n* a kind of scarf worn instead of a tie round the neck.

crave [kreiv] *v* **1** to beg for. **2** to long for, desire extremely.
'**craving** *n* a desire or longing: *a craving for adventure*.

craven ['kreivən] *adj* cowardly.

crawfish *see* **crayfish**.

crawl [kro:l] *v* **1** to move slowly along the ground: *The injured dog crawled away*. **2** (of people) to move on hands and knees or with the front of the body on the ground: *The baby can't walk yet, but she crawls everywhere*. **3** to move slowly: *The traffic was crawling along at ten kilometres per hour*. **4** to be covered with crawling things: *His hair was crawling with lice*. – *n* **1** a very slow movement or speed: *We drove along at a crawl*. **2** a style of swimming in which the arms make alternate overarm movements: *She's better at the crawl than she is at the breaststroke*.

crayfish ['kreifiʃ] – *pl* '**crayfish** – (*also, esp Amer*, **crawfish** ['kro:fiʃ] – *pl* '**crawfish**) a type of edible shellfish.

crayon ['kreiən] *n* a coloured pencil or stick of chalk *etc* for drawing with. – *v* to use crayons to draw a picture *etc*.

craze [kreiz] *n* a (*usu* temporary) fashion; great (but temporary) enthusiasm: *the current craze for cutting one's hair extremely short*.
'**crazy** *adj* **1** insane: *He must be going crazy*; *a crazy idea*. **2** very enthusiastic: *She's crazy about her boyfriend*. '**crazily** *adv*. '**craziness** *n*.

creak [kri:k] *v* to make a sharp grating sound: *That chair is creaking beneath your weight*. – *n* such a sound: *The strange creaks in the old house kept the girl awake*. '**creaky** *adj*. '**creakiness** *n*.

cream [kri:m] *n* **1** the yellowish-white oily substance that forms on the top of milk, and from which butter and cheese are made. **2** any of many substances made of, or similar to, cream: *ice-cream*; *face-cream*. **3** the best part; the top people: *the cream of the medical profession*. **4** (*also adj*) (of) a yellowish-white colour: *cream paint*. – *v* **1** to make into a cream-like mixture: *Cream the eggs, butter and sugar together*. **2** to take the cream off: *She creamed the milk*. **3** (with **off**) to select (the best): *The best pupils will be creamed off for special training*.
'**creamy** *adj* **1** full of, or like, cream: *creamy milk*. **2** smooth and white: *a creamy complexion*. '**creaminess** *n*.

crease [kri:s] *n* **1** a mark made by folding or doubling something: *a smart crease in his*

trousers; *My dress was full of creases after being in my suitcase*. **2** in cricket, a line showing the position of the batsman or bowler. – *v* to make or become creased: *You've creased my newspaper*; *This fabric creases easily*.

create [kri'eit] *v* **1** to cause to exist; to make: *How was the earth created?*; *The circus created great excitement*. **2** to give (a rank *etc* to): *Sir John was created a knight in 1958*.
cre'ation *n* **1** the act of creating: *the creation of the world*. **2** something created: *The dress designer is showing his latest creations*.
cre'ative [-tiv] *adj* having or showing the power and imagination to create: *a creative dress-designer*. **cre'atively** *adv*. **cre'ativeness**, ,**crea'tivity** [kri:ə-] *ns*.
cre'ator *n* a person who creates.
the Creator God.

creature ['kri:tʃə] *n* **1** an animal or human being: *all God's creatures*. **2** a term of contempt or pity: *The poor creature could hardly stand*.

crèche [kreʃ] *n* a nursery for babies whose mothers are at work *etc*: *Some factories have crèches for the children of their workers*.

credible ['kredəbl] *adj* that may be believed: *The story he told was barely credible*. '**credibly** *adv*. ,**credi'bility** *n*.

credit ['kredit] *n* **1** time allowed for payment of goods *etc* after they have been received: *We don't give credit at this shop*. **2** money loaned (by a bank). **3** trustworthiness regarding ability to pay for goods *etc*: *Your credit is good*. **4** (an entry on) the side of an account on which payments received are entered: *Our credits are greater than our debits*. **5** the sum of money which someone has in an account at a bank: *Your credit amounts to 2014 dollars*. **6** belief or trust: *This theory is gaining credit*. **7** (*Amer*) a certificate to show that a student has completed a course which counts towards his degree. – *v* **1** to enter (a sum of money) on the credit side (of an account): *This cheque was credited to your account last month*. **2** (with **with**) to think of (a person or thing) as having: *He was credited with magical powers*. **3** to believe (something) to be possible: *Well, would you credit that!*
'**creditable** *adj* bringing honour or respect: *creditable effort*. '**creditably** *adv*.
'**creditor** *n* a person to whom a debt is owed.
'**credits** *n pl* the list of names of the actors, producer, director *etc* given at the beginning or end of a film.
credit card a card which allows the holder to buy goods *etc* on credit: *to pay by credit card*.
be a credit to (someone), do (someone) credit

to bring honour or respect to (someone or something): *Your son is a credit to his school*; *Your honesty does you credit*.

give (someone) credit (for something) to acknowledge and praise (someone for a good piece of work): *He was given credit for completing the work so quickly*.

on credit payment being made after the date of sale: *Do you sell goods on credit?*

take (the) credit (for something) to accept the praise given (for something): *I did all the work, and he took all the credit*.

credulous ['kredjuləs, (*Amer*) -dʒu-] *adj* believing too easily. **'credulousness, cre'dulity** [-'dju:-] *ns*.

creed [kri:d] *n* (a short statement of) one's (*esp* religious) beliefs.

creek [kri:k] *n* **1** a small inlet, *esp* off a river. **2** (*Amer*) a small river.

creep [kri:p] – *pt, ptp* **crept** [krept] – *v* **1** to move slowly, quietly or secretly: *He crept into the bedroom*. **2** to move on hands or knees or with the body close to the ground: *The cat crept towards the bird*. **3** (of plants) to grow along the ground, up a wall *etc*.
'creeper *n* a creeping plant.
'creepy *adj* causing feelings of fear *etc*: *The house is rather creepy at night*. **'creepily** *adv*.
'creepiness *n*.
,creepy-'crawly – *pl* ,creepy-'crawlies – *n* a small creeping insect.
creep up on to approach slowly and stealthily: *Old age creeps up on us all*.
make someone's flesh creep to scare or horrify someone.

cremate [kri'meit] *v* to burn dead (human) bodies: *He asked to be cremated, not buried*.
cre'mation *n*.
crematorium [kremə'tɔ:riəm] *n* a place where cremation is carried out.

crêpe [kreip] *n, adj* (of) a thin silk-like fabric with a wrinkled surface.
crêpe paper paper with a similar surface.

crept *see* creep.

crescendo [kri'ʃendou] – *pl* cres'cendos – *n* (*esp* in music) a gradual and continuous increase in loudness.

crescent ['kresnt] *n* **1** (*also adj*) (having) the curved shape of the growing moon: *the crescent moon*; *crescent-shaped earrings*. **2** (*abbrev* **Cres.** when written in street-names) a curved street.

cress [kres] *n* any of several edible plants with sharp-tasting leaves used in salads.

crest [krest] *n* **1** the comb or tuft on the head of a cock or other bird. **2** the summit or highest part: *the crest of a wave*. **3** feathers on the top of a helmet. **4** a badge or emblem: *the family crest*.
'crested *adj* having a tuft on the head.

crestfallen ['krestfɔ:lən] *adj* very disappointed: *He was crestfallen at his failure*.

cretin ['kretin] *n* **1** a person who is mentally subnormal and physically deformed. **2** an idiot, used as a term of contempt and abuse.

crevasse [kri'vas] *n* a very deep crack or split in a glacier.

crevice ['krevis] *n* a crack or narrow opening (in a wall, rock *etc*): *Plants grew in the crevices*.

crew¹ [kru:] *n* **1** the group of people who work or operate a ship, aeroplane, bus *etc*. **2** used jokingly, a group of people: *What an odd crew!* – *v* (*usu with* **for**) to act as a crew member (for someone).
'crewcut *n* a very short hairstyle.

crew² *see* crow.

crib [krib] *n* **1** a cradle. **2** (*Amer*) a child's cot. **3** a translation used when studying a text in a foreign language. **4** a manger. – *v* – *pt, ptp* **cribbed** – to copy: *She cribbed the answer from her friend's work*.

*cricket¹ ['krikit] *n* an outdoor game played with bats, a ball and wickets, between two sides of eleven each. **'cricketer** *n*.
not cricket unfair; not sportsmanlike.

cricket² ['krikit] *n* an insect related to the grasshopper, the male of which makes a chirping noise.

crime [kraim] *n* **1** act(s) punishable by law: *Murder is a crime*; *Crime is on the increase*. **2** something wrong though not illegal: *What a crime to cut down those trees!*

criminal ['kriminl] *adj* **1** concerned with crime: *criminal law*. **2** against the law: *Theft is a criminal offence*. **3** very wrong; wicked: *a criminal waste of food*. – *n* a person who has been found guilty of a crime.
'criminally *adv*.

crimson ['krimzn] *n, adj* (of) a deep red colour: *He went crimson with embarrassment*.

cringe [krindʒ] *v* to shrink back in fear, terror *etc*: *The dog cringed when his cruel master raised his hand to strike him*.

crinkle ['kriŋkl] *v* to (cause to) wrinkle or curl: *The paper crinkled in the heat of the sun*.
'crinkly *adj*: *grey crinkly hair*.

cripple ['kripl] *v* **1** to make lame or disabled: *He was crippled by a fall from a horse*. **2** to make less strong, less efficient *etc*: *The war has crippled the country's economy*. – *n* a lame or disabled person: *He's been a cripple since the car accident*.

crisis ['kraisis] – *pl* **'crises** [-si:z] – *n* **1** a deciding moment or turning-point (*esp* of an illness): *Although she is still very ill, she has passed the crisis*. **2** a time of great danger or difficulty: *a crisis such as the recent flooding*; *You can rely on her in a crisis*.

* see illustration on p. 206

crisp [krisp] *adj* 1 stiff and dry enough to break easily: *crisp biscuits.* 2 (of vegetables *etc*) firm and fresh: *a crisp lettuce.* 3 (of manner, speech *etc*) firm and clear. – *n* short for **potato crisp**.
'crisply *adv*. 'crispness *n*. 'crispy *adj*.
criss-cross ['kriskros] *adj* made of lines which cross each other repeatedly: *a criss-cross pattern.*
criterion [krai'tiəriən] – *pl* cri'teria [-ə] – *n* a standard used or referred to in judging something: *What are your criteria for deciding which words to include in this dictionary?*
critic ['kritik] *n* 1 a person who judges or comments on books, art *etc*: *He is the book critic for the local newspaper.* 2 a person who finds fault: *His critics would say that he is unsuitable for the job.*
'critical *adj* 1 judging and analysing: *He has written several critical works on Shakespeare.* 2 fault-finding: *He tends to be critical of his children.* 3 of, at or having the nature of, a crisis; very serious: *a critical shortage of food; After the accident, his condition was critical.* 'critically *adv*.
'criticize, -ise [-saiz] *v* 1 to find fault (with): *He's always criticizing her.* 2 to give an opinion of or judgement on a book *etc*. 'criticism *n*.
croak [krouk] *v* to utter a low hoarse sound like that of a frog: *I could hear the frogs croaking.* – *n* such a sound.
crochet ['krouʃei, (*Amer*) krou'ʃei] – *prp* 'crocheting: *pt, ptp* 'crocheted – *v* to knit using a single small needle with a hooked end (a **crochet hook**). – *n* work done in this way: *She enjoys doing crochet.*
crock [krok] *n* 1 an earthenware pot or jar. 2 an old and decrepit person or thing: *That car's an old crock.*
crockery ['krokəri] *n* earthenware and china dishes, *eg* plate, cups, saucers *etc*: *I've washed the crockery but the cutlery is still dirty.*
crocodile ['krokədail] *n* a large reptile found in the rivers of Asia, Africa, South America and northern Australia.
crocodile tears pretended tears of grief.
crocus ['kroukəs] *n* a plant growing from a bulb and having brilliant yellow, purple or white flowers.
croissant ['krwa:sã] *n* a crescent-shaped bread roll.
crony ['krouni] – *pl* 'cronies – *n* a close companion: *He spent the evening drinking with his cronies.*
crook [kruk] *n* 1 a (shepherd's or bishop's) stick, bent at the end. 2 a criminal: *The two crooks stole the old woman's jewels.* 3 the inside of the bend (of one's arm at the elbow): *She held the puppy in the crook of her arm.* – *v* to bend (*esp* one's finger) into

the shape of a hook: *She crooked her finger to beckon him.*
'crooked [-kid] *adj* 1 badly shaped: *a crooked little man.* 2 not straight: *That picture is crooked* (=not horizontal). 3 dishonest: *a crooked dealer.* 'crookedly [-kid-] *adv*. 'crookedness [-kid-] *n*.
croon [kru:n] *v* 1 to sing or hum in a low voice: *She crooned a lullaby.* 2 to sing in a quiet, sentimental style. 'crooner *n*.
crop [krop] *n* 1 a plant which is farmed and harvested: *a fine crop of rice; We grow a variety of crops, including cabbages, wheat and barley.* 2 a short whip used when horse-riding. 3 a (short) haircut: *a crop of red hair.* 4 (of certain birds) the first stomach, which hangs like a bag from the neck. – *v* – *pt, ptp* cropped – to cut or nibble short: *The sheep crop the grass.*
crop up to happen unexpectedly: *I'm sorry I'm late, but something important cropped up.*
croquet ['kroukei, (*Amer*) krou'kei] *n* a game in which wooden balls are driven by mallets through a series of hoops stuck in the ground.
cross¹ [kros] *adj* angry: *I get very cross when I lose something.* 'crossly *adv*.
cross² [kros] – *pl* 'crosses – *n* 1 a symbol formed by two lines placed across each other, *eg* + or ×. 2 two wooden beams placed thus (†), on which Christ was nailed. 3 the symbol of the Christian religion. 4 a lasting cause of suffering *etc*: *Your rheumatism is a cross you will have to bear.* 5 the result of breeding two varieties of animal or plant: *This dog is a cross between an alsatian and a labrador.* 6 a monument in the shape of a cross. 7 any of several types of medal given for bravery *etc*: *the Victoria Cross.* – *v* 1 to go from one side to the other: *Let's cross* (*the street*); *This road crosses the swamp.* 2 (*neg* un-) to place (two things) across each other: *He sat down and crossed his legs.* 3 to go or be placed across (each other): *The roads cross in the centre of town.* 4 to meet and pass: *Our letters must have crossed in the post.* 5 to put a line across: *Cross your 't's'.* 6 to make (a cheque or postal order) payable only through a bank by drawing two parallel lines across it. 7 to breed (something) from two different varieties: *I've crossed two varieties of rose.* 8 to go against the wishes of: *If you cross me, you'll regret it!*
cross- 1 going or placed across: *cross-winds; cross-pieces.* 2 of mixed variety: *a cross-breed.*
'crossing *n* 1 a place where a road *etc* may be crossed: *a pedestrian-crossing; a level-crossing.* 2 a journey over the sea: *I was seasick as it was a very rough crossing.*

'**crossbow** *n* a medieval type of bow fixed to a shaft with a mechanism for pulling back and releasing the string.

'**cross-breed** *n* an animal bred from two different breeds. '**cross-bred** *adj*.

cross-'**country** *adj* across fields *etc*, not on roads: *a cross-country run*.

,cross-ex'**amine** *v* in a court of law, to test or check the previous evidence of (a witness) by questioning him. '**cross-ex,ami'nation** *n*.

,cross-'**eyed** *adj* having a squint.

'**cross-fire** *n* the crossing of lines of gunfire from two or more points.

at cross-**purposes** of two or more people, confused about what they are saying or doing because of misunderstanding one another: *I think we're talking at cross-purposes*.

,cross-re'**fer** *v* to give a cross-reference (to): *In this dictionary* went *is cross-referred to* go.

,cross-'**reference** *n* a reference from one part of a book, list *etc* to another, *eg* crept *see* creep.

'**crossroads** *n sing* a place where two or more roads cross or meet: *At the crossroads we'll have to decide which road to take*.

,cross-'**section** *n* 1 (a drawing *etc* of) the area or surface made visible by cutting through something, *eg* an apple. 2 a sample as representative of the whole: *He interviewed a cross-section of the audience to get their opinion of the play*.

crossword (**puzzle**) a square word-puzzle in which the blanks in a pattern of blank and solid checks are to be filled with words reading across and down, the words being found from clues.

cross one's **fingers** to place a finger across the one next to it, for good luck.

cross out to draw a line through: *He crossed out all her mistakes*.

crotch [krotʃ], crutch [krʌʃ] *ns* in humans, the place where the legs meet together and join the body.

crotchet ['krotʃit] *n* in music, a note equal to half a minim.

crotchety ['krotʃəti] *adj* bad-tempered.

crouch [krautʃ] *v* 1 to stand with the knees well bent; to squat: *He crouched behind the bush*. 2 (of animals) to lie close to the ground, in fear, readiness for action *etc*: *The tiger was crouching ready to spring on its prey*.

croupier ['kru:piei] *n* a person who takes and pays bets at a gambling table in a casino *etc*.

croûton ['kru:ton] *n* a small piece of fried or toasted bread, served in soup *etc*.

crow [krou] *n* 1 the name given to a number of large birds, generally black. 2 the cry of a cock. – *v* 1 (*pt* crew) to utter the cry of a

cock. 2 to utter a cry of delight *etc*: *The baby crowed with happiness*.

,crow's-'**nest** *n* a shelter at the masthead of a ship, used as a lookout post.

crowbar ['krouba:] *n* a large iron stake with a bend at the end, used to lift heavy stones *etc*.

crowd [kraud] *n* 1 a number of persons or things gathered together: *A crowd of people gathered in the street*. 2 a group of friends, *usu* known to one another: *John's friends are a nice crowd*. – *v* 1 to gather in a large group: *They crowded round the injured motorcyclist*. 2 to fill too full by coming together in: *Sightseers crowded the building*.

'**crowded** *adj* having or containing a lot of people or things: *crowded buses*.

crown [kraun] *n* 1 a circular, often jewelled, head-dress, *esp* one worn as a mark of royalty or honour: *the queen's crown*. 2 (*with cap*) the king or queen or governing power in a monarchy: *revenue belonging to the Crown*. 3 the top *eg* of a head, hat, hill *etc*: *We reached the crown of the hill*. 4 (an artificial replacement for) the part of a tooth which can be seen. – *v* 1 to make (someone) king or queen by placing a crown on his or her head: *The archbishop crowned the queen*. 2 to form the top part of (something): *an iced cake crowned with a cherry*. 3 to put an artificial crown on (a tooth). 4 to hit (someone) on the head: *If you do that again, I'll crown you!*

crown prince the heir to the throne.

crown princess 1 the wife of a crown prince. 2 the female heir to the throne.

crucial ['kru:ʃəl] *adj* involving a big decision; of the greatest importance: *He took the crucial step of asking her to marry him; The next game is crucial – if we lose it we lose the match*.

crucible ['kru:sibl] *n* a pot in which metals *etc* may be melted: *He heated the chemicals in a crucible in the laboratory*.

crucify ['kru:sifai] *v* to put to death by fixing the hands and feet to a cross: *Christ was crucified*.

'**crucifix** [-fiks] *n* a figure of Christ on the cross.

,cruci'**fixion** [-'fikʃən] *n* (a) death on the cross, *esp* that of Christ.

crude [kru:d] *adj* 1 unrefined: *crude oil*. 2 rough or primitive: *a crude shelter*. '**crudeness** *n*. '**crudity** *n*.

cruel ['kru:əl] *adj* 1 pleased at causing pain; merciless: *He was cruel to his dog*. 2 causing distress: *a cruel disappointment*. '**cruelly** *adv*. '**cruelty** *n*.

cruet ['kru:it] *n* 1 a small jar or bottle for salt, pepper, vinegar *etc*. 2 (*also* '**cruet-stand**) a holder for such jars *etc*, often with them on it.

cruise [kru:z] *v* **1** to sail for pleasure: *We're going cruising in the Mediterranean.* **2** to go at a steady, comfortable speed: *The plane is cruising at an altitude of 10 000 metres.* – *n* a voyage from place to place made for pleasure and relaxation: *They went on a cruise.* **'cruiser** *n* **1** a high-speed battleship. **2** (*also* **'cabin-cruiser**) a motor yacht with living quarters.

crumb [krʌm] *n* a tiny piece, *esp* of bread: *She puts crumbs for the birds on her window-sill.*

crumble ['krʌmbl] *v* to break into crumbs or small pieces: *She crumbled the bread*; *The building had crumbled into ruins*; *Her hopes of success finally crumbled.* **'crumbly** *adj.*

crumple ['krʌmpl] *v* to make or become wrinkled or creased: *This material crumples easily*; *She crumpled up the piece of paper.*

crunch [krʌntʃ] *v* to crush noisily (something hard), with the teeth, feet *etc*: *She crunched sweets all through the film.* – *n*: *the crunch of gravel under the car wheels.* **'crunchy** *adj*: *thick crunchy biscuits.*

crusade [kru:'seid] *n* **1** in medieval times, a military expedition of Christians to win back the Holy Land from the Turks. **2** a campaign in support of a good cause: *the crusade against cigarette advertising.* – *v* to take part in a crusade. **cru'sader** *n.*

crush [krʌʃ] *v* **1** to squash by squeezing together *etc*: *The car was crushed between the two trucks.* **2** to crease: *That material crushes easily.* **3** to defeat: *He crushed the rebellion.* **4** to push, press *etc* together: *We (were) all crushed into the tiny room.* – *n* squeezing or crowding together: *There's always a crush in the supermarket on Saturdays.* **'crushing** *adj* overwhelming: *a crushing defeat.*

crust [krʌst] **1** (a piece of) the hard outside coating of bread: *The child would not eat the crusts.* **2** (*Amer*) pastry: *She makes excellent crust.* **3** a hard surface *esp* the outer layer of the earth. **'crusty** *adj* **1** having a crust: *crusty bread.* **2** surly or irritable. **'crustily** *adv.* **'crustiness** *n.*

crustacean [krʌ'steiʃən] *n, adj* (of) any of a group of animals, including crabs, lobsters, shrimps *etc*, whose bodies are covered with a hard shell.

crusty *see* **crust.**

crutch[1] *see* **crotch.**

crutch[2] [krʌtʃ] *n* a stick with a bar at the top to support a lame person: *He can walk only by using crutches.*

crux [krʌks] – *pl* **'cruxes** – *n* a difficult or essential point: *That is the crux of the matter.*

cry [krai] *v* **1** to let tears come from the eyes; to weep: *She cried when she heard of the old man's death.* **2** (*often with* **out**) to shout out (a loud sound): *She cried out for help.* – *n* –*pl* **cries** – **1** a shout: *a cry of triumph.* **2** a time of weeping: *The baby had a little cry before he went to sleep.* **3** the sound made by some animals: *the cry of a wolf.*

a far cry a long way (from): *Our modern clothes are a far cry from the animal skins worn by our ancestors.*

cry off to cancel (an engagement or agreement).

crypt [kript] *n* an underground chapel beneath a church.

cryptic ['kriptik] *adj* intentionally very difficult to understand or make sense of: *a cryptic message.*

crystal ['kristl] *n* **1** a small part of a solid substance (*eg* salt or ice). which has a regular shape. **2** a special kind of very clear glass: *This bowl is made of crystal.* **'crystalline** [-lain] *adj* (of minerals *etc*) formed into crystals: *Salt is a crystalline substance.* **'crystallize, -ise** *v* **1** to form (into) crystals: *He crystallized the salt from the sea water.* **2** to cover with a coating of sugar crystals: *crystallized fruits.* **3** to make or become definite or clear: *He tried to crystallize his ideas.* **,crystalli'zation, -s-** *n.*

crystal ball a glass ball used in fortune-telling.

crystal clear absolutely clear: *My instructions were crystal clear.*

cub [kʌb] *n* **1** the young of certain animals such as foxes, lions *etc*: *a bear cub.* **2** (*with cap*: *short for* **Cub Scout**) a member of the junior branch of the Scouts.

cubby-hole ['kʌbihoul] *n* a very small room, cupboard *etc.*

*****cube** [kju:b] *n* **1** a solid body having six equal square faces. **2** the result of multiplying a number by itself twice: *The cube of $4 = 4 \times 4 \times 4 = 4^3 = 64.$* – *v* **1** to calculate the cube of (a number): *If you cube 2, you will get the answer 8.* **2** to make into a cube or cubes: *She cubed the beef.* **'cubic** *adj* shaped like a cube.

cube root the number of which a given number is the cube: *The cube root of 64 is 4.*

cubic centimetre (*abbrev* cc), **metre** *etc* the volume of, or the volume equivalent to, a cube whose sides measure one centimetre, metre *etc*: *This jug holds 500 cubic centimetres.*

cubicle ['kju:bikl] *n* a small room *etc* closed off in some way from a larger one: *Please use the (changing-)cubicle to change into your swimming trunks.*

cuckoo ['kuku:] – *pl* **'cuckoos** – *n* a bird, named after its call, which lays eggs in the nests of other birds.

cucumber ['kju:kʌmbə] *n* a type of creeping

plant with long green edible fruit, often used in salads *etc*.

cud [kʌd]: **chew the cud** (of cows *etc*) to bring food from the stomach back into the mouth and chew it again.

cuddle ['kʌdl] *v* to hug affectionately: *The mother cuddled the child until he fell asleep.* – *n* an affectionate hug.

'**cuddly** *adj*: *a cuddly teddy-bear*.

cudgel ['kʌdʒəl] *n* a heavy stick or club. – *v* – *pt, ptp* '**cudgelled**, (*Amer*) '**cudgeled** – to beat with a cudgel.

cue[1] [kjuː] *n* the last words of another actor's speech *etc*, serving as a sign to an actor to speak *etc*: *Your cue is '– whatever the vicar says!'*

cue[2] [kjuː] *n* a stick which gets thinner towards one end and the point of which is used to strike the ball in playing billiards.

cuff[1] [kʌf] *n* the end of the sleeve (of a shirt, coat *etc*) near the wrist: *Does your shirt have buttons on the cuffs?* **2** (*esp Amer*) the turned-up part of a trouser leg.

'**cufflinks** *n pl* two ornamental buttons *etc* joined by a small bar, chain *etc* used to fasten a shirt cuff.

cuff[2] [kʌf] *n* a blow with the open hand: *a cuff on the ear*. – *v* to give such a blow: *He cuffed him on the head*.

cuisine [kwi'ziːn] *n* style of cookery: *French cuisine*.

cul-de-sac ['kʌldəsak] *n* a street closed at one end.

culinary ['kʌlinəri] *adj* of or used ·in the kitchen or in cookery: *culinary herbs*.

cull [kʌl] *v* **1** to gather or collect. **2** to select and kill (surplus animals): *They are culling the seals*. – *n* an act of killing surplus animals.

culminate ['kʌlmineit] *v* (*with* **in**) to reach the highest or most important point: *The celebrations culminated in a firework display in the local park*. ,**culmi'nation** *n*.

culotte [kjuː'lot] *n* (*usu in pl*) women's knee-length trousers cut so as to look like a skirt.

culpable ['kʌlpəbl] *adj* deserving blame; guilty: *She was the one who committed the crime but he was culpable also*. ,**culpa'bility** *n*.

culprit ['kʌlprit] *n* a person responsible for something wrong, unpleasant *etc*: *As soon as he saw the broken window he began to look for the culprit*.

cult [kʌlt] *n* a particular system of (religious) belief or worship: *a strange new religious cult*; *Physical fitness has become a cult with him*.

cultivate ['kʌltiveit] *v* **1** to prepare (land) for crops. **2** to grow (a crop in a garden, field *etc*): *He cultivates mushrooms in the cellar*. '**cultivated** *adj* **1** (of fields *etc*) prepared for crops; used for growing crops: *cultivated land*. **2** grown in a garden *etc*; not wild: *a cultivated variety of raspberries*. **3** having good manners; educated: *a cultivated young lady*; *He has cultivated tastes in music*. ,**culti'vation** *n*.

'**cultivator** *n* a tool or machine for breaking up ground and removing weeds.

culture ['kʌltʃə] *n* **1** a form or type of civilization of a certain race or nation: *the Jewish culture*. **2** improvement of the mind *etc* by education *etc*: *He was an enthusiastic seeker of culture*. **3** educated taste in art, literature, music *etc*: *He thinks that anyone who dislikes Bach is lacking in culture*. **4** (a) cultivated growth of bacteria *etc*. **5** the commercial rearing of fish, certain plants *etc*. '**cultural** *adj*.

'**cultured** *adj* (*neg* **un-**) well-educated.

cumbersome ['kʌmbəsəm] *adj* (of things) heavy and clumsy: *a cumbersome piece of furniture*.

cumulative ['kjuːlmjuətiv] *adj* becoming greater by stages or additions: *This drug has a cumulative effect*.

cunning ['kʌniŋ] *adj* **1** sly; clever in a deceitful way: *cunning tricks*. **2** clever: *a cunning device*. – *n* slyness or deceitful cleverness: *full of cunning*. '**cunningly** *adv*: *cunningly disguised*.

cup [kʌp] *n* **1** a *usu* round hollow container to hold liquid for drinking, often with a handle: *a teacup*; *a cup of tea*. **2** an ornamental vessel, *usu* of silver or other metal, given as a prize in sports events *etc*: *They won the Football League Cup*. – *v*– *pt, ptp* **cupped** – **1** to form (one's hands) into the shape of a cup: *He cupped his hands round his mouth and called*. **2** to hold (something) in one's cupped hands: *He cupped the egg in his hands*. '**cupful** *n*: *three cupfuls of water*.

cupboard ['kʌbəd] *n* (*Amer* '**closet**) a cabinet of any size up to that of a small room for storing anything: *Put the food in the cupboard*; *a broom cupboard*.

cup final the final match in a football competition in which the prize is a cup.

'**cup-tie** *n* one of a series of games in a football competition in which the prize is a cup.

one's cup of tea the sort of thing one likes or prefers: *Classical music is not my cup of tea*.

cur [kəː] *n* a dog of mixed breed.

curable *see* **cure**.

curate ['kjuərət] *n* a clergyman in the Church of England assisting a rector or vicar.

curative *see* **cure**.

curator [kjuə'reitə] *n* a person in charge of a museum *etc*.

curb [kəːb] *n* **1** something which restrains or controls: *We'll have to put a curb on his enthusiasm*. **2** (*Amer*) a kerb. – *v* to hold back, restrain or control: *You must curb your spending.*

'curbstone *n* (*Amer*) a kerbstone.

curd [kə:d] *n* (*also* **curds** *n pl*) the solid substance formed when milk turns sour, used in making cheese.

curdle ['kə:dl] *v* to turn into curd: *The heat has curdled the milk*; *This milk has curdled.*

cure [kjuə] *v* 1 to make better: *That medicine cured me*; *That will cure him of his bad habits.* 2 to get rid of (an illness *etc*): *That pill cured my headache.* 3 to preserve (bacon *etc*) by drying, salting *etc.* – *n* something which cures: *They're trying to find a cure for cancer.*

'curable *adj* able to be cured: *a curable form of cancer.*

curative ['kjuərətiv] *adj* intended to, or likely to, cure: *curative treatment.*

curfew ['kə:fju:] *n* an order forbidding people to be in the streets after a certain hour: *There's a curfew in force from ten o'clock tonight.*

curio ['kjuəriou] – *pl* **'curios** – *n* an article valued for its oddness or its rareness.

curious ['kjuəriəs] *adj* 1 strange; odd: *a curious habit.* 2 anxious or interested (to learn): *I'm curious (to find out) whether he passed his exams.* **'curiously** *adv.*

,curi'osity [-'o-] – *pl* **,curi'osities** – *n* 1 eagerness to learn: *She was very unpopular because of her curiosity about other people's affairs.* 2 something strange and rare: *That old chair is quite a curiosity.*

curl [kə:l] *v* 1 to twist or turn (*esp* hair) into small coils or rolls: *My hair curls easily.* 2 (*sometimes with* **up**) to move in curves; to bend or roll: *The paper curled* (*up*) *at the edges.* – *n* 1 a coil of hair *etc.* 2 the quality of being curled: *My hair has very little curl in it.*

'curler *n* an object round which hair is rolled to make it curl, fastened in the hair. **'curly** *adj*: *curly hair.* **'curliness** *n.*

curl up to move or roll into a position or shape: *The hedgehog curled* (*itself*) *up into a ball.*

currant ['kʌrənt, (*Amer*) 'kə:-] *n* 1 a small black raisin or dried seedless grape: *This cake has currants in it.* 2 any of several types of small berry: *a redcurrant/blackcurrant.*

currency ['kʌrənsi, (*Amer*) 'kə:-] – *pl* **'currencies** – *n* the money (notes and coins) of a country: *the currencies of the world*; *foreign currency.*

current ['kʌrənt, (*Amer*) 'kə:-] *adj* of or belonging to the present: *current affairs*; *the current month*; *the current temperature.* – *n* 1 (the direction of) a stream of water or

air: *the current of a river.* 2 (a) flow of electricity: *an electrical current.*

'currently *adv* at the present time: *John is currently working as a bus-driver.*

current account an account with a bank from which money may be withdrawn by cheque.

curriculum [kə'rikjuləm] – *pl* **cur'ricula** [-lə] – *n* a course, *esp* of study at school or university: *They are changing the curriculum.*

curry[1] ['kʌri, (*Amer*) 'kə:ri] – *pl* **'curries** – *n* (an *orig* Indian dish of) meat, vegetables *etc* cooked with spices: *chicken curry.* – *v* to cook in this way: *Are you going to curry this meat?*

'curried *adj*: *curried chicken.*

curry powder a selection of spices ground together and used in making a curry.

curry[2] ['kʌri, (*Amer*) 'kə:ri] *v* to rub down or comb and clean (a horse).

curry favour (*with* **with**) to seek (a) favour by flattery: *She's currying favour with the boss.*

curse [kə:s] *v* 1 to wish that evil may fall upon: *I curse the day that I was born!*; *The witch cursed him.* 2 to use violent language; to swear: *He cursed* (*at his own stupidity*) *when he dropped the hammer on his toe.* – *n* 1 an act of cursing, or the words used: *the witch's curse.* 2 a thing or person which is cursed: *Having to work is the curse of my life.*

cursed with having the misfortune to have: *She's cursed with a troublesome mother-in-law.*

cursive ['kə:siv] *adj* (of handwriting) with letters joined.

cursory ['kə:səri] *adj* hurried: *a cursory glance.* **'cursorily** *adv.*

curt [kə:t] *adj* rudely brief: *a curt reply.* **'curtly** *adv.* **'curtness** *n.*

curtail [kə'teil] *v* make less, shorter *etc* (than was originally intended): *I've had to curtail my visit.*

cur'tailment *n.*

curtain ['kə:tn] *n* a piece of material hung up to act as a screen at a window, on a theatre stage *etc*: *The maid drew the curtains*; *The curtain came down at the end of the play.*

curtain call an appearance by actors, singers *etc* after a performance for the purpose of receiving applause: *After the play the actors took ten curtain calls.*

curtain off to separate or enclose with a curtain: *She curtained off the alcove.*

curtsy, curtsey ['kə:tsi] – *pl* **'curtsies** – *n* a bow made by women by bending the knees. – *v* to make a curtsy: *She curtsied to the queen.*

curvature ['kə:vətʃə, (*Amer*) -tʃuər] *n* the

condition or extent of being curved: *the curvature of the earth.*

curve [kə:v] *n* **1** a line which is not straight at any point, like part of the edge of a circle. **2** anything shaped like this: *a curve in the road.* – *v* to bend in a curve: *The road curves east.*

curved *adj*: *a curved blade.*

'curvy *adj.*

cushion ['kuʃən] *n* **1** a bag of cloth *etc* filled with soft material, *eg* feathers *etc*, used for support or to make a seat more comfortable: *I'll sit on a cushion on the floor.* **2** any similar support: *A hovercraft travels on a cushion of air.* – *v* to lessen the force of a blow *etc*: *The soft sand cushioned his fall.*

cushy ['kuʃi] *adj* easy and comfortable: *a cushy job.*

custard ['kʌstəd] *n* **1** milk, eggs *etc* cooked together and flavoured. **2** a sauce made of milk, sugar and cornflour for sweet dishes.

custody ['kʌstədi] *n* **1** care or keeping: *The mother was awarded custody of the children by the court.* **2** the care of police or prison authorities: *The accused man is in custody.*

cu'stodian [-'stou-] *n* a person who guards or takes care of something: *the custodian of an art collection.*

custom ['kʌstəm] *n* **1** what a person *etc* is in the habit of doing or does regularly: *It's my custom to go for a walk on Saturday mornings; religious customs.* **2** the regular buying of goods at the same shop *etc*; trade or business: *The new supermarkets take away custom from the small shops.*

'customary *adj* habitual; usually done *etc*: *It is customary to eat turkey for Christmas dinner.* **'customarily** *adv.*

'customer *n* **1** a person who buys from a shop *etc*: *our regular customers.* **2** used jokingly for a person: *a strange customer.*

'customs *n pl* **1** (the government department that collects) taxes paid on goods coming into a country: *Did you have to pay customs on those watches?; He works for the customs;* (*also adj*) *customs duty.* **2** the place at a port *etc* where these taxes are collected: *I was searched when I came through customs at the airport.*

cut [kʌt] – *prp* **'cutting**: *pt, ptp* **cut** – *v* **1** to make an opening in, *usu* with something with a sharp edge: *He cut the paper with a pair of scissors.* **2** to separate or divide by cutting: *She cut a slice of bread; The child cut out the pictures; She cut up the meat into small pieces.* **3** to make by cutting: *She cut a hole in the cloth.* **4** to shorten by cutting; to trim: *to cut hair; I'll cut the grass.* **5** to reduce: *They cut my wages by ten per cent.* **6** to remove: *They cut several passages from the film.* **7** to wound or hurt by breaking the skin (of): *I cut my hand on a piece of glass.*

8 to divide (a pack of cards). **9** to stop: *When the actress said the wrong words, the director ordered 'Cut!'* **10** to take a short route or way: *He cut through/across the park on his way to the office; A van cut in in front of me on the motorway.* **11** to meet and cross (a line or geometrical figure): *An axis cuts a circle in two places.* **12** to stay away from (a class, lecture *etc*): *He cut school and went to the cinema.* **13** (also **cut dead**) to ignore completely: *She cut me dead in the High Street.* – *n* **1** the result of an act of cutting: *a cut on the head; a power-cut* (= stoppage of electrical power); *a haircut; a cut in prices.* **2** the way in which something is tailored, fashioned *etc*: *the cut of the jacket.* **3** a piece of meat cut from an animal: *a cut of beef.*

'cutter *n* **1** a person or thing that cuts: *a wood-cutter; a glass-cutter.* **2** a type of small sailing ship.

'cutting *n* **1** a piece of plant cut off and replanted to form another plant. **2** an article cut out from a newspaper *etc*: *She collects cuttings about the Royal Family.* **3** a trench dug through a hillside *etc*, in which a railway, road *etc* is built. – *adj* insulting or offending: *a cutting remark.*

'cut-price cheaper than normal: *cut-price goods; a cut-price store.*

'cut-throat *n* a murderer. – *adj* fierce; ruthless: *cut-throat business competition.*

a cut above (obviously) better than: *He's a cut above the average engineer.*

cut and dried fixed and definite: *cut-and-dried opinions.*

cut back to reduce considerably: *The government cut back (on) public spending (n* **'cutback**).

cut both ways to affect both parts of a question, both people involved, good and bad points *etc*: *That argument cuts both ways!*

cut a dash to have a smart or striking appearance: *He cuts a dash in his purple suit.*

cut down 1 to cause to fall by cutting: *He has cut down the apple tree.* **2** to reduce (an amount taken *etc*): *I haven't given up smoking but I'm cutting down.*

cut in to interrupt: *She cut in with a remark.*

cut it fine to allow barely enough time, money *etc* for something that must be done.

cut no ice to have no effect: *This sort of flattery cuts no ice with me.*

cut off 1 to interrupt or break a telephone connection: *I was cut off in the middle of the telephone call.* **2** to separate: *They were cut off from the rest of the army.* **3** to stop or prevent delivery of: *They've cut off our supplies of coal.*

cut one's losses to decide to spend no more

money, effort *etc* on something which is proving unprofitable.

cut one's teeth to grow one's first teeth: *The baby's cutting his first tooth.*

cut out 1 to stop working, sometimes because of a safety device: *The engines cut out* (*n* '**cut-out**). **2** to stop: *I've cut out smoking.*

cut short 1 to make shorter than intended: *He cut short his holiday to deal with the crisis.* **2** to cause (someone) to stop talking by interrupting them: *I tried to apologize but he cut me short.*

cute [kju:t] *adj* **1** (*esp Amer*) attractive or pleasing in any way: *a cute baby.* **2** cunningly clever: *You think you're pretty cute, don't you!*

cuticle ['kju:tikl] *n* the dead skin at the inner edge of a fingernail or toenail.

cutlass ['kʌtləs] *n* a short, broad, slightly curved sword with one cutting edge.

cutlery ['kʌtləri] *n* knives, forks and spoons.

cutlet ['kʌtlit] *n* a small slice of meat (mutton, veal, pork) on a rib or other bone: *lamb cutlets.*

cutter, cutting *see* cut.

cuttlefish ['kʌtlfiʃ] – *pl* '**cuttlefish** – *n* a sea-creature like the squid, able to squirt an inky liquid.

cyanide ['saiənaid] *n* a deadly type of poison.

cycle[1] ['saikl] *v* to go by bicycle: *He cycles to work every day.* – *n* shortened form of **bicycle**: *They bought the child a cycle for his birthday.*

'**cyclist** *n* a person who rides a bicycle.

cycle[2] ['saikl] *n* **1** a number of events happening one after the other in a certain order:

the life-cycle of the butterfly. **2** a series of poems, songs *etc* written about one main event *etc*: *a song cycle.* **3** (of alternating current, radio waves *etc*) one complete series of changes in a regularly varying supply, signal *etc*. '**cyclic** *adj*. '**cyclically** *adv*.

cyclist *see* cycle[1].

cyclone ['saikloun] *n* a violent wind-storm: *The cyclone ripped the roofs off houses and tore up trees.*

cygnet ['signit] *n* a young swan: *a swan with three cygnets.*

***cylinder** ['silində] *n* **1** a solid shape or object with a circular base and top and straight sides. **2** any of several pieces of machinery of this shape, solid or hollow: *The brake cylinder of his car is leaking.* **3** a container in the shape of a cylinder: *two cylinders of oxygen.*

cy'lindrical *adj* shaped like a cylinder: *A beer-can is cylindrical.*

cymbal ['simbəl] *n* a brass musical instrument like a plate with a hollow in the centre, two of which are struck together to produce a noise: *The cymbals clashed.*

cynical ['sinikəl] *adj* inclined to believe the worst, *esp* about people: *a cynical attitude.* '**cynically** *adv*.

'**cynic** *n* a person who believes the worst about everyone: *He is a cynic – he thinks no-one is really unselfish.*

'**cynicism** [-sizəm] *n*.

cypress ['saipris] *n* a type of evergreen tree.

cyst [sist] *n* a kind of liquid-filled blister on an internal part of the body or just under the skin.

czar *see* tsar.

Dd

dab [dab] – *pt, ptp* **dabbed** – *v* to touch gently with something soft or moist: *He dabbed the wound gently with cottonwool.* – *n* **1** a small lump of anything soft or moist: *a dab of butter.* **2** a gentle touch: *a dab with a wet cloth.*

dabble ['dabl] *v* **1** to play, or trail, in water: *He dabbled his feet in the river.* **2** to do anything in a half-serious way or as a hobby: *He dabbles in chemistry.*

dachshund ['dakshund, (*Amer*) 'da:ks-] *n* a type of small dog with a long body and very short legs.

dad [dad], **daddy** ['dadi] (*pl* '**daddies**) *n* children's words for father: *Where is your daddy?; What are you doing, Daddy?*

daffodil ['dafədil] *n* a kind of yellow spring flower which grows from a bulb.

dagger ['dagə] *n* a knife or short sword for stabbing.

daily ['deili] *adj* happening *etc* every day: *a daily walk; This is part of our daily lives.* – *adv* every day: *Our cream is fresh daily.* – *n* – *pl* '**dailies** – **1** a newspaper published every day: *We take three dailies.* **2** (*also* **daily help**) a person who is paid to come regularly and help with housework: *Our daily (help) comes on Mondays.*

dainty ['deinti] *adj* small or fragile and attractive: *a dainty little girl.* '**daintily** *adv*. '**daintiness** *n*.

dairy ['deəri] – *pl* '**dairies** – *n* **1** a shop supplying milk, butter, cheese *etc*: *We*

* see illustration on p. 476

bought milk at the dairy. **2** the place on a farm *etc* where milk is kept and butter and cheese are made.

dairy cow – *pl* **dairy cows/cattle** – a cow kept for its milk.

dairy farm a farm specializing in producing milk and milk products.

daisy ['deizi] – *pl* **'daisies** – *n* a type of small common flower with a yellow centre and *usu* white petals: *The field was full of daisies.*

dally ['dali] *v* to go *etc* slowly: *Don't dally – do hurry up!*

dam [dam] *n* **1** a bank or wall of earth, concrete *etc* to keep back water: *A new dam was being built at the mouth of the valley.* **2** the water kept back. – *v* – *pt, ptp* **dammed** – *v* (*sometimes with* **up**) to hold back by means of a dam: *The river has been dammed up.*

damage ['damidʒ] *n* **1** injury or hurt, *esp* to a thing: *The storm did/caused a lot of damage; She suffered brain-damage as a result of the accident.* **2** (*in pl*) payment for loss or injury suffered: *The court awarded him $5,000 damages.* – *v* to make less effective or less usable *etc*; to spoil: *The bomb damaged several buildings; The book was damaged in the post.*

'damaged *adj* (*neg* **un-**): *a damaged table.*

dame [deim] *n* **1** (the status of) a lady of the same rank as a knight: *There were several dames at the royal wedding.* **2** (*Amer*) a woman.

dammed *see* **dam**.

damn [dam] *v* **1** to sentence to unending punishment in hell: *His soul is damned.* **2** to cause to be condemned as bad, unacceptable *etc*: *That film was damned by the critics.* – *interj* expressing anger, irritation *etc*: *Damn! I've forgotten my purse.* – *n* something unimportant or of no value: *It's not worth a damn; I don't give a damn!* (= I don't care in the least).

damned *adj* **1** sentenced to unending punishment in hell. **2** annoying, greatly disliked *etc*: *Get that damned dog out of here!*

'damning *adj* showing faults, sins *etc*: *The evidence was damning.*

damp [damp] *adj* slightly wet: *This towel is still damp.* – *n* slight wetness, *esp* in the air: *The walls were brown with (the) damp.*

'dampen *v* **1** to make damp. **2** to make or become less fierce or strong (interest *etc*): *The rain dampened everyone's enthusiasm considerably.*

'damper *n* **1** something which lessens the strength of enthusiasm, interest *etc*: *Her presence cast a damper on the proceedings.* **2** a movable plate for controlling the draught *eg* in a stove.

'dampness *n* slight wetness.

damp down 1 to make (a fire) burn more slowly. **2** to reduce, make less strong: *He was trying to damp down their enthusiasm.*

damsel ['damzəl] *n* a young girl: *a damsel in distress.*

'damselfly *n* an insect with a long thin body found near water.

dance [daːns] *v* **1** to move in time to music by making a series of rhythmic steps: *She began to dance; Can you dance the waltz?* **2** to move quickly up and down: *The father was dancing the baby on his knee.* – *n* **1** a series of fixed steps made in time to music: *Have you done this dance before?*; (*also adj*) *dance music.* **2** a social gathering at which people dance: *We're going to a dance next Saturday.*

'dancer *n*: *a ballet dancer.*

'dancing *n*: *She likes dancing*; (*also adj*) *dancing shoes.*

dandelion ['dandilaiən] *n* a kind of common wild plant with jagged leaves and a yellow flower.

dandruff ['dandrʌf] *n* dead skin under the hair which falls off in small pieces.

danger ['deindʒə] *n* **1** something that may cause harm or injury: *The canal is a danger to children.* **2** a state or situation in which harm may come to a person or thing: *He is in danger; The bridge is in danger of collapse.*

'dangerous *adj* very unsafe and likely to be the cause of danger: *a dangerous road; a dangerous enemy.*

dangle ['dangl] *v* to (cause to) hang loosely: *She dangled her scarf out of the car window.*

dare [deə] – *neg short form* **daren't** – *v* **1** to be brave enough (to do something): *I daren't go; I don't dare (to) go; He wouldn't dare do a thing like that; Don't you dare say such a thing again!* **2** to challenge: *I dare you to do it.* – *n* a challenge: *He went into the lion's cage for a dare.*

'daring *adj* bold; courageous: *He was a daring pilot; a daring attempt to rescue the climber.* – *n* boldness: *We admired his daring.*

'dare-devil *n* a bold or reckless person. – Also *adj*: *a dare-devil motorcyclist.*

I dare say (*also* **I ˌdare'say**) I suppose (so): *I dare say you're right; 'Will you be there?' 'Oh, I daresay.'*

dark [daːk] *adj* **1** without light: *a dark room; It's getting dark; the dark* (= not cheerful) *side.* **2** blackish or closer to black than white: *a dark red colour; a dark* (= not very white or fair) *complexion; Her hair is dark.* **3** evil and *usu* secret: *dark deeds; a dark secret.* – *n* absence of light: *in the dark; afraid of the dark; He never goes out after dark; We are in the dark* (= we have no knowledge) *about what is happening.*

'darken v to make or become dark or darker.

'darkness n the state of being dark.

keep it dark to keep something a secret: *They're engaged to be married but they want to keep it dark.*

darling ['da:liŋ] n **1** a dearly loved person (often used as a term of endearment): *Is that you, darling?* **2** a lovable person: *Mary really is a darling! – adj* **1** much loved: *My darling child!* **2** lovable; pretty and appealing: *What a darling little girl!*

dart [da:t] n **1** a pointed arrow-like weapon for throwing or shooting: *a poisoned dart.* **2** a sudden and quick movement. – v to move suddenly and quickly: *The mouse darted into a hole.*

darts n sing a game in which darts are thrown at a board (**'dart-board**) which has a series of numbers on it by which one scores: *a game of darts; (also adj) a darts match.*

dash [daʃ] v **1** to move with speed and violence: *A man dashed into a shop.* **2** to knock, throw etc violently, esp so as to break: *He dashed the bottle to pieces against the wall.* **3** to bring down suddenly and violently or to make very depressed: *Our hopes were dashed.* – n **1** a sudden rush or movement: *The child made a dash for the door.* **2** a small amount of something, esp liquid: *whisky with a dash of soda.* **3** (in writing) a short line (—) to show a break in a sentence etc. **4** energy and enthusiasm: *All his activities showed the same dash and spirit.*

'dashing adj smart and lively: *a dashing young man; She looks very dashing in her new clothes.*

dash off 1 to write quickly: *to dash off a letter.* **2** to leave hastily: *to dash off to the shops.*

dashboard ['daʃbo:d] n a board etc with dials, switches etc in front of the driver's seat in a car.

data ['deitə] n pl or n sing facts or information (esp the information given to a computer): *All the data has/have been fed into the computer.*

'data-bank n a large amount of information which is stored in a computer.

,data-'processing n the handling and processing of information by computer.

date[1] [deit] n **1** (a statement on a letter etc giving) the day of the month, the month and year: *I can't read the date on this letter.* **2** the day and month and/or the year in which something happened or is going to happen: *What is your date of birth?* **3** an appointment or engagement, esp a social one with a member of the opposite sex: *He asked her for a date.* – v **1** to have or put a date on: *This letter isn't dated.* **2** (with **from** or **back**) to belong to; to have been made, written etc at (a certain time): *Their quarrel dates back to last year.* **3** to become obviously old-fashioned: *His books haven't dated much.*

'dated adj old-fashioned: *Her clothes looked very dated.*

'dateline n a north–south line drawn on maps through the Pacific Ocean, east and west of which the date is different.

out of date 1 old-fashioned: *This coat is out of date.* **2** no longer able to be (legally) used; no longer valid: *Your ticket is out of date/very out-of-date; an out-of-date directory.*

to date up to the present time: *This is the best entry we've received to date.*

up to date 1 completed etc up to the present time: *Is the catalogue up to date?; an up-to-date catalogue.* **2** modern and in touch with the latest ideas: *This method is up to date/very up-to-date; an up-to-date method.*

date[2] [deit] n the brown, sticky fruit of the **date palm**, a kind of tree growing in the tropics.

daughter ['do:tə] n a female child (when spoken of in relation to her parents): *That is Mary's daughter; She has two daughters.*

'daughter-in-law – pl **'daughters-in-law** – n a son's wife.

dawdle ['do:dl] v to waste time esp by moving slowly: *Hurry up, and don't dawdle!* **'dawdler** n. **'dawdling** n.

dawn [do:n] v (esp of daylight) to begin to appear: *A new day has dawned. – See also* **dawn on** below. – n **1** the very beginning of a day; very early morning: *We must get up at dawn.* **2** the very beginning of something: *the dawn of civilization.*

'dawning n the act of beginning: *the dawning of a new day/a new age.*

dawn on to become suddenly clear to (a person): *It suddenly dawned on me what he had meant.*

day [dei] n **1** the period from sunrise to sunset: *She worked all day; The days are warm but the nights are cold.* **2** a part of this period eg that part spent at work: *How long is your working day?; The school day ends at 3 o'clock; I see him every day.* **3** the period of twenty-four hours from one midnight to the next: *How many days are in the month of September?* **4** (often in pl) the period of, or of the greatest activity, influence, strength etc of (something or someone): *in my grandfather's day; in the days of steampower.*

'daybreak n dawn; the first appearance of light: *We left at daybreak.*

'day-dream n a dreaming or imagining of pleasant events; the making of unreal plans etc while awake. – v: *She often day-dreams.*

'**daylight** *n* **1** (*also adj*) (of) the light given by the sun: *daylight hours*. **2** dawn: *To get there on time we must leave before daylight*.

day school a school whose pupils attend only during the day and live at home.

'**day-time** *n* the time when it is day.

call it a day to bring (something) to an end; to stop (*eg* working): *I'm so tired that I'll have to call it a day*.

day by day every day: *He's getting better day by day*.

day in, day out *see* **in**.

make someone's day to make someone very happy: *That baby's smile made my day*.

one day 1 at some time in the future: *He hopes to to to America one day*. **2** on a day in the past: *I saw him one day last week*.

some day at some time in the future: *She hopes to get married some day*.

the other day not long ago: *I saw Mr Smith the other day*.

daze [deiz] *v* to make confused (*eg* by a blow or a shock): *She was dazed by the news.* – *n* a bewildered or absent-minded state: *She's been going around in a daze all day*.

dazed *adj* confused (by a blow *etc*): *He came in looking dazed with shock*.

dazzle ['dazl] *v* **1** (of a strong light) to prevent from seeing properly: *I was dazzled by the car's headlights*. **2** to affect the ability of making correct judgements: *She was dazzled by his charm*.

'**dazzling** *adj* **1** extremely bright: *a dazzling light*. **2** colourful; impressive: *a dazzling display of wit*.

dead [ded] *adj* **1** without life; not living: *a dead body*; *Throw out those dead flowers*. **2** not working and not giving any sign of being about to work: *The phone/engine is dead*. **3** absolute or complete: *There was dead silence at his words*; *He came to a dead stop.* – *adv* completely: *dead drunk*.

'**deaden** *v* to lessen, weaken or make less sharp, strong *etc*: *That will deaden the pain*.

'**deadly** *adj* **1** causing death: *a deadly poison*. **2** very great: *He is in deadly earnest* (= He is completely serious). **3** very dull or uninteresting: *What a deadly job this is.* – *adv* (*inf*) extremely: *deadly dull*; *deadly serious*.

dead end a road closed off at one end.

'**dead-end** *adj* leading nowhere: *a dead-end job*.

dead heat a race, or a situation happening in a race, in which two or more competitors cross the finishing line together.

dead language a language no longer spoken, *eg* Latin.

'**deadline** *n* a time by which something must be done or finished: *Monday is the deadline for handing in this essay*.

'**deadlock** *n* a situation in which no further progress towards an agreement is possible: *Talks between the two sides ended in deadlock*.

to set a **deadline** (not **dateline**) for finishing a job.

deaf [def] *adj* **1** unable to hear: *She has been deaf since birth*. **2** (*with* **to**) refusing to understand or to listen: *He was deaf to all arguments*. '**deafness** *n*.

'**deafen** *v* to make hearing difficult; to have an unpleasant effect on the hearing: *I was deafened by the noise in there!*

'**deafening** *adj* very loud: *the deafening roar of the engine*.

‚**deaf-'mute** *n* a person who is deaf and dumb.

fall on deaf ears (of a warning *etc*) to be ignored.

turn a deaf ear to deliberately to ignore: *They turned a deaf ear to my advice*.

deal [di:l] *n* **1** a bargain or arrangement: *a business deal*. **2** the act of dividing cards among players in a card game. – *v* – *pt, ptp* **dealt** [delt] – **1** to do business, *esp* to buy and sell: *I think he deals in stocks and shares*. **2** to distribute (cards).

'**dealer** *n* **1** a person who buys and sells: *a dealer in antiques*. **2** the person who distributes the cards in a card game.

'**dealing** *n* (*usu in pl*) contact (often in business), bargaining, agreement *etc* made (between two or more people or groups): *fair/honest dealing*; *dealing on the Stock Market*; *I have no dealings with him*.

deal with 1 to be concerned with: *This book deals with methods of teaching English*. **2** to take action about, *esp* in order to solve a problem, get rid of a person, complete a piece of business *etc*: *She deals with all the inquiries*.

a good deal/a great deal much or a lot: *They made a good deal of noise*; *She spent a great deal of money on it*.

dean [di:n] *n* **1** the chief clergyman in a cathedral church. **2** an important official in a university.

dear [diə] *adj* **1** high in price: *Cabbages are very dear this week*. **2** very lovable: *He is such a dear little boy*. **3** (*with* **to**) much loved: *She is very dear to me*. **4** used as a polite way of addressing someone, *esp* in a letter: *Dear Sir.* – *n* **1** a person who is lovable or charming: *He is such a dear!* **2** a person who is loved or liked (*esp* used to address someone): *Come in, dear*.

'**dearly** *adv* very much or very strongly: *I would dearly like to see you*; *She loved him dearly*.

dear, dear!/oh dear! mild expressions of regret, sorrow, pity *etc*: *Oh dear! I've forgotten my key*.

death 119 decide

death [deθ] n 1 the act of dying: *There have been several deaths in the town recently*; *Most people fear death.* 2 something which causes one to die: *Smoking too much was the death of him.* 3 the state of being dead: *eyes closed in death.*
'**deathly** adj, adv as if caused by death: *a deathly silence*; *It was deathly quiet.*
'**death-bed** n the bed in which a person dies.
'**death certificate** an official piece of paper signed by a doctor stating the cause of someone's death.
at death's door on the point of dying.
put to death to cause to be killed: *The criminal was put to death by hanging.*
to death very greatly: *I'm sick to death of you.*

debate [di'beit] n a discussion or argument, *esp* a formal one in front of an audience: *a Parliamentary debate.* – v 1 to hold a formal discussion (about): *Parliament will debate the question tomorrow.* 2 to think about or talk about something before coming to a decision: *We debated whether to go by bus or train.*
de'batable adj doubtful; able to be argued about: *a debatable point.*

debauched [di'bɔːtʃt] adj inclined to debauchery.
de'bauchery n too much indulgence in pleasures *usu* considered immoral, *esp* sexual activity and excessive drinking: *a life of debauchery.*

debilitate [di'biliteit] v to make weak.
de'bility n bodily weakness: *Despite his debility, he leads a normal life.*

debit ['debit] n an entry on the side of an account which records what is owed: *His debits outnumbered his credits.* – v – pt, ptp '**debited** – to enter or record on this side of an account.

debris ['deibriː, (Amer) də'briː] n 1 the remains of something broken, destroyed *etc*: *The fireman found a corpse among the debris.* 2 rubbish: *There was a lot of debris in the house after the builder had left.*

debt [det] n what one person owes to another: *His debts amount to over $3,000*; *a debt of gratitude.*
'**debtor** n a person who owes a debt.
in debt owing money.

debut, début ['deibjuː, (Amer) dei'bjuː] n a first public appearance on the stage *etc*: *She made her stage debut at the age of eight.*

decade ['dekeid, di'keid] n a period of ten years: *the first decade of this century* (= 1900–09).

decadence ['dekədəns] n 1 a falling from high to low standards in morals or the arts: *the decadence of the late Roman empire.* 2 the state of having low or incorrect standards of behaviour; immorality: *He lived a life of decadence.*
'**decadent** adj: *a decadent young man.*

decapitate [di'kapiteit] v to cut the head from (*esp* a person): *He was decapitated in the accident.* de,capi'tation n.

decay [di'kei] v to (cause to) become rotten or ruined: *Sugar makes your teeth decay.* – n the act or process of decaying: *tooth decay*; *in a state of decay.*

deceased [di'siːst] adj dead: *His parents, now deceased, were very wealthy.*
the deceased in law, the dead person already mentioned, *esp* one who has recently died: *Were you a friend of the deceased?*

deceit [di'siːt] n (an act of) deceiving: *She was too honest to be capable of deceit.*
de'ceitful adj deceiving or insincere: *She's such a deceitful child!* **de'ceitfully** adv. **de'ceitfulness** n.

deceive [di'siːv] v to mislead or cause to make mistakes, *usu* by giving or suggesting false information: *He was deceived by her innocent appearance.*

decelerate [diː'seləreit] v to slow down, *esp* in a car *etc*: *You must decelerate before a crossroads.* de,cele'ration n.

December [di'sembə] n the twelfth month of the year, the month following November.

decent ['diːsnt] adj 1 fairly good; of fairly good quality: *a decent standard of living.* 2 kindly, tolerant or likeable: *He's a decent enough fellow.* 3 not vulgar or immoral; modest: *Keep your language decent!*
'**decency** n (the general idea of) what is proper, fitting, moral *etc*; the quality or act of being decent: *In the interests of decency, we have banned nude bathing*; *He had the decency to admit that it was his fault.*
'**decently** adv in a manner acceptable to the general idea of what is proper or suitable: *You're not going out unless you're decently dressed.*

deception [di'sepʃən] n (an act of) deceiving: *Deception is difficult in these circumstances.*
de'ceptive [-tiv] adj deceiving; misleading: *Appearances may be deceptive.*
de'ceptively adj: *She is deceptively shy.*

decibel ['desibel] n (abbrev **db**) the main unit of measurement of the loudness of a sound: *Traffic noise is measured in decibels.*

decide [di'said] v 1 to (cause to) make up one's mind: *I have decided to retire*; *What decided you against going?* 2 to settle or make the result (of something) *etc* certain: *The last goal decided the match.*

deciduous [di'sidjuəs, (*Amer*) -dʒuəs] *adj* (of trees) having leaves that fall in autumn: *Oaks are deciduous trees.*

decilitre ['desili:tə] *n* a measure of (liquid) capacity equal to one-tenth of a litre.

decimal ['desiməl] *adj* numbered by tens: *the decimal system.* – *n* a decimal fraction: *Convert these fractions to decimals.*

decimal currency a system of money in which each coin or note is either a tenth of or ten times another in value.

decimal fraction a fraction expressed as so many tenths, hundredths, thousandths *etc* and written with a decimal point, like this: 0·1 (= $^1/_{10}$), 2·33 (= $2^{33}/_{100}$).

decimate ['desimeit] *v* (of disease, battle *etc*) to reduce greatly in number: *The population was decimated by the plague.* ˌdeci'mation *n*.

decipher [di'saifə] *v* 1 to translate (writing in code) into ordinary language: *They deciphered the spy's letter.* 2 to make out the meaning of (something which is difficult to read): *I can't decipher his handwriting.*

decision [di'siʒən] *n* the act of deciding; a judgement: *a time/moment of decision*; *I think you made the wrong decision.*

decisive [di'saisiv] *adj* 1 final; putting an end to a contest, dispute *etc*: *The battle was decisive.* 2 showing decision and firmness: *He's very decisive.* **de'cisiveness** *n*.
de'cisively *adj*: *He acted very decisively.*

deck [dek] *n* 1 a platform extending from one side of a ship *etc* to the other and forming the floor: *The cars are on the lower deck.* 2 a floor in a bus: *Let's go on the top deck.* 3 a pack of playing-cards: *The gambler used his own deck of cards.*
'deck-chair *n* a light collapsible chair: *They were sitting in deck-chairs on the beach.*

declaim [di'kleim] *v* to make (a speech) in an impressive and dramatic manner: *She declaimed against immorality.*

declare [di'kleə] *v* 1 to announce publicly or formally: *War was declared this morning.* 2 to say firmly: *'I don't like him at all,' she declared.* 3 to make known (goods on which duty must be paid, income on which tax should be paid *etc*): *He decided to declare his untaxed earnings to the tax-office.*
declaration [deklə'reiʃən] *n* a formal announcement: *a declaration of marriage/war.*

decline [di'klain] *v* 1 to say 'no' to (an invitation *etc*); to refuse: *We declined his offer of a lift.* 2 to become less strong or less good *etc*: *His health has declined recently*; *Our profits have temporarily declined.* – *n* a gradual lessening or worsening (of health, standards, quantity *etc*): *There has been a gradual decline in the birthrate.*

decode [di:'koud] *v* to translate (a coded message) into ordinary understandable language.

decompose [di:kəm'pouz] *v* (of vegetable or animal matter) to (cause to) decay or rot: *Corpses decompose quickly in heat.*
decomposition [di:kompə'ziʃən] *n*.
ˌdecom'poser *n* something that causes a substance to rot or break up into simpler parts.

décor ['deikɔ:, (*Amer*) dei'kɔ:r] *n* the decoration of a room *etc* and the arrangement of the objects in it: *It was a comfortable room but I didn't like the décor.*

decorate ['dekəreit] *v* 1 to add some kind of ornament *etc* to (something) to make more beautiful, striking *etc*: *We decorated the Christmas tree with glass balls.* 2 to put paint, paper *etc* on the walls, ceiling and woodwork of (a room): *He spent a week decorating the living-room.* 3 to give a medal or badge to (someone) as a mark of honour: *He was decorated for his bravery.*
ˌdeco'ration *n* 1 something used to decorate: *Christmas decorations.* 2 the act of decorating: *The decoration of the house will be a long job.*
'decorative [-rətiv] *adj* ornamental or beautiful (*esp* if not useful): *a decorative arrangement of flowers.*
'decorator *n* a person who decorates rooms, houses *etc*: *He was a painter and decorator.*

decorous ['dekərəs] *adj* (behaving in a manner which is) acceptable, *esp* quiet and dignified: *behaving in a decorous manner.*
'decorously *adv*.
decorum [di'kɔ:rəm] *n* quiet, dignified and proper behaviour: *The man behaved with decorum in the old lady's presence.*

decoy ['di:kɔi] *n* anything intended to lead someone or something into a trap: *The policewoman acted as a decoy when the police were trying to catch the murderer.*

decrease [di'kri:s] *v* to make or become less: *Their numbers had decreased over the previous year.* – ['di:kri:s] *n* a growing less: *a decrease of fifty per cent*; *a gradual decrease in unemployment.*

decree [di'kri:] *n* 1 an order or law: *a decree forbidding hunting.* 2 a ruling of a court of civil law. – *v* – *pt, ptp* **de'creed** – to order, command or decide (something): *The court decreed that he should pay the fine in full.*

dedicate ['dedikeit] *v* 1 to give up wholly to; to devote to: *He dedicated his life to good works.* 2 to set apart, *esp* for a holy or sacred purpose: *He decided to dedicate a chapel to his wife's memory.* 3 (of an author *etc*) to state that (a book *etc*) is in honour of someone: *He dedicated the book to his father*; *He dedicated that song to her.*
'dedicated *adj* spending a great deal of one's time and energy on a subject, one's job *etc*:

She's a dedicated teacher; *He is dedicated to music.*

,dedi'cation *n* **1** the quality of being dedicated; the act of dedicating: *dedication to duty*; *the dedication of the church.* **2** the words dedicating a book to someone: *We can put the dedication at the top of the page.*

deduce [di'dju:s] *v* to work out from facts one knows or guesses: *From the height of the sun I deduced that it was about ten o'clock.*

deduction¹ [di'dʌkʃən] *n* **1** the act of deducing. **2** something that has been deduced: *Is this deduction accurate?*

deduct [di'dʌkt] *v* to subtract; to take away: *They deducted the expenses from his salary.*

de'duction² [-ʃən] *n* something that has been deducted: *There were a lot of deductions from my salary this month.*

deem [di:m] *v* to judge or think: *He deemed it unwise to tell her the truth.*

deed [di:d] *n* something done; an act: *a good deed.*

deep [di:p] *adj* **1** going or being far down or far into: *a deep lake*; *a deep wound.* **2** going or being far down by a named amount: *a hole six feet deep.* **3** occupied or involved to a great extent: *He is deep in debt.* **4** intense; strong: *The sea is a deep blue colour*; *They are in a deep sleep.* **5** low in pitch: *His voice is very deep.* – *adv.* far down or into: *deep into the wood.*

'deepen *v* **1** to make or become deeper: *He deepened the hole.* **2** to increase: *His troubles were deepening.*

'deeply *adv* very greatly: *We are deeply grateful to you.*

'deepness *n* the quality of being deep.

,deep-'freeze *n* a type of refrigerator which freezes food quickly and can keep it for a long time. – *v* to freeze and keep (food) in this.

'deep-sea *adj* of, for, or in the deeper parts of the sea: *deep-sea diving*; *deep-sea fishing.*

in deep water in difficulties or trouble: *He found himself in deep water when he took over the management of the firm.*

*deer [diə] – *pl* **deer** – *n* a kind of large, grass-eating animal, the male of which sometimes has antlers: *a herd of deer.*

deface [di'feis] *v* to spoil the appearance of: *The statue had been defaced with red paint.*

defeat [di'fi:t] *v* to win a victory over: *They defeated our team by three goals*; *We will defeat the enemy eventually.* – *n* the loss of a game, battle, race *etc*: *His defeat in the last race depressed him*; *We suffered yet another defeat.*

de'feated *adj* (*neg* **un-**): *a defeated enemy.*

de'featism *n* a state of mind in which one expects and accepts defeat too easily: *The defeatism of the captain affects the rest of the players.*

de'featist *n, adj* (of) a person who gives up too easily and is too easily discouraged: *She is such a defeatist*; *She has a defeatist attitude to life.*

defect ['di:fekt] *n* a fault or flaw: *It was a basic defect in her character*; *a defect in the china.* – [di'fekt] *v* to leave a country, political party *etc* to go and join another; to desert: *He defected to the West.*

de'fection [-ʃən] *n* (an act of) desertion.

de'fective [-tiv] *adj* having a fault or flaw: *a defective machine*; *He is mentally defective.*

defence, (*Amer*) **defense** [di'fens] *n* **1** the act or action of defending against attack: *the defence of Rome*; *He spoke in defence of the plans.* **2** the method or equipment used to guard or protect: *The walls will act as a defence against flooding.* **3** a person's answer to an accusation *esp* in a law-court: *What is your defence?*

de'fenceless *adj* helpless or without protection.

the defence the case on behalf of a person who is accused in a law court: *the counsel for the defence.*

defend [di'fend] *v* **1** to guard or protect against attack: *The soldiers defended the castle*; *I am prepared to defend my opinions.* **2** to conduct the defence of (a person) in a law-court.

de'fendant *n* a person accused or sued in a law-court.

de'fender *n* a person who defends (someone or something): *the defenders of the castle.*

de'fensive [-siv] *adj* protective or resisting attack: *a defensive attitude*; *defensive action.*

defer¹ [di'fə:] – *pt, ptp* **de'ferred** – *v* to put off to another time: *They can defer their departure.*

defer² [di'fə] – *pt, ptp* **de'ferred** – *v* (*with* **to**) to act according to the wishes or opinions of another or the orders of authority: *I defer to your greater knowledge of the matter.*

deference ['defərəns] *n* **1** willingness to consider the wishes *etc* of others: *He always treats his mother with deference.* **2** the act of deferring.

in deference to showing respct for: *I let him speak first, in deference to his authority.*

defiance [di'faiəns] *n* open disobedience; challenging or opposition: *He went in defiance of my orders.*

de'fiant *adj* hostile; showing or feeling defiance: *a defiant attitude.* **de'fiantly** *adv.*

deficient [di'fiʃənt] *adj* lacking in what is needed: *Their food is deficient in vitamins.*

de'ficiency – *pl* **de'ficiencies** – *n* (a) shortage or absence of what is needed.

deficit ['defisit] *n* the amount by which an amount (of money *etc*) is less than the amount required: *a deficit of several hundred dollars.*

define [di'fain] *v* to fix or state the exact meaning of: *Words are defined in a dictionary.* **de'finable** *adj.*

definition [defi'niʃən] *n* an explanation of the exact meaning of a word or phrase: *Is that definition accurate?*

definite ['definit] *adj* clear; fixed or certain: *I'll give you a definite answer later.*
'definitely *adv* clearly or certainly: *She definitely said I wasn't to wait; Her dress is definitely not red.*
definite article the name given to the word **the.**

definition *see* **define.**

deflate [di'fleit] *v* 1 to let gas out of (a tyre *etc*). 2 to reduce (a person's) importance, self-confidence *etc*: *He was completely deflated by his failure.* **de'flation** *n.*

deflect [di'flekt] *v* to turn aside (from a fixed course or direction): *He deflected the blow with his arm.* **de'flection** [-ʃən] *n.*

deform [di'fo:m] *v* to spoil the shape of: *Heat deforms plastic.*
de'formed *adj* twisted out of the correct shape: *His foot was deformed.*
de'formity – *pl* **de'formities** – *n* 1 the state of being badly shaped or formed: *Drugs can cause deformity.* 2 a part which is not the correct shape: *A twisted foot is a deformity.*

defrost [di:'frost] *v* 1 to remove frost or ice from (*eg* a refrigerator): *I keep forgetting to defrost the freezer.* 2 (of frozen food *etc*) to thaw (out): *Make sure you defrost the chicken thoroughly.*

deft [deft] *adj* skilful, quick and neat: *his deft handling of the situation.* **'deftly** *adv.* **'deftness** *n.*

defuse [di:'fju:z] *v* 1 to remove the fuse from (a bomb *etc*). 2 to make harmless or less dangerous: *He succeeded in defusing the situation.*

defy [di'fai] *v* 1 to dare (someone to act); to challenge: *I defy you to try and stop me!* 2 to resist boldly or openly: *Are you defying my authority?*

degenerate [di'dʒenərət] *adj* having become immoral or inferior: *the degenerate son of well-respected parents.* – *n* a person, plant *etc* that is degenerate. – [-reit] *v* to become much less good or admirable: *The discussion degenerated into insults.*

degrade [di'greid] *v* to disgrace or make contemptible: *He felt degraded by having to ask for money.*
de'grading *adj* tending to make lower in rank *etc* or to disgrace: *a degrading occupation.*

degree [di'gri:] *n* 1 (an) amount or extent: *There is still a degree of uncertainty; The degree of skill varies considerably from per-*

son to person. 2 a unit of temperature: *20°* (= 20 degrees) *Celsius.* 3 a unit by which angles are measured: *at an angle of 90°* (= 90 degrees). 4 a title or certificate given by a university *etc*: *He took a degree in chemistry.*
by degrees gradually: *We reached the desired standard of efficiency by degrees.*
to a degree to a small extent: *I agree with you to a degree,* but I have doubts about your conclusions.

dehydrate [di:hai'dreit] *v* to remove water from or dry out (*esp* foodstuffs): *Vegetables take up less space if they have been dehydrated.* **dehy'dration** *n.*

deity ['deiəti, (*Amer*) 'di:əti] – *pl* **'deities** – *n* a god or goddess: *Bacchus was one of the Roman deities.*

deity is spelt with **-ei-**.

dejected [di'dʒektid] *adj* gloomy or miserable: *He looked rather dejected.* **de'jectedly** *adv.* **de'jection** [-ʃən] *n.*

delay [di'lei] *v* 1 to put off to another time: *We have delayed publication of the book till the spring.* 2 to keep or stay back or slow down: *I was delayed by the traffic.* – *n* (something which causes) keeping back or slowing down: *He came without delay; My work is subject to delays.*

delegate ['deləgeit] *v* to give (a piece of work, power *etc*) to someone else: *He delegates a great deal of work to his assistant.* – [-gət, (*Amer*) -geit] *n* an elected representative (to a conference, Parliament, committee *etc*): *The delegates met in the conference room.*
dele'gation *n* a body of delegates.

delete [di'li:t] *v* to rub or strike out (*eg* a piece of writing): *Delete his name from the list.* **de'letion** *n.*

deliberate [di'libərət] *adj* 1 intentional and not by accident: *That was a deliberate insult.* 2 cautious and not hurried: *He had a very deliberate way of walking.*
de'liberately [-rət-] *adv* 1 on purpose: *You did that deliberately!* 2 carefully and without hurrying: *He spoke quietly and deliberately.*

delicate ['delikət] *adj* 1 requiring special treatment or careful handling: *delicate china; a delicate situation/problem.* 2 of fine texture *etc*; dainty: *a delicate pattern ; the delicate skin of a child.* 3 able to do fine, accurate work: *a delicate instrument.* 4 subtle: *a delicate wine; a delicate shade of blue.*
'delicately *adv.*
'delicacy – *pl* **'delicacies** – *n* 1 the state or quality of being delicate. 2 something delicious and special to eat: *Caviare is a delicacy.*

delicatessen [delikə'tesn] *n* (a shop selling)

foods prepared ready for the table, *esp* cooked meats and *usu* unusual and foreign foods: *I bought some smoked sausage at the delicatessen.*

delicious [di'liʃəs] *adj* highly pleasing to the taste: *a delicious meal.* **de'liciously** *adv.* **de'liciousness** *n.*

delight [di'lait] *v* **1** to please greatly: *I was delighted by/at the news; They were delighted to accept the invitation.* **2** to have or take great pleasure (from): *He delights in teasing me.* – *n* (something which causes) great pleasure: *Peacefulness is one of the delights of country life.*
de'lightful *adj* causing delight: *a delightful person/party.* **de'lightfully** *adv.*

delirious [di'liriəs] *adj* **1** wandering in the mind and talking complete nonsense (*usu* as a result of fever): *The sick man was delirious and nothing he said made sense.* **2** wild with excitement: *She was delirious with happiness at the news.*
de'liriously *adv*: *deliriously happy.*

deliver [di'livə] *v* **1** to give or hand over (something) to the person for whom it is intended: *The postman delivers letters.* **2** to give: *He delivered a long speech.* **3** to assist (a woman) at the birth of (a child): *The doctor delivered the twins safely.*
de'livery – *pl* **de'liveries** – *n* **1** (an act of) handing over (letters, parcels *etc*): *There are two parcel deliveries a week.* **2** the process of the birth of a child: *the delivery of the twins.*

delta ['deltə] *n* a roughly triangular area of land formed at the mouth of a river which reaches the sea in two or more branches: *the delta of the Nile.*

delude [di'lu:d] *v* to deceive or mislead (*usu* without actually telling lies): *She deluded herself into thinking he cared for her.*
de'lusion [-ʒən] *n* a false belief, *esp* as a symptom of mental illness: *The young man was suffering from delusions.*

deluge ['delju:dʒ] *n* a great quantity of water: *Few people survived the deluge.* – *v* to fill or overwhelm with a great quantity: *We've been deluged with orders for our new book.*

delusion *see* delude.

de luxe [də'luks] *adj* very luxurious or elegant; special (*esp* with extra qualities not found in an ordinary version of something): *a de luxe model of a car.*

demand [di'ma:nd] *v* **1** to ask or ask for firmly and sharply: *I demanded an explanation.* **2** to require or need: *This demands careful thought.* – *n* **1** a request made so that it sounds like a command: *They refused to meet the workers' demands for more money.* **2** an urgent claim: *The children make demands on my time.* **3** willingness or desire to buy or obtain (certain goods *etc*); a need

for (certain goods *etc*): *There's no demand for books of this kind.*
de'manding *adj* requiring a lot of effort, ability *etc*: *a demanding job.*
on demand when asked for: *I'm expected to supply meals on demand.*

demeanour, (*Amer*) **demeanor** [dimi:nə] *n* manner; bearing; the way one behaves.

demo *see* demonstration.

democracy [di'mokrəsi] – *pl* **de'mocracies** – *n* (a country having) a form of government in which the people freely elect representatives to govern them: *Which is the world's largest democracy?; He believes in democracy.*
democrat ['deməkrat] *n* one who believes in democracy as a principle: *She likes to pretend she's a democrat.*
democratic [demə'kratik] *adj* (*neg* **un-**) **1** belonging to, governed by or typical of democracy: *a democratic country.* **2** believing in equal rights and privileges for all: *The boss is very democratic.*
democratically [demə'kratikəli] *adv* (*neg* **un-**) following democratic principles: *The issue was decided democratically by taking a general vote.*

demolish [di'moliʃ] *v* to pull or tear down: *They're demolishing the old buildings in the centre of town.* **demo'lition** [demə-] *n.*

demon ['di:mən] *n* an evil spirit; a devil: *demons from Hell.*

demonstrate ['demənstreit] *v* **1** to show clearly: *This demonstrates his ignorance of the situation.* **2** to show how (something) works: *He demonstrated the new vacuum cleaner.* **3** to express an opinion (*usu* political) by marching, showing banners *etc* in public: *A crowd collected to demonstrate against the new taxes.*
demon'stration *n* **1** a display or exhibition (of how something works *etc*): *I'd like a demonstration of this dishwasher.* **2** (*also* **'demo** ['demou] – *pl* **'demos**) a public expression of opinion by holding meetings and processions, showing placards *etc.*
'demonstrator *n* **1** a person who takes part in a public demonstration. **2** a teacher or assistant who helps students with practical work.
demonstrative adjective/pronoun any one of the words **this, that, these** or **those.**

demoralize, -ise [di'morəlaiz] *v* to take away the confidence and courage of: *The army was demoralized by its defeat.*

demote [di'mout] *v* to reduce to a lower rank: *He was demoted for misconduct.* **de'motion** *n.*

demure [di'mjuə] *adj* quiet, shy, modest and well behaved (sometimes deceptively): *She looked too demure ever to do such a bold thing.* **de'murely** *adv.* **de'mureness** *n.*

den [den] n **1** the home of a wild beast: *a lion's den*. **2** a private room for working in etc.

denial *see* **deny**.

denigrate ['denigreit] v to attack the reputation etc of: *I'm not trying to denigrate her achievement*. ˌdeni'gration n.

denim ['denim] n, adj (of) a kind of cotton cloth, often blue, used for making jeans, overalls etc.
'**denims** n pl clothes, esp jeans, made of denim: *She wore blue denims*; *a pair of denims*.

denomination [dinomi'neiʃən] n **1** a value (of a stamp, coin etc): *banknotes of all denominations*. **2** a group of people with the same religious beliefs: *This service is open to people of all denominations*.

denote [di'nout] v to be the sign of or to mean: *Do you think his silence denotes guilt?*

denounce [di'nauns] v to accuse publicly (of a crime etc): *He was denounced as a murderer*. **denunciation** [dinʌnsi'eiʃən] n.

dense [dens] adj **1** thick and close: *We made our way through dense forest*; *The fog was so dense that we could not see anything*. **2** very stupid: *He's so dense I have to tell him everything twice*.
'**densely** adv very closely together: *The crowd was densely packed*.
'**density** n **1** the number or items, people etc found in a given area compared with other areas esp if large: *the density of the population*. **2** the quantity of matter in each unit of volume: *the density of a gas*.

dent [dent] n a small hollow made by pressure or a blow: *My car has a dent where it hit a tree*. – v to make such a hollow in: *The car was dented when it hit a wall*.

dental ['dentl] adj of or for the teeth: *Regular dental care is essential for healthy teeth*.

dentist ['dentist] n a person who cares for diseases etc of the teeth, by filling or removing them etc: *Our dentist is very careful*; *I hate going to the dentist*.
'**dentistry** n a dentist's work.

dentures ['dentʃəz] n pl a set of artificial teeth: *Do you wear dentures?*

denunciation *see* **denounce**.

deny [di'nai] v **1** to declare not to be true: *He denied the charge of theft*. **2** to refuse (to give or grant someone something); to say 'no' to: *He was denied admission to the house*.
de'nial n **1** (an act of) declaring that something is not true: *Do you accept her denial?* **2** (an act of) refusing someone something: *a denial of his request*.

deodorant [di:'oudərənt] n a substance that destroys or conceals unpleasant (body) smells: *She perspires a lot – she should use (a) deodorant*.

depart [di'pa:t] v **1** to go away: *The tour departed from the station at 9 a.m.* **2** (with from) to cease to follow (a course of action): *We departed from our original plan*.
de'parture [-tʃə] n an act of departing: *The departure of the train was delayed*.

department [di'pa:tmənt] n a part or section of a government, university, office or shop: *The Department of Justice*; *the sales department*.
ˌdepart'mental adj: *a departmental manager*.
department store a large shop with many different departments selling a wide variety of goods.

department (not **departmental**) store.

departure *see* **depart**.

depend [di'pend] v (with on) **1** to rely on: *You can't depend on his arriving on time*. **2** to rely on receiving necessary (financial) support from: *The school depends for its survival on money from the Church*. **3** (of a future happening etc) to be decided by: *Our success depends on everyone working hard*.
de'pendable adj (neg **un-**) trustworthy or reliable: *I know he'll remember to get the wine – he's very dependable*.
de'pendant n a person who is kept or supported by another: *He has five dependants to support – a wife and four children*.
de'pendent adj **1** relying on (someone etc) for (financial) support: *He is totally dependent on his parents*. **2** (of a future happening etc) to be decided by: *Whether we go or not is dependent on whether we have enough money*.
it/that depends, it all depends what happens, is decided etc, will be affected by something else: *I don't know if I'll go to the party – it all depends*.

to look after one's **dependants** (not **dependents**).
to be **dependent** (not **dependant**) on one's parents.

depict [di'piktk] v **1** to paint, draw etc. **2** to describe: *Her novel depicts the life of country people*.

deplete [di'pli:t] v to make smaller in amount, number etc; *Our supplies of food are rather depleted*. **de'pletion** n.

deplore [di'plo:] v to express disapproval and regret about (something): *We all deplore the actions of murderers*.
de'plorable adj very bad: *deplorable behaviour*.

deport [di'po:t] v (of a government etc) to send (a person) out of the country eg because he has committed a crime or because he is not officially supposed to be there: *He is being deported on a charge of murder*. ˌdepor'tation [di:po:-] n.

depose [di'pouz] *v* to remove from a high position (*eg* from that of a king): *They have deposed the emperor.*

deposit [di'pozit] *v* 1 to put or set down: *She deposited her shopping-basket in the kitchen.* 2 to put in for safe keeping: *He deposited the money in the bank.* – *n* 1 an act of putting money in a bank *etc*: *She made several large deposits at the bank during that month.* 2 an act of paying money as a guarantee that money which is or will be owed will be paid: *We have put down a deposit on a house in the country.* 3 the money put into a bank or paid as a guarantee in this way: *We decided we could not afford to go on holiday and managed to get back the deposit which we had paid.* 4 a quantity of solid matter that has settled at the bottom of a liquid, or is left behind by a liquid: *The flood-water left a yellow deposit over everything.* 5 a layer (of coal, iron *etc*) occurring naturally in rock: *rich deposits of iron ore.*

depot ['depou, (*Amer*) 'di:-] *n* 1 the place where railway engines, buses *etc* are kept and repaired: *a bus depot.* 2 a storehouse or warehouse. 3 a military station or headquarters.

depress [di'pres] *v* 1 to make sad or gloomy: *I am always depressed by wet weather.* 2 to make less active: *This drug depresses the action of the heart.*
de'pressed *adj* 1 sad or unhappy: *The news made me very depressed.* 2 made less active: *the depressed state of the stock market.*
de'pressing *adj* tending to make one sad or gloomy: *What a depressing piece of news!*
de'pression [-ʃən] *n* 1 a state of sadness and low spirits: *She was treated by the doctor for depression.* 2 lack of activity in trade: *the depression of the 1930s.* 3 an area of low pressure in the atmosphere: *The bad weather is caused by a depression.* 4 a hollow.

deprive [di'praiv] *v* (*with* **of**) to take something away from: *They deprived him of food and drink.*
deprivation [depri'veiʃən] *n* 1 (a condition of) loss, hardship, *etc*. 2 (an) act of depriving.
de'prived *adj* suffering from hardship *etc*, under-privileged: *deprived areas of the city.*

depth [depθ] *n* 1 the distance from the top downwards or from the surface inwards *esp* if great: *Coal is mined at a depth of 1000m.* 2 intensity or strength *esp* if great: *The depth of colour was astonishing; The depth of his feeling prevented him from speaking.*
depths *n pl* a part far under the surface or in the middle of something: *the depths of the sea; the depths of winter.*

'in-depth *adj* (of a survey *etc*) deep and thorough: *an in-depth report on alcoholism.*
in depth deeply and thoroughly: *I have studied the subject in depth.*

depute [di'pju:t] *v* 1 to appoint a person to take over a task *etc*. 2 to hand over (a task *etc*) to someone else to do for one.
,depu'tation [depju-] *n* a group of people appointed to represent others: *The miners sent a deputation to the Prime Minister.*
deputize, -ise ['depju-] *v* to act as a deputy: *She deputized for her father at the meeting.*
deputy ['depjuti] *n* someone appointed to help a person and take over some of his jobs if necessary: *While the boss was ill, his deputy ran the office.*

deranged [di'reindʒd] *adj* insane: *His mind had become deranged as a result of his ordeal; mentally deranged.* **de'rangement** *n*.

derelict ['derilikt] *adj* abandoned and left to fall to pieces: *a derelict airfield.*

deride [di'raid] *v* to laugh at; to mock.
derision [di'riʒən] *n* mockery or laughter which shows scorn and contempt: *His remarks were greeted with shouts of derision.*
de'risive [-siv] *adj* 1 mocking; showing scorn: *derisive laughter.* 2 causing or deserving scorn: *The salary they offered me was derisive.*
de'risory [-səri] *adj* ridiculous: *His attempts were derisory.*

derive [di'raiv] *v* (with **from**) 1 to come or develop from: *The word derives/is derived from an old French word.* 2 to draw or take from (a source or origin): *We derive comfort from his presence.*
,deri'vation [deri-] *n* 1 the source or origin (of a word *etc*). 2 the process of deriving.
derivative [di'rivətiv] *adj* derived from something else and not original. – *n* a word, substance *etc* formed from another word, substance *etc*: *'Reader' is a derivative of 'read'.*

derrick ['derik] *n* an apparatus like a mechanical crane for lifting weights: *The ship was unloaded, using the large derricks on the quay.*

descend [di'send] *v* 1 to go or climb down from a higher place or position: *He descended the staircase.* 2 to slope downwards: *The hills descend to the sea.* 3 (with **on**) to make a sudden attack on: *The soldiers descended on the helpless villagers.*
de'scendant *n* the child, grandchild, great-grandchild *etc* of a person: *This is a photograph of my grandmother with all her descendants.*
de'scent [-t] *n* 1 the act of descending: *The descent of the hill was quickly completed.* 2 a slope: *That is a steep descent.* 3 family; ancestry: *She is of royal descent.*
be descended from to be a descendant of.

the noun **descendant** ends in **-ant** (not **-ent**).

describe [di'skraib] *v* **1** to give an account of in words: to tell in words what something or someone is like: *He described what had happened*; *Would you describe her as beautiful?* **2** to say that one is something: *He describes himself as a salesman.*

de'scription [-'skrip-] *n* **1** (an) act of describing: *I recognized him from your description.* **2** an account of anything in words: *He gave a description of his holiday.* **3** a sort or kind: *He carried a gun of some description.*

to **describe** (not **describe about**) a scene.

desert¹ [di'zə:t] *v* **1** to go away from and leave without help *etc*; to leave or abandon: *Why did you desert us?* **2** to run away, *usu* from the army: *He was shot for trying to desert.* **de'serted** *adj* **1** with no people *etc*: *The streets are completely deserted.* **2** abandoned: *his deserted wife and children.*

de'serter *n* a man who deserts from the army *etc*.

de'sertion [-ʃən] *n* (an) act of deserting.

desert² ['dezət] *n* an area of barren country, *usu* hot, dry and sandy, where there is very little rain: *Parts of the country are almost desert*; (*also adj*) *desert plants.*

the Sahara **desert** (not **dessert**).

deserve [di'zə:v] *v* to have earned as a right by one's actions; to be worthy of: *He deserves recognition of his achievements.*

de'serving *adj* (*neg* **un-**) **1** worthy or suitable (to be given charity *etc*): *I only give money to deserving causes.* **2** (*with* **of**) worthy of: *He is deserving of better treatment than this.*

desiccated ['desikeitid] *adj* completely dried out: *desiccated coconut.*

design [di'zain] *v* to invent and prepare a plan of (something) before it is built or made: *A famous architect designed this building.* – *n* **1** a sketch or plan produced before something is made: *a design for a dress.* **2** style; the way in which something has been made or put together: *It is very modern in design*; *I don't like the design of that building.* **3** a pattern *etc*: *The curtains have a flower design on them.* **4** a plan formed in the mind; (an) intention: *Our holidays coincided by design and not by accident.*

de'signer *n* a person who makes designs or patterns: *He is the designer of the yacht.*

de'signing *n* the art of making designs or patterns: *dress-designing.*

designate ['dezigneit] *v* **1** to call or name: *It was designated a conservation area.* **2** to point out or identify: *He has been designated our next Prime Minister.* – *adj* (placed *immediately after noun*) appointed to an office *etc* but not yet having begun it: *the ambassador designate.*

,desig'nation *n* a name or title.

designer *etc see* **design**.

desire [di'zaiə] *n* a wish or longing: *I have a sudden desire for a bar of chocolate*; *I have no desire ever to see him again.* – *v* to long for or feel desire for: *After a day's work, all I desire is a hot bath.*

de'sirable *adj* pleasing or worth having: *a desirable residence.*

de,sira'bility *n* the extent to which something is desirable.

desk [desk] *n* a piece of furniture, often like a table, for sitting at while writing, reading *etc*: *She kept the pile of letters in a drawer in her desk.*

desolate ['desələt] *adj* **1** (of landscapes, areas *etc*) very lonely or barren: *desolate moorland.* **2** (of people) very sad, lonely and unhappy. **deso'lation** *n*.

despair [di'speə] *v* to lose hope (of): *I despair of ever teaching my son anything.* – *n* **1** the state of having given up hope: *He was filled with despair at the news.* **2** (*with* **the**) something which causes someone to despair: *He is the despair of his mother.*

desperate ['despərət] *adj* **1** (*sometimes used loosely*) despairingly reckless or violent: *She was desperate to get into university*; *a desperate criminal.* **2** very bad or almost hopeless: *We are in a desperate situation.* **3** urgent and despairing: *He made a desperate appeal for help.* **'desperately** *adv.*

,despe'ration *n*: *In desperation we asked the police for help.*

despise [di'spaiz] *v* **1** to look upon with scorn and contempt: *I know he despises me for being stupid.* **2** to refuse to have, use *etc*; to scorn: *She despises such luxuries as fur boots.*

despicable [di'spikəbl] *adj* contemptible, worthless and deserving to be despised: *His behaviour was despicable.* **de'spicably** *adv.*

despite [di'spait] *prep* in spite of: *He didn't get the job despite all his qualifications.*

despondent [di'spondənt] *adj* feeling miserable, unhappy, gloomy *etc*: *She was utterly despondent at her failure.* **de'spondently** *adv.* **de'spondency** *n.*

despot ['despot, (*Amer*) -pət] *n* a person (*usu* the king or ruler of a country) with absolute power, often a tyrant. **de'spotic** *adj.* **de'spotically** *adv.*

'despotism [-pə-] *n* absolute power or tyranny.

dessert [di'zə:t] *n* **1** the sweet course in a meal; pudding: *We had ice-cream for dessert.* **2** fruits, sweets *etc* served at the end of dinner.

to eat a **dessert** (not **desert**).

destination [desti'neiʃən] n the place to which
someone or something is going: I think
we've arrived at our destination at last.

destined ['destind] adj 1 (having a future)
organized or arranged beforehand (by a
person or by fate): She was destined for
success. 2 bound or heading (for a place):
destined for Singapore.

destiny ['destəni] – pl 'destinies – n the power
which appears or is thought to control
events; fate: We are all subject to the tricks
played by destiny.

destitute ['destitju:t] adj in great need of food,
shelter etc: They were left destitute when he
died.

destroy [di'stroi] v 1 to put an end to or make
useless; to ruin: Vandals destroyed the
painting. 2 to kill (animals): This poison
destroys rats.
  de'stroyer n a type of small fast warship:
  naval destroyers.

destruction [di'strʌkʃən] n 1 the act or process of destroying or being destroyed: the
destruction of the city. 2 the state of being
destroyed; ruin: a scene of destruction.
  des'tructive [-tiv] adj 1 causing or able to
  cause destruction: Small children can be
  very destructive. 2 (of criticism etc)
  pointing out faults etc without suggesting
  improvements. de'structively adv.
  de'structiveness n.

detach [di'tatʃ] v to unfasten or remove
(from): I detached the bottom part of the
form and sent it back.
  de'tachable adj able to be detached.
  de'tached adj 1 standing etc apart or by
  itself: a detached house. 2 not personally
  involved or showing no emotion or prejudice: a detached attitude to the problem.
  de'tachment n 1 the state of not being influenced by emotion or prejudice. 2 the act of
  detaching. 3 a group (esp of soldiers): A
  detachment was sent to guard the supplies.

detail ['di:teil, (Amer also) di'teil] n 1 a
small part or an item: She paid close attention to the small details. 2 all the small
features and parts considered as a whole:
Look at the amazing detail in this drawing!
  'detailed adj giving many details with nothing left out: His instructions were very detailed.
  in detail item by item, giving attention to
  the details: I'll tell you the story in detail.

detain [di'tein] v 1 to hold back and delay: I
won't detain you – I can see you're in a
hurry. 2 (of the police etc) to keep under
guard: Three suspects were detained at the
police station.
  detai'nee n a person who is detained (by the
  police etc).

de'tention [-'ten-] the state of being imprisoned: The criminals are in detention.

detect [di'tekt] v to notice or discover: She
thought she could detect a smell of gas.
  de'tective [-tiv] n a person who tries to find
  criminals or watches suspected persons:
  She was questioned by detectives.

detention see detain.

deter [di'tə:] – pt, ptp de'terred – v to make
less willing or prevent by frightening: She
was not deterred by his threats.
  de'terrent [-'te-, (Amer) -'tə:-] n, adj
  (something) that deters: The possession of
  nuclear weapons by nations is thought to be a
  deterrent against nuclear war itself; a deterrent effect.

detergent [di'tə:dʒənt] n a (soapless) substance used for cleaning: She poured detergent into the washing-machine.

deteriorate [di'tiəriəreit] v to grow worse: His
work has deteriorated recently. de,terio'ration n.

determine [di'tə:min] v 1 to fix or settle; to
decide: He determined his course of action.
2 to find out exactly: He tried to determine
what had gone wrong.
  de,termi'nation n 1 firmness of character or
  stubbornness: She showed her determination
  by refusing to give way. 2 the act of deter-
  mining.
  de'termined adj 1 having one's mind made
  up: She is determined to succeed. 2 stubborn: He's very determined. 3 fixed or settled: Our route has already been determined.

deterrent see deter.

detest [di'test] v to hate intensely: I detest
cruelty.
  de'testable adj extremely hateful.

detonate ['detəneit] v to (cause to) explode
violently: This device detonates the bomb.
  deto'nation n an explosion.
  'detonator n something (esp a piece of
  equipment) that sets off an explosion.

detour ['di:tuə] n a wandering from the direct
way: We made a detour through the mountains.

detriment ['detrimənt] n harm, damage or
disadvantage: to the detriment of his health.
  detri'mental [-'men-] adj causing harm or
  damage.

devalue [di:'valju:] v to reduce the value of
(esp a currency): The government devalued
the dollar.
  devalu'ation [di:val-] n the act of devalu-
  ing.

devastate ['devəsteit] v 1 to leave in ruins:
The fire devastated the countryside. 2 to
overwhelm (a person) with grief: She was
devastated by the terrible news.
  'devastating adj overwhelming: a devastating flood; The news was devastating.

develop [di'veləp] – pt, ptp de'veloped – v 1 to

(cause to) grow bigger or to a more advanced state: *The plan developed slowly in his mind*; *It has developed into a very large city.* **2** to acquire gradually: *He developed the habit of getting up early.* **3** to become active, visible *etc*; *Spots developed on her face.* **4** to use chemicals to make (a photograph) visible: *My brother develops all his own films.*

de'velopment *n* **1** the process or act of developing: *a crucial stage in the development of a child.* **2** something new which is the result of developing: *important new developments in science.*

deviate ['di:vieit] *v* to turn aside, *esp* from a right, normal or standard course: *She will not deviate from her routine.* **,devi'ation** *n*.

device [di'vais] *n* **1** something made for a purpose, *eg* a tool or instrument: *a device for opening cans.* **2** a plan or system of doing something, sometimes involving trickery: *This is a device for avoiding income-tax.*

device, unlike **advice**, can be used in the plural: *ingenious devices.*
devise is a verb: *to devise a scheme.*

devil ['devl] *n* **1** the spirit of evil; Satan: *He does not worship God – he worships the Devil.* **2** any evil or wicked spirit or person: *That woman is a devil!* **3** a person who is bad or disapproved of: *She's a lazy devil.* **4** an unfortunate person for whom one feels pity: *Poor devils! I feel really sorry for them.*

devious ['di:viəs] *adj* not direct; not straightforward: *We climbed the hill by a devious route*; *He used devious methods to get what he wanted.* **'deviously** *adv*. **'deviousness** *n*.

devise [di'vaiz] *v* to invent; to put together: *A shelter/new scheme was hurriedly devised.*

devoid [di'void] *adj* (*with* **of**) free from or lacking: *That is devoid of any meaning.*

devote [di'vout] *v* (*with* **to**) to give up wholly to or use entirely for: *She devotes her life to music.*

de'voted *adj* **1** (*sometimes with* **to**) loving and loyal: *a devoted friend*; *I am devoted to him.* **2** (*with* **to**) given up (to): *He is devoted to his work.*

devotee [devə'ti:] *n* a keen follower; an enthusiast: *a devotee of football.*

de'votion *n* **1** great love: *her undying devotion for her children.* **2** the act of devoting or of being devoted: *devotion to duty.*

devour [di'vauə] *v* to eat up greedily: *He was devoured by a lion*; *She devoured the chocolates.*

devout [di'vaut] *adj* **1** earnest or sincere: *Please accept my devout thanks.* **2** religious: *a devout Christian.*

dew [dju:] *n* tiny drops of moisture coming

from the air as it cools, *esp* at night: *The grass is wet with early-morning dew.*

dexterity [dek'sterəti] *n* skill and/or quickness, *esp* with the hands: *She showed her dexterity with a needle and thread.*
'dext(e)rous *adj* skilful, *esp* with the hands: *He is a very dexterous surgeon.*

dhobi ['doubi] *n* an Indian washerman.

dhoti ['douti] *n* the loincloth worn by Hindus.

diabetes [daiə'bi:ti:z] *n* a disease in which there is usually too much sugar in the blood.
,dia'betic [-'be-] *n* a person who suffers from diabetes: *He is a diabetic.* – *adj* relating to or suffering from diabetes: *a diabetic patient.*

diagnose [daiəg'nouz, (*Amer*) -'nous] *v* to say what is wrong (with a sick person *etc*) after making an examination; to identify (an illness *etc*): *The doctor diagnosed her illness as flu.*
,diag'nosis [-sis] – *pl* **diag'noses** [-si:z] – *n* a conclusion reached by diagnosing: *What diagnosis did the doctor make?*

diagonal [dai'agənl] *n* a line going from one corner to the opposite corner: *The two diagonals of a rectangle cross at the centre.*
di'agonally *adv* in a diagonal line: *He walked diagonally across the field.*

diagram ['daiəgram] *n* a drawing used to explain something that is difficult to understand: *This book has diagrams showing the parts of a car engine.*

dial ['daiəl] *n* **1** the face of a watch or clock: *My watch has a dial you can see in the dark.* **2** the turning disc over the numbers on a telephone. **3** any disc *etc* bearing numbers *etc* used to give information: *the dial on a radio.* – *v* – *pt, ptp* **'dialled** – to turn a telephone dial to get a number: *She dialled the wrong number.*

dialect ['daiəlekt] *n* a way of speaking found only in a certain area or among a certain group or class of people: *They were speaking in dialect.*

dialogue, (*Amer*) **dialog(ue)** ['daiəlog] *n* (a) talk between two or more people, *esp* in a play or novel.

diameter [dai'amitə] *n* (the length of) a straight line drawn from side to side of a circle, passing through its centre: *Could you measure the diameter of that circle?*

diamond ['daiəmənd] *n* **1** a very hard, colourless precious stone: *Her brooch had three diamonds in it*; (*also adj*) *a diamond ring.* **2** a piece of diamond (often artificial) used as a tip on *eg* a record-player stylus. **3*** a kind of four-sided figure or shape; ◇: *There was a a pattern of red and yellow diamonds on the floor.* **4** one of the playing-cards of the suit diamonds, which have red symbols of this shape on them.

* see illustration on p. 476

'**diamonds** *n pl* (sometimes treated as *n sing*) one of the four card suits: *the five of diamonds.*

diaper ['daiəpə] *see* **nappy.**

diarrhoea, (*Amer*) **diarrhea** [daiə'riə] *n* too much liquid in and too frequent emptying of the bowels: *He has diarrhoea.*

diary ['daiəri] – *pl* '**diaries** – *n* a (small book containing a) record of daily happenings: *The explorer kept a diary of his adventures.*

dice [dais] – *pl* **dice** – *n* (*Amer* **die** [dai]) a small cube, *usu* with numbered sides or faces, used in certain games: *It is your turn to throw the dice.* – *v* **1** to cut (vegetables *etc*) into small cubes: *She diced the carrots for the soup.* **2** to compete (with someone) at throwing dice; to gamble.

'**dicey** *adj* uncertain; risky: *a dicey situation.*

dice with death to do something very risky (and dangerous): *He diced with death every time he took a short cut across the main railway line.*

the die is cast the decisive step has been taken – there is no going back.

dictate [dik'teit, (*Amer*) 'dikteit] *v* **1** to say or read out (something) for someone else to write down: *He always dictates his letters (to his secretary).* **2** to state officially or with authority: *He dictated the terms of our offer.* **3** to give orders to; to command: *I certainly won't be dictated to by you* (= I won't do as you say).

dic'tation *n* something read for another to write down: *The secretary is taking dictation.*

dic'tator *n* an all-powerful ruler: *As soon as he became dictator, he made all political parties illegal and governed the country as he liked.*

dic'tatorship *n* **1** the authority of a dictator: *His dictatorship is threatened by the terrorists.* **2** a state ruled by a dictator: *That country is a dictatorship now.*

diction ['dikʃən] *n* the manner of speaking: *Her diction is always very clear.*

dictionary ['dikʃənəri] – *pl* '**dictionaries** – *n* **1** a book containing the words of a language alphabetically arranged, with their meanings *etc*: *This is an English dictionary.* **2** a book containing other information alphabetically arranged: *a dictionary of place-names.*

did *see* **do.**

didn't *see* **do.**

die¹ [dai] – *prp* **dying** ['daiiŋ] : *pt, ptp* **died** – *v* **1** to lose life; to stop living and become dead: *Those flowers are dying*; *She died of old age.* **2** to fade; to disappear: *The daylight was dying fast.* **3** to have a strong desire (for something or to do something): *I'm dying for a drink*; *I'm dying to see her.*

'**diehard** *n* a person who resists new ideas.

die away to fade from sight or hearing: *The sound died away into the distance.*

die down to lose strength or power: *I think the wind has died down a bit.*

die hard to take a long time to disappear: *Old habits die hard.*

die off to die quickly or in large numbers: *Herds of cattle were dying off because of the drought.*

die out to cease to exist anywhere: *The custom died out during the last century.*

die² [dai] *n* a stamp or punch for making raised designs on money, paper *etc.*

die³ *see* **dice.**

diesel engine ['di:zəl] an internal-combustion engine in lorries *etc*, in which a heavy form of oil is used.

diesel fuel/oil heavy oil used as a fuel for a diesel engine.

diet ['daiət] *n* food, *esp* a course of recommended foods, for losing weight or as treatment for an illness *etc*: *a diet of fish and vegetables*; *a salt-free diet*; *She went on a diet to lose weight.* – *v* to eat certain kinds of food to lose weight: *She has to diet to stay slim.*

differ ['difə] – *pt, ptp* '**differed** – *v* **1** (*often with* **from**) to be not like or alike: *Our views differ*; *Her house differs from mine.* **2** to disagree (with): *I think we will have to agree to differ.*

difference ['difrəns] *n* **1** what makes one thing unlike another: *I can't see any difference between these two pictures*; *It doesn't make any difference to me whether you go or stay*; *There's not much difference between them.* **2** an act of differing, *esp* a disagreement: *We had a difference of opinion*; *Have they settled their differences?* (= Have they stopped arguing?) **3** the amount by which one quantity or number is greater than another: *If you buy it for me I'll give you $6 now and make up the difference later.*

'**different** *adj* (*often with* **from**) not the same: *These gloves are not a pair – they're different*; *My ideas are different from his.*

,**diffe'rentiate** [-'renʃieit] *v* **1** to see or be able to tell a difference (between): *I cannot even differentiate a blackbird and a starling.* **2** (*with* **between**) to treat differently: *She does not differentiate between her two children although one is adopted.* '**diffe,renti'ation** *n.*

difficult ['difikəlt] *adj* **1** hard to do or understand; not easy: *difficult sums*; *a difficult task*; *It is difficult to know what to do for the best.* **2** hard to deal with or needing to be treated *etc* in a special way: *a difficult child.*

'difficulty – *pl* **'difficulties** – *n* **1** the state or quality of being hard (to do) or not easy: *I have difficulty in understanding him.* **2** an obstacle or objection: *He has a habit of foreseeing difficulties.* **3** (*esp in pl*) trouble, *esp* money trouble: *The firm was in difficulties.*

diffident ['difidənt] *adj* not confident. **'diffidently** *adv*. **'diffidence** *n*.

diffuse [di'fju:z] *v* to (cause to) spread in all directions.

dig [dig] – *prp* **'digging** : *pt, ptp* **dug** [dʌg] – *v* **1** to turn up (earth) with a spade *etc*: *to dig the garden.* **2** to make (a hole) in this way: *The child dug a tunnel in the sand.* **3** to poke: *He dug his brother in the ribs with his elbow.* – *n* **1** a poke: *a dig in the ribs; I knew that his remarks about women drivers were a dig at me* (= a joke directed at me).
'digger *n* a machine for digging.
dig out 1 to get out by digging: *We had to dig the car out of the mud.* **2** to find by searching: *I'll see if I can dig out that photo.*
dig up *We dug up that old tree; They dug up a skeleton; They're digging up the road yet again.*

digest [dai'dʒest] *v* **1** to break up (food) in the stomach *etc* and turn it into a form which the body can use: *The invalid had to have food that was easy to digest.* **2** to take in and think over (information *etc*): *It took me some minutes to digest what he had said.*
di'gestible *adj* able to be digested: *This food is scarcely digestible.*
di'gestion [-tʃən] *n* **1** the act of digesting food. **2** the ability of one's body to digest food: *poor digestion.*
di'gestive [-tiv] *adj* of digestion: *the human digestive system.*

digit ['didʒit] *n* **1** any of the figures 0 to 9: *105 is a number with three digits.* **2** a finger or toe.
'digital *adj* (of a computer *etc*) using the numbers 0–9.
digital clock/watch a clock or watch which shows the time in numbers instead of on a dial.

dignified ['dignifaid] *adj* (*neg* **un-**) stately, serious or showing dignity: *She decided that it would not be dignified to run for the bus.*

dignitary ['dignitəri] – *pl* **'dignitaries** – *n* a person who has a high rank or office.

dignity ['dignəti] *n* **1** stateliness or seriousness of manner: *Holding her head high, she retreated with dignity.* **2** importance or seriousness: *the dignity of the occasion.* **3** a privilege *etc* indicating rank: *He had risen to the dignity of an office of his own.* **4** one's personal pride: *He had wounded her dignity.*

digress [dai'gres] *v* to wander from the point, or from the main subject in speaking or writing. **di'gression** [-ʃən] *n*.

dilate [dai'leit] *v* to make or become larger: *The sudden darkness made the pupils of his eyes dilate.*

dilemma [di'lemə] *n* a position or situation giving two choices, neither pleasant: *His dilemma was whether to leave the party early so as to get a lift in his friend's car, or to stay and walk eight kilometres home.*

diligent ['dilidʒənt] *adj* conscientious; hard-working: *a diligent student.* **'diligently** *adv*. **'diligence** *n*.

dilly-dally [dili'dali] *v* to waste time *esp* by stopping often: *She's always dilly-dallying on the way to school.*

dilute [dai'lju:t] *v* to lessen the strength *etc* of by mixing *esp* with water: *You are supposed to dilute that lime juice with water.* – *adj* reduced in strength; weak: *dilute acid.* **di'lution** *n*.

dim [dim] *adj* **1** not bright or distinct: *a dim light in the distance; a dim memory.* **2** (of a person) not intelligent: *She's a bit dim!* – *v* – *pt, ptp* **dimmed** – to make or become dim: *Tears dimmed her eyes; He dimmed the lights in the theatre.*
'dimly *adv*. **'dimness** *n*.

dime [daim] *n* the tenth part of an American dollar; 10 cents.

dimension [di'menʃən] *n* a measurement in length, breadth, or thickness: *The dimensions of the box are 20 cm by 10 cm by 4 cm.*
-dimensional of (a certain number of) dimensions: *a three-dimensional figure.*

diminish [di'miniʃ] *v* to make or become less: *Our supplies are diminishing rapidly.* **di'minished** *adj* (*neg* **un-**).

diminution [dimi'nju:ʃən] *n* lessening: *a diminution in the birth rate.*

diminutive [di'minjutiv] *adj* very small: *a diminutive child.*

dimple ['dimpl] *n* a small hollow *esp* on the surface of the skin: *She has a dimple in her cheek when she smiles.*

din [din] *n* a loud continuous noise: *What a terrible din that machine makes!*

dine [dain] *v* to have dinner: *We shall dine at half-past eight.*
'diner *n* **1** a person who dines: *The diners ran from the restaurant when the fire started.* **2** a restaurant car on a train.
'dining-room *n* a room used mainly for eating in.
'dining-table *n* a table round which people sit to eat.
dine on to have for one's dinner: *They dined on lobster and champagne.*
dine out to have dinner somewhere other than one's own house *eg* in a restaurant or at the house of friends *etc*.

ding-dong ['diŋdoŋ] *adj* (of an argument, fight *etc*) vigorous, with first one side then the other seeming to win. – *n* a noisy argument.

dinghy ['diŋgi] – *pl* '**dinghies** – *n* 1 a small boat carried on a larger boat to take passengers ashore. 2 a small sailing or rowing boat.

dingo ['diŋgou] – *pl* '**dingoes** – *n* a type of wild dog found in Australia.

dingy ['dindʒi] *adj* dull; faded and dirty-looking: *This room is so dingy.* '**dinginess** *n*.

dinner ['dinə]·*n* 1 the main meal of the day eaten *usu* in the evening: *Is it time for dinner yet?* 2 a formal party in the evening, when such a meal is eaten: *They asked me to dinner*; *He was the guest of honour at the dinner*; (*also adj*) *a dinner party.*

'**dinner-jacket** *n* a man's formal jacket for wear in the evening.

dinosaur ['dainəsɔ:] *n* any of several types of extinct giant reptile.

dint [dint] *n* a hollow made by a blow; a dent.
by dint of by means of: *He succeeded by dint of sheer hard work.*

diocese ['daiəsis] *n* the district over which a bishop has authority.

dip [dip] – *pt, ptp* **dipped** – *v* 1 to lower into any liquid for a moment: *He dipped his bread in the soup.* 2 to slope downwards: *The road dipped just beyond the crossroads.* 3 to lower the beam of (car headlights): *He dipped his lights as the other car approached.* 4 (of a flag) to lower (a flag) briefly in salute. – *n* 1 a hollow (in a road *etc*): *The car was hidden by a dip in the road.* 2 a soft, savoury mixture in which a biscuit *etc* can be dipped: *a cheese dip.* 3 a short swim: *a dip in the sea.*
dip into 1 to withdraw amounts from (a supply, *eg* of money): *I've been dipping into my savings recently.* 2 to look briefly at (a book) or to study (a subject) in a casual manner: *I've dipped into his book on Shakespeare, but I haven't read it right through.*

diphtheria [dif'θiəriə] *n* an infectious disease of the throat.

diphthong ['difθoŋ] *n* two vowel sounds pronounced as one syllable: *The vowel sound in 'out' is a diphthong.*

diploma [di'ploumə] *n* a written statement saying that one has passed a certain examination *etc*: *She has a diploma in teaching.*

diplomacy [di'plouməsi] *n* 1 the business of making agreements, treaties *etc* between countries; the business of looking after the affairs of one's country *etc* in a foreign country. 2 skill and tact in dealing with people, persuading them *etc*: *Use a little diplomacy and she'll soon agree to help.*

diplomat ['dipləmat] *n* a person engaged in diplomacy: *He is a diplomat at the American embassy.*

diplomatic·[diplə'matik] *adj* 1 concerning

diplomacy: *a diplomatic mission.* 2 tactful: *a diplomatic remark.* ˌdiplo'matically *adv*.

dire ['daiə] *adj* dreadful; perilous.

direct [di'rekt] *adj* 1 straight; following the quickest and shortest way: *Is this the most direct route?* 2 (of manner *etc*) straightforward and honest: *a direct answer.* 3 occurring as an immediate result: *His dismissal was a direct result of his rudeness to the manager.* 4 exact; complete: *Her opinions are the direct opposite of his.* 5 in an unbroken line of descent from father to son *etc*: *He is a direct descendant of Napoleon.* – *v* 1 to point, aim or turn in a particular direction: *He directed my attention towards the notice.* 2 to show the way to: *She directed him to the station.* 3 to order or instruct: *We will do as you direct.* 4 to control or organize: *A policeman was directing the traffic; to direct a film.*

di'rection [-ʃən] *n* 1 (the) place or point to which one moves, looks *etc*: *What direction did he go in?*; *They were heading in my direction* (= towards me); *I'll find my way all right – I've a good sense of direction.* 2 guidance: *They are under your direction.* 3 (*in pl*) instructions (*eg* on how to get somewhere, use something *etc*): *We asked the policeman for directions; I have lost the directions for this washing-machine.* 4 the act of aiming or turning (something or someone) towards a certain point. **di'rectional** *adj*.

di'rective [-tiv] *n* a general instruction from a higher authority about what is to be done *etc*.

di'rectly *adv* 1 in a direct manner: *I went directly to the office.* 2 almost at once: *He will be here directly.* **di'rectness** *n*.

di'rector *n* a person or thing that directs, *eg* one of a group of persons who manage the affairs of a business or a person who is in charge of the making of a film, play *etc*: *He is on the board of directors of our firm; The producer and the director quarrelled about the film.*

di'rectory – *pl* **di'rectories** – *n* a type of book giving names and addresses *etc*: *a telephone directory.*

dirt [də:t] *n* any unclean substance, such as mud, dust, dung *etc*: *His shoes are covered in dirt.*
'**dirty** *adj* 1 not clean: *dirty clothes.* 2 mean or unfair: *a dirty trick.* 3 offensive; obscene: *dirty books.* 4 (of weather) stormy. – *v* to make or become dirty: *He dirtied his hands/shoes.* '**dirtiness** *n*.
ˌdirt-'cheap *adj, adv* very cheap.
dirt track an earth-track for motor-racing.

disable [dis'eibl] *v* to reduce the ability or strength of; to cripple: *He was disabled during the war.*

disability [disə'biləti] – *pl* **disa'bilities** – *n* something which disables: *He has a disability which prevents him from walking very far.* **dis'abled** *adj* lacking ability or strength; crippled: *a disabled soldier.* **dis'ablement** *n.*

disadvantage [disəd'va:ntidʒ] *n* something which makes a difficulty or which is an unfavourable circumstance: *There are several disadvantages to this plan.* **disadvantageous** [disadvən'teidʒəs] *adj.* **at a disadvantage** in an unfavourable position: *His power was strengthened by the fact that he had us all at a disadvantage.*

disagree [disə'gri:] *v* 1 (*sometimes with* **with**) to hold different opinions *etc* (from someone else): *We disagree about everything; I disagree with you on that point.* 2 to quarrel: *We never meet without disagreeing.* 3 (*with* **with**) (of food) to be unsuitable (to someone) and cause pain: *Onions disagree with me.* **,disa'greeable** *adj* unpleasant: *a disagreeable task; a most disagreeable person.* **,dis-a'greeably** *adv.* **,disa'greement** *n* 1 disagreeing: *disagreement between the two witnesses to the accident.* 2 a quarrel: *a violent disagreement.*

disallow [disə'lau] *v* to refuse to allow (a claim *etc*).

disappear [disə'piə] *v* 1 to vanish from sight: *The sun disappeared slowly below the horizon.* 2 to fade out of existence: *This custom had disappeared by the end of the century.* 3 to go away so that other people do not know where one is: *A search is being carried out for the boy who disappeared from his home on Monday.* **,disap'pearance** *n.*

disappoint [disə'point] *v* to fail to fulfil the hopes or expectations of: *London disappointed her after all she had heard about it.* **,disap'pointed** *adj: I was disappointed to hear that the party had been cancelled; a group of disappointed children.* **disap'pointing** *adj: disappointing results.* **,disap'pointment** *n: Her disappointment was obvious from her face; His failure was a great disappointment to his wife.*

disapprove [disə'pru:v] *v* to have an unfavourable opinion (of): *Her mother disapproved of her behaviour.* **,disap'proval** *n: She frowned to show her disapproval.* **,disap'proving** *adj: a disapproving look.* **,disap'provingly** *adv.*

disarm [dis'a:m] *v* 1 to, take away weapons from: *He crept up from behind and managed to disarm the gunman.* 2 to get rid of weapons of war: *Not until peace was made did the victors consider it safe to disarm.* 3 to make less hostile; to charm.

dis'armament *n* the act of doing away with war-weapons. **dis'arming** *adj* charming: *a disarming smile.* **dis'armingly** *adv.*

disarrange [disə'reindʒ] *v* to throw out of order; to make untidy: *The strong wind had disarranged her hair.* **,disar'rangement** *n.*

disarray [disə'rei] *n* disorder: *The army was in complete disarray after the battle.*

disaster [di'za:stə] *n* a terrible event, *esp* one that causes great damage, loss *etc*: *The earthquake was the greatest disaster the country had ever experienced.* **di'sastrous** *adj.* **di'sastrously** *adv.*

disband [dis'band] *v* to (cause a group, *eg* a military force to) break up: *The regiment disbanded at the end of the war.*

disbelieve [disbi'li:v] *v* not to believe: *He was inclined to disbelieve her story.* **,disbe'lief** [-f] *n* the state of not believing: *She stared at him in disbelief.*

disc, disk [disk] *n* 1 a flat, thin, circular object: *From the earth, the full moon looks like a silver disc.* 2 a gramophone record. 3 in computing, a disc-shaped file. **disc jockey** a person employed to present a programme of music (*usu* pop-music) on the radio *etc*, from gramophone records.

discard [di'ska:d] *v* to throw away as useless: *They discarded the empty bottles.*

discern [di'sə:n] *v* to see or realize; to notice: *We could discern from his appearance that he was upset.*

discharge [dis'tʃa:dʒ] *v* 1 to allow to leave; to dismiss: *The prisoner was at last discharged; She was discharged from hospital.* 2 to fire (a gun): *He discharged his gun at the policeman.* 3 to perform (a task *etc*): *He discharges his duties well.* 4 to pay (a debt). 5 to (cause to) let or send out: *The chimney was discharging clouds of smoke; The drain discharged into the street.* – ['distʃa:dʒ] *n* 1 (an) act of discharging: *He was given his discharge from the army; the discharge of one's duties.* 2 pus *etc* coming from *eg* a wound.

disciple [di'saipl] *n* a person who believes in the teaching of another, *esp* one of the original followers of Christ: *Jesus and his twelve disciples.*

discipline ['disiplin] *n* 1 training in an orderly way of life: *All children need discipline.* 2 strict self-control (amongst soldiers *etc*). – *v* 1 to bring under control: *You must discipline yourself so that you do not waste time.* 2 to punish: *The students who caused the disturbance have been disciplined.* **'disciplinary** *adj* 1 of discipline. 2 intended as, punishment: *disciplinary action.*

disclaim [dis'kleim] *v* to refuse to have anything to do with; to deny: *I disclaimed all responsibility.*

disclose [dis'klouz] v to uncover, reveal or make known: *He refused to disclose his identity.* **dis'closure** [-ʒə] n.

disco ['diskou] short for **discotheque**.

discolour, (*Amer*) **discolor** [dis'kʌlə] v to (cause to) change colour or become stained: *The paintwork had discoloured with the damp.* **dis,colou'ration** n.

discomfit [dis'kʌmfit] v to embarrass: *He realized that his remarks had succeeded in discomfiting her.* **dis'comfiture** [-tʃə] n.

discomfort [dis'kʌmfət] n **1** the state of being uncomfortable; pain: *Her broken leg caused her great discomfort.* **2** something that causes lack of comfort: *the discomforts of living in a tent.*

disconcert [diskən'səːt] v to embarrass or take aback: *He was disconcerted by the amount he had to pay.*

disconnect [diskə'nekt] v to separate; to break the connection (*esp* electrical) with: *Our phone has been disconnected.* **,discon'nection** [-ʃən] n.

discontent [diskən'tent] n the state of not being contented; dissatisfaction: *There is a lot of discontent among young people.*
,discon'tented adj dissatisfied or not happy: *She's discontented with her life; a discontented expression.* **,discon'tentedly** adv. **,discon'tentment** n.

discontinue [diskən'tinju] v to stop or put an end to: *I have discontinued my visits there.* **'discon,tinu'ation** n.

discord ['diskoːd] n **1** disagreement or quarrelling. **2** in music, a group of notes played together which give a jarring sound. **dis'cordant** adj.

discotheque ['diskətek] n (*usu abbrev* **disco** ['diskou]) a place, or a type of entertainment, at which recorded music is played for dancing.

discount ['diskaunt] n a (small) sum taken off the price of something: *He gave me a discount of 20%.* – [dis'kaunt] v to leave aside as something not to be considered: *You can discount most of what he says – it's nearly all lies!*

discourage [dis'kʌridʒ, (*Amer*) -'kəː-] v **1** to take away the confidence, hope *etc* of: *His lack of success discouraged him.* **2** to try to prevent (by showing disapproval *etc*): *She discouraged all his attempts to get to know her.* **3** (*with* **from**) to persuade against: *The rain discouraged him from going camping.* **dis'couragement** n.

discourteous [dis'kəːtiəs] adj not polite; rude: *a discourteous remark.* **dis'courtesy** [-təsi] n.

discover [dis'kʌvə] v **1** to find by chance, *esp* for the first time: *Columbus discovered America; Marie Curie discovered radium.* **2** to find out: *Try to discover what's going on!*

dis'covery – pl **dis'coveries** – n: *a voyage of discovery; She made several startling discoveries.*

We **discover** something that existed but was not yet known: *He discovered a cave.* We **invent** something that was not in existence: *They invented a new machine.*

discredit [dis'kredit] n (something that causes) loss of good reputation. – v **1** to show (a story *etc*) to be false. **2** to disgrace. **dis'creditable** adj bringing discredit or disgrace. **dis'creditably** adv.

discreet [dis'kriːt] adj wise, cautious and not saying anything which might cause trouble: *My secretary won't let the secret out – she's very discreet.* **di'screetness** n. **di'scretion** [-'skre-] n **1** discreetness: *A secretary needs discretion and tact.* **2** personal judgement: *I leave the arrangements entirely to your discretion; The money will be distributed at the discretion of the management.*

discrepancy [di'skrepənsi] – pl **di'screpancies** – n disagreement or difference.

discretion see **discreet**.

discriminate [di'skrimineit] v **1** (*with* **between**) to make or see a difference between: *It is difficult to discriminate between real and pretended cases of poverty.* **2** (often with **against**) to treat a certain kind of people differently: *He was accused of discriminating against women employees.* **dis,crimi'nation** n.

discus ['diskəs] n a heavy disc of metal *etc* thrown in a type of athletic competition.

discuss [di'skʌs] v to talk about: *We had a meeting to discuss our plans for the future.* **di'scussion** [-ʃən] n (an act of) talking about something: *I think there has been too much discussion of this subject; Discussions between the heads of state took place in strict security.*

to **discuss** (not **discuss about**) a problem.

disdain [dis'dein] n scorn or pride: *a look of disdain.* – v **1** to be too proud (to do something). **2** to look down on (something): *She disdains our company.* **dis'dainful** adj. **dis'dainfully** adv.

disease [di'ziːz] n (an) illness: *She's suffering from a disease of the kidneys; poverty and disease.*

disembark [disim'baːk] v to (cause to) go from a ship on to land: *We disembarked soon after breakfast.* **,disembar'kation** n.

disembodied [disim'bodid] adj (of *eg* a spirit, soul *etc*) separated from the body: *A disembodied voice.*

disengage [disin'geidʒ] v to separate or free (one thing from another): *to disengage the gears; He disengaged himself from her embrace.*

disentangle [disin'taŋgl] v to free from being tangled; to unravel: *The bird could not disentangle itself from the net.* ˌdisen'tanglement n.

disfavour, (*Amer*) **disfavor** [dis'feivə] n **1** the state of being out of favour: *He was in disfavour because he had stayed out late.* **2** displeasure or disapproval.

disfigure [dis'figə, (*Amer*) -'figjər] v to spoil the beauty of: *That scar will disfigure her for life.* **dis'figurement** n.

disgorge [dis'go:dʒ] v to bring up from the stomach; to throw out or up: *The chimney was disgorging clouds of black smoke.*

disgrace [dis'greis] n **1** the state of being out of favour: *He is in disgrace because of his behaviour.* **2** a state of being without honour and regarded without respect: *There seemed to be nothing ahead of him but disgrace and shame.* **3** something which causes or ought to cause shame: *Your clothes are a disgrace!* – v **1** to bring shame upon: *Did you have to disgrace me by appearing in those clothes?* **2** to dismiss from a position of importance: *He was publicly disgraced.*
dis'graceful adj very bad or shameful: *disgraceful behaviour; The service in that hotel was disgraceful.* **dis'gracefully** adv.

disgruntled [dis'grʌntld] adj sulky and dissatisfied.

disguise [dis'gaiz] v **1** to hide the identity of by altering the appearance *etc*: *He disguised himself as a policeman; She disguised her voice with a foreign accent.* **2** to hide (*eg* one's intentions *etc*): *He tried hard to disguise his feelings.* – n **1** a disguised state: *He was in disguise.* **2** a set of clothes, make-up *etc* which disguises: *He was wearing a false beard as a disguise.*

disgust [dis'gʌst] v to cause feelings of dislike or sickness in: *The smell of that soup disgusts me; She was disgusted by your behaviour.* – n the state or feeling of being disgusted: *She left the room in disgust.*
dis'gusting adj: *What a disgusting smell!; Her house is in a disgusting mess.* **dis'gustingly** adv.

dish [diʃ] n **1** a plate, bowl *etc* in which food is brought to the table: *a large shallow dish.* **2** food mixed and prepared for the table: *She served us an interesting dish containing chicken and almonds.*
'dish-washing n the job of washing used dishes.
'dishwater n water that has been used for this job.
dish out to distribute or give to people: *He dished out the potatoes.*

dishearten [dis'ha:tn] v to take courage or hope away from: *The failure of her first attempt disheartened her.*

dishevelled, disheveled [di'ʃevəld] adj untidy: *She had been gardening and looked rather dishevelled.*

dishonest [dis'onist] adj not honest; deceitful: *She was dishonest about her qualifications when she applied for the job.* **dis'honestly** adv.
dis'honesty n the state or quality of being dishonest: *I would not have expected such dishonesty from him.*

dishonour [dis'onə] n disgrace; shame. – v to cause shame to: *You have dishonoured your family by your actions!*
dis'honourable adj: *a dishonourable action.* **dis'honourably** adv.

disillusion [disi'lu:ʒən] v to destroy the false but pleasant beliefs held by (a person): *I thought his job sounded interesting, but he soon disillusioned me.* **disil'lusionment** n.

disinclination [disinkli'neiʃən] n unwillingness: *a disinclination to work.*
ˌdisin'clined [-'klaind] adj unwilling (to do something): *I am disinclined to help.*

disinfect [disin'fekt] v to destroy disease-causing germs in: *This sink should be disinfected regularly.*
ˌdisin'fectant n a substance that destroys germs.

disintegrate [dis'intigreit] v to (cause to) fall to pieces: *The paper bag was so wet that the bottom disintegrated and all the groceries fell out.* disˌinte'gration n.

disinterested [dis'intristid] adj not influenced by private feelings or selfish motives: *a disinterested judgement.*

disk *see* **disc**.

dislike [dis'laik] v not to like; to have strong feelings against: *I know he dislikes me.* – n strong feeling directed against a thing, person or idea: *He doesn't go to football matches because of his dislike of crowds; He has few dislikes.*
take a dislike to to begin to dislike: *The boss has taken a dislike to me.*

dislocate ['disləkeit, (*Amer*) -lou-] v to put (a bone) out of joint; to displace: *She dislocated her hip when she fell.* ˌdislo'cation n.

dislodge [dis'lodʒ] v to knock out of place: *He accidentally dislodged a stone from the wall.*

disloyal [dis'loiəl] adj unfaithful or not loyal: *He has been very disloyal to his friends.* **dis'loyally** adv. **dis'loyalty** n.

dismal ['dizməl] adj gloomy: *dismal news; Don't look so dismal!* **'dismally** adv.

dismantle [dis'mantl] v to pull down or take to pieces: *The wardrobe was so large we had to dismantle it to get it down the stairs.*

dismay [dis'mei] v to shock or upset: *We were dismayed by the bad news.* – n the state of being shocked and upset: *a shout of dismay.*

dismiss [dis'mis] v **1** to send or put away: *She dismissed him with a wave of the hand;*

Dismiss the idea from your mind! **2** to remove from office or employment: *He was dismissed from his post for being lazy.* **3** to stop or close (a law-suit *etc*): *Case dismissed!* **dis'missal** *n.*

dismount [dis'maunt] *v* to get off a horse, bicycle *etc*: *He dismounted and pushed his bicycle up the hill.*

disobey [disə'bei] *v* to fail or refuse to do what is commanded: *He disobeyed my orders not to go into the road*; *He disobeyed his mother.* **diso'bedience** [-'bi:djəns] *n* failing or refusing to obey: *You must be punished for your disobedience!*

diso'bedient [-'bi:djənt] *adj* failing or refusing to obey: *a disobedient child.* **diso'bediently** *adv.*

disorder [dis'o:də] *n* **1** lack of order; confusion or disturbance: *The strike threw the whole country into disorder*; *scenes of disorder and rioting.* **2** a disease: *a disorder of the lungs.*

dis'orderly *adj* **1** not neatly arranged; in confusion: *His clothes lay in a disorderly heap.* **2** lawless; causing trouble: *a disorderly group of people.*

disorganized, -s- [dis'o:gənaizd] *adj* in confusion or not organized: *a disorganized person*; *The meeting was very disorganized.* **dis,organi'zation, -s-** *n.*

disown [dis'oun] *v* to refuse to acknowledge as belonging to oneself: *to disown one's son.*

dispatch [di'spatʃ] *v* **1** to send off: *He dispatched several letters asking for financial help.* **2** to finish off or deal with quickly: *She dispatched several pieces of business within the hour.* – *n* **1** a written official report: *a dispatch from the commanding officer.* **2** an act of sending away. **3** haste. **dispatch rider** a carrier of military dispatches by motor-cycle.

dispel [di'spel] – *pt, ptp* **di'spelled** – *v* to drive away: *His words dispelled her fears.*

dispense [di'spens] *v* **1** to give or deal out. **2** to prepare (medicines, *esp* prescriptions) for giving out.
di'spensary – *pl* **di'spensaries** – *n* a place *esp* in a hospital where medicines are given out. **di'spenser** *n.*
dispense with to get rid of or do without: *We could economize by dispensing with two assistants.*

disperse [di'spə:s] *v* **1** to (cause to) scatter in all directions: *Some seeds are dispersed by the wind.* **2** to (cause to) spread (news *etc*): *Information is dispersed by volunteers who distribute leaflets.* **3** to (cause to) vanish: *By this time the crowd had dispersed.*
di'spersal *n.*

dispirited [di'spiritid] *adj* sad and discouraged.

displace [dis'pleis] *v* **1** to disarrange or put

out of place. **2** to take the place of: *The dog had displaced her doll in the little girl's affections.* **dis'placement** *n.*
displaced person a person forced to leave his own country as a result of war *etc.*

display [di'splei] *v* **1** to set out for show: *The china was displayed in a special cabinet.* **2** to show: *She displayed a talent for mimicry.* – *n* **1** (an) act of showing or making clear: *a display of military strength.* **2** an entertainment *etc* intended to show the ability *etc* of those taking part: *a dancing display.* **3** something which shows or sets out something else: *an advertising display.*

displease [dis'pli:z] *v* to offend or annoy: *The children's behaviour displeased their father.* **dis'pleased** *adj*: *She was displeased with him for being late.*
displeasure [dis'pleʒə] *n* disapproval: *She showed her displeasure by leaving at once.*

dispose [di'spouz] *v* **1** to make inclined: *I am not disposed to help him.* **2** to arrange or settle.
di'sposable *adj* intended to be thrown away or destroyed after use: *disposable cups/plates.*
di'sposal *n* the act of getting rid of something: *the disposal of waste paper.*
at one's disposal available for one's use: *They put a car at his disposal during his stay.*
dispose of to get rid of: *I've disposed of your old coat.*

disposition [dispə'ziʃən] *n* personality: *He has a naturally calm disposition.*

dispossess [dispə'zes] *v* to take (property) away from: *He was dispossessed of all his lands.*

disproportionate [disprə'po:ʃənət] *adj* (*often with* **to**) too large or too small in relation to something else: *His head looks disproportionate (to his body).* **,dispro'portionately** *adv.*

disprove [dis'pru:v] *v* to prove to be false or wrong: *His theories have been disproved by modern scientific research.*

dispute [di'spju:t] *v* **1** to argue against or deny: *I'm not disputing what you say.* **2** to argue (about): *They disputed the ownership of the land for years.* – *n* (an) argument or quarrel: *a dispute over wages.*
di'sputable *adj* able to be argued about: *Whether this change was an improvement is disputable.*
,dispu'tation *n* a formal argument.

disqualify [dis'kwolifai] *v* **1** to put out of a competition *etc* for breaking rules: *She was disqualified for being too young.* **2** to make unfit for some purpose: *His colour-blindness disqualified him for the Air Force.* **dis,qualifi'cation** [-fi-] *n.*

disquiet [dis'kwaiət] *n* uneasiness: *a feeling of disquiet.* – *v* to make uneasy.

disregard [disrə'ga:d] *v* to ignore: *He disregarded my warnings.* – *n* lack of concern: *He has a complete disregard for his own safety.*

disrepair [disrə'peə] *n* the state of needing repair: *The old house has fallen into disrepair.*

disrepute [disrə'pju:t] *n* bad reputation: *He has brought the family into disrepute.*

dis'reputable [-'repju-] *adj* **1** not respectable, *esp* in appearance: *a disreputable old coat.* **2** of bad reputation: *He's rather a disreputable character.*

disrespect [disrə'spekt] *n* rudeness or lack of respect: *He spoke of his parents with disrespect.*

,disre'spectful *adj* showing disrespect: *Never be disrespectful to older people.* **,disre'spectfully** *adv.*

disrupt [dis'rʌpt] *v* to break up or put into a state of disorder: *Rioters disrupted the meeting; Traffic was disrupted by floods.* **dis'ruption** [-ʃən] *n.*

dis'ruptive [-tiv] *adj* causing disorder: *a disruptive child.*

dissatisfy [di'satisfai] *v* to fail to satisfy or to displease: *The teacher was dissatisfied with the pupil's work.* **dis,satis'faction** [-'fakʃən] *n.*

dissect [di'sekt] *v* to cut (*eg* an animal's body) into parts for (scientific) examination. **dis'section** [-ʃən] *n.*

dissent [di'sent] *n* disagreement: *There was a murmur of dissent.* – *v* (with **from**) to disagree: *I dissent from the general opinion.* **dis'sension** [-ʃən] *n* disagreement: *The proposal caused a great deal of dissension.*

dissertation [disə'teiʃən] *n* a long formal talk or piece of writing (for a university degree *etc*).

disservice [dis'sə:vis] *n* an action which is not helpful.

dissident ['disidənt] *n, adj* (a person) disagreeing, *esp* with a ruling group or form of government: *a demonstration by a large number of dissidents.* **'dissidence** *n.*

dissimilar [di'similə] *adj* unlike or unalike: *The two cases are not dissimilar; The sisters have very dissimilar characters.* **dis,simi'larity** [-'la-] *n.*

dissociate [di'sousieit] *v* **1** to separate, *esp* in thought. **2** to refuse to connect (oneself) (any longer) with: *I'm dissociating myself completely from their actions.*

dissolute ['disəlu:t] *adj* bad or immoral: *dissolute behaviour.* **'dissoluteness** *n.*

dissolution *see* **dissolve.**

dissolve [di'zolv] *v* **1** to (cause to) melt or break up, *esp* by putting in a liquid: *He dissolved the pills in water; The pills dissolved easily in water.* **2** to put an end to (a parliament, a marriage *etc*).

dissolution [disə'lu:ʃən] *n: the dissolution of Parliament.*

dissuade [di'sweid] *v* to stop (from doing something) by advice or persuasion: *I tried to dissuade him from his foolish intention.* **dis'suasion** [-ʒən] *n.*

distance ['distəns] *n* **1** the space between things, places *etc*: *Some of the children have to walk long distances to school; It's quite a distance to the bus stop; It is difficult to judge distance when driving at night; What's the distance from here to London?* **2** a far-off place or point: *We could see the town in the distance; He disappeared into the distance; The picture looks better at a distance.*

'distant *adj* **1** far away or far apart, in place or time: *the distant past; a distant country; Our house is two kilometres distant from the school.* **2** not close: *a distant relation.* **3** not friendly: *Her manner was rather distant.*

distaste [dis'teist] *n* dislike (of something unpleasant): *She looked at the untidy room with distaste.*

dis'tasteful *adj* disagreeable: *a distasteful job.* **dis'tastefully** *adv.* **dis'tastefulness** *n.*

distended [di'stendəd] *adj* stretched; swollen.

distil, (*Amer*) **distill** [di'stil] – *pt, ptp* **di'stilled** – *v* **1** to get (a liquid) in a pure state by heating to steam or a vapour and cooling again. **2** to obtain alcoholic spirit from anything by this method: *Whisky is distilled from barley.* **,distil'lation** *n.*

di'stiller *n* a person or firm that distils and makes spirits: *a firm of whisky-distillers.*

di'stillery – *pl* **di'stilleries** – *n* a place where distilling (of whisky, brandy *etc*) is carried on.

distinct [di'stiŋkt] *adj* **1** easily seen, heard or noticed: *There are distinct differences between the two; Her voice is very distinct.* **2** separate or different: *Those two birds are quite distinct – you couldn't confuse them.*

di'stinctly *adv: He pronounces his words very distinctly; I distinctly heard him tell you to wait!* **di'stinctness** *n.*

di'stinction [-ʃən] *n* **1** (the making of) a difference: *He makes no distinction between male and female employees with regard to pay.* **2** a grade awarded that indicates outstanding ability or achievement: *She passed her exams with distinction.*

di'stinctive [-tiv] *adj* different and easily identified: *I recognized her from a long way off – she has a very distinctive walk!* **di'stinctively** *adv.*

distinguish [di'stiŋgwiʃ] *v* **1** (*often with* **from**) to mark as different: *What distinguishes this café from all the others?* **2** to identify or make out: *He could just distinguish the figure of a man running away.* **3** (*sometimes with* **between**) to recognize a difference: *I can't distinguish (between) the two types –*

they both look the same to me. **4** to make (oneself) noticed through one's achievements: *He distinguished himself at school by winning a prize in every subject.* **di'stinguishable** *adj.*

di'stinguished *adj* famous or outstanding: *a distinguished scientist.*

distort [di'sto:t] *n* **1** to make or become twisted out of shape: *Her face was distorted with pain; Metal distorts under stress.* **2** to make (sound) indistinct and unnatural: *Her voice sounded distorted on the telephone.* **di'stortion** [-ʃən] *n.*

distract [di'strakt] *v* to draw aside (the mind or attention of): *He was constantly being distracted from his work by the noisy conversation of his colleagues.*

di'stracted *adj* **1** turned aside (from what one is doing or thinking): *He had slipped out while her attention was distracted.* **2** out of one's mind; mad: *a distracted old woman.* **3** distressed: *The distracted mother couldn't reach her child in the burning house.* **di'straction** [-ʃən] *n* **1** something that takes the mind off other *esp* more serious affairs: *There are too many distractions here to allow one to work properly.* **2** anxiety and confusion: *in a state of complete distraction.*

distraught [di'stro:t] *adj* very worried and upset.

distress [di'stres] *n* **1** great sorrow, trouble or pain: *She was in great distress over his disappearance; Is your leg causing you any distress?; The loss of all their money left the family in acute distress.* **2** a cause of sorrow: *My inability to draw has always been a distress to me.* − *v* to cause pain or sorrow to: *I'm distressed by your lack of interest.* **di'stressing** *adj.* **di'stressingly** *adv.*

distribute [di'stribjut] *v* **1** to divide (something) among several (people); to deal out: *He distributed sweets to all the children in the class.* **2** to spread out widely: *Our shops are distributed all over the city.* ˌdistri'bution [-'bju:-] *n.*

district ['distrikt] *n* an area of a country, town etc: *He lives in a poor district of London; Public transport is often infrequent in country districts.*

distrust [dis'trʌst] *n* suspicion; lack of trust or faith: *He has always had a distrust of electrical gadgets.* − *v* to have no trust in: *He distrusts his own judgement.* **dis'trustful** *adj.* **dis'trustfully** *adv.* **dis'trustfulness** *n.*

disturb [di'stə:b] *v* **1** to interrupt or take attention away from: *I'm sorry, am I disturbing you?* **2** to worry or make anxious: *This news has disturbed me very much.* **3** to stir up or throw into confusion: *A violent storm disturbed the surface of the lake.* **di'sturbance** *n* **1** a noisy or disorderly happening: *He was thrown out of the meeting*

for causing a disturbance. **2** an interruption: *I've done quite a lot of work, despite several disturbances.* **3** an act of disturbing: *He was arrested for disturbance of the peace.*

disuse [dis'ju:s] *n* the state of not being used: *The canal fell into disuse.*

dis'used [-'ju:zd] *adj: a disused warehouse.*

ditch [ditʃ] *n* a long narrow hollow dug in the ground *esp* one to drain water from a field, road *etc: He climbed over the fence and fell into a ditch.* − *v* to get rid of: *The stolen car had been ditched by the thieves several miles away.*

ditty ['diti] − *pl* **'ditties** − *n* a simple little song.

divan [di'van, (*Amer*) 'daivan] *n* a long, low couch without back or arms, *usu* able to be used as a bed.

dive [daiv] *v* **1** to plunge headfirst into water or down through the air: *He dived off a rock into the sea.* **2** to go quickly and suddenly out of sight: *She dived down a back street and into a shop.* − *n* an act of diving: *She did a beautiful dive into the deep end of the pool.* **'diver** *n* a person who dives, *esp* one who works under water using special breathing equipment.

'diving-board *n* a platform from which to dive, erected beside a swimming-pool.

great diving beetle a water insect that carries a bubble of air under its wing cover for breathing when it is under water.

diverge [dai'və:dʒ] *v* **1** to separate and go in different directions: *The roads diverge three kilometres further on.* **2** to differ (from someone or something else); to go away (from a standard): *This is where our opinions diverge.* **di'vergence** *n.* **di'vergent** *adj.*

diverse [dai'və:s] *adj* different; of various kinds. **di'versely** *adv.* **di'verseness** *n.* **di'versify** [-fai] *v* to make or become varied or different.

di'versity *n* variety.

diversion [dai'və:ʃən, (*Amer*) -ʒən] *n* **1** an alteration to a traffic route: *There's a diversion at the end of the road.* **2** (an act of) diverting attention. **3** (an) amusement.

diversity *see* **diverse.**

divert [dai'və:t] *v* **1** to cause to turn aside or change direction: *Traffic had to be diverted because of the accident.* **2** to amuse or entertain.

divide [di'vaid] *v* **1** to separate into parts or groups: *The wall divided the garden in two; The group divided into three when we got off the bus; We are divided (= We do not agree) as to where to spend our holidays.* **2** (with **between** or **among**) to share: *We divided the sweets between us.* **3** to find out how many times one number contains another: *6 divided by 2 equals 3.*

di'viders *n pl* a measuring instrument used in geometry.

divisible [di'vizəbl] *adj* able to be divided: *100 is divisible by 4.*

division [di'viʒən] *n* **1** (an) act of dividing. **2** something that separates; a dividing line: *a ditch marks the division between their two fields.* **3** a part or section (of an army *etc*): *He belongs to B division of the local police force.* **4** (a) separation of thought; disagreement. **5** the finding of how many times one number is contained in another. **divisional** [di'viʒənl] *adj* of a division: *The soldier contacted divisional headquarters.*

dividend ['dividend] *n* the interest paid on shares *etc*: *a dividend of 2%.*

divine [di'vain] *adj* **1** of or belonging to God or a god: *divinè wisdom.* **2** very good or excellent: *What divine weather!* − *v* to find out by keen understanding: *I· managed to divine the truth.* ˌ**divi'nation** [divi-] *n*.

di'viner *n* a person who has or claims a special ability to find hidden water or metals.

di'vining *n* discovering the presence of underground water, metal *etc* by holding a **di'vining-rod** which moves when held directly above the water *etc*: *water-divining.*

di'vinity [-'vi-] − *pl* **di'vinities** − *n* **1** religious studies. **2** a god or goddess: *The ancient Greeks worshipped many divinities.* **3** the state of being divine: *the divinity of God.*

divisible, division *etc see* **divide.**

divorce [di'vo:s] *n* the legal ending of a marriage: *Divorce is becoming more common nowadays.* − *v* **1** to end one's marriage (with): *He's divorcing her for desertion; They were divorced two years ago.* **2** to separate: *You can't divorce these two concepts.*

dizzy ['dizi] *adj* **1** giddy or confused: *If you spin round and round like that, you'll make yourself dizzy.* **2** causing dizziness: *dizzy heights.* '**dizzily** *adv.* '**dizziness** *n*.

do [du:] − *3rd pers sing prt* **does** [dʌz]: *pt* **did** [did]: *ptp* **done** [dʌn]: *neg short forms* **don't** [dount], **doesn't** ['dʌznt], **didn't** ['didnt] − *v* **1** used with a more important verb in questions and negative statements: *Do you smoke?; I don't know him.* **2** used with a more important verb for emphasis: *I do think you should apologise; I did see him after all.* **3** used to avoid repeating a verb which comes immediately before: *I thought she wouldn't come, but she did.* **4** used with a more important verb after **seldom, rarely** and **little**: *Little did he know what was in store for him.* **5** to carry out or perform: *What shall I do?; That was a terrible thing to do.* **6** to manage to finish or complete: *When you've done that, you can start on this; We did a hundred kilometres in an hour.* **7** to perform some obvious action concerning: *to do the washing; to do the garden/the*

windows. **8** to be enough or suitable for a purpose: *Will this piece of fish do two of us?; That'll do nicely; Do you want me to look for a blue one or will a pink one do?; Will next Saturday do for our next meeting?* **9** to work at or study: *She's doing sums; He's at university doing science.* **10** to manage or prosper: *How's your wife doing?; My son is doing well at school.* **11** to put in order or arrange: *She's doing her hair.* **12** to act or behave: *Why don't you do as we do?* **13** to give or show: *The whole town gathered to do· him honour.* **14** to cause: *What damage did the storm do?; It won't do him any harm.* **15** to see everything and visit everything in: *They tried to do London in four days.* − *n* − *pl* **do's** − an affair or a festivity, *esp* a party: *The school is having a do for Christmas.*

'**doer** *n* a person who does something: *an evildoer; a doer of good deeds.*

'**doings** *n pl* the things which a person does: *He tells me about all your doings.*

done [dʌn] *adj* **1** finished or complete: *That's that job done at last.* **2** (of food) completely cooked and ready to eat: *I don't think the meat is quite done yet.* **3** socially accepted: *the done thing.*

ˌ**do-it-your'self** *n, adj* (of) the art or practice of doing one's own decorating, repairs *etc*: *I've just bought a book on do-it-yourself so I can try to tile the bathroom; a do-it-yourself job.*

to-'do a fuss: *a tremendous to-do about the missing papers.*

I, he *etc* **could be doing with/could do with** it would be better if I, he *etc* had or did (something): *I could do with a cup of coffee.*

do away with to get rid of: *They did away with uniforms at that school years ago.*

do for to kill or cause the end of: *That attack of flu almost did for him.*

done for ruined, defeated or about to be killed *etc*: *The police are coming − run for it or we're done for!*

done in exhausted.

do out to clean thoroughly: *The room's tidy − I did it out yesterday.*

do out of to prevent from getting, *esp* by using dishonest methods: *My boss tried to do me out of a day's holiday.*

do's and don'ts [dounts] rules or advice for action: *If you want to lose weight, I can give you a list of do's and don'ts.*

do without to manage without and accept the lack of: *We'll just have to do without a phone; If you're too lazy to fetch the ice-cream you can just do without; I can do without your opinion, if you don't mind.*

to do with 1 (*with* **have**) to have dealings with: *I never had anything to do with the neighbours.* **2** (*with* **have**) to be involved in, *esp* to be (partly) responsible for: *Did you have anything to do with her death?* **3** (*with* **have**) to be connected with: *Has this decision anything to do with what I said yesterday?* **4** (*with* **be** *or* **have**) to be about or concerned with: *This letter is/has to do with Bill's plans for the summer.* **5** (*with* **have**) to be the concern of: *I'm sorry, but that question has nothing to do with me; What has that (got) to do with him?*

what are you *etc* **doing with 1** why or how have you *etc* got: *What are you doing with my umbrella?* **2** what action are you *etc* taking about: *What are they doing with the children during the day if they're both working?*

docile ['dousail, (*Amer*) 'dosl] *adj* (of a person or animal) quiet and easy to manage: *a docile child/pony.* **'docilely** *adv.* **do'cility** [də'si-] *n.*

dock[1] [dok] *n* **1** a deepened part of a harbour *etc* where ships go for loading, unloading, repair *etc*: *The ship was in dock for three weeks.* **2** the area surrounding this: *He works down at the docks.* **3** the box in a law court where the accused person sits or stands. – *v* to (cause to) enter a dock and tie up alongside a quay: *The liner docked in Southampton this morning.*

'docker *n* a person who works in the docks.
'dockyard *n* a naval harbour with docks, stores *etc.*

dock[2] [dok] *v* to cut short or remove part from: *The dog's tail had been docked; His wages were docked to pay for the broken window.*

dockyard *see* **dock**[1].

doctor ['doktə] *n* **1** (*often abbrev* **Dr** when written in titles) a person who is trained to treat ill people: *Doctor Davidson; You should call the doctor if you are ill; I'll have to go the doctor.* **2** (*often abbrev* **Dr** when written in titles) a person who has gained the higest university degree in any subject. – *v* **1** to interfere with; to add something to: *Someone had doctored her drink.* **2** to treat with medicine *etc*: *I'm doctoring my cold with aspirin.*

'doctorate [-rət] *n* the degree of Doctor.

doctrine ['doktrin] *n* a belief or set of beliefs which is taught: *religious doctrines.*

document ['dokjumənt] *n* a written statement giving information, proof, evidence *etc*: *She signed several legal documents relating to the sale of her house.*

,docu'mentary [-'men-] *adj* of or found in documents: *documentary evidence.* – *n* – *pl* **docu'mentaries** – a film, programme *etc* giving information on a certain subject: *a documentary on the political situation in Argentina.*

dodge [dodʒ] *v* to avoid (something) by a

sudden and/or clever movement: *She dodged the blow; He dodged round the corner out of sight; Politicians are very good at dodging difficult questions.* – *n* **1** an act of dodging. **2** a trick: *You'll never catch him – he knows every dodge there is.*

'dodgy *adj* **1** difficult or risky: *Catching the 5.15 train after the meeting will be rather dodgy.* **2** (of a person, organization *etc*) not trustworthy or safe, financially or otherwise: *I think the whole business sounds a bit dodgy.*

doe [dou] *n* the female of certain deer, and of the rabbit, hare *etc.*

doer, does, doesn't *see* **do**.

dog [dog] *n* a domestic, meat-eating animal related to the wolf and fox. – *adj* (*usu* of members of the dog family) male: *a dog-fox.* – *v* – *pt, ptp* **dogged** – to follow closely as a dog does: *She dogged his footsteps.*

dogged ['dogid] *adj* keeping on at what one is doing in a determined and persistent manner: *his dogged perseverance.*

'doggedly [-gid-] *adv*: *He went doggedly on with his work despite the interruptions.* **'doggedness** [-gid-] *n.*

'dog-biscuit *n* a small hard biscuit fed to dogs.

'dog collar a stiff round collar worn by a clergyman.

'dog-eared *adj* (of a book) having the pages turned down at the corner: *dog-eared volumes; Several pages were dog-eared.*

,dog-'tired *adj* very tired: *I'm dog-tired this morning after sitting up all night in the train.*

a dog's life a wretched existence: *He leads a dog's life.*

go to the dogs to be ruined, *esp* to ruin oneself.

in the doghouse in disgrace: *He forgot his wife's birthday, so he's in the doghouse.*

not a dog's chance no chance at all: *He hasn't a dog's chance of getting a ticket.*

dogged *see* **dog**.

doggerel ['dogərəl] *n* bad poetry.

doggo ['dogou]: **to lie doggo** to remain in hiding without giving any sign of one's presence.

dogma ['dogmə] *n* opinions settled or fixed by an authority, *eg* the Church.

dogmatic [dog'matik] *adj* tending to force one's own opinions on other people: *He's very dogmatic on this subject.* **dog'matically** *adv*.

doings *see* **do**.

dole [doul] *v* (*usu with* **out**) to hand or give out shares of: *She doled out the food.* – *n* (*with* **the**) a slang word for the payment made by the state to an unemployed person: *He's on the dole.*

doleful ['doulful] *adj* sorrowful: *a doleful expression.* **'dolefully** *adv*. **'dolefulness** *n.*

doll [dol] *n* a toy in the shape of a small human being: *a china doll.*

dollar ['dolə] *n* (*usu abbrev* $ *when written*) the standard unit of currency in several countries, *eg* the US, Australia, Singapore; *It costs ten dollars/$10.*

dolly ['doli] – *pl* '**dollies** – *n* a child's word for a doll.

dolphin ['dolfin] *n* a type of sea-animal about two and a half to three metres long, closely related to the porpoise.

domain [də'mein] *n* **1** an old word for the lands which belong to a person: *the king's domains.* **2** one's area of interest or of knowledge: *That question is outside my domain.*

dome [doum] *n* a roof shaped like half a ball: *the dome of the cathedral.*

  domed *adj* having or resembling a dome: *a domed forehead.*

domestic [də'mestik] *adj* **1** of or in the house or home: *a domestic servant*; *domestic utensils.* **2** concerning one's private life or family: *domestic problems.* **3** (of animals) tame and living with or used by people. **4** not foreign: *the Government's domestic policy.*

  do'mesticated [-keitid] *adj* **1** (of animals) accustomed to living near and being used by people: *Cows and sheep have been domesticated for many thousands of years.* **2** good at doing jobs associated with running a house: *My husband has become very domesticated since I've been ill.* **do,mesti'cation** *n*.

  domesticity [doume'stisəti] *n* (fondness for) home life.

  domestic help (a person paid to give) assistance with housework *etc*.

dominant ['dominənt] *adj* ruling; most important; strongest: *the dominant group in society*; *Green was the dominant colour in the room.* '**dominance** *n*.

  '**dominate** [-neit] *v* **1** to have command or influence (over): *The stronger man dominates the weaker.* **2** to be most strong or most noticeable *etc* (in): *The skyline is dominated by the castle.* ,**domi'nation** *n*.

domineering [domi'niəriŋ] *adj* tending to order people about: *a domineering older brother.*

dominion [də'minjən] *n* **1** rule or power: *There was no-one left to challenge his dominion.* **2** a self-governing country of the British Commonwealth: *the Dominion of Canada.*

domino ['dominou] – *pl* '**dominoes** – *n* an oblong piece of wood *etc* marked with spots with which the game of '**dominoes** is played.

donate [də'neit, (*Amer*) 'douneit] *v* to give to a fund *etc*: *He donated $100 to the fund.*

  do'nation *n* a gift of money or goods to a fund or collection: *All donations are welcome.*

donor ['dounə] *n* a giver of a gift or of a part of the body used to replace a diseased part of someone else's body: *The new piano in the hall is the gift of an anonymous donor*; *a kidney-donor*; *a blood-donor.*

done *see* **do**.

donkey ['doŋki] *n* **1** a domesticated animal with long ears related to the horse but smaller. **2** a stupid person: *Don't be such a donkey!*

  '**donkey-work** *n* hard, uninteresting work: *We have a computer now, which saves us a lot of donkey-work.*

  donkey's years/ages a very long time: *It's donkey's years since I was last there.*

donor *see* **donate**.

don't *see* **do**.

doodle ['du:dl] *v* to make meaningless drawings and scribbles, *usu* while thinking, talking on the telephone *etc*. – *n* a drawing of this sort.

doom [du:m] *n* fate, *esp* something terrible and final which is about to happen (to one): *The whole place had an atmosphere of doom*; *His doom was inevitable.* – *v* to condemn; to make certain to come to harm, fail *etc*: *His crippled leg doomed him to long periods of unemployment*; *The project was doomed to failure*; *He was doomed from the moment he first took drugs.*

door [do:] *n* **1** the *usu* hinged barrier, *usu* of wood, which closes the entrance of a room, house *etc*: *He knocked loudly on the door.* **2** a means of achieving something: *the door to success.*

  '**doorknob** *n* a knob-shaped handle for opening and closing a door.

  '**doorman** *n* a man on duty at the door of a hotel, store *etc*.

  '**doormat** *n* a mat kept in front of the door for people to wipe their feet on.

  '**doorstep** *n* a raised step just outside the door of a house.

  '**doorway** *n* the space usually filled by a door: *He was standing in the doorway.*

  on one's doorstep very close to where one lives: *The Welsh mountains are on our doorstep.*

dope [doup] *n* any drug or drugs: *He was accused of stealing dope from the chemist.* – *v* to drug: *They discovered that the race-horse had been doped.*

  '**dopey** *adj* made stupid (as if) by drugs: *I was dopey from lack of sleep.*

dormant ['do:mənt] *adj* not dead but not active: *a dormant volcano.*

dormitory ['do:mitri] – *pl* '**dormitories** – *n* a room used for sleeping in, with many beds.

dorsal ['do:səl] *adj* of the back: *a shark's dorsal fin.*

dose [dous] *n* **1** the quantity of medicine *etc* to be taken at one time: *It's time you had a* *dose of your medi ine.* **2** an unpleasant thing (*esp* an illness) which one is forced to suffer: *a nasty dose of flu. – v* to give medicine to: *She dosed him with aspirin.*

'dosage [-sidʒ] *n* the size of, or method of giving, a dose of medicine *etc*: *What is the dosage for a child of five?*

dossier ['dosiei] *n* a set of papers containing information *etc* about a person or a particular matter.

dot [dot] *n* a small, round mark: *She marked the paper with a dot.*

'dotted *adj* **1** consisting of dots: *a dotted line.* **2** having dots: *dotted material.*

dote [dout]: **dote on** to be fond of to an extent which is foolish: *He just dotes on that child!*

dotted *see* **dot.**

double ['dʌbl] *adj* **1** of twice the (usual) weight, size *etc*: *A double whisky, please.* **2** two of a sort together or occurring in pairs: *double doors.* **3** consisting of two parts or layers: *a double thickness of paper; a double meaning.* **4** for two people: *a double bed. – adv* **1** twice: *I gave her double the usual quantity.* **2** in two: *The coat had been folded double. – n* **1** a double quantity: *Whatever the women earn, the men earn double.* **2** someone who is exactly like another: *He is my father's double.* **– 1** to (cause to) become twice as large or numerous: *He doubled his income in three years; Road accidents have doubled since 1960.* **2** to have two jobs or uses: *This sofa doubles as a bed.*

'doubles *n sing* or *n pl* in tennis *etc*, a kind of match with two players on each side: *I enjoy playing doubles;* (*also adj*) *a doubles match.*

double agent a spy paid by each of two countries hostile to each other.

double bass [beis] a type of large stringed instrument, the largest and deepest in sound of the violin family.

double-'bedded *adj* containing a double bed: *a double-bedded room.*

double-'cross *v* to betray (someone for whom one has already arranged to do something deceitful).

double-'dealing *n* cheating and deceitfulness. *– adj* cheating: *You double-dealing liar!*

* **double-'decker** *n* a bus *etc* having two decks or levels. *– Also adj*: *a double-decker bus.*

double-'Dutch *n* nonsense: *You're talking double-Dutch!*

double figures the numbers between 10 and 99: *The number of times you have been late is well into double figures.*

double-'quick *adj, adv* very quick(ly): *Get here double-quick/in double-quick time!*

at the double very quickly: *He came up the road at the double and rushed into the house.*

double back to turn and go back the way one came: *The fox doubled back and went down a hole.*

double up 1 to (cause to) bend or collapse suddenly at the waist: *We (were) doubled up with laughter; He received a blow in the stomach which doubled him up.* **2** to join up in pairs: *There weren't enough desks, so some pupils had to double up.*

see double to see two images of everything instead of only one: *When I first met the twins, I thought I was seeing double, they were so alike.*

doubt [daut] *v* **1** to feel uncertain about, but inclined not to believe: *I doubt if he'll come now; He might have a screwdriver, but I doubt it.* **2** not to be sure of the reliability of: *Sometimes I doubt your intelligence! – n* a feeling of not being sure and sometimes of being suspicious: *There is some doubt as to what happened; I have doubts about that place.*

'doubtful *adj* **1** feeling doubt; uncertain what to think, expect *etc*: *He is doubtful about the future of the school.* **2** able to be doubted; not clear: *The meaning is doubtful; a doubtful result.* **3** uncertain but rather unlikely, unhopeful *etc*: *It is doubtful whether this will work; a doubtful improvement.* **4** suspicious: *He's rather a doubtful character.* **'doubtfully** *adv.* **'doubtfulness** *n.*

'doubtless *adv* probably: *John has doubtless told you about me.*

beyond doubt certain(ly): *Beyond doubt, they will arrive tomorrow; His honesty is beyond doubt.*

in doubt uncertain: *The result of the dispute is still in doubt.*

no doubt surely; probably: *No doubt you would like to see your bedroom; He will come back again tomorrow, no doubt.*

dough [dou] *n* a mass of flour moistened and kneaded but not baked.

'doughnut [-nʌt, (*Amer*) -nət] *n* a ring-shaped cake, with a hole in the middle, fried in fat.

dove [dʌv] *n* a kind of pigeon.

dowdy ['daudi] *adj* (of dress *etc*) not smart; unfashionable.

down[1] [daun] *adv* **1** towards or in a low or lower position, level or state: *He climbed down to the bottom of the ladder.* **2** on or to the ground: *The little boy fell down and cut his knee.* **3** from earlier to later times: *The recipe has been handed down in our family for years.* **4** from a greater to a smaller size, amount *etc*: *Prices have been going down steadily.* **5** towards or in a place thought of as being lower, *esp* southward or away from a centre: *We went down from Glasgow to Bristol. – prep* **1** in a lower position on: *Their house is halfway down the hill.* **2** to a lower position on, by, through or along: *Water poured down the drain.* **3** along: *The teacher's gaze travelled slowly down the line of children.* – *v* to finish (a drink) very quickly, *esp* in one gulp: *He downed a pint of beer.*

'**downward** *adj* leading, moving *etc* down: *a downward curve.*

'**downward(s)** *adv* towards a lower position or state: *The path led downward(s) towards the sea.*

down-and-'out *n, adj* (a person) having no money and no means of earning a living: *a hostel for down-and-outs.*

,**down-at-'heel** *adj* shabby, untidy and not well looked after or well-dressed.

'**downcast** *adj* (of a person) depressed; in low spirits: *a downcast expression.*

'**downfall** *n* a disastrous fall, *esp* a final failure or ruin: *the downfall of our hopes.*

,**down'grade** *v* to reduce to a lower level, *esp* of importance: *His job was downgraded.*

,**down'hearted** *adj* depressed and in low spirits, *esp* lacking the inclination to carry on with something: *Don't be downhearted!* – *we may yet win.*

,**down'hill** *adv* **1** down a slope: *The road goes downhill all the way from our house to yours.* **2** towards a worse and worse state: *We expected him to die, I suppose, because he's been going steadily downhill for months.*

,**down-in-the-'mouth** *adj* miserable; in low spirits.

down payment a payment in cash, *esp* to begin the purchase of something for which further payments will be made over a period of time.

'**downpour** *n* a very heavy fall of rain.

'**downright** *adv* plainly; there's no other word for it: *I think he was downright rude!* – *adj*: *He is a downright nuisance!*

'**downstairs** *adj,* ,**down'stairs** *adv* on or towards a lower floor: *He walked downstairs; I left my book downstairs; a downstairs flat.*

,**down'stream** *adv* further along a river towards the sea: *We found/rowed the boat downstream.*

,**down-to-'earth** *adj* practical and not concerned with theories, ideals *etc*: *She is a sensible, down-to-earth person.*

'**downtown** *adj* (*Amer*) the part (of a city) containing the main centres for business and shopping: *downtown Manhattan.* – ,**down'town** *adv* (also **down town**) in or towards this area: *to go downtown; I was down town yesterday.*

'**down-trodden** *adj* badly treated; treated without respect: *a down-trodden wife.*

be/go down with to be or become ill with: *The children all went down with measles.*

down on one's luck having bad luck.

down tools to stop working: *When the man was sacked his fellow workers downed tools and walked out.*

down with get rid of: *Down with the dictator!*

get down to to begin working seriously at or on: *I must get down to some letters!*

suit (someone) down to the ground to suit perfectly: *That arrangement will suit me down to the ground.*

down² [daun] *n* small, soft feathers: *a quilt filled with down.*

downie® *see* **duvet.**

'**downy** *adj* soft, like feathers: *the baby's downy hair.*

dowry ['dauəri] – *pl* '**dowries** – *n* money and property brought by a woman to her husband when they marry.

doze [douz] *v* to sleep lightly for short periods: *The old lady dozed in her chair.* – *n* a short sleep.

doze off to go into a light sleep.

dozen ['dʌzn] – *pls* '**dozens**, (after a number or a word signifying a quantity) '**dozen** – *n* a group of twelve: *two dozen handkerchiefs; These eggs are 50 cents a dozen; Half-a-dozen eggs, please.*

dozens (of) very many: *I've been there dozens of times.*

drab [drab] *adj* dull and uninteresting, *esp* in colour: *drab clothes.* '**drably** *adv.* '**drabness** *n.*

drachma ['drakmə] *n* the standard unit of Greek currency.

draft [dra:ft] *n* **1** a rough sketch or outline of something, *esp* written: *a rough draft of my speech.* **2** a group (of soldiers *etc*) taken from a larger group. **3** an order (to a bank *etc*) for the payment of money: *a draft for $80.* **4** (*Amer*) conscription: *He emigrated to avoid the draft.* – *v* **1** to make in the form of a rough plan: *Could you draft a report on this?* **2** (*Amer*) to conscript into the army *etc*: *He was drafted into the Navy.*

draftsman *see* **draughtsman.**

drag [drag] – *pt, ptp* **dragged** – *v* **1** to pull, *esp* by force or roughly: *She was dragged screaming from her car.* **2** to pull (something) slowly (*usu* because heavy): *He dragged the heavy table across the floor.* **3** to (cause to) move along the ground: *His coat was so long it dragged on the ground at the back.* **4** to search (the bed of a lake *etc*) by using a net or hook: *Police are dragging the canal to try to find the body.* **5** to be slow-moving and boring: *The evening dragged a bit.* – *n* **1** something which slows something down: *He felt that his lack of education was a drag on his progress.* **2** an act of drawing in smoke from a cigarette *etc*: *He took a long drag at his cigarette.* **3** something or someone that is dull and boring: *Washing* up is a drag. **4** a slang word for women's clothes when worn by men.

dragon ['dragən] *n* a mythical beast, a *usu* large, winged, fire-breathing reptile: *St George and the dragon*.

dragonfly ['dragənflai] *n* a kind of insect with a long body and double wings.

drain [drein] *v* **1** to clear (land) of water by the use of ditches and pipes: *There are plans to drain the marsh.* **2** (of water) to run away: *The water drained away/off into the ditch.* **3** to pour off the water *etc* from or allow the water *etc* to run off from: *Would you drain the vegetables?*; *He drained the petrol tank*; *The blood drained from her face.* **4** to drink everything contained in: *He drained his glass.* **5** to use up completely (the money, strength *etc* of): *The effort drained all his energy.* – *n* **1** something (a ditch, trench, waterpipe *etc*) designed to carry away water: *The heavy rain has caused several drains to overflow.* **2** something which slowly exhausts a supply, *esp* of one's money or strength: *His car is a constant drain on his money.*

'drainage [-nidʒ] *n* the process, method or system of carrying away extra water: *The town's drainage is very efficient.*

'draining-board *n* the area at the side of a sink grooved and sloping to allow water from dishes to drain away.

'drainpipe *n* a pipe which carries water from the roof of a building to the ground.

down the drain wasted: *We had to scrap everything and start again – six months' work down the drain!*

drake [dreik] *n* a male duck.

drama ['dra:mə] *n* **1** a play for acting on the stage: *He has just produced a new drama.* **2** plays for the stage in general: *modern drama.* **3** the art of acting in plays: *He studied drama at college.* **4** exciting events: *Life here is full of drama.*

dramatic [drə'matik] *adj* **1** of or in the form of a drama: *a dramatic entertainment.* **2** vivid or striking: *a dramatic improvement*; *She made a dramatic entrance.* **3** (of a person) showing (too) much feeling or emotion: *She's very dramatic about everything.* **dra'matically** *adv*.

'dramatist ['dra-] *n* a writer of plays.

'dramatize, -ise ['dra-] *v* **1** to turn into the form of a play: *She dramatized the novel for television.* **2** to make real events seem like things that happen in a play: *She dramatizes everything so!* **dramati'zation** *n*.

drank *see* **drink**.

drape [dreip] *v* **1** to hang cloth in folds (about): *We draped the sofa in red velvet.* **2** to hang in folds: *We draped sheets over the boxes to hide them.*

'draper *n* a person who sells cloth, clothing *etc*.

'drapery – *pl* **'draperies** – *n* **1** a draper's business. **2** cloth used for draping: *walls hung with blue drapery.*

drapes *n pl* (*Amer*) curtains.

drastic ['drastik] *adj* violent, severe and having a wide effect: *At this point they decided to take drastic action.* **'drastically** *adv*.

draught, (*Amer*) **draft** [dra:ft] *n* **1** a movement of air, *esp* one which causes discomfort in a room or which helps a fire to burn: *We increase the heat in the furnace by increasing the draught*; *There's a dreadful draught in this room!* **2** a quantity of liquid drunk at once without stopping: *He took a long draught of beer.* **3** the amount of water a ship requires to float it: *a draught of half a metre.*

draughts, (*Amer* **'checkers**) *n* **1** *sing* a game for two people, played on a board (a **'draughtboard**, (*Amer*) **'checkerboard**) exactly like a chessboard, with twenty-four discs. **2** *pl* the discs.

'draughty *adj* full of draughts of air: *a draughty room.*

draughtsman, (*esp Amer*) **draftsman** ['dra:ftsmən] – *pl* **'draughtsmen, 'draftsmen** – *n* a person who is good at or employed in making drawings: *My son is a draughtsman in a firm of engineers.*

draw [drɔ:] – *pt* **drew** [dru:]; *ptp* **drawn** – *v* **1** to make a picture or pictures (of), *usu* with a pencil, crayons *etc*: *During his stay in hospital he drew a great deal*; *Shall I draw a cow?*; **2** to pull along, out or towards oneself: *She drew the child towards her*; *He drew a gun suddenly and fired*; *All water had to be drawn from a well*; *The cart was drawn by a pony.* **3** to move (towards or away from someone or something): *The car drew away from the kerb*; *Christmas is drawing closer.* **4** to play (a game) in which neither side wins: *The match was drawn/We drew at 1-1.* **5** to obtain (money) from a fund, bank *etc*: *to draw a pension/an allowance.* **6** to open or close (curtains). **7** to attract: *She was trying to draw my attention to something.* – *n* **1** a drawn game: *The match ended in a draw.* **2** an attraction: *The acrobats' act should be a real draw.* **3** the selecting of winning tickets in a raffle, lottery *etc*: *a prize draw.* **4** an act of drawing, *esp* a gun: *He's quick on the draw.*

'drawing *n* (the art of making) a picture made with a pencil, crayon *etc*: *the drawings of Leonardo da Vinci*; *I am no good at drawing.*

drawn *adj* **1** (of curtains) pulled together or closed: *The curtains were drawn, although it was still daylight.* **2** (of a game *etc*) neither won nor lost: *a drawn match.* **3** (of a blade

etc) pulled out of its sheath: *a drawn sword*.
4 (of a person) strained and tired: *His face was pale and drawn*.

'**drawback** *n* a disadvantage: *There are several drawbacks to his plan*.

'**drawbridge** *n* a bridge (at the entrance to a castle) which can be pulled up or let down.

'**drawing-pin** *n* (*Amer* '**thumbtack**) a pin with a broad, flat head used for fastening paper to a board *etc*.

'**drawstring** *n* a cord threaded through the top of a bag *etc* for closing it.

draw a blank to be unsuccessful in a search, inquiry *etc*.

draw a conclusion from to come to a conclusion after thinking about (what one has learned): *Don't draw any hasty conclusions from what I've said!*

draw in (of a car *etc*) to come to a halt at the side of the road.

draw the line to fix a limit *esp* for what one is prepared to do.

draw/cast lots to decide who is to do *etc* something by drawing names out of a box *etc*: *Five of us drew lots for the two pop-concert tickets*.

draw off to pour out (liquid) from a large container: *The barman drew off a pint of beer*.

draw on[1] to use (money, strength, memory *etc*) as a source: *I'll have to draw on my savings*.

draw on[2] 1 to pull on: *He drew on his gloves*. 2 to come nearer: *Night drew on*.

draw out 1 to take (money) from a bank: *I drew out $40 yesterday*. 2 to make longer: *We drew out the journey as much as we could but we still arrived early*. 3 (of a car *etc*) to move into the middle of the road from the side.

draw up 1 (of a car *etc*) to stop: *We drew up outside their house*. 2 to arrange in an acceptable form or order: *They drew up the soldiers in ·line*; *The solicitor drew up a contract for them to sign*. 3 to move closer: *Draw up a chair!* 4 to extend (oneself) into an upright position: *He drew himself up to his full height*.

long drawn out going on for a long time: *The meeting was long drawn out*; *a long-drawn-out meeting/scream*.

drawer [drɔ:] *n* a sliding box without a lid which fits into a chest, table *etc*: *the bottom drawer of my desk*.

drawing *see* draw.

drawing-room ['drɔ:iŋrum] *n* a sitting-room.

drawl [drɔ:l] *v* to speak or say in a slow, lazy manner: *He drawled his words in an irritating manner*. – *n* a slow, lazy manner of speaking: *She spoke in a drawl*.

drawn, drawstring *see* draw.

dread [dred] *n* great fear: *She lives in dread of* her child being drowned in the canal; *His voice was husky with dread*. – *v* to fear greatly: *We were dreading his arrival*.

'**dreadful** *adj* 1 terrible: *a dreadful accident*. 2 very bad or annoying: *What dreadful children!*. '**dreadfulness** *n*.

'**dreadfully** *adv* extremely: *dreadfully ill*; *dreadfully clever*.

dream [dri:m] *n* 1 thoughts and pictures in the mind that come mostly during sleep: *I had a terrible dream last night*. 2 a state of being completely occupied by one's own thoughts: *Don't sit there in a dream!* 3 something perfect or very beautiful: *Your house is a dream!* 4 an ambition or hope: *It's my dream to win a Nobel Prize*. – *v* – *pts*, *ptps* **dreamed, dreamt** [dremt] – (*sometimes with* **of**) to see visions and pictures in the mind, *esp* when asleep: *For years I dreamed of being a great artist*; *I dreamt last night that the house had burnt down*.

'**dreamer** *n* a person who is often occupied with his thoughts: *I'm afraid my son is a bit of a dreamer and not very practical*.

'**dreamless** *adj* (of sleep) sound; not disturbed by dreams.

'**dreamy** *adj* as if of a person who is not quite awake: *a dreamy smile*; *She is too dreamy*. '**dreamily** *adv*. '**dreaminess** *n*.

dream up to invent: *I'm sure she'll dream up some silly plan*.

dreary ['driəri] *adj* 1 gloomy: *What dreary weather!* 2 very dull: *I've got to go to another dreary meeting tomorrow*. '**drearily** *adv*. '**dreariness** *n*.

dredge[1] [dredʒ] *v* to deepen or clear the bed of (a river *etc*) by bringing up mud.

'**dredger** *n* a boat with apparatus for dredging.

dredge[2] [dredʒ] *v* to sprinkle (food with sugar *etc*): *pancakes dredged with sugar*.

dregs [dregʒ] *n pl* 1 the solid matter which is left at the bottom of a container when the liquid is all used up: *the dregs of the wine*. 2 anything worthless: *the dregs of society*.

drench [drentʃ] *v* to soak completely: *They went out in the rain and were drenched to the skin*.

dress [dres] *v* 1 to put clothes or a covering on: *We dressed in a hurry and my wife dressed the children*. 2 to prepare (food *etc*) to be eaten: *She dressed a salad*. 3 to treat and bandage (wounds): *He was sent home from hospital after his burns had been dressed*. – *n* 1 what one is wearing or dressed in: *He has strange tastes in dress*. 2 a piece of women's clothing with a top and skirt in one piece: *Shall I wear a dress or a blouse and skirt?*

dressed *adj* wearing (clothes): *Don't come in – I'm not dressed!*; *She was dressed in black*;

Get dressed immediately; *a well-dressed man.*

'**dresser** *n* a kitchen sideboard for holding dishes.

'**dressing** *n* **1** something put on as a covering: *We gave the rose-bed a dressing of manure.* **2** a sauce added *esp* to salads: *oil and vinegar dressing.* **3** a bandage *etc* used to dress a wound: *He changed the patient's dressing.*

'**dressing-gown** *n* a loose garment worn over pyjamas *etc.*

'**dressing-room** *n* a room (in a theatre *etc*) for actors *etc* to change in.

'**dressing-table** *n* a table in a bedroom with a mirror and drawers.

'**dressmaker** *n* a person who makes clothes for women.

dress rehearsal a full rehearsal of a play *etc* with costumes *etc.*

dress up to put on special clothes, *eg* fancy dress: *He dressed up as a clown for the party.*

drew *see* **draw.**

dribble ['dribl] *v* **1** to fall in small drops: *Water dribbled out of the tap.* **2** (of a baby *etc*) to allow saliva to run from the mouth. **3** in football, hockey *etc* to kick or hit (the ball) along little by little: *He dribbled up the field.* – *n* a small quantity of liquid: *A dribble ran down his chin.*

dried, drier *see* **dry.**

drift [drift] *n* **1** a heap of something driven together, *esp* snow: *His car stuck in a snowdrift.* **2** the direction in which something is going; the general meaning: *I couldn't hear you clearly, but I did catch the drift of what you said.* – *v* **1** to (cause to) float or be blown along: *Sand drifted across the road; The boat drifted down the river.* **2** (of people) to wander or live aimlessly: *She drifted from job to job.*

'**drifter** *n* **1** a fishing-boat that uses a net which floats near the surface of the water. **2** a person who drifts.

'**driftwood** *n* wood floating on or cast up on the shore by the sea: *We made a fire with driftwood.*

drill [dril] *v* **1** to make (a hole) with a drill: *He drilled holes in the wood; to drill for oil.* **2** (of soldiers *etc*) to exercise or be exercised: *The soldiers drilled every morning.* – *n* **1*** a tool for making holes: *a hand-drill; an electric drill.* **2** exercise or practice, *esp* of soldiers: *We do half-an-hour of drill after tea.*

drily *see* **dry.**

drink [driŋk] – *pt* **drank** [draŋk]: *ptp* **drunk** [drʌŋk] – *v* **1** to swallow (a liquid): *She drank a pint of water; He drank from a bottle.* **2** to take alcoholic liquids, *esp* in too great a quantity. – *n* **1** (an act of drinking)

a liquid suitable for swallowing: *He had/ took a drink of water; Lemonade is a refreshing drink.* **2** (a glassful *etc* of) alcoholic liquor: *He likes a drink when he returns home from work; Have we any drink in the house?*

drink in to take in eagerly: *They listened eagerly, drinking in every detail.*

drink to/drink (to) the health of to offer good wishes to, or wish well, while drinking: *to drink someone's health; Raise your glasses and drink to the bride and groom.*

drink up to finish by drinking: *Drink up your milk!*

drip [drip] – *pt, ptp* **dripped** – *v* to (cause to) fall in single drops: *Rain dripped off the roof; His hand was dripping blood.* – *n* **1** a small quantity (of liquid) falling in drops: *A drip of water ran down her arm.* **2** the noise made by dripping: *I can hear a drip somewhere.* **3** an apparatus for passing a liquid slowly and continuously into a vein of the body.

'**dripping** *n* fat obtained from meat while it is roasting *etc.*

,**drip-'dry** *adj* (of a garment *etc*) requiring no ironing if allowed to dry by hanging up. – *v* to dry in this manner.

drive [draiv] – *pt* **drove** [drouv]: *ptp* **driven** ['drivn] – *v* **1** to control or guide (a car *etc*): *Do you want to drive (the car), or shall I?* **2** to take, bring *etc* in a car: *My mother is driving me to the airport.* **3** to force or urge along: *Two men and a dog were driving a herd of cattle across the road.* **4** to hit hard: *He drove a nail into the door; He drove a golf-ball from the tee.* **5** to cause to work by providing the necessary power: *This mill is driven by water.* – *n* **1** a journey in a car, *esp* for pleasure: *We decided to go for a drive.* **2** a private road leading from a gate to a house *etc*: *The drive is lined with trees.* **3** energy and enthusiasm: *I think he has the drive needed for this job.* **4** a special effort: *We're having a drive to save electricity.* **5** in sport, a hard stroke (with a golf-club, a cricket bat *etc*).

'**driver** *n* a person who drives a car *etc*: *a bus-driver.*

'**drive-in** *adj* (of a cinema, café etc, *esp* in North America) catering for people who remain in their cars while watching a film, eating *etc*: *a drive-in movie.*

be driving at to be trying to say or suggest: *I don't know what you're driving at.*

drive off 1 to leave or go away in a car *etc*: *He got into a van and drove off.* **2** to keep away: *to drive off flies.* **3** in golf, to make the first stroke from the tee.

drive on 1 to carry on driving a car *etc*: *Drive on – we haven't time to stop!* **2** to urge

---

* see illustration on p. 566

strongly forward: *It was ambition that drove him on.*

drizzle ['drizl] *v* (*only with* it *as subject*) to rain in small drops. – *n* fine, light rain.

dromedary *see* **camel**.

drone [droun] *n* **1** the male of the bee. **2** a person who is lazy and idle. **3** a deep, humming sound: *the distant drone of traffic.* – *v* **1** to make a low, humming sound: *An aeroplane droned overhead.* **2** to speak in a dull, boring voice: *The lecturer droned on and on.*

droop [dru:p] *v* **1** to (cause to) hang down: *The willows drooped over the pond.* **2** (of a plant) to flop from lack of water: *a vase of drooping flowers.*

drop [drop] *n* **1** a small round or pear-shaped blob of liquid, *usu* falling: *a drop of rain.* **2** a small quantity (of liquid): *If you want more wine, there's a drop left.* **3** an act of falling: *a drop in temperature.* **4** a vertical descent: *From the top of the mountain there was a sheer drop of a thousand feet.* – *v* – *pt, ptp* **dropped** – **1** to let fall, *usu* accidentally: *She dropped a box of pins all over the floor.* **2** to fall: *The coin dropped through the grating*; *The cat dropped* (=jumped down) *on to its paws.* **3** to give up (a friend, a habit *etc*): *I think she's dropped the idea of going to London.* **4** to set down from a car *etc*: *The bus dropped me at the end of the road.* **5** to say or write in an informal and casual manner: *I'll drop her a note.*

'droplet [-lit] *n* a tiny drop: *droplets of rain.*

'droppings *n pl* excrement (of animals or birds).

'drop-out *n* a person who withdraws, *esp* from a course at a university *etc* or the normal life of society.

drop a brick/drop a clanger unknowingly to say or do something extremely tactless.

drop back to slow down; to fall behind: *I was at the front of the crowd but I dropped back to speak to Bill.*

drop by to visit someone casually and without being invited: *I'll drop by at his house on my way home.*

drop in to arrive informally to visit someone: *Do drop in (on me) if you happen to be passing!*

drop off 1 to become separated or fall off: *The door-handle dropped off*; *This button dropped off your coat.* **2** to fall asleep: *I was so tired I dropped off in front of the television.* **3** to allow to get off a vehicle: *Drop me off at the corner.*

drop out (*often with* of) to withdraw from a group, from a course at university, or from the normal life of society: *There are only two of us going to the theatre now Mary has dropped out*; *She's dropped out of college.*

drought [draut] *n* (a period of) lack of rain:

The reservoir dried up completely during the drought.

drown [draun] *v* **1** to (cause to) sink in water and so suffocate and die: *He drowned in the river*; *He tried to drown the cat.* **2** to cause (a sound) not to be heard by making a louder sound: *His voice was drowned by the roar of the traffic.*

drowsy ['drauzi] *adj* sleepy: *drowsy children.*

'drowsily *adv.* **'drowsiness** *n.*

drudge [drʌdʒ] *v* to do dull, very hard or humble work. – *n* a person who does such work.

'drudgery *n* hard or humble work.

drug [drʌg] *n* **1** any substance used in medicine: *She has been prescribed a new drug for her stomach-pains.* **2** a substance, sometimes one used in medicine, taken by some people to achieve a certain effect, *eg* great happiness or excitement: *I think she takes drugs*; *He behaves as though he is on drugs.* – *v* – *pt, ptp* **drugged** – to make to lose consciousness by giving a drug: *She drugged him and tied him up.*

'druggist *n* (*Amer*) a person who sells medicines *etc*; a chemist; a pharmacist.

'drug-addict *n* a person who has formed the habit of taking drugs.

'drugstore *n* (*Amer*) a shop which sells various articles (*eg* cosmetics, newpapers and soft drinks) as well as medicines.

drum [drʌm] *n* **1** a musical instrument constructed of skin *etc* stretched on a round frame and beaten with a stick: *He plays the drums.* **2** something shaped like a drum, *esp* a container: *an oil-drum.* **3** an eardrum. – *v* – *pt, ptp* **drummed** – **1** to beat a drum. **2** to tap continuously *esp* with the fingers: *Stop drumming (your fingers) on the table!* **3** to make a sound like someone beating a drum: *The rain drummed on the metal roof.*

'drummer *n* a person who plays the drums.

'drumstick *n* **1** a stick used for beating a drum. **2** the lower part of the leg of a cooked chicken *etc*.

drum in/into to force someone to remember (something) by repeating it constantly: *You never remember anything unless I drum it in/into you.*

drunk [drʌŋk] *v see* **drink**. – *adj* overcome by having too much alcohol: *A drunk man fell off the bus*; *drunk with success.* – *n* a drunk person, *esp* one who is often drunk.

'drunkard [-kəd] *n* a person who is often drunk: *I'm afraid he's turning into a drunkard.*

'drunken *adj* **1** drunk: *drunken soldiers.* **2** caused by being drunk: *a drunken sleep.*

'drunkenness *n.*

dry [drai] *adj* **1** having little, or no, moisture, sap, rain *etc*: *The ground is very dry*; *The leaves are dry and withered*; *I need to find* *dry socks for the children.* **2** uninteresting and not lively: *a very dry book.* **3** (of humour or manner) quiet, restrained: *a dry wit.* **4** (of wine) not sweet. – *v* – *pt, ptp* **dried** – to (cause to) become dry: *I prefer drying dishes to washing them*; *The clothes dried quickly in the sun.*

dried *adj* (of food) having had moisture removed for the purpose of preservation.

'drier, 'dryer *n* a machine *etc* that dries: *a spin-drier; a hair-dryer.*

'drily, 'dryly *adv* in a quiet, restrained (and humorous) manner: *He commented drily on the untidiness of the room.*

'dryness *n.*

,dry-'clean *v* to clean (clothes *etc*) with chemicals, not with water.

dry land the land as opposed to the sea *etc*.

dry off to make or become completely dry: *She climbed out of the swimming-pool and dried off in the sun.*

dry up 1 to lose water; to cease running *etc* completely: *All the rivers dried up in the heat.* **2** to become used up: *Supplies of bandages have dried up.* **3** to make dry: *The sun dried up the puddles in the road.* **4** (of a speaker) to forget what he is going to say: *He dried up in the middle of his speech.*

dual ['djuəl] *adj* double; twofold; made up of two: *a gadget with a dual purpose*; *The driving instructor's car has dual controls.*

dual carriageway a road divided by a central strip of land *etc* with each side used by traffic moving in one direction.

dub[1] [dʌb] – *pt, ptp* **dubbed** – *v* **1** to give (a film) a new sound-track (*eg* in a different language). **2** to add sound effects or music to (a film *etc*). **'dubbing** *n.*

dub[2] [dʌb] – *pt, ptp* **dubbed** – *v* to nickname: *He was dubbed Shorty because of his size.*

dubious ['dju:biəs] *adj* **1** doubtful: *I am dubious about the wisdom of this action.* **2** probably not honest: *dubious behaviour.* **dubiety** [dju'baiəti], **'dubiousness** *ns.*

ducal *see* **duke.**

duchess ['dʌtʃis] *n* **1** the wife of a duke. **2** a woman of the same rank as a duke.

duck[1] [dʌk] *v* **1** to push briefly under water: *They splashed about, ducking each other.* **2** to lower the head suddenly as if to avoid a blow: *He ducked as the ball came at him.*

duck[2] [dʌk] – *pls* **ducks, duck** – *n* **1** a kind of wild or domesticated water-bird with short legs and a broad flat beak. **2** a female duck. – *See also* **drake.** **3** in cricket, a score by a batsman of nil: *He was out for a duck.* **'duckling** [-liŋ] *n* a baby duck.

duct [dʌkt] *n* a tube or pipe for fluids *etc*: *a ventilation duct.*

ductile ['dʌktail] *adj* (of metals) able to be drawn out into wire *etc*.

dud [dʌd] *n* something which is useless, does

not work *etc*: *This light-bulb is a dud.* – *adj* useless or not working: *a dud battery.*

due [dju:] *adj* **1** owed: *I think I'm still due some pay*; *Our thanks are due to the doctor.* **2** expected according to timetable, promise *etc*: *The bus is due in three minutes.* **3** proper: *Take due care.* – *adv* directly: *sailing due east.* – *n* **1** what is owed, *esp* what one has a right to: *I'm only taking what is my due.* **2** (*in pl*) charge, fee or toll: *He paid the dues on the cargo.*

'duly *adv* properly; as expected: *The bus duly arrived.*

'due to brought about by: *His success was due to hard work.*

give (someone) his due to be fair to someone.

see also **owe.**

duel ['djuəl] *n* **1** a fight (with swords or pistols) between two people over a matter of honour *etc*. **2** any contest between two people or two sides: *a duel for first place.* – *v* – *pt, ptp* **'duelled** – to fight a duel.

duet [dju'et] *n* a musical piece for two singers or players: *a piano duet.*

duffel-coat, duffle-coat ['dʌfəlkout] *n* a coat of coarse woollen cloth *usu* with a hood.

duffel bag a large bag with a round bottom, straight sides and drawstring.

dug *see* **dig.**

duke [dju:k] *n* a nobleman of the highest rank. **ducal** ['dju:kəl] *adj.*

'dukedom *n* the rank or territories of a duke.

dull [dʌl] *adj* **1** slow to learn or to understand: *The clever children help the dull ones.* **2** not bright or clear: *a dull day.* **3** not exciting or interesting: *a very dull book.* **'dully** *adv.* **'dullness** *n.*

duly *see* **due.**

dumb [dʌm] *adj* **1** without the power of speech: *She was born deaf and dumb*; *We were struck dumb with astonishment.* **2** silent: *On this point he was dumb.* **3** (*esp* Amer) very stupid: *What a dumb thing to do!* **'dumbness** *n.* **'dumbly** *adv.*

dum(b)found [dʌm'faund] *v* to make speechless with amazement: *I'm completely dumbfounded!*

dummy ['dʌmi] – *pl* **'dummies** – *n* **1** an artificial substitute looking like the real thing: *The packets of cigarettes on display were dummies.* **2** a model of a human used for displaying clothes *etc*: *a dressmaker's dummy.* **3** an artificial teat put in a baby's mouth to comfort it.

dump [dʌmp] *v* **1** to set (down) heavily: *She dumped the heavy shopping-bag on the table.* **2** to unload and leave (*eg* rubbish): *People dump things over our wall.* – *n* a place for leaving or storing unwanted things: *a rubbish dump.*

dumpiness *see* **dumpy.**

dumpling ['dʌmpliŋ] n (a) thick pudding or ball of cooked dough: *stewed beef and dumplings.*

dumpy ['dʌmpi] adj short and thick or fat: *a dumpy little woman.* '**dumpiness** n.

dunce [dʌns] n a person who is slow at learning or stupid: *I was an absolute dunce at school.*

dune [dju:n] n (also '**sand-dune**) a low hill of sand.

dung [dʌŋ] n the waste matter passed out of an animal's body, *esp* when used as manure.

dungarees [dʌŋgə'ri:z] n pl trousers with a bib: *a pair of dungarees.*

dungeon ['dʌndʒən] n a dark underground prison.

dupe [dju:p] n a person who is cheated or deceived: *She had been the dupe of a dishonest rogue.* – v to deceive or trick: *He duped me into thinking he had gone home.*

duplicate ['dju:plikət] adj exactly the same as something else: *a duplicate key.* – n 1 another thing of exactly the same kind: *He managed to find a perfect duplicate of the ring she had lost.* 2 an exact copy of something written: *She gave everyone a duplicate of her report.* – [-keit] v to make an exact copy or copies of: *He duplicated the letter.* ,**dupli'cation** n.
'**duplicator** [-kei-] n a machine for making copies.

durable ['djuərəbl] adj 1 lasting or able to last: *a durable peace.* 2 wearing well: *durable material.* ,**dura'bility** n.

duration [dju'reiʃən] n the length of time anything continues: *We all had to stay indoors for the duration of the storm.*

durian ['du:riən] n a large green fruit with a hard, prickly rind and seeds covered with cream-coloured pulp.

during ['djuəriŋ] prep 1 throughout the time of: *We couldn't get cigarettes during the war.* 2 at a particular time within: *He died during the war.*

dusk [dʌsk] n (the time of) partial darkness after the sun sets; twilight.
'**dusky** adj dark-coloured. '**duskiness** n.

dust [dʌst] n 1 fine grains of earth, sand *etc*: *The furniture was covered in dust.* 2 anything in the form of fine powder: *gold-dust; sawdust.* – v to free (furniture *etc*) from dust: *She dusts* (*the house*) *once a week.*
'**duster** n a cloth for removing dust.
'**dusty** adj: *a dusty floor.* '**dustiness** n.
dustbin ['dʌstbin] n (*Amer* '**garbage-can** or '**trash-can**) a container for household rubbish.
dust-jacket ['dʌstdʒakit] n the loose paper cover of a book.
dustman ['dʌstmən] n a person employed to remove household rubbish.

dustpan ['dʌstpan] n a type of flat container with a handle, used for holding dust swept from the floor.
'**dust-up** n a quarrel: *There was a bit of a dust-up between the two men.*
dust down to remove the dust from with a brushing action: *She picked herself up and dusted herself down.*
throw dust in someone's eyes to try to deceive someone.

duty ['dju:ti] – pl '**duties** – n 1 what one ought morally or legally to do: *He acted out of duty; I do my duty as a responsible citizen.* 2 an action or task requiring to be done, *esp* one attached to a job: *I had a few duties to perform in connection with my job.* 3 (a) tax on goods: *You must pay duty when you bring wine into the country.*
'**dutiable** adj (of goods) on which tax is to be paid.
'**dutiful** adj (*neg* **un-**) careful to do what one should: *a dutiful daughter.*
,**duty-'free** adj free from tax: *duty-free wines.*
off duty not actually working and not liable to be asked to do so: *The doctor's off duty this weekend;* (*also adj*) *She spend her off-duty hours at home.*
on duty carrying out one's duties or liable to be asked to do so during a certain period: *I'm on duty again this evening.*

duvet ['du:vei] n (*also* **downie**® ['dauni]) a type of quilt stuffed with feathers, down *etc*, used on a bed instead of blankets.

dwarf [dwɔ:f] – pls **dwarfs**, (*rare*) **dwarves** [dwɔ:vz] – n 1 an animal, plant or person much smaller than normal. 2 in fairy tales *etc*, a creature like a tiny man, with magic powers: *Snow White and the seven dwarfs.* – v to make to appear small: *The cathedral was dwarfed by the surrounding skyscrapers.*

dwell [dwel] – pts, ptps **dwelt** [-t], **dwelled** – v to live (in a place): *She dwelt in the middle of a dark forest.*
'**dwelling** n a house, flat *etc*.
dwell on to think or speak about something for a long time: *It isn't a good thing to dwell on your problems.*

dwindle ['dwindl] v to grow less: *His money dwindled away.*

dye [dai] – pt, ptp **dyed**: prp '**dyeing** – v to give a permanent colour to (clothes, cloth *etc*): *I've just dyed my coat green; I'm sure she dyes her hair.* – n a powder or liquid for colouring: *a bottle of green dye.*

dying see **die**[1].

dyke, dike [daik] n an embankment built as a barrier against the sea *etc*.

dynamic [dai'namik] adj 1 concerned with force. 2 (of a person) forceful and very energetic. **dy'namically** adv.

dy'namics *n sing* the science that deals with movement and force.

dynamite ['dainəmait] *n* a type of powerful explosive.

dynamo ['dainəmou] – *pl* '**dynamos** – *n* a machine that produces electric currents.

dynasty ['dinəsti, (*Amer*) 'dai-] – *pl* '**dynasties** – *n* a succession or series of rulers of the same family: *the Ming dynasty*. **dy'nastic** [-'nas-] *adj*.

dysentery ['disəntri] *n* an infectious disease with severe diarrhoea.

Ee

each [iːʃ] *adj* every (thing, person *etc*) of two or more, considered separately: *each house in this street*. – *pron* every single one, of two or more: *They each have 50 cents*. – *adv* to or for each one; apiece; *I gave them an apple each*.

each other used as the object when an action takes place between two (loosely, more than two) people *etc*: *They wounded each other*.

each is singular: *Each of them has* (not *have*) *a bag in his hand*.

eager ['iːgə] *adj* full of desire, interest *etc*; keen; enthusiastic: *He is always eager to win*. '**eagerness** *n*. '**eagerly** *adv*.

eagle ['iːgl] *n* a kind of large bird of prey noted for its good eyesight.

ear[1] [iə] *n* **1** the part of the head by means of which we hear, or its external part only: *Her new hair-style covers her ears*. **2** the sense or power of hearing *esp* the ability to hear the difference between sounds: *sharp ears*; *He has a good ear for music*.

'**earache** *n* pain in the inner part of the ear.
'**eardrum** *n* the layer of tissue separating the inner from the outer ear.
'**earmark** *v* to set aside (for a particular purpose): *This money is earmarked for our holiday*.
'**earring** *n* an ornament worn attached to the ear: *silver earrings*.
'**earshot** *n* the distance at which sound can be heard: *He did not hear her last remark as he was out of earshot*.
be all ears to listen with keen attention. *The children were all ears when their father was describing the car crash*.
go in one ear and out the other not to make any lasting impression: *I keep telling that child to work harder but my words go in one ear and out the other*.
play by ear to play (music) without looking at and without having memorized printed music.
up to one's ears (in) deeply involved (in): *I'm up to my ears in work*.

ear[2] [iə] *n* the part of a cereal plant which contains the seed: *ears of corn*.

earl [əːl] *n* a British nobleman between a marquis and a viscount in rank.

early ['əːli] *adv* **1** near the beginning (of a period of time *etc*): *early in my life*; *early in the afternoon*. **2** sooner than others; sooner than usual; sooner than expected or than the appointed time: *He arrived early*; *She came an hour early*. – *adj* **1** belonging to, or happening, near the beginning of a period of time *etc*: *early morning*; *in the early part of the century*. **2** belonging to the first stages of development: *early musical instruments*. **3** happening *etc* sooner than usual or than expected: *the baby's early arrival*; *It's too early to get up yet*. **4** prompt: *I hope for an early reply to my letter*. '**earliness** *n*.

early bird someone who gets up early or who acts before others do.

earmark *see* **ear**[1].

earn [əːn] *v* **1** to gain (money, wages, one's living) by working: *He earns $200 a week*; *He earns his living by cleaning shoes*; *You can afford a car now that your're earning*. **2** to deserve: *I've earned a rest*.

'**earnings** *n pl* money *etc* earned: *His earnings are not sufficient to support his family*.

earnest ['əːnist] *adj* **1** serious or over-serious: *an earnest student*; *She wore an earnest expression*. **2** showing determination, sincerity or strong feeling: *He made an earnest attempt to improve his work*. '**earnestness** *n*. **earnestly** *adv*.

in earnest 1 serious; not joking: *I am in earnest when I say this*. **2** seriously; with energy and determination: *He set to work in earnest*.

earring, earshot *see* **ear**[1].

earth [əːθ] *n* **1** the third planet in order of distance from the Sun; the planet on which we live: *Is Earth nearer the Sun than Mars is?*; *the geography of the earth*. **2** the world as opposed to heaven: *heaven and earth*. **3** soil: *Fill the plant-pot with earth*. **4** dry land; the ground: *the earth, sea and sky*. **5** a burrow or hole of an animal, *esp* of a fox. **6** (a wire that provides) an electrical connection with the earth. – *v* to connect to earth electrically: *Is your washing-machine properly earthed?*

'**earthen** *adj* (of a floor *etc*) made of earth.

'**earthly** *adj* 1 of or belonging to this world; not heavenly or spiritual: *this earthly life.* 2 possible: *This car is no earthly use.*

'**earthenware** *n, adj* (of) a kind of pottery coarser than china: *an earthenware dish.*

'**earthquake** *n* a shaking of the earth's surface: *The village was destroyed by an earthquake.*

'**earthworm** *n* (*usu* **worm**) a kind of small animal with a ringed body and no backbone, living in damp earth.

on earth used for emphasis: *What on earth are you doing?*; *the stupidest man on earth.*

run to earth to find (something or someone) after a long search: *He ran his friend to earth in the pub.*

earwig ['iəwig] *n* a kind of insect with pincers at the end of its body.

ease [i:z] *n* 1 freedom from pain or from worry or hard work: *a lifetime of ease.* 2 freedom from difficulty: *He passed his exam with ease.* 3 naturalness: *ease of manner.* – *v* 1 to free from pain, trouble or anxiety: *A hot bath eased his tired limbs.* 2 (*often with* **off**) to make or become less strong, less severe, less fast *etc*: *The pain has eased* (*off*); *The driver eased off as he approached the town.* 3 to move (something heavy or awkward) gently or gradually in or out of position: *They eased the wardrobe carefully up the narrow staircase.*

'**easily** *adv* 1 without difficulty: *She won the race easily.* 2 by far: *This is easily the best book I've read this year.* 3 very probably: *It may easily rain tomorrow.*

'**easiness** *n.*

'**easy** *adj* 1 not difficult: *This is an easy job* (*to do*). 2 free from pain, trouble, anxiety *etc*: *He had an easy day at the office.* 3 friendly: *an easy manner/smile.* 4 relaxed; leisurely: *The farmer walked with an easy stride.* – *interj* a command to go or act gently: *Easy! You'll fall if you run too fast.*

easy chair a chair that is soft and comfortable, *eg* an armchair.

,**easy-'going** *adj* not inclined to worry.

at ease free from anxiety or embarrassment: *He is completely at ease among strangers.*

easier said than done more difficult than it at first seems: *Getting seats for the theatre is easier said than done.*

go easy on to be careful with: *Go easy on the wine – there won't be enough for the rest of the guests.*

stand at ease (*eg* soldiers) to stand with legs apart and hands clasped behind the back.

take it easy not to work *etc* hard or ener-

getically; to avoid using much effort: *The doctor told him to take it easy.*

take one's ease to make oneself comfortable; to relax: *There he was – taking his ease in his father's chair!*

easel ['i:zl] *n* a (hinged) stand for supporting a blackboard, an artist's picture *etc*.

east [i:st] *n* 1 the direction from which the sun rises, or any part of the earth lying in that direction: *The wind is blowing from the east*; *The village is to the east of Canton*; *in the east of England.* 2 (*also* **E**) one of the four main points of the compass: *He took a direction 10° E of N/east of north.* – *adj* 1 in the east: *the east coast.* 2 from the direction of the east: *an east wind.* – *adv* towards the east: *The house faces east.*

'**easterly** *adj* 1 (of a wind, breeze *etc*) coming from the east: *an easterly wind.* 2 looking, lying *etc* towards the east: *We are travelling in an easterly direction.*

'**eastern** *adj* of the east or the East: *an eastern custom.*

'**easternmost** *adj* being furthest east: *the easternmost city in America.*

'**eastward** *adj* towards the east: *in an eastward direction.*

'**eastward(s)** *adv* towards the east: *They are travelling eastwards.*

the East 1 the countries east of Europe: *the Middle/Far East.* 2 (*sometimes without* **the**) the USSR, the countries of Eastern Europe, and the People's Republic of China: *the different political systems of* (*the*) *East and* (*the*) *West.*

Easter ['i:stə] *n* a Christian festival held in the spring, to celebrate Christ's coming back to life after the Crucifixion.

Easter egg a decorated egg, *esp* one made of chocolate, eaten at Easter.

easy *see* **ease.**

eat [i:t] – *pt* **ate** [et, eit; (*Amer*) eit]: *ptp* '**eaten** – *v* to (chew and) swallow; to take food: *They are forbidden to eat meat*; *They ate up all the cakes*; *We must eat to live.*

'**eatable** (*neg* **un-**) *adj* fit to be eaten: *The meal was scarcely eatable.* – *n* (*in pl*) food: *Cover all eatables to keep mice away.*

eat into to destroy or waste gradually: *Acid eats into metal*; *The school fees have eaten into our savings.*

eat one's words to admit humbly that one was mistaken in saying something: *I'll make him eat his words!*

eau-de-cologne [oudəkə'loun] (*also* **co'logne**) *n* a type of perfume first made at Cologne.

eaves [i:vz] *n pl* the edge of the roof sticking out beyond the wall: *There are birds nesting under the eaves.*

eavesdrop ['i:vzdrop] – *pt, ptp* '**eavesdropped** – *v* (*with* **on**) to listen in order to overhear a private conversation: *The child eaves-*

ebb

edit

dropped on her parents' discussion. **'eaves-dropper** *n.*

ebb [eb] **1** (of the tide) to go out from the land: *The tide began to ebb.* **2** to become less: *His strength was ebbing fast.*

ebb tide the ebbing tide: *They sailed on the ebb tide.*

at a low ebb in a poor or depressed state: *She was at a low ebb after the operation.*

on the ebb ebbing or getting less: *His power is on the ebb.*

ebony ['ebəni] **1** *n, adj* (of) a type of wood, *usu* black and almost as heavy and hard as stone. **2** *adj* black as ebony.

eccentric [ik'sentrik] *adj* (of a person, his behaviour *etc*) odd; unusual: *He is growing more eccentric every day; He had an eccentric habit of collecting stray cats.* – *n* an eccentric person. **ec'centrically** *adv.*
eccentricity [eksen'trisəti] *n* oddness of behaviour or an example of this.

echo ['ekou] – *pl* **'echoes** – *n* the repeating of a sound caused by its striking a surface and coming back: *The children shouted loudly in the cave so that they could hear the echoes.* – *v* – *pt* **'echoed** – **1** to send back an echo or echoes: *The cave was echoing with shouts; The hills echoed his shout.* **2** to repeat (a sound or a statement): *She always echoes her husband's opinion.*

eclair [i'kleə] *n* a long iced cake *usu* with cream filling and chocolate icing.

eclipse [i'klips] *n* the disappearance of the whole or part of the sun when the moon comes between it and the earth, or of the moon when the earth's shadow falls across it: *When was the last total eclipse of the sun?* – *v* **1** to obscure or cut off the light or sight of (the sun or moon): *The sun was partially eclipsed at 9 a.m.* **2** to be much better than: *His great success eclipsed his brother's achievements.*

eco- [i:kou] (*as part of a word*) concerned with living things in relation to their environment: *the eco-system.*

ecology [i'kolədʒi] *n* (the study of) living things considered in relation to their environment: *Pollution has a disastrous effect on the ecology of a region.* **e'cologist** *n.* **,eco'logical** [i:-] *adj.* **,eco'logically** *adv.*

economy [i'konəmi] *n* **1** the thrifty, careful management of money *etc* to avoid waste: *Please use the water with economy; We must make economies in household spending.* **2** organization of money and resources: *the country's economy; household economy.*
economic [i:kə'nomik] *adj* **1** of or concerned with (an) economy: *the country's economic future.* **2** likely to bring a profit: *an economic rent.*
economical [i:kə'nomikəl] *adj* thrifty; not

economics [i:kə'nomiks] *n sing* the study of production and distribution of money and goods: *He is studying economics.*
e'conomist *n* a person who is an expert in economics.
e'conomize, -ise *v* to spend money or goods carefully: *We must economize on fuel.*

ecstasy ['ekstəsi] – *pl* **'ecstasies** – *n* (a feeling of) very great joy or other overwhelming emotion.
ec'static [-'sta-] *adj: an ecstatic mood.* **ec'statically** *adv.*

eczema ['eksimə] *n* a type of skin disease in which there is an itchy rash.

eddy ['edi] – *pl* **'eddies** – *n* a current of water or air running back against the main stream or current. – *v* to move round and round: *The water eddied round the pier; The crowds eddied to and fro in the square.*

edge [edʒ] *n* **1** the part farthest from the middle of something; a border: *Don't put that cup so near the edge of the table – it will fall off; the edge of the lake; the water's edge.* **2** the cutting side of something sharp, *eg* a knife or weapon: *the edge of the sword.* **3** keenness; sharpness: *The chocolate took the edge off his hunger.* – *v* **1** to form a border to: *a handkerchief edged with lace.* **2** to move or push little by little: *He edged his chair nearer to her; She edged her way through the crowd.*
'edging *n* a border or fringe round a garment: *gold edging.*
'edgy *adj* irritable: *That actress is always edgy before a performance.*
'edgily *adv.* **'edginess** *n.*
have the edge on/over to have an advantage over: *he had the edge over his opponent.*
on edge uneasy; nervous: *She was on edge when waiting for her exam results.*

edible ['edəbl] *adj* fit to be eaten: *Are these berries edible?* **,edi'bility** *n.*

edict ['i:dikt] *n* an order or command from someone in authority; a decree.

edification *see* **edify.**

edifice ['edifis] *n* a building: *The new cathedral is a magnificent edifice.*

edit ['edit] *v* to prepare (a book, manuscript, newspaper, programme, film etc) for publication, or for broadcasting *etc, esp* by correcting, altering, shortening *etc.*
edition [i'difən] *n* a number of copies of a book *etc* printed at a time, or the form in which they are produced: *the third edition of the book; a paperback edition; the evening edition of the newspaper.*
'editor *n* **1** a person who edits books *etc: a dictionary editor.* **2** a person who is in charge of (part of) a newspaper, journal

etc: *The editor of The Times; She has been appointed fashion editor.*

,edi'torial [-'tɔ:-] *adj* of or belonging to editors: *editorial work/staff.* – *n* the leading article in a newspaper.

educate ['edjukeit] *v* to train and teach: *He was educated at a private school.*

,edu'cation *n* instruction and teaching, *esp* of children and young people in schools, universities *etc*: *His lack of education prevented him from getting a good job.*

,edu'cational *adj* **1** of education: *educational methods.* **2** providing information: *Our visit to the zoo was educational as well as enjoyable.*

,edu'cation(al)ist *n* an expert in methods of educating.

eel [i:l] *n* a kind of fish with a long smooth cylindrical or ribbon-shaped body.

eerie ['iəri] *adj* causing fear; weird: *an eerie silence.* **'eerily** *adv.* **'eeriness** *n*.

efface [i'feis] *v* **1** to rub out; to remove: *You must try to efface the event from your memory.* **2** to avoid drawing attention to (oneself): *She did her best to efface herself at parties.*

effect [i'fekt] *n* **1** a result or consequence: *He is suffering from the effects of over-eating; His discovery had little effect at first.* **2** an impression given or produced: *The speech did not have much effect (on them); a pleasing effect.*– *v* to make happen; to bring about: *He tried to effect a reconciliation between his parents.*

ef'fective [-tiv] *adj* **1** having power to produce, or producing, a desired result: *These new teaching methods have proved very effective.* **2** striking or pleasing: *an effective display of flowers.* **3** in operation; working; active: *The new law becomes effective next week.* **ef'fectively** [-tivli] *adv.*

ef'fects *n pl* **1** property; goods: *She left few personal effects when she died.* **2** in drama *etc*, devices for producing suitable sounds, lighting *etc* to accompany a play *etc*: *sound effects.*

ef'fectual [-tʃuəl] *adj* successful in producing the desired results: *He was not very effectual as an organiser.*

come into effect (of a law *etc*) to begin to operate: *The law came into effect last month.*

for effect for the sake of making an impression: *You don't mean that – you only said it for effect.*

in effect 1 (of a rule *etc*) in operation: *That law is no longer in effect.* **2** in truth or in practical terms: *In effect our opinions differed very little.*

put into effect to put (a law *etc*) into operation: *He has begun to put his theories into effect.*

take effect to begin to work; to come into force: *When will the drug take effect?*

effeminate [i'feminət] *adj* (of a man) unmanly or womanish.

effervesce [efə'ves] *v* to give off bubbles of gas; to fizz: *The champagne effervesced in the glasses.* **,effer'vescence** *n.* **,effer'vescent** *adj.*

efficacious [efi'keiʃəs] *adj* producing the result intended: *The medicine was most efficacious.* **efficacy** ['efikəsi] *n.*

efficient [i'fiʃənt] *adj* **1** (of a person) capable; skilful: *a very efficient secretary.* **2** (of an action, tool *etc*) producing (quick and) satisfactory results: *The new bread knife is much more efficient than the old one.* **ef'ficiently** *adv.* **ef'ficiency** *n.*

effigy ['efidʒi] *n* a likeness of a person, animal *etc* (in wood, stone *etc*): *effigies of Buddha.*

effluent ['efluənt] *n* (a flowing out of) waste matter from a factory *etc*.

effort ['efət] *n* **1** hard work; energy: *Learning a foreign language requires effort. The effort of climbing the hill made the old man very tired.* **2** a trying hard; a struggle: *The government's efforts to improve the economy were unsuccessful; Please make every effort to be punctual.* **3** the result of an attempt: *Your drawing was a good effort.*

'effortless *adj* done without (apparent) effort: *The dancer's movements looked effortless.* **'effortlessly** *adv.*

effusive [i'fju:siv] *adj* showing too much feeling; emotional: *an effusive letter.* **ef'fusively** *adv.*

egg¹ [eg] *n* **1** an oval object *usu* covered with shell, laid by a bird, reptile *etc*, from which a young one is hatched: *The female bird is sitting on the eggs in the nest.* **2** such an object laid by a hen, used as food: *Would you rather have boiled, fried or scrambled eggs?* **3** in the female mammal, the cell from which the young one is formed; the ovum: *The egg is fertilized by the male sperm.*

'egg-cup *n* a small cup-shaped container for holding a boiled egg while it is being eaten.

'eggplant *n* a dark purple fruit used as a vegetable.

'eggshell *n* the fragile covering of an egg.

put all one's eggs in one basket to depend entirely on the success of one scheme, plan *etc*: *You should apply for more than one job – don't put all your eggs in one basket.*

teach one's grandmother to suck eggs to try to show someone more experienced than oneself how to do something.

egg² [eg]: **egg on** to urge (somebody) on (to do something): *He egged his friend on to steal the radio.*

ego ['i:gou] *n* **1** personal pride: *His criticism*

wounded my ego. **2** the part of a person that is conscious and thinks; the self.

egocentric [egə'sentrik, (*Amer*) i:gou-] *adj* interested in oneself only.

'egoism ['e-, (*Amer*) i:-] *n* selfishness. **'egoist** ['e-, (*Amer*) 'i:-] *n*. ,**ego'istic,** **ego'istical** *adjs*.

eight [eit] *n* **1** the number or figure 8: *Four and four are/is/make eight.* **2** the age of 8: *children of eight and over.* **3** the crew of an eight-oared racing boat: *Did the Cambridge eight win?* – *adj* **1** 8 in number: *eight people*; *He is eight years old.* **2** aged 8: *He is eight today.*

eight- having eight (of something): *an eight-sided figure.*

eighth [eitθ] *n* **1** one of eight equal parts: *They each received an eighth of the money.* **2** (*also adj*) (the) last of eight (people, things *etc*); (the) next after the seventh: *His horse was eighth in the race*; *Are you having another cup of coffee? That's your eighth (cup) this morning*; *Henry VIII* (said as 'Henry the Eighth').

'eight-year-old *n* a person or animal that is eight years old: *Is this game suitable for an eight-year-old?* – *adj*: *an eight-year-old child.*

eighteen [ei'ti:n] *n* **1** the number or figure 18. **2** the age of 18: *a girl of eighteen.* – *adj* **1** 18 in number: *eighteen horses.* **2** aged 18: *He is eighteen now.*

eighteen- having eighteen: *an eighteen-page booklet.*

,**eigh'teenth** *n* **1** one of eighteen equal parts: *seventeen eighteenths.* **2** (*also adj*) (the) last of eighteen (people, things *etc*); (the) next after the seventeenth: *He was eighteenth in the competition*; *the eighteenth storey.*

,**eigh'teen-year-old** *n*: *He is married to an eighteen-year-old.* – *adj*: *an eighteen-year-old girl.*

eighty ['eiti] *n* **1** the number or figure 80. **2** the age of 80. – *adj* **1** 80 in number. **2** aged 80.

'eighties *n pl* **1** the period of time between one's eightieth and ninetieth birthdays: *He is in his eighties.* **2** the range of temperatures between eighty and ninety degrees: *It was in the eighties yesterday.* **3** the period of time between the eightieth and ninetieth years of a century: *life in the 'eighties/'80s.*

'eightieth *n* **1** one of eighty equal parts: *eleven eightieths.* **2** (*also adj*) (the) last of eighty (people, things *etc*); (the) next after the seventy-ninth.

eighty- having eighty: *an eighty-page book.* **'eighty-year-old** *n*: *a lively eighty-year-old.* – *adj*: *an eighty-year-old widow.*

either [(*esp Brit*) 'aiðə, (*esp Amer*) 'i:ðə(r)] *pron* the one or the other of two: *You may borrow either of these books*; *I offered him*

coffee or tea, but he didn't want either. – *adj* **1** the one or the other (of two things, people *etc*): *He can write with either hand.* **2** the one and the other (of two things, people *etc*); both: *at either side of the garden.* – *adv* **1** used for emphasis: *If you don't go, I won't either.* **2** moreover; besides: *I used to sing, and I hadn't a bad voice, either.*

either ... or introducing alternatives: *Either you must go to see him or send an apology.*

either way in the one case or the other: *Either way he wins.*

either ... or the verb usually matches the noun or pronoun that comes closest to it: *Either John or Mary is to blame* / *Either John or his brothers are going to the show.*

ejaculate [i'dʒakjuleit] *v* to utter or exclaim suddenly. **e,jacu'lation** *n*.

eject [i'dʒekt] *v* **1** to throw out with force; to force to leave: *They were ejected from their house for not paying the rent.* **2** to leave an aircraft in an emergency by causing one's seat to be ejected: *The pilot had to eject when his plane caught fire.* **e'jection** [-ʃən] *n*.

eke [i:k]: **eke out 1** to make (a supply of something) last longer *eg* by adding something else to it: *You could eke out the meat with potatoes.* **2** to manage with difficulty to make (a living, livelihood *etc*): *The artist could scarcely eke out a living from his painting.*

elaborate [i'labəreit] *v* **1** to work out or describe (a plan *etc*) in detail: *He elaborated his theory.* **2** (*esp with on*) to discuss details: *She elaborated on the next day's menu.* – [-rət] *adj* **1** very detailed or complicated: *an elaborate design.* **2** carefully planned: *elaborate plans for escape.* **e'laborately** *adv*. **e,labo'ration** *n*.

elapse [i'laps] *v* (of time) to pass: *A month had elapsed since our last meeting.*

elastic [i'lastik] *adj* **1** (of a material or substance) able to return to its original shape or size after being pulled or pressed out of shape: *an elastic bandage*; *Rubber is an elastic substance.* **2** able to be changed or adapted: *This is a fairly elastic arrangement.* – *n* a type of cord containing strands of rubber: *Her hat was held on with a piece of elastic.*

elasticity [i:la'stisəti, (*Amer*) ilas-] *n*.

elastic band (*also* **rubber band**) a small thin piece of rubber for holding things together or in place: *He put an elastic band round the papers.*

elated [i'leitid] *adj* very cheerful: *She felt elated after winning.* **e'lation** *n*.

elbow ['elbou] *n* the joint where the arm bends: *He leant forward on his elbows.* – *v* to push with the elbow: *He elbowed his way through the crowd.*

'elbow-room *n* space enough for doing something: *Get out of my way and give me some elbow-room!*

at one's elbow close to one: *The journalist always works with a dictionary at his elbow.*

elder[1] ['eldə] *adj* 1 (often of members of a family) older; senior: *He has three elder sisters; He is the elder of the two.* – *n* 1 a person who is older: *Take the advice of your elders.* 2 an office-bearer in Presbyterian churches.

'elderly *adj* (rather) old: *an elderly lady.*

'eldest *adj* oldest: *She is the eldest of the three children.*

the elderly people who are (rather) old: *It is important for the elderly to take some exercise.*

elder[2] ['eldə] *n* a kind of shrub or tree with purple-black fruit (**'elderberries**).

elect [i'lekt] *v* 1 to choose by vote: *He was elected chairman; elected to the committee.* 2 to choose (to do something): *They elected to go by taxi.* – *adj* (*placed immediately after noun*) chosen for office but not yet in it: *the president elect.*

e'lection [-ʃən] *n* the choosing, or choice, (*usu* by vote) of person(s) for office: *When do the elections take place?; He is standing for election again.*

e'lector *n* a person who has the right to vote at an election: *Not all the electors bothered to vote.*

e'lectoral *adj* of elections or electors: *The names of all electors are listed in the electoral roll.*

e'lectorate [-rət] *n* all electors taken together: *Half of the electorate did not vote.*

electricity [elek'trisəti] *n* a form of energy used to give heat, light, power *etc*: *worked by electricity; Don't waste electricity.*

electric [ə'lektrik] *adj* 1 of, produced by, or worked by electricity: *electric light.* 2 full of excitement: *The atmosphere in the theatre was electric.*

e'lectrical *adj* related to electricity: *electrical engineering; electrical goods; an electrical fault.*

e'lectrically *adv*: *Is this machine electrically operated?*

elec'trician [-ʃən] *n* a person whose job is to make, install, repair *etc* electrical equipment: *The electrician mended the electric fan.*

e'lectrified [-faid] *adj* supplied or charged with electricity: *an electrified fence.*

e'lectrify [-fai] *v* 1 to convert (a railway *etc*) to the use of electricity as the moving power. 2 to excite or astonish: *The news electrified us.* e,lectrifi'cation [-fi] *n.*

e'lectrifying *adj*: *an electrifying speech.*

electric chair a chair used to execute criminals by sending a powerful electric current through them.

electrocute [i'lektrəkjuːt] *v* 1 to kill (a person *etc*) accidentally by electricity: *The child was electrocuted when he touched an uncovered electric wire.* 2 to put (a person) to death by means of electricity.

electrode [i'lektroud] *n* a conductor through which a current of electricity enters or leaves a battery *etc*.

electromagnetic waves [ilektrəməg'netik] waves of energy travelling through space *etc, eg* light waves, X-rays, radio waves.

electron [i'lektron] *n* a very small particle within the atom.

electronic [elək'tronik] *adj* 1 worked or produced by devices built or made according to the principles of electronics: *an electronic calculator.* 2 concerned or working with such machines: *an electronic engineer.*

electronics [elək'troniks] *n sing* the branch of science that deals with the study of the movement and effects of electrons and with their application to machines *etc*.

elegant ['eligənt] *adj* having or showing stylishness: *elegant clothes; You look elegant today.* **'elegance** *n.*

elegy ['elidʒi] *n* a song or poem of mourning.

element ['eləmənt] *n* 1 an essential part of anything: *Sound teaching of grammar is one of the elements of a good education.* 2 a substance that cannot be split by chemical means into simpler substances: *Hydrogen, chlorine, iron and uranium are elements.* 3 surroundings necessary for life: *Water is a fish's natural element.* 4 a slight amount: *an element of doubt.* 5 the heating part in an electric kettle *etc*.

ele'mentary [-'men-] *adj* very simple; not advanced: *elementary mathematics.*

'elements *n pl* 1 the first things to be learned in any subject: *the elements of musical theory.* 2 the forces of nature, as wind and rain.

elephant ['elifənt] *n* a very large type of animal with very thick skin, a trunk and two tusks.

elevate ['eliveit] *v* 1 to raise to a higher position or to a higher rank *etc*: *elevated to the post of manager.* 2 to improve (a person's mind *etc*): *an elevating book.*

ele'vation *n* 1 the act of elevating, or state of being elevated. 2 height above sea-level: *at an elevation of 1500 metres.* 3 an architect's drawing of one side of a building.

'elevator *n* 1 (*esp Amer*) a lift or machine for raising persons, goods *etc* to a higher floor: *There is no elevator in this shop – you will have to climb the stairs.* 2 a tall storehouse for grain.

eleven [i'levn] *n* 1 the number or figure 11.

2 the age of 11. **3** in football *etc*, a team of eleven players: *He plays for the school's first eleven.* – *adj* **1** 11 in number. **2** aged 11.
eleven- having eleven (of something): *an eleven-page booklet.*
e'leventh *n* **1** one of eleven equal parts. **2** (*also adj*) (the) last of eleven (people, things *etc*); (the) next after the tenth.
e'leven-year-old *n* a person or animal that is eleven years old. – *adj* (of a person, animal or thing) that is eleven years old.
at the eleventh hour at the last possible moment; only just in time: *The child was saved from the kidnappers at the eleventh hour.*

elf [elf] – *pl* **elves** [elvz] – *n* a tiny and mischievous fairy.
'elfin *adj* of or like an elf.

elicit [i'lisit] *v* to succeed in getting (information *etc*) from a person, *usu* with difficulty.

eligible ['elidʒəbl] *adj* **1** suitable or worthy to be chosen: *the most eligible candidate.* **2** qualified or entitled: *Is he eligible to join the Scouts?* ,**eligi'bility** *n*.

eliminate [i'limineit] *v* to get rid of; to omit or exclude: *He was eliminated from the tennis match in the first round.* **e,limi'nation** *n*.

élite [ei'liːt, (*Amer*) i-] *n* (with **the**) the best or most important people *esp* within society.

elixir [i'liksə] *n* a liquid that would supposedly make people able to go on living for ever, or a substance that would turn the cheaper metals into gold: *the elixir of life.*

elk [elk] – *pls* **elks, elk** – *n* the largest of all deer, found in the north of Europe and Asia.

ellipse [i'lips] *n* a geometrical figure that is a regular oval. **el'liptical** *adj*.

elocution [elə'kjuːʃən] *n* the art of speaking clearly and effectively.

elongated ['iːloŋgeitid, (*Amer*) i'loːŋgeitid] *adj* (made) long and narrow; stretched out: *An oval looks like an elongated circle.* ,**elon'gation** *n*.

elope [i'loup] *v* to run away secretly, *esp* with a lover. **e'lopement** *n*.

eloquence ['eləkwəns] *n* the power of expressing feelings or thoughts in words that impress or move other people: *a speaker of great eloquence.*
'eloquent *adj*: *an eloquent speaker/speech.*
'eloquently *adv*.

else [els] *adj*, *adv* besides; other than that already mentioned: *What else can I do? Can we go anywhere else?*; *He took someone else's pencil.*
,**else'where** *adv* in, or to, another place; somewhere or anywhere else: *You must look elsewhere if you want a less tiring job.*
or else otherwise: *He must have missed the train – or else he's ill.*

elucidate [i'luːsideit] *v* to explain. **e,luci'dation** *n*.

elude [i'luːd] *v* **1** to escape or avoid by quickness or cleverness: *He eluded his pursuers.* **2** to be too difficult *etc* for (a person) to understand or remember: *The meaning of this poem eludes me.*
e'lusive [-siv] *adj* escaping or vanishing, often or cleverly: *an elusive criminal.*

elves *see* **elf**.

emaciated [i'meisieitid] *adj* having become very thin (through illness, starvation *etc*). **e,maci'ation** *n*.

emanate ['eməneit] *v* to flow out; to come out (from some source). ,**ema'nation** *n*.

emancipate [i'mansipeit] *v* to set free from slavery or other strict or unfair control. **e,manci'pation** *n*.

embalm [im'baːm] *v* to preserve (a dead body) from decay by treatment with spices or drugs: *The Egyptians embalmed the corpses of their kings.*

embankment [im'baŋkmənt] *n* a bank or ridge made *eg* to keep back water or to carry a railway over low-lying places *etc*.

embargo [im'baːgou] – *pl* **em'bargoes** – *n* an official order forbidding something, *esp* trade with another country.

embark [im'baːk] *v* to go, or put, on board ship: *Passengers should embark early.* ,**embar'kation** [em-] *n*.
embark on to start or engage in: *She embarked on a new career.*

embarrass [im'barəs] *v* **1** to cause to feel uneasy or self-conscious: *She was embarrassed by his praise.* **2** to involve in (*esp* financial) difficulties: *embarrassed by debts.*
em'barrassment *n*.
em'barrassed *adj*: *He was embarrassed when the teacher asked him to read his essay to the class.*
em'barrassing *adj*: *an embarrassing question.*

embassy ['embəsi] – *pl* **'embassies** – *n* (the official residence of) an ambassador and his staff: *the American embassy in London.*

embed [im'bed] – *pt*, *ptp* **em'bedded** – *v* to fix deeply (in something): *The bullet was embedded in the wall.*

embellish [im'beliʃ] *v* **1** to increase the interest of (a story *etc*) by adding (untrue) details: *The soldier embellished the story of his escape.* **2** to make beautiful with ornaments *etc*: *uniform embellished with gold braid.*
em'bellishment *n*.

embers ['embəz] *n pl* the sparking or glowing remains of a fire.

embezzle [im'bezl] *v* to take dishonestly (money that has been entrusted to oneself): *As the firm's accountant, he embezzled $20 000 in two years.*
em'bezzlement *n*. **em'bezzler** *n*.

embitter [im'bitə] *v* to make bitter and resentful: *embittered by poverty and failure.*

emblem ['embləm] *n* an object chosen to represent an idea, a quality, a country *etc*: *The dove is the emblem of peace.* ,emble'matic [-'matik] *adj.*

embody [im'bodi] *v* to represent. em'bodiment *n.*

embossed [im'bost] *adj* (of metal, leather *etc*) ornamented with a raised design: *an embossed silver spoon.*

embrace [im'breis] *v* to take (a person *etc*) in the arms; to hug: *She embraced her brother warmly.*– *n* a clasping in the arms; a hug: *a loving embrace.*

embroider [im'broidə] *v* to decorate with designs in needlework: *The child embroidered her name on her handkerchief; an embroidered tablecloth.*
em'broidery *n*: *Embroidery is one of her hobbies; What a beautiful piece of embroidery!*

embroil [im'broil] *v* to involve (a person) in a quarrel or in a difficult situation: *I do not wish to become embroiled in their family quarrels.*

embryo ['embriou] – *pl* 'embryos – *n* 1 a young animal or plant in its earliest stages in seed, egg or womb: *An egg contains the embryo of a chicken*; (*also adj*) *the embryo child.* 2 (*also adj*) (of) the beginning stage of anything: *The project is still at the embryo stage.*
,embry'ology [-'olədʒi] *n* the science of the formation and development of the embryo. ,embryo'logical [-'lo-] *adj.* ,embry'ologist *n.* ,embry'onic [-'onik] *adj* in an early stage of development.

emerald ['emərəld] *n* 1 a type of precious stone, green in colour. 2 (*also* emerald green) its colour (*also adj*): *She has an emerald (green) coat.*

emerge [i'mə:dʒ] *v* 1 to come out; to come into view: *The swimmer emerged from the water; He was already thirty before his artistic talent emerged.* 2 to become known: *It emerged that they had had a disagreement.* e'mergence *n.*
e'mergent *adj* being in the process of emerging or developing: *the emergent nations.*

emergency [i'mə:dʒənsi] – *pl* e'mergencies – *n* an unexpected, *esp* dangerous happening or situation: *Call the doctor – it's an emergency; You must save some money for emergencies;* (*also adj*) *an emergency exit.*
emergent *see* emerge.

emery ['eməri] *n* a very hard kind of mineral, used as a powder *etc* for polishing.
emery board a small flat strip of wood or card coated with emery powder and used for filing the fingernails.

emigrate ['emigreit] *v* to leave one's country and settle in another: *Many doctors have emigrated from Britain to America.*
'emigrant *n, adj* (a person) emigrating or having emigrated: *The numbers of emigrants are increasing; emigrant doctors.* ,emi'gration *n.*

eminent ['eminənt] *adj* outstanding; distinguished; famous: *an eminent lawyer.*
'eminence 1 distinction; fame. 2 a title of honour used to or of a cardinal: *His Eminence Cardinal Kelly.*
'eminently *adv* very: *eminently suitable.*

emission *see* emit.

emit [i'mit] – *pt, ptp* e'mitted – *v* to give out (light, heat, a sound, a smell *etc*). e'mission [-ʃən] *n.*

emolument [i'moljumənt] *n* profit made from employment, salary, fees *etc.*

emotion [i'mouʃən] *n* 1 a (strong) feeling of any kind: *Fear, joy, anger, love, jealousy are all emotions.* 2 the moving or upsetting of the mind or feelings: *He was overcome by/with emotion.*
e'motional *adj* 1 of the emotions: *Emotional problems are affecting her work.* 2 (*neg* un-) causing or showing emotion: *an emotional farewell.* 3 (*neg* un-) (of a person) easily affected by joy, anger, grief *etc*: *She is a very emotional person; She is very emotional.* e'motionally *adv.*

emperor ['empərə] – *fem* 'empress – *n* the head of an empire: *Charlemagne was emperor of a large part of the world; the Emperor Napoleon.*

emphasis ['emfəsis] – *pl* 'emphases [-si:z] – *n* 1 stress put on certain words in speaking *etc*; greater force of voice used in words or parts of words to make them more noticeable: *In writing we sometimes underline words to show emphasis.* 2 force; firmness: *'I do not intend to go,' he said with emphasis.* 3 importance given to something: *He placed great emphasis on this point.*
'emphasize, -ise *v* to lay or put emphasis on: *You emphasize the word 'too' in the sentence 'Are you going too?'; He emphasized the importance of working hard.*
em'phatic [-'fa-] *adj* (*neg* un-) expressed with emphasis; firm and definite: *an emphatic denial; He was most emphatic about the importance of arriving on time.* em'phatically *adv.*

to **emphasize** (not **emphasize on**) a point.

empire ['empaiə] *n* 1 a group of states *etc* under a single ruler or ruling power: *the Roman empire.* 2 a large industrial organization controlling many firms: *He owns a washing-machine empire.*

employ [im'ploi] *v* 1 to give (*esp* paid) work to: *He employs three typists; She is employed as a teacher.* 2 to occupy the time or attention of: *She was busily employed (in) writing letters.* **3** to make use of: *You should employ your time better.*

em'ployed *adj* having a job; working.

em'ployee, ,employ'ee [em-] *n* a person employed for wages, a salary *etc*: *That firm has fifty employees.*

em'ployer *n* a person who employs others: *His employer dismissed him.*

em'ployment *n* the act of employing or state of being employed: *She was in my employment*; *This will give employment to more men.*

emporium [em'po:riəm] *n* **1** a trading centre. **2** a large shop.

empty ['empti] *adj* **1** having nothing inside: *an empty box*; *an empty cup.* **2** unoccupied: *an empty house.* **3** (*with* of) completely without: *a street quite empty of people.* **4** having no practical result; (likely to be) unfulfilled: *empty threats.* – *v* **1** to make or become empty: *He emptied the jug*; *The cinema emptied quickly at 10.30*; *He emptied out his pockets.* **2** to tip, pour, or fall out of a container: *She emptied the milk into a pan*; *The rubbish emptied on to the ground.* – *n* an empty bottle *etc*: *Take the empties back to the shop.*

'emptiness *n.*

,empty-'handed *adj* carrying nothing: *I went to collect my wages but returned empty-handed.*

,empty-'headed *adj* brainless: *an empty-headed young girl.*

emu ['i:mju:] *n* a type of Australian bird which cannot fly.

emulate ['emjuleit] *v* to try hard to equal or be better than. **,emu'lation** *n.*

emulsion [i'mʌlʃən] *n* a milky liquid prepared by mixing *eg* oil and water.

emulsion paint a paint mixed with water rather than oil.

enable [i'neibl] *v* to make able by giving means, power or authority (to do something): *The money I inherited enabled me to go on a world cruise.*

enact [i'nakt] *v* to act (a rôle, scene, *etc*) not necessarily on stage. **e'nactment** *n.*

enamel [i'naməl] *n* **1** a variety of glass applied as coating to a metal or other surface and made hard by heating: *This pan is covered with enamel*; (*also adj*) *an enamel plate.* **2** the coating of the teeth. **3** a glossy paint. – *v* – *pt, ptp* **e'namelled**, (*Amer*) **e'nameled** – to cover or decorate with enamel.

enamoured [i'naməd]: **enamoured of/with** delighted with: *I am not enamoured of the idea of going abroad.*

encampment [in'kampmənt] *n* a place where troops *etc* are settled in or camp.

encase [in'keis] *v* to enclose (as if) in a case:

The nuts were encased in hard outer coverings.

enchant [in'tʃa:nt] *v* **1** to delight: *I was enchanted by the children's concert.* **2** to put a magic spell on: *A wizard had enchanted her.* **en'chanted** *adj*: *an enchanted castle.*

en'chanter – *fem* **en'chantress** – *n* a person who enchants.

en'chantment *n* **1** the act of enchanting or state of being enchanted: *a look of enchantment on the children's faces.* **2** a magic spell. **3** charm; attraction: *the enchantment(s) of a big city.*

encircle [in'sə:kl] *v* to surround: *Enemies encircled him.*

enclose [in'klouz] *v* **1** to put inside a letter or its envelope: *I enclose a cheque for $4.00.* **2** to shut in: *The garden was enclosed by a high wall.*

en'closure [-ʒə] *n* **1** the act of enclosing. **2** land surrounded by a fence or wall: *He keeps a donkey in that enclosure.* **3** something put in along with a letter: *I received your enclosure with gratitude.*

encore ['oŋko:] *n, interj* (a call from an audience for) a repetition of a performance, or (for) a further performance: *The audience cried 'Encore!'*; *The singer gave two encores.*

encounter [in'kauntə] *v* **1** to meet *esp* unexpectedly: *She encountered the manager in the hall.* **2** to meet with (difficulties *etc*): *I expect to encounter many difficulties in the course of this job.* – *n* **1** a meeting: *I feel that I know him quite well, even after a brief encounter.* **2** a fight: *The encounter between the armies was fierce.*

encourage [in'kʌridʒ, (*Amer*) -'kə:-] *v* **1** to give support, confidence or hope to: *The general tried to encourage the troops*: *You should not encourage him in his extravagance*; *I felt encouraged by his praise.* **2** to urge (a person) to do something: *You must encourage him to try again.* **en'couraging** *adj.* **en'couragingly** *adv.*

en'couragement *n*: *words of encouragement*; *He must be given every encouragement.*

the opposite of **encourage** is **discourage**.

encroach [in'kroutʃ]: **en'croach on** to advance into; invade: *to encroach on someone's land/rights.* **en'croachment** *n.*

encyclop(a)edia [insaiklə'pi:diə] *n* a reference work containing information on every branch of knowledge, or on one particular branch: *an encyclopaedia of jazz*; *If you do not know the capital city of Hungary, look it up in an encyclopaedia.* **en,cyclo'p(a)edic** *adj.*

end [end] *n* **1** the last or farthest part of the length of something: *the house at the end of the road*; *both ends of the room*; *Put the tables end to end* (= *with the end of one*

touching the end of another); (also adj) We live in the end house. 2 the finish or conclusion: the end of the week; The talks have come to an end; The affair is at an end; He is at the end of his strength; They fought bravely to the end; If she wins the prize we'll never hear the end of it (= she will often talk about it). 3 death: The soldiers met their end bravely. 4 an aim: What end have you in view? 5 a small piece left over: cigarette ends. – v to bring or come to an end: The scheme ended in disaster; How does the play end?; How should I end (off) this letter?
'ending n the end, esp of a story, poem etc: Fairy stories have happy endings.
'endless adj 1 going on for ever or for a very long time: endless arguments. 2 continuous, because of having the two ends joined: an endless chain.
at a loose end with nothing to do: He went to the cinema because he was at a loose end.
end up 1 to reach or come to an end, usu unpleasant: I knew that he would end up in prison. 2 to do something in the end: He refused to believe her but he ended up apologizing.
in the end finally: He had to work very hard but he passed his exam in the end.
make (both) ends meet not to get into debt: The widow and her four children found it difficult to make ends meet.
no end (of) very much: I feel no end of a fool.
on end 1 upright; erect: Stand the table on end; The cat's fur stood on end. 2 continuously; without a pause: For days on end we had hardly anything to eat.
put an end to to cause to finish; to stop: The government put an end to public execution.
the end the limit (of what can be borne or tolerated): His behaviour is the end!
endanger [in'deindʒə] v to put in danger: Drunk drivers endanger the lives of others.
endear [in'diə] v to make dear or more dear (to): His loyalty endeared him to me.
en'dearing adj arousing feelings of affection: his endearing innocence.
en'dearment n a word of love.
endeavour [in'devə] v to attempt; to try (to do something): He endeavoured to attract the waiter's attention. – n an attempt: He succeeded in his endeavour to climb Everest.
endemic [en'demik] adj (of a disease etc) regularly found in people or a district owing to local conditions: Malaria is endemic in/to certain tropical countries.
endorse [in'dɔ:s] v 1 to write one's signature on the back of (a cheque). 2 to make a note of an offence on (a driving licence). 3 to give one's approval to (a decision, statement etc): The court endorsed the judge's decision. en'dorsement n.

endow [in'dau] v to provide: She was endowed with great beauty. en'dowment n.
endure [in'djuə] v 1 to bear patiently; to tolerate: She endures her troubles bravely; I can endure her rudeness no longer. 2 to remain firm; to last: You must endure to the end; The memory of her great acting has endured.
en'durable adj (neg un-) able to be borne or tolerated: This pain is scarcely endurable.
en'durance n the power or ability to bear or to last: He has amazing (power of) endurance; Her rudeness is beyond endurance; (also adj) endurance tests.
enema ['enəmə] n the injection of a liquid into the rectum: He was given an enema to clean out the bowels before his operation.
enemy ['enəmi] – pl 'enemies – n 1 a person who hates or wishes to harm one: She is so good and kind that she has no enemies. 2 (also n pl) troops, forces, a nation etc opposed to oneself in war etc: He's one of the enemy; The enemy was/were encamped on the hillside; (also adj) enemy forces.
energy ['enədʒi] – pl 'energies – n 1 the ability to act, or the habit of acting, strongly and vigorously: He has amazing energy for his age; That child has too much energy; I must devote my energies to gardening today. 2 the power, eg of electricity, of doing work: electrical energy; nuclear energy.
,ener'getic [-'dʒetik] adj 1 vigorous; very active: an energetic child. 2 requiring energy: an energetic walk. ,ener'getically adv.
enforce [in'fɔ:s] v to cause (a law, a command, one's own will etc) to be carried out: There is a law against dropping litter but it is rarely enforced. en'forcement n.
engage [in'geidʒ] v 1 to begin to employ (a workman etc): He engaged him as his assistant. 2 to book; to reserve: He has engaged an entertainer for the children's party. 3 to take hold of or hold fast; to occupy: to engage someone's attention. 4 to join battle with: The two armies were fiercely engaged. 5 to (cause part of a machine etc to) fit into and lock with another part: The driver engaged second gear.
en'gaged adj 1 bound by promise (esp to marry): She became engaged to John. 2 (with in) employed or occupied: She is engaged in social work. 3 busy; not free; occupied: Please come if you are not already engaged for that evening; The room/telephone line is engaged.
en'gagement n: the engagement of three new assistants; When shall we announce our engagement?; (also adj) an engagement ring; Have you any engagements tomorrow?; a naval engagement (= battle).
en'gaging adj attractive: an engaging smile.
engine ['endʒin] n 1 a machine in which heat

or other energy is used to produce motion:
The car has a new engine. **2** a railway
engine: *He likes to sit in a seat facing the
engine.*

'**engine-driver** *n* a person who drives a railway engine.

,**engi'neer** *n* **1** a person who designs, makes,
or works with, machinery: *an electrical
engineer.* **2** (*usu* **civil engineer**) a person who
designs, constructs, or maintains roads,
railways, bridges, sewers *etc.* **3** an officer
who manages a ship's engines. **4** (*Amer*) an
engine-driver. – *v* to arrange by skill or by
cunning means: *He engineered my promotion.*

,**engi'neering** *n* the art or profession of an
engineer: *He is studying engineering at university.*

English ['ingliʃ] *adj* of England or its inhabitants: *three English people*; *the English language.* – *n* the main language of England
and the rest of Britain, North America, a
great part of the British Commonwealth
and some other countries: *He speaks
English.*

Englishman – *fem* '**Englishwoman** – *n* a
person born in England.

engrave [in'greiv] *v* **1** to cut (letters or designs) on stone, wood, metal *etc*: *They
engraved his initials on the silver cup.* **2** to
decorate (metal *etc*) in this way: *He engraved the silver cup.* **en'graver** *n.*

engrossed [in'groust] *adj* (*often with* **in**) having one's attention and interest completely
taken up: *He is completely engrossed in his
work.*

engulf [in'gʌlf] *v* (of waves, flames *etc*) to
swallow up completely: *Flames engulfed
him.*

enhance [in'ha:ns] *v* to make to appear
greater or better.

enigma [i'nigmə] *n* anything difficult to
understand; a mystery.

enigmatic [enig'matik] *adj* puzzling; mysterious: *an enigmatic smile.* ,**enig'matically**
adv.

enjoy [in'dʒoi] *v* **1** to find pleasure in: *He
enjoyed the meal.* **2** to experience; to be in
the habit of having (*esp* a benefit): *he
enjoyed good health all his life.*

en'joyable *adj*: *an enjoyable book*; *That was
most enjoyable.*

en'joyment *n*: *the enjoyment of life.*

enjoy oneself to experience pleasure or happiness: *She enjoyed herself at the party.*

> **enjoy** must be followed by an object: *He
> enjoys reading* | *We enjoyed ourselves.*

enlarge [in'la:dʒ] *v* **1** to make larger: *He
enlarged the garden.* **2** to reproduce on a
larger scale (a photograph *etc*): *We had the
photograph enlarged.*

en'largement *n* **1** something enlarged, *esp* a
photograph. **2** the act of enlarging or state
of being enlarged: *Enlargement of the
glands in the neck is usually a sign of illness.*

enlarge on to speak, write *etc* in more
detail: *Would you like to enlarge on your
original statement?*

enlighten [in'laitn] *v* to give more information
to (a person): *Will someone please enlighten
me as to what is happening?*

en'lightened *adj* wise through knowledge;
free from prejudice: *an enlightened headmaster*; *an enlightened decision.* **en'lighten-
ment** *n.*

enlist [in'list] *v* **1** to join an army *etc*: *My
father enlisted on the day after war was
declared.* **2** to obtain the support and help
of: *He has enlisted George to help him
organize the party.* **3** to obtain (support and
help) from someone: *They enlisted the support of five hundred people for their campaign.*

enliven [in'laivn] *v* to make (more) lively: *I
tried to think of something that might enliven
the class.*

enmity ['enməti] *n* unfriendliness; hatred.

enormous [i'nɔ:məs] *adj* very large: *The new
building is enormous*; *We had an enormous
lunch.* **e'normousness** *n.*

e'normity *n* **1** great wickedness. **2** hugeness.

enough [i'nʌf] *adj* in the number or quantity
etc needed: *Have you enough money to pay
for the books?*; *food enough for everyone.* –
pron the amount needed: *He has had
enough to eat*; *I've had enough of her rudeness.* – *adv* **1** to the degree needed: *Is it hot
enough?*; *He swam well enough to pass the
test.* **2** one must admit; you must agree:
She's pretty enough, but not beautiful; *Oddly
enough, it isn't raining.*

enquire, enquiry *see* **inquire.**

enrage [in'reidʒ] *v* to make very angry: *His
son's rudeness enraged him.*

enrapture [in'raptʃə] *v* to give delight to.

enrich [in'ritʃ] *v* to improve the quality of:
Fertilizers enrich the soil; *Reading enriches
the mind*; *an enriching* (= useful and enjoyable) *experience.*

enrol, (*Amer*) **enroll** [in'roul] – *pt*, *ptp* **en-
'rolled** – *v* to add (someone), or have
oneself added, to a list (as a pupil at a
school, a member of a club *etc*): *Can we
enrol for this class?*; *You must enrol your
child before the start of the school term.*
en'rolment *n.*

> **enrolment** is spelt with one **-l-**.

en route [ã'ru:t, (*Amer*) on-] *adv* on the way:
I'm en route for my office; *en route from
London to Edinburgh.*

ensemble [ãn'sãblə, (*Amer*) on'sombl] *n* **1** a
woman's complete outfit of clothes. **2** in

opera *etc*, a passage performed by all the singers, musicians *etc* together. **3** a group of musicians performing regularly together. **4** all the parts of a thing taken as a whole.

ensnare [in'sneə] *v* to trap: *He was ensnared by her beauty.*

ensue [in'sju:] *v* to come after; to result (from): *the panic that ensued from the false news report.*

en'suing *adj* coming after; happening as a result: *She was killed in the ensuing riots.*

ensure [in'ʃuə] *v* to make sure: *Ensure that your television set is switched off at night.*

entail [in'teil] *v* to bring as a result; to require: *These alterations will entail great expense.*

entangle [in'taŋgl] *v* to cause (something) to become twisted or tangled with something else: *Her long scarf entangled itself in the bicycle wheel; entangled in an unhappy love affair.* **en'tanglement** *n*.

enter ['entə] *v* **1** to go or come in: *Enter by this door.* **2** to come or go into (a place): *He entered the room.* **3** to give the name of (another person or oneself) for a competition *etc*: *He entered for the race; I entered my pupils for the examination.* **4** to write (one's name *etc*) in a book *etc*: *Did you enter your name in the visitors' book?* **5** to start in: *She entered his employment last week.*

enter into 1 to take part in: *He entered into an agreement with the film director.* **2** to take part enthusiastically in: *They entered into the Christmas spirit.* **3** to begin to discuss: *We cannot enter into the question of salaries yet.* **4** to be a part of: *The price did not enter into the discussion.*

enter on/upon to begin: *We have entered upon the new term.*

to enter (not enter into) a room.

enterprise ['entəpraiz] *n* **1** something that is attempted or undertaken (*esp* if it requires boldness or courage): *business enterprises; a completely new enterprise.* **2** willingness to try new lines of action: *We need someone with enterprise and enthusiasm.*

'enterprising *adj* (*neg* **un-**) full of enterprise; adventurous.

entertain [entə'tein] *v* **1** to receive, and give food *etc* to (guests): *They entertained us to dinner.* **2** to amuse: *His stories entertained us for hours.* **3** to hold in the mind: *He entertained the hope that he would one day be Prime Minister.*

enter'tainer *n* one who gives amusing performances professionally.

,enter'taining *adj* amusing: *entertaining stories.*

,enter'tainment *n* **1** something that entertains, *eg* a theatrical show *etc*. **2** the act of entertaining. **3** amusement; interest: *There*

is no lack of entertainment in the city at night.

enthral, (*Amer*) **enthrall** [in'θrɔ:l] – *pt, ptp* **en'thralled** – *v* to delight greatly: *His stories enthralled the children.* **en'thralling** *adj*. **en'thralment** *n*.

enthrone [in'θroun] *v* to place on a throne; to crown (as a king, queen, bishop *etc*): *The queen was enthroned with great ceremony.* **en'thronement** *n*.

enthuse [in'θju:z] *v* **1** to be enthusiastic. **2** to fill with enthusiasm.

enthusiasm [in'θju:ziazəm] *n* strong or passionate interest: *He has a great enthusiasm for travelling; He did not show any enthusiasm for our new plans.*

en'thusiast *n* a person filled with enthusiasm: *a computer enthusiast.*

en,thusi'astic *adj* (*neg* **un-**) full of enthusiasm or approval: *an enthusiastic mountaineer.* **en,thusi'astically** *adv*.

entice [in'tais] *v* to attract or tempt: *Goods are displayed in shop windows to entice people into the shop.* **en'ticement** *n*.

en'ticing *adj* attractive: *an enticing smell.*

entire [in'taiə] *adj* whole: *I spent the entire day on the beach.*

en'tirely *adv* completely: *a house entirely hidden by trees; not entirely satisfactory; entirely different.*

en'tirety [-rəti] *n* completeness.

entitle [in'taitl] *v* **1** to give (a person) a right (to, or to do, something): *You are not entitled to free school lunches; He was not entitled to borrow money from the cash box.* **2** to give to (a book *etc*) as a title or name: *a story entitled 'The White Horse'.* **en'title-ment** *n*.

entourage [ontu'ra:ʒ] *n* a group of followers, *esp* of a person of high rank.

entrails ['entreilz] *n pl* the internal parts of the body, *esp* the intestines: *a chicken's entrails.*

entrance¹ ['entrəns] *n* **1** a place of entering, *eg* an opening, a door *etc*: *the entrance to the tunnel; The church has an impressive entrance.* **2** (an) act of entering: *Hamlet now makes his second entrance.* **3** the right to enter: *He has applied for entrance to university; (also adj) an entrance exam.*

'entrant *n* one who enters (*eg* a competition): *There were sixty entrants for the musical competition.*

entrance² [in'tra:ns] *v* to fill with great delight: *The audience were entranced by her singing.*

entrant *see* entrance¹.

entreat [in'tri:t] *v* to ask (a person) earnestly and seriously (to do something).

en'treaty – *pl* **en'treaties** – *n* (an) earnest request or plea.

entrée ['ontrei] *n* a dish served at dinner as, or before, the main course.

entrepot ['ontrəpou] *n* a seaport through which exports and imports pass without incurring duty: *Singapore is an entrepot.*

entrepreneur [ontrəprə'nə:] *n* a person who starts or organizes a business company, *esp* one involving risk: *What this company needs is a real entrepreneur.*

entrust [in'trʌst] *v* to give into the care of another; to trust (somebody with something): *I entrusted this secret to her*; *I entrusted her with the duty of locking up.*

entry ['entri] – *pl* **'entries** – *n* **1** (an) act of coming in or going in: *They were silenced by the entry of the headmaster*; *Britain's entry into the European Common Market.* **2** the right to enter: *We can't go in – the sign says 'No Entry'.* **3** place of entrance, *esp* a passage or small entrance hall: *Don't bring your bike in here – leave it in the entry.* **4** a person or thing entered for a competition *ect*: *There are forty-five entries for the painting competition.* **5** something written in a list in a book *etc*: *Some of the entries in the cash-book are inaccurate.*

entwine [in'twain] *v* to wind round.

enumerate [i'nju:məreit] *v* to give a list of: *He enumerated my faults – laziness, vanity etc.* **e,nume'ration** *n.*

enunciate [i'nʌnsieit] *v* to pronounce clearly and distinctly: *He carefully enunciated each syllable of the word.* **e,nunci'ation** *n.*

envelop [in'veləp] – *pt, ptp* **en'veloped** – *v* to cover by wrapping; to surround completely: *She enveloped herself in a long cloak.*

envelop, without an -e, is a verb.
envelope, with an -e is a noun.

envelope ['envəloup] *n* a thin, flat wrapper or cover, *esp* for a letter: *The letter arrived in a long envelope.*

enviable, envious *see* **envy.**

environment [in'vaiərənmənt] *n* (a set of) surrounding conditions, *esp* those influencing development or growth: *An unhappy home environment may drive a teenager to crime*; *We should protect the environment from destruction by modern chemicals etc.* **en,viron'mental** [-'men-] *adj.*

envisage [in'vizidʒ] *v* to picture in one's mind and consider: *This was the plan that we envisaged for the future.*

envoy ['envoi] *n* a messenger, *esp* one sent to deal with a foreign government: *He was sent to France as the king's envoy.*

envy ['envi] *n* a feeling of discontent at another's good fortune or success: *She could not conceal her envy of me/at my success.* – *v* **1** to feel envy towards (someone): *He envied me*; *She envied him his money.* **2** to feel envy because of: *I've always envied that dress of yours.*

'enviable *adj* (*neg* **un-**) that is to be envied: *She spoke in public with enviable ease.*

'envious *adj* feeling or showing envy: *I'm envious of her talents.*

the envy of something envied by: *Her piano-playing was the envy of her sisters.*

epic ['epik] *n* **1** a long poem telling a story of great deeds. **2** a long story, film *etc* telling of great deeds *esp* historic.

epidemic [epi'demik] *n* an outbreak of a disease that spreads rapidly and attacks very many people: *an epidemic of measles/influenza.*

epilepsy ['epilepsi] *n* a disease of the nervous system causing attacks of unconsciousness, *usu* with violent movements of the body. **,epi'leptic** [-tik] *n, adj* (a person who is) suffering from epilepsy. – *adj* of, or caused by, epilepsy: *She has epileptic fits.*

epilogue, (*Amer*) **epilog** ['epilog] *n* the closing section of a book, programme *etc.*

episode ['episoud] *n* **1** an incident, or series of events, occurring in a longer story *etc*: *The episode of/about the donkeys is in Chapter 3*; *That is an episode in her life that she wishes to forget.* **2** a part of a radio or television serial that is broadcast at one time: *This is the last episode of the serial.*

epistle [i'pisl] *n* a letter, *esp* in the Bible from an apostle: *The epistles of St Paul.*

epitaph ['epita:f] *n* something written or said about a dead person, *esp* something written on a tombstone.

epoch ['i:pok, (*Amer*) 'epək] *n* (the start of) a particular period of history, development *etc*: *The invention of printing marked an epoch in the history of education.*

equal ['i:kwəl] *adj* the same in size, amount, value *etc*: *four equal slices*; *coins of equal value*; *Are these pieces equal in size? Women want equal wages with men.* – *n* one of the same age, rank, ability *etc*: *I am not his equal at running.* – *v* – *pt, ptp* **'equalled**, (*Amer*) **'equaled** – to be the same in amount, value, size *etc*: *I cannot hope to equal him*; *She equalled his score of twenty points*; *Five and five equals ten.*

equality [i'kwoləti] *n* the state of being equal: *Women want equality of opportunity with men.*

'equalize, -ise *v* to make or become equal: *Our team were winning by one goal – but the other side soon equalized.*

'equally *adv*: *All are equally good*; *He divided his chocolate equally between us.*

equal to fit or able for: *I didn't feel equal to telling him the truth.*

equate [i'kweit] *v* to regard as the same in some way: *He equates money with happiness.*

e'quation [-ʒən] *n* **1** a statement that two things are equal or the same: $xy + xy = 2xy$

is an equation. **2** a formula expressing the action of certain substances on others: $2H_2 + O_2 = 2H_2O$ *is an equation.*

equator [i'kweitə] *n* (*with* **the**) an imaginary line (or one drawn on a map *etc*) passing round the globe, at an equal distance from the North and South poles: *Singapore is almost on the equator.*

equatorial [ekwə'to:riəl] *adj* of or near the equator: *an equatorial climate.*

equestrian [i'kwestriən] *adj* of the art of horse-riding.

equilateral [i:kwi'latərəl] *adj* having all sides equal: *an equilateral triangle.*

equilibrium [i:kwi'libriəm] *n* a state of equal balance between weights, forces *etc.*

equinox ['ekwinoks] *n* the time when the sun crosses the equator, about March 21 and September 23.

equip [i'kwip] – *pt, ptp* **e'quipped** – *v* to fit out or provide with everything needed: *He was fully equipped for the journey; The school is equipped with four computers.*

e'quipment *n* **1** the clothes, machines, tools *etc* necessary for a particular kind of work, activity *etc*: *The mechanic could not repair the car because he did not have the right equipment; The boy could not afford the equipment necessary for mountaineering.* **2** the act of equipping.

equitable ['ekwitəbl] *adj* fair and just. **'equitably** *adv.*

equity ['ekwəti] *n* fairness; justice.

equivalent [i'kwivələnt] *adj* equal in value, power, meaning *etc*: *A metre is not quite equivalent to a yard; Would you say that 'bravery' and 'courage' are exactly equivalent?* – *n* something or someone that is equivalent to something or someone else: *This word has no equivalent in French.*

era ['iərə] *n* **1** a number of years counting from an important point in history: *the Victorian era.* **2** a period of time marked by an important event or events: *an era of social reform.*

eradicate [i'radikeit] *v* to get rid of completely: *Smallpox has almost been eradicated.* **e,radi'cation** *n.*

erase [i'reiz, (*Amer*) i'reis] *v* to rub out (pencil marks *etc*): *The typist tried to erase the error.*

e'raser *n* (*esp Amer*) something that erases, *esp* a piece of india-rubber *etc* for erasing pencil *etc.*

erect [i'rekt] *adj* upright: *He held his head erect.* – *v* **1** to set up; to put up or to build: *They erected a statue in his memory; They plan to erect an office block there.* **2** to set upright (a mast *etc*). **e'rection** [-ʃən] *n.* **e'rectly** *adv.* **e'rectness** *n.*

erode [i'roud] *v* to eat or wear away (metals *etc*); to destroy gradually: *Acids erode cer-*

tain metals; Water has eroded the rock; The individual's right to privacy is being eroded. **e'rosion** [-ʒən] *n.*

erotic [i'rotik] *adj* of, or arousing, sexual love or desire.

err [ə:] *v* to make a mistake; to be wrong; to do wrong.

err on the side of to be guilty of what might be seen as a fault in order to avoid an opposite and greater fault: *It is better to err on the side of leniency when punishing a child.*

errand ['erənd] *n* **1** a short journey made in order to get something or do something *esp* for someone else: *He has sent the child on an errand; The child will run errands for you.* **2** the purpose of such a journey: *She accomplished her errand.*

erratic [i'ratik] *adj* inclined to be irregular; not dependable: *His behaviour/work is erratic.* **er'ratically** *adv.*

erratum [i'ra:təm] – *pl* **er'rata** [-tə] – *n* an error in writing or printing: *The errata are listed at the beginning of the book.*

erroneous [i'rouniəs] *adj* (not used of a person) wrong; incorrect: *an erroneous statement.* **er'roneously** *adv.* **er'roneousness** *n.*

error ['erə] *n* a mistake: *His written work is full of errors.* **2** the state of being mistaken: *I did it in error.*

erupt [i'rʌpt] *v* (of a volcano) to throw out lava *etc*: *When did Mount Etna last erupt?; The demonstration started quietly but suddenly violence erupted.* **e'ruption** [-ʃən] *n.*

escalate ['eskəleit] *v* to increase or enlarge rapidly: *Prices are escalating.* **,esca'lation** *n.*

escalator ['eskəleitə] *n* a moving staircase in a shop, underground railway *etc.*

escapade [eskə'peid] *n* a daring or adventurous act, often one that is disapproved of by others: *Have you heard about his latest escapade?*

escape [i'skeip] *v* **1** to gain freedom: *He escaped from prison.* **2** to manage to avoid (punishment, disease *etc*): *She escaped the infection.* **3** to avoid being noticed or remembered by; to avoid (the observation of): *The fact escaped me/my notice; His name escapes me/my memory.* **4** (of a gas, liquid *etc*) to leak; to find a way out: *Gas was escaping from a hole in the pipe.* – *n* (act of) escaping; state of having escaped: *Make your escape while the guard is away; There have been several escapes from that prison; Escape was impossible; The explosion was caused by an escape of gas.*

e'scapism *n* the tendency to escape from unpleasant reality into day-dreams *etc.* **e'scapist** *n, adj.*

escort ['esko:t] *n* person(s), ship(s) *etc* accompanying for protection, guidance, courtesy *etc*: *He offered to be my escort round* the city; *The transport supplies were under military/police escort.* – [i'skɔ:t] – *v* to accompany or attend as escort: *He offered to escort her to the dance; Four police motorcyclists escorted the president's car along the route.*

especial [i'speʃəl] *adj* more than the ordinary; particular: *You must treat this with especial care.*

e'specially *adv* particularly: *These insects are quite common, especially in hot countries.*

espionage ['espiəna:ʒ] *n* the activity of spying: *He has never been involved in espionage.*

esplanade [esplə'neid] *n* a level space for walking or driving *esp* at the seaside: *Our hotel is on the esplanade and overlooks the sea.*

essay ['esei] *n* a written composition; a piece of written prose: *The examination consists of four essays; Write an essay on/about your holiday.*

essence ['esns] **1** the most important part or quality: *Tolerance is the essence of friendship.* **2** a substance obtained from a plant, drug *etc*: *vanilla essence.*

essential [i'senʃəl] *adj* absolutely necessary: *Strong boots are essential for mountaineering; It is essential that you arrive punctually.* – *n* a thing that is fundamental or necessary: *Everyone should learn the essentials of first aid; Is a television set an essential?*

es'sentially *adv* basically: *She is an essentially selfish person.*

establish [i'stabliʃ] *v* **1** to settle firmly in a position (*eg* a job, business *etc*): *He established himself (in business) as a jeweller.* **2** to found; to set up (*eg* a university, a business): *How long has the firm been established?* **3** to show to be true; to prove: *The police established that he was guilty.*

e'stablished *adj* settled or accepted: *established customs.*

e'stablishment *n* **1** the act of establishing. **2** an institution or organization: *All employees of this establishment get a bonus at New Year.* **3** a person's residence or household: *a bachelor's establishment.*

estate [i'steit] *n* **1** a large piece of land owned by one person or a group of people *etc*: *They have an estate in Ireland.* **2** a piece of land developed for building *etc*: *a housing/industrial estate.* **3** a person's total possessions (property, money *etc*): *His estate was divided among his sons.*

estate agent a person whose job is to sell houses and land.

e'state-car *n* (*Amer* **station wagon**) a car with a large area behind the seats for luggage *etc*, and a rear door.

esteem [i'sti:m] *v* to value or respect. – *n* favourable opinion; respect: *His foolish*

behaviour lowered him in my esteem; He was held in great esteem by his colleagues.

esthetic *see* **aesthetic**.

estimate ['estimeit] *v* **1** to judge size, amount, value *etc*, *esp* roughly or without measuring: *He estimated that the journey would take two hours.* **2** to form an idea or judgement of how good *etc* something is: *I did not estimate my chances of escape very highly.* – [-mət] *n* a calculation (*eg* of the probable cost *etc* of something): *He gave us an estimate of the cost of repairing the stonework; a rough estimate.*

,esti'mation *n* judgement; opinion: *In my estimation, he is the more gifted artist of the two.*

estuary ['estjuəri] – *pl* **'estuaries** – *n* the wide lower part of a river up which the tide flows: *the Thames estuary.*

et cetera [it'setrə, (*Amer*) et-] (*usu abbrev* **etc** or **&c** *when written*) a Latin phrase meaning 'and the rest', 'and so on': *The refugees need food, clothes, blankets etc.*

etch [etʃ] *v* to make (designs) on metal, glass *etc* using an acid to eat out the lines.

eternal [i'tə:nl] *adj* **1** without end; lasting for ever; unchanging: *God is eternal; eternal life.* **2** never ceasing: *I am tired of your eternal complaints.* **e'ternally** *adv*.

e'ternity *n* **1** time without end. **2** a seemingly endless time: *He waited for an eternity.* **3** the state or time after death.

ether ['i:θə] *n* a colourless liquid used to dissolve fats *etc*, and, medically, as an anaesthetic.

ethics ['eθiks] *n sing* the study or the science of morals. – *n pl* rules or principles of behaviour.

'ethical *adj* **1** of or concerning morals, justice or duty. **2** (*neg* **un-**) morally right. **'ethically** *adv*.

ethnic ['eθnik] *adj* of nations or races of mankind or their customs, dress, food *etc*: *ethnic groups/dances.*

etiquette ['etiket] *n* rules for correct or polite behaviour between people, or within certain professions: *medical/legal etiquette.*

eucalyptus [ju:kə'liptəs] – *pls* **,euca'lyptuses**, **,euca'lypti** [-tai] – a type of large Australian evergreen tree, giving timber, gum and an oil that is used in the treatment of colds.

eulogy ['ju:lədʒi] – *pl* **'eulogies** – *n* (a speech or piece of writing containing) high praise.

euphemism ['ju:fəmizəm] *n* a pleasant name for something that is unpleasant: *'Pass on' is a euphemism for 'die'.* **euphe'mistic** *adj*.

euthanasia [ju:θə'neiziə] *n* the painless killing of someone who is suffering from a painful and incurable illness: *Many old people would prefer euthanasia to the suffering they have to endure.*

evacuate [i'vakjueit] *v* **1** to leave or withdraw

from (a place), *esp* because of danger: *The troops evacuated their position because of the enemy's advance.* **2** to cause (inhabitants *etc*) to leave a place, *esp* because of danger: *Children were evacuated from the city to the country during the war.* **e͵vacu'ation** *n.*

evade [i'veid] *v* to escape or avoid by *eg* trickery or skill. **e'vasion** [-ʒən] *n.*

e'vasive [-siv] *adj* **1** having the purpose of evading. **2** not frank and direct: *He gave evasive answers.* **e'vasively** *adv.* **e'vasiveness** *n.*

evaluate [i'valjueit] *v* **1** to form an idea of the worth of: *It is difficult to evaluate him as a writer.* **2** to work out the numerical value of: *If $x = 1$ and $y = 2$ we can evaluate $x^2 + y^2$.* **e͵valu'ation** *n.*

evangelical [i:van'dʒelikəl] *adj* seeking to convert people, *esp* to Christianity.

e'vangelist [i-] *n* a person who preaches Christianity *esp* at large public meetings.

evaporate [i'vapəreit] *v* to (cause to) change into vapour and disappear: *The small pool of water evaporated in the sunshine*; *His enthusiasm soon evaporated.*

e'vaporated *adj* having had some moisture removed by evaporation: *evaporated milk.* **e͵vapo'ration** *n.*

evasion, evasive *see* **evade**.

eve [i:v] *n* **1** the day or evening before a festival: *Christmas Eve*; *New Year's Eve.* **2** the time just before an event: *on the eve of (the) battle.* **3** evening.

even¹ [i:vən] *adj* **1** level; the same in height, amount *etc*: *Are the table-legs even?*; *an even temperature.* **2** smooth: *Make the path more even.* **3** regular: *He has a strong, even pulse.* **4** divisible by 2 *with no remainder*: *2, 4, 6, 8, 10 etc are even numbers.* **5** equal (in number, amount *etc*): *The teams have scored one goal each and so they are even now.* **6** (of temperament *etc*) calm: *She has a very even temper.* – *v* – *pt, ptp* **'evened** – **1** to make equal: *Smith's goal evened the score.* **2** to make smooth or level.

'evenly *adv.* **'evenness** *n.*

be/get even with to be revenged on: *He tricked me, but I'll get even with him.*

an even chance *see* **chance**.

even out 1 to become level or regular: *The road rose steeply and then evened out*; *His pulse began to even out.* **2** to make smooth: *He raked the soil to even it out.* **3** to make equal: *If Jane would do some of Mary's typing, that would even the work out.*

even up to make equal: *John did better in the maths exam than Jim and that evened up their marks.*

even² [i:vən] *adv* **1** used to point out something unexpected in what one is saying: *'Have you finished yet?' 'No, I haven't even*

started.'; *Even the winner got no prize.* **2** yet; still: *My boots were dirty, but his were even dirtier.*

even if no matter whether: *Even if I leave now, I'll be too late.*

even so in spite of that: *It rained, but even so we enjoyed the day.*

even though in spite of the fact that: *I like the job even though it's badly paid.*

evening [i:vniŋ] *n* **1** the part of the day between the afternoon and the night: *He leaves the house in the morning and returns in the evening*; *summer evenings*; *tomorrow evening*; *on Tuesday evening*; *early evening*; *(also adj) the evening performance.* **2** the last part (of one's life *etc*): *in the evening of her life.*

evening dress 1 clothes worn for formal occasions in the evening. **2** a formal dress worn by a woman in the evening.

event [i'vent] *n* **1** something that happens; an incident or occurrence: *That night a terrible event occurred.* **2** an item in a programme of sports *etc*: *The long-jump was to be the third event.*

e'ventful *adj* (*neg* **un-**) full of events; exciting: *We had an eventful day.*

at all events/at any event in any case: *At all events, we can't make things worse than they already are.*

in that event if that happens: *In that event you must do as he says.*

in the event in the end, as it happened/happens/may happen: *In the event, I did not need to go to hospital.*

in the event of if (something) occurs: *In the event of his death, you will inherit his money.*

eventual [i'ventʃuəl] *adj* happening in the end: *their quarrel and eventual reconciliation.*

e͵ventu'ality [-'a-] – *pl* **eventu'alities** – *n* a possible happening: *We are ready for all eventualities.*

e'ventually *adv* finally; at length: *I thought he would never ask her to marry him, but he did eventually.*

ever ['evə] *adv* **1** at any time: *Nobody ever visits us*; *She hardly ever writes*; *Have you ever ridden on an elephant?*; *If I ever/If ever I see him again I shall get my revenge*; *better than ever*; *the brightest star they had ever seen.* **2** always; continually: *They lived happily ever after*; *I've known her ever since she was a baby.* **3** used for emphasis: *The new doctor is ever so gentle*; *What ever shall I do?*

ever- always; continually: *the ever-increasing traffic.*

'evergreen *adj* (of trees *etc*) having green leaves all the year round: *Holly is evergreen.* – *n* an evergreen tree: *Firs and pines are evergreens.*

ever'lasting *adj* endless; continual; unchanging: *I'm tired of your everlasting
grumbles*; *everlasting life/flowers*. **‚ever'last-
ingly** *adv*.

‚ever'more *adv* for all time: *He said that he
would love her (for) evermore*.

for ever/for'ever *adv* **1** continually: *He was
forever looking at this watch*. **2** for all time:
I'll love you for ever (and ever).

every ['evri] *adj* **1** each one of or all (of a
certain number): *Every room is painted
white*; *Not every family has a car*. **2** each (of
an indefinite number or series): *Every hour
brought the two countries nearer war*; *He
attends to her every need*. **3** the most absolute or complete possible: *We have every
reason to believe that she will get better*.
4 used to show repetition after certain
intervals of time or space: *I go to the
supermarket every four or five days*; *Every
second house in the row was bright pink*;
*'Every other day' means 'every two days' or
'on alternate days'*.

'everybody, 'everyone *pron* every person:
Everyone thinks I'm mad.

'everyday *adj* **1** happening, done used *etc*
daily: *her everyday duties*. **2** common or
usual: *an everyday event*.

'everything *pron* all things; *Have you everything you want*?

'everywhere *adv* (in or to) every place: *The
flies are everywhere*; *Everywhere I go, he
follows me*.

every bit as just as: *You're every bit as clever
as he is*.

**every now and then/every now and again/
every so often** occasionally: *We get a letter
from him every now and then*.

every time 1 always; invariably: *We use this
method every time*. **2** whenever: *Every time
he comes, we quarrel*.

everybody, everyone are singular: *Everybody is* (not *are*) *tired* / *Everyone should
buy his own ticket*.
see also **their**.

evict [i'vikt] *v* to put out from house or land
esp by force of law. **e'viction** [-ʃən] *n*.

evidence ['evidəns] *n* **1** information *etc* that
gives reason for believing something; proof
(*eg* in a law case): *Have you enough evidence (of his guilt) to arrest him*? **2** (an)
indication; a sign: *Her bag on the table was
the only evidence of her presence*.

evident ['evidənt] *adj* clearly to be seen or
understood: *his evident satisfaction*; *It is
evident that you have misunderstood me*.

'evidently *adv* **1** as far as can be seen:
Evidently he disagrees. **2** clearly or obviously: *He was quite evidently furious*.

evil ['iːvl] *adj* very bad; wicked; sinful: *evil
intentions*; *an evil man*; *He looks evil*; *evil

deeds*; *an evil tongue*. – *n* **1** wrong-doing,
harm or wickedness: *He tries to ignore all
the evil in the world*; *Do not speak evil of
anyone*. **2** anything evil, *eg* crime, misfortune *etc*: *London in the eighteenth century
was a place of crime, filth, poverty and other
evils*.

evil-: *evil-minded*; *evil-smelling*.

'evilly *adv*.

'evilness *n*.

‚evil-'doer *n* a wicked or sinful person.

evocation, evocative *see* **evoke**.

evoke [i'vouk] *v* **1** to cause or produce (*esp* a
response, reaction *etc*): *His letter in the
newspaper evoked a storm of protest*. **2** to
bring into the mind: *A piece of music can
sometimes evoke (memories of) the past*.

‚evo'cation [evə-] *n*.

evocative [i'vokətiv] *adj* tending to evoke
memories *etc*.

evolution, evolutionary *see* **evolve**.

evolve [i'volv] *v* to (cause to) develop gradually: *Man evolved from the apes*.

evolution [iːvə'luːʃən, (*Amer*) e-] *n* **1** gradual working out or development: *the evolution of our form of government*. **2** the development of the higher kinds of animals (*eg*
man), plants *etc*, from the lower kinds:
Darwin's theory of evolution. **evolutionary**
[iːvə'luːʃənəri, (*Amer*) e-] *adj*.

ewe [juː] *n* a female sheep: *The ewe had two
lambs*.

exact [ig'zakt] *adj* **1** absolutely accurate or
correct in every detail; the same in every
detail; precise: *What are the exact measurements of the room?*; *For this recipe the
quantities must be absolutely exact*; *an exact
copy*; *What is the exact time?*; *He walked in
at that exact moment*. **2** (of a person, his
mind *etc*) capable of being accurate over
small details: *Accountants have to be very
exact*. – *v* to force the payment of or giving
of: *We should exact fines from everyone who
drops litter on the streets*.

ex'acting *adj* requiring much effort or work
from a person: *a very exacting job*.

ex'actly *adv* **1** just; quite; absolutely: *He's
exactly the right man for the job*. **2** in accurate detail; precisely: *Work out the prices
exactly*; *What exactly did you say?* **3** used
as a reply meaning 'I quite agree'. **ex'act-
ness** *n*.

exaggerate [ig'zadʒəreit] *v* **1** to make (something) appear to be, or describe it as,
greater *etc* than it really is: *You seem to be
exaggerating his faults*; *That dress exaggerates her thinness*. **2** to go beyond the truth
in describing something *etc*: *You can't trust
her. She always exaggerates*.

ex‚agge'ration *n* **1** the act of exaggerating.
2 an exaggerated description, term *etc*: *To

say she is beautiful is an exaggeration, but she does have nice eyes.

exalted [ig'zo:ltid] *adj* high in rank, position *etc*; noble; important.

exam *see* **examine**.

examine [ig'zamin] *v* **1** to look at closely; to inspect closely: *They examined the animal tracks and decided that they were those of a fox.* **2** (of a doctor) to inspect the body of thoroughly to check for disease *etc*: *The doctor examined the child and said she was healthy.* **3** to consider carefully: *The police must examine the facts.* **4** to test the knowledge or ability of (students *etc*): *She examines pupils in mathematics.* **5** to question: *The lawyer examined the witness in the court case.*

ex,ami'nation *n* **1** (a) close inspection: *Make a thorough examination of the area where the crime took place*; *On examination the patient was discovered to have appendicitis.* **2** (*also* **ex'am**) a test of knowledge or ability: *school examinations*; *She is to take a French/dancing exam*; (*also adj*) *examination/exam papers*; *He failed/passed the English exam.* **3** (a) formal questioning (*eg* of a witness).

ex'aminer *n* a person who examines.

example [ig'za:mpl] *n* **1** something that represents other things of the same kind; a specimen: *an example of his handwriting.* **2** something that shows clearly or illustrates a fact *etc*: *Can you give me an example of how this word is used?* **3** a person or thing that is a pattern to be copied: *She was an example to the rest of the class.* **4** a warning to be heeded: *Let this be an example to you, and never do it again!*

for example (*often abbrev* **eg** [iː'dʒiː]) for instance; as an example: *Several European countries have no sea-coast - for example, Switzerland and Austria.*

make an example of to punish as a warning to others: *The judge decided to make an example of the young thief and sent him to prison for five years.*

set (someone) an example to act in such a way that other people will copy one's behaviour: *Teachers must set a good example to their pupils.*

exasperate [ig'za:spəreit] *v* to irritate (someone) very much indeed: *He was exasperated by the continual interruptions.*

ex,aspe'ration *n*: *She hit the child in exasperation.*

excavate ['ekskəveit] *v* **1** to dig up (a piece of ground *etc*) or to dig out (a hole) by doing this. **2** in archaeology, to uncover or open up (a structure *etc* remaining from earlier times) by digging: *The archaeologist excavated an ancient fortress.* **,exca'vation** *n*.

'excavator *n* a machine or person that excavates.

exceed [ik'siːd] *v* to go beyond; to be greater than: *His expenditure exceeds his income*; *He exceeded the speed limit on the motorway.*

ex'ceedingly *adv* very: *exceedingly nervous.*

excel [ik'sel] - *pt, ptp* **ex'celled** - *v* **1** to stand out beyond others (in some quality *etc*); to do very well (in or at some activity): *He excelled in mathematics/at football.* **2** to be better than: *She excels them all at swimming.*

'excellence ['ek-] *n* unusual goodness or worth: *this man's excellence as a teacher.*

'Excellency ['ek-] - *pl* **'Excellencies** - *n* (*with* **His, Your** *etc*) a title of honour, used *eg* for ambassadors: *His/Your Excellency*; *Their Excellencies.*

'excellent ['ek-] *adj* unusually good: *an excellent plan.* **'excellently** *adv*.

except [ik'sept] *prep* leaving out; not including: *They're all here except him*; *Your essay was good except that it was too long.* - *v* to leave out or exclude.

ex'ception [-ʃən] *n* **1** something or someone not included: *They all work hard, without exception*; *With the exception of Jim we all went home early.* **2** something not according to the rule: *We normally eat nothing at lunchtime, but Sunday is an exception.*

ex'ceptional *adj* (*neg* **un-**) unusual; remarkable: *exceptional loyalty*; *His ability is exceptional.*

ex'ceptionally *adv* unusually: *exceptionally stupid.*

except for 1 apart from: *We enjoyed the holiday except for the expense.* **2** except: *Except for John, they all arrived punctually.*

take exception to/at to object to: *The old lady took exception to the rudeness of the children.*

excerpt ['eksə:pt] *n* a part taken from a book *etc*: *I heard an excerpt from his latest novel on the radio.*

excess [ik'ses] *n* **1** the (act of) going beyond normal or suitable limits: *He ate well, but not to excess.* **2** an abnormally large amount: *He had consumed an excess of alcohol.* **3** an amount by which something is greater than something else: *He found he had paid an excess of $5.00 over what was actually on the bill.* - *adj* extra; additional (to the amount needed, allowed or usual): *He had to pay extra for his excess baggage on the aircraft.*

ex'cessive [-siv] *adj* beyond what is right and proper: *The manager expects them to do an excessive amount of work.* **ex'cessively** *adv*. **ex'cessiveness** *n*.

in excess of more than: *His salary is in excess of $25 000 a year.*

exchange [iks'tʃeindʒ] v **1** to give, or give up, in return for something else: *Can you exchange a dollar note for two 50-cent pieces?* **2** to give and receive in return: *They exchanged amused glances.* – n **1** the giving and taking of one thing for another: *He gave me a pencil in exchange for the marble; An exchange of opinions is helpful.* **2** a conversation or dispute: *An angry exchange took place between the two brothers when their father's will was read.* **3** the act of exchanging the money of one country for that of another. **4** the difference between the value of money in different countries: *What is the rate of exchange between the U.S dollar and the mark?* **5** a place where business shares are bought and sold or international financial dealings carried on. **6** (*also* **telephone exchange**) a central telephone system where lines are connected. **ex'changeable** *adj.*

excise¹ ['eksaiz] n the tax on goods *etc* made and sold within a country.

excise² [ik'saiz] v to cut out or off. **excision** [ik'siʒən] n.

excite [ik'sait] v **1** to cause or rouse strong feelings of expectation, happiness *etc* in: *The children were excited at the thought of the party.* **2** to cause or rouse (feelings, emotions *etc*): *The book did not excite my interest.* **ex'citable** *adj* easily becoming excited or upset. **ex,cita'bility** n. **ex'cited** *adj*. **ex'citedly** *adv*. **ex'citement** n: *His arrival caused great excitement; the excitement of travel.* **ex'citing** *adj*: *an exciting adventure.*

exclaim [ik'skleim] v to call out, or say, suddenly and loudly: *'Good!' he exclaimed; She exclaimed in astonishment.* **exclamation** [eksklə'meiʃən] n an expression of surprise or other sudden feeling: *He gave an exclamation of anger.* **exclamation mark** the mark (!) following and showing an exclamation.

exclude [ik'sklu:d] v **1** to prevent (someone) from sharing or taking part in something: *They excluded her from the meeting.* **2** to shut out; to keep out: *Fill the bottle to the top so as to exclude all air.* **3** to leave out of consideration: *We cannot exclude the possibility that he was lying.* **ex'clusion** [-ʒən] n. **ex'cluding** *prep* not counting; without including: *The club's expenses, excluding the cost of stationery, amounted to $251.*

exclusive [ik'sklu:siv] *adj* **1** tending to exclude. **2** (of a group *etc*) not easily or readily mixing with others or allowing others in: *a very exclusive club.* **3** given to only one individual or group *etc*: *The story is exclusive to this newspaper.* **4** fashionable and expensive: *exclusive shops/restaurants.* **ex'clusively** *adv*. **ex'clusiveness** n.

exclusive of excluding: *That is the price of the meal exclusive of service charge.*

excrement ['ekskrəmənt] n matter, *esp* solid, discharged from the body; faeces; dung: *The streets are filthy with dogs' excrement.*

excrete [ik'skri:t] v to discharge (waste matter) from the body. **ex'cretion** [-ʃən] n.

excruciating [ik'skru:ʃieitiŋ] *adj* causing extreme bodily or mental pain: *an excruciating headache.*

excursion [ik'skə:ʃən, (*Amer*) -ʒən] n a trip; an outing: *an excursion to the seaside.*

excuse [ik'skju:z] v **1** to forgive or pardon: *Excuse me – can you tell me the time?; I'll excuse your carelessness this time.* **2** to free (someone) from a task, duty *etc*: *May I be excused from writing this essay?* – [ik'skju:s] n a reason (given by oneself) for being excused, or a reason for excusing: *He has no excuse for being so late.* **excusable** [ik'skju:zəbl] *adj* pardonable.

execute ['eksikju:t] v **1** to put to death by order of the law: *After the war many traitors were executed.* **2** to carry out (instructions etc). **3** to perform (a movement *etc usu* requiring skill). **,exe'cution** [-ʃən] n **1** (an act of) killing by law: *The judge ordered the execution of the murderer.* **2** the act of executing (orders or skilled movements *etc*). **,exe'cutioner** n a person whose duty is to put to death condemned persons.

executive [ig'zekjutiv] *adv* **1** (in a business organization *etc*) concerned with management: *executive skills.* **2** concerned with the carrying out of laws *etc*: *executive powers.* – n **1** the branch of the government that puts the laws into effect. **2** a person or body of people in an organization *etc* that has power to direct or manage: *He is an executive in an insurance company.*

executor [ig'zekjutə] n a person appointed to see to the carrying out of what is stated in a will: *His two brothers are his executors.*

exemplary [ig'zempləri] *adj* worth following as an example: *His behaviour is always exemplary.*

exemplary is spelt with **-em-** (not **-am-**).

exemplify [ig'zemplifai] v to be an example of; to show by means of an example: *His originality as a composer is exemplified by the following group of songs.*

exempt [ig'zempt] v to free (a person) from a duty that other people have to carry out: *He was exempted from military service.* – *adj* free (from a duty *etc*): *Children under 16 are exempt from the usual charges for dental treatment.* **ex'emption** [-ʃən] n.

exercise ['eksəsaiz] n **1** training or use (*esp* of

the body) through action or effort: *Swimming is one of the healthiest forms of exercise*; *Take more exercise.* **2** an activity intended as training: *ballet exercises*; *spelling exercises.* **3** a series of tasks, movements *etc* for training troops *etc*: *His battalion is on an exercise in the mountains.* – *v* **1** to train or give exercise to: *Dogs should be exercised frequently*; *I exercise every morning.* **2** to use; to make use of: *She was given the opportunity to exercise her skill as a pianist.*

exert [ig'zɔːt] *v* **1** to bring forcefully into use or action: *He likes to exert his authority.* **2** to force (oneself) to make an effort: *Please exert yourselves.*

ex'ertion [-ʃən] *n* **1** the act of bringing forcefully into use: *the exertion of one's influence.* **2** (an) effort: *They failed in spite of their exertions.*

exhale [eks'heil] *v* to breathe out. **exhalation** [eksə'leiʃən] *n.*

exhaust [ig'zɔːst] *v* **1** to make very tired: *She was exhausted by her long walk.* **2** to use all of; to use completely: *We have exhausted our supplies*; *You're exhausting my patience.* **3** to say all that can be said about (a subject *etc*): *We've exhausted that topic.* – *n* (an outlet from the engine of a car, motorcycle *etc* for) fumes and other waste.

ex'hausted *adj* extremely tired.

ex'haustion *n*: *He collapsed from exhaustion.*

ex'haustive [-tiv] *adj* complete; very thorough: *an exhaustive search.*

exhibit [ig'zibit] *v* **1** to show; to display to the public: *My picture is to be exhibited in the art gallery.* **2** to show (a quality *etc*): *He exhibited a complete lack of concern for others.* – *n* **1** an object displayed publicly (*eg* in a museum): *One of the exhibits is missing.* **2** an object or document produced in court as part of the evidence: *The bloodstained scarf was exhibit number one in the murder trial.*

exhibition [eksi'biʃən] *n* a public display (*eg* of works of art, industrial goods *etc*): *an exhibition of children's books.* **2** an act of showing or revealing: *What an exhibition of bad temper!*

ex'hibitor *n* a person who provides an exhibit for a display *etc*: *He is one of the exhibitors at the flower show.*

exhilarate [ig'ziləreit] *v* to make (a person) feel happy and lively: *He was exhilarated by the walk.* **ex,hila'ration** *n.*

ex'hilarating *adj*: *an exhilarating walk.*

exhort [ig'zɔːt] *v* to urge strongly and earnestly. **,exhor'tation** [egzɔː-] *n.*

exhume [ig'zjuːm] *v* to dig out (*esp* a body from a grave). **exhumation** [eksju'meiʃən] *n.*

exile ['eksail] *n* **1** a person who lives outside his own country either from choice or because he is forced to do so: *an exile from his native land.* **2** a (*usu* long) stay in a foreign land (*eg* as a punishment): *He was sent into exile.* – *v* to send away or banish (a person) from his own country.

exist [ig'zist] *v* **1** to be something real or actual: *Do ghosts really exist?* **2** to stay alive; to continue to live: *It is possible to exist on bread and water.*

ex'istence *n* **1** the state of existing: *He does not believe in the existence of God*; *How long has this rule been in existence?* **2** (a way of) life: *an uneventful existence.*

exit ['egzit] *n* **1** a way out of a building *etc*: *the emergency exit.* **2** an actor's departure from the stage: *Macbeth's exit.* **3** an act of going out or departing: *She made a noisy exit.* – *v* (used as a stage direction to one person) (he/she) goes off the stage: *Exit Hamlet.*

exodus ['eksədəs] *n* a going away of many people: *There was a general exodus from the room.*

exorbitant [ig'zɔːbitənt] *adj* (of prices or demands) very high or unreasonable. **ex'orbitantly** *adv.* **ex'orbitance** *n.*

exorcize,-ise ['eksɔːsaiz] *v* to drive away (an evil spirit); to rid (a house *etc*) of an evil spirit.

'exorcism *n* (an) act of exorcizing.

'exorcist *n* a person who exorcizes.

exotic [ig'zotik] *adj* **1** unusual or colourful: *exotic clothes.* **2** brought or introduced from a foreign country: *exotic plants.*

expand [ik'spand] *v* to make or grow larger; to spread out wider: *Metals expand when heated*; *He does exercises to expand his chest*; *The school's activities have expanded to include climbing and mountaineering.*

ex'panse [-s] *n* a wide area or extent: *an expanse of water.*

ex'pansion [-ʃən] *n* the act or state of expanding: *the expansion of metals.*

expatriate [eks'peitriət] *n, adj* (a person) living outside his own country.

expect [ik'spekt] *v* **1** to think of as likely to happen or come: *I'm expecting a letter today*; *We expect her on tomorrow's train.* **2** to think or believe (that something will happen): *He expects to be home tomorrow*; *I expect that he will go*; 'Will she go too?' 'I expect so'/'I don't expect so'/'I expect not.' **3** to require: *They expect high wages for skilled work*; *You are expected to tidy your own room.* **4** to suppose or assume: *I expect (that) you're tired.*

ex'pectancy *n* the state of expecting or hoping: *a feeling/look/air of expectancy.*

ex'pectant *adj* **1** full of hope or expectation: *the expectant faces of the audience.* **2** ex-

pecting (a baby): *an expectant mother.*
ex'pectantly *adv.*

,expec'tation [ekspek-] *n* **1** the state of expecting: *In expectation of a wage increase, he bought a washing-machine.* **2** what is expected: *contrary to expectation, contrary to expectation(s); Did the concert come up to your expectations?*

expedient [ik'spi:diənt] *adj* convenient or advisable: *It would not be expedient to pay him what he asks.* **ex'pedience, ex'pediency** *ns.*

expedite ['ekspidait] *v* to hasten or speed up (a work process *etc*).

,expe'ditious [-'diʃəs] *adj* quick (and efficient). **expe'ditiously** *adv.*

expedition [ekspi'diʃən] *n* **1** an organized journey with a purpose: *an expedition to the South Pole.* **2** a group making such a journey: *He was a member of the expedition which climbed Mount Everest.*

expe'ditionary *adj* (*esp* of troops) forming, or sent on, an expedition *eg* to fight abroad.

expel [ik'spel] – *pt, ptp* **ex'pelled** – *v* **1** to send away in disgrace (a person from a school *etc*): *The child was expelled for stealing.* **2** to get rid of: *an electric fan for expelling kitchen smells.*

expulsion [ik'spʌlʃən] *n*: *Any child found disobeying this rule will face expulsion from the school.*

expend [ik'spend] *v* to use or spend (supplies *etc*).

ex'penditure [-tʃə] the act of spending: *the expenditure of money and resources; His expenditure(s) amounted to $500.*

ex'pense [-s] *n* **1** the spending of money *etc*; cost: *I've gone to a lot of expense to educate you well.* **2** a cause of spending: *What an expense clothes are!*

ex'penses [-siz] *n pl* money spent in carrying out a job *etc*: *His firm paid his travelling expenses.*

ex'pensive [-siv] *adj* costing a great deal: *expensive clothes.*

at the expense of 1 being paid for by; at the cost of: *He equipped the expedition at his own expense; At the expense of his health he finally completed the work.* **2** making (a person) appear ridiculous: *He told a joke at his wife's expense.*

experience [ik'spiəriəns] *n* **1** (knowledge, skill or wisdom gained through) practice in some activity, or the doing of something: *Learn by experience – don't make the same mistake again; Has she had experience in teaching?* **2** an event that affects or involves a person *etc*: *The earthquake was a terrible experience.* – *v* to have experience of; to feel: *I have never before experienced such rudeness!*

ex'perienced *adj* having gained knowledge

from experience; skilled: *an experienced mountaineer.*

experiment [ik'sperimənt] *n* a test done in order to find out something, *eg* if an idea is correct: *He performs chemical experiments; experiments in traffic control; We shall find out by experiment.* – *v* (*with* on *or* with) to try to find out something by making tests: *He experimented with various medicines to find the safest cure; The doctor experiments on animals.*

ex,peri'mental [-'mentl] *adj* of, or used for an experiment: *experimental teaching methods.* **ex,peri'mentally** *adv.*

ex,perimen'tation *n* the practice of making experiments.

expert ['ekspə:t] *adj* (*with* at *or* on) skilled through training or practice: *an expert car designer; I'm expert at map-reading; Get expert advice on plumbing.* – *n* a person who is an expert: *an expert in political history/on ancient pottery.* **'expertly** *adv.* **'expertness** *n.*

expire [ik'spaiə] *v* **1** (of a limited period of time) to come to an end: *His three weeks' leave expires tomorrow.* **2** (of a ticket, licence *etc*) to go out of date: *My driving licence expired last month.* **3** to die. **expiration** [ekspi'reiʃən] *n.*

ex'piry *n* the end of a period of time or of an agreement *etc* with a time limit: *The date of expiry is shown on your driving licence.*

explain [ik'splein] *v* **1** to make (something) clear or easy to understand: *Can you explain the railway timetable to me?; Did she explain why she was late?* **2** to give, or be, a reason for: *I cannot explain his failure; That explains his silence.*

explanation [eksplə'neiʃən] *n* **1** the act or process of explaining: *Let me give a few words of explanation.* **2** a statement or fact that explains: *There are several possible explanations for the explosion.*

ex'planatory [-'splanə-] *adj* giving an explanation: *There are explanatory notes in this book.*

explain away to get rid of (difficulties *etc*) by clever explaining: *She could not explain away the missing money.*

explicable [ek'splikəbl] *adj* capable of being explained.

explicit [ik'splisit] *adj* stated, or stating, fully and clearly: *explicit instructions; Can you be more explicit?* **ex'plicitly** *adv.* **ex'plicitness** *n.*

explode [ik'sploud] *v* **1** to (cause to) blow up with a loud noise: *The bomb exploded; The police exploded the bomb where it could cause no damage.* **2** suddenly to show strong feeling: *The teacher exploded with anger; The children exploded into laughter.* **3** to prove (a theory *etc*) wrong.

ex'plosion [-ʒən] *n* **1** a blowing up, or the

noise caused by this: *a gas explosion*: *The explosion could be heard a long way off.* **2** the action of exploding: *the explosion of the atom bomb.* **3** a sudden showing of strong feelings *etc*: *an explosion of laughter.* **4** a sudden great increase: *an explosion in food prices.*

ex'plosive [-siv] *adj* likely to explode: *Hydrogen is a dangerously explosive gas.* – *n* (a) material that is likely to explode: *gelignite and other explosives.*

exploit ['eksploit] *n* a (daring) deed or action: *stories of his military exploits.* – [ik'sploit] *v* **1** to make good or advantageous use of: *to exploit the country's natural resources.* **2** to use (*eg* a person) unfairly for one's own advantage.

,exploi'tation *n*.

explore [ik'splo:] *v* **1** to search or travel through (a place) for the purpose of discovery: *The oceans have not yet been fully explored*; *Let's go exploring in the caves.* **2** to examine carefully: *I'll explore the possibilities of getting a job here.*

exploration [eksplə'reiʃən] *n*: *a journey of exploration.*

ex'ploratory [-'splorə-] *adj* for the purpose of exploration or investigation: *an exploratory expedition.*

ex'plorer *n* a person who explores unknown regions: *explorers in space.*

explosion, explosive *see* **explode**.

expo *see* **exposition**.

exponent [ik'spounənt] *n* **1** a person able to demonstrate skilfully a particular art or activity: *She was an accomplished exponent of Bach's flute sonatas.* **2** a person who explains and supports (a theory or belief *etc*): *He was one of the early exponents of Marxism.*

export [ek'spo:t] *v* to send (goods) to another country for sale: *Jamacia exports bananas to Britain.* – ['ekspo:t] *n* **1** the act or business of exporting: *the export of rubber.* **2** something which is exported: *Paper is an important Swedish export.*

,expor'tation [ek-] *n*.

ex'porter *n* a person who exports goods: *His father was a tobacco exporter.*

expose [ik'spouz] *v* **1** to uncover; to leave unprotected from (*eg* weather, danger, observation *etc*): *Paintings should not be exposed to direct sunlight*; *Don't expose children to danger.* **2** to discover and make known (*eg* criminals or their activities): *It was a newspaper that exposed his spying activities.* **3** by releasing the camera shutter, to allow light to fall on (a photographic film).

ex'posure [-ʒə] *n* **1** (an) act of exposing or state of being exposed: *Prolonged exposure of the skin to hot sun can be harmful.* **2** one frame of a photographic film *etc*: *I have two exposures left.*

exposition [ekspə'ziʃən] *n* **1** a detailed explanation (of a subject). **2** (*abbrev* **'expo**) an exhibition: *a trade exposition.*

exposure *see* **expose**.

expound [ik'spaund] *v* to explain in detail.

express [ik'spres] *v* **1** to put into words: *He expressed his ideas very clearly.* **2** (with **oneself** *etc*) to put one's own thoughts into words: *You haven't expressed yourself clearly.* **3** to show (thoughts, feelings *etc*) by looks, actions *etc*: *She nodded to express her agreement.* **4** to send by fast (postal) delivery: *Will you express this letter, please?* – *adj* **1** travelling, carrying goods *etc*, especially fast: *an express train*; *express delivery.* **2** clearly stated: *You have disobeyed my express wishes.* – *adv* by express train or fast delivery service: *Send your letter express.* – *n* **1** an express train: *the London to Cardiff express.* **2** the service provided *eg* by the post office for carrying goods *etc* quickly: *The parcel was sent by express.*

ex'pressly *adv* in clear, definite words: *I expressly forbade you to do that.*

ex'pression [-ʃən] *n* **1** a look on one's face that shows one's feelings: *He always has a bored expression.* **2** a word or phrase: *'Dough' is a slang expression for 'money'.* **3** (a) showing of thoughts or feelings by words, actions *etc*: *This poem is an expression of his grief.* **4** the showing of feeling when *eg* reciting, reading aloud or playing a musical instrument: *Put more expression into your playing!*

ex'pressionless *adj* (of a face or voice) showing no feeling: *a cold, expressionless tone.*

ex'pressive [-siv] *adj* showing meaning or feeling clearly: *She has an expressive face.*

ex'pressiveness *n*. **ex'pressively** *adv*.

ex'pressway *n* a divided highway; a motorway.

expulsion *see* **expel**.

exquisite ['ekskwizit] *adj* very beautiful or skilful: *exquisite embroidery.* **'exquisitely** *adv*.

extend [ik'stend] *v* **1** to make longer or larger: *He extended his vegetable garden.* **2** to reach or stretch: *The school grounds extend as far as this fence.* **3** to hold out or stretch out (a limb *etc*): *He extended his hand to her.* **4** to offer: *May I extend a welcome to you all?*

ex'tension [-ʃən] *n* **1** an added part: *He built an extension to his house*; *a two-day extension to the holiday*; *He has telephone extensions* (= telephones) *in every bedroom.* **2** the process of extending.

ex'tensive [-siv] *adj* large in area or amount: *extensive plantations*; *He suffered extensive injuries in the accident.*

ex'tent [-t] *n* **1** the area or length to which something extends: *The bird's wings measured 20 centimetres at their fullest extent*; *The garden is nearly a kilometre in extent*; *A vast extent of grassland.* **2** amount; degree: *What is the extent of the damage?*; *To what extent can we trust him?* **to a certain extent/to some extent** partly but not completely.

exterior [ik'stiəriə] *adj* on or from the outside; outer: *an exterior wall of a house.* – *n* the outside (of something or someone): *On the exterior she was charming, but she was known to have a violent temper.*

exterminate [ik'stə:mineit] *v* to get rid of or destroy completely: *Rats must be exterminated from a building or they will cause disease.* **ex,termi'nation** *n.*

external [ik'stə:nl] *adj* of, for, from, or on, the outside: *Chemists often label skin creams 'For external use only'.* **ex'ternally** *adv.*

extinct [ik'stiŋkt] *adj* **1** (of a type of animal *etc*) no longer in existence: *Mammoths became extinct in prehistoric times.* **2** (of a volcano) no longer active: *That volcano was thought to be extinct until it suddenly erupted ten years ago.*

extinction [ik'stiŋkʃən] *n* **1** making or becoming extinct: *the extinction of the species.* **2** the act of putting out or extinguishing (fire, hope *etc*).

extinguish [ik'stiŋgwiʃ] *v* to put out (a fire *etc*): *Please extinguish your cigarettes.* **ex'tinguisher** *n* a spraying apparatus containing chemicals for putting out fire.

extol [ik'stoul] – *pt, ptp* **ex'tolled** – *v* to praise highly.

extort [ik'sto:t] *v* to obtain (from a person) by threats or violence: *They extorted a confession from him by torture.* **ex'tortion** [-ʃən] *n.* **ex'tortionate** [-nət] *adj* (of a price) much too high: *That restaurant's prices are extortionate!*

extra ['ekstrə] *adj* additional; more than usual or necessary: *They demand an extra $10 a week*; *We need extra men for this job.* – *adv* unusually: *an extra-large box of chocolates.* – *pron* an additional amount: *The book costs $6.90 but we charge extra for postage.* – *n* **1** something extra, or something for which an extra price is charged: *The college fees cover teaching only – stationery and other equipment are extras.* **2** in cinema or television, an actor employed in a small part, *eg* as a person in a crowd. **3** a special edition of a newspaper containing later or special news.

extract [ik'strakt] *v* **1** to pull out, or draw out, *esp* by force or with effort: *I have to have a tooth extracted*; *Did you manage to extract the information from her?* **2** to select

(passages from a book *etc*). **3** to take out (a substance forming part of something else) by crushing or by chemical means: *Vanilla essence is extracted from vanilla beans.* – ['ekstrakt] *n* **1** a passage selected from a book *etc*: *a short extract from his novel.* **2** a substance obtained by an extracting process: *beef/yeast extract*; *extract of malt.* **ex'traction** [-ʃən] *n* **1** race or parentage: *He is of Greek extraction.* **2** (an) act of extracting *eg* a tooth.

extradite ['ekstrədait] *v* to give (someone) up to the police of another country (for a crime committed there). **,extra'dition** [-'di-] *n.*

extramural [ekstrə'mjuərəl] *adj* **1** (of teaching, lectures *etc*) for people who are not full-time students at a college *etc*: *extramural lectures.* **2** separate from or outside the area of one's studies (in a university *etc*): *extramural activities.*

extraordinary [ik'stro:dənəri] *adj* surprising; unusual: *What an extraordinary thing to say!*; *She wears the most extraordinary clothes.* **extraordinarily** [ik'stro:dənərəli, (*Amer*) ikstrə:rdə'nerəli] *adv.*

extraterrestrial [ekstrətə'restriəl] *n, adj* person *etc*) not living on or coming from the planet Earth.

extravagant [ik'stravəgənt] *adj* **1** using or spending too much; wasteful: *He's extravagant with money*; *an extravagant use of materials/energy.* **2** (of ideas, emotions *etc*) exaggerated or too great: *extravagant praise.* **ex'travagantly** *adv.* **ex'travagance** *n*: *His wife's extravagance reduced them to poverty*; *Food is a necessity, but wine is an extravagance.*

extreme [ik'stri:m] *adj* **1** very great, *esp* much more than usual: *extreme pleasure*; *He is in extreme pain.* **2** very far or furthest in any direction, *esp* out from the centre: *the extreme south-western tip of England*; *Politically, he belongs to the extreme left.* **3** very violent or strong; not ordinary or usual: *He holds extreme views on education.* – *n* **1** something as far, or as different, as possible from something else: *the extremes of sadness and joy.* **2** the greatest degree of any state, *esp* if unpleasant: *The extremes of heat in the desert make life uncomfortable.* **ex'tremely** *adv* very: *extremely kind.* **ex'tremism** *n* the holding of views which are as far from being moderate as possible. **ex'tremist** *n, adj.* **ex'tremity** [-'stre-] – *pl* **ex'tremities** – *n* **1** the farthest point: *The two poles represent the extremities of the earth's axis.* **2** an extreme degree; the quality of being extreme: *Their suffering reached such extremities that many died.* **3** a situation of great danger or distress: *They need help in this extremity.* **4** the parts of the body furthest from the middle *eg* the hands and feet.

in the extreme very: *dangerous in the extreme.*

to extremes very far, *esp* further than is thought to be reasonable: *She can never express an opinion without going to extremes.*

extricate ['ekstrikeit] *v* to set free: *He extricated her from her difficulties.* ‚extri'cation *n.*

extrovert ['ekstrəvə:t] *n, adj* (a person) more interested in what happens around him than his own ideas and feelings: *An extrovert (person)is usually good company.*

exuberant [ig'zju:bərənt] *adj* happy and excited or in high spirits: *an exuberant mood.* ex'uberance *n.*

exude [ig'zju:d] *v* to give off (eg sweat) or show (a quality *etc*) strongly.

exult [ig'zʌlt] *v* (*with* **in** or **at**) to be very happy; to rejoice: *They exulted in their victory/at the news of their victory.*

ex'ultant *adj* very happy (at a victory or success *etc*): *exultant football fans.* ‚exul'tation [eg-] *n.*

eye [ai] *n* **1** the part of the body with which one sees: *Open your eyes; She has blue eyes.* **2** anything like or suggesting an eye, *eg* the hole in a needle, the loop or ring into which a hook connects *etc.* **3** a talent for noticing and judging a particular type of thing: *She has an eye for detail/colour/beauty.* – *v* to look at, observe: *The boys were eyeing the girls at the dance; The thief eyed the policeman warily.*

'eyeball *n* **1** the whole rounded structure of the eye. **2** the part of the eye between the eyelids.

'eyebrow *n* the curved line of hair above each eye.

'eye-catching *adj* striking or noticeable, *esp* if attractive: *an eye-catching advertisement.*

'eyelash *n* one of the (rows of) hairs that grow on the edge of the eyelids: *She looked at him through her eyelashes.*

'eyelet [-lit] *n* a small hole in fabric *etc* for a cord *etc.*

'eyelid *n* the movable piece of skin that covers or uncovers the eye.

'eye-opener *n* something that reveals an unexpected fact *etc*: *Our visit to their office was a real eye-opener – they are so inefficient!*

'eye-piece *n* the part of a telescope *etc* to which one puts one's eye.

'eyeshadow *n* a kind of coloured make-up worn around the eyes.

'eyesight *n* the ability to see: *I have good eyesight.*

'eyesore *n* something (*eg* a building) that is ugly to look at.

'eye-witness *n* a person who sees something (*eg* a crime) happen: *Eye-witnesses were questioned by the police.*

before/under one's very eyes in front of one, *usu* with no attempt at concealment: *It happened before my very eyes.*

be up to the eyes in to be very busy or deeply involved in or with: *She's up the eyes in work.*

close one's eyes to to ignore (*esp* something wrong): *She closed her eyes to the children's misbehaviour.*

in the eyes of in the opinion of: *You've done no wrong in my eyes.*

keep an eye on 1 to watch closely: *Keep an eye on the patient's temperature.* **2** to look after: *Keep an eye on the baby while I am out!*

lay/set eyes on to see, *esp* for the first time: *I wish I'd never set eyes on her!*

raise one's eyebrows to (lift one's eyebrows in order to) show surprise.

see eye to eye to be in agreement: *We've never seen eye to eye about this matter.*

with an eye to something with something as an aim. *He's doing this with an eye to promotion.*

with one's eyes open with full awareness of what one is doing: *I knew what the job would involve – I went into it with my eyes open.*

Ff

fable ['feibl] *n* **1** a story (*usu* about animals) that teaches a lesson about human behaviour: *Aesop's fables.* **2** a legend or untrue story: *fact or fable?*

fabulous ['fabjuləs] *adj* **1** wonderful: *a fabulous idea.* **2** existing (only) in a fable: *The phoenix is a fabulous bird.* 'fabulously *adv.*

fabric ['fabrik] *n* **1** (a type of) cloth or material: *Nylon is a man-made fabric.*

fabricate ['fabrikeit] *v* to make up something that is not true (a story, accusation *etc*): *to fabricate an excuse.*

‚fabri'cation *n* **1** a lie: *Her account of the accident was a complete fabrication.* **2** the act of fabricating.

fabulous see **fable.**

façade [fə'sa:d] *n* **1** the front of a building: *the façade of the temple.* **2** a pretended show: *In spite of his bold façade, he was very frightened.*

face [feis] *n* **1** the front part of the head, from forehead to chin: *a beautiful face.* **2** a surface *esp* the front surface: *a rock face.* **3** in mining, the end of a tunnel *etc* where work is being done: *a coal face.* – *v* **1** to be opposite to: *My house faces the park.* **2** to turn, stand *etc* in the direction of: *She faced him across the desk.* **3** to meet or accept boldly: *to face one's fate.*

-faced *adj* having a face of a certain kind: *a baby-faced man.*

facial ['feiʃəl] *adj* of the face: *facial expressions.*

facing *prep* opposite: *The hotel is facing the church.*

'facelift *n* **1** an operation to smooth and firm the face: *She has had a facelift.* **2** a process intended to make a building *etc* look better: *This village will be given a facelift.*

'face-powder *n* a type of make-up in the form of a fine powder: *She put on face-powder to stop her nose shining.*

'face-saving *adj* of something which helps a person not to look stupid or not to appear to be giving in: *He agreed to everything we asked and as a face-saving exercise we offered to consult him occasionally.*

face value the value stated on the face of a coin *etc*: *Some old coins are now worth a great deal more than their face value.*

at face value as being as valuable *etc* as it appears: *You must take this offer at face value.*

face the music to accept punishment or responsibility for something one has done: *The child had to face the music after being rude to the teacher.*

face to face in person; in the actual presence of one another: *I'd like to meet him face to face some day – I've heard so much about him.*

face up to to meet or accept boldly: *He faced up to his difficult situation.*

in the face of having to deal with and in spite of: *He succeeded in the face of great difficulties.*

lose face to suffer a loss of respect or reputation: *You will really lose face if you are defeated.*

make/pull a face to twist one's face into a strange expression: *He pulled faces at the baby to make it laugh.*

on the face of it as it appears at first glance, *usu* deceptively: *On the face of it, the problem was easy.*

put a good face on it to give the appearance of being satisfied *etc* with something when one is not: *Now it's done we'll have to put a good face on it.*

save one's face to avoid appearing stupid or wrong: *I refuse to accept the reponsibility for that error just to save your face – it's your fault.*

facet ['fasit] *n* **1** a side of a many-sided object, *esp* a cut jewel: *the facets of a diamond.* **2** an aspect or view of a subject: *There are several facets to this question.*

facetious [fə'siːʃəs] *adj* not serious; intended to be funny or humorous: *a facetious remark.* **fa'cetiously** *adv.* **fa'cetiousness** *n.*

facial *see* **face.**

facility [fə'siləti] *n* **1** ease or quickness: *He showed great facility in learning languages.* **2** a skill: *He has a great facility for always being right.* – *n pl* **fa'cilities** the means to do something: *There are facilities for cooking.*

facing *see* **face.**

facsimile [fak'siməli] *n* an exact copy. – *adj*: *a facsimile edition of an eighteenth-century book.*

fact [fakt] *n* **1** something known or believed to be true: *It is a fact that smoking is a danger to health.* **2** reality: *fact or fiction.* **factual** ['faktʃuəl] *adj* of or containing facts: *a factual account.* **'factually** *adv.*

as a matter of fact, in fact, in point of fact actually or really: *She doesn't like him much – in fact I think she hates him!*

faction ['fakʃən] *n* a group or party that belongs to, and *usu* dissents from, a larger group.

factor ['faktə] *n* **1** something, *eg* a fact, which has to be taken into account or which affects the course of events: *There are various factors to be considered.* **2** a number which exactly divides into another: *3 is a factor of 6.*

factory ['faktəri] – *pl* **'factories** – *n* a workshop where manufactured articles are made in large numbers: *a car factory*; (*also adj*) *a factory worker.*

factual *see* **fact.**

faculty ['fakəlti] – *pl* **'faculties** – *n* **1** a power of the mind: *the faculty of reason.* **2** a natural power of the body: *the faculty of hearing.* **3** ability or skill: *He has a faculty for saying the right thing.* **4** (*often with cap*) a section of a university: *the Faculty of Arts/Science.*

fade [feid] *v* to (make something) lose strength, colour, loudness *etc*: *The noise gradually faded (away).*

faeces, (*Amer*) **feces** ['fiːsiːz] *n pl* solid waste matter passed out from the body.

fag [fag] *n* **1** hard or boring work: *It was a real fag to clean the whole house.* **2** a slang word for a cigarette: *I'm dying for a fag.*

fag-end *n* the small, useless piece of a cigarette that remains after it has been smoked: *The ashtray was full of fag-ends; the fag-end of the conversation.*

fagged out very tired: *I'm completely fagged out after that long walk.*

Fahrenheit ['farənhait] *adj* (*often abbrev* **F** *when written*) as measured on a Fahrenheit thermometer: *fifty degrees Fahrenheit* (*50°F*).

fail [feil] *v* **1** to be unsuccessful (in); not to manage (to do something): *They failed in their attempt*; *I failed my exam*; *I failed to post the letter.* **2** to break down or cease to work: *The brakes failed.* **3** to be insufficient or not enough: *His courage failed (him).* **4** (in a test, examination *etc*) to reject (a candidate): *The examiner failed half the class.* **5** to disappoint: *They did not fail him in their support.*

'**failing** *n* a fault or weakness: *He may have his failings, but he has always treated his children well.* – *prep* if (something) fails or is lacking: *Failing his help, we shall have to try something else.*

'**failure** [-jə] *n* **1** the state or act of failing: *She was upset by her failure in the exam*; *failure of the electricity supply.* **2** an unsuccessful person or thing: *He felt he was a failure.* **3** inability, refusal *etc* to do something: *his failure to reply.*

without fail definitely or certainly: *I shall do it tomorrow without fail.*

faint [feint] *adj* **1** lacking in strength, brightness, courage *etc*: *The sound grew faint*; *a faint light.* **2** physically weak and about to lose consciousness: *Suddenly he felt faint.* – *v* to lose consciousness: *She fainted on hearing the news.* – *n* loss of consciousness: *Her faint gave everybody a fright.*

'**faintly** *adv* **1** in a faint manner: *A light shone faintly.* **2** slightly; rather: *She looked faintly surprised.* '**faintness** *n.*

fair[1] [feə] *adj* **1** light-coloured; with light-coloured hair and skin: *fair hair*; *Scandinavian people are often fair.* **2** just; not favouring one side: *a fair test.* **3** (of weather) fine; without rain: *a fair afternoon.* **4** quite good; neither bad nor good: *His work is only fair.* **5** quite big, long *etc*: *a fair size.* **6** beautiful: *a fair maiden.* '**fairness** *n.*

'**fairly** *adv* **1** justly; honestly: *fairly judged.* **2** quite or rather: *The work was fairly hard.*

fair play honest treatment; an absence of cheating, biased actions *etc*: *He's not involved in the contest – he's only here to see fair play.*

fair[2] [feə] *n* **1** a collection of entertainments that travels from town to town: *She won a large doll at the fair.* **2** a large market held at fixed times: *A fair is held here every spring.* **3** an exhibition of goods from different countries, firms *etc*: *a trade fair.*

fairy ['feəri] – *pl* '**fairies** – *n* an imaginary creature in the form of a very small (often winged) human, with magical powers: *Children often believe in fairies*; (*also adj*) *fairy-land.*

'**fairy-story** *n* **1** an old, or children's, story of fairies, magic *etc*: *a book of fairy-stories.* **2** an untrue statement; a lie: *I don't want to hear any fairy-stories!*

'**fairy-tale** *n* a fairy-story: *to tell fairy-tales*; (*also adj*) *the fairy-tale appearance of the countryside.*

faith [feiθ] *n* **1** trust or belief: *He had faith in his ability.* **2** religious belief: *Years of hardship had not caused him to lose his faith.* **3** loyalty to one's promise: *to keep/break faith with someone.*

'**faithful** *adj* **1** loyal and true; not changing: *a faithful friend*; *faithful to his promise.* **2** true or exact: *a faithful account of what had happened.* '**faithfully** *adv.* '**faithfulness** *n.* '**faithless** *adj.* '**faithlessness** *n.*

in (all) good faith sincerely: *She made the offer in good faith.*

fake [feik] *n* **1** a worthless imitation (*esp* intended to deceive); a forgery: *That picture is a fake.* **2** a person who pretends to be something he is not: *He pretended to be a doctor, but he was a fake.* – *adj* **1** made in imitation of something more valuable, *esp* with the intention of deceiving: *fake diamonds.* **2** pretending to be something one is not: *a fake clergyman.* – *v* to pretend or imitate in order to deceive: *to fake a signature.*

falcon ['fo:lkən, (*Amer*) 'fal-] *n* a kind of bird of prey sometimes used for hunting.

fall [fo:l] – *pl* fell [fel]: *ptp* '**fallen** – *v* **1** to go down from a higher level *usu* unintentionally: *The apple fell from the tree*; *Her eye fell on an old book.* **2** (*often with* **over**) to go down to the ground *etc* from an upright position, *usu* by accident: *She fell (over).* **3** to become lower or less: *The temperature is falling.* **4** to happen or occur: *Easter falls early this year.* **5** to enter a certain state or condition: *He fell asleep*; *They fell in love.* **6** (*formal*: *only with* **it** *as subject*) to come as one's duty *etc*: *It falls to me to take care of the children.* – *n* **1** the act of falling: *He had a fall.* **2** (a quantity of) something that has fallen: *a fall of snow.* **3** capture or (political) defeat: *the fall of Rome.* **4** (*Amer*) the autumn: *Leaves change colour in the fall.*

falls *n pl* a waterfall: *the Niagara Falls.*

'**fallout** *n* radioactive dust from a nuclear explosion *etc.*

his, her *etc* **face fell** he, she *etc* looked suddenly disappointed.

fall away 1 to become less in number: *The crowd began to fall away.* **2** to slope downwards: *The ground fell away steeply.*

fall back to move back or stop moving forward.

Family Tree

GRANDFATHER = GRANDMOTHER

GRANDMOTHER = GRANDFATHER

AUNT = UNCLE

MOTHER-IN-LAW = FATHER-IN-LAW

MOTHER = FATHER

COUSINS

MARY'S HUSBAND = MARY
(Mary is his wife)

SISTER-IN-LAW = BROTHER

SISTER = BROTHER-IN-LAW

NEPHEW   NIECE

SON-IN-LAW = DAUGHTER

DAUGHTER-IN-LAW = SON

GRANDDAUGHTER   GRANDSON

This plan shows
<u>Mary's</u> relations

The sign = means
'married to'.

fall back on to use, or to go to for help, finally when everything else has been tried: *Whatever happens you have your father's money to fall back on.*

fall behind 1 to be slower than (someone else): *Hurry up! You're falling behind* (*the others*); *He is falling behind in his schoolwork.* **2** (*with* with) to become late in regular payment, letter-writing *etc*: *Don't fall behind with the rent!*

fall down (*sometimes with* on) to fail (in): *He's falling down on his job.*

fall flat (*esp* of jokes *etc*) to fail completely or to have no effect: *His joke fell flat.*

fall for 1 to do be deceived by (something): *I made up a story to explain why I had not been at work and he fell for it.* **2** to fall in love with (someone): *He has fallen for your sister.*

fall in with 1 to join with (someone) for company: *On the way home we fell in with some friends.* **2** to agree with (a plan, idea *etc*): *They fell in with our suggestion.*

fall off *vi* to become smaller in number or amount: *Audiences often fall off during the summer.*

fall on/upon to attack: *He fell on the old man and beat him; They fell hungrily upon the food.*

fall out (*sometimes with* with) to quarrel: *I have fallen out with my brother.*

fall short (*often with* of) to be not enough or not good enough *etc*: *The money we have falls short of what we need.*

fall through (of plans *etc*) to fail or come to nothing: *Our plans fell through.*

fallacy ['faləsi] – *pl* **'fallacies** – *n* a wrong idea or belief, *usu* one that is generally believed to be true; false reasoning: *That belief is just a fallacy.*
fallacious [fə'leiʃəs] *adj* wrong, mistaken or showing false reasoning: *a fallacious argument.*

fallible ['faləbl] *adj* able or likely to make mistakes: *Human beings are fallible.*

fallow ['falou] *adj* (of land) left to its own natural growth and not planted with seeds: *We will let this field lie fallow for a year; fallow fields.*

false [fo:ls] *adj* **1** not true; not correct: *He made a false statement to the police.* **2** not genuine; intended to deceive: *He has a false passport.* **3** artificial: *false teeth.* **4** not loyal: *false friends.*
'falsehood *n* (the telling of) a lie: *He is incapable of (uttering a) falsehood.*
'falsify [-fai] *v* to make false: *He falsified the accounts.* **,falsifi'cation** [-fi-] *n.*
'falsity *n.*
false alarm a warning of something which in fact does not happen.

false start in a race, a start which is declared not valid and therefore has to be repeated.
falter ['fo:ltə] *v* **1** to stumble or hesitate: *She walked without faltering.* **2** to speak with hesitation: *His voice faltered.* **'faltering** *adj.* **'falteringly** *adv.*
fame [feim] *n* the quality of being well-known: *His novels brought him fame.*
'famous *adj* well-known (for good or worthy reasons): *He is famous for his strength.*
'famously *adv* very well.
familiar [fə'miljə] *adj* **1** well-known: *The house was familiar to him; He looks very familiar* (*to me*). **2** (*with* with) knowing about: *Are you familiar with the plays of Shakespeare?* **3** too friendly: *You are much too familiar with my wife!* **fa'miliarly** *adv.*
fa,mili'arity [-li'a-] – *pl* **fa,mili'arities** – *n* **1** the state of being familiar: *I was surprised by his familiarity with our way of life.* **2** an act of (too) friendly behaviour: *You must not allow such familiarities.*
fa'miliarize, -ise *v* (*with* with) to make something well known to (someone): *You must familiarize yourself with the rules.* **fa,miliari'zation, -s-** *n.*
family ['faməli] – *pl* **'families** – *n* **1** (*sing or pl*) a man, his wife and their children: *These houses were built for families; The* (*members of the*) *Smith family are all very athletic;* (*also adj*) *a family holiday.* **2** a group of people related to each other, including cousins, grandchildren *etc*: *He comes from a wealthy family;* (*also adj*) *the family home.* **3** the children of a man and his wife: *When I get married I should like a large family.* **4** a group of plants, animals, languages *etc* that are connected in some way: *In spite of its name, a koala bear is not a member of the bear family.*
family planning controlling or limiting the number of children that people have *esp* by using a means of contraception: *a family planning clinic.*
*****family tree** (a plan showing) a person's ancestors and relations.
famine ['famin] *n* (a) great lack or shortage *esp* of food: *Some parts of the world suffer regularly from famine.*
famished ['famiʃt] *adj* very hungry: *I was famished after my long walk.*
famous, famously *see* fame.
fan[1] [fan] *n* **1** a flat instrument held in the hand and waved to direct a current of air across the face in hot weather: *Ladies used to carry fans to keep themselves cool.* **2** a mechanical instrument causing a current of air: *She has had a fan fitted in the kitchen for extracting smells.* – *v* – *pt, ptp* **fanned** – **1** to cool (as if) with a fan: *She sat in the corner, fanning herself.* **2** to increase or strengthen

(a fire) by directing air towards it with a fan *etc*: *They fanned the fire until it burst into flames.*

fan² [fan] *n* an enthusiastic admirer of a sport, hobby or well-known person: *I'm a great fan of his*; *football fans*; (*also adj*) *fan mail/letters* (= letters *etc* sent by admirers).

fanatic [fə'natik] *n* a person who is (too) enthusiastic about something: *a religious fanatic.*

fa'natic(al) *adj* (too) enthusiastic: *He is fanatical about physical exercise.* **fa'natically** *adv.*

fa'naticism [-sizəm] *n* (too) great enthusiasm, *esp* about religion: *Fanaticism is the cause of most religious hatred.*

fancy ['fansi] – *pl* **'fancies** – *n* **1** a sudden (often unexpected) liking or desire: *The pregnant woman had many peculiar fancies.* **2** the power of the mind to imagine things: *She had a tendency to indulge in flights of fancy.* **3** something imagined: *He had a sudden fancy that he could see Spring approaching.* – *adj* decorated; not plain: *fancy cakes.* – *v* **1** to like the idea of having or doing something: *I fancy a cup of tea.* **2** to think or have a certain feeling or impression (that): *I fancied (that) you were angry.* **3** to have strong sexual interest in (a person): *He fancies her a lot.*

'fanciful *adj* **1** inclined to have fancies, *esp* strange, unreal ideas: *She's a very fanciful girl.* **2** imaginary or unreal: *That idea is rather fanciful.* **'fancifully** *adv.*

fancy dress clothes representing a particular character, nationality, historical period *etc*: *He went to the party in fancy dress*; (*also adj*) *a fancy-dress party.*

take a fancy to to become fond of, often suddenly or unexpectedly: *He bought that house because his wife took a fancy to it.*

take one's fancy to be liked or wanted by (someone): *When my wife goes shopping she just buys anything that takes her fancy.*

fanfare ['fanfeə] *n* a short piece of music played by trumpets *etc* at the entry of a king or queen during a ceremony *etc.*

fang [faŋ] *n* **1** a long pointed tooth *esp* of a fierce animal: *The wolf bared its fangs.* **2** the poison-tooth of a snake.

fantasy ['fantəsi] – *pl* **'fantasies** – *n* an imaginary (*esp* not realistic) scene, story *etc*: *She was always having fantasies about becoming rich and famous*; (*also adj*) *She lived in a fantasy world.*

fantastic [fan'tastik] *adj* **1** unbelievable and like a fantasy: *She told me some fantastic story about her father being a Grand Duke!* **2** wonderful; very good: *You look fantastic!* **fan'tastically** *adv.*

far [faː] *adv* **1** indicating distance, progress *etc*: *How far is it from here to his house?*

2 at or to a long way away: *He went far away/off.* **3** very much: *He was a far better swimmer than his friend (was).* – *adj* **1** distant; a long way away: *a far country.* **2** more distant (*usu* of two things): *He lives on the far side of the lake.*

farther, farthest *see* **further.**

'faraway *adj* **1** distant: *faraway places.* **2** not paying attention; dreamy: *She had a faraway look in her eyes.*

,far-'fetched *adj* very unlikely: *a far-fetched story.*

as far as 1 to the place or point mentioned: *We walked as far as the lake.* **2** (*also* **so far as**) as great a distance as: *He did not walk as far as his friends.* **3** (*also* **so far as**) to the extent that: *As far as I know he is well.*

by far by a large amount: *They have by far the largest family in the village.*

far and away by a very great amount: *He is far and away the cleverest boy in the class!*

far from 1 not only not, but: *Far from liking him, I hate him.* **2** not at all: *He was far from helpful.*

so far 1 until now: *So far we have been quite successful.* **2** up to a certain point: *We can get so far but no further without more help.*

farce [faːs] *n* **1** a (kind of) comic play in which both the characters and the events shown are improbable and ridiculous: *The play is a classic farce.* **2** any funny or stupid situation in real life: *The meeting was an absolute farce.*

farcical ['faːsikəl] *adj* completely ridiculous, and therefore *usu* humorous: *The whole idea was farcical.*

fare [feə] *n* **1** the price of a journey on a train, bus, ship *etc*: *He hadn't enough money for his bus fare.* **2** a paying passenger in a hired vehicle, *esp* in a taxi: *The taxi-driver was asked by the police where his last fare got out.*

farewell [feə'wel] *n* an act of saying goodbye: *They said their farewells at the station*; (*also adj*) *a farewell dinner.* – *interj* goodbye: *'Farewell for ever!' she cried.*

farm [faːm] *n* **1** an area of land, including buildings, used for growing crops, breeding and keeping cows, sheep, pigs *etc*: *Much of England is good agricultural land and there are many farms.* **2** the farmer's house and the buildings near it in such a place: *We visited the farm*; (*also adj*) *a farm kitchen.* – *v* to cultivate (the land) in order to grow crops, breed and keep animals *etc*: *He farms (5000 acres) in the south.*

'farmer *n* the owner or tenant of a farm who works on the land *etc*: *How many farm-workers does that farmer employ?*

'farming *n* the business of owning or running a farm: *There is a lot of money involved in farming*; (*also adj*) *farming communities.*

'farmhouse *n* the house in which a farmer lives.

'farmyard *n* the open area surrounded by the farm buildings: *There were several hens loose in the farmyard*; (*also adj*) *farmyard animals.*

farther, farthest *see* **further.**

fascinate ['fasineit] *v* to charm; to attract or interest very strongly: *She was fascinated by the strange clothes and customs of the country people.*

'fascinating *adj* very charming, attractive or interesting: *a fascinating story.*

,fasci'nation *n* **1** the act of fascinating or state of being fascinated: *the look of fascination on the children's faces.* **2** the power of fascinating or something that has this: *Old books have/hold a fascination for him.*

fashion ['faʃən] *n* **1** the style and design of clothes: *Are you interested in fashion?*; (*also adj*) *a fashion magazine.* **2** the way of behaving, dressing *etc* which is popular at a certain time: *Fashions in music and art are always changing.* **3** a way of doing something: *She spoke in a very strange fashion.*

'fashionable *adj* following, or in keeping with, the newest style of dress, way of living *etc*: *a fashionable woman*; *a fashionable part of town.* **'fashionably** *adv.*

after a fashion in a way, but not very well: *He can speak French after a fashion*

all the fashion very fashionable: *Long skirts were all the fashion last year.*

in fashion fashionable: *Tweed jackets are in fashion.*

out of fashion not fashionable: *Long skirts are out of fashion at present.*

fast¹ [fa:st] *adj* **1** quick-moving: *a fast car.* **2** quick: *a fast worker.* **3** (of a clock, watch *etc*) showing a time in advance of the correct time: *My watch is five minutes fast.* – *adv* quickly: *She speaks so fast I can't understand her.* **'fastness** *n.*

fast food(s) food that can be quickly prepared, *eg* hamburgers *etc.*

fast² [fa:st] *v* to go without food, *esp* for religious or medical reasons: *Muslims fast during the festival of Ramadan.* – *n* a time or act of fasting: *He has just finished two days' fast.* **'fasting** *n.*

fast³ [fa:st] *adj* **1** (of a dye) fixed; that will not come out of a fabric when it is washed. **2** firm; fixed: *He made his end of the rope fast to a tree.*

fast asleep completely asleep: *The baby fell fast asleep in my arms.*

fasten ['fa:sn] *v* to fix or join (together): *Fasten the gate!*; *She fastened a flower to the front of her dress*; *He fastened his eyes upon her face.*

'fastener *n* something that fastens things (together): *a zip-fastener.*

fastidious [fə'stidiəs, (*Amer*) fa-] *adj* very critical and difficult to please: *She is so fastidious about her food that she will not eat in a restaurant.* **fa'stidiously** *adv.* **fa'stidiousness** *n.*

fat [fat] *n* **1** an oily substance made by the bodies of animals and by some plants: *This meat has got a lot of fat on it.* **2** a kind of such substance, used *esp* for cooking: *There are several good cooking fats on the market.* – *adj* **1** having a lot of fat on one's body; large, heavy and round in shape: *He was a very fat child.* **2** large or abundant: *His business made a fat profit*; *A fat lot of good that is!* (=That is no good at all). **'fatness** *n.*

'fatten *v* (*often with* **up**) to make or become fat: *They are fattening up a chicken to eat at Christmas.*

'fatty *adj* containing, or like, fat: *This meat is very fatty.* **'fattiness** *n.*

'fat-head *n* a stupid person.

fatal ['feitl] *adj* **1** causing death: *a fatal accident.* **2** disastrous: *She made the fatal mistake of not inviting him to the party.* **'fatally** *adv.*

fatality [fə'taləti] – *pl* **fa'talities** – *n* (an accident causing) death: *fatalities on the roads.*

fate [feit] *n* **1** (*sometimes with cap*) the supposed power. that controls events: *Who knows what fate has in store* (=waiting for us in the future)? **2** a destiny or doom, *eg* death: *A terrible fate awaited her.*

'fatalism *n* the belief that fate controls everything, and man cannot change it.

'fatalist *n* a person who believes in fatalism: *He is a complete fatalist – he just accepts everything that happens to him.* **,fata'listic** *adj.*

'fated *adj* controlled or intended by fate: *He seemed fated to arrive late wherever he went.*

'fateful *adj* involving important decisions, results *etc*: *At last the fateful day arrived.*

father ['fa:ðə] *n* **1** a male parent, *esp* human: *Mr Smith is her father.* **2** (*with cap*) the title of a (*usu* Roman Catholic) priest: *I met Father Sullivan this morning.* **3** a person who begins, invents or first makes something: *King Alfred was the father of the English navy.* – *v* to be the father of: *King Charles II fathered a number of children.*

'fatherhood *n* the state or condition of being a father: *Now that the children are older I am enjoying fatherhood.*

'fatherly *adj* like a father: *He showed a fatherly interest in his friend's child.*

'father-in-law *n* the father of one's wife or husband.

fathom ['faðəm] *n* a measure of depth of water (6 feet or 1.8 metres): *The water is 8 fathoms deep* . – *v* to understand (a mystery *etc*): *I cannot fathom why she should have left home.*

fatigue [fə'ti:g] *n* **1** great tiredness (caused *esp* by hard work or effort): *He was suffering from fatigue.* **2** (*esp* in metals) weakness caused by continual use: *metal fatigue.*
fa'tigued *adj* made very tired: *He was fatigued by the constant questioning.*

fatten, fatty see **fat.**

fault [fo:lt] *n* **1** a mistake; something for which one is to blame: *The accident was your fault.* **2** an imperfection; something wrong: *There is a fault in this machine; a fault in his character.* **3** a crack in the rock surface of the earth: *faults in the earth's crust.* – *v* to find fault with: *I couldn't fault him/his piano-playing.*
'faultless *adj* without fault; perfect: *a faultless performance.* **'faultlessly** *adv.*
'faulty *adj* (*usu* of something mechanical) not made or working correctly.'
at fault wrong or to blame: *She was at fault.*
find fault with to criticize or complain of: *She is always finding fault with the way he eats.*
to a fault to too great an extent: *He was generous to a fault.*

faun [fo:n] *n* an imaginary creature, half man and half goat.

fauna ['fo:nə] *n* the animals of a district or country as a whole: *He is interested in South American fauna.*

favour, (*Amer*) **favor** ['feivə] *n* **1** a kind action: *Will you do me a favour and lend me your car?* **2** kindness or approval: *She looked on him with great favour.* **3** preference or too much kindness: *By doing that he showed favour to the other side.* **4** a state of being approved of: *He was very much in favour with the Prime Minister.* – *v* to support or show preference for: *Which side do you favour?*
'favourable *adj* **1** showing approval: *Was his reaction favourable or unfavourable?* **2** helpful or advantageous: *a favourable wind.* **'favourably** *adv.*
'favourite [-rit] *adj* best-liked; preferred: *his favourite city.* – *n* a person or thing that one likes best: *Of all his paintings that is my favourite.*
'favouritism [-ri-] *n* preferring or supporting one person *etc* more than another: *I can't be accused of favouritism – I voted for everyone!*
in favour of in support of: *I am in favour of higher pay.*
in one's favour to one's benefit or advantage: *The wind was in our favour.*

> **favour,** noun, ends in **-our.**
> The adjective **favourable** is also spelt with **-our-.**

fawn[1] [fo:n] *n* **1** a young deer. **2** (*also adj*)

(of) its colour, a light yellowish brown: *a fawn sweater.*

fawn[2] [fo:n] *v* **1** (of dogs) to show affection (by wagging the tail, rolling over *etc*). **2** (*with upon*) to be too humble or to flatter (someone) in a servile way: *The courtiers fawned upon the king.*

fear [fiə] *n* (a) feeling of great worry or anxiety caused by the knowledge of danger: *The soldier tried not to show his fear; fear of water.* – *v* **1** to feel fear because of (something): *She feared her father when he was angry; I fear for my father's safety* (= I am worried because I thing he is in danger). **2** to regret: *I fear you will not be able to see him today.*
'fearful *adj* **1** afraid: *a fearful look.* **2** terrible: *The lion gave a fearful roar.* **3** very bad: *a fearful mistake!* **'fearfully** *adv.*
'fearless *adj* without fear; brave: *a fearless soldier.* **'fearlessly** *adv.*
for fear of so as not to: *She would not go swimming for fear of catching a cold.*
in fear of in a state of being afraid of: *He lived in fear of his father.*

feasible ['fi:zəbl] *adj* able to be done: *a feasible solution to the problem.* **feasi'bility** *n.*

feast [fi:st] *n* **1** a large and rich meal, *usu* eaten to celebrate some occasion: *The king invited them to a feast in the palace.* **2** (*sometimes with cap*) a particular day on which some (*esp* religious) person or event is remembered and celebrated: *Today is the feast of St Stephen.* – *v* to eat (as if) at a feast: *We feasted all day.*

feather ['feðə] *n* one of the things that grow from a bird's skin that form the covering of its body: *They cleaned the oil off the sea-gull's feathers.* – *v* to line, cover or decorate with feathers: *The eagle feathers its nest with down from its own breast.* **'feathered** *adj.*
'feathery *adj* **1** of, like, or covered in, a feather or feathers: *a feathery hat.* **2** soft and light: *a feathery touch.*
a feather in one's cap something one can be proud of: *Winning the race was quite a feather in his cap.*

feature ['fi:tʃə] *n* **1** a mark by which anything is known; a quality: *The use of bright colours is one of the features of his painting.* **2** one of the parts of one's face (eyes, nose *etc*): *She has very regular features.* **3** a special article in a newspaper: *'The Times' is doing a feature on holidays.* **4** the main film in a cinema programme *etc*: *The feature begins at 7.30;* (*also adj*) *a feature film.* – *v* to give or have a part (*esp* an important one): *That film features the best of the British actresses.*

February ['februəri] *n* the second month of the year, the month following January.

feces *see* **faeces**.

fed *see* **feed**.

federal ['fedərəl] *adj* (of a government or group of states) joined together, *usu* for national and external affairs only: *the federal government of the United States of America.*

'**federated** [-rei-] *adj* joined by a treaty, agreement *etc*.

ˌ**fede'ration** *n* people, societies, unions, states *etc* joined together for a common purpose: *the International Federation of Actors.*

fee [fi:] *n* the price paid for work done by a doctor, lawyer *etc* or for some special service or right: *the lawyer's fee; an entrance fee; university fees.*

feeble ['fi:bl] *adj* weak: *The old lady has been rather feeble since her illness; a feeble excuse.* '**feebly** *adv*.

feed [fi:d] – *pt, ptp* **fed** [fed] – *v* 1 to give food to: *He fed the child with a spoon.* 2 (*with* **on**) to eat: *Cows feed on grass.* – *n* 1 food *esp* for a baby or animals: *Have you given the baby his feed?; cattle feed.*

fed up tired; bored and annoyed: *I'm fed up with all this work!*

feel [fi:l] – *pt, ptp* **felt** [felt] – *v* 1 to become aware of (something) by the sense of touch: *She felt his hand on her shoulder.* 2 to find out the shape, size, texture *etc* of something by touching, *usu* with the hands: *She felt the parcel carefully.* 3 to experience or be aware of (an emotion, sensation *etc*): *He felt a sudden anger.* 4 to think (oneself) to be: *She feels sick; How does she feel about her work?* 5 to believe or consider: *She feels that the firm treated her badly.*

'**feeler** *n* (in certain animals, insects *etc*) an organ for touching, *esp* one of the two thread-like parts on an insect's head.

'**feeling** *n* 1 power and ability to feel: *I have no feeling in my little finger.* 2 something that one feels physically: *a feeling of great pain.* 3 (*usu in pl*) something that one feels in one's mind: *His angry words hurt my feelings; a feeling of happiness.* 4 an impression or belief: *I have a feeling that the work is too hard.* 5 affection: *He has no feeling for her now.* 6 emotion: *He spoke with great feeling.*

feel as if/as though to have the sensation (physical or mental) or feeling that: *I feel as if I am going to be sick; She feels as though she has known him for years.*

feel like 1 to have the feelings that one would have if one were: *I feel like a princess in this beautiful dress; He felt like an idiot* (= He felt very foolish). 2 to feel that one would like to (have, do *etc*): *I feel like a drink; Do you feel like going to the cinema?*

feel one's way to find one's way by feeling: *I had to feel my way to the door in the dark.*

get the feel of to become accustomed to: *to get the feel of a new job.*

feet *see* **foot**.

feign [fein] *v* to pretend to feel: *He feigned illness.*

feigned *adj* pretend: *feigned happiness.*

felicity [fə'lisəti] *n* happiness.

fe,lici'tations *n pl* congratulations.

feline ['fi:lain] *adj* of or like a cat: *a feline appearance.*

fell[1] *see* **fall**.

fell[2] [fel] *v* to cut or knock down to the ground: *They are felling all the trees in this area.*

fellow ['felou] *n* 1 a man: *He's quite a nice fellow but I don't like him.* 2 (*often as part of a word*) a companion and equal: *She is playing with her schoolfellows.* – *adj* belonging to the same group, country *etc*: *a fellow student; a fellow music-lover.*

'**fellowship** *n* 1 an association (of people with common interests): *a youth fellowship* (= a club for young people). 2 friendliness.

ˌ**fellow-'feeling** *n* sympathy (*esp* for someone in a similar situation, of similar tastes *etc*): *I had a fellow-feeling for the broken leg.*

felon ['felən] *n* a person who is guilty of a serious crime.

'**felony** – *pl* '**felonies** – *n* a serious crime: *He committed a felony.*

felt[1] *see* **feel**.

felt[2] [felt] *n, adj* (of) a type of cloth made of wool that has been pressed together not woven: *She bought a metre of felt to recover the card table* (= table for playing cards on); *a felt hat.*

female ['fi:meil] *n, adj* 1 (a person, animal *etc*) of the sex that gives birth to children, produces eggs *etc*: *a female blackbird; the female of the species.* 2 (a plant) that produces seeds.

feminine ['feminin] *adj* 1 of a woman: *a feminine voice.* 2 with all the essential qualities of a woman: *She was a very feminine person.* 3 in certain languages, of one of *usu* two or three genders of nouns *etc*.

ˌ**femi'ninity** *n* the quality of being feminine: *She used her femininity to win the argument.*

'**feminism** *n* the thought and actions of people who want to make women's (legal, political, social *etc*) rights equal to those of men.

'**feminist** *n* a supporter of feminism.

femur ['fi:mə] *n* the thigh bone.

fen [fen] *n* a area of low marshy land often covered with water.

fence[1] [fens] *n* a line of wooden or metal posts joined by wood, wire *etc* to stop people, animals *etc* moving on to or off a piece of land: *The garden was surrounded by a wooden fence.* – *v* to enclose (an area of land) with a fence *eg* to prevent people, animals *etc* from getting in: *We fenced off the lake.*

'fencing[1] *n* (the material used for) a fence: *a hundred metres of fencing.*

fence[2] [fens] *v* **1** to fight with (blunted) swords as a sport. **2** to avoid answering questions: *He fenced with me for half an hour before I got the truth.*

'fencing[2] *n* the sport of fighting with (blunted) swords: *I used to be very good at fencing.*

fend [fend]: **fend for oneself** to look after oneself: *He is old enough to fend for himself.*

ferment [fə'ment] *v* **1** to (make something) go through a particular chemical change (as when yeast is added to dough in the making of bread): *Grape juice must be fermented before it becomes wine.* **2** to excite or be excited: *He is the kind of person to ferment trouble.* – ['fə:ment] *n* a state of excitement: *The whole city was in a ferment.*

ˌfermen'tation [fə:men-] *n* the chemical change occurring when something ferments or is fermented.

fern [fə:n] *n* a kind of plant with no flowers and delicate feather-like leaves.

ferocious [fə'rouʃəs] *adj* fierce or savage: *a ferocious animal.* **fe'rociously** *adv.* **ferocity** [fə'rosəti] *n.*

ferret ['ferit] *n* a type of small, weasel-like animal used to chase rabbits out of their holes.

ferret (about) *v* to search busily and persistently: *He ferreted about in the cupboard.*

ferro- [ferou] of or containing iron: *ferro-concrete.*

ferry ['feri] *v* to carry (people, cars *etc*) from one place to another by boat (or plane): *He ferried us across the river in a small boat.* – *n* – *pl* 'ferries – a boat which ferries people, cars *etc* from one place to another: *We took the cross-channel ferry.*

fertile ['fə:tail] *adj* **1** producing a lot: *fertile fields*; *a fertile mind/imagination.* **2** able to produce fruit, children, young animals *etc*: *fertile seed.*

fer'tility [-'ti-] *n* the state or condition of being fertile.

fertilize, -ise [-ti-] *v* to make fertile: *He fertilized his fields with manure*; *An egg must be fertilized before it can develop.* ˌfertili'zation, -s- *n.*

'fertilizer, -s- [-ti-] *n* a substance (manure, chemicals *etc*) used to make land (more) fertile.

fervent ['fə:vənt] *adj* enthusiastic and very sincere: *fervent hope.* '**fervently** *adv.*

fervour (*Amer* fervor) ['fə:və] *n* enthusiasm

and strength of emotion: *He spoke with fervour.*

fester ['festə] *v* (of an open injury *eg* a cut or sore) to become infected: *The wound began to fester.*

festival ['festəvəl] *n* **1** an occasion of public celebration: *In Italy, each village holds a festival once a year.* **2** a season of musical, theatrical *etc* performances: *Every three years the city holds a drama festival*; (*also adj*) *a festival programme.*

festive ['festiv] *adj* happy and (as if) celebrating: *a festive atmosphere.*

fe'stivity [-'sti-] – *pl* **fe'stivities** – *n* a celebration: *Come and join in the festivities.*

fetal *see* foetus.

fetch [fetʃ] *v* **1** to go and get (something or someone) and bring it: *Fetch me some bread.* **2** to be sold for (a certain price): *The picture fetched $100.*

see also **bring**.

fête [feit] *n* an entertainment, *esp* in the open air, with competitions, displays, the selling of goods *etc usu* to raise money, *esp* for charity: *We are holding a summer fête in aid of charity.*

fetid ['fi:tid] *adj* having a bad smell; stinking: *a fetid pool of water.*

fetish ['fetiʃ] *n* **1** an object worshipped, *esp* because a spirit is supposed to lodge in it. **2** something which is regarded with too much reverence or given too much attention: *It is good to dress well, but there is no need to make a fetish of it.*

fetter ['fetə] *n* a chain that holds the foot or feet of a prisoner, animal *etc* to prevent running away: *The prisoner was in fetters.* – *v* to fasten with a fetter: *He fettered the horse.*

fetus *see* foetus.

feud [fju:d] *n* a long-lasting quarrel or war between families, tribes *etc*: *There has been a feud between our two families for two hundred years.*

feudal ['fju:dl] *adj* of the system by which people gave certain services *eg* military support to a more powerful man in return for lands, protection *etc.* '**feudalism** *n.*

fever ['fi:və] *n* (an illness causing) high body temperature and quick heart-beat: *She is in bed with a fever*; *a fever of excitement.*

'feverish *adj* **1** having a slight fever: *She seems a bit feverish tonight.* **2** restlessly excited: *a feverish air.*

'feverishly *adv* quickly and excitedly: *He wrote feverishly.*

at fever pitch at a level of great excitement: *The crowd's excitement was at fever pitch as they waited for the filmstar to appear.*

few [fju:] *adj, pron* not many (emphasizing the smallness of the number): *Few people visit me nowadays; every few minutes* (=very frequently); *Such opportunites are few.*

a few a small number (emphasizing that there are indeed some): *There are a few books in this library about geology; We have only a few left.*

few and far between very few: *Interesting jobs are few and far between.*

> **few** means 'not many'.
> **a few** means 'some'.
> see also **less**.

fez [fez] *n* a type of brimless hat with a tassel, *usu* red and worn by some Muslims.

fiancé [fiãsei, (*Amer*) fiːənˈsei] – *fem* **fiˈancée** – *n* a person to whom one is engaged to be married.

fiasco [fiˈaskou] – *pl* **fiˈascos** – *n* a complete failure: *The party was a fiasco.*

fib [fib] *n* an unimportant lie: *to tell fibs.* – *v* – *pt, ptp* **fibbed** – to tell a fib: *She fibbed about her age.*

fibre, (*Amer*) **fiber** [ˈfaibə] *n* 1 a fine thread or something like a thread: *a nerve fibre.* 2 a material made up of fibres: *coconut fibre.* 3 character: *A man of strong moral fibre.* **ˈfibrous** *adj.*

ˈfibreglass *n, adj* 1 (of) very fine threadlike pieces of glass, used for insulation, in materials *etc*: *fibreglass curtains.* 2 (of) a plastic material reinforced with such glass, used for many purposes *eg* building boats.

fickle [ˈfikl] *adj* always changing (one's mind, likes and dislikes *etc*): *Men think that women are fickle.* **ˈfickleness** *n.*

fiction [ˈfikʃən] *n* stories *etc* which tell of imagined, not real, characters and events: *I prefer reading fiction to hearing about real events.* **ˈfictional** *adj.*

fictitious [fikˈtiʃəs] *adj* 1 not true: *a fictitious account.* 2 not real or based on fact: *All the characters in the book are fictitious.*

fiddle [ˈfidl] *n* 1 a violin: *He played the fiddle.* 2 a dishonest business arrangement: *He's working a fiddle over his taxes.* – *v* 1 to play a violin: *He fiddled while they danced.* 2 (*with* **with**) to make restless, aimless movements: *Stop fiddling with your pencil!* 3 to manage (money, accounts *etc*) dishonestly: *He has been fiddling the accounts for years.* **ˈfiddler** *n.*

fiddler crab a small crab, the male of which has an enlarged claw.

on the fiddle dishonest: *He's always on the fiddle.*

fidelity [fiˈdeləti] *n* faithfulness or loyalty: *his fidelity to his wife; fidelity to a promise.*

fidget [ˈfiʒit] – *pt, ptp* **ˈfidgeted** – *v* to move (the hands, feet *etc*) restlessly: *Stop fidgeting while I'm talking to you!* – *n* a person who fidgets: *She's a terrible fidget!*

the fidgets nervous restlessness.

field [fiːld] *n* 1 a piece of land enclosed for growing crops, keeping animals *etc*: *Our house is surrounded by fields.* 2 a wide area: *playing fields* (=an area for games, sports *etc*). 3 a piece of land *etc* where minerals or other natural resources are found: *an oilfield; a coalfield.* 4 an area of knowledge, interest, study *etc*: *in the fields of literature/economic development; his main fields of interest.* 5 an area affected, covered or included by something: *a magnetic field; in his field of vision.* 6 an area of battle: *the field of Waterloo.* – *v* (*also adj*) *a field-gun.* – *v* (in cricket, basketball *etc*) to catch (the ball) and return it.

ˈfielder, ˈfieldsman [ˈfiːldz-] *ns* a person who fields in cricket *etc.*

ˈfield-glasses *n pl* binoculars.

ˈfieldwork *n* work done outside the laboratory, office *etc* (*eg* collecting information).

fiend [fiːnd] *n* 1 a devil: *the fiends of hell.* 2 a wicked or cruel person: *She's an absolute fiend when she's angry.* 3 a person who is very enthusiastic about something: *a fresh air fiend; a fiend for work.*

ˈfiendish *adj* 1 wicked or devilish: *a fiendish temper.* 2 very difficult, clever *etc*: *a fiendish plan.*

ˈfiendishly *adv* 1 wickedly. 2 very: *fiendishly difficult.*

fierce [fiəs] *adj* 1 very angry and likely to attack: *a fierce dog; a fierce expression.* 2 intense or strong: *fierce rivals.* **ˈfiercely** *adv.*

fiery [ˈfaiəri] *adj* 1 like fire: *a fiery light.* 2 angry: *a fiery temper.*

fiesta [fiˈestə] *n* 1 a (religious) holiday, *esp* in Roman Catholic countries. 2 a festival or celebration.

fife [faif] *n* a type of small flute.

fifteen [fifˈtiːn] *n* 1 the number or figure 15. 2 the age of 15. 3 a team containing fifteen members: *a rugby fifteen.* – *adj* 1 15 in number. 2 aged 15.

fifteen- having fifteen (of something): *a fifteen-page report.*

ˈfifˈteenth *n* 1 one of fifteen equal parts. 2 (*also adj*) (the) last of fifteen (people, things etc); (the) next after the fourteenth.

ˈfifˈteen-year-old *n* a person or animal that is fifteen years old. – *adj* (of a person, animal or thing) that is fifteen years old.

fifth [fifθ] *n* 1 one of five equal parts. 2 (*also adj*) the last of five (people *etc*); the next after the fourth.

fifty [ˈfifti] *n* 1 the number or figure 50. 2 the age of 50. – *adj* 1 50 in number. 2 aged 50.

ˈfifties *n pl* 1 the period of time between one's fiftieth and sixtieth birthdays. 2 the range of temperatures between fifty and sixty degrees. 3 the period of time between the fiftieth and sixtieth years of a century.

fig   183   fill

'fiftieth *n* **1** one of fifty equal parts. **2** (*also adj*) (the) last of fifty (people, things *etc*); (the) next after the forty-ninth.

fifty- having fifty (of something): *a fifty-page book*.

'fifty-year-old *n* a person or animal that is fifty years old. – *adj* (of a person, animal or thing) that is fifty years old.

,fifty-'fifty *adv* half and half: *We'll divide the money fifty-fifty*. – *adj* equal: *a fifty-fifty chance*.

fig [fig] *n* a type of soft pear-shaped fruit, often eaten dried.

fight [fait] – *pt, ptp* **fought** [fo:t] – *v* **1** to act against (someone or something) with physical violence: *The two boys are fighting over* (= because of) *some money they found*. **2** to resist strongly; to take strong action to prevent: *to fight a fire*; *We must fight against any attempt to deprive us of our freedom*. **3** to quarrel: *His parents were always fighting*. – *n* **1** an act of physical violence between people, countries *etc*: *There was a fight going on in the street*. **2** a struggle; action involving effort: *the fight for freedom of speech*; *the fight against disease*. **3** the will or strength to resist: *There was no fight left in him*. **4** a boxing-match.

'fighter *n* **1** a person who fights. **2** a small fast aircraft designed to shoot down other aircraft.

fight back to defend oneself against an attack, or attack in return.

fight it out to fight on to a decisive end: *Although they were both exhausted the armies fought it out until the attackers were victorious at dawn*; *Fight it out among yourselves which of you is to go*.

fight off to drive away by fighting: *He managed to fight off his attacker*; *I'll fight this cold off by going to bed early*.

fight one's way to make one's way with difficulty: *He fought his way through the crowd*.

fight shy of to avoid: *He fought shy of introducing her to his wife*.

put up a good fight to fight well and bravely.

figment ['figmənt] *n*: **a figment of the/one's imagination** something one has imagined and which has no reality.

figure ['figə, (*Amer*) 'figjər] *n* **1** the form or shape of a person: *A mysterious figure came towards me*; *That girl has got a good figure*. **2** a (geometrical) shape: *The page was covered with a series of triangles, squares and other geometrical figures*. **3** a symbol representing a number: *a six-figure telephone number*. **4** a diagram or drawing to explain something: *The parts of a flower are shown in figure 3*. – *v* **1** to appear (in a story *etc*): *He figures largely in the story*. **2** to

think, estimate or consider: *I figured that you would arrive before half past eight*.

'figurative [-rətiv] *adj* of or using figures of speech: *figurative language*. **'figuratively** *adv*.

'figurehead *n* **1** a person who is officially a leader but who does little or has little power: *She is the real leader of the party – he is only a figurehead*. **2** an ornamental figure (*usu* of carved wood) attached to the front of a ship.

figure of speech one of several devices (*eg* metaphor, simile) for using words not with their ordinary meanings but to make a striking effect.

figure out to understand: *I can't figure out why he said that*.

figurine ['figjəri:n] *n* a small statue of a person: *china figurines of Spanish ladies*.

filament ['filəmənt] *n* something very thin shaped like a thread, *esp* the thin wire in an electric light bulb.

file¹ [fail] *n* a line of soldiers *etc* walking one behind the other. – *v* to walk in a file: *They filed across the road*.

in single file (moving along) singly, one behind the other: *They went downstairs in single file*.

file² [fail] *n* **1** a folder, loose-leaf book *etc* to hold papers. **2** a collection of papers on a particular subject (kept in such a folder). **3** in computing, a collection of data stored *eg* on a disc. – *v* **1** to put (papers *etc*) in a file: *He filed the letter under P*. **2** to bring (a suit) before a law court: *to file (a suit) for divorce*.

'filing cabinet *n* a piece of furniture with drawers *etc* for holding papers.

***file³** [fail] *n* a steel tool with a rough surface for smoothing or rubbing away wood, metal *etc*. – *v* to cut or smooth with a file: *She filed her nails*.

'filings *n pl* pieces of wood, metal *etc* rubbed off with a file: *iron filings*.

filial ['filiəl] *adj* of or suitable to a son or daughter: *filial piety*.

fill [fil] *v* **1** to put (something) into (until there is no room for more); to make full: *to fill a cupboard with books*; *The news filled him with joy*. **2** to become full: *Her eyes filled with tears*. **3** to satisfy (a condition, requirement *etc*): *Does he fill all our requirements?* **4** to put something in a hole (in a tooth *etc*) to stop it up: *The dentist filled two of my teeth yesterday*. – *n* as much as fills or satisfies someone: *He ate his fill*.

filled *adj* having been filled.

'filler *n* **1** a tool or instrument used for filling something, *esp* for conveying liquid into a bottle. **2** material used to fill cracks in a wall *etc*.

'filling *n* anything used to fill: *The filling has*

* see illustration on p. 566

come out of my tooth; *She put an orange filling in the cake.*

'filling-station *n* a place where petrol is sold.

fill in 1 to add or put in (whatever is needed to make something complete): *to fill in the details.* **2** to complete (forms, application *etc*) by putting in the information required: *Have you filled in your tax form yet?* **3** to give (someone) all the necessary information: *I've been away – can you fill me in on what has happened?* **4** to occupy (time): *He had several drinks in the bar to fill in time until the train left.* **5** to do another person's job temporarily: *I'm filling in for his secretary.*

fill up to make or become completely full: *Fill up the petrol tank, please.*

fillet ['filit] *n* a piece of meat or fish without bones: *fillet of veal*; *cod fillet*; (*also adj*) *fillet steak.* – *v* – *pt, ptp* **'filleted** – to remove the bones from (meat or fish).

filly ['fili] – *pl* **'fillies** – *n* a young female horse.

film [film] *n* **1** (a thin strip of) celluloid made sensitive to light on which photographs are taken: *photographic film.* **2** a story, play *etc* shown as a motion picture in a cinema, on television *etc*: *to make a film*; (*also adj*) *a film version of the novel.* **3** a thin skin or covering: *a film of dust.* – *v* **1** to make a motion picture (of): *They are going to film the race.* **2** (*usu with* **over**) to cover with a film: *Her eyes gradually filmed (over) with tears.*

'filmstar *n* a famous actor or actress in films.

filter ['filtə] *n* **1** a strainer or other device through which liquid, gas, smoke *etc* can pass, but not solid material: *A filter is used to make sure that the oil is clean and does not contain any dirt*; (*also adj*) *filter paper.* **2** a kind of screening plate used to change or correct certain colours: *If you are taking photographs in sun and snow, you should use a blue filter.* – *v* **1** (of liquids) to (become) clean by passing through a filter: *The rainwater filtered into a tank.* **2** to come bit by bit or gradually: *The news filtered out.*

filter-'tip *n* (a cigarette with) a filter.

filth [filθ] *n* anything very dirty or foul: *Look at that filth on your boots!*

'filthy *adj* **1** very dirty: *The whole house is absolutely filthy.* **2** obscene: *a filthy story.*

fin [fin] *n* **1** a thin movable part on a fish's body by which it balances, moves, changes direction *etc.* **2** anything that looks or is used like a fin: *the tail-fin of an aeroplane.*

final ['fainl] *adj* **1** the very last: *the final chapter of the book.* **2** (of a decision *etc*) definite; decided and not to be changed: *The judge's decision is final.* – *n* the last part of a competition: *The first parts of the*

competition will take place throughout the country, but the final will be in London.

'finally *adv* **1** as the last (of many): *The soldiers rode past, then came the Royal visitors, and finally the Queen.* **2** at last, after a long time: *The train finally arrived.*

'finalist *n* a person who reaches the final stage in a competition: *It was difficult to decide which of the two finalists was the better tennis player.*

fi'nality [-'na-] *n.*

'finalize, -ise *v* to make a final decision about plans, arrangements *etc*: *We must finalize the arrangements by Friday.* **finali-'zation, -s-** *n.*

'finals *n pl* the last examinations for a university degree *etc*: *I am sitting/taking my finals in June.*

finale [fi'na:li] *n* the last part of anything, *esp* a concert, opera, musical show *etc*: *The whole cast of the concert appeared in the finale.*

finance [fai'nans] *n* **1** (the study or management of) money affairs: *He is an expert in finance.* **2** (*often in pl*) the money one has to spend: *The government is worried about the state of the country's finances.* – *v* to give money for (a plan, business *etc*): *Will the company finance your trip abroad?*

fi'nancial [-ʃəl] *adj* concerning money: *financial affairs.* **fi'nancially** *adv.*

fi'nancier [-siə, (*Amer*) fainan'siər] *n* a person who manages large sums of money.

finch [fintʃ] *n* one of several kinds of small bird: *a greenfinch.*

find [faind] – *pt, ptp* **found** [faund] – *v* **1** to come upon or meet with accidentally or after searching: *Look what I've found!* **2** to discover: *I found that I couldn't do the work.* **3** to consider; to think (something) to be: *I found the British weather very cold.* – *n* something found, *esp* something of value or interest: *That old book is quite a find!*

find one's feet to become able to cope with a new situation: *She found the new job difficult at first but she soon found her feet.*

find out 1 to discover: *I found out what was troubling her.* **2** to discover the truth (about someone), *usu* that he has done wrong: *He had been stealing for years, but eventually they found him out.*

fine[1] [fain] *adj* **1** (*usu* of art *etc*) very good; of excellent quality: *fine paintings*; *a fine performance.* **2** (of weather) bright; not raining: *a fine day.* **3** well; healthy: *I was ill yesterday but I am feeling fine today!* **4** thin or delicate: *a fine material.* **5** careful; detailed: *Fine workmanship is required for such delicate embroidery.* **6** made of small pieces, grains *etc*: *fine sand*; *fine rain.* **7** slight; delicate: *a fine balance*; *a fine distinction.* **8** perfectly satisfactory: *There's* *nothing wrong with your work – it's fine. –* adv satisfactorily: *This arrangement suits me fine. – interj* good; well done *etc: You've finished already – fine!* **'finely** adv.

'finery n beautiful clothes, jewellery *etc: She arrived in all her finery.*

fine art art that appeals immediately to the senses, *eg* painting, sculpture, music *etc: Painting is one of the fine arts.*

fine² [fain] n money which must be paid as a punishment: *I had to pay a fine. – v* to make (someone) pay a fine: *He was fined £10.*

finesse [fines] n cleverness and skill in dealing with a situation *etc: She managed that situation with great finesse.*

finger ['fiŋgə] n **1** one of the five end parts of the hand, sometimes excluding the thumb: *She pointed a finger at the thief.* **2** the part of a glove into which a finger is put. **3** anything made, shaped, cut *etc* like a finger: *a finger of toast. – v* to touch or feel with the fingers: *She fingered the material.*

'fingernail n the nail at the tip of the finger.

'fingerprint n the mark made by the tip of the finger, often used by the police *etc* as a means of identification: *The thief wiped his fingerprints off the safe.*

'fingertip n the very end of a finger: *She burnt her fingertips on the stove.*

be all fingers and thumbs/my *etc* **fingers are all thumbs** to be very awkward or clumsy in handling or holding things: *He was so excited that his fingers were all thumbs and he dropped the cup.*

have (something) at one's fingertips to know all the details of (a subject) thoroughly: *He has the history of the firm at his fingertips.*

have a finger in the pie/in every pie to be involved in everything that happens: *She likes to have a finger in every pie in the village.*

put one's finger on to point out or describe exactly; to identify: *He put his finger on the cause of our financial trouble.*

finicky ['finiki] adj too much concerned with detail: *She is a very finicky person.*

finish ['finiʃ] v **1** to bring or come to an end: *She's finished her work; The music finished.* **2** to use, eat, drink *etc* the last of: *Have you finished your tea? – n* **1** the last touch (of paint, polish *etc*) that makes the work perfect: *The wood has a beautiful finish.* **2** the last part (of a race *etc*): *It was a close finish.*

'finished adj **1** ended: *Her chances of success are finished.* **2** (neg **un-**) done; completed: *a finished product.* **3** having been completely used, eaten *etc: The food is finished – there's none left.*

finish off 1 to complete: *He finished off the job yesterday.* **2** to use, eat *etc* the last of: *We've finished off the cake.* **3** to kill (a

person): *His last illness nearly finished him off.*

finish up 1 to use, eat *etc* the last of; to finish: *Finish up your meal as quickly as possible.* **2** to end: *It was no surprise to me when he finished up in jail; The car finished up in the dump.*

finite ['fainait] adj **1** having an end or limit: *Human knowledge is finite, divine knowledge infinite.* **2** (of a verb) having a subject: *He speaks; I ran; She fell.*

fir [fə:] n a kind of evergreen tree that bears cones (**'fir-cones**) and is often grown for its wood.

fire ['faiə] n **1** anything that is burning, whether accidentally or not: *a warm fire in the kitchen; Several houses were destroyed in a fire.* **2** an apparatus for heating: *a gas fire; an electric fire.* **3** the heat and light produced by burning: *Fire is one of man's greatest benefits.* **4** enthusiasm: *with fire in his heart.* **5** attack by gunfire: *The soldiers were under fire. –v* **1** (of china, pottery *etc*) to heat in an oven, or kiln, in order to harden and strengthen: *The pots must be fired.* **2** to make (someone) enthusiastic; to inspire: *The story fired his imagination.* **3** to operate (a gun *etc*) by discharging a bullet *etc* from it: *He fired his revolver three times.* **4** to send out or discharge (a bullet *etc*) from a gun *etc: He fired three bullets at the target.* **5** (often with **at** or **on**) to aim and operate a gun at; to shoot at: *They suddenly fired on us; He fired at the target.* **6** to send away someone from his/her job; to dismiss: *He was fired from his last job for being late.*

fire alarm an apparatus (*eg* a bell) to give warning of a fire: *Everyone had to leave the building when the fire alarm rang.*

'firearm n any type of gun: *In certain countries you need a licence to keep firearms.*

'fire-cracker n a kind of firework which makes a loud noise.

'fire-brigade n a company of firemen: *Call the fire-brigade!*

'fire-engine n a vehicle carrying firemen and their equipment.

'fire-escape n a means of escape from a building in case of fire, *usu* in the form of a metal staircase on the outside of the building: *Hotels should have fire-escapes.*

'fire-extinguisher n an apparatus (*usu* containing chemicals) for putting out fires: *There must be fire-extinguishers in every room.*

'fire-guard n a metal framework placed in front of a fireplace for safety.

'fireman n a man whose job is to put out accidental fires or those caused deliberately as a criminal act.

'fireplace n a space in a room (*usu* in a wall)

with a chimney above, for a fire: *a wide stone fireplace.*

'fireside *n* a place beside a fireplace: *The old man slept by the fireside;(also adj) a fireside chair.*

'fire-station *n* the building or buildings where fire-engines and other pieces of equipment used by firemen are kept.

'firewood *n* wood that is suitable for burning as fuel: *He went into the garden to cut firewood.*

'firework *n* a small exploding device giving off a colourful display of lights: *Rockets are my favourite fireworks; (also adj) a firework display; If your father finds out, there'll be fireworks* (= a display of anger)!

'firing-squad *n* a group of soldiers with guns, to execute a prisoner: *He must face the firing-squad.*

catch fire to begin to burn: *Dry wood catches fire easily.*

on fire burning: *The building is on fire!*

open fire (*usu with* **on**) to begin shooting at: *The enemy opened fire (on us).*

play with fire to do something dangerous or risky: *Putting all your money into that business is playing with fire!*

set fire to (something)/set (something) on fire to cause (something) to begin burning *usu* accidentally or deliberately as a criminal act: *They set fire to the ambassador's house; He has set the house on fire.*

under fire 1 being shot at: *We have been under fire from the enemy all day.* 2 being criticized or blamed: *The government is under fire.*

firm[1] [fəːm] *adj* 1 (fixed) strong and steady: *a firm handshake.* 2 decided; not changing one's mind: *a firm refusal.* **'firmly** *adv.*

firm[2] [fəːm] *n* a business company: *an engineering firm.*

firmament ['fəːməmənt] *n* the sky; the heavens: *The stars shine in the endless firmament.*

first [fəːst] *adj, adv* before all others in place, time or rank: *the first person to arrive; The boy spoke first.* – *adv* before doing anything else: *'Shall we eat now?' 'Wash your hands first!'* – *n* the person, animal *etc* that does something before any other person, animal *etc*: *the first to arrive.*

'firstly *adv* in the first place: *I have three reasons for not going – firstly, it's cold, secondly, I'm tired, and thirdly, I don't want to!*

first aid treatment of a wounded or sick person before the doctor's arrival: *We should all learn first aid; (also adj) first-aid treatment.*

'first-born *adj, n* (one's) oldest (child).

,first-'class *adj* 1 of the best quality: *a first-class hotel.* 2 very good: *This food is first-class!* 3 (for) travelling in the best and most

expensive part of the train, plane, ship *etc*: *a first-class passenger ticket; (also adv) He always travels first-class.*

,first-'hand *adj, adv* (of a story, description *etc*) obtained directly, not through various other people: *a first-hand account; I heard the story first-hand.*

,first-'rate *adj* of the best quality: *He is a first-rate architect.*

at first at the beginning: *At first I didn't like him.*

at first hand obtained *etc* directly: *I was able to acquire information at first hand.*

first and foremost first of all.

first of all to begin with; the most important thing is: *First of all, let's clear up the mess; First of all, the scheme is impossible – secondly, we can't afford it.*

fish [fiʃ] – *pls* **fish**, (*rare*) **'fishes** – *n* 1 a kind of creature that lives in water and breathes through gills: *There are plenty of fish around the coast.* 2 its flesh eaten as food: *Do you prefer meat or fish?* – *v* 1 to (try to) catch fish (in): *He likes fishing; He fished the river all day.* 2 (*usu with* **for**) to search for: *She fished around in her handbag for a handkerchief.* 3 (*usu with* **for**) to try to get by indirect means: *She is always fishing for compliments.*

'fishy *adj* 1 of or like a fish: *a fishy smell.* 2 odd or suspicious: *There's something fishy about that man.*

'fishball *n* mashed fish shaped into a ball and cooked.

'fisherman *n* a man who fishes either as a job or as a hobby.

fish farmer a person who breeds fish.

'fishing-line *n* a fine strong thread, now *usu* made of nylon, used with a rod, hooks *etc* for catching fish.

'fishing-rod *n* a long thin flexible rod used with a fishing-line and hooks *etc* for catching fish.

fish merchant a fishmonger.

'fishmonger *n* 1 a person who sells fish. 2 a shop that sells mainly fish: *I must go down to the fishmonger.*

feel like a fish out of water to feel uncomfortable or out of place in a situation.

fish out to pull something out with some difficulty: *At last he fished out the letter he was looking for.*

The plural **fish** is never wrong, but sometimes **fishes** is used in talking about different individuals or species: *How many fish did you catch?; the fishes of the Indian Ocean; the story of two little fishes.*

fist [fist] *n* a tightly closed hand: *He shook his fist at me in anger.*

fit[1] [fit] *adj* 1 in good health: *I am feeling very fit.* 2 suitable; correct for a particular purpose or person: *a dinner fit for a king.* – *n* the right size or shape for a particular person, purpose *etc*: *Your dress is a very good fit.* – *v* – *pt, ptp* '**fitted** – **1** to be the right size or shape (for someone or something): *The coats fits (you) very well.* **2** to be suitable for: *His speech fitted the occasion.* **3** to put (something) in position: *You must fit a new lock on the door.* **4** to supply with; to equip with: *He fitted the cupboard with shelves.*

'**fitter** *n* a person who puts the parts of a machine together.

'**fitting** *adj* suitable: *a fitting occasion.* – *n* **1** something, *eg* a piece of furniture, which is fixed, *esp* in a house *etc*: *kitchen fittings.* **2** the trying-on of a dress *etc* and altering to make it fit: *I am having a fitting for my wedding-dress tomorrow.*

fit in (*often with* **with**) to be able to live, exist *etc* in agreement or harmony: *She doesn't fit in with the other children.*

fit out to provide with everything necessary (clothes, equipment *etc*): *The shop fitted them out with everything they needed for their journey.*

see/think fit to consider that some action is right, suitable *etc*: *You must do as you see fit (to do).*

fit² [fit] *n* **1** a sudden attack of illness, *esp* epilepsy: *She suffers from fits.* **2** something which happens as suddenly as this: *a fit of laughter/coughing.*

by fits and starts irregularly; often stopping and starting again: *He did his work by fits and starts.*

five [faiv] *n* **1** the number or figure 5. **2** the age of 5. – *adj* **1** 5 in number. **2** aged 5. **five-** having five (of something): *a five-apartment house.*

'**fiver** *n* (a banknote worth) £5 or $5: *It cost me a fiver.*

'**five-year-old** *n* a person or animal that is five years old. – *adj* (of a person, animal or thing) that is five years old.

fix [fiks] *v* **1** to make firm or steady: *He fixed the post firmly in the ground; He fixed his eyes on the door.* **2** to attach; to join: *He fixed the shelf to the wall.* **3** to mend or repair: *He has succeeded in fixing my watch.* **4** to direct (attention, a look *etc*) at: *She fixed all her attention on me.* **5** (*often with* up) to arrange; to settle: *to fix a price; We fixed (up) a meeting.* **6** to make (something) permanent by the use of certain chemicals: *to fix a photgraphic print.* **7** to prepare; to get ready: *I'll fix dinner tonight.* – *n* trouble; a difficulty: *I'm in a terrible fix!*

fix'ation *n* a strong idea or opinion for or against something that one does not or cannot change: *She has a fixation about travelling alone.*

fixed *adj* **1** arranged in advance; settled: *a fixed price.* **2** steady; not moving: *a fixed gaze/stare.* **3** arranged illegally or dishonestly: *The result was fixed.*

fixedly ['fiksidli] *adv* ṣteadily: *He stared fixedly.*

fixture ['fikstʃə] *n* **1** a fixed piece of furniture *etc*: *We can't move the cupboard – it's a fixture.* **2** an event, *esp* sporting, arranged for a certain time: *The football team has a fixture on Saturday.*

fix on to decide on, choose: *Have you fixed on a date for the wedding?*

fix (someone) up with (something) to provide (someone) with (something): *Can you fix me up with a car for tomorrow?*

fizz [fiz] *v* (of a liquid) to release or give off many small bubbles: *I like the way champagne fizzes.* – *n* the sound made or the feeling in the mouth produced by this: *This lemonade has lost its fizz.* '**fizzy** *adj*.

fizzle ['fizl]: **fizzle out** to fail, to come to nothing: *The fire fizzled out.*

flabbergasted ['flabəga:stid] *adj* very surprised: *She was quite flabbergasted when we told her.*

flabby ['flabi] *adj* loose and fat; not firm: *flabby cheeks.*

flag¹ [flag] *n* a piece of cloth with a particular design representing a country, party, association *etc*: *the French flag.*

'**flag-pole/**'**flagstaff** *ns* the pole on which a flag is hung.

flag down – *v* – *pt, ptp* **flagged** – to wave at (a car *etc*) in order to make it stop: *We flagged down a taxi.*

flag² [flag] – *pt, ptp* **flagged** – *v* to become tired or weak: *Halfway through the race he began to flag.*

flagrant ['fleigrənt] *adj* (*usu* of something bad) very obvious; easily seen: *flagrant injustice.* '**flagrantly** *adv.* '**flagrancy** *n.*

flair [fleə] *n* a natural ability or cleverness for (doing) something: *She has flair for (learning) languages.*

flake [fleik] *n* a very small piece: *a snowflake.* – *v* (*usu with* off) to come off in flakes: *The paint is flaking.* '**flaky** *adj.*

flamboyant [flam'boiənt] *adj* intended to attract notice: *flamboyant clothes.* **flam'boyance** *n.*

flame [fleim] *n* the bright light of something burning: *A small flame burned in the lamp.* – *v* **1** to burn with flames: *His eyes flamed with anger.* **2** to become very hot, red *etc*: *Her cheeks flamed with embarrassment.* '**flaming** *adj.*

flammable ['flaməbl] *adj* able or likely to burn: *flammable material.*

*flame of the forest a tropical tree with large bright-red flowers and long brown pods.

see also inflammable.

flamingo [flə'miŋgou] – pl fla'mingo(e)s – n a type of long-legged wading bird, pink or bright red in colour.

flank [flaŋk] n the side of anything esp an animal's body or an army: the horse's flank; They marched around the enemy's flank. – v 1 to be at the side of: The prisoner appeared, flanked by two policemen. 2 to come around the side of: The troops flanked the enemy forces.

flannel ['flanl] n loosely woven woollen cloth: blankets made of flannel; (also adj) a flannel petticoat.

flap [flap] n 1 anything broad or wide that hangs loosely: a flap of canvas. 2 the sound made when such a thing moves: We could hear the flap of the flag bowing in the wind. 3 great confusion or panic: They are all in a terrible flap. – v – pt, ptp flapped – 1 to (make something) move with the sound of a flap: the leaves were flapping in the breeze; The bird flapped its wings. 2 to become confused; to get into a panic: There is no need to flap.

flare [fleə] v 1 to burn with a bright unsteady light: The firelight flared. 2 (of a skirt, trousers etc) to become wider at the bottom edge: a flared skirt.

flare up suddenly to burn strongly: A quarrel flared up between them (n 'flare-up).

flash [flaʃ] n 1 a quick showing of a bright light: a flash of lightning. 2 a moment; a very short time: He was with her in a flash. 3 a flashlight (def 2). 4 (often 'newsflash) a brief news report sent by radio, television etc: Did you hear the flash about the king's death? – v 1 (of a light) to (cause to) shine quickly: He flashed a torch. 2 (usu with by or past) to pass quickly: The days flashed by; The cars flashed past. 3 to show; to display: He flashed a card and was allowed to pass.

'flashing adj: flashing lights.

'flashy adj big, bright etc but cheap and of poor quality: flashy clothes. 'flashily adv.

'flashlight n 1 a (battery) torch. 2 (often abbrev flash) an instrument which produces a sudden bright light for taking photographs.

flask [flɑːsk] n 1 a container in which drinks can be carried: a flask of whisky. 2 a vacuum flask: The workmen carried flasks of tea. 3 a bottle, usu with a narrow neck.

flat [flat] adj 1 level; without rise or fall: a flat surface. 2 dull; without interest: She spent a very flat weekend. 3 (of something said, decided etc) definite; emphatic: a flat denial. 4 (of a tyre) not inflated, having lost

most of its air: His car had a flat tyre. 5 (of drinks) no longer fizzy: flat lemonade; (also adv) My beer has gone flat. 6 slightly lower than a musical note should be: That last note was flat; (also adv) The choir went very flat. – adv stretched out: She was lying flat on her back. – n 1 (Amer a'partment) a set of rooms on one floor, with kitchen and bathroom, in a larger building or block: Do you live in a house or a flat? 2 (in musical notation) a sign (♭) which makes a note a semitone lower. 3 a level, even part: the flat of her hand. 4 (usu in pl) an area of flat land, esp beside the sea, a river etc: mud flats.

'flatly adv definitely; emphatically: She flatly denied it.

'flatten v (often with out) to make or become flat: The countryside flattened out as they came near the sea.

flat rate a fixed amount, esp one that is the same in all cases: He charged a flat rate for the work.

flat out as fast, energetically etc as possible: She worked flat out.

flatter ['flatə] v 1 to praise too much or insincerely: Flatter him by complimenting him on his singing. 2 to show, describe etc someone or something as being better than someone etc really is: The photograph flatters him. 3 to be pleased to say about (oneself) (that one can do something): I flatter myself that I can speak French perfectly. 'flatterer n.

'flattery n insincere praise.

flaunt [flɔːnt] v to show off in order to attract attention to oneself: She flaunted her expensive clothes.

flavour, (Amer) flavor ['fleivə] n 1 taste: The tea has a wonderful flavour. 2 atmosphere; quality: an Eastern flavour. – v to give flavour to: She flavoured the cake with lemon.

'flavouring n anything used to give a particular taste: lemon flavouring.

flaw [flɔː] n a fault; something which makes something not perfect: a flaw in the material.

flawed adj having a flaw: This china is flawed.

'flawless adj perfect: her flawless beauty.

flea [fliː] n a type of small blood-sucking insect that jumps instead of flying and lives on the bodies of animals or people.

fleck [flek] n a spot: a fleck of dust.

flecked adj marked with spots: a flecked pattern.

fled see flee.

fledg(e)ling ['fledʒliŋ] n a young bird ready to fly.

flee [fliː] v – pt, ptp fled [fled] – v to run away (from danger): He fled the danger.

* see illustration on p. 573

fleece [fliːs] *n* a sheep's coat of wool. – *v* to cut wool from (sheep).
'**fleecy** *adj* soft and woolly: *a fleecy blanket*.

fleet [fliːt] *n* **1** a number of ships or boats under one command or sailing together: *a fleet of fishing boats*. **2** the entire navy of a country: *the British fleet*.

flesh [fleʃ] *n* **1** the soft substance (muscles *etc*) that covers the bones of animals. **2** the soft part of fruit: *the golden flesh of a peach*.
'**fleshy** *adj* fat: *a fleshy face*.
flesh and blood 1 relations; family: *She is my own flesh and blood*. **2** human nature: *It is more than flesh and blood can tolerate*.
in the flesh actually present: *I have seen him on television, but never in the flesh*.

flew *see* **fly**[2].

flex [fleks] *v* to bend, *esp* in order to test: *to flex one's joints*. – *n* (a piece of) thin insulated wire for carrying electricity: *That lamp has a long flex*.
'**flexible** *adj* **1** that can be bent easily: *flexible metal*. **2** able or willing to change according to circumstances *etc*: *My holiday plans are very flexible*. ˌflexi'bility *n*.

flick [flik] *n* a quick, sharp movement: *a flick of the wrist*. – *v* to make this kind of movement (to or with something): *He flicked open a packet of cigarettes*.

flicker ['flikə] *v* **1** to burn unsteadily: *the candle flickered*. **2** to move quickly and unsteadily: *A smile flickered across her face*. – *n* an unsteady light or flame: *the flicker of an oil lamp*.

flier *see* **fly**[2].

flight[1] [flait] *n* **1** act of flying: *the flight of a bird*. **2** a journey in a plane: *How long is the flight to New York?* **3** a number of steps or stairs: *A flight of steps*. **4** a number of birds *etc* flying or moving through the air: *a flight of geese; a flight of arrows*.
'**flighty** *adj* (*usu* of girls and women) with easily changed ideas; not thinking deeply; always looking for amusement.
flight deck 1 the upper deck of an aircraft carrier where planes take off or land. **2** the forward part of an aeroplane where the pilot and crew sit.
in flight flying: *Have you seen the geese in flight?*
See also **fly**[2].

flight[2] [flait] *n* the act of fleeing or running away from an enemy, danger *etc*: *The general regarded the flight of his army as a disgrace*.
put to flight to cause (someone) to flee or run away: *the army put the rebels to flight*.

flimsy ['flimzi] *adj* **1** thin and light: *You'll be cold in those flimsy clothes*. **2** not very well made; likely to break: *a flimsy boat*.

flinch [flintʃ] *v* to make a sudden movement back or away in fear, pain *etc*: *He flinched away from the sudden heat*.

fling [fliŋ] – *pt, ptp* **flung** [flʌŋ] – *v* **1** to throw with great force: *He flung a brick through the window*. **2** to rush: *He flung out of the house*. – *n* a lively Scottish dance: *They danced a Highland fling*.

flint [flint] *n* **1** (*also adj*) (of) a kind of very hard stone: *Prehistoric man used flint knives*. **2** a piece of hard mineral from which sparks can be struck: *I must buy a new flint for my cigarette-lighter*.

flip [flip] – *pt, ptp* **flipped** – *v* **1** to throw (something) in the air (so that it turns): *They flipped a coin to see which side it landed on*. **2** (*sometimes with* **over**) to turn over quickly: *She flipped over the pages of the book*. – *n* an act of flipping.

flippant ['flipənt] *adj* not serious enough about important matters: *a flippant reply*.
flip'pantly *adv*. '**flippancy** *n*.

flipper ['flipə] *n* **1** a limb for swimming, *esp* of a seal, walrus *etc*. **2** a kind of rubber or plastic shoe, worn when swimming, which is shaped like the flipper of a seal *etc*.

flirt [fləːt] *v* (*often with* **with**) to behave (towards someone) as though one were in love but without serious intentions: *She flirts with every man she meets*. – *n* a person, *esp* a woman, who behaves in this way.
flir'tation *n* act of flirting. **flir'tatious** [-ʃəs] *adj*. **flir'tatiously** *adv*.

flit [flit] – *pt, ptp* '**flitted** – *v* to move quickly and lightly from place to place: *Butterflies flitted around in the garden*. '**flitting** *n*.

float [flout] *v* to (make something) stay on the surface of a liquid: *A piece of wood was floating in the stream*. – *n* **1** something that floats on a fishing-line: *If the float moves, there is probably a fish on the hook*. **2** a vehicle for transporting certain things: *a milk-float; a cattle-float*.
floating population a section of the population not permanently resident in a place.
floating restaurant a restaurant on a boat or other floating structure.

flock [flok] *n* a number of certain animals or birds together: *a flock of sheep*. – *v* (*with* **to**, **into** *etc*) to gather or go somewhere together in a group or crowd: *People flocked to the cinema*.

flog [flog] – *pt, ptp* **flogged** – *v* to beat; to whip: *You will be flogged for stealing the money*. '**flogging** *n*.
flog a dead horse to try to create interest in something after all interest in it has been lost.

flood [flʌd] *n* **1** a great overflow of water: *If it continues to rain like this, we shall have floods*. **2** any great quantity: *a flood of letters*. – *v* to (cause something to) overflow with water: *She left the water running and flooded the kitchen.*

'**floodlight** *n* a kind of very strong light often used to light up the outside of buildings *etc*: *There were floodlights in the sports stadium.* − *v* − *pt, ptp* '**floodlit** [-lit] − to light with floodlights. '**floodlighting** *n*. '**floodlit** *adj*.

,**flood-'tide** *n* the rising tide.

floor [flo:] *n* **1** the surface in a room *etc* on which one stands or walks. **2** all the rooms on the same level in a building: *My office is on the third floor.* − *v* **1** to make or cover a floor: *We've floored the kitchen with plastic tiles.* **2** to knock down: *He floored him with a powerful blow.*

-**floored** having a floor or floors (of a particular kind): *a stone-floored kitchen.*

'**floorboard** *n* one of the narrow boards used to make a floor.

'**flooring** *n* material for making or covering floors.

flop [flop] − *pt, ptp* **flopped** − *v* **1** to fall or sit down suddenly and heavily: *She flopped into an armchair.* **2** to hang or swing about loosely: *Her hair flopped over her face.* **3** (of a theatrical production) to fail; to be unsuccessful: *the play flopped.* − *n* **1** (a) flopping movement. **2** a failure: *The show was complete flop.*

'**floppy** *adj* tending to flop; flopping: *a floppy hat.*

flora ['flo:rə] *n* the plants of a district or country as a whole: *the flora and fauna of Borneo.*

floral ['flo:rəl] *adj* made of, or having a pattern of, flowers: *floral decorations*; *a floral dress.*

florist ['florist] *n* a person who (grows and) sells flowers.

flotilla [flə'tilə] *n* a fleet of small ships: *A flotilla of yachts.*

flounce[1] [flauns] *v* (*usu with* **out, away** *etc*) to move (away) in anger, impatience *etc*: *She flounced out of the room.*

flounce[2] [flauns] *n* a decorative strip of material *usu* frilled: *There are flounces at the bottom of her evening skirt.*

flounced *adj* decorated with a flounce.

flounder ['flaundə] *v* to move one's legs and arms violently and with difficulty (in water, mud *etc*): *She floundered helplessly in the mud.*

flour ['flauə] *n* wheat, or other cereal, ground into a powder and used for cooking, baking *etc.*

flourish ['flʌriʃ, (*Amer*) 'flə:-] *v* **1** to be healthy; to grow well; to thrive: *My plants are flourishing.* **2** to be successful or active: *His business is flourishing.* **3** to hold or wave something as a show, threat *etc*: *He flourished his sword.* − *n* **1** an ornamental stroke of the pen in writing: *His writing was full of*

flourishes. **2** an impressive, sweeping movement (with the hand or something held in it): *He bowed and made a flourish with his hat.* **3** an ornamental passage of music: *There was a flourish on the trumpets.*

'**flourishing** *adj* **1** successful: *a flourishing business.* **2** growing well : *flourishing crops.*

flout [flaut] *v* to refuse to respect or obey: *He flouted the headmaster's authority.*

flow [flou] *v* **1** to move along in the way that water does: *The river flowed into the sea.* **2** (of the tide) to rise: *The boat left the harbour when the tide began to flow.* − *n* the act of flowing: *a flow of blood*; *the flow of traffic.*

flower ['flauə] *n* the part of a plant or tree from which fruit or seed grows, often brightly coloured and sometimes including the stem on which it grows: *a bunch of flowers.* − *v* (of plants *etc*) to produce flowers: *This plant flowers in early May.*

'**flowered** *adj* having a pattern of flowers: *flowered material.*

'**flowery** *adj* **1** having, or decorated with, flowers: *a flowery hat.* **2** (of language) using ornamental words and phrases; poetic: *a flowery speech.*

'**flower-bed** *n* a piece of earth prepared and used for the growing of plants.

'**flower-pot** *n* a container made of earthenware, plastic *etc* in which a plant is grown.

in flower (of a plant) having flowers in bloom: *These trees are in flower in May.*

flown *see* **fly**.

flu [flu:] short for **influenza**.

fluent ['fluənt] *adj* **1** (of a language *etc*) smoothly and skilfully spoken: *He spoke fluent French.* **2** (of a person) able to express oneself easily: *He is fluent in English.*

'**fluency** *n* ease in speaking or expressing: *Her fluency surprised her colleagues.*

'**fluently** *adv*: *He speaks Spanish fluently.*

fluff [flʌf] *n* small pieces of soft, wool-like material from blankets *etc*: *My coat is covered with fluff.* − *v* **1** (*often with* **out** *or* **up**) to make full and soft like fluff: *The bird fluffed out its feathers*; *Fluff up the pillows and make the invalid more comfortable.* **2** to make a mistake in doing (something): *The actress fluffed her lines*; *The golfer fluffed his stroke.*

'**fluffy** *adj* **1** soft and woolly: *a fluffy kitten.* **2** soft, light and full of air: *She cooked a fluffy omelette.*

fluid ['fluid] *n* **1** a substance (liquid or gas) whose particles can move about freely. **2** any liquid substance: *cleaning fluid.* − *adj* **1** able to flow like a liquid: *a fluid substance.* **2** smooth and graceful: *fluid movements.* **3** (of arrangements, plans *etc*) able to be changed easily: *My holiday plans are fluid.* **flu'idity** *n*.

fluke [flu:k] *n* a chance success: *Passing the exam was a fluke – I had done no work.*

flung *see* **fling**.

flunk [flʌŋk] *v* a slang word for to fail in an examination: *I flunked* (*maths*).

fluorescent [fluə'resnt] *adj* giving off a certain kind of light: *fluorescent light*; *fluorescent paint.* **fluo'rescence** *n*.

fluoride ['fluəraid] *n* any of several substances containing fluorine, *esp* one which helps to prevent tooth decay.

fluorine ['fluəri:n] *n* an element, a pale greenish-yellow gas.

flurry ['flʌri, (*Amer*) 'flə:ri] – *pl* **'flurries** – *n* **1** a sudden rush (of wind *etc*): *A flurry of wind made the door bang.* **2** a confusion: *She was in a flurry.*

flush [flʌʃ] *n* **1** a flow of blood to the face, making it red: *A slow flush covered her face.* **2** (the device that works) a rush of water which cleans a toilet: *a flush toilet.* – *v* **1** to become red in the face: *She flushed with embarrassment.* **2** to clean by a rush of water: *to flush a toilet.* **3** (*usu* with **out**) to cause (an animal *etc*) to leave a hiding place: *The police flushed out the criminal.* **flushed** *adj* red in the face: *You look very flushed.*

(in) the first flush of (in) the early stages of (something) when a person is feeling fresh, strong, enthusiastic *etc*: *in the first flush of youth.*

fluster ['flʌstə] *n* excitement and confusion caused by hurry: *She was in a terrible fluster when unexpected guests arrived.* – *v* to cause to be worried or nervous; to agitate: *Don't fluster me!*

flute [flu:t] *n* a type of high-pitched woodwind musical instrument.

flutter ['flʌtə] *v* **1** to (cause to) move quickly: *A leaf fluttered to the ground.* **2** (of a bird, insect *etc*) to move the wings rapidly and lightly: *The moth fluttered round the light.* – *n* **1** a quick irregular movement (of a pulse *etc*): *She felt a flutter in her chest.* **2** nervous excitement: *She was in a great flutter.*

flux [flʌks] *n* continual change: *Events are in a state of flux.*

fly[1] [flai] – *pl* **flies** – *n* **1** a type of small winged insect. **2** a fish hook made to look like a fly so that a fish will take it in its mouth: *Which fly should I use to catch a trout?* **3** (*often in pl*) a piece of material with buttons or a zip, *esp* at the front of trousers.

a fly in the ointment something that spoils one's enjoyment.

fly[2] [flai] – *pt* **flew** [flu:]: *ptp* **flown** [floun] – *v* **1** to (make something) go through the air on wings *etc* or in an aeroplane: *The pilot*

flew (*the plane*) *across the sea.* **2** to run away (from): *He flew* (*the country*). **3** (of time) to pass quickly: *The days flew past.*

'flyer, 'flier *n* a person who flies an aeroplane *etc*.

flying saucer a strange flying object thought possibly to come from another planet.

flying visit a very short, often unexpected, visit: *She paid her mother a flying visit.*

'flyleaf *n* a blank page at the beginning or end of a book.

'flyover *n* a road *etc* which is built up so as to cross above another: *a flyover across the motorway.*

fly in the face of to oppose or defy; to treat with contempt: *He flew in the face of danger.*

fly into suddenly to get into (a rage, a temper *etc*).

fly off the handle to lose one's temper.

get off to a flying start to have a very successful beginning: *Our new shop has got off to a flying start.*

let fly (*often with* **at**) to throw, shoot or send out violently: *He let fly* (*an arrow*) *at the target.*

send (someone/something) flying to hit or knock someone or something so that he or it falls down or falls backwards: *She hit him and sent him flying.*

foal [foul] *n* a young horse. – *v* to give birth to a foal: *The mare should foal this week.*

foam [foum] *n* a mass of small bubbles on the surface of liquids *etc*. – *v* to produce foam: *the beer foamed in the glass.*

foam rubber a form of rubber with a sponge-like appearance, used for stuffing chairs *etc*.

fob [fob]: **fob (someone) off with (something)** to get (someone) to accept (something worthless): *He fobbed me off with promises.*

focus ['foukəs] – *pls* **'focuses, foci** ['fousai] – *n* **1** the point at which rays of light meet after passing through a lens. **2** a point to which light, a look, attention *etc* is directed: *She was the focus of everyone's attention.* – *v* – *pt, ptp* **'focus(s)ed** – **1** to adjust (a camera, binoculars *etc*) in order to get a clear picture: *Remember to focus the camera/the picture before taking the photograph.* **2** to direct (attention *etc*) to one point: *The accident focussed public attention on the danger.* **'focal** *adj*.

in, out of focus giving or not giving a clear picture: *These photographs are out of focus.*

fodder ['fodə] *n* food for farm animals.

foe [fou] *n* an enemy: *He fought against the foe.*

foetus, (*Amer*) fetus ['fi:təs] *n* a young human being, animal, bird *etc* in the early stages of development before it is born or hatched.

'**foetal**, (*Amer*) '**fetal** *adj* of a foetus: *in a foetal position.*

fog [fog] *n* a thick cloud of moisture or water vapour in the air which makes it difficult to see: *I had to drive very slowly because of the fog.* – *v* – *pt*, *ptp* **fogged** – (*usu with* **up**) to cover with fog: *Her glasses were fogged up with steam.*

'**foggy** *adj* full of, or covered with, fog: *It is very foggy tonight.*

'**fog-bound** *adj* unable to move or function because of fog: *The plane is fog-bound.*

'**fog-horn** *n* a horn used as a warning to or by ships in fog.

foil[1] [foil] *v* to defeat; to disappoint: *She was foiled in her attempt to become President.*

foil[2] [foil] *n* **1** extremely thin sheets of metal that resemble paper: *silver foil.* **2** a dull person or thing against which someone or something else seems brighter: *She acted as a foil to her beautiful sister.*

foil[3] [foil] *n* a blunt sword with a button at the end, used in the sport of fencing.

fold[1] [fould] *v* **1** to double over (material, paper *etc*): *She folded the paper in half.* **2** to lay one on top of another: *She folded her hands in her lap.* **3** to bring in (wings) close to the body: *The bird folded its wings.* – *n* **1** a doubling of one layer of material, paper *etc* over another: *Her dress hung in folds.* **2** a mark made *esp* on paper *etc* by doing this; a crease: *There was a fold in the page.*

'**folded** *adj*.

'**folder** *n* a cover for keeping loose papers together: *He kept the notes for his speech in a folder.*

'**folding** *adj* that can be folded: *a folding chair.*

fold[2] [fould] *n* a place surrounded by a fence or wall, in which sheep are kept: *a sheep fold.*

foliage ['fouliidʒ] *n* leaves: *This plant has dark foliage.*

folio ['fouliou] – *pl* '**folios** – *n* **1** a sheet of paper folded once. **2** a book in which the pages are made of sheets of paper folded once: *Shakespeare's plays were first printed in folio.*

folk [fouk] *n pl* (*esp Amer* **folks**) people: *The folk in this town are very friendly.* – *adj* (of the traditions) of the common people of a country: *folk customs*; *folk dance*; *folk music.*

folks *n pl* one's family: *My folks all live nearby.*

'**folklore** *n* the study of the customs, beliefs, stories, traditions *etc* of a particular people: *the folklore of the American Indians.*

follow ['folou] *v* **1** to go or come after: *I will follow* (*you*). **2** to go along (a road, river *etc*): *Follow this road.* **3** to understand: *Do*

you follow (*my argument*)? **4** to act according to: *I followed his advice.*

'**follower** *n* a person who follows, *esp* the philosophy, ideas *etc* of another person: *He is a follower of Plato* (= Plato's theories).

'**following** *n* supporters: *He has a great following among the poorer people.* – *adj* **1** coming after: *the following day.* **2** about to be mentioned: *You will need the following things.* – *prep* after; as a result of: *Following his illness, his hair turned white.* – *pron* things about to be mentioned: *You must bring the following – pen, pencil, paper and rubber.*

'**follow-up** *n* further reaction or response: *Was there any follow-up to the letter you wrote to the newspaper?*

follow up 1 to go further in doing something: *The police are following up a clue.* **2** to find out more about (something): *I followed up the news.*

folly ['foli] – *pl* '**follies** – *n* foolishness: *the follies of youth.*

fond [fond] *adj* **1** loving: *fond looks*; *a fond husband.* **2** (of wishes, hopes *etc*) unlikely to be fulfilled: *His fond ambition was to be a film star.* '**fondly** *adv*.

'**fondness** *n* (*esp with* **for**) affection; liking: *her fondness for children.*

fond of having a liking for: *He is very fond of dogs.*

fondle ['fondl] *v* to touch, stroke *etc* affectionately: *He fondled the dog's ears.*

food [fu:d] *n* what living things eat: *Horses and cows eat different food from dogs.*

food centre, food stall a place where, a stall at which, food can be bought.

'**foodstuff** *n* a material used for food: *frozen foodstuffs.*

fool [fu:l] *n* a person without sense or intelligence: *He is such a fool he never knows what to do.* – *v* **1** to deceive: *She completely fooled me with her story.* **2** (*often with* **about** *or* **around**) to act like a fool or playfully: *Stop fooling about!*

'**foolish** *adj* **1** having no sense: *He is a foolish young man.* **2** ridiculous: *He looked very foolish.* '**foolishly** *adv*. '**foolishness** *n*.

'**foolhardy** *adj* taking foolish risks; rash: *He made a foolhardy attempt to climb the mountain in winter.* '**foolhardiness** *n*.

'**foolproof** *adj* unable to go wrong: *His new plan seems completely foolproof.*

make a fool of to make (someone) appear ridiculous or stupid: *He made a real fool of her by promising to marry her and then leaving her when he had spent all her money.*

make a fool of oneself to act in such a way that people consider one ridiculous or stupid: *She made a fool of herself at the party.*

play the fool to act in a foolish manner, *esp* with the intention of amusing other people:

He always played the fool when the teacher left the classroom.

foolscap ['fu:lskap] *n* a large size of paper for writing or printing.

foot [fut] – *pl* **feet** [fi:t] – *n* **1** the part of the leg on which a person or animal stands or walks: *My feet are very sore from walking so far.* **2** the lower part of anything: *at the foot of the hill.* **3** (*pl* often **foot**; *often abbrev* **ft** *when written*) a measure of length equal to twelve inches (30.48 cm): *He is five feet/foot six inches tall; a four-foot wall.*

'**footing** *n* **1** balance: *It was difficult to keep his footing on the narrow path.* **2** foundation: *The business is now on a firm footing.*

'**football** *n* **1** a game played by kicking a large ball: *The children played football*; (*also adj*) *a football fan.* **2** the ball used in this game.

'**foothill** *n* a small hill at the foot of a mountain: *the foothills of the Alps.*

'**foothold** *n* a place to put one's feet when climbing: *to find footholds on the slippery rock.*

'**footlight** *n* (in a theatre) a light which shines on the actors *etc* from the front of the stage.

'**footmark** *n* a footprint: *He left dirty footmarks.*

'**footnote** *n* a note at the botom of a page: *The footnotes referred to other chapters of the book.*

'**footpath** *n* a path or way for walking, not for cars, bicycles *etc*: *You can go by the footpath.*

'**footprint** *n* the mark or impression of a foot: *She followed his footprints through the snow.*

'**footsore** *adj* with painful feet from too much walking: *He arrived, tired and footsore.*

'**footstep** *n* the sound of a foot: *She heard his footsteps on the stairs.*

'**footwear** *n* boots, shoes, slippers *etc*: *He always buys expensive footwear.*

follow in someone's footsteps to do the same as someone has done before one: *When he joined the police force he was following in his father's footsteps.*

foot the bill to be the person who pays the bill.

on foot walking: *She arrived at the house on foot.*

put one's foot down to be firm about something: *I put my foot down and refused.*

put one's foot in it to say or do something stupid: *I really put my foot in it when I asked about his wife – she has just run away with his friend!*

for [fo:] *prep* **1** to be given or sent to: *This letter is for you.* **2** towards; in the direction of: *We set off for London.* **3** through a certain time or distance: *for three hours; for three miles.* **4** in order to have, get, be *etc*: *He asked me for some money; Go for a walk.* **5** in return; as payment: *He paid £2 for his ticket.* **6** in order to be prepared: *He's getting ready for the journey.* **7** representing: *He is the member of parliament for Hull.* **8** on behalf of: *Will you do it for me?* **9** in favour of: *Are you for or against the plan?* **10** because of: *for this reason.* **11** having a particular purpose: *He gave her money for her bus fare.* **12** indicating an ability or an attitude to: *a liking for peace; an ear for music.* **13** as being: *They mistook him for someone else.* **14** considering what is used in the case of: *It is quite warm for January* (=considering that it is January when it is *usu* cold). **15** in spite of: *For all his money, he didn't seem happy.* – *conj* because: *It must be late, for I have been here a long time.*

forage ['forid3] *v* (*often with* **about**) to search thoroughly: *He foraged about in the cupboard; He foraged for food in the cupboard.* – *n* food for horses and cattle.

forbade see **forbid**.

for'bearance [fə'beərəns] *n* patience; control of temper: *She showed great forbearance.*

for'bearing *adj* patient: *a patient and forbearing friend.*

forbears see **forebears**.

forbid [fə'bid] – *pt* **forbade** [fə'bad]: *ptp* **for'bidden** – *v* to tell (someone) not to do something: *She forbade him to go.*

for'bidden *adj* not allowed: *Smoking is forbidden.*

for'bidding *adj* rather frightening: *a forbidding appearance.*

force [fo:s] *n* **1** strength or power that can be felt: *the force of the wind.* **2** a person or thing that has great power: *the forces of Nature.* **3** (*sometimes with* **cap**) a group of men prepared for action: *the police force; the Royal Air Force.* – *v* **1** to make (someone or something) do something, go somewhere *etc*, often against his *etc* will: *He forced me to give him money.* **2** to achieve by strength or effort: *He forced a smile despite his grief.*

forced *adj* done with great effort: *a forced march.*

'**forceful** *adj* powerful: *a forceful argument.*

'**forcefully** *adv.*

'**forces** *n pl* the army, navy and air force considered together: *The Forces played a large part in the parade.*

in, into force in or into operation; working or effective: *The new law is now in force.*

forceps ['fo:seps] *n pl* a medical instrument used for holding things firmly: *a pair of forceps.*

ford [fo:d] *n* a shallow crossing-place in a

river. – *v* to cross (water) on foot *etc*: *They forded the river.*

forearm ['fo:ra:m] *n* the lower part of the arm (between wrist and elbow).

forebears, forbears ['fo:beəz] *n pl* ancestors: *My forebears lived in that castle.*

forecast ['fo:ka:st] – *pt, ptp* **'forecast** *or* **'forecasted** – *v* to tell about (something) before it happens: *He forecast good weather for the next three days.* – *n* a statement about what is going to happen; a prediction: *forecasts about the economy.*

forefathers ['fo:fa:ðəz] *n pl* ancestors: *His forefathers emigrated to America.*

forefinger ['fo:fiŋgə] *n* the finger next to the thumb.

forefront ['fo:frʌnt]: **in the 'forefront** at or in the very front: *in the forefront of the battle.*

foregone ['fo:gon]: **a foregone conclusion** a result that is so obvious that it can be seen before it happens: *It is a foregone conclusion who will win.*

foreground ['fo:graund] *n* the part of a view or picture nearest to the person looking at it: *a landscape, with two horses in the foreground.*

forehand ['fo:hand] *n* in tennis *etc*, (the ability to make) a stroke or shot with the palm of one's hand turned towards the ball: *a strong forehand*; (*also adj*) *a forehand stroke.*

forehead ['forid] *n* the part of the face above the eyebrows and below the hairline; the brow: *Her hair covers her forehead.*

foreign ['forən] *adj* **1** belonging to a country other than one's own: *a foreign passport.* **2** (*with* **to**) not naturally part of: *Anger was foreign to her nature.*

'foreigner *n* **1** a person from another country. **2** an unfamiliar person.

foreleg ['fo:leg] *n* an animal's front leg.

foreman ['fo:mən] – *pl* **'foremen** – *n* the supervisor or leader of a group, *esp* of workmen or a jury: *The foreman here is in charge of twenty workmen.*

foremost ['fo:moust] *adj* most famous or important: *the foremost modern artist.*

forensic [fə'rensik] *adj* of or concerning courts of law: *forensic medicine.*

forerunner ['fo:rʌnə] *n* a person or thing which is a sign of what is to follow: *Penicillin was the forerunner of modern antibiotics.*

foresee [fo:'si:] – *pt* **fore'saw** [-'so:]; *ptp* **fore'seen** – *v* to see or know about before or in advance: *He could foresee the difficulties.*

fore'seeable *adj* able to be foreseen: *in the foreseeable future* (= soon; within a short space of time).

'foresight [-sait] *n* the ability to see in advance what may happen and to plan for it: *She had the foresight to drive carefully in case the roads were icy.*

foreskin ['fo:skin] *n* the skin that covers the end of the penis.

forest ['forist] *n* **1** (a large piece of) land covered with trees. **2** an area of land in which animals, *esp* deer, are kept: *a deer forest.*

'forested *adj* covered with forest.

'forester *n* a person who works in a forest or is involved in forestry.

'forestry *n* (the science of) growing and looking after forests. – *adj*: *a forestry worker.*

foretaste ['fo:teist] *n* a small sample or experience of something before it happens: *This cold weather is just a foretaste of winter.*

foretell [fo:'tel] – *pt, ptp* **fore'told** [-'tould] – *v* to tell (about something) before it has happened: *to foretell the future from the stars.*

forethought ['fo:θo:t] *n* thought about, or concern for, the future: *They acted without sufficient forethought.*

forever *see* **ever.**

foreword ['fo:wə:d] *n* a piece of writing as an introduction at the beginning of a book; a preface: *The foreword was written by a famous scholar.*

to write a **foreword** (not **forward**) to a book.

forfeit ['fo:fit] *n* something that must be given up because one has done something wrong, *esp* in games: *If you lose the game you will have to pay a forfeit.* – *v* to lose (something) because one has done something wrong: *He forfeited our respect by telling lies.* – *adj* forfeited: *His former rights are forfeit now.*

forgave *see* **forgive.**

forge[1] [fo:dʒ] *n* a very hot oven in which metals are melted *etc*; a furnace: *Steel is manufactured in a forge.* – *v* to shape metal by heating and hammering: *He forged a horse-shoe out of an iron bar.*

forge[2] [fo:dʒ] *v* to copy (*eg* a letter or a signature) and pretend that it is genuine, *usu* for illegal purposes: *He forged my signature.*

'forgery – *pl* **'forgeries** – *n* **1** (the crime of) copying pictures, documents, signatures *etc* and pretending they are genuine: *He was sent to prison for forgery.* **2** a picture, document *etc* copied for this reason: *The painting was a forgery.*

forge[3] [fo:dʒ] *v* to move steadily: *they forged ahead with their plans.*

forget [fə'get] – *pt* **forgot** [fə'got]; *ptp* **forgotten** [fə'gotn] – *v* **1** to fail to remember: *He has forgotten my name.* **2** to leave behind accidentally: *She has forgotten her handbag.* **3** to lose control of (oneself), act in an undignified manner: *She forgot herself so far as to criticize her boss.*

for'getful *adj* often forgetting: *She is a very forgetful person*. **for'getfully** *adv*.

forgive [fə'giv] – *pt* **forgave** [fə'geiv]: *ptp* **for'given** – **1** to stop being angry with (someone who has done something wrong): *He forgave her for stealing his watch*. **2** to stop being angry about (something that someone has done): *He forgave her angry words*.

forgiveness [fə'givnis] *n* **1** the act of forgiving: *He showed great forgiveness towards them*. **2** readiness to forgive: *He showed great forgiveness towards them*.

for'giving *adj* ready to forgive (often): *a forgiving person*.

forgot, forgotten *see* **forget**.

fork [fo:k] *n* **1** an instrument with two or more pointed pieces for piercing and lifting things: *We usually eat with a knife, fork and spoon*. **2** the point at which a road, river *etc* divides into two or more branches or divisions: *a fork in the river*. **3** one of the branches or divisions of a road, river *etc* into which the road, river *etc* divides: *Take the left fork (of the road)*. – *v* **1** (of a road, river *etc*) to divide into (*usu* two) branches or divisions: *The main road forks here*. **2** (of a person or vehicle) to follow one of the branches or divisions into which a road has divided: *The car forked left*. **3** to lift or move with a fork: *The farmer forked the hay*.

forked *adj* divided into two branches or divisions: *A snake has a forked tongue*.

fork-lift truck a small power-driven machine with an arrangement of steel prongs which can lift, raise up high and carry heavy packages and stack them where required.

fork out to pay or give *esp* unwillingly: *You have to fork out (money) for so many charities these days*.

forlorn [fə'lo:n] *adj* pitiful; unhappy because left alone: *She seems rather forlorn since he left*. **for'lornly** *adv*.

form¹ [fo:m]] *n* **1** (a) shape; outward appearance: *He saw a strange form in the darkness*. **2** a kind, type or variety: *What form of ceremony usually takes place?* **3** a document containing certain questions, the answers to which must be written on it: *an application form*. **4** a fixed way of doing things: *forms and ceremonies*. **5** a school class: *He is in the sixth form*. – *v* **1** to make; to cause to take shape: *They decided to form a drama group*. **2** to come into existence; to take shape: *An idea slowly formed in his mind*. **3** to organize or arrange (oneself or other people) into a particular order: *The women formed (themselves) into three groups*. **4** to be; to make up: *These lectures form part of the medical course*.

for'mation *n* **1** the act of forming or making: *He agreed to the formation of a music society*. **2** (a) particular arrangement or order: *The planes flew in formation*.

be in good form to be in good spirits or health: *She's in good form after her holiday*.

in the form of having the shape, character, style *etc* of: *He wrote a novel in the form of a diary*.

form² [fo:m] *n* a long, *usu* wooden seat: *The children were sitting on forms*.

formal ['fo:məl] *adj* **1** done *etc* according to a fixed and accepted way: *a formal letter*. **2** suitable or correct for occasions when things are done according to a fixed and accepted way: *You must wear formal dress*. **3** (of behaviour, attitude *etc*) not relaxed and friendly: *formal behaviour*. **4** (of language) exactly correct by grammatical *etc* rules but not conversational: *Her English was very formal*. **5** (of designs *etc*) precise and following a fixed pattern rather than occuring naturally: *formal gardens*. **'formally** *adv*.

for'mality [-'ma-] *n* **1** something which is done for appearance but has little meaning: *The chairman's speech was only a formality*. **2** unrelaxed correctness of behaviour: *His formality made him appear unfriendly*.

format ['fo:mat] *n* shape and size, *eg* that of a book, magazine *etc*.

former ['fo:mə] *adj* of an earlier time: *In former times people did not travel so much*. **'formerly** *adv* in earlier times: *Formerly this large town was a small village*.

the former the first of two things mentioned: *We visited America and Australia, staying longer in the former than in the latter*.

formidable ['fo:midəbl] *adj* **1** rather frightening: *a formidable appearance*. **2** very difficult to overcome: *formidable difficulties*. **'formidably** *adv*.

formula ['fo:mjulə] – *pls* **'formulae** [-li:], **'formulas** – *n* **1** an arrangement of signs or letters used in chemistry, arithmetic *etc* to express an idea briefly: *the formula for water is H_2O*. **2** a recipe or set of instructions for making something: *The shampoo was made to a new formula*.

forsake [fə'seik] – *pt* **forsook** [fə'suk]: *ptp* **for'saken** – *v* to leave alone; to abandon: *He was forsaken by his friends*.

forswear [fo:'sweə] – *pt* **forswore** [fo:'swo:]: *ptp* **forsworn** [fo:'swo:n] – *v* to give up; to stop: *He has forsworn all his bad habits*.

fort [fo:t] *n* a building which is built so that it can be defended against an enemy.

forth [fo:θ] *adv* forward; onward: *They went forth into the desert*.

back and forth first in one direction and then in the other; backwards and forwards:

We had to go back and forth many times before we moved all our furniture to the new house.

forthcoming [fo:θ'kʌmiŋ] *adj* **1** happening or appearing soon: *forthcoming events.* **2** (of a person) open and willing to talk: *She wasn't very forthcoming about her work; not a very forthcoming personality.*

forthright ['fo:θrait] *adj* honest and straightforward: *He is a very forthright young man.*

fortify ['fo:tifai] *v* **1** to prepare (a building, city *etc*) for an attack by strengthening and arming it: *The king fortified the castle against the attacking armies.* **2** to strengthen or enrich (*eg* food, drink): *Sherry is a fortified wine.*

,**fortifi'cation** [-fi-] *n* **1** walls *etc* built to strengthen an army, city, nation *etc* against attack: *Fortifications surrounded the city.* **2** the act of fortifying.

fortitude ['fo:titju:d] *n* courage and endurance: *He showed great fortitude during his long illness.*

fortnight ['fo:tnait] *n* two weeks: *It's a fortnight since I last saw her.*

'**fortnightly** *adj, adv* every fortnight: *a fortnightly visit; He is paid fortnightly.*

fortress ['fo:tris] *n a (usu* large) fort or fortified building.

fortune ['fo:tʃən] *n* **1** whatever happens by chance or (good or bad) luck: *whatever fortune may bring.* **2** a large amount of money: *That ring must be worth a fortune!* '**fortunate** [-nət] *adj* having good fortune; lucky: *It was fortunate that no-one was killed in the accident.* '**fortunately** *adv.*

'**fortune-teller** *n* someone who tells fortunes.

tell (someone's) fortune to foretell what will happen to someone in the future: *The gypsy told my fortune.*

forty ['fo:ti] *n* **1** the number or figure 40. **2** the age of 40. – *adj* **1** 40 in number. **2** aged 40.

'**forties** *n pl* **1** the period of time between one's fortieth and fiftieth birthdays. **2** the range of temperatures between forty and fifty degrees. **3** the period of time between the fortieth and fiftieth years of a century. '**fortieth** *n* **1** one of forty equal parts. **2** (*also adj*) the last of forty (people, things *etc*); the next after the thirty-ninth.

forty- having forty (of something): *a forty-page index.*

'**forty-year-old** *n* a person or animal that is forty years old. – *Also adj.*

forty winks a short sleep: *He always has forty winks after dinner.*

forum ['fo:rəm] *n* **1** any public place in which discussions take place, speeches are made *etc*: *In modern times the television studio is* as much a forum for public opinion as the market-places of ancient Rome used to be. **2** a market-place in ancient Roman cities and towns.

forward ['fo:wəd] *adj* **1** moving on; advancing: *a forward movement.* **2** at or near the front: *The forward part of a ship is called the 'bows'.* – *adv* **1** (*also* '**forwards**) moving towards the front: *A pendulum swings backward(s) and forward(s).* **2** to a later time: *from this time forward.* – *n* (in certain team games, *eg* football, hockey) a player in a forward position. – *v* to send (letters *etc*) on to another address: *I have asked the post office to forward my mail.*

bring forward **1** (*also* **put forward**) to bring to people's attention; to cause to be discussed *etc*: *They will consider the suggestions which you have brought/put forward.* **2** to make to happen at an earlier date; to advance in time: *They have brought forward the date of their wedding by one week.*

fossil ['fosl] *n* the hardened remains of an animal or vegetable found in rock: *Fossils have been found here which may be a million years old.*

'**fossilize, -ise** *v* to change into a fossil: *Time had fossilized the animal remains in the riverbed.*

foster ['fostə] *v* **1** to look after for a period of time; to bring up a child that is not one's own: *She fostered the children for several months.* **2** to encourage or give help to (ideas *etc*): *She fostered the child's talents.* '**foster-brother,** '**foster-sister** *ns* a child that has been fostered in another child's family. '**foster-child** *n* a child fostered by a family. '**foster-parent** ('**foster-father,** '**foster= mother**) *n* a person who looks after a child not his or her own.

fought *see* **fight**.

foul [faul] *adj* **1** (*esp* of smell or taste) causing disgust: *a foul smell.* **2** very unpleasant; nasty: *a foul mess.* – *n* an action *etc* which breaks the rules of a game: *The other team committed a foul.* – *v* **1** to break the rules of a game (against): *He fouled his opponent.* **2** to make dirty, *esp* with faeces: *Dogs often foul the pavement.*

foul play a criminal act, *esp* involving murder: *A man has been found dead and the police suspect foul play.*

found[1] *see* **find**.

found[2] [faund] *v* **1** to start or establish: *The school was founded by the king.* **2** (*with* **on/upon**) to base on: *The story was founded upon fact.* '**founding** *n.*

foun'dation *n* **1** the act of founding: *the foundation of a new university.* **2** the base on which something is built: *First they laid the* *foundations, then they built the walls.* **3** an amount of money to be used for a special purpose or the organization that manages it: *The British Foundation for Cancer Research.*

'founder *n* a person who founds a school, college, organization *etc*: *We commemorate the founder of the school.*

foundry ['faundri] – *pl* **'foundries** – *n* a place where metal or glass is formed by melting and pouring into moulds.

fountain ['fauntin] *n* **1** an often ornamental structure which produces a spring of water that rises into the air: *Rome is famous for its beautifully carved stone fountains.* **2** the water coming from such a structure: *It was so hot that he stood under the fountain to get cool.* **3** a source: *God is the fountain of all goodness.*

fountain pen a kind of pen with a nib and containing a supply of ink which is released as one writes.

four [fo:] *n* **1** the number or figure 4. **2** the age of 4. – *adj* **1** 4 in number. **2** aged 4.

four- having four (of something): *a four-man team.*

fourth *n* **1** one of four equal parts. **2** (*also adj*) the last of four (people, things *etc*); the next after the third.

'foursome *n* a group of four people, *esp* for playing games, *eg* .golf: *We'll play in a foursome.*

'four-year-old *n* a person or animal that is four years old. – *adj* (of a person, animal or thing) that is four years old.

on all fours on hands and knees: *He went up the steep path on all fours.*

fourteen [fo:'ti:n] *n* **1** the number or figure 14. **2** the age of 14. – *adj* **1** 14 in number. **2** aged 14.

fourteen- having fourteen (of something): *a fourteen-volume encyclopaedia.*

four'teenth *n* **1** one of fourteen equal parts. **2** (*also adj*) the last of fourteen (people things *etc*); the next after the thirteenth.

,four'teen-year-old *n* a person or animal that is fourteen years old. – *adj* (of a person, animal or thing) that is fourteen years old.

fowl [faul] – *pls* **fowl, fowls** – *n* a bird, *esp* domestic, *eg* hens, ducks, geese *etc*: *He keeps fowls and a few pigs.*

fox [foks] – *pl* **'foxes** – *n* a type of reddish-brown wild animal which looks like a dog. – *adj*: *fox-fur.* – *v* to puzzle or confuse: *She was completely foxed.*

'foxy *adj* **1** clever in a deceitful way: *He's a foxy fellow.* **2** like a fox: *She had rather foxy features.*

'foxhound *n* a kind of dog trained to chase foxes.

fox terrier a kind of dog formerly trained to drive foxes out of their holes in the ground.

foyer ['foiei, (*Amer*) 'foiər] *n* an entrance hall to a theatre, hotel *etc*: *I'll meet you in the foyer.*

fraction ['frakʃən] *n* **1** a part; not a whole number *eg* ½, ⅔, ⅞ *etc*. **2** a small part: *She has only a fraction of her brother's intelligence.*

'fractional *adj* very small: *a fractional amount.*

fracture ['fraktʃə] *n* a break of anything hard, *esp* a bone: *a fracture of the left thigh-bone.* – *v* to break: *The metal pipes (were) fractured.*

fragile ['fradʒail] *adj* easily broken: *a fragile glass vase.* **fra'gility** [-'dʒi-] *n*.

fragment ['fragmənt] *n* **1** a piece broken off: *The floor was covered with fragments of glass.* **2** something which is not complete: *a fragment of poetry.* – [frag'ment, (*Amer*) 'fragmənt] *v* to break into pieces: *The glass is very strong but will fragment if hit by something sharp.*

'fragmentary *adj* made of pieces; incomplete: *a fragmentary account of what happened.*

fragrant ['freigrənt] *adj* having a sweet smell: *fragrant flowers.*

'fragrance *n* (a) sweet smell: *all the fragrance(s) of the East.*

a fragrant (not flagrant) plant.

frail [freil] *adj* weak, *esp* in health: *a frail old lady.*

'frailty – *pl* **'frailties** – *n* physical weakness or (a) moral failing: *She loved him in spite of his frailties.*

frame [freim] *n* **1** a hard main structure round which something is built or made: *the steel frame of the aircraft.* **2** something made to enclose something: *a picture-frame; a window-frame.* **3** the human body: *He has a slight frame.* – *v* **1** to put a frame around: *to frame a picture.* **2** to act as a frame for: *Her hair framed her face.* **3** to arrange false evidence so as to make (someone) seem guilty of a crime *etc* (*n* **'frame-up**).

'framework *n* the basic supporting structure of anything: *The building will be made of concrete on a steel framework.*

frame of mind mental state: *He is in a strange frame of mind.*

franc [fraŋk] *n* the standard unit of currency in France, Belgium, Switzerland and several other countries, *eg* in some parts of Africa where French is spoken.

franchise ['frantʃaiz] *n* the right to vote: *Women did not get the franchise until the twentieth century.*

Franco- ['fraŋkou] (*as part of a word*) French: *,Franco-'Scottish.*

frank [fraŋk] *adj* saying or showing openly what is in one's mind; honest: *a frank* *person*; *a frank reply*. – *v* to mark a letter by machine to show that postage has been paid. '**frankly** *adv*.

frankfurter ['fraŋkfə:tə] *n* a kind of smoked sausage.

frantic ['frantik] *adj* **1** anxious or very worried: *The frantic mother searched for her child*. **2** wildly excited: *the frantic pace of modern life*. '**frantically** *adv*.

fraternal [frə'tə:nl] *adj* of or like a brother: *a fraternal greeting*. **fra'ternally** *adv*.

fra'ternity – *pl* **fra'ternities** – *n* **1** a company of people who regard each other as equals, *eg* monks. **2** a company of people with the same interest, job *etc*: *the banking fraternity*.

fraud [fro:d] *n* **1** (an act of) dishonesty: *He was sent to prison for fraud*. **2** a person who pretends to be something that he isn't: *That man is not a famous writer, he's a fraud*. '**fraudulent** [-djulənt, (*Amer*) -dʒulənt] *adj* dishonest or intending to deceive: *fraudulent behaviour*. '**fraudulently** *adv*. '**fraudulence** *n*.

fray [frei] *v* (of cloth, rope *etc*) to make or become worn at the ends or edges, so that the threads or fibres come loose: *This material frays easily*.

freak [fri:k] *n* **1** an unusual or abnormal event, person or thing: *A storm as bad as that one is a freak of nature*; (*also adj*) *a freak result*. **2** a person who is wildly enthusiastic about something: *a film-freak*.

freak out to become very excited, *esp* because of having taken drugs (*n* '**freak-out**).

freckle ['frekl] *n* a small brown spot on the skin: *In summer her face was always covered with freckles*. – *v* to cover with small brown spots. '**freckled**, '**freckly** *adjs*.

free [fri:] *adj* **1** allowed to move where one wants; not shut in, tied, fastened *etc*: *The prison door opened, and he was a free man*. **2** not forced or persuaded to act, think, speak *etc* in a particular way: *free speech*; *You are free to think what you like*. **3** (*with* **with**) generous: *He is always free with his money/advice*. **4** frank, open and ready to speak: *a free manner*. **5** costing nothing: *a free gift*. **6** not working or having another appointment; not busy: *I shall be free at five o'clock*. **7** not occupied, not in use: *Is this table free*? **8** (*with* **of** *or* **from**) without or no longer having (*esp* something or someone unpleasant *etc*): *She is free from pain now*; *free of charge*. – *v* – *pt*, *ptp* **freed** – **1** to make or set (someone) free: *He freed all the prisoners*. **2** (*with* **from** *or* **of**) to rid or relieve (someone) of something: *She was able to free herself of her debts by working very hard*.

'**freedom** *n* the state of not being under

control and being able to do whatever one wishes: *The prisoner was given his freedom*.

'**freely** *adv* **1** in a free manner: *to give freely to charity*; *to speak freely*. **2** willingly; readily: *I freely admit it was my fault*.

,**free-for-'all** *n* a contest, debate *etc* in which anyone can take part.

'**freehand** *adj*, *adv* (of a drawing *etc*) (done) without any instruments (*eg* a ruler) to guide the hand.

'**freehold** *adj* (of land, property *etc*) belonging completely to the owner, not just for a certain time.

'**freelance** *n*, *adj* (of or done by) a person who is working on his own, not for any one employer: *a freelance journalist*; *freelance work*. – *v* to work in this way: *He is freelancing now*.

free speech the right to express an opinion freely: *I believe in free speach*.

free trade trade with foreign countries without customs duties, taxes *etc*.

'**freeway** *n* a motorway.

free will the ability to choose and act freely: *He did it of his own free will*.

a free hand freedom to do whatever one likes: *He gave her a free hand with the servants*.

set free to make (someone) free: *The soldiers set the terrorists' prisoners free*.

freeze [fri:z] – *pt* **froze** [frouz]: *ptp* **frozen** ['frouzn] – *v* **1** to make into or become ice: *It's so cold that the river has frozen over*. **2** (of weather) to be at or below freezing-point: *If it freezes again tonight all my plants will die*. **3** to make or be very cold: *If you had stayed out all night in the snow you might have frozen to death* (= died of exposure to cold). **4** to make (food) very cold in order to preserve it: *You can freeze the rest of that food and eat it later*. **5** to make or become stiff, still or unable to move (with fear *etc*): *She froze when she heard the strange noise*. **6** to fix prices, wages *etc* at a certain level: *If the situation does not improve, wages will be frozen again*. – *n* a period of very cold weather when temperatures are below freezing-point: *How long do you think the freeze will last*?

'**freezer** *n* a cabinet for keeping food at, or bringing it down to, a temperature below freezing-point.

'**freezing** *adj* very cold: *This room's freezing*. '**frozen** *adj*.

'**freezing-point** *n* the temperature at which a liquid becomes solid: *The freezing-point of water is 0° centigrade*.

freeze up to stop moving or functioning because of extreme cold: *The car engine froze up*.

freight [freit] *n* **1** goods being carried from place to place: *air-freight*; (*also adj*) *a* *freight train*. **2** the money charged for carrying such goods: *He charged me $100 freight.*

'freighter *n* a ship (or aircraft) that carries freight rather than passengers.

French [frentʃ]: **French fries** [fraiz] potato chips; **French beans*** the long green edible pods of a type of bean.

frenzy ['frenzi] – *pl* **'frenzies** – *n* a state of great excitement, fear *etc*: *She waited in a frenzy of anxiety.* **'frenzied** *adj*. **'frenziedly** *adv*.

frequent ['fri:kwənt] *adj* happening often: *He made frequent journeys.* – [fri'kwent] *v* to visit often: *He used to frequent the George Hotel.*

'frequency – *pl* **'frequencies** – *n* **1** the state of happening often: *The frequency of her visits surprised him.* **2** (in electricity, radio *etc*) the number of waves, vibrations *etc* per second: *At what frequency does the sound occur?* **3** a set wavelength on which radio stations regularly broadcast: *All the radio stations changed their frequencies.* **'frequently** *adv* often: *He frequently arrived late.*

fresco ['freskou] – *pl* **'fresco(e)s** – *n* a picture painted on a wall while the plaster is still wet.

fresh [freʃ] *adj* **1** newly made, gathered, arrived *etc*: *fresh fruit* (= fruit that is not tinned, frozen *etc*); *fresh flowers.* **2** (of people *etc*) healthy; not tired: *You are looking very fresh this morning.* **3** another; different; not already used, begun, worn, heard *etc*: *a fresh piece of paper; fresh news.* **4** (of weather *etc*) cool; refreshing: *a fresh breeze; fresh air.* **5** (of water) without salt: *The swimming-pool has fresh water in it, not sea water.*

'freshen *v* **1** to become fresh or cool: *The wind began to freshen.* **2** (*often with* **up**) to (cause to) become less tired or untidy looking: *I must freshen up before dinner.*

'freshly *adv* newly; recently: *freshly gathered plums; freshly arrived.*

'fresh-water *adj* of inland rivers or lakes; not of the sea: *fresh-water fish.*

fret [fret] – *pt, ptp* **'fretted** – *v* to worry or show anxiety or dicontentment: *She was always fretting about something or other.*

'fretful *adj* cross; discontented: *fretful children.*

friction ['frikʃən] *n* **1** the rubbing together of two things: *The friction between the head of the match and the matchbox causes a spark.* **2** the resistance felt when one object is moved against another (or through liquid or gas): *There is friction between the wheels of a car and the road-surface.* **3** quarrelling; disagreement: *There seems to be some friction between the workmen and the manager.*

Friday ['fraidei] *n* the sixth day of the week, the day following Thursday: *She arrived on Friday*; (*also adj*) *Friday evening.*

fridge [fridʒ] short for **refrigerator**.

friend [frend] *n* **1** someone who knows and likes another person very well: *He is my best friend.* **2** a person who acts in a friendly and generous way to people *etc* he or she does not know: *a friend to animals.*

'friendless *adj* without friends: *alone and friendless.*

'friendly *adj* kind and willing to make friends: *She is very friendly to everybody.*

'friendship *n* **1** the state of being friends: *Friendship is a wonderful thing.* **2** a particular relationship between two friends: *Our friendship grew through the years.*

make friends (with) to start a friendly relationship; to become friends with someone: *The child tried to make friends with the dog.*

frieze [fri:z] *n* a narrow strip around the walls of a room, building *etc* near the top, *usu* decorated with pictures, carving *etc*: *The walls were decorated with a frieze of horses.*

fright [frait] *n* **1** a sudden fear: *the noise gave me a terrible fright.* **2** a person who looks ridiculous: *She looks a fright in those clothes.*

'frighten *v* to make (someone) afraid: *She was frightened by a large dog.* **'frightened** *adj*.

'frightful *adj* **1** terrible or frightening: *I had a frightful experience.* **2** very bad: *He is a frightful liar.* **'frightening** *adj*.

'frightfully *adv* very: *He's frightfully clever.*

take fright to become frightened *usu* suddenly and quickly: *She took fright and ran away.*

frigid ['fridʒid] *adj* **1** cold and unemotional: *He behaves in a frigid manner.* **2** frozen: *the frigid zones of the world* (= the Arctic and Antarctic). **'frigidly** *adv.* **fri'gidity** *n.*

frill [fril] *n* **1** a decorative edging to a piece of cloth, made of a strip of cloth gathered along one side and sewn on: *She sewed a frill along the bottom of the skirt.* **2** (*often in pl*) something unnecessary added as decoration: *the frills of business* (= having expensive dinners, *etc*).

frilled, 'frilly *adjs* decorated with frills: *a frilled curtain; a frilly dress.*

fringe [frindʒ] *n* **1** a border of loose threads on a carpet, shawl *etc*: *Her red shawl has a black fringe.* **2** hair cut to hang over the forehead: *You should have your fringe cut before it covers your eyes.* **3** the outer area; the edge; the part farthest from the main part or centre of something: *on the fringe of the city.* – *v* to make or be a border around: *Trees fringed the pond.*

frisk [frisk] *v* to jump about playfully: *The lambs are frisking in the fields.* **'frisky** *adj.* **'friskily** *adv.*

---

* see illustration on p. 594

fritter ['fritə] v (often with **away**) to throw away or waste gradually: He frittered (away) all his money on gambling.

frivolous ['frivələs] adj not serious; playful: He wasted his time on frivolous pleasures. **'frivolously** adv. **'frivolousness** n.

fri'volity [-'vo-] – pl **fri'volities** – n 1 frivolousness: The frivolity of his behaviour. 2 a frivolous action or thought: I have no time for frivolities.

frizz [friz] v to (cause hair to) form a mass of tight curls: The hairdresser frizzed her hair. **'frizzy** adj (of hair) in very small curls: He had frizzy red hair.

frock [frok] n a woman's or girl's dress: She wore a summer frock.

frog [frog] n a small jumping animal, without a tail, that lives on land and in water. **'frogman** n an underwater swimmer who uses breathing apparatus and flippers.

frolic ['frolik] – pt, ptp **'frolicked** – v (of children young animals etc) to play happily: The puppies frolicked in the garden.

from [from] prep 1 used before the place, thing, person, time etc that is the point at which an action, journey, period of time etc begins: from Europe to Asia; from Monday to Friday; a letter from her father. 2 used to indicate that from which something or someone comes: a quotation from Shakespeare. 3 used to indicate separation: Take it from him. 4 used to indicate a cause or reason: He is suffering from a cold.

front [frʌnt] n 1 the part of anything (intended to be) nearest the person who sees it; usu the most important part of anything: the front of the house; the front of the picture; (also adj) the front page. 2 the foremost part of anything in the direction in which it moves: the front of the ship; (also adj) the front seat of the bus. 3 the part of a city or town that faces the sea: We walked along the (sea) front. 4 (in war) the line of soldiers nearest the enemy: They are sending more soldiers to the front. 5 a boundary separating two masses of air of different temperatures: A cold front is approaching from the Atlantic. 6 an outward appearance: He put on a brave front. 7 a name sometimes given to a political movement: the Popular Front for Liberation. **'frontage** [-tidʒ] n the front part of a building etc. **'frontal** adj from the front: a frontal attack. **at the front of** (standing etc) in the front part of something: at the front of the house; They stood at the front of the crowd. **in front (of)** (placed, standing, moving etc) outside something on its front or forward-facing side: There is a garden in front (of the house).

frontier ['frʌntiə, (Amer) frʌn'tiər] n 1 a boundary between countries: We crossed the frontier; (also adj) a frontier town. 2 the farthest area of land on which people live and work, before the country becomes wild and deserted: Many families went to make a new life on the frontier. 3 the limits or boundaries (of knowledge etc): the frontiers of scientific knowledge.

frost [frost] n 1 frozen dew, vapour etc: The ground was covered with frost this morning. 2 the coldness of weather needed to form ice: There'll be (a) frost tomorrow. – v (often with **over** or **up**) to become covered with frost: The windscreen of my car frosted up last night. **'frosty** adj 1 covered with frost: the frosty countryside. 2 of behaviour, very unfriendly: a frosty manner. **'frostily** adv. **frostbite** n injury caused to the body by very great cold: He was suffering from frostbite in his feet. **'frostbitten** adj.

froth [froθ] n a mass of small bubbles on the top of a liquid etc: Some types of beer have more froth than others. – v to have or produce froth: Mad dogs froth at the mouth. **'frothy** adj 1 containing froth: frothy beer. 2 light, like froth: frothy silk dresses.

frown [fraun] v to make the forehead wrinkle and the eyebrows move down (as a sign of worry, disapproval, deep thought etc): He frowned at her bad behaviour. – n such a movement of the forehead and eyebrows: a frown of disapproval. **frown on/upon** to disapprove of (something): My family frowns (up)on smoking and drinking.

froze, frozen see **freeze**.

fruit [fru:t] n 1 the part of a plant that produces the seed, esp when eaten as food: The fruit of the vine is the grape. 2 a result; something gained as a result of hard work etc: the fruit of his hard work. – v to produce fruit: This tree fruits early. **'fruitful** adj producing (good) results: a fruitful meeting. **fruition** [fru'iʃən] n an actual result; the happening of something that was thought of, hoped for etc: Her dreams came to fruition. **'fruitless** adj useless; with no results: a fruitless attempt. **'fruitlessly** adv. **'fruity** adj of or like fruit: a fruity taste; a fruity drink.

> **fruit** is a collective noun taking a singular verb: Fruit is good for you; The tree bears fruit (not fruits).
> The plural **fruits** is used in talking about different types of fruit: oranges, mangoes and other fruits.

frustrate [frʌ'streit, (Amer) 'frʌstreit] v 1 to make (someone) feel disappointed, useless

Fruits

Key

1 Pomelo	**5** Water-melon	**9** Starfruit
2 Longan	**6** Mango	**10** Avocado
3 Pomegranate	**7** Soursop	**11** Lime
4 Guava	**8** Jack fruit	**12** Lychee

etc: *Staying at home all day frustrated her.*
2 to make useless: *His efforts were frustrated.* **frus'tration** *n.*

frus'strated *adj* **1** disappointed; unhappy; not satisfied: *She is very unhappy and frustrated as a teacher.* **2** unable to have the kind of job, career *etc* that one would like: *Literary critics are often frustrated writers.*

fry[1] [frai] *v* to cook in hot oil or fat: *Shall I fry the eggs or boil them?*

'frying-pan, (*Amer*) **'fry-pan** *n* a shallow pan, *usu* with a long handle, for frying food in.

out of the frying-pan into the fire from a difficult or dangerous situation into a worse one: *His first marriage was unhappy but his second was even more unhappy – it was a real case of out of the frying-pan into the fire.*

fry[2] [frai] *n* a swarm of young, *esp* of fish.
small fry unimportant people or things: *The local politicians are just small fry.*

fudge [fʌdʒ] *n* a type of soft, sugary sweet: *chocolate fudge; Would you like a piece of fudge?*

fuel ['fjuəl] *n* any substance by which a fire, engine *etc* is made to work (*eg* coal, oil, petrol): *The machine ran out of fuel.* – *v* – *pt, ptp* **'fuelled,** (*Amer*) **fueled** – to give or take fuel: *The tanker will leave when it has finished fuelling/being fuelled.*

fugitive ['fjuːdʒətiv] *n* a person who is running away (from the police *etc*): *a fugitive from justice.*

fulfil [ful'fil] – *pt, ptp* **ful'filled** – *v* **1** to carry out or perform (a task, promise *etc*): *He always fulfils his promises.* **2** to satisfy (requirements): *He fulfilled all the requirements for the job.*

ful'filled *adj* (of a person) satisfied, having achieved everything he or she needs to have and to do: *With her family and her career, she is a very fulfilled person.* **ful'filment** *n.*

fulfil begins with **ful-** (not **full-**) and ends with **-fil** (not **-fill**); the past tense is **fulfilled** and present participle **fulfilling**.

full [ful] *adj* **1** holding or containing as much as possible: *My basket is full.* **2** complete: *a full year; a full account of what happened.* **3** (of clothes) containing a large amount of material: *a full skirt.* – *adv* **1** completely: *Fill the petrol tank full; a full-length novel.* **2** exactly; directly: *She hit him full in the face.*

'fully *adv* **1** completely: *He was fully aware of what was happening; fully-grown dogs.* **2** quite; at least: *It will take fully three days.*

,full-'length *adj* **1** complete; of the usual or standard length: *a full-length novel.* **2** down to the feet: *a full-length portrait.*

full moon (the time of) the moon when it

appears at its most complete: *There is a full moon tonight.*

,full-'scale *adj* (of a drawing *etc*) of the same size as the subject: *a full-scale drawing of a flower.*

full stop a written or printed point (.) marking the end of a sentence; a period.

,full-'time *adj, adv* occupying one's working time completely: *a full-time job; She works full-time now.*

fully-fledged *adj* **1** (as in bird) having grown its feathers and ready to fly. **2** fully trained, qualified *etc*: *He's now a fully-fledged teacher.*

full of 1 filled with; containing or holding very much or very many: *The bus was full of people.* **2** completely concerned with: *She rushed into the room full of the news.*

in full completely: *Write your name in full; He paid his bill in full.*

to the full to the greatest possible extent: *to enjoy life to the full.*

fumble ['fʌmbl] *v* to use one's hands awkwardly and with difficulty: *He fumbled with the key; She fumbled about in her bag for her key.*

fume [fjuːm] *n* smoke or vapour which can be seen or smelled: *He smelled the petrol fumes.* – *v* to be very angry whilst trying not to show it: *He was fuming (with rage).*

fun [fʌn] *n* enjoyment; a good time: *They had a lot of fun at the party; Isn't this fun!*

'funny *adj* **1** amusing; making one laugh: *a funny story.* **2** strange; peculiar: *I heard a funny noise.* **'funnily** *adv.*

for fun as a joke; for amusement: *The children threw stones for fun.*

in fun as a joke; not seriously: *I said it in fun.*

make fun of to laugh at (someone, *usu* unkindly): *They made fun of her.*

function ['fʌŋkʃən] *n* a special job, use or duty (of a machine, part of the body, person *etc*): *The function of the brake is to stop the car.* – *v* (of a machine *etc*) to work; to operate: *This typewriter isn't functioning very well.*

'functional *adj* **1** designed to be useful rather than to look beautiful: *functional clothes; a functional building.* **2** able to operate: *It's an old car, but it's still functional.*

fund [fʌnd] *n* **1** a sum of money for a special purpose: *Have you given money to the repair fund?* **2** a store or supply: *He has a fund of funny stories.*

funds *n pl* money ready to spend: *Have you enough funds for your journey?*

fundamental [fʌndə'mentl] *adj* of great importance; essential; basic: *Respect for law and order is fundamental to a peaceful society.* – *n* a basic or essential part of anything: *Learning to read is one of the fundamentals of education.*

,funda'mentally *adv*: *He was fundamentally honest.*

funeral ['fjuːnərəl] *n* the ceremony before the burying or cremation of a dead body: *A large number of people attended the president's funeral*; (*also adj*) *a funeral procession.*

funereal [fjuːˈniəriəl] *adj* mournful; suitable for a funeral: *to speak in funereal tones.*

fungus ['fʌŋgəs] – *pls* **'fungi** [-gai], **'funguses** – *n* any of several kinds of soft spongy plants without any leaves or green part: *edible fungi*; *That tree has a fungus growing on it.*
'fungicide [-fisaid] *n* a substance used to kill fungus.

funk [fʌŋk] *n* (a state of) fear: *He was in a funk over his exam.* – *v* not to do (something) because one is afraid: *She funked the appointment.*

funnel ['fʌnl] *n* **1** a wide-mouthed tube through which liquid can be poured into a narrow bottle *etc*: *You will need a funnel if you are going to pour petrol into that can.* **2** a chimney on a ship *etc* through which smoke escapes.

funnily, funny *etc see* **fun.**

fur [fəː] *n* **1** the thick, short, fine hair of certain animals. **2** the skin(s) of these animals, often used to make or decorate clothes *etc* for people: *a hat made of fur*; (*also adj*) *a fur coat.* **3** a coat, cape *etc* made of fur: *She was wearing her fur.*
furrier ['fʌriə, (*Amer*) 'fəː-] *n* a person who (makes and) sells furs.
'furry *adj* **1** covered with fur: *a furry animal.* **2** like fur: *furry material.*

furious, furiously *see* **fury.**

furl [fəːl] *v* to roll up (a flag, sail or umbrella).

furnace ['fəːnis] *n* a very hot oven or closed-in fireplace for melting iron ore, making steam for heating *etc.*

furnish ['fəːniʃ] *v* **1** to provide (a house *etc*) with furniture: *We spent a lot of money on furnishing our house.* **2** to give (what is necessary); to supply: *They furnished the library with new books.*
'furnished *adj*: *a furnished flat.*
'furnishings *n pl* furniture, equipment *etc*: *The office had very expensive furnishings.*
'furniture [-tʃə] *n* things in a house *etc* such as tables, chairs, beds *etc*: *modern furniture.*

furniture is a collective noun taking a singular verb: *His furniture is rather old.*

furrier *see* **fur.**

furrow ['fɔrou, (*Amer*) 'fəː-] *n* **1** a line cut into the earth by a plough: *The farmer planted potatoes in the furrows.* **2** a line in the skin of the face; a wrinkle: *The furrows in her forehead made her look older.* – *v* to

make furrows in: *Her face was furrowed with worry.* **'furrowed** *adj.*

furry *see* **fur.**

further ['fəːðə] *adv* (*sometimes* **'farther** ['faː-]) at or to a great distance or degree: *I cannot go any further.* – *adv, adj* more; in addition: *I cannot explain further*; *There is no further news.* – *v* to help (something) to proceed or go forward quickly: *He furthered our plans.*
,further'more [-'mɔː] *adv* in addition (to what has been said): *Furthermore, I should like to point out ...*
'furthest *adv* (*also* **'farthest** ['faː-]) at or to the greatest distance or degree: *Who lives furthest away?*

furtive ['fəːtiv] *adj* secretive; avoiding attention: *a furtive action/look.*

fury ['fjuəri] – *pl* **'furies** – *n* very great anger; rage: *She was in a terrible fury.*
'furious *adj* **1** very angry: *She was furious with him about it.* **2** violent: *a furious argument.*
like fury with great effort, enthusiasm *etc*: *She drove like fury.*

fuse[1] [fjuːz] *v* **1** to melt (together) as a result of great heat: *Copper and tin fuse together to make bronze.* **2** (of an electric circuit or appliance) to (cause to) stop working because of the melting of a fuse: *Suddenly all the lights fused*; *She fused all the lights.* – *n* a piece of easily-melted wire included in an electric circuit so that a dangerously high electric current will break the circuit and switch itself off: *She mended the fuse.*
fusion ['fjuːʒən] *n* **1** the act of melting together: *fusion of the metal pieces.* **2** a very close joining of things: *the fusion of his ideas.*

fuse[2] [fjuːz] *n* a piece of material, a mechanical device *etc* which makes a bomb *etc* explode at a particular time: *He lit the fuse and waited for the explosion.*

fuselage ['fjuːzəlaːʒ, (*Amer*) -sə-] *n* the body of an aeroplane: *Repairs were needed to the fuselage.*

fusion *see* **fuse**[1].

fuss [fʌs] *n* unnecessary excitement, worry or activity, often about something unimportant: *Don't make such a fuss.* – *v* to be too concerned with or pay too much attention to (unimportant) details: *She fusses over children.*
'fussy *adj* **1** too concerned with details; too particular; difficult to satisfy: *She is very fussy about her food.* **2** (of clothes *etc*) with too much decoration: *a very fussy hat.*
'fussily *adv.*
make a fuss of to pay a lot of attention to: *He always makes a fuss of his grandchildren.*

futile ['fjuːtail] *adj* useless; having no effect: *a futile attempt.*

fu'tility [-'ti-] *n* uselessness: *He realized the futility of trying to continue his journey.*

future ['fjuːtʃə] *n* **1** (what is going to happen in) the time to come: *He was afraid of what the future might bring*; (*also adj*) *his future wife.* **2** (a verb in) the future tense. – *adj* (of a tense of a verb) indicating an action which will take place at a later time.

in future *adv* after this; from now on: *Don't do that in future.*

fuzz *n* [fʌz] a mass of soft, light material such as fine light hair *etc*: *The peaches were covered with fuzz.*
'fuzzy *adj* **1** covered with fuzz: *fuzzy material.* **2** indistinct; blurred; not clear: *The television picture was fuzzy.* **'fuzzily** *adv.* **'fuzziness** *n.*

Gg

gabble ['gabl] *v* to talk very quickly and not very clearly. – *n* fast, incoherent talk.

gable ['geibl] *n* the triangular part of the side wall of a building between the sloping parts of the roof.
'gabled *adj*: *a gabled roof.*

gad [gad] – *pt, ptp* **'gadded** – **gad about/around** *v* to go around to one place after another (*usu* in order to amuse oneself): *She's forever gadding about now that the children are at school.*

gadget ['gadʒit] *n* a *usu* small tool, machine *etc*: *a useful gadget for loosening bottle lids.*

gaffe [gaf] *n* something which ought to have been said, done *etc*, a blunder.

gag [gag] – *pt, ptp* **gagged** – *v* **1** to prevent (a person) talking or making a noise, by putting something in or over his mouth: *The guards tied up and gagged the prisoners.* **2** to choke and almost be sick. – *n* something which is put in or over a person's mouth to prevent him talking or making a noise.

gage *see* **gauge.**

gaiety, gaily *see* **gay.**

gain [gein] *v* **1** to obtain: *He quickly gained experience.* **2** (*often with* **by** *or* **from**) to get (something good) by doing something: *What have I to gain by staying here?* **3** to have an increase in (something): *He gained strength after his illness.* **4** (of a clock or watch) to go too fast: *This clock gains (four minutes a day).* – *n* **1** an increase (in weight *etc*): *a gain of one kilo.* **2** profits, advantage, wealth *etc*: *His loss was my gain*; *He'd do anything for gain.*

gain ground 1 to make progress. **2** to become more influential: *His views were once unacceptable but are now gaining ground rapidly.*

gain on to get or come closer to (a person, thing *etc* that one is chasing): *Drive faster – the police car is gaining on us.*

gait [geit] *n* (*pl rare*) the way in which a person or animal walks: *the old man's shuffling gait.*

gala ['gaːlə, 'geilə; (*Amer*) 'geilə] *n* **1** an occasion of entertainment and enjoyment out of doors: *a children's gala.* **2** a meeting for certain sports: *a swimming gala.*

galaxy ['galəksi] – *pl* **'galaxies** – *n* **1** a very large group of stars. **2** a large group of famous, impressive *etc* people, things *etc*: *a galaxy of entertainers*; *a galaxy of new cars.*
the Galaxy *see* **the Milky Way** *under* **milk.**

gale [geil] *n* a strong wind: *Many trees were blown down in the gale.*
gale force the speed or strength of a gale: *The winds reached gale force*; (*also adj*) *gale-force winds.*

gall [goːl] *n* **1** a bitter liquid which is stored in the gall bladder. **2** impudence: *He had the gall to say he was my friend after being so rude to me.* – *v* to annoy (a person) very much: *It galls me to think that he is earning so much money.*
gall bladder an organ of the body attached to the liver, in which gall is stored.
'gallstone *n* a small hard object that is sometimes formed in the gall bladder.

gallant ['galənt] **1** *adj* brave: *a gallant soldier.* **2** *adj* which looks splendid or fine: *a gallant ship.* **'gallantly** *adv.*
'gallantry *n* **1** bravery: *He won a medal for gallantry.* **2** politeness and attention to ladies: *The young man was noted for gallantry.*

galleon ['galiən] *n* in former times, a large, *usu* Spanish, sailing-ship.

gallery ['galəri] – *pl* **'galleries** – *n* **1** a large room or building in which paintings, statues *etc* are on show: *an art gallery.* **2** an upper floor of seats in a church, theatre *etc, esp* (in a theatre) the top floor. – *Also adj*: *gallery seats.*

galley ['gali] *n* **1** in former times, a long low ship with one deck, moved by oars (and often sails). **2** a ship's kitchen.

gallon ['galən] *n* a measure for liquids, eight

gallop 205 gargle

pints (in Britain, 4.546 litres; in the US, 3.785 litres).

gallons (of) (*loosely*) a large amount (of something liquid): *The children drank gallons of orange juice.*

gallop ['galəp] *n* (a period of riding at) the fastest pace of a horse: *He took the horse out for a gallop; The horse went off at a gallop.* – *v* **1** (of a horse) to move at a gallop: *The horse galloped round the field.* **2** (*with* **through**) to do, say *etc* (something) very quickly: *He galloped through the work.* **'galloping** *adj* increasing very quickly: *galloping inflation.*

gallows ['galouz] *n sing* a wooden frame on which criminals were hanged.

galore [gə'lɔ:] *adj* (*placed immediately after noun*) in large amounts, numbers: *There are book-shops galore in this town.*

galvanize, -ise ['galvənaiz] *v* **1** to cover (iron or steel) with a thin layer of zinc to prevent it rusting. **2** (*with* **into**) to cause or move (a person) to do something: *The threat of losing their jobs galvanized the men into action.*

gambit ['gambit] *n* **1** a first move in a game, *esp* chess. **2** (*usu* **opening gambit**) a starting remark in a conversation.

gamble ['gambl] *v* to risk losing money on the result of a horse-race *etc.* – *n* (something which involves) a risk: *The whole business was a bit of a gamble.* **'gambler** *n.* **'gambling** *n.*

take a gamble to do something risky in the hope that it will succeed.

gambol ['gambl] – *pt, ptp* **'gambolled,** (*Amer*) **'gamboled** – *v* (*usu* only of lambs) to jump around playfully.

game [geim] *n* **1** an enjoyable activity, which *eg* children play: *a game of pretending.* **2*** a competitive form of activity, with rules: *Football, tennis and chess are games.* **3** a match or part of a match: *a game of tennis; winning (by) three games to one.* **4** (the flesh of) certain birds and animals which are killed for sport: *He's very fond of game;* (*also adj*) *a game bird.* – *adj* brave; willing; ready: *a game old guy; game for anything.* **'gamely** *adv* courageously.

games *n pl* an athletic competition, sometimes with other sports: *the Olympic Games.*

'gamekeeper *n* a person who looks after game.

game point a winning point.

game reserve an area of land set aside for the protection of animals.

game warden a person who looks after a game reserve or, in the US, game.

the game is up the plan or trick has failed or has been found out.

gamma ['gamə] : **gamma rays** a powerful form of radiation.

gammon ['gamən] *n* the meat of the leg of a pig, salted and smoked.

gander ['gandə] *n* a male goose.

gang [gaŋ] *n* **1** a number (of workmen *etc*) working together: *a gang of men working on the railway.* **2** a group (of people), *usu* formed for a bad purpose: *a gang of jewel thieves.*

'gangster *n* a member of a gang of criminals.

gang up on to join or act with a person *etc* against (some other person *etc*).

gang up with to join or act with.

gangling ['gaŋgliŋ] *adj* tall, very thin and *usu* awkward.

gangplank ['gaŋplaŋk] *n* (*also* **'gangway**) a movable bridge by which to get on or off a boat.

gangster *see* **gang**.

gantry ['gantri] – *pl* **'gantries** – *n* a bridge-like structure which supports a crane, railway signals *etc.*

gaol, gaoler *see* **jail, jailer**.

see also **goal**.

gap [gap] *n* a break or open space: *a gap between his teeth.*

gape [geip] *v* to stare with open mouth, *eg* in surprise: *The children gaped at the monkeys.* **'gaping** *adj* wide open: *a gaping hole.*

garage ['gara:ʒ, (*Amer*) gə'ra:ʒ] *n* **1** a building in which a car *etc* is kept: *a house with a garage.* **2** a building where cars are repaired and *usu* petrol, oil *etc* is sold: *He has taken his car to the garage to be repaired.*

garbage ['ga:bidʒ] *n* (*esp Amer*) rubbish. – Also *adj*: *There is a garbage chute at the end of the corridor.*

garbage can (*Amer*) a dustbin.

garbled ['ga:bld] *adj* (of a story *etc*) mixed up: *The child gave a garbled account of the accident.*

garden ['ga:dn] *n* a piece of ground on which flowers, vegetables *etc* are grown: *a small garden at the front of the house;* (*also adj*) *a garden slug.* – *v* to work in a garden, *usu* as a hobby: *The old lady does not garden much.*

'gardener *n* a person who works in, and looks after, a garden.

'gardening *n* the work of looking after a garden: *Gardening is his favourite hobby;* (*also adj*) *gardening clothes/tools.*

'gardens *n sing or pl* a park, *esp* one where animals are kept or special trees or flowers are grown: *zoological/botanical gardens.*

garden party a large (*usu* formal) party, held in the garden of a house *etc.*

gargle ['ga:gl] *v* to wash the throat *eg* with a

Games

Key

1 Squash	2 Table tennis	3 Baseball
4 Tennis	5 Cricket	6 Rugby
		7 Volleyball

soothing liquid, by letting the liquid lie in the throat and breathing out against it.

garish ['geəriʃ] *adj* unpleasantly bright or showy: *His shirts are very garish.* **'garishly** *adv.* **'garishness** *n.*

garland ['ga:lənd] *n* flowers or leaves tied or woven into a circle: *The islanders wore garlands of flowers round their heads.*

garlic ['ga:lik] *n* a plant with a bulb shaped like an onion, which has a strong taste and smell and is used in cooking: *The sauce is flavoured with garlic.*

garment ['ga:mənt] *n* an article of clothing: *This shop sells ladies' garments.*

garnish ['ga:niʃ] *v* to decorate (a dish of food): *Parsley is often used to garnish salads.* – *n* (an) edible decoration added to food.

garret ['garət] *n* a *usu* small and sometimes dark room just under the roof of a house: *He was poor and lived in a garret.*

garrison ['garisn] *n* a number of soldiers, for guarding a fortress, town *etc*. – *Also adj: a garrison town.* – *v* to supply (a town *etc*) with troops to guard it.

garrulous ['garələs] *adj* fond of talking: *a garrulous old man.* **'garrulously** *adv.* **gar'rulity** [-'ru:-], **'garrulousness** *ns.*

gas [gas] *n* **1** a substance like air: *Oxygen is a gas.* **2** any gas which is used for heating, cooking *etc.* **3** a gas which is used by dentists as an anaesthetic. **4** a poisonous or irritating gas used in war *etc*: *The police used tear gas to control the riot.* – *v* – *pt, ptp* **gassed** – to poison or kill (a person or animal) with gas: *He was gassed during World War I.*

gaseous ['gasiəs] *adj* of or like (a) gas: *a gaseous substance.*

'gassy *adj* full of gas: *gassy lemonade.* **'gassiness** *n.*

gas chamber a room in which people are killed by means of gas: *Many people were sent to the gas chamber in World War II.*

gas mask something which is used to cover the face to prevent a person breathing poisonous gas.

gas meter an instrument which measures the amount of gas which is used.

gasoline, gasolene ['gasəli:n] *n* (*Amer: also* **gas**) petrol.

gas station (*Amer*) a petrol station.

'gasworks *n sing* a place where gas is made: *The gasworks is rather an ugly building.*

gash [gaʃ] *n* a deep, open cut or wound: *a gash on his cheek.*

gasolene *etc see* **gas**.

gasp [ga:sp] *n* the sound made by suddenly breathing in, *eg* because of surprise or sudden pain: *a gasp of fear.* – *Also v: He gasped with pain.*

be gasping for to want (something) very much: *I'm gasping for a cigarette.*

gastric ['gastrik] *adj* of the stomach: *a gastric ulcer.*

gastronomic [gastrə'nomik] *adj* of good food: *the gastronomic delights of France.*

gate [geit] *n* (a metal, wooden *etc* doorlike object which closes) the opening in a wall, fence *etc* through which people *etc* pass: *I'll meet you at the park gate(s).*

'gate-crash *v* to enter or go to (a party, meeting *etc*) without being invited or without paying. **'gate-crasher** *n.*

'gate-post *n* a post to which a gate is fixed.

'gateway *n* an opening or entrance into a city *etc*, which contains a gate.

gather ['gaðə] *v* **1** to (cause to) come together in one place: *A crowd of people gathered near the accident.* **2** to learn (from what has been seen, heard *etc*): *I gather you are leaving tomorrow.* **3** to collect or get: *She gathered flowers.* **4** to pull (material) into small folds and stitch together: *She gathered the skirt at the waist.* – *n* a fold in material, a piece of clothing *etc.*

'gathering *n* a meeting of people: *a family gathering.*

gather round to come together around a person, thing *etc*: *Will everyone please gather round?*

gather together to come or bring together, in a group: *He gathered his books and papers together.*

gauche [gouʃ] *adj* awkward and clumsy: *a gauche young woman.*

gaudy ['go:di] *adj* very bright in colour: *a bird's gaudy plumage; gaudy clothes.*

gauge, (*also, esp Amer*) **gage** [geidʒ] *v* **1** to measure (something) very accurately: *They gauged the hours of sunshine.* **2** to estimate, judge: *Can you gauge her willingness to help?* – *n* **1** an instrument for measuring amount, size, speed *etc*: *a petrol gauge.* **2** a standard size (of wire, bullets *etc*): *38 gauge wire.* **3** the distance between the rails of a railway line.

gaunt [go:nt] *adj* (of a person) thin or thin-faced: *a gaunt old woman.* **'gauntness** *n.*

gauze [go:z] *n* thin cloth used *eg* to cover wounds: *a length of gauze;* (*also adj*) *a gauze bandage.*

gave *see* **give**.

gawky ['go:ki] *adj* (of a person) looking clumsy or awkward: *She is tall and gawky.*

gay [gei] *adj* **1** happy or making people happy: *The children were gay and cheerful; gay music.* **2** bright: *gay colours.* **'gaily** *adv.* **gaiety** ['geiəti] *n* **1** (an occasion of) fun or happiness: *They joined in the gaiety.* **2** the state of being gay: *the gaiety of the music.*

gaze [geiz] *v* to look steadily (at) for some

time, *usu* in surprise, out of interest *etc.* –
n a long steady look.

gazelle [gəˈzel] – *pls* **ga'zelles, ga'zelle** – *n* a
type of small antelope.

gazette [gəˈzet] *n* a type of newspaper that has
lists of government notices.

gear [giə] *n* 1 (*usu in pl*) a set of toothed
wheels which act together to carry motion:
a car with automatic gears. 2 a combination
of these wheels, *eg* in a car: *The car is in
first gear.* 3 a mechanism used for a particular purpose: *an aeroplane's landing-gear.*
4 the things needed for a particular job,
sport *etc*: *sports gear.*
'**gearbox** *n* the part of a car *etc* which has
the gears in it.
gear lever/change/stick (*Brit*), **gear shift**
(*Amer*) the apparatus in a car *etc* which is
used to change gear.

geese *see* **goose.**

geisha [ˈgeiʃə] *n* (*often* **geisha girl**) a Japanese
girl trained to entertain (men) by her conversation, dancing *etc.*

gelatine [ˈdʒelətiːn, (*Amer*) -tin] *n* a jelly-like
substance made from hooves, animal bones
etc and used in food.

gem [dʒem] *n* 1 a precious stone *esp* when cut
into a particular shape, *eg* for a ring or
necklace. 2 anything or anyone thought to
be especially good: *This picture is the gem
of my collection.*
'**gemstone** *n* a precious or semi-precious
stone *esp* before it is cut into shape.

†**gender** [ˈdʒendə] *n* any of a number of
classes into which nouns and pronouns can
be divided (*eg* masculine, feminine, neuter).

gene [dʒiːn] *n* any of the basic elements of
heredity, passed from parents to their
offspring: *If the children are red-haired, one
of their parents must have a gene for red
hair.*
genetic [dʒəˈnetik] *adj* of genes or genetics:
a genetic abnormality.
genetics [dʒəˈnetiks] *n sing* the science of
heredity.

general [ˈdʒenərəl] *adj* 1 of, involving *etc* all,
most or very many people, things *etc*: *The
general feeling is that he is stupid*; *His
general knowledge is good although he is not
good at mathematics.* 2 covering a large
number of cases: *a general rule.* 3 without
details: *I'll just give you a general idea of the
plan.* 4 (as part of an official title) chief: *the
Postmaster General.* – *n* in the British army,
(a person of) the rank next below field
marshal: *General Smith.*
'**generalize, -ise** *v* 1 to make a general rule
etc that can be applied to many cases, based
on a number of cases: *He's trying to generalize from only two examples.* 2 to talk
(about something) in general terms: *We

should stop generalizing and discuss each
problem separately.* ,**generali'zation, -s-** *n.*
'**generally** *adv* usually; by most people; on
the whole: *He is generally disliked*; *He
generally wins.*
general election an election in which the
voters in every constituency are involved.
general store a shop that sells a wide range
of goods.
as a general rule usually; in most cases: *As a
general rule, we don't employ unskilled
workers.*
in general usually; in most cases; most of (a
group of people *etc*): *People in general were
not very sympathetic*; *People were in general
not very sympathetic.*
the general public the people of a town,
country *etc*, considered as a group.

generate [ˈdʒenəreit] *v* to cause or produce:
This machine generates electricity; *His suggestions generated a lot of ill-feeling.*
gene'ration *n* 1 one stage in the descent of a
family: *All three generations – children,
parents and grandparents – lived together
quite happily.* 2 people born at about the
same time: *People of my generation all think
the same way about this.*
'**generator** *n* a machine which produces
electricity, gas *etc*: *The hospital has an
emergency generator.*

generic [dʒəˈnerik] *adj* (of a name, term *etc*)
referring to several similar objects *etc*: *'Furniture' is a generic term for chairs, tables etc.*

generous [ˈdʒenərəs] *adj* (*neg* **un-**) 1 willing to
give a lot of money, time *etc* for some
purpose: *a generous giver*; *It is very generous of you to pay for our holiday.* 2 large;
larger than necessary: *a generous sum of
money*; *a generous piece of cake.* 3 kind,
willing to forgive: *Try to be generous and
forgive*; *a person's generous nature/remarks.*
'**generously** *adv.* ,**gene'rosity** [-ˈrosəti] *n.*

genetic, genetics *see* **gene.**

genial [ˈdʒiːniəl] *adj* kindly; friendly; good-
natured: *a genial person.* '**genially** *adv.*
,**geni'ality** [-ˈa-] *n.*

genitive [ˈdʒenitiv] *n* (the case or form of) a
noun, pronoun *etc* which shows possession:
*In John's hat, 'John's' is in the genitive/is a
genitive*; (*also adj*) *the genitive case.*

genius [ˈdʒiːnjəs] – *pl* '**geniuses** – *n* a person
who is very clever: *The new professor of
mathematics has been described as a genius.*

genocide [ˈdʒenəsaid] *n* the deliberate killing
of a race of people.

gent, gents *see* **gentleman.**

genteel [dʒənˈtiːl] *adj* acting, talking *etc* with a
very great (often too great) attention to the
rules of polite behaviour: *She was laughed
at for being too genteel.* **gen'teelly** *adv.*
gen'teelness *n.*

† see Grammatical Notes on pp. 627–632

gentility [dʒən'tiləti] *n* good manners, often to too great an extent: *She was laughed at for her gentility*.

gentle ['dʒentl] *adj* 1 (of people) behaving, talking *etc* in a mild, kindly, pleasant way: *a gentle old lady*; *The doctor was very gentle*. 2 not strong or rough: *a gentle breeze*. 3 (of hills) rising gradually: *a gentle slope*. **'gently** *adv*. **'gentleness** *n*.

gentleman ['dʒentlmən] – *pl* **'gentlemen** – *n* (*abbrev* **gent**) 1 a polite word for a man: *Two gentlemen arrived this morning*. 2 a polite, well-mannered man: *He's a real gentleman*.
'gentlemanly *adj* (of men) polite; well-mannered: *gentlemanly behaviour*.
gents *n* (*usu with* **the**) a public toilet for men: *Where's the nearest gents?*

gently *see* **gentle**.

genuine ['dʒenjuin] *adj* 1 real; not fake or artificial: *a genuine pearl*; *a genuine antique*. 2 honest; sincere: *He shows a genuine desire to improve*.
'genuinely *adv*: *He was genuinely pleased to see her*.

geography [dʒi'ogrəfi] *n* the science that describes the surface of the Earth and its inhabitants: *He is studying geography*.
ge'ographer *n* a person who studies geography.
geographic(al) [dʒiə'grafik(əl)] *adj*: *a geographical study of the area*. **,geo'graphically** *adv*.

geology [dʒi'olədʒi] *n* the science of the history and development of the Earth as shown by rocks *etc*: *He is studying geology*.
geological [dʒiə'lodʒikəl] *adj*: *a geological survey*. **,geo'logically** *adv*.
ge'ologist *n*.

geometry [dʒi'omətri] *n* a branch of mathematics dealing with the study of lines, angles *etc*: *He is studying geometry*.
geometric(al) [dʒiə'metrik(əl)] *adj* made up of lines, circles *etc* and with a regular shape: *a geometrical design on wallpaper*. **,geo'metrically** *adv*.

germ [dʒəːm] *n* 1 a very tiny animal or plant that causes disease: *Disinfectant kills germs*. 2 the small beginning (of anything): *the germ of an idea*.

germinate ['dʒəːmineit] *v* to (cause *eg* a seed to) begin to grow. **,germi'nation** *n*.

gesticulate [dʒe'stikjuleit] *v* to wave one's hands and arms about when speaking: *He gesticulates wildly when he is angry*.

gesture ['dʒestʃə] *n* a movement of the head, hand *etc* to express an idea, *etc*: *The speaker emphasized his words with violent gestures*. – *v* to make a gesture or gestures: *He gestured to her to keep quiet*.

get [get] – *pt* **got** [got]: *ptp* **got**, (*Amer*) **gotten** ['gotn] – *v* 1 to receive or obtain: *I got a*
letter this morning. 2 to bring or buy: *Please get me some food*. 3 to (manage to) move, go, take, put *etc*: *He couldn't get across the river*; *I got the book down from the shelf*. 4 to cause to be in a certain condition *etc*: *You'll get me into trouble*. 5 to become: *You're getting old*. 6 to persuade: *I'll try to get him to go*. 7 to arrive: *When did they get home?* 8 to succeed (in doing) or to happen (to do) something: *I'll soon get to know the neighbours*; *I got the book read last night*. 9 to catch (a disease *etc*): *She got measles last week*. 10 to catch (someone): *The police will soon get the thief*. 11 to understand: *I didn't get the point of his story*.

'getaway *n* an escape: *The thieves made their getaway in a stolen car*; (*also adj*) *a getaway car*.

'get-together *n* an informal meeting.

'get-up *n* clothes, *usu* odd or unattractive: *She wore a very strange get-up at the party*.

be getting on for to be close to (a particular age, time *etc*): *He must be getting on for sixty at least*.

get about 1 (of stories, rumours *etc*) to become well known: *I don't know how the story got about that she was leaving*. 2 to be able to move or travel about, often of people who have been ill: *She didn't get about much after her operation*.

get across to be or make (something) understood: *This is something which rarely gets across to the general public*.

get after to follow: *If you want to catch him, you had better get after him at once*.

get ahead to make progress; to be successful: *If you want to get ahead, you must work hard*.

get along (*often with* **with**) to be friendly or on good terms (with someone): *I get along very well with him*; *The children just cannot get along together*.

get around 1 (of stories, rumours *etc*) to become well known: *I don't know how the story got around that she was getting married*. 2 (of people) to be active or involved in many activities: *He really gets around, doesn't he!*

get around to *see* **get round to**.

get at 1 to reach (a place, thing *etc*): *The farm is very difficult to get at*. 2 to suggest or imply (something): *What are you getting at?* 3 to point out (a person's faults) or make fun of (a person): *He's always getting at me*.

get away 1 to (be able to) leave: *I usually get away (from the office) at four-thirty*. 2 to escape: *The thieves got away in a stolen car*.

get away with to do (something bad) without being punished for it: *Murder is a*

serious crime and one rarely gets away with
it.

get back 1 to move away: *The policeman
told the crowd to get back.* **2** to retrieve: *She
eventually got back the book she had lent
him.*

get by to manage: *I can't get by on such a
small salary.*

get down to make (a person) sad: *Working
in this place really gets me down.*

get down to to begin to work (hard) at: *I
must get down to work tonight, as the exams
start next week.*

get in to send for (a person): *The television
is broken – we'll need to get a man in to
repair it.*

get into 1 to put on (clothes *etc*): *Get into
your pyjamas.* **2** to begin to be in a particular state or behave in a particular way: *He
got into a temper.* **3** to affect strangely: *I
don't know what has got into him* (= I don't
know why he is behaving the way he is).

get nowhere to make no progress: *You'll get
nowhere if you follow his instructions.*

get off 1 to take off or remove (clothes,
marks *etc*): *I can't get my boots off; I'll
never get these stains off* (*my dress*). **2** to
change (the subject which one is talking,
writing *etc* about): *We've rather got off the
subject.*

get on 1 to make progress or be successful:
How are you getting on in your new job? **2** to
work, live *etc* in a friendly way: *We get on
very well together; I get on well with him.*
3 to grow old: *Our doctor is getting on a bit
now.* **4** to put (clothes *etc*) on: *Go and get
your coat on.* **5** to continue doing something: *I must get on, so please don't interrupt
me; I must get on with my work.*

get on at to criticize (a person) continually
or frequently: *My wife is always getting on
at me.*

get out 1 to leave or escape: *No-one knows
how the lion got out.* **2** (of information) to
become known: *I've no idea how word got
out that you were leaving.*

get out of to (help a person *etc* to) avoid
doing something: *I wonder how I can get out
of washing the dishes; How can I get him out
of going to the party?*

get over 1 to recover from (an illness, surprise, disappointment *etc*): *I've got over my
cold now; I can't get over her leaving so
suddenly.* **2** to manage to make (oneself or
something) understood: *We must get our
message over to the general public.* **3** (*with
with*) to do (something one does not want
to do): *I'm not looking forward to this
meeting, but let's get it over* (*with*).

get round 1 to persuade (a person *etc*) to do
something to one's own advantage: *She can
always get round her grandfather by giving

him a big smile.* **2** to solve (a problem *etc*):
We can easily get round these few difficulties.

get (a)round to to manage to (do something): *I don't know when I'll get round to*
(*painting*) *the door.*

get there to succeed or make progress:
*There have been a lot of problems but we're
getting there.*

get through 1 to finish (work *etc*): *We got
through a lot of work today.* **2** to pass (an
examination). **3** to arrive, *usu* with some
difficulty: *The food got through to the fort
despite the enemy's attempts to stop it.* **4** to
make oneself understood: *I just can't get
through to her any more.*

get together to meet: *We usually get together once a week.*

get up 1 to (cause to) get out of bed: *I got
up at seven o'clock; Get John up at seven
o'clock.* **2** to stand up. **3** to increase (*usu*
speed). **4** to arrange, organize or prepare
(something): *We must get up some sort of
celebration for him when he leaves.*

get up to to do (something bad): *He's
always getting up to mischief.*

geyser ['giːzə] *n* **1** an underground spring that
produces and sends out hot water and
steam: *There are geysers in Iceland and New
Zealand.* **2** a small gas or electric water
heater in a bathroom, kitchen *etc*.

ghastly ['gaːstli] *adj* **1** very bad, ugly *etc*: *a
ghastly mistake.* **2** horrible; terrible: *a
ghastly murder; a ghastly experience.* **3** ill;
upset: *I felt ghastly when I had flu.* **'ghastli-
ness** *n*.

ghetto ['getou] – *pl* **'ghetto(e)s** – *n* a (poor)
part of a city *etc* in which a certain group of
people (*esp* immigrants) lives: *Large cities
like New York have many ghettoes.*

ghost [goust] *n* a spirit, *usu* of a dead person:
*Do you believe in ghosts?; Hamlet thought
he saw his father's ghost.*

'ghostly *adj* of or like a ghost or ghosts: *a
ghostly figure.*

give up the ghost to die.

giant ['dʒaiənt] – *fem* **'giantess** – *n* **1** (in fairy
stories *etc*) a huge person: *Jack met a giant
when he climbed the beanstalk.* **2** a person of
unusually great height and size. **3** a person
of very great ability or importance: *Einstein
is one of the giants of twentieth-century
science.* – *adj* of unusually great height or
size: *a giant cod; a giant fern.*

gibber ['dʒibə] *v* to make meaningless noises:
He was gibbering with fear.

'gibberish [-riʃ] *n* nonsense: *His explanations are just gibberish to me.*

*****gibbon** ['gibən] *n* a type of ape with long
arms.

gibe *see* jibe.

giblets ['dʒiblits] *n pl* the eatable parts from
inside a chicken *etc*, *eg* heart and liver.

* see illustration on p. 17

giddy ['gidi] *adj* feeling that one is going to fall over, or that everything is spinning round: *I was dancing round so fast that I felt quite giddy*; *a giddy feeling*. '**giddily** *adv*. '**giddiness** *n*.

gift [gift] *n* **1** something given willingly, *eg* as a present: *a birthday gift*. **2** a natural ability: *She has a gift for music.* – *v* to give or present as a gift: *This painting was gifted by our former chairman.*
'**gifted** *adj* having very great natural ability: *a gifted musician/child.*
gift of the gab the ability to talk fluently and persuasively.

gigantic [dʒai'gantik] *adj* very large: *a gigantic wave.*

giggle ['gigl] *v* to laugh in a nervous or silly way. – *n* a laugh of this kind. '**giggler** *n*.
'**giggly** *adj* giggling often: *a giggly young girl.*

gild [gild] *v* to cover with gilt: *We could gild the frame of that picture.*

gill [gil] *n* **1** one of the openings on the side of a fish's head through which it breathes. **2** a leaf-like structure on the lower side of the top of a mushroom.
gill cover a fold of skin protecting the gills.

gilt [gilt] *n* a gold or gold-like substance: *a tiny vase covered with gilt*; *(also adj)* *a gilt brooch.*
,**gilt-'edged** *adj* safe to invest in and certain to produce interest: *gilt-edged stocks.*

gimmick ['gimik] *n* something used to attract attention to something or someone: *an advertising gimmick.* '**gimmicky** *adj*.

gin [dʒin] *n* a type of alcoholic drink made from grain and flavoured with juniper berries.

ginger ['dʒindʒə] *n* a hot-tasting root which is used as a spice. – *adj* **1** flavoured with ginger. **2** reddish-brown in colour: *a ginger cat.*
ginger ale, ginger beer a type of non-alcoholic drink flavoured with ginger.
'**gingerbread** *n* (a) cake flavoured with treacle and ginger.

gingerly ['dʒindʒəli] *adv* very gently and carefully: *He gingerly moved his injured foot.*

gipsy *see* **gypsy**.

giraffe [dʒi'raːf] – *pls* **gi'raffes, gi'raffe** – *n* an African animal with a very long neck, long legs and spots.

giraffe is spelt with one r and two fs.

girder ['gəːdə] *n* a large beam of steel *etc*, *eg* to support a road or bridge: *The girders of the bridge have collapsed.*

girdle ['gəːdl] *n* a belt or cord worn round the waist: *She wore a girdle round her tunic.*

girl [gəːl] *n* **1** a female child: *Her new baby is a girl.* **2** a young *usu* unmarried woman.
'**girlish** *adj* of or like a girl: *girlish laughter.*
'**girl-friend** *n* a girl or woman who is often in the company of a particular man or boy: *He is taking his girl-friend to the cinema tonight.*
Girl Guide (*also* **Guide**), (*Amer*) **Girl Scout** (*also no caps*) a member of an organization for girls which is aimed at developing character *etc*.

girth [gəːθ] *n* **1** the measurement round a tree, a person's waist *etc*. **2** the strap that holds a saddle on a horse.

gist [dʒist]: **the gist** the main points (of an argument *etc*): *Just give me the gist of what he said.*

give [giv] – *pt* **gave** [geiv]: *ptp* '**given** – *v* **1** to cause to have: *My aunt gave me a book for Christmas*; *Can you give me an opinion on this?* **2** to produce (something): *Cows give milk but horses do not*; *He gave a talk on his travels.* **3** to yield, bend, break *etc*: *This lock looks solid, but it will give under pressure.* **4** to organize (some event *etc*): *We're giving a party next week.* – *n* the ability to yield or bend under pressure: *This chair has a lot of give in it.*
'**given** *adj* **1** stated: *to do a job at a given time.* **2** (*with* **to**) in the habit of (doing) something: *He's given to making stupid remarks.* **3** taking (something) as a fact: *Given that x equals three, x plus two equals five.*
given name (*Amer*) a personal or christian name.
give and take willingness to allow someone something in return for being allowed something oneself.
give away **1** to give *etc* (something) to someone (*eg* because one no longer wants it): *I'm going to give all my money away.* **2** to cause or allow (information *etc*) to become known *usu* accidentally: *He gave away our hiding-place* (*n* '**give-away**: *the lingering smell was a give-away*).
give back to return something: *She gave me back the book that she borrowed last week.*
give in **1** to stop fighting and admit defeat; to yield: *The soldiers were outnumbered and gave in to the enemy.* **2** to hand or bring (something) to someone (often a person in authority): *Do we have to give in our books at the end of the lesson?*
give off to produce: *That fire is giving off a lot of smoke.*
give or take allowing for the addition or subtraction of: *I weigh sixty-five kilos, give or take a little* (=approximately sixty-five kilos).
give out **1** to give, *usu* to several people: *The headmaster's wife gave out the school prizes.* **2** to come to an end: *My patience gave out.* **3** to produce: *The fire gave out a lot of heat.*
give rise to to cause: *This gives rise to a large number of problems.*

give up 1 to stop, abandon: *I must give up smoking*; *They gave up the search.* **2** to stop using *etc*: *You'll have to give up cigarettes*; *I won't give up all my hobbies for you.* **3** to hand over (*eg* oneself or something that one has) to someone else. **4** to devote (time *etc*) to doing something: *He gave up all his time to gardening.* **5** (*often with* **as** *or* **for**) to consider (a person, thing *etc*) to be: *You took so long to arrive that we had almost given you up (for lost).*

give way 1 to stop in order to allow *eg* traffic to pass: *Give way to traffic coming from the right.* **2** to break, collapse *etc* under pressure: *The bridge will give way any day now.* **3** to agree against one's will: *I have no intention of giving way to demands like that.*

glacé ['glasei, (*Amer*) gla'sei] *adj* iced or sugared: *glacé cherries.*

glacier ['glasiə, (*Amer*) 'gleiʃər] *n* a mass of ice, formed from the snow on mountains.

glad [glad] *adj* **1** pleased or happy: *I'm very glad that you are here*; *the glad smiles of the children.*

'**gladden** *v* to make glad: *The news gladdened her.*

'**gladly** *adv*: *I'd gladly help but I have too many other things to do.* '**gladness** *n*.

glad rags a person's best clothes, worn for special occasions: *I'll get my glad rags on for the party.*

gladiator ['gladieitə] *n* in ancient Rome, a man trained to fight with other men or with animals for the amusement of spectators.

glamour, (*Amer*) **glamor** ['glamə] *n* **1** the often false or superficial beauty or charm which attracts: *the glamour of a career in films.* **2** great beauty or charm, achieved with the aid of make-up, beautiful clothes *etc*: *the glamour of film stars.*

'**glamorize, -ise** *v* to make glamorous: *This film attempts to glamorize war.*

'**glamorous** *adj* having glamour. '**glamorously** *adv*.

glance [gla:ns] *v* to look very quickly: *He glanced at the book*; *He glanced over the accounts.* – *n* a brief or quick look: *I had a glance at the books last night.*

'**glancing** *adj* which hits and glances off: *a glancing blow.*

at a glance at once: *I could tell at a glance that something was wrong.*

glance off to hit and bounce off to one side: *The ball glanced off the edge of his bat.*

gland [gland] *n* a part of the body that takes substances from the blood and stores them for use or in order that the body may get rid

of them: *a sweat gland*; *He has swollen glands in his neck.*

'**glandular** [-djulə, (*Amer*) -dʒulər] *adj* of the glands: *glandular fever.*

glare [gleə] *v* **1** to stare fiercely and angrily: *She glared at the little boy.* **2** to shine very brightly, *usu* to an unpleasant extent: *The sun glared down on us as we crossed the desert.* – *n* **1** a fierce or angry look: *a glare of displeasure.* **2** unpleasantly bright light: *the glare of the sun.*

'**glaring** *adj* **1** unpleasantly bright; too bright: *the glaring sun*; *glaring colours.* **2** obvious: *a glaring error.* '**glaringly** *adv*.

glass [gla:s] *n* **1** a hard *usu* breakable transparent substance: *The bottle is made of glass*; (*also adj*) *a glass bottle.* **2** a *usu* tall hollow object made of glass, used for drinking: *There are six glasses on the tray*; *sherry-glasses.* **3** (*also* '**looking-glass**) a mirror. **4** a barometer, or the atmospheric pressure shown by one: *The glass is falling.*

'**glasses** *n pl* spectacles.

'**glassful** *n* the amount that a drinking-glass will hold: *Pour in two glassfuls of water.*

'**glassy** *adj* **1** not showing any expression: *a glassy stare.* **2** like glass: *a glassy sea.* '**glassiness** *n*.

glaze [gleiz] *v* **1** to fit glass into: *to glaze a window.* **2** to cover with glass or a glaze: *The potter glazed the vase.* **3** (of eyes) to become blank or dull. – *n* **1** a glassy coating put on pottery *etc*: *a pink glaze on the grey vase.* **2** a shiny coating *eg* of sugar on fruit *etc*.

'**glazier** [-ziə, (*Amer*) -ʒər] *n* a person who puts glass in window frames *etc*.

gleam [gli:m] *v* to shine faintly: *a light gleaming in the distance.* – *n* **1** a faint glow: *the gleam of her eyes.* **2** a slight sign or amount: *a gleam of hope.*

glean [gli:n] *v* to collect or pick up (news, facts *etc*).

glee [gli:] *n* great delight: *The children shouted with glee when they saw their presents.*

'**gleeful** *adj* '**gleefully** *adv*.

glib [glib] *adj* **1** speaking persuasively but *usu* without sincerity: *The salesman was a very glib talker.* **2** (of a reply *etc*) quick and ready, but showing little thought: *glib excuses.* '**glibly** *adv*.

glide [glaid] *v* **1** to move smoothly and easily: *The dancers glided across the floor.* **2** to travel by or fly a glider. – *n* a gliding movement.

'**glider** *n* a small, light aeroplane which has no engine.

'gliding *n* the flying of gliders: *I enjoy gliding.*

glimmer ['glimə] *v* to shine faintly: *A single candle glimmered in the darkness.* – *n* **1** a faint light. **2** a slight sign or amount: *a glimmer of hope.*

glimpse [glimps] *n* a very brief look: *He caught a glimpse of the burglar.* – *v* to get a brief look at.

glint [glint] *v* to gleam or sparkle: *The windows glinted in the sunlight.* – *n* a gleam or sparkle: *the glint of steel; a glint of anger in her eyes.*

glisten ['glisn] *v* to shine faintly or sparkle: *His skin glistened with sweat.*

glitter ['glitə] *v* to sparkle: *Her diamonds glittered in the light.* – *n* the quality of glittering: *the glitter of her diamonds.*
'glittering *adj: glittering jewels.*

gloat [glout] *v* to look at or think about with wicked pleasure: *He gloated over his rival's failure.*

globe [gloub] *n* **1** (*usu with* **the**) the Earth: *I've travelled to all parts of the globe.* **2** a ball with a map of the Earth on it. **3** an object shaped like a globe: *The chemicals were crushed in a large metal globe.*
'global *adj* affecting the whole world: *War is now a global problem.* **'globally** *adv.*
globular ['globjulə] *adj* shaped like a globe.
'globe-trotter *n* a person who goes sightseeing all over the world. **'globe-trotting** *n.*

gloom [glu:m] *n* **1** a state of not quite complete darkness: *I could not tell the colour of the car in the gloom.* **2** sadness: *The king's death cast a gloom over the whole country.*
'gloomy *adj* **1** sad or depressed: *Don't look so gloomy.* **2** depressing: *gloomy news.* **3** dim; dark: *gloomy rooms.* **'gloominess** *n.*

glory ['glo:ri] – *pl* **'glories** – *n* **1** fame or honour: *glory on the field of battle; He took part in the competition for the glory of the school.* **2** a source of pride, fame *etc*: *This building is one of the many glories of Venice.* **3** the quality of being magnificent: *The sun rose in all its glory.* – *v* to take great pleasure in: *He glories in his work as an architect.*
'glorify [-fai] *v* **1** to make (something) seem better than it is: *That book glorified war.* **2** to praise. **glorifi'cation** [-fi-] *n.*
'glorious *adj* **1** splendid; deserving great praise: *a glorious career/victory.* **2** very pleasant; delightful: *glorious weather; Isn't the sunshine glorious?* **'gloriously** *adv.*

gloss [glos] *n* brightness or shininess on the surface: *Her hair has a lovely gloss;* (*also adj*) *gloss paint.*
'glossary [-səri] – *pl* **'glossaries** – *n* a list of words *etc* with their meanings: *a glossary of technical terms; a Shakespeare glossary.*

'glossy *adj* smooth and shining: *The dog has a glossy coat.* **'glossiness** *n.*

gloss over to try to hide (a mistake *etc*): *He glossed over the fact that he had forgotten the previous appointment by talking about his accident.*

glove [glʌv] *n* a covering for the hand: *a pair of gloves.*
fit like a glove to fit perfectly: *This suit fits like a glove.*

glow [glou] *v* **1** to give out heat or light without any flame: *The coal was glowing in the fire.* **2** to have red cheeks because of heat, cold, emotion *etc*: *The little boy glowed with pride.* – *n* the state of glowing: *the glow of the coal in the fire.*
'glowing *adj: glowing colours.*
'glow-worm *n* a kind of beetle whose tail glows in the dark.

glower ['glauə] *v* to stare angrily: *He glowered at me.*
'glowering *adj* angry; threatening: *a glowering look.* **'gloweringly** *adv.*

glucose ['glu:kous] *n* a kind of sugar found in the juice of fruit.

glue [glu:] *n* a substance used for sticking things together: *That glue will not stick plastic to wood.* – *v* to join (things) with glue.

glum [glʌm] *adj* gloomy and sad: *a glum expression.* **'glumly** *adv.* **'glumness** *n.*

glut [glʌt] *n* too great a supply: *There has been a glut of apples this year.*

glutinous ['glu:tinəs] *adj* sticky, like glue: *glutinous rice.*

glutton ['glʌtən] *n* **1** a person who eats too much: *That child is fat because he is such a glutton.* **2** a person who is always eager for more of something *usu* unpleasant: *He's a glutton for work.*
'gluttony *n* greediness in eating.

glycerin(e) ['glisəri:n, (*Amer*) -rin] *n* a sweet, sticky, colourless liquid.

gnarled [na:ld] *adj* (of trees, branches *etc*) twisted.

gnash [naʃ] *v* to rub (the teeth) together in anger *etc.*

gnat [nat] *n* a very small, *usu* blood-sucking, fly.

gnaw [no:] *v* to bite or chew with a scraping movement: *The dog was gnawing a large bone; The mice have gnawed holes in the walls of this room.*

gnu [nu:] – *pls* **gnus, gnu** – *n* a type of large African antelope.

go [gou] – *3rd pers sing prt* **goes**: *pt* **went** [went]: *ptp* **gone** [gon] – *v* **1** to walk, travel, move *etc*: *He is going across the field; Go straight ahead; When did he go out?* **2** to be sent, passed on *etc*: *Complaints have to go through the proper channels.* **3** to be given, sold *etc*: *The prize goes to John Smith; The* *table went for $100.* **4** to lead to: *Where does this road go?* **5** to visit, to attend: *He goes to school every day; I decided not to go to the movie.* **6** to be destroyed *etc*: *This wall will have to go.* **7** to proceed, be done: *The meeting went very well.* **8** to move away: *I think it is time you were going.* **9** to disappear: *My purse has gone!* **10** to do (some action or activity): *I'm going for a walk; I'm going hiking next week-end.* **11** to fail *etc*: *I think the clutch on this car has gone.* **12** to be working *etc*: *I don't think that clock is going.* **13** to become: *These apples have gone bad.* **14** to be: *Many people in the world regularly go hungry.* **15** to be put: *Spoons go in that drawer.* **16** to pass: *Time goes quickly when you are enjoying yourself.* **17** to be used: *All her pocket-money goes on sweets.* **18** to be acceptable *etc*: *Anything goes in this office.* **19** to make a particular noise: *Dogs go woof, not miaow.* **20** to have a particular tune *etc*: *How does that song go?* **21** to become successful *etc*: *She always makes a party go.* – *n* – *pl* **goes** – **1** an attempt: *I'm not sure how to do it, but I'll have a go.* **2** energy: *She's full of go.*

'going *n* **1** an act of leaving, moving away *etc*: *the comings and goings of the people in the street.* **2** the conditions under which something is done: *Walking was heavy going because of all the mud.* – *adj* **1** successful: *That shop is still a going concern.* **2** in existence at present: *the going rate for typing manuscripts.*

'go-ahead *adj* successful and progressive: *His firm is very go-ahead.* – *n* permission: *We'll start as soon as we get the go-ahead.*

,go-'getter *n* a person with a great deal of energy, ability *etc* who gets what he wants.

,going-'over *n* a study or examination: *He gave the accounts a thorough going-over.*

,goings-'on *n pl* (*usu* strange) happenings or behaviour.

,no-'go *adj* (of a district *etc*) which a person *etc* is not allowed to enter: *a no-go area.*

all go very busy: *It's all go in this office today.*

be going on (for) to be near or close to (a time, age *etc*): *He must be going on (for) eighty.*

be going strong to be successful, healthy *etc*: *Our business/grandfather is still going strong.*

from the word go from the very beginning.

get going to get started: *If you want to finish that job you'd better get going.*

give the go-by to ignore in an unfriendly way: *I think we'll give all his stupid suggestions the go-by.*

go about 1 to (begin to) work at: *I don't*

know the best way to go about the job! **2** (of a ship) to change direction or turn around.

go after 1 to try to win: *He's going after that prize.* **2** to follow or chase: *Go after him and apologize.*

go against 1 to oppose or refuse to act on: *A child should never go against his parents' wishes.* **2** to be unacceptable to: *This goes against my conscience.*

go along 1 to go: *I think I'll go along to that meeting.* **2** to proceed or progress: *Check your work as you go along.*

go along with to agree with: *I'm afraid I can't go along with you on that.*

go around (of stories, rumours *etc*) to be passed from one person to another: *There's a rumour going around that you are leaving.*

go around with to be friendly with: *I don't like the group of friends you're going around with.*

go at 1 to attack: *The little boys went at each other with their fists.* **2** to do with enthusiasm: *He really went at the job of painting the wall.*

go back to return to an earlier time, topic of conversation *etc*: *Let's go back for a minute to what we were talking about earlier.*

go back on to fail to do (something one has promised to do): *I never go back on my promises.*

go by 1 to base an opinion on: *We can't go by what he says.* **2** to be guided by: *I always go by the instructions.*

go down 1 (*with* **well/badly**) to be approved or disapproved of: *The story went down well (with them).* **2** (of a ship) to sink: *They were lost at sea when the ship went down.* **3** (of the sun or moon) to go below the horizon. **4** to be remembered: *Your bravery will go down in history.* **5** (of places) to become less desirable: *This part of town has gone down in the last twenty years.*

go far to be successful: *If you keep on working as hard as this, I'm sure you'll go far.*

go for to attack physically or in words: *The two dogs went for each other as soon as they met.*

go in (of the sun or moon) to become covered by cloud.

go in for 1 to take part in: *I'm not going in for the 1000 metres race.* **2** to do (something) as a hobby, career *etc*: *My son is going in for medicine; She goes in for collecting postcards.*

go into 1 to make a careful study of (something): *We'll need to go into this plan in detail.* **2** to discuss in detail: *I don't want to go into the problems at the moment.*

go off 1 (of a bomb *etc*) to explode: *The little boy was injured when the firework went off in his hand.* **2** (of an alarm) to ring:

When the alarm went off the thieves ran away. **3** to leave: *He went off yesterday.* **4** to begin to dislike: *I've gone off cigarettes.* **5** to become rotten: *That meat has gone off.* **6** to stop working: *The fan has gone off.*

go on 1 to continue: *Go on reading – I won't disturb you.* **2** to talk a great deal, *usu* too much: *She goes on and on about her health.* **3** to happen: *What is going on here?* **4** to base one's investigations *etc* on: *The police had very few clues to go on in their search for the murderer.*

go on at to nag at: *Her mother went on at her for coming home late after the dance.*

go out 1 to become extinguished: *The light has gone out.* **2** to go to parties, concerts, meetings *etc*: *We don't go out as much as we did when we were younger.* **3** to be frequently in the company of (a person, *usu* of the opposite sex): *I've been going out with her for months.*

go over 1 to study or examine carefully: *I want to go over the work you have done before you do any more.* **2** to repeat (a story *etc*): *I'll go over the whole lesson again.* **3** to list: *He went over all her faults.* **4** (of plays, behaviour *etc*) to be received (well or badly): *The play didn't go over at all well the first night.*

go round to be enough for everyone: *Is there enough food to go round?*

go slow (of workers in a factory *etc*) to work less quickly than usual, *eg* as a form of protest.

go steady to have a close friendly relationship with someone of the opposite sex: *My girl-friend and I have been going steady for a year.*

go through 1 to search in: *I've gone through all my pockets but I still can't find my key.* **2** to suffer: *You have no idea what I went through to get this finished in time.* **3** to use up: *We went through a lot of money on holiday.* **4** to complete: *to go through certain formalities.* **5** to be completed: *After long hours of negotiations, the deal went through.*

go through with to finish doing: *I'm going to go through with this in spite of what you say.*

go too far to do something which is so bad as to be unacceptable.

go towards to help to buy *etc*: *The money we collect will go towards a new roof.*

go up 1 to increase in size, value *etc*: *The temperature/price has gone up.* **2** to be built: *There are office blocks going up all over town.*

go up in smoke/flames to catch fire; to be destroyed or damaged by fire *etc*: *The building across the street went up in flames.*

go with 1 to be sold with, be part of *etc*: *The carpets will go with the house.* **2** to look *etc*

well with: *The carpet goes with the wallpaper.*

go without to manage without: *If you can't afford a new dress, you'll have to go without (one).*

keep going to continue doing what one is doing; to survive: *The snow was falling heavily, but we had to keep going; Business is bad at the moment, but we'll manage to keep going.*

make a go (of something) to make a success (of something): *He has never owned a shop before, but I think he'll make a go of it.*

on the go very busy or active: *He's always on the go, from morning to night.*

goad [goud] *v* to urge or force (a person *etc*) to do something by annoying (him *etc*): *I was goaded into being rude to him.* – *n* a sharp-pointed stick used for driving cattle *etc*.

goal [goul] *n* **1** in football, rugby, hockey *etc* the act of kicking, hitting *etc* a ball between the goalposts; the point gained by doing this: *He scored six goals.* **2** an aim or purpose: *My goal in life is to write a book.* '**goalkeeper** *n* a player, *eg* in hockey or football, whose job is to prevent members of the other team from scoring goals. '**goalpost** *n* one of the two upright posts which form the goal in football, rugby, hockey *etc*.

> to score a **goal** (not **gaol**).
> to put a criminal in **gaol** (not **goal**).

goat [gout] *n* an animal of the sheep family, with horns and a long-haired coat.

gobble ['gobl] *v* **1** to swallow food *etc* quickly: *You'll be sick if you keep gobbling your meals like that.* **2** (of turkeys) to make a noise in the throat: *We could hear the turkeys gobbling in the farmyard.*

goblet ['goblit] *n* a drinking-cup with a thin stem: *He served the wine in goblets.*

goblin ['goblin] *n* a mischievous, ugly spirit: *a frightening fairy-story about goblins.*

goby ['goubi] – *pls* '**gobies**, '**goby** – *n* a bony coastal fish with fins that form a sucker by which it clings to rocks.

god [god] *n* **1** (*with cap*) the creator and ruler of the world (in the Christian, Jewish *etc* religions). **2** (*fem* '**goddess**) a supernatural being who is worshipped: *the gods of Greece and Rome.* '**godly** *adj* religious: *a godly man/life.* '**godliness** *n*. '**godchild**, '**goddaughter**, '**godson** *ns* a child who has a godparent or godparents. '**godfather**, '**godmother**, '**godparent** *ns* a person who, at a child's baptism, promises to make sure that the child is brought up according to the beliefs of the Christian church.

'**godsend** *n* a very welcome piece of unexpected good luck: *Your cheque was an absolute godsend.*

godown [gou'daun] *n* in India and East Asia, a warehouse, or a storehouse for goods at a port.

goggle ['gogl] *v* to have wide, staring eyes (*eg* because of surprise): *He goggled at the amount of money he received.*

goggles ['goglz] *n pl* a type of spectacles used to protect the eyes from dust, water *etc*: *Many swimmers wear goggles in the water.*

gold [gould] *n* 1 an element, a precious yellow metal used for making jewellery *etc*: *This watch is made of gold*; (*also adj*) *a gold watch.* 2 coins, jewellery *etc* made of gold. 3 the colour of the metal: *the browns and golds of autumn leaves*; (*also adj*) *a gold carpet.*

'**golden** *adj* 1 of gold or the colour of gold: *golden hair.* 2 (of a wedding anniversary, jubilee *etc*) fiftieth: *They will celebrate their golden wedding* (*anniversary*) *next month.*

'**goldfish** – *pl* '**goldfish** – *n* a small golden-yellow fish often kept as a pet: *The child kept a goldfish in a bowl.*

,**gold-'leaf** *n* gold beaten into a very thin sheet: *a brooch made of gold-leaf.*

gold medal in competitions, the medal awarded as first prize.

'**gold-mine** *n* 1 a place where gold is mined. 2 a source of wealth or profit: *That clothes shop is an absolute gold-mine.*

'**gold-rush** *n* a rush of people to a part of a country where gold has been discovered.

'**goldsmith** *n* a person who makes jewellery, ornaments *etc* of gold.

as good as gold very well-behaved.

golden opportunity a very good opportunity.

golf [golf] *n* a game in which a small white ball is hit across open ground and into small holes by means of golf-clubs: *He plays golf every Sunday.* – *v* to play golf. '**golfing** *n*.

'**golfer** *n* a person who plays golf: *a keen golfer.*

'**golf-club** *n* the long thin stick used to hit the ball in golf: *He bought a new set of golf-clubs.*

golf club a society of people who play golf, or the place where they meet: *the local golf club.*

golf course the place where golf is played.

gondola ['gondələ] *n* 1 a long narrow boat used on the canals of Venice. 2 a kind of safety cage for people who are working on the outside of a tall building to stand in.

gondo'lier [-'liə] *n* a person who rows a gondola.

gone *see* go.

gong [goŋ] *n* a metal plate which, when struck, gives a ringing sound: *a dinner gong.*

good [gud] – *compar* **better** ['betə]: *superl* **best** [best] – *adj* 1 well-behaved; not causing trouble *etc*: *Be good!*; *She's a good baby.* 2 correct, desirable *etc*: *She was a good wife*; *good manners*; *good English.* 3 of high quality: *good food/literature*; *His singing is very good.* 4 skilful; able to do something well: *a good doctor*; *good at tennis*; *good with children.* 5 kind: *You've been very good to him*; *a good father.* 6 helpful; beneficial: *What a good night's sleep!*; *Cheese is good for you.* 7 pleased, happy *etc*: *in a good mood today.* 8 pleasant; enjoyable: *to read a good book*; *Ice-cream is good to eat.* 9 considerable; enough: *a good salary*; *She talked a good deal of nonsense.* 10 suitable: *a good man for the job.* 11 sound, fit: *good health*; *good eyesight*; *a car with good brakes.* 12 sensible: *Can you think of one good reason for doing that?* 13 showing approval: *We've had very good reports about you.* 14 thorough: *a good clean.* 15 well: *I don't feel very good this morning.* – *n* 1 advantage or benefit: *He worked for the good of the poor*; *for your own good*; *What's the good of a broken-down car?* 2 goodness: *I always try to see the good in people.* – *interj* an expression of approval, gladness *etc*.

'**goodness** *n* the state of being good. – *interj* (*also* **my goodness**) an expression of surprise *etc*.

goods *n pl* 1 objects *etc* for sale, products: *leather goods.* 2 articles sent by rail, not road, sea or air: *This station is for passengers and goods*; (*also adj*) *a goods train/station.*

'**goody** – *pl* '**goodies** – *n* (*usu in pl*) any food (*eg* cake, ice-cream) which is particularly enjoyable to eat: *the goodies at a children's party.*

good'bye [-'bai] *interj, n* an expression used when leaving someone: *Goodbye – it was good of you to visit us*; *sad goodbyes.*

good-day, good evening *see* **good morning**.

good-for-'nothing *adj, n* (a person who is) useless or lazy: *That boy's a lazy good-for-nothing* (*rascal*).

good humour kindliness and cheerfulness.

good-'humoured *adj*: *a good-humoured smile.* **good-'humouredly** *adv*.

good-'looking *adj* handsome; attractive: *a good-looking girl*; *He is very good-looking.*

good morning, good afternoon, good-'day, good evening, good night *interjs, ns* words used (depending on the time of day) when meeting or leaving someone: *Good morning, Mrs Brown*; *Good night, everyone – I'm going to bed.*

good-'natured adj pleasant; not easily made angry: a good-natured fellow.

,good'will, good will n 1 the good reputation and trade with customers that a business firm has: We are selling the goodwill along with the shop. 2 friendliness: He has always shown a good deal of goodwill towards us.

good works n pl acts of charity: He is known throughout the city for his good works.

as good as almost: The job's as good as done.

be as good as one's word to keep one's promises.

be up to no good to be doing something wrong: I'm sure he's up to no good.

deliver the goods to do what one has promised to do.

for good (sometimes **for good and all**) permanently: He's not going to France for a holiday – he's going for good.

for goodness' sake an expression of annoyance: For goodness' sake, will you stop that noise!

good for 1 certain to last: These houses are good for another hundred years at least. **2** certain to pay (a sum of money): He's good for $50. **3** certain to cause: That story is always good for a laugh.

good for you, him etc an expression of approval: You've passed your exam – good for you!

Good Friday the Friday before Easter Sunday: Christ was crucified on Good Friday.

good gracious, good heavens expressions of surprise.

goodness gracious, goodness me expressions of surprise.

good old an expression used to show approval etc: Good old Fred! I knew he would help us out.

make good 1 to be successful: Through hard work and ability, he soon made good. **2** to repair or compensate for (loss, damages etc): The damage you caused to my car must be made good.

no good useless; pointless: It's no good crying for help – no-one will hear you; This penknife is no good – the blades are blunt.

put in a good word for to praise or recommend: Put in a good word for me when you see the boss.

take (something) in good part not to be upset, offended or annoyed (eg by a joke, remark etc): John took the jokes about his accident with the pot of paint all in good part.

thank goodness an expression used to show that a person is glad that something is all right: Thank goodness it isn't raining.

to the good richer: After buying and selling some of these paintings, we finished up $500 to the good.

goose [gu:s] – pl **geese** [gi:s] – n a web-footed animal like a duck, but larger: The farmer's wife keeps geese.

'goose-flesh n, **'goosepimples** n pl small bumps on the skin caused by cold or fear.

he etc wouldn't say boo to a goose he etc is very timid.

gooseberry ['guzbəri, (Amer) 'gu:s-] – pl **'gooseberries** – n a round, whiskery, edible green berry.

gore [go:] n blood (esp when it is thick and solid): After the battle, the knight was covered in gore. – v (of an animal) to pierce with its horns, tusks etc: The bull gored the farmer to death.

'gory adj with a lot of blood or bloodshed: a gory battle; a gory tale.

gorge [go:dʒ] n a deep narrow valley: A river ran along the bottom of the gorge. – v to eat greedily until one is full: He gorged himself on fruit at the party.

gorgeous ['go:dʒəs] adj **1** beautiful; splendid: a gorgeous dress; gorgeous plumage; These colours are gorgeous. **2** very pleasant: a gorgeous meal.

gorilla [gə'rilə] n the largest type of ape: Two gorillas have escaped from the zoo.

gory see **gore**.

gosh [goʃ] interj an expression of surprise.

gosling ['gozliŋ] n a young goose.

gospel ['gospəl] n (one of the four descriptions in the Bible of) the life and teaching of Christ: the Gospel according to St Luke; The parable of the sower is in one of the gospels.

gossamer ['gosəmə] n the fine threads made by a spider which float in the air or lie on bushes. – adj like gossamer: a blouse of a gossamer material.

gossip ['gosip] n **1** talk about other people's affairs, not always truthful: I never pay any attention to gossip. **2** a chat: She dropped in for a cup of coffee and a gossip. **3** a person who listens to and passes on gossip: She's a dreadful gossip. – v **1** to pass on gossip. **2** to chat:

'gossipy adj fond of gossiping: gossipy neighbours.

gossip column an article in a newspaper etc containing gossip about famous people.

got, gotten see **get**.

gouge [gaudʒ] v **1** to make (a groove or hole) with a tool: He gouged (out) a hole in the wood. **2** to take or force out: The tyrant gouged out the prisoner's eyes. – n a type of chisel for making grooves etc.

gourd [guəd, (Amer) go:rd] n a type of large fruit, or the plant on which it grows.

gourmet ['guəmei] n a person who enjoys and knows a lot about good food and wines.

govern ['gʌvən] v **1** to rule: The emperor governed (the country) wisely and well. **2** to

government and grammar

government [ˈgʌvəmənt] n 1 the people who rule a country or state: *the British Government*. 2 the way in which a country or state is ruled: *Democracy is one form of government*. 3 the act or process of governing. **governmental** [gʌvnˈmentl] adj.

'**governor** n 1 in the US, the head of a state: *the Governor of Ohio*. 2 a member of the committee of people who govern a school, hospital etc: *He is on the board of governors*. 3 a person who governs a province or colony. '**governorship** n.

gown [gaun] n 1 a woman's dress, esp one of high quality for dances, parties etc. 2 a loose robe worn by clergymen, lawyers, teachers etc.

grab [grab] – pt, ptp **grabbed** – v 1 to seize, grasp or take suddenly: *He grabbed a biscuit*. 2 to get by rough or illegal means: *Many people tried to grab land when oil was discovered in the district*. – n a sudden attempt to grasp or seize: *He made a grab at the boy*.

grab at to try to grasp, seize or take, not necessarily successfully: *He grabbed at the boy; He grabbed at the chance to leave*.

grace [greis] n 1 beauty of form or movement: *The dancer's movements had very little grace*. 2 a sense of what is right: *At least he had the grace to leave after his dreadful behaviour*. 3 a short prayer of thanks for a meal. 4 a delay allowed as a favour: *You should have paid me today but I'll give you a week's grace*. 5 the title of a duke, duchess or archbishop: *Your/His Grace*. 6 mercy: *by the grace of God*. '**graceful** adj having or showing beauty of form or movement: *a graceful dancer*. '**gracefully** adv. '**gracefulness** n.

'**gracious** [-ʃəs] adj 1 kind or polite: *a gracious smile*. 2 (of God) merciful. – interj an exclamation of surprise. '**graciously** adv: *She smiled graciously*. '**graciousness** n.

with (a) good/bad grace (un)willingly: *She accepted his apology with good grace*.

grade [greid] n 1 one level in a scale of qualities, sizes etc: *several grades of sandpaper; a high-grade ore*. 2 (*Amer*) (the pupils in) a class or year at school: *We're in the fifth grade now*. 3 a mark for, or level in, an examination etc: *He always got good grades at school*. 4 (*esp Amer*) the slope of a railway etc; gradient. – v 1 to sort into grades: *to grade eggs*. 2 to move through different stages: *Red grades into purple as blue is added*.

gradation [grəˈdeiʃən] n 1 (one stage or degree in) a series of gradual and successive stages: *There are various gradations of col-*

our between red and purple. 2 the act or process of grading.

make the grade to do as well as necessary: *That new apprentice will never make the grade as a trained mechanic*.

gradient [ˈgreidiənt] n 1 the amount of slope (*eg* of a road, a railway): *a gradient of 1 in 4*. 2 a slope.

gradual [ˈgradjuəl] adj happening gently and slowly: *a gradual rise in temperature*. '**gradually** adv: *His health is gradually improving*.

graduate [ˈgradjueit] v 1 to receive a degree, diploma etc: *He graduated in German and French*. 2 to mark out with regular divisions: *A thermometer is graduated in degrees*. – [-ət] n a person who has been awarded a degree or diploma: *a graduate in French*.

,**gradu'ation** n 1 the act or ceremony of graduating from a college, university etc: *The graduation will be held in the large hall*; (*also adj*) *a graduation ceremony*. 2 a marked division: *the graduations on a thermometer*.

graffiti [grəˈfiːti] n pl or n sing words or drawings scratched or painted on a wall etc.

graft¹ [graːft] v to fix (skin, bone etc) from one part of the body on to or into another part of the body: *The doctor treated her burns by grafting skin from her leg on to her back*. – n a piece of skin, bone etc which is grafted: *a skin graft*.

graft² [graːft] n 1 dishonesty in obtaining profit or good position. 2 hard work.

grain [grein] n 1 a seed of wheat, oats etc. 2 corn in general: *Grain is ground into flour*. 3 a very small, hard particle: *a grain of sand*. 4 the way in which the lines of fibre run in wood, leather etc. 5 a very small amount: *There isn't a grain of truth in that story*.

go against the grain to be against a person's wishes, feelings etc: *It goes against the grain for me to tell lies*.

gram see **gram(me)**.

grammar [ˈgramə] n 1 the rules for forming words and for combining words to form sentences: *He's an expert on French grammar*. 2 a description or collection of the rules of grammar: *Could you lend me your Latin grammar?*; (*also adj*) *a grammar book*. 3 a person's use of grammatical rules: *This essay is full of bad grammar*. **gram'matical** [-ˈma-] adj 1 (neg **un-**) correct according to the rules of grammar: *a grammatical sentence*. 2 of (a) grammar: *a grammatical rule*. **gram'matically** adv.

grammar school 1 a type of secondary school. 2 (*Amer*) a primary school.

grammar ends in **-ar** (not **-er**).

gram(me) [gram] *n* the basic unit of weight in the metric system.

gramophone ['graməfoun] *n* (*Amer* 'phono-graph) the old name for a record-player.

granary ['granəri] – *pl* 'granaries – *n* a store-house for grain.

grand [grand] *adj* 1 splendid; magnificent: *a grand procession.* 2 proud: *She gives herself grand airs.* 3 very pleasant: *a grand day at the seaside.* 4 highly respected: *a grand old man.* – *n* – *pl* grand – a slang term for $1000 or £1000: *I paid five grand for that car.*

grand finale the final act or scene in a show *etc, usu* with all the actors, singers *etc* on the stage.

grand piano a type of piano with a large flat top shaped like a harp.

'grandstand *n* rows of raised seats at a sports ground *etc*: *We watched the sports meeting from the grandstand;* (*also adj*) *grandstand seats; We had a grandstand* (= a very good) *view of the parade.*

grand total the final total; the total of several smaller totals.

grandchild ['grantʃaild], **grand-daughter** ['grandɔːtə], **grandson** ['gransʌn] *ns* the child, daughter or son, of one's son or daughter.

grandad ['grandad] *n* a grandfather.

grand-daughter *see* grandchild.

grandeur ['grandʒə] *n* great and impressive beauty: *the grandeur of the Alps.*

grandfather ['granfaːðə], **grandmother** ['granmʌðə], **grandparent** ['granpeərənt] *ns* the father or mother of one's father or mother.

grandfather clock a clock with a tall *usu* wooden case which stands on the floor.

grandiose ['grandious] *adj* impressive to an excessive or foolish degree: *He produced several grandiose schemes for a holiday resort but no resort was ever built.*

grandmother *see* grandfather.

grandparent *see* grandfather.

grandson *see* grandchild.

granite ['granit] *n, adj* (of) a type of hard *usu* grey or red rock used for building: *buildings of granite: granite hills.*

granny (*pl* 'grannies), **grannie** ['grani] *n* a grandmother: *I have two grannies; Hallo, Granny!*

grant [graːnt] *v* 1 to agree to, to give: *Would you grant me one favour; He granted the man permission to leave.* 2 to agree or admit: *I grant (you) that it was a stupid thing to do.* – *n* money given for a particular purpose: *He was awarded a grant for studying abroad.*

'granted, 'granting (even) if; assuming: *Granted that you are right, we will have to move fast.*

take for granted 1 to assume without check-ing: *I took it for granted that you had heard the story.* 2 to treat casually: *People take electricity for granted until their supply is cut off.*

granule ['granjuːl] *n* a very small particle: *a granule of sugar.* **'granular** *adj.*

'granulated [-lei-] *adj* broken into tiny par-ticles: *granulated sugar.*

grape [greip] *n* a green or black smooth-skinned eatable berry from which wine is made.

'grapevine *n* 1 an informal means of passing news from person to person: *I hear through the grapevine that he is leaving.* 2 a vine.

sour grapes saying or pretending that some-thing is not worth having because one cannot obtain it.

grapefruit ['greipfruːt] – *pls* 'grapefruit, 'grapefruits – *n* (the flesh of) a large yellow-skinned fruit similar to an orange.

graph [graf] *n* a diagram consisting of a line or lines drawn to show changes in some quantity: *a graph of temperature changes.*

'graphic *adj* 1 vivid: *a graphic description of an accident.* 2 of painting, drawing *etc*: *the graphic arts.* **'graphically** *adv.*

graph paper paper covered in small squares used for drawing graphs on.

graphite ['grafit] *n* a form of carbon used in the leads of pencils.

grapple ['grapl] *v* (with **with**) 1 to grasp and fight with: *He grappled with the thief.* 2 to (try to) deal with (a problem *etc*): *He enjoys grappling with riddles.*

grasp [graːsp] *v* 1 to take hold of *esp* by putting one's fingers or arm(s) round: *He grasped the rope; He grasped the opportun-ity to ask for a higher salary.* 2 to under-stand: *I can't grasp what he's getting at.* – *n* 1 a grip with one's hand *etc*: *Have you got a good grasp on that rope?* 2 the ability to understand: *His ideas are quite beyond my grasp.*

'grasping *adj* greedy (*esp* for money): *a grasping old man.*

grass [graːs] *n* 1 the green plant which covers fields, garden lawns *etc.* 2 any species of grass, including also corn and bamboo: *He studies grasses.*

'grassy *adj*: *a grassy bank/slope.*

'grasshopper *n* a type of insect which jumps and which makes a noise by rubbing its wings.

'grassland *n* land covered with grass, used as pasture for animals.

grate[1] [greit] *n* a framework of iron bars for holding a fire in a fireplace.

grate[2] [greit] *v* 1 to rub (cheese, vegetables *etc*) into small pieces by means of a grater. 2 to irritate: *His voice grates on me.*

'grater *n* an instrument with a rough surface on which cheese, vegetables *etc* can be grated.

'grating[1] *adj* (of sounds) unpleasant.

grateful ['greitful] *adj* feeling thankful: *I am grateful to you for your help.*

'gratefully *adv*: *She accepted his offer gratefully.*

gratified ['gratifaid] *adj* pleased: *I was gratified at the response to my letter.*

'gratifying *adj* causing pleasure or satisfaction: *a gratifying result.*

grating[1] *see* **grate**[2].

grating[2] ['greitiŋ] *n* a framework of iron *etc* bars: *a grating in the road.*

gratitude ['gratitju:d] *n* the state of feeling grateful: *I wish there was some way of showing my gratitude for all you have done for me.*

gratuity [grə'tjuəti] – *pl* **gra'tuities** – *n* a small sum of money given as a reward for good service; a tip.

gra'tuitous *adj* 1 (*derog*) done, said *etc* without good reason or excuse or when not wanted: *gratuitous insults.* 2 done, given *etc* without payment: *gratuitous advice.*

gra'tuitously *adv*. **gra'tuitousness** *n*.

grave[1] [greiv] *n* a plot of ground, or the hole dug in it, in which a dead person is buried: *He laid flowers on the grave.*

'gravedigger *n* a person whose job is digging graves.

'gravestone *n* a stone placed at a grave on which the dead person's name *etc* is written.

'graveyard *n* a place where the dead are buried.

grave[2] [greiv] *adj* 1 important: *a grave responsibility*; *grave decisions.* 2 serious, dangerous: *grave news.* 3 serious, sad: *a grave expression.* **'gravely** *adv*.

'gravity ['gra-] *n*: *The gravity of the situation was clear to us all.*

gravel ['gravəl] *n* very small stones: *gravel for the garden path.*

gravity[1] *see* **grave**[2].

gravity[2] ['gravəti] *n* the force which attracts things towards the Earth and causes them to fall to the ground.

gravy ['greivi] – *pl* **'gravies** – *n* (a sauce made from) the juices from meat that is cooking.

gray *see* **grey**.

graze[1] [greiz] *v* (of animals) to eat grass *etc* which is growing.

graze[2] [greiz] *v* 1 to scrape the skin from (a part of the body): *I've grazed my hand on that stone wall.* 2 to touch lightly in passing: *The bullet grazed the car.* – *n* the slight wound caused by grazing a part of the body: *a graze on one's hand.*

grease [gri:s] *n* 1 soft, thick, animal fat. 2 any thick, oily substance: *She put grease on the squeaking hinge.* – *v* to put grease on, over or in: *The mechanic greased the car's axle.*

'greasy *adj* 1 of or like grease: *greasy food.* 2 covered in grease: *greasy hands.* 3 slippery, as if covered in grease: *greasy roads.*

'greasiness *n*.

great [greit] *adj* 1 of a better quality than average; important: *a great writer*; *Churchill was a great man.* 2 very large, larger *etc* than average: *a great crowd of people at the football match.* 3 of a high degree: *Take great care of that book.* 4 very pleasant: *We had a great time at the party.* 5 clever and expert: *John's great at football.*

'greatly *adv*: *I was greatly impressed by her singing.*

'greatness: *her greatness as an athlete.*

great- [greit] separated by one generation more than (an uncle, grandfather *etc*): *A great-uncle is one's father's or mother's uncle*; *a great-grandchild.*

greed [gri:d] *n* a (too) great desire for food, money *etc*: *Eating five cakes is just sheer greed.*

'greedy *adj*. **'greedily** *adv*. **'greediness** *n*.

green [gri:n] *adj* 1 of the colour of growing grass or the leaves of most plants: *a green hat.* 2 not ripe: *green bananas.* 3 without experience: *Only someone as green as you would believe a story like that.* 4 looking as if one is about to be sick; very pale: *He was green with envy* (= very jealous). – *n* 1 the colour of grass or the leaves of plants: *the green of the trees in summer.* 2 something (*eg* paint) green in colour: *I've used up all my green* 3 an area of grass: *a village green.* 4 an area of grass on a golf course with a small hole in the centre.

'greenish *adj* close to green: *a greenish dress.*

greens *n pl* green vegetables: *Children are often told that they must eat their greens.*

'greenfly – *pl* **'greenfly** – *n* a type of small, green insect: *The leaves of this rose tree have been eaten by greenfly.*

'greengrocer *n* a person who sells fruit and vegetables.

'greenhouse *n* a building *usu* of glass, in which plants are grown.

the green light permission to begin: *We can't start until he gives us the green light.*

greet [gri:t] *v* to welcome: *She greeted me when I arrived.*

'greeting *n* friendly words or actions used in welcome.

'greetings *n pl* a friendly message: *Christmas greetings.*

gregarious [gri'geəriəs] *adj* 1 liking the company of other people: *a gregarious person.* 2 (of animals, birds *etc*) living in groups: *Geese are gregarious.*

grenade [grə'neid] *n* a small bomb, *esp* one thrown by hand.

grew *see* **grow**.

grey, (*esp Amer*) **gray** [grei] *adj* 1 of a mixture of colour between black and white: *a grey dress.* 2 grey-haired: *He's turning/going* grey. – n **1** (any shade of) a colour between black and white: *Grey is rather a dull colour.* **2** something grey in colour: *I never wear grey.* – v to become grey or grey-haired.

'**greyish** *adj* close to grey: *a greyish dress.*

greyhound ['greihaund] *n* a breed of dog which can run very fast: *He breeds greyhounds for racing;* (*also adj*) *greyhound racing.*

grid [grid] *n* **1** a set of vertical and horizontal lines drawn on a map. **2** a framework of iron bars.

grief [gri:f] *n* great sorrow or unhappiness: *She was filled with grief at the news of her sister's death.*

'**grief-stricken** *adj* overcome by very great grief: *the grief-stricken widow.*

come to grief to meet disaster; to fail: *The project came to grief.*

grievance ['gri:vəns] *n* a cause or reason for complaint: *a list of grievances.*

grieve [gri:v] *v* **1** to cause to feel great sorrow: *Your wickedness grieves me deeply.* **2** to feel sorrow.

'**grievous** *adj* severe or very bad; *He was found guilty of inflicting grievous bodily harm* (= very serious injuries) *on the old man.*

grill [gril] *v* **1** to cook directly under heat: *to grill the chops.* **2** to question (a person) closely: *The police grilled the man they thought was the murderer.* – n **1** the part of a cooker used for grilling. **2** a frame of metal bars for grilling food on. **3** a dish of grilled food: *a mixed grill.*

grim [grim] *adj* **1** horrible; very unpleasant: *The soldiers had a grim task looking for bodies in the wrecked houses.* **2** angry; fierce-looking: *The boss looks a bit grim this morning.* **3** stubborn, unyielding: *grim determination.* '**grimness** *n.*

'**grimly** *adv*: *He held on grimly to the rope.*

like grim death with great determination.

grime [graim] *n* dirt which is difficult to remove.

'**grimy** *adj*: *grimy buildings.*

grin [grin] – *pt, ptp* **grinned** – v to smile broadly: *The children grinned happily for the photographer.* – n a broad smile.

grin and bear it to put up with something unpleasant without complaining: *He doesn't like his present job but he'll just have to grin and bear it till he finds another.*

grind [graind] – *pt, ptp* **ground** [graund] – v **1** to crush into powder or small pieces: *This machine grinds coffee.* **2** to rub together, *usu* producing an unpleasant noise: *He grinds his teeth.* **3** to rub into or against something else: *He ground his heel into the earth.* – n boring hard work: *Learning vocabulary is a bit of a grind.*

'**grinder** *n* a person or machine that grinds: *a coffee-grinder.*

'**grinding** *adj* **1** with a sound of grinding: *The train came to a grinding stop.* **2** severe: *grinding poverty.*

'**grindstone** *n* a wheel-shaped stone against which knives are sharpened as it turns.

grind down to crush: *She was ground down by poverty.*

grind up to grind into powder or small pieces: *This machine grinds up rocks.*

keep (some)one's nose to the grindstone to (force someone to) work hard, without stopping.

grip [grip] – *pt, ptp* **gripped** – v to take a firm hold of: *He gripped his stick; The speaker gripped* (*the attention of*) *his audience.* – n **1** a firm hold: *He had a firm grip on his stick; He has a very strong grip; in the grip of the storm.* **2** a bag used by travellers: *He carried his sports equipment in a large grip.* **3** understanding: *He has a good grip of the subject.*

'**gripping** *adj* which holds the attention: *a gripping story.*

come to grips with to deal with (a problem, difficulty *etc*).

lose one's grip to lose understanding or control.

grisly ['grizli] *adj* horrible: *a grisly sight.*

gristle ['grisl] *n* a tough, rubbery substance found in meat: *There's too much gristle in this steak.* '**gristly** *adj.*

grit [grit] *n* **1** very small pieces of stone: *She's got a piece of grit in her eye.* **2** courage: *He's got a lot of grit.* – v – *pt, ptp* **gritted** – to keep (the teeth) tightly closed together: *He gritted his teeth to stop himself crying out in pain.*

'**gritty** *adj*: *a gritty substance.*

grizzly ['grizli] – *pl* '**grizzlies** – n (*usu* **grizzly bear**) a large fierce N American bear.

groan [groun] *v* to produce a deep sound (because of pain, unhappiness *etc*): *He groaned when he heard that he had failed his exam; The table was groaning with food* (= there was a great deal of food on it). – n a deep sound: *a groan of despair.*

grocer ['grousə] *n* a person who sells certain kinds of food and household supplies.

'**groceries** *n pl* food *etc* sold in a grocer's shop.

groggy ['grogi] *adj* weak and walking unsteadily: *I'm not seriously hurt – I just feel a bit groggy.* '**grogginess** *n.*

groin [groin] *n* the part of the front of the body where the inner part of the thigh joins the rest of the body.

groom [gru:m] *n* **1** a person who looks after horses: *a groom at the stables.* **2** a bridegroom. – v **1** to clean, brush *etc* a horse's coat: *The horses were groomed for the horse* *show.* **2** to prepare for some task, purpose *etc*: *He's being groomed as a possible successor to our head of department.*

groove [gru:v] *n* a long, narrow cut made in a surface: *the groove in a record.*
grooved *adj*: *grooved edges.*

grope [group] *v* to search for something by feeling with one's hands: *He groped his way through the smoke*; *He groped for the door.*

gross [grous] *adj* **1** very bad: *gross errors/indecency.* **2** vulgar: *gross behaviour/language.* **3** too fat: *a large, gross woman.* **4** total: *The gross weight of a parcel is the total weight of the contents, the box, the wrapping etc.* – *n* the total amount (of several things added together).
'grossly *adv*: *grossly underpaid*; *He behaved grossly.*

grotesque [grə'tesk] *adj* very strange-looking: *a grotesque figure.* **gro'tesquely** *adv.*

grouch [grautʃ] *v* to complain: *He's quite happy in his job although he's always grouching (about it).* – *n* **1** a person who complains. **2** a complaint. **'grouchy** *adj.*

ground[1] *see* grind.

ground[2] [graund] *n* **1** the solid surface of the Earth: *lying on the ground*; *high ground.* **2** a piece of land used for some purpose: *a football ground.* – *v* **1** to base: *His argument is grounded on a series of wrong assumptions.* **2** to (cause a ship to) hit the seabed or shore and remain stuck. **3** to prevent (an aeroplane, pilot) from flying: *All planes have been grounded because of the fog.*
'grounding *n* the teaching of the basic facts of a subject: *a good grounding in mathematics.*
'groundless *adj* without reason: *Your fears are groundless.*
grounds *n pl* **1** the garden or land round a large house *etc*: *the castle grounds.* **2** good reasons: *Have you any grounds for calling him a liar?* **3** the powder which remains in a cup (*eg* of coffee) which one has drunk: *coffee grounds.*
ground floor *the rooms of a building which are at street level*: *My office is on the ground floor*; (*also adj*) *a ground-floor flat.*
groundnut *see* peanut.
'groundwork *n* work done in preparation for beginning a project *etc.*
break new ground to deal with a subject for the first time.
cover ground to deal with a certain amount of work *etc*: *We've covered a lot of ground at this morning's meeting.*
get (something) off the ground to get (a project *etc*) started.
hold one's ground to refuse to move back or retreat when attacked: *Although many were killed, the soldiers held their ground.*
lose ground to (be forced to) move back or

retreat: *The general sent in reinforcements when he saw that his troops were losing ground.*

group [gru:p] *n* **1** a number of persons or things together: *a group of boys.* **2** a group of people who play or sing together: *a pop group*; *a folk group.* – *v* to form into a group or groups: *The children grouped round the teacher.*

grouse[1] [graus] – *pl* **grouse** – *n* a kind of game bird.

grouse[2] [graus] *v* to complain: *He's grousing about his job again.* – *n* a complaint.

grovel ['grovl] – *pt, ptp* **'grovelled,** (*Amer*) **'groveled** – *v* to make oneself (too) humble: *He grovelled before his leader.*

grow [grou] – *pt* **grew** [gru:] : *ptp* **grown** – *v* **1** (of plants) to develop: *Carrots grow well in this soil.* **2** to become bigger, longer *etc*: *My hair has grown too long*; *Our friendship grew as time went on.* **3** to cause or allow to grow: *He has grown a beard.* **4** (with **into**) to change into, in becoming mature: *Your daughter has grown into a beautiful woman.* **5** to become: *It's growing dark.*
'grower *n* a person who grows (plants *etc*): *a tomato-grower.*
grown *adj* adult: *a grown man*; *fully grown.*
growth [-θ] *n* **1** the act or process of growing, increasing, developing *etc*: *the growth of trade unionism.* **2** something that has grown: *a week's growth of beard.* **3** the amount by which something grows: *to measure the growth of a plant.* **4** something unwanted which grows: *a cancerous growth.*
'grown-'up *n* an adult.
grown up mature; adult; fully grown: *Her children are grown up now*; *a grown-up daughter.*
grow on to gradually become liked: *I didn't like the painting at first, but it has grown on me.*
grow up to become an adult: *I'm going to be an engine-driver when I grow up.*

growl [graul] *v* to make a deep, rough sound: *The dog growled angrily (at the postman)*; *He growled out a command.* – *n* a deep, rough sound.

grown, growth *see* grow.

grub [grʌb] *n* **1** the form of an insect after it hatches from its egg: *A caterpillar is a grub.* **2** a slang term for food: *Have we enough grub to eat?* – *v* – *pt, ptp* **grubbed** – to search by digging: *The pigs were grubbing around for roots.*
grubby ['grʌbi] *adj* dirty: *a grubby little boy*; **'grubbiness** *n.*
grudge [grʌdʒ] *v* **1** to be unwilling to do, give *etc*; to do, give *etc* unwillingly: *I grudge wasting time on this, but I suppose I'll have to do it*; *She grudges the dog even the little food she gives it.* **2** to feel resentment

against (someone) for: *I grudge him his success.* – *n* a feeling of anger *etc*: *He has a grudge against me.*
'grudging *adj* said, done *etc* unwillingly: *grudging admiration.* **'grudgingly** *adv.*
gruelling, (*Amer*) **grueling** ['gruəliŋ] *adj* exhausting: *a gruelling race.*
gruesome ['gruːsəm] *adj* horrible: a gruesome sight.
gruff [grʌf] *adj* **1** deep and rough: *a gruff voice.* **2** (seeming to be) unfriendly: *a gruff old man.* **'gruffly** *adv.* **'gruffness** *n.*
grumble ['grʌmbl] *v* **1** to complain in a bad-tempered way: *He grumbled at the way he had been treated.* **2** to make a low and deep sound: *Thunder grumbled in the distance.* – *n* **1** a complaint made in a bad-tempered way. **2** a low, deep sound: *the grumble of thunder.*
grumpy ['grʌmpi] *adj* bad-tempered: *a grumpy old man.*
'grumpily *adv.* **'grumpiness** *n.*
grunt [grʌnt] *v* **1** to make a low, rough sound: *The pigs grunted when the farmer brought their food.* **2** (of people) to say in a way that sounds like grunting: *He grunted that he was too busy to talk to me.* – *n* a low, rough sound: *a grunt of disapproval.*
guarantee [garən'tiː] *n* **1** a statement by the maker that something will work for a certain period of time: *This guarantee is valid for one year.* **2** a thing that makes something likely or certain: *It is no guarantee against failure.* – *v* **1** to act as, or give, a guarantee: *This watch is guaranteed for six months.* **2** to state that something is true, definite *etc*: *I can't guarantee that what he told me is correct.*
guard [gaːd] *v* **1** to protect from danger or attack: *The soldiers were guarding the king/palace.* **2** to prevent (a person) escaping, (something) happening: *The soldiers guarded their prisoners; to guard against mistakes.* – *n* **1** someone who or something which protects: *a guard round the king; a guard in front of the fire.* **2** someone whose job is to prevent (a person) escaping: *There was a guard with the prisoner every hour of the day.* **3** (*Amer* **conductor**) a person in charge of a train. **4** the act or duty of guarding.
'guarded *adj* cautious: *He gave guarded replies.* **'guardedly** *adv.*
guard of honour soldiers or other people who are lined up as an honour to someone important: *A guard of honour greeted the President at the airport.*
keep guard (on): *The soldiers kept guard (on the prisoner).*
off guard unprepared: *He hit me while I was off guard; to catch someone off guard.*

on guard prepared: *Be on your guard against his tricks.*
stand guard to be on duty as a guard: *He stood guard at the gates.*
guardian ['gaːdiən] *n* **1** a person who has the legal right to take care of a child (*usu* an orphan): *He became the child's guardian when her parents died.* **2** a person who looks after something: *the guardian of the castle.*
'guardianship *n* the state or duty of being a guardian.
***guava** ['gwaːvə] *n* the yellow pear-shaped fruit of a type of tropical tree.
guer(r)illa [gə'rilə] *n* a member of a small group of fighters who make sudden attacks on an enemy. – *Also adj*: *guerrilla warfare.*
guess [ges] *v* **1** to say what is likely to be the case: *I'm trying to guess the height of this building; If you don't know the answer, just guess.* **2** (*esp Amer*) to suppose: *I guess I'll have to leave now.* – *n* an opinion, answer *etc* got by guessing: *My guess is that he's not coming.*
'guesswork *n* the process or result of guessing: *I got the answer by guesswork.*
anybody's guess a matter of complete uncertainty: *Who will win is anybody's guess.*
guest [gest] *n* a visitor received in a house, in a hotel *etc*: *We are having guests for dinner;* (*also adj*) *a guest bedroom.*
'guesthouse *n* a small hotel.
guffaw [gə'fɔː] *v* to laugh loudly. – *n* a loud laugh.
guide [gaid] *v* **1** to lead, direct or show the way: *I don't know how to get to your house – I'll need someone to guide me; Your comments guided me in my final choice.* **2** to control the movement of: *The teacher guided the child's hand as she wrote.* – *n* **1** a person who shows the way to go, points out interesting things *etc*: *A guide will show you round the castle.* **2** (*also* **'guidebook**) a book which contains information for tourists: *a guide to Rome.* **3** (*usu with cap*) a Girl Guide. **4** something which informs, directs or influences.
'guidance *n* advice towards doing something: *a project prepared under the guidance of the professor.*
'guideline *n* (*usu in pl*) an indication as to how something should be done.
guided missile an explosive rocket which can be guided to its target by radio waves.
guilder ['gildə] *n* the standard unit of Dutch currency.
guile [gail] *n* the ability to deceive or trick people: *She used guile to get him to propose to her.*
'guileless *adj* honest; sincere: *a guileless person/smile.* **'guilelessly** *adv.* **'guilelessness** *n.*
guillotine ['gilətiːn] *n* **1** in France, an instru-

ment for cutting criminals' heads off. **2** a machine for cutting paper. – *v* to cut the head off (a person) or to cut (paper) with a guillotine.

guilt [gilt] *n* **1** a sense of shame: *a feeling of guilt.* **2** the state of having done wrong: *Fingerprints proved the murderer's guilt.*
'**guilty** *adj* having, feeling, or causing guilt: *The jury found the prisoner guilty; a guilty conscience.* '**guiltiness** *n*.
'**guiltily** *adv*: *He looked at his mother guiltily.*

guinea-pig ['ginipig] *n* **1** a small animal, like a rabbit, with short ears and often kept as a pet. **2** a person used as the subject of an experiment: *He was used as a guinea-pig for the new drug.*

guise [gaiz] *n* a disguised or false appearance: *The thieves entered the house in the guise of workmen.*

guitar [gi'ta:] *n* a type of musical instrument with *usu* six strings. **gui'tarist** *n*.

gulf [gʌlf] *n* a part of the sea with land round a large part of it: *the Gulf of Mexico.*

gull [gʌl] *n* (*often* '**seagull**) a type of web-footed sea bird, *usu* black and white or grey and white.

gullet ['gʌlit] *n* the tube by which food passes from the mouth to the stomach.

gullible ['gʌləbl] *adj* easily tricked or fooled: *He is so gullible that he believes everything you tell him.* ,**gulli'bility** *n*.

gully ['gʌli] – *pl* '**gullies** – *n* a channel worn by running water *eg* on a mountain side.

gulp [gʌlp] *v* **1** to swallow eagerly or in large mouthfuls: *He gulped down a sandwich.* – *n* **1** a swallowing movement: *'There's a ghost out there,' he said with a gulp.* **2** the amount of food swallowed: *a gulp of coffee.*

gum[1] [gʌm] *n* (*usu in pl*) the firm flesh in which the teeth grow.
'**gumboil** *n* a painful swelling in the gum.

gum[2] [gʌm] *n* **1** a sticky juice got from some trees and plants. **2** a glue: *We can stick these pictures into the book with gum.* **3** a type of sweet: *a fruit gum.* **4** chewing-gum: *He chews gum when he is working.* – *v* – *pt, ptp* **gummed** – to glue with gum: *I'll gum this bit on to the other one.*
'**gummy** *adj.* '**gumminess** *n*.

gun [gʌn] *n* any weapon which fires bullets or shells: *He fired a gun at the burglar.*
'**gunboat** *n* a small warship with large guns.
'**gunfire** *n* the firing of guns: *I could hear the sound of gunfire in the distance.*
'**gunman** *n* a criminal who uses a gun to kill or rob people: *Three gunmen robbed the bank.*
'**gunpowder** *n* an explosive in the form of a powder.
'**gunshot** *n* the sound of a gun firing: *I heard a gunshot and a man dropped dead.* – *adj*

caused by the bullet from a gun: *a gunshot wound.*
stick to one's guns to hold to one's position in an argument *etc*: *No-one believed her story but she stuck to her guns.*

guppy ['gʌpi] – *pl* '**guppies** – *n* a small brightly-coloured fresh-water fish, often kept in aquariums.

gush [gʌʃ] *v* **1** (of liquids) to flow out suddenly and in large amounts: *Blood gushed from his wound.* **2** to exaggerate one's enthusiasm *etc* while talking: *The lady kept gushing about her husband's success.* – *n* a sudden flowing (of a liquid): *a gush of water.*
'**gushing** *adj* speaking or spoken in an exaggerated manner: *gushing remarks; She's a bit too gushing for me.* '**gushingly** *adv*.

gust [gʌst] *n* a sudden blast (of wind): *gusts of wind of up to eighty kilometres an hour.*
'**gusty** *adj*: *a gusty day.* '**gustily** *adv*. '**gustiness** *n*.

gusto ['gʌstou] *n* enthusiasm or enjoyment: *The boy was blowing his trumpet with great gusto.*

gut [gʌt] *n* **1** the tube in the lower part of the body through which food passes. **2** a strong thread made from the gut of an animal, used for violin strings *etc*. – *v* – *pt, ptp* '**gutted** – **1** to take the guts out of: *Her job was to gut fish.* **2** to destroy completely, except for the outer frame: *The fire gutted the house.*
guts *n pl* **1** the gut, liver, kidneys *etc*. **2** courage: *He's got a lot of guts.*

gutter ['gʌtə] *n* a channel for carrying away water, *esp* at the edge of a road or roof: *The gutters are flooded with water.*

guy [gai] *n* **1** a man: *I don't know the guy you're talking about.* **2** (*also* '**guy-rope**) a rope which keeps a tent *etc* steady.

gym [dʒim] short for **gymnasium** and **gymnastics**: *The children have gym on Thursdays; (also adj) a gym teacher.*
gym shoe a light, canvas *usu* rubber-soled shoe worn for gymnastics.

gymnasium [dʒim'neiziəm] – *pls* **gym'nasiums, gym'nasia** [-ə] – *n* a building or room with equipment for physical exercise.
gymnast ['dʒimnast] *n* a person who does gymnastics.
gym'nastic [-'nas-] *adj* of gymnastics.
gym'nastics [-'nas-] *n sing* physical exercises *usu* done in a gymnasium with certain types of equipment.

gynaecology, (*Amer*) **gynecology** [gainə'kolədʒi] *n* the branch of medicine which deals with the diseases of women. ,**gynae'cologist** *n*.

gypsy, gipsy ['dʒipsi] – *pls* '**gypsies, 'gipsies** – *n* a member of a race of wandering people. *Also adj*: *a gypsy caravan.*

Hh

ha! [ha, ha:] *interj* an expression of surprise, triumph *etc*: *Ha! I've found it!*
See also **ha! ha!**

habit ['habit] *n* **1** something which a person does usually or regularly: *the habit of going for a walk before bed; an irritating habit of interrupting.* **2** a tendency to do the same things that one has always done: *I did it out of habit.* **3** clothes: *a monk's habit.*
habitual [hə'bitjuəl] *adj* **1** having a habit of doing, being *etc* (something): *He's a habitual drunkard.* **2** done *etc* regularly: *He took his habitual walk before bed.* **habitually** [hə'bitjuəli] *adv.*
from force of habit because one is used to doing (something): *I took the cigarette from force of habit.*
get (someone) into, out of the habit of to make (a person) start or stop doing (something) as a habit: *I wish I could get out of the habit of biting my nails; You must get your children into the habit of cleaning their teeth.*
habitable ['habitəbl] *adj* (*neg* **un-**) (*usu* of buildings) fit to be lived in: *The house is no longer habitable – the roof is collapsing.*
'habitat [-tat] *n* the natural home of an animal or plant: *The Antarctic is the penguin's natural habitat.*
habi'tation *n* the act of living in (a building *etc*): *These houses are not fit for human habitation.*
habitual *see* **habit.**

hack [hak] **1** to cut or chop up roughly: *The butcher hacked the beef into large pieces.* **2** to cut (a path *etc*) roughly: *He hacked his way through the jungle; He hacked (out) a path through the jungle.* – *n* **1** a rough cut made in something: *He marked the tree by making a few hacks on the trunk.* **2** a horse, or in the US, a car, for hire.
'hacking *adj* (of a cough) rough and dry: *He has had a hacking cough for weeks.*
*'hacksaw *n* a saw for cutting metals.
hackles ['haklz] *n pl* the hair on a dog's neck or the feathers on the neck of a farmyard cock.
hackney ['hakni]: **hackney carriage/cab** *n* a taxi.
hacksaw *see* **hack.**
had *see* **have.**
hadn't *see* **have.**
haemoglobin, (*Amer*) **hemoglobin** [hi:mə'gloubin] *n* the oxygen-carrying substance in red blood cells.
haemorrhage, (*Amer*) **hemorrhage** ['heməridʒ] *n* bleeding in large amounts, from damaged blood-vessels.
hag [hag] *n* an ugly old woman.
haggard ['hagəd] *adj* (of a person) looking very tired and thin-faced, because of pain, worry *etc*: *She looked haggard after a sleepless night.*

haggle ['hagl] *v* to argue about the price of something, or about the terms of an agreement.

ha! ha! [ha:'ha:] *interj* an expression of laughter, sometimes used as a sneer: *Ha! ha! That's a good joke!*

hail¹ [heil] *n* **1** small balls of ice falling from the clouds: *There was some hail during the rainstorm last night.* **2** a shower (of things): *a hail of arrows.* – *v* to shower hail: *It was hailing as I drove home.*
'hailstone *n* a ball of hail: *Hailstones battered against the window.*

hail² [heil] *v* **1** to shout to in order to attract attention: *We hailed a taxi; The captain hailed the passing ship.* **2** to greet or welcome (a person, thing *etc*) as something: *His discoveries were hailed as a great step forward in medicine.* – *n* a shout (to attract attention): *Give that ship a hail.* – *interj* an old word of greeting: *Hail, O King!*
hail from to come from or belong to (a place): *He hails from Texas.*

hair [heə] *n* **1** one of the mass of thread-like objects that grow from from the skin: *He brushed the dog's hairs off his jacket.* **2** the mass of these, *esp* on a person's head: *He's got brown hair.*
-haired having (a certain kind of) hair: *a fair-haired girl.*
'hairy *adj* covered in hair or having a lot of hair: *a hairy chest.* **'hairiness** *n.*
'hair('s)-breadth *n* a very small distance: *That knife missed me by a hair's-breadth.*
'hairbrush *n* a brush for arranging and smoothing the hair.
'haircut *n* the act or style of cutting a person's hair: *Go and get a haircut.*
'hair-do – *pls* **'hair-dos, 'hair-do's** – *n* a hairstyle: *I like her new hair-do.*
'hairdresser *n* a person who cuts, washes, styles *etc* a person's hair. **'hairdressing** *n.*
'hair-drier *n* an electrical apparatus which dries a person's hair by blowing hot air over it.
'hairline *n* the line along the forehead where the hair begins to grow.
'hair-oil *n* a scented, oily lotion for smoothing down the hair.
'hairpin *n* a bent wire for keeping a woman's hair in place. – *adj* (of a bend in a road) sharp and U-shaped, *esp* on a mountain or a hill.
'hair-raising *adj* terrifying: *hair-raising stories.*

* see illustration on p. 566

'hairstyle *n* the result of cutting, styling *etc* a person's hair: *a simple hairstyle*.

keep one's hair on to remain calm and not become angry.

let one's hair down to behave in a free and relaxed manner.

make (someone's) hair stand on end to terrify (a person).

(not to) turn a hair to remain calm: *He put his finger in the flame without turning a hair*.

split hairs to worry about unimportant details.

tear one's hair to show great irritation or despair.

half [ha:f] – *pl* **halves** [ha:vz] – *n* **1** one of two equal parts of anything: *He tried to stick the two halves together again*; *half a kilo of sugar*; *a kilo and a half of sugar*; *one and a half kilos of sugar*. **2** one of two equal parts of a game (*eg* in football, hockey) *usu* with a break between them: *Rangers scored three goals in the first half*. – *adj* **1** being (equal to) one of two equal parts (of something): *a half bottle of wine*. **2** being made up of two things in equal parts: *A centaur is a mythical creature, half man and half horse*. **3** not full or complete: *a half smile*. – *adv* **1** to the extent of one half: *This cup is only half full*; *It's half empty*. **2** almost; partly: *I'm half hoping he won't come*; *half dead from hunger*.

half-: *a half-dozen*; *a half-kilo of tea*.

halve [ha:v] *v* **1** to divide (something) into two equal parts: *He halved the apple*. **2** to make half as great as before; to reduce by half: *By going away early in the year, we nearly halved the cost of our holiday*.

half-and-'half *adv, adj* in equal parts: *We can split the costs between us half-and-half*.

'half-back *n* in football, hockey *etc*, (a player in) a position directly behind the forwards.

'half-brother, 'half-sister *ns* a brother or sister by one parent only: *My father has been married twice, and I have two half-brothers*.

'half-caste *n* a person whose father and mother are of different races, *esp* white and black.

half-'hearted *adj* not eager; done without enthusiasm: *a half-hearted cheer/attempt*.

half-'heartedly *adv*. **half-'heartedness** *n*.

half-'holiday *n* a part of a day (*usu* the afternoon) during which no work is done: *the school-children were given a half-holiday to celebrate the football team's success*.

half-'hourly *adj, adv* done *etc* every half-hour: *at half-hourly intervals*; *The buses to town run half-hourly*.

half-'time *n* a short rest between two halves of a game (of football *etc*): *the players ate oranges at half-time*.

half-'way *adj, adv* of or at a point equally far from the beginning and the end: *We have reached the half-way point*; *We are half-way through the work now*.

'half-wit *n* a fool or idiot.

half-'witted *adj* foolish or idiotic.

half-'yearly *adj, adv* done *etc* every six months: *a half-yearly report*; *We balance our accounts half-yearly*.

at half mast (of flags) flying at a position half-way up a mast *etc* to show that someone of importance has died: *The flags are (flying) at half mast*.

by half by a long way: *He's too clever by half*.

do thing by halves to do thing in an incomplete way: *He never does things by halves*.

go halves with to share the cost with.

half past three, four, seven *etc*, (*Amer*) **half after three** *etc* at thirty minutes past the hour stated: *I'm leaving at half past six*.

in half in(to) two equal parts: *He cut the cake in half*; *The pencil broke in half*.

not half a slang expression for very much: *'Are you enjoying yourself?' 'Not half!'*

hall [ho:l] *n* **1** a room or passage at the entrance to a house: *We left our coats in the hall*. **2** (a building with) a large public room, used for concerts, meetings *etc*: *a community hall*. **3** a building with offices where the administration of a town *etc* is carried out: *a town hall*; (*Amer*) *the city hall*. **4** (*Amer*) a passageway through a building; a corridor. **5** a building of a university, college *etc*, *esp* one in which students *etc* live.

'hallmark *n* a mark put on gold and silver articles to show the quality of the gold or silver.

'hallway *n* a hall or passage.

hallo *see* **hello**.

hallowed ['haloud] *adj* holy: *hallowed ground*.

hallucination [həlu:si'neiʃən] *n* the seeing of something that is not really there: *He had hallucinations after he took drugs*.

hallway *see* **hall**.

halo ['heilou] – *pls* **halo(e)s** – *n* **1** a ring of light round the sun or moon. **2** a similar ring of light round the head of a holy person in a picture *etc*.

halt [ho:lt] *v* to (cause to) stop walking, marching, running *etc*: *The driver halted the train*; *The train halted at the signals*. – *n* **1** a complete stop: *the train came to a halt*. **2** a short stop (on a march *etc*). **3** a small railway station.

call a halt (to) to stop; to put an end (to): *It's time to call a halt to these stupid arguments*.

halter ['ho:ltə] *n* a rope for holding and leading a horse by its head.

halve, halves *see* **half**.

ham [ham] *n* **1** the top of the back leg of a pig, salted and dried.

,ham-'fisted *adj* clumsy: *He can't tie a knot in that rope – he's too ham-fisted.*

hamburger ['hambə:gə] *n* **1** a round cake of minced beef, *usu* fried. **2** a bread roll containing one of these.

*****hammer** ['hamə] *n* **1** a tool with a heavy *usu* metal head, used for driving nails into wood, breaking hard substances *etc*: *a joiner's hammer.* **2** the part of a bell, piano, clock *etc* that hits against some other part, so making a noise. **3** in sport, a metal ball on a long steel handle for throwing. – *v* **1** to hit, beat, break *etc* (something) with a hammer: *He hammered the nail into the wood.* **2** to teach a person (something) with difficulty, by repetition: *Grammar was hammered into us at school.*

give (someone) a hammering to hammer (=beat) (a person): *His father gave him a hammering for stealing.*

hammer home to make great efforts to make a person realize: *We'll have to hammer home to them the importance of secrecy.*

hammer out to produce (an agreement *etc*) with a great deal of effort and discussion: *to hammer out a solution.*

hammock ['hamək] *n* a long piece of netting, canvas *etc* hung up by the corners and used as a bed, *eg* in a ship.

hamper ['hampə] *v* to make it difficult for (someone) to do something: *I tried to run away but I was hampered by my long dress.* – *n* a large basket with a lid: *a picnic hamper.*

hamster ['hamstə] *n* a small animal, rather like a fat rat without a tail, often kept as a pet.

hand [hand] *n* **1** the part of the body at the end of the arm. **2** a pointer on a clock, watch *etc*: *Clocks usually have an hour hand and a minute hand.* **3** a person employed as a helper, crew member *etc*: *a farm hand; All hands on deck!* **4** help; assistance: *Can I lend a hand?; Give me a hand with this box, please.* **5** a set of playing-cards dealt to a person: *I had a very good hand so I thought I had a chance of winning.* **6** a measure (*approx* 10 centimetres) used for measuring the height of horses: *a horse of 14 hands.* **7** handwriting: *written in a neat hand.* – *v* (often with **back, down, up** *etc*) **1** to give (something) to someone by hand: *I handed him the book; He handed it back to me; I'll go up the ladder, and you can hand the tools up to me.* **2** to pass, transfer *etc* into another's care *etc*: *That is the end of my report from Paris. I'll now hand you back to Fred Smith in the television studio in London.*

'handful *n* **1** as much as can be held in one hand: *a handful of sweets.* **2** a small num-

ber: *Only a handful of people came to the meeting.* **3** a person *etc* difficult to control: *Her three children are a (bit of a) handful.*

'handbag *n* (*Amer usu* **purse**) a small bag carried by women, for personal belongings.

'handbill *n* a small printed notice.

'handbook *n* a small book giving information about (how to do) something: *a handbook of European birds; a bicycle-repair handbook.*

'handbrake *n* (in a car, bus *etc*) a brake operated by the driver's hand.

'handcuff *v* to put handcuffs on (a person): *The police handcuffed the criminal.*

'handcuffs *n pl* steel rings, joined by a short chain, put round the wrists of prisoners: *a pair of handcuffs.*

'hand-lens *n* a magnifying-glass held in the hand.

,hand'made *adj* made with a person's hands or with tools held in the hands, rather than by machines: *hand-made furniture.*

hand-'operated *adj*: *hand-operated switches.*

'hand-out *see* **hand out** below.

,hand-'picked *adj* chosen very carefully: *a hand-picked team of workers.*

'handshake *n* the act of grasping (a person's) hand *eg* as a greeting.

'handstand *n* the gymnastic act of balancing one's body upright in the air with one's hands on the ground.

'handwriting *n* **1** writing with a pen or pencil: *Today we will practise handwriting.* **2** the way in which a person writes: *Your handwriting is terrible!*

'handwritten *adj*: *The letter was handwritten, not typed.*

at hand 1 (*with* **close** *or* **near**) near: *The bus station is close at hand.* **2** available: *Help is at hand.*

at the hands of from, or by the action of: *He received very rough treatment at the hands of the terrorists.*

be hand in glove (with someone) to be very closely associated with someone, *esp* for a bad purpose.

by hand 1 with a person's hand or tools held in the hands, rather than with machinery: *furniture made by hand.* **2** not by post but by a messenger *etc*: *This parcel was delivered by hand.*

fall into the hands (of someone) to be caught, found, captured *etc* by someone: *He fell into the hands of bandits; The documents fell into the wrong hands* (=were found, captured *etc* by someone who was not supposed to see them).

force someone's hand to force someone to do something either which he does not want to do or sooner than he wants to do it.

get one's hands on 1 to catch: *If I ever get my hands on him, I'll make him sorry for* *what he did!* **2** to get or obtain: *I'd love to get my hands on a car like that.*

give/lend a helping hand to help or assist: *I'm always ready to give/lend a helping hand.*

hand down to pass on from one generation to the next: *These customs have been handed down from father to son since the Middle Ages.*

hand in to give or bring to a person, place *etc*: *The teacher told the children to hand in their exercise-books.*

hand in hand with one person holding the hand of another: *The boy and girl were walking along hand in hand; Poverty and crime go hand in hand.*

hand on to give to someone: *When you have finished reading these notes, hand them on to me.*

hand out 1 to give to several people; to distribute: *The teacher handed out books to all the pupils; They were handing out leaflets in the street. – n* **'hand-out** a leaflet.

hand over to give or pass; to surrender: *We know you have the jewels, so hand them over; They handed the thief over to the police.*

hand over fist in large amounts, *usu* quickly: *He's making money hand over fist.*

hands down very easily: *You'll win hands down.*

hands off! do not touch!

hands up! raise your hands above your head: *'Hands up!' shouted the gunman.*

hand to hand with one individual fighting another at close quarters: *The soldiers fought the enemy hand to hand;* (*also adj*) *hand-to-hand fighting.*

have a hand in (something) to be one of the people who have caused, done *etc* (something): *Did you have a hand in the building of this boat/in the success of the project?*

have/get/gain the upper hand to (begin to) win, beat the enemy *etc*: *The enemy made a fierce attack but failed to get the upper hand.*

hold hands (with someone) to be hand in hand with someone: *The boy and girl walked along holding hands (with each other).*

in good hands receiving care and attention: *The patient is in good hands.*

in hand 1 not used *etc*; remaining: *We still have $10 in hand.* **2** being dealt with: *We have received your complaint and the matter is now in hand.*

in the hands of being dealt with by: *This matter is now in the hands of my solicitor.*

keep one's hand in to remain good or skilful at doing something. by doing it occasionally: *I still sometimes play a game of billiards, just to keep my hand in.*

off one's hands no longer needing to be looked after *etc*: *You'll be glad to get the children off your hands for a couple of weeks.*

on hand near; present; ready for use *etc*: *We always keep some candles on hand in case there's a power failure.*

(on the one hand) … on the other hand an expression used to introduce two opposing parts of an argument *etc*: *(On the one hand) we could stay and help you, but on the other hand, it might be better if we went to help him instead.*

out of hand unable to be controlled: *The angry crowd was getting out of hand.*

shake hands with (someone)/shake someone's hand to grasp a person's (*usu* right) hand, in one's own (*usu* right) hand, as a form of greeting, as a sign of agreement *etc*.

a show of hands at a meeting, debate *etc*, a vote expressed by people raising their hands.

take in hand to look after, discipline or train.

handicap ['handikap] *n* **1** something that makes doing something more difficult: *The loss of a finger would be a handicap for a pianist.* **2** (in a race, competition *etc*) a disadvantage of some sort (*eg* having to run a greater distance in a race) given to the best competitors so that others have a better chance of winning. **3** a race, competition *etc* in which this happens. **4** (a form of) physical or mental disability: *children with physical handicaps. – v – pt, ptp* **'handicapped** – to make something (more) difficult for: *He wanted to be a pianist, but was handicapped by his deafness.* **'handicapped** *adj*: *He is physically handicapped and cannot walk; a handicapped child.*

handicraft ['handikra:ft] *n* skilled work done by hand, *eg* knitting, pottery, model-making *etc*.

handiwork ['handiwə:k] *n* **1** thing(s) made by hand: *Examples of the pupils' handiwork were on show.* **2** something bad caused by a particular person: *The broken window was Simon's handiwork.*

handkerchief ['haŋkətʃif] – *pls* **'handkerchiefs, 'handkerchieves** [-tʃi:vz] – *n* (*abbrev* **hanky** (*pl* **'hankies**), **hankie** ['haŋki]) a small *usu* square piece of cloth or paper tissue used for wiping or blowing one's nose into.

handle ['handl] *n* the part of an object by which it may be held or grasped: *I've broken the handle off this cup; You've got to turn the handle in order to open the door. – v* **1** to touch or hold with the hand: *Please wash your hands before handling food.* **2** to control, manage or deal with: *He'll never make a good teacher – he doesn't know how to handle children.* **3** to buy or sell; to deal in: *I'm afraid we do not handle such goods in* *this shop.* **4** to treat in a particular way: *Never handle animals roughly.*

-handled: *a long-handled knife.*

'handler *n* a person who trains and controls an animal (*esp* a dog): *a police dog and its handler.*

'handlebars *n pl* the bar at the front of a bicycle *etc* which is held by the rider and by which the bicycle *etc* is steered: *The cyclist was thrown over the handlebars when the bike crashed.*

handsome ['hansəm] *adj* **1** (*usu* of men) good-looking: *a handsome prince.* **2** very large; generous: *He gave a handsome sum of money to charity.* **'handsomely** *adv.* **'handsomeness** *n.*

handstand, handwriting *see* **hand.**

handy ['handi] *adj* **1** ready (to use); in a convenient place: *I like to keep my tools handy; This house is handy for the shops.* **2** easy to use; useful: *a handy tool.* **'handiness** *n.*

'handyman ['man] *n* a man who does jobs, for himself or other people, *esp* around the house.

come in handy to be useful: *I'll keep these bottles – they might come in handy.*

hang [haŋ] – *pt, ptp* **hung** [hʌŋ] – *v* **1** to put or fix, or to be put or fixed, above the ground *eg* by a hook: *We'll hang the picture on that wall; The picture is hanging on the wall.* **2** to fasten (something), or to be fastened, at the top or side so that it can move freely but cannot fall: *A door hangs by its hinges.* **3** (*pt, ptp* **hanged**) to kill, or to be killed, by having a rope put round the neck and being allowed to drop: *Murderers used to be hanged in the United Kingdom, but no-one hangs for murder now.* **4** (*often with* **down** or **out**) to be bending, drooping or falling downwards: *The dog's tongue was hanging out; Her hair was hanging down.* **5** to bow (one's head): *He hung his head in shame.*

'hanger *n* (*usu* **'coat-hanger**) a shaped metal, wooden or plastic frame with a hook on which jackets, dresses *etc* are hung up.

'hanging *n* the (act of) killing a criminal by hanging.

'hangings *n pl* curtains or material hung on walls for decoration.

'hangman *n* a man whose job it is to hang criminals.

'hangover *n* the unpleasant effects of having had too much alcohol: *He woke up with a hangover.*

get the hang of to learn or begin to understand how to do (something): *It may seem difficult at first, but you'll get the hang of it after a few weeks.*

hang about/around 1 to stand around, doing nothing: *I don't like to see all these youths hanging about* (*street-corners*). **2** to

be close to (a person) frequently: *I don't want you hanging around my daughter.*

hang back to hesitate or be unwilling: *The soldiers all hung back when the sergeant asked for volunteers.*

hang in the balance to be in doubt: *The success of this project is hanging in the balance.*

hang on 1 to wait: *Will you hang on a minute – I'm not quite ready.* **2** (*often with* **to**) to hold: *Hang on to that rope.* **3** to keep; to retain: *He likes to hang on to his money.*

hang together to agree or be consistent: *His statements just do not hang together.*

hang up 1 to hang (something) on something: *Hang up your coat in the cupboard.* **2** (*often with* **on**) to put the receiver back after a telephone conversation: *I tried to talk to her, but she hung up* (*on me*).

She **hung** the picture up.
The murderer was **hanged**.

hangar ['haŋə] *n* a shed for aeroplanes.

hank [haŋk] *n* a coil or loop of rope, wool, string *etc*: *hanks of knitting-wool.*

hanker ['haŋkə] *v* (*with* **after** *or* **for**) to want (something): *He was hankering after the bright lights of the city.*

have a hankering for: *I have a hankering for a strawberry ice-cream.*

hankie, hanky ['haŋki] short for **handkerchief.**

haphazard [hap'hazəd] *adj* depending on chance; without planning or system: *a haphazard arrangement.* **hap'hazardly** *adv.*

happen ['hapən] *v* **1** to take place or occur; to occur by chance: *What happened next?; It just so happens/As it happens, I have the key in my pocket.* **2** (*usu with* **to**) to be done to (a person, thing *etc*): *She's late – something must have happened to her.* **3** to do or be by chance: *I happened to find him; He happens to be my friend.*

'happening *n* an occurrence: *strange happenings.*

happen (up)on to find by chance: *He happened upon the perfect solution to the problem just as he was about to give up his research.*

happy ['hapi] *adj* **1** having or showing a feeling of pleasure or contentment: *a happy smile; I feel happy today.* **2** willing: *I'd be happy to help you.* **3** lucky: *By a happy chance I have the key with me.* **'happiness** *n.*

'happily *adv*: *The child smiled happily; Happily,* (= *Fortunately,*) *she arrived home safely.*

,happy-go-'lucky *adj* not worrying about what might happen: *cheerful and happy-go-lucky.*

happy medium a sensible middle course between two extreme positions: *I need to* *find the happy medium between starving and over-eating.*

harangue [həˈraŋ] *n* a long loud speech: *a harangue from the headmaster on good behaviour.* – *v* to give a harangue to.

harass [ˈharəs, (*esp Amer*) həˈras] *v* 1 to annoy or trouble (a person) constantly or frequently: *The children have been harassing me all morning.* 2 to make frequent sudden attacks on (an enemy): *The army was constantly harassed by groups of terrorists.*
ˈharassed *adj*: *a harassed mother.*
ˈharassment *n*: *He complained of harassment by the police.*

harbour, (*Amer*) **harbor** [ˈhaːbə] *n* a place of shelter for ships: *All the ships stayed in (the) harbour during the storm.* – *v* 1 to give shelter or refuge to (a person): *It is against the law to harbour criminals.* 2 to have (*usu* bad) thoughts in one's head: *He harbours a grudge against me.*
ˈharbour-master *n* the official in charge of a harbour.

hard [haːd] *adj* 1 firm; solid; not easy to break, scratch *etc*: *The ground is too hard to dig.* 2 not easy to do, learn, solve *etc*: *Is English a hard language to learn?*; *He is a hard man to please.* 3 not feeling or showing kindness: *a hard master.* 4 (of weather) severe: *a hard winter.* 5 having or causing suffering: *a hard life; hard times.* 6 (of water) containing many chemical salts and so not easily forming bubbles when soap is added: *The water is hard in this part of the country.* – *adv* 1 with great effort: *He works very hard; Think hard.* 2 with great force; heavily: *Don't hit him too hard; It was raining hard.* 3 with great attention: *He stared hard at the man.* 4 to the full extent; completely: *The car turned hard right.*
ˈharden *v* to make or become hard: *Don't touch the toffee till it hardens; Try to harden your heart against him.*
ˈhardness *n*.
ˈhardship *n* (something which causes) pain, suffering *etc*: *a life full of hardship.*
ˈhard-and-fast *adj* (of rules) that can never be changed or ignored.
ˈhard-back *n* a book with a hard cover: *Hard-backs are more expensive than paperbacks.*
ˌhard-ˈboiled *adj* (of eggs) boiled until the white and the yolk are solid.
ˈhard-earned *adj* earned by hard work or with difficulty: *I deserve every penny of my hard-earned wages.*
ˌhard-ˈheaded *adj* practical; shrewd; not influenced by emotion: *a hard-headed businessman.*
ˌhard-ˈhearted *adj* not feeling or showing pity or kindness: *a hard-hearted employer.*

ˈhardware *n* metal goods such as pots, tools *etc*: *This shop sells hardware.*
ˌhard-ˈwearing *adj* that will not wear out easily: *a hard-wearing fabric.*
be hard on 1 to punish or criticize severely: *Don't be too hard on the boy – he's too young to know that he was doing wrong.* 2 to be unfair to: *If you punish all the children for the broken window it's a bit hard on those who had nothing to do with it.*
hard at it busy doing (something): *I've been hard at it all day, trying to get this report finished.*
hard done by unfairly treated: *You should complain to the headmaster if you feel hard done by.*
hard lines/luck bad luck: *Hard lines/luck! I'm afraid you haven't won this time; It's hard luck that he broke his leg.*
hard of hearing rather deaf: *He is a bit hard of hearing now.*
a hard time (of it) trouble, difficulty, worry *etc*: *The audience gave the speaker a hard time of it at the meeting; The speaker had a hard time (of it) trying to make himself heard.*
hard up not having much *esp* money: *I'm a bit hard up at the moment; I'm hard up for envelopes.*

hardly [ˈhaːdli] *adv* 1 almost no, none, never *etc*: *Hardly any small businesses are successful nowadays; I hardly ever go out.* 2 only just; almost not: *My feet are so sore, I can hardly walk; I had hardly got on my bicycle when I got a puncture.* 3 probably not: *He's hardly likely to forgive you after what you said about him.*

hardship, hardware see **hard**.

hardy [ˈhaːdi] *adj* tough; strong; able to bear cold, tiredness *etc*: *He's very hardy – he takes a cold shower every morning.*
ˈhardiness *n*.

hare [heə] *n* an animal with long ears, like a rabbit but slightly larger.

harem [ˈheərəm] *n* 1 the part of a Muslim house occupied by the women. 2 the women themselves.

hark! [haːk] *interj* listen!

harm [haːm] *n* damage; injury; distress: *I'll make sure you come to no harm; He meant no harm; It'll do you no harm to go.* – *v* to cause (a person) harm: *There's no need to be frightened – he won't harm you.*
ˈharmful *adj* doing harm: *Medicines can be harmful if you take too much of them.*
ˈharmless *adj* not dangerous or liable to cause harm: *Don't be frightened of that snake – it's harmless.* **ˈharmlessly** *adv*.
ˈharmlessness *n*.
out of harm's way in a safe place: *I'll put this glass vase out of harm's way, in case it gets broken.*

harmonic see **harmony**.

harmonica [ha:'mɔnikə] n a kind of small musical instrument played with the mouth.

harmony ['ha:məni] – pl **'harmonies** – n 1 (of musical sounds, colours etc) (the state of forming) a pleasing combination: The singers sang in harmony. 2 the agreement of people's feelings, opinions etc: Few married couples live in perfect harmony.

har'monic [-'mɔ-] adj of, or concerned with, esp musical harmony.

har'monious [-'mou-] adj 1 pleasant-sounding: a harmonious melody. 2 pleasant to the eye: a harmonious colour scheme. 3 without disagreement or bad feeling: a harmonious relationship. **har'moniously** adv. **har'moniousness** n.

'harmonize, -ise v 1 to sing or play musical instruments in harmony. 2 to add different parts to (a melody) to form harmonies. 3 to (cause to) be in harmony or agreement: The colours in this room harmonize nicely. **harmoni'zation, -s-** n.

harness ['ha:nis] n the leather straps etc by which a horse is attached to a cart etc which it is pulling and by means of which it is controlled. – v 1 to put the harness on (a horse). 2 to make use of (a source of power, eg a river) for some purpose, eg to produce electricity or to drive machinery: Attempts are now being made to harness the sun as a source of heat and power.

harp [ha:p] n a usu large musical instrument which is held upright, and which has many strings which are plucked with the fingers. **'harpist** n.

harp on (about) to keep on talking about: He's forever harping on (about his low wages); She keeps harping on his faults.

harpoon [ha:'pu:n] n a spear fastened to a rope, used esp for killing whales. – v to strike with a harpoon: He has harpooned the whale.

harpsichord ['ha:psikɔ:d] n a type of early keyboard musical instrument.

harrowing ['harouiŋ] adj extremely distressing: a harrowing experience.

harry ['hari] v to torment or worry frequently.

harsh [ha:ʃ] adj 1 (of people, discipline etc) very strict; cruel: That is a very harsh punishment to give a young child. 2 rough and unpleasant to hear, see, taste etc: a harsh voice; harsh colours. **'harshly** adv. **'harshness** n.

harvest ['ha:vist] n the gathering in of ripened crops: the rice harvest. – v to gather in (crops etc): We harvested the apples yesterday.

'harvester n a person or machine that harvests corn.

has, has-been see **have**.

hashish ['haʃi:ʃ] n (a drug made from) the dried leaves, flowers etc of the hemp plant, usu smoked or chewed; cannabis.

hasn't see **have**.

hassle ['hasl] n 1 trouble or fuss: It's such a hassle to get to work on time: Travelling with children is such a hassle. 2 a fight or argument: I got into a bit of a hassle with a couple of thugs. – v 1 to argue or fight: It seemed pointless to hassle over such a small matter. 2 to annoy (a person): I don't like people hassling me.

haste [heist] n (too much) speed: Your work shows signs of haste – there are too many mistakes in it.

hasten ['heisn] v 1 to (cause to) move with speed: He hastened towards me; We must hasten the preparations. 2 to do at once: He hastened to add an explanation.

'hasty adj 1 done etc in a hurry: a hasty snack. 2 acting or done with too much speed and without thought: She is too hasty – she should think carefully before making such an important decision; a hasty decision. 3 easily made angry: a hasty temper. **'hastily** adv. **'hastiness** n.

in haste in a hurry; quickly: I am writing in haste before leaving for the airport.

make haste to hurry.

hat [hat] n a covering for the head, usu worn out of doors: He raised his hat as the lady approached.

'hatter n a person who makes or sells hats.

hat trick (in football) three goals scored by one player in a match.

keep (something) under one's hat to keep (something) secret: Keep it under your hat but I'm getting married next week.

pass/send round the hat to ask for or collect money on someone's behalf.

take one's hat off to to admire (someone) for doing something.

talk through one's hat to talk nonsense.

hatch[1] [hatʃ] n (the door or cover of) an opening in a wall, floor, ship's deck etc: There are two hatches between the kitchen and dining-room for serving food.

'hatchway n an opening, esp in a ship's deck.

hatch[2] [hatʃ] v 1 to produce (young birds etc) from eggs: My hens have hatched ten chicks. 2 to break out of the egg: These chicks hatched this morning. 3 to become young birds: Four of the eggs have hatched. 4 to plan (something, usu bad) in secret: to hatch a plot.

hatchet ['hatʃit] n a small axe held in one hand.

hatchway see **hatch**[1].

hate [heit] v to dislike very much: I hate them for their cruelty to my father; I hate getting up in the morning. – n 1 great dislike: a look of hate. 2 something disliked: Getting up in the morning is one of my pet (=particular) hates.

'hateful adj very bad; very unpleasant: That was a hateful thing to do to her; What a hateful person! **'hatefully** adv. **'hatefulness** n.

hatred ['heitrid] n great dislike: There was a look of hatred in his eyes; I have a deep-seated hatred of liars.

hatter see **hat**.

.haughty ['ho:ti] adj very proud: a haughty look; a haughty young woman. **'haughtily** adv. **'haughtiness** n.

haul [ho:l] v 1 to pull with great effort or difficulty: Horses are used to haul barges along canals. 2 to carry by some form of transport: Coal is hauled by road and rail. – n 1 a strong pull: He gave the rope a haul. 2 the amount of anything, esp fish, that is got at one time: The fishermen had a good haul; The thieves got away from the jeweller's with a good haul.

a long haul a long or tiring job, journey etc.

haunch [ho:ntʃ] n 1 (usu in pl) the fleshy part of the hip: The children were squatting on their haunches. 2 the leg and lower part of the body of a deer etc, as meat: a haunch of venison.

haunt [ho:nt] v 1 (of a ghost) to inhabit: A ghost is said to haunt this house. 2 (of an unpleasant memory) to keep coming back into the mind of: Her look of misery haunts me. 3 to visit very often: He haunts that café. – n a place one often visits: This is one of my favourite haunts.

'haunted adj inhabited by ghosts: a haunted castle; The old house is said to be haunted.

have [hav] – 3rd pers sing prt **has** [haz]: pt, ptp **had** [had]: short forms **I've** [aiv] **(I have)**, **you've** [ju:v] **(you have)**, **he's** [hi:z] **(he has)**, **she's** [ʃi:z] **(she has)**, **it's** [its] **(it has)**, **we've** [wi:v] **(we have)**, **they've** [ðeiv] **(they have)**, **I'd** [aid] **(I had)**, **you'd** [ju:d] **(you had)**, **he'd** [hi:d] **(he had)**, **she'd** [ʃi:d] **(she had)**, **it'd** ['itəd] **(it had)**, **we'd** [wi:d] **(we had)**, **they'd** [ðeid] **(they had)**: neg short forms **hadn't** ['hadnt] **(had not)**, **hasn't** ['haznt] **(has not)**, **haven't** ['havnt] **(have not)** – v 1 used with ptp of other verbs to show that an action is in the past and has been completed: I've bought a new dictionary; Has he gone yet? – 2 (also **have got**) to hold or possess (something which belongs to oneself or to someone else): I have a book of yours at home; He's got your book; I don't have any books by Sir Walter Scott. 3 (also **have got**) to possess something as part of oneself or in some way connected with oneself: She has blue eyes; Our house has six rooms; I've got a pain in my stomach. 4 (sometimes with **back**) to receive or get: Have you had any news of your brother?; Thank you for lending me the book – you can

have it back next week. 5 to produce: He does have some good ideas; She has had a baby. 6 to cause to be done: I'm having a tooth (taken) out; Have Smith come and see me. 7 to enjoy or suffer: We had a lovely holiday. 8 to do or take: I'll have a drink; Let me have a try. 9 to allow: I will not have you wearing clothes like that! 10 (with **back, in, round** etc) to ask to one's house as a guest or to do a job: We're having friends round for dinner; We're having someone in to paint this room. 11 to think or feel: I have some doubts about this project. 12 to trick: You've been had!

'has-been n a person who is no longer famous and important.

have done with to stop or put an end to: Let's have done with all this quarrelling.

have had it to be dead, ruined etc: The bullet went into his brain – he's had it, I'm afraid.

have it in oneself etc to have the courage or ability to do something: I hear she told her boss to stop shouting at her – I didn't think she had it in her.

have it out (often with **with**) to argue with (a person) in order to put an end to some disagreement: I'm going to have it out with her once and for all.

have on 1 (also **have got on**) to wear: That's a nice suit you have on. 2 to fool (someone): You're having me on – that's not really true, is it? 3 (also **have got on**) to be busy with: Have you (got) anything on this afternoon?

have to (also **have got to**) to be obliged to (do something): I don't want to do this, but I have to; Do you have to go so soon?; I've got to leave soon; You didn't have to do that, did you?

have to do with (a person or thing), (also **have got to do with**) to be of importance or concern to (a person or thing): What have these letters to do with you?; Your remarks have (got) nothing to do with the subject we are discussing.

have what it takes, (also **have got what it takes**) to have the qualities or ability that one needs to do something: He has (got) what it takes to make a good officer.

I have it!, (also **I've got it!**) I have found the answer (to a problem etc).

haven ['heivn] n a harbour; a place of safety or rest.

haven't see **have**.

haversack ['havəsak] n a bag worn over one shoulder by a walker etc for carrying food etc.

havoc ['havək] n great destruction or damage: The hurricane created havoc over a wide area.

hawk[1] [ho:k] n a type of bird of prey.

'hawk-'eyed adj having very good eye-sight.

hawk² [ho:k] *v* to carry goods round for sale. **'hawker** *n*.

hawser ['ho:zə] *n* a thick rope or a steel cable for towing ships or tying them to a dock *etc*.

hay [hei] *n* grass, cut and dried, used as food for cattle *etc*.
hay-'fever *n* an illness like a bad cold, caused by the pollen of flowers *etc*.
'hayrick [-rik], **'hay-stack** *ns* hay built up into a large pile.
'haywire *adj* in a state of disorder; crazy: *Our computer has gone haywire.*

hazard ['hazəd] *n* (something which causes) a risk of harm or danger: *the hazards of mountain-climbing.* – *v* **1** to risk; to be prepared to do (something, the result of which is uncertain): *Are you prepared to hazard your life for the success of this mission?* **2** to put forward (a guess *etc*).
'hazardous *adj* dangerous: *a hazardous journey.* **'hazardousness** *n*.

haze [heiz] *n* a thin mist: *The mountains were dim through the haze.*
'hazy *adj* **1** misty: *a hazy view of the mountains.* **2** not clear or certain: *a hazy idea; I'm a bit hazy about what happened.* **'haziness** *n*.

hazel ['heizl] *n* a kind of small tree on which nuts grow. – *adj* of a light-brown colour: *hazel eyes.*
'hazel-nut *n* the edible nut of the hazel.

H-bomb ['eitʃbom] short for **hydrogen bomb**.

he [hi:] *pron* (used as the subject of a verb) **1** a male person or animal already spoken about: *When I spoke to John, he told me he had seen you.* **2** any (male) person: *He who hesitates is lost.* – *n* a male person or animal: *Is a cow a he or a she?*
he- male: *a he-goat.*
'he-man [-man] – *pl* **'he-men** – *n* a very strong, powerful man.

head [hed] *n* **1** the top part of the human body, containing the eyes, mouth, brain *etc*; the same part of an animal's body: *The stone hit him on the head; He scratched his head in amazement.* **2** a person's mind: *An idea came into my head last night.* **3** the height or length of a head: *The horse won by a head.* **4** the chief or most important person (of an organization, country *etc*): *Kings and presidents are heads of state; (also adj) a head waiter; the head office.* **5** anything that is like a head in shape or position: *the head of a pin; The boy knocked the heads off the flowers.* **6** the place where a river, lake *etc* begins: *the head of the Nile.* **7** the top, or the top part, of anything: *Write your address at the head of the paper; the head of the table.* **8** the front part: *He walked at the head of the procession.* **9** a particular ability or tolerance: *He has no*

head for heights; She has a good head for figures. **10** a headmaster or headmistress: *You'd better ask the Head.* **11** (for) one person: *This dinner costs $10 a head.* **12** a headland: *Beachy Head.* **13** the foam on the top of a glass of beer *etc*. – *v* **1** to go at the front of or at the top of (something): *The procession was headed by the band; Whose name headed the list?* **2** to be in charge of; to be the leader of: *He heads a team of scientists investigating cancer.* **3** (*often with* **for**) to (cause to) move in a certain direction: *The explorers headed south; The boys headed for home; You're heading for disaster!* **4** to put or write something at the begining of: *His report was headed 'Ways of Preventing Industrial Accidents'.* **5** (in football) to hit the ball with the head: *He headed the ball into the goal.*
-headed having (a certain number or type of) head(s): *a two-headed monster; a bald-headed man.*
'header *n* **1** a fall or dive forwards: *He slipped and took a header into the mud.* **2** (in football) the act of hitting the ball with the head: *He scored with a great header.*
'heading *n* what is written at the top of a page *etc*: *The teacher said that essays must have a proper heading.*
heads *n, adv* (on) the side of a coin with the head of a king, president *etc* on it: *He tossed the penny and it came down heads.*
'headache *n* **1** a pain in the head: *Bright lights give me a headache.* **2** something worrying: *Lack of money is a real headache.*
'headband *n* a strip of material worn round the head to keep one's hair off one's face.
'head-dress *n* something, *usu* ornamental, which is worn on, and covers, the head: *The tribesmen were wearing head-dresses of fur and feathers.*
head'first *adv* with one's head in front or bent forward: *He fell headfirst into a pool of water.*
'headgear *n* anything that is worn on the head: *Hats, caps and helmets are headgear.*
'headlamp *n* a headlight.
'headland *n* a point of land which sticks out into the sea.
'headlight *n* a powerful light at or on the front of a car, lorry, train, ship, aeroplane *etc*: *As it was getting dark, the driver switched on his headlights.*
'headline *n* the words written in large letters at the top of newspaper articles: *I never read a paper in detail – I just glance at the headlines.*
'headlines *n pl* a brief statement of the most important items of news, on television or radio: *the news headlines.*
'headlong *adj, adv* **1** moving fowards or downwards, with one's head in front: *a*

headlong dive into the pool of water; *He fell headlong into a pool of water.* **2** (done) without thought or delay, often foolishly: *a headlong rush*; *He rushes headlong into disaster.*

head louse a type of louse that infests the human head.

head'master – *fem* **head'mistress** – *n* the person in charge of a school; the principal.

head-'on *adv, adj* (*usu* of cars *etc*) with the front of one car *etc* hitting the front of another car *etc*: *a head-on collision*; *The two cars crashed head-on.*

'headphones *n pl* (*also* **'earphones**) a pair of electronic instruments held over a person's ears, by a metal band over the head, which are connected to a radio: *a set of headphones.*

head'quarters *n sing or pl* (*often abbrev* **HQ** [eitʃ'kjuː] *n*) the place from which the chief officers or leaders of an organization (*esp* an army) direct and control the activities of that organization: *During the election, his house was used as the campaign headquarters.*

'headrest *n* a sort of small cushion which supports a person's head, *eg* as fitted to a dentist's chair, a car seat.

'headscarf, 'headsquare *ns* a *usu* square scarf worn by women over or round the head.

'headstone *n* a stone put at a grave, *usu* with the name of the dead person on it, the date of his birth and death *etc.*

'headstrong *adj* (of people) difficult to persuade or control; always doing or wanting to do what they themselves want: *a headstrong, obstinate child.*

'headwind *n* a wind which is blowing towards one.

above someone's head too difficult (for someone) to understand: *His lecture was well above their heads.*

go to someone's head 1 (of alcohol) to make someone slightly drunk: *Champagne always goes to my head.* **2** (of praise, success *etc*) to make someone arrogant, foolish *etc*: *Don't let success go to your head.*

head off 1 to make (a person, animal *etc*) change direction: *One group of the soldiers rode across the valley to head the bandits off.* **2** to go in some direction: *He headed off towards the river.*

head over heels 1 completely: *He fell head over heels in love.* **2** turning over completely; headfirst: *He fell head over heels into a pond.*

heads or tails? used when tossing a coin, *eg* to decide which of two people does, gets *etc* something: *Heads or tails? Heads you do the dishes, tails I do them.*

keep one's head to remain calm and sensible in a crisis *etc.*

lose one's head to become angry or excited, or to act foolishly in a crisis.

make head or tail of to understand: *I can't make head or tail of these instructions.*

make headway to make progress: *We're not making much headway with this new scheme.*

off one's head mad: *You must be off your head to work for nothing.*

heal [hiːl] *v* (*often with* **up**) (*esp* of cuts, wounds *etc*) to make or become healthy; to (cause to) return to a normal state or condition: *That scratch will heal (up) in a couple of days*; *this ointment will soon heal your cuts.*

'healer *n* a person or thing that heals: *Time is the great healer.*

health [helθ] *n* **1** the state of being well or ill: *He is in good/poor health.* **2** the state of being well: *I may be getting old, but so long as I keep my health, I'll be happy.*

'healthy *adj* **1** (generally) having good health: *I'm rarely ill – I'm really a very healthy person*; *My bank balance is healthier than it was.* **2** causing or helping to produce good health: *a healthy climate.* **3** resulting from good health: *a healthy appetite.* **4** showing a sensible concern for one's own well-being *etc*: *He shows a healthy respect for the law.* **'healthiness** *n.*

health service (the organization which runs) all the medical services of a country which are available to the public.

drink (to) someone's health to drink a toast to someone, wishing him good health.

heap [hiːp] *n* **1** a large amount or a large number, in a pile: *a heap of sand/apples.* **2** (*usu in pl with* **of**) many, much or plenty: *We've got heaps of time*; *I've done that heaps of times.* – *v* **1** to put, throw *etc* in a heap: *I'll heap these stones (up) in a corner of the garden.* **2** to fill or cover with a heap: *He heaped his plate with vegetables*; *He heaped insults on his opponent.*

heaped *adj* having enough (of something) on it to form a heap: *A heaped spoonful of sugar.*

hear [hiə] – *pt, ptp* **heard** [həːd] – *v* **1** to (be able to) receive (sounds) by ear: *I don't hear very well*; *Speak louder – I can't hear you*; *I didn't hear you come in.* **2** to listen for some purpose: *A judge hears court cases*; *Part of a manager's job is to hear workers' complaints.* **3** to receive information, news *etc*, not only by ear: *I've heard that story before*; *I hear that you're leaving*; *'Have you heard from your sister?' 'Yes, I got a letter from her today'*; *I've never heard of him – who is he? This is the first I've heard of the plan.*

'hearing *n* **1** the ability to hear: *My hearing is not very good.* **2** the distance within which something can be heard: *I don't want to tell* *you when so many people are within hearing*; *I think we're out of hearing now.* **3** an act of listening: *We ought to give his views a fair hearing.* **4** a court case: *The hearing is to-morrow.*

'**hearing-aid** *n* a small electronic instrument which helps deaf people to hear better by making sounds louder by means of an amplifier.

'**hearsay** [-sei] *n* that which one has been told about by others but for which one has otherwise no evidence: *I never trust any-thing that I learn by hearsay.*

hear! hear! a shout to show that one agrees with what a speaker has said (*eg* in Parlia-ment or at a meeting).

I, he *etc* **will, would not hear of** I; he *etc* will or would not allow: *He would not hear of her going home alone, and insisted on going with her.*

hearsay *see* **hear**.

hearse [hə:s] *n* a car used for carrying a dead body in a coffin to a cemetery *etc*.

heart [ha:t] *n* **1** the organ which pumps blood through the body: *How fast does a person's heart beat?*; (*also adj*) *heart disease; a heart specialist.* **2** the central part: *I live in the heart of the city; in the heart of the forest; the heart of a lettuce; Let's get straight to the heart of the matter/problem.* **3** the part of the body where one's feelings, *esp* of love, conscience *etc* are imagined to arise: *She has a kind heart; You know in your heart that you ought to go; She has no heart* (= She is not kind). **4** courage and enthusiasm: *The sol-diers were beginning to lose heart.* **5** a symbol supposed to represent the shape of the heart; ♥: *a white dress with little pink hearts on it; heart-shaped.* **6** one of the playing-cards of the suit hearts, which have red symbols of this shape on them.
-hearted: *kind-hearted; hard-hearted; broken-hearted.*

'**hearten** *v* to encourage or cheer up: *We were greatly heartened by the good news.*

'**heartless** *adj* cruel; very unkind: *a heartless remark.* '**heartlessly** *adv.* '**heartlessness** *n.*

hearts *n pl* (sometimes treated as *n sing*) one of the four card suits: *the two of hearts.*

'**hearty** *adj* **1** very friendly: *a hearty wel-come.* **2** enthusiastic: *a hearty cheer.* **3** very cheerful; too cheerful: *a hearty person/laugh.* **4** (of meals) large: *He ate a hearty breakfast.* **5** (of a person's appetite) large. '**heartily** *adv.* '**heartiness** *n.*

'**heartache** *n* (a feeling of) great sadness.

heart attack a sudden failure of the heart to function correctly, sometimes causing death: *My father has had a slight heart attack.*

'**heartbeat** *n* (the sound of) the regular movement of the heart.

'**heartbreak** *n* (something which causes) great sorrow: *I have suffered many heart-breaks in my life.*

'**heartbroken** *adj* feeling very great sorrow: *a heartbroken widow.*

'**heartburn** *n* a burning feeling in the chest caused by indigestion: *She suffers from heartburn after meals.*

heart failure the sudden stopping of the heart's beating: *the old man died of heart failure.*

'**heartfelt** *adj* sincere: *heartfelt thanks.*

,**heart-to'heart** *adj* open and sincere, *usu* in private: *I'm going to have a heart-to-heart talk with him.* – *n* an open and sincere talk, *usu* in private: *After our heart-to-heart I felt more cheerful.*

'**heart-warming** *adj* causing a person to feel pleasure: *It was heart-warming to see the happiness of the children.*

at heart really; basically: *He seems rather stern but he is at heart a very kind man.*

break someone's heart to cause someone great sorrow: *If you leave her, it'll break her heart.*

by heart from memory; by memorizing: *The children know their multiplication tables by heart; Actors must learn their speeches (off) by heart.*

from the bottom of one's heart very sin-cerely: *She thanked him from the bottom of her heart.*

have a change of heart to change a decision *etc, usu* to a better, kinder one: *He's had a change of heart – he's going to help us after all.*

have a heart! show some pity!

have at heart to have a concern for or interest in: *He has the interest of his workers at heart.*

heart and soul with all one's attention and energy: *She devoted herself heart and soul to caring for her husband.*

lose heart to become discouraged.

not have the heart to not to want or be unkind enough to (do something unpleas-ant): *I don't have the heart to tell him that everyone laughed at his suggestions.*

set one's heart on/have one's heart set on to want very much: *He had set his heart on winning the prize; He had his heart set on winning.*

take heart to become encouraged or more confident.

take to heart 1 to be made very sad or upset by: *You mustn't take his unkind remarks to heart.* **2** to pay attention to : *He's taken my criticism to heart – his work has improved.*

to one's heart's content as much as one wants: *She could play in the big garden to her heart's content.*

with all one's heart very willingly or sincerely: *I hope with all my heart that you will be happy.*

heartily *etc see* **heart**.

heat [hi:t] *n* **1** the amount of hotness (of something), *esp* of things which are very hot: *Test the heat of the water before you bath the baby.* **2** the warmth from something which is hot: *The heat from the fire will dry your coat; the effect of heat on metal; the heat of the sun.* **3** the hottest time: *the heat of the day.* **4** anger or excitement: *He didn't mean to be rude – he just said that in the heat of the moment.* **5** in a sports competition *etc*, one of two or more contests from which the winners go on to take part in later stages of the competition: *Having won his heat he is going through to the final.* – *v* (*sometimes with* **up**) to make or become hot or warm: *We'll heat* (*up*) *the soup; The day heats up quickly once the sun has risen.*

'heated *adj* **1** having been made hot: *a heated swimming-pool.* **2** showing anger, excitement *etc*: *a heated argument.* **'heatedly** *adv*. **'heatedness** *n*.

'heater *n* an apparatus which gives out heat in order to warm a room *etc*, or which heats water *etc* eg in a water-tank.

'heating *n* the system of heaters *etc* which heat a room, building *etc*: *We turn the heating off in the summer.*

heat wave a period of very hot weather.

in/on heat (of female animals) in a condition for mating.

See also **hot**.

heathen ['hi:ðən] *n, adj* (of) a person who believes in a less advanced form of religion, *esp* one with many gods: *Missionaries tried to convert the heathens to Christianity.*

heather ['heðə] *n* a plant with small purple or white flowers growing *eg* in hilly parts of Britain.

heave [hi:v] *v* **1** to (try to) lift or to pull, with great effort: *They heaved with all their strength, but could not move the rock; They heaved the wardrobe up into the lorry.* **2** to throw (something heavy): *Someone heaved a stone through my window.* **3** to rise, or rise and fall again several times: *The earthquake made the ground heave.* – *n* the act of heaving: *He gave one heave and the rock moved; the heave of the waves.*

heave a sigh to sigh: *He heaved a sigh of relief when he reached safety.*

heave to – *pt, ptp* **hove** [houv] – (of a ship) to (cause to) stop while at sea: *The ship hove to.*

heaven ['hevn] *n* **1** in some religions, the place where God or the gods live, and where good people go when they die. **2** the sky: *He raised his eyes to heaven/the heavens.* **3** (something which brings) great happiness: *'This is heaven', she said, lying on the beach in the sun.*

'heavenly *adv* **1** very pleasant; beautiful: *What a heavenly colour!* **2** of or from heaven. **'heavenliness** *n*.

'heavens (*also* **good heavens**) (*interj*) an expression of surprise, dismay *etc*: *Heavens! I forgot to buy your birthday present.*

heavenly bodies the sun, moon, planets, stars.

heaven-'sent *adj* very lucky or convenient: *a heaven-sent opportunity.*

for heaven's sake an expression used to show anger, surprise *etc*: *For heaven's sake, stop making that noise!*

heaven knows 1 I don't know: *Heaven knows what he's trying to do.* **2** certainly: *Heaven knows I've tried to help.*

thank heavens an expression used to show that a person is glad something has (not) happened: *Thank heavens he isn't coming!; Thank heavens for that!*

heavy ['hevi] *adj* **1** having great weight; difficult to lift or carry: *a heavy parcel.* **2** having a particular weight: *I wonder how heavy our little baby is.* **3** of very great amount, force *etc*: *heavy rain; a heavy blow; The ship capsized in the heavy seas; heavy taxes.* **4** doing something to a great extent: *He's a heavy smoker/drinker.* **5** dark and dull; looking or feeling stormy: *a heavy sky/atmosphere.* **6** difficult to read, do, understand *etc*: *Books on philosophy are too heavy for me.* **7** (of food) hard to digest: *rather heavy pastry.* **8** noisy and clumsy: *heavy footsteps.* **'heavily** *adv*. **'heaviness** *n*.

‚heavy-'duty *adj* made to stand up to very hard wear or use: *heavy-duty tyres.*

heavy industry industries such as coal-mining, ship-building *etc* which involve the use of large or heavy machines or which produce large or heavy products.

'heavyweight *adj, n* (a person) in the heaviest of the various classes into which competitors in certain sports (*eg* boxing, wrestling) are divided according to their weight: *a heavyweight boxer.*

heavy going difficult to make any progress with: *I found this book very heavy going.*

a heavy heart a feeling of sadness: *He obeyed with a heavy heart.*

make heavy weather of to find surprising difficulty in doing: *He said he'd finish the job in half an hour, but he's making rather heavy weather of it.*

hectare ['hekta:, (*Amer*) -teər] *n* a metric unit of area, 10 000 square metres.

hectic ['hektik] *adj* very busy; rushed: *Life is hectic these days.*

he'd *see* **have, would**.

hedge [hedʒ] *n* a line of bushes *etc* planted so closely together that their branches form a solid mass, grown round the edges of gardens, fields *etc.* – *v* **1** to avoid giving a clear answer to a question. **2** (with **in** or **off**) to enclose (an area of land) with a hedge.

'**hedgehog** *n* a small brown prickly-backed animal.

'**hedgerow** [-rou] *n* a row of bushes forming a hedge, *esp* in the country.

heed [hi:d] *v* to pay attention to: *He refused to heed my warning; Heed what I say!*

'**heedful** *adj* (with **of**) paying attention to; responding to: *heedful of danger.*

'**heedless** *adj* (*esp* with **of**) careless; paying no attention: *Heedless of the danger, he ran into the burning building to rescue the girl.* '**heedlessly** *adv.*

pay heed to, take heed of: *Take heed of my warning; He paid no heed to me.*

heel [hi:l] *n* **1** the back part of the foot: *I have a blister on my heel.* **2** the part of a sock *etc* that covers this part of the foot: *I have a hole in the heel of my sock.* **3** the part of a shoe, boot *etc* under or round the heel of the foot: *The heel has come off this shoe.* – *v* **1** to put a heel on (a shoe *etc*). **2** (*usu* with **over**) (of ships) to lean to one side: *The boat heeled over in the strong wind.*

-heeled: *high-heeled shoes.*

at/on one's heels close behind one: *The thief ran off with the policeman close on his heels.*

kick one's heels to be kept waiting: *I was left kicking my heels for half an hour.*

take to one's heels to run away: *The thief took to his heels.*

to heel (of dogs *etc*) at a person's heel: *You must teach your dog to walk to heel in a busy street.*

turn on one's heel to turn one's back (and walk off).

hefty ['hefti] *adj* **1** (of people) big and strong: *Her husband is pretty hefty.* **2** (of punches *etc*) powerful: *a hefty kick.*

heifer ['hefə] *n* a young cow.

height [hait] *n* **1** the distance from the bottom to the top of something: *What is the height of this building?; He is 1.75 metres in height.* **2** the highest, greatest, strongest *etc* point: *He is at the height of his career; The storm was at its height.* **3** the peak or extreme: *dressed in the height of fashion; His actions were the height of folly.* **4** a high place: *We looked down from the heights at the valley beneath us.*

'**heighten** *v* **1** to make or become higher: *to heighten the garden wall.* **2** to increase (an effect *etc*).

heir [eə] – *fem* '**heiress** – *n* a person who by law receives wealth, property *etc* when the owner dies: *A person's eldest son is usually his heir; A king's eldest son is the heir to the throne.*

'**heirloom** [-lu:m] *n* something valuable that

has been handed down in a family from generation to generation: *This brooch is a family heirloom.*

held *see* **hold.**

helicopter ['helikoptə] *n* a flying-machine kept in the air by large propellors fixed on top of it which go round very fast.

helium ['hi:liəm] *n* an element, a very light gas which does not burn and which is used *eg* in balloons.

hell [hel] *n* (according to some religions) the place or state of punishment of the wicked after death with much pain, misery *etc.*

for the hell of it for no particular reason; just for fun: *The boys said they had set fire to the house just for the hell of it.*

,**hell'bent on** determined on: *I've told him it will be dangerous, but he's hellbent on going.*

he'll *see* **will.**

hello, hallo, hullo [hə'lou] *interjs, ns* a word used as a greeting, to attract attention, or to express surprise: *Say hello to your aunt; 'Hullo,' I said to myself, 'What's going on here?'*

helm [helm] *n* the wheel or handle by which a ship is steered: *He asked me to take the helm* (= steer the ship).

'**helmsman** ['helmz-] *n* a person who steers a ship.

helmet ['helmit] *n* a metal, leather *etc* covering to protect the head: *Soldiers wear helmets when fighting.*

help [help] *v* **1** to do something with or for someone that he cannot do alone, or that he will find useful: *Will you help me with this translation?; Will you please help me (to) translate this poem?; Can I help?; He fell down and I helped him up.* **2** to play a part in something; to improve or advance: *Bright posters will help to attract the public to the exhibition; Good exam results will help his chances of a job.* **3** to make less bad: *An aspirin will help your headache.* **4** to serve (a person) in a shop: *Can I help you, sir?* **5** (with **can(not), could(not)**) to be able not to do something or to prevent something: *He looked so funny that I couldn't help laughing; Can I help it if it rains?* – *n* **1** the act of helping, or the result of this: *Can you give me some help?; Your digging the garden was a big help; Can I be of help to you?* **2** someone or something that is useful: *You're a great help to me.* **3** a servant, farmworker *etc*: *She has hired a new help.* **4** (*usu* with **no**) a way of preventing something: *Even if you don't want to do it, the decision has been made – there's no help for it now.*

'**helper** *n*: *We need several helpers for this job.*

'**helpful** *adj*: *a very helpful boy; You may find*

this book helpful. **'helpfully** *adv.* **'helpfulness** *n.*

'helping *n* the amount of food one has on one's plate: *a large helping of pudding.*

'helpless *adj* needing the help of other people; unable to do anything for oneself: *A baby is almost completely helpless.* **'helplessly** *adv.* **'helplessness** *n.*

help oneself 1 (*with* **to**) to give oneself or take (food *etc*): *Help yourself to another cake;* '*Can I have a pencil?*' '*Certainly – help yourself;* *He helped himself to* (= stole) *my jewellery.* **2** (*with* **cannot, could not**) to be able to stop (oneself): *I burst out laughing when he told me – I just couldn't help myself.*

help out to help (a person), *usu* for a short time because the person is in some difficulty: *I help out in the shop from time to time;* *Could you help me out by looking after the baby?*

helter-skelter ['heltə'skeltə] *adv* in great hurry and confusion.

hem [hem] *n* the border of a piece of clothing, folded over and sewn. – *v* – *pt, ptp* **hemmed** – to make a hem on (a piece of clothing): *I've hemmed the skirt.*

hem in to surround (someone): *The soldiers were hemmed in on all sides by the enemy.*

hemisphere ['hemisfiə] *n* one half of the Earth: *Singapore and the British Isles are in the northern hemisphere.*

,hemi'spherical [-'sfe-] *adj* like half a ball in shape.

hemoglobin *see* **haemoglobin**.

hemorrhage *see* **haemorrhage**.

hemp [hemp] *n* (a plant from which is obtained) a coarse fibre used to make rope, bags, sails *etc* and the drug cannabis (hashish or marijuana).

hen [hen] *n* **1** the female farmyard fowl: *Hens lay eggs.* **2** the female of any bird: *The hen is sitting on the nest;* (*also adj*) *a hen blackbird.*

'henpecked [-pekt] *adj* (of a man) ruled by his wife: *a henpecked husband.*

hence [hens] *adv* **1** for this reason: *Hence, I shall have to stay.* **2** from this time: *a year hence.* **3** away from this place.

hence'forth *adv* from now on: *Henceforth I shall refuse to work with him.*

henchman ['hentʃmən] – *pl* **'henchmen** – *n* a loyal supporter: *a politician/gangster and his henchmen.*

henpecked *see* **hen**.

her [həː] *pron* (used as the object of a verb or preposition) a female person or animal already spoken about: *I'll ask my mother when I see her;* *He came with her.* – *adj* belonging to such a person or animal: *My mother bought his car, so it's her car;* *a cat and her kittens.*

hers [həːz] *pron* something which belongs to

a female person or animal already spoken about: *It's not your book – it's hers;* *Hers is on that shelf.*

her'self *pron* **1** used as the object of a verb or preposition when a female person or animal is the object of an action she performs: *The cat licked herself;* *She looked at herself in the mirror.* **2** used to emphasize **she, her,** or the name of a female person or animal: *She herself played no part in this;* *Mary answered the letter herself.* **3** without help *etc*: *She did it all herself.*

herald ['herəld] *n* formerly, a person who carries and reads important messages or notices (*eg* from a king): *The king sent out heralds to announce the new law.* – *v* to announce or be a sign of: *A sharp wind often heralds a storm.*

he'raldic [-ral-] *adj* of heraldry.

'heraldry *n* the study of coats of arms, crests *etc* and of the history of the families who have the right to use them.

herb [həːb] *n* a *usu* small plant used to flavour food or to make medicines: *herbs and spices.*

'herbal *adj* of herbs, *esp* herbs used to make medicines: *a herbal remedy.*

'herbalist *n* a person who deals in herbs, *esp* those used to make medicines.

herd [həːd] *n* a group of animals of one kind that stay, or are kept, together: *a herd of cattle;* *a herd of elephant(s).* – *v* to gather together, or be brought together, in a group: *The dogs herded the sheep together;* *The tourists were herded into a tiny room.*

-herd a person who looks after a herd of certain kinds of animals: *a goat-herd.*

'herdsman ['həːdz-] *n* a person who looks after a herd of animals.

the herd instinct the tendency to behave, think *etc* like everyone else.

here [hiə] *adv* **1** (at, in or to) this place: *He's here;* *Come here;* *He lives not far from here;* *Here they come;* *Here is/Here's your lost book.* **2** at this time; at this point in an argument: *Here she stopped speaking to wipe her eyes;* *Here is where I disagree with you.* **3** beside one: *My colleague here will deal with the matter.* – *interj* **1** a shout of surprise, disapproval *etc*: *Here! what do you think you're doing?* **2** a shout used to show that one is present: *Shout 'Here!' when I call your name.*

,herea'bout(s) *adv* near this place: *He lives somewhere hereabouts.*

,here'by *adv esp* in legal language, now, by means of (*eg* this statement): *I hereby declare that I will not be responsible for any of her debts.*

here'with *adv* with this (letter *etc*): *I am returning your passport herewith.*

here and there in, or to, various places: *Books were scattered here and there.*

here goes I'm going to do something now: *I've never tried diving before, but here goes!*

here's to *interj* used as a toast to the health, success *etc* of someone or something: *Here's to the success of the new company.*

here, there and everywhere in, or to, a larger number of places; in all directions: *People were running around here, there and everywhere.*

here you are here is what you want *etc*: *Here you are. This is the book you were looking for.*

neither here nor there not important: *His opinion is neither here nor there.*

heredity [hi'redəti] *n* the passing on of qualities (*eg* appearance, intelligence) from parents to children.

he'reditary *adj* (able to be) passed on in this way: *Is musical ability hereditary?*

herein *see* **here.**

heresy ['herəsi] *n* (the holding or teaching of) a (*esp* religious) opinion which differs from the official opinion.

'heretic [-tik] *n* a person who holds or teaches such an opinion. **heretical** [hə'retikl] *adj*.

heritage ['heritidʒ] *n* things (*esp* valuable things such as buildings, literature *etc*) which are passed on from one generation to another: *We must all take care to preserve our national heritage.*

hermit ['hɜːmit] *n* a person who lives alone, *esp* to devote himself to religion.

'hermitage [-tidʒ] *n* the place where a hermit lives.

hermit crab a soft-bodied crab that inhabits the empty shells of other creatures.

hero ['hiərou] – *pl* **'heroes**: *fem* **heroine** ['herouin] – *n* **1** a man or boy admired (by many people) for his brave deeds: *The boy was regarded as a hero for saving his friend's life.* **2** the chief male person in a story, play *etc*: *The hero of this book is a young American boy called Tom Sawyer.*

heroic [hi'rouik] *adj* **1** very brave: *heroic deeds.* **2** of heroes: *heroic tales.* **he'roically** *adv*.

heroism ['herouizm] *n* great bravery: *The policeman was given a medal in recognition of his heroism.*

'hero-worship *n* very great, sometimes too great, admiration for a person. – *v* to show such admiration for (someone): *The boy hero-worshipped the footballer.*

the **heroine** (not **heroin**) of the story.

heroin ['herouin] *n* a drug obtained from opium.

to take **heroin** (not **heroine**).

heroine, heroism *see* **hero.**

heron ['herən] *n* a type of large water-bird, with long legs and a long neck.

herring ['heriŋ] – *pls* **'herring, 'herrings** – *n* a small, edible kind of sea fish.

hers, herself *see* **her.**

hertz [hɜːts] – *pl* **hertz** – *n* (*often abbrev* **Hz** *when written*) a unit of frequency used of radio waves *etc*.

he's *see* **be, have.**

hesitate ['heziteit] *v* **1** to pause briefly *eg* because of uncertainty: *He hesitated before answering; The diver hesitated for a minute on the diving-board.* **2** to be unwilling (to do something) *eg* because one is not sure it is right: *I hesitate to say he lied but he certainly misled me; Don't hesitate to tell me if you have any complaints.*

'hesitancy *n* the tendency to hesitate.

'hesitant *adj* making or having frequent hesitations: *a hesitant speaker; I'm hesitant to tell her she's wrong.* **'hesitantly** *adv*.

hesi'tation *n* **1** an act of hesitating. **2** unwillingness or uncertainty.

hew [hjuː] – *pt* **hewed**; *ptp* **hewed, hewn** [hjuːn] – *v* **1** to cut with an axe, sword *etc*: *He hewed down the tree.* **2** to cut out or shape with an axe, sword *etc*: *He hewed a path through the forest.*

*****hexagon** ['heksəgən] *n* a six-sided figure.

hey [hei] *interj* a shout expressing joy, or a question, or used to attract attention: *Hey! What are you doing there?*

heyday ['heidei] *n* the time when a particular person or thing had great importance and popularity: *The 1950's were the heyday of rock and roll.*

hi [hai] *interj* a word of greeting: *Hi! How are you?*

hibernate ['haibəneit] *v* (of certain animals, *eg* hedgehogs) to pass the winter in a condition like sleep. **,hiber'nation** *n*.

hibiscus [hi'biskəs] *n* a tropical plant with brightly-coloured flowers.

hiccup, hiccough ['hikʌp] *n* **1** (the sound caused by) a sudden brief stopping of the breath caused by *eg* eating or drinking too much, too quickly. **2** (*in pl*) the frequent repetition of this, at intervals of a few seconds: *an attack of hiccoughs; I've got the hiccups.* – *v* – *pt, ptp* **'hiccuped** (*Amer also* **'hiccupped**) – to make a hiccup or hiccups.

hide[1] [haid] – *pt* **hid** [hid]; *ptp* **hidden** ['hidn] – *v* to put (a person, thing *etc*) in a place where it cannot be seen or easily found: *I'll hide the children's presents; You hide, and I'll come and look for you; She hid from her father; He tries to hide his feelings.* – *n* a small concealed hut *etc* from which birds *etc* can be watched, photographed *etc*.

'hidden *adj* (made in such a way as to be) difficult to see or find: *a hidden door; a hidden meaning.*

***** see illustration on p. 476

hide-and-seek *n* a children's game in which one person searches for other people who have hidden themselves.

'hide-out *n* a place where one can hide or is hiding: *The police searched for the bandits' hide-out.*

'hiding[1] *n*: *He has gone into hiding because he knows the police are looking for him*; *Is he still in hiding?*; *The burglar came out of hiding when the police car drove off.*

'hiding-place *n* a place where a person or thing can be or is hidden: *We'll have to find a safe hiding-place for our jewels.*

hide[2] [haid] *n* the skin of an animal: *He makes coats out of animal hides*; **cow-hide.**

'hiding[2] *n* a beating on the buttocks (*usu* of a child as punishment): *He got a good hiding.*

hideous ['hidiəs] *adj* extremely ugly: *a hideous vase.* **'hideously** *adv.* **'hideousness** *n.*

hierarchy ['haiəra:ki] *n* (an) arrangement (of *usu* people in a group, also things *etc*) in order of rank, importance *etc*. **hie'rarchical** [-'ra:-] *adj.*

> Notice the second **r** in **hierarchy**.

hieroglyphics [haiərə'glifiks] *n pl* a form of writing used *eg* in ancient Egypt, in which pictures represent words and sounds.

hi-fi ['haifai] (short for **high fidelity**) *n* (a record-player *etc* producing) high quality and great accuracy in the reproduction of sound. – *adj*: *hi-fi equipment.*

high [hai] *adj* **1** at, from, or reaching up to, a great distance from ground-level, sea-level *etc*: *a high mountain*; *a high dive*; *a dive from the high diving-board.* **2** having a particular height: *This building is about 20 metres high*; *a little man only one metre high*; *My horse is fifteen hands high.* **3** great; large; considerable: *The car was travelling at high speed*; *He has a high opinion of her work*; *They charge high prices*; *high hopes*; *The child has a high fever/temperature.* **4** most important; very important: *the high altar in a church*; *Important criminal trials are held at the High Court*; *a high official.* **5** noble; good: *high ideals.* **6** (of a wind) strong: *The wind is high tonight.* **7** (of sounds) at or towards the top of a (musical) range: *a high note.* **8** (of voices) like a child's voice (rather than like a man's): *He still speaks in a high voice.* **9** (of food, *esp* meat) beginning to go bad. **10** having great value: *Aces and kings are high cards.* – *adv* at, or to, a great distance from ground-level, sea-level *etc*: *The plane was flying high in the sky*; *He'll rise high in his profession.*

'highly *adv* **1** very; very much: *highly delighted*; *highly paid*; *I value the book highly.* **2** with approval: *He thinks/speaks very highly of you.*

'highness *n* **1** the state or quality of being high. **2** a title of a prince, princess *etc*: *Your Highness*; *Her Highness.*

'high-chair *n* a chair with long legs, used by a baby or young child at mealtimes.

high-'class *adj* of high quality: *This is a high-class hotel.*

higher education education beyond the level of secondary school education, *eg* at a university.

high fidelity high quality and great accuracy (in the reproduction of sound). – *See also* **hi-fi.**

high-'handed *adj* done, acting, without consultation of, or consideration for, other people: *a high-handed decision*; *A new headmaster should try not to be too high-handed.* **high-'handedly** *adv.* **high-'handedness** *n.*

high jump a sports contest in which people jump over a bar which is raised until no-one can jump over it.

'highlands *n pl* a mountainous part of certain countries, *esp* (*with cap*) of Scotland.

'high-level *adj* involving important people: *high-level talks.*

'highlight *n* the best or most memorable event, experience, part of something *etc*: *The highlight of our holiday was a trip to a brewery.* – *v* to draw particular attention to (a person, thing *etc*).

highly-'strung *adj* very nervous; very easily upset or excited.

high-'minded *adj* having or showing good or noble ideals, principles *etc*. **high-'mindedness** *n.*

high-'pitched *adj* (of sounds, voices *etc*) high, sharp: *a high-pitched, childish voice.*

high-'powered *adj* (with an engine which is) very powerful: *a high-powered motorboat/engine.*

'high-rise *adj* with many storeys: *She does not like living in a high-rise flat as the children cannot get out to play easily.*

'highroad *n* a main road.

high school a secondary school: *She goes to high school next year.*

high-'spirited *adj* showing high spirits: *a high-spirited horse.*

high spirits enthusiasm, cheerfulness and energy: *He's in high spirits today.*

high street (*with cap when used as a name*) the main street of a town *etc*, *usu* with shops *etc.*

high tide the time when the tide is farthest up the shore: *High tide today is at 15.46*; *They set sail at high tide.*

high treason *see* **treason.**

high water the time at which the tide or other water (*eg* a river) is at its highest point.

'highway *n* a road, *esp* a large or main road.

Highway Code in Britain, (a booklet containing) a set of official rules for road users.

'highwayman – pl **'highwaymen** – n in earlier times, a man usu on horseback, who attacked and robbed people travelling in coaches etc on public roads.

high wire see wire.

high and dry 1 (of boats) on the shore; out of the water: The boat was left high and dry of the beach. **2** in difficulties: Her husband has left her high and dry without any money.

high and low everywhere: I've searched high and low for that book.

high and mighty behaving as if one thinks one is very important: Don't be so high and mighty – you're no-one special.

the high seas the open seas; far from land.

it is etc **high time** something ought to be done or have been done etc by now: It is high time that this job was finished; It's high time someone spanked that child.

see also **tall.**

hijack ['haidʒak] v **1** to take control of (an aeroplane) while it is moving and force the pilot to fly to a particular place. **2** to stop and rob (a vehicle): Thieves hijacked a lorry carrying $20 000 worth of whisky. **3** to steal (something) from a vehicle: Thieves hijacked $20 000 worth of whisky from a lorry. – n the act of hijacking. **'hijacker** n.

hike [haik] n a long walk, usu in the country: twenty-mile hike. – v to go on a hike or hikes: He has hiked all over Britain. **'hiker** n.

hilarious [hi'leəriəs] adj very funny: a hilarious comedy. **hi'lariously** adv.

hi'larity [-'la-] n amusement; laughter.

hill [hil] **1** n a piece of high land, smaller than a mountain: We went for a walk in the hills yesterday. **2** a slope on a road: This car has difficulty going up steep hills.

'hillock [-lək] n a small hill.

'hilly adj having many hills: hilly country.

'hillside n the side or slope of a hill: The hillside was covered with new housing.

hilt [hilt] n the handle, esp of a sword.

him [him] pron (used as the object of a verb or preposition) a male person or animal already spoken about: I saw him yesterday; I gave him a book; I came with him.

him'self pron **1** used as the object of a verb or preposition when a male person or animal is the object of an action he performs: He kicked himself; He looked at himself in the mirror. **2** used to emphasize **he, him** or the name of a male person or animal: John himself played no part in this. **3** without help etc: He did it himself.

See also **he, his.**

hind¹ [haind] n a female deer, esp of the red deer.

hind² [haind] adj at the back (usu of an animal): a hind leg.

hinder ['hində] v to delay or prevent; to make difficult: All these interruptions hinder my work; All the interruptions hinder me from working.

'hindrance [-drəns] n a person, thing etc that hinders: I know you are trying to help but you're just being a hindrance.

hindquarters ['haindkwo:təz] n pl (of an animal) the back legs and the part of the body above them: I think our dog has injured its hindquarters – it is limping.

hindrance see hinder.

hindsight ['haindsait] n wisdom or knowledge got only after something (usu bad) has happened.

Hindu [hin'du:] n, adj (of) a person who believes in, and lives according to the rules of, the religion of **'Hinduism.**

hinge [hindʒ] n the joint by means of which a door is fastened to a door-frame, a lid is fastened to a box etc and on which the door, lid etc turns when it opens or closes: I must oil the hinges.

hinge on to depend on: The result of the whole competition hinges on the last match.

hint [hint] n **1** a statement that passes on information without giving it openly or directly: He didn't actually say he wanted more money, but he dropped a hint. **2** a helpful suggestion: I can give you some useful gardening hints. **3** a very small amount; a slight impression: There was a hint of fear in his voice. – v to (try to) pass on information without stating it openly or directly: He hinted that he would like more money; He hinted at possible changes.

take a/the hint to understand a hint and act on it: I keep making jokes to my secretary about her coming to work late every day, but she never takes the hint.

hinterland ['hintəland] n the district lying inland from the coast.

hip [hip] n **1** (the bones in) either of the two sides of the body just below the waist: She fell and broke her left hip. **2** (the measurement round) the body at the level of the hips and buttocks: This exercise is good for the hips; What (size of) hip are you?

hippie, hippy ['hipi] – pl **'hippies** – n, adj (of) a usu young person who does not wish to live by the normal rules of society and who shows his rejection of these rules by his unusual clothes, habits etc: The farm cottage was bought by a group of young hippies; (also adj) hippy clothes.

hippopotamus [hipə'potəməs] n a large African animal with very thick skin living in or near rivers.

hire ['haiə] v **1** (often with from) to get the use of by paying money: He's hiring a car (from *us) for the week.* **2** (*often with* **out**) to give (someone) the use of in exchange for money: *Will you hire me your boat for the week-end?*; *Does this firm hire out cars?* **3** (*esp Amer*) to employ (a workman *etc*): *They have hired a team of labourers to dig the road.* – *n* (money paid for) hiring: *Is this hall for hire?*; *How much is the hire of the hall?*; *We don't own this crane – it's on hire.* **'hirer** *n.*

hire-'purchase *n* (*also abbrev* **HP** [eitʃ'piː]) a way of buying an article by paying the price in several weekly or monthly parts: *I got this television on hire-purchase*; (*also adj*) *a hire-purchase agreement.*

his [hiz] *adj, pron* belonging to a male person already spoken about: *John says it's his book*; *He says the book is his*; *No, his is on the table.*

hiss [his] *v* (of snakes, geese, people *etc*) to make a sound like that of the letter *s* [s], *eg* to show anger or displeasure: *The children hissed (at) the witch when she came on stage*; *The geese hissed at the dog.* – *n* such a sound: *The speaker ignored the hisses of the angry crowd.*

history ['histəri] – *pl* **'histories** – *n* **1** the study of events *etc* that happened in the past: *She is studying British history*; (*also adj*) *a history lesson/book.* **2** a description *usu* in writing of past events, ways of life *etc*: *I'm writing a history of Scotland.* **3** (the description of) the *usu* interesting events *etc* associated with (something): *This desk/word has a very interesting history.*
hi'storian [-'stoː-] *n* a person who studies (and writes about) history.
hi'storic [-'stoː-] *adj* famous or important in history: *a historic battle.*
hi'storical [-'stoː-] *adj* **1** of or about history; of or about people or events from history: *historical research*; *historical novels.* **2** that actually happened or existed, not legendary or mythical: *Was Shakespeare's character Macbeth a historical person?* **hi'storically** [-'stoː-] *adv.*
make history to do something very important, *esp* to be the first to do something: *The Wright brothers made history when they were the first to fly an aeroplane.*

hit [hit] – *prp* **'hitting**: *pt, ptp* **hit** – *v* **1** to (cause or allow to) come into hard contact with: *The ball hit him on the head*; *He hit his head on/against a low branch*; *The car hit a lamp-post*; *He hit me on the head with a bottle*; *He was hit by a bullet*; *That boxer can certainly hit hard!* **2** to make hard contact with (something), and force or cause it to move in some direction: *The batsman hit the ball (over the wall).* **3** to cause to suffer: *The farmers were badly hit by the lack of rain*; *Her husband's death hit*

her hard. **4** to find; to succeed in reaching: *His second arrow hit the bull's-eye*; *Take the path across the fields and you'll hit the road*; *She used to be a famous soprano but she cannot hit the high notes now.* – *n* **1** the act of hitting: *That was a good hit.* **2** a point scored by hitting a target *etc*: *He scored five hits.* **3** something which is popular or successful: *The play/record is a hit*; (*also adj*) *a hit song.*

hit-and-'run *adj* **1** (of a driver) causing injury to a person and driving away without stopping or reporting the accident. **2** (of an accident) caused by such a driver.
hit-or-'miss *adj* without any system or planning; careless: *hit-or-miss methods.*
hit back to hit (someone) by whom one has been hit): *He hit me, so I hit him back.*
hit below the belt to hit in an unfair way.
hit it off to become friendly: *We hit it off as soon as we met*; *I hit it off with him.*
hit on to find (an answer *etc*): *We've hit on the solution at last.*
hit out (*often with* **against** *or* **at**) to attempt to hit: *The injured man hit out blindly at his attackers.*
make a hit with to make oneself liked or approved of by: *That young man has made a hit with your daughter.*

hitch [hitʃ] *v* **1** to fasten to something: *He hitched his horse to the fence-post*; *He hitched his car to his caravan.* **2** to hitch-hike: *I can't afford the train-fare – I'll have to hitch.* – *n* **1** an unexpected problem or delay: *The job was completed without a hitch.* **2** a kind of knot. **3** a sudden, short pull upwards: *She gave her skirt a hitch.*
'hitch-hike *v* to travel by means of free rides in other people's cars: *He has hitch-hiked all over Britain.* **'hitch-hiker** *n.*
hitch a lift/ride to get a free ride in someone else's car.
hitch up to pull up or raise with a sudden short pull: *He hitched up his trousers.*

hither ['hiðə] *adv* to this place.
hither'to *adv* up to this time: *Hitherto, this information has been kept secret.*
hither and thither in various directions: *People were running hither and thither.*

hive [haiv] *n* **1** a box *etc* where bees live and store up honey: *He's building a hive so that he can keep bees.* **2** the bees that live in such a place: *The whole hive flew after the queen bee.*

hoard [hoːd] *n* a (sometimes hidden) store (of treasure, food *etc*): *When she was supposed to be on a diet she secretly kept a hoard of potato crisps in a cupboard.* – *v* to store up or keep large quantities of (something), often in secret: *His mother told him to stop hoarding old newspapers.* **'hoarder** *n.*
hoarding ['hoːdiŋ] *n* **1** a temporary fence of

boards, *eg* round a place where a building is being knocked down or built. **2** a *usu* large wooden board on which advertisements, posters *etc* are stuck.

hoarse [ho:s] *adj* **1** (of voices, shouts *etc*) rough; harsh: *a hoarse cry; His voice sounds hoarse.* **2** having a hoarse voice, *usu* because one has a cold or cough, or because one has been shouting: *You sound hoarse – have you a cold?; The spectators shouted themselves hoarse.* **'hoarseness** *n*.

hoax [houks] *n* a trick played to deceive people: *There was not a bomb in the school at all – it was just a hoax. – v* to trick: *They found that they had been hoaxed.*

play a hoax on to carry out a trick on.

hob [hob] *n* the flat framework on top of a cooker, on which pots are placed to be heated: *A pan of stew was simmering on the hob.*

hobble ['hobl] *v* to walk with difficulty, *usu* taking short steps (*eg* because one is lame or because one's feet are sore): *The old lady hobbled along with a stick.*

hobby ['hobi] – *pl* **'hobbies** – *n* something a person enjoys doing (*usu* frequently) in his spare time: *Stamp-collecting is a popular hobby.*

hobo ['houbou] – *pl* **'hobo(e)s** – *n* (*Amer*) a tramp.

hock [hok] *n* a joint on the hind leg of an animal, below the knee: *The horse has an injured hock.*

hockey ['hoki] *n* a game for two teams of eleven players, played with clubs which are bent at one end (**'hockey-sticks**) and a ball, or in **ice hockey**, a round flat disc called a puck.

hocus-pocus [houkəs'poukəs] *n* trickery; words, actions *etc* which are intended to deceive or mislead (someone): *The people were not deceived by the political hocus-pocus of the prospective candidate.*

hoe [hou] *n* a long-handled tool with a metal blade used for removing or destroying weeds *etc. – v – prp* **'hoeing** – to use a hoe *eg* to remove or destroy weeds: *This morning I hoed the garden/weeds.*

hog [hog] *n* (*esp Amer*) a pig. – *v – pt, ptp* **hogged** – **1** to gobble up greedily. **2** to take or use more of than one ought to; to keep or use longer than one ought to: *She's hogging the mirror and no-one else can use it.* **'hogwash** *n* (*esp Amer*) nonsense.

go the whole hog to do something completely: *I've bought a new dress – I think I'll go the whole hog and buy a complete outfit.*

hoist [hoist] *v* **1** to lift (something heavy): *he hoisted the sack on to his back; He hoisted the child up on to his shoulders.* **2** to raise or lift by means of some apparatus, a rope *etc*: *The cargo was hoisted on to the ship: They hoisted the flag. – n* **1** an apparatus for lifting *usu* heavy objects: *a luggage hoist.* **2** a lift or push up: *Give me a hoist over this wall, will you!*

hold¹ [hould] – *pt, ptp* **held** [held] – *v* **1** to have in one's hand(s) or between one's hands:. *He was holding a knife; Hold that dish with both hands; He held the little boy's hand; He held the mouse by its tail.* **2** to have in a part, or between parts, of the body, or between parts of a tool *etc*: *He held the pencil in his teeth; She was holding a pile of books in her arms; Hold the stamp with tweezers.* **3** to support or keep from moving, running away, falling *etc*: *What holds that shelf up?; He held the door closed by leaning against it; Hold you hands above your head; Hold his arms so that he can't struggle.* **4** to remain in position, fixed *etc* when under strain: *I've tied the two pieces of string together, but I'm not sure the knot will hold; Will the anchor hold in a storm?* **5** to keep (a person) in some place or in one's power: *The police are holding a man for questioning in connection with the murder; He was held captive.* **6** to (be able to) contain: *This jug holds two pints; You can't hold water in a handkerchief; This drawer holds all my shirts.* **7** to cause to take place: *The meeting will be held next week; We'll hold the meeting in the hall.* **8** to keep (oneself), or to be, in a particular state or condition: *We'll hold ourselves in readiness in case you send for us; She holds herself very erect.* **9** to have or to be (a job *etc*): *He held the position of company secretary for five years.* **10** to think strongly; to believe; to consider or regard: *I hold that this was the right decision; He holds me (to be) responsible for everyone's mistakes; He is held in great respect; He holds certain very odd beliefs.* **11** to continue to be valid or apply: *Our offer will hold until next week; These rules hold under all circumstances.* **12** (*with* **to**) to force (a person) to do something he has promised to do: *I intend to hold him to his promises.* **13** to defend: *They held the castle against the enemy.* **14** not to be beaten by: *The general realized that the soldiers could not hold the enemy for long.* **15** to keep (a person's attention). **16** to celebrate: *The festival is held on 24 June.* **17** to be the owner of: *He holds shares in this company.* **18** (of good weather) to continue: *I hope the weather holds until after the school sports.* **19** (*also* **hold the line**) (of a person who is making a telephone call) to wait: *Mr Brown is busy at the moment – will you hold or would you like him to call you back?* **20** to continue to sing: *Please hold that note for four whole beats.* **21** to keep (something): *They'll hold your luggage at* *the station until you collect it.* **22** (of the future) to be going to produce: *I wonder what the future holds for me?* – *n* **1** the act of holding: *He caught/got/laid/took hold of the rope and pulled; Keep hold of that rope.* **2** power; influence: *He has a strange hold over that girl.* **3** (in wrestling *etc*) a manner of holding one's opponent: *The wrestler invented a new hold.*

-holder a person or thing that holds something: *a pen-holder; a ticket-holder* (= a person who has a ticket for something).

'hold-all *n* a (*usu* large) bag with a zip for packing clothes *etc* into.

get hold of 1 to manage to speak to: *I've been trying to get hold of you by phone all morning.* **2** to get, buy or obtain: *I've been trying to get hold of a copy of that book for years.*

hold back 1 to refuse to tell someone (something): *The police were convinced the man was holding something back.* **2** to prevent from happening, being seen *etc*, with an effort: *The little girl succeeded in holding back her tears.* **3** to prevent from making progress: *I meant to finish cleaning the house but the children have held me back all morning.*

hold down to keep or be allowed to stay in (a job): *He is incapable of holding down a job.*

hold forth to talk or give one's opinions, often loudly, at great length: *The prime minister held forth for hours on the success of his government.*

hold good to be true or valid; to apply: *Does that rule hold good in every case?*

hold it to stop or wait: *Hold it! Don't start till I tell you to.*

hold off 1 (of weather) to stay away: *I hope the rain holds off.* **2** to keep off; to fight successfully against: *The soldiers managed to hold off the enemy.*

hold on 1 (*often with* **to**) to keep (a grip on) (something): *She held on to me to stop herself slipping; I couldn't hold on any longer, so I let go of the rope.* **2** to stop or wait: *Hold on – I'm not quite ready yet; The telephonist asked the caller to hold on while she connected him.*

hold out 1 to continue to survive *etc* until help arrives: *The rescue team hoped the men in the boat could hold out till they arrived.* **2** to continue to fight against an enemy attack: *The soldiers held out for eight days.* **3** to be enough to last: *Will our supplies hold out till the end of the month?*

hold one's own to be as successful in a fight, argument *etc* as one's opponent: *His opponents tried to prove his arguments wrong but he managed to hold his own.*

hold one's tongue to remain silent or stop

talking: *There were a lot of things I wanted to say, but I thought I'd better just hold my tongue.*

hold up 1 to stop or slow the progress of: *I'm sorry I'm late – I got held up at the office.* **2** to stop and rob: *The bandits held up the stagecoach.* – *n* **'hold-up.**

hold with to approve of: *He doesn't hold with smoking.*

hold² [hould] *n* (in ships) the place, below the deck, where cargo is stored.

hole [houl] *n* **1** an opening or gap in or through something: *a hole in the fence; holes in my socks.* **2** a hollow in something solid: *a hole in my tooth; Many animals live in holes in the ground.* **3** (in golf) (the point scored by the player who takes the fewest strokes to hit his ball over) any one of the *usu* eighteen sections of the golf course between the tees and the holes in the middle of the greens: *He won by two holes; We played nine holes.* – *v* **1** to make a hole in: *The ship was badly holed when it hit the rock.* **2** to hit (a ball *etc*) into a hole: *The golfer holed his ball from twelve metres away.*

holiday ['holədi] *n* **1** a day when one does not have to work: *Next Monday is a holiday.* **2** (*often in pl*) a period of time when one does not have to work: *The summer holidays will soon be here; We're going to Sweden for our holiday(s); I'm taking two weeks' holiday in June;* (*also adj*) *holiday clothes.*

'holidaymaker *n* a person who has gone *eg* to the seaside for a holiday.

on holiday not working; having a holiday: *Mr Smith has gone on holiday; She is on holiday in France.*

holler ['holə] *v* to shout: *He hollered at the boy to go away; He's hollering about the cost of petrol again.*

holiness *see* **holy.**

hollow ['holou] *adj* **1** having an empty space in it: *a hollow tree; Bottles, pipes and tubes are hollow.* **2** (of a sound) strangely deep, as if made in something hollow: *a hollow voice.* – *n* **1** something hollow: *hollows in her cheeks.* **2** a small valley; a dip in the ground: *You can't see the farm from here because it's in a hollow.* **'hollowness** *n*.

beat hollow to beat thoroughly at a game *etc*: *The local team were beaten hollow by eight goals to one on Saturday.*

hollow out to make hollow: *They hollowed out a tree-trunk to make a boat.*

holly ['holi] *n* a type of evergreen tree or bush with prickly leaves and red berries.

holocaust ['holəkɔːst] *n* great destruction, *usu* by fire, *esp* of people's lives.

holster ['houlstə] *n* the *usu* leather case for a pistol, *usu* worn on a person's hips.

holy ['houli] *adj* **1** (worthy of worship or

respect because) associated with God, Jesus, a saint *etc*; sacred: *the Holy Bible*; *holy ground*. **2** good; pure; following the rules of religion: *a holy life*.

'holiness *n* **1** the state of being holy. **2** (*with cap*: with **His, Your** *etc*) a title of the Pope. **the Holy Father** the Pope.

homage ['homidʒ] *n* (a sign of) great respect shown to a person: *We pay homage to this great man by laying a wreath yearly on his grave*.

home [houm] *n* **1** the house, town, country *etc* where a person *etc usu* lives: *I work in London but my home is in Bournemouth*; *When I retire, I'll make my home in Bournemouth*; *Africa is the home of the lion*; *We'll have to find a home for the kitten*. **2** the place from which a person, thing *etc* comes originally: *America is the home of jazz*. **3** a place where children without parents, old people, people who are ill *etc* live and are looked after: *an old folk's home*; *a nursing home*. **4** a place where people stay while they are working: *a nurses' home*. **5** a house: *Crumpy Construction build fine homes for fine people*; *He invited me round to his home.* – *adj* **1** of a person's home or family: *home comforts*. **2** of the country *etc* where a person lives: *home produce*. **3** (in football) playing or played on a team's own ground: *the home team*; *a home game.* – *adv* **1** to a person's home: *I'm going home now*; *Hallo – I'm home!* **2** completely; to the place, position *etc* a thing is intended to be: *He drove the nail home*; *Few of his punches went home*; *These photographs of the war brought home to me the suffering of the soldiers*.

'homeless *n pl, adj* (people) without a place to live in: *This charity was set up to help the homeless*; *homeless people*.

'homely *adj* **1** simple but pleasant: *homely food*. **2** making a person feel he is at home: *a homely atmosphere*. **3** (*Amer*) (of a person) not attractive; ugly. **'homeliness** *n*.

'homing *adj* **1** (of pigeons *etc*) which (can) fly home when set free a long way from home. **2** able to take a missile *etc* to its target: *These torpedoes have homing devices in their noses*.

'home-coming *n* the return home of a person (who has been away for some time): *We had a party to celebrate his home-coming*.

home-'grown *adj* grown in one's own garden or in one's own country: *These tomatoes are home-grown*.

'homeland *n* a person's native land: *Immigrants often weep for their homeland*.

home-'made *adj* made by a person at home; not professionally made: *home-made jam*; *home-made furniture*.

home rule the government of a country or part of a country by its own citizens.

'homesick *adj* missing one's home: *When the boy first went to boarding-school he was very homesick*. **'homesickness** *n*.

'homestead [-sted] *n* a house, *esp* a farm, with the land and other buildings (*eg* barns) which belong to it, *esp* in the US, Australia *etc*.

home truth a plain statement of something which is unpleasant but true (about a person, his behaviour *etc*) said directly to the person: *It's time someone told him a few home truths*.

'homeward *adj* going home: *his homeward journey*.

'homeward(s) *adv* towards home: *his journey homeward*; *He journeyed homewards*.

'homework *n* work or study done at home, *esp* by a school pupil: *Finish your homework!*

at home 1 in one's home: *I'm afraid he's not at home*. **2** (in football *etc*) in one's own ground: *The team is playing at home today*.

be/feel at home to feel as relaxed as one does in one's own home or in a place or situation one knows well: *I always feel at home in France*; *He's quite at home with cows – he used to live on a farm*.

home in on to move towards (a target *etc*): *The missile is designed to home in on aircraft*.

leave home 1 to leave one's house: *I usually leave home at 7.30 a.m.* **2** to leave one's home to go and live somewhere else: *He left home at the age of fifteen to get a job in Australia*.

make oneself at home to make oneself as comfortable and relaxed as one would at home: *Make yourself at home!*

nothing to write home about not very good: *The concert was nothing to write home about*.

homicide ['homisaid] *n* the killing of one person by another: *He has been found guilty of homicide*. **homi'cidal** *adj*.

homonym ['homənim] *n* a word having the same sound as another word, but a different meaning: *The words 'there' and 'their' are homonyms*.

homosexual [homə'sekʃuəl] *adj, n* (a person, *esp* a man, who is) sexually attracted to people of the same sex. **2** *adj* of or concerning a homosexual or homosexuals: *a homosexual relationship*. **'homo,sexu'ality** [-'a-] *n*.

honest ['onist] *adj* **1** (of people or their behaviour, statements *etc*) truthful; not cheating, stealing *etc*: *My secretary is absolutely honest*; *Give me an honest opinion*. **2** (of a person's appearance) suggesting that he is honest: *an honest face*. **3** (of wealth *etc*) not

gained by cheating, stealing *etc*: *to earn an honest living*.
'**honestly** *adv* **1** in an honest way: *He gained his wealth honestly*. **2** used to stress the truth of what a person is saying: *Honestly, that's exactly what he said*; *I honestly don't think it's possible*. – *interj* used to express mild anger *etc*: *Honestly! That was a stupid thing to do!*
'**honesty** *n*: *Surely, if you own up to something, you should be praised for your honesty, not punished*.
honey ['hʌni] *n* **1** a sweet, thick fluid made by bees from the nectar of flowers: *bread and honey*. **2** (*esp Amer*) darling (used when speaking to someone one loves).
'**honeybee** *n* a bee in a hive, bred for producing honey.
'**honeycomb** *n* the mass formed by rows of wax cells in which bees store their honey.
'**honeymoon** *n* a holiday spent immediately after one's marriage: *We went to London for our honeymoon*; (*also adj*) *a honeymoon couple*.
honk [hoŋk] *n* (a sound like) the cry of a goose or the sound of a motor-car horn. – *v* to make such a noise: *Don't honk that horn any more – you'll disturb the neighbours*.
honorary *see* **honour**.
honour, (*Amer*) **honor** ['onə] *n* **1** respect for truth, honesty *etc*: *a man of honour*. **2** (the keeping or increasing of) a person's, country's *etc* good reputation: *We must fight for the honour of our country*. **3** fame; glory: *He won honour on the field of battle*. **4** respect: *This ceremony is being held in honour of those who died in the war*. **5** something which a person feels to be a reason for pride *etc*: *It is a great honour to be asked to address this meeting*. **6** a title, degree *etc* given to a person as a mark of respect for his services, work, ability *etc*: *He has received many honours for his research into cancer*. **7** (*with cap*: *with* **His**, **Your** *etc*) a title of respect used when talking to or about judges, mayors *etc*: *My client wishes to plead guilty, Your Honour*. – *v* **1** to show great respect to (a person, thing *etc*): *We should honour the Queen*. **2** to do, say *etc* something which is a reason for pride, satisfaction *etc* to: *Will you honour us with your presence at the meeting?* **3** to give (someone) a title, degree *etc* as a mark of respect for his ability *etc*: *He was honoured for his work with the mentally handicapped*. **4** to fulfil (a promise *etc*): *We'll honour our agreement*.
'**honorary** *adj* **1** (*often abbrev* **Hon.** *in writing*) (of an official position) not having any payment: *the Honorary Secretary of the Darts Association*. **2** given to a person as a

mark of respect for his ability *etc*: *an honorary degree*.
'**honourable** *adj* having, showing, bringing or deserving honour: *an honourable man*.
'**honours** *n pl* **1** (*sometimes with cap*: *sometimes abbrev* **Hons** *when written*) a degree awarded by universities, colleges *etc* to students who achieve good results in their final degree examinations, or who carry out specialized study or research; the course of study leading to the awarding of such a degree: *He got First Class Honours in French*; (*also adj*) *an honours degree*, (*Amer*) *an honors course*. **2** ceremony, when given as a mark of respect: *The dead soldiers were buried with full military honours*.
(**in**) **honour bound** forced (to do something) not by law, but because one knows it is right: *I said I would go if he sent for me, and I feel honour bound to do as I promised*.
on one's honour an expression used to emphasize the truth and solemnity of something which is said: *Do you swear, on your honour, never to reveal what you see here?*
word of honour a promise which cannot be broken without loss of honour: *I give you my word of honour that I'll do it*.

honour, noun, ends in -our.
honorary, adjective, drops the u.
honourable, adjective, keeps the u.

hood [hud] *n* **1** a *usu* loose covering for the whole head, often attached to a coat, cloak *etc*: *The monk pulled his hood over his head*. **2** a folding cover on a car, pram *etc*: *Put the hood of the pram up – the baby is getting wet*. **3** (*Amer*) the bonnet of a car: *He raised the hood to look at the engine*. **4** a fold of cloth representing a hood, worn by university graduates over their gowns on ceremonial occasions: *The professors and lecturers all wore their gowns and hoods for the graduation ceremony*.
'**hooded** *adj* fitted with, or wearing, a hood.
hoodlum ['hu:dləm] *n* **1** a destructive person. **2** (*esp Amer*) a criminal.
hoodwink ['hudwiŋk] *v* to trick or deceive.
hoof [hu:f, (*Amer*) huf] – *pls* **hooves** [hu:vz, (*Amer*) huvz], **hoofs** – *n* the horny part of the feet of horses, cows *etc*: *That horse has an injured hoof*.
hook [huk] *n* **1** a small piece of metal shaped like a J fixed at the end of a fishing-line used for catching fish *etc*: *a fish-hook*. **2** a bent piece of metal *etc* used for hanging coats, cups *etc* on, or a smaller one sewn on to a garment, for fastening it: *Hang your jacket on that hook behind the door*; *hooks and eyes*. **3** in boxing, a kind of punch with the elbow bent: *a left hook*. – *v* **1** to catch (a fish *etc*) with a hook: *He hooked a large salmon*. **2** to fasten or to be fastened by a

hook or hooks: *He hooked the ladder on* (*to the branch*); *This bit hooks on to that bit*; *Could you hook my dress up down the back?* **3** in golf, to hit (the ball) far to the left of where it should be (or to the right if one is left-handed).

hooked *adj* **1** curved like a hook: *a hooked nose.* **2** (*with on*) slang for very interested in, or showing a great liking for; addicted to: *He's hooked on modern art*; *He's hooked on marijuana.*

by hook or by crook by some means or another; in any way possible: *I'll get her to marry me, by hook or by crook.*

off the hook free from some difficulty or problem: *If he couldn't keep the terms of the contract, he shouldn't have signed it – I don't see how we can get him off the hook now.*

hooligan ['huːligən] *n* a young violent, destructive or badly-behaved person.

'hooliganism *n* violent or destructive behaviour *esp* by young people.

hoop [huːp] *n* a thin ring of metal, wood *etc*: *At the circus we saw a dog jumping through a hoop.*

hooping-cough *see* **whooping-cough.**

hoorah, hooray *see* **hurrah.**

hoot [huːt] *v* **1** to sound the horn of a car *etc*: *The driver hooted* (*his horn*) *at the old lady.* **2** (of car *etc* horns, sirens *etc*) to make a loud noise, as a warning, signal *etc*: *You can't leave the factory till the siren hoots.* **3** (of owls) to call out: *An owl hooted in the wood.* **4** (of people) to make a loud noise of laughter or disapproval: *They hooted with laughter.* – *n* **1** the sound of a car *etc* horn, a siren *etc*. **2** the call of an owl. **3** a loud shout of laughter or disapproval.

'hooter *n* an instrument which makes a hooting sound: *the factory hooter.*

not care a hoot/two hoots not to care in the least: *He doesn't care two hoots what anyone thinks of him.*

hooves *see* **hoof.**

hop¹ [hop] – *pt*, *ptp* **hopped** – *v* **1** (of people) to jump on one leg: *The children had a competition to see who could hop the farthest*; *He hopped about in pain when the hammer fell on his foot.* **2** (of certain small birds, animals and insects) to jump on both or all legs: *The sparrow/frog hopped across the lawn.* **3** to jump: *He hopped* (*over*) *the fence and ran away*; *He hopped out of bed.* **4** (*with in*(*to*), *out* (*of*)) to get into or out of a car *etc*: *The car stopped and the driver told the hikers to hop in*; *I'll hop out of the car at the next crossroads.* – *n* **1** a short jump on one leg. **2** (of certain small birds, animals and insects) a short jump on both or all legs: *The sparrow crossed the lawn in a series of hops.*

'hopscotch [-skotʃ] *n* a game played *usu* by

children in which they hop into a series of squares drawn on the ground: *The children are playing hopscotch on the pavement.*

catch (**someone**) **on the hop** to do something to (someone) when he is not prepared.

keep (**someone**) **on the hop** to keep (someone) busy, active, *etc*.

hop² [hop] *n* a climbing plant, the bitter fruits of which (**hops**) are used in brewing beer.

hope [houp] *v* to want something to happen and have some reason to believe that it will or might happen: *He's very late, but we are still hoping he will come*; *I hope to be in London next month*; *We're hoping for some help from other people*; *It's unlikely that he'll come now, but we keep on hoping*; *'Do you think it will rain?' 'I hope so/not'.* – *n* **1** (any reason or encouragement for) the state of feeling that what one wants will or might happen: *He has lost all hope of becoming the president*; *He came to see me in the hope that I would help him*; *He has hopes of winning a scholarship*; *The rescuers said there was no hope of finding anyone alive in the mine.* **2** a person, thing *etc* that one is relying on for help *etc*: *He's my last hope – there is no-one else I can ask.* **3** something hoped for: *My hope is that he will get married and settle down soon.*

'hopeful *adj* **1** (*neg* **un-**) full of hope: *The police are hopeful that they will soon find the killer*; *hopeful faces*; *He is hopeful of success.* **2** giving a reason or encouragement for hope: *That's a hopeful sign – perhaps he is going to change his mind after all.* **3** likely to be pleasant, successful *etc*: *The future looks quite hopeful.* **'hopefulness** *n*.

'hopefully *adv* **1** in a hopeful way: *The dog looked hopefully at the joint of meat.* **2** it is to be hoped that: *Hopefully, that will never happen.*

'hopeless *adj* **1** not likely to be successful: *It's hopeless to try to persuade him*; *a hopeless attempt*; *The future looks hopeless.* **2** (*with at*) not good: *I'm a hopeless housewife*; *He's hopeless at French.* **3** unable to be stopped, cured *etc*: *The doctors considered the patient's case hopeless*; *He's a hopeless liar/idiot.* **'hopelessly** *adv*. **'hopelessness** *n*.

hope against hope to continue hoping when there is no (longer any) reason for hope.

hope for the best to hope that something will succeed, that nothing bad will happen *etc*.

not (**have**) **a hope** (to be) completely unlikely (to succeed in something): *He hasn't a hope of getting the job*; *'Will he get the job?' 'Not a hope!'*

raise someone's hopes to cause someone to hope, *usu* when there is no good reason to.

horde [hoːd] *n* a crowd or large number (of

people *etc*): *Hordes of tourists thronged the temple.*

horizon [hə'raizn] *n* the line at which the earth and the sky seem to meet: *The sun went down below the horizon; A ship could be seen on the horizon.*

horizontal [hori'zontl] *adj* at right angles to vertical; parallel to the horizon; lying level or flat: *a horizontal line; a horizontal surface.* ,**hori'zontally** *adv.*

hormone ['ho:moun] *n* a substance produced by certain glands of the body, which makes some organ of the body active: *Adrenalin is a hormone.*

horn [ho:n] *n* **1** a hard object which grows (*usu* in pairs) on the head of a cow, sheep *etc*: *A ram has horns.* **2** the material of which this is made: *spoons made of horn;* (*also adj*) *horn spoons.* **3** something which is made of horn: *a shoehorn.* **4** something which looks like a horn in shape: *a snail's horns.* **5** the apparatus in a car *etc* which gives a warning sound: *The driver blew his horn.* **6** an instrument, formerly an animal's horn but now made of brass, that is blown to produce a musical sound: *a hunting-horn.* **7** (*also* **French horn**) the type of coiled brass horn that is played in orchestras *etc.*

horned *adj* having a horn or horns: *a horned animal.*

-horned: *a long-horned antelope.*

'**horny** *adj* **1** like horn: *a horny substance.* **2** as hard as horn: *horny hands.*

hornet ['ho:nit] *n* a kind of large wasp.

horoscope ['horəskoup] *n* the prediction of a person's future based on the position of the stars and planets at the time of his birth.

horrible, horrid *etc see* **horror.**

horror ['horə] *n* **1** great fear or dislike: *She has a horror of spiders; She looked at me in horror.* **2** a disagreeable person or thing: *Her little boy is an absolute horror.*

'**horrible** *adj* **1** causing horror; dreadful: *a horrible sight.* **2** unpleasant: *What a horrible day!* '**horribleness** *n.* '**horribly** *adv.*

'**horrid** [-rid] *adj* **1** unpleasant: *That was a horrid thing to say.* **2** dreadful: *a horrid shriek.*

horrific [hə'rifik] *adj* **1** terrible; terrifying: *a horrific accident; a horrific journey.*

'**horrify** [-fai] *v* to shock greatly: *Mrs Smith was horrified to find that her son had grown a beard.* '**horrifying** *adj.*

horse [ho:s] *n* **1** a large four-footed animal which is used to pull carts *etc* or to carry people *etc.* **2** a piece of apparatus used for jumping, vaulting *etc* in a gymnasium.

'**horse-box** *n* an enclosed vehicle *etc* used for carrying horses.

'**horsefly** *n* a large fly that bites horses *etc.*

'**horsehair** *n, adj* (of) the hair from a horse's mane or tail: *The mattress is stuffed with horsehair; a horsehair mattress.*

'**horseman** – *fem* '**horsewoman** – *n* a rider, *esp* a skilled one: *She is a very competent horsewoman.* '**horsemanship** *n.*

'**horseplay** *n* rough and noisy behaviour or play.

'**horsepower** (*usu abbrev* **h.p.** *when written*) *n* a standard unit used to measure the power of engines, cars *etc.*

horseshoe ['ho:ʃʃu:] *n* **1** a curved iron shoe for a horse. **2** something in the shape of a horseshoe: *The bride was presented with a lucky silver horseshoe.*

on horseback riding on a horse: *The soldiers rode through the town on horseback.*

(**straight**) **from the horse's mouth** from a well-informed and reliable source: *I got that story straight from the horse's mouth.*

horticulture ['ho:tikʌltʃə] *n* the science and art of gardening. ,**horti'cultural** *adj.*

hose [houz] **1** (*also* '**hosepipe**) a rubber, plastic *etc* tube which bends and which is used to carry water *etc*: *a garden hose; a fireman's hose.* **2** an older word for stockings or socks: *woollen hose.* – *v* to apply water to by means of a hose: *I'll go and hose the garden/car.*

hosiery ['houziəri] *n* knitted goods, *esp* stockings, socks and tights.

hose reel a revolving drum for carrying hoses.

hose down to clean (*eg* a car) by means of water brought by a hose.

hospitable [hə'spitəbl] *adj* showing kindness to guests: *She is one of the most hospitable people I know.* **ho'spitably** *adv.* **ho'spitableness** *n.*

hospitality [hospi'taləti] *n* a friendly welcome for guests or strangers, which often includes offering them food, drink *etc.*

hospital ['hospitl] *n* a building or group of buildings where people who are ill or injured are given treatment: *After the train crash, the injured people were taken to hospital.*

'**hospitalize, -ise** *v* (*esp Amer*) to keep (a person) in hospital for treatment. ,**hospitali'zation, -s-** *n.*

host[1] [houst] *n* **1** (*fem* '**hostess**) a person who entertains someone else as his guest, *usu* in his own house: *Our host/hostess introduced us at the party.* **2** an animal or plant on which another lives as a parasite.

host[2] [houst] *n* a very large number of people or things.

hostage ['hostidʒ] *n* a person who is held prisoner in order to ensure that the captor's demands *etc* will be carried out: *The terrorists took three people with them as hostages; They took/were holding three people hostage.*

take, hold (someone) hostage to take or keep (someone) as a hostage: *The police were unable to attack the terrorists because they were holding three people hostage.*

hostel ['hostəl] *n* **1** a building with simple accommodation, *esp* for young people, hikers *etc*: *a youth hostel.* **2** a building where students *etc* may live: *a nurses' hostel.*

hostess *see* **host.**

hostile ['hostail] *adj* **1** unfriendly; warlike: *hostile tribesmen.* **2** belonging to an enemy: *a hostile army.* **3** showing dislike or opposition to something: *a hostile attitude.*

ho'stilities [-'sti-] *n pl* acts of war; battles: *The two countries were engaged in hostilities.*

ho'stility [-'sti-] *n* unfriendliness; opposition.

hot [hot] *adj* **1** having or causing a great deal of heat: *a hot oven; That water is hot.* **2** very warm: *a hot day; Running makes me feel hot.* **3** (of food) having a sharp, burning taste: *a hot curry.* **4** easily made angry: *a hot temper.* **5** recent; fresh: *hot news.*

'hotly *adv* **1** eagerly; quickly: *The thieves were hotly pursued by the police.* **2** angrily; passionately: *The accusations were hotly denied.*

hot air boastful words, promises that will not be kept *etc*: *Most of what he said was just hot air.*

hot-'blooded *adj* passionate; having strong feelings: *hot-blooded young men.*

hot dog a hot sausage sandwich.

'hotfoot *adv* in a great hurry: *He arrived hotfoot from the meeting.*

'hothead *n* a hotheaded person.

hot'headed *adj* easily made angry; inclined to act suddenly and without sufficient thought.

'hothouse *n* a glass-house kept warm for growing plants in: *He grows orchids in his hothouse.*

'hot-plate *n* **1** the part of a cooker on which food is heated for cooking. **2** a portable heated plate of metal *etc* for keeping plates of food *etc* hot.

be in, get into hot water to be in or get into trouble.

hot up – *pt, ptp* **'hotted** – *v* to increase; to become more exciting *etc*.

in hot pursuit chasing as fast as one can: *The thief ran off, with the shopkeeper in hot pursuit.*

like hot cakes very quickly: *These books are selling like hot cakes.*

hotel [hə'tel] *n* a *usu* large house or building where travellers, holidaymakers *etc* may receive food, lodging *etc* in return for payment: *The new hotel has over five hundred bedrooms.*

ho'telier [-liə] *n* a person who owns, and sometimes manages, a hotel.

hound [haund] *n* a hunting-dog: *The fox threw the hounds off the scent and escaped.* – *v* to pursue or hunt (someone): *The film star was constantly hounded by newspaper reporters.*

hour ['auə] *n* (*sometimes abbrev* **hr** when written) **1** sixty minutes, the twenty-fourth part of a day: *He spent an hour trying to start the car this morning; She'll be home in half an hour; a five-hour delay.* **2** the time at which a particular thing happens: *when the hour for action arrives; He helped me in my hour of need; You can consult him during business hours.*

'hourly *adj, adv* (happening or done) every hour: *Take his temperature hourly; hourly reports.*

'hour-glass *n* a device that measures time in hours by passing sand from one glass container through a narrow tube into a lower container.

hour hand the smaller of the two hands of a watch or clock, which shows the time in hours.

at all hours at irregular times, *esp* late at night: *He comes home at all hours.*

for hours for a very long time: *We waited for hours for the train.*

on the hour at exactly one, two, three *etc* o'clock: *Buses leave here for London on the hour until 10 o'clock in the evening.*

house [haus] – *pl* **houses** ['hauziz] – *n* **1** a building in which people, *esp* a single family, live: *Houses have been built on the outskirts of the town for the workers in the new industrial estate.* **2** a place or building used for a particular purpose: *a hen-house; a public house.* **3** a theatre, or the audience in a theatre: *There was a full house for the first night of the play.* **4** a family, *usu* important or noble, including its ancestors and descendants: *the house of David.* – [hauz] *v* **1** to provide with a house, accommodation or shelter: *All these people will have to be housed; The animals are housed in the barn.* **2** to store or keep somewhere: *The generator for the electricity is housed in the garage.*

'housing [-ziŋ] *n* **1** houses: *These flats will provide housing for the immigrants.* **2** the hard cover round a machine *etc*.

house agent (*Amer* **'real-estate agent**) a person who arranges the sale or letting of houses.

house arrest a type of arrest in which a person is not allowed to leave his own house: *He was kept under house arrest.*

'houseboat *n* a type of boat, *usu* with a flat bottom, which is built to be lived in.

'housebreaker *n* a person who breaks into a house in order to steal. **'housebreaking** *n*.

'house-fly n the common fly, found throughout the world.

'household n the people who live together in a house, including their servants: How many people are there in this household?

'householder n the person who owns a house or pays the rent for it.

household word something which is well-known to everyone: His name is a household word throughout the country.

'housekeeper n a person, usu a woman, who is paid to look after the management of a house.

'housekeeping n the management of a house.

'houseman n a recently qualified doctor who is living in a hospital while working there to complete his training.

'house-warming n a party given after moving into a new house. – Also adj: a house-warming party.

'housewife – pl 'housewives – n a woman who looks after her house, her husband and her family, and who usu does not have a job outside the home.

'housework n the work of keeping a house clean and tidy: My mother has a woman to help her with the housework.

like a house on fire 1 very well: The two children got on with each other like a house on fire. 2 very quickly: I'm getting through this job like a house on fire.

hovel ['hovəl, (Amer) 'hʌ-] n a small, dirty house.

hover ['hovə, (Amer) 'hʌ-] v 1 (of a bird, insect etc) to remain in the air without moving in any direction. 2 to move around while still remaining near a person etc: I wish she'd stop hovering round me and go away. 3 (with between) to be undecided: She hovered between leaving and staying.

*'hovercraft n a vehicle which is able to move over land or water, supported by a cushion of air.

how [hau] adv, conj 1 in what way: How do you make bread? 2 to what extent: How do you like my new hat?; How far is Paris from London? 3 by what means: I've no idea how he came here. 4 in what condition: How are you today?; How do I look? 5 for what reason: How is it that I am the last to know about this?

how'ever adv 1 in spite of that: It would be .nice if we had more money. However, I suppose we'll manage with what we have. 2 (also how ever) in what way; by what means: However did you get here?; However did you do that? 3 to no matter what extent: However hard I try, I still can't do it. – conj in no matter what way: This painting still looks wrong however you look at it.

how about 1 I would like to suggest: 'Where

shall we go tonight?' 'How about the cinema?' 2 what is he, are you etc going to do?; what does he, do you etc think?: We're going to the cinema tonight. How about you?; I rather like that picture. How about you?

how come for what reason: How come I didn't get any cake?

'how do you do? words that are said by a person to someone he is being introduced to: 'How do you do? My name is Smith,' he said, shaking her hand.

however see how.

howl [haul] v 1 to make a long, loud cry: The wolves howled; He howled with pain; We howled with laughter. 2 (of wind) to make a similar sound: The wind howled through the trees. – n such a cry: a howl of pain; howls of laughter.

'howler n a mistake so bad as to be funny: an exam paper full of howlers.

hub [hʌb] n 1 the centre of a wheel. 2 a centre of activity or business.

hubbub ['hʌbʌb] n 1 a confused noise of many sounds esp voices. 2 uproar; protest.

huddle ['hʌdl] v 1 (often with together) to crowd closely together: The cows (were) huddled together in the corner of the field. 2 to curl up in a sitting position: The old man (was) huddled near the fire to keep warm. – n a number of people, things etc crowded together: a huddle of people round the injured man.

hue [hju:] n colour: flowers of many hues.

huff [hʌf]: in(to) a huff being or becoming silent because one is angry, displeased etc: He is in a huff; He went into a huff.

'huffy adj 1 in a huff. 2 easily offended, and likely to go into a huff. 'huffily adv. 'huffiness n.

hug [hʌg] – pt, ptp hugged – v 1 to hold close to oneself with the arms, esp to show love: She hugged her son when he returned from the war. 2 to keep close to: During the storm, the ships all hugged the shore. – n a tight grasp with the arms, esp to show love: As they said good-bye she gave him a hug.

huge [hju:dʒ] adj very large: a huge dog; a huge sum of money; Their new house is huge. 'hugeness n.

'hugely adv very much; greatly.

hulk [hʌlk] n 1 the body of an old ship from which everything has been taken away. 2 something or someone enormous and clumsy.

hull [hʌl] n the frame or body of a ship: The hull of the ship was painted black.

hullo see hello.

hullabaloo [hʌləbə'lu:] n 1 an uproar: The teacher told the pupils to stop making such a hullabaloo. 2 a loud public protest.

hum [hʌm] – pt, ptp hummed – v 1 to make a

* see illustration on p. 595

musical sound with closed lips: *He was humming a tune to himself.* **2** to make a similar sound: *The bees were humming round the hive.* **3** to be active: *Things are really humming round here.* – *n* a humming sound: *I could hear the hum of the machines; a hum of conversation.*
'humming-bird *n* a small brightly-coloured American bird which makes a humming sound with its wings.

human ['hju:mən] *adj* of, natural to, concerning, or belonging to, mankind: *human nature; The dog was so clever that he seemed almost human.* – *n* a person: *Humans are not as different from animals as we might think.*
'humanly *adv* within human power: *If it is humanly possible, he will do it.*
human being a person: *Animals may behave like that, but human beings shouldn't.*

humane [hju'mein] *adj* kind; not cruel: *a humane man; a humane way to kill rats and mice.* **hu'manely** *adv.* **hu'maneness** *n.*

humanity [hju'manəti] *n* **1** kindness: *a man of great humanity.* **2** people in general: *all humanity.*
See also **humane**.

humble ['hʌmbl] *adj* **1** not having a high opinion of oneself *etc*: *You have plenty of ability but you're too humble.* **2** unimportant; having a low position in society *etc*: *a man of humble origins.* – *v* to make (someone) humble: *He was humbled by his failure.*
'humbly *adv.* **'humbleness** *n.*
See also **humility**.

humdrum ['hʌmdrʌm] *adj* dull: *a humdrum life.*

humid ['hju:mid] *adj* damp: *a humid climate.* **hu'midity** *n.*

humiliate [hju'milieit] *v* to make (someone) feel ashamed: *He was humiliated to find that his girlfriend could run faster than he could.* **hu'miliating** *adj.* **hu,mili'ation** *n.*

humility [hju'miləti] *n* modesty; humbleness: *Despite his powerful position in the government, he was still a man of great humility.*
See also **humble**.

humour, (*Amer*) **humor** ['hju:mə] *n* **1** the ability to amuse people; quickness to spot a joke: *He has a great sense of humour.* **2** the quality of being amusing: *the humour of the situation.* – *v* to please (someone) by agreeing with him or doing as he wishes: *There is no point in telling him he is wrong – just humour him instead.*
'humorist *n* a person who writes or tells amusing stories, jokes *etc*.
'humorous *adj* funny; amusing: *a humorous situation/remark.* **'humorously** *adv.* **'humorousness** *n.*
-humoured having, or showing, feelings or a

personality of a particular sort: *a good-humoured person; an ill-humoured remark.*

humour, noun, ends in **-our**.
humorous, adjective, drops the **u**.

hump [hʌmp] *n* **1** a large lump on the back of an animal, person *etc*: *a camel's hump.* **2** part of a road *etc* which rises and falls in the shape of a hump.
'humpback *n* a back with a hump. – *adj* rising and falling in the shape of a hump: *a humpback bridge.*
'humpbacked *adj* having a hump on the back.

humus ['hju:məs] *n* a substance like earth, made of decayed plants, leaves *etc*.

hunch [hʌntʃ] *n* an idea or belief based on one's feelings or suspicions rather than on clear evidence: *I have a hunch he'll be late.*
'hunchback *n* a person with a hump on his back.
'hunchbacked *adj* having a hump on one's back.
hunched up with one's back and shoulders bent forward: *He sat hunched up near the fire.*

hundred ['hʌndrəd] *n* **1** (*pl* **'hundred**) the number 100: *Ten times ten is a hundred; more than one/a hundred; There must be at least six hundred of them here.* **2** the figure 100. **3** the age of 100: *She's over a hundred; a man of a hundred.* **4** (*pl* **'hundred**) a hundred pounds or dollars: *I lost several hundred at the casino last night.* – *adj* **1** 100 in number: *six hundred people; a few hundred pounds.* **2** aged 100: *He is a hundred today.*
'hundred-: *a hundred-dollar bill.*
'hundredfold *adj, adv* one hundred times as much or as great: *Production has increased a hundredfold.*
'hundredth *n* **1** one of a hundred equal parts. **2** (*also adj*) (the) last of a hundred (people, things *etc*) or (the person, thing *etc*) in an equivalent position.
'hundreds of **1** several hundred: *He has hundreds of pounds in the bank.* **2** very many: *I've got hundreds of things to do.*

hung *see* **hang**.

hunger ['hʌŋgə] *n* **1** the desire for food: *A cheese roll won't satisfy my hunger.* **2** the state of not having enough food: *Poor people in many parts of the world are dying of hunger.* **3** any strong desire: *a hunger for love.* – *v* (*usu with* **for**) to long for (*eg* affection, love).
'hungry *adj* wanting or needing food *etc*: *a hungry baby; I'm hungry – I haven't eaten all day; He's hungry for adventure.* **'hungrily** *adv.* **'hungriness** *n.*
hunger strike a refusal to eat, as a form of protest or to force (someone) to agree to certain demands *etc*: *The prisoners went on*

hunger strike as a protest against prison discipline.

hunk [hʌŋk] *n* a lump of something broken or cut off from a larger peice: *a hunk of cheese/bread.*

hunt [hʌnt] *v* **1** to chase (animals *etc*) for food or for sport: *He spent the whole day hunting (deer).* **2** to pursue or drive out: *The murderer was hunted from town to town.* − *n* **1** the act of hunting animals *etc*: *a tiger hunt.* **2** a search: *I'll have a hunt for that lost necklace.*

'**hunter** − *fem* '**huntress** − *n* a person who hunts.

'**hunting** *n* the activity of chasing animals *etc* for food or for sport.

'**huntsman** ['hʌnts-] *n* a hunter.

hunt down to search for (someone or something) until found: *The police hunted down the escaped prisoner.*

hunt for to search for: *I've been hunting for that shoe all morning.*

hunt high and low to search everywhere.

hunt out to search for (something that has been put away) until it is found: *I'll hunt out that old photograph for you.*

hurdle ['hə:dl] *n* **1** a frame to be jumped in a race. **2** a problem or difficulty: *There are several hurdles to be got over in this project.* − *v* to run in a race in which hurdles are used: *He has hurdled since he was twelve.* '**hurdler** *n*. '**hurdling** *n*.

hurl [hə:l] *v* to throw violently: *He hurled himself to the ground; They hurled rocks/insults at their attackers.*

hurrah, hurray, hoorah, hooray [hu'rei] *n, interj* a shout of joy, enthusiasm *etc*: *Hurrah! We're getting an extra day's holiday!*

hurricane ['hʌrikən, (*Amer*) 'hə:rikein] *n* a violent storm with winds blowing at over 120 kilometres per hour.

hurry ['hʌri, (*Amer*) 'hə:ri] *v* **1** to (cause to) move or act quickly, often too quickly: *You'd better hurry if you want to catch that bus; If you hurry me, I'll make mistakes.* **2** to convey quickly: *After the accident, the injured man was hurried to the hospital.* − *n* **1** the act of doing something quickly, often too quickly: *In his hurry to leave, he fell and broke his arm.* **2** the need to do something quickly: *Is there any hurry for this job?*

'**hurried** *adj* **1** done quickly, often too quickly: *This was a very hurried piece of work.* **2** (*neg* **un-**) forced to do something quickly, often too quickly: *I hate feeling hurried.* '**hurriedly** *adv*.

in a hurry 1 acting quickly: *I did this in a hurry.* **2** wishing or needing to act quickly: *I'm in a hurry.* **3** soon; easily: *You won't untie this knot in a hurry.* **4** eager: *I'm in a hurry to see my new house.*

hurry up to (cause to) move quickly: *Hurry him up, will you; Do hurry up!*

hurt [hə:t] − *pt, ptp* **hurt** − *v* **1** to injure or cause pain to: *I hurt my hand on that broken glass.* **2** to upset (a person or his feelings): *He hurt me/my feelings by ignoring me.* **3** to be painful: *My tooth hurts.* **4** to do harm (to) or have a bad effect (on): *It wouldn't hurt you to work late just once.* − *adj* **1** upset; distressed: *She felt very hurt at/by his behaviour; her hurt feelings.* **2** injured: *Are you badly hurt?*

'**hurtful** *adj* causing distress: *a hurtful remark.* '**hurtfully** *adv*. '**hurtfulness** *n*.

hurtle ['hə:tl] *v* to move very quickly and violently: *The car hurtled down the hill at top speed.*

husband ['hʌzbənd] *n* a man to whom a woman is married. − *v* to spend or use carefully, a little at a time: *He needs to husband his strength.*

'**husbandry** *n* management, *esp* of a farm or animals.

hush [hʌʃ] *interj* be quiet; silence: *Hush! Don't wake the baby.* − *n* silence: *A hush came over the room.*

hushed *adj* silent, still: *a hushed room/crowd.*

hush up to prevent from becoming known to the general public: *The affair was hushed up.*

husk [hʌsk] *n* the dry thin covering of certain fruits and seeds: *coconut husk.* − *v* to remove the husk from (a fruit or seed).

husky[1] ['hʌski] *adj* (of a voice) rough in sound: *You sound husky − have you a cold?* '**huskiness** *n*. '**huskily** *adv*.

husky[2] ['hʌski] − *pl* '**huskies** − *n* a N American dog used for pulling sledges.

hustle ['hʌsl] *v* **1** to push quickly and roughly: *The man was hustled out of the office.* **2** to make (someone) act quickly: *Don't try to hustle me into making a sudden decision.* − *n* quick and busy activity.

hut [hʌt] *n* a small house or shelter, *usu* made of wood.

hutch [hʌtʃ] *n* a box with a wire front in which rabbits are kept.

hyacinth ['haiəsinθ] *n* a plant, a member of the lily family, growing from a bulb and having a sweet-smelling flower.

hyaena *see* **hyena**.

hydrant ['haidrənt] *n* a pipe connected to the main water supply *esp* in a street, to which a hose can be attached in order to draw water off *eg* to put out a fire.

hydraulic [hai'dro:lik] *adj* **1** worked by the pressure of water or some other liquid: *hydraulic brakes.* **2** relating to hydraulics: *a hydraulic engineer.* **hy'draulically** *adv*.

hy'draulics *n sing* the study of the behaviour of moving liquids (*eg* of water in pipes).

hydrilla [hai'drilə] *n* an aquatic plant with fine leaves, commonly found in ponds.

hydroelectricity ['haidrouelek'trisəti] *n* electricity produced by means of water-power. **,hydroe'lectric** [-'lek-] *adj*: *hydroelectric power stations.*

hydrogen ['haidrədʒən] *n* an element, the lightest gas, which burns and which, when combined with oxygen, produces water. **hydrogen bomb** (*also* **H-bomb** ['eitʃbom]) a very powerful bomb in which the explosion is caused by turning hydrogen into helium at a very high temperature.

hyena, hyaena [hai'i:nə] *n* a dog-like animal with a howl which sounds like human laughter.

hygiene['haidʒi:n] *n* (the rules or science of) cleanliness whose aim is to preserve health and prevent the spread of disease. **hy'gienic** [-'dʒi:-, (*Amer*) -'dʒe-] *adj* (*neg* **un-**) free from germs or dirt: *Hygienic conditions are essential in a hospital.* **hy'gienically** [-'dʒi:-, (*Amer*) -'dʒe-] *adv.*

hymn [him] *n* a (*usu* religious) song of praise.

hyphen ['haifən] *n* a short stroke (-) which is used to join two parts of a word or phrase, as in *co-exist*; *a sleeping-bag*; *a well-thought-out plan.*

hypnosis [hip'nousis] *n* a sleep-like state caused by the action of another person who can then make the sleeper obey his commands. **hyp'notic** [-'no-] *adj.*

'hypnotize, -ise *v* **1** to put in a state of hypnosis: *The hypnotist hypnotized three people from the audience.* **2** to fascinate completely: *Her beauty hypnotized him.*

'hypnotism *n* the art of producing hypnosis. **'hypnotist** *n.*

hypocrisy [hi'pokrəsi] *n* the act or state of pretending to be better than one is or to have feelings or beliefs which one does not actually have.

hypocrite ['hipəkrit] *n* a person who is guilty of hypocrisy. **,hypo'critical** [hipə'kri-] *adj.* **,hypo'critically** *adv.*

hypodermic [haipə'də:mik] *n, adj* (an instrument) used for injecting a drug under the skin.

hypothesis [hai'poθəsis] – *pl* **hy'potheses** [-si:z]– *n* an unproved theory or point of view put forward, *eg* for the sake of argument.

hypothetical [haipə'θetikəl] *adj* imaginary; supposed.

hypothetically [haipə'θetikəli] *adv.*

hysteria [hi'stiəriə] *n* **1** a severe nervous upset which causes *eg* uncontrolled laughing or crying, imaginary illnesses *etc.* **2** uncontrolled excitement, *eg* of a crowd of people: *mass hysteria.*

hy'sterical [-'ste-] *adj* of or suffering from hysteria. **hy'sterically** [-'ste-] *adv.*

hy'sterics [-'ste-] *n pl* a fit of hysteria.

Ii

I [ai] *pron* (only as the subject of a verb) the word used by a speaker or writer in talking about himself or herself: *I can't find my book*; *John and I have always been friends.*

ice [ais] *n* **1** frozen water: *The pond is covered with ice.* **2** an ice-cream: *Three ices, please.* – *v* to cover with icing: *She iced the cake.*

'icing *n* a mixture of sugar, white of egg, water *etc* used to cover or decorate cakes.

'icy *adj* **1** very cold: *icy winds.* **2** covered with ice: *icy roads.* **3** unfriendly: *an icy tone of voice.* **'icily** *adv.* **'iciness** *n.*

ice age a time when a great part of the earth's surface was covered with ice.

ice axe a type of axe used by mountain climbers to cut holds in ice for their hands and feet.

'iceberg *n* a huge mass of ice floating in the sea.

ice box (*Amer*) a refrigerator.

,ice-'cream *n* cream or a mixture of creamy substances, flavoured and frozen.

'ice-cube *n* a small cube of ice used for cooling drinks *etc.*

ice rink a large room or building with a floor of ice for skating.

ice tray a metal or plastic tray for making ice-cubes in a refrigerator.

ice over/up to become covered with ice: *The pond iced over during the night*; *The windows have iced up.*

icicle ['aisikl] *n* a long hanging piece of ice formed by the freezing of dripping water: *icicles hanging from the roof.*

icing *see* ice.

icon, ikon ['aikon] *n esp* in the Orthodox Churches, a painting *etc* of Christ or a saint.

icy *see* ice.

I'd *see* have, would.

idea [ai'diə] *n* **1** opinion; belief: *I have an idea that it won't work.* **2** a plan: *I've an idea for* *solving this problem.* **3** mental picture: *This will give you an idea of what I mean.*

ideal [ai'diəl] *adj* perfect: *This tool is ideal for the job I have in mind.* – *n* **1** a person, thing *etc* that is looked on as being perfect: *She was clever and beautiful – in fact she was his ideal of what a wife should be.* **2** a person's standard of behaviour *etc*: *a man of high ideals.*

i'dealist *n* a person having (too) high ideals of behaviour *etc.* **i'dealism** *n.* **,idea'listic** [aidiə-] *adj.*

i'dealize, -ise *v* to regard as perfect: *Children tend to idealize their parents.* **i,deali'zation, -s-** *n.*

i'deally *adv* **1** perfectly: *He is ideally suited to this job.* **2** under perfect conditions: *Ideally, we should check this again, but we haven't enough time.*

identical [ai'dentikəl] *adj* **1** the same in every detail: *They wore identical dresses.* **2** the very same: *That is the identical car that I saw outside the bank just before the robbery.* **i'dentically** *adv.* **i'denticalness** *n.*

identify [ai'dentifai] *v* **1** to recognize as being a certain person *etc*: *Would you be able to identify the man who robbed you?*; *He identified the coat as his brother's.* **2** to think of as being the same: *He identifies beauty with goodness.* **i,dentifi'cation** [-fi] *n.*

i'dentify with to feel in sympathy with (*eg* a character in a story).

i'dentify oneself with/be i'dentified with to be associated with or give one's full support or interest to (a political party *etc*).

identity [ai'dentəti] *n* who or what a person is: *The police are still uncertain of the murderer's identity.*

i'dentity card a named card (often with a photograph) which is carried by a person to show or prove who he is.

idiocy *see* **idiot.**

idiom ['idiəm] *n* **1** an expression with a meaning that cannot be guessed from the meanings of the individual words: *His mother passed away* (= died) *this morning.* **2** the expressions of a language in general: *English idiom.*

,idio'matic [-'matik] *adj* (*neg* **un-**) **1** using an idiom: *an idiomatic use of this word.* **2** using appropriate idioms: *We try to teach idiomatic English.* **,idio'matically** *adv.*

idiot ['idiət] *n* **1** a foolish person: *She was an idiot to give up such a good job.* **2** a person with very low intelligence. **'idiocy** *n.* **,idi'otic** [-'otik] *adj.* **,idi'otically** *adv.*

idle ['aidl] *adj* **1** not working; not in use: *ships lying idle in the harbour.* **2** lazy: *He has work to do, but he's idle and just sits around.* **3** having no effect or result: *idle threats.* **4** unnecessary; without good reason or foundation: *idle fears*; *idle gossip.* – *v* **1** to

be idle or do nothing: *On holiday they just idled from morning till night.* **2** of an engine *etc*, to run gently without doing any work: *They kept the car engine idling while they checked their position with the map.*

'idler *n* a lazy person.

'idleness *n.* **'idly** *adv.*

idle away to spend (time) doing nothing: *idling the hours away.*

idol ['aidl] *n* **1** an image of a god, which is worshipped: *The tribesmen bowed down before their idol.* **2** a greatly loved person, thing *etc*: *The singer was the idol of thousands of teenagers.*

idolatry [ai'dolətri] *n* **1** the worship of idols. **2** too great admiration, *esp* of a person. **i'dolatrous** *adj.* **i'dolatrously** *adv.*

'idolize, -ise *v* to love or admire a person *etc* greatly or too much: *She idolized her older brother.*

if [if] *conj* **1** in the event that; on condition that: *He will have to go into hospital if his illness gets any worse*; *I'll only stay if you can stay too.* **2** supposing that: *If he were to come along now, we would be in trouble.* **3** whenever: *If I sneeze, my nose bleeds.* **4** although: *They are happy, if poor.* **5** whether: *I don't know if I can come or not.*

if 'only I wish that: *If only I were rich!*

igloo ['iglu:] – *pl* **'igloos** – *n* an Eskimo hut, *usu* built of blocks of snow.

ignite [ig'nait] *v* to (cause to) catch fire: *Petrol is easily ignited.*

ignition [ig'niʃən] *n* **1** the instrument in a car *etc* which ignites the petrol in the engine: *He switched on the car's ignition.* **2** the act of igniting.

ignoble [ig'noubl] *adj* shameful: *an ignoble action.* **ig'nobleness** *n.* **ig'nobly** *adv.*

ignorant ['ignərənt] *adj* **1** knowing very little: *He's really very ignorant – he ought to read more*; *I'm ignorant about money matters.* **2** (*with* **of**) unaware: *He continued on his way, ignorant of the dangers which lay ahead.* **'ignorantly** *adv.* **'ignorance** *n.*

ignore [ig'no:] *v* to take no notice of: *He ignored all my warnings.*

iguana [i'gwa:na] *n* a tropical American lizard that lives in trees.

ikon *see* **icon.**

ill [il] – *compar* **worse** [wə:s]: *superl* **worst** [wə:st] – *adj* **1** not in good health; not well: *She was ill for a long time.* **2** bad: *ill health*; *These pills have no ill effects.* **3** evil or unlucky: *ill luck.* – *adv* not easily: *We could ill afford to lose that money.* – *n* **1** evil: *I would never wish anyone ill.* **2** trouble: *all the ills of this world.*

ill- badly: *ill-equipped*; *ill-used.*

'illness *n* a state or occasion of being unwell: *There is a lot of illness in the village just now*; *childhood illnesses.*

,ill-at-'ease *adj* uncomfortable; embarrassed: *She feels ill-at-ease at parties.*

,ill-'fated *adj* ending in, or bringing, disaster: *an ill-fated expedition.*

,ill-'feeling *n* (an) unkind feeling (towards another person): *The two men parted without any ill-feeling(s).*

,ill-'mannered/,ill-'bred *adjs* having bad manners: *He's an ill-mannered young man.*

,ill-'tempered/,ill-'natured *adjs* having or showing bad temper: *Don't be so ill-natured just because you're tired.*

,ill-'treat *v* to treat badly or cruelly: *She often ill-treated her children.* ,ill-'treatment *n*.

,ill-'use [-'juːz] *v* to ill-treat.

,ill-'will *n* unkind feeling: *I bear you no ill-will.*

be taken ill to become ill: *He was taken ill at the party and was rushed to hospital.*

> ill means unwell: *He was very ill when he had pneumonia.*
> sick means vomiting or inclined to vomit: *He was sick twice in the car; I feel sick.*

I'll *see* will, shall.

illegal [i'liːgəl] *adj* not allowed by the law; not legal: *It is illegal to park a car here.* il'legally *adv*. illegality [ili'galəti] *n*.

illegible [i'ledʒəbl] *adj* (almost) impossible to read; not legible: *His writing is illegible.* il'legibly *adv*. il,legi'bility *n*.

illegitimate [ili'dʒitəmət] *adj* 1 born of parents-not married to each other. 2 unacceptable or not allowed (*esp* by law). ,ille'gitimately *adv*. ,ille'gitimacy *n*.

illicit [i'lisit] *adj* unlawful or not permitted. il'licitly *adv*. il'licitness *n*.

illiterate [i'litərət] *adj* 1 unable to read and write. 2 having little or no education. il'literacy *n*.

illness *see* ill.

illogical [i'lodʒikəl] *adj* not logical; not based on, or showing, sound reasoning. il'logically *adv*. il,logi'cality [-'ka-] *n*.

illuminate [i'luːmineit] *v* to light up: *The gardens were illuminated by rows of lamps.* il'luminated *adj* (of a manuscript) decorated with ornamental lettering or illustrations. il'luminating *adj* helping to make something clear: *an illuminating discussion.* il,lumi'nation *n* 1 the act of illuminating. 2 (*in pl*) the decorative lights in a town *etc*: *Go to Blackpool and see the illuminations.*

illusion [i'luːʒən] *n* (something that produces) a false impression, idea or belief: *an optical illusion.*
il'lusionist *n* a conjuror.

illustrate ['iləstreit] *v* 1 to provide (a book, lecture *etc*) with pictures, diagrams *etc*. 2 to make (a statement *etc*) clearer by providing examples *etc*: *Let me illustrate my point; This diagram will illustrate what I mean.*

'illustrated *adj* having pictures *etc*: *an illustrated catalogue.*

,illu'stration 1 a picture: *coloured illustrations.* 2 an example. 3 the act of illustrating.

'illustrative [-strətiv, (*Amer*) i'lʌstrətiv] *adj*.

'illustrator *n* a person who draws pictures *etc* for books *etc*.

illustrious [i'lʌstriəs] *adj* of a very high quality, ability *etc*; famous: *an illustrious career; He is the most illustrious of a famous family.* il'lustriousness *n*.

I'm *see* be.

image ['imidʒ] *n* 1 a likeness or copy of a person *etc* made of wood, stone *etc*: *images of the saints.* 2 a close likeness: *She's the very image of her sister.* 3 reflection: *She looked at her image in the mirror.* 4 mental picture: *I have an image of the place in my mind.* 5 the general opinion that people have about a person, company *etc*: *our public image.*

imagine [i'madʒin] *v* 1 to form a mental picture of (something): *I can imagine how you felt.* 2 to see or hear *etc* (something which is not true or does not exist): *Children often imagine that there are frightening animals under their beds; You're just imagining things!* 3 to think; to suppose: *I imagine (that) he will be late.*

i'maginary *adj* existing only in the mind or imagination; not real: *Her illnesses are usually imaginary.*

i,magi'nation *n* 1 (the part of the mind which has) the ability to form mental pictures: *I can see it all in my imagination.* 2 the creative ability of a writer *etc*: *This book shows a lot of imagination.* 3 the seeing *etc* of things which do not exist: *There was no-one there – it was just your imagination.*

i'maginative [-nətiv, (*Amer*) -neitiv] *adj* (*neg* un-) having, or created with, imagination: *an imaginative writer; This essay is interesting and imaginative.*

imbecile ['imbəsiːl, (*Amer*) -sl] *n* 1 a stupid person; a fool. 2 a person of very low intelligence who cannot look after himself. ,imbe'cility [-'si-] *n*.

imitate ['imiteit] *v* to (try to) be, behave or look the same as (a person *etc*): *Children imitate their friends rather than their parents; He could imitate the song of many different birds.*

,imi'tation *n* 1 the act of imitating: *Children learn how to speak by imitation.* 2 a copy: *an imitation of an ancient statue.* – *adj* made to look like something else: *imitation wood.*
'imitative [-tətiv] *adj*. 'imitativeness *n*.
'imitator *n* a person who imitates.

immaculate [i'makjulət] *adj* 1 perfectly clean; spotless. 2 perfectly correct; faultless.

immature [imə'tjuə] *adj* **1** childish and behaving like someone much younger. **2** not fully grown or fully developed; not ripe. ‚imma'turity *n.*

immeasurable [i'meʒərəbl] *adj* **1** very great. **2** too great *etc* to be able to be measured. im'measurably *adv.*

immediate [i'mi:diət] *adj* **1** happening at once and without delay: *an immediate response.* **2** without anyone *etc* coming between: *His immediate successor was Bill Jones.* **3** close: *our immediate surroundings.*
im'mediately *adv* at once: *He answered immediately.* – *conj* as soon as: *You may leave immediately you finish your work.*

immense [i'mens] *adj* very large or very great: *an immense forest; immense amounts of money.* im'mensely *adv.* im'mensity *n.*

immerse [i'mə:s] *v* to put completely under the surface of a liquid: *She immersed the vegetables in boiling water.* im'mersion [-ʃən, (*Amer*) -ʒən] *n.*
immersion heater an electric water-heater which is immersed in water which is to be heated, *usu* inside a hot-water tank.

immigrant ['imigrənt] *n, adj* (a person) who has come into a foreign country to live there permanently, not as a tourist or visitor: *The eastern part of the city is inhabited by immigrants; the immigrant population.*
‚immi'gration *n* the act of entering a country in order to settle there.

imminent ['iminənt] *adj* (*esp* of something unpleasant) likely to happen *etc* very soon: *A storm is imminent.* 'imminence *n.*

immobile [i'moubail] *adj* **1** not able to move or be moved: *His leg was put in plaster and he was immobile for several weeks.* **2** not moving; motionless: *He crouched there immobile until they had gone.* ‚immo'bility [-'bi-] *n.*
im'mobilize, -ise [-bi-] *v* to make immobile: *He immobilized the car by removing part of the engine.*

immodest [i'modist] *adj* shameless or indecent; not modest. im'modestly *adv.* im'modesty *n.*

immoral [i'morəl] *adj* wrong or wicked: *immoral conduct.* im'morally *adv.* ‚immo'rality [-'ra-] *n.*

immortal [i'mo:tl] *adj* living for ever and never dying: *A person's soul is said to be immortal; the immortal works of Shakespeare.* ‚immor'tality [-'ta-] *n.*
im'mortalize, -ise *v* to make (a person *etc*) famous for ever: *He wrote a song immortalizing the battle.*

immovable [i'mu:vəbl] *adj* **1** impossible to move: *an immovable object.* **2** not allowing one's feelings or attitude to be changed.

immune [i'mju:n] *adj* (*with to* or *from*) protected against, or naturally resistant to, *eg* a disease: *immune to measles; immune from danger.* im'munity *n.*

'**immunize, -ise** ['imju-] *v* to make immune to a disease, *esp* by an injection of a weak form of the disease. ‚immuni'zation, -s- *n.*

imp [imp] *n* **1** a small devil or wicked spirit. **2** a mischievous child: *Her son is a little imp.* 'impish *adj.*

impact ['impakt] *n* **1** (the force of) one object *etc* hitting against another: *The bomb exploded on impact.* **2** a strong effect or impression: *The film had quite an impact on television viewers.*

impair [im'peə] *v* to damage, weaken or make less good: *He was told that smoking would impair his health.* im'pairment *n.*

impale [im'peil] *v* to fix on, or pierce with, a long pointed object such as a spear *etc.*

impart [im'pa:t] *v* to give (*eg* information): *She said she had vital information to impart.*

impartial [im'pa:ʃəl] *adj* not favouring one person *etc* more than another: *an impartial judge.* im'partially *adv.* im‚parti'ality [-ʃi'a-] *n.*

impassable [im'pa:səbl] *adj* not able to be passed through or travelled along: *The road is impassable because of flooding.*

impassive [im'pasiv] *adj* not feeling or showing emotion: *an impassive face.* im'passively *adv.*

impatient [im'peiʃənt] *adj* not willing to wait or delay; not patient: *Don't be so impatient – it will soon be your turn.* im'patience *n.* im'patiently *adv.*

impede [im'pi:d] *v* to prevent or delay the start or progress of: *Progress on the building of the road was impeded by a fall of rock.*
impediment [im'pedimənt] *n* **1** something that delays or prevents. **2** a small fault in a person's speech: *A stammer is a speech impediment.*

impel [im'pel] – *pt, ptp* im'pelled – *v* to urge or force: *Hunger impelled the boy to steal.*

impenetrable [im'penitrəbl] *adj* **1** that cannot be penetrated, entered or passed through: *impenetrable jungle.* **2** impossible to understand: *an impenetrable mystery.*

imperative [im'perətiv] *n, adj* used of verbs that are expressing a command: *In the sentence 'Come here!', 'come' is an imperative (verb).*

imperfect [im'pə:fikt] *adj* **1** having a fault: *This coat is being sold at half-price because it is imperfect.* **2** (*also n*) (a verb) of the tense expressing an action or state in the past which is not completed: *The verb 'go' in 'I was going' is in the imperfect tense.* im'perfectly *adv.*
‚imper'fection [-'fekʃən] *n* (the state of having) a fault or defect.

imperial [im'piəriəl] *adj* of an empire or an emperor: *the imperial crown.*
im'perialism *n* (belief in) the policy of hav-

ing or extending control over the territory of other nations. **im'perialist** *n, adj.*

imperious [im'piəriəs] *adj* proud, behaving as if expecting to be obeyed: *an imperious manner.* **im'periousness** *n.*

impersonal [im'pə:sənl] *adj* **1** not showing, or being affected by, personal feelings: *His manner was formal and impersonal.* **2** (of a verb) having a subject which does not refer to a person, thing *etc*: *'It is raining' is an example of an impersonal verb.* **im'personally** *adv.* **im,perso'nality** [-'na-] *n.*

impersonate [im'pə:səneit] *v* to copy the behaviour *etc* of or pretend to be (another person), sometimes in order to deceive: *The comedian impersonated the prime minister.* **im,perso'nation** *n.*

impertinent [im'pə:tinənt] *adj* impudent or rude: *She was impertinent to her teacher.* **im'pertinently** *adv.* **im'pertinence** *n.*

impetuous [im'petjuəs] *adj* acting in a hasty manner and without thinking. **im'petuously** *adv.* **im,petu'osity** [-'o-] *n.*

impetus ['impətəs] *n* the force or energy with which something moves.

implacable [im'plakəbl] *adj* not able to be satisfied or won over: *an implacable enemy.* **im'placably** *adv.*

implant [im'pla:nt] *v* **1** to put (ideas *etc*) into a person's mind. **2** to put (*eg* human tissue, a device *etc*) permanently into a part of the body. **implan'tation** *n.*

implement ['implimənt] *n* a tool or instrument: *kitchen/garden implements.*

implicit [im'plisit] *adj* unquestioning; complete: *implicit obedience.* **im'plicitly** *adv.*

implore [im'plo:] *v* to ask earnestly: *She implored her husband to give up his life of crime; She implored his forgiveness.* **im'ploringly** *adv.*

imply [im'plai] *v* to suggest or hint without actually stating: *Are you implying that I am a liar?* **impli'cation** *n.*

impolite [impə'lait] *adj* not polite; rude: *You must not be impolite to the teacher.* **,impo'litely** *adv.* **,impo'liteness** *n.*

import [im'po:t] *v* to bring in (goods *etc*) from abroad *usu* for sale: *We import wine from France.* – ['impo:t] *n* **1** something which is imported from abroad: *Our imports are greater than our exports.* **2** the act of bringing in goods from abroad: *the import of wine.* **,impor'tation** *n.* **im'porter** *n.*

important [im'po:tənt] *adj* (*neg* **un-**) having great value, influence or effect: *an important book/person/occasion; It is important that you arrive here on time.* **im'portantly** *adv.* **im'portance** *n: matters of great importance.*

impose [im'pouz] *v* **1** to place (a tax, fine, task *etc*) on someone or something: *The government have imposed a new tax on cigarettes.* **2** to force (oneself, one's opinions *etc*) on a

person: *The headmaster liked to impose his authority on the teachers.* **3** (*often with* **on**) to ask someone to do something which he should not be asked to do or which he will find difficult to do: *I hope I'm not imposing (on you) by asking you to help.* **imposition** [impə'ziʃən] *n.*

imposing [im'pouziŋ] *adj* making a great impression; large and handsome: *an imposing building.*

impossible [im'posəbl] *adj* **1** that cannot be or be done: *It is impossible to sing and drink at the same time; an impossible task.* **2** hopelessly bad or wrong: *That child's behaviour is quite impossible.* **im'possibly** *adv.* **im,possi-'bility** *n.*

impostor [im'postə] *n* a person who pretends to be someone else, or to be something he is not, in order to deceive another person.

impoverish [im'povəriʃ] *v* to make poor. **im'poverishment** *n.*

impracticable [im'praktikəbl] *adj* not able to be put into practice, used, done *etc*: *a completely impracticable idea.* **im,practica-'bility** *n.*

impractical [im'praktikəl] *adj* lacking common sense: *an impractical person/ suggestion.*

imprecise [impri'sais] *adj* not clear; vague: *Her directions were so imprecise that we lost our way.* **,impre'cision** *n.*

impress [im'pres] *v* **1** to cause feelings of admiration *etc* in (a person): *I was impressed by his good behaviour.* **2** (*with* **on** or **upon**) to stress (something to someone): *I must impress upon you the need for silence.* **3** to fix (a fact *etc* in the mind): *She re-read the plans in order to impress the details on her memory.* **4** make (a mark) on something by pressing: *a footprint impressed in the sand.*

im'pression [-ʃən] *n* **1** the idea or effect produced in someone's mind by a person, experience *etc*: *The film made a great impression on me.* **2** a vague idea: *I have the impression that he's not pleased.* **3** the mark left by an object on another object: *The dog left an impression of its paws in the wet cement.* **4** a single printing of a book *etc.* **im'pressive** [-siv] *adj* (*neg* **un-**) making a great impression on a person's mind, feelings *etc*: *an impressive ceremony.* **im'pressively** *adv.* **im'pressiveness** *n.*

be under the impression (that) to have the (often wrong) feeling or idea that: *I was under the impression that you were paying for this meal.*

imprint ['imprint] *n* a mark made by pressure: *She saw the imprint of a foot in the sand.* – [im'print] *v* to make (a mark) on something by pressure; to fix permanently (in the mind or memory).

imprison [im'prizn] *v* to put in prison; to take or keep prisoner: *He was imprisoned for twenty years for his crimes.* **im'prisonment** *n*.

improbable [im'probabl] *adj* **1** not likely to happen or exist; not probable: *Although death at his age was improbable, he had already made his will.* **2** hard to believe. *an improbable explanation.* **im'probably** *adv.* **im,proba'bility** *n*.

impromptu [im'promptju:] *adj, adv* (made or done) without preparation beforehand: *an impromptu speech; He spoke impromptu for ten minutes.*

improper [im'propə] *adj* (of behaviour *etc*) not acceptable; indecent; wrong: *improper suggestions.* **impropriety** [imprə'praiəti] *n*. **improper fraction** a fraction which is larger than 1: $\frac{7}{5}$ *is an improper fraction.*

improve [im'pru:v] *v* to (cause to) become better, of higher quality *etc*: *His work has greatly improved; They recently improved the design of that car.*
im'provement *n* **1** the state or act of improving or being improved: *There has been a great improvement in her work; The patient's condition shows some improvement.* **2** something which improves, or adds beauty, value *etc*: *I've made several improvements to the house.*
improve on to produce something which is better, more useful *etc* than: *I think I can improve on that suggestion.*

improvise ['imprəvaiz] *v* **1** to compose and perform (a poem, tune *etc*) without preparation: *The pianist forgot his music and had to improvise.* **2** to make (something) from materials that happen to be available, often materials that are not normally used for that purpose: *They improvised a shelter from branches and blankets.* **,improvi'sation** *n*.

imprudent [im'pru:dənt] *adj* not having or showing good sense; unwise. **im'prudently** *adv.* **im'prudence** *n*.

impudent ['impjudənt] *adj* rude; disrespectful: *an impudent child/suggestion.* **'impudently** *adv.* **'impudence** *n*.

impulse ['impʌls] *n* **1** a sudden desire to do something, without thinking about the consequences: *I bought the dress on impulse – I didn't really need it.* **2** a sudden force or stimulation: *an electrical impulse.*
im'pulsive [-siv] *adj* done, or likely to act, suddenly, without careful thought: *an impulsive action; You're far too impulsive!* **im'pulsively** *adv.* **im'pulsiveness** *n*.

impure [im'pjue] *adj* dirty, with other substances mixed in; not pure: *impure air; The water is impure.*
im'purity *n* **1** something which is mixed into another substance, but which should not be: *There are too many impurities in this steel.* **2** the state of being impure: *Com-*

plaints were made about the impurity of the milk.

in [in] *prep* **1** describing the position of a thing *etc* which is surrounded by something else: *My mother is in the house; in London; in bed.* **2** showing the direction of movement: *He put his hand in his pocket.* **3** describing the time at, after or within which something happens: *in the morning; I'll be back in a week.* **4** indicating amount or relative number: *They arrived in large numbers.* **5** expressing circumstances, state, manner *etc* of an event, person *etc*: *dressed in a brown coat; walking in the rain; in a hurry; written in English; He is in the army; books tied up in bundles; She is in her sixties.*
– *adv, adj* **1** expressing the position of a person *etc, usu* at or to a place where the person *etc* is expected to be, *eg* home, office, station: *Is Mr Smith in?; Is the train in yet?; Is he coming in today?* **2** describing something which is fashionable or popular: *Short skirts are in at the moment.* **3** (of the tide) with the water at, or moving to, its highest level: *The tide is (coming) in.*
-in describing an activity *usu* carried out by groups of people as a form of protest *etc*: *a sit-in; a work-in.*
inmost *see* **innermost** *under* **inner.**
day *etc* **in, day** *etc* **out** day *etc* after day *etc* without a break: *I do the same boring job day in, day out; Last summer it rained week in, week out.*
in for likely to experience (*esp* something bad): *We're in for some bad weather; You're in for it if you broke that window!*
ins and outs the complex details of a plan *etc*: *He knows all the ins and outs of this scheme.*
insofar as, in so far as to the degree or extent that: *I gave him the details insofar as I knew them.*
in that because; from the fact that: *This is not a good plant for your garden in that its seeds are poisonous.*

inability [inə'biləti] *n* the lack of power, means, ability *etc* (to do something): *I was surprised at his inability to read.*

inaccessible [inək'sesəbl] *adj* not able to be (easily) approached, reached or obtained: *The village is inaccessible by car because of flooding.* **'inac,cessi'bility** [-sesə] *n*.

inaccurate [in'akjurət] *adj* containing errors; not correct or accurate: *inaccurate translation/addition.* **in'accuracy** *n* (*pl* **in'accuracies**).

inactive [in'aktiv] *adj* (*formal*) **1** not taking much exercise: *You're fat because you're so inactive.* **2** no longer working, functioning, etc; not active: *an inactive volcano.* **in'action, inac'tivity** *ns*.

inadequate [in'adikwət] *adj* not sufficient; not

adequate: *inadequate supplies*; *Our equipment is inadequate for this job*. **in'adequacy** *n*.

inadmissible [inəd'misəbl] *adj* not allowable. **'inad,missi'bility** *n*.

inadvertent [inəd'və:tənt] *adj* not done on purpose: *an inadvertent insult*. **,inad'vertently** *adv*.

inadvisable [inəd'vaizəbl] *adj* unwise; not advisable: *It would be inadvisable for you to go alone*. **'inad,visa'bility** [-vai-] *n*.

inanimate [in'animət] *adj* not living: *A rock is an inanimate object*.

inappropriate [inə'proupriət] *adj* (*sometimes with* **to** *or* **for**) not appropriate or suitable: *inappropriate clothes (for a wedding)*; *His speech was inappropriate to the occasion*. **,inap'propriateness** *n*.

inattentive [inə'tentiv] *adj* not paying attention; not attentive: *This pupil is very inattentive in class*; *an inattentive audience*. **,inat'tention**, **,inat'tentiveness** *ns*.

inaudible [in'o:dəbl] *adj* not loud or clear enough to be heard: *Her voice was inaudible because of the noise*. **in'audibly** *adv*. **in,audi'bility** *n*.

inaugurate [i'no:gjureit] *v* **1** to place (a person) in an official position with great ceremony: *to inaugurate a president*. **2** to make a ceremonial start to: *This meeting is to inaugurate our new Social Work scheme*. **3** to open (a building, exhibition *etc*) formally to the public: *The Queen inaugurated the new university buildings*. **i,naugu'ration** *n*. **i'naugural** *adj*.

inborn ['in'bo:n] *adj* natural; possessed by a person from birth: *an inborn ability to paint*.

incalculable [in'kalkjuləbl] *adj* not able to be calculated; very great.

incandescent [inkan'desnt] *adj* glowing white with heat.

incantation [inkan'teiʃən] *n* words said or sung as a spell.

incapable [in'keipəbl] *adj* (*with* **of**) not able (to do something): *incapable of learning anything*. **in,capa'bility** *n*.

incarnate [in'ka:nət] *adj* (of God, the devil *etc*) having taken human form: *a devil incarnate*. **incarnation** [inka:'neiʃən] *n* (the) human form taken by a divine being *etc*: *Most Christians believe that Christ was the incarnation of God*.

incautious [in'ko:ʃəs] *adj* acting or done without thinking; not cautious: *an incautious action/remark/person*. **in'cautiousness** *n*.

incendiary [in'sendiəri] *adj* used for setting (a building *etc*) on fire: *an incendiary bomb*. – *n* – *pl* **in'cendiaries** – **1** a person who sets fire to buildings *etc* unlawfully. **2** an incendiary bomb.

incense ['insens] *n* a substance which is

burned *esp* in religious services, and which gives off a pleasant smell.

incentive [in'sentiv] *n* something that encourages *etc*: *Hope of promotion was an incentive to hard work*.

incessant [in'sesnt] *adj* going on without stopping: *incessant noise*. **in'cessantly** *adv*.

inch [intʃ] *n* **1** (*often abbrev* **in** *when written*) a measure of length, the twelfth part of a foot (2·54 centimetres). **2** a small amount: *There is not an inch of room to spare*. – *v* to move slowly and carefully: *He inched (his way) along the narrow ledge*.

within an inch of almost; very near(ly): *He came within an inch of failing the exam*.

incident ['insidənt] *n* an event or happening: *There was a strange incident in the supermarket today*.

,inci'dental [-'den-] *adj* **1** occurring *etc* by chance in connection with something else: *an incidental remark*. **2** accompanying (something) but not forming part of it: *He wrote the incidental music for the play*.

,inci'dentally [-'den-] *adv* by the way: *Incidentally, where were you last night?*

incinerate [in'sinəreit] *v* to burn to ashes. **in,cine'ration** *n*.

in'cinerator *n* a furnace or other container for burning rubbish *etc*.

incision [in'siʒən] *n* **1** a cut, *esp* one made in a person's body by a surgeon. **2** the act of cutting *esp* by a surgeon.

incisor [in'saizə] *n* one of the four front cutting teeth in the upper or lower jaw.

incite [in'sait] *v* **1** to urge (someone) to do something: *He incited the people to rebel against the king*. **2** to stir up or cause: *They incited violence in the crowd*. **in'citement** *n*.

incivility [insi'viləti] *n* impoliteness.

incline [in'klain] *v* to bow (one's head *etc*). – ['inklain] *n* a slope.

inclination [inklə'neiʃən] *n* **1** a tendency or slight desire to do something: *Has he any inclinations towards engineering?*; *I felt an inclination to hit him*. **2** (an act of) bowing (the head *etc*).

be inclined to 1 to have a tendency to (do something): *He is inclined to be a bit lazy*. **2** to have a slight desire to (do something): *I am inclined to accept their invitation*.

include [iŋ'klu:d] *v* to take in or consider along with (other people, things *etc*) as part of a group, set *etc*: *Am I included in the team?*; *Your duties include making the tea*. **in'clusion** [-ʒən] *n*.

including *prep*: *The whole family has been ill, including the baby*.

in'clusive [-siv] *adj* counting both the first and last in a series: *May 7 to May 9 inclusive is three days*.

incognito [iŋkog'ni:tou] *adv*, *adj* without letting people know who one is, *eg* by using a false name: *He travelled incognito to Paris.*

incoherent [inkə'hiərənt] *adj* talking, writing *etc* in a way which is not easy to follow: *He was quite incoherent with rage.* ˌinco'herently *adv.* ˌinco'herence *n.*

incombustible [inkəm'ʌstəbl] *adj* not able to be burned: *That new building material is quite incombustible.*

income ['iŋkəm] *n* money received by a person as wages *etc*: *He cannot support his family on his income.*

income tax a tax paid on income over a certain amount.

incoming ['inkʌmiŋ] *adj* which is coming in; approaching: *the incoming tide*; *incoming telephone calls.*

incomparable [in'kompərəbl] *adj* without equal; not comparable: *incomparable skill.* in'comparably *adv.*

incompatible [inkəm'patəbl] *adj* 1 (of people) certain to disagree, fight *etc*. 2 (of statements *etc*) not in agreement with one another. ˌincom‚pati'bility *n.*

incompetent [in'kompitənt] *adj* not good enough at doing a job *etc*: *a very incompetent mechanic.* in'competence *n.*

incomplete [inkəm'pli:t] *adj* not complete or finished; with some part missing: *His novel was incomplete when he died*; *an incomplete pack of cards.*

incomprehensible [inkompri'hensəbl] *adj* impossible to understand: *an incomprehensible statement.*

inconceivable [inkən'si:vəbl] *adj* not able to be imagined or believed: *inconceivable wickedness.*

inconclusive [inkən'klu:siv] *adj* not leading to a definite decision, result *etc*: *inconclusive evidence.*

incongruous [iŋ'koŋgruəs] *adj* unsuitable or out of place; odd: *Boots would look incongruous with an evening dress.* incon'gruity, in'congruousness *ns.*

inconsiderate [inkən'sidərət] *adj* not showing thought for the feelings, rights *etc* of other people; thoughtless: *It was inconsiderate of you to arrive without telephoning first.* ˌincon'siderateness *n.*

inconsistent [inkən'sistənt] *adj* 1 (*often with* with) contradictory in some way; not in agreement: *What you're saying today is quite inconsistent with the statement you made yesterday.* 2 changeable, *eg* in standard: *His work is inconsistent.* ˌincon'sistency *n* (*pl* incon'sistencies).

inconsolable [inkən'souləbl] *adj* not able to be comforted: *the inconsolable widow.*

inconspicuous [inkən'spikjuəs] *adj* not noticeable or conspicuous: *The detective tried to be as inconspicuous as possible.* ˌincon'spicuousness *n.*

inconstant [in'konstənt] *adj* (of people) having feelings, intentions *etc* which change frequently.

inconvenient [inkən'vi:njənt] *adj* causing trouble or difficulty; awkward: *He has come at a very inconvenient time.*

ˌincon'venience *n* (something which causes) trouble or difficulty: *He apologized for the inconvenience caused by his late arrival.* – *v* to cause trouble or difficulty to: *I hope I haven't inconvenienced you.*

incorporate [in'ko:pəreit] *v* to contain or include as part of the whole: *The shopping centre incorporates a library and a bank.*

in'corporated *adj* (*often abbrev* Inc., inc.) formed into a company, corporation *etc*: *The name of our company is 'Field Services, Incorporated'.*

incorrect [inkə'rekt] *adj* 1 not accurate or correct; wrong: *incorrect translation of a word.* 2 (of behaviour *etc*) not acceptable; wrong. ˌincor'rectness *n.*

incorrigible [in'koridʒəbl] *adj* too bad to be corrected or improved.

incorruptible [inkə'rʌptəbl] *adj* not able to be bribed; honest: *The police should be incorruptible.* 'incor‚rupti'bility *n.*

increase [in'kri:s] *v* to (cause to) grow in size, number *etc*: *The number of children in this school has increased greatly in recent years.* – ['inkri:s] *n* (the amount, number *etc* added by) growth: *There has been some increase in business*; *The increase in the population over the last ten years was 40 000.*

in'creasingly *adv* more and more: *It became increasingly difficult to find helpers.*

on the increase becoming more frequent or becoming greater: *Acts of violence are on the increase.*

incredible [in'kredəbl] *adj* 1 hard to believe: *He does an incredible amount of work.* 2 impossible to believe; not credible: *I found his story incredible.* in'credibly *adv.* in‚credi'bility *n.*

incredulous [in'kredjuləs, (*Amer*) -dʒu-] *adj* unwilling to believe: *She listened to him with an incredulous expression.* ˌincre'dulity [-'dju:-] *n.*

increment ['iŋkrəmənt] *n* an increase *esp* in salary.

incriminate [in'krimineit] *v* (of evidence) to show the involvement of (someone) in a crime *etc*. in'criminating *adj.* in‚crimi'nation *n.*

incubate ['iŋkjubeit] *v* 1 to produce (young birds) from eggs by sitting on them or by keeping them warm by some other means. 2 (of germs or disease) to develop until signs of the disease appear: *How long does chickenpox take to incubate?* ˌincu'bation *n.* 'incubator *n* a heated box-like apparatus for hatching eggs or a similar one for rearing premature babies *etc.*

incur [in'kə:] – *pt, ptp* **in'curred** – *v* **1** to bring (something unpleasant) on oneself: *to incur someone's displeasure.* **2** to become liable to pay (a debt): *to incur enormous debts.*

incurable [in'kjuərəbl] *adj* not able to be cured or corrected; not curable: *an incurable disease/habit.*

indebted [in'detid] *adj* (*with* **to**) having reason to be grateful to: *I am indebted to you for your help.* **in'debtedness** *n.*

indecent [in'di:snt] *adj* offending against accepted standards of sexual or moral behaviour; not modest: *indecent clothing.* **in'decency** *n.*

indecision [indi'siʒən] *n* the state of not being able to decide; hesitation.

,**inde'cisive** [-'saisiv] *adj* **1** not producing a clear decision or a definite result: *an indecisive battle.* **2** unable to make firm decisions: *indecisive person.*

indeed [in'di:d] *adv* **1** really; in fact; as you say; of course *etc*: *'He's very talented, isn't he?' He is indeed; 'Do you remember your grandmother?' 'Indeed I do!'* **2** used for emphasis: *Thank you very much indeed; He is very clever indeed.* – *interj* used to show surprise, interest *etc*: *'John said your idea was stupid.' 'Indeed!'*

indefinite [in'definit] *adj* **1** not fixed or exact; without clearly marked outlines or limits: *She invited her mother to stay for an indefinite length of time.* **2** vague; uncertain: *His plans are indefinite at the moment.* **in'definiteness** *n.*

in'definitely *adv* for an indefinite period of time: *The match was postponed indefinitely.*

indefinite article the name given to the words **a** and **an.**

indelible [in'deləbl] *adj* (making a mark) that cannot be removed: *indelible ink; The events of that day have left an indelible impression on my mind.*

indent [in'dent] *v* to begin (a line of writing) farther in from the margin than the other lines. – ['indent] *n* (*also* ,**inden'tation**) the space left at the beginning of a line, *eg* the first line of a paragraph.

,**inden'tation** [inden-] *n* **1** a V-shaped cut (in the edge or outline of an object). **2** an indent. **3** a deep inward curve in a coastline.

in'dented *adj* having an edge, outline *etc* with V-shaped cuts or inward curves.

independent [indi'pendənt] *adj* **1** not controlled by other people, countries *etc*: *an independent country; That country is now independent of Britain.* **2** not willing to accept help: *an independent old lady.* **3** having enough money to support oneself: *She is completely independent and receives no*

money *from her family; She is now independent of her parents.* **4** not relying on, or affected by, something or someone else: *an independent observer; to arrive at an independent conclusion.* **inde'pendence** *n.* **inde'pendently** *adv.*

index ['indeks] *n* **1** an alphabetical list of names, subjects *etc eg* at the end of a book. **2** (*pl* **indices** ['indisi:z]) in mathematics the figure which indicates the number of times a figure *etc* must be multiplied by itself *etc*: *In 6^3 and 7^5, the figures 3 and 5 are the indices.*

index finger the finger next to the thumb: *She pointed at the map with her index finger.*

Indian ['indiən] *n* **1** a native inhabitant of North America (see also **Red Indian** at **red**), Central or South America. **2** a person born in India or having Indian citizenship. – *adj* of India or of Indians.

india-rubber [indiə'rʌbə] *n* rubber, *esp* a piece for rubbing out pencil marks *etc.*

indicate ['indikeit] *v* to point out or show: *We can paint an arrow here to indicate the right path.*

,**indi'cation** *n*: *There are clear indications that the war will soon be over; He had given no indication that he was intending to resign.*

indicative [in'dikətiv] *adj, n* describing verbs which occur as parts of statements and questions: *In 'I ran home' and 'Are you going?' ran and are going are indicative (verbs).*

'**indicator** *n* a pointer, sign, instrument *etc* which indicates something or gives information about something: *the indicator on the petrol gauge of a car.*

indices *see* **index.**

indifferent [in'difrənt] *adj* **1** (*often with* **to**) showing no interest in or not caring about (opinions, events *etc*): *She is quite indifferent to other people's suffering.* **2** not very good: *He is a rather indifferent card-player.* **in'differently** *adv.*

in'difference *n* the state of showing no interest in, or concern about, something: *She showed complete indifference to the cries of the baby.*

indigestion [indi'dʒestʃən] *n* (discomfort or pain which is caused by) difficulty in digesting food: *She suffers from indigestion after eating fatty food.*

,**indi'gestible** *adj* not easily disgested: *This food is quite indigestible.* '**indi,gesti'bility** *n.*

indignant [in'dignənt] *adj* angry, *usu* because of some wrong that has been done to oneself or others: *I feel most indignant at the rude way I've been treated; The indignant customer complained to the manager.* **in'dignantly** *adv*: *'Take your foot off my toe!' she said indignantly.* ,**indig'nation** *n.*

indirect [indi'rekt] *adj* **1** not leading straight to the destination; not direct: *We arrived late because we took rather an indirect route.* **2** not straightforward: *I asked her several questions but she kept giving me indirect answers.* **3** not intended; not directly aimed at: *an indirect result.* ,indi'rectness *n.*

indirect object the word in a sentence which stands for the person or thing to or for whom something is given, done *etc*: *In 'Give me the book', 'Tell the children a story', 'Boil John an egg', me, the children and John are indirect objects.*

indirect speech a person's words as they are reported rather than in the form in which they were said: *He said that he would come is the form in indirect speech of He said 'I will come'.*

indiscipline [in'disəplin] *n* bad behaviour; unwillingness to obey orders.

indiscreet [indi'skri:t] *adj* **1** giving too much information away: *an indiscreet remark.* **2** not wise or cautious: *indiscreet behaviour.* ,indi'scretion [-'skreʃən] *n.*

indispensable [indi'spensəbl] *adj* necessary; that cannot be done without: *A dictionary should be considered an indispensable possession.*

indisposed [indi'spouzd] *adj* (slightly) ill: *The princess is indisposed and has cancelled her engagements.* 'in,dispo'sition *n.*

indisputable [indi'spju:təbl] *adj* not able to be denied.

indistinct [indi'stiŋkt] *adj* not clear to the eye, ear or mind; not distinct: *an indistinct outline of a ship; His speech is rather indistinct.* ,indi'stinctly *adv.* ,indi'stinctness *n.*

indistinguishable [indi'stiŋgwiʃəbl] *adj* not able to be seen as different or separate: *This copy is indistinguishable from the original; The twins are almost indistinguishable.*

individual [indi'vidjuəl] *adj* **1** single; separate: *Put price labels on each individual item.* **2** intended for, used by *etc* one person *etc*: *Customers in shops should be given individual attention.* **3** special to one person *etc*, showing or having special qualities: *Her style of dress is very individual.* – *n* **1** a single person in contrast to the group to which he belongs: *the rights of the individual in society.* **2** a person: *He's an untidy individual.* 'indi,vidu'ality [-'a-] *n* the qualities that distinguish one person *etc* from others. ,indi'vidually *adv* each separately: *I'll deal with each question individually.*

indivisible [indi'vizəbl] *adj* not able to be divided or separated. 'indi,visi'bility *n.*

indoor ['indo:] *adj* used, done *etc* inside a building: *indoor games; an indoor swimming-pool.* ,in'doors *adv* in or into a building: *Stay indoors till you've finished your homework; He went indoors when the rain started.*

indulge [in'dʌldʒ] *v* **1** to allow (a person) to do or have what he wishes: *You shouldn't indulge that child.* **2** to follow (a wish, interest *etc*): *He indulges his love of food by dining at expensive restaurants.* **3** to allow (oneself) a luxury *etc* : *Life would be very dull if we never indulged (ourselves).* in'dulgence *n.*

in'dulgent *adj* willing to allow people to do or have what they wish (often to too great an extent): *an indulgent parent.*

indulge in to give way to (an inclination, emotion *etc*): *She indulged in tears/in a fit of temper.*

industry ['indəstri] – *pl* 'industries – *n* **1** (any part of) the business of producing or making goods: *the ship-building industry; The government should invest more money in industry.* **2** hard work or effort: *He owed his success to both ability and industry.*

in'dustrial [-'dʌs] *adj* having, concerning *etc* industries or the making of goods: *That area of the country is industrial rather than agricultural.*

in'dustrialist [-'dʌs-] *n* a person who takes part in the running of a large industrial organization: *a wealthy industrialist.*

in'dustrialized, -ised [-'dʌs] *adj* (of a country) having a large number of industries. in,dustriali'zation, -s- *n.*

in'dustrious [-'dʌs-] *adj* busy and hardworking: *industrious pupils.*

industrial estate an area of a town *etc* set aside for (the building of) factories.

industrial relations the relationship between the management and the workers in a factory *etc.*

inedible [in'edibl] *adj* not fit or suitable to be eaten: *The meal was inedible.*

ineffective [ini'fektiv] *adj* useless; not producing any result or the result desired: *ineffective methods.* ,inef'fectiveness *n.*

ineffectual [ini'fektʃuəl] *adj* **1** not producing any result or the desired result: *His attempts to keep order in the classroom were quite ineffectual.* **2** (of a person) not confident or able to lead people; not able to get things done: *an ineffectual teacher.* ,inef'fectualness *n.*

inefficient [ini'fiʃənt] *adj* not working or producing results *etc* in the best way and so wasting time, energy *etc*: *an inefficient workman; old-fashioned, inefficient machinery.* ,inef'ficiently *adv.* ,inef'ficiency *n.*

inelegant [in'eligənt] *adj* not graceful; not elegant: *She was sprawled in a chair in a most inelegant fashion.* in'elegantly *adv.* in'elegance *n.*

ineligible [in'elidʒəbl] *adj* not eligible: *Children under eighteen years of age are ineligible to vote in elections.* in,eligi'bility *n.*

inequality [iniˈkwɒləti] n (a case of) the existence of differences in size, value etc between two or more objects etc: There is bound to be inequality between a manager's salary and a workman's wages.

inert [iˈnəːt] adj 1 without the power to move: A stone is an inert object. 2 (of people) not wanting to move, act or think: lazy, inert people. iˈnertness n.
iˈnertia [-ʃiə] n the state of being inert: It was difficult to overcome the feeling of inertia that the wine and heat had brought on.

inescapable [iniˈskeipəbl] adj (formal) that cannot be avoided: an inescapable conclusion.

inessential [inəˈsenʃəl] n, adj (something) which is not essential: We have no money for inessentials; inessential luxuries.

inevitable [inˈevitəbl] adj that cannot be avoided; certain to happen, be done, said, used etc: The Prime Minister said that war was inevitable. inˌevitaˈbility n.
inˈevitably adv as you might expect: Inevitably the train was late.

inexact [inigˈzakt] adj not quite correct, exact or true: an inexact description. ˌinexˈactness n.

inexcusable [inikˈskjuːzəbl] adj too bad etc to be excused or justified; not excusable: inexcusable rudeness. ˌinexˈcusably adv.

inexhaustible [inigˈzɔːstəbl] adj very large; not likely to be used up: an inexhaustible supply; Her energy seems inexhaustible. ˌinexˈhaustibly adv. ˌinexˌhaustiˈbility n.

inexpensive [inikˈspensiv] adj not costly; not expensive: inexpensive clothes. ˌinexˈpensively adv.

inexperience [inikˈspiəriəns] n lack of experience or skilled knowledge: He seems good at the job in spite of his youth and inexperience.
ˌinexˈperienced adj lacking knowledge, skill and experience: Inexperienced climbers should not attempt this route.

inexpert [inˈekspəːt] adj unskilled or clumsy: inexpert attempts at dressmaking. inˈexpertly adv.

inexplicable [inikˈsplikəbl] adj impossible to explain or understand: His inexplicable absence worried all of us. ˌinexˈplicably adv.

inexpressible [inikˈspresəbl] adj that cannot be expressed or described: inexpressible delight. ˌinexˈpressibly adv.

infallible [inˈfaləbl] adj 1 (of a person or his judgement etc) never making a mistake. 2 (of a remedy etc) always successful: infallible cures. inˌfalliˈbility n. inˈfallibly adv.

infamous [ˈinfəməs] adj 1 (of something bad) well-known; notorious. 2 disgraceful.
ˈinfamy n.

infant [ˈinfənt] n a baby or very young child: the baptism of infants; (also adj) an infant school.
ˈinfancy n the state or time of being a baby: They had two children who died in infancy.

infantry [ˈinfəntri] n or n pl (the part of an army consisting of) foot-soldiers: The infantry was/were sent on ahead, with the artillery following in the rear.

infect [inˈfekt] v to fill with germs that cause disease; to give a disease to: You must wash that cut on your knee in case it becomes infected; She had a bad cold last week and has infected the rest of the class.
inˈfection [-ʃən] n 1 the process of infecting or state of being infected: You should wash your hands after handling raw meat to avoid infection. 2 a disease: a throat infection.
inˈfectious [-ʃəs] adj likely to spread to others: Measles is an infectious disease. inˈfectiously adv.

infer [inˈfəː] – pt, ptp inˈferred – v to judge (from facts or evidence): I inferred from your silence that you were angry. ˈinference n.

inferior [inˈfiəriə] adj (sometimes with to) 1 of poor, or poorer, quality etc: This carpet is inferior to that. 2 lower in rank: Is a colonel inferior to a brigadier? inˌferiˈority [-ˈo-] n.

infertile [inˈfəːtail] adj 1 (of soil etc) not fertile or producing good crops: The land was stony and infertile. 2 (of persons or animals) unable to have young. inferˈtility [-ˈti-] n.

infest [inˈfest] v (of something bad) to swarm over and cover or fill: The dog was infested with fleas. infeˈstation [infe-] n.

infidelity [infiˈdeləti] n disloyalty or unfaithfulness (eg to one's husband or wife).

infiltrate [ˈinfiltreit] v 1 (of soldiers) to get through enemy lines a few at a time: to infiltrate (into) enemy territory. 2 (of a group of persons) to enter (an organization) gradually so as to be able to influence decisions etc.

infinite [ˈinfinit] adj 1 without end or limits: We believe that space is infinite. 2 very great: Infinite damage could be caused by such a mistake.
ˈinfinitely adv extremely; to a very great degree: The time at which our sun will finally cease to burn is infinitely far away.
ˈinfiniteness n.
inˈfinity [-ˈfi-] n 1 space, time or quantity that is without limit, or is immeasurably great or small. 2 in mathematics, an indefinitely large number, quantity or distance: Parallel lines meet at infinity.

infinitive [inˈfinitiv] n the part of the verb used in English with or without to, that expresses an action but has no subject: The sentence 'You need not stay if you want to go' contains two infinitives, stay and go.

infinity *see* **infinite**.

infirm [in'fə:m] *adj* (of a person) weak or ill: *elderly and infirm people*.

in'firmary – *pl* **in'firmaries** – *n* a name given to some hospitals.

in'firmity – *pl* **in'firmities** – *n* weakness or illness.

inflame [in'fleim] *v* to cause (feelings *etc*) to become violent.

in'flamed *adj* hot and red *esp* because of infection: *Her throat was very inflamed*.

inflammable [in'flaməbl] *adj* easily set on fire: *Paper is highly inflammable*. **in,flamma'bility** *n*.

inflammation [inflə'meiʃən] *n* (a place in the body where there is) development of heat with pain, redness and swelling: *Tonsillitis is inflammation of the tonsils*.

inflammable means the same as flammable: *a highly inflammable gas*.

inflate [in'fleit] *v* to blow up or expand (*esp* a balloon, tyre or lungs with air): *He used a bicycle pump to inflate the ball*.

in'flatable *adj* (of *eg* a cushion, ball *etc*) that can be filled with air for use: *an inflatable beach ball*.

in'flation *n* **1** the process of inflating or being inflated. **2** a situation in country's economy where prices and wages keep forcing each other to increase.

in'flationary *adj* relating to economic inflation.

inflexible [in'fleksəbl] *adj* **1** (of a person) never yielding or giving way. **2** not able to bend. **in'flexibly** *adv*. **in,flexi'bility** *n*.

inflict [in'flikt] *v* (*with* on) to give or impose (something unpleasant and unwanted): *Was it necessary to inflict such a punishment on him?*; *She is always inflicting her company on me*. **in'fliction** [-ʃən] *n*.

influence ['influəns] *n* **1** the power to affect people, actions or events: *He used his influence to get her the job*; *He should not have driven the car while under the influence of alcohol*. **2** a person or thing that has this power: *She is a bad influence on him*. – *v* to have an effect on: *The weather seems to influence her moods*.

,influ'ential [-'enʃəl] *adj* having much influence: *He is in quite an influential job*; *He was influential in getting the plan accepted*. **,influ'entially** *adv*.

influenza [influ'enzə] (*usu abbrev* **flu** *or* **'flu** [flu:]) *n* a type of infectious illness *usu* causing headache, fever, a cold *etc*.

influx ['inflʌks] *n* an arrival of something in great quantities or numbers: *an influx of tourists*.

inform [in'fo:m] *v* **1** to tell; to give knowledge to: *Please inform me of your intentions in this matter*; *I was informed that you were absent*

from the office. **2** (*with* **against** *or* **on**) to tell facts to *eg* the police about (a criminal *etc*): *He informed against his fellow thieves*.

in'formant *n* someone who tells or informs: *He passed on the news to us, but would not say who his informant had been*.

,infor'mation *n* facts told or knowledge gained or given: *Can you give me any information about this writer?*; *the latest information on the progress of the war*; *He is full of interesting bits of information*.

in'formative [-mətiv] *adj* giving useful information: *an informative book*.

in'former *n* a person who informs against a criminal *etc*.

information does not have a plural: *some information*; *any information*.

informal [in'fo:ml] *adj* **1** not formal or official; friendly and relaxed: *The two prime ministers will meet for informal discussions today*; *Will the party be formal or informal?*; *friendly, informal manners*. **2** (of speech or vocabulary) used in conversation but not *usu* when writing formally, speaking in public *etc*: *'Won't' and 'can't' are informal forms of 'will not' and 'cannot'*. **,infor'mality** [-'ma-] *n*. **in'formally** *adv*.

infra-red [infrə'red] *adj* (of rays) below the red end of the spectrum.

infrequent [in'fri:kwənt] *adj* not frequent: *His visits grew infrequent*. **in'frequency** *n*.

infringe [in'frindʒ] *v* to break (a law *etc*) or interfere with (a person's freedom or rights). **in'fringement** *n*.

infuriate [in'fjuərieit] *v* to make very angry: *I was infuriated by his words*.

in'furiating *adj*: *I find his silly jokes infuriating*. **in'furiatingly** *adv*.

ingenious [in'dʒi:njəs] *adj* **1** (of a person or his personality *etc*) clever at inventing: *He was ingenious at making up new games for the children*. **2** (of an object or idea) cleverly made or thought out: *an ingenious plan/machine*. **in'geniously** *adv*. **in'geniousness, ingenuity** [indʒə'njuəti] *ns*.

ingot ['iŋgət] *n* a mass of metal (*eg* gold or silver) cast in a mould: *The gold was transported as ingots*.

ingratitude [in'gratitju:d] *n* lack of gratitude: *I felt hurt by his ingratitude*.

ingredient [in'gri:diənt] *n* one of the things that go into a mixture: *Could you give me a list of the ingredients of the cake?*

inhabit [in'habit] *v* (of people, animals *etc*) to live in (a region *etc*): *Polar bears inhabit the Arctic region*; *That house is now inhabited by a Polish family*.

in'habitable *adj* (*neg* **un-**) fit to be lived in: *The building was no longer inhabitable*.

in'habitant *n* a person or animal that lives permanently in a place: *the inhabitants of* the village; *tigers, leopards and other inhabitants of the jungle.*

inhale [in'heil] *v* to breathe in: *He inhaled deeply; It is very unpleasant to have to inhale the smoke from other people's cigarettes.*
inhalation [in(h)ə'leiʃən] *n.*

in'haler *n* a *usu* small apparatus by means of which people inhale certain medicines.

inherit [in'herit] *v* **1** to receive (property *etc* belonging to someone who has died): *He inherited the house from his father; She inherited four thousand dollars from her father.* **2** to have (qualities) the same as one's parents *etc*: *She inherits her quick temper from her mother.*
in'heritance *n* **1** money *etc* inherited: *He spent most of his inheritance on drink.* **2** the act of inheriting: *The property came to him by inheritance.*

inhibit [in'hibit] *v* to stop or hinder (*eg* someone from doing something).
in'hibited *adj* unable to relax and express one's feelings in an open and natural way.
inhibition [ini'biʃən] *n.*

inhospitable [inhə'spitəbl] *adj* not welcoming guests; not friendly towards strangers: *She could not refuse to invite them in without seeming inhospitable.*

inhuman [in'hju:mən] *adj* extremely cruel or brutal; not seeming to be human: *His treatment of his children was quite inhuman.*
,inhu'manity [-'ma-] *n* cruelty or lack of pity.

inhumane [inhju'mein] *adj* unkind or cruel: *inhumane treatment of prisoners-of-war.*
,inhu'manely *adv.*

iniquity [i'nikwiti] – *pl* **i'niquities** – *n* (an act of) wickedness.

initial [i'niʃəl] *adj* of, or at, the beginning: *There were difficulties during the initial stages of building the house.* – *n* the letter that begins a word, *esp* a name: *The picture was signed with the initials JJB, standing for John James Brown.* – *v* – *pt, ptp* **i'nitialled** – to mark or sign with initials of one's name: *Any alteration on a cheque should be initialled.*
i'nitially *adv* at the beginning; at first: *This project will cost a lot of money initially but will eventually make a profit.*

i'nitiate[1] [-ʃeit] *v* **1** to start (*eg* a plan, scheme, changes, reforms *etc*): *He initiated a scheme for helping old people with their shopping.* **2** to take (a person) into a society *etc*, *esp* with secret ceremonies: *No-one who had been initiated into the society ever revealed the details of the ceremony.*
i'nitiate[2] [-ʃiət] *n* a person who has been initiated (into a society *etc*).
i,niti'ation [-ʃi'ei-] *n* the act of initiating or process of being initiated.
i'nitiative [-ʃətiv] *n* **1** a first step or move

that leads the way: *He took the initiative in organizing a search party to look for the girl; A move to start peace talks is sometimes called a peace initiative.* **2** the ability to lead or make decisions for oneself: *He is quite good at his job, but lacks initiative; My son actually went to the hairdresser's on his own initiative!*

inject [in'dʒekt] *v* to force (a liquid *etc*) into the body of (a person) by means of a needle and syringe: *The doctor injected the antibiotic into her arm; He has to be injected twice daily with an antibiotic.*
in'jection [-ʃən] *n*: *The medicine was given by injection; She has regular injections of insulin.*

injure ['indʒə] *v* to harm or damage: *He injured his arm when he fell; They were badly injured when the car crashed; A story like that could injure his reputation; His pride has been injured.*
'injured *adj* **1** (also *n*) (people who have been) wounded or harmed: *The injured (people) were all taken to hospital after the accident.* **2** (of feelings, pride *etc*) hurt: *'Why didn't you tell me before?' he said in an injured voice.*
injurious [in'dʒuəriəs] *adj* (*with* **to**) harmful: *Smoking is injurious to one's health.*
'injury – *pl* **'injuries** – *n* (an instance of) harm or damage: *Badly designed chairs can cause injury to the spine; The motorcyclist received severe injuries in the crash.*

injustice [in'dʒʌstis] *n* (an instance of) unfairness or the lack of justice: *He complained of injustice in the way he had been treated; They agreed that an injustice had been committed.*
do (someone) an injustice to treat or regard (someone) unfairly: *You do me an injustice if you think I could tell such a lie.*

ink [iŋk] *n* a black or coloured liquid used in writing, printing *etc*: *Please sign your name in ink rather than pencil; I spilt red ink all over my dress.*
'inky *adj* **1** covered with ink: *inky fingers; Don't touch that wall – your hands are inky.* **2** like ink; black or very dark: *inky blackness.*
'inkpot, 'inkwell *ns* a small pot for ink.

inkling ['iŋkliŋ] *n* a slight idea or suspicion (about something that is happening): *I had no inkling of what was going on until she told me all about it.*

inky *see* **ink.**

inlaid *see* **inlay.**

inland ['inlənd] *adj* **1** not beside the sea: *inland areas.* **2** done *etc* inside a country: *inland trade.* – [in'land] *adv* in, or towards, the parts of the land away from the sea: *These flowers grow better inland.*

in-law ['inlɔ:] – *pl* **'in-laws** – *n* a person related to one by marriage *eg* one's brother-in-law, mother-in-law *etc*.

inlay ['inlei] *n* material set into the surface of *eg* a table to form a design: *The top of the table had an inlay of ivory.*

in'laid *adj* decorated in this way: *an inlaid table.*

inlet ['inlit] *n* a small bay in the coastline of a sea, lake *etc*: *There are several pretty inlets suitable for bathing.*

inmate ['inmeit] *n* one of the people living in an institution, *esp* a prison or mental hospital.

inmost *see* **innermost** *under* **inner**.

inn [in] *n* **1** a name given to some small hotels or public houses *esp* in villages or the countryside. **2** in former times, a house providing food and lodging for travellers. **'innkeeper** *n* a person who owned or ran such a house.

inner ['inə] *adj* **1** placed *etc* on the inside or further in: *The inner tube of his tyre was punctured.* **2** (of feelings *etc*) secret or hidden: *I could not guess what his inner thoughts might be.* **'innermost** *adj* **1** placed *etc* furthest from the edge or outside: *the innermost parts of the castle.* **2** (*also* **inmost**) most secret or hidden: *his innermost feelings; in the inmost corners of his heart.*

innings ['iniŋz] – *pl* **'innings** – *n* in a game of cricket, a team's turn at batting: *At the end of their second innings, the West Indian team was 279 runs ahead.* **'inning** *n* in a game of baseball, any of the nine periods in which each team bats.

innocent ['inəsnt] *adj* **1** not guilty (of a crime, misdeed *etc*): *A man should be presumed innocent of a crime until he is proved guilty; They hanged an innocent man.* **2** (of an action *etc*) harmless or without harmful or hidden intentions: *innocent games and amusements; an innocent remark.* **3** free from, or knowing nothing about, evil *etc*: *an innocent child; You can't be so innocent as to believe what advertisements say!* **'innocently** *adv.* **'innocence** *n*: *He at last managed to prove his innocence; the innocence of a child.*

innocuous [i'nɔkjuəs] *adj* harmless: *This drug was at first mistakenly thought to be innocuous.*

innovation [inə'veiʃən] *n* (the act of making) a change or a new arrangement *etc*: *The new system in the school canteen was a welcome innovation.* **'innovator** *n*.

innumerable [i'nju:mərəbl] *adj* too many to be counted; a great many: *innumerable difficulties.*

inoculate [i'nɔkjuleit] *v* to give (a person *etc*) a mild form of a disease, *usu* by injecting germs into his body, so as to prevent him

from catching a more serious form: *Has he been inoculated against diphtheria?* **i,nocu'lation** *n*.

inoffensive [inə'fensiv] *adj* harmless; not likely to offend: *an inoffensive remark.*

inoperable [in'ɔpərəbl] *adj* not suitable for a surgical operation: *inoperable cancer.*

inorganic [inɔː'ganik] *adj* not having the special characteristics of living bodies; not organic: *Stone, metal and other minerals are inorganic.*

in-patient ['inpeiʃənt] *n* a patient living in, as well as receiving treatment in, a hospital.

input ['input] *n* **1** something, *eg* an amount of electrical energy, that is supplied to a machine *etc*. **2** information put into a computer for processing.

inquest ['inkwest] *n* a legal inquiry into a case of sudden and unexpected death.

inquire, enquire [in'kwaiə] *v* **1** to ask: *He inquired the way to the art gallery; She inquired what time the bus left.* **2** (*with* **about**) to ask for information about: *They inquired about trains to London.* **3** (*with* **after**) to ask for information about the state of (*eg* a person's health): *He enquired after her mother.* **4** (*with* **for**) to ask to see or talk to (a person): *Someone rang up inquiring for you, but you were out.* **5** (*with* **for**) to ask for (goods in a shop *etc*): *Several people have been inquiring for the new catalogue.* **6** (*with* **into**) to try to discover the facts of: *The police are inquiring into the matter.* **in'quiry** [*Amer also* 'inkwəri], **en'quiry** [*Amer also* 'enkwəri] – *pl* **inquiries, enquiries** – *n* **1** (an act of) asking or investigating: *His inquiries led him to her hotel;* (*also adj*) *All questions will be dealt with at the inquiry desk.* **2** an investigation: *An inquiry is being held into her disappearance.* **make inquiries** to ask for information.

inquisitive [in'kwizətiv] *adj* eager to find out about other people's affairs: *He was rather inquisitive about the cost of our house; inquisitive neighbours.* **in'quisitively** *adv.* **in'quisitiveness** *n*.

insane [in'sein] *adj* **1** mad; mentally ill. **2** extremely foolish: *It was insane to think he would give you the money.* **in'sanity** [-'sa-] *n*.

insanitary [in'sanətəri] *adj* so dirty as to be a danger to health: *living in crowded, insanitary conditions.* **in'sanitariness** *n*.

insatiable [in'seiʃəbl] *adj* not able to be satisfied: *an insatiable desire for adventure.* **in'satiably** *adv.* **in'satiableness** *n*.

inscribe [in'skraib] *v* to carve or write: *The monument was inscribed with the names of the men who died in the war; He carefully inscribed his name in his new book.* **inscription** [in'skripʃən] *n* something written, *eg* on a gravestone or on a coin: *The* *coin was so worn that the inscription could scarcely be read.*

insect ['insekt] *n* any of many kinds of small six-legged creatures with wings and a body divided into sections: *We were bothered by flies, wasps and other insects.*

insecticide [in'sektisaid] *n* a substance (*usu* in powder or liquid form) for killing insects.

insec'tivorous [-'tivərəs] *adj* (of plants or animals) feeding (mainly) on insects.

insecure [insi'kjuə] *adj* **1** unsure of oneself or lacking confidence: *Whenever he was in a crowd of people he felt anxious and insecure.* **2** not safe or firmly fixed: *This chair-leg is insecure; an insecure lock.* **inse'curely** *adv.* ˌinse'curity *n.*

insensible [in'sensəbl] *adj* unconscious: *He lay on the floor insensible.*

insensitive [in'sensətiv] *adj* (*with* to) **1** not noticing or not sympathetic towards (*eg* others' feelings): *He was insensitive to her grief.* **2** (*with* to) not feeling or not reacting to (touch, light *etc*): *The dentist's injection numbed the nerves and made the tooth insensitive to the drill.* inˌsensi'tivity *n.*

inseparable [in'sepərəbl] *adj* not to be separated or parted: *inseparable companions.*

insert [in'sə:t] *v* to put or place (something) in: *He inserted the money in the parking meter; An extra chapter has been inserted into the book; They inserted the announcement in the newspaper.* **in'sertion** [-ʃən] *n.*

inset ['inset] *n* a small map, picture *etc* that has been put in the corner of a larger one: *In a map of a coastline, there may be an inset to show offshore islands.*

inshore [in'ʃo:] *adv* near or towards the shore. – ['inʃo:] *adj* near the shore: *inshore fishing.*

inside [in'said] *n* **1** the inner side, or the part or space within: *The inside of this apple is quite rotten.* **2** the stomach and bowels: *He ate too much and got a pain in his inside(s).* – ['insaid] *adj* being on or in the inside: *the inside pages of the newspaper; The inside traffic lane is the one nearest to the kerb.* – [in'said] *adv* **1** to, in, or on, the inside: *The door was open and he went inside; She shut the door but left her key inside by mistake.* **2** in a house or building: *You should stay inside in such bad weather.* – ['in'said] *prep* **1** (*sometimes* (*esp Amer*) *with* **of**) within; to or on the inside of: *She is inside the house; He went inside the shop.* **2** (*sometimes with* **of**) in less than, or within, a certain time: *He finished the work inside (of) two days.*

inside out 1 with the inner side out: *Haven't you got your shirt on inside out?* **2** very thoroughly: *He knows the plays of Shakespeare inside out.*

insight ['insait] *n* (the quality of having) an understanding of something: *He shows remarkable insight (into children's problems).*

insignia [in'signiə] *n pl* symbols worn or carried as a mark of high office: *The crown and sceptre are the insignia of a king.*

insignificant [insig'nifikənt] *adj* of little value or importance; not significant: *They paid me an insignificant sum of money; an insignificant person.* ˌinsig'nificance *n.*

insincere [insin'siə] *adj* not sincere; not genuine: *His praise was insincere; insincere promises.* ˌinsin'cerely *adv.* ˌinsin'cerity [-'se-] *n.*

insist [in'sist] *v* **1** (*with* **that** *or* **on**) to state, emphasize, or hold firmly to (an opinion, plan *etc*): *He insists that I was to blame for the accident; I insisted on driving him home.* **2** (*often with* **on** *or* **that**) to demand or urge: *He insists on punctuality/obedience; She insisted on coming with me; He insisted that I should go.*

in'sistence *n* (the act of) insisting: *She went to see the doctor at her husband's insistence.* **in'sistent** *adj.*

insofar as *see* **in.**

insolent ['insələnt] *adj* (of a person or his behaviour) insulting or offensive: *an insolent stare/remark.* **'insolently** *adv.* **'insolence** *n.*

insoluble [in'soljubl] *adj* **1** (of a substance) impossible to dissolve: *This chemical is insoluble (in water).* **2** (of a problem or difficulty) impossible to solve. **insolu'bility** *n.*

insomnia [in'somniə] *n* inability to sleep: *She takes sleeping-pills as she suffers from insomnia.*

in'somniac [-ak] *n, adj* (of) a person who suffers from insomnia.

inspect [in'spekt] *v* **1** to look at, or examine, carefully or formally: *He inspected the bloodstains.* **2** to visit (*eg* a restaurant or school) officially, to make sure that it is properly run: *Cafés must be regularly inspected to find out if they are kept clean.* **3** to look at (troops *etc*) ceremonially: *The Queen will inspect the regiment.* **in'spection** [-ʃən] *n.*

in'spector *n* **1** a person appointed to inspect: *a school inspector.* **2** a police officer below a superintendent and above a sergeant in rank.

inspire [in'spaiə] *v* **1** to encourage by filling with *eg* confidence, enthusiasm *etc*: *The players were inspired by the loyalty of their supporters and played better football than ever before.* **2** to be the origin or source of a poetic or artistic idea: *An incident in his childhood inspired the poem.* **inspiration** [inspə'reiʃən] *n.*

instability [instə'biləti] *n* lack of stability or steadiness *eg* of personality.

install [in'sto:l] *v* **1** to put in place ready for use: *When was the telephone/electricity in-*

stalled (*in this house*)? **2** to put (a thing, oneself or another person) in a place or position: *He was installed as president yesterday; They soon installed themselves in the new house.*

installation [instə'leiʃən] *n* **1** the act of installing. **2** a piece of equipment that has been installed: *The cooker, fridge and other electrical installations are all in working order.*

in'stalment *n* **1** one payment out of a number of payments into which an amount of money, *esp* a debt, is divided: *The new carpet is being paid for by monthly instalments.* **2** a part of a story that is printed one part at a time *eg* in a weekly magazine, or read in parts on the radio: *Did you hear the final instalment last week?*

instance ['instəns] *n* an example, *esp* of a condition or circumstance: *As a social worker, he saw many instances of extreme poverty.*

for instance for example: *Some birds, penguins for instance, cannot fly at all.*

instant ['instənt] *adj* **1** immediate: *Anyone disobeying these rules will face instant dismissal; His latest play was an instant success.* **2** (of food *etc*) able to be prepared *etc* almost immediately: *instant coffee/potato.* – *n* **1** a point in time: *He climbed into bed and at that instant the telephone rang; He came the instant* (*that*) *he heard the news.* **2** a moment or very short time: *It all happened in an instant; I'll be there in an instant.*

'instantly *adv* immediately: *He went to bed and instantly fell asleep.*

this instant straight away; at this very moment: *Give it back this instant!*

instantaneous [instən'teiniəs] *adj* done, happening or acting in an instant or very quickly: *The effect of this poison is instantaneous.* **,instan'taneously** *adv.*

instead [in'sted] *adv* as a substitute; in place of something or someone: *I don't like coffee. Could I please have tea instead?*

instead of in place of: *Please take me instead of him; You should have been working instead of watching television.*

instep ['instep] *n* the arched upper part of the foot: *The strap of that shoe is too tight across the instep.*

instigate ['instigeit] *v* to suggest and encourage (a wrong action, a rebellion *etc*). **insti'gation** *n.*

instil [in'stil] – *pt, ptp* **in'stilled** – *v* to put (ideas *etc*) into the mind of a person: *The habit of punctuality was instilled into me early in life.*

instinct ['instiŋkt] *n* a natural tendency to behave or react in a particular way, without thinking and without having been taught: *As winter approaches, swallows fly south*

from Britain by instinct; He has an instinct for saying the right thing.

in'stinctive [-tiv] *adj* arising from instinct or from a natural ability: *Blinking our eyes is an instinctive reaction when something suddenly comes close to them; I couldn't help putting my foot on the brake when I saw the other car coming towards me – it was instinctive.* **in'stinctively** *adv.*

institute ['institjuːt] *n* a society or organization, or the building it uses: *There is a lecture at the Philosophical Institute tonight.* – *v* to start or establish: *When was the Red Cross instituted?*

,insti'tution *n* **1** the act of instituting or process of being instituted. **2** (the building used by) an organization *etc* founded for a particular purpose, *esp* care of people, or education: *schools, hospitals, prisons and other institutions.* **,insti'tutional** *adj.*

instruct [in'strʌkt] *v* **1** to teach or train (a person in a subject or skill): *Girls as well as boys should be instructed in woodwork.* **2** to order or direct (a person *esp* to do something): *He was instructed to come here at nine o'clock; I have already instructed you how to cook the meat.*

in'struction [-ʃən] *n* **1** the act of instructing (*esp* in a school subject or a skill) or the process of being instructed: *She sometimes gives instruction in gymnastics.* **2** an order or direction: *You must learn to obey instructions.* **3** (*in pl*) (a book *etc* giving) directions, *eg* about the use of a machine *etc*: *Could I look at the instructions, please?*

in'structive [-tiv] *adj* giving knowledge or information: *He gave an instructive talk about electrical repair work.* **in'structively** *adv.* **in'structiveness** *n.*

in'structor – *fem* **in'structress** – *n* a person who gives instruction (in a skill *etc*): *a ski-instructor.*

instrument ['instrəmənt] *n* **1** a tool, *esp* if used for delicate scientific or medical work: *medical/surgical/mathematical instruments.* **2** (*also* **musical instrument**) an apparatus for producing musical sounds: *He can play the piano, violin and several other instruments.*

,instru'mental [-'men-] *adj* performed on, or written for, musical instrument(s) rather than voices: *She likes instrumental music.*

,instru'mentalist [-'men-] *n* a person who plays a musical instrument: *There are three instrumentalists and one singer in the group.*

insubordinate [insə'bɔːdənət] *adj* (of a person or his behaviour) disobedient or rebellious: *an insubordinate employee.* **'insu,bordi'nation** [-bɔː-] *n.*

insufficient [insə'fiʃənt] *adj* not enough: *The prisoner was released because the police had* *insufficient proof of his guilt.* ,insuf'ficiently *adv.* ,insuf'ficiency *n.*

insular ['insjulə] *adj* of, or belonging to, an island or islands: *There are some plants that grow only in an insular climate.*

insulate ['insjuleit] *v* to cover, protect or separate (something) with a material that does not let *esp* electrical currents or heat *etc* pass through it: *Rubber and plastic are used for insulating electric wires and cables.* ,insu'lation *n.*

insulin ['insjulin] *n* a substance used in the treatment of the disease diabetes.

insult [in'sʌlt] *v* to treat (a person) rudely or contemptuously: *He insulted her by telling her she was not only ugly but stupid too.* – ['insʌlt] *n* (a) comment or action that insults: *She took it as an insult that he did not shake hands with her.*
in'sulting *adj* contemptuous or offensive: *insulting words.*

insuperable [in'sju:pərəbl] *adj* (of a problem *etc*) that cannot be overcome: *insuperable difficulties.*

insure [in'ʃuə] *v* to arrange for the payment of a sum of money in the event of the loss of (something) or accident or injury to (someone): *Is your car insured?*; *Employers have to insure employees against accident.*
in'surance *n* the promise of a sum of money in event of loss *eg* by fire or other disaster, given in compensation by a company *etc* in return for regular payments: *Have you paid the insurance on your jewellery?*; (*also adj*) *insurance companies.*
insurance policy (a document setting out) an agreement with an insurance company.

insurgent [in'sə:dʒənt] *adj* risng up in rebellion: *an insurgent population.* – *n* a rebel: *the leading insurgents.*

intact [in'takt] *adj* undamaged or whole: *The box was washed up on the beach with its contents still intact.*

intake ['inteik] *n* **1** the thing or quantity taken in: *This year's intake of students is smaller than last year's.* **2** a place at which *eg* water is taken into a channel *etc*: *The ventilation system broke down when something blocked the main air intake.* **3** the act of taking in: *an intake of breath.*

integrate ['intigreit] *v* to (cause to) mix freely with other groups in society *etc*: *The immigrants are not finding it easy to integrate into the life of our cities.* ,inte'gration *n.*

integrity [in'tegrəti] *n* honesty: *He is a man of absolute integrity.*

intellect ['intilekt] *n* the thinking power of the mind: *He was a person of great intellect.*
,intel'lectual [-'lektʃuəl] *adj* of, or appealing to, the intellect: *He does not play football – his interests are mainly intellectual.*

intelligent [in'telidʒənt] *adj* (*neg* **un-**) **1** clever

and quick at understanding: *an intelligent child*; *That dog is so intelligent.* **2** showing these qualities: *an intelligent question.* **in'telligently** *adv.*

in'telligence *n* **1** the quality of being intelligent: *It requires a high degree of intelligence to do this job well.* **2** news or information given. **3** a department of state or of the army *etc* which deals with secret information: *He works in Intelligence.*

intelligible [in'telidʒəbl] *adj* (*neg* **un-**) able to be understood: *His answer was barely intelligible because he was speaking through a mouthful of food.* in,telligi'bility *n.*
in'telligibly *adv.*

intend [in'tend] *v* **1** to mean or plan (to do something or that someone else should do something): *Do you still intend to go?*; *Do you intend them to go?*; *Do you intend that they should go too?* **2** to mean (something) to be understood in a particular way: *His remarks were intended to be a compliment.* **3** (with **for**) to direct at: *That letter/bullet was intended for me.*

in'tent [-t] *adj* **1** (with **on**) meaning, planning or wanting to do (something): *He's intent on going*; *He's intent on marrying the girl.* **2** (with **on**) concentrating hard on: *He was intent on the job he was doing.* – *n* purpose; what a person means to do: *He broke into the house with intent to steal.*

in'tention [-ʃən] *n* what a person plans or intends to do: *He has no intention of leaving*; *He went to see the boss with the intention of asking for a pay rise*; *If I have offended you, it was quite without intention*; *good intentions.*

in'tentional [-ʃənl] *adj* (*neg* **un-**) done, said *etc* deliberately and not by accident: *I'm sorry I offended you – it wasn't intentional*; *intentional cruelty.* **in'tentionally** *adv.*

in'tently *adv* with great concentration: *He was watching her intently.*

intense [in'tens] *adj* very great: *intense heat*; *intense hatred.*
in'tensely *adv* very much: *I dislike that sort of behaviour intensely.*
in'tenseness *n.*
in'tensity *n* the quality of being intense: *the intensity of the heat.*
in'tensive [-siv] *adj* very great; showing or having great care *etc*: *The police began an intensive search for the murderer*; *The hospital has just opened a new intensive care unit.* **in'tensively** *adv.* **in'tensiveness** *n.*

intent, intention *etc see* **intend.**

inter [in'tə:] – *pt, ptp* **in'terred** – *v* to bury (a person *etc*). **in'terment** *n.*

interact [intər'akt] *v* (of two or more people, things *etc*) to act, or have some effect, on each other. ,inter'action [-ʃən] *n.*

intercede [intə'si:d] *v* **1** to try to put an end to

a fight, argument *etc* between two people, countries *etc*: *All attempts to intercede between the two nations failed.* **2** to try to persuade someone not to do something to someone else: *The condemned murderer's family interceded (with the President) on his behalf.* ,inter'cession [-'seʃən] *n*.

intercept [intə'sept] *v* to stop or catch (a person, thing *etc*) before he, it *etc* arrives at the place to which he, it *etc* is going, being sent *etc*: *The messenger was intercepted on his way to the king.* ,inter'ception *n*.

intercession *see* intercede.

interchange ['intətʃeindʒ] *n* **1** a place where two or more main roads or motorways at different levels are joined by means of several small roads, so allowing cars *etc* to move from one road to another. **2** (an) exchange: *an interchange of ideas.*
,inter'changeable *adj* able to be used, put *etc* in the place of each other without a difference in effect, meaning *etc*: *'Great' and 'big' are not completely interchangeable.*

intercom ['intəkom] *n* a system of communication within an aeroplane, factory *etc usu* by means of microphones and loudspeakers: *The pilot spoke to the passengers over the intercom.*

intercourse ['intəko:s] *n* **1** sexual intercourse. **2** conversation, business dealings, trade *etc* between two or more people, countries *etc.*

interest ['intrəst] *n* **1** curiosity; attention: *That newspaper story is bound to arouse interest.* **2** a matter, activity *etc* that is of special concern to one: *Gardening is one of my main interests.* **3** money paid in return for borrowing a *usu* large sum of money: *The (rate of) interest on this loan is eight per cent; (also adj) the interest rate.* **4** (a share in the ownership of) a business firm *etc*: *He bought an interest in the night-club.* **5** a group of connected businesses which act together to their own advantage: *I suspect that the scheme will be opposed by the banking interest* (=all the banks acting together). – *v* **1** to arouse the curiosity and attention of; to be of importance or concern to: *Political arguments don't interest me at all.* **2** (with **in**) to persuade to do, buy *etc*: *Can I interest you in (buying) this dictionary?*
'interested *adj* **1** (*often with* **in**) showing attention or having curiosity: *He's not interested in politics; Don't tell me any more – I'm not interested; I'll be interested to see what happens next week.* **2** (*often with* **in**) willing, or wanting, to do, buy *etc*: *Are you interested in (buying) a second-hand car?* **3** personally involved in a particular business, project *etc* and therefore likely to be anxious about decisions made regarding it:

You must consult the other interested parties (=the other people involved).
'interesting (*neg* **un-**) *adj*: *an interesting book.* 'interestingly *adv*.
in one's (own) interest bringing, or in order to bring, advantage, benefit, help *etc* to oneself *etc*: *It would be in our own interest to help him, as he may be able to help us later.*
in the interest(s) of in order to get, achieve, increase *etc*: *The political march was banned in the interests of public safety.*
lose interest to stop being interested: *He used to be very active in politics, but he's lost interest now.*
take an interest to be interested: *I take a great interest in everything they do.*

interfere [intə'fiə] *v* **1** (*often with* **in**, **with**) to (try to) become involved in *etc*, when one's help *etc* is not wanted: *I wish you would stop interfering (with my plans); Don't interfere in other people's business!* **2** (*with* **with**) to prevent, stop or slow down the progress of: *He doesn't let anything interfere with his game of golf on Saturday mornings.*
,inter'ference *n* **1** the act of interfering: *She was infuriated by his mother's interference in their holiday arrangements.* **2** (the spoiling of radio or television reception by) the noise caused by programmes from another station, bad weather *etc*: *This television set picks up a lot of interference.*
,inter'fering *adj*: *an interfering old woman.*

interior [in'tiəriə] *adj* on, of *etc*, the inside of (something): *the interior walls of a building.* – *n* **1** the inside of a building *etc*: *The interior of the house was very attractive.* **2** the part of a country away from the coast, borders *etc*: *The explorers landed on the coast, and then travelled into the interior.*
interior decoration the art and process of designing, decorating, furnishing *etc* the insides of houses, offices *etc.*
interior decorator a person who does interior decoration.

interjection [intə'dʒekʃən] *n* **1** a word or words, or some noise, used to express surprise, dismay, pain or other feelings and emotions: *Oh dear! I think I've lost my key; Ouch! That hurts!* **2** the act of interjecting something.
,inter'ject *v* to say (something) which interrupts what one, or someone else, is saying.

interlock [intə'lok] *v* (of two or more pieces or parts) to fit or fasten together: *The pieces of a jigsaw puzzle interlock; 400 interlocking pieces.*

interlude ['intəlu:d] *n* a *usu* short period or gap, *eg* between the acts of a play: *We bought an ice-cream during the interlude; an interlude of calm during the violence.*

intermarry [intə'mari] *v* (of tribes, families *etc*) to marry one another: *The invaders* *intermarried with the local population*; *The two families intermarried.* ˌinter'**marriage** [-ridʒ] *n.*

intermediary [intə'mi:diəri] – *pl* inter'**mediaries** – *n* a person who takes messages from one person to another in a dispute *etc, esp* in order to settle the dispute.

intermediate [intə'mi:diət] *adj* in the middle; placed between two things, stages *etc*: *An intermediate English course is more advanced than a beginners' course, but not as difficult as an advanced course.*

interment *see* **inter**.

intermission [intə'miʃən] *n* a *usu* short pause or gap between two (television or radio) programmes, parts of a programme, play *etc.*

intermittent [intə'mitənt] *adj* happening occasionally; stopping for a while and then starting again: *an intermittent pain.* ˌinter'**mittently** *adv.*

intern[1] [in'tə:n] *v* during a war, to keep (someone who belongs to an enemy nation but who is living in one's own country) a prisoner. in'**ternment** *n.*

intern[2] ['intə:n] *n* (*Amer*) (*also* **interne**) a junior doctor resident in a hospital.

internal [in'tə:nl] *adj* 1 of, on or in the inside of something (*eg* a person's body): *The man suffered internal injuries in the accident.* 2 concerning what happens within a country *etc*, rather than its relationship with other countries *etc*: *The prime ministers agreed that no country should interfere in another country's internal affairs.* in'**ternally** *adv.*

internal combustion a means of producing power *eg* in the engine of a motor car by the burning of a fuel gas (*eg* petrol vapour) inside the cylinder(s) of the engine.

international [intə'naʃənl] *adj* involving, or done by, two or more nations: *international trade*; *an international football match.* – *n* 1 a football *etc* match played between teams from two countries. 2 (*also* ˌinter'**nationalist**) a player in such a match. ˌinter'**nationally** *adv.*

interne *see* **intern**[2].

internment *see* **intern**[1].

interpret [in'tə:prit] *v* 1 to translate a speaker's words, while he is speaking, into the language of his hearers: *He spoke to the audience in French and she interpreted.* 2 to explain the meaning of: *How do you interpret these lines of the poem?* 3 to show or bring out the meaning of (*eg* a piece of music) in one's performance of it: *The sonata was skilfully interpreted by the pianist.* in,terpre'**tation** *n.*

in'**terpreter** *n* a person who translates the words of a speaker into the language of his hearers.

interrogate [in'terəgeit] *v* to question (a person) thoroughly: *The police spent five hours interrogating the prisoner.* in,terro'**gation** *n.* in'**terrogator** *n.*

interrogative [intə'rogətiv] *adj, n* (a word) that asks a question: *'Who?' is an interrogative* (*pronoun*).

interrupt [intə'rʌpt] *v* 1 to stop a person while he is saying or doing something, *esp* by saying *etc* something oneself: *He interrupted her while she was speaking*; *He interrupted her speech*; *Listen to me and don't interrupt!* 2 to stop or make a break in (an activity *etc*): *He interrupted his work to eat his lunch*; *You interrupted my thoughts.* 3 to cut off (a view *etc*): *A block of flats interrupted their view of the sea.*

ˌinter'**ruption** [-ʃən] *n* 1 the act of interrupting or state of being interrupted: *His failure to complete the job was due to constant interruption.* 2 something that interrupts: *I get too many interruptions in my work.*

intersect [intə'sekt] *v* to divide (*eg* lines or roads) by cutting or crossing: *The line AB intersects the line CD at X*; *Where do the two roads intersect?*

ˌinter'**section** [-ʃən] *n* 1 the act of intersecting. 2 a place where lines, roads *etc* intersect: *The crash occurred at the intersection* (*between the two roads*).

interval ['intəvəl] *n* 1 a time or space between: *He returned home after an interval of two hours.* 2 a short break in a play, concert *etc*: *We had ice-cream in the interval.*

at intervals here and there; now and then: *Trees grew at intervals along the road.*

intervene [intə'vi:n] *v* 1 to interfere in a quarrel: *He intervened in the dispute.* 2 to be or come between, in place or time: *A week intervened before our next meeting.*

ˌinter'**vention** [-'venʃən] *n* (an) act of intervening (in a quarrel *etc*).

interview ['intəvju:] *n* a formal meeting and discussion with someone, *eg* a person applying for a job, or a person with information to broadcast on radio or television. – *v* to question (a person) in an interview: *They interviewed seven people for the job*; *He was interviewed by reporters about his policies.* '**interviewer** *n.*

intestine [in'testin] *n* (*often in pl*) the lower part of the food passage in man and animals. **intestinal** [intes'tainl], (*esp Amer*) in'testinl] *adj.*

intimate ['intimət] *adj* 1 close and affectionate: *intimate friends.* 2 private or personal: *the intimate details of his correspondence.* 3 (of knowledge of a subject) deep and thorough. – *n* a close friend. – [-meit] *v* to give information or announce. ˌinti'**mation** [-'mei-] *n.*

'**intimacy** [-məsi] *n* **1** the quality of being intimate. **2** close friendship.
'**intimately** [-mət-] *adv*.
intimidate [in'timideit] *v* to frighten *eg* by threatening violence. **in,timi'dation** *n*.
into ['intu] *prep* **1** to or towards the inside of; to within: *The eggs were put into the box*; *They disappeared into the mist*. **2** against: *The car ran into the wall*. **3** to the state or condition of: *A tadpole turns into a frog*; *I've sorted the books into piles*. **4** expressing the idea of division: *Two into four goes twice*.
intolerable [in'tolərəbl] *adj* that cannot be endured or borne: *intolerable pain*; *This delay is intolerable*. **in'tolerably** *adv*.
in'tolerant *adj* (*often with* **of**) unwilling to endure or accept *eg* people whose ideas *etc* are different from one's own, members of a different race or religion *etc*: *an intolerant attitude*; *He is intolerant of others' faults*.
in'tolerance *n*.
intonation [intə'neiʃən] *n* the rise and fall of the voice in speech.
intoxicate [in'toksikeit] *v* to make drunk.
in,toxi'cation *n*. **in'toxicating** *adj*.
intransitive [in'transitiv] *adj* (of a verb) that does not have an object: *The baby lay on the floor and kicked*; *Go and fetch the book!*
in'transitively *adv*.
intrepid [in'trepid] *adj* bold and fearlesss: *an intrepid explorer*. **in'trepidly** *adv*. **,intre'pidity** [-'pi-] *n*.
intricate ['intrikət] *adj* complicated: *an intricate knitting pattern*; *intricate details*. '**intricately** *adv*. '**intricacy** – *pl* '**intricacies** – *n*.
intrigue [in'triːg, 'intriːg] *n* the activity of plotting or scheming: *a plot or scheme*: *He became president as a result of* (*a*) *political intrigue*. – [in'triːg] *v* **1** to fascinate, arouse the curiosity of or amuse: *The book intrigued me*. **2** to plot or scheme.
in'triguing *adj* curious or amusing: *an intriguing idea*.
introduce [intrə'djuːs] *v* **1** (*often with* **to**) to make (people) known by name to each other: *He introduced the guests* (*to each other*); *Let me introduce you to my mother*; *May I introduce myself? I'm John Brown*. **2** (*often with* **into**) to bring in (something new): *Grey squirrels were introduced into Britain from Canada*; *Why did you introduce such a boring subject* (*into the conversation*)? **3** to propose or put forward: *He introduced a bill in Parliament for the abolition of income tax*. **4** (*with* **to**) to cause (a person) to get to know (a subject *etc*): *Children are introduced to algebra at about the age of eleven*.
,intro'duction [-'dʌkʃən] *n* **1** the act of introducing, or the process of being introduced: *the introduction of new methods*.

2 an act of introducing one person to another: *The hostess made the introductions and everyone shook hands*. **3** something written at the beginning of a book explaining the contents, or said at the beginning of a speech *etc*.
,intro'ductory [-'dʌktəri] *adj* giving an introduction: *He made a few introductory remarks about the film before showing it*.
introvert ['intrəvəːt] *n* a person who is more concerned with his own thoughts and feelings than with other people or happenings outside him.
intrude [in'truːd] *v* (*sometimes with* **on**) to enter, or cause (something) to enter, when unwelcome or unwanted: *He opened her door and said 'I'm sorry to intrude'*; *I'm sorry to intrude on your time*.
in'truder *n* a person who intrudes, *eg* a burglar: *Fit a good lock to your door to keep out intruders*.
in'trusion [-ʒən] *n* (an) act of intruding: *Please forgive this intrusion*.
intuition [intju'iʃən] *n* **1** the power of understanding or realizing something without thinking it out: *She knew by intuition that he was telling her the truth*. **2** something understood or realized by this power: *Her intuitions are always right*.
intuitive [in'tjuːətiv] *adj*.
inundate ['inəndeit] *v* to flood (a place, building *etc*). **,inun'dation** *n*.
invade [in'veid] *v* (of an enemy) to enter (a country *etc*) with an army: *Britain was twice invaded by the Romans*.
in'vader *n* a person, or (*sometimes in sing with* **the**) an armed force *etc*, that invades: *Our armies fought bravely against the invader*(s).
in'vasion [-ʒən] *n*.
invalid¹ [in'valid] *adj* (of a document or agreement *etc*) having no legal force; not valid: *Your passport is out of date and therefore invalid*.
in'validate [-deit] *v* to make invalid.
invalidity [invə'lidəti] *n*.
invalid² ['invəlid] *n* a person who is ill or diabled: *During his last few years, he was a permanent invalid*. – [-liːd] *v* **1** (*with* **out**) to remove (*esp* a soldier) from service, because of illness: *He was invalided out of the army*. **2** to cause (*esp* a soldier) to be disabled: *He was invalided in the last war*.
invaluable [in'valjuəbl] *adj* of value too great to be estimated: *Thank you for your invaluable help*.
invariable [in'veəriəbl] *adj* unchanging; not variable.
in'variably *adv* always: *They invariably quarrel when he comes home*.
invasion *see* **invade**.
invent [in'vent] *v* **1** to be the first person to

make or use (*eg* a machine, method *etc*): *Who invented the microscope?*; *When was printing invented?* **2** to make up or think of (*eg* an excuse or story): *I'll have to invent some excuse for not going with him.*

in'vention [-ʃən] *n* **1** the act of inventing or the ability to invent: *He had great powers of invention.* **2** something invented: *What a marvellous invention the sewing-machine was!*

in'ventive [-tiv] *adj* good at inventing: *an inventive mind.* **in'ventiveness** *n*.

in'ventor *n* a person who invents: *Alexander Graham Bell was the inventor of the telephone.*

see also **discover**.

inventory ['invəntri] – *pl* **'inventories** – *n* a formal and detailed list of goods *eg* house furniture.

invert [in'vəːt] *v* to turn upside down or reverse the order of. **in'version** [-ʃən] *n*.

inverted commas single or double commas, the first (set) of which is turned upside down (" ", ' '), used in writing to show where direct speech begins and ends: *"It is a lovely day," she said.*

invertebrate [in'vəːtibrət] *adj, n* (an animal *eg* a worm or insect) not having a backbone.

invest¹ [in'vest] *v* (*with* **in**) to put (money) into (a firm or business) *usu* by buying shares in it, in order to make a profit: *He invested (two hundred dollars) in a building firm.*

in'vestment *n* **1** the act of investing. **2** a sum of money invested.

in'vestor *n* a person who invests money.

invest² [in'vest] *v* to establish (a person) officially in a position of authority *etc*: *The governor will be invested next week.*

in'vestiture [-titʃə] *n* (a ceremony of) giving (the robes *etc* of) high rank or office to someone.

investigate [in'vestigeit] *v* to examine or inquire into carefully: *The police are investigating the mystery.* **in,vesti'gation** *n*.

in'vestigator *n* a person, *eg* a detective, who investigates.

investment see **invest¹**.

invigilate [in'vidʒileit] *v* to supervise students while they are doing an examination: *I am going to invigilate (the candidates) (at) the English exam.*
in,vigi'lation *n*. **in'vigilator** *n*.

invigorate [in'vigəreit] *v* to strengthen or refresh: *The shower invigorated her.*
in'vigorating *adj*.

invincible [in'vinsəbl] *adj* that cannot be overcome or defeated: *That general thinks that his army is invincible.*
in'vincibly *adv*. **in,vinci'bility** *n*.

invisible [in'vizəbl] *adj* not able to be seen:

Only in stories can people make themselves invisible. **in'visibly** *adv*. **in,visi'bility** *n*.

invite [in'vait] *v* **1** to ask (a person) politely to come (*eg* to one's house, to a party *etc*): *They have invited us to dinner tomorrow.* **2** to ask (a person) politely to do something: *He was invited to speak at the meeting.* **3** to ask for (another person's suggestions *etc*): *He invited proposals from members of the society.*

invitation [invi'teiʃən] *n* **1** a (written) request to come or go somewhere: *Have you received an invitation to their party?*; *We had to refuse the invitation to the wedding.* **2** the act of inviting: *He attended the committee meeting on the invitation of the chairman.*

in'viting *adj* (*neg* **un-**) attractive or tempting: *There was an inviting smell coming from the kitchen.*

invocation see **invoke**.

invoice ['invois] *n* a list sent with goods giving details of price and quantity.

invoke [in'vouk] *v* to appeal to (some power, *eg* God, the law *etc*) for help *etc*. **invocation** [invə'keiʃən] *n*.

involuntary [in'voləntəri] *adj* (of an action *etc*) not intentional: *He gave an involuntary cry.* **in'voluntarily** *adv*.

involve [in'volv] *v* **1** to require; to bring as a result: *His job involves a lot of travelling.* **2** (*often with* **in** or **with**) to cause to take part in or to be mixed up in: *He has always been involved in/with the theatre*; *Don't ask my advice – I don't want to be/get involved.* **in'volved** *adj* complicated: *My timetable for Friday is becoming very involved.* **in'volvement** *n*.

inward ['inwəd] *adj* **1** being within, *esp* in the mind: *his inward thoughts.* **2** moving towards the inside: *an inward curve in the coastline.*

'inward, 'inwards *advs* towards the inside or the centre: *When one of the eyes turns inwards, we call the effect a squint.*

'inwardly *adv* in one's thoughts; secretly: *He was inwardly pleased when she failed*; *She was laughing/groaning inwardly.*

iodine ['aiədiːn, (*Amer*) -dain] *n* **1** an element used in medicine and photgraphy, forming black crystals. **2** a liquid form of the element used as an antiseptic.

irascible [i'rasibl] *adj* irritable; easily made angry. **i'rascibly** *adv*. **i,rasci'bility** *n*.

irate [ai'reit] *adj* angry.

iridescent [iri'desnt] *adj* shining or glittering with the colours of the rainbow: *Soap bubbles are iridescent.* **,iri'descence** *n*.

iris ['aiəris] *n* **1** the coloured part of the eye. **2** a kind of brightly-coloured flower with sword-shaped leaves.

iron ['aiən] *n* **1** (*also adj*) (of) an element that is the most common metal, is very hard, and is widely used for making tools *etc*: *Steel is made from iron*; *The ground is as hard as iron*; *iron railings*; *iron determination* (= very strong determination). **2** a flat-bottomed instrument that is heated up and used for smoothing clothes *etc*: *I've burnt a hole in my dress with the iron.* **3** a type of golf-club. – *v* to smooth (clothes *etc*) with an iron: *This dress needs to be ironed*; *I've been ironing all afternoon.*

'**ironing** *n* clothes *etc* waiting to be ironed, or just ironed: *What a huge pile of ironing!*

'**irons** *n pl* formerly, a prisoner's chains: *They put him in irons.*

'**ironing-board** *n* a padded board on which to iron clothes.

'**ironmonger** *n* a dealer in articles of metal *eg* tools, locks *etc* and other goods.

'**ironmongery** *n* the business or goods of an ironmonger.

have several, too many *etc* **irons in the fire** to be involved in, or doing, several *etc* things at the same time.

iron out 1 to get rid of (creases *etc*) by ironing. **2** to get rid of (difficulties *etc*) so that progress becomes easier.

strike while the iron is hot to act *etc* while the situation is favourable.

irony ['aiərəni] – *pl* '**ironies** – *n* **1** a form of deliberate mockery in which one says the opposite of what is obviously true. **2** seeming mockery in a situation, words *etc*: *The irony of the situation was that he stole the money which she had already planned to give him.* **ironic(al)** [ai'ronik(l)] *adj.* **i'ronically** *adv.*

irregular [i'regjulə] *adj* **1** not happening *etc* regularly: *His attendance at classes was irregular.* **2** not formed smoothly or evenly: *irregular handwriting.* **3** contrary to rules. **4** (in grammar) not formed *etc* in the normal way: *irregular verbs.* **ir'regularly** *adv.* **ir'regu'larity** [-'la-] *n* (*pl* **irregu'larities**).

irrelevant [i'relivənt] *adj* not connected with the subject that is being discussed *etc*: *irrelevant comments.* **ir'relevantly** *adv.* **ir'relevance, ir'relevancy** *ns.*

irreparable [i'repərəbl] *adj* (of damage *etc*) that cannot be put right. **ir'reparably** *adv.*

irreplaceable [iri'pleisəbl] *adj* too good, rare *etc* to be able to be replaced if lost or damaged.

irrepressible [iri'presəbl] *adj* not able to be subdued; very cheerful.

irresistible [iri'zistəbl] *adj* too strong, delightful, tempting *etc* to be resisted: *He had an irresistible desire to hit her.* ˌ**irre'sistibly** *adv.* '**irreˌsisti'bility** *n.*

irrespective [iri'spektiv]: **irrespective of** without consideration of: *The pupils are all taught together, irrespective of age or ability.*

irresponsible [iri'sponsəbl] *adj* (of a person or his behaviour) not reliable, trustworthy or sensible; not responsible: *irresponsible parents/conduct.* '**irreˌsponsi'bility** *n.* ˌ**irre'sponsibly** *adv.*

irreverent [i'revərənt] *adj* showing no respect or reverence (*eg* for holy things, or people and things generally considered important). **ir'reverently** *adv.* **ir'reverence** *n.*

irreversible [iri'vɔːsəbl] *adj* that cannot be reversed or changed back; (of damage) permanent.

irrigate ['irigeit] *v* to supply water to (land), *esp* by canals or other artificial means. ˌ**irri'gation** *n.*

irritate ['iriteit] *v* **1** to annoy or make angry: *The children's chatter irritated him.* **2** to make (a part of the body) sore, red, itchy *etc*: *Soap can irritate a baby's skin.* '**irritable** *adj* easily annoyed: *He was in an irritable mood.* '**irritably** *adv.* ˌ**irrita'bility**, '**irritableness** *ns.* '**irritating** *adj*: *She has an irritating voice.* ˌ**irri'tation** *n.*

is *see* **be.**

Islam ['izlɑːm] *n* the Muslim religion. **Is'lamic** [-'la-] *adj* of Islam: *Islamic festivals.*

island ['ailənd] *n* **1** a piece of land surrounded by water: *The island lay a mile off the coast.* **2** (*also* **traffic island**) a traffic-free area, built in the middle of a street, for pedestrians to stand on. '**islander** *n.*

isle [ail] *n* (*used mostly in place-names*) an island: *the Isle of Wight.*

isn't *see* **be.**

isolate ['aisəleit] *v* to separate, cut off or keep apart from others: *Several houses have been isolated by the flood water*; *A child with an infectious disease should be isolated.* '**isolated** *adj* lonely; standing alone. ˌ**iso'lation** *n.*

issue ['iʃuː] *v* **1** to give or send out, or to distribute, *esp* officially: *The police issued a description of the criminal*; *Rifles were issued to the troops.* **2** to flow or come out (from something): *A strange noise issued from the room.* – *n* **1** the act of issuing or process of being issued: *Stamp collectors like to buy new stamps on the day of issue.* **2** one number in the series of a newspaper, magazine *etc*: *Have you seen the latest issue of that magazine?* **3** a subject for discussion and argument: *The question of pay is not an important issue at the moment.*

isthmus ['isməs] *n* a narrow strip of land joining two larger pieces: *the Isthmus of Panama.*

it [it] *pron* **1** (used as the subject of a verb or object of a verb or preposition) the thing spoken of, used *esp* of lifeless things and of

situations, but also of animals and babies:
If you find my pencil, please give it to me;
The dog is in the garden, isn't it?; *I picked up
the baby because it was crying*; *He decided
to run a mile every morning but he couldn't
keep it up*. **2** used as a subject in certain
kinds of sentences *eg* in talking about the
weather, distance or time: *Is it raining very
hard?*; *It's cold*; *It is five o'clock*; *Is it the
fifth of March?*; *It's two miles to the village*;
Is it your turn to make the tea?; *It is
impossible for him to finish the work*; *It was
nice of you to come*; *Is it likely that he would
go without us?* **3** (*usu* as the subject of the
verb **be**) used to give emphasis to a certain
word or phrase: *It was you* (*that*) *I wanted
to see, not Mary*. **4** used with some verbs as
a direct object with little meaning: *The car
broke down and we had to walk it*; *Oh,
bother it!*

its *adj* belonging to it: *The bird has hurt its
wing*.

itself *pron* **1** used as the object of a verb or
preposition when an object, animal *etc* is
the object of an action it performs: *The cat
looked at itself in the mirror*; *The cat
stretched itself by the fire*. **2** used to emphasize **it** or the name of an object, animal *etc*:
*The house itself is quite small, but the garden
is big*. **3** without help *etc*: *'How did the dog
get in?' 'Oh, it can open the gate itself.'*

its is an adjective or pronoun expressing
possession: *a cat and its kittens*.
it's is short for **it is** or **it has**: *It's raining
heavily.*

italic [i'talik] *adj* (of print) of the sloping kind
used *eg* to show emphasis and for the

examples in this dictionary: *This example is
printed in italic type*.
i'talicize, -ise [-saiz] *v* to put (words) in
italics.
i'talics *n pl* italic print: *This example is
printed in italics*.

itch [itʃ] *n* an irritating feeling in the skin that
makes one want to scratch: *He had an itch
in the middle of his back and could not
scratch it easily.* – *v* **1** to have an itch: *Some
plants can cause the skin to itch*. **2** to have a
strong desire (for something, or to be something): *I was itching to slap the child*.
'itchy *adj* itching: *an itchy rash*; *I feel itchy
all over*. **'itchiness** *n*.
it'd *see* **have, would**.
item ['aitəm] *n* **1** a separate object, article *etc*,
esp one of a number named in a list: *He
ticked the items as he read through the list*.
2 a separate piece of information or news:
*Did you see the item about dogs in the
newspaper?*
itinerant [i'tinərənt] *adj* travelling from place
to place, *eg* on business: *an itinerant
preacher*.
itinerary [ai'tinərəri] *n* a route for a journey.
it'll *see* **will**.
its, itself *see* **it**.
it's *see* **be, have**.
I've *see* **have**.
ivory ['aivəri] *n, adj* (of) the hard white
substance forming the tusks of an elephant,
walrus *etc*: *Ivory was formerly used to make
piano keys*; *ivory chessmen*.
ivy ['aivi] *n* a type of climbing evergreen plant
with small shiny leaves that grows up trees
and walls.
ixora ['iksərə] *n* a garden shrub with large
round clusters of red or yellow flowers.

Jj

jab [dʒab] – *pt, ptp* **jabbed** – *v* to poke or
prod: *He jabbed me in the ribs with his
elbow*; *She jabbed the needle into her finger*.
– *n* a sudden hard poke or prod: *He gave
me a jab with his finger*; *a jab of pain*.
jabber ['dʒabə] *v* to talk idly, rapidly and
indistinctly: *The women are always jabber-
ing with one another*.
jack [dʒak] *n* **1** an instrument for lifting up a
motor car or other heavy weight: *You
should always keep a jack in the car in case
you need to change a wheel*. **2** the playing-
card between the ten and queen, sometimes
called the **knave**: *The jack, queen and king
are the three face cards*.

jack up to raise (a motor car *etc*) and keep
it supported, with a jack: *You need to jack
up the car before you try to remove the
wheel*.
jackal ['dʒako:l, (*Amer*) -kl] *n* a type of wild
animal similar to a dog or wolf.
jackass ['dʒakas] *n* **1** a male ass. **2** a stupid
person: *the silly jackass!*
laughing jackass a type of Australian bird
that sounds as if it is laughing.
jackboot ['dʒakbu:t] *n* a type of tall *esp*
military boot that reaches above the knee.
jackdaw ['dʒakdo:] *n* a type of bird of the
crow family that sometimes steals bright
objects.

jacket ['dʒakit] *n* **1** a short coat: *He wore brown trousers and a blue jacket.* **2** a covering, *esp* a loose paper cover for a book: *I like the design on this (book-)jacket.*

*jackfruit ['dʒakfruːt] *n* a tropical tree with large oval fruit, the yellow flesh and seeds of which are edible.

jack-in-the-box ['dʒakinðəboks] *n* a toy consisting of a figure, fixed to a spring inside a box, which comes out suddenly when the lid is opened.

jack-knife ['dʒaknaif] *n* a large folding knife. – *v* (of *eg* a lorry and its trailer) to swing together so that the trailer is at a sharp angle to the cab: *The lorry skidded and jack-knifed, blocking the road.*

jackpot ['dʒakpot] *n* in playing cards, some competitions *etc*, a fund of prize-money that goes on increasing until it is won.

hit the jackpot to win or obtain a lot of money or success: *He must have hit the jackpot with the sales of his last gramophone record.*

jade [dʒeid] *n, adj* (of) a type of hard stone, *usu* green in colour: *a piece of jade*; *jade ornaments.*

jaded ['dʒeidid] *adj* (of *eg* a person or his interest, appetite *etc*) worn out and made tired and dull.

jagged ['dʒagid] *adj* having rough or sharp and uneven edges: *jagged rocks.* **'jaggedly** *adv.* **'jaggedness** *n.*

jaguar ['dʒagjuə, (*Amer*) 'dʒagwaːr] *n* a South American beast of prey of the cat family, resembling the leopard.

jail, gaol [dʒeil] *n* (a) prison: *You ought to be sent to jail for doing that.* – *v* to put in prison: *He was jailed for two years.* **'jailer, 'jailor, 'gaoler** *n* a person who has charge of a jail or of prisoners: *The jailer was knocked unconscious in the riot.* **'jailbird, 'gaolbird** *n* a person who is or has often been in jail.

to put a criminal in **jail** or **gaol** (not **goal**).

jam[1] [dʒam] *n* a thick sticky substance made of fruit *etc* preserved by being boiled with sugar: *raspberry jam*; (*also adj*) *a jam sandwich.*

jammy *adj* covered with jam: *jammy fingers.*

jam[2] [dʒam] – *pt, ptp* **jammed** – *v* **1** to crowd full: *The gateway was jammed with angry people.* **2** to squeeze, press or wedge tightly or firmly: *He jammed his foot in the doorway.* **3** to stick and (cause to) be unable to move: *The door/steering-wheel has jammed.* **4** (of a radio station) to cause interference with (another radio station's broadcast) by sending out signals on a similar wavelength. – *n* **1** a crowding together of vehicles, people *etc* so that movement is difficult or impossible: *traffic-jams.* **2** a difficult situa-

tion: *I'm in a bit of a jam – I haven't got enough money to pay for this meal.*

jam on to put (brakes *etc*) on with force and haste: *When the dog ran in front of his car he jammed on his brakes and skidded.*

jamboree [dʒambə'riː] *n* **1** a large and lively gathering. **2** a rally of Boy Scouts, Girl Guides *etc.*

jammed *see* **jam**[2].

jammy *see* **jam**[1].

jangle ['dʒaŋgl] *v* to (cause to) give a harsh (ringing) sound: *The bell jangled noisily.*

janitor ['dʒanitə] – *fem* **'janitress** – *n* a caretaker or a doorkeeper.

January ['dʒanjuəri] *n* the first month of the year, the month following December.

jar[1] [dʒaː] *n* a kind of bottle made of glass or pottery, with a wide mouth: *She poured the jam into large jars*; *jam-jars.*

jar[2] [dʒaː] – *pt, ptp* **jarred** – *v* **1** (*with* **on**) to have a harsh and startling effect (on): *Her sharp voice jarred on my ears.* **2** to give a shock to: *The car accident had jarred her nerves.*

'jarring *adj* startling or harsh: *The orange curtains with the purple carpet had a jarring effect.*

jargon ['dʒaːgən] *n* special words or phrases used within a group, trade or profession *etc*: *legal jargon*; *medical jargon*; *Thieves use a special jargon in order to confuse passing hearers.*

jarred, jarring *see* **jar**[2].

jaundice ['dʒoːndis] *n* a diseased state of the body in which the skin and whites of the eyes become yellow.

jaunt [dʒoːnt] *n* a brief trip or journey made for pleasure: *Did you enjoy your jaunt to Paris?*

jaunty ['dʒoːnti] *adj* cheerful, bright, lively: *a jaunty mood/hat.* **'jauntily** *adv.* **'jauntiness** *n.*

javelin ['dʒavəlin] *n* a light spear for throwing *eg* as an event in an athletic competition.

jaw [dʒoː] *n* **1** either of the two bones of the mouth in which the teeth are set: *the upper/lower jaw*; *His jaw was broken in the fight.* **2** (*in pl*) the mouth (*esp* of an animal): *The crocodile's jaws opened wide.*

jaywalker ['dʒeiwoːkə] *n* a person who walks carelessly among traffic: *She never looks to see if there's a car coming before she crosses the road – she's a jaywalker.*

'jaywalking *n*: *The police were concerned about the number of accidents involving jaywalking.*

jazz [dʒaz] *n* popular music of American Negro origin: *She prefers jazz to classical music*; (*also adj*) *a jazz musician.*

'jazzy *adj* **1** bright or bold in colour or design: *a jazzy shirt.* **2** of or like jazz: *jazzy music.*

jealous ['dʒeləs] *adj* **1** (*with* **of**) feeling or

showing envy: *She is jealous of her sister.*
2 having feelings of dislike for any possible
rivals (*esp* in love): *a jealous husband.*
'jealously *adv.* **'jealousy** *n.*

jeans [dʒi:nz] *n pl* trousers, *usu* tight-fitting,
made of denim.

'jeep [dʒi:p] *n* a kind of small motor vehicle
used *esp* by the armed forces.

jeer [dʒiə] *v* **1** to shout at or laugh at rudely or
mockingly: *He was jeered as he tried to
speak to the crowds.* **2** (*with* **at**) to make fun
of (someone) rudely: *He's always jeering at
her stupidity.* – *n* a rude or mocking shout:
the jeers and boos of the audience.
'jeering *adj* mocking or scornful. **'jeeringly**
adv.

jelly ['dʒeli] – *pl* **'jellies** – *n* **1** the juice of fruit
boiled with sugar until it is firm, used like
jam, or served with meat. **2** a transparent,
smooth food, *usu* fruit-flavoured: *I've made
raspberry jelly for the party.* **3** any jelly-like
substance: *Frogs' eggs are enclosed in a kind
of jelly.* **4** (*Amer*) same as **jam**[1].
'jellyfish – *pls* **'jellyfish**, **'jellyfishes** – *n* a kind
of sea animal with a jelly-like body: *The
child was stung by a jellyfish.*

jelutong ['jelutoŋ] *n* (a tree yielding) a material used as a rubber substitute *etc.*

jeopardy ['dʒepədi] *n* danger.
'jeopardize, -ise *v* to put in danger: *Bad
spelling could jeopardize your chances of
passing the exam.*

jerk [dʒə:k] *n* a short, sudden movement: *We
felt a jerk as the train started.* – *v* to move
with a jerk or jerks: *He grasped my arm and
jerked me round; The car jerked to a halt.*
'jerky *adj* jerking; full of jerks: *a jerky
movement; a jerky way of speaking.* **'jerkily**
adv. **'jerkiness** *n.*

jersey ['dʒə:zi] *n* a sweater or pullover.

jest [dʒest] *n* a joke; something done or said
to cause amusement. – *v* to joke.
'jester *n* in former times, a man employed in
the courts of kings, nobles *etc* to amuse
them with jokes *etc.*
in jest as a joke; not seriously: *speaking in
jest.*

jet[1] [dʒet] *n, adj* (of) a hard black mineral
substance, used for ornaments *etc*: *The
beads are made of jet; a jet brooch.*
jet-'black *adj* very black: *jet-black hair.*

jet[2] [dʒet] *n* **1** a sudden, strong stream or flow
(of liquid, gas, flame or steam), forced
through a narrow opening: *Firemen have to
be trained to direct the jets from their hoses
accurately.* **2** a narrow opening in an apparatus through which a jet comes: *This gas
jet is blocked.* **3** an aeroplane driven by jet
propulsion: *We flew by jet to America.*
'jet-lag *n* symptoms such as tiredness and
lack of concentration caused by flying a
long distance in a short period of time.

jet-pro'pelled *adj* driven by jet propulsion:
jet-propelled racing-cars.
jet propulsion a method of producing very
fast forward motion (for aircraft, missiles
etc) by sucking air or liquid *etc* into a **jet
engine** and forcing it out from behind.

jettison ['dʒetisn] *v* to throw (cargo *etc*) overboard to lighten a ship, aircraft *etc* in times
of danger: *When one of the engines failed,
the aeroplane crew jettisoned the luggage.*

jetty ['dʒeti] – *pl* **'jetties** – *n* a small pier for
use as a landing-place.

jewel ['dʒu:əl] *n* a precious stone: *rubies,
emeralds and other jewels.*
'jewelled, (*Amer*) **'jeweled** *adj* ornamented
with jewels: *a jewelled crown.*
'jeweller, (*Amer*) **'jeweler** *n* a person who
makes, or deals in, ornaments and other
articles made of precious stones and metals.
'jewellery, (*Amer*) **'jewelry** *n* articles made
or sold by a jeweller, and worn for personal
adornment, *eg* bracelets, necklaces,
brooches, rings *etc.*

jib [dʒib] *n* **1** a three-cornered sail on the
front mast of a ship. **2** the jutting-out arm
of a crane.

jibe, gibe [dʒaib] *n* a cruel or unkind remark
or taunt: *cruel jibes.* – *v* (*with* **at**) to make
fun (of) unkindly.

jiffy ['dʒifi] *n* a moment: *I'll be back in a jiffy.*

jig [dʒig] *n* (a piece of music for) a type of
lively dance. – *v* – *pt, ptp* **jigged** – to
jump (about): *Stop jigging about and
stand still!*

jiggle ['dʒigl] *v* to (cause to) jump (about) or
move jerkily: *The television picture kept
jiggling up and down.*

jigsaw (puzzle) ['dʒigso:] *n* a puzzle made up
of many differently-shaped pieces that fit
together to form a picture.

jilt [dʒilt] *v* to reject or send away (someone
with whom one has been in love): *After
being her boyfriend for two years, he suddenly jilted her.*

jingle ['dʒiŋgl] *n* **1** a slight metallic ringing
sound (made *eg* by coins or by small bells):
*The dog pricked up its ears at the jingle of its
master's keys.* **2** a simple rhyming verse or
tune: *nursery rhymes and other little jingles;
advertising jingles.* – *v* to (cause to) make a
clinking or ringing sound; *He jingled the
coins in his pocket.*

jittery ['dʒitəri] *adj* very nervous and easily
upset: *She has become very jittery since her
accident.*

job [dʒob] *n* **1** a person's daily work or employment: *She has a job as a bank-clerk;
Some of the unemployed men have been out
of a job for four years.* **2** a piece of work or
a task: *I have several jobs to do before going
to bed.*

a good job a lucky or satisfactory state of affairs: *It's a good job that she can't hear what you're saying; He has lost his trumpet, and a good job too!*

have a job to have difficulty: *You'll have a job finishing all this work tonight.*

just the job entirely suitable: *These gloves are just the job for gardening.*

make the best of a bad job to do one's best in difficult circumstances.

jockey ['dʒɒki] *n* a person employed to ride horses in races.

jog [dʒɒg] – *pt, ptp* **jogged** – *v* **1** to push, shake or knock gently: *He jogged my arm and I spilt my coffee; I have forgotten, but something may jog my memory later on.* **2** to travel slowly: *The cart jogged along the rough track.* **3** to run at a gentle pace, *esp* for the sake of exercise: *She jogs/goes jogging round the park for half an hour every morning.*

at a jog-trot at a gentle running pace: *Every morning he goes down the road at a jog-trot.*

join [dʒɔin] *v* **1** (*often with* **up, on** *etc*) to put together or connect: *The electrician joined the wires (up) wrongly; You must join this piece (on) to that piece; He joined the two stories together to make a play; The island is joined to the mainland by a sandbank at low tide.* **2** to connect (two points) *eg* by a line, as in geometry: *Join point A to point B.* **3** to become a member of (a group): *Join our club!* **4** (*sometimes with* **up**) to meet and come together (with): *This lane joins the main road; Do you know where the two rivers join?; They joined up with us for the remainder of the holiday.* **5** to come into the company of: *I'll join you later in the restaurant.* – *n* a place where two things are joined: *You can hardly see the joins in the material.*

join forces to come together for united work or action: *We would do better if we joined forces (with each other).*

join hands to clasp one another's hands (*eg* for dancing): *Join hands with your partner; They joined hands in a ring.*

join in to take part (in): *We're playing a game – do join in!; He would not join in the game.*

join up to become a member of an armed force: *He joined up in 1940.*

joiner ['dʒɔinə] *n* a skilled worker in wood who puts doors, stairs *etc* into buildings.

'joinery *n* the work of a joiner.

joint [dʒɔint] *n* **1** the place where two or more things join: *The plumber tightened up all the joints in the pipes.* **2** a part of the body where two bones meet but are able to move in the manner of *eg* a hinge: *The shoulders, elbows, wrists, hips, knees and ankles are joints.* **3** a piece of meat for cooking containing a bone:

A leg of mutton is a fairly large joint. – *adj* **1** united; done together: *the joint efforts of the whole team.* **2** shared by, or belonging to, two or more: *She and her husband have a joint bank account.* – *v* to divide (an animal *etc* for cooking) at the, or into, joints: *Joint the chicken before cooking it.*

'jointed *adj* **1** having (*esp* movable) joints: *a jointed doll.* **2** (of an animal *etc* for cooking) divided into joints or pieces: *a jointed chicken.*

'jointly *adv* together: *They worked jointly on this book.*

out of joint (of a limb *etc*) not in the correct place; dislocated: *He put his shoulder out of joint when he moved the wardrobe.*
See also **join**.

joke [dʒouk] *n* **1** anything said or done to cause laughter: *He told/made the old joke about the elephant in the refrigerator; He dressed up as a ghost for a joke; He played a joke on us and dressed up as a ghost.* **2** something that causes laughter or amusement: *The children thought it a huge joke when the cat stole the fish.* – *v* **1** to make a joke or jokes: *They joked about my mistake for a long time afterwards.* **2** to talk playfully and not seriously: *Don't be upset by what he said – he was only joking.*

'joker *n* **1** in a pack of playing-cards, an extra card (*usu* having a picture of a jester) used in some games. **2** a person who enjoys telling jokes, playing tricks *etc*.

'jokingly *adv*: *He looked out at the rain and jokingly suggested a walk.*

it's no joke it is a serious or worrying matter: *It's no joke when water gets into the petrol tank.*

joking apart/aside let us stop joking and talk seriously: *I feel like going to Timbuctoo for the weekend – but, joking apart, I do need a rest!*

take a joke to be able to accept or laugh at a joke played on oneself: *The trouble with him is that he can't take a joke.*

jolly ['dʒɒli] *adj* merry and cheerful: *He's in quite a jolly mood today.* – *adv* very: *Taste this – it's jolly good!* **'jolliness, 'jollity** *ns*.

jolt [dʒoult] *v* **1** to move jerkily: *The bus jolted along the road.* **2** to shake or move suddenly: *I was violently jolted as the train stopped.* – *n* **1** a sudden movement or shake: *The car gave a jolt and started.* **2** a shock: *He got a jolt when he heard the bad news.*

joss stick ['dʒɒsstik] a stick of incense used *eg* to give a sweet smell to a room.

jostle ['dʒɒsl] *v* to push roughly: *We were jostled by the crowd; I felt people jostling against me in the dark.*

jot [dʒɒt] *n* a small amount: *I haven't a jot of sympathy for him.* – *v* – *pt, ptp* **'jotted** – (*usu* *with* **down**) to write briefly or quickly: *He jotted* (*down*) *the telephone number in his notebook.*

'jotter *n* a notebook or notepad, *esp* used in school.

journal ['dʒɜːnl] *n* **1** a magazine or other regularly published paper (*eg* of a society): *the British Medical Journal.* **2** a diary giving an account of each day's activities.

'journalism *n* the business of running, or writing for, newspapers or magazines.

'journalist *n* a writer for a newspaper, magazine *etc.*

journa'listic *adj* (of style of writing) like that of a journalist, colourful and racy.

journey ['dʒɜːni] *n* a distance travelled, *esp* over land; an act of travelling: *By train, it is a two-hour journey from here to the coast*; *I'm going on a long journey.* – *v* to travel.

jovial ['dʒouviəl] *adj* full of good humour: *He seems to be in a very jovial mood this morning.* **jovi'ality** [-'a-] *n.* **'jovially** *adv.*

joy [dʒoi] *n* **1** great happiness: *The children jumped for joy when they saw the new toys.* **2** a cause of great happiness: *Our son is a great joy to us.*

'joyful *adj* filled with, showing or causing joy; *a joyful mood*; *joyful faces/news.* **'joyfully** *adv.* **'joyfulness** *n.*

'joyous *adj* joyful. **'joyously** *adv.*

jubilant ['dʒuːbilənt] *adj* showing and expressing triumphant joy: *Jubilant crowds welcomed the victorious team home.* **'jubilantly** *adv.*

jubi'lation [-'lei-] *n* (*sometimes in pl*) **1** (triumphant) rejoicing: *There was great jubilation over the victory*; *The jubilations went on till midnight.*

jubilee ['dʒuːbiliː] *n* a celebration of a special anniversary (*esp* the 25th, 50th or 60th) of some event, *eg* the succession of a king or queen: *The king celebrated his golden jubilee* (=fiftieth anniversary of his succession) *last year.*

judge [dʒʌdʒ] *v* **1** to hear and try (cases) in a court of law: *Who will be judging this murder case?* **2** to decide which is the best in a competition *etc*: *Is she going to judge the singing competition again?*; *Who will be judging the vegetables at the flower show?*; *Who is judging at the horse show?* **3** to consider and form an idea of; to estimate: *You can't judge a man by his appearance*; *Watch how a cat judges the distance before it jumps*; *She couldn't judge whether he was telling the truth.* **4** to criticize for doing wrong: *We have no right to judge him – we might have done the same thing ourselves.* – *n* **1** a public officer who hears and decides cases in a law court: *The judge asked if the jury had reached a verdict.* **2** a person who decides which is the best in a competition

etc: *The judge's decision is final* (=you cannot argue with the judge's decision); *He was asked to be on the panel of judges at the beauty contest.* **3** a person who is skilled at deciding how good *etc* something is: *He says she's honest, and he's a good judge of character*; *He seems a very fine pianist to me, but I'm no judge.*

'judg(e)ment *n* **1** the decision of a judge in a court of law: *It looked as if he might be acquitted but the judgement went against him.* **2** the act of judging or estimating: *Faulty judgement in overtaking is a common cause of traffic accidents.* **3** the ability to make right or sensible decisions: *You showed good judgement in choosing this method.* **4** (an) opinion: *In my judgement, he is a very good actor.*

judging from/to judge from if one can use (something) as an indication: *Judging from the sky, there'll be a storm soon.*

pass judgement (on) to criticize or condemn: *Do not pass judgement* (*on others*) *unless you are perfect yourself.*

judicial [dʒuː'diʃəl] *adj* of a judge or court of law: *judicial powers*; *He might bring judicial proceedings against you.* **ju'dicially** *adv.*

judicious [dʒuː'diʃəs] *adj* showing wisdom and good sense: *a judicious choice of words.* **ju'diciously** *adv.* **ju'diciousness** *n.*

judo ['dʒuːdou] *n* a Japanese form of wrestling: *He learns judo at the sports centre.*

jug [dʒʌg] *n* a deep container for liquids, *usu* with a handle and a shaped lip for pouring: *a milk-jug.*

juggle ['dʒʌgl] *v* to keep throwing in the air and catching a number of objects (*eg* balls or clubs): *He entertained the audience by juggling with four balls and four plates at once.* **'juggler** *n.*

juice [dʒuːs] *n* **1** the liquid part of fruits or vegetables: *She squeezed the juice out of the orange*; *tomato juice.* **2** (*often in pl*) the fluid contained in meat: *Roasting meat in tin foil helps to preserve the juices.* **3** (*in pl*) fluid contained in the organs of the body, *eg* to help digestion: *digestive/gastric juices.* **'juicy** *adj.* **'juiciness** *n.*

juke-box ['dʒuːkbɔks] *n* a machine that plays selected records automatically when coins are put into it.

July [dʒu'lai] *n* the seventh month of the year, the month following June.

jumble ['dʒʌmbl] *v* (*often with* **up** *or* **together**) to mix or throw together without order: *In this puzzle, the letters of all the words have been jumbled* (*up*); *His shoes and clothes were all jumbled* (*together*) *in the cupboard.* – *n* **1** a confused mixture: *He found an untidy jumble of things in the drawer.* **2** unwanted possessions suitable for a jumble sale: *Have you any jumble to spare?*

jumble sale a sale of unwanted possessions, *eg* used clothing, *usu* to raise money for a charity *etc*.

jump [dʒʌmp] *v* 1 to (cause to) go quickly off the ground with a springing movement: *He jumped off the wall/across the puddle/over the fallen tree/into the swimming-pool*; *Don't jump the horse over that fence!* 2 to rise; to move quickly (upwards): *She jumped to her feet*; *He jumped into the car*. 3 to make a startled movement: *The noise made me jump*. 4 to pass over (a gap *etc*) by bounding: *He jumped the stream easily.* – *n* 1 an act of jumping: *She crossed the stream in one jump*. 2 an obstacle to be jumped over: *Her horse fell at the third jump*. 3 a jumping competition: *the high jump*. 4 a startled movement: *She gave a jump when the door suddenly banged shut*. 5 a sudden rise, *eg* in prices: *There has been a jump in the price of potatoes*.

'jumpy *adj* nervous; easily upset: *He has been very jumpy and irritable lately.*

jump at to take or accept eagerly: *He jumped at the chance to go to Germany for a fortnight.*

jump for joy to show great pleasure.

jump on to make a sudden attack on: *He was waiting round the corner and jumped on me in the dark.*

jump the gun to start before the proper time: *We shouldn't be going on holiday till tomorrow, but we jumped the gun and caught today's last flight.*

jump the queue to move ahead of others in a queue without waiting for one's proper turn: *Many wealthy or important people try to jump the queue for hospital beds.*

jump to conclusions/jump to the conclusion that to form an idea without making sure of the facts: *He saw my case in the hall and jumped to the conclusion that I was leaving.*

jump to it to hurry up: *If you don't jump to it you'll miss the train.*

jumper ['dʒʌmpə] *n* 1 a sweater or jersey. 2 (*Amer*) a pinafore dress.

junction ['dʒʌŋkʃən] *n* a place at which things (*eg* railway lines) join: *a railway junction*; *There was an accident at the junction of Park Road and School Lane.*

juncture ['dʒʌŋktʃə]: **at this/that juncture** at this or that moment or point: *At this juncture the chairman declared the meeting closed.*

June [dʒuːn] *n* the sixth month of the year, the month following May.

jungle ['dʒʌŋgl] *n* a thick growth of trees and plants in tropical areas: *the Amazon jungle*; *Tigers are found in the jungles of Asia*; (*also adj*) *soldiers trained in jungle warfare.*

junior ['dʒuːnjə] *n, adj* (a person who is) younger in years or lower in rank or authority: *He is two years my junior*; *The school sent two juniors and one senior to take part*; *junior pupils*; *He is junior to me in the firm*; *the junior school.* – *adj* (*often abbrev* **Jnr, Jr** *or* **Jun.** *when written*) used to indicate the son of a person who is still alive and who has the same name: *John Jones Junior.* – *n* (*esp Amer*) a name for the child (*usu* a son) of a family: *Do bring Junior!*

younger than but junior to.

junk[1] [dʒʌŋk] *n* unwanted or worthless articles; rubbish: *That cupboard is full of junk*; (*also adj*) *This vase was bought in a junk shop* (= a shop that sells junk).

junk[2] [dʒʌŋk] *n* a Chinese flat-bottomed sailing ship, high in the bow and stern.

junta ['dʒʌntə] *n* a group of army officers that has taken over the administration of a country by force.

jurisdiction [dʒuəris'dikʃən] *n* legal power; authority.

jury ['dʒuəri] – *pl* **'juries** – *n* 1 a group of people legally selected to hear a case and to decide what are the facts, *eg* whether or not a prisoner accused of a crime is guilty: *The verdict of the jury was that the prisoner was guilty of the crime*. 2 a group of judges for a competition, contest *etc*: *The jury recorded their votes for the song contest.*

'juror, 'juryman *ns* a member of a jury in a law court.

just[1] [dʒʌst] *adj* 1 right and fair: not favouring one more than another: *a fair and just decision*. 2 reasonable; based on one's rights: *He certainly has a just claim to the money*. 3 deserved: *He got his just reward when he crashed the stolen car and broke his leg.*

'justly *adv*: *He was justly blamed for the accident.*

'justness *n*.

just[2] [dʒʌst] *adv* 1 (*often with* **as**) exactly or precisely: *This penknife is just what I needed*; *He was behaving just as if nothing had happened*; *The house was just as I'd remembered it*. 2 (*with* **as**) quite: *This dress is just as nice as that one*. 3 very lately or recently: *He has just gone out of the house*. 4 on the point of; in the process of: *She is just coming through the door*. 5 at the particular moment: *The telephone rang just as I was leaving*. 6 (*often with* **only**) barely: *We have only just enough milk to last till Friday*; *I just managed to escape*; *You came just in time*. 7 only; merely: *They waited for six hours just to get a glimpse of the Queen*; *'Where are you going?' 'Just to the post office'*; *Could you wait just a minute?* 8 used for emphasis, *eg* with commands: *Just look at that mess!*; *That just isn't true!*; *I just don't know what to do*. 9 absolutely: *The weather is just marvellous.*

just about more or less: *Is your watch just about right?*

just now 1 at this particular moment: *I can't do it just now.* 2 a short while ago: *She fell and banged her head just now, but she feels better again.*

just then 1 at that particular moment: *He was feeling rather hungry just then.* 2 in the next minute: *She opened the letter and read it. Just then the door bell rang.*

justice ['dʒʌstis] *n* 1 fairness or rightness in the treatment of other people: *Everyone has a right to justice; I don't deserve to be punished – where's your sense of justice?* 2 the law or the administration of it: *Their dispute had to be settled in a court of justice.* 3 a judge.

bring to justice to arrest, try and sentence (a criminal): *The murderer escaped but was finally brought to justice.*

do (someone/something) justice/do justice to (someone/something) 1 to treat fairly or properly: *It would not be doing him justice to call him lazy when he's so ill.* 2 to fulfil the highest possibilities of; to get the best results from; to show fully or fairly: *I was so tired that I didn't do myself justice in the exam.*

in justice to (him, her *etc***)/to do (him, her** *etc***) justice** if one must be fair (to him, her *etc*): *To do her justice, I must admit that she was only trying to help when she broke the cup.*

justify ['dʒʌstifai] *v* 1 to prove or show (a person, action, opinion *etc*) to be just, right, desirable or reasonable: *How can the government justify the spending of millions of pounds on weapons when there is so much poverty in the country?* 2 to be a good excuse for: *Your state of anxiety does not justify your being so rude to me.*

justi'fiable *adj* (*neg* **un-**) able to be justified: *Is dishonesty ever justifiable?*

justifi'cation [-fi-] *n* 1 (the act of) justifying or excusing. 2 something that justifies: *You have no justification for criticizing him in that way.*

jut [dʒʌt] – *pt, ptp* '**jutted** – *v* (*usu with* **out**) to stick out or project: *His top teeth jut out.*

jute [dʒuːt] *n, adj* (*of*) the fibre of certain plants found in Pakistan and India, used for making sacks *etc.*

jutted *see* **jut.**

juvenile ['dʒuːvənail] *adj* 1 (*also n*) (a person who is) young or youthful: *She will not be sent to prison – she is still a juvenile; juvenile offenders.* 2 *adj* childish: *juvenile behaviour.*

Kk

kaftan *see* **caftan.**

kaleidoscope [kə'laidəskoup] *n* a tube-shaped toy in which loose coloured pieces of glass *etc* reflected in two mirrors form changing patterns.

ka,leido'scopic [-'sko-] *adj* with many changing colours, sights, impressions *etc.*

kampung ['kampoŋ] *n* a Malay village, usually consisting of wooden houses on stilts.

kangaroo [kaŋgə'ruː] – *pl* **kanga'roos** – *n* a type of large Australian animal with very long hind legs and great power of leaping, the female of which carries her young in a pouch on the front of her body.

kapok ['keipok] *n* a very light waterproof fibre fluff obtained from a type of tropical tree and used to stuff toys *etc.*

karate [kə'raːti] *n* a Japanese form of unarmed fighting, using blows and kicks.

kayak ['kaiak] *n* an open canoe, *esp* àn Eskimo canoe made of sealskins stretched over a frame.

kebab [ki'bab] *n* small pieces of meat *etc, usu* cooked on a skewer: *They ate kebabs and rice in the Indian restaurant.*

keel [kiːl] *n* the long supporting piece of a ship's frame that lies lengthways along the bottom: *The boat's keel stuck in the mud near the shore.*

keel over to fall over *usu* suddenly or unexpectedly *eg* in a faint.

be/keep on an even keel to be, keep or remain in a calm and untroubled state.

keen [kiːn] *adj* 1 eager or enthusiastic: *He is a keen golfer; I'm keen to succeed.* 2 sharp: *Her eyesight is as keen as ever.* 3 (of wind *etc*) very cold and biting. '**keenly** *adv*. '**keenness** *n*.

keen on very enthusiastic about, interested in or fond of: *She's keen on sailing; She's been keen on that boy for years.*

keep [kiːp] – *pt, ptp* **kept** [kept] – *v* 1 to have for a very long or indefinite period of time: *He gave me the picture to keep.* 2 not to give or throw away; to preserve: *I kept the most interesting books; Can you keep a secret?* 3 to (cause to) remain in a certain state or position: *I keep this gun loaded; How do you keep cool in this heat?; Will you keep me informed of what happens?* 4 to go on (performing or repeating a certain action): *He kept walking.* 5 to have in store: *I always*

keep a tin of baked beans for emergencies.
6 to look after or care for: *She keeps the garden beautifully*; *I think they keep hens.*
7 to remain in good condition: *That meat won't keep in this heat unless you put it in the fridge.* **8** to make entries in (a diary, accounts *etc*): *She keeps a diary to remind her of her appointments*; *He kept the accounts for the club.* **9** to hold back or delay: *Sorry to keep you.* **10** to provide food, clothes, housing for (someone): *He has a wife and child to keep.* **11** to act in the way demanded by: *She kept her promise.* **12** to celebrate: *to keep Christmas.* – *n* food and lodging: *She gives her mother money every week for her keep*; *Our cat really earns her keep – she kills all the mice in the house.*

'keeper *n* a person who looks after something, *eg* animals in a zoo: *The lion has killed its keeper.*

'keeping *n* care or charge: *The money had been given into his keeping.*

,keep-'fit *n* a series or system of exercises, *usu* simple, intended to improve the physical condition of ordinary people, *esp* women: *She's very keen on keep-fit but it doesn't do her much good*; *(also adj) keep-fit exercises.*

'keepsake [-seik] *n* something given or taken to be kept in memory of the giver: *She gave him a piece of her hair as a keepsake.*

for keeps permanently: *You can have this necklace for keeps.*

in keeping with suited to: *He has moved to a house more in keeping with his position as a headmaster.*

keep away to (cause to) remain at a distance: *Keep away – it's dangerous!*

keep back 1 not to (allow to) move forward: *She kept the child back on the edge of the crowd*; *Everybody keep back from the door!* **2** not to tell or make known: *I feel he's keeping the real story back for some reason.* **3** not to give or pay out: *Part of my allowance is kept back to pay for my meals*; *Will they keep it back every week?*

keep one's distance to stay quite far away: *The deer did not trust us and kept their distance.*

keep down 1 not to (allow to) rise up: *Keep down – they're shooting at us!* **2** to control or put a limit on: *They are taking steps to keep down the rabbit population.* **3** to digest without vomiting: *He has eaten some food but he won't be able to keep it down.*

keep one's end up to perform one's part in something just as well as all the others who are involved.

keep from to stop oneself from (doing something): *I could hardly keep from hitting him.*

keep going to go on doing something despite difficulties.

keep hold of not to let go of: *Keep hold of those tickets!*

keep house (for) to do the cooking, housework *etc* (for): *She keeps house for her brother.*

keep in 1 not to allow to go or come out or outside: *The teacher kept him in till he had finished the work.* **2** to stay close to the side of a road *etc.*

keep in mind to remember and take into consideration later.

keep it up to carry on doing something at the same speed or as well as one is doing it at present: *Your work is good – keep it up!*

keep off to stay away: *There are notices round the bomb warning people to keep off*; *The rain kept off and we had sunshine for the wedding.* **2** to prevent from getting to or on to (something): *This umbrella isn't pretty, but it keeps off the rain.*

keep on to continue (doing something or moving): *He just kept on writing*; *They kept on until they came to a petrol station.*

keep oneself to oneself to tell others very little about oneself, and not to be very friendly or sociable.

keep out not to (allow to) enter: *The notice at the building site said 'Keep out!'*; *This coat keeps out the wind.*

keep out of not to become involved in: *Do try to keep out of trouble!*

keep time (of a clock *etc*) to show the time accurately: *Does this watch keep (good) time?*

keep to not to leave or go away from: *Keep to this side of the park!*; *We kept to the roads we knew.*

keep (something) to oneself not to tell anyone (something): *He kept his conclusions to himself.*

keep up 1 to continue, or cause to remain, in operation: *I enjoy our friendship and try to keep it up.* **2** *(often with* **with***)* to move fast enough not to be left behind (by): *Even the children managed to keep up*; *Don't run – I can't keep up with you.*

keep up with the Joneses ['dʒounziz] to have everything one's neighbours have: *She didn't need a new cooker – she just bought one to keep up with the Joneses.*

keep watch to have the task of staying alert and watching for danger.

kennel ['kenl] *n* **1** a type of small hut for a dog. **2** *(usu in pl)* a place where dogs can be looked after.

kept *see* **keep.**

kerb [kə:b] *n* *(esp Amer* **curb***)* an edging, *usu* of stone, round a raised area, *esp* a pavement: *The old lady stepped off the kerb right in front of a car.*

'**kerbstone** *n* a stone used as part of a kerb.

kernel ['kə:nl] *n* **1** the softer substance inside the shell of a nut, or the stone of a fruit such as a plum, peach *etc*. **2** the central, most important part of a matter.

kerosene ['kerəsi:n] *n* paraffin oil, obtained from petroleum or from coal: *The jet plane refuelled with kerosene*; (*also adj*) *a kerosene lamp/stove*.

ketchup ['ketʃəp] *n* a flavouring sauce made from tomatoes or mushrooms *etc*.

kettle ['ketl] *n* a metal pot, *usu* with a special part for pouring and a lid, for heating liquids: *a kettle full of boiling water*.

'**kettledrum** *n* a type of drum made of a brass or copper bowl covered with a stretched skin *etc*.

key [ki:] *n* **1** an instrument or tool by which something (*eg* a lock or a nut) is turned: *Have you the key for this door?* **2** in musical instruments, one of the small parts pressed to sound the notes: *piano keys*. **3** in a typewriter, calculator *etc*, one of the parts which one presses to cause a letter *etc* to be printed, displayed *etc*. **4** the scale in which a piece of music is set: *What key are you singing in?*; *the key of F*. **5** something that explains a mystery or gives an answer to a mystery, a code *etc*: *the key to the whole problem*. **6** in a map *etc*, a table explaining the symbols *etc* used in it. – *adj* most important: *key industries*; *He is a key man in the firm*.

'**keyboard** *n* the keys in a piano, typewriter *etc* arranged along or on a flat board: *The pianist sat down at the keyboard and began to play*; *A computer keyboard looks like that of a typewriter*; (*also adj*) *harpsichords and other early keyboard instruments*.

'**keyhole** *n* the hole in which a key of a door *etc* is placed: *The child looked through the keyhole to see if his teacher was still with his parents*.

'**keynote** *n* **1** the chief note in a musical key. **2** the chief point or theme (of a lecture *etc*).

keyed up excited; tense.

khaki ['ka:ki] *n*, *adj* (of) a dull brownish or greenish yellow: *a khaki uniform*; *The café was full of men in khaki*.

kick [kik] *v* **1** to hit or strike out with the foot: *The child kicked his brother*; *He kicked the ball into the next garden*; *He kicked at the locked door*; *He kicked open the gate*. **2** (of a gun) to jerk or spring back violently when fired. – *n* **1** a blow with the foot: *The boy gave him a kick on the ankle*; *He was injured by a kick from a horse*. **2** the springing back of a gun after it has been fired. **3** a pleasant thrill: *She gets a kick out of making people happy*.

kick about/around to treat badly or bully:

The bigger boys are always kicking him around.

kick off to start a football game by kicking the ball: *We kick off at 2.30*. (*n* '**kick-off**: *The kick-off is at 2.30*).

kick up to cause or start off (a fuss *etc*).

kid¹ [kid] *n* **1** a popular word for a child or teenager: *They've got three kids now, two boys and a girl*; *More than a hundred kids went to the disco last night*; (*also adj*) *his kid brother* (= younger brother). **2** a young goat. **3** (*also adj*) (of) the leather made from its skin: *slippers made of kid*; *kid gloves*.

kid² [kid] – *pt, ptp* '**kidded** – *v* to deceive or tease, *esp* harmlessly: *We were kidding him about the girl who keeps ringing him up*; *He kidded his wife into thinking he'd forgotten her birthday*; *He didn't mean that – he was only kidding!*

kidnap ['kidnap] – *pt, ptp* '**kidnapped**, (*Amer*) '**kidnaped** – *v* to carry off (a person) by force, often demanding money in exchange for his safe return: *He is very wealthy and lives in fear of his children being kidnapped*. '**kidnapper** *n*.

kidney ['kidni] *n* one of a pair of organs in the body which remove waste matter from the blood and produce urine: *The kidneys of some animals are used as food*.

kill [kil] *v* to cause the death of: *He killed the rats with poison*; *The outbreak of typhoid killed many people*; *The flat tyre killed our hopes of getting home before midnight*. – *n* an act of killing: *The hunter was determined to make a kill before returning to the camp*. '**killer** *n* a person, animal *etc* that kills: *There is a killer somewhere in the village*; (*also adj*) *a killer disease*.

kill off to destroy completely: *So many deer have been shot that the species has almost been killed off*.

kill time to find something to do to use up spare time: *I'm just killing time until I hear whether I've got a job or not*.

kiln [kiln] *n* a type of large oven for baking pottery or bricks, drying grain *etc*.

kilogram(me) ['kiləgram] (*often abbrev* **kilo** ['ki:lou] – *pl* '**kilos**) *n* a unit of weight equal to 1000 gram(me)s.

kilometre, (*Amer*) **kilometer** ['kiləmi:tə, ki-'lomitə] *n* a unit of length, equal to 1000 metres.

kilowatt ['kiləwot] *n* (*often abbrev* **kW** when *written*) a measure of power, 1000 watts.

kilt [kilt] *n* an item of Scottish national dress, a pleated tartan skirt reaching to the knees and traditionally worn by men.

kimono [ki'mounou, (*Amer*) -nə] – *pl* **ki'monos** – *n* a loose Japanese robe, fastened with a sash.

kin [kin] *n pl* persons of the same family; one's relations. – *adj* related.

'**kinsfolk** ['inz-] *n pl* one's relations.

'**kinsman** ['kinz-], '**kinswoman** ['kinz-] – *pls* '**kinsmen**, '**kinswomen** – *ns* a man or a woman of the same family as oneself.

next of kin one's nearest relative(s).

kind[1] [kaind] *n* a sort or type: *What kind of car is it?*; *He is not the kind of man who would be cruel to children.*

kind[2] [kaind] *adj* ready or anxious to do good to others; friendly: *He's such a kind man*; *It was very kind of you to look after the children yesterday.*

'**kindly** *adv* **1** in a kind manner: *She kindly lent me a handkerchief.* **2** please: *Would you kindly stop talking!* – *adj* having or showing a gentle and friendly nature: *a kindly smile*; *a kindly old lady.* '**kindliness** *n*.

'**kindness** *n* the quality of being kind: *I'll never forget her kindness*; *Thank you for all your kindness.*

‚**kind-'hearted** *adj* having or showing kindness: *She is too kind-hearted to hurt an animal.*

kindergarten ['kindəga:tn] *n* a school for very young children.

kindle ['kindl] *v* to (cause to) catch fire: *I kindled a fire using twigs and grass*; *The fire kindled easily*; *His speech kindled the anger of the crowd.*

'**kindling** *n* dry wood *etc* for starting a fire.

kindliness, kindly, kindness *see* kind.

kindred ['kindrid] *n pl* one's relatives. – *adj* of the same sort: *climbing and kindred sports.*

kinetic [ki'netik] *adj* of motion.

king [kiŋ] *n* **1** a male ruler of a nation, who inherits his position by right of birth: *He became king when his father died*; *King Charles III.* **2** the playing-card with the picture of a king: *I have two cards – the ten of spades and the king of diamonds.* **3** the most important piece in chess.

'**kingdom** *n* **1** a state having a king (or queen) as its head: *The United Kingdom of Great Britain and Northern Ireland*; *He rules over a large kingdom.* **2** any of the three great divisions of natural objects: *the animal, vegetable and mineral kingdoms.*

'**kingly** *adj* of, relating to, or suitable for a king: *kingly robes*; *a kingly feast.* '**kingliness** *n*.

'**kingfisher** *n* a type of bird with brilliant blue feathers which feeds on fish.

'**king-size(d)** *adj* of a large size; larger than normal: *a king-size(d) bed*; *king-size cigarettes.*

kink [kiŋk] *n* a twist or bend, *eg* in a string, rope *etc*.

kinsman, kinswoman *etc see* kin.

kiosk ['ki:osk] *n* **1** a small roofed stall, either out of doors or in a public building *etc*, for the sale of newspapers, confectionery *etc*: *I bought a magazine at the kiosk at the station.* **2** a public telephone box: *She phoned from the kiosk outside the post-office*; *a telephone-kiosk.*

kiss [kis] *v* to touch with the lips as a sign of affection: *She kissed him when he arrived home*; *The child kissed his parents good-night*; *The film ended with a shot of the lovers kissing.* – *n* an act of kissing: *He gave her a kiss.*

kiss of life a mouth-to-mouth method of restoring breathing.

kit [kit] **1** (an outfit of) tools, clothes *etc* for a particular purpose: *He carried his tennis kit in a bag*; *a repair kit for mending punctures in bicycle tyres.* **2** a collection of the materials *etc* required to make something: *He bought a model aeroplane kit.*

'**kitbag** *n* a strong bag for holding (*usu* a soldier's) kit.

kit out – *pt, ptp* '**kitted** – to provide with all the clothes, tools *etc* necessary for a particular purpose: *The money was spent on kitting out the school football team.*

kitchen ['kitʃin] *n* a room where food is cooked: *A smell of burning was coming from the kitchen*; *(also adj)* *a kitchen table.*

‚**kitche'nette** [-'net] *n* a small kitchen.

kite [kait] *n* a light frame covered with paper or other material, and with string attached, for flying in the air: *The children were flying their kites in the park.*

kitted *see* kit.

kitten ['kitn] *n* a young cat: *The cat had five kittens last week.*

'**kittenish** *adj* playful.

kitty ['kiti] – *pl* '**kitties** – *n* (a container holding) a sum of money kept for a particular purpose, to which members of a group jointly contribute: *The three friends shared a flat and kept a kitty for buying food.*

kiwi ['ki:wi:] *n* a type of bird which is unable to fly, found in New Zealand.

knack [nak] *n* the ability to do something skilfully and easily: *It took me some time to learn the knack of making pancakes.*

knapsack ['napsak] *n* a small bag for food, clothes *etc* slung on the back.

knave [neiv] *n* a jack in a pack of playing-cards: *the knave of diamonds.*

knead [ni:d] *v* to press together and work (dough *etc*) with the fingers: *His mother was kneading (dough) in the kitchen.*

knee [ni:] *n* **1** the joint at the bend of the leg: *He fell and cut his knee*; *The child sat on her father's knee*; *She was on her knees weeding the garden*; *He fell on his knees and begged for mercy.* **2** the part of an article of clothing covering this joint: *He has a hole in the knee of his trousers.*

'kneecap n the flat, round bone on the front of the knee joint.

,knee-'deep adj reaching up to, or covered up to, one's knees: knee-deep water; He is knee-deep in water.

kneel [ni:l] – pt, ptp **knelt** [nelt] – v (often with **down**) to be in, or move into, a position in which both the foot and the knee of one or both legs are on the ground: She knelt (down) to fasten the child's shoes; She was kneeling on the floor cutting out a dress pattern.

knell [nel] n the sound of a bell giving warning of a death or funeral.

knelt see **kneel**.

knew see **know**.

knickers ['nikəz] n pl women's and girls' pants, esp if loose-fitting and gathered in at the thigh.

knife [naif] – pl **knives** [naivz] – n 1 an instrument for cutting: He carved the meat with a large knife. 2 such an instrument used as a weapon: She stabbed him with a knife. – v to stab with a knife: He knifed her in the back.

knight [nait] n 1 in earlier times, a man of noble birth who is trained to fight, esp on horseback: King Arthur and his knights. 2 a man of rank, having the title 'Sir': Sir John Brown was made a knight in 1969. 3 a piece used in chess, usu shaped like a horse's head. – v to make (a person) a knight: He was knighted for his services to industry.

'knighthood n the rank or title of a knight: He received a knighthood from the Queen.

knit [nit] – pt, ptp **'knitted** – v 1 to form (a garment) from yarn (of wool etc) by making and connecting loops, using knitting-needles: She is teaching children to knit and sew; She knitted him a sweater for Christmas. 2 (of broken bones) to grow together: The bone in his arm took a long time to knit.

'knitter n: She's a very good knitter.

'knitting n 1 the work of a knitter: She was occupied with her knitting. 2 the material made by knitting: a piece of knitting.

'knitting-needle n a thin rod of steel or plastic etc, used in knitting.

knit one's brows to frown.

knives see **knife**.

knob [nob] n 1 a hard rounded part standing out from the main part: a bedstead with brass knobs on. 2 a rounded handle on or for a door or drawer: wooden door-knobs.

'knobbly adj having knobs or lumps: a knobbly walking-stick.

knock [nok] v 1 to make a sharp noise by hitting or tapping, esp on a door etc to attract attention: Just then, someone knocked at the door. 2 to cause to move, esp to fall, by hitting (often accidentally): She knocked a vase on to the floor while she was

dusting. 3 to put into a certain state or position by hitting: He knocked the other man senseless. 4 (often with **against, on**) to strike against or bump into: She knocked against the table and spilt his cup of coffee; I knocked my head on the car door. – n 1 an act of knocking or striking: She gave two knocks on the door; He had a nasty bruise from a knock he had received playing football. 2 the sound made by a knock, esp on a door etc: Suddenly they heard a loud knock.

'knocker n a piece of metal etc fixed to a door and used for knocking.

knock about/around 1 to treat in a rough and unkind manner, esp to hit repeatedly: I've heard that her husband knocks her about. 2 to move about (in) a casual manner without a definite destination or purpose: He spent six months knocking around before getting a job. 3 (with **with**) to be friendly with: I don't like the boys he knocks about with.

knock back to drink, esp quickly and in large quantities: He knocked back three pints of beer in ten minutes.

knock down 1 to cause to fall by striking: He was so angry with the man that he knocked him down; The old lady was knocked down by a van as she crossed the street. 2 to reduce the price of (goods): She bought a coat that had been knocked down to half-price.

knock off to stop working: I knocked off at six o'clock after studying for four hours; What time do you knock off in this factory?

knock out 1 to make unconscious by a blow, or (in boxing) unable to recover within the required time: The boxer knocked his opponent out in the third round. 2 to defeat and cause to retire from a competition: That team knocked us out in the semi-finals (n **'knock-out**).

knock over to cause to fall from an upright position: The dog knocked over a chair as it rushed past.

knock up (of opponents in a tennis match) to have a short practice before starting on the match (n **'knock-up**).

knot [not] n 1 a lump or join made in string, rope etc by twisting the ends together and drawing tight the loops formed: She fastened the string round the parcel, tying it with a knot. 2 a lump in wood at the join between a branch and the trunk: This wood is full of knots. 3 a group or gathering: a small knot of people. 4 a measure of speed for ships (about 1·85 km per hour) – v – pt, ptp **'knotted** – to tie in a knot: He knotted the rope around the post.

'knotty adj 1 containing knots. 2 (of a problem etc) difficult: a knotty problem.

know [nou] – pt **knew** [nju:]; ptp **known** – v

1 to be aware of or to have been informed about: *He knows everything*; *I know he is at home because his car is in the drive*; *He knows all about it*; *I know of no reason why you cannot go.* 2 to have learned and to remember: *He knows a lot of poetry.* 3 to be aware of the identity of; to be friendly with: *I know Mrs Smith — she lives near me.* 4 to (be able to) recognize or identify: *You would hardly know her now — she has become very thin*; *He knows a good car when he sees one.*

'knowing *adj* showing secret understanding: *She gave him a knowing look.*

'knowingly *adv* 1 in a knowing manner: *She smiled knowingly.* 2 deliberately or on purpose: *He would not knowingly insult her.*

'know-all *n* an unkind name for a person who thinks he knows everything.

'know-how *n* the practical knowledge and skill to deal with something: *She has acquired a lot of know-how about cars.*

in the know having information possessed only by a small group of people: *People in the know tell me that she is the most likely person to get the job.*

know backwards to know extremely well or perfectly: *He knows his history backwards.*

know better to be too wise or well-taught (to do something): *She should know better*

at her age!*; *He should have known better than to trust them.*

know how to to have learned the way to: *She already knew how to read when she went to school.*

know the ropes to understand the detail and procedure of a job *etc.*

knowledge ['nolidʒ] *n* 1 the fact of knowing: *She was greatly encouraged by the knowledge that she had won first prize in the competition.* 2 information or what is known: *He had a vast amount of knowledge about boats.* 3 the whole of what can be learned or found out: *Science is a branch of knowledge about which I am rather ignorant.*

'knowledgeable *adj* having a great deal of information: *He is very knowledgeable about the history of the city.*

general knowledge knowledge about a wide range of subjects: *The teacher sometimes tests our general knowledge.*

known *see* know.

knuckle ['nʌkl] *n* a joint of a finger: *She hit her hand against the wall and grazed her knuckles.*

koala (bear) [kou'aːlə] *n* a type of Australian tree-climbing animal like a small bear, the female of which carries her baby in a pouch.

Koran [ko'raːn, (*Amer*) kou-] *n* the holy book of the Muslims.

Ll

lab *see* laboratory.

label ['leibl] *n* a small written note fixed on or near anything to tell its contents, owner *etc*: *luggage labels*; *The label on the blouse said 'Do not iron'.* – *v* – *pt*, *ptp* 'labelled, *Amer* 'labeled – *v* to attach a label to: *She labelled all the boxes of books carefully.*

laboratory [lə'borətəri, (*Amer*) 'labrətoːri] – *pl* la'boratories – *n* (*abbrev* lab [læb]) a place where scientific experiments are carried on or where drugs *etc* are prepared: *Samples of her blood were sent to the hospital lab(oratory) for testing.*

labour, (*Amer*) labor ['leibə] *n* 1 hard work: *The building of the cathedral involved considerable labour over two centuries*; *People engaged in manual labour are often badly paid.* 2 workmen on a job: *The firm is having difficulty hiring labour.* 3 (in a pregnant woman *etc*) the process of childbirth: *She was in labour for several hours before the baby was born.* 4 used (*with cap*) as a name for the Socialist party in the UK. – *v* 1 to be employed to do hard and unskilled

work: *He spends the summer labouring on a building site.* 2 to move or work *etc* slowly or with difficulty: *They laboured through the deep undergrowth in the jungle*; *the car engine labours a bit on steep hills.*

laborious [lə'boːriəs] *adj* difficult; requiring hard work: *Moving house is always a laborious process.* la'boriously *adv.* la'boriousness *n.*

'labourer *n* a workman who is employed to do heavy work requiring little skill: *the labourers on a building site.*

'labour-saving *adj* intended to lessen work: *washing-machines and other labour-saving devices.*

labyrinth ['labərinθ] *n* a place full of long, winding passages; a maze.

lace [leis] *n* 1 a string or cord for fastening shoes *etc*: *I need a new pair of laces for my tennis shoes.* 2 delicate net-like decorative fabric made with fine thread: *Her dress was trimmed with lace*; (*also adj*) *a lace shawl.* – to fasten or be fastened with a lace which is threaded through holes: *Lace (up) your boots firmly.*

lack [lak] *v* to have too little or none of: *He lacked the courage to join the army.* – *n* the state of not having any or enough: *our lack of money.*
  be lacking (*with* **in**) **1** to be without or not to have enough: *He is lacking in intelligence.* **2** to be absent; to be present in too little an amount: *Money for the project is not lacking but enthusiasm is.*

lacquer ['lakə] *n* **1** a type of varnish: *He painted the iron table with black lacquer.* **2** a sticky liquid sprayed on the hair to keep it in place. – *v* to cover with lacquer.

lad [lad] *n* a boy or a youth: *I knew him when he was a lad.*

ladder ['ladə] *n* **1** a set of rungs or steps between two long supports, for climbing up or down: *She was standing on a ladder painting the ceiling; the ladder of success.* **2** (*Amer* **run**) a long, narrow flaw caused by the breaking of a stitch in a stocking or other knitted fabric. – *v* to (cause to) develop such a flaw: *I laddered my best pair of tights today; Fine stockings ladder very easily.*

laden ['leidn] *adj* carrying a lot; heavily loaded (with): *People left the shops laden with purchases; Several laden lorries turned out of the yard.*

ladle ['leidl] *n* a bowl-like spoon with a long handle fixed to it at right angles, for lifting out liquid from a container: *a soup ladle.* – *v* to lift and deal out with a ladle: *He ladled soup into the plates.*
  'ladleful *n*: *two ladlefuls of soup.*

lady ['leidi] *n* **1** a more polite form of **woman**: *Tell that child to stand up and let that lady sit down; The lady in the flower shop said that roses are expensive just now; Ladies' shoes are upstairs in this shop;* (*also adj*) *a lady doctor.* **2** a woman of good manners and refined behaviour: *Be quiet! – Ladies do not shout in public.* **3** in the UK, used as the title of, or a name for, a woman of noble rank: *Sir James and Lady Brown; lords and ladies.*
  'ladylike *adj* like a lady in manners: *She is too ladylike to swear.*
  'Ladyship *n* (*with* **Her, Your** *etc*) a word used in speaking to, or about, a woman with the title 'Lady': *Thank you, Your Ladyship; Ask Her Ladyship for permission.*
  'ladybird *n* (*Amer* **'ladybug**) a type of little round beetle, usually red with black spots.
  ***lady's fingers** *n pl* the long sticky green pods of a tropical plant, used as a vegetable.

lag [lag] – *pt, ptp* **lagged** – *v* (often with **behind**) to move too slowly and become left behind: *We waited for the smaller children, who were lagging behind the rest.* – *n* an act of lagging or the amount by which one thing is later than another: *There is some-*

times a time-lag of several seconds between our seeing the lightning and our hearing the thunder.

lagoon [lə'gu:n] *n* a shallow stretch of water separated from the sea by sandbanks, coral reefs *etc.*

laid *see* **lay**[1].

lain *see* **lie**[2].

lair [leə] *n* the den of a wild beast: *The bear had its lair among the rocks at the top of the valley.*

lake [leik] *n* a large area of water surrounded by land: *They go swimming in/sailing on the lake; Lake Michigan.*

lallang ['la:la:ŋ] *n* a tall coarse tropical grass.

lamb [lam] *n* **1** a young sheep: *The ewe has had three lambs.* **2** its flesh eaten as food: *a roast leg of lamb.* **3** a lovable or gentle person, *usu* a child.
  'lambskin *n, adj* (of) the skin of a lamb with the wool left on it: *a lambskin coat.*
  'lambswool ['lamz-] *n, adj* (of) a fine type of wool obtained from a lamb: *a lambswool sweater.*

lame [leim] *adj* **1** unable to walk properly: *He was lame for weeks after his fall.* **2** not satisfactory; unacceptable: *a lame excuse.* – *v* to make unable to walk properly: *He was lamed by a bullet in the ankle.* **'lamely** *adv.* **'lameness** *n.*

lament [lə'ment] *v* to feel or express regret for: *We all lament his death; He sat lamenting over his past failures.* – *n* **1** a poem or piece of music which laments something: *This song is a lament for those killed in battle.* **2** a show of grief, regret *etc*: *I'm not going to sit listening to her laments all day.*
  lamen'tation [lamən-] *n* (an) act of lamenting: *the lamentations of the widow.*

lamp [lamp] *n* a (glass-covered) light: *an oil-lamp; a table lamp; a street-lamp.*
  'lamp-post *n* the pillar supporting a street-lamp.
  'lampshade *n* a cover for a light-bulb, made of *eg* cloth, paper or metal, which lessens, softens or directs the light coming from it.

lance [la:ns] *n* a weapon of former times with a long shaft or handle of wood, a spearhead and often a small flag. – *v* to cut open (a boil *etc*) with a knife: *The doctor lanced the boil on my neck.*

land [land] *n* **1** the solid part of the surface of the Earth which is covered by the sea: *We had been at sea a week before we saw land.* **2** a country: *foreign lands.* **3** the ground or soil: *He never made any money at farming as his land was poor and stony.* **4** an estate: *He owns land/lands in Scotland.* – *v* **1** to come or bring down from the air upon the land: *The plane landed in a field; They managed to land the helicopter safely; She fell twenty feet, but landed without injury.* **2** to come or

* see illustration on p. 594

bring from the sea on to the land: *After being at sea for three months, they landed at Plymouth*; *He landed the big fish with some help*. **3** to (cause to) get into a particular (*usu* unfortunate) situation: *Don't drive so fast – you'll land (yourself) in hospital/trouble!*

'**landing** *n* **1** (an act of) coming or bringing to shore or to ground: *an emergency landing*; (*also adj*) *a landing place*. **2** a place for coming ashore. **3** the level part of a staircase between flights of steps: *Her room was on the first floor, across the landing from mine*.

'**landing-gear** *n* the parts of an aircraft that carry the load when it lands: *The accident was caused by the failure of the plane's landing-gear*.

'**landing-stage** *n* a platform, fixed or floating, on which to land passengers or goods from a boat.

'**landlocked** *adj* enclosed by land: *a landlocked bay*; *That area is completely landlocked*.

'**landlord** – *fem* '**landlady** (*pl* '**landladies**) – *n* **1** a person who has tenants or lodgers: *My landlady has just put up my rent*. **2** a person who keeps a public house: *The landlord of the 'Swan' is Mr Smith*.

'**landmark** *n* **1** an object on land that serves as a guide to seamen or others: *The church-tower is a landmark for sailors because it stands on the top of a cliff*. **2** an event of great importance.

land mine a mine laid on or near the surface of the ground, which is set off by something passing over it.

'**landowner** *n* a person who owns land, *esp* a lot of land.

'**Landrover**® [-rouvə] *n* a type of strong motor vehicle used for driving over rough ground.

'**landslide** *n* a piece of land that falls down from the side of a hill: *His car was buried in the landslide*.

land up to get into a particular, *usu* unfortunate, situation, *esp* through one's own fault: *If you go on like that, you'll land up in jail*.

land with to burden (someone) with (an unpleasant task): *She was landed with the job of telling him the bad news*.

landscape ['landskeip] *n* **1** the area of land that a person can look at all at the same time: *He stood on the hill surveying the landscape*. **2** a picture showing a view of the countryside: *He paints landscapes*. – *v* to do landscape gardening on: *We are having our back garden landscaped*.

landscape gardening the art of planning and laying out gardens, parks *etc*. **landscape gardener** *n*.

landslide *see* **land**.

lane [lein] **1** a narrow road or street: *a winding lane*. **2** used in the names of certain roads or streets: *His address is 12 Penny Lane*. **3** a division of a road for one line of traffic: *The new motorway has three lanes in each direction*. **4** a regular course across the sea taken by ships: *a regular shipping lane*.

language ['laŋgwidʒ] *n* **1** human speech: *the development of language in children*. **2** the speech of a particular nation: *She is very good at (learning) languages*; *Russian is a difficult language*. **3** the words and way of speaking, writing *etc* usually connnected with a particular group of people *etc*: *the language of journalists*; *medical language*.

bad language *n* swearing.

languid ['laŋgwid] *adj* without liveliness or energy. '**languidly** *adv*.

languish ['laŋgwiʃ] *v* to grow weak; to waste away.

lank [laŋk] *adj* (of hair) straight, thin, and *usu* greasy.

'**lanky** *adj* thin, tall and not elegant: *He is tall and lanky*. '**lankiness** *n*.

lantana [lan'tɑːnə] *n* a tropical shrub with prickly stems and small yellow or red flowers.

lantern ['lantən] *n* a case for holding or carrying a light.

lap¹ [lap] – *pt, ptp* **lapped** – *v* **1** to drink by licking with the tongue: *The cat lapped milk from a saucer*. **2** (of a liquid) to wash or flow (against): *Water lapped the side of the boat*.

lap up to drink eagerly by lapping: *The dog lapped up the water*.

lap² [lap] *n* **1** the part from waist to knees of a person who is sitting: *The baby was lying in its mother's lap*. **2** one round of a racecourse or other competition track: *The runners have completed five laps, with three still to run*.

lap dog a small pet dog.

the lap of luxury very luxurious conditions: *living in the lap of luxury*.

lapel [lə'pel] *n* the part of a coat joined to the collar and folded back against the chest: *Narrow lapels are in fashion*.

lapse [laps] *v* **1** to cease to exist, often because of lack of effort: *His insurance policy had lapsed and was not renewed*. **2** to slip, fall, be reduced: *As he could think of nothing more to say, he lapsed into silence*; *I'm afraid our standards of tidiness have lapsed*. – *n* **1** a mistake or failure (in behaviour, memory *etc*): *a lapse of memory*. **2** a passing away (of time): *I saw him again after a lapse of five years*.

lard [lɑːd] *n* the melted fat of the pig, used in cooking. – *v* **1** to put lard on; to cover with lard.

larder ['la:də] *n* a room or cupboard where food is stored in a house.

large ['la:dʒ] *adj* great in size, amount *etc*; not small: *a large number of people*; *a large house*; *a large family*; *This house is too large for two people*.

'**largely** *adv* mainly; to a great extent: *This success was largely due to her efforts*; *Our methods have been largely successful*.

'**largeness** *n*.

at large 1 (of prisoners *etc*) free: *Despite the efforts of the police, the escaped prisoner is still at large.* **2** in general: *the country/the public at large*.

lark[1] [la:k] *n* a general name for several types of singing-bird, *esp* the skylark, which flies high into the air as it sings.

lark[2] [la:k] *n* a piece of fun or mischief.

lark about/around to play about in a rough and *usu* noisy manner.

larva ['la:və] – *pl* '**larvae** [-vi:] – *n* a developing insect in its first stage after coming out of the egg; a grub or caterpillar. '**larval** *adj*.

laser ['leizə] *n* (an instrument that produces) a narrow and very intense beam of light: *The men were cutting the sheets of metal with a laser*; (*also adj*) *a laser beam*.

lash [laʃ] *n* **1** an eyelash: *She looked at him through her thick lashes.* **2** a stroke with a whip *etc*: *The sailor was given twenty lashes as a punishment.* **3** a thin piece of rope or cord, *esp* of a whip: *a whip with a long, thin lash.* – *v* **1** to strike with a lash: *He lashed the horse with his whip.* **2** to fasten with a rope or cord: *All the equipment had to be lashed to the deck of the ship.* **3** to make a sudden or restless movement (with) (a tail): *The tiger crouched in the tall grass, its tail lashing from side to side.* **4** (of rain) to come down very heavily.

lash out (*often with* at) to hit out violently: *He lashed out with his fists.*

lass [las] *n* a girl.

lasso [la'su:] – *pl* **las'so(e)s** – *n* a long rope with a loop which tightens when the rope is pulled, used for catching wild horses *etc*. – *v* – *prt* **las'soes**: *pt*, *ptp* **las'soed** – to catch with a lasso: *The cowboy lassoed the horse*.

last[1] [la:st] *adj* **1** coming at the end: *We set out on the last day of November*; *He was last in the race*; *He caught the last bus home.* **2** most recent; next before the present: *Our last house was much smaller than this*; *last year/month/week.* **3** coming or remaining after all the others: *He was the last guest to leave.* – *adv* at the end of or after all the others: *He took his turn last.*

'**lastly** *adv* finally: *Lastly, I would like to thank you all for listening so patiently to what I have been saying.*

at (long) last in the end, *esp* after a long delay: *Oh, there he is at (long) last!*

hear, see *etc* **the last of** to be finished with, be able to forget: *You haven't heard the last of this!*

the last person a person who is very unlikely or unwilling to do a particular thing, or to whom it would be unwise or dangerous to do a particular thing: *I'm the last person to make a fuss, but you should have told me all the same*; *He's the last person you should offend.*

the last straw a fact, happening *etc* which, when added to all other facts or happenings, makes a situation finally impossible to bear.

the last thing something very unlikely, unwanted, not intended *etc*: *It's the last thing you would think of looking for*; *The last thing I want is to hurt anyone.*

the last word 1 the final remark in an argument *etc*: *She always must have the last word!* **2** the final decision: *The last word rests with the chairman.* **3** something very fashionable or up-to-date: *Her hat was the last word in elegance.*

to the last until the very end: *He kept his courage to the last.*

last[2] [la:st] *v* **1** to continue to exist: *This situation lasted until she got married*; *I hope this fine weather lasts.* **2** to remain in good condition or supply: *This carpet has lasted well*; *The bread won't last another two days – we'll need more*; *This coat will last me until I die.*

'**lasting** *adj*: *A good education is a lasting benefit.*

last out to be or have enough to survive or continue to exist (until the end of): *I hope the petrol lasts out until we reach a garage*; *They could only last out another week on the little food they had*; *The sick man was not expected to last out the night.*

latch [latʃ] *n* a catch of wood or metal used to fasten a door *etc*: *She lifted the latch and walked in.*

'**latchkey** *n* a small front-door key: *She put her latchkey in the lock.*

late [leit] *adj* **1** coming *etc* after the expected or usual time: *The train is late tonight*; *I try to be punctual but I am always late.* **2** far on in the day or night: *late in the day*; *late at night*; *It was very late when I got to bed.* **3** dead, *esp* recently: *the late king.* **4** recently, but no longer, holding an office or position: *Mr Allan, the late chairman, made a speech.* – *adv* **1** after the expected or usual time: *He arrived late for his interview.* **2** far on in the day or night: *They always go to bed late.* '**lateness** *n*.

'**lately** *adv* in the recent past or not long ago: *Have you seen her lately?*

later on at a later time: *He hasn't arrived yet but no doubt he'll be here later on.*

of late lately: *He thought she had been less friendly of late.*

later *see* **latter.**

latent ['leitənt] *adj* hidden or undeveloped, but capable of being developed: *a latent talent for music.*

lateral ['latərəl] *adj* of, at, to or from the side: *lateral movement.* **'laterally** *adv.*

latex ['leiteks] *n* the milky juice of some plants *esp* rubber trees.

lathe [leið] *n* a machine for shaping wood, metal *etc*, which turns the piece of wood *etc* which is to be shaped round and round against a tool kept steady by the operator.

lather ['la:ðə] *n* **1** foam made up of soap bubbles: *Add the detergent to the water and work up a good lather.* **2** a foam of sweat appearing *eg* on a horse's neck.

Latin ['latin] *n, adj* **1** (of) the language spoken in ancient Rome: *We studied Latin at school; a Latin lesson.* **2** (a person) who speaks a language derived from Latin.
Latin America the countries of Central and South America, where the official language is usually a form of either Spanish or Portuguese. **Latin American** *n, adj.*

latitude ['latitju:d] *n* **1** the distance, measured in degrees on the map, that a place is north or south of the Equator: *What is the latitude of London?* **2** freedom of choice or action.

latrine [lə'tri:n] *n* a lavatory, *esp* one used by soldiers *etc.*

latter ['latə] *adj* towards the end: *the latter part of our holiday.*
'latterly *adv* **1** recently; lately. **2** towards the end.
the latter the second of two things *etc* mentioned: *John and Mary arrived, the latter wearing a green wool dress.*

to choose the second or **latter** (not **later**) of two alternatives.

laudable ['lo:dəbl] *adj* worthy of being praised: *a laudable effort.* **'laudably** *adv.*

laugh [la:f] *v* to make sounds with the voice in showing happiness, amusement, scorn *etc*: *We laughed at the funny photographs; Children were laughing in the garden as they played.* – *n* an act or sound of laughing: *He gave a laugh; a loud laugh.*
'laughable *adj* **1** ridiculous or deserving scorn: *Her attempts at drawing were laughable.* **2** amusing; comical. **'laughably** *adv.*
'laughingly *adv* as a joke: *She suggested laughingly that he should try it himself.*
'laughter *n* the act or sound of laughing: *We could hear laughter/the sound of laughter from the next room.*
'laughing-stock *n* someone who is laughed

at: *If I wear that hat, I'll be a laughing-stock.*
laugh at to make it obvious that one regards something or someone as humorous, ridiculous or deserving scorn: *Everyone will laugh at me if I wear that dress!; The others laughed at his fears.*

launch¹ [lo:ntʃ] *v* **1** to make (a boat or ship) slide into the water or (a rocket) leave the ground: *As soon as the alarm was given, the lifeboat was launched; The Russians have launched a rocket.* **2** to start (a person, project *etc*) off on a course: *His success launched him on a brilliant career.* **3** to throw. – *n* (an) act of launching.
'launching-pad *n* a platform from which a rocket can be launched.
launch into to begin eagerly: *He launched into an enthusiastic description of the play.*
launch out to throw oneself freely into some new activity (often involving spending money).

launch² [lo:ntʃ] *n* a large, power-driven boat, *usu* used for short trips or for pleasure: *We cruised round the bay in a motor launch.*

launder ['lo:ndə] *v* to wash and iron: *to launder clothes.*
laund(e)rette [lo:n'dret] *n* a shop where customers may wash clothes in washing-machines.
'laundress *n* a woman employed to launder.
'laundry – *pl* **laundries** – *n* **1** a place where clothes *etc* are washed, *esp* in return for payment: *She took the sheets to the laundry; a hospital laundry.* **2** clothes *etc* which have been, or are to be, washed: *a bundle of laundry.*

laurel ['lorəl] *n* a type of tree, once used for making wreaths to crown winners of races or competitions *etc.*
rest on one's laurels to depend too much on one's past successes and therefore make no further effort.

lava ['la:və] *n* liquid, melted rock *etc* thrown out from a volcano and becoming solid as it cools.

lavatory ['lavətəri] – *pl* **'lavatories** – *n* (a room containing) a receptacle for waste matter from the body.

lavender ['lavində] *n* **1** a type of plant with sweet-smelling pale bluish-purple flowers. **2** (*also adj*) (of) the colour of the flowers: *a lavender dress.*

lavish ['laviʃ] *v* to spend or give very freely: *She lavishes too much money on that child.* – *adj* **1** (of a person) spending or giving generously and sometimes too freely: *a lavish host; You have certainly been lavish with the brandy in this cake.* **2** given generously or too freely: *lavish gifts.* **'lavishly** *adv.* **'lavishness** *n.*

law [lo:] *n* **1** the collection of rules according

to which people live or a country *etc* is governed: *Such an action is against the law*; *law and order*. **2** any one of such rules: *A new law has been passed by Parliament*. **3** (in science) a rule that says that under certain conditions certain things always happen: *the law of gravity*.

'**lawful** *adj* **1** (*neg* **un-**) allowed by law: *He was attacked while going about his lawful business*. **2** just or rightful: *She is the lawful owner of the property*. '**lawfully** *adv*.

'**lawless** *adj* paying no attention to, and not keeping, the law: *In its early days, the American West was full of lawless men*. '**lawlessly** *adv*. '**lawlessness** *n*.

'**lawyer** ['lɔ:jə] *n* a person whose work it is to know about and give advice and help to others concerning the law: *If you want to make your will, consult a lawyer*.

'**law-abiding** *adj* obeying the law: *a law-abiding citizen*.

'**law court** (*also* **court of law**) a place where people accused of crimes are tried and legal disagreements between people are judged.

'**lawsuit** *n* a quarrel or disagreement taken to a court of law to be settled.

be a law unto oneself to be inclined not to obey rules or follow the usual customs and conventions.

the law the police: *The thief was still in the building when the law arrived*.

the law of the land the established law of a country.

lay down the law to state something in a way that indicates that one expects one's opinion and orders to be accepted without argument.

lawn [lɔ:n] *n* an area of smooth, short grass, *esp* as part of a garden: *He is mowing the lawn*.

lax [laks] *adj* careless or not strict in discipline or morals: *Pupils have been rather lax about some of the school rules recently*. '**laxity**, '**laxness** *ns*.

laxative ['laksətiv] *n, adj* (a medicine) which makes it easier to pass waste matter from the bowels.

lay¹ [lei] – *pt, ptp* **laid** [leid] – *v* **1** to place, set or put (down), often carefully: *She laid the clothes in a drawer/on a chair*; *He laid down his pencil*; *She laid her report before the committee*. **2** to place in a lying position: *She laid the baby on his back*. **3** to put in order or arrange: *She went to lay the table for dinner*; *to lay one's plans/a trap*. **4** to flatten: *The animal laid back its ears*; *The wind laid the corn flat*. **5** to cause to disappear or become quiet: *to lay a ghost/ doubts*. **6** (of a bird) to produce (eggs): *The hen laid four eggs*; *My hens are laying well*. **7** to bet: *I'll lay five pounds that you don't succeed*.

'**layer** *n* **1** a thickness or covering: *The ground was covered with a layer of snow*; *There was a layer of clay a few feet under the ground*. **2** something which lays, *esp* a hen: *a good layer*. – *v* to put, cut or arrange in layers: *She had her hair layered by the hairdresser*.

'**layabout** *n* a lazy, idle person.

'**layout** *n* the manner in which something is displayed or laid out: *the layout of the building*.

laid up ill in bed: *When I caught flu, I was laid up for a fortnight*.

lay aside to put away or to one side, *esp* to be used or dealt with at a later time: *She laid the books aside for later use*.

lay bare to show clearly; to expose to view: *They dug up the road and laid bare the water-pipe*; *Shy people don't like to lay bare their feelings*.

lay by to put away for future use: *She laid by a store of tinned vegetables*.

lay down 1 to give up: *They laid down their arms*; *The soldiers laid down their lives in the cause of peace*. **2** to order or instruct: *The rule book lays down what should be done in such a case*. **3** to store: *My father laid down a good stock of wine which I am now drinking*.

lay (one's) hands on 1 to find or be able to obtain: *I wish I could lay (my) hands on that book!* **2** to catch: *The police had been trying to lay hands on the criminal for months*.

lay in to get and store a supply of: *I've laid in an extra stock of drinks for Christmas*.

lay low to make ill: *I was laid low by flu, just before my exams*.

lay off to dismiss (employees) temporarily: *Because of a shortage of orders, the firm has laid off a quarter of its workforce*.

lay on to provide: *The staff laid on a tea party for the pupils*.

lay out 1 to arrange over a wide area (*esp* according to a plan): *He was the architect who laid out the public gardens*. **2** to spread so as to be easily seen: *He laid out the contents of the box on the table*. **3** to knock unconscious. **4** to spend (money). **5** to prepare (a dead body) to be buried.

lay up 1 to keep or store: *We laid up a good supply of apples this year from our own trees*. **2** to put (a ship) out of use in a dock.

lay waste to make (a piece of land) into barren country by burning and plundering.

lay needs an object and has **laid** as its past tense and past participle: *He (had) laid his book down*; *He will be laying his proposals before the committee tomorrow*. **lie** takes no object and has **lying** as its present participle, **lay** as its past tense and **lain** as its past participle: *Please lie*

down; He lay down; He had lain there for hours.
lie, to be untruthful, has **lying** as its present participle, and **lied** as its past tense and past participle: *She (has always) lied about her age.*

lay² *see* **lie²**.

lay³ [lei] *adj* **1** not a member of the clergy: *lay preachers.* **2** not an expert or a professional (in a particular subject): *Doctors tend to use words that lay people don't understand.*
  '**layman** *n* a lay person.

layer *see* **lay¹**.

layman *see* **lay³**.

layout *see* **lay¹**.

lazy ['leizi] *adj* too inclined to avoid hard work, exercise *etc*: *I take the bus to work as I'm too lazy to walk; Lazy people tend to become fat.* '**lazily** *adv.* '**laziness** *n.*
  '**lazy-bones** *n* a name for a lazy person.

lead¹ [li:d] – *pt, ptp* **led** [led] – *v* **1** to guide or direct or cause to go in a certain direction: *Follow my car and I'll lead you to the motorway; She took the child by the hand and led him across the road; He was leading the horse into the stable; The sound of hammering led us to the garage; You led us to believe that we would be paid!* **2** to go or carry to a particular place or along a particular course: *A small path leads through the woods.* **3** (*with* **to**) to cause or bring about a certain situation or state of affairs: *The heavy rain led to serious floods.* **4** to be first (in): *An official car led the procession; He is still leading in the competition.* **5** to live (a certain kind of life): *She leads a pleasant existence on a Greek island.* – *n* **1** the front place or position: *He has taken over the lead in the race.* **2** the state of being first: *We have a lead over the rest of the world in this kind of research.* **3** the act of leading: *We all followed his lead.* **4** the amount by which one is ahead of others: *He has a lead of twenty metres (over the man in second place).* **5** a leather strap or chain for leading a dog *etc*: *All dogs must be kept on a lead.* **6** a piece of information which will help to solve a mystery *etc*: *The police have several leads concerning the identity of the thief.* **7** a leading part in a play *etc*: *Who plays the lead in that film?*
  '**leader** *n* **1** a person who is in front or goes first: *The fourth runner is several miles behind the leaders.* **2** a person who is the head of, organizes or is in charge (of something): *The leader of the expedition is a scientist.* **3** an article in a newspaper *etc* written to express the opinions of the editor.
  '**leadership** *n* **1** the state of being a leader: *He took over the leadership of the Labour*

party two years later. **2** the quality of being able to be a leader: *The post requires a person who combines leadership and energy.*
  lead on 1 to deceive with false expectations. **2** to go first; to show the way: *Lead on!*
  lead up the garden path to deceive.
  lead up to to progress towards; to contribute to: *to lead up to a climax; the events leading up to the First World War.*
  lead the way to go first (*esp* to show the way): *She led the way upstairs.*

lead² [led] *n* **1** (*also adj*) (of) an element, a soft, heavy, bluish-grey metal: *lead pipes; Are these pipes made of lead or copper?* **2** the part of a pencil that leaves a mark: *The lead of my pencil has broken.*
  '**leaden** *adj* **1** lead-coloured: *leaden skies.* **2** made of lead.

leaf [li:f] – *pl* **leaves** [li:vz] – *n* **1** a part of a plant growing from the side of a stem, *usu* green, flat and thin, but of various shapes depending on the plant: *Many trees lose their leaves in autumn.* **2** something thin like a leaf, *esp* the page of a book: *Several leaves had been torn out of the book.* **3** an extra part of a table, either attached to one side with a hinge or added to the centre when the two ends are apart.
  '**leaflet** [-lit] *n* a small, printed sheet containing information *etc*.
  '**leafy** *adj* having many leaves: *a leafy plant.*
  turn over a new leaf to begin a new and better way of behaving, working *etc*.

league¹ [li:g] *n* **1** a union of persons, nations *etc* for the benefit of each other: *the League for the Protection of Shopkeepers.* **2** a grouping of sports clubs for games.
  be in league with to be allied to.

league² [li:g] *n* an old measure of distance (about 4.8 km).

leak [li:k] *n* **1** a crack or hole through which liquid or gas escapes: *Water was escaping through a leak in the pipe.* **2** the passing of gas, water *etc* through a crack or hole: *a gas-leak.* **3** a giving away of secret information: *a leak of Government plans.* – *v* **1** to have a leak: *This bucket leaks; The boiler leaked hot water all over the floor.* **2** to (cause something to) pass through a leak: *Gas was leaking from the cracked pipe; He was accused of leaking secrets to the enemy.*
  '**leakage** [-kidʒ] *n* (an act of) leaking: *Leakages in several water-mains had been reported; a leakage of information.*
  '**leaky** *adj*: *a leaky boat.*

lean¹ [li:n] – *pts, ptps* **leant** [lent], **leaned** – *v* **1** to slope over to one side; not to be upright: *The lamp-post had slipped and was leaning across the road.* **2** to rest (against, on): *She leaned the ladder against the wall; Don't lean your elbows on the table; He leant on the gate.*

'leaning n a liking or preference: *She has a leaning towards the arts.*

lean[2] [li:n] adj **1** thin; not fat: *a tall, lean man.* **2** not containing much fat: *lean meat.* **3** poor; not producing much: *a lean harvest.* **'leanness** n.

leant see **lean**[1].

leap [li:p] – pts, ptps **leapt** [lept], (esp Amer) **leaped** – v **1** to jump: *He leapt into the boat.* **2** to jump over: *The dog leapt the wall.* **3** to rush eagerly: *She leaped into his arms.* – n an act of leaping: *The cat jumped from the roof and reached the ground in two leaps.*

'leap-frog n a game in which one person vaults over another's bent back, pushing off from his hands.

leap year every fourth year, which consists of 366 days, February having 29, ie 1976, 1980, 1984 etc.

by leaps and bounds extremely rapidly and successfully: *improving by leaps and bounds.*

learn [lə:n] – pts, ptps **learned, learnt** – v **1** to get to know: *It was then that I learned that she was dead.* **2** to gain knowledge or skill (in): *A child is always learning; to learn French; She is learning (how) to swim.*

'learned [-nid] adj having or showing great learning: *a learned professor.*

'learner n a person who is in process of learning: *Be patient – I'm only a learner; (also adj) a learner driver.*

'learning n knowledge which has been gained by learning: *The professor was a man of great learning.*

lease [li:s] n (the period of) an agreement giving the use of a house etc on payment of rent: *We signed the lease yesterday; a twenty-year lease.* – v to give or acquire a house etc in this way: *He leases the land from the local council.*

leash [li:ʃ] n a strip of leather or piece of chain attached to a collar round its neck by which a dog etc is held.

least [li:st] adj, pron (something) which is the smallest or the smallest amount that exists, is possible etc: *I think the least you can do is apologize!; She wanted to know how to do it with the least amount of bother.* – adv (sometimes with **the**) to the smallest or lowest degree: *I like her (the) least of all the girls; That is the least important of our problems.*

at least at any rate; anyway: *I think she's well – at least she was when I saw her last.*

not in the least not at all: *You're not disturbing me in the least!*

leather ['leðə] n, adj (of) the skin of an animal prepared for making clothes, luggage etc: *shoes made of leather; a leather jacket/case.* **'leathery** adj like leather, esp tough: *The plant had broad, leathery leaves.*

leave[1] [li:v] – pt, ptp **left** [left] v **1** to go away

or depart from, often without intending to return: *He left the room for a moment; They left at about six o'clock; I have left that job.* **2** to go without taking: *She left her gloves in the car; He left his children behind when he went to France.* **3** to allow to remain in a particular state or condition: *She left the job half-finished.* **4** to let (a person or a thing) do something without being helped or attended to: *I'll leave the meat to cook for a while.* **5** to allow to remain for someone to do, make etc: *Leave that job to the experts!* **6** to make a gift of in one's will: *She left all her property to her son.*

leave alone not to disturb, upset or tease: *Why can't you leave your little brother alone?*

leave out not to include or put in: *You've left out a word in that sentence.*

left over not used; extra: *When everyone took a partner there was one person left over; We divided out the left-over food.*

leave[2] [li:v] n **1** permission to do something, eg to be absent: *Have I your leave to go?* **2** (esp of soldiers, sailors etc) a holiday: *He is home on leave at the moment.*

take one's leave (of) to say goodbye (to): *I took my leave (of the others) and went out.*

leavened ['levnd] adj (neg **un-**) containing yeast to make it rise: *leavened bread.*

leaves see **leaf**.

lectern ['lektən] n a stand for holding a book etc to be read from, esp for a lecture or in a church.

lecture ['lektʃə] n **1** a formal talk given to students or other audiences: *a history lecture.* **2** a long and boring or irritating speech, warning or scolding: *The teacher gave the children a lecture for running in the corridor.* – v to give a lecture: *He lectures on Roman Art; She lectured him on good behaviour.*

'lecturer n a person who lectures, esp to students: *He is a lecturer in the English department.*

led see **lead**[1].

ledge [ledʒ] n a shelf or an object that sticks out like a shelf: *He keeps plant-pots on the window-ledge; They stopped on a ledge halfway up the cliff.*

ledger ['ledʒə] n the book of accounts of an office or shop.

lee [li:] n the sheltered side, away from the wind: *We sat in the lee of the rock.*

'leeway n **1** the drifting of a ship etc away from its true course, or the amount of this. **2** lost time: *He has a lot of leeway to make up at school after being away ill.* **3** extra space, time etc allowed: *Book the later flight so as to allow yourself some leeway in case you're delayed.*

leech [li:tʃ] n a kind of blood-sucking worm.

leek [li:k] *n* a type of vegetable related to the onion with green leaves and a white base.

leer [liə] *n* an unpleasant kind of smile. – *v* to give this kind of smile.

left[1] *see* **leave**[1].

left[2] [left] *adj* on, for, or belonging to, the side of the body that in most people has the less skilful hand (the side of a person or thing which is toward the west when that person or thing is facing north–opposite to **right**): *She wore an engagement ring on her left hand*; *They drive on the left side of the road in Britain.* – *adv* to or towards this side: *He turned left at the end of the road.* – *n* **1** the left side, part *etc*: *He sat on her left*; *She turned to her left*; *Take the first road on the left*; *Keep to the left!* **2** within a political party, Parliament *etc*, the most radical or socialist group.

'left-hand *adj* **1** at the left; to the left of something else: *the bottom left-hand drawer of the desk.* **2** towards the left: *a left-hand bend in the road.*

left-'handed *adj* having the left hand more skilful than the right. **left-'handedness** *n*.

leg [leg] *n* **1** one of the limbs by which animals and man walk: *The horse injured a front leg*; *She stood on one leg.* **2** the part of an article of clothing that covers one of these limbs closely: *He has torn the leg of his trousers.* **3** a long, narrow support of a table *etc*: *One of the legs of the chair was broken.* **4** one stage in a journey, competition *etc*: *the last leg of the trip*; *the second leg of the contest.*

-legged [legid] *adj*: *a long-legged girl*; *a four-legged animal.*

pull someone's leg to try as a joke to make someone believe something which is not true: *Your haven't really got a black mark on your face – he's only pulling your leg.*

legacy ['legəsi] – *pl* **'legacies** – *n* something left in a will by someone who has died: *He was left a legacy by his great-aunt.*

legal ['li:gəl] *adj* **1** lawful; allowed by the law: *Is it legal to bring gold watches into the country?*; *a legal contract.* **2** concerned with or used in the law: *the legal profession.*
'legally *adv.* **le'gality** [-'ga-] *n*.
'legalize, -ise *v* to make legal or lawful.

legation [li'geiʃən] *n* (the headquarters of) an official group of people acting on behalf of the government of their own country *etc* in another country.

legend ['ledʒənd] *n* a myth or traditional story, handed down from one generation to another: *the legend of St George.*
'legendary *adj* **1** mentioned *etc* in legend: *legendary heroes.* **2** very famous because very great, good *etc*: *His generosity is legendary.*

legible ['ledʒəbl] *adj* clear enough to be read:

The writing was faded but still legible.
'legibly *adv.* **legi'bility** *n*.

legion ['li:dʒən] *n* **1** in ancient Rome, a body of from three to six thousand soldiers. **2** a great many or a very large number.

legislate ['ledʒisleit] *v* to make laws: *The government plan to legislate against the import of foreign cars.*
legi'slation *n* **1** the act of legislating. **2** a law or group of laws.
'legislative [-lətiv] *adj* law-making: *a legislative assembly*; *legislative powers.*
'legislator *n* a person who makes laws.
'legislature [-lətʃə] *n* the part of the government which has the power of making laws.

legitimate [li'dʒitimət] *adj* **1** lawful: *Is this procedure perfectly legitimate?* **2** (of a child) born to parents who are married to each other. **le'gitimately** *adv.* **le'gitimacy** *n*.

leisure ['leʒə, (*Amer*) 'li:ʒər] *n* time which one can spend as one likes, *esp* when one does not have to work: *I seldom have leisure to watch television.*
'leisurely *adj, adv* not hurrying; taking plenty of time: *She had a leisurely bath.*

lemon ['lemən] *n, adj* **1** (of) a type of oval, juicy, citrus fruit with pale yellow skin and very sour juice: *She added the juice of a lemon to the pudding*; *a lemon drink.* **2** (of) the colour of this fruit: *a pale lemon dress.*
lemo'nade [-'neid] *n* a (fizzy) drink flavoured with lemons.

lemon grass a tough grass with a strong scent, used to flavour food.

lend [lend] – *pt, ptp* **lent** [lent] – *v* **1** to give (someone) the use of a thing for a time: *She had forgotten her umbrella so I lent her mine to go home with.* **2** to give or add (a quality) to: *Desperation lent him strength.*

lend itself to to be suitable for or adapt easily to: *The play lends itself to performance by children.*

see also **borrow**.

length [leŋθ] *n* **1** the distance from one end to the other of an object, period of time *etc*: *What is the length of your car?*; *Please note down the length of time it takes you to do this.* **2** a piece of something, *esp* cloth: *I bought a (3-metre) length of silk.* **3** in racing, the measurement from end to end of a horse, boat *etc*: *He won by a length*; *The other boat is several lengths in front.*
'lengthen *v* to make or become longer: *I'll have to lengthen this skirt*; *The days are lengthening now that the spring has come.*
'lengthways/'lengthwise *advs* in the direction of the length: *She folded the towels lengthways.*
'lengthy *adj* of great, often too great, length: *This essay is interesting but lengthy.*
at length 1 in detail; taking a long time: *She*

told us at length about her accident. **2** at last: *At length the walkers arrived home.*

go to any lengths to do anything, no matter how extreme, dishonest, wicked *etc*, to achieve a particular aim: *She'd go to any lengths to get herself promoted.*

lenient ['li:niənt] *adj* merciful or punishing only lightly: *You are much too lenient with wrongdoers.* **'leniently** *adv.*
'lenience, 'leniency *ns.*

lens [lenz] *n* **1** a piece of glass *etc* curved on one or both sides and used in spectacles, microscopes, cameras *etc*: *I need new lenses in my spectacles; The camera lens is dirty.* **2** a similar part of the eye: *The disease has affected the lens of his left eye.*

lens is singular; the plural is lenses.

lent *see* **lend.**

lentil ['lentil] *n* the small orange seed of a pod-bearing plant, used in soups *etc.*

leopard ['lepəd] *n* a type of large spotted animal of the cat family.

leotard ['liəta:d] *n* a kind of tight-fitting garment worn for dancing, gymnastics *etc.*

leper ['lepə] *n* a person who has leprosy.
'leprosy [-rəsi] *n* a contagious skin disease, causing serious and permanent damage to the body, including loss of fingers, nose *etc.*

less [les] *adj* (*often with* **than**) not as much (as): *Think of a number less than forty; He drank his tea and wished he had put less sugar in it; The salary for that job will be not less than $20 000.* – *adv* not as much or to a smaller extent: *I like her less every time I see her; You should smoke less if you want to remain healthy.* – *pron* a smaller part or amount: *He has less than I have.* – *prep* minus: *He earns $180 a week less $60 income tax.*
'lessen *v* to make or become less: *The fan lessened the heat a little; When the children left, the noise lessened considerably.*
'lesser *adj* smaller or not as important: *the lesser of the two towns.* – *adv* less: *the lesser-known streets of London.*

the less ... the less/more *etc*: *The less I see of him, the better (pleased I'll be)!; The less I practise, the less confident I become; The less I try, the more I succeed.*

no less a person *etc* **than**: as great a person *etc* as: *I had tea with no less a person than the Prime Minister (= with the Prime minister himself).*

less is used in speaking about quantity or amount: *People should eat less fat; I've less than $100 in the bank.*
fewer sould be used in speaking about numbers of individual things or people: *I've fewer books than he has; There were fewer than 50 people at the meeting.*

lesson ['lesn] *n* **1** something which is learned or taught: *The lesson which we learned from the experience was never to trust anyone.* **2** a period of teaching: *during the French lesson.* **3** a part of the Bible read in church: *He was asked to read the lesson on Sunday morning.*

lest [lest] *conj* in case: *He was scared lest he should fail his exam.*

let¹ [let] – *prp* **'letting**: *pt, ptp* **let** – *v* **1** to allow or permit: *She refused to let her children go out in the rain; Let me see your drawing.* **2** to cause to: *I will let you know how much it costs.* **3** used for giving orders or suggestions: *If they will not work, let them starve;* *Let's (= let us) leave right away!*

let alone not to mention; without taking into consideration: *There's no room for all the adults, let alone the children.*

let (someone or something) alone/be to leave alone; not to disturb or worry: *Why don't you let him be when he's not feeling well!; Do let your father alone.*

let down 1 to lower: *She let down the blind.* **2** to disappoint or fail to help when necessary *etc*: *You must give a film show at the party – you can't let the children down (n* **'let-down**); *She felt he had let her down by not coming to see her perform.* **3** to make flat by allowing the air to escape: *When he got back to his car, he found that some children had let his tyres down.* **4** to make longer: *She had to let down the child's skirt.*

let fall to drop: *She was so startled she let fall everything she was carrying.*

let go (of) to stop holding (something): *Will you let go of my coat!; When he was nearly at the top of the rope he suddenly let go and fell.*

let in, out: to allow to come in, go out: *Let me in!; I let the dog out.*

let in for to involve (someone) in: *I didn't know what I was letting myself in for when I agreed to do that job.*

let in on to allow to share (a secret *etc*): *We'll let her in on our plans.*

let off 1 to fire (a gun) or cause (a firework *etc*) to explode: *He let the gun off accidentally.* **2** to allow to go without punishment *etc*: *The policeman let him off (with a warning).*

let up to become less strong or violent; to stop: *I wish the rain would let up (n* **'let-up**).

let² [let] – *prp* **'letting**: *pt, ptp* **let** – *v* to give the use of (a house *etc*) in return for payment: *He lets his house to visitors in the summer.*

to let for letting: *house to let.*

let to, rent (out) to mean to allow the use of (a house *etc* that one owns) to (someone) in return for payment: *to let/rent (out) one's flat to visitors.*

rent from means to give payment for one's use of (a house *etc*) to (the owner): *I rent my flat from a landlord who lives abroad.*

lethal ['li:θəl] *adj* causing death; enough to kill: *a lethal dose of poison.*

lethargy ['leθədʒi] *n* lack of interest or energy. **le'thargic** [-'θa:-] *adj.*

letter ['letə] *n* **1** a mark expressing a sound: *the letters of the alphabet.* **2** a written message, *esp* sent by post in an envelope: *She slowly took the letter from its envelope; Did you post my letter?*
'lettering *n* **1** the way in which letters are formed: *the art of lettering.* **2** letters which have been drawn, painted *etc*: *He repainted the lettering over the shop door.*
'letterbox *n* **1** a slit in a door (sometimes with a box behind it) through which mail from the post is put: *He put the card through the letterbox.* **2** a postbox.
to the letter precisely; according to every detail: *He followed his father's instructions to the letter.*

lettuce ['letis] *n* a type of green plant with large leaves used as a salad.

leukaemia, (*Amer*) **leukemia** [luːˈkiːmiə] *n* a disease that causes white blood cells to multiply abnormally in the body.

level ['levl] *n* **1** height, position, strength, rank *etc*: *The level of the river rose; a high level of intelligence.* **2** a horizontal division or floor: *the third level of the multi-storey car park.* **3** a kind of instrument for showing whether a surface is level: *a spirit level.* **4** a flat, smooth surface or piece of land: *It was difficult running uphill but he could run fast on the level.* – *adj* **1** flat, even, smooth or horizontal: *a level surface; a level spoonful* (= an amount which just fills the spoon to the top of the sides). **2** of the same height, standard *etc*: *The top of the kitchen sink is level with the window-sill; The scores of the two teams are level.* **3** steady, even and not rising or falling much: *a calm, level voice.* – *v* – *pt, ptp* **'levelled**, (*Amer*) **'leveled** – **1** to make flat, smooth or horizontal: *He levelled the soil.* **2** to make equal: *His goal levelled the scores of the two teams.* **3** (*usu* with **at**) to aim (a gun *etc*): *He levelled his pistol at the target.* **4** to pull down: *The bulldozer levelled the block of flats.*
'levelness *n.*
level crossing a place where a road crosses a railway without a bridge.
level-'headed *adj* calm and sensible.
do one's level best to do one's very best.
level off to make or become flat, even, steady *etc*: *After rising for so long, prices have now levelled off.*

level out to make or become level: *The road levels out as it comes down to the plain.*
on a level with level with: *His eyes were on a level with the shop counter.*
on the level fair; honest.

lever ['liːvə, (*Amer*) 'levər] *n* **1** a bar of wood, metal *etc* used to lift heavy weights: *A crowbar is a kind of lever; You must use a coin as a lever to get the lid of that tin off.* **2** a bar or handle for operating a machine *etc*: *This is the lever that switches on the power.* – *v* to move with or as if with a lever: *He levered the lid off with a coin.*
'leverage [-ridʒ] *n* the power gained by the use of a lever.

levy ['levi] *v* to raise or collect (*esp* an army or a tax): *A tax was levied on tobacco.* – *n* – *pl* **'levies** – **1** soldiers or money collected by order: *a levy on imports.* **2** the act of levying.

lexicon ['leksikən, (*Amer*) -kon] *n* a dictionary.

liable ['laiəbl] *adj* **1** (with **to**) tending to have, get, suffer from *etc*: *This road is liable to flooding; He is liable to pneumonia.* **2** possibly or probably about (to do something or to happen): *Watch the milk – it's liable to boil over.* **lia'bility** *n.*

liaison [liːˈeizon, (*Amer*) 'liːeizon] *n* a contact or communication: *liaison between parents and teachers;* (*also adj*) a liason officer.
liaise [liːˈeiz] *v* to communicate or make contact (with) *esp* as an official duty.

liar *see* **lie**[1].

libel ['laibəl] *n* the legal term for something written which is harmful to a person's reputation. – *v* – *pt, ptp* **'libelled**, (*Amer*) **'libeled** – to damage the reputation of (someone) by libel.
'libellous *adj.* **'libellously** *adv.*

liberal ['libərəl] *adj* **1** generous: *She gave me a liberal helping of apple pie; She was very liberal with her money.* **2** tolerant; not criticizing or disapproving: *The headmaster is very liberal in his attitude to young people.* **3** (*also n*) (*esp* with *cap*) in politics, (a person belonging to a party) favouring liberty for the individual. **libe'rality** [-'ra-] *n.* **'liberally** *adv.*

liberate ['libəreit] *v* to set free: *The prisoners were liberated by the new government.* **libe'ration** *n.* **'liberator** *n.*

liberty ['libəti] *n* **1** freedom from captivity or from slavery: *He ordered that all prisoners should be given their liberty.* **2** freedom to do as one pleases: *Children have a lot more liberty now than they used to.* **3** (*esp* with **take**) too great freedom of speech or action: *I think it was* (*taking*) *a liberty to ask her such a question!*
'liberties *n pl* privileges, rights *etc*: *civil liberties.*

take the liberty of to do without permission: *I took the liberty of moving the papers from your desk – I hope you don't mind.*

library ['laibrəri] – *pl* **'libraries** – *n* (a building or room containing) a collection of books or of gramophone records *etc*: *He works in the public library*; *She has a fine library of books about art.*

li'brarian [-'breə-] *n* a person who is employed in a library.

lice *see* **louse**.

licence, (*Amer*) **license** ['laisəns] *n* **a** (a printed) form giving permission to do something (*eg* to keep a television set *etc*, drive a car, sell alcohol *etc*): *a driving licence.*

'license *v* to give a licence to or permit: *He is licensed to sell alcohol.*

'licensed *adj* (of a shop, hotel *etc*) legally allowed to sell alcohol to customers: *a licensed grocer.*

licen'see *n* a person to whom a licence (*esp* to keep a licensed hotel or public house) has been given.

licence is a noun: a licence (not license) to sell alcohol.
license is a verb: licensed (not licenced) to drive a goods vehicle.

lichee *see* **lychee**.

lichen ['laikən] *n* any of a large group of tiny plants which grow over stones, trees *etc*.

lick [lik] *v* to pass the tongue over: *The dog licked her hand.* – *n* **1** an act of licking: *The child gave the ice-cream a lick.* **2** a hasty application (of paint): *These doors could do with a lick of paint.*

lick into shape to put into a better or more efficient form.

lid [lid] *n* **1** a cover for a pot, box *etc*: *He lifted the lid of the box and looked inside.* **2** an eyelid: *The infection has not affected the eye itself although the lid is swollen.*

lie¹ [lai] *n* a false statement made with the intention of deceiving: *It would be a lie to say I knew, because I didn't.* – *v* – *prp* **'lying**; *pt, ptp* **lied** – to say *etc* something which is not true, with the intention of deceiving: *There's no point in asking her – she'll just lie about it.*

liar ['laiə] *n* a person who tells lies, *esp* as a habit: *You can't trust what she says – she's such a liar.*

see also lay¹.

lie² [lai] – *prp* **'lying**: *pt* **lay** [lei]; *ptp* **lain** [lein] – *v* **1** to be in or take a more or less flat position: *She went into the bedroom and lay on the bed*; *The book was lying in the hall.* **2** to be situated; to be in a particular place *etc*: *The farm lay three miles from the sea*; *His interest lies in farming.* **3** to remain in a certain state: *The shop is lying empty now.*

4 (*with* **in**) (of feelings, impressions *etc*) to be caused by or contained in: *His charm lies in his honesty.*

lie back to lean back on a support: *He lay back against the pillows and went to sleep.*

lie down to take a flat or horizontal position: *The man lay down*; *My hair won't lie down.*

lie in to stay in bed late in the morning: *I like to lie in until nine on a Saturday.*

lie in wait (for) to be waiting to catch or attack: *They lay in wait at the corner of the street and attacked him on his way home.*

lie low to stay quiet or hidden: *The criminal lay low until the police stopped looking for him.*

lie with (of a choice, duty *etc*) to be the responsibility of: *The decision lies with you.*

take lying down to accept or suffer (something) without arguing, complaining or trying to avoid it.

see also lay¹.

lieutenant [ləf'tenənt], (*Amer*) lu:-] *n* (*often abbrev* **Lt.**, **Lieut.**, *when written*) **1** in the army, the rank next below captain. **2** in the navy, the rank next below lieutenant-commander.

life [laif] – *pl* **lives** [laivz] – *n* **1** the quality belonging to plants and animals which distinguishes them from rocks, minerals *etc* and things which are dead: *Doctors are fighting to save the child's life.* **2** the period between birth and death: *He had a long and happy life.* **3** liveliness: *She was full of life and energy.* **4** a manner of living: *She lived a life of ease and idleness.* **5** the period during which any particular state exists: *He had many different jobs during his working life.* **6** living things: *It is now believed that there is no life on Mars*; *animal life.* **7** the story of a life: *He has written a life of Churchill.* **8** life imprisonment: *He was given life for murder.*

'lifeless *adj* **1** dead: *a lifeless body.* **2** not lively; uninteresting: *The actress gave a lifeless performance.*

'lifelike *adj* like a living person, animal *etc*: *The statue was very lifelike*; *a lifelike portrait.*

life-and-'death *adj* serious and deciding between life and death: *a life-and-death struggle.*

'lifebelt *n* a ring or belt filled with air or made of a material which floats, for keeping a person afloat.

'lifeboat *n* a boat for saving shipwrecked people.

'lifebuoy *n* a buoy intended to support a person in the water till he can be rescued.

'life-cycle *n* the various stages through

which a living thing passes: *the life-cycle of the snail.*

life expectancy the (average) length of time a person can expect to live.

'**lifeguard** *n* a person employed to protect and rescue swimmers at a swimming-pool, beach *etc.*

'**life-jacket** *n* a sleeveless jacket filled with material that will float, for keeping a person afloat.

'**lifeline** *n* a rope for support in dangerous operations or thrown to rescue a drowning person.

'**lifelong** *adj* lasting the whole length of a life: *a lifelong friendship.*

'**life-saving** *n* the act or skill of rescuing people from drowning: *The boy is being taught life-saving.*

'**life-size(d)** *adj, adv* (of a copy, drawing *etc*) as large as the original: *a life-sized statue.*

'**lifetime** *n* the period of a person's life: *He saw many changes in his lifetime.*

as large as life in person; actually: *I went to the party and there was John as large as life.*

bring to life to make lively or interesting: *His lectures really brought the subject to life.*

come to life to become lively or interesting: *The play did not come to life until the last act.*

for life until death: *They became friends for life.*

the life and soul of the party a person who is very active, enthusiastic, amusing *etc* at a party.

not for the life of me not even if it was necessary in order to save my life: *I couldn't for the life of me remember his name!*

not on your life! certainly not!: *'Will you get married?' 'Not on your life!'*

take life to kill: *It is a sin to take life.*

take one's life to kill oneself.

take one's life in one's hands to take the risk of being killed.

to the life exactly (like): *When he put on that uniform, he was Napoleon to the life.*

lift [lift] *v* **1** to raise or bring to a higher position: *The box was so heavy I couldn't lift it.* **2** to take and carry away: *He lifted the table through into the kitchen.* **3** (of mist *etc*) to disappear: *By noon, the fog was beginning to lift.* **4** to rise: *The aeroplane lifted into the air.* – *n* **1** the act of lifting: *a lift of the eyebrows.* **2** (*Amer* '**elevator**) a small enclosed platform *etc* that moves up and down between floors carrying goods or people: *Since she was too tired to climb the stairs, she went up in the lift.* **3** a ride in someone's car *etc*: *Can I give you a lift into town?* **4** a raising of the spirits: *Her success in the exam gave her a great lift.*

lift off (of a rocket *etc*) to leave the ground (*n* '**lift-off**).

ligament ['ligǝmǝnt] *n* a piece of tough substance that joins together the bones of the body: *She pulled a ligament in her knee when she fell.*

light¹ [lait] *n* **1** the brightness given by the sun, a flame, lamps *etc* that makes things able to be seen: *It was nearly dawn and the light was getting stronger; Sunlight streamed into the room.* **2** something which gives light (*eg* a lamp): *Suddenly all the lights went out.* **3** something which can be used to set fire to something else; a flame: *Have you got a light* (= a match *etc*) *for my cigarette?* **4** a way of viewing or regarding: *He regarded her action in a favourable light.* – *adj* **1** having light; not dark: *The studio was a large, light room.* **2** (of a colour) pale; closer to white than black: *light green.* – *v* – *pt, ptp* **lit** [lit], '**lighted** – **1** to give light to: *The room was lit only by candles.* **2** to (make something) catch fire: *She lit the gas; I think this match is damp, because it won't light.*

'**lightness¹** *n.*

'**lighten¹** *v* to make or become brighter: *The white ceiling lightened the room; The sky was lightening.*

'**lighter** *n* something used for lighting (a cigarette *etc*).

'**lighting** *n* a means of providing light: *The lighting was so bad in the restaurant that we could hardly see.*

lighthouse *n* a building built on rocks, coastline *etc* with a (flashing) light to guide or warn ships.

'**light-year** *n* the distance light travels in a year (nearly 9.5 million million kilometres).

bring to light to reveal or cause to be noticed: *The scandal was brought to light by the investigations of a journalist.*

come to light to be revealed or discovered: *The manuscript came to light in a box of books at an auction.*

in the light of taking into consideration (*eg* new information): *The theory has been abandoned in the light of more recent discoveries.*

light up 1 to begin to give out light: *Evening came and the streetlights lit up.* **2** to make, be or become full of light: *The powerful searchlight lit up the building; She watched the house light up as everyone awoke.* **3** to make or become happy: *Her face lit up when she saw him; A sudden smile lit up her face.*

see the light 1 to be born, discovered, produced *etc*: *After many problems his invention finally saw the light (of day).* **2** to be converted to someone else's point of view *etc.*

set light to to cause to begin burning: *He set light to the pile of rubbish in his garden.*

light² [lait] *adj* **1** easy to lift or carry; of little weight: *I bought a light suitcase for plane journeys.* 2 easy to bear, suffer or do: *Next time the punishment will not be so light.* 3 (of food) easy to digest: *a light meal.* 4 of less weight than it should be: *The load of grain was several kilos light.* 5 of little weight: *Aluminium is a light metal.* 6 lively or agile: *She was very light on her feet.* 7 cheerful; not serious: *light music.* 8 little in quantity; not intense, heavy, strong *etc*: *light rain.* 9 (of soil) containing a lot of sand. **'lightly** *adv.* **'lightness²** *n.*

'lighten² *v* to make or become less heavy: *She lightened her suitcase by taking out several pairs of shoes; The postman's bag of parcels lightened as he went from house to house.*

,light-'fingered *adj* inclined to steal things.

,light-'headed *adj* dizzy and giddy.

,light-'hearted *adj* happy and free from anxiety; not grave or serious: *a light-hearted mood.*

'lightweight *adj* light in weight: *a lightweight raincoat.*

get off lightly to escape or be allowed to go without severe punishment *etc*.

make light of to treat (problems *etc*) as unimportant.

travel light to travel with little luggage.

light³ [lait]: **light on** – *pt, ptp* **lit** [lit] – to find by chance: *While wandering round the town, we lit on a very cheap restaurant.*

lighten *see* light¹, light².

lighter *see* light¹.

lightning ['laitniŋ] *n* a flash of electricity between clouds or from a cloud to earth during a storm, *usu* followed by thunder: *The house was struck by lightning.*

a flash of **lightning** (not **lightening**). **lightening** is the present participle of **lighten**, to make or become lighter.

like¹ [laik] *adj* the same or similar: *They're as like as two peas.* – *prep* the same as or similar to; in the same or a similar way as: *He climbs like a cat; She is like her mother.* – *n* someone or something which is the same or as good *etc* as another: *You won't see his like/their like again.* – *conj* (*esp Amer*) in the same or a similar way as: *No-one does it like he does.*

'likely *adj* 1 probable: *the likely result; It's likely that she'll succeed.* 2 looking *etc* as if it might be good, useful, suitable *etc*: *a likely spot for a picnic; She's the most likely person for the job.*

'likelihood *n* probability.

'liken *v* to think or speak of as being similar; to compare: *He likened the earth to an apple.*

'likeness *n* 1 (a) similarity or resemblance: *The likeness between them is amazing.* 2 a

representation of a a person *etc* in a photographic or painted portrait *etc*: *That photo of Mary is a good likeness.*

'likewise *adv* 1 in the same or a similar manner: *He ignored her, and she ignored him likewise.* 2 also: *Mrs. Brown came, likewise Mrs. Smith.*

like-'minded *adj* having a similar opinion or purpose.

a likely story! I don't believe it!

as likely as not probably: *As likely as not, he won't remember to come.*

be like someone to be typical of someone: *It isn't like him to be late.*

feel like to be inclined, willing or anxious to (do or have something): *I don't feel like going out; I expect he feels like a cup of tea.*

he etc is likely to it is probable that he *etc* will: *He is likely to fail.*

look like 1 to appear similar to: *She looks very like her mother.* 2 to show the effects, signs or possibility of: *It looks like rain.*

not likely! certainly not!: *'Would you put your head in a lion's mouth?' 'Me? Not likely!'*

like² [laik] *v* 1 to be pleased with; to find pleasant or agreeable: *I like him very much; I like the way you've decorated this room.* 2 to enjoy: *I like gardening.*

'lik(e)able *adj* (of a person) agreeable or attractive.

'liking *n* 1 a taste or fondness (for): *He has too great a liking for chocolate.* 2 satisfaction: *Is the meal to your liking?*

should/would like want: *I would like to say thank you; Would you like a cup of tea?*

take a liking to to begin to like: *I've taken a liking to him.*

lilac ['lailǝk] *n* 1 a type of small tree with bunches of white or pale purple flowers. 2 (*also adj*) (of) a pale, *usu* pinkish, purple colour: *lilac sheets.*

lilt [lilt] *n* (a tune *etc* with) a strong rhythm.

lily ['lili] – *pl* **'lilies** – *n* a type of tall plant grown from a bulb, with white or coloured flowers.

limb [lim] *n* 1 an arm or leg. 2 a branch.

out on a limb on one's own and in a dangerous or disadvantageous position.

limber ['limbǝ]: **limber up** to exercise so as to become able to move easily.

lime¹ [laim] *n* the white substance left after heating limestone, used in making cement. **'limestone** *n* a kind of rock. **'limelight: in the limelight** attracting the public's attention.

***lime²** [laim] *n* 1 a type of small, very sour, yellowish-green citrus fruit related to the lemon. 2 (*also adj*) (of) the colour of this fruit: *lime walls.*

***lime³** [laim] *n* a tree with rough bark and small heart-shaped leaves.

* see illustrations on pp. 201, 573

limelight *see* **lime**[1].

limerick ['limərik] *n* a type of humorous poem with five lines, the third and fourth lines being shorter than the others.

limit ['limit] *n* **1** the farthest point or place; the boundary: *There was no limit to his ambition.* **2** a restriction: *We must put a limit on our spending.* – *v* to set a restriction on: *We must limit the amount of time we spend on this work.*

limi'tation *n* **1** an act of limiting. **2** a lack, *eg* of a particular facility, ability *etc*: *We all have our limitations.*

'limited *adj* **1** (*neg* **un-**) not very great, large *etc*; restricted: *My experience is rather limited.* **2** (*with cap, abbrev* **Ltd.** *when written*) a word used in the titles of certain companies: *W. and R. Chambers Ltd.*

'limitless *adj*.

limousine ['limuzi:n] *n* a kind of large motor car *esp* one with a screen separating the front seat from the back.

limp[1] [limp] *adj* lacking stiffness or strength; drooping: *a limp lettuce; a limp excuse.*

limp[2] [limp] *v* to walk in an uneven manner (*usu* because one has hurt one's foot or leg): *He twisted his ankle and came limping home.* – *n* the act of limping: *He walks with a limp.*

limpet ['limpit] *n* a type of small, cone-shaped shellfish that fastens itself very firmly to rocks.

line[1] [lain] *n* **1** (a piece of) thread, cord, rope *etc*: *She hung the washing on the line; a fishing-rod and line.* **2** a long, narrow mark, streak or stripe: *She drew straight lines across the page; a dotted/wavy line.* **3** outline or shape *esp* relating to length or direction: *The ship had very graceful lines; A dancer uses a mirror to improve his line.* **4** a groove on the skin; a wrinkle. **5** a row or group of objects or persons arranged side by side or one behind the other: *The children stood in a line; a line of trees.* **6** a short letter: *I'll drop him a line.* **7** a series or group of persons which come one after the other *esp* in the same family: *a line of kings.* **8** a track or direction: *He pointed out the line of the new road; a new line of research.* **9** the railway or a single track of the railway: *Passengers must cross the line by the bridge only.* **10** a continuous system (*esp* of pipes, electrical or telephone cables *etc*) connecting one place with another: *a pipeline; a line of communication; All (telephone) lines are engaged.* **11** a row of written or printed words: *The letter contained only three lines; a poem of sixteen lines.* **12** a regular service of ships, aircraft *etc*: *a shipping line.* **13** a group or class (of goods for sale) or a field of activity, interest *etc*: *This has been a very popular new line; Computers are not really my line.* **14** an

arrangement of troops, *esp* when ready to fight: *fighting in the front line.* – *v* **1** to form lines along: *Crowds lined the pavement to see the Queen.* **2** to mark with lines.

lineage ['liniidʒ] *n* ancestry.

linear ['liniə] *adj* of, consisting of or like a line or lines.

lined[1] *adj* having lines: *lined paper; a lined face.*

'liner[1] *n* a ship or aircraft of a regular line or company: *They sailed to America in a large liner.*

lines *n pl* the words an actor has to say: *He had difficulty remembering his lines.*

'linesman ['lainz-] *n* in sport, a judge or umpire at a boundary line.

in line for likely to get or to be given something: *He is in line for promotion.*

in, out of line with in or out of agreement with: *His views are out of line with those of his colleagues.*

line up 1 to form a line: *The children lined up ready to leave the classroom; She lined up the chairs.* **2** to collect and arrange in readiness: *We've lined up several interesting guests to appear on the programme* (*n* **'line-up**).

read between the lines to understand something (from a piece of writing *etc*) which is not actually stated.

line[2] [lain] *v* **1** to cover on the inside: *She lined the box with newspaper.* **2** to put a lining in: *She lined the dress with silk.*

lined[2] *adj* (*neg* **un-**) having a lining: *a lined skirt.*

'liner[2] *n* something used for lining: *a dustbin liner; a nappy liner.*

'lining *n* **1** (a) covering on the inside: *The basket had a padded lining.* **2** a fairly exact copy (of a piece of clothing) attached to the inside to help keep its shape *etc*: *The lining of my jacket is torn.*

linen ['linin] *n* **1** (*also adj*) (of) cloth made of flax used to make sheets, tablecloths, tea-towels *etc*: *This handkerchief is made of linen; linen sheets.* **2** articles made of linen or, now more usually, cotton: *table-linen; bed-linen.*

liner *see* **line**[1], **line**[2].

linger ['liŋɡə] *v* **1** to remain, last or continue for a long time or after the expected time: *The smell of the bad fish lingered for days.* **2** to proceed slowly or delay: *We lingered in the hall, looking at the pictures.*

lingerie ['lãʒəri:] *n* women's underwear.

linguist ['liŋɡwist] *n* a person who studies language and/or is good at languages.

lin'guistic *adj* of languages.

lin'guistics *n sing* the science of languages.

lining *see* **line**[2].

link [liŋk] *n* **1** a ring of a chain: *There was a worn link in the chain and it broke; an important link in the chain of the evidence.*

2 anything connecting two things: *His job was to act as a link between the government and the press.* – *v* to connect as by a link: *The new train service links the suburbs with the heart of the city.*

link up to join or be joined closely or by a link: *An electrician called to link up our house to the mains electricity supply* (*n* **'link-up**).

links [liŋks] *n pl* **1** a stretch of more or less flat ground along a seashore. **2** (*often with sing verb*) a golf course.

linoleum [li'nouliəm] *n* (*abbrev* **lino** ['lainou]) a type of smooth, hard-wearing covering for floors.

lint [lint] *n* **1** linen in the form of a soft fluffy material for putting over wounds. **2** very small pieces of fluff from cotton *etc*.

lion ['laiən] – *fem* **'lioness** – *n* a type of large, flesh-eating animal of the cat family, the male of which has a long, coarse mane.

the lion's share the largest share.

lip [lip] *n* **1** either of the folds of flesh which form the edge of the mouth: *She bit her lip.* **2** the edge of something: *the lip of a cup.*
-lipped: *a thin-lipped mouth.*

'lip-read *v* (of a deaf person) to understand what a person is saying by watching the movement of his lips.

'lipstick *n* (a stick of) colouring for the lips.

pay lip-service to to show respect to, or approval of, in word only, without sincerely feeling it.

liquefy *see* **liquid**.

liqueur [li'kjuə, (*Amer*) -'kəːr] *n* a strong, very sweet alcoholic drink.

liquid ['likwid] *adj* able to flow; not solid, but not a gas: *liquid nitrogen; The ice-cream has become liquid.* – *n* a substance which flows, like water: *a clear liquid.*

liquefy ['likwifai] *v* to make or become liquid: *The butter had liquefied in the heat.*

'liquidate [-deit] *v* **1** to close, and finish the affairs of (a business *etc* that has no money to continue). **2** to get rid of. ˌ**liqui'dation** *n*.
'liquidator *n*.

'liquidize, -ise *v* to make (food *etc*) into a liquid or semi-liquid substance by grinding it up in a liquidizer.

'liquidizer, -s- *n* an electrical device used in cookery to grind up food.

liquor ['likə] *n* strong alcoholic drink.

lira ['liərə] – *pl* **lire** ['liərei] – *n* the standard unit of Italian currency.

list¹ [list] *n* a series *eg* of names, numbers, prices *etc* written down or said one after the other: *a shopping-list; We have a long list of people who are willing to help.* – *v* to place in a list: *He listed the things he had to do.*

list² [list] *v* to lean over to one side: *The ship is listing.* – *n*: *The ship had a heavy list.*

listen ['lisn] *v* **1** (*often with* **to**) to give attention so as to hear (what someone is saying *etc*): *I*

told her three times, but she wasn't listening; *Do listen to the music!* **2** (*with* **to**) to follow the advice of: *If she'd listened to me, she wouldn't have got into trouble.*

listen in on to listen intentionally to (a private conversation *etc*).

listless ['listlis] *adj* tired and without energy or interest: *listless children.* **'listlessly** *adv.* **'listlessness** *n*.

lit *see* **light¹, light³**.

liter *see* **litre**.

literacy *see* **literate**.

literal ['litərəl] *adj* **1** following the exact meaning with no exaggeration: *the literal truth.* **2** understanding the meaning by taking one word at a time: *a literal translation.* **'literalness** *n*.

'literally *adv*: *We had literally a minute to catch the train.*

literary ['litərəri] *adj* **1** concerning literature or the writing of books: *a literary magazine.* **2** (of a person) knowledgeable about books.

literate ['litərət] *adj* **1** able to read and write. **2** clever and having read a great deal. **'literacy** *n*.

literature ['litrətʃə] *n* poems, novels, plays *etc* in verse or prose, *esp* if of fine quality.

lithe [laið] *adj* (used *esp* of the human body) bending easily; flexible: *as lithe as a cat.* **'litheness** *n*.

litigation [liti'geiʃən] *n* a private law-suit.

litre, (*Amer*) liter ['liːtə] *n* a measure of (*usu* liquid) capacity: *a litre of wine.*

litter ['litə] *n* **1** an untidy mess of paper, rubbish *etc*: *Put your litter in that bin.* **2** a heap of straw *etc* for animals to lie on *etc* **3** a number of animals born to the same mother at the same time: *a litter of kittens.* – *v* to cover (the ground *etc*) with scattered objects: *Papers littered the table.*

little ['litl] *adj* **1** small in size: *He is only a little boy; when she was little* (= a child). **2** small in amount; not much: *He has little knowledge of the difficulties involved.* **3** not important: *I did not expect her to make a fuss about such a little thing.* – *pron* (only) a small amount: *He knows little of the real world.* – *adv* **1** not much: *I go out little nowadays.* **2** only to a small degree: *a little-known fact.* **3** not at all: *He little knows how ill he is.*

a little 1 a short time or distance: *Move a little to the right!* **2** a small quantity of something: *He has a little money to spare; 'Is there any soup left?' 'Yes, a little.'* **3** slightly: *She was a little frightened.*

little by little gradually: *Little by little we began to get to know him.*

make little of 1 to treat as unimportant *etc*: *He made little of his injuries.* **2** not to be able to understand: *I could make little of his instructions.*

little means 'not much': *You have little reason to boast.*
a little means 'some', 'a small quantity': *There's a little milk left.*

live¹ [liv] *v* **1** to have life; to be alive: *This poison is dangerous to everything that lives.* **2** to survive: *The doctors say he is very ill, but they think he will live*; *It was difficult to believe that she had lived through such an experience.* **3** to have one's home or dwelling (in a particular place): *She lives next to the church*; *They went to live in Bristol/in a huge house.* **4** to pass (one's life): *He lived a life of luxury*; *She lives in fear of being attacked.* **5** (*with* **by**) to make enough money *etc* to feed and house oneself: *He lives by fishing.*
-lived *adj* having (a certain type of) life: *long-lived.*
'living *adj* **1** having life; being alive: *a living creature*; *The aim of the project was to discover if there was anything living on Mars.* **2** now alive: *the greatest living artist.* – *n* the money *etc* needed to feed and house oneself and keep oneself alive: *He earns his living driving a taxi*; *She makes a good living as an author.*
'living-room *n* the room of a house *etc* in which the occupants of the house usually sit during their leisure time.
live and let live to tolerate other people's actions and expect them to tolerate one's own.
live down to live through the shame of (a foolish act *etc*) till it is forgotten.
live in, out to have one's home at, away from, the place where one works: *All the hotel staff live in*; *The nurse chose to live out.*
live on 1 to keep oneself alive by eating: *He lives on fish and potatoes.* **2** to be supported (financially) by: *He lives on $40 a week.*
live up to to behave in a manner worthy of: *He found it difficult to live up to his reputation as a hero.*
(with)in living memory within a period recent enough to be remembered by someone still alive: *It was the worst harvest in living memory.*
live² [laiv] *adj* **1** having life; not dead: *a live mouse.* **2** (of a radio or television broadcast *etc*) heard or seen as the event takes place; not recorded: *I watched a live performance of my favourite opera on television*; *Was the performance live or recorded?* **3** full of energy, and capable of becoming active: *a live bomb.* **4** burning: *a live coal.* – *adv* (of a radio or television broadcast *etc*) as the event takes place: *The competition will be broadcast live.*
'lively *adj* active; full of life, high spirits or

movement: *She took a lively interest in us*; *The music is bright and lively.* **'liveliness** *n.*
'livestock *n* domestic animals, *esp* horses, cattle, sheep, and pigs.
live wire 1 a wire charged with electricity. **2** a person who is full of energy and enthusiasm: *He is very quiet, but his sister is a real live wire.*
livelihood ['laivlihud] *n* a means of living, *esp* of earning enough money to feed oneself *etc.*
liveliness, lively *see* **live².**
liver ['livə] *n* **1** a large organ in the body which purifies the blood. **2** this organ in certain animals used as food.
lives *see* **life.**
livestock *see* **live².**
living *see* **live¹.**
lizard ['lizəd] *n* any of several types of *usu* small, four-footed reptile.
lo [lou]: **lo and behold** an expression indicating surprise *etc* at seeing or finding something.
load [loud] *n* **1** something which is being carried: *The lorry had to stop because its load had fallen off*; *She was carrying a load of groceries.* **2** as much as can be carried at one time: *two lorry-loads of earth.* **3** a large amount: *He talked a load of rubbish*; *We ate loads of ice-cream.* **4** the power carried by an electric circuit: *The wires were designed for a load of 15 amps.* – *v* **1** to take or put on what is to be carried (*esp* if heavy): *They loaded the luggage into the car*; *The lorry was loading when they arrived.* **2** to put ammunition into (a gun): *He loaded the revolver and fired.* **3** to put film into (a camera).
'loaded *adj* **1** carrying a load: *a loaded van.* **2** (of a gun) containing ammunition: *a loaded pistol.* **3** (of a camera) containing film.
loaf¹ [louf] – *pl* **loaves** [louvz] – *n* a shaped mass of bread: *a sliced loaf.*
loaf² [louf] *v* (*with* **about** *or* **around**) to pass time without doing anything in particular: *They were loafing about (the street).*
'loafer *n: an idle loafer.*
loan [loun] *n* **1** anything lent, *esp* money: *I shall ask the bank for a loan.* **2** the act of lending: *I gave him the loan of my bicycle.* – *v* (*esp Amer*) to lend: *Can you loan me a pen?*
loathe [louð] *v* to hate very much.
'loathing *n* great dislike and disgust.
'loathsome *adj* horrible.
loaves *see* **loaf¹.**
lob [lob] *n* a slow, high throw, hit *etc* of a ball *etc.* – *v* – *pt, ptp* **lobbed** – to throw or strike (a ball *etc*) so that it moves high and slowly: *He lobbed the ball over the net.*
lobby ['lobi] – *pl* **'lobbies** – *n* **1** a (small)

entrance-hall: *a hotel lobby*. 2 a group of people who try to influence the Government *etc* in a certain way or for a certain purpose. – *v* to try to influence (the Government *etc*).

lobe [loub] *n* 1 the soft lower part of the ear. 2 a division of the lungs, brain *etc*.

lobster ['lobstə] *n* a type of shellfish with large claws.

local ['loukəl] *adj* belonging to a certain place or district: *The local shops are very good*; *local problems*. '**locally** *adv*.
  locality [lə'kaləti] – *pl* **lo'calities** – *n* a district: *Public transport is a problem in this locality*.
  locate [lə'keit, (*Amer*) 'loukeit] *v* 1 to set in a particular place or position: *The kitchen is located in the basement*. 2 to find the place or position of: *He located the street he was looking for on the map*.
  lo'cation [-'keiʃən] *n* 1 position or situation. 2 the act of locating.
  on location (of filming) in natural surroundings outside the studio.

lock¹ [lok] *n* 1 a mechanism for fastening doors *etc*: *He put the key in the lock*. 2 a closed part of a canal for raising or lowering boats to a higher or lower part of the canal. 3 the part of a gun by which it is fired. 4 a tight hold (in wrestling *etc*). – *v* to fasten or become fastened with a lock: *She locked the drawer*; *This door doesn't lock*.
  '**locker** *n* a small cupboard, *esp* for sports equipment.
  '**locket** [-kit] *n* a little ornamental case hung round the neck: *a gold locket containing a piece of his hair*.
  '**locksmith** *n* a person who makes and mends locks.
  lock in to prevent from getting out of a building *etc* by using a lock: *She found she was locked in, and had to climb out of the window*.
  lock out to prevent from getting into a building *etc* by using a lock: *Don't lock yourself out (of the house) by forgetting to take your key with you*.
  lock up 1 to confine or prevent from leaving or being taken away by using a lock: *to lock up a prisoner/one's jewellery*. 2 to lock whatever should be locked: *He locked up and left the shop about 5.30 p.m.*

lock² [lok] *n* 1 a piece of hair: *She cut off a lock of his hair*. 2 (*in pl*) hair: *curly brown locks*.

locomotive [loukə'moutiv] *n* a railway engine.
  ,**loco'motion** [-'mouʃən] *n* the process of moving from place to place.

locum ['loukəm] *n* a person who takes the place of another (*esp* a doctor, dentist *etc*) for a time.

locust ['loukəst] *n* a type of large insect of the grasshopper family, found in Africa and Asia, which moves in very large groups and destroys growing crops by eating them.

lodge [lodʒ] *n* 1 a small house, *esp* one at a gate to the grounds of a large house. 2 a room at a college gate *etc* for an attendant: *the porter's lodge*. – *v* 1 to live in rooms for which one pays, in someone else's house: *He lodges with the Smiths*. 2 to make or become fixed: *The bullet was lodged in his spine*. 3 to make (an objection, an appeal *etc*) formally or officially.
  '**lodger** *n* a person who lives in a room or rooms, for which he pays, in someone else's house: *She rented a room to a lodger*.
  '**lodging** 1 (*often in pl*) a room or rooms hired in someone else's house: *She lives in lodgings*. 2 a place to stay: *He paid the landlady for board and lodging*.

loft [loft] *n* a room or space under a roof: *They kept a lot of spare furniture in the loft*.
  '**lofty** *adj* 1 very high: *a lofty building*. 2 haughty or proud: *a lofty attitude*.
  '**loftily** *adv*. '**loftiness** *n*.

log [log] *n* 1 a thick piece of unshaped wood: *The trees were sawn into logs and taken to the sawmill*. 2 a logbook: *The captain of the ship entered the details in the log*. – *v* – *pt*, *ptp* **logged** – to write down or record in a logbook (*esp* the distance covered during a journey).
  '**logbook** *n* an official record of the journey of a ship or aeroplane: *All the details of the flight were entered in the logbook*.

logarithm ['logəriðəm] *n* (*abbrev* **log** [log]) the number of times *eg* 10 must be multiplied by itself to produce a particular number: $10 \times 10 \times 10$ or $10^3 = 1000$, so 3 is here the logarithm of 1000.

loggerheads ['logəhedz]: **at loggerheads** quarrelling: *They're always at loggerheads with their neighbours*.

logic ['lodʒik] *n* (the study and art of) reasoning correctly.
  '**logical** *adj* (thinking or acting) according to the rules of logic: *It is logical to assume that you will get a higher salary if you are promoted*; *She is always logical in her thinking*. '**logically** *adv*.

loin [loin] *n* the back of an animal when cut into pieces for food.
  '**loincloth** *n* a piece of cloth worn round the hips, *esp* in India.

loiter ['loitə] *v* to proceed, work *etc* slowly or to stand doing nothing in particular: *They were loitering outside the ship*.

loll [lol] *v* 1 to sit or lie lazily: *to loll in a chair*; *You'll get nothing done if you loll about all day*. 2 (of the tongue) to hang down or out: *The dog lay down with his tongue lolling*.

lollipop ['lolipop] *n* a large sweet on a stick for sucking.

lolly ['loli] – *pl* **'lollies** – *n* **1** a lollipop, or a similar type of sweet made of ice-cream *etc*: *an ice-lolly.* **2** a slang word for money.

lone [loun] *adj* solitary, without companions, by itself *etc*: *a lone figure on the beach.*
'lonely *adj* **1** lacking or wanting companionship: *Aren't you lonely, living by yourself?* **2** (of a place) far away from busy places, having few people: *a lonely island.* **'loneliness** *n.*
'lonesome *adj* (*esp Amer*) lonely; solitary: *She feels lonesome when her brothers are at school.* **'lonesomeness** *n.*

long¹ [loŋ] *adj* **1** measuring a great distance from one end to the other: *a long journey*; *a long road*; *long legs.* **2** having a great period of time from the first moment to the last: *The book took a long time to read*; *a long conversation*; *a long delay.* **3** measuring a certain amount in distance or time: *The wire is two centimetres long*; *The television programme was just over an hour long.* **4** away, doing or using something *etc* for a great period of time: *Will you be long?* **5** reaching to a great distance in space or time: *She has a long memory.* – *adv* **1** a great period of time: *This happened long before you were born.* **2** for a great period of time: *Have you been waiting long?*
'longways *adv* in the direction of the length: *The planks had to go into the lorry longways.*
,long-'distance *adj*: *long-distance races*; *a long-distance lorry-driver.*
,long-drawn-'out *adj* taking a needlessly long time: *long-drawn-out discussions.*
'longhand *n* ordinary writing as opposed to shorthand.
long house in tribal societies, a long rectangular dwelling shared by several families, *esp* in south-east Asia and amongst North American Indians.
long jump a sports contest in which people jump as far as possible.
long-playing record (*usu abbrev* **LP**) a gramophone record which plays for a long time.
,long-'range *adj* **1** able to reach a great distance: *long-range rockets.* **2** taking into consideration a long period of time: *a long-range weather forecast.*
,long-'sighted *adj* having difficulty in seeing close objects clearly. **,long-'sightedness** *n.*
,long-'suffering *adj* patiently enduring a great deal of trouble.
,long-'winded *adj* (of a speaker or his speech) tiresomely long.
as long as/so long as 1 provided only that: *As/So long as you're happy, it doesn't matter what you do.* **2** while; during the time that: *As long as he's here I'll have more work to do.*
before (very) long soon: *Come in and wait – he'll be here before long!*

in the long run in the end: *We thought we would save money, but in the long run our spending was about the same as usual.*
the long and the short of it whole story in a few words.
no longer not now as in the past: *This cinema is no longer used.*
so long! goodbye!

long² [loŋ] *v* (*often with* for) to wish very much: *He longed to go home*; *I am longing for a drink.*
'longing *n* a great desire or wish for something: *She looked at the cakes with longing.*
'longingly *adv*: *She looked longingly at the chocolate.*

*longan ['loŋgan] *n* a small round brown-skinned edible fruit with a dark brown seed.

longevity [lon'dʒevəti] *n* great length of life.

longitude ['loŋgitjuːd] *n* the distance, measured in degrees on the map, that a place is east or west of a standard north-south line, *usu* that which passes through Greenwich: *What is the latitude and longitude of that town?* **,longi'tudinal** *adj.*
,longi'tudinally *adv.*

look [luk] *v* **1** to turn the eyes in a certain direction so as to see, to find, to express, *etc*: *He looked out of the window*; *I've looked everywhere, but I can't find him*; *He looked at me (angrily).* **2** to seem: *It looks as if it's going to rain*; *She looks sad.* **3** to face: *The house looks west.* – *n* **1** the act of looking or seeing: *Let me have a look!* **2** a glance: *a look of surprise.* **3** appearance: *The house had a look of neglect.*
-looking having a certain appearance: *good-looking*; *strange-looking.*
looks *n pl* (attractive) appearance: *She lost her looks as she grew older*; *good looks.*
,looker-'on *n* a person who is watching something happening; an onlooker.
'looking-glass *n* a mirror.
'lookout *n* **1** a careful watch: *a sharp lookout*; (*also adj*) *a lookout post.* **2** a place from which such a watch can be kept. **3** a person who has been given the job of watching: *There was a shout from the lookout.* **4** concern, responsibility: *If he catches you leaving early, that's your lookout!*
by the look(s) of judging from the appearance of (someone or something) it seems likely or probable: *By the looks of him, he won't live much longer*; *It's going to rain by the look of it.*
look after to attend to or take care of: *to look after the children.*
look ahead to consider what will happen in the future.
look down one's nose at to regard with contempt.
look down on to regard as inferior: *She looks down on her husband's relations.*

* see illustration on p. 201

look for to search for: *She lost her handbag and wasted ten minutes looking for it.*

look forward to to wait with pleasure for: *I am looking forward to seeing you/to the holidays.*

look here! give your attention to this: *Look here! Isn't that what you wanted?*; *Look here, Mary, you're being unfair!*

look in on to visit briefly: *I decided to look in on Paul and Carol on my way home.*

look into to inspect or investigate closely: *The manager will look into your complaint.*

look on 1 to watch something: *No, I don't want to play – I'd rather look on.* 2 (*with* **as**) to think of or consider: *I have lived with my aunt since I was a baby, and I look on her as my mother.*

look out 1 (*usu with* **for**) to watch: *She was looking out for him from the window.* 2 to find by searching: *I've looked out these books for you.*

look out! beware! take care!

look over to examine: *We have been looking over the new house.*

look through to look at or study briefly: *I've looked through your notes.*

look up 1 to improve: *Things have been looking up lately.* 2 to pay a visit to: *I looked up several old friends.* 3 to search for in a book of reference: *You should look the word up (in a dictionary).* 4 to consult (a reference book): *I looked up the encyclopedia.*

look up to to respect the conduct, opinions etc of: *He has always looked up to his father.*

loom¹ [lu:m] *n* a machine in which thread is woven into a fabric.

loom² [lu:m] *v* (*often with* **up**) to appear indistinctly, often threateningly: *A huge ship loomed (up) in the fog.*

loony *see* **lunatic.**

loop [lu:p] *n* 1 a doubled-over part of a piece of rope, chain *etc*: *She made a loop in the string.* 2 a U-shaped bend in a river *etc*. – *v* to fasten with, or form into, a loop or loops: *He looped the rope round a post.*

loose [lu:s] *adj* 1 not tight; not firmly stretched: *a loose coat*; *This belt is loose.* 2 not firmly fixed: *This button is loose.* 3 not tied; free: *The horses are loose in the field.* 4 not packed; not in a packet: *loose biscuits.* **'loosely** *adv.* **'looseness** *n.*

'loosen *v* 1 to make or become loose: *She loosened the string*; *The screw had loosened and fallen out.* 2 to relax (*eg* a hold): *He loosened his grip.*

loose-'leaf *adj* (of a notebook *etc*) made so that pages can easily be added or removed.

break loose to escape: *The prisoner broke loose.*

let loose to free from control: *The circus trainer has let the lions loose.*

a loose (not lose) screw.

loot [lu:t] something which is stolen: *The thieves got away with a lot of loot.* – *v* to rob or steal from (a place): *The soldiers looted the shops of the captured town.*

lop [lop] – *pt, ptp* **lopped** – *v* to cut off (parts) from *eg* a tree: *We lopped several branches from the tree*; *He lopped a dollar off the price.*

lope [loup] *v* to run with long steps.

lord [lo:d] *n* 1 a master; a man or animal that has power over others or over an area: *The lion is lord of the jungle.* 2 (*with cap when used in titles*) in the UK *etc* a nobleman or man of rank. 3 (*with cap*) in the UK, used as part of several official titles: *the Lord Mayor.*

'lordly *adj* grand or proud: *a lordly attitude.* **'lordliness** *n.*

'Lordship *n* (*with* **His, Your** *etc*) a word used in speaking to, or about, a man with the title 'Lord' and also certain judges who do not have this title: *Thank you, Your Lordship.*

the Lord God; Christ.

lord it over to act like a lord or master towards: *Don't think you can lord it over us.*

lore [lo:] *n* knowledge handed down on a subject: *the lore of the sea.*

*lorry ['lori] *n* (*Amer* **truck**) a motor vehicle for carrying heavy loads: *He has a licence to drive a lorry*; *a coal-lorry.*

'lorry-driver *n.*

lose [lu:z] – *pt, ptp* **lost** [lost] – *v* 1 to stop having; to have no longer: *She has lost interest in her work*; *I have lost my watch*; *He lost hold of the rope.* 2 to have taken away from one (by death, accident *etc*): *She lost her father last year*; *The ship was lost in the storm*; *He has lost his job.* 3 to put (something) where it cannot be found: *My secretary has lost your letter.* 4 not to win: *I always lose at cards*; *She lost the race.* 5 to waste or use more (time) than is necessary: *He lost no time in informing the police of the crime.*

'loser *n* a person who loses: *The losers congratulated the winners.*

loss [los] *n* 1 the act or fact of losing: *suffering from loss of memory*; *the loss (=death) of our friend.* 2 something which is lost: *It was only after he was dead that we realized what a loss he was.* 3 the amount (*esp* of money) which is lost: *a loss of £500.*

lost *adj* 1 missing; no longer to be found: *a lost ticket.* 2 not won: *The game is lost.* 3 wasted; not used properly: *a lost opportunity.* 4 no longer knowing where one is, or in which direction to go: *I don't know whether to turn left or right – I'm lost.*

at a loss not knowing what to do, say *etc*:

* see illustration on p. 595

He was at a loss for words to express his gratitude.

a bad, good loser someone who behaves badly or well when he loses a game *etc.*

lose one's memory to stop being able to remember things.

lose out to suffer loss or be at a disadvantage.

lost in having one's attention wholly taken up by: *She was lost in thought.*

lost on wasted, having no effect, on: *The joke was lost on her.*

to **lose** (not **loose**) the match.

lot [lot] *n* **1** a person's fortune or fate: *It seemed to be her lot to be always unlucky.* **2** a separate part: *She gave one lot of clothes to a jumble sale and threw another lot away.* **3** one article or several, sold as a single item at an auction: *Are you going to bid for lot 28?*

lots *n pl* a large quantity or number: *lots of people*; *She had lots and lots of food left over from the party.*

a lot a large quantity or number: *What a lot of letters!*

draw/cast lots *see* **draw.**

lotion ['loʃən] *n* a liquid for soothing or cleaning the skin: *hand-lotion.*

lottery ['lotəri] – *pl* '**lotteries** – *n* the sharing out of money or prizes won by chance, through drawing lots: *They held a public lottery in aid of charity.*

lotus ['loutəs] *n* a type of waterlily found in Egypt and India.

loud [laud] *adj* **1** making a great sound; not quiet: *a loud voice*; *loud music.* **2** showy; too bright and harsh: *loud colours*; *a loud shirt.* '**loudly** *adv.* '**loudness** *n.*

'**loud-'hailer** *n* a simple type of loudspeaker: *The police used a loud-hailer to tell the crowd to get back.*

'**loud'speaker** *n* **1** an instrument for increasing the loudness of sounds so that they can be heard further away: *The politician addressed the crowds from his car through a loudspeaker.* **2** a speaker in a radio, record-player *etc.*

lounge [laundʒ] *v* **1** to lie back in a casual manner: *lounging on a sofa.* **2** to move about lazily; to be inactive: *I spent the day lounging about the house.* – *n* a sitting-room, *eg* in a hotel: *They watched television in the hotel lounge.*

lounge suit *n* a man's suit for everyday formal wear.

lour *see* **lower**[1].

louse [laus] – *pl* **lice** [lais] – *n* a type of wingless, bood-sucking insect, sometimes found on the bodies of animals and people.

lousy ['lauzi] *adj* **1** having lice. **2** really terrible: *I'm a lousy cook.* '**lousiness** *n.*

lout [laut] *n* a clumsy, ill-mannered boy or man. '**loutish** *adj.*

love [lʌv] *n* **1** a feeling of great fondness or enthusiasm for a person or thing: *She has a great love of music*; *her love for her children.* **2** strong attachment with sexual attraction: *They are in love with one another.* **3** a person or thing that is thought of with (great) fondness (used also as a term of affection): *Ballet is the love of her life*; *Goodbye, love!* **4** a score of nothing in tennis: *The present score is fifteen love* (written 15-0). – *v* **1** to be (very) fond of: *She loves her children dearly.* **2** to take pleasure in: *They both love dancing.*

'**lovable** *adj* (*neg* **un-**) easy to love or like; attractive: *a lovable child.*

'**lovely** *adj* **1** (*neg* **un-**) beautiful; attractive: *She is a lovely girl*; *She looked lovely in that dress.* **2** delightful: *Someone told me a lovely joke last night, but I can't remember it*; *a lovely meal.* '**loveliness** *n.*

'**lover** *n* **1** a person who enjoys or admires or has a special affection for something: *an art-lover*; *He is a lover of sport*; *an animal-lover.* **2** a person who is having a love affair with another.

'**loving** *adj.* '**lovingly** *adv.*

love affair a (temporary and often sexual) relationship between two people who are in love but not married.

'**love-letter** *n* a letter expressing love.

'**lovesick** *adj* sad because of being in love: *a lovesick youth*; *lovesick glances.*

fall in love (with) to develop feelings of love and sexual attraction (for): *He fell in love with her straightaway.*

for love or money in any way at all: *We couldn't get a taxi for love or money.*

make love to have sexual intercourse.

there's no love lost between them they dislike one another.

low[1] [lou] *adj* **1** not at or reaching up to a great distance from the ground, sea-level *etc*: *low hills*; *a low ceiling*; *This chair is too low for the child.* **2** making little sound; not loud: *She spoke in a low voice.* **3** at the bottom of the range of musical sounds: *That note is too low for a female voice.* **4** small: *a low price.* **5** not strong; weak or feeble: *The fire was very low.* **6** near the bottom in grade, rank, class *etc*: *low temperatures*; *the lower classes.* – *adv* in or to a low position, manner or state: *The ball flew low over the net.*

'**lower** *v* **1** to make or become less high: *She lowered her voice.* **2** to let down: *He lowered the blinds.*

'**lowly** *adj* of low rank; humble. '**lowliness** *n.*

'**low-down** *adj* mean; contemptible: *a low-down thief.*

'lowland adj of or concerning lowlands: lowland districts.

'lowlander n a person who lives in the lowlands.

'lowlands n pl land which is low compared with other, higher land.

'low-lying adj (of land) at a height not much above sea-level.

low tide/water the time when the sea is lowest at a particular place during ebb-tide: There is three feet of water in the harbour, even at low water.

be low on not to have enough of: I'll have to go to the supermarket – we're low on coffee and sugar.

low² [lou] v to make the noise of cattle; to moo: The cows were lowing.

lower¹, lour ['lauə] v (of the sky·etc) to become dark or threatening. 'lowering adj.

lower² see low¹.

loyal ['loiəl] adj faithful: a loyal friend. 'loyally adv. 'loyalty n.

lozenge ['lozindʒ] n 1 a small sweet for sucking: peppermint lozenges. 2 a diamond-shaped figure.

lubricate ['lu:brikeit] v to oil (a machine etc) to make it move more easily and smoothly. ˌlubriˈcation n.

'lubricant n something (oil etc) which lubricates.

luck [lʌk] n 1 the state of happening by chance: Whether you win or not is just luck – there's no skill involved. 2 something good which happens by chance: She has all the luck!

'luckless adj unfortunate: luckless children.

'lucky adj 1 having good luck: He was very lucky to escape alive. 2 bringing good luck: a lucky number; a lucky charm. 'luckily adv. 'luckiness n.

lucky dip a form of amusement at a fair etc in which prizes are drawn from a container without the taker seeing what he is getting.

bad luck! an expression of sympathy for someone who has failed or been unlucky.

good luck! an expression of encouragement made to someone who is about to take part in a competition, sit an exam etc: She wished him good luck.

lucrative ['lu:krətiv] adj (of a job etc) bringing in a lot of money; profitable.

ludicrous ['lu:dikrəs] adj completely ridiculous. 'ludicrously adv. 'ludicrousness n.

ludo ['lu:dou] n a game played (usu by children) with counters on a board.

lug [lʌg] – pt, ptp lugged – v to drag with difficulty: She lugged the heavy trunk across the floor.

luggage ['lʌgidʒ] n the suitcases, trunks etc of a traveller: He carried her luggage to the train; (also adj) a luggage compartment.

lukewarm ['lu:kwo:m] adj 1 slightly warm: lukewarm water. 2 (of eg interest, support etc) not very enthusiastic.

lull [lʌl] v to make calm or quiet: The sound of the waves lulled him to sleep. – n a temporary period of calm.

lullaby ['lʌləbai] – pl 'lullabies [-baiz] – n a song sung to make children go to sleep.

lumbago [lʌm'beigou] n pain in the lower part of the back.

lumber¹ ['lʌmbə] n 1 old unwanted furniture etc. 2 timber sawn up. – v to give (someone) an unwanted responsibility: to lumber someone with a job.

'lumberjack [-dʒak] n a person employed to cut down, saw up and move trees.

lumber² ['lʌmbə] v to move about heavily and clumsily.

luminous ['lu:minəs] adj giving out light; faintly shining so as to be visible in the dark: a luminous clock-face. ˌlumiˈnosity [-'no-].n.

lump [lʌmp] n 1 a small solid mass of no particular shape: The custard was full of lumps and no-one would eat it. 2 a swelling: She had a lump on her head where she had hit it. 3 a small cube-shaped mass of sugar. – v (usu with together) to treat or think of as (all) alike.

'lumpy adj containing lumps: lumpy custard. 'lumpiness n.

lump sum an amount of money given all at once, not in parts over a period of time.

if you don't like it, you can lump it whether you like the situation or not, you will have to endure it.

lunacy ['lu:nəsi] n insanity; madness.

'lunatic [-tik] adj, n (abbrev (usu unkind) loony ['lu:ni] – pl 'loonies) (a person who is) insane or crazy: Only a lunatic would do such a thing!

lunar adj of the moon: a lunar eclipse.

lunatic see lunacy.

lunch [lʌntʃ], also luncheon ['lʌntʃən] n a meal eaten in the middle of the day. – v to eat this meal: We lunched on the train.

'lunchtime n the time between 12.00 p.m. and 2.00 p.m., when people eat lunch.

lung [lʌŋ] n one of the pair of organs of breathing, in man and other animals.

lunge [lʌndʒ] v to make a sudden strong or violent forward movement: Her attacker lunged at her with a knife. – n a movement of this sort: He made a lunge at her.

lurch [lə:tʃ] v to move suddenly or unevenly forward; to roll to one side. – n such a movement: The train gave a lurch and started off.

leave in the lurch to leave (a person etc) in a difficult situation and without help.

lure [luə] n attraction; something very attractive or tempting: The lure of his mother's good cooking brought him back home. – v to tempt or attract: *The bright lights of the city lured him away from home.*

lurid ['luərid] *adj* **1** (too) brightly coloured or vivid: *a lurid dress/painting/sky.* **2** unpleasantly shocking: *the lurid details of his accident.* **'luridly** *adv.* **'luridness** *n.*

lurk [ləːk] *v* to wait in hiding *esp* with a dishonest or criminal purpose: *She saw someone lurking in the shadows.*

luscious ['lʌʃəs] *adj* very sweet, juicy and delicious: *a luscious peach.* **'lusciousness** *n.*

lush [lʌʃ] *adj* green and fertile: *lush meadows.*

lust [lʌst] *n* (a) very strong desire: *a lust for power.* **'lustful** *adj.* **'lustfully** *adv.*
'lusty *adj* **1** strong and loud: *The baby gave a lusty yell.* **2** strong and healthy: *a lusty young man.* **'lustily** *adv.* **'lustiness** *n.*

lustre, (*Amer*) **luster** ['lʌstə] *n* shininess or brightness: *Her hair had a brilliant lustre.* **'lustrous** [-trəs] *adj.*

lusty *see* lust.

luxury ['lʌkʃəri] *n* – *pl* **'luxuries** – **1** great comfort *usu* amongst expensive things: *They live in luxury;* (*also adj*) *gold jewellery and other luxury goods.* **2** something pleasant but not necessary, and often rare and expensive: *We're going to give up all those luxuries and only spend money on essentials.* **luxurious** [lʌg'zjuəriəs] *adj* supplied with luxuries: *a really luxurious flat/life.* **lu'xuriously** *adv.* **lu'xuriousness** *n.*

*****lychee, lichee** ['laitʃiː, 'liː-] *n* (a Chinese tree bearing) a small round fruit with white juicy pulp.

lying *see* lie[1], lie[2].

lyric ['lirik] *adj* (of poetry) expressing the poet's personal feeling. – *n* **1** a lyric poem. **2** (*in pl*) the words of a song: *The tune is good, but I don't like the lyrics.*

Mm

macabre [mə'kaːbr] *adj* weird, unearthly or horrible: *macabre horror stories.*

macaroni [makə'rouni] *n* a form of pasta, pressed out to form tubes, and dried: *The macaroni is over-cooked.*

mace[1] [meis] *n* **1** a metal or metal-headed war club, often with spikes. **2** an ornamental rod used as a mark of authority on ceremonial occasions.

mace[2] [meis] *n* a type of spice obtained from the same fruit as nutmeg.

machine [mə'ʃiːn] *n* **1** a working arrangement of wheels, levers or other parts, driven *eg* by human power, electricity *etc*, or operating electronically, producing power and/or motion for a particular purpose: *a sewing-machine.* **2** a vehicle, *esp* a motorbike: *That's a fine machine you have!* – *v* **1** to shape, make or finish with a power-driven tool: *The articles are machined to a smooth finish.* **2** to sew with a sewing-machine: *You should machine the seams.*

ma'chinery *n* **1** machines in general: *Many products are made by machinery rather than by hand.* **2** the workings or processes: *the machinery of government.*

ma'chinist *n* a person skilled in the use of machines, *eg* a sewing-machine, or electrical tools: *She's a machinist in a clothes factory.*

ma'chine-gun *n* an automatic gun that fires very rapidly. – Also *v*: *He machine-gunned a crowd of defenceless villagers.*

machine tool a power-driven machine that shapes metal, wood, or plastics by cutting, pressing, or drilling.

machinery does not have a plural.

mackerel ['makrəl] – *pls* **'mackerel, 'mackerels** – *n* **1** a type of edible sea-fish, bluish green with wavy markings: *They are fishing for mackerel; two mackerels.* **2** its flesh as food: *fried mackerel.*

mackintosh ['makintoʃ] *n* a waterproof overcoat, *esp* made of plastic material.

macramé [mə'kraːmi] *n* the craft of tying thread, string *etc* in decorative knots.

mad [mad] *adj* **1** mentally disturbed or insane: *Ophelia went mad; You must be mad.* **2** (*sometimes with* at *or* with) very angry: *She was mad at me for losing my keys.* **3** (*with* about) having a great liking or desire for: *I'm just mad about Harry.* **'madly** *adv.* **'madness** *n.*
'madden *v* to make mad or very angry: *The animal was maddened by the pain.*
'maddening *adj* likely to cause anger: *maddening delays.* **'maddeningly** *adv.*
'madman – *pl* **'madmen**: *fem* **'madwoman** – *pl* **'madwomen** – *n* a person who is insane: *He drove/fought like a madman.*
like mad wildly, desperately, very quickly *etc*: *struggling/trying/running like mad.*

madam ['madəm] – *pls* **mesdames** [mei'dam] – *n* a polite form of address to a woman.

madden, maddening, maddeningly *see* mad.

made *see* make.

Madonna [mə'donə] *n* (*with* the) the Virgin

Mary, mother of Christ, *esp* as shown in works of art: *a painting of the Madonna and Child.*

maestro ['maistrou] – *pl* '**maestros** – *n* (a title given to) a master in one of the arts, *esp* a musical composer or conductor.

magazine [magə'zi:n, (*Amer*) 'magəzi:n] *n* **1** (*abbrev* **mag** [mag]) a publication issued regularly containing articles, stories, *etc* by various writers: *women's magazines*; (*also adj*) *a magazine article.* **2** a compartment in or on a gun that holds cartridges. **3** a storeroom for ammunition, explosives *etc*.

maggot ['magət] *n* the worm-like grub or larva of a fly, *esp* a bluebottle.

magic ['madʒik] *n* **1** (the charms, spells *etc* used in) the art or practice of using supernatural forces: *The prince was turned by magic into a frog.* **2** the art of producing illusions by tricks: *The conjuror's magic delighted the children.* **3** fascination or great charm: *the magic of Turner's paintings.* – *adj* used in or using magic: *a magic wand*; *a magic spell.*
'**magical** *adj* **1** produced by, or as if by, the art of magic: *magical power.* **2** fascinating; charming or very beautiful: *a magical experience.* '**magically** *adv*.
ma'gician [mə'dʒiʃən] *n* a person skilled in the art of magic: *They hired a magician to entertain the children.*

magistrate ['madʒistreit] *n* a person who has power to put the laws into force and sentence those guilty of lesser crimes.

magnanimous [mag'nanıməs] *adj* noble and generous: *a magnanimous gesture.* **mag'nanimously** *adv*. **magnanimity** [magnə'nimiti] *n*.

magnate ['magneit] *n* a man of wealth or power: *He is a rich shipping magnate.*

magnesium [mag'ni:ziəm] *n* a silver-white metallic element that burns with a bright, white light.

magnet ['magnit] *n* a piece of iron, or of certain other materials, that attracts or repels other pieces of iron *etc*.
mag'netic [-'ne-] *adj* **1** of, or having the powers of, or operating by means of, a magnet or magnetism: *magnetic force.* **2** strongly attractive: *a magnetic personality.* **mag'netically** *adv*.
'**magnetism** *n* **1** power of attraction: *his personal magnetism.* **2** (the science of) magnets and their power of attraction: *the magnetism of the earth.*
'**magnetize, -ise** *v* **1** to make magnetic: *You can magnetize a piece of iron.* **2** to attract or influence strongly: *She's the kind of person who can magnetize others.*
magnetic field the area in which the pull of a magnet, or thing acting like a magnet, is felt: *the earth's magnetic field.*

magnetic north the direction, either east or west of the true north, in which a magnetized needle points.

magnificent [mag'nifisnt] *adj* great and splendid: *a magnificent costume*; *a magnificent performance.* **mag'nificently** *adv*. **mag'nificence** *n*.

magnify ['magnifai] *v* to cause to appear greater: *A telescope magnifies an image*; *to magnify one's troubles.*
,**magnifi'cation** [-fi-] *n* **1** the act of magnifying (something). **2** the power of magnifying: *the magnification of a pair of binoculars.* **3** the extent to which something (*eg* a photograph) has been magnified: *The magnification is ten times* (*10* ×).
'**magnifying-glass** *n* a piece of glass with curved surfaces that makes an object looked at through it appear larger: *This print is so small that I need a magnifying-glass to read it.*

magnitude ['magnitju:d] *n* **1** importance: *a decision of great magnitude.* **2** size: *a star of great magnitude.*

magpie ['magpai] *n* a black-and-white bird of the crow family, known for its habit of collecting shiny objects.

mahjong(g) [ma:'dʒoŋ] *n* an old Chinese game played with small painted tiles.

mahogany [mə'hogəni] *n* **1** the wood of a tropical American tree, much used for making furniture: *This table is made of mahogany*; (*also adj*) *a mahogany table.* **2** (*also adj*) (of) its dark brown colour. **3** (*also* **mahogany tree**) the tree.

maid [meid] *n* a female servant: *The maid answered the door.*

maiden ['meidən] *n* a (young) unmarried woman: *the village maidens.*
maiden name a woman's surname before her marriage: *Mrs Johnson's maiden name was Scott.*
maiden voyage a ship's first voyage.

mail [meil] *n* letters, parcels *etc* by post: *His secretary opens his mail.* – *v* to send by post.
'**mailbag** *n* a bag for letters *etc*: *The letters are put into mailbags and sent to London by train.*
'**mailbox** *n* a postbox.
'**mailman** [-man] *n* (*Amer*) a postman.

maim [meim] *v* to injure badly, *esp* with permanent effects: *The hunter was maimed for life.*

main [mein] *adj* chief, principal or most important: *the main purpose*; *the main character in the story.* – *n* (*also* **mains**) the chief pipe or cable in a branching system of pipes or cables: *The water's been turned off at the main(s)*; (*also adj*) *the mains electricity supply.*
'**mainly** *adv* more (of) the thing mentioned

than anything else; mostly or largely: *This skirt is mainly dark grey.*

'**mainland** *n* a large piece of land as compared with neighbouring islands: *Britain is not part of the mainland of Europe.*

'**mainspring** *n* the chief spring, *esp* the spring that causes the wheels to move in a watch or clock.

'**mainstream** *n* the chief direction or trend of a system of theories, developments *etc*: *the mainstream of traditional art.*

maintain [mein'tein] *v* 1 to continue: *How long can you maintain this silence?* 2 to keep in good condition: *He maintains his car very well.* 3 to pay the expenses of: *How can you maintain a wife and three children on your small salary?* 4 to continue to argue or believe (that): *I maintain that the theory is true.*

'**maintenance** [-tənəns] *n* 1 the process of keeping something in good condition: *car maintenance.* 2 the act of maintaining (a point of view *etc*).

maisonette [meizə'net] *n* (used *esp* by estate agents) a flat or apartment on two floors or stories.

maize [meiz] *n* (*Amer* **corn, Indian corn**) an important cereal, grown *esp* in America.

majesty ['madʒəsti] – *pl* '**majesties** – *n* 1 greatness; impressive dignity: *the majesty of God.* 2 (*with cap*: *with* **His, Your** *etc*) a title used when speaking to or of a king or queen: *Her Majesty the Queen: Their Majesties: Your Majesty.*

ma'jestic [-'dʒes-] *adj* having great dignity: *He looked truly majestic.* **ma'jestically** *adv.*

major ['meidʒə] *adj* great, or greater, in size, importance *etc*: *major and minor roads; a major discovery.* – *n* (*often abbrev* **Maj.** *when written*) the rank next below lieutenant-colonel.

ma'jority [mə'dʒɔ-] – *pl* **ma'jorities** – *n* 1 the greater number: *The majority of people.* 2 the difference between a greater and a smaller number: *The Democratic Party won by/with a majority of six hundred votes.*

,**major-'general** *n* (*often abbrev* **Maj.-Gen,** *when written*) in the British army, (a person of) the rank next below lieutenant-general.

make [meik] – *pt, ptp* **made** [meid] – *v* 1 to create, form or produce: *God made the Earth; She makes all her own clothes; He made it out of paper; to make a muddle/mess of the job; to make lunch/coffee; We made an arrangement / agreement / deal / bargain.* 2 to compel, force or cause (a person or thing to do something): *They made her do it; He made me laugh.* 3 to cause to be: *I made it clear; You've made me very unhappy.* 4 to gain or earn: *He makes $100 a week; to make a profit.* 5 (of numbers *etc*)

to add up to; to amount to: *2 and 2 make(s) 4.* 6 to become, turn into, or be: *He'll make an excellent teacher.* 7 to estimate as: *I make the total 483.* 8 to appoint, or choose, as: *He was made manager.* 9 used with many nouns to give a similar meaning to that of the verb from which the noun is formed: *He made several attempts* (= attempted several times); *They made a left turn* (= turned left); *He made* (= offered) *a suggestion/proposal/bid; Have you any comments to make?* – *n* a (*usu* manufacturer's) brand: *What make is your new car?*

'**maker** *n* a person who makes: *a toolmaker; a dressmaker.*

'**making** *n* the process of producing or forming something: *glassmaking*; (*also adj*) *the road-making industry.*

,**make-be'lieve** *n* the act or art of pretending and imagining: *a world of make-believe;* (*also adj*) *a make-believe world.*

'**makeshift** *adj* temporary and *usu* of poor quality: *a makeshift garden shed.*

'**make-up** *n* 1 cosmetics applied to the face *etc*: *She never wears any make-up.* 2 the set, or combination, of characteristics or ingredients that together form something, *eg* a personality; composition: *Violence is just not part of his make-up.*

have the makings of to have the clear ability for becoming: *Your son has the makings of an engineer.*

in the making being made or formed at this very moment: *A revolution is in the making.*

make a/one's bed to tidy and straighten the sheets, blankets *etc* on a bed after it has been used: *The children make their own beds every morning.*

make believe to pretend (that): *The children made believe they were animals.*

make do (*with* **with**) to use something as a poor-quality or temporary alternative to the real thing: *There's no meat, so we'll have to make do with potatoes.*

make for to go towards: *We're making for home.*

make it to be successful: *After twenty years, we've finally made it.*

make it up 1 to become friends again after a quarrel: *It's time you two made it up* (*with each other*). 2 to give compensation or make amends for something: *I'm sorry – I'll make it up to you somehow.*

make (something) of (something) to understand (something) by or from (something): *What do you make of all this?*

make out 1 to see, hear or understand: *He could make out a ship in the distance.* 2 to make it seem that: *He made out that he was earning a huge amount of money.* 3 to write or fill in: *The doctor made out a prescription.*

make up 1 to invent: *He made up the whole*

story. **2** to compose or be part(s) of: *The group was made up of doctors and lawyers.* **3** to complete: *We need one more player – will you make up the number(s)?* **4** to apply cosmetics to (the face): *I don't like to see women making up (their faces) in public.* **5** to become friends again (after a quarrel etc): *They've finally made up (their disagreement).*

make up for to supply a reward, substitute etc for disappointment, damage, loss (of money or time) etc: *Next week we'll try to make up for lost time.*

make up one's mind to make a decision: *He finally made up his mind about the job.*

make up to to try to gain the favour or love of by flattery etc: *She's always making up to the teacher by bringing him presents.*

made of is used in speaking of the material from which an object is constructed etc: *This table is made of wood/plastic/steel.*
made from is used in speaking of the raw material from which something has been produced by a process of manufacture: *Paper is made from wood/rags.*

malady ['malədi] – *pl* **'maladies** – *n* an illness or disease: *He is suffering from some strange malady.*

malaria [mə'leəriə] *n* a fever caused by the bite of a certain type of mosquito.

male [meil] *n*, *adj* **1** (a person, animal etc) of the sex having testes or an organ or organs performing a similar function; not (of) the sex which carries the young until birth etc: *the male of the species; the male rabbit.* **2** (a plant) having flowers with stamens which can fertilize female flowers.

malevolent [mə'levələnt] *adj* wishing evil to others: *The wicked old woman gave a malevolent smile.* **ma'levolently** *adv.* **ma'levolence** *n.*

malfunction [mal'fʌŋkʃən] *n* faulty performance or a faulty process: *There's a malfunction in the main engine.*

malice ['malis] *n* the wish to harm other people etc: *There was no malice intended in what she said.*

mal'icious [-ʃəs] *adj*: *She took a malicious pleasure in hurting others.* **ma'liciously** *adv.*

malign [mə'lain] *v* to say unpleasant things about (someone or something), *esp* without reason: *He's always maligning his wife when she isn't there.*

malignant [mə'lignənt] *adj* **1** (of people, their actions etc) intending, or intended, to do harm: *a malignant remark.* **2** (of a tumour, disease etc) likely to become worse and cause death: *She died of a malignant tumour.* **ma'lignantly** *adv.*

malinger [mə'liŋgə] *v* to pretend to be unwell

eg in order to avoid work: *He says he's ill, but I think he's just malingering.* **ma'lingerer** *n.*

*****mallet** ['malit] *n* **1** a type of small wooden hammer: *We hammered the tent pegs into the ground with a mallet.* **2** a long-handled wooden hammer for playing croquet or polo.

malnutrition [malnjuː'triʃən] *n* (a medical condition resulting from) eating too little or getting too little nourishing food: *About half of the population is suffering from malnutrition.*

malt [moːlt] *n* **1** barley or other grain soaked in water, allowed to sprout, and dried in a kiln, used in making beer, whisky etc. **2** a variety of malt whisky: *This pub sells fifteen different malts.*

mamma, mama [mə'maː] *n* a (name for one's) mother.

mammal ['maməl] *n* any member of the class of animals (including man) in which the females feed the young with their own milk: *Monkeys are mammals.* **mam'malian** [-'mei-] *adj.*

mammary ['maməri] *adj* of the breasts or milk glands: *the mammary glands.*

mammoth ['maməθ] *n* a large hairy elephant of a kind no longer found living. – *adj* very large (and often very difficult): *a mammoth project/task.*

man [man] – *pl* **men** [men] – *n* **1** an adult male human being: *Hundreds of men, women and children; a four-man team.* **2** human beings taken as a whole; the human race: *the development of man.* **3** obviously masculine male person: *He's independent, tough, strong, brave – a real man!* **4** a word sometimes used in speaking informally or giving commands to someone: *Get on with your work, man, and stop complaining!* **5** an ordinary soldier, who is not an officer: *officers and men.* **6** a piece used in playing chess or draughts: *I took three of his men in one move.* – *v* – *pt, ptp* **manned** – to supply with men (*esp* soldiers): *The colonel manned the guns with soldiers from our regiment.*

-man [-mən, -man] a person (formerly *usu* used for either sex; currently, often replaced by **-person** when the person referred to can be of either sex) who performs a particular activity, as in **postman, milkman, chairman** etc.

'manhood *n* **1** (of a male) the state of being adult, physically (and mentally) mature etc: *He died before he reached manhood.* **2** manly qualities: *He took her refusal to marry him as an insult to his manhood.*

man'kind *n* the human race as a whole: *He worked for the benefit of all mankind.*

'manly *adj* having the qualities thought desirable in a man, *ie* strength, determination, courage *etc*: *He is strong and manly.* '**manliness** *n.*

manned *adj* supplied with men: *a manned spacecraft.*

'**man-eating** *adj* which will eat people: *a man-eating tiger.* '**man-eater** *n.*

man'handle *v* **1** to move, carry *etc* by hand: *When the crane broke down, they had to manhandle the crates on to the boat.* **2** to treat roughly: *You'll break all the china if you manhandle it like that!*

'**manhole** *n* a hole (*usu* in the middle of a road or pavement) through which someone may go to inspect sewers *etc.*

,**man-'made** *adj* made, happening or formed by man, not by natural means: *a man-made lake.*

'**manpower** *n* the number of people available for employment *etc*: *There's a shortage of manpower in the building industry.*

'**manservant** – *pl* '**menservants** – *n* a male servant (*esp* one employed as a valet): *He has only one manservant.*

'**mansize(d)** *adj* of a size suitable for a man; large: *a mansized breakfast.*

'**manslaughter** *n* the crime of killing someone, without intending to do so: *He was found guilty of manslaughter.*

'**menfolk** *n pl* male people, *esp* male relatives: *The wives accompanied their menfolk.* '**menswear** ['menz-] *n* clothing for men: *Do you sell menswear?*

as one man simultaneously; together: *They rose as one man to applaud his speech.*

the man in the street the ordinary, typical, average man: *The man in the street often has little interest in politics.*

man of letters a writer and/or scholar: *Shakespeare was perhaps Britain's greatest man of letters.*

man to man as one man to another; openly or frankly: *They talked man to man about their problems*; (*also adj*) *a man-to-man discussion.*

to a man every one, without exception: *They voted to a man to accept the proposal.*

manage ['manidʒ] *v* **1** to be in control or charge of: *My lawyer manages all my legal affairs/money.* **2** to be manager of: *James manages the local football team.* **3** to deal with, or control: *She's good at managing people.* **4** to be able to do something; to succeed or cope: *Will you manage to repair your bicycle?; Can you manage (to eat) some more meat?*

'**manageable** *adj* (*neg* **un-**) **1** that can be controlled: *The children are not very manageable.* **2** that can be done: *Are you finding this work manageable?* ,**manage- a'bility** *n.*

'**management** *n* **1** the art of managing: *The management of this company is a difficult*

task. **2** *or n pl* the managers of a firm *etc* as a group: *The management has/have agreed to pay the workers more.*

'**manager** – *fem* ,**manage'ress** – *n* a person who is in charge of *eg* a business, football team *etc*: *the manager of the new store.*

mandarin ['mandərin] *n* **1** (*also* **mandarin orange**) a type of small orange. **2** an official of high rank in the Chinese Empire.

mandolin, mandoline ['mandəlin] *n* a musical instrument similar to a guitar: *He played a tune on the mandolin.*

mane [mein] *n* the long hair on the back of the neck of a horse, lion *etc*: *The male of the lion has a mane.*

maneuver *see* **manoeuvre.**

manger ['meindʒə] *n* a box or trough in which food for horses and cattle is placed.

mangle ['maŋgl] *v* **1** to crush to pieces: *The car was badly mangled in the accident.* **2** to spoil (*eg* a piece of music) by bad mistakes *etc*: *He mangled the music by his terrible playing.* **3** to put (clothing *etc*) through a mangle. – *n* a machine with rollers for squeezing water out of wet clothes *etc.*

mango ['maŋgou] – *pl* 'mango(e)s** – *n* **1** the yellowish fruit of an Indian tropical tree. **2** (*also* **mango tree**) the tree.

mangosteen ['maŋgəstiːn] *n* **1** the dark brown, orange-shaped fruit of an East Indian tree. **2** the tree.

mangrove ['maŋgrouv] *n* a tropical evergreen tree growing in or near water.

mania ['meiniə] *n* **1** a form of mental illness in which the sufferer is over-active, over-excited, and unreasonably happy. **2** an unreasonable enthusiasm for something: *He has a mania for fast cars.*

'**maniac** [-ak] *n* an insane (and dangerous) person; a madman: *He drives like a maniac.* **manic** ['manik] *adj* **1** of, or suffering from, mania: *She's in a manic state.* **2** extremely energetic, active and excited: *The new manager is one of those manic people who can't rest even for a minute.*

manicure ['manikjuə] *v* to care for (the hands and nails): *She manicures her nails every night.* – *n* a treatment for the hands and nails: *I'm going for a manicure.* '**mani- curist** *n.*

manifest ['manifest] *v* to show (clearly): *He manifested his character in his behaviour.* – *adj* easily seen by the eye or understood by the mind; obvious: *manifest stupidity.* '**manifestly** *adv.*

,**manife'station** *n* **1** an obvious or clear example: *This is another manifestation of his ignorance.* **2** the act of showing clearly.

manipulate [mə'nipjuleit] *v* **1** to handle *esp* skilfully: *I watched him manipulating the controls of the aircraft.* **2** to manage or influence cleverly (and dishonestly): *A*

* see illustration on p. 201

clever lawyer can manipulate a jury.
ma‚nipu'lation *n.* ma'nipulator *n.*

manner ['manə] *n* **1** a way in which anything is done *etc*: *She greeted me in a friendly manner.* **2** the way in which a person behaves, speaks *etc*: *I don't like her manner.* **3** (*in pl*) (polite) behaviour, *usu* towards others: *Why doesn't she teach her children (good) manners?*
-'**mannered** having, or showing, manners of a certain kind: *a well-/bad-mannered person.*
'**mannerism** *n* an odd and obvious habit in a person's behaviour, speech *etc*: *He scratches his ear when he talks and has other mannerisms.*
all manner of all kinds of: *He has all manner of problems.*
in a manner of speaking in a certain way: *I suppose, in a manner of speaking, I am an engineer.*

manoeuvre, (*Amer*) **maneuver** [mə'nu:və] *n* **1** a planned movement (of troops, ships, aircraft, vehicles *etc*): *Can you perform all the manoeuvres required by the driving test?* **2** a skilful or cunning plan or action: *His appointment was the result of many cunning manoeuvres.* – *v* to (cause to) perform manoeuvres: *She had difficulty manoeuvring her car into the narrow space.*

mansion ['manʃən] *n* a large (luxurious) house: *They own a country mansion.*

manual ['manjuəl] *adj* **1** of the hand or hands: *manual skills/labour.* **2** working with the hands: *a manual worker.* **3** worked or operated by the hand: *a car with a manual gearbox.* – *n* **1** a handbook *eg* of technical information about a machine *etc*: *an instruction manual.* **2** a keyboard of an organ *etc.*
'**manually** *adv* by hand: *You have to operate this sewing-machine manually – it is not electric.*

manufacture [manju'faktʃə] *v* **1** to make, *orig* by hand but now *usu* by machinery and in large quantities: *This firm manufactures cars at the rate of two hundred per day.* **2** to invent (something false): *He manufactured an excuse for being late.* – *n* the process of manufacturing: *the manufacture of glass.*
‚manu'facturer *n* a person or firm that manufactures goods: *He is a carpet manufacturer.*

manure [mə'njuə] *n* a mixture containing animal dung, spread on soil to help produce better crops *etc*: *The farmer is putting manure on his fields.* – *v* to treat (soil or plants) with manure: *The farmer has been manuring the fields.*

manuscript ['manjuskript] *n* **1** the handwritten or typed material for a book *etc, usu* prepared for printing: *The publishers have lost the manuscript of my book.* **2** a book or document written by hand: *a collection of manuscripts and printed books.*

many ['meni] – *compar* **more** [mo:]: *superl* **most** [moust] – *adj* a great number of: *Many languages are spoken in Africa; There weren't very many people; You've made a great/good many mistakes.* – *pron* a great number: *A few people survived, but many died.*
many- having a great number of (something): *many-coloured; many-sided.*
many a a great number of: *I've told him many a time to be more polite.*

> **many** means a great number (of): *many cars; Some are full, but many are empty.*
> **much** means a great amount (of): *much effort; She doesn't say much.*

map [map] *n* **1** a drawing or plan, in outline, of (any part of) the surface of the earth, with various features shown (*usu* roads, rivers, seas, towns *etc*): *a map of the world; a road map.* **2** a similar type of drawing showing *eg* the surface of the moon, the position of the stars in the sky *etc.* – *v* – *pt, ptp* **mapped** – to make a map of (an area): *Africa was mapped by many different explorers.*
map out to plan (a route, course of action *etc*) in detail: *to map out a route/journey.*

mar [ma:] – *pt, ptp* **marred** – *v* to spoil or damage (enjoyment, beauty *etc*): *Her beauty was marred by a scar on her cheek.*

marathon ['marəθən, (*Amer*) -θon] *n* a long-distance footrace, *usu* 42 km 195 m (26 miles 385 yd): *He came third in the marathon;* (*also adj*) *a marathon race/discussion.*

marble ['ma:bl] *n* **1** a kind of hard, *usu* highly polished stone, cold to the touch: *This table is made of marble;* (*also adj*) *a marble statue.* **2** a small hard ball of glass used in children's games: *The little boy rolled a marble along the ground.*
'**marbled** *adj* having irregular streaks of different colours, like some types of marble: *marbled stonework.*
'**marbles** *n sing* any of several games played with marbles: *The boys were playing marbles.*

March [ma:tʃ] *n* the third month of the year, the month following February.

march [ma:tʃ] *v* **1** to (cause to) walk at a constant rhythm, and often in step with others: *Soldiers were marching along the street.* **2** to go on steadily: *Time marches on.* – *n* **1** (the) act of marching: *a long march; the march of time.* **2** a piece of music for marching to: *The band played a march.*

mare [meə] *n* a female horse.

margarine ['ma:dʒəri:n] *n* (*abbrev* **marge** [ma:dʒ]) a butter-like substance made mainly from vegetable fats: *We use margarine instead of butter.*

margin ['ma:dʒin] *n* 1 the blank edge round a page of writing or print: *Please write your comments in the margin.* 2 an edge or border: *the margin of the lake.* 3 something extra, beyond what should be needed: *Leave a wide margin for error!*

'marginal *adj* small and almost non-existent or unimportant: *a marginal improvement.*

marijuana, marihuana [mari'wa:nə] *n* a type of drug (illegal in many countries) made from the dried flowers and leaves of the hemp plant.

marine [mo'ri:n] *adj* of the sea: *marine animals*; *marine law.* – *n* a soldier serving on board a ship: *He has joined the marines.*

mariner ['marinə] *n* a sailor: *a master mariner.*

marionette [mariə'net] *n* a type of puppet moved by strings.

marital ['maritl] *adj* of marriage: *marital relations* (= the relationship between a married couple).

maritime ['maritaim] *adj* 1 of the sea, shipping *etc*: *maritime law.* 2 lying near the sea, and therefore having a navy, merchant shipping *etc*: *a maritime nation.*

mark[1] [ma:k] *n* 1 (*also* **Deutsche Mark, Deutschmark** ['doitʃma:k]) the standard unit of currency in the Federal Republic of Germany. 2 the standard unit of currency in the German Democratic Republic.

mark[2] [ma:k] *n* 1 a sign or spot that can be seen, *eg* on a person's or animal's body: *My dog has a white mark on his nose.* 2 a point given as a reward for good work *etc*: *She got good marks in the exam.* 3 a stain: *That spilt coffee has left a mark on the carpet.* 4 a sign used as a guide to position *etc*: *There's a mark on the map showing where the church is.* 5 a cross or other sign used instead of a signature: *He couldn't sign his name, so he made his mark instead.* 6 an indication or sign of a particular thing: *a mark of respect.* – *v* 1 to put a mark or stain on, or to become marked or stained: *Every pupil's coat must be marked with his name*; *That coffee has marked the tablecloth*; *This white material marks easily.* 2 to give marks to (a piece of work): *I have forty exam-papers to mark tonight.* 3 to show; to be a sign of: *X marks the spot where the treasure is buried.* 4 to note: *Mark it down in your notebook.* 5 (in football *etc*) to keep close to (an opponent) so as to prevent his getting the ball: *Your job is to mark the centre-forward.*

marked *adj* obvious or easily noticeable: *There has been a marked improvement in her work.*

'markedly [-kid-] *adv* noticeably: *It's markedly easier to do it by this method.*

'marker *n* 1 a person who marks *eg* the score at games. 2 something used for marking, *eg* in scoring, showing the position of something *etc*: *The area is indicated by large green markers.* 3 a type of pen, *usu* with a thick point.

'marksman ['ma:ks-] – *pl* **'marksmen** – *n* a person who shoots well: *The police marksman did not kill the criminal – he wounded him in the leg to prevent him escaping.*

'marksmanship *n* a person's skill as a marksman.

leave/make one's mark to make a permanent or strong impression: *The horrors of the war have left their mark on the children.*

mark out 1 to mark the boundary of (*eg* a football pitch) by making lines *etc*: *The pitch was marked out with white lines.* 2 to select or choose for some particular purpose *etc* in the future: *He had been marked out for an army career from early childhood.*

mark time to move the feet up and down as if marching, but without going forward: *He's only marking time in this job till he gets a better one.*

market ['ma:kit] *n* 1 a public place where people meet to buy and sell or the public event at which this happens: *He has a clothes stall in the market.* 2 (a place where there is) a demand for certain things: *There is a market for cotton goods in hot countries.* – *v* to (attempt to) sell: *I produce the goods and my brother markets them all over the world.*

'marketable *adj* wanted by the public and therefore able to be sold: *a marketable product.*

'marketing *n* (the study of) the processes by which anything may be sold: *He is in charge of marketing*; (*also adj*) *marketing methods.*

,market-'garden *n* a garden where fruit and vegetables are grown for sale.

'market-place, ,market-'square *n* the open space or square in a town in which a market is held.

market price/value the price at which a thing is being sold at a particular time: *What's the current market price of gold?*

market research investigation of the habits and preferences of the public in choosing what goods to buy: *She does market research for a cosmetics firm.*

be on the market to be for sale: *Her house has been on the market for months.*

marmalade ['ma:məleid] *n* a type of jam made from oranges, lemons or grapefruit.

maroon[1] [mə'ru:n] *n* a dark brownish-red colour: *a deep shade of maroon*; (*also adj*) *a large maroon car.*

maroon[2] [mə'ru:n] *v* 1 to put (someone) on shore on a lonely island from which he cannot escape. 2 to leave (someone) in a helpless, lonely or uncomfortable position: *I was marooned on a lonely country road.*

marquee [ma:'ki:] *n* a very large tent used for circuses, parties *etc*: *They hired a marquee for their party.*

marriage ['maridʒ] *n* **1** the ceremony by which a man and woman become husband and wife: *Their marriage took place last week*; (*also adj*) *the marriage ceremony.* **2** the state of being married; married life: *Their marriage lasted for thirty happy years.* **3** a close joining together: *the marriage of his skill and her judgement.*

'**marriageable** *adj* suitable, or at a proper age, for marriage: *He has four marriageable daughters*; *marriageable age.*

marriage licence a paper giving official permission for a marriage to take place.

marrow *n* **1** the soft substance in the hollow parts of bones: *Beef marrow is needed for this dish.* **2** (*Amer* **squash**) a large, green, thick-skinned vegetable, or its flesh as food.

marry ['mari] *v* **1** to take (a person) as one's husband or wife: *John married my sister*; *They married in church.* **2** (of a clergyman *etc*) to perform the ceremony of marriage between (two people): *The priest married them.* **3** to give (a son or daughter) as a husband or wife: *He married his son to a rich woman.*

'**married** *adj*: *She has two married daughters.*

marsh [ma:ʃ] *n* (an area of) soft wet land: *The heavy rainfall turned the land into a marsh.* '**marshy** *adj*. '**marshiness** *n*.

marshal ['ma:ʃəl] *n* **1** an official who arranges ceremonies, processions *etc*. **2** (*Amer*) an official with certain duties in the lawcourts. **3** (*Amer*) the head of a police or fire department. – *v* – *pt, ptp* '**marshalled**, (*Amer*) '**marshaled** – **1** to arrange (forces, facts, arguments *etc*) in order: *Give me a minute to marshal my thoughts.* **2** to lead or show the way to: *We marshalled the whole group into a large room.*

marsupial [ma:'sju:piəl] *n, adj* (an animal) having a pouch in which to carry its young: *The kangaroo is a marsupial.*

martial ['ma:ʃəl] *adj* **1** warlike or fond of fighting: *a martial nation.* **2** belonging to or suitable for war: *martial music.*

martial law the ruling of a country by the army in time of war or great national emergency, when ordinary law does not apply: *The country is now under martial law.*

martyr ['ma:tə] *n* **1** a person who suffers death or hardship for what he or she believes: *St Joan is said to have been a martyr.* **2** a person who continually suffers from a disease, difficulty *etc*: *She is a martyr to rheumatism.* – *v* to put (someone) to death or cause (him) to suffer greatly for his

beliefs: *Saint Joan was martyred by the English*

'**martyrdom** *n* the suffering or death of a martyr.

marvel ['ma:vəl] *n* something or someone astonishing or wonderful: *the marvels of the circus*; *She's a marvel at producing delicious meals.* – *v* – *pt, ptp* '**marvelled**, (*Amer*) '**marveled** – (*often with* **at**) to feel astonishment or wonder (at): *They marvelled at the fantastic sight.*

'**marvellous**, (*Amer*) '**marvelous** *adj* **1** wonderful: *The Alps are a marvellous sight.* **2** very good in some way; excellent: *a marvellous idea.* '**marvellously** *adv*.

mascot ['maskət] *n* a person, animal or thing supposed to bring good luck.

masculine ['maskjulin] *adj* **1** of the male sex: *masculine qualities.* **2** in certain languages, of one of *usu* two or three genders of nouns *etc*: *Is the French word for 'door' masculine or feminine?* ,**mascu'linity** *n*.

mash [maʃ] *v* to crush into small pieces or a soft mass: *Put in some butter when you mash the potatoes.* – *n* mashed potato: *sausage and mash.*

mask [ma:sk] *n* **1** something, *eg* a covering resembling a face, used for hiding or protecting the whole or part of the face: *The thief wore a black mask*; *Her face was a mask*; *under the mask of friendship.* – *v* to hide or disguise: *He managed to mask his feelings.*

mason ['meisn] *n* (*usu* '**stonemason**) a skilled worker or builder in stone.

'**masonry** *n* stone(work): *He was killed by falling masonry.*

masquerade [maskə'reid] *n* (a) pretence or disguise: *Her show of friendship was (a) masquerade.* – *v* (*with* **as**) to pretend to be, *usu* intending to deceive: *The criminal was masquerading as a respectable businessman.*

mass[1] [mas] *n* **1** a large lump or quantity, gathered together: *a mass of concrete/people.* **2** a large quantity: *I've masses of work/things to do.* **3** the bulk, principal part or main body: *The mass of people are in favour of peace.* **4** (a) measure of the quantity of matter in an object: *The mass of the rock is 500 kilos.* – *v* to bring or come together in large numbers or quantities: *The troops massed for an attack.* – *adj* of large quantities or numbers: *mass murder*; *a mass meeting.*

,**mass-pro'duced** *adj* (of goods) all exactly the same and produced in great numbers or quantity: *mass-produced plastic toys.* ,**mass-pro'duce** *v*. ,**mass-pro'duction** *n*.

the mass media those channels of communication (TV, radio, newspapers *etc*) that reach large numbers of people.

mass[2] [mas] *n* **1** (a) celebration, *esp* in the

Roman Catholic church, of Christ's last meal (**Last Supper**) with his disciples: *What time do you go to Mass?* **2** a setting to music of some of the words used in this service.

massacre ['masəkə] *n* **1** the killing of a large number of (*usu* people, *esp* with great cruelty. **2** a very bad defeat: *That last game was a complete massacre.* – *v* to kill (large numbers) cruelly.

massage ['masɑːʒ, (*Amer*) mə'sɑːʒ] *v* to treat (a person's body or part of it) by rubbing *etc* to ease and remove pain or stiffness: *She massaged my sore back.* – *n* (a) treatment by massaging: *His ankle was treated by massage.*

masseur [ma'sɜː] – *fem* **masseuse** [ma'sɜːz, (*Amer also*) mə'suːz] – *n* a person who gives massage.

massive ['masiv] *adj* huge or heavy: *a massive building*; *a massive burden of taxation.* '**massively** *adv.* '**massiveness** *n.*

mast [mɑːst] *n* a long upright pole *esp* for carrying the sails of a ship, an aerial, flag *etc*: *The sailor climbed the mast.*

-masted having (a certain number of) masts: *single-masted; four-masted.*

master ['mɑːstə] – *fem* **mistress** ['mistris] – *n* **1** a person or thing that commands or controls: *I'm master in this house!* **2** an owner (of a slave, dog *etc*): *The dog ran to its master.* **3** a male teacher: *the Maths master.* **4** the commander of a merchant ship: *the ship's master.* **5** a person very skilled in an art, science *etc*: *He's a real master at painting.* **6** (*with cap*) a polite title for a boy, in writing or in speaking: *Master John Smith.* – *adj* (of a person in a job) fully qualified, skilled and experienced: *a master builder/mariner/plumber.* – *v* **1** to overcome (an opponent, handicap *etc*): *She has mastered her fear of heights.* **2** to become skilful in: *I don't think I'll ever master arithmetic.*

'**masterful** *adj* showing the power, authority or determination of a master: *a masterful man.* '**masterfully** *adv.* '**masterfulness** *n.*

'**masterly** *adj* showing the skill of a master: *His handling of the situation was masterly.* '**masterliness** *n.*

'**mastery** *n* (*usu with* **over** *or* **of**) control, great skill or knowledge: *We have gained mastery over the enemy.*

master key a key which opens a number of locks.

'**mastermind** *n* the person planning and controlling an undertaking or scheme: *He was the mastermind behind the scheme.* – *v* to plan (such a scheme): *Who masterminded the robbery?*

'**masterpiece** *n* a piece of work or art worthy (to be called the greatest achievement) of a

master: *He considers this picture his masterpiece.*

master stroke a very clever thing to do: *This sudden, unexpected attack was a master stroke.*

master switch a switch for controlling a number of other switches: *There is a master switch that controls all the electricity.*

master of ceremonies (*abbrev* **MC**) a person who announces the various stages of an entertainment, formal social gathering, series of speakers at a dinner *etc*: *The master of ceremonies introduced the speaker.*

mat [mat] *n* a flat piece of material (rushes, rubber, carpet, cork *etc*) for wiping shoes on, covering a floor, or various other purposes: *Wipe your shoes on the doormat; a table mat.*

'**matted** *adj* in a thick untidy mess: *matted hair.*

'**matting** *n* a material used for making mats: *coconut matting.*

matador ['matədɔː] *n* the man who kills the bull in a bullfight.

match[1] [matʃ] *n* a short piece of wood or other material tipped with a substance that catches fire when rubbed against a rough or specially-prepared surface: *He struck a match.*

'**matchbox** *n* a box for holding matches.

match[2] [matʃ] *n* **1** a contest or game: *a football/rugby/chess match.* **2** a thing that is similar to or the same as another in some way(s) *eg* in colour or pattern: *These trousers are not an exact match for my jacket.* **3** a person who is able to equal another: *She has finally met her match at arguing.* **4** a marriage or an act of marrying: *She hoped to arrange a match for her daughter.* – *v* **1** to be equal or similar to something or someone in some way *eg* in colour or pattern: *That dress matches her red hair.* **2** to set (two things, people *etc*) to compete: *He matched his skill against the champion's.*

matched *adj* paired or joined together, *eg* in marriage, or as contestants in a competition *etc*: *a well-matched couple; The competitors were evenly matched.*

'**matchless** *adj* having no equal: *a woman of matchless beauty.*

'**matchmaker** *n* a person who tries to arrange marriages between people.

mate [meit] *v* **1** to come, or bring (animals *etc*), together for breeding: *The bears have mated and produced a cub.* **2** (*chess*) to checkmate (someone). – *n* **1** an animal *etc* with which another is paired for breeding: *Some birds sing in order to attract a mate.* **2** a husband or wife. **3** a companion or friend: *We've been mates for years.* **4** a fellow workman or assistant: *a carpenter's mate.* **5** a merchant ship's officer under the master or captain: *the first mate.* **6** in chess, checkmate.

material [məˈtiəriəl] *n* **1** anything out of which something is, or may be, made: *Tables are usually made from solid material such as wood.* **2** cloth: *I'd like three metres of blue woollen material.* – *adj* **1** consisting of solid(s), liquid(s), gas(es) or any combination of these: *the material world.* **2** belonging to the world; not spiritual: *He wanted material things like money, possessions and power.* **3** essential or important: *evidence that is material to his defence.*

ma'terially *adv* to a great or important extent: *Circumstances have changed materially.*

ma'terialize, -ise *v* **1** to take solid or bodily form: *The figure materialized as we watched with astonishment.* **2** (of something expected or hoped for) to happen: *I don't think her plans will materialize.*

ma,teriali'zation, -s- *n.*

maternal [məˈtəːnl] *adj* **1** of or like a mother: *maternal feelings.* **2** related on the mother's side of the family: *my maternal grandfather.*

ma'ternally *adv.*

maternity [məˈtəːnəti] *n* (*usu as adj*) the state of being or becoming a mother: *a maternity hospital*; *maternity clothes.*

mathematics [maθəˈmatiks] *n sing* (*abbrev* **maths** [maθs], (*Amer*) **math** [maθ]) the science or branch of knowledge dealing with measurements, numbers and quantities.

,mathe'matical *adj* **1** of or done by mathematics: *mathematical tables.* **2** very exact or accurate: *mathematical precision.* **,mathe'matically** *adv.*

,mathema'tician [-ˈtiʃən] *n* **1** a person who is good at mathematics: *For a young boy, he's quite a mathematician!* **2** someone who works in mathematics: *He is a mathematician with a local engineering firm.*

matinée [ˈmatinei, (*Amer*) matəˈnei] *n* a performance at a theatre, circus, cinema *etc* held in the afternoon or morning.

matriarch [ˈmeitriaːk] *n* a woman who is head and ruler of her family or of a tribe.

,matri'archal *adj* of, like, ruled by *etc* a matriarch or matriarchs: *a matriarchal society* (= a society dominated by women).

matrimony [ˈmatriməni, (*Amer*) -mouni] *n* the state of being married: *holy matrimony.* **,matri'monial** [-ˈmou-] *adj.*

matron [ˈmeitrən] *n* **1** a senior nurse in charge of a hospital. **2** a dignified married woman: *Her behaviour shocked all the middle-class matrons in the neighbourhood.*

'matronly *adj* **1** dignified and calm. **2** rather fat: *a matronly figure.*

matter [ˈmatə] *n* **1** solids, liquids and/or gases

in any form, from which everything physical is made: *The entire universe is made up of different kinds of matter.* **2** a subject or topic (of discussion *etc*): *a private matter*; *money matters.* **3** pus: *The wound was infected and full of matter.* – *v* to be important: *That car matters a great deal to him*; *It doesn't matter.*

,matter-of-'fact *adj* keeping to the actual facts; not fanciful, emotional or imaginative: *a matter-of-fact account/statement/opinion/attitude.*

be the matter (*often with* **with**) to be the/a trouble, difficulty or thing that is wrong: *Is anything the matter?*; *What's the matter with you?*

a matter of course something that one expects to happen, be done *etc*: *You don't have to ask her – she'll do it as a matter of course.*

a matter of opinion something about which different people have different opinions or views: *Whether she's clever or not is a matter of opinion.*

no matter it is not important: *'He's not here.' 'No matter, I'll see him later.'*

no matter who, what, where *etc* whoever, whatever, wherever *etc*: *No matter what happens, I'll go.*

mattress [ˈmatris] *n* a thick, firm layer of padding, covered in cloth *etc*, for lying on, *usu* as part of a bed.

mature [məˈtjuə] *adj* **1** (having the qualities of someone who, or something that, is) fully grown or developed: *a very mature person.* **2** (of cheese, wine *etc*) ready for eating or drinking: *a mature cheese.* – *v* **1** to make or become mature: *She matured early.* **2** (of an insurance policy) to become due to be paid: *My insurance policy matures when I reach sixty-five.* **ma'turely** *adv.*

ma'turity, ma'tureness *ns.*

maul [moːl] *v* (*esp* of an animal) to injure (a person or animal) *usu* badly: *He was badly mauled by an angry lion.*

mausoleum [moːsəˈliəm] *n* a very fine tomb, often with a monument: *They buried the duke in the mausoleum.*

mauve [mouv] *n, adj* (of) a pale purple colour.

maxim [ˈmaksim] *n* a saying, general truth or rule giving a guide to good behaviour: *'He who hesitates is lost' is a well-known maxim.*

maximum [ˈmaksiməm] *adj* greatest: *This requires maximum effort/the maximum amount of effort.* – *n* – *pls* **'maximums, 'maxima** [-mə] – the greatest number or quantity or the highest point or degree: *Two hundred an hour is the maximum we can produce.*

may [mei] – *neg short form* **mayn't** [ˈmeiənt] – **1** to have the permission to: *You may go home now.* **2** used to express a possibility in the present or future: *He may be here, I don't know.* **3** used to express a wish: *May you live a long and happy life.*

may as well might as well.

may have used to express a possibility in the past: *He may have been here, but we cannot be sure.*

May [mei] *n* the fifth month of the year, the month following April.

May Day the first day of May, an *esp* socialist holiday or festival in many countries.

maybe ['meibiː] *adv* it is possible (that); perhaps: *Maybe he'll come, and maybe he won't.*

mayday ['meidei] *n* the international distress signal sent out by ships and aircraft: *The ship sent out a mayday (signal) before it sank.*

mayonnaise [meiə'neiz, (*Amer*) 'meiəneiz] *n* a thick sauce made of egg yolk, oil, vinegar or lemon and seasoning, and often used on salads.

mayor [meə, (*Amer*) 'meiər] *n* (*esp* in England, Ireland and the United States) the chief public official of a city, town or borough.

'**mayoress** *n* **1** a mayor's wife: *The mayor and mayoress attended the dinner.* **2** a female mayor: *She has just been elected mayoress.*

lord mayor in Britain the mayor of some capital and other cities: *The Lord Mayor of London.*

maze [meiz] *n* a deliberately confusing series of paths, often surrounded by walls or hedges, from which it's difficult to find the way out: *I'm lost in a maze of rules and regulations.*

me [miː] *pron* (used as the object of a verb or preposition and sometimes instead of **I**) the word used by a speaker or writer when referring to himself: *He hit me; Give that to me; It's me; He can go with John and me.*

meadow ['medou] *n* (*often in pl*) a field of grass, *usu* on low ground: *There were cows in the meadow.*

meagre, (*Amer*) **meager** ['miːgə] *adj* poor or not enough: *meagre strength.*

'**meagrely** *adv.* '**meagreness** *n.*

meal[1] [miːl] *n* the food taken at one time: *She eats three meals a day.*

meal[2] [miːl] *n* the edible parts of grain ground to a coarse powder: *a sack of meal*; *oatmeal.*

'**mealy** *adj* like, or containing, meal.

mean[1] [miːn] *adj* **1** not generous (with money *etc*): *He's very mean (with his money/over pay).* **2** likely or intending to cause harm or annoyance: *It is mean to tell lies.* **3** (*esp Amer*) bad-tempered, vicious or cruel: *a*

mean mood. **4** (of a house *etc*) of poor quality; humble: *a mean dwelling.* '**meanly** *adv.* '**meanness** *n.*

mean[2] [miːn] *adj* **1** (of a statistic) having the middle position between two points, quantities *etc*: *the mean value on a graph.* **2** average: *the mean annual rainfall.* – *n* something that is midway between two opposite ends or extremes: *Three is the mean of the series one to five.*

mean[3] [miːn] – *pt, ptp* **meant** [ment] – *v* **1** to (intend to) express, show or indicate: *'Vacation' means 'holiday'*; *What do you mean by (saying/doing) that?* **2** to intend: *I meant to go to the exhibition but forgot*; *For whom was that letter meant?*; *He means* (= is determined) *to be a rich man some day.*

'**meaning** *n* the sense in which a statement, action, word *etc* is (intended to be) understood: *What is the meaning of this phrase?*; *What is the meaning of his behaviour?* – *adj* (of a look, glance *etc*) showing a certain feeling or giving a certain message: *The teacher gave the boy a meaning look when he arrived late.*

'**meaningful** *adj* (often used loosely) important in some way: *a meaningful statement/relationship.*

'**meaningless** *adj* without meaning or reason; of no importance: *meaningless chatter.*

be meant to to be required or supposed; to have to: *The child is meant to be asleep!*

mean well to have good intentions: *He meant well by what he said.*

meander [mi'andə] *v* **1** (of a river) to flow slowly along with many bends and curves: *The stream meandered through the meadows.* **2** (of people *etc*) to wander about in various directions: *His writing meanders all over the page.*

means[1] [miːnz] *n sing or pl* the instrument(s), method(s) *etc* by which a thing is, or may be, done or made to happen: *By what means can we find out?*

by all means yes, of course: *If you want to use the telephone, by all means do.*

by means of using: *We escaped by means of a secret tunnel.*

by no means 1 definitely not: *'Can I go home now?' 'By no means!'* **2** (*also* **not by any means**) not at all: *I'm by no means certain to win.*

means[2] [miːnz] *n pl* money available or necessary for living *etc*: *She's a person of considerable means* (= She has plenty of money).

a man of means a wealthy or rich man.

meantime ['miːntaim] *adv, n* (in the) time or period between: *I'll hear her account of the matter later – meantime, I'd like to hear yours.*

meanwhile ['mi:nwail] *adv* during this time; at the same time: *The child had gone home. Meanwhile, his mother was searching for him in the street.*

measles ['mi:zlz] *n sing* an infectious disease accompanied by red spots on the skin: *People usually get measles in childhood.*

measure ['meʒə] *n* **1** an instrument for finding the size, amount *etc* of something: *a glass measure for liquids*; *a tape-measure.* **2** a unit: *The metre is a measure of length.* **3** a system of measuring: *dry/liquid/square measure.* **4** a plan of action or something done: *We must take* (= use, or put into action) *certain measures to stop the increase in crime.* **5** a certain amount: *a measure of sympathy.* – *v* **1** to find the size, amount *etc* of (something): *He measured the table.* **2** to show the size, amount *etc* of: *A thermometer measures temperature.* **3** (*with* **against**, **besides** *etc*) to judge in comparison with: *She measured her skill in cooking against her friend's.* **4** to be a certain size: *This table measures two metres by one metre.*

'measurement *n* **1** size, amount *etc* found by measuring: *What are the measurements of this room?* **2** the sizes of various parts of the body, *usu* the distance round the chest, waist and hips: *What are your measurements, madam?* **3** the act of measuring: *We can find the size of something by means of measurement.*

beyond measure very great: *I'm offering you riches beyond measure!*

for good measure as something extra or above the minimum necessary: *The shopkeeper weighed out the sweets and put in a few more for good measure.*

full measure (no less than) the correct amount: *We must ensure that customers get full measure.*

made to measure (of clothing) made to fit the measurements of a particular person: *Was your jacket made to measure?*; (*also adj*) *a made-to-measure suit.*

measure out to mark (off), weigh (out) a certain distance, amount: *He measured out a kilo of sugar.*

measure up (*often with* **to**) to reach a certain required standard: *John's performance doesn't measure up (to the others).*

meat [mi:t] *n* the flesh of animals or birds used as food: *She does not eat meat*; (*also adj*) *What did you have for the meat course?*

'meaty *adj* **1** full of (animal) meat: *a meaty soup/stew.* **2** (tasting, smelling *etc*) like meat: *This smells meaty.*

mechanic [mi'kanik] *n* a skilled worker who repairs or maintains machinery.

me'chanical *adj* **1** having to do with machines: *mechanical engineering.* **2** worked or done by machinery: *a mechanical*

sweeper. **3** done *etc* without thinking, from force of habit: *a mechanical action.* **me'chanically** *adv.*

me'chanics *n sing* **1** the science of the action of forces on objects: *He is studying mechanics.* **2** the art of building machines: *He applied his knowledge of mechanics to designing a new wheelchair.* – *n pl* the ways in which something works or is applied: *the mechanics of the legal system.*

'mechanism ['me-] *n* a (*usu* small) piece of machinery: *a watch mechanism.*

'mechanize, -ise ['me-] *v* to introduce machinery into (an industry *etc*): *We've mechanized the entire process.* **2** to supply (troops) with motor vehicles. **,mechani'zation, -s- n.**

medal ['medl] *n* a piece of metal with a design, inscription *etc* stamped on it, given as a reward for bravery, long service, excellence *etc*, or made to celebrate a special occasion: *He won a medal in the War.*

'medallist, (*Amer*) **'medalist** *n* a person who has won a medal in a competition *etc*:

meddle ['medl] *v* to interfere: *She was always trying to meddle.* **'meddler** *n.*

'meddlesome *adj* fond of meddling: *a meddlesome old woman.*

mediate ['mi:dieit] *v* to try to settle a dispute between people who are disagreeing: *The United States is trying to mediate (in the dispute) between these two countries.* **,medi'ation** *n.* **'mediator** *n.*

medical ['medikəl] *adj* of healing, medicine or doctors: *medical care*; *medical insurance.* – *n* a medical examination. **'medically** *adv.*

medicated ['medikeitid] *adj* having a healing or health-giving substance mixed in: *Medicated shampoo.*

medicine ['medsin] *n* **1** a substance, *esp* a liquid for swallowing, that is used to treat or keep away disease or illness: *a dose of medicine.* **2** the science of curing people who are ill, or making their suffering less (*esp* by means other than surgery): *He is studying medicine.*

medicinal [mə'disinl] *adj* **1** having the power to heal and used as a medicine: *medicinal substances.* **2** of healing: *for medicinal purposes.* **me'dicinally** *adv.*

medieval, mediaeval [medi'i:vəl, (*Amer*) mi:-] *adj* of, or belonging to, the Middle Ages: *medieval plays/music.*

mediocre [mi:di'oukə] *adj* not very good or great; ordinary: *a mediocre performance/effort.* **medi'ocrity** ['-o-] *n.*

meditate ['mediteit] *v* **1** to think deeply: *He was meditating on his troubles.* **2** to spend short, regular periods in deep (*esp* religious) thought: *He meditates twice a day.* **,medi'tation** *n.*

'meditative [-tətiv, (*Amer*) -teitiv] *adj*

thoughtful: *a meditative mood.* '**meditatively** *adv.*

medium ['mi:diəm] – *pls* **media** [-diə], **mediums** – *n* **1** something by or through which an effect is produced: *Air is the medium through which sound is carried.* **2** (*esp in pl*) a means (*esp* radio, television and newspapers) by which news *etc* is made known: *the news media.* **3** a person through whom spirits of dead people are said to speak: *I know a medium who says she can communicate with Napoleon.* **4** a substance in which specimens are preserved, bacteria grown *etc.* – *adj* middle or average in size, quality *etc*: *Would you like the small, medium or large packet?*

medley ['medli] *n* a piece of music put together from a number of other pieces: *She sang a medley of old songs.*

meek [mi:k] *adj* humble and not likely to complain, argue, react strongly *etc*: *a meek little man.* '**meekly** *adv.* '**meekness** *n.*

meet [mi:t] – *pt, ptp* **met** [met] – *v* **1** to come face to face with (*eg* a person whom one knows), by chance: *She met a man on the train.* **2** (*sometimes, esp Amer, with* **with**) to come together with (a person *etc*), by arrangement: *The committee meets every Monday.* **3** to be introduced to (someone) for the first time: *Come and meet my wife.* **4** to join: *Where do the two roads meet?* **5** to be equal to or satisfy (*eg* a person's needs, requirements *etc*): *Will there be sufficient stocks to meet the public demand?* **6** to come into the view, experience or presence of: *A terrible sight met him/his eyes when he opened the door.* **7** to come to or be faced with: *He met his death in a car accident.* **8** (*with* **with**) to experience or suffer; to receive a particular response: *She met with an accident; The scheme met with their approval.* **9** to answer or oppose: *We will meet force with greater force.* – *n* a gathering, *esp* of sportsmen: *The local huntsmen are holding a meet this week.*

'**meeting** *n* **1** an act of meeting: *The meeting between my mother and my husband was not friendly.* **2** a gathering of people for discussion or another purpose: *to attend a committee meeting.*

meet (someone) halfway to respond to (someone) by making an equal effort or a compromise: *I'll invest £5 000 in this idea if you meet me halfway and do the same.*

mega- [megə] **1** a million, as in **megaton.** **2** (*also* **megalo-** [megəlou]) large or great, as in **megalomania.**

megalomania [megələ'meiniə] *n* the idea, *usu* false, that one is great or powerful, combined with a passion for more greatness or power.

megalo'maniac [-ak] *adj, n* (of) a person having megalomania: *That country is in the power of a dangerous megalomaniac.*

megaphone ['megəfoun] *n* a funnel-shaped device for speaking through, that causes sounds to be made louder and/or sent in a given direction: *He shouted instructions to the crowd through a megaphone.*

megaton ['megətən] *adj* (*usu with a number*) (of a bomb) giving an explosion as great as that of a million tons of TNT: *a five-megaton bomb.*

melancholy ['melənkəli] *n* depression or sadness: *He was overcome by a feeling of melancholy.* – *adj* sad; showing or causing sadness: *melancholy eyes.*

mellow ['melou] *adj* **1** (of character) made softer and more mature, relaxed *etc* by age and/or experience: *Her personality became more mellow as middle age approached.* **2** (of sound, colour, light *etc*) soft, not strong or unpleasant: *The lamplight was soft and mellow.* **3** (of wine, cheese *etc*) kept until the flavour has developed fully: *a mellow burgundy.* – *v* to make or become softer or more mature: *Old age has mellowed him.* '**mellowness** *n.*

melodrama ['melədra:mə] *n* **1** a (type of) play in which emotions and the goodness or wickedness of the characters are exaggerated greatly. **2** (an example of) behaviour similar to a play of this sort: *He makes a melodrama out of everything that happens.* ,**melodra'matic** [-drə'ma-] *adj.* ,**melo-dra'matically** *adv.*

melody ['melədi] – *pl* '**melodies** – *n* **1** a tune: *He played Irish melodies on the harp.* **2** the principal part in a piece of harmonized music: *The sopranos sang the melody, and the other voices added the harmony.*

me'lodic [-'lo-] *adj* of melody: *a melodic style.*

me'lodious ['lou-] *adj* pleasing to the ear; tuneful: *melodious tunes.* **me'lodiously** *adv.* **me'lodiousness** *n.*

melon ['melən] *n* **1** a large, sweet fruit with many seeds. **2** its firm yellow or red flesh as food: *We started the meal with melon;* (*also adj*) *a melon seed.*

melt [melt] *v* to (cause to) become soft or liquid, or to lose shape, *usu* by heating/being heated: *The ice has melted; My heart melted when I saw how sorry he was.*

'**melting-point** *n* the temperature at which a given solid melts: *The melting-point of ice is 0° centigrade.*

member ['membə] *n* **1** a person who belongs to a group, club, society, trade union *etc*: *The association has three thousand members.* **2** short for **Member of Parliament.**

'**membership** *n* **1** the state of being a member: *membership of the Communist Party.* **2** a group of members: *a society with a* *large membership.* **3** the amount of money paid to a society *etc* in order to become a member: *The membership has increased to $5 this year.*

membrane ['membrein] *n* a thin film or layer of tissue that covers or lines parts of the body, forms the outside of cells *etc*.

memento [mə'mentou] – *pl* me'mento(e)s – *n* something kept or given as a reminder or souvenir: *They gave her a small gift as a memento.*

memo ['memou] short for **memorandum**.

memoirs ['memwa:z] *n pl* a person's written account of his own life; an autobiography: *When I retire, I'm going to write my memoirs.*

memorable ['memərəbl] *adj* worthy of being remembered: *a memorable event.*

memorandum [memə'randəm] – *pls* ,memo-'randums, ,memo'randa [-də] *n (often abbrev* **memo** ['memou] – *pl* 'memos –) **1** a note to help one to remember: *He wrote a memo*; (*also adj*) *a memo pad.* **2** a (brief) written statement about a particular matter, often passed around between colleagues: *a memorandum on Thursday's meeting.*

memorial [mi'mo:riəl] *n* something (*eg* a monument) that honours or commemorates people or events of the past: *a memorial to Sir Winston Churchill*; *a war memorial.*

memory ['memori] – *pl* 'memories – *n* **1** the power to remember things: *a good memory for details.* **2** the mind's store of remembered things: *Her memory is full of interesting stories.* **3** something remembered: *memories of her childhood.* **4** the time as far back as can be remembered: *the greatest fire in memory.*

'memorize, -ise *v* to learn (something) so well that one can remember all of it without looking: *She memorized the directions.*

from memory by remembering; without using a book *etc* for reference: *He said the whole poem from memory.*

in memory of/to the memory of as a reminder or memorial of: *They built a monument in memory of their dead leader.*

menace ['menəs] *n* **1** something likely to cause injury, damage *etc*: *Traffic is a menace on narrow roads.* **2** a threat or show of hostility: *His voice was full of menace.* – *v* to threaten: *menaced by danger.*

'menacing *adj* threatening to harm: *a menacing weapon.* **'menacingly** *adv.*

menagerie [mi'nadʒəri] *n* (a place for keeping) a collection of wild animals.

mend [mend] *v* **1** to put (something broken, torn *etc*) into good condition again; to repair: *Can you mend this broken chair?* **2** to grow better, *esp* in health: *My broken*

leg is mending very well. – *n* a repaired place: *This shirt has a mend in the sleeve.*

'mending *n* **1** the act of repairing: *the mending of the chair.* **2** things needing to be mended, *esp* by sewing: *Put your torn shirt with my pile of mending!*

meningitis [menin'dʒaitis] *n* a serious disease in which there is inflammation of the membranes round the brain or spinal cord.

menstruate ['menstrueit] *v* to discharge blood monthly from the uterus: *Many girls begin to menstruate at the age of 12 or 13.* ,men-stru'ation *n.*

mental ['mentl] *adj* **1** of the mind: *mental illnesses/disorders.* **2** done or made by the mind: *mental arithmetic*; *a mental picture.* **3** for those who are ill in mind: *a mental hospital.* **4** suffering from an illness of the mind: *a mental patient.*

men'tality [-'ta-] *n* (a level of) mental power: *low mentality.*

'mentally *adv* in the mind: *She's mentally incapable of understanding*; *He is mentally ill.*

menthol ['menθəl] *n* a sharp-smelling substance got from peppermint oil used to help give relief from colds *etc*: *If you have a cold put some menthol in boiling water and breathe in the steam*; *Some cigarettes contain menthol.*

'mentholated [-leitid] *adj* containing menthol: *mentholated cigarettes.*

mention ['menʃən] *v* **1** to speak of or refer to: *He mentioned the plan.* **2** to remark or say *usu* briefly or indirectly: *She mentioned (that) she might be leaving.* – *n (often with* **of**) a (*usu* brief) remark (about): *No mention was made of this matter.*

not to mention used to emphasize something important or to excuse oneself for mentioning something relatively unimportant: *He is rich and clever, not to mention handsome.*

menu ['menju:] *n* (a card with) a list of dishes that may be ordered at a meal: *What's on the menu today?*

mercenary ['mə:sinəri] *adj* too strongly influenced by desire for money: *a mercenary attitude.* – *n* – *pl* 'mercenaries – a soldier from one country who hires his services to another country: *Mercenaries are fighting in Africa.*

merchandise ['mə:tʃəndaiz] *n* goods to be bought and sold: *This store sells merchandise from all over the world.*

merchant ['mə:tʃənt] *n* a trader, *esp* wholesale, in goods of a particular kind: *timber/tea/wine merchants.*

merchant marine, navy, service the ships of a country that are employed in trading, and their crews: *His son has joined the merchant navy.*

merchant ship a ship involved in trade.

mercury ['mə:kjuri] *n* an element, a poisonous, silvery, liquid metal used *esp* in thermometers *etc*.

mercy ['mə:si] – *pl* 'mercies – *n* **1** kindness towards a person, *esp* an enemy, who is in one's power: *He showed his enemies no mercy*. **2** a piece of good luck or something for which one should be grateful: *It was a mercy that it didn't rain*.
'**merciful** *adj* willing to forgive or to punish only lightly: *a merciful judge*. '**mercifully** *adv*.
'**merciless** *adj* without mercy; cruel: *merciless criticism*. '**mercilessly** *adv*.
at the mercy of wholly in the power of, liable to be harmed by: *A sailor is at the mercy of the sea*.
have mercy on to give kindness to (an enemy *etc* who is in one's power): *Have mercy on me!*

mere [miə] *adj* no more than or no better than: *a mere child*; *the merest suggestion of criticism*.
'**merely** *adv* simply or only: *I was merely asking a question*.

merge [mə:dʒ] *v* **1** to (cause to) combine or join: *The sea and sky appear to merge at the horizon*. **2** (*with* into) to change gradually into something else: *Summer slowly merged into autumn*. **3** (*with* into *etc*) to disappear into (*eg* a crowd, back-ground *etc*): *He merged into the crowd*.
'**merger** *n* a joining together of business firms: *There's been a merger between two companies*.

meridian [mə'ridiən] *n* an imaginary line on the earth's surface passing through the poles and any given place; any line of longitude.

meringue [mə'raŋ] *n* (a cake made from) a crisp cooked mixture of sugar and white of eggs.

merit ['merit] *n* **1** the quality of worth, excellence or praiseworthiness: *He reached his present position through merit*. **2** a good point or quality: *His speech had at least the merit of being short*. – *v* to deserve as reward or punishment: *Your case merits careful consideration*.
,**meri'torious** [-'tɔ:-] *adj* deserving reward or praise: *a meritorious performance*.

mermaid ['mə:meid] – *masc* 'merman [-man] – *n* an imaginary sea creature with a human body down to the waist and a fish's tail.

merry ['meri] *adj* **1** cheerful; noisily or laughingly lively *etc*: *merry children*; *a merry party*. **2** slightly drunk: *He's been getting merry on whisky*. '**merrily** *adv*. '**merriness** *n*.
'**merriment** *n* fun and laughter: *There was a great deal of merriment at the party*.
'**merry-go-round** *n* (*Amer* ,**carou'sel**) a re-

volving ring of toy horses *etc* on which children ride at a fair.
'**merrymaking** *n* cheerful celebration: *all the merrymaking at Christmas*. '**merrymaker** *n*.

mesdames *see* **madam**.

mesh [meʃ] *n* **1** (one of) the openings between the threads of a net: *a net of* (*a*) *very fine* (=small) *mesh*. **2** (*often in pl*) a network: *A fly was struggling in the meshes of the spider's web*. – *v* (of teeth on *eg* gear wheels) to become engaged with each other: *The teeth on these two cogwheels mesh when they go round*.

mesmerize, -ise ['mezməraiz] *v* to hypnotize: *The child was mesmerized* (=fascinated) *by the television screen*. '**mesmerism** *n*.

mess [mes] *n* a state of disorder or confusion; an untidy, dirty or unpleasant sight or muddle: *This room is in a terrible mess!*; *She looked a mess*; *The spilt food made a mess on the carpet*. – *v* (*with* with) to meddle, or to have something to do with: *She's always messing with the television set*.
'**messy** *adj* dirty: *a messy job*. '**messily** *adv*. '**messiness** *n*.
'**mess-up** *n* a muddle or state of confusion: *There has been a mess-up in the timetable*.
make a mess of 1 to make dirty, untidy or confused: *The heavy rain has made a real mess of the garden*. **2** to do badly: *He made a mess of his essay*. **3** to spoil or ruin (*eg* one's life): *He made a mess of his life by drinking too much*.
mess about/around 1 to behave in a foolish or annoying way: *The children were shouting and messing about*. **2** to work with no particular plan in a situation that involves mess: *I love messing about in the kitchen*. **3** (*with* with) to meddle or interfere with: *Who's been messing about with my papers?* **4** to upset or put into a state of disorder or confusion: *The wind messed her hair about*.
mess up to spoil; to make a mess of: *Don't mess the room up!*

message ['mesidʒ] *n* **1** a piece of information spoken or written, passed from one person to another: *I have a message for you from Mr Johnston*. **2** the instruction or teaching of a moral story, religion, prophet *etc*: *What message is this story trying to give us?*
'**messenger** [-sindʒə] *n* a person who carries letters, information *etc* from place to place: *The king's messenger brought news of the army's defeat*.

Messiah [mə'saiə] *n* (*with* the) Jesus Christ.

metal ['metl] *n*, *adj* **1** (of) any of a group of substances, *usu* shiny, that can conduct heat and electricity and can be hammered into shape, or drawn out in sheets, bars *etc*: *Gold, silver and iron are all metals*. **2** (of) a combination of more than one of such

substances: *Brass is a metal made from copper and zinc.*

me'tallic [-'ta-] *adj* **1** made of metal: *a metallic element.* **2** like a metal (*eg* in appearance or sound): *metallic blue; a metallic noise.*

metamorphosis [metə'mɔːfəsis] – *pl* ‚meta'morphoses [-siːz] – *n* (a) marked change of form, appearance, character *etc*: *a caterpillar's metamorphosis into a butterfly.*

metaphor ['metəfə] *n* a form of expression (not using 'like' or 'as') in which a quality or characteristic is given to a person or thing by using a name, image, adjective *etc* normally used of something else which has similar qualities *etc*: *'He's a tiger when he's angry' is an example of (a) metaphor.* ‚meta'phoric(al) [-'fo-] *adj* of, like or using metaphors: *metaphorical language.* ‚meta'phorically *adv.*

meteor ['miːtiə] *n* (*also* **shooting star**) a small mass or body travelling very quickly through space which appears very bright after entering the earth's atmosphere. ‚mete'oric [-'o-] *adj* (of success *etc*) rapid and often only lasting for a short time: *a meteoric rise to fame.* 'meteorite [-rait] *n* a small meteor that has fallen to earth.

meteorology [miːtiə'rolədʒi] *n* the study of weather and climate. ‚meteo'rologist *n.* ‚meteoro'logical [-'lo-] *adj*: *meteorological charts.*

meter ['miːtə] *n* **1** an instrument for measuring, *esp* quantities of electricity, gas, water *etc*: *If you want to know how much electricity you have used you will have to look at the meter.* **2** (*Amer*) *see* **metre¹, metre².** – *v* to measure (*esp* electricity *etc*) by using a meter: *This instrument meters rainfall.*

method ['meθəd] *n* **1** the way in which one does something: *I don't like his methods of training workers.* **2** an orderly or fixed series of actions for doing something: *Follow the method set down in the instruction book.* **3** good sense and a definite plan: *Her work seems to lack method.* **me'thodical** [-'θo-] *adj* (*neg* **un-**) **1** arranged or done in an orderly manner or according to a plan: *a methodical search.* **2** (in the habit of) acting in a planned, orderly way: *a methodical person/nature.* **me'thodically** *adv.*

meticulous [mi'tikjuləs] *adj* very careful, almost too careful (about small details): *He paid meticulous attention to detail.* **me'ticulously** *adv.*

metre¹, (*Amer*) **meter** ['miːtə] *n* (*often abbrev* **m** *when written*) the chief unit of length in the metric system, equal to 39.37 inches: *This table is one metre broad.*

metric ['metrik] *adj* of the metre or metric system: *Are these scales metric?* **the metric system** a system of weights and measures based on multiples of ten (*eg* 1 metre = 100 centimetres, 1 centimetre = 10 millimetres *etc*).

metre², (*Amer*) **meter** ['miːtə] *n* (in poetry) the regular arrangement of syllables that are stressed or unstressed, long or short: *The metre of this passage is typical of Shakespeare.* 'metrical ['me-] *adj* of or in poetry: *The translation is not metrical – it is in prose.*

metronome ['metrənoum] *n* an instrument that can be set to make a ticking noise at different speeds to mark musical time.

metropolis [mə'tropəlis] *n* a large city, *esp* the chief city of a country: *London is England's metropolis.* **metropolitan** [metrə'politən] *adj* of or in a capital city: *the metropolitan area/police.*

mew [mjuː] *v* to make the cry of a (young) cat: *The kittens mewed.* – *n* such a cry.

mezzo ['metsou], **mezzo-soprano** [metsou-sə'praːnou] – *pls* 'mezzos, ‚mezzo-so'pranos – *n* (a person having) a singing voice between soprano and alto.

miaow [mi'au] *v* to make the cry of a cat: *The cat miaowed all night.* – *n* such a cry.

mice *see* **mouse.**

micro- [maikrou] **1** very small: *microcomputer; microprint; micro-organism.* **2** one millionth part: *microvolt* (= one millionth of a volt).

microbe ['maikroub] *n* a very tiny living thing invisible to the naked eye, *esp* a germ causing disease.

microcomputer [maikroukəm'pjuːtə] *n* a very small computer containing tiny pieces of silicon *etc* ('**microchips**) designed to act as complex electronic circuits.

microfilm ['maikrəfilm] *n* film on which documents, books *etc* are recorded very much smaller than actual size.

microphone ['maikrəfoun] *n* (*abbrev* **mike** [maik]) an electronic instrument for picking up sound waves to be broadcast, recorded or amplified as in radio, the telephone, a tape-recorder *etc*: *Speak into the microphone.*

microscope ['maikrəskoup] *n* an instrument which makes very small objects able to be seen magnifying them greatly: *Germs are very small, and can only be seen with the aid of a microscope.* ‚micro'scopic [-'sko-] *adj* seen only by the aid of a microscope: *microscopic bacteria.* ‚micro'scopically *adv.*

mid [mid] *adj* at, or in, the middle of: *a midweek football match; in mid air; a mid-air collision between two aircraft.*

'mid-'fielders in football *etc*, the players in the middle area of the pitch.

midday [mid'dei] *n* the middle of the day; twelve o'clock: *We'll meet you at midday*; (*also adj*) *a midday meal*.

middle ['midl] *n* 1 the central point or part: *the middle of a circle*. 2 the central area of the body; the waist: *You're getting rather fat round your middle.* – *adj* equally distant from both ends: *the middle seat in a row*.

'**middling** *adj* average: *He's neither tall nor short, but of middling height*.

middle age the years between youth and old age: *She is well into middle age.* ,**middle=** '**aged** *adj*.

Middle Ages (*with the*) the time between the end of the Roman Empire and the Renaissance.

Middle East (*with the*) Egypt and the countries of Asia west of Pakistan.

'**middleman** [-man] *n* a dealer who buys goods from the person who makes or grows them, and sells them to shopkeepers or to the public; a wholesaler: *You can save money by buying direct from the factory and cutting out the middleman*.

be in the middle of (doing) something to be busily occupied doing something: *Please excuse my appearance. I was in the middle of washing my hair*.

midget ['midʒit] *n* a person who is fully developed but has not grown to normal height.

midnight ['midnait] *n* twelve o'clock at night: *I'll go to bed at midnight*; (*also adj*) *a midnight attack*.

midriff ['midrif] *n* the middle of the body just below the ribs.

midst [midst]: **in the midst of** 1 among or in the centre of: *in the midst of a crowd of people*. 2 at the same time as: *in the midst of all these troubles*.

in our, your, their midst among, or in the same place as, us, you or them: *Large buildings keep rising in our midst*.

midsummer [mid'sʌmə] *n* the middle of summer: *It happened in midsummer*; (*also adj*) *a midsummer day*.

midway [mid'wei] *adj, adv* in the middle of the distance or time between two points; halfway: *the midway point*.

midwife ['midwaif] – *pl* '**midwives** [-waivz] – *n* a person (*usu* a trained nurse) who helps at the birth of children. **mid'wifery** [mid'wi-, (*Amer*) 'midwai-] *n*.

midwinter [mid'wintə] *n* the middle of winter: *He arrived in midwinter*; (*also adj*) *on a midwinter day*.

might[1] [mait] – *neg short form* **mightn't** ['maitnt] – 1 *pt* of **may**: *I thought I might find you here*; *He might come if you offered him a meal*. 2 used instead of 'may', *eg* to

make a possibility seem less likely, or a request for permission more polite: *He might win if he tries hard*; *Might I speak to you for a few minutes, please?* 3 used in suggesting that a person is not doing what he should: *You might help me clean the car!*

might as well used to suggest that there is no good reason for not doing something: *I might as well do it all at once*.

might have 1 used to suggest that something would have been possible if something else had been the case: *You might have caught the bus if you had run*. 2 used to suggest that a person has not done what he should: *You might have told me!* 3 used to show that something was a possible action *etc* but was in fact not carried out or done: *I might have gone, but I decided not to*. 4 used when a person does not want to admit to having done something: *'Have you seen this man?' 'I might have.'*

I *etc* **might have known** (often used in annoyance) **I** *etc* ought to have known, thought, guessed *etc* that something was or would be the case: *I might have known you would lose the key!*

might[2] [mait] *n* power or strength: *The might of the opposing army was too great for us*.

'**mighty** *adj* having great power: *a mighty nation*. '**mightily** *adv*. '**mightiness** *n*.

migraine ['mi:grein, (*Amer*) 'mai-] *n* (an attack of) a type of very severe headache, often accompanied by vomiting and difficulty in seeing: *She suffers from migraine*.

migrate [mai'greit, (*Amer*) 'maigreit] *v* 1 (of certain birds and animals) to travel from one region to another at certain times of the year: *Many birds migrate in the early winter*. 2 (of people) to change one's home to another country or (regularly) from place to place: *The Gothic peoples who overwhelmed the Roman Empire migrated from the East*. **mi'gration** *n*.

'**migrant** [(*Brit and Amer*) 'mai-] *n* a person, bird or animal that migrates or has migrated: *The swallow is a summer migrant to Britain*; (*also adj*) *migrant workers*.

'**migratory** [(Brit and Amer) 'maigrə-] *adj*.

mike *see* **microphone**.

mild [maild] *adj* 1 (of a person or his personality) gentle in temper or behaviour: *such a mild man*. 2 (of punishment *etc*) not severe: *a mild sentence*. 3 (of weather *esp* if not in summer) not cold; rather warm: *a mild spring day*. 4 (of spices, spiced foods *etc*) not hot: *a mild curry*. '**mildly** *adv*. '**mildness** *n*.

mile [mail] *n* (*sometimes abbrev* **m** *when written*) a measure of length equal to 1760 yards (1.61 km): *We walked ten miles today*; *70 miles per hour* (sometimes written **mph**); *a ten-mile hike*.

'milestone *n* **1** a stone set up to show distances in miles to various places. **2** a very important event: *The discovery of penicillin was a milestone in medical history.*

military ['militəri] *adj* of soldiers or armed forces generally, or war: *military supplies/discipline/power.*

milk [milk] *n* a white liquid produced by female mammals as food for their young: *The commonest source of milk is the cow.* – *v* to obtain milk from: *The farmer milks his cows each day.*

'milky *adj* **1** containing milk: *milky coffee.* **2** like milk in appearance: *A milky substance.* 'milkiness *n.*

'milkmaid *n* formerly, a woman employed to milk cows by hand.

'milkman *n* a man who delivers milk.

'milkshake *n* a drink made by shaking up milk and a particular flavouring: *I'd like a chocolate/strawberry milkshake.*

milk tooth one of the first set of a baby's teeth: *The child's milk teeth started to come out when he was six years old.*

the Milky Way (*also* the Galaxy) a huge collection of stars stretching across the sky.

mill [mil] *n* **1** a machine, sometimes now electrical, for grinding coffee, pepper *etc* by crushing it between rough, hard surfaces: *a coffee-mill; a pepper-mill.* **2** a building where grain is ground: *The farmer took his corn to the mill.* **3** a building where certain types of things are manufactured: *A woollen-mill; a steel-mill.* – *v* **1** to grind or press: *This flour was milled locally.* **2** (*usu with* about or around) (of crowds) to move about in a disorganized way: *There's a huge crowd of people milling around outside.*

'miller *n* a person who works a grain mill.

'millstone *n* **1** one of the two large, heavy stones used in an old-fashioned mill for grinding grain. **2** (*usu with* round one's/the neck) something that is a heavy burden or responsibility, and prevents easy progress: *He regarded his brother as a millstone round his neck.*

millennium [mi'leniəm] – *pl* mil'lennia [-niə] – *n* a period of a thousand years: *Almost two millennia have passed since the birth of Christ.*

millet ['milit] *n* a type of grain used as food: *The farmer grows millet.*

million ['miljən] – *pls* 'million (**1, 3**), 'millions (**2, 3**) – *n* **1** (preceded by a, a number, or a word signifying a quantity) the number 1 000 000: *a million; one million; five million.* **2** the figure 1 000 000. **3** a million pounds or dollars: *Her fortune amounts to several million(s).* – *adj* (preceded by a, a number, or a word signifying a quantity) 1 000 000 in number: *six million people.*

'million- having a million (of something): *a million-pound banknote.*

,millio'naire [-'neə] – *fem* millio'nairess – *n* a person having a million pounds, dollars *etc* or more.

'millionth *n* **1** one of a million equal parts. **2** the last of a million (people, things *etc*) or (the person, thing *etc*) in an equivalent position: *the millionth (car).*

millipede ['milipi:d] *n* a small many-legged creature with a long round body.

mime [maim] *n* **1** the art of using movement to perform the function of speech, *esp* in drama: *She is studying mime.* **2** a play in which no words are spoken and the actions tell the story: *The children performed a mime.* **3** an actor in such a play; someone who practises this art: *Marcel Marceau is a famous mime.* – *v* to act, *eg* in such a play, using movements rather than words: *He mimed his love for her by holding his hands over his heart.*

mimic ['mimik] – *pt, ptp* 'mimicked – *v* to imitate (someone or something), *esp* with the intention of making him or it appear ridiculous or funny: *The comedian mimicked the Prime Minister's way of speaking.* – *n* a person who mimics: *Children are often good mimics.* 'mimicry *n.*

mimosa [mi'mouzə] *n* a plant with small flowers and fern-like leaves which close when touched (also called sensitive plant).

minaret [minə'ret] *n* a tower on a mosque from which the call to prayer is sounded.

mince [mins] *v* **1** to cut into small pieces or chop finely: *Would you like me to mince the meat for you?* **2** to walk with short steps, in an unpleasantly dainty or delicate way: *She minced over to him.* – *n* meat (*usu* beef) chopped up into small pieces: *mince and potatoes.*

'mincer *n* a machine for mincing meat *etc*: *Could you put the meat in the mincer?*

'mincing *adj* too dainty or prim: *He walked with little mincing steps.* 'mincingly *adv.*

'mincemeat *n* a mixture of raisins, other fruits *etc, usu* with suet (used in baking ,mince-'pies).

mind [maind] the power by which one thinks *etc*; the intelligence or understanding: *The child already has the mind of an adult.* – *v* **1** to look after or supervise (*eg* a child): *mind the baby.* **2** to be upset by; to object to: *You must try not to mind when he criticizes your work.* **3** to be careful of: *Mind* (= be careful not to trip over) *the step!* **4** to pay attention to or obey: *You should mind your parents' words/advice.* – *interj* be careful!: *Mind! There's a car coming!*

-minded having a (certain type of) mind, as in narrow-minded, like-minded.

'**mindless** *adj* stupid and senseless: *mindless violence*. '**mindlessly** *adv*. '**mindlessness** *n*.

'**mindreader** *n* a person who claims to know other people's thoughts.

be out of one's mind to be mad: *He must be out of his mind!*

do you mind! used to show annoyance, stop someone doing something *etc*: *Do you mind! That's my foot you're standing on!*

have a good mind to to feel very much inclined to (do something): *I've a good mind to tell your father what a naughty girl you are!*

have (half) a mind to to feel (slightly) inclined to (do something): *I've half a mind to take my holidays in winter this year.*

in one's mind's eye in one's imagination: *If you try hard, you can see the room in your mind's eye.*

in one's right mind sane: *No-one in his right mind would behave like that.*

keep one's mind on to give all one's attention to: *Keep your mind on what you're doing!*

know one's own mind (*usu in neg*) to know what one really thinks, wants to do *etc*: *She doesn't know her own mind yet about abortion.*

make up one's mind to decide: *They've made up their minds to stay in Africa.*

mind one's own business to attend to one's own affairs, not interfering in other people's: *Go away and mind your own business!*

never mind don't bother; it's all right: *Never mind, I'll do it myself.*

one one's mind making one anxious, worried *etc*: *She has a lot on her mind.*

put (someone) in mind of to remind (someone) of: *This place puts me in mind of a book I once read.*

speak one's mind to say frankly what one means or thinks: *You must allow me to speak my mind.*

take/keep one's mind off to turn one's attention from; to prevent one from thinking about: *A good holiday will take your mind off your troubles.*

to my mind in my opinion: *To my mind, you're better off working here than in most other places.*

mine[1] [main] *pron* something which belongs to me: *Are these pencils yours or mine? He is a friend of mine* (= one of my friends).

mine: *This pencil isn't yours – it's mine* (not *my one*).

mine[2] [main] *n* **1** a place (*usu* underground) from which metals, coal, salt *etc* are dug: *a coalmine*; *My father worked in the mines*. **2** a type of bomb used underwater or placed just beneath the surface of the ground: *The ship has been blown up by a mine*. – *v* **1** to dig (for metals *etc*) in a mine:

Coal is mined near here. **2** to place explosive mines in: *They've mined the mouth of the river.* **3** to blow up with mines: *His ship was mined.*

'**miner** *n* a person who works in a mine, in Britain *usu* a coalminer. '**mining** *n*.

'**minefield** *n* an area of ground or water which is full of explosive mines.

mineral ['minərəl] *n* a substance (metals, gems, coal, salt *etc*) found naturally in the earth and mined: *What minerals are mined in that country?*; (*also adj*) *mineral ores*.

mineral water **1** a type of water containing small quantities of health-giving minerals. **2** a fizzy, non-alcoholic drink such as lemonade.

mingle ['miŋgl] *v* to mix: *He mingled with the crowd*. '**mingled** *adj*.

mini ['mini] *n* **1** short for **miniskirt**. **2** (*with cap*: ®) a type of small car. – *adj* (*or part of a word*) small: *a mini dictionary*; *a minibus*.

miniature ['minitʃə] *adj* smaller than normal, often very small: *a miniature radio*. – *n* **1** a very small painting of a person. **2** a copy or model of something, made on a small scale.

minibus ['minibʌs] *n* a small bus, *usu* with only a dozen seats or so: *The school choir hired a minibus*.

minim ['minim] *n* a musical note roughly equal to a slow walking step in length.

minimum ['miniməm] *adj* smallest or lowest (possible, obtained, recorded *etc*): *the minimum temperature last night*. – *n* – *pls* '**minimums**, '**minima** [-mə] – the smallest possible number, quantity *etc* or the lowest level: *Tickets will cost a minimum of $20.*

'**minimal** *adj* very small indeed: *minimal expense*.

'**minimize, -ise** *v* **1** to make as little as possible: *to minimize the danger*. **2** to cause to seem little or unimportant: *He minimized the help he had received.*

minion ['minjən] *n* a slave-like follower or employee.

miniskirt ['miniskə:t] *n* (*abbrev* **mini** ['mini]) a short skirt the hem of which is well above the knees.

minister ['ministə] *n* **1** a clergyman in certain branches of the Christian Church: *He is a minister in the Presbyterian church*. **2** (the title of) the head of any of the divisions or departments of a government: *the Minister for Education*. – *v* (*with* **to**) to give help (to): *She ministered to his needs.*

ministerial [mini'stiəriəl] *adj* of or concerning ministers: *ministerial duties*.

'**ministry** – *pl* '**ministries** – *n* **1** the profession, duties or period of service of a minister of religion: *His ministry lasted for fifteen years*. **2** a department of government or the building where its employees work: *the Transport Ministry*.

mink [miŋk] *n* **1** a small weasel-like kind of animal. **2** its fur: *a hat made of mink*; (*also adj*) *a mink coat*. **3** a mink coat: *She wore her new mink.*

minor ['mainə] *adj* less, or little, in importance, size *etc*: *Always halt when driving from a minor road on to a major road*; *She has to go into hospital for a minor operation.* – *n* a person who is not yet legally an adult.
mi'nority [mi'no-, mai'no-] *n* a small number; less than half: *Only a minority of people live in the countryside*; *a racial/political minority.*
be in the minority to be in the smaller of two groups: *Women were in the minority* (=There were more men than women) *at the meeting.*

minstrel ['minstrəl] *n* a musician who went about the country in medieval times, reciting or singing poems.

mint¹ [mint] *n* a place where money is made by the government. – *v* to manufacture (money): *When were these coins minted?*
in mint condition fresh; unused; in perfect condition.

mint² [mint] *n* **1** a plant with strong-smelling leaves, used as a flavouring. **2** (*also* '**peppermint**') (a sweet with) the flavour of these leaves: *a box of mints*; (*also adj*) *mint chocolate.*

minus ['mainəs] *prep* used to show subtraction: *Ten minus two equals eight* (10−2=8). – *n* (*also* **minus sign**) a sign (−) used to show subtraction or negative quality. – *adj* negative or less than zero: *a minus number*; *Twelve from ten equals minus two* (10−12=−2).

minute¹ ['minit] *n* **1** the sixtieth part of an hour; sixty seconds: *It is twenty minutes to eight*; *The journey takes thirty minutes*; *a ten-minute delay.* **2** in measuring an angle, the sixtieth part of a degree; sixty seconds: *an angle of 47° 50'* (=forty-seven degrees, fifty minutes). **3** a very short time: *Wait a minute*; *It will be done in a minute.* **4** a particular point in time: *At that minute, the telephone rang.* **5** (*in pl*) the notes taken at a meeting recording what was said: *The chairman asked for this decision to be recorded in the minutes.*
minute hand the larger of the two pointers on a clock or watch, which shows the time in minutes past the hour.
the minute (that) as soon as: *Telephone me the minute he arrives!*
to the minute (of time) exactly; precisely: *The cooking time must be correct to the minute.*
up to the minute most modern or recent: *Her clothes are always right up to the minute*; *up-to-the-minute clothes.*

minute² [mai'nju:t] *adj* **1** very small: *The diamonds in the brooch were minute.* **2** paying attention to the smallest details: *minute care.* **mi'nutely** *adv.* **mi'nuteness** *n.*

miracle ['mirəkl] *n* **1** something which man is not normally capable of making happen and which is therefore thought to be done by a god or God: *Christ's turning of water into wine was a miracle.* **2** a fortunate happening that has no obvious natural cause or explanation: *It's a miracle he wasn't killed in the plane crash.*
mi'raculous [-'rakju-] *adj*: *a miraculous recovery.* **mi'raculously** *adv.*

mirage ['mira:ʒ, (*esp Amer*) mi'ra:ʒ] *n* an illusion of an area of water in the desert or on a road *etc.*

mirror ['mirə] *n* a piece of glass or metal having a surface that reflects an image: *She spends a lot of time looking in the mirror.* – *v* to reflect as a mirror does: *The smooth surface of the lake mirrored the surrounding mountains.*

mirth [mɔ:θ] *n* laughter or amusement.

misadventure [misəd'ventʃə] *n* an unlucky happening or accident.

misapprehension [misapri'henʃən] *n* misunderstanding.

misbehave [misbi'heiv] *v* to behave badly: *If you misbehave, I'll send you to bed.* ,**misbe'haviour** [-'heivjə] *n.*

miscalculate [mis'kalkjuleit] *v* to calculate or estimate wrongly: *I miscalculated the bill.* **mis,calcu'lation** *n.*

miscarriage ['miskaridʒ] **1** in pregnancy, the loss of the baby from the womb before it is able to survive. **2** a failure: *a miscarriage of justice* (=a wrong judgement).

miscellaneous [misə'leiniəs] *adj* composed of several kinds; mixed: *a miscellaneous collection of pictures.*
miscellany [mi'seləni, (*Amer*) 'misəleini] – *pl* **miscellanies** – *n* a collection or mixture of things.

mischance [mis'tʃa:ns] *n* (a piece of) bad luck.

mischief ['mistʃif] *n* **1** action or behaviour (*esp* of children) that causes small troubles or annoyance to others: *That boy is always up to some mischief.* **2** evil, damage or harm.
'**mischievous** [-vəs] *adj*: *a mischievous child.* '**mischievously** *adv.*
make mischief to cause trouble *etc.*

misconception [miskən'sepʃən] *n* a wrong idea or impression.

misconduct [mis'kondʌkt] *n* bad behaviour.

misdeed [mis'di:d] *n* a bad deed.

misdirect [misdi'rekt, -dai-] *v* to direct wrongly: *She was misdirected, and ended up in the wrong street.*

miser ['maizə] *n* a mean person who lives very poorly in order to store up wealth: *That old*

miser won't give you a cent! **'miserly** *adj.*
'miserliness *n.*

miserable ['mizərəbl] *adj* **1** very unhappy;
She's been miserable since he went away.
2 very poor in quantity or quality: *The
house was in a miserable condition.*
'miserably *adv.*

misery ['mizəri] – *pl* **'miseries** – *n* (something
that causes) unhappiness: *the misery of the
fatherless children; Forget your miseries and
· come out with me!*

misfire [mis'faiə] *v* **1** (of a gun, bomb *etc*) to
fail to explode or catch fire. **2** (of a motor
engine) to fail to ignite properly. **3** (of a
plan *etc*) to go wrong.

misfit ['misfit] *n* a person who is not able to
live or work happily with others.

misfortune [mis'fo:tʃən] *n* (a piece of) bad
luck: *I had the misfortune to break my leg.*

misgiving [mis'giviŋ] *n* (*esp in pl*) (a feeling
of) fear or doubt.

mishap ['mishap] *n* an unlucky accident.

misinform [misin'fo:m] *v* to give wrong information to.

misjudge [mis'dʒʌdʒ] *v* to have an unfairly
low opinion of (a person).

mislay [mis'lei] – *pt, ptp* **mis'laid** – *v* to lose: *I
seem to have mislaid my wallet.*

mislead [mis'li:d] – *pt, ptp* **mis'led** [-'led] – *v*
to give a wrong idea to: *Her friendly atti-
tude misled me into thinking I could trust
her.*
mis'leading *adj: a misleading remark.*

misplace [mis'pleis] *v* **1** to lose, mislay. **2** to
give (trust, love) to the wrong person: *Your
trust in him was misplaced.*

misprint ['misprint] *n* a mistake in printing:
This newspaper is full of misprints.

mispronounce [misprə'nauns] *v* to pronounce
(words *etc*) wrongly. **'mispro,nunci'ation**
[-nʌnsi-] *n.*

Miss [mis] *n* **1** a polite title given to an
unmarried female, either in writing or in
speech: *Miss Wilson; the Misses Wilson;
Could you ask Miss Smith to type this
letter?; Excuse me, miss. Could you tell me
how to get to Princess Road?* **2** a girl or
young woman: *She's a cheeky little miss!*

miss [mis] *v* **1** to fail to hit, catch *etc*: *The
arrow missed the target.* **2** to fail to arrive in
time for: *He missed the 8 o'clock train.* **3** to
fail to take advantage of: *You've missed
your opportunity.* **4** to feel sad because of
the absence of: *You'll miss your friends
when you go to live abroad.* **5** to notice the
absence of: *I didn't miss my purse till several
hours after I'd dropped it.* **6** to fail to hear or
see: *He missed what you said because he
wasn't listening.* **7** to fail to go to: *I'll have
to miss my lesson next week, as I'm going to
the dentist.* **8** to fail to meet: *We missed you
in the crowd.* **9** to avoid: *The thief only just*

missed being caught by the police. **10** (of an
engine) to misfire. – *n* a failure to hit, catch
etc: *two hits and two misses.*

missing *adj* not in the usual place or not able
to be found: *The child has been missing since
Tuesday; I've found those missing papers.*
go missing to be lost: *A group of climbers
has gone missing in the Himalayas.*

miss out **1** to omit or fail to include: *I
missed her out (of the list).* **2** (*often with* on)
to be left out of something: *George missed
out (on all the fun) because of his broken leg.*
miss the boat to be left behind, miss an
opportunity *etc*: *I meant to send her a
birthday card but I missed the boat – her
birthday was last week.*

misshapen [miʃ'ʃeipən] *adj* badly formed: *a
misshapen tree.*

missile ['misail] *n* **1** a weapon or object which
is thrown or fired from a gun, bow *etc*. **2** a
rocket-powered weapon carrying an explosive charge: *a ground-to-air missile.*
guided missile a rocket-powered missile
which is directed to its target by a built-in
device or by radio waves *etc*.

missing *see* **miss**.

mission ['miʃən] *n* **1** a purpose for which a
person or group of people is sent: *His
mission was to seek help.* **2** the purpose for
which (one feels) one was born: *He regards
it as his mission to help the cause of world
peace.* **3** a group of people sent to have
political and/or business discussions: *a
Chinese trade mission.* **4** a place where missionaries live. **5** a group of missionaries: *a
Catholic mission.*
'missionary – *pl* **'missionaries** – *n* a person
who is sent to teach and spread a particular
religion.

misspell [mis'spel] – *pts, ptps* **,mis'spelt,
,mis'spelled** – *v* to spell wrongly.

mist [mist] *n* a cloud of moisture in the air but
very close to the ground, which makes it
difficult to see any distance: *The hills are
covered in thick mist.* **'mistily** *adv.* **'misty** *adj.*
'mistiness *n.*
mist over, up to become covered (as if) with
mist: *The mirror misted over; The windscreen misted up.*

mistake [mi'steik] – *pt* **mi'stook** [-'stuk]: *ptp*
mi'staken – *v* **1** (*with* for) to think that (one
person or thing) is another: *I mistook you
for my brother in this bad light.* **2** to make
an error about: *They mistook the date, and
arrived two days early.* – *n* a wrong act or
judgement: *a spelling mistake; It was a
mistake to trust him; I took your umbrella by
mistake – it looks like mine.*
mi'staken *adj* wrong: *You are mistaken if
you think he's clever.* **mi'stakenly** *adv.*

Mister ['mistə] *n* (*abbrev* **Mr** *when written*) a
polite title given to a male adult, either in

writing or in speech: *Good mòrning, Mr Smith*; *Ask Mr Jones*.

mistletoe ['misltou] *n* a plant with white berries, used in Christmas decorations.

mistress ['mistris] *n* 1 a woman who is the lover of a man to whom she is not married. 2 a female teacher: *the games mistress*. 3 a woman who commands, controls or owns: *a dog and his mistress*. 4 a female employer (of a servant): *The servant stole her mistress's jewellery*.

mistrust [mis'trʌst] *v* to have no confidence or trust in. – *n* lack of confidence in something. ,mis'trustful *adj*. ,mis'trustfully *adv*.

misty *see* mist.

misunderstand [misʌndə'stand] – *pt, ptp* ,misunder'stood [-'stud] – *v* to take a wrong meaning from: *She misunderstood what I said*.
,misunder'standing *n* 1 (a) confusion or mistake: *a misunderstanding about the date of the meeting*. 2 a slight quarrel.

misuse [mis'juːs] *n* (a) wrong or bad use: *the misuse of company money*; *The machine was damaged by misuse*.
,mis'use [-'juːz] *v* 1 to use wrongly. 2 to treat badly.

mite [mait] *n* 1 a tiny person or child. 2 a type of very small insect.

miter *see* mitre.

mitre, (*Amer*) **miter** ['maitə] *n* a type of headdress worn by archbishops and bishops.

mitten ['mitn] *n* (*also* **mitt** [mit]) 1 a kind of glove with two sections, one for the thumb and the other for the fingers: *a pair of mittens*. 2 a type of glove with separate sections for each finger, reaching only to halfway down the fingers.

mix [miks] *v* 1 to put or blend together to form one mass: *She mixed the butter and sugar together*; *He mixed the blue paint with the yellow paint to make green paint*. 2 to prepare or make by doing this: *She mixed the cement in a bucket*. 3 to go together or blend successfully to form one mass: *Oil and water don't mix*. 4 to go together socially: *People of different races were mixing together happily*. – *n* 1 the result of mixing things or people together: *London has an interesting racial mix*. 2 a collection of ingredients used to make something: (*a*) *cake-mix*.
mixed *adj* 1 consisting of different kinds: *I have mixed feelings about leaving home*; *mixed races*; *a mixed population*. 2 done, used *etc* by people of different sexes: *mixed tennis*.
'mixer *n* a person or thing that mixes; a thing which is used for mixing: *an electric food-mixer*.
mixture ['mikstʃə] *n* 1 the result of mixing things or people together: *a mixture of eggs, flour and milk*. 2 a number of things mixed together and used for a given purpose: *The doctor gave the baby some cough mixture*. 3 the act of mixing.
'mix-up *n* a confused situation *etc*: *a mix-up over the concert tickets*.
be mixed up (in, with) to be involved: *He was mixed up in that burglary/with some drug-takers*.
mix up 1 to blend together: *I need to mix up another tin of paint*. 2 to confuse or muddle: *I'm always mixing the twins up*. 3 to confuse or upset: *You've mixed me up completely with all this information*.

moan [moun] *v* 1 to make a low sound of grief, pain *etc*: *The wounded soldier moaned*. 2 to complain: *She's always moaning about how hard she has to work*. – *n* a sound (as if) of grief, pain *etc*: *a moan of pain*; *the moan of the wind*.

moat [mout] *n* a deep ditch, dug round a castle *etc*, *usu* filled with water.

mob [mob] *n* a noisy, violent or disorderly crowd of people: *He was attacked by an angry mob*. – *v* – *pt, ptp* **mobbed** – (of a crowd) to surround and push about in a disorderly way: *The singer was mobbed by a huge crowd of his fans*.

mobile ['moubail] *adj* 1 able to move: *The van supplying country districts with library books is called a mobile library*; *The old lady is no longer mobile – she has to stay in bed all day*. 2 able to move or be moved quickly or easily: *Most of the furniture is very light and mobile*. 3 (of someone's features or face) changing easily in expression.
mo'bility [-'bi-] *n*.
'mobilize, -ise [-bi-] *v* to make (*esp* troops, an army *etc*), or become, ready for use or action. ,mobili'zation, -s-[-bi-] *n*.

moccasin ['mokəsin] *n* a type of shoe, made of soft leather, worn by American Indians; an imitation of it.

mock [mok] *v* to laugh at or cause to seem ridiculous: *They mocked her efforts at cooking*. – *adj* pretended or not real: *a mock battle*; *He looked at me in mock horror*.
'mockery *n* an act of making fun of something: *She could not bear the mockery of the other children*.
'mocking *adj*: *a mocking laugh*. 'mockingly *adv*.

mode [moud] *n* 1 a manner of doing something: *an unusual mode of expression*. 2 a kind or type: *modes of transport*. 3 a fashion: *Large hats are the latest mode*.
'modish *adj* fashionable and smart. 'modishly *adv*.

model ['modl] *n* 1 a copy or representation of something *usu* on a much smaller scale: *a model of the Taj Mahal*; (*also adj*) *a model* *aeroplane*. **2** a particular type or design of something, *eg* a car, that is manufactured in large numbers: *Our Renault car is the 1983 model*. **3** a person who wears clothes *etc* so that possible buyers can see them being worn: *He has a job as a male fashion model*. **4** a person who is painted, sculpted, photographed *etc* by an artist, photographer *etc*: *I work as an artist's model*. **5** something that can be used to copy from. **6** a person or thing which is an excellent example: *She is a model of politeness*; (*also adj*) *model behaviour*. – *v* – *pt*, *ptp* '**modelled**, (*Amer usu*) '**modeled** – **1** to wear (clothes *etc*) to show them to possible buyers: *They model (underwear) for a living*. **2** to work or pose as a model for an artist, photographer *etc*: *She models at the local art school*. **3** to make models (of things or people): *to model (the heads of famous people) in clay*. **4** to form (something) into a (particular) shape: *She modelled the clay into the shape of a penguin*; *She models herself on her older sister*. '**modelling**, (*Amer*) '**modeling** *n*.

moderate ['mɔdəreit] *v* to make or become less extreme: *He was forced to moderate his demands*; *Gradually the pain moderated*. – [-rət] *adj* **1** keeping within reasonable limits; not extreme: *The prices were moderate*; *moderate opinions*. **2** medium or average; not particularly good: *workmanship of moderate quality*. – *n* a person whose views are not extreme: *Politically, she's a moderate*. '**moderately** *adv*. '**moderateness** [-rət-] *n*. ‚mode'**ration** *n* **1** the quality of being moderate: *Alcohol isn't harmful if it's taken in moderation*. **2** (an) act of moderating: *There has been some moderation in the force of the gale*.

modern ['mɔdən] *adj* belonging to the present or to recent times; not old or ancient: *modern furniture/clothes*. **mo'dernity** [-'dɔ:-], '**modernness** *ns*. '**modernize**, **-ise** *v* to bring up to date: *We should modernize the education system*. ‚moderni'**zation**, **-s-** *n*. **modern language** a language spoken nowadays (as opposed to ancient Greek, Latin *etc*).

modest ['mɔdist] *adj* **1** not having, or showing, too high an opinion of one's abilities *etc*: *He's very modest about his success*. **2** decent, or showing good taste; not shocking: *modest clothing*. **3** not very large; moderate: *She's a person of modest ambitions*. '**modestly** *adv*. '**modesty** *n*.

modicum ['mɔdikəm] *n* a small quantity.

modify ['mɔdifai] *v* to change the form or quality of, *usu* slightly: *We had to modify the original design*. ‚modifi'**cation** [-fi-] *n*.

modish *see* **mode**.

module ['mɔdju:l] *n* a self-contained unit

forming *eg* part of a building, spacecraft *etc*: *a lunar module*.

mohair ['mouheə] *n* **1** the long silken hair of a type of goat. **2** (*also adj*) (of) a type of cloth or wool made from it: *a mohair jersey*.

moist [moist] *adj* damp; slightly wet: *moist, fertile soil*. '**moistly** *adv*. '**moistness** *n*.

moisten ['moisn] *v* to wet slightly: *He moistened* (= licked) *his lips*.

moisture ['moistʃə] *n* (the quality of) dampness: *This soil needs moisture*. '**moisturize**, **-ise** [-stʃə-] *v* to keep the moisture in (skin): *This cream is used to moisturize the skin*. '**moisturizer**, **-s-** *n*.

molar ['moulə] *n* a back tooth which is used for grinding food.

molasses [mə'lasiz] *n* (*Amer*) treacle.

mold *see* **mould**.

mole[1] [moul] *n* a small, permanent, *usu* dark, spot on the skin.

mole[2] [moul] *n* a small burrowing animal with very small eyes and soft fur. '**molehill** *n* a little heap of earth dug up by a mole while tunnelling.

make a mountain out of a molehill to exaggerate the importance of a problem *etc*.

molecule ['molikju:l] *n* the group of atoms that is the smallest unit into which a substance can be divided without losing its basic nature or identity. **mo'lecular** [-'le-] *adj*.

molehill *see* **mole**[2].

molest [mə'lest] *v* to annoy or interfere with: *The children kept molesting her*.

mollify ['molifai] *v* to calm, soothe or lessen the anger of. ‚mollifi'**cation** [-fi-] *n*.

molten [moultən] *adj* (of a solid) in a liquid state, having been melted: *molten rock*.

moment ['moumənt] *n* **1** a very short space of time: *I'll be ready in a moment*; *after a few moments' silence*. **2** a particular point in time: *At that moment, the telephone rang*. '**momentary** *adj* lasting for only a moment: *a momentary feeling of fear*. '**momentarily** [(*Amer*) moumən'te-] *adv*. **mo'mentous** [-'men-] *adj* of great importance: *a momentous event*. **mo'mentously** *adv*. **at the moment** at this particular time; now: *She's rather busy at the moment*. **the moment (that)** exactly when: *I want to see him the moment he arrives*.

momentum [mə'mentəm] *n* the amount or force of motion in a moving body.

monarch ['monək] *n* a king, queen, emperor, or empress. '**monarchy** – *pl* '**monarchies** – *n* (a country *etc* that has) government by a monarch.

monastery ['monəstəri] – *pl* '**monasteries** – *n* a house in which a community of monks lives.

mo'nastic [-'na-] *adj* of, or like, monks or monasteries: *the monastic way of life.*

Monday ['mʌndi] *n* the second day of the week, the day following Sunday.

monetary ['mʌnitəri] *adj* of, or consisting of, money: *monetary problems.*

money ['mʌni] *n* coins or banknotes used in trading: *Have you any money in your purse?*; *The desire for money is a cause of much unhappiness.*

'**money-box** *n* a box for saving money in.

'**moneylender** *n* a person who lends money and charges interest.

lose, make money to make a loss or a profit: *This film is making a lot of money in America.*

mongrel ['mʌŋgrəl] *n adj* (an animal, *esp* a dog) bred from different types.

monitor ['monitə] *n* **1** a senior pupil who helps to see that school rules are kept. **2** any of several kinds of instrument *etc* by means of which something can be constantly checked, *esp* a small screen in a television studio showing the picture which is being transmitted at any given time. – *v* to act as, or to use, a monitor; to keep a careful check on: *These machines/technicians monitor the results constantly.*

monk [mʌŋk] *n* a member of a male religious group, who lives in a monastery, away from the rest of society.

monkey ['mʌŋki] *n* **1** an animal of the type most like man, *esp* those which are small and have long tails (*ie* not the apes). **2** a mischievous child: *Their son is a little monkey.* – *v* (*esp with* **with**) to meddle or interfere: *Who's been monkeying (about) with the television set?*

monkey business michievous or illegal happenings *etc.*

monkey nut *see* **peanut**.

mono ['monou] *adj* (of records, record-playing equipment *etc*) using one channel only; not stereo.

monocle ['monəkl] *n* a lens or eyeglass for one eye only.

monogram ['monəgram] *n* a single design made up of several letters (often a person's initials).

monologue ['monəlog] *n* a long speech by one person *eg* in a film, play *etc.*

monoplane ['monəplein] *n* an aeroplane (*usu* small) with one set of wings.

monopoly [mə'nopəli] – *pl* **mo'nopolies** – *n* the sole right of making or selling something *etc*: *This firm has a local monopoly of soap-manufacturing.*

mo'nopolize, -ise *v* **1** to have a monopoly of or over: *They've monopolized the fruit-canning industry.* **2** to take up the whole of (*eg* someone's attention): *She tries to monopolize the teacher's attention.*

monorail ['monəreil] *n* a system of railways with trains which run hanging from, or along the top of, one rail.

monotonous [mə'notənəs] *adj* lacking in variety; dull: *a monotonous piece of music.* **mo'notonously** *adv.* **mo'notony** *n.*

monsoon [mon'su:n] *n* **1** a wind that blows in Southern Asia, from the SW in summer, fron the NE in winter. **2** the rainy season caused by the SW monsoon.

monster ['monstə] *n* **1** (*also adj*) (something) of unusual size, form or appearance: *a monster tomato.* **2** a huge and/or horrible creature: *prehistoric monsters.* **3** a very evil person: *The man must be a monster to treat his children so badly!*

'**monstrous** *adj* **1** huge and often unpleasant. **2** shocking: *a monstrous lie.* '**monstrously** *adv.*

month [mʌnθ] *n* one of the twelve divisions of the year (January, February *etc*), varying in length between 28 and 31 days.

'**monthly** *adj* happening, being published *etc* once a month: *a monthly magazine.* – *adv* once a month: *The magazine is published monthly.*

monument ['monjumənt] *n* something built in memory of a person or event, *eg* a building, tomb *etc*: *They erected a monument in his honour.*

,**monu'mental** [-'men-] *adj* of great size or scale: *a monumental achievement.*

moo [mu:] – *3rd pers sing prt* **moos**: *pt, ptp* **mooed** – *v* to make the sound of a cow. – *n* such a sound.

mood [mu:d] *n* the state of a person's feelings, temper, mind *etc* at a particular time: *What kind of mood is she in?*; *I'm in a bad mood today.*

'**moody** *adj* often bad-tempered: *a moody child.* '**moodily** *adv.* '**moodiness** *n.*

moon [mu:n] *n* **1** the heavenly body that moves once round the earth in a month and reflects light from the sun: *The moon was shining brightly*; *Spacemen landed on the moon.* **2** any of the similar bodies moving round the other planets: *the moons of Jupiter.*

'**moonless** *adj* (of a night) dark and having no moonlight.

'**moonbeam** *n* a beam of light reflected from the moon.

'**moonlight** *n, adj* (made with the help of) the light reflected by the moon: *The sea looked silver in the moonlight*; *a moonlight raid.*

'**moonlit** *adj* lit by the moon: *a moonlit hillside.*

moon about/around to wander around as if dazed, *eg* because one is in love.

moor[1] [muə] *n* a large stretch of open, un-farmed land with poor soil often covered with heather, coarse grass *etc*.

'**moorland** *n* a stretch of moor.

moor[2] [muə] *v* to fasten (a ship *etc*) by a rope, cable or anchor: *We moored (the yacht) in the bay.*

'**mooring** *n* the act, or a means, of fastening a ship: *The mooring broke.*

'**moorings** *n pl* the place where a ship is anchored or fastened.

moose [muːs] – *pl* **moose** – *n* a type of large deer found in North America, and also in northern Europe where it is known as the elk.

mop [mop] *n* 1 a pad of sponge, or a bunch of pieces of coarse string or yarn *etc*, fixed on a handle, for washing floors, dishes *etc*. 2 a thick mass of hair: *a mop of dark hair.* 3 an act of mopping: *He gave the floor a quick mop.* – *v* – *pt*, *ptp* **mopped** – 1 to rub or wipe with a mop: *She mopped the kitchen floor.* 2 to wipe or clean (*eg* a face covered with sweat): *He mopped his brow.*

mop up to clean away using a mop, cloth *etc*: *He mopped up the mess with his hand-kerchief.*

mope [moup] *v* to be depressed and mournful.

moped ['mouped] *n* a pedal-cycle which has a small motor.

moral ['morəl] *adj* of, or relating to, character or behaviour *esp* right behaviour: *high moral standards*; *He leads a very moral* (=good) *life.* – *n* the lesson to be learned from something that happens, or from a story: *The moral of this story is that crime doesn't pay.*

'**morally** *adv*. **mo'rality** *n*.

morals *n pl* one's principles and behaviour: *He has no morals and will do anything for money.*

morale [mə'raːl] *n* the level of courage and confidence in *eg* an army, team *etc*: *In spite of the defeat, morale was still high.*

morass [mə'ras] *n* a bog or swamp.

more [moː] – *compar of* **many**, **much** – *adj* 1 a greater number or quantity of: *I've more pencils than he has.* 2 an additional number or quantity of: *We need some more milk.* – *adv* 1 used to form the comparative of many adjectives and adverbs, *esp* those of more than two syllables: *She can do it more easily that I can*; *He is much more intelligent than they are.* 2 to a greater degree or extent: *I'm exercising a little more now than I used to.* 3 again: *We'll play it once more.* – *pron* 1 a greater number or quantity: *'Are there a lot of people?' 'There are far more than we expected.'* 2 an additional number or amount: *We've run out of paint. Will you go and get some more?*

more'over *adv* also; what is more import-ant: *I don't like the idea, and moreover, I think it's illegal.*

any more any longer; nowadays: *He doesn't go any more, but he used to go twice a week.*

more and more increasingly: *It's becoming more and more difficult to see.*

more or less approximately or almost: *They've more or less finished the job*; *The distance is ten kilometres, more or less.*

the more … the more/less: *The more I see her, the more/less I like her.*

what is/what's more moreover: *He came home after midnight, and what's more, he was drunk.*

morgue [moːg] *n* a building where people who have been found dead are laid until they are identified *etc*.

morn [moːn] *n* morning.

morning ['moːniŋ] *n* the first part of the day, approximately up to noon: *this morning*; *tomorrow morning.*

morning glory any of various vines with funnel-shaped purple, blue, pink or white flowers that bloom early in the day.

morose [mə'rous] *adj* angry and silent.

mo'rosely *adv*. **mo'roseness** *n*.

morphia ['moːfiə] , **morphine** ['moːfiːn] *ns* a drug used to cause sleep or deaden pain.

Morse [moːs] *n* a code for signalling and telegraphy in which each letter is made up of dots and dashes, or short and long sounds or flashes of light.

morsel ['moːsəl] *n* a small piece of something, *esp* food: *a tasty morsel of fish for the cat.*

mortal ['moːtl] *adj* 1 liable to die; unable to live for ever: *Man is mortal.* 2 of or causing death: *a mortal illness*; *mortal enemies* (=enemies willing to fight each other till death); *mortal combat.* – *n* a human being: *All mortals must die sometime.*

mor'tality [-'ta-] *n* 1 the state of being mortal. 2 (*also* **mortality rate**) the number of deaths in proportion to the population; the death rate: *infant mortality.*

'**mortally** *adv* in such a way as to cause death: *He has been mortally wounded.*

mortal sin (*esp* in Roman Catholicism) a very serious sin, as a result of which the soul is damned for ever.

mortar[1] ['moːtə] *n* a mixture of cement, sand and water, used in building *eg* to hold bricks in place.

mortar[2] ['moːtə] *n* a type of short gun for firing shells upwards, in close-range at-tacks.

mortar[3] ['moːtə] *n* a dish in which to grind substances, *esp* with a pestle.

mortar-board ['moːtəboːd] *n* a type of cap with a square flat top, worn on formal occasions at universities.

mortgage ['moːgidʒ] *n* a legal agreement by which a sum of money is lent for the purpose of buying buildings, land *etc*. – *v* to offer (buildings *etc*) as security for a loan.

mortuary [mɔːtʃuəri] – *pl* '**mortuaries** – *n* a building or room *eg* in a hospital, where dead bodies are kept before burial or cremation.

mosaic [mə'zeiik] *n* (the art of making) a design formed by fitting together small pieces of coloured marble, glass *etc*.

Moslem *see* **Muslim**.

mosque [mosk] *n* a Muslim place of worship.

mosquito [mə'skiːtou] – *pl* **mo'squito(e)s** – *n* any of several types of small insect, which suck blood from animals and people and in this way transmit diseases such as malaria.

moss [mos] *n* (any variety of) a type of small flowerless plant, found in damp places, forming a soft green covering on tree trunks *etc*: *The bank of the river was covered in moss*. '**mossy** *adj*.

most [moust] – *superl of* **many, much** (*often with* **the**) – *adj* **1** (the) greatest number or quantity of: *Which of the students has read the most books?*; *Reading is what gives me most enjoyment*. **2** the majority or greater part of: *Most boys like playing football*; *Most modern music is difficult to understand*. – *adv* **1** used to form the superlative of many adjectives and adverbs, *esp* those of more than two syllables: *Of all the women I know, she's the most beautiful*; *the most delicious cake I've ever tasted*; *We see her mother or father sometimes, but we see her grandmother most frequently*. **2** to the greatest degree or extent: *They like sweets and biscuits but they like ice-cream most of all*. **3** very or extremely: *I'm most grateful to you for everything you've done*; *a most annoying child*. **4** (*Amer*) almost: *Most everyone I know has read that book*. – *pron* **1** the greatest number or quantity: *I ate two cakes, but Mary ate more, and John ate* (*the*) *most*. **2** the greatest part; the majority: *He'll be at home for most of the day*; *Most of these students speak English*; *Everyone is leaving – most have gone already*.

'**mostly** *adv* to the greatest degree or extent, or for most of the time; mainly: *The air we breathe is mostly nitrogen and oxygen*; *Mostly I go to the library rather than buy books*.

at (the) most taking the greatest estimate: *There were no more than fifty people in the audience at* (*the*) *most*.

for the most part mostly: *For the most part, the passengers on the ship were Swedes*.

make the most of (something) to take advantage of (an opportunity *etc*) to the greatest possible extent: *You'll only get one chance, so you'd better make the most of it!*

motel [mou'tel] *n* a hotel which caters particularly for motorists.

moth [moθ] – *pl* **moths** [moθs, (*Amer*) mɔːðz] – *n* **1** any of a large number of insects, rather like butterflies but with wider bodies, seen mostly at night and attracted by light. **2** a clothes moth: *The moths have been at my evening dress*.

clothes moth a type of moth whose larva feeds on cloth and makes holes.

'**mothball** *n* a small ball of a chemical used to protect clothes from clothes moths.

'**moth-eaten** *adj* (of cloth) eaten by moths: *a moth-eaten blanket*.

mother ['mʌðə] *n* **1** a female parent, *esp* human: *John's mother lives in Manchester*; (*also adj*) *The mother bird feeds her young*. **2** (*often with cap*: *also* **Mother Superior**) the female leader of a group of nuns. – *v* to care for as a mother does; to protect (sometimes too much): *His wife tries to mother him*.

'**motherhood** *n* the state of being a mother.

'**motherless** *adj* having no mother: *The children were left motherless by the accident*.

'**motherly** *adj* like a mother; of, or suitable to, a mother: *a motherly woman*; *motherly love*. '**motherliness** *n*.

'**mother-country/'motherland** [-land] *ns* the country where one was born.

'**mother-in-law** – *pl* '**mothers-in-law** – *n* the mother of one's husband or wife.

,**mother-of-'pearl** *n, adj* (of) the shining, hard, smooth substance on the inside of certain shells.

'**mother-tongue** *n* a person's native language: *My mother-tongue is Hindi*.

motion ['mouʃən] *n* **1** the act or state of moving: *the motion of the planets*; *He lost the power of motion*. **2** a single movement or gesture: *He summoned the waiter with a motion of the hand*. **3** a proposal put before a meeting: *She was asked to speak against the motion in the debate*. – *v* to make a movement or sign *eg* directing a person or telling him to do something: *He motioned* (*to*) *her to come nearer*.

'**motionless** *adj* not moving: *a motionless figure*.

motion picture a cinema film.

in motion moving: *Don't jump on the bus while it is in motion*.

motive ['moutiv] *n* something that makes a person choose to act in a particular way; a reason: *What was his motive for murdering the old lady?*

'**motivate** [-veit] *v* to cause to act in a particular way: *He was motivated by jealousy*. **moti'vation** *n*.

motor ['moutə] *n* a machine, *usu* a petrol engine or an electrical device, that gives motion or power: *a washing-machine has an electric motor*; (*also adj*) *a motor boat/ vehicle*. – *v* to travel by car: *We motored down to my mother's house at the weekend*.

'**motorist** *n* a person who drives a motor car: *The motorist could not avoid hitting the dog.*

'**motorize, -ise** *v* 1 to fit a motor to (*eg* a bicycle). 2 to supply (*eg* troops) with motor vehicles: *Many army units have been motorized.*

'**motorcade** [-keid] *n* a procession in which everyone goes by car.

'**motorway** *n* a road specially made for fast traffic: *They are building a new motorway to link the two cities.*

*'**motorbike, 'motorcycle** *ns* any of several types of *usu* heavy bicycle moved by a motor.

'**motor car** a vehicle on four wheels, moved by a motor, but not a lorry or van; an automobile, car.

'**motorcyclist** *n* a person who rides a motorbike: *The motorcyclist was injured in the road accident.*

mottled ['motld] *adj* marked with spots or patches of many colours or shades: *mottled leaves.*

motto ['motou] – *pl* '**mottoes** – *n* 1 (a short sentence or phrase which expresses) a principle of behaviour *etc*: *'Honesty is the best policy' is my motto; a school motto.* 2 a printed saying *etc*, often found inside a Christmas cracker.

mould¹, (*Amer*) **mold**¹ [mould] *n* 1 (soil which is full of) rotted leaves *etc*. 2 a growth on stale food *etc*: *This bread is covered with mould.*

'**mouldy** *adj* (of food *etc*) covered with mould: *mouldy cheese; The bread has gone mouldy.* '**mouldiness** *n*.

mould², (*Amer*) **mold**² [mould] *n* 1 a shape into which a substance in liquid form is poured so that it may take on that shape when it cools and hardens: *a jelly mould.* 2 something, *esp* a food, formed in a mould. – *v* 1 to form in a mould: *The metal is moulded into long bars.* 2 to work into a shape: *He moulded the clay into a ball.* 3 to make the shape of (something): *She moulded the figure out of/in clay.*

moult, (*Amer*) **molt** [moult] *v* (of birds, dogs or cats, snakes *etc*) to shed feathers, hair, a skin *etc*.

mound [maund] *n* a small hill or heap of earth *etc*: *a grassy mound; a mound of rubbish.*

mount [maunt] *v* 1 to get or climb up (on or on to): *He mounted the platform; She mounted (the horse) and rode off.* 2 to rise in level: *Prices are mounting steeply.* 3 to put (a picture *etc*) into a frame, or stick it on to card *etc*. 4 to hang or put up on a stand, support *etc*: *He mounted the tiger's head on the wall.* 5 to organize: *The army mounted an attack; to mount an exhibition.* – *n* 1 a thing or animal that one rides, *esp* a horse.

2 a support or backing on which anything is placed for display: *Would this picture look better on a red mount or a black one?*

'**mounted** *adj* on horseback: *mounted policemen.*

Mount [maunt] *n* a mountain: *Mount Everest.*

mountain [mauntən] *n* a high hill: *Mount Everest is the highest mountain in the world*; (*also adj*) *a mountain stream.*

,**mountai'neer** *n* a person who climbs mountains, *esp* with skill, or as his occupation.

,**mountai'neering** *n* mountain-climbing.

'**mountainous** *adj* full of mountains: *The country is very mountainous.*

'**mountain-side** *n* the slope of a mountain: *The avalanche swept the climbers down the mountain-side.*

'**mountain-top** *n* the summit of a mountain.

mourn [mo:n] *v* to have or show great sorrow *eg* for a person who has died: *She mourned (for) her dead son.*

'**mourner** *n*: *The mourners stood round the graveside.*

'**mournful** *adj* feeling or showing sorrow: *a mournful expression.* '**mournfully** *adv*.

'**mourning** *n* 1 grief shown *eg* because of someone's death. 2 black or dark-coloured clothes suitable for a mourner: *She was wearing mourning.*

mouse [maus] *pl* **mice** [mais] – *n* any of several types of small furry gnawing animal with a long tail, found in houses and in fields.

'**mousy** *adj* 1 (of hair) dull brown in colour. 2 timid; uninteresting: *a mousy little woman.*

'**mousehole** *n* a hole made or used by mice.

'**mousetrap** *n* a mechanical trap for a mouse.

moustache, (*esp Amer*) **mustache** [mə'sta:ʃ, (*Amer*) 'mʌstaʃ] *n* the hair on the upper lip of a man: *The young man has grown a moustache.*

mouth [mauθ] – *pl* **mouths** [mauðz] – *n* 1 the opening in the head by which a human or animal eats and speaks or makes noises: *What has the baby got in its mouth?* 2 the opening or entrance *eg* of a bottle, river *etc*: *the mouth of the harbour.* – [mauð] *v* to move the lips as if forming (words), but without making any sound: *He mouthed the words to me so that no-one could overhear.*

'**mouthful** *n* as much as fills the mouth: *a mouthful of soup; He ate the cake in two mouthfuls.*

'**mouth-organ** *n* a small musical instrument played by blowing or sucking air through its metal pipes.

'**mouthpiece** *n* 1 the piece of a musical instrument *etc* which is held in the mouth: *the mouthpiece of a horn.* 2 the part of a telephone *etc* into which one speaks.

'**mouthwash** *n* an antiseptic liquid used for cleaning out the mouth.

move [mu:v] v **1** to (cause to) change position or go from one place to another: *He moved his arm*; *Don't move!*; *Please move your car.* **2** to change houses: *We're moving on Saturday.* **3** to affect the feelings or emotions of: *I was deeply moved by the film.* – n **1** (in board games) an act of moving a piece: *You can win this game in three moves.* **2** an act of changing homes: *How did your move go?* **'movable, 'moveable** *adjs.*

'movement n **1** (an act of) changing position or going from one point to another: *The animal turned sideways with a swift movement.* **2** activity: *In this play there is a lot of discussion but not much movement.* **3** the art of moving gracefully or expressively: *She teaches movement and drama.* **4** an organization or association: *the Scout movement.* **5** the moving parts of a watch, clock etc.* **6** a section of a large-scale piece of music: *the third movement of Beethoven's Fifth Symphony.* **7** a general tendency towards a habit, point of view etc: *There's a movement towards simple designs in clothing these days.*

movie [-vi] n (esp Amer) **1** a cinema film: *a horror movie.* **2** (in pl: with **the**) the cinema and films in general: *to go to the movies.*

'moving adj having an effect on the emotions etc: *a very moving speech.* **'movingly** adv.

get a move on to hurry or move quickly: *Get a move on, or you'll be late!*

make a move 1 to move at all: *If you make a move, I'll shoot you!* **2** (with **for** or **towards**) to move (in the direction of): *He made a move for the door.*

move along to keep moving, not staying in one place: *The police told the crowd to move along.*

move heaven and earth to do everything that one possibly can.

move house to change one's home or place of residence: *They're moving house next week.*

move in to go into and occupy a house etc: *We can move in on Saturday.*

move off (of vehicles etc) to begin moving away: *The bus moved off just as I got to the bus stop.*

move out to leave, cease to live in, a house etc: *She has to move out before the new owners arrive.*

move up to move in any given direction so as to make more space: *Move up and let me sit down, please.*

on the move 1 moving from place to place: *With his kind of job, he's always on the move.* **2** advancing or making progress: *The frontiers of scientific knowledge are always on the move.*

movie see **move**.

mow [mou] – pt **mowed**: ptps **mowed, mown** – v to cut (grass etc) with a scythe or mower: *He mowed the lawn.*

'mower n a machine for cutting grass.

mow down to kill in large numbers: *Our troops were mown down by machine-gun fire.*

Mr see **Mister**.

Mrs ['misiz] n a polite title given to a married woman, in writing or in speaking: *Please come in, Mrs Anderson.*

Ms [miz] n a polite title given, esp in writing, to a woman, whether married or unmarried: *Ms Johnson.*

much [mʌtʃ] – compar **more** [mo:]: superl **most** [moust] – adj a (great) amount or quantity of: *This job won't take much effort*; *I found it without much difficulty*; *How much sugar is there left?*; *There's far too much salt in my soup*; *He ate so much ice-cream that he was sick*; *Take as much money as you need*; *After much discussion they decided to go.* – pron a large amount; a great deal: *He didn't say much about it*; *Much of this trouble could have been prevented*; *Did you eat much?*; *not much*; *too much*; *as much as I wanted*; *How much did you eat?*; *Only this/that/so much*; *How much is* (=What is the price of) *that fish?*; *Please tidy your room – it isn't much to ask.* – adv **1** (by) a great deal; (by) far: *She's much prettier than I am*; *He isn't much older than you*; *How much further must we walk?*; *much more easily*; *He's much the best person to ask.* **2** to a great extent or degree: *He will be much missed*; *We don't see her much* (=often); *I thanked her very much*; *much too late*; *I've much too much to do*; *The accident was as much my fault as his*; *Much to my dismay, she began to cry.*

be not much of a to be not a very good thing of a particular kind: *I'm not much of a photographer*; *That wasn't much of a lecture.*

be not up to much to be not very good: *The dinner wasn't up to much.*

be too much for to overwhelm; to be too difficult etc for: *Is the job too much for you?*

make much of 1 to make a fuss of (a person) or about (a thing). **2** to make sense of; to understand: *I couldn't make much of the film.*

much as although: *Much as I should like to come, I can't.*

much the same not very different: *The patient's condition is still much the same.*

nothing much nothing important, impressive etc: *'What are you doing?' 'Nothing much.'*

not much nothing important, impressive etc: *My car isn't much to look at but it's fast.*

so much for that's all that can be said about: *So much for that – let's talk about something* *else*; *He arrived half an hour late – so much for his punctuality!*

think too much of to have too high an opinion of: *He thinks too much of himself.*
without so much as without even: *He took my umbrella without so much as asking.*

see also **many**.

muck [mʌk] *n* dung, filth, rubbish *etc*: *farmyard muck.* '**mucky** *adj*.
muck about/around 1 to do things without any definite plan. **2** to fool around.
muck out to clean (a stable).
mucus ['mju:kəs] *n* the fluid from the nose.
mud [mʌd] *n* wet soft earth.
'**muddy** *adj* covered with or containing mud: *muddy boots/water.* – *v* to make muddy: *You've muddied the floor!*
'**mudflat** *n* (*often in pl*) an area of muddy seaside land which is covered with water at high tide.
'**mudguard** *n* a shield or guard over the wheel of a car, bicycle *etc* to keep mud, rainwater *etc* from splashing upwards.
'**mudskipper** *n* a small fish found in shallow coastal waters, able to jump about and climb low rocks to look for food.
muddle ['mʌdl] *v* to confuse or mix up: *Don't talk while I'm counting, or you'll muddle me.* – *n* a state of confusion: *These papers keep getting in a muddle.*
'**muddled** *adj*: *muddled thinking.*
'**muddle-headed** *adj* incapable of clear thinking: *Men think that all women are muddle-headed.*
muddle along/through to progress in spite of one's unsatisfactory methods and foolish mistakes.
muddle up to confuse (*eg* two different things): *I'm always muddling the twins up*; *I've muddled up these book orders.*
muffin ['mʌfin] *n* a type of round, flat cake eaten hot with butter.
muffle ['mʌfl] *v* to deaden the sound of: *They used a gag to muffle his cries.*
'**muffler** *n* **1** a scarf worn round the neck. **2** (*Amer*) a silencer on a motor vehicle.
mug[1] [mʌg] *n* a type of cup with *usu* tall, more or less vertical sides: *a mug of coffee.*
'**mugful** *n*: *two mugfuls of coffee.*
mug[2] [mʌg] *n* a slang word for the face.
mug[3] [mʌg] – *pt, ptp* **mugged** – *v* to attack and *usu* rob: *He was mugged when coming home late at night.*
'**mugger** *n* a person who attacks others in this way.
mulberry ['mʌlbəri] – *pl* '**mulberries** – *n* **1** a type of tree on whose leaves silkworms feed. **2** its (*usu* purple) fruit.
mule[1] [mju:l] *n* an animal whose parents are a horse and an ass, known for its habit of being stubborn.

'**mulish** *adj* stubborn.
mule[2] [mju:l] *n* a loose, backless slipper.
mullet ['mʌlit] *n* an edible fish found in coastal waters.
multicoloured, (*Amer*) **multicolored** [mʌlti'kʌləd] *adj* having many colours: *a multicoloured shirt.*
multimillionaire [mʌltimiljə'neə] *n* a person who has wealth valued at several million pounds, dollars *etc*.
multiple ['mʌltipl] *adj* **1** having, or affecting, many parts: *She suffered multiple injuries when she fell out of the window.* **2** involving many things of the same sort: *Fifteen vehicles were involved in the multiple crash on the motorway.* – *n* a number that contains another number an exact number of times: *65 is a multiple of 5.*
multiply ['mʌltiplai] *v* **1** to add a number to itself a given number of times and find the total: *4+4+4 or 4 multiplied by 3 or 4×3=12.* **2** to (cause to) increase in number, *esp* by breeding: *Rabbits multiply very rapidly.*
,**multipli'cation** [-pli-] *n* the act of multiplying numbers.
multiracial [mʌlti'reiʃəl] *adj* including, for, or of, people of many races: *Britain is becoming more and more multiracial.*
multi-storey, multi-story [mʌlti'stɔ:ri] *adj* having many floors or storeys: *a multi-storey car park.*
multitude ['mʌltitju:d] *n* a great number or crowd: *a multitude of reasons*; *multitudes of people.*
mum, mummy[1] (*pl* '**mummies**) ['mʌm(i)] *n* a child's name for his or her mother: *Goodbye, Mum(my)!*; *Where's your mum(my), John?*
mumble ['mʌmbl] *v* to speak (words) in such a way that they are difficult to hear: *The old man mumbled (a few words) quietly to himself.*
mummy[1] see **mum**.
mummy[2] ['mʌmi] – *pl* '**mummies** – *n* a dead human body preserved *eg* by the ancient Egyptians by wrapping in bandages and treating with spice, wax *etc*.
mumps [mʌmps] *n sing* a contagious disease causing painful swelling at the sides of the neck and face.
munch [mʌntʃ] *v* to chew (something) with the lips closed: *He was munching his breakfast.*
municipal [mju'nisipəl] *adj* of, or controlled or owned by, the government of a city or town: *the municipal buildings.* **mu'nicipally** *adv*.
munitions [mju'niʃənz] *n pl* weapons and ammunition used in war.
mural ['mjuərəl] *n* a painting that is painted directly on to a wall.

murder ['məːdə] *n* **1** (an act of) killing a person on purpose and illegally: *The police are treating his death as a case of murder; an increase in the number of murders.* **2** any killing or causing of death that is considered as bad as this: *the murder of innocent people by terrorists.* – *v* to kill (a person) on purpose and illegally: *He murdered two children.*

'murderer – *fem* **'murderess** – *n*: *Murderers are no longer hanged in Britain.*

'murderous *adj* intending, or capable of, murder: *There was a murderous look in his eye.* **'murderously** *adv.*

murmur ['məːmə] *n* a quiet, indistinct sound, *eg* that of running water or low voices: *the murmur of the sea; There was a low murmur among the crowd.* – *v* to make such a sound: *The child murmured (something) in his sleep.* **'murmuring** *adj.*

muscle ['mʌsl] *n* any of the bundles of fibres in the body which, by contracting or relaxing, cause movement of the body: *He has well-developed muscles in his arms.*

muscular ['mʌskjulə] *adj* **1** of, or relating to, muscle(s): *great muscular strength.* **2** having well-developed muscles; strong: *She is tall and muscular.*

muscle in (*often with* **on**) to gain entry, or gain a share of something by force: *The large firms have muscled in on all the important contracts.*

muse [mjuːz] *v* to think about a matter *usu* without serious concentration.

museum [mjuˈziəm] *n* a place where collections of things of artistic, scientific or historic interest are set out for show.

mush [mʌʃ] *n* something soft and wet: *The potatoes have turned to mush after being boiled for so long.* **'mushy** *adj.*

mushroom ['mʌʃrum] *n* a type of fungus, *usu* shaped like an umbrella, many varieties of which are, edible. – *v* to grow in size very rapidly: *The town has mushroomed since all the new industry was brought in.*

music ['mjuːzik] *n* **1** the art of arranging and combining sounds able to be produced by the human voice or by instruments: *She prefers classical music to popular music; She is studying music; (also adj) a music lesson.* **2** the written form in which such tones *etc* are set down: *The pianist has forgotten to bring her music.*

'musical *adj* **1** of or producing music: *a musical instrument.* **2** like music, *esp* in being pleasant to hear: *a musical voice.* **3** (of a person) having a talent for music: *Their children are all musical.* – *n* a film or play that includes a large amount of singing, dancing *etc.* **'musically** *adv.*

musician [mjuˈziʃən] *n* **1** a person who is skilled in music: *The conductor of this or-* chestra is a fine musician. **2** a person who plays a musical instrument: *This show has ten singers, twenty dancers and fifty musicians.*

musket ['mʌskit] *n* an old type of gun once carried by foot-soldiers. **,muske'teer** *n* a soldier armed with a musket.

Muslim ['muzlim], **Moslem** ['mozləm] *n, adj* (a person) of the religion known as Islam.

muslin ['mʌzlin] *n, adj* (of) a type of fine soft cotton cloth.

mussel ['mʌsl] *n* a variety of edible shellfish with a shell in two parts.

must [mʌst] – *neg short form* **'mustn't** [-snt] – *v* **1** used with another verb to express need: *We must go to the shops to get milk.* **2** used, *usu* with another verb, to suggest a probability: *They must be finding it very difficult to live in such a small house.* **3** used, *usu* with another verb, to express duty, an order, rule *etc*: *You must come home before midnight; All competitors must be under 15 years of age.* – *n* something necessary, essential, or not to be missed: *This new tent is a must for the serious camper.*

must have used to state a probability about something in the past: *She must have been very young when she got married.*

mustache *see* **moustache.**

mustard ['mʌstəd] *n* a type of seasoning with a hot taste made from the seeds of the mustard plant.

muster ['mʌstə] *v* **1** to gather together (*esp* soldiers for duty or inspection). **2** to gather (courage, energy *etc*): *He mustered his energy for a final effort.*

mustn't *see* **must.**

musty ['mʌsti] *adj* damp or stale in smell or taste: *musty old books.*

mute [mjuːt] *adj* **1** unable to speak; dumb. **2** silent: *She gazed at him in mute horror.* **3** (of a letter) not sounded in certain words: *The word 'dumb' has a mute 'b' at the end.* **'mutely** *adv.*

mutiny ['mjuːtini] – *pl* **'mutinies** – *n* (a) refusal to obey one's senior officers in the navy or other armed services: *There has been a mutiny on HMS Tigress; The sailors were found guilty of mutiny.* – *v* (of sailors *etc*) to refuse to obey commands from those in authority: *The sailors mutinied because they did not have enough food.*

muti'neer *n* a person who mutinies.

'mutinous *adj*: *mutinous sailors.*

mutter ['mʌtə] *v* to utter words in a quiet voice *esp* when grumbling *etc.* – *n* such a sound: *He spoke in a mutter.*

mutton ['mʌtn] *n* the flesh of sheep, used as food.

mutual ['mjuːtʃuəl] *adj* **1** given *etc* by each of

two or more to the other(s): *mutual help*; *Their dislike was mutual.* **2** common to, or shared by, two or more: *a mutual friend.* **'mutually** *adv.*

muzzle ['mʌzl] *n* **1** the jaws and nose of an animal such as a dog. **2** an arrangement of straps *etc* round the muzzle of an animal to prevent it from biting. **3** the open end of the barrel of a gun *etc.* – *v* to put a muzzle on (a dog *etc*).

my [mai] *adj* of or belonging to me: *That is my book*; *I hurt my leg*; *She borrowed my pen.* – *interj* used to express surprise: *My, how you've grown!*

my'self *pron* **1** used as the object of a verb or preposition when the speaker or writer is the object of an action he or she performs: *I cut myself while shaving*; *I looked at myself in the mirror.* **2** used to emphasize **I, me** or the name of the speaker or writer: *I myself can't tell you, but my friend will*; *I don't intend to go myself.*

see also **mine**[1].

mynah ['mainə] *n* a small tropical bird that can mimic human speech.

myopia [mai'oupiə] *n* short-sightedness: *She suffers from myopia.*
my'opic [-'o-] *adj*: *a myopic old lady*; *a myopic condition*; *She's slightly myopic.*

myself *see* **my.**

mystery ['mistəri] – *pl* **'mysteries** – *n* **1** something that cannot be, or has not been, explained: *the mystery of how the universe was formed*; *the mystery of his disappearance*; *How she passed her exam is a mystery to me.* **2** the quality of being impossible to explain, understand *etc*: *Her death was surrounded by mystery.*

my'sterious [-'stiəriəs] *adj* difficult to understand or explain, or full of mystery: *mysterious happenings*; *He's being very mysterious* (= refuses to explain fully) *about what his work is.* **my'steriously** *adv.*

mystify ['mistifai] *v* to be impossible (for someone) to explain or understand: *I was mystified by his behaviour.*

myth [miθ] *n* an ancient, fictional story, *esp* one dealing with gods, heroes *etc*.
'mythical *adj.* **'mythically** *adv.*
mythology [mi'θolədʒi] *n* (a collection of) myths. **mytho'logical** [-'lo-] *adj.*

Nn

nab [nab] – *pt*, *ptp* **nabbed** – *v* to take, catch or get hold of: *The police nabbed the thief.*

nag [nag] – *pt*, *ptp* **nagged** – *v* (*often with* **at**) to complain or criticize continually: *She nags (at) her husband about their lack of money.*
'nagging *adj* continuously troublesome: *a nagging worry/pain.*

nail [neil] *n* **1** a piece of horn-like substance which grows over the ends of the fingers and toes to protect them: *I've broken my nail*; *toe-nails*; *Don't bite your finger-nails.* **2** a thin pointed piece of metal used to fasten pieces of wood *etc* together: *He hammered a nail into the wall and hung a picture on it.* – *v* to fasten with nails: *He nailed the picture to the wall.*
'nail-brush *n* a small brush used for cleaning one's nails.
'nail-file *n* a small instrument with a rough surface, used for smoothing or shaping the edges of one's finger-nails.
'nail-polish, 'nail-varnish *ns* a substance used to colour and/or varnish one's nails.
'nail-scissors *n pl* scissors for trimming one's nails.
hit the nail on the head to be absolutely accurate (in one's description of something or someone, in an estimate of something *etc*).

naïve, naive [nai'i:v] *adj* **1** simple and straightforward in one's way of thinking, speaking *etc*. **2** ignorantly simple. **na'ïvely** *adv.*

naked ['neikid] *adj* **1** without clothes: *a naked child.* **2** openly seen, not hidden: *the naked truth.* **3** (of a flame *etc*) uncovered or unprotected: *Naked lights are dangerous.*
'nakedly *adv.* **'nakedness** *n.*
the naked eye the eye unaided by any artificial means such as a telescope, microscope *etc*: *Germs are too small to be seen by the naked eye.*

name [neim] *n* **1** a word by which a person, place or thing is called: *My name is Rachel*; *She knows all the flowers by name.* **2** reputation; fame: *He has a name for honesty.* – *v* **1** to give a name to: *They named the child Thomas.* **2** to speak of or list by name: *He could name all the kings of England.*
'nameless *adj* **1** not having a name: *a nameless fear.* **2** not spoken of by name: *The author of the book shall be nameless.*
'namely *adv* that is: *Only one student passed the exam, namely John.*
'nameplate *n* a piece of metal, plastic *etc* with a name on it: *You will know his office by the nameplate on the door.*

'**namesake** n a person with the same name as oneself.

call (someone) names to insult (someone) by applying rude names to him.

in the name of by the authority of: *I arrest you in the name of the Queen.*

make a name for oneself to become famous, get a (*usu* good) reputation *etc*: *He made a name for himself as a concert pianist.*

name after, (*Amer*) **name for** to give (a child or a thing) the name of (another person): *Peter was named after his father.*

nanny ['nani] – *pl* '**nannies** – *n* a children's nurse.

nanny-goat ['nanigout] *n* a female goat.

nap [nap] *n* a short sleep: *She always has a nap after lunch.*

catch (someone) napping to catch (someone) unprepared for a particular emergency *etc*.

napalm ['neipa:m] *n* petrol in a jelly-like form, used in bombs to cause fire.

nape [neip] *n* the back of the neck: *His hair curled over the nape of his neck.*

napkin ['napkin] *n* 1 (*also* **table napkin**) a small piece of cloth or paper for protecting the clothes from drips *etc* and for wiping the lips at meals. 2 full form of **nappy**.

nappy ['napi] – *pl* '**nappies** – *n* (*Amer* '**diaper**) a piece of cloth or paper put between a baby's legs to soak up urine *etc*.

narcotic [na:'kotik] *n* a type of drug that stops pain or makes one sleep, often addictive when taken in large doses.

narrate [nə'reit] *v* to tell (a story): *He narrated the events of the afternoon.* **nar'ra-tion** *n*.

narrative ['narətiv] *n* a story: *an exciting narrative.*

nar'rator *n* a person who tells a story.

narrow ['narou] *adj* 1 having or being only a small distance from side to side: *a narrow road*; *The bridge is too narrow for large lorries to cross.* 2 only just managed: *a narrow escape.* 3 (of ideas, interests or experience) not extensive enough. – *v* to make or become narrow: *The road suddenly narrowed.*

'**narrowly** *adv* closely; only just: *The ball narrowly missed his head.*

'**narrows** *n pl* a narrow sea-passage; a channel or strait.

,**narrow-'minded** *adj* unwilling to accept ideas different from one's own.

nasal ['neizəl] *adj* 1 of the nose: *a nasal infection.* 2 sounding through the nose: *a nasal voice.*

nasty ['na:sti] *adj* 1 unpleasant to the senses: *a nasty smell.* 2 unfriendly or unpleasant in manner: *The man was very nasty to me.* 3 wicked; evil: *He has a nasty temper.* 4 (of weather) very poor, cold, rainy *etc*. 5 (of a wound, cut *etc*) serious: *That dog gave her a*

nasty bite. 6 awkward or very difficult: *a nasty situation.* '**nastily** *adv*. '**nastiness** *n*.

nation ['neiʃən] *n* 1 a group of people living in a particular country, forming a single political and economic unit. 2 a large number of people who share the same history, ancestors, culture *etc* (whether or not they all live in the same country): *the Jewish nation.*

national ['naʃənəl] *adj* of or belonging to a particular nation: *national government*; *national pride.* '**nationally** *adv*.

'**nationalism** ['na-] *n* 1 a sense of pride in the history, culture, achievements *etc* of one's nation. 2 the desire to bring the people of one's nation together under their own government. '**nationalist** ['na-] *n*. ,**nationa'listic** *adj*.

nationality [naʃə'naləti] – *pl* **natio'nalities** – *n* (the state of belonging to) a particular nation: *'What nationality are you?' 'I'm German'*; *You can see (people of) many nationalities in London.*

'**nationalize, -ise** ['na-] *v* to make (*esp* an industry) the property of the nation as a whole rather than the property of an individual. ,**nationali'zation, -s-** *n*.

national anthem a nation's official song or hymn.

national service in some countries, a period of compulsory service in the armed forces.

,**nation-'wide** *adj*, *adv* (happening *etc*) throughout the whole nation: *a nation-wide broadcast*; *They travelled nation-wide.*

native ['neitiv] *adj* 1 where one was born: *my native land.* 2 belonging to that place: *my native language.* 3 belonging by race to a country: *a native Englishman.* 4 belonging to a person naturally: *native intelligence.* – *n* 1 a person born in a certain place: *a native of Scotland*; *a native of London.* 2 one of the original inhabitants of a country *eg* before the arrival of explorers, immigrants *etc*: *Columbus thought the natives of America were Indians.*

native speaker a person who has spoken a particular language ever since he was able to speak at all: *I am a native speaker of English*; *a native Spanish speaker.*

native to (of plants and animals) belonging originally to a particular place: *These birds are native to Australia.*

the Nativity [nə'tivəti] the birth of Christ.

natter ['natə] *v* to chatter or talk continuously, *usu* about unimportant things.

natural ['natʃərəl] *adj* 1 of or produced by nature, not made by men: *Coal, oil etc are natural resources*; *Wild animals are happier in their natural state than in a zoo.* 2 born in a person: *natural beauty*; *He had a natural ability for music.* 3 (of manner) simple, without pretence: *a nice, natural smile.* 4 normal; as one would expect: *It's quite*

natural for a boy of his age to be interested in girls. **5** of a musical note, not sharp or flat: *G natural is lower in pitch than G sharp.* – *n* **1** a person who is naturally good at something. **2** in music (a sign (♮) indicating) a note which is not to be played sharp or flat.
'naturalist *n* a person who studies animal and plant life.
'naturally *adv* **1** of course; as one would expect: *Naturally I didn't want to risk missing the train.* **2** by nature; as a natural characteristic: *She is naturally kind.* **3** normally; in a relaxed way: *Although he was nervous, he behaved quite naturally.*
natural gas gas suitable for burning, found underground or under the sea.
natural history the study of plants and animals.
natural resources sources of energy, wealth *etc* which occur naturally and are not made by man, *eg* coal, oil, forests *etc*.
nature ['neitʃə] *n* **1** the physical world, *eg* trees, plants, animals, mountains, rivers *etc*, or the power which made them: *the beauty of nature*; *the forces of nature*; *the study of nature.* **2** the qualities born in a person; personality: *She has a generous nature.* **3** quality; what something is or consists of: *What is the nature of your work?* **4** a kind, type *etc*: *bankers and other people of that nature.*
-natured having a certain type of personality: *good-natured*; *ill-natured.*
in the nature of having the qualities of: *His words were in the nature of a threat.*
naught [nɔːt] *n* nothing.
naughty ['nɔːti] *adj* (*usu* of children) badly-behaved: *a naughty boy*; *It is naughty to kick other children.* **'naughtily** *adv*. **'naughtiness** *n*.
nausea ['nɔːziə, (*Amer*) -ʃə] *n* a feeling of sickness.
nauseate ['nɔːzieit, (*Amer*) -ʒi-] *v* to make (someone) feel nausea.
nautical ['nɔːtikəl] *adj* of ships or sailors: *nautical language.*
naval *see* **navy.**
nave [neiv] *n* the middle or main part of a church.
navel [neivəl] *n* the small hollow in the front of the abdomen, just below the middle of the waist.
navigate ['navigeit] *v* **1** to direct, guide or move (a ship, aircraft *etc*) in a particular direction: *He navigated the ship through the dangerous rocks.* **2** to find or follow one's route when in a ship, aircraft, car *etc*: *If I drive will you navigate?*
'navigable *adj* (*neg* **un-**) able to be travelled along: *a navigable river.*
navi'gation *n* the art or skill of navigating.
'navigator *n* a person who navigates.

navy ['neivi] – *pl* **'navies** – *n* **1** a country's warships and the people who work in and with them: *Russia has one of the largest navies in the world*; *I joined the navy fifteen years ago.* **2** (*also adj*) (*also* **navy blue**) (of) a dark blue colour: *a navy (blue) jersey.*
'naval *adj* of the navy: *naval uniform*; *naval officer.*
near [niə] *adj* **1** not far away in place or time: *The station is quite near*; *Christmas is getting near.* **2** not far away in relationship: *He is a near relation.* – *adv* **1** to or at a short distance from here or the place mentioned: *He lives quite near.* **2** (*with* **to**) close to: *Don't sit too near to the window.* – *prep* at a very small distance from (in place, time *etc*): *She lives near the church*; *It was near midnight when they arrived.* – *v* to come near (to): *The roads became busier as they neared the town*; *as evening was nearing.*
'nearly *adv* not far from; almost: *nearly one o'clock*; *He has nearly finished.*
'nearness *n*.
nearby [niə'bai] *adv* close to here or the place mentioned: *He lives nearby*; *a cottage with a stream running nearby.*
'nearside *adj* (of the side of a vehicle *etc*) furthest from the centre of the road.
,near-'sighted *adj* short-sighted.
a near miss something that is almost a hit, success *etc*.
neat [niːt] *adj* **1** tidy; well-ordered, with everything in the right place: *a neat house*; *She is very neat and tidy.* **2** skilfully done: *He has made a neat job of the repair.* **3** (of drink, *esp* alcoholic) without added water: *neat whisky.* **'neatness** *n*.
'neatly *adv* tidily or skilfully: *Please write neatly.*
necessary ['nesisəri] *adj* needed; essential: *Is it necessary to sign one's name?*; *I shall do all that is necessary.* **,neces'sarily** [-'se-] *adv*.
necessitate [ni'sesiteit] *v* to make necessary: *Re-building the castle would necessitate spending a lot of money.*
necessity [ni'sesəti] – *pl* **ne'cessities** – *n* something needed or essential: *Food is one of the necessities of life.*
neck [nek] *n* **1** the part of the body between the head and chest: *She wore a scarf around her neck.* **2** the part of an article of clothing that covers that part of the body: *The neck of that shirt is dirty.* **3** anything like a neck in shape or position: *the neck of a bottle.*
'necklace [-ləs] *n* a string of jewels, beads *etc* worn around the neck: *a diamond necklace.*
'neckline *n* the edge of a piece of clothing at or around a person's neck: *The dress has a very low neckline.*
'necktie *n* (*Amer*) a man's tie.
neck and neck (in a race) exactly equal: *The*

horses were neck and neck as they came up to the finish.

nectar ['nektə] *n* **1** the sweet liquid collected by bees to make honey. **2** a delicious drink.

née [nei] *adj* born; used to state what a woman's name was before she married: *Mrs Jane Brown, née Black.*

need [ni:d] – *neg short form* **needn't** ['ni:dnt] – *v* **1** to require: *This page needs to be checked again; This page needs checking again; Do you need any help?* **2** to be obliged: *You need to work hard if you want to succeed; They don't need to come until six o'clock; She needn't have given me such an expensive present.* – *n* **1** something essential, that one must have: *Food is one of our basic needs.* **2** poverty or other difficulty: *Many people are in great need.* **3** a reason: *There is no need for panic.*

'**needless** *adj, adv* unnecessary: *You are doing a lot of needless work; Needless to say, he couldn't do it.* '**needlessly** *adv.*

'**needy** *adj* poor: *You must help needy people.*

a need for a lack of; a requirement for: *There is an urgent need for teachers in this city.*

in need of requiring; having a lack of: *We're in need of more money; You're badly in need of a haircut.*

needle ['ni:dl] *n* **1** a small, sharp piece of steel with a hole (called an eye) at one end for thread, used in sewing *etc*: *a sewing needle.* **2** any of various instruments of a long narrow pointed shape: *a knitting needle; a hypodermic needle.* **3** (in a compass *etc*) a moving pointer. **4** the thin, sharp-pointed leaf of a pine, fir *etc.*

'**needlework** *n* work done with a needle *ie* sewing, embroidery *etc.*

needn't *see* **need**.

negative ['negətiv] *adj* **1** meaning or saying 'no'; denying something: *a negative answer.* **2** expecting to fail: *a negative attitude.* **3** less than zero: *−4 is a negative or minus number.* **4** having more electrons than normal: *The battery has a negative and a positive terminal.* – *n* **1** a word *etc* by which something is denied: *'No' and 'never' are negatives.* **2** the photographic film, from which prints are made, on which light and dark are reversed: *I gave away the print, but I still have the negative.*

'**negatively** *adv.*

neglect [ni'glekt] *v* **1** to treat carelessly or not give enough attention to: *He neglected his work.* **2** to fail (to do something): *He neglected to answer the letter.* – *n* lack of care and attention: *The garden is suffering from neglect.*

negligence ['neglidʒəns] *n* carelessness: *The*

accident was caused by the driver's negligence. '**negligent** *adj.* '**negligently** *adv.*

negotiate [ni'gouʃieit] *v* **1** to bargain or discuss a subject in order to agree. **2** to arrange (a treaty, payment *etc*), *usu* after a long discussion. **3** to get past (an obstacle or difficulty). **ne'gotiator** *n.*

ne,goti'ation *n*: *Negotiations ended without any settlement being reached; The dispute was settled by negotiation.*

Negro ['ni:grou] – *fem* '**Negress**; *pl* '**Negroes** – *n* a name for a person belonging to or descended from the black-skinned race from the area of Africa south of the Sahara.

neigh [nei] *v* to utter the cry of a horse: *They could hear the horses neighing.* – *n* such a cry: *The horse gave a neigh.*

neighbour, (*Amer*) **neighbor** ['neibə] *n* a person who lives near oneself: *my next-door neighbour.*

'**neighbourhood** *n* **1** a district or area, *esp* in a town or city: *a poor neighbourhood.* **2** a district or area surrounding a particular place: *He lives somewhere in the neighbourhood of the station.*

'**neighbouring** *adj* near or next in place: *France and Belgium are neighbouring countries.*

'**neighbourly** *adj* (*neg* **un-**) friendly: *a very neighbourly person.*

neither ['naiðə, (*esp Amer*) 'ni:ðə(r)] *adj, pron* not the one nor the other (of two things or people): *Neither window faces the sea; Neither of them could understand Italian.*

neither...nor used to introduce alternatives which are both negative: *Neither John nor David could come; He can neither read nor write.*

> As with **either ... or**, the verb usually follows the noun or pronoun that comes closest to it: *Neither John nor I am responsible; Neither she nor her children speak English.*

neon ['ni:on] *n* an element, a colourless gas used in certain forms of electric lighting, *eg* advertising signs.

nephew ['nefju:] – *fem* **niece** [ni:s] – *n* the son or daughter of a brother or sister: *My sister's two sons are my nephews, and I am their uncle.*

nerve [nə:v] *n* **1** one of the cords which carry messages between all parts of the body and the brain. **2** courage: *He must have needed a lot of nerve ot do that; He lost his nerve.* **3** rudeness: *What a nerve!* – *v* to force (oneself) to have enough courage (to do something): *He nerved himself to climb the high tower.*

nerves *n pl* the condition of being too easily excited or upset: *She suffers from nerves.*

'**nervous** *adj* 1 of the nerves: *the nervous system*. 2 rather afraid: *She was nervous about travelling by air*; *a nervous old lady*. '**nervously** *adv*. '**nervousness** *n*.

'**nervy** *adj* excitable: *The horse is rather nervy*. '**nerviness** *n*.

'**nerve-racking** *adj* causing great anxiety or nervousness: *a nerve-racking experience*.

nervous breakdown a period of mental illness caused by a time of great strain.

nervous system the brain, spinal cord and nerves of a person or animal.

get on someone's nerves to irritate someone: *Her behaviour really gets on my nerves*.

nest [nest] *n* a structure or place in which birds (and some animals and insects) hatch or give birth to and look after their young: *The swallows are building a nest under the roof of our house*; *a wasp's nest*. – *v* to build a nest and live in it: *A pair of robins are nesting in that bush*.

'**nestling** [-liŋ] *n* a young bird (still in the nest).

'**nest-egg** *n* a sum of money saved up for the future.

feather one's (own) nest *see* **feather**.

nestle ['nesl] *v* 1 to lie close together as if in a nest: *The children nestled together for warmth*. 2 to settle comfortably: *She nestled into the cushions*.

nestling *see* **nest**.

net[1] [net] *n* (any of various devices for catching creatures, *eg* fish, or for any of a number of other purposes, consisting of) a loose open material made of knotted string, thread, wire *etc*: *a fishing-net*; *a hair-net*; *a tennis-net*; (*also adj*) *a net curtain*. – *v* – *pt*, *ptp* '**netted** – to catch in a net: *They netted several tons of fish*.

'**netting** *n* material made in the form of a net: *wire netting*.

'**netball** *n* a team-game in which a ball is thrown into a net hanging high up on a pole.

'**network** *n* 1 anything in the form of a net, *ie* with many lines crossing each other: *A network of roads covered the countryside*. 2 a widespread organization: *a radio network*.

net[2], **nett** [net] *adj* 1 (of a profit *etc*) remaining after all expenses *etc* have been paid: *The net profit from the sale was $200*. 2 (of the weight of something) not including the packaging or container: *The sugar has a net weight of 1 kilo*; *The sugar weighs one kilo net*.

netball *see* **net**[1].

nett *see* **net**[2].

netting *see* **net**[1].

nettle ['netl] *n* a type of plant covered with hairs that cause a painful rash if touched.

network *see* **net**[1].

neuter ['nju:tə] *adj* 1 in certain languages, of the gender which is neither masculine nor feminine: *a neuter noun*. 2 without sex: *Worker bees are neuter, being neither male nor female*.

neutral ['nju:trəl] *adj* 1 not taking sides in a quarrel or war: *A neutral country was asked to help settle the dispute*. 2 (of colour) not strong or definite: *Grey is a neutral colour*. 3 (in electricity) neither positively nor negatively charged. – *n* 1 (a person belonging to) a nation that takes no part in a war or quarrel. 2 the position of the gear of an engine in which no power passes to the wheels *etc*: *I put the car into neutral*.

neu'trality [-'tra-] *n* the state of being neutral.

'**neutralize, -ise** *v* to make useless or harmless *usu* by causing an opposite effect.

neutron ['nju:tron] *n* one of the particles which make up the nucleus of an atom.

never ['nevə] *adv* not ever; at no time: *I shall never go there again*; *Never have I been so angry*; *his never-failing kindness*.

,**never'more** *adv* never again.

,**neverthe'less** [-ðə'les] *adv* in spite of that: *I am feeling ill, but I shall come with you nevertheless*.

new [nju:] *adj* 1 having only just happened, been built, made, bought *etc*: *She is wearing a new dress*; *We are building a new house*. 2 only just discovered, experienced *etc*: *Flying in an aeroplane was a new experience for her*. 3 changed: *He is a new man*. 4 just arrived *etc*: *The schoolchildren teased the new boy*. – *adv* freshly: *new-laid eggs*.

'**newly** *adv* only just; recently: *She is newly married*; *Her hair is newly cut*.

'**newcomer** *n* a person who has just arrived: *He is a newcomer to this district*.

,**new'fangled** [-'faŋgld] *adj* (of things, ideas *etc*) too new to be considered reliable: *newfangled machines*.

new to having no previous experience of: *He's new to this kind of work*.

news [nju:z] *n sing* a report of, or information about, recent events: *You can hear the news on the radio at 9 o'clock*; *Is there any news about your friend?*; (*also adj*) *a news broadcast*.

'**newsy** *adj* full of news: *a newsy letter*.

'**newsagent** *n* (*Amer* **news dealer**) a person who has a shop selling newspapers (and *usu* other goods).

'**newscast** *n* a broadcast of news in a radio or television programme.

'**newscaster** *n* a person who presents a news broadcast.

'**newsletter** *n* a sheet containing news issued to members of a group, organization *etc*.

'**newspaper** *n* a paper, printed daily or

weekly, containing news *etc*: *a daily newspaper.*

newt [njuːt] *n* a type of small animal which lives on land and in water.

next [nekst] *adj* nearest in place, time *etc*: *When you have called at that house, go on to the next one; The next person to arrive late will be sent away; Who is next on the list?* – *adv* immediately after in place or time: *John arrived first and Jane came next.* – *pron* the person or thing nearest in place, time *etc*: *Finish one question before you begin to answer the next; One minute he was sitting beside me – the next he was lying on the ground.*

next best, biggest, oldest *etc* the one immediately after the best, biggest, oldest *etc*: *I can't go to Paris so London is the next best place.*

next door *adv* in the next house: *I live next door (to Mrs Smith).*

next to 1 beside: *She sat next to me.* **2** closest to: *In height, George comes next to me.* **3** more or less; pretty well: *His writing is next to illegible.*

nib [nib] *n* (*also* **'pen-nib**) the pointed, metal part of a fountain-pen or other pen from which the ink flows.

-nibbed: *a fine-nibbed pen.*

nibble ['nibl] *v* to take very small bites (of): *She was nibbling (at) a biscuit.* – *n* a small bite: *Have a nibble of this cake.*

nice [nais] *adj* **1** pleasant; agreeable: *nice weather; a nice person.* **2** used jokingly: *We're in a nice mess now.* **3** exact; precise: *a nice sense of timing.* **'nicely** *adv.*

nicety ['naisəti] – *pl* **'niceties** – *n* a precise or delicate detail.

to a nicety exactly: *He judged the distance to a nicety.*

niche [nitʃ, niːʃ] *n* **1** a hollow in a wall for a statue, ornament *etc*. **2** a suitable place in life: *He found his niche in engineering.*

Nichrome® ['naikroum] *n* an alloy consisting of 60% nickel, 16% chromium and 24% iron.

nick [nik] *n* a small cut: *There was a nick in the doorpost.* – *v* to make a small cut in something: *He nicked his chin while he was shaving.*

in the nick of time at the last possible moment; just in time: *He arrived in the nick of time.*

nickel ['nikl] *n* **1** an element, a greyish-white metal used *esp* for mixing with other metals and for plating. **2** (*Amer*) a five-cent coin.

nickname ['nikneim] *n* an informal name given in affection, admiration, dislike *etc*: *Wellington's nickname was 'the Iron Duke'.* – *v* to give a nickname to: *We nicknamed him 'Foureyes' because he wore spectacles.*

nicotine ['nikətiːn] *n* a harmful substance contained in tobacco.

niece *see* **nephew**.

niggardly ['nigədli] *adj* not generous; unwilling to give or spend money: *He's niggardly with his money; a niggardly gift.*

nigger ['nigə] *n* an impolite name for a Negro.

nigh [nai] *adv* an old word for near.

'well-nigh nearly; almost: *It was well-nigh midnight when he arrived.*

night [nait] *n* **1** the period from sunset to sunrise: *We sleep at night; They talked all night (long); He travelled by night and rested during the day; The days were warm and the nights were cool;* (*also adj*) *He is doing night work.* **2** the time of darkness: *In the Arctic in winter, night lasts for twenty-four hours out of twenty-four.*

'nightly *adj, adv* every night: *a nightly news programme; He goes there nightly.*

'night-club *n* a club open at night for drinking, dancing, entertainment *etc*.

'nightdress, 'nightgown *n* a garment for wearing in bed.

'nightfall *n* the beginning of night; dusk.

'nightmare *n* a frightening dream: *I had a nightmare about being strangled.* **'nightmarish** *adj.*

'night-school *n* (a place providing) educational classes held in the evenings for people who are at work during the day.

'night shift 1 (a period of) work during the night: *He's on (the) night shift this week.* **2** the people who work during this period: *We met the night shift leaving the factory.*

'night-time *n* the time when it is night: *Owls are usually seen at night-time.*

,night-'watchman *n* a person who looks after a building *etc* during the night.

nightingale ['naitingeil, (*Amer*) -tən-] *n* a type of small bird with a beautiful song.

nil [nil] *n* (in scoring) nothing; zero: *Leeds United won two-nil/by two goals to nil.*

nimble ['nimbl] *adj* quick and light in movement: *a nimble jump.* **'nimbly** *adv.*

nine [nain] *n* **1** the number or figure 9. **2** the age of 9. – *adj* **1** 9 in number. **2** aged 9.

nine- having nine (of something): *a nine-page booklet.*

ninth *n* **1** one of nine equal parts. **2** (*also adj*) the last of nine (people, things *etc*); the next after the eighth.

'nine-year-old *n* a person or animal that is nine years old. – *adj* (of a person, animal or thing) that is nine years old.

ninepins ['nainpinz] *n sing* a game in which nine bottle-shaped objects are knocked over with a ball: *a game of ninepins; Ninepins is a very good game.*

nineteen [nain'tiːn] *n* **1** the number or figure

19. **2** the age of 19. – *adj* **1** 19 in number.
2 aged 19.

nineteen- having nineteen (of something): *a nineteen-page document*.

‚**nine'teenth** *n* **1** one of nineteen equal parts. **2** (*also adj*) the last of nineteen (people, things *etc*); the next after the eighteenth.

‚**nine'teen-year-old** *n* a person or animal that is nineteen years old. – *adj* (of a person, animal or thing) that is nineteen years old.

talk nineteen to the dozen to talk (to one another) continually or for a long time.

ninety ['nainti] *n* **1** the number or figure 90. **2** the age of 90. – *adj* **1** 90 in number. **2** aged 90.

'**nineties** *n pl* **1** the period of time between one's ninetieth and one hundredth birthdays. **2** the range of temperatures between ninety and one hundred degrees. **3** the period of time between the ninetieth and one hundredth years of a century.

'**ninetieth** *n* **1** one of ninety equal parts. **2** (*also adj*) the last of ninety (people, things *etc*); the next after the eighty-ninth.

ninety- having ninety (of something): *a ninety-dollar fine*.

'**ninety-year-old** *n* a person or animal that is ninety years old. – *adj* (of a person, animal or thing) that is ninety years old.

nip [nip] – *pt, ptp* **nipped** – *v* **1** to press between the thumb and a finger, or between claws or teeth, causing pain; to pinch or bite: *A crab nipped her toe*; *The dog nipped her ankle*. **2** to cut with such an action: *He nipped the wire with the pliers*; *He nipped off the heads of the flowers*. **3** to sting: *Iodine nips when it is put on a cut*. **4** to move quickly; to make a quick, *usu* short, journey: *I'll just nip into this shop for cigarettes*; *He nipped over to Paris for the week-end*. **5** to stop the growth of (plants *etc*): *The frost has nipped the roses*. – *n* **1** the act of pinching or biting: *His dog gave her a nip on the ankle*. **2** a sharp stinging quality, or coldness in the weather: *a nip in the air*. **3** a small drink, *esp* of spirits.

'**nippy** *adj* **1** (of the weather) cold. **2** quick-moving; nimble: *a nippy little car*.

nip (something) in the bud to stop (something) as soon as it starts: *The managers nipped the strike in the bud*.

nipah ['ni:pə] *n* a tropical palm tree with large feathery leaves used for thatching, mats *etc*.

nipple ['nipl] *n* **1** the darker, pointed part of a woman's breast from which a baby sucks milk; the equivalent part of a male breast. **2** (*Amer*) the rubber mouth-piece of a baby's feeding-bottle; a teat.

nippy *see* **nip**.

nit [nit] *n* the egg of a louse or other small insect (*eg* found in a person's hair).

nitrate *see* **nitrogen**.

nitrogen ['naitrədʒən] *n* an element, a type of gas making up nearly four-fifths of the air we breathe.

'**nitrate** *n* any of several substances containing nitrogen often used as soil fertilizers.

no [nou] *adj* **1** not any: *We have no food*; *No other person could have done it*. **2** not allowed: *No smoking*. **3** not a: *He is no friend of mine*; *This will be no easy task*. – *adv* not (any): *He is no better at golf than swimming*; *He went as far as the shop and no further*. – *interj* a word used for denying, disagreeing, refusing *etc*: *'Do you like travelling?' 'No, (I don't).'*; *No, I don't agree*; *'Will you help me?' 'No, I won't.'* – *pl* **noes** – *n* **1** a refusal: *She answered with a definite no*. **2** a vote against something: *The noes have won*.

'**nobody** *pron* no person; no-one: *Nobody likes him*. – *n* a very unimportant person: *She's just a nobody*.

'**no-one** *pron* no person; nobody: *She will see no-one*; *No-one is to blame*.

there's no saying, knowing *etc* it is impossible to say, know *etc*: *There's no denying it*; *There's no knowing what she will say*.

nobility *see* **noble**.

noble ['noubl] *adj* **1** honourable; unselfish: *a noble mind*; *a noble deed*. **2** of high birth or rank: *a noble family*; *of noble birth*. – *n* a person of high birth: *The nobles planned to murder the king*.

no'bility [-'bi-] *n* **1** the state of being noble: *the nobility of his mind/birth*. **2** nobles *ie* dukes, earls *etc*: *The nobility supported the king during the revolution*.

'**nobly** *adv*: *He worked nobly for the cause of peace*.

'**nobleman** – *fem* '**noblewoman** – *n* a noble: *The king was murdered by a nobleman at his court*.

nobody *see* **no**.

nocturnal [nok'tə:nl] *adj* **1** active at night: *The owl is a nocturnal bird*. **2** happening at night: *a nocturnal encounter*.

nod [nod] – *pt, ptp* '**nodded** – *v* **1** to make a quick forward and downward movement of the head to show agreement, as a greeting *etc*: *I asked him if he agreed and he nodded (his head)*; *He nodded to the man as he passed him in the street*. **2** to let the head fall forward and downward when sleepy: *Grandmother sat nodding by the fire*. – *n* a nodding movement of the head: *He answered with a nod*.

nod off to fall asleep: *He nodded off while she was speaking to him*.

node [noud] *n* **1** a small swelling *eg* in an organ of the body. **2** a place, often swollen, where a leaf is attached to a stem.

Noel, Nowell, Noël [nou'el] *n* an old word for Christmas.

noise [noiz] *n* **1** a sound: *I heard a strange noise outside*; *the noise of gunfire*. **2** an unpleasantly loud sound: *I hate noise.*
'**noiseless** *adj* without any sound: *noiseless footsteps.* '**noiselessly** *adv.*
'**noisy** *adj* making a loud noise: *noisy children*; *a noisy engine.* '**noisily** *adv.*

nomad ['noumad] *n* one of a group of people with no permanent home who travel about with their sheep, cattle *etc: Many of the people of central Asia are nomads.* **no'madic** *adj.* **no'madically** *adv.*

no-man's-land ['noumanzland] *n* land which no-one owns or controls, *esp* between opposing armies.

nominal ['nominəl] *adj* **1** in name only, not in reality: *He is only the nominal head of the firm.* **2** very small: *He had to pay only a nominal fine.*

nominate ['nomineit] *v* to name (someone) for possible election to a particular job *etc: They nominated him as captain.*
,**nomi'nation** *n* **1** the act of nominating: *the nomination of a president.* **2** a suggestion of a particular person for a post *etc: We've had four nominations for the job.*
,**nomi'nee** *n* a person who is nominated for a job *etc.*

non- [non] used with many words to change their meanings to the opposite; not.

nonagenarian [nonədʒi'neəriən] *n* a person who is between ninety and ninety-nine years old.

non-alcoholic ['nonalkə'holik] *adj* (of a drink) not containing any alcohol.

nonchalant ['nonʃələnt, (*Amer*) nonʃə'lont] *adj* feeling or showing no excitement, fear or other emotion. '**nonchalantly** *adv.* '**nonchalance** *n.*

non-commissioned [nonkə'miʃənd] *adj* not holding a commission (*ie* in the army, below the rank of second lieutenant).

non-conductor [,nonkən'dʌktə] *n* a substance *etc* that does not easily conduct heat or electricity.

nondescript ['nondiskript] *adj* having no noticeable, interesting or memorable characteristics: *a nondescript sort of building.*

none [nʌn] *pron* not one; not any: '*How many tickets have you got?*' '*None*'; *He asked me for some food but there was none in the house*; *None of us have/has seen him*; *None of your cheek!* (=Don't be cheeky!). – *adv* not at all: *He is none the worse for his accident.*
none but only: *None but the brave deserve our respect.*
,**nonethe'less, none the less** nevertheless; in spite of this: *He had a headache, but he wanted to come with us nonetheless.*

none can be followed by a singular or plural verb: *None of the children like(s) the new teacher.*

nonetheless *see* **none.**

non-existent [nonig'zistənt] *adj* not existing; not real; *He is afraid of some non-existent monster.* ,**non-ex'istence** *n.*

non-fiction [non'fikʃən] *n* books, magazines *etc* giving facts, information *etc, ie* not stories, novels, plays, poetry: *I read a lot of non-fiction.*

non-flammable [non'flaməbl] *adj* non-inflammable: *Babies' clothes should be non-flammable.*

non-inflammable [nonin'flaməbl] *adj* not able to burn or be set alight: *non-inflammable material*; *Asbestos is non-inflammable.*

nonplussed [non'plʌst] *adj* completely puzzled; bewildered.

non-resident [non'rezidənt] *adj* not living in (a school *etc): We have several non-resident members of staff.*

nonsense ['nonsəns, (*Amer*) -sens] *n* foolishness; foolish words, actions *etc*; something that is ridiculous: *He's talking nonsense*; *The whole book is a lot of nonsense*; *What nonsense!* ,**non'sensical** [-'sen-] *adj.*

non-starter [non'sta:tə] *n* a horse or person that, though entered for a race, does not run.

non-stick [non'stik] *adj* (of a pan *etc*) treated, *usu* by covering with a special substance, so that food *etc* will not stick to it: *a non-stick frying-pan.*

non-stop [non'stop] *adj* continuing without a stop: *non-stop entertainment*; *Is this train non-stop?*

non-violence [non'vaiələns] *n* the refusal to use any violent means in order to gain political, social *etc* aims. ,**non-'violent** *adj.*

noodle ['nu:dl] *n* a strip of paste *usu* made with water, flour and egg: *fried noodles.*

nook [nuk] *n* a quiet, dark corner or place.
every nook and cranny everywhere: *They searched in every nook and cranny.*

noon [nu:n] *n* twelve o'clock midday: *They arrived at noon.*

noose [nu:s] *n* **1** a loop in rope, wire *etc* that becomes tighter when pulled. **2** such a loop in a rope used for hanging a person.

nor [no:] *conj* and not: *He did not know then what had happened, nor did he ever find out*; *I'm not going, nor is John.*

normal ['no:məl] *adj* usual; without any special characteristics or circumstances: *How much work do you do on a normal day?*; *normal people*; *His behaviour is not normal.* **nor'mality** [-'ma-] *n.*
normally *adv* **1** in a usual, ordinary way: *He was behaving quite normally yesterday.* **2** usually; most often: *I normally go home at 4 o'clock.*

north [no:θ] *n* **1** the direction to the left of a person facing the rising sun, or any part of the earth lying in that direction: *He faced towards the north*; *The wind is blowing from the north*; *I used to live in the north of England.* **2** (*also* **N**) one of the four main points of the compass. – *adj* **1** in the north: *on the north bank of the river.* **2** from the direction of the north: *a north wind.* – *adv* towards the north: *The stream flows north.*

'northerly [-ðə-] *adj* **1** (of a wind *etc*) coming from the north: *a northerly breeze.* **2** looking, lying *etc* towards the north: *in a northerly direction.*

'northern [-ðən] *adj* of the north or the North.

'northerner [-ðə-] *n* a person who lives, or was born, in a northern region or country.

'northernmost [-ðən-] *adj* being furthest north: *the northernmost point of the coast.*

'northward *adj* towards the north: *in a northward direction.*

'northward(s) *adv* towards the north: *They were travelling northwards.*

'northbound *adj* travelling northwards: *the northbound railway-line.*

‚north-'east/‚north-'west *ns, adjs* (in or from) the direction midway between north and east or north and west, or any part of the earth lying in that direction: *the north-east counties*; *a north-west wind.* – *advs* towards the north-east or north-west: *The building faces north-west.*

‚north-'easterly/‚north-'westerly *adjs* **1** (of a wind *etc*) coming from the north-east or north-west: *a north-easterly wind.* **2** looking, lying *etc* towards the north-east or north-west: *a north-westerly direction.*

‚north-'eastern/‚north-'western *adjs* of the north-east or north-west.

the North Pole the northern end of the imaginary line through the earth, round which it turns.

nose [nouz] *n* **1** the part of the face by which people and animals smell and *usu* breathe: *She held the flower to her nose*; *He punched the man on the nose.* **2** the sense of smell: *Police dogs have good noses and can follow criminals' trails.* **3** the part of anything which is like a nose in shape or position: *the nose of an aeroplane.* – *v* **1** to make a way by pushing carefully forward: *The ship nosed (its way) through the ice.* **2** to look or search as if by smelling: *He nosed about (in) the cupboard.*

-nosed: *a long-nosed dog.*

'nos(e)y *adj* taking too much interest in other people and what they are doing: *She is a very nos(e)y person.* **'nosily** *adv.* **'nosiness** *n.*

'nose-bag *n* food-bag for horses, hung over the head.

'nosedive *n* a dive or fall with the head or nose first: *The aeroplane did a nosedive into the sea.* – *v* to make such a dive: *Suddenly the plane nosedived.*

follow one's nose to go straight forward.

lead by the nose to make (a person) do whatever one wants.

nose out to find (as if) by smelling: *The dog nosed out its master's glove.*

pay through the nose to pay a lot, or too much.

turn up one's nose at to treat with contempt: *He turned up his nose at the school dinner.*

under (a person's) (very) nose right in front of (a person): *The book was right under my very nose*; *He stole the money from under my very nose.*

nostalgia [no'staldʒə] *n* a longing for past times: *She felt a great nostalgia for her childhood.* **no'stalgic** *adj.* **no'stalgically** *adv.*

nostril ['nostril] *n* one of the two openings in the nose through which one breathes, smells *etc.*

not [not] *adv* **1** (often abbrev **n't**) a word used for denying, forbidding, refusing, or expressing the opposite of something: *I did not see him*; *I didn't see him*; *He isn't here*; *Isn't he coming?*; *They told me not to go*; *Not a single person came to the party*; *We're going to London, not Paris*; *That's not true!* **2** used with certain verbs such as **hope, seem, believe, expect** and also with **be afraid**: *'Have you got much money?' 'I'm afraid not'*; *'Is he going to fail his exam?' 'I hope not'.*

not at all it does not matter; it is not important *etc*: *'Thank you for helping me.' 'Not at all.'*

notable *etc see* **note.**

notation [nə'teiʃən] *n* (the use of) a system of signs representing numbers, musical sounds *etc*: *musical/mathematical notation.*

notch [notʃ] *n* a small V-shaped cut: *He cut a notch in his stick.* – *v* to make a notch in.

note [nout] *n* **1** a piece of writing to call attention to something: *He left me a note about the meeting.* **2** (*in pl*) ideas for a speech, details from a lecture *etc* written down in short form: *The students took notes on the professor's lecture.* **3** a written or mental record: *Have you kept a note of his name?* **4** a short explanation: *There is a note at the bottom of the page about that difficult word.* **5** a short letter: *She wrote a note to her friend.* **6** (*Amer* **bill**) a piece of paper used as money; a bank-note: *a five-dollar note.* **7** a musical sound: *The song ended on a high note.* **8** a written or printed symbol representing a musical note. **9** an impression or feeling: *The conference ended on a note of hope.* – *v* **1** (*often with* **down**) to write down: *He noted (down) her telephone* *number in his diary.* **2** to notice; to be aware of: *He noted a change in her behaviour.*

'**notable** *adj* worth taking notice of; important: *There were several notable people at the meeting.* ,**nota'bility** *n.*

'**notably** *adv* **1** in particular: *Several people offered to help, notably Mrs Brown.* **2** in a noticeable way: *Her behaviour was notably different from usual.*

'**noted** *adj* well-known: *a noted author*; *This town is noted for its cathedral.*

'**notelet** [-lit] *n* a small piece of notepaper, often folded like a card and with a picture on it, used for short letters.

'**notebook** *n* a small book in which to write notes.

'**notecase** *n* a case for bank-notes, carried in the pocket.

'**notepaper** *n* paper for writing letters.

'**noteworthy** *adj* worthy of notice; remarkable. '**noteworthiness** *n.*

take note of to notice and remember: *He took note of the change in her appearance.*

nothing ['nʌθiŋ] *pron* no thing; not anything: *There was nothing in the cupboard*; *I have nothing new to say.* – *n* the number 0; nought: *a telephone number with three nothings in it.* – *adv* not at all: *He's nothing like his father.*

'**nothingness** *n* the state of being nothing or of not existing; emptiness.

come to nothing to fail: *His plans came to nothing.*

for nothing 1 free; without payment: *I'll do that job for you for nothing.* **2** without result; in vain: *I've been working on this book for six years, and all for nothing!*

have nothing to do with 1 to avoid completely: *After he came out of prison, many of his friends would have nothing to do with him.* **2** (also **be nothing to do with**) to be something that a person ought not to be interested in: *This letter has/is nothing to do with you.*

make nothing of not to understand: *I can make nothing of this letter.*

mean nothing to not to be understandable to: *These mathematical figures mean nothing to me.*

next to nothing almost nothing: *The child was wearing next to nothing.*

nothing but just; only: *The fellow's nothing but a fool!*

nothing doing! an expression used to show a strong or emphatic refusal: *'Would you like to go to the meeting instead of me?' 'Nothing doing!'*

there is nothing to it it is easy: *You'll soon see how to do this job – there's nothing to it!*

think nothing of not to consider difficult, unusual *etc*: *My father thought nothing of*

walking 8 kilometres to school when he was a boy.

to say nothing of as well as; and in addition: *When her mother comes to stay with us, she brings all her clothes with her, to say nothing of her three dogs.*

notice ['noutis] *n* **1** a written or printed statement to announce something publicly: *He stuck a notice on the door, saying that he had gone home*; *They put a notice in the paper announcing the birth of their daughter.* **2** attention: *His skill attracted their notice*; *I'll bring the problem to his notice as soon as possible.* **3** warning given *esp* before leaving a job or dismissing someone: *Her employer gave her a month's notice*; *The cook gave in her notice*; *Please give notice of your intentions.* – *v* to see, observe, or keep in one's mind: *I noticed a book on the table*; *He noticed her leave the room*; *Did he say that? I didn't notice.*

'**noticeable** *adj* (likely to be) easily noticed: *There's a slight stain on this dress but it's not really noticeable.*

'**noticeably** *adv*: *This ball of wool is noticeably darker than these others.*

'**noticed** *adj* (*neg* **un-**).

'**notice-board** (*Amer* '**bulletin board**) *n* a *usu* large board *eg* in a hall, school *etc* on which notices are put.

at short notice without much warning time for preparation *etc*: *He had to make the speech at very short notice when his boss suddenly fell ill.*

take notice of to pay attention to: *He never takes any notice of what his father says*; *Take no notice of gossip.*

notify ['noutifai] *v* to inform or warn about something: *He notified the headmaster of his intentions*; *If there has been an accident you must notify the police.* ,**notifi'cation** [-fi-] *n.*

notion ['nouʃən] *n* **1** understanding: *I've no notion what he's talking about.* **2** an uncertain belief; an idea: *He has some very odd notions.* **3** a desire for something or to do something: *He had a sudden notion to visit his aunt.*

notorious [nə'tɔ:riəs] *adj* well-known for badness or wickedness: *a notorious murderer.* **notoriety** [noutə'raiəti] *n.* **no'toriously** *adv.*

notwithstanding [notwið'standiŋ] *prep* in spite of: *Notwithstanding the bad weather, the ship arrived on time.*

nougat ['nʌgət, 'nu:ga:] *n* a sticky kind of sweet containing nuts *etc*.

nought [nɔ:t] *n* **1** nothing. **2** the figure 0: *The number contained five noughts.*

noughts and crosses a game in which the players try to make a line of three noughts or crosses between vertical and horizontal lines.

†**noun** [naun] *n* a word used as the name of a

person, animal, place, state or thing: *The words 'boy', 'James' and 'happiness' are all nouns.*

nourish ['nʌriʃ, (*Amer*) 'nə:-] *v* to cause or help to grow, become healthy *etc*.

'**nourishing** *adj* giving the body what is necessary for health and growth: *nourishing food.*

'**nourishment** *n* something that nourishes; food: *Plants draw nourishment from the earth.*

novel[1] ['novəl] *n* a book telling a long story in prose: *the novels of Charles Dickens.*

'**novelist** *n* the writer of a novel; *Dickens was a great novelist.*

novel[2] ['novəl] *adj* new and strange: *a novel idea.*

'**novelty** – *pl* '**novelties** – *n* **1** newness and strangeness: *It took her a long time to get used to the novelty of her surroundings.* **2** something new and strange: *Snow is a novelty to people from hot countries.* **3** a small, cheap manufactured thing sold as a toy or souvenir: *a stall selling novelties.*

November [nə'vembə] *n* the eleventh month of the year, the month following October.

novice ['novis] *n* **1** a beginner in any skill *etc*. **2** a monk or nun who has not yet taken all his or her vows.

now [nau] *adv* **1** (at) the present period of time: *I am now living in England.* **2** at once; immediately: *I can't do it now – you'll have to wait.* **3** (at) this moment: *He'll be at home now*; *From now on, I shall be more careful about what I say to her.* **4** (in stories) then; at that time: *We were now very close to the city.* **5** because of what has happened *etc*: *I now know better than to trust her.* **6** a word in explanations, warnings, commands, or to show disbelief: *Now this is what happened*; *Stop that, now!*; *Do be careful, now.* – *conj* (*often with* **that**) because or since something has happened, is now true *etc*: *Now that you are here, I can leave*; *Now you have left school, you will have to find a job.*

'**nowadays** *adv* at the present period of time: *Food is very expensive nowadays.*

for now: *That will be enough for now – we'll continue our conversation tomorrow.*

just now a moment ago: *I saw him just now in the street.*

(every) now and then/again sometimes; occasionally: *We go to the theatre (every) now and then.*

now, now! an expression used to warn or rebuke: *Now, now! Behave yourself!*

now then an expression used for calming people *etc*: *'Now then,' said the policeman, 'what's going on here?'*

Nowell *see* **Noel**.

nowhere ['nouweə] *adv* in or to no place; not

anywhere: *It was nowhere to be found*; *'Where have you been?' 'Nowhere in particular.'*

nowhere near not nearly: *We've nowhere near enough money to buy a car.*

nozzle ['nozl] *n* a narrow end-piece fitted to a pipe, tube *etc*: *The fireman pointed the nozzle of the hose-pipe at the fire.*

-n't *see* **not**.

nucleus ['nju:kliəs] – *pl* '**nuclei** [-kliai] – *n* **1** the central part of an atom. **2** the part of a plant or animal cell that controls its development.

nuclear ['nju:kliə] *adj* **1** using atomic energy: *a nuclear power station.* **2** of a nucleus.

nuclear disarmament the act of ceasing to store atomic weapons.

nuclear energy atomic energy.

nuclear reactor an apparatus for producing nuclear energy.

nude [nju:d] *adj* without clothes; naked. – *n* a photograph, picture *etc* of an unclothed human figure.

'**nudism** *n* the practice of not wearing clothes *usu* because it is thought to be healthy. '**nudist** *n*.

'**nudity** *n* the state of not wearing clothes.

in the nude without clothes.

nudge [nʌdʒ] *n* a gentle push *usu* with the elbow: *He gave her a nudge.* – *v* to hit gently, *usu* with the elbow: *She nudged him in the ribs.*

nudism *etc see* **nude**.

nugget ['nʌgit] *n* a lump, *esp* of gold.

nuisance ['nju:sns] *n* a person or thing that is annoying or troublesome: *That child is a terrible nuisance.*

numb [nʌm] *adj* not able to feel or move: *My arm has gone numb*; *She was numb with cold.* – *v* to make numb: *The cold numbed her fingers.* '**numbly** *adv*. '**numbness** *n*.

number ['nʌmbə] *n* **1** (*sometimes abbrev* **no** – *pl* **nos** – *when written in front of a figure*) a word or figure showing *eg* how many of something there are, or the position of something in a series *etc*: *Seven was often considered a magic number*; *Answer nos 1–10 of exercise 2.* **2** a (large) quantity or group (of people or things): *He has a number of records*; *There were a large number of people in the room.* **3** one issue of a magazine: *the autumn number.* **4** a popular song or piece of music: *He sang his most popular number.* – *v* **1** to put a number on: *He numbered the pages in the top corner.* **2** to include: *He numbered her among his closest friends.* **3** to come to in total: *The group numbered ten.*

'**numberless** *adj* very many.

'**number-plate** *n* one of the metal plates carried on the front and back of a motor vehicle showing the registration number of the vehicle.

his *etc* **days are numbered** he *etc* won't last much longer.

without number very many: *I've told him times without number* (= very often) *not to do that.*

a number of, meaning 'several', is plural: *A number of boys are absent today.*
the number of, meaning 'the total quantity of' is singular: *The number of girls in the class is small.*

numeral ['nju:mərəl] *n* a figure used to express a number: *1, 10, 50 are Arabic numerals; I, X, L are Roman numerals.*
nu'merical [-'me-] *adj* of, using or consisting of numbers: *a numerical code.*
nu'merically *adv.*
numerate ['nju:mərət] *adj* having a basic understanding of mathematics and science.
numerical *etc see* **numeral.**
numerous ['nju:mərəs] *adj* very many: *His faults are too numerous to mention.*
nun [nʌn] *n* a member of a female religious community.
'nunnery – *pl* **'nunneries** – *n* a house in which a group of nuns live; a convent.
nuptial ['nʌpʃəl] *adj* of marriage.
nurse [nə:s] *n* **1** a person who looks after sick or injured people in hospital: *She wants to be a nurse.* **2** a person, *usu* a woman, who looks after small children: *The children have gone out with their nurse.* – *v* **1** to look after sick or injured people, *esp* in a hospital: *He was nursed back to health.* **2** to give (a baby) milk from the breast. **3** to hold with care: *She was nursing a kitten.* **4** to have or encourage (feelings *eg* of anger or hope) in oneself.
'nursery – *pl* **'nurseries** – *n* **1** a room *etc* for young children. **2** a place where young plants are grown.
'nursing *n* the profession of a nurse who cares for the sick.
'nursemaid *n* a nurse who looks after small children.

'nurseryman *n* a person who runs, or works in, a nursery for plants.
nursery rhyme a short, simple poem for children.
nursery school a school for very young children.
'nursing-home *n* a small private hospital.
nurture ['nə:tʃə] *v* to encourage the growth and development of (a child, plant *etc*). – *n* care; help in growing or developing.
nut [nʌt] *n* **1** a fruit consisting of a single seed in a hard shell: *a hazel-nut; a walnut.* **2** a small round piece of metal with a hole through it, for screwing on the end of a bolt to hold pieces of wood, metal *etc* together: *a nut and bolt.*
'nutty *adj* **1** containing, or tasting of, nuts: *a nutty flavour.* **2** a slang word for mad: *He's quite nutty.*
'nutcracker *n* (*usu in pl*) an instrument for cracking nuts open: *a pair of nutcrackers.*
'nutshell *n* the hard covering of a nut.
in a nutshell expressed, described *etc* very briefly: *I'll tell you the story in a nutshell.*
nutmeg ['nʌtmeg] *n* a hard seed ground into a powder and used as a spice in food.
nutritious [nju'triʃəs] *adj* valuable as food; nourishing.
nutrient ['nju:triənt] *n* a substance which gives nourishment: *This food contains important nutrients.*
'nutriment *n* nourishment; food.
nu'trition *n* (the act of giving or getting) nourishment, or the scientific study of this.
nu'tritional *adj.*
nutshell, nutty *see* **nut.**
nuzzle ['nʌzl] *v* to press, rub or caress with the nose: *The horse nuzzled (against) her cheek.*
nylon ['nailən] *n, adj* (of) a type of material made from chemicals and used for clothes, ropes, brushes *etc*: *a nylon shirt.*
'nylons *n pl* stockings made of nylon: *three pairs of nylons.*
nymph [nimf] *n* a goddess or spirit of the rivers, trees *etc.*

Oo

o [ou] *interj* an expression used when speaking to a person, thing *etc.*
See also **oh.**
oaf [ouf] *n* a stupid or clumsy person: *That stupid oaf is always knocking things over.*
'oafish *adj.*
oak [ouk] *n* a type of large tree with hard wood. – *Also adj*: *trees in an oak wood; a room with oak panelling.*

oar [o:] *n* a long piece of wood with a flat end for rowing a boat.
oasis [ou'eisis] – *pl* **o'ases** [-si:z] – *n* an area in a desert where water is found: *The travellers stopped at an oasis.*
oath [ouθ] – *pl* **oaths** [ouðs, ouðz] – *n* **1** a solemn promise: *He swore an oath to support the king.* **2** a word or phrase used when swearing: *curses and oaths.*

on/under oath having sworn an oath to tell the truth in a court of law: *The witness is on/under oath.*

oats [outs] *n pl or sing* a type of cereal plant or its grain (seeds): *a field of oats; Horses eat oats.*

obedience, obedient *see* obey.

obese [ə'bi:s] *adj* (of people) very fat.
o'besity *n*: *Obesity is a danger to health.*

obey [ə'bei, (*Amer*) ou-] *v* to do what one is told to do: *I obeyed the order.*
obedience [ə'bi:djəns] *n* 1 the act of obeying: *obedience to an order.* 2 willingness to obey: *She showed great obedience.*
o'bedient *adj*: *an obedient and well-behaved child.* **o'bediently** *adv.*

obituary [ə'bitjuəri] – *pl* **o'bituaries** – *n* a notice (*eg* in a newspaper) of a person's death, often with an account of his life and work.

object[1] ['obdʒikt] *n* 1 a thing that can be seen or felt: *There were various objects on the table.* 2 an aim or intention: *His main object in life was to become rich.* 3 the word or words in a sentence or phrase which represent(s) the person or thing affected by the action of the verb: *He hit me; You can eat what you like.*

object[2] [əb'dʒekt] *v* (*often with* to) to feel or express dislike or disapproval: *He wanted us to travel on foot but I objected (to that).*
objection [əb'dʒekʃən] *n* 1 an expression of disapproval: *He raised no objection to the idea.* 2 a reason for disapproving: *My objection is that he is too young.*
ob'jectionable [-'dʒekʃə-] *adj* unpleasant: *a very objectionable person.* **ob'jectionably** *adv.*

objective [əb'dʒektiv] *n* a thing aimed at: *Our objective is freedom.* – *adj* not influenced by personal opinions *etc*: *He tried to take an objective view of the situation.*
ob'jectively *adv*: *He considered the problem objectively.*

oblige [ə'blaidʒ] *v* 1 to force to do something: *She was obliged to go; The police obliged him to leave.* 2 to do (someone) a favour or service: *Could you oblige me by carrying this, please?*
obligation [obli'geiʃən] *n* a promise or duty: *You are under no obligation to buy this.*
obligatory [ə'bligətəri] *adj* compulsory: *Attendance at tonight's meeting is obligatory.*
o'bligatorily *adv.*
o'bliging *adj* willing to help other people: *He'll help you – he's very obliging.*
o'bligingly *adv.*

oblique [ə'bli:k] *adj* 1 sloping: *He drew an oblique line from one corner of the paper to the other.* 2 not straight or direct: *He made*

an oblique reference to his work. **o'bliquely** *adv.*

obliterate [ə'blitəreit] *v* 1 to cover, to prevent from being visible: *The sand-storm obliterated his footprints.* 2 to destroy completely: *The town was obliterated by the bombs.*

oblivious [ə'bliviəs] *adj* unaware of or not paying attention to: *He was oblivious of what was happening; He was oblivious to our warnings.* **o'bliviously** *adv.*

oblong ['oblon] *n* a two-dimensional, rectangular figure, but with one pair of opposite sides longer than the other pair. – *adj* shaped like this: *an oblong table.*

obnoxious [əb'nokʃəs] *adj* offensive: *an obnoxious man; The smell of that mixture is really obnoxious.* **ob'noxiously** *adv.*

oboe ['oubou] *n* a type of high-pitched woodwind musical instrument. **'oboist** *n.*

obscene [əb'si:n] *adj* disgusting, *esp* sexually: *obscene photographs.* **ob'scenely** *adv.*
obscenity [-'se-] – *pl* **ob'scenities** – *n* an obscene act or word(s): *He shouted obscenities at the police.*

obscure [əb'skjuə] *adj* 1 not clear; difficult to see: *an obscure corner of the library.* 2 not well-known: *an obscure author.* 3 difficult to understand: *an obscure poem.* – *v* to make obscure: *A large tree obscured the view.* **ob'scurely** *adv.* **ob'scurity** *n.*

observe [əb'zə:v] *v* 1 to notice: *I observed her late arrival.* 2 to watch carefully: *She observed his actions with interest.* 3 to obey: *We must observe the rules.* 4 to make a remark: 'It's a lovely day', he observed.
ob'servance *n* 1 the act of obeying rules *etc*: *the observance of the law.* 2 the act of observing (a tradition *etc*): *the observance of religious holidays.*
ob'servant *adj* quick to notice: *An observant boy remembered the car's registration number.*
,obser'vation [ob-] *n* 1 the act of noticing or watching: *She is in hospital for observation.* 2 a remark.
ob'servatory – *pl* **ob'servatories** – *n* a place for observing and studying the stars, weather *etc.*
ob'server *n* a person who observes.

obsess [əb'ses] *v* to occupy (someone's mind) too much: *He is obsessed by the fear of death.*
ob'session [-ʃən] *n*: *an obsession about motorbikes.*
ob'sessional [-ʃə-] *adj*: *obsessional behaviour.*
ob'sessive [-siv] *adj*: *obsessive about cleanliness.* **ob'sessively** *adv.* **ob'sessiveness** *n.*

obsolescent [obsə'lesnt] *adj* going out of use: *obsolescent slang.* **,obso'lescence** *n.*

obsolete ['obsəli:t, (*Amer also*) obsə'li:t] *adj* no longer in use: *obsolete weapons.*

obstacle ['obstəkl] *n* something which prevents progress: *His inability to learn foreign languages was an obstacle to his career.*

obstacle race a race in which runners have to climb over, crawl through *etc* obstacles such as tyres, nets *etc*.

obstetrics [ob'stetriks] *n sing* the science of helping women before, during, and after, the birth of babies.

obstetrician [obstə'triʃən] *n* a doctor who specializes in obstetrics.

obstinate ['obstinət] *adj* refusing to yield, obey *etc*: *She won't change her mind – she's very obstinate.* **'obstinacy** [-nəsi] *n*.
'obstinately *adv*.

obstruct [əb'strʌkt] *v* 1 to block or close: *The road was obstructed by a fallen tree.* 2 to stop (something) moving past or making progress: *The crashed lorry obstructed the traffic.*
ob'struction [-ʃən] *n* something that obstructs: *an obstruction in the pipe.*
ob'structive *adj* inclined to cause trouble and difficulties: *an obstructive personality.*

obtain [əb'tein] *v* to get; to become the possessor of: *He obtained a large sum of money by buying and selling houses.*
ob'tainable *adj* (*neg* **un-**).

obtrusive [əb'truːsiv] *adj* (*neg* **un-**) too noticeable: *Loud music can be very obtrusive.*
ob'trusively *adv*. **ob'trusiveness** *n*.

obtuse [əb'tjuːs] *adj* (of an angle) greater than a right-angle.

obvious ['obviəs] *adj* easily seen or understood; evident: *It was obvious that she was ill; an obvious improvement.*
'obviously *adv* it is obvious (that something is the case): *Obviously, I'll need some help.*

occasion [ə'keiʒən] *n* 1 a particular time: *I've heard him speak on several occasions.* 2 a special event: *The wedding was a great occasion.*
oc'casional *adj* happening, done *etc* now and then: *I take an occasional trip to London.*
oc'casionally *adv* now and then: *I occasionally go to the theatre.*

occult [ə'kʌlt]: **the occult** supernatural practices, ceremonies *etc*: *He has made a study of witches, magic and the occult.*

occupy ['okjupai] *v* 1 to be in or fill (time, space *etc*): *A table occupied the centre of the room.* 2 to live in: *The family occupied a small flat.* 3 to capture: *The soldiers occupied the town.*
'occupant *n* a person who occupies (a house *etc*), not necessarily the owner of the house.
,occu'pation *n* 1 a person's job or work. 2 the act of occupying (a house, town *etc*). 3 the period of time during which a town, house *etc* is occupied: *During the occupation, there was a shortage of food.*

,occu'pational *adj* of, or caused by, a person's job: *an occupational disease.*
'occupier *n* an occupant.

occur [ə'kəː] – *pt, ptp* **oc'curred** – *v* 1 to take place: *The accident occurred yesterday morning.* 2 (*with* **to**) to come into one's mind: *An idea occurred to him; It occurred to me to visit my parents.* 3 to be found: *Oil occurs under the sea.*
oc'currence [-'kʌ-, (*Amer*) -'kəː-] *n*: *a strange occurrence.*

occurrence, occurred and occurring have two **rs**.

ocean ['ouʃən] *n* 1 the salt water that covers most of the earth's surface. 2 one of its five main divisions: *the Atlantic Ocean.*

o'clock [ə'klok] *adv* used, in stating the time, to refer to a particular hour: *It's five o'clock.* – *Also adj*: *the three o'clock train.*

*octagon ['oktəgən, (*Amer*) -gon] *n* two-dimensional figure with eight sides.
octagonal [ok'tagənl] *adj* having eight sides: *an octagonal figure.*

octave ['oktiv] *n* in music, a series or range of eight notes.

octet [ok'tet] *n* a group of eight musicians, eight lines in a poem *etc*.

October [ok'toubə] *n* the tenth month of the year, the month following September.

octogenarian [oktədʒi'neəriən] *n* a person between eighty and eighty-nine years old.

octopus ['oktəpəs] *n* a type of sea-creature with eight tentacles.

oculist ['okjulist] *n* a doctor who specializes in diseases of the eyes.

odd [od] *adj* 1 unusual; strange: *He's wearing very odd clothes; a very odd young man.* 2 (of a number) that cannot be divided exactly by 2: *5 and 7 are odd* (*numbers*). 3 not one of a pair, set *etc*: *an odd shoe.* 4 occasional; free: *odd moments.*
'oddity – *pl* **'oddities** – *n* a strange person or thing: *He's a bit of an oddity.*
'oddly *adv* strangely: *He is behaving very oddly.*
'oddment *n* a piece left over from something: *an oddment of material.*
odds *n pl* 1 chances; probability: *The odds are that he will win.* 2 a difference in strength, in favour of one side: *They are fighting against heavy odds.*
odd jobs (*usu* small) jobs of various kinds, often done for other people: *He's unemployed, but earns some money by doing odd jobs for old people.*
odd job man a person employed to do such jobs.
be at odds to be quarrelling: *He has been at odds with his brother for years.*
make no odds to be unimportant: *We*

haven't got much money, but that makes no odds.

oddly enough it is strange or remarkable (that): *I saw John this morning. Oddly enough, I was just thinking I hadn't seen him for a long time.*

odd man out/odd one out 1 a person or thing that is different from others: *In this test, you have to decide which of these three objects is the odd one out.* **2** a person or thing that is left over when teams *etc* are made up: *When they chose the two teams, I was the odd man out.*

odds and ends small objects *etc* of different kinds: *There were various odds and ends lying about on the table.*

what's the odds? it's not important; it doesn't matter: *We didn't win the competition but what's the odds?*

ode [oud] *n* a poem written to a person or thing: *'Ode to a Nightingale' was written by John Keats.*

odious ['oudiəs] *adj* hateful; disgusting: *She is an odious young woman.* **'odiously** *adv.* **'odiousness** *n.*

odour, (*Amer*) **odor** ['oudə] *n* a smell (*usu* particularly good or bad): *the sweet odour of roses.* **'odourless** *adj.*

o'er [oː] *adv, prep* short for **over**: *o'er the sea.*

of [ov] *prep* **1** belonging to: *a friend of mine.* **2** away from (a place *etc*); after (a given time): *within five miles of London; within a year of his death.* **3** written *etc* by: *the plays of Shakespeare.* **4** belonging to or forming a group: *He is one of my friends.* **5** showing: *a picture of my father.* **6** made from; consisting of: *a dress of silk; a collection of pictures.* **7** used to show an amount, measurement of something: *a gallon of petrol; five bags of coal.* **8** about: *an account of his work.* **9** containing: *a box of chocolates.* **10** used to show a cause: *She died of hunger.* **11** used to show a loss or removal: *She was robbed of her jewels.* **12** used to show the connection between an action and its object: *the smoking of a cigarette.* **13** used to show character, qualities *etc*: *a man of courage.* **14** (*Amer*) (of time) a certain number of minutes before (the hour): *It's ten minutes of three.*

off [of] *adv* **1** away (from a place, time *etc*): *He walked off; She cut her hair off; The holidays are only a week off; She took off her coat.* **2** not working; not giving power *etc*: *The water's off; Switch off the light.* **3** not at work: *He's taking tomorrow off; He's off today.* **4** completely: *Finish off your work.* **5** not as good as usual, or as it should be: *His work has gone off recently; (also adj) an off day.* **6** (of food) rotten: *This milk has gone off – we can't drink it; (also adj) That meat is certainly off.* **7** out of a vehicle, train

etc: The bus stopped and we got off. **8** cancelled: *The marriage is off.* – *prep* **1** away from; down from: *It fell off the table; a mile off the coast; He cut about five centimetres off my hair.* **2** not wanting or allowed to have (food *etc*): *The child is off his food.* **3** out of (a vehicle, train *etc*): *We got off the bus.*

ˌoff-'chance *n* a slight chance: *We waited, on the off-chance (that) he might come.*

ˌoff-'colour, (*Amer*) ˌoff-'color *adj* not very well: *She's a bit off-colour this morning.*

ˌoff'hand *adj* acting or speaking so casually that one is being rude: *offhand behaviour.* – *adv* without thinking about something first: *I can't tell you the answer offhand.* ˌoff'handedly *adv.* ˌoff'handedness *n.*

ˌoff'shore *adj* **1** in or on the sea, not far from the coast: *offshore oil-wells.* **2** (of winds) blowing away from the coast, out to sea.

ˌoff'side *adv* (in football, hockey *etc*) in a position (not allowed by the rules) between the ball and the opponents' goal: *The referee disallowed the goal because one of the players was offside.* – *adj* (of a vehicle *etc*) on the side nearest to the centre of the road: *the front offside wheel.*

ˌoff-'white *adj* not quite white, *eg* slightly yellow *etc*: *an off-white dress.*

badly, well off poor, rich: *The family was quite well off.*

be off with you! go away!

in the offing about to happen: *He has a new job in the offing.*

off and on/on and off sometimes; occasionally: *I see him off and on at the club.*

the off season the period, at a hotel, holiday resort *etc*, when there are few visitors: *It's very quiet here in the off season; (also adj) off-season rates.*

offal ['ofəl] *n* the parts of an animal *eg* the heart, liver *etc* which are considered as food for people.

offend [ə'fend] *v* **1** to make feel upset or angry: *If you don't go to her party she will be offended; His criticism offended her.* **2** to be unpleasant or disagreeable: *Cigarette smoke offends me.*

of'fence, (*Amer*) of'fense *n* **1** (any cause of) anger, displeasure, hurt feelings *etc*: *That rubbish dump is an offence to the eye.* **2** a crime: *The police charged him with several offences.*

of'fender *n* a person who offends, *esp* against the law.

of'fensive [-siv] *adj* **1** insulting: *offensive remarks.* **2** disgusting: *an offensive smell.* **3** used to attack: *an offensive weapon.* – *n* an attack: *They launched an offensive against the invading army.*

of'fensively *adv.* of'fensiveness *n.*

be on the offensive to be making an attack: *She always expects people to criticize her and so she is always on the offensive.*

take offence (*with* **at**) to be offended (by something): *He took offence at what she said.*

offer ['ofə] – *pt, ptp* **'offered** – *v* **1** to put forward (a gift, suggestion *etc*) for acceptance or refusal: *She offered the man a cup of tea; He offered her $20 for the picture.* **2** to say that one is willing: *He offered to help.* – *n* **1** an act of offering: *an offer of help.* **2** an offering of money as the price of something: *They made an offer of $50 000 for the house.*

'offering *n* **1** a gift: *a birthday offering.* **2** money given during a religious service: *a church offering.*

on offer for sale, often cheaply: *That shop has chairs on offer at $20 each.*

office ['ofis] *n* **1** the room or building in which the business of a firm is done: *The firm's head offices are in New York*; (*also adj*) *office furniture.* **2** the room in which a particular person works: *the bank manager's office.* **3** a room or building used for a particular purpose: *Train tickets are bought at the ticket-office.* **4** a position of authority, *esp* in or as a government: *Our party has not been in office for years; the office of mayor.*

'officer *n* **1** a person holding a commission in the army, navy or air force: *a naval officer.* **2** a person who carries out a public duty: *a police-officer.*

official [ə'fiʃəl] *adj* **1** of or concerning a position of authority: *official powers; official uniform.* **2** done or confirmed by people in authority *etc*: *the official result of the race.* – *n* a person who holds a position of authority: *a government official.*

officially [ə'fiʃəli] *adv* **1** (*neg* **un-**) as an official: *He attended the ceremony officially.* **2** formally: *The new library was officially opened yesterday.* **3** according to what is announced publicly (though not necessarily true in fact): *Officially he is on holiday – actually he is working on a new book.*

officiate [ə'fiʃieit] *v* to do the duty or service of an office or official position: *The new clergyman officiated at the wedding.*

officious [ə'fiʃəs] *adj* offering help *etc* in order to interfere: *His mother-in-law is so officious that he does not let her visit his house.* **of'ficiously** *adv.* **of'ficiousness** *n.*

'office-bearer *n* a person who holds a position of authority in a society *etc*.

through the (kind) offices of with the help of: *I got the job through the kind offices of a friend.*

often ['ofn] *adv* many times: *I often go to the theatre; I should see him more often.*

every so often sometimes; occasionally: *I meet him at the club every so often.*

ogre ['ougə] *n* in fairy stories, a frightening, cruel giant.

oh [ou] *interj* an expression of surprise, admiration *etc*: *Oh, what a lovely present!* See also **o.**

oil [oil] *n* a *usu* thick liquid that will not mix with water, obtained from plants, animals and minerals: *olive oil; whale oil; vegetable oil; cooking oil; He put some oil on the hinges of the door; The car's engine is in need of oil.* – *v* to put oil on or into: *The machine will work better if it's oiled.*

oils *n pl* oil paint: *He paints in oils.*

'oily *adj* **1** of, like or covered with oil: *an oily liquid; an oily rag.* **2** trying to be too friendly or polite: *The waiters in that restaurant are too oily.*

'oilfield *n* a place where mineral oil is found: *There are oilfields in the North Sea.*

oil paint paint made with oil: *Some artists prefer to use oil paint(s).*

oil painting a picture painted with oil paints.

*oil palm a palm tree whose fruit and seeds yield oil.

'oil-rig *n* a structure used to drill oil-wells: *The ship sailed past an enormous oil-rig.*

'oil-tanker *n* a ship used for carrying oil: *An oil-tanker has run aground near here.*

'oil-well *n* a hole drilled into the earth or the sea-bed to obtain petroleum.

strike oil to find oil under the ground: *After drilling for several months, they finally struck oil; We've struck oil* (=found what we have been looking for) *in our search for a suitable house.*

ointment ['ointmənt] *n* any greasy substance rubbed on the skin to heal injuries *etc*.

O.K., okay [ou'kei] *interj, adj, adv* all right: *Will you do it? O.K., I will; Is my dress O.K.?; That's O.K. with/by me* (=I agree). – *n* approval: *He gave the plan his O.K.*

old [ould] *adj* **1** advanced in age: *an old man; He is too old to live alone.* **2** having a certain age: *He is thirty years old.* **3** having existed for a long time: *an old building; Those trees are very old.* **4** no longer useful: *She threw away the old shoes.* **5** belonging to times long ago: *old civilizations like that of Greece.*

old age the later part of a person's life: *He wrote most of his poems in his old age.*

old boy/girl a former pupil (of a school): *The new prime minister is an old boy of our school.*

,old-'fashioned *adj* in a style common some time ago: *old-fashioned clothes; Her hairstyle is very old-fashioned.*

old hand a person who is very experienced: *He's an old hand at this sort of job.*

* see illustration on p. 573

olive 354 one

old maid an unmarried woman who is past the usual age of marriage.

the old old people: *hospitals for the old.*

olive ['oliv] *n* **1** a type of edible fruit which is used as a garnish *etc* and which gives oil used for cooking: *He put an olive in her cocktail*; *(also adj) an olive tree*; *(also adj) olive oil.* **2** the tree on which it grows: *a grove of olives.* **3** *(also* **olive-green)** the brownish-green or yellowish-green colour of the fruit: *They painted the room olive*; *(also adj) She wore an olive-green hat.* **4** *(also* '**olive-wood)** the wood of the tree.

olive branch a sign of a wish for peace: *The government held out the olive branch to its opponents.*

Olympic [ə'limpik]: **the Olympic Games** *(also* **the Olympics)** a sports competition held once every four years for amateur competitors from all parts of the world.

ombudsman ['ombudzmən] *n* an official appointed to look into complaints *esp* against a government.

omelette, omelet ['omlit] *n* eggs beaten and fried sometimes with vegetables, meat *etc*: *a mushroom omelette.*

omen ['oumən] *n* a sign of a future event: *Long ago, storms were regarded as bad omens.*

ominous ['ominəs] *adj* giving a suggestion or warning about something bad that is going to happen: *an ominous cloud*; *an ominous silence.* '**ominously** *adv.*

omit [ə'mit] – *pt, ptp* o'**mitted** – *v* **1** to leave out: *You can omit the last chapter of the book.* **2** not to do: *I omitted to tell him about the meeting.*
o'**mission** [-ʃən] *n* **1** something that has been left out: *I have made several omissions in the list of names.* **2** the act of omitting: *the omission of his name from the list.*

omitted and **omitting** have two ts.

omnibus ['omnibəs] *n* **1** a large book containing a number of books, stories *etc*: *a Jane Austen omnibus*; *(also adj) an omnibus edition of Jane Austen's novels.* **2** an old word for a bus.

omnipotent [om'nipətənt] *adj* having absolute, unlimited power: *the omnipotent power of God.* om'**nipotently** *adv.* om'**nipotence** *n.*

on [on] *prep* **1** touching, fixed to, covering *etc* the upper or outer side of: *The book was lying on the table*; *He was standing on the floor*; *She wore a hat on her head.* **2** in or into (a vehicle, train *etc*): *We were sitting on the bus*; *I got on the wrong bus.* **3** at or during a certain day, time *etc*: *on Monday*; *On his arrival, he went straight to bed.* **4** about: *a book on the theatre.* **5** in the state or process of: *He's on holiday.* **6** supported by: *She was standing on one leg.*

7 receiving, taking: *on drugs*; *on a diet.* **8** taking part in: *He is on the committee*; *Which detective is working on this case?* **9** towards: *They marched on the town.* **10** near or beside: *a shop on the main road.* **11** by means of: *He played a tune on the violin*; *I spoke to him on the telephone.* **12** being carried by: *The thief had the stolen jewels on him.* **13** when (something is, or has been, done): *On investigation, there proved to be no need to panic.* **14** followed by: *disaster on disaster.* – *adv* **1** *(esp* of something being worn) so as to be touching, fixed to, covering *etc* the upper or outer side of: *She put her hat on.* **2** used to show a continuing state *etc*, onwards: *She kept on asking questions*; *They moved on.* **3** *(also adj)* (of electric light, machines *etc*) working: *The television is on*; *Turn/Switch the light on.* **4** *(also adj)* (of films *etc*) able to be seen: *There's a good film on at the cinema this week.* **5** *(also adj)* in or into a vehicle, train *etc*: *The bus stopped and we got on.* – *adj* **1** in progress: *The game was on.* **2** not cancelled: *Is the party on tonight?*

'**oncoming** *adj* approaching: *oncoming traffic.*

'**ongoing** *adj* continuing: *an ongoing argument.*

'**onward(s)** *adv* moving forward (in place or time): *They marched onward(s).*

be on to (someone) to have discovered (a person's) trick, secret *etc*: *The thieves realized that the police were on to them.*

on and on used with certain verbs to emphasize the length of an activity: *She kept on and on asking questions.*

on time at the right time: *He got here on time.*

on to/'onto to a position on: *He lifted it onto the table.*

once [wʌns] *adv* **1** a single time: *He did it once*; *If I could see her once again I would be happy.* **2** at a time in the past: *I once wanted to be a dancer.* – *conj* when; as soon as: *Once (it had been) unlocked, the door opened easily.*

at once immediately: *Go away at once!*

(just) for once as an exception: *Why can't you be nice to her for once?*

once and for all once and finally: *Once and for all, I refuse!*

once in a while occasionally: *I meet him once in a while at the club.*

oncoming *see* **on.**

one [wʌn] *n* **1** the number or figure 1: *One and one is two (1+1=2).* **2** the age of 1: *Babies start to talk at one.* – *pron* **1** a single person or thing: *She's the one I like the best*; *I'll buy the red one.* **2** anyone; any person: *One can see the city from here.* – *adj* **1** **1** in number: *one person*; *He took one book.*

2 aged 1: *The baby will be one tomorrow.* **3** of the same opinion *etc*: *We are one in our love of freedom.*

one- having one (of something): *a one-legged man.*

one'self *pron* **1** used as the object of a verb, the subject of which is **one**: *One should wash oneself every morning.* **2** used in emphasis: *One always has to do these things oneself.*

one-'off *n, adj* (something) made, intended *etc* for one occasion only: *It's just a one-off arrangement.*

one-'sided *adj* **1** with one person or side having a great advantage over the other: *a one-sided contest.* **2** representing only one aspect of a subject: *a one-sided discussion.*

one-'way *adj* **1** in which traffic can move in one direction only: *a one-way street.* **2** (*esp Amer*) valid for travel in one direction only: *a one-way ticket.*

one-year-old *n* a person or animal that is one year old. – *adj* (of a person, animal or thing) that is one year old.

all one just the same: *It's all one to me what she does.*

be one up on (a person) to have an advantage over (someone): *We brought out a book on this before our rivals so we're one up on them.*

not be oneself to look or feel ill, anxious *etc*: *I'd better go home – I'm not myself today.*

one and all all (of a group): *This was agreed by one and all.*

one another used as the object of a verb when an action takes place between people *etc*: *They hit one another.*

one by one (of a number of people, things *etc*) one after the other: *He examined all the vases one by one.*

one or two a few: *I don't want a lot of nuts – I'll just take one or two.*

one of is followed by a plural noun or pronoun, but takes a singular verb: *One of the girls works as a hairdresser*; *One of them is ill.*

onerous ['ounərəs] *adj* hard to bear or do: *an onerous task.*

ongoing *see* **on.**

onion ['ʌnjən] *n* a type of vegetable with an eatable bulb which has a strong taste and smell: *pickled onions*; *Put plenty of onion in the stew.*

onlooker ['onlukə] *n* a person who watches something happening: *A crowd of onlookers had gathered round the two men who were fighting.*

only ['ounli] *adj* without any others of the same type: *He has no brothers or sisters – he's an only child; the only book of its kind.* – *adv* **1** not more than: *We have only two cups left*; *He lives only a mile away.* **2** alone:

Only you can do it. **3** showing the one action done, in contrast to other possibilities: *I only scolded the child – I did not smack him.* **4** not longer ago than: *I saw him only yesterday.* **5** showing the one possible result of an action: *If you do that, you'll only make him angry.* – *conj* except that, but: *I'd like to go, only I have to work.*

only too very: *I'll be only too pleased to come.*

onset ['onset] *n* a beginning: *the onset of a cold.*

onslaught ['onslo:t] *n* a fierce attack: *an onslaught on the enemy troops.*

onus ['ounəs] *n* the responsibility: *The onus is on him to prove his theory.*

onward(s) *see* **on.**

onyx ['oniks] *n* a type of precious stone with layers of different colours: *The ashtray is made of onyx*; (*also adj*) *an onyx ashtray.*

ooze [u:z] *v* **1** to flow slowly: *The water oozed through the sand.* **2** to have (something liquid) flowing slowly out: *His arm was oozing blood.* – *n* liquid, slippery mud: *The river bed was thick with ooze.* **'oozy** *adj.*

opacity *see* **opaque.**

opal ['oupəl] *n* a type of *usu* bluish-white or milky white precious stone, with slight traces or streaks of various other colours: *There are three opals in her brooch*; (*also adj*) *an opal necklace.*

opaque [ə'peik, (*Amer*) ou-] *adj* not transparent: *an opaque liquid.* **o'paqueness, opacity** [ə'pasəti] *ns.*

open ['oupən] *adj* **1** not shut, allowing entry or exit: *an open box*; *The gate is wide open.* **2** allowing the inside to be seen: *an open book.* **3** ready for business *etc*: *The shop is open on Sunday afternoons*; *After the fog had cleared, the airport was soon open again*; *The gardens are open to the public.* **4** not kept secret: *an open show of affection.* **5** frank: *He was very open with me about his work.* **6** still being considered *etc*: *Leave the matter open.* **7** empty, with no trees, buildings *etc*: *I like to be out in the open country*; *an open space.* – *v* **1** to make or become open: *He opened the door*; *The door opened*; *The new shop opened last week.* **2** to begin: *He opened the meeting with a speech of welcome.*

'opener *n* something that opens (something): *a tin-opener.*

'opening *n* **1** a hole; a clear or open space: *an opening in the fence/forest.* **2** a beginning: *the opening of the film*; (*also adj*) *the chairman's opening remarks.* **3** the act of becoming or making open, the ceremony of making open: *the opening of a flower/shop/door*; *the opening of the new theatre.* **4** an opportunity for work: *There are good openings in the automobile industry.*

'openly adv frankly: *She talked very openly about it.*

'open-air adj outside: *an open-air meeting.*

,open-'minded adj willing to consider new ideas: *an open-minded approach to the problem.*

,open-'plan adj (of a building) built with few walls inside: *an open-plan office.*

be an open secret to be known to many people although supposed to be a secret: *It's an open secret that she's getting married next week.*

bring (something) out into the open to make (something) public: *This affair has been kept a secret for too long – it's time it was brought out into the open.*

in the open outside; in the open air: *It's very healthy for children to be able to play in the open.*

in the open air not in a building: *If it doesn't rain, we'll have the party in the open air.*

keep/have an open mind to have a willingness to listen to or accept new ideas, other people's suggestions *etc* (*eg* before making a decision): *It doesn't seem to be a very good plan, but I think we should keep an open mind about it for the time being.*

open on to (of a door *etc*) to open towards: *Our front door opens straight on to the street.*

the open sea any area of sea far from land: *When they reached the open sea, they were faced with large waves.*

open to 1 likely or willing to receive: *open to charges of corruption*; *open to suggestions from any member of staff.* **3** possible: *There are only two courses of action open to us.*

open up 1 to open (a shop *etc*): *I open up the shop at nine o'clock every morning.* **2** to open (a box *etc*) completely: *He opened up the parcel.* **3** to open the (main) door of a building *etc*: *'Open up!' shouted the policeman. 'We know you are in there!'*

with open arms in a very friendly way: *They received their visitors with open arms.*

opera ['opərə] n a musical drama in which the dialogue is sung: *an opera by Verdi.*

,ope'ratic [-'ra-] adj of, or relating to, opera: *an operatic society*; *an operatic singer.*

opera glasses binoculars for use in a theatre.

'opera-house n a theatre in which operas are performed.

operate ['opəreit] v **1** to act or work: *The sewing-machine isn't operating properly.* **2** to do or perform a surgical operation: *The surgeon operated on her for appendicitis.* **,ope'ration** n **1** an action or process, *esp* when planned: *a rescue operation.* **2** the process of working: *Our plan is now in operation.* **3** the act of surgically cutting a part of the body in order to cure disease: *an operation for appendicitis.* **4** (*often in pl*) the

movement, fighting *etc* of armies: *The general was in command of operations in the north.*

,ope'rational adj in good working order.

'operative [-rətiv, (*Amer*) -reitiv] adj in action, having effect: *Many old laws are still operative.*

'operator n **1** a person who works a machine: *a lift operator.* **2** a person who connects telephone calls: *Ask the operator to connect you to that number.*

'operating-theatre n (*sometimes* **theatre**) the room in a hospital in which operations are performed.

opiate *see* **opium.**

opinion [ə'pinjən] n **1** what a person thinks or believes: *My opinions about education have changed.* **2** a (professional) judgement, *usu* of a doctor, lawyer *etc*: *He wanted a second opinion on his illness.* **3** what one thinks of the worth or value of someone or something: *I have a very high opinion of his work.*

be of the opinion (that) to think: *He is of the opinion that nothing more can be done.*

in my, your *etc* **opinion** according to what I, you *etc* think: *In my opinion, he's right.*

a matter of opinion something about which different people (may) have different opinions: *Whether it is better to marry young or not is a matter of opinion.*

opium ['oupiəm] n a drug made from the dried juice of a type of poppy.

opiate ['oupiət] n any drug containing opium, used to make a person sleep: *The doctor gave him an opiate.*

opponent [ə'pounənt] n a person who opposes: *an opponent of the government*; *He beat his opponent by four points.*

opportunity [opə'tju:nəti] – *pl* **oppor'tunities** – n a chance to do or a time for doing (something): *an opportunity to go to Rome*; *You've had several opportunities to ask him.*

oppor'tune adj coming at the right time: *an opportune remark.* **oppor'tunely** adv. **oppor'tuneness** n.

oppor'tunist n a person who takes advantage of any circumstance which will help him personally: *a political opportunist.* **oppor'tunism** n.

oppose [ə'pouz] v **1** to resist or fight against (someone or something) by force or argument: *We oppose the government on this matter.* **2** to act or compete against: *Who is opposing him in the election?*

as opposed to separate or distinct from; in contrast with: *It happened in the late afternoon, as opposed to the evening.*

opposite ['opəzit] adj **1** being on the other side of: *on the opposite side of town.* **2** completely different: *The two men walked off in opposite directions. – prep, adv* on the opposite side of (something) in relation to something else: *He lives in the house opposite (mine).* – *n* something that is completely different: *Hate is the opposite of love.*

opposition [opə'ziʃən] *n* **1** the act of resisting or fighting against by force or argument: *There is a lot of opposition to his ideas.* **2** the people who are fighting or competing against: *In war and business, one should always get to know one's opposition.*

oppress [ə'pres] *v* **1** to govern cruelly: *The king oppressed his people.* **2** to worry or depress: *The thought of leaving her oppressed me.*

op'pression [-ʃən] *n*: *After five years of oppression, the peasants revolted.*

op'pressive [-siv] *adj* oppressing; cruel; hard to bear: *oppressive laws.*

op'pressively *adj.* **op'pressiveness** *n.*

op'pressor *n* a ruler who oppresses his people; a tyrant.

opt [opt] *v*: **opt out** (*often with* **of**) to choose or decide not to do something or take part in something: *You promised to help us, so you can't opt out (of it) now.*

optician [op'tiʃən] *n* a person who makes and sells spectacles and optical instruments: *The optician mended my spectacles.*

optical ['optikəl] *adj* of or concerning sight or what one sees: *The two objects in the picture appear to be the same size, but this is just an optical illusion* (= they are not actually the same size); *microscopes and other optical instruments.*

optics ['optiks] *n sing* the science of light.

optimism ['optimizəm] *n* a state of mind in which one always hopes or expects that something good will happen: *Even when it was obvious to the others that he was not going to succeed he was full of optimism.*

'optimist *n.*

opti'mistic *adj* always hoping or believing that something good will happen: *an optimistic person/attitude.* **opti'mistically** *adv.*

option ['opʃən] *n* choice: *You have no option but to obey him.*

'optional *adj* a matter of choice: *Music is optional at our school; an optional subject.*

opulent ['opjulənt] *adj* luxurious; rich: *They lived in opulent surroundings.* **'opulence** *n.*

or [oː] *conj* **1** used to show an alternative: *Is that your book or is it mine?* **2** because if not: *Hurry or you'll be late.*

or so about; approximately: *I bought a dozen or so* (*books*).

oracle ['orəkl] *n* **1** a very knowledgeable person: *I don't know the answer to this problem, so I'd better go and ask the oracle.* **2** in former times, a holy place where a god was believed to give answers to questions: *the oracle at Delphi.*

oral ['oːrəl] *adj* **1** spoken, not written: *an oral*

examination. **2** of or by the mouth: *oral hygiene; an oral contraceptive.* – *n* a spoken examination: *He passed the written exam, but failed his oral.*

'orally *adv*: *medicine to be taken orally.*

orange ['orindʒ] *n* **1** a type of juicy citrus fruit with a thick reddish-yellow skin: *I'd like an orange;* (*also adj*) *an orange tree.* **2** the colour of this fruit. – *adj* **1** of the colour orange: *an orange dress.* **2** with the taste of orange juice: *an orange drink.*

*orang-utan** ['oːraŋ'uːtan] *n* a type of large, man-like ape.

oration [ə'reiʃən] *n* a formal, public speech, *esp* in fine, beautiful language: *a funeral oration.*

orator ['orətə] *n* a person who makes public speeches, *esp* very eloquent ones.

'oratory ['orə-] *n* the art of speaking well in public. **ora'torical** *adj.*

*orbit** ['oːbit] *n* the path in which something moves around a planet, star *etc, eg* the path of the Earth round the Sun or of a spacecraft round the Earth: *The spaceship is in orbit round the moon.* – *v* to go round in space: *The spacecraft orbits the Earth every 24 hours.*

orchard ['oːtʃəd] *n* a garden or other area in which fruit trees are grown: *a cherry orchard.*

orchestra ['oːkəstrə] *n* a (*usu* large) group of musicians playing together, led by a conductor.

or'chestral [-'kes-] *adj* for, or given by, an orchestra: *orchestral music; an orchestral concert.*

orchid ['oːkid] *n* a kind of plant *usu* having brightly-coloured or unusually-shaped flowers.

ordain [oː'dein] *v* to make (someone) a priest, minister *etc, usu* by a church ceremony: *He was ordained a priest.*

ordeal [oː'diːl] *n* a difficult, painful experience: *Being kidnapped was an ordeal for the child.*

order ['oːdə] *n* **1** a statement (by a person in authority) of what someone must do; a command: *He gave me my orders.* **2** an instruction to supply something: *orders from Germany for special gates.* **3** something supplied: *Your order is nearly ready.* **4** a tidy state: *The house is in (good) order.* **5** a system or method: *I must have order in my life.* **6** an arrangement (of people, things *etc*) in space, time *etc*: *in alphabetical order; in order of importance.* **7** a peaceful condition: *law and order.* **8** a written instruction to pay money: *a banker's order.* **9** a group, class, rank or position: *This is a list of the various orders of plants; the social order.* **10** a religious society, *esp* of monks: *the Benedictine order.* – *v* **1** to tell (someone) to do something (from a position of authority): *He ordered me to stand up.* **2** to give an instruction to supply: *I have ordered some new furniture from the shop*; *He ordered a steak.* **3** to put in order: *Should we order these alphabetically?*

'**orderly** *adj* well-behaved; quiet: *an orderly queue of people.* – *n* – *pl* '**orderlies** – **1** a hospital attendant who does routine jobs. **2** a soldier who carries an officer's orders and messages. '**orderliness** *n.*

'**order-form** *n* a form on which a customer's order is written.

in order 1 correct according to what is regularly done, *esp* in meetings *etc*: *It is quite in order to end the meeting now.* **2** in a good efficient state: *Everything is in order for the party.*

in order (that) so that: *He checked all his figures again in order that the report might be as accurate as possible.*

in order to for the purpose of: *I went home in order to change my clothes.*

made to order made when and how a customer wishes: *curtains made to order.*

on order having been ordered but not yet supplied: *We don't have any copies of this book at the moment, but it's on order.*

order about to keep on giving orders (to someone): *I'm tired of him ordering me about all the time.*

out of order 1 not working (properly): *The machine is out of order.* **2** not correct according to what is regularly done, *esp* in meetings *etc*: *He was out of order in saying that.*

a tall order a difficult job or task: *Asking us to finish this by Friday is a bit of a tall order.*

ordinal ['oːdinl]: **ordinal numbers** the numbers which show order in a series *ie* first, second, third *etc.*
See also **cardinal.**

ordinary ['oːdənəri] *adj* **1** usual; normal: *She was behaving in a perfectly ordinary manner.* **2** not unusually good *etc*: *Some people like his poetry but I think it's rather ordinary.* '**ordinarily** *adv* usually.

out of the ordinary unusual: *I don't consider her behaviour at all out of the ordinary.*

ore [oː] *n* any mineral, rock *etc* from which a metal is obtained: *iron ore.*

organ[1] ['oːgən] *n* **1** a part of the body or of a plant which has a special purpose: *the reproductive organs.* **2** a means of spreading information, *eg* a newspaper: *an organ of the Communist Party.*

or'ganic [-'ga-] *adj* **1** of or concerning the organs of the body: *organic diseases.* **2** of, found in, or produced by, living things: *Organic compounds all contain carbon.* **3** (of food) grown without the use of articial fertilizers. **or'ganically** *adv.*

organ[2] ['oːgən] *n* **1** a *usu* large musical instrument similar to a piano, with or without pipes: *He plays the organ*; *an electric organ.* '**organist** *n* a person who plays the organ: *the organist in the church.*

organic *see* **organ**[1].

organism ['oːgənizəm] *n* a *usu* small living animal or plant: *A pond is full of organisms.*

organize, -ise ['oːgənaiz] *v* **1** to arrange or prepare (something), *usu* requiring some time or effort: *They organized a conference.* **2** to make into a society *etc*: *He organized the workers into a trade union.* '**organizer, -s-** *n.*

,**organi'zation, -s-** *n* **1** a group of people working together for a purpose: *a business organization.* **2** the act of organizing: *Efficiency depends on the organization of one's work.* **3** the state of being organized: *This report lacks organization.*

'**organized, -s-** *adj* **1** efficient: *She's a very organized person.* **2** well-arranged: *an organized report.* **3** having been planned: *an organized protest.*

orgy ['oːdʒi] – *pl* '**orgies** – *n* a wild party or celebration: *a drunken orgy.*

Orient ['oːriənt]: **the Orient** the east (China, Japan *etc*): *the mysteries of the Orient.*

,**ori'ental** [-'en-] *adj* in or from the east: *oriental art.* – *n* a person who comes from the east.

orientate ['oːriənteit], (*Amer*) **orient** ['oːriənt] *v* **1** to get (oneself) used to unfamiliar surroundings, conditions *etc.* **2** to find out one's position in relation to something else: *The hikers tried to orientate themselves before continuing their walk.* ,**orien'tation** *n.*

origin ['oridʒin] *n* the place or point from which anything first comes; the cause: *the origin(s) of the English language*; *the origin of the disagreement.*

o'riginal [ə'ri-] *adj* **1** existing at the beginning; first: *This part of the house is new but the rest is original.* **2** (able to produce ideas which are) new, fresh or not thought of before: *original ideas*; *He has a very original mind.* **3** (of a painting *etc*) by the artist *etc*, from which copies may be made: *The original painting is in the museum, but there are hundreds of copies.* – *n* **1** the earliest version: *This is the original – all the others are copies.* **2** a model from which a painting *etc* is made: *She is the original of the famous portrait.*

o,rigi'nality [əridʒi'na-] *n*: *His writing shows originality.*

o'riginally *adv.*

originate [ə'ridʒineit] *v* to bring or come into being: *That style of painting originated in China.*

'**origins** *n pl* a person's place of birth, family, background *etc*: *He tried to hide his origins.*

ornament ['ɔ:nəmənt] *n* something decorative, intended to make a room *etc* more beautiful: *china ornaments.* – [ɔ:nə'ment] *v* to decorate: *The church was richly ornamented.* ,ornamen'tation *n*.

,orna'mental [-'men-] *adj* used for ornament: *an ornamental pool in the garden.*

ornate [ɔ:'neit] *adj* with a lot of ornament: *an ornate doorway.* or'nately *adv.* or'nateness *n*.

orphan ['ɔ:fən] *n* a child who has lost both parents (rarely only one parent): *That little girl is an orphan*; (*also adj*) *an orphan child.* 'orphanage [-nidʒ] *n* a home for orphans.

orthodox ['ɔ:θədɔks] *adj* 1 (of beliefs *etc*) generally accepted: *orthodox views.* 2 (of people) holding such beliefs: *She is very orthodox in her approach to grammar.*

orthop(a)edics [ɔ:θə'pi:diks] *n sing* the branch of medicine which concerns diseases and injuries of the bones: *He specialized in orthopaedics.*

ortho'p(a)edic *adj.*

ostensible [o'stensəbl] *adj* (of reasons *etc*) apparent, but not necessarily true: *Illness was the ostensible reason for his absence, but in fact he was just lazy.* o'stensibly *adv.*

ostentatious [osten'teiʃəs] *adj* behaving, done *etc* in such a way as to be seen by other people and to impress them: *Their style of living is very ostentatious.* ,osten'tation, ,osten'tatiousness *ns.*

,osten'tatiously *adv.*

ostracize, -ise ['ostrəsaiz] *v* to refuse to accept (someone) in society or a group: *His former friends ostracized him because of his rudeness.* 'ostracism *n*.

ostrich ['ostritʃ] *n* a type of large bird which cannot fly.

other ['ʌðə] 1 *adj, pron* the second of two: *I have lost my other glove*; *I've got one of my gloves but I can't find the other* (one). 2 *adj, pron* those people, things *etc* not mentioned, present *etc*; additional: *Some of them have arrived – where are the others?*; *The baby is here and the other children are at school.* 3 *adj* (*with* **day, week** *etc*) recently past: *I saw him just the other day/morning.* 'otherwise *adv* 1 in every other way except this: *She has a big nose but otherwise she is very good-looking.* 2 doing, thinking *etc* something else: *I am otherwise engaged this evening.* – *conj* or else; if not: *Take a taxi – otherwise you'll be late.*

no/none other than the very same person as: *The man who had sent the flowers was none other than the man she had spoken to the night before.*

other than except: *There was no-one there other than an old woman.*

somehow or other in some way or by some means not known or decided: *I'll finish this job on time somehow or other.*

someone/something or other a person or thing that is not known: *Someone or other broke that window.*

somewhere or other in one place if not in another; in some place not known or decided: *He must have hidden it somewhere or other.*

***otter** ['tə] *n* a type of small furry river animal that eats fish.

ought [ɔ:t] – *neg short form* **oughtn't** ['ɔ:tnt] – *v* (*usu with* **to**) 1 used to indicated duty; should: *You ought to help them*; *He oughtn't to have done that.* 2 used to indicate something that one could reasonably expect; should: *He ought to have been able to do it.*

ounce [auns] *n* (*usu abbrev* **oz** *when written*) a unit of weight, 28·35 grammes.

our [auə] *adj* belonging to us: *This is our house.*

ours [auəz] *pron* the one(s) belonging to us: *The house is ours.*

our'selves *pron* 1 used as the object of a verb when the person speaking and other people are the object of an action *etc* they perform: *We saw ourselves in the mirror.* 2 used to emphasize **we, us** or the names of the speaker and other people performing an action *etc*: *We ourselves played no part in this.* 3 without help *etc*: *We'll just have to finish the job ourselves.*

oust [aust] *v* to force out (and take the place of): *She ousted him as leader of the party.*

out [aut] 1 *adv, adj* not in a building *etc*; from inside a building *etc*; in(to) the open air: *The children are out in the garden*; *They went out for a walk.* 2 *adv* from inside (something): *He opened the desk and took out a pencil.* 3 *adv, adj* away from home, an office *etc*: *We had an evening out*; *The manager is out.* 4 *adv, adj* far away: *The ship was out at sea*; *He went out to India.* 5 *adv* loudly and clearly: *He shouted out the answer.* 6 *adv* completely: *She was tired out.* 7 *adv, adj* not correct: *My calculations seem to be out.* 8 *adv, adj* free, known, available *etc*: *He let the cat out*; *The secret is out.* 9 *adv, adj* (in games) having been defeated: *The batsman was* (*caught*) *out.* 10 *adv, adj* on strike: *The men came out in protest.* 11 *adv, adj* no longer in fashion: *Long hair is definitely out.* 12 *adv, adj* (of the tide) with the water at or going to its lowest level: *The tide is* (*going*) *out.* 13 *adj* unacceptable: *That suggestion is right out.* – (*as part of a word*) 1 not inside or near, as in **outlying.** 2 indicating outward movement, as in **outburst.** 3 indicating that the action goes further or beyond a normal action, as in **outshine.**

'**outer** adj outside; far from (the centre of) something: *outer space*.

'**outermost** adj nearest the edge, outside *etc*: *the outermost ring on the target*.

'**outing** n a *usu* short trip, made for pleasure: *an outing to the seaside*.

'**outward** adj 1 on or towards the outside; able to be seen: *Judging by his outward appearance, he's not very rich*; *no outward sign of unhappiness*. 2 (of a journey) away from: *The outward journey will be by sea, but they will return home by air*.

'**outwardly** adv in appearance: *Outwardly he is cheerful, but he is really a very unhappy person*.

'**outwards** adv towards the outside edge or surface: *Moving outwards from the centre of the painting, we see that the figures become smaller*.

'**out-and-out** adj very bad: *an out-and-out liar*.

out-of-date *see* date.

,**out-of-the-'way** adj difficult to reach or arrive at: *an out-of-the-way place*.

be out for to be wanting or intending to get: *She is out for revenge*.

be out to to be determined to: *He is out to win the race*.

out of 1 from inside: *He took it out of the bag*. 2 not in: *Mr Smith is out of the office*; *out of danger*; *out of sight*. 3 from among: *Four out of five people like this song*. 4 having none left: *She is quite out of breath*. 5 because of: *He did it out of curiosity/spite*. 6 from: *He drank the lemonade straight out of the bottle*.

out of doors outside: *We like to eat out of doors in summer*.

out of it 1 not part of a group, activity *etc*: *I felt a bit out of it at the party*. 2 no longer involved in something: *That was a crazy scheme – I'm glad to be out of it*.

out of the way unusual: *There was nothing out of the way about what she said*.

outboard ['autbɔ:d]: **outboard motor/engine** a motor or engine fixed on to the outside of a boat.

outbreak ['autbreik] n a sudden beginning (*usu* of something unpleasant): *the outbreak of war*.

outburst ['autbɔ:st] n an explosion, *esp* of angry feelings: *a sudden outburst (of rage)*.

outcast ['autka:st] n a person who has been driven away from friends, *etc*: *an outcast from society*.

outcome ['autkʌm] n the result: *What was the outcome of your discussion?*

outcry ['autkrai] n a show of disapproval *etc*, *esp* by the general public: *There was a great outcry about the inadequate train service*.

outdo [aut'du:] – *pt* **out'did** [-'did]: *ptp* **out'done** [-'dʌn] – v to do better than: *He*

worked very hard as he did not want to be outdone by anyone.

outdoor ['autdɔ:] adj done, for use *etc* outside, not in a building: *outdoor shoes*.

out'doors adv outside; not in a building *etc*: *We spend a lot of time outdoors*.

outer, outermost *see* out.

outfit ['autfit] n a set of clothes, *esp* for a particular occasion: *a wedding outfit*.

outgoing [aut'gouiŋ] adj 1 friendly: *a very outgoing personality*. 2 going out; leaving: *the outgoing president*.

outgrow [aut'grou] – *pt* **out'grew** [-'gru:]: *ptp* **out'grown** – v to grow too big or too old for: *My son has outgrown all his clothes*.

outing *see* out.

outlaw ['autlɔ:] n a criminal, *esp* one who is punished by being refused the protection of the law. – v to make (someone) an outlaw.

outlay ['autlei] n money spent: *an outlay of $500 on furniture*.

outlet ['autlit] n 1 a way or passage outwards or for releasing: *That pipe is an outlet from the main tank*; *an outlet for his energy*.

outline ['autlain] n 1 the line forming, or showing, the outer edge of something: *He drew the outline of the face first, then added the features*. 2 a short description of the main details of a plan *etc*: *Don't tell me the whole story, just give me an outline*. – v to draw or give the outline of.

outlook ['autluk] n 1 a view: *Their house has a wonderful outlook*. 2 a person's view of life *etc*: *He has a strange outlook (on life)*. 3 what is likely to happen in the future: *The weather outlook is bad*.

outlying ['autlaiiŋ] adj distant, far from a city *etc*: *outlying villages*.

outnumber [aut'nʌmbə] v to be more (in number) than: *The boys in the class outnumber the girls*.

out-of-date *see* date.

out-patient ['autpeiʃənt] n a person who comes to hospital for treatment but does not stay there overnight. – *Also adj*: *an out-patient department*.

outpost ['autpoust] n a distant place: *The island was an outpost of the nation*.

output ['autput] n the quantity of goods, amount of work produced: *The output of this factory has increased by 20%*; *His output is poor*.

outrage ['autreidʒ] n a wicked act, *esp* of great violence: *the outrages committed by the soldiers*; *The decision to close the road is a public outrage*. – v to hurt, shock or insult: *She was outraged by his behaviour*.

out'rageous adj 1 noticeably terrible: *an outrageous hat*; *outrageous behaviour*. **out'rageously** adv. **out'rageousness** n.

outright [aut'rait] adv 1 honestly: *I told him outright what I thought*. 2 immediately: *He* *was killed outright.* – ['autrait] *adj* without any exception or doubt: *He is the outright winner.*

outset ['autset] *n* the beginning of something: *We have to get quite clear from the outset what out policy is.*

outshine [aut'ʃain] – *pt, ptp* **out'shone** [-'ʃon] – *v* to be brighter than: *She outshone all the other students.*

outside ['autsaid] *n* the outer surface: *The outside of the house was painted white.* – ['autsaid] *adj* **1** of, on, or near the outer part of anything: *the outside door.* **2** not part of (a group, one's work *etc*): *We shall need outside help; She has a lot of outside interests.* **3** (of a chance *etc*) very small. –[aut'said] *adv* **1** out of, not in a building *etc*: *He went outside; He stayed outside.* **2** on the outside: *The house looked beautiful outside.* – [aut'said] *prep* on the outer part or side of; not inside or within: *He stood outside the house; He did that outside working hours.*

out'sider *n* **1** a person who is not part of a group *etc*. **2** (in a race *etc*) a runner who is not expected to win: *The race was won by a complete outsider.*

outside in turned so that the inside and outside change places: *You're wearing your jersey outside in.*

outsize ['autsaiz] *adj* (for people who are) bigger than usual: *outsize clothes.*

outskirts ['autskə:ts] *n pl* the outer parts or area, *esp* of a town: *I live on the outskirts of London.*

outspoken [aut'spoukən] *adj* saying exactly what one thinks: *She's a very outspoken person.*

outstanding [aut'standiŋ] *adj* **1** excellent; very good: *an outstanding student.* **2** not yet paid, done *etc*: *You must pay all outstanding bills.*

out'standingly *adv*: *outstandingly good.*

outstrip [aut'strip] – *pt, ptp* **out'stripped** – *v* to go much faster than: *He outstripped the other runners.*

outward(s), outwardly *see* **out.**

outweigh [aut'wei] *v* to be greater or more than: *The advantages outweigh the disadvantages.*

outwit [aut'wit] – *pt, ptp* **out'witted** – *v* to defeat (someone) by being cleverer than he is: *She managed to outwit the police and escape.*

ova *see* **ovum.**

***oval** ['ouvəl] *adj* shaped like an egg: *an oval table.* – *n* an oval shape: *He drew an oval.*

ovary ['ouvəri] – *pl* **'ovaries** – *n* the part of the female body in which eggs are formed.

ovation [ə'veiʃən, (*Amer*) ou-] *n* cheering or applause *etc* to express approval, welcome

etc: *They gave the president a standing ovation* (= They stood and applauded him).

oven ['ʌvn] *n* a closed box-like space, *usu* part of a cooker, which is heated for cooking food: *She put the cake into the oven.*

over ['ouvə] *prep* **1** higher than; above in position, number, authority *etc*: *Hang that picture over the fireplace; He's over 90 years old.* **2** from one side to another, on or above the top of; on the other side of: *He jumped over the gate; She fell over the cat; My friend lives over the street.* **3** covering: *He put his handkerchief over his face.* **4** across: *You find people like him all over the world.* **5** about: *a quarrel over money.* **6** by means of: *He spoke to her over the telephone.* **7** during: *Over the years, she grew to hate her husband.* **8** while having *etc*: *He fell asleep over his dinner.* – *adv* **1** higher, moving *etc* above: *The plane flew over about an hour ago.* **2** used to show movement, change of position: *He rolled over on his back; He turned over the page.* **3** across: *He went over and spoke to them.* **4** downwards: *He fell over.* **5** higher in number: *for people aged twenty and over.* **6** remaining: *There are two cakes for each of us, and two over.* **7** through from beginning to end, carefully: *Read it over; Talk it over between you.* – *adj* finished: *The affair is over now.* – *n* (in cricket) a certain number of balls bowled from one end of the wicket: *He bowled thirty overs in the match.* – (*as part of a word*) **1** too (much), as in **overdo.** **2** in a higher position, as in **overhead.** **3** covering, as in **overcoat.** **4** down from an upright position, as in **overturn.** **5** completely, as in **overcome.**

over again once more: *Play the tune over again.*

over all *see* **overall** *below.*

over and done with finished; no longer important: *He has behaved very wickedly in the past but that's all over and done with now.*

overall ['ouvərɔ:l] *n* a garment worn over ordinary clothes to protect them from dirt *etc*: *She wears an overall when cleaning the house.* – *adj* complete, including everything: *What is the overall cost of the scheme?* – [ouvər'ɔ:l] *adv* (*also* **over all**) complete, including everything: *What will the scheme cost overall?*

'overalls *n pl* a type of trousers or suit made of hard-wearing materials worn *usu* over ordinary clothes by workmen *etc* to protect them from dirt *etc*: *The painter put on his overalls before starting work; I'll need a clean pair of overalls tomorrow.*

* see illustration on p. 476

overarm ['ouvəra:m] *adj, adv* (of a throw) with the hand and arm moving round above the shoulder: *He bowled overarm*; *an overarm throw.*

overbalance [ouvə'baləns] *v* to lose balance and fall: *He overbalanced on the edge of the cliff and fell into the sea below.*

overbearing [ouvə'beəriŋ] *adj* too sure that one is right: *I disliked her overbearing manner.*

overboard ['ouvəbo:d] *adv* over the side of a ship or boat into the water: *He jumped overboard.*

overcast [ouvə'ka:st] *adj* cloudy: *on a slightly overcast day.*

overcharge [ouvə't∫a:dʒ] *v* to charge too much: *I have been overcharged for these goods.*

overcoat ['ouvəkout] *n* a *usu* heavy coat worn over all other clothes *esp* in winter.

overcome [ouvə'kʌm] *adj* helpless; defeated by emotion *etc*: *overcome with grief*; *I felt quite overcome.* − *v* − *pt* ,**over'came** [-'keim]: *ptp* ,**over'come** − to defeat or conquer: *She finally overcame her fear of the dark.*

overcrowded [ouvə'kraudid] *adj* having too many people on or in: *overcrowded buses/cities.*
,**over'crowding** *n* the state of being overcrowded: *There is often overcrowding in cities.*

overdo [ouvə'du:] − *pt* ,**over'did** [-'did] : *ptp* **over'done** [-'dʌn] − *v* **1** to do, say (something) in an exaggerated way *etc*: *They overdid the sympathy.* **2** to cook for too long: *The meat was rather overdone.*

overdose ['ouvədous] *n* too great an amount (of medicine): *an overdose of sleeping-pills.*

overdraft ['ouvədra:ft] *n* the amount of money by which a bank account is overdrawn: *a large overdraft.*

overdrawn [ouvə'dro:n] *adj* having taken more money out of one's account than it had in it: *His account is overdrawn.*

overdue [ouvə'dju:] *adj* **1** late: *The train is overdue.* **2** (of bills, work *etc*) not yet paid, done, delivered *etc*, although the date for doing this has passed: *overdue library books.*

overestimate [ouvər'estimeit] *v* to estimate, judge *etc* (something) to be greater, larger or more important than it is: *He overestimates his own ability.*

overflow [ouvə'flou] *v* to flow over the edge or limits (of): *The river overflowed (its banks)*; *The crowd overflowed into the next room.* − ['ouvəflou] *n* **1** a flowing over of liquid: *I put a bucket under the pipe to catch the overflow*; *(also adj) an overflow pipe.* **2** an overflow pipe.

overgrown [ouvə'groun] *adj* **1** full of plants that have grown too large or thick: *Our garden is overgrown with weeds.* **2** grown too large: *an overgrown puppy.*

overhaul [ouvə'ho:l] *v* to examine carefully and repair: *I had my car overhauled at the garage.* − ['ouvəho:l] *n*: *a complete overhaul.*

overhead [ouvə'hed] *adv, adj* above; over one's head: *The plane flew overhead*; *an overhead bridge.*

overhear [ouvə'hiə] − *pt, ptp* ,**over'heard** [-'hə:d] − *v* to hear (what one was not intended to hear): *She overheard two people talking in the next room.*

overjoyed [ouvə'dʒoid] *adj* full of joy; very glad: *She was overjoyed to hear of his safe arrival.*

overlap [ouvə'lap] − *pt, ptp* ,**over'lapped** − *v* to extend over and cover a part of: *The pieces of cloth overlapped (each other).* − ['ouvəlap] *n: an overlap of two centimetres.*

overload [ouvə'loud] *v* to fill with too much of something: *The lorry overturned because it had been overloaded.*

overlook [ouvə'luk] *v* **1** to look down on: *The house overlooked the river.* **2** to take no notice of: *We shall overlook your lateness this time.*

overnight [ouvə'nait] *adj, adv* **1** for or during the night: *an overnight bag.* **2** very quick(ly): *He was an overnight success.*

overpass ['ouvəpa:s] *n* a bridge-like part of a road *etc* which passes over another road, a railway *etc*.

overpower [ouvə'pauə] *v* to defeat or make helpless or captive by a greater strength: *The police overpowered the thieves.*
,**over'powering** *adj* very strong: *That smell is quite overpowering.*

overrate [ouvə'reit] *v* to think that something is better, stronger, more valuable *etc* than it really is: *Her beauty is overrated.*

overreact [ouvəri'akt] *v* to react too much: *She overreacts to criticism.* ,**overre'action** [-∫ən] *n*.

overrule [ouvə'ru:l] *v* to go against a judgement that has already been made: *The judge overruled the previous decision.*

overrun [ouvə'rʌn] − *prp* ,**over'running**: *pt* ,**over'ran** [-'ran]: *ptp* ,**over'run** − *v* **1** to fill, occupy or take possession of: *The house was overrun with mice.* **2** to continue longer than intended: *The programme overran by five minutes.*

overseas ['ouvəsi:z] *adj,* [ouvə'si:z] *adv* across the sea; abroad: *He went overseas*; *overseas trade.*

oversee [ouvə'si:] − *pt* ,**over'saw** [-'so:]: *ptp* ,**over'seen** − *v* to supervise: *He oversees production at the factory.*
overseer ['ouvəsiə] *n: The overseer reported her for being late.*

overshadow ['ouvə'ʃadou] v to make less important esp by being much better than: *With her beauty and wit she quite overshadowed her sister.*

overshoot ['ouvə'ʃuːt] – pt, ptp **over'shot** [-'ʃot] – v to go farther than (the point one was aiming at): *The plane overshot the runway.*

oversight ['ouvəsait] n a failure to notice: *Due to an oversight, we have not paid the bill.*

oversleep ['ouvə'sliːp] – pt, ptp **over'slept** [-'slept] – v to sleep longer than one intended: *He overslept and missed the train.*

overspend ['ouvə'spend] – pt, ptp **over'spent** [-t] – v to spend too much money: *He overspent on his new house.*

overt [ou'vəːt] adj not hidden or secret: *overt opposition to a plan.* **o'vertly** adv.

overtake ['ouvə'teik] – pt **over'took** [-'tuk] – ptp **over'taken** – v to pass (a car etc) while driving etc: *He overtook a police-car.*

overtax ['ouvə'taks] v to put too great a strain on: *He overtaxed his strength.*

overthrow ['ouvə'θrou] – pt **over'threw** [-'θruː]: ptp **over'thrown** – v to defeat and force out of power: *The government has been overthrown.*

overtime ['ouvətaim] n time spent in working beyond one's set number of hours etc: *He did five hours' overtime this week.*

overtones ['ouvətounz] n pl suggestions; hints: *There were overtones of discontent in his speech.*

overture ['ouvətjuə] n a piece of music played as an introduction to an opera etc.

overturn ['ouvə'təːn] v to turn over: *They overturned the boat; The car overturned.*

overweight ['ouvə'weit] adj too heavy; too fat: *If I eat too much I soon get overweight.*

overwhelm ['ouvə'welm] v to defeat or overcome: *He was overwhelmed with work/grief.* **over'whelming** adj very great: *an overwhelming victory.*

overwork ['ouvə'wəːk] n the act of working too hard: *It's overwork that made him ill.* **over'worked** adj made to work too hard: *His staff are overworked.*

ovum ['ouvəm] – pl **ova** ['ouvə] – n the egg from which the young of people and animals develop.

owe [ou] v to be in debt to: *I owe (him) $10.* **'owing** adj still to be paid: *There is some money still owing (to us).* **owing to** because of: *Owing to the rain, the football has been cancelled.*

owing to is used to mean 'because of': *The shop is closed owing to* (not *due to*) *the manager's illness.*
due to is used to mean 'caused by': *The accident was believed to be due to his negligence.*

owl [aul] n a type of bird that flies at night and feeds on small birds and animals.

own [oun] v 1 to have as a possession: *I own a car.* 2 to admit that something is true: *I own that I have not been working very hard.* – adj, pron belonging to (the person stated): *The house is my own; I saw it with my own eyes.* **'owner** n a person who owns something: *Are you the owner of that car?* **'ownership** n. **get one's own back** to revenge oneself: *He has beaten me this time, but I'll get my own back (on him).*
own up (often with to) to admit that one has done something: *He owned up to having broken the window.*

ox [oks] – pl **'oxen** – n 1 a castrated bull used (formerly in Britain and still in some countries) to pull carts, ploughs etc: *an ox-drawn cart.* 2 any bull or cow.

oxygen ['oksidʒən] n an element, a gas without taste, colour or smell, forming part of the air: *He died from lack of oxygen.* **oxygen mask** a mask through which a person can breathe oxygen.

oyster ['oistə] n a type of shellfish eaten as food, and from which pearls are got. **oyster bed** a place in the sea where oysters breed or are bred.

ozone ['ouzoun] n 1 fresh (sea) air. 2 a type of oxygen.

Pp

pace [peis] n 1 a step: *He took a pace forward.* 2 speed of movement: *a fast pace.* – v to walk backwards and forwards (across): *He paced up and down.* **'pacemaker** n 1 an electronic device to make the heart beats regular or stronger. 2 a person who sets the speed of a race. **keep pace with** to go as fast as: *He kept pace with the car on his motorbike.*

pace out to measure by walking along, across etc with even steps: *She paced out the room.*
put someone etc through his etc paces to make someone etc show what he etc can do: *He put his new car through its paces.*
set the pace to go forward at a particular speed which everyone else has to follow: *Her experiments set the pace for future research.*

show one's paces to show what one can do:
They made the horse show its paces.

pacify ['pasifai] *v* to make calm or peaceful:
She tried to pacify the quarrelling children.
,pacifi'cation [-fi-] *n*.

'**pacifism** *n* the belief that all war is wrong
and that one must not take part in it.

'**pacifist** *n* a person who believes in
pacifism: *As a pacifist he refused to fight in
the war.*

pack [pak] *n* **1** things tied up together or put
in a container, *esp* to be carried on one's
back: *He carried his luggage in a pack on his
back.* **2** a set of (fifty-two) playing-cards: *a
pack of cards.* **3** a number or group of
certain animals: *a pack of wolves/a wolf-
pack.* **4** a packet: *a pack of cigarettes.* – *v*
1 to put (clothes *etc*) into a bag, suitcase or
trunk for a journey: *I've packed all I need
and I'm ready to go.* **2** to come together in
large numbers in a small space: *They
packed into the hall to hear his speech.*

'**packing** *n* **1** the act of putting things in
bags, cases *etc*: *He has done his packing
tonight as he is leaving in the morning.* **2** the
materials (paper, string *etc*) used to wrap
things for posting *etc*: *He unwrapped the
vase and threw away the packing.*

'**packing-case** *n* a (large) wooden box in
which goods are packed and sent from
place to place.

packed (out) containing as many people as
possible: *The theatre/meeting was packed
(out).*

pack off to send away, *usu* quickly and
without wasting time: *They packed the children off to bed early.*

pack up 1 to put into containers in order to
take somewhere else: *She packed up the
contents of her house.* **2** to stop working or
operating: *We'd only gone five miles when
the engine packed up.*

package ['pakidʒ] *n* things wrapped up and
tied (for posting *etc*); a parcel: *a package of
books.* – *v* to wrap up into a package: *He
packaged (up) the clothes.*

package holiday, package tour a holiday or
tour for which one pays the organizer a
fixed price which includes everything
(travel, hotel, food *etc*): *It is cheaper to go
on a package holiday.*

packet ['pakit] *n* a small *often* flat, *usu* paper
or cardboard container, especially one in
which food is sold or in which small objects
are sent through the post: *a packet of
biscuits.*

pact [pakt] *n* an agreement, *esp* if formal
and/or between the representatives of
nations: *They made a pact to help each other.*

pad[1] [pad] *n* **1** a soft, cushion-like object
made of or filled with a soft material, used
to prevent damage by knocking, rubbing

etc: *She knelt on a pad to clean the floor.*
2 sheets of paper fixed together: *a writing-
pad.* **3** a platform from which rockets are
sent off: *a launching-pad.* – *v* – *pt, ptp*
'**padded** – to put a pad in or on (for
protection, to make big enough *etc*): *The
shoes were too big so she padded them with
cottonwool.*

'**padding** *n* material used to make a pad to
protect, fill *etc*: *He used old blankets as
padding.*

pad out to fill with a soft material to make
the right size: *The actor's costume was
padded out to make him look fat.*

pad[2] [pad] – *pt, ptp* '**padded** – *v* to walk softly:
The dog padded along the road.

paddle[1] ['padl] *v* to walk about in shallow
water: *The children went paddling in the sea.*

paddle[2] ['padl] *n* a short, light oar, often with
a blade at each end of the shaft, used in
canoes *etc*. – *v* to move with a paddle: *He
paddled the canoe along the river.*

'**paddle-steamer** *n* a boat driven by paddle-
wheels.

'**paddle-wheel** *n* a large wheel fitted with flat
pieces of wood, attached to the side or stern
of a boat and turned to make it move
through the water.

to paddle (not pedal) a canoe.

paddock ['padək] *n* a small field, containing
grass and *usu* near a house or stable, in
which horses *etc* are often kept.

paddy-field ['padifiːld] *n* a field, often flooded
with water, in which rice is grown.

padlock ['padlok] *n* a (*usu* metal) movable
lock with a U-shaped bar which can be
passed through a ring, chain *etc* and locked:
He has put a padlock on the gate. – *v* to fasten
with a padlock: *She padlocked her bike.*

paediatrics, (*Amer*) **pediatrics** [piːdi'atriks] *n*
sing the study of the illnesses of children.
,paedi'atric *adj*: *paediatric illnesses.*

,paedia'trician [-ʃən] *n* a doctor who specializes in treating and studying children's
illnesses.

pagan ['peigən] *adj* not belonging to any of
the major world religions: *pagan tribes;
pagan gods.* – *n* a person who does not
belong to any of the major world religions.
'**paganism** *n*.

page[1] [peidʒ] *n* one side of a sheet of paper in
a book, magazine *etc*: *page ninety-four; a
three-page letter.*

page[2] [peidʒ] *n* **1** (in hotels) a boy who takes
messages, carries luggage *etc*. **2** (*also* '**page=
boy**) a boy servant. – *v* to try to find
someone in a public place by calling out his
name (often through a loud-speaker system): *I could not see my friend in the hotel,
so I had him paged.*

pageant ['padʒənt] *n* **1** a dramatic perfor-

mance made up of different, *usu* historical scenes, often performed during a procession: *The children performed a historical pageant.* **2** any fine show or display: *a pageant of colour.*
'pageantry *n* splendid and colourful show or display: *I love the pageantry of royal processions.*
pagoda [pə'goudə] *n* a Chinese temple, built in the shape of a tall tower, each storey of which has its own narrow strip of overhanging roof.
paid *see* pay.
pail [peil] *n* a bucket: *Fetch a pail of water.*
pain [pein] *n* hurt or suffering of the body or mind: *a pain in the chest.* – *v* to cause suffering or upset to (someone): *It pained her to admit that she was wrong.*
pained *adj* showing or expressing pain: *a pained expression.*
'painful *adj* causing pain: *a painful injury.*
'painfully *adv.*
'painless *adj* without pain: *painless childbirth.* 'painlessly *adv.*
'painkiller *n* a drug *etc* which lessens or removes pain.
'painstaking ['peinz-] *adj* going to great trouble and taking great care: *a painstaking student.*
a pain in the neck a person who is constantly annoying: *People who are always complaining are a pain in the neck.*
take pains to take great trouble and care (to do something): *He took great pains to make sure we enjoyed ourselves.*
paint [peint] *n* a colouring substance in the form of liquid or paste: *The artist's clothes were covered in paint;* (*also adj*) *a paint pot.* – *v* **1** to spread paint carefully on (wood, walls *etc*): *He is painting the kitchen.* **2** to make a picture (of something or someone) using paint: *She painted her mother and father.*
'painter *n* **1** a person whose job is to put paint on things, *esp* walls, doors *etc* in houses: *We employed a painter to paint the outside of the house.* **2** an artist who makes pictures in paint: *Who was the painter of this portrait?*
'painting *n* **1** the act or art of using paint: *Painting is very relaxing.* **2** a painted picture: *There were four paintings (hanging) on the wall.*
'paint-box *n* a (small) box containing different paints for making pictures.
'paint-brush *n* a brush used for putting on paint.
pair [peə] *n* **1** a set of two of the same thing which are (intended to be) used *etc* together: *a pair of shoes/gloves.* **2** a single thing made up of two parts: *a pair of scissors; a pair of pants.* **3** two people,

animals *etc*, often one of either sex, who are thought of together for some reason: *a pair of giant pandas; John and James are the guilty pair.* – *v* to make into a pair: *She was paired with my brother in the tennis match.*

pair is singular: *That pair of trousers needs mending; There is a pair of gloves on the table.*

pajamas *see* pyjamas.
pal [pal] *n* an informal word for a friend: *My son brought a pal home for tea.*
'pally *adj* friendly: *They've become very pally.*
palace ['paləs] *n* a large and magnificent house, *esp* one lived in by a king or queen: *Buckingham Palace.*
palatial [pə'leiʃəl] *adj* large and magnificent, as (in) a palace: *They lived in a palatial house; palatial rooms.*
palate ['palət] *n* **1** the top of the inside of the mouth. **2** the ability to tell good wine, food *etc* from bad: *He has a good palate for wine.*
palatial *see* palace.
pale [peil] *adj* **1** (of a person, his face *etc*) having less colour than normal: *a pale face; She went pale with fear.* **2** (of a colour) closer to white than black; not dark: *pale green.* – *v* to become pale: *She paled at the bad news.*
'paleness *n.*
palette ['palit] *n* a small flat piece of wood *etc*, with a hole for the thumb, on which an artist mixes his colours.
pall¹ [po:l] *n* the (*usu* dark-coloured) cloth which covers a coffin at a funeral: *a pall of purple-velvet; A pall of smoke hung over the town.*
pall² [po:l] *v* to become boring or uninteresting: *Loud music soon palls.*
pallid ['palid] *adj* unpleasantly pale (*usu* suggesting ill-health): *He looked pallid and sickly.*
'pallor *n* unpleasant paleness: *an unhealthy pallor.*
pally *see* pal.
palm¹ [pa:m] *n* the inner surface of the hand between the wrist and the fingers: *She held the mouse in the palm of her hand.*
palm² [pa:m] *n* (*also* palm tree) a kind of tall tree, with broad, spreading leaves, which grows in hot countries: *a coconut palm.*
palpitate ['palpiteit] *v* (of the heart) to beat rapidly.
,palpi'tations *n pl* an attack of rapid beating of the heart.
pamper ['pampə] *v* to treat with great kindness and give a great many special things to (a person): *The child was pampered by his parents.*
pamphlet ['pamflit] *n* a small paper-covered book *usu* giving information, expressing an

opinion on a popular subject *etc*: *a political pamphlet*.

pan¹ [pan] *n* a metal pot used for cooking food: *a frying-pan*; *a saucepan*.
'**pancake** *n* a thin cake *usu* made of milk, flour and eggs and fried in a pan *etc*.

pan² [pan] – *pt*, *ptp* **panned** – *v* to move (a film or television camera) so as to follow a moving object or show a wide view: *The camera panned slowly across to the other side of the street*.

pan- [pan] all; whole: *pan-American*.

panama [panə'maː, (*Amer*) 'panəmaː] *n* (*often* **panama hat**) a hat made of straw-like material, worn in hot weather.

pancreas ['paŋkriəs] *n* a part of the body which helps in the digestion of food.

panda ['pandə] *n* (*often* **giant panda**) a large black and white bear-like animal of the raccoon family, which lives in the mountains of China.

pandemonium [pandi'mouniəm] *n* a state of noise and confusion: *There was pandemonium in the classroom before the teacher arrived*.

pander ['pandə]: **pander to** to give in to (a desire, *esp* if unworthy): *Some newspapers pander to people's interest in crime and violence*.

pane [pein] *n* a flat piece of glass: *a window-pane*.

panel ['panl] *n* **1** a flat, straight-sided piece of wood, fabric *etc* such as is put into a door, wall, dress *etc*: *a door-panel*. **2** a group of people chosen for a particular purpose *eg* to judge a contest, take part in a quiz or other game: *I will ask some questions and the panel will try to answer them*.
'**panelled** *adj* made of or surrounded with panels (*usu* of wood): *a panelled door*; *oak-panelled*.
'**panelling** *n* (wood used for) panels covering the walls of a room *etc*: *oak panelling*.

pang [paŋ] *n* a sudden sharp pain: *a pang of hunger/grief/regret*.

panic ['panik] *n* (a) sudden great fear, *esp* that spreads through a crowd *etc*: *The fire caused a panic in the city*. – *v* – *pt*, *ptp* '**panicked** – to make or become so frightened that one loses the power to think clearly: *He panicked at the sight of the audience*.
'**panicky** *adj* inclined to panic: *She gets panicky in an exam*; *in a panicky mood*.

panorama [panə'raːmə] *n* a wide view, of a landscape *etc*: *There is a wonderful panorama from that hill*.
,**pano'ramic** [-'ra-] *adj* of or like a panorama: *a panoramic view*.

pant [pant] *v* **1** to gasp for breath: *He was panting heavily as he ran*. **2** to say while

gasping for breath: *'Wait for me!' she panted*.

panther ['panθə] *n* **1** a leopard, *esp* a large one. **2** (*Amer*) a puma.

panties *see* **pants**.

pantomime ['pantəmaim] *n* a play performed at Christmas time, *usu* based on a popular fairy tale, with music, dancing, comedy *etc*.

pantry ['pantri] – *pl* '**pantries** – *n* a room for storing food: *The house had a large kitchen with a pantry*.

pants [pants] *n pl* **1** (*also* '**panties**) a short undergarment worn on the lower part of the body: *a pair of pants*. **2** (*Amer*) trousers.

papa [pə'paː, (*Amer*) 'paːpə] *n* a father: *You must ask your papa*; *Where are you, Papa?*

papal ['peipl] *adj* of the pope: *papal authority*.

papaya [pə'paiə] *n* a tropical tree or its fruit.

paper ['peipə] *n* **1** the material on which these words are written, made from wood, rags *etc* and used for writing, printing, wrapping parcels *etc*: *I need paper and a pen to write a letter*; (*also adj*) *a paper bag*. **2** a single (often printed or typed) piece of this: *There were papers all over his desk*. **3** a newspaper: *Have you read the paper?* **4** a group of questions for a written examination: *The Latin paper was very difficult*. **5** (*in pl*) documents proving one's identity, nationality *etc*: *The policeman demanded my papers*.
'**papery** *adj* like paper: *papery leaves*.
'**paperback** *n* a book with a paper cover. – *adj*: *paperback novels*.
'**paper-clip** *n* a small, *usu* metal clip for holding papers together: *She attached her note to the papers with a paper-clip*.
'**paper-knife** *n* a knife used for opening envelopes *etc*.
paper sculpture the art of modelling with folded paper.
'**paperweight** *n* a small, heavy object which can be put on top of pieces of paper to keep them in place, also used as an ornament.
'**paperwork** *n* the part of a job which consists of keeping files, writing letters *etc*: *I spend most of my time on paperwork*.

papier-mâché [papiei'maʃei, (*Amer*) peipər-mə'ʃei] *n*, *adj* (of) a substance consisting of paper mixed together with some kind of glue, which can be made into models, bowls, boxes *etc*.

paprika ['paprikə, (*esp Amer*) pə'priːkə] *n* a type of red pepper powder used in cooking.

par [paː] *n* the normal level, standard, value *etc*.
below par/not up to par not up to the usual standard: *Your work is not up to par this week*.

on a par with equal to: *As a writer he is on a par with the great novelists.*

parable ['parəbl] *n* a story (*esp* in the Bible) which is intended to teach a lesson: *Jesus told parables.*

parachute ['parəʃuːt] *n* an umbrella-shaped piece of light, strong cloth *etc* beneath which a person *etc* is tied with ropes so that he *etc* can come slowly down to the ground from a great height: *They made the descent from the plane by parachute*; (*also adj*) *a parachute-jump.* – *v* to come down to the ground using a parachute: *The troops parachuted into France.*

'parachutist *n* a person who uses a parachute.

parade [pə'reid] *n* **1** a line of people, vehicles *etc* moving forward in order often as a celebration of some event: *a circus parade.* **2** an arrangement of soldiers in a particular order: *The troops are on parade.* – *v* **1** to march in a line moving forward in order: *They paraded through the town.* **2** to arrange soldiers in order: *The colonel paraded his soldiers.* **3** to show or display in an obvious way: *She paraded her new clothes in front of her friends.*

paradise ['parədais] *n* **1** a place or state of great happiness: *It's paradise to be by a warm fire on a cold night.* **2** (*with cap*) heaven: *When we die, we go to Paradise.*

paradox ['parədoks] *n* a statement *etc* that seems to contradict itself but which is nevertheless true: *If your birthday is on February 29 you could state the paradox that you are thirteen years old although you have only had three birthdays.* ,para'doxical *adj.* ,para'doxically *adv.*

paraffin ['parəfin] *n* a kind of oil which is used as a fuel: *This heater burns paraffin*; (*also adj*) *a paraffin lamp.*

paragon ['parəgən, (*Amer*) -gon] *n* a perfect example of a good quality *etc*: *She is a paragon of virtue.*

paragraph ['parəgraːf] *n* a part of a piece of writing, marked by beginning the first sentence on a new line and *usu* leaving a short space at the beginning of the line: *There are a couple of paragraphs about football on page three of today's paper.*

parallel ['parəlel] *adj* **1** (of straight lines) going in the same direction and always staying the same distance apart: *The road is parallel to/with the river.* **2** alike (in some way): *There are parallel passages in the two books.* – *adv* in the same direction but always about the same distance away: *We sailed parallel to the coast for several days.* – *n* **1** a line parallel to another: *Draw a parallel to this line.* **2** a likeness or state of being alike: *Is there a parallel between the British Empire and the Roman Empire?* **3** a line drawn

from east to west across a map *etc* at a fixed distance from the equator: *The border between Canada and the United States follows the forty-ninth parallel.* – *v* to be equal to: *His stupidity can't be paralleled.*

para'llelogram [-əgram] *n* a four-sided figure with opposite sides equal and parallel.

paralysis [pə'raləsis] *n* a loss of the ability to move: *The paralysis affects his legs.*

paralyse, (*Amer*) **paralyze** ['parəlaiz] *v* to make unable to move: *paralysed with fear.*

paralytic [parə'litik] *adj.*

paranoia [parə'noiə] *n* a type of mental illness in which a person has fixed and unreasonable ideas that he is very important, or that other people are being unfair or unfriendly to him.

,para'noiac [-'noːik], ,paranoid [-noid] *ns, adjs.*

parapet ['parəpit] *n* a low wall along the edge of a bridge, balcony *etc.*

paraphernalia [parəfə'neiliə] *n* a (large) collection of (small) objects, often the tools *etc* for a job or hobby: *a photographer's paraphernalia.*

paraphrase ['parəfreiz] *v* to repeat, in speech or writing, in different words: *He paraphrased the poem in modern English.* – *n* something which repeats something else in different words: *He made a paraphrase of the poem.*

parasite ['parəsait] *n* an animal or plant that lives on another animal or plant without giving anything in return: *Fleas are parasites*; *He is a parasite on society.* ,para'sitic *adj.*

parasol ['parəsol] *n* a light umbrella used as a protection against the sun.

paratroops ['parətruːps] *n pl* soldiers who are trained to drop by parachute into enemy territory. **'paratrooper** *n.*

parcel ['paːsl] *n* thing(s) wrapped and tied, *usu* to be sent by post: *I got a parcel in the post today.*

parch [paːtʃ] *v* to make hot and very dry: *The sun parched the earth.*

parched *adj* **1** hot and dry: *Nothing could grow in the parched land.* **2** thirsty: *Can I have a cup of tea – I'm parched!*

parchment ['paːtʃmənt] *n* a (piece of a) material used for writing on, made from animal skin: *Medieval men often wrote on parchment.*

pardon ['paːdn] *v* **1** to forgive: *Pardon my asking, but can you help me?* **2** to free (from prison, punishment *etc*): *The king pardoned the prisoners.* – *n* **1** forgiveness: *He prayed for pardon for his wickedness.* **2** a (document) freeing from prison or punishment: *He was granted a pardon.* – *interj* used to indicate that one has not heard properly what was said: *Pardon? Could you repeat that last sentence?*

beg someone's pardon to say one is sorry (*usu* for having offended someone else *etc*): *I've come to beg (your) pardon for being so rude this morning.*

I beg your pardon I'm sorry: *I beg your pardon – what did you say? I wasn't listening.*

pardon me *interj* expressing a polite apology, *esp* for not agreeing with someone: *Pardon me for interrupting you.*

parent ['peərənt] *n* **1** one of the two persons *etc* (one male and one female) who are jointly the cause of one's birth. **2** a person with the legal position of a mother or father *eg* by adoption.

'**parentage** [-tidʒ] *n* family or ancestry: *a man of unknown parentage.*

parental [pə'rentl] *adj*: *parental responsibility.*

'**parenthood** *n* the state of being a parent.

parenthesis [pə'renθəsis] – *pl* **pa'rentheses** [-si:z] – *n* **1** a word or group of words within a sentence, which gives a comment *etc* and *usu* separates from the rest of the sentence by brackets, dashes *etc*: *I asked John (my friend John Smith) to come and see me.* **2** a round bracket used to mark the seperate part of such a sentence. **parenthetical** [parən'θetikəl] *adj*: *a parenthetical remark.*

in parentheses said, written *etc* as a parenthesis.

pariah [pə'raiə] *n* a person driven out of a group or community; an outcast: *Because of his political beliefs he became a pariah in the district.*

parish ['pariʃ] *n* a district or area with a particular church and priest or minister: *Our house is in the parish of St Mary('s)*; (*also adj*) *parish affairs.*

park [pa:k] *n* **1** a public piece of ground with grass and trees: *The children go to the park every morning to play.* **2** the land surrounding a large country house: *Deer run wild in the park surrounding the mansion.* – *v* **1** to stop and leave (a motor car *etc*) for a time: *He parked in front of our house.*

'**parking-lot** *n* (*Amer*) a car park.

'**parking-meter** *n* a coin-operated meter beside which a car may be parked for the number of minutes or hours shown on the meter.

parliament ['pa:ləmənt] *n* the highest law-making council of a nation – in Britain, the House of Commons and the House of Lords, considered together: *an Act of Parliament.* ,**parlia'mentary** [-'men-] *adj.*

parlour, (*Amer*) **parlor** ['pa:lə] *n* **1** a room in a (*usu* small) house used for sitting in and for entertaining guests. **2** room(s) for cus-

tomers *usu* of firms providing particular services: *a beauty parlo(u)r*; *a funeral parlo(u)r.*

'**parlour-maid** *n* a female servant who opens the door to visitors, serves tea *etc.*

parody ['parədi] – *pl* '**parodies** – *n* **1** an amusing imitation of a serious author's style of writing: *He writes parodies of John Donne's poems.* **2** a very bad imitation: *a parody of the truth.* – *v* to make a parody of (something or someone).

parquet ['pa:kei, (*Amer*) pa:r'kei] *n* a type of floor-covering made of pieces of wood arranged in a design: *flooring made of parquet*; (*also adj*) *a parquet floor.*

parrot ['parət] *n* a kind of bird found in warm countries, *esp* in South America, with a hooked bill and *usu* brightly-coloured feathers, that can be taught to imitate human speech.

parsley ['pa:sli] *n* a kind of herb used in cookery to decorate or add flavour to food.

parsnip ['pa:snip] *n* a plant with a yellowish-white root used as a vegetable. **2** the root.

parson ['pa:sn] *n* **1** the priest, minister *etc* of a parish, *usu* of the Church of England. **2** any priest, minister *etc.*

'**parsonage** [-nidʒ] *n* the house in which the parson of a parish lives.

part [pa:t] *n* **1** something which, together with other things, makes a whole; a piece: *We spent part of the time at home and part at the seaside.* **2** an equal division: *He divided the cake into three parts.* **3** a character in a play *etc*: *She played the part of the queen.* **4** the words, actions *etc* of a character in a play *etc*: *He learned his part quickly.* **5** in music, the notes to be played or sung by a particular instrument or voice: *the violin part.* **6** a person's share, responsibility *etc* in doing something: *He played a great part in the government's decision.* – *v* to separate; to divide: *They parted (from each other) at the gate.*

'**parting** *n* **1** the act of leaving someone, saying goodbye *etc*: *Their final parting was at the station.* **2** a line dividing hair brushed in opposite directions on the head.

'**partly** *adv* to a certain extent but not completely: *She was tired, partly because of the journey and partly because of the heat.*

,**part-'time** *adj, adv* not taking one's whole time; for only a few hours or days a week: *a part-time job*; *She works part-time.*

in part partly: *He agreed that he was in part responsible for the accident.*

part company 1 to go in different directions: *We parted company at the bus-stop.* **2** to leave each other or end a friendship, partnership *etc.*

part of speech one of the groups into which

words are divided (*eg* noun, verb, adjective *etc*).

part with to give away or be separated from: *He doesn't like parting with money.*

take in good part to accept without being hurt or offended: *He took their jokes in good part.*

take someone's part to support someone (in an argument *etc*): *She always takes his part.*

take part in to be one of a group of people doing something, to take an active share in (*eg* playing a game, performing a play, holding a discussion *etc*): *He never took part in arguments.*

partake [pa:'teik] – *pt* **partook** [-'tuk]: *ptp* **par'taken** – *v* to take part: *They all partook in the final decision.*

partial ['pa:ʃəl] *adj* 1 not complete; in part only: *a partial success; partial payment.* 2 having a liking for (a person or thing): *He is very partial to cheese.*

,parti'ality [-ʃi'aləti] *n* 1 a liking for: *He has a partiality for cheese.* 2 the preferring of one person or side more than another: *He could not help showing his partiality for/towards his own team.*

participate [pa:'tisipeit] *v* to be one of a group of people actively doing something: *Did you participate in the discussion?* **par,tici'pation** *n*.

par'ticipant, par'ticipator *ns* a person who participates (in a particular activity): *the participants in the Olympic Games.*

particle ['pa:tikl] *n* a very small piece: *a particle of dust.*

particular [pə'tikjulə] *adj* 1 of a single definite person, thing *etc* thought of separately from all others: *this particular man/problem.* 2 more than ordinary: *Please take particular care of this letter.* 3 difficult to please: *He is very particular about his food.* **par'ticularly** *adv* more than usually: *He was particularly pleased to see his brother.*

par'ticulars *n pl* facts or details: *You must give them all the particulars about the accident.*

in particular more than others: *I liked this book in particular.*

partition [pə'tiʃən] *n* 1 something that divides, *eg* a light, often temporary, wall between rooms: *The office was divided in two by a wooden partition.* 2 the act of dividing; the state of being divided: *the partition of India.* – *v* to divide: *They partitioned the room (off) with a curtain.*

partner ['pa:tnə] *n* 1 a person who shares the ownership of a business *etc* with one or more others: *She was made a partner in the firm.* 2 one of two people who dance, play in a game *etc* together: *a tennis/dancing partner.* – *v* to be a partner to (someone): *He partnered his wife in the last dance.*

'partnership *n* 1 the state of being or becoming partners: *a business partnership; He entered into partnership with his brother.* 2 people playing together in a game: *The champions were defeated by the partnership of Jones and Smith in the men's doubles.*

party ['pa:ti] – *pl* **'parties** – *n* 1 a meeting of guests for entertainment, celebration *etc*: *a birthday party; She's giving/having a party tonight;* (*also adj*) *a party dress.* 2 a group of people with a particular purpose: *a party of tourists.* 3 a group of people with the same ideas and purposes, *esp* political: *a political party.*

pass [pa:s] *v* 1 to move towards and then beyond (something, by going past, through, by, over *etc*): *I pass the shops on my way to work; The procession passed along the corridor.* 2 to move, give *etc* from one person, state *etc* to another: *They passed the photographs around; The tradition is passed (on/down) from father to son.* 3 to go or be beyond: *This passes my understanding.* 4 (of vehicles *etc* on a road) to overtake: *The sports car passed me at a dangerous bend in the road.* 5 to spend (time): *They passed several weeks in the country.* 6 (of an official group, government *etc*) to accept or approve: *The government has passed a resolution.* 7 to give or announce (a judgement or sentence): *The magistrate passed judgement on the prisoner.* 8 to end or go away: *His sickness soon passed.* 9 (to judge to) be successful in (an examination *etc*): *I passed my driving test.* – *n* 1 a narrow path between mountains: *a mountain pass.* 2 a ticket or card allowing a person to do something, *eg* to travel free or to get in to a building: *You must show your pass before entering.* 3 a successful result in an examination, *esp* when below a distinction, honours *etc*: *There were ten passes and no fails.* 4 (in ball games) a throw, kick, hit *etc* of the ball from one player to another: *The centre-forward made a pass towards the goal.*

'passable *adj* 1 fairly good: *a passable tennis player.* 2 (of a river, road *etc*) able to be passed, travelled over *etc*: *The mud has made the roads no longer passable.*

'passing *adj* 1 going past: *a passing car.* 2 lasting only a short time: *a passing interest.* 3 (of something said) casual and not made as part of a serious talk about the subject: *a passing reference.*

,passer-'by – *pl* **,passers-'by** – *n* a person who is going past a place when something happens: *He asked the passers-by if they had seen the accident.*

'password *n* a secret word by which those who know it can recognize each other and be allowed to go past, enter *etc*: *He was not* allowed into the army camp because he did not know the password.

in passing while doing or talking about something else; without explaining fully what one means: *He told her the story, and said in passing that he did not completely believe it.*

let (something) pass to ignore something rather than take the trouble to argue: *I'll let that pass.*

pass as/for to be mistaken for or accepted as: *Some man-made materials could pass as silk; His nasty remarks pass for wit among his admirers.*

pass away to die: *Her grandmother passed away last night.*

pass the buck to give the responsibility or blame for something to someone else: *She always passes the buck if she is asked to do anything.*

pass by to go past (a particular place): *I was passing by when the bride arrived at the church; She passed by the hospital on the way to the library.*

pass off (of sickness, an emotion *etc*) to go away: *By the evening, his sickness had passed off and he felt better.*

pass (something or someone) off as to pretend that (something or someone) is (something or someone else): *He passed himself off as a journalist.*

pass on 1 to give to someone else (*usu* something which one has been given by a third person): *I passed on his message.* **2** to die: *His mother passed on yesterday.*

pass out 1 to faint: *I feel as though I'm going to pass out.* **2** to give to several different people: *The teacher passed out books to her class.*

pass over to ignore or overlook: *They passed him over for promotion.*

pass up not to accept (a chance, opportunity *etc*): *He passed up the offer of a good job.*

passed is the past tense of **to pass**: *He passed the scene of the accident.*
past means up to and beyond: *She walked past the shops.*

passage ['pasidʒ] *n* **1** a long narrow way through, *eg* a corridor through a building: *There was a dark passage leading down to the river between tall buildings.* **2** a part of a piece of writing or music: *That is my favourite passage from the Bible.* **3** (*usu* of time) the act of passing: *the passage of time.* **4** a journey by boat: *He paid for his passage by working as a steward.*

passenger ['pasindʒə] *n* a person who travels in any vehicle, boat, aeroplane *etc* (not the driver or anyone working there): *a passenger on a train;* (*also adj*) *a passenger train.*

passion ['paʃən] *n* very strong feeling, *esp* of

anger or love: *He argued with great passion; He has a passion for chocolate.*

'passionate [-nət] *adj* having very strong feelings; intense or emotional: *a passionate woman; passionate hatred.*

passive ['pasiv] *adj* **1** showing no interest, emotion *etc*, or not resisting an attack *etc*: *The villagers showed passive resistance to the enemy* (= They opposed their authority by disobedience *etc*, not by active opposition). **2** of the form of the verb used when the subject receives the action of the verb: *The boy was bitten by the dog.* **'passively** *adv*. **'passiveness, pas'sivity** *ns*.

passport ['pa:spo:t] *n* a document of identification, necessary for foreign travel: *a British passport.*

past [pa:st] *adj* **1** just finished: *the past year.* **2** over, finished or ended, of an earlier time than the present: *The time for discussion is past.* **3** (of the tense of a verb) indicating action in the past: *In 'He did it', the verb is in the past tense.* – *prep* **1** up to and beyond; by: *He ran past me.* **2** after: *It's past six o'clock.* – *adv* up to and beyond (a particular place, person *etc*): *The soldiers marched past.* – *n* **1** a person's earlier life or career, *esp* if secret or not respectable: *He never spoke about his past.* **2** the past tense: *a verb in the past.*

the past the time which was before the present: *In the past, houses were built of wood or stone.*

see also **passed**.

pasta ['pastə, (*Amer*) 'pa:-] *n* a dough used in Italian cooking for making spaghetti, macaroni *etc*.

paste [peist] *n* **1** a soft, damp mixture, *esp* one made up of glue and water and used for sticking pieces of paper *etc* together. **2** a mixture of flour, fat *etc* used for making pies, pastry *etc*. **3** a mixture made from some types of food: *almond paste.*

pastel ['pastəl, (*Amer*) pa'stel] *adj* (of colours) pale, containing a lot of white: *a soft pastel green.* – *n* **1** a kind of coloured pencil, made with chalk, which makes a pale colour. **2** a picture drawn with this kind of pencil.

pasteurize, -ise ['pastʃəraiz] *v* to heat food, *esp* milk, for a time to kill germs in it. **,pasteuri'zation, -s-** *n*.

pastille ['pastəl, (*Amer*) pa'sti:l] *n* a small sweet often containing medicine (*usu* for infections of the mouth or throat *etc*): *throat pastilles.*

pastime ['pa:staim] *n* an occupation which one enjoys and takes part in in one's spare time; a hobby: *Playing chess is his favourite pastime.*

pastor ['pa:stə] *n* a minister of religion, *esp* of the Protestant church.
'**pastoral** *adj* of country life: *a pastoral scene.* 2 of a pastor, or his work: *pastoral responsibilities.*

pastry ['peistri] – *pl* '**pastries** – *n* 1 flour paste used in making pies, tarts *etc.* 2 a pie, tart *etc* made with this: *Danish pastries.*

pasture ['pa:stʃə] *n* a field or area of ground covered with grass for cattle *etc* to eat: *The horses were out in the pasture.*

pat [pat] *n* 1 a light, gentle blow or touch, *usu* with the palm of the hand and showing affection: *She gave the child a pat on the head.* 2 (of butter) a small piece; a lump. – *v* – *pt, ptp* '**patted** – to strike gently with the palm of the hand, *usu* as a sign of affection: *He patted the horse's neck.* – *adv* (*often* **off pat**) memorized, prepared and ready to be said: *He had the answer (off) pat.*

patch [patʃ] *n* 1 a piece of material sewn on to cover a hole: *She sewed a patch on the knee of her jeans.* 2 a small piece of ground: *a vegetable patch.* – *v* to mend (clothes *etc*) by sewing on pieces of material: *She patched the (hole in the) child's trousers.*
'**patchy** *adj* not all the same; varying in quality: *patchy work.* '**patchiness** *n.*
'**patchwork** *n* cloth made by sewing small pieces of material together: *a skirt made of patchwork*; (*also adj*) *a patchwork quilt.*
patch up 1 to mend, *esp* quickly and temporarily: *He patched up the roof with bits of wood.* 2 to settle (a quarrel): *They soon patched up their disagreement.*

patent ['peitənt, (*Amer*) 'pa-] *n* an official licence from the government giving one person or business the right to make and sell a particular article and to prevent others from doing the same: *She took out a patent on her design*; (*also adj*) *a patent process.* – *v* to obtain a patent for; *He patented his new invention.*

paternal [pə'tə:nl] *adj* 1 of or like a father: *paternal feelings.* 2 among one's father's relatives: *Her paternal grandmother.*
pa'ternity *n* the fact or state of being a father.

path [pa:θ] – *pl* **paths** [pa:ðz] – *n* 1 a way made across the ground by the passing of people or animals: *There is a path through the fields; a mountain path.* 2 (any place on) the line along which someone or something is moving: *She stood right in the path of the bus.*
'**pathway** *n* a path.

pathetic [pə'θetik] *adj* 1 causing pity: *The lost dog was a pathetic sight.* 2 weak and useless: *a pathetic attempt.* **pa'thetically** *adv.*

pathology [pə'θolədʒi] *n* the science of diseases. **pa'thologist** *n.* ,**patho'logical** *adj.* ,**patho'logically** *adv.*

patient ['peiʃənt] *adj* suffering delay, pain, irritation *etc* quietly and without complaining: *It will be your turn soon – you must just be patient!* – *n* a person who is being treated by a doctor, dentist *etc*: *The hospital had too many patients.*
'**patiently** *adv.*
'**patience** *n* 1 the ability or willingness to be patient: *Patience is a virtue.* 2 a card game *usu* played by one person: *She often plays patience.*

patrial ['peitriəl] *n* a citizen of the UK, a British colony or the British Commonwealth, who for certain reasons (*eg* because one of his parents was born in the UK) has the right to enter and stay in the UK. ,**patri'ality** [-'a-] *n.*

patriarch ['peitria:k] *n* 1 the male head of a family or tribe. 2 *esp* in the Eastern Orthodox Church, a high-ranking bishop. ,**patri'archal** *adj* of, like, ruled by *etc* a patriarch or patriarchs: *a patriarchal society/church.*

patricide ['patrisaid] *n* 1 the act of killing one's father. 2 a person who does such an act.

patrimony ['patriməni] *n* property passed on to a person by his or her father or ancestors: *This farm is part of my patrimony.*

patriot ['peitriət] *n* a person who loves (and serves) his country: *Many terrorists consider themselves to be patriots fighting for freedom.*
patriotic [patri'otik, (*esp Amer*) pei-] *adj* (*neg* **un-**) having or showing great love for one's country: *He is so patriotic that he refuses to buy anything made abroad.* ,**patri'otically** *adv.*
'**patriotism** ['pa-, (*esp Amer*) 'pei-] *n* (the showing of) great love for one's country.

patrol [pə'troul] – *pt, ptp* **pa'trolled** – *v* to watch or protect (an area) by moving continually around or through it: *Soldiers patrolled the streets.* – *n* 1 a group of people *etc* who patrol an area: *They came across several army patrols in the hills.* 2 the act of watching or guarding by patrolling: *The soldiers went out on patrol*; (*also adj*) *patrol duty.*

patron ['peitrən] *n* 1 a person who supports (often with money) an artist, musician, writer, form of art *etc*: *He's a patron of the arts.* 2 a (regular) customer of a shop *etc*: *The manager said that he knew all his patrons.*
patronage ['patrənidʒ, (*Amer*) 'pei-] *n* the support given by a patron.
'**patronize, -ise** ['pa-, (*Amer*) 'pei-] *v* 1 to behave towards (someone) in a way which is kind and friendly but which nevertheless shows that one thinks oneself to be more important, clever *etc* than that person: *He's*

a nice fellow but he does patronize his assistants. **2** to visit (a shop, theatre, society *etc*) regularly: *That's not a shop I patronize nowadays.* '**patronizing, -s-** *adj.* '**patronizingly, -s-** *adv.*

patron saint a saint who protects a particular person, group of people, country *etc*: *St Andrew is the patron saint of Scotland.*

patter ['patə] *v* (of rain, footsteps *etc*) to make a quick, tapping sound: *She heard the mice pattering behind the walls.* – *n* the sound made in this way: *the patter of rain on the roof.*

pattern ['patən] *n* **1** a model or guide for making something: *a dress-pattern.* **2** a repeated decoration or design on material *etc*: *The dress is nice but I don't like the pattern.* **3** an example suitable to be copied: *the pattern of good behaviour.*

'**patterned** *adj* with a decoration or design on it; not plain: *Is her new carpet patterned?*

paunch [pɔ:ntʃ] *n* a large, round stomach: *He developed quite a paunch.*

'**paunchy** *adj* having a paunch: *He's become quite paunchy.*

pauper ['pɔ:pə] *n* a very poor person: *Her husband died a pauper.*

pause [pɔ:z] *n* **1** a short stop, break or interval (while doing something): *There was a pause in the conversation.* **2** the act of making a musical note or rest slightly longer than normal, or a mark showing that this is to be done. – *v* to stop talking, working *etc* for a short time: *They paused for a cup of tea.*

pave [peiv] *v* to cover (a street, path *etc*) with (*usu* large) flat stones, concrete *etc* to make a flat surface for walking on *etc*: *He wants to pave the garden.*

'**pavement** *n* (*Amer* '**sidewalk**) a paved surface, *esp* a paved footpath along the sides of a road for people to walk on.

'**paving-stone** *n* a large flat stone or piece of concrete used for paving.

pavilion [pə'viljən] *n* a building on a sports ground in which players change their clothes, store equipment *etc*: *a cricket pavilion.*

paw [pɔ:] *n* the foot of an animal with claws or nails: *The dog had a thorn in its paw.* – *v* **1** (of an animal) to touch, hit *etc* (*usu* several times) with a paw or paws: *The cat was pawing (at) the dead mouse.* **2** (of an animal) to hit (the ground, *usu* several times) with a hoof, *usu* a front hoof: *The horse pawed (at) the ground.*

pawn [pɔ:n] *v* to give (an article of value) to a pawnbroker in exchange for money (which may be repaid at a later time to get the article back): *I had to pawn my watch to pay the bill.* – *n* **1** in chess, one of the small pieces of lowest rank. **2** a person who is

used by another person for his own gain, advantage *etc*: *She was a pawn in his ambitious plans.*

'**pawnbroker** *n* a person who lends money in exchange for pawned articles.

'**pawnshop** *n* a pawnbroker's place of business.

in pawn having been pawned: *His watch is in pawn.*

pay [pei] – *pt, ptp* **paid** – *v* **1** to give (money) to (someone) in exchange for goods, services *etc*: *He paid $5 for the book.* **2** to return (money that is owed): *It's time you paid your debts.* **3** to suffer punishment (for): *You'll pay for that remark!* **4** to be useful or profitable (to): *Crime doesn't pay.* **5** to give (attention, homage, respect *etc*): *Pay attention!*; *to pay one's respects.* – *n* money given or received for work *etc*; wages: *How much pay do you get?*

'**payable** *adj* which may be or must be paid: *The account is payable at the end of the month.*

pay'ee *n* a person to whom money is (to be) paid.

'**payment** *n* **1** money *etc* paid: *The radio can be paid for in ten weekly payments.* **2** the act of paying: *He gave me a book in payment for my kindness.*

'**pay-packet** *n* an envelope containing a person's wages: *The manager handed out the pay-packets.*

'**pay-roll** *n* **1** a list of all the workers in a factory *etc*: *We have 450 people on the payroll.* **2** the total amount of money to be paid to all the workers: *The thieves stole the payroll.*

pay back 1 to give back (to someone something that one has borrowed): *I'll pay you back as soon as I can.* **2** to punish: *I'll pay you back for that!*

pay off 1 to pay in full and discharge (workers) because they are no longer needed: *Hundreds of steel-workers have been paid off.* **2** to have good results: *His hard work paid off.*

pay up to give (money) to someone, *eg* in order to pay a debt: *You have three days to pay up* (= You must pay up within three days).

pea [pi:] *n* **1** the round seed of a kind of climbing plant, eaten as a vegetable: *We had roast beef, potatoes and peas for dinner.* **2** the plant which produces these seeds: *We planted peas and beans this year.*

peace [pi:s] *n* **1** (*sometimes with* **a**) (a time of) freedom from war; (a treaty or agreement which brings about) the end or stopping of a war: *Does our country want peace or war?*; (*also adj*) *a peace treaty.* **2** freedom from disturbance; quietness: *I need some peace and quiet.*

'peaceable *adj* liking peace; not fighting, quarrelling *etc*: *He's a peaceable person.* **'peaceably** *adv.*

'peaceful *adj* quiet; calm; without worry or disturbance: *It's very peaceful in the country.* **'peacefully** *adv.* **'peacefulness** *n.*

'peacemaker *n* a person who tries to make peace between enemies, people who are quarrelling *etc*: *When my brother and sister quarrel I act as peacemaker.*

'peace-offering *n* something offered or given to make peace: *She took him a drink as a peace-offering.*

'peacetime *n* a time when there is no war: *Even in peacetime, a soldier's life is hard.*

at peace not at war; not fighting: *The two countries were at peace.*

in peace 1 without disturbance: *Why can't you leave me in peace?* **2** not wanting to fight: *They said they came in peace.*

make peace to agree to end a war: *The two countries finally made peace* (*with each other*).

peace of mind freedom from worry *etc.*

peach [piːtʃ] *n* **1** a kind of juicy, soft-skinned fruit: *She doesn't like peaches*; (*also adj*) *a peach tree.* **2** (*also adj*) (of) the orange-pink colour of the fruit: *Would you call that colour peach?*; *The walls are painted peach.*

peacock ['piːkok] – *fem* **'peahen** [-hen] – *n* a kind of large bird, the male of which is noted for its magnificent tail-feathers.

peak [piːk] *n* **1** the pointed top of a mountain or hill: *snow-covered peaks.* **2** the highest, greatest, busiest *etc* point, time *etc*: *He was at the peak of his career.* **3** the front part of a cap which shades the eyes: *The boy wore a cap with a peak.* – *v* to reach the highest, greatest, busiest *etc* point, time *etc*: *Prices peaked in July and then began to fall.*

peaked *adj* having a peak: *a peaked cap.*

'peaky *adj* looking pale and unhealthy: *You look peaky today.*

peal [piːl] *n* **1** the ringing of (a set of) bells. **2** a set of (*usu* church) bells. **3** a loud noise: *peals of laughter/thunder.* – *v* to (cause to) ring or sound loudly: *Thunder pealed through the valley.*

peanut ['piːnʌt] *n* (*also* **'groundnut** *or* **monkey nut**) a type of nut that looks rather like a pea.

pear [peə] *n* a type of fruit of the apple family, round at the bottom and narrowing towards the stem or top: *She's very fond of pears*; (*also adj*) *a pear tree.*

'pear-shaped *adj.*

pearl [pəːl] *n* a valuable, hard, round object formed by oysters and several other shellfish: *The necklace consists of three strings of pearls*; (*also adj*) *a pearl necklace.*

'pearly *adj* like pearls: *pearly teeth.*

'pearl-diver, 'pearl-fisher *ns* a person who dives or fishes for pearls.

peasant ['peznt] *n* a person who lives and works on the land, *esp* in a poor, primitive or underdeveloped area: *Many peasants died during the drought*; (*also adj*) *a peasant farmer.*

'peasantry *n* peasants as a group; the peasants of a particular place: *What part did the peasantry play in the Russian revolution?*

pebble ['pebl] *n* a small, *usu* smooth stone: *small pebbles on the beach.* **'pebbly** *adj.*

peck [pek] *v* **1** (of birds) to strike or pick up with the beak, *usu* in order to eat: *The birds pecked at the corn*; *The bird pecked his hand.* **2** to eat very little: *She just pecks (at) her food.* **3** to kiss quickly and briefly: *She pecked her mother on the cheek.* – *n* **1** a tap or bite with the beak: *The bird gave him a painful peck on the hand.* **2** a brief kiss: *a peck on the cheek.*

'peckish *adj* rather hungry: *I feel a bit peckish.*

pectoral ['pektərəl] *adj* of or on the breast or chest: *the pectoral muscles.*

peculiar [pi'kjuːljə] *adj* **1** strange; odd: *peculiar behaviour.* **2** belonging to one person, place or thing in particular and to no other: *customs peculiar to France.* **pe,culi'arity** [-'a-] – *pl* **pe,culi'arities** – *n.* **pe'culiarly** *adv.*

pedal ['pedl] *n* a lever worked by the foot, as on a bicycle, piano, organ *etc*: *the brake pedal in a car.* – *v* – *pt, ptp* **'pedalled,** (*Amer*) **'pedaled** – to move (something) by means of pedals: *He pedalled (his bicycle) down the road.*

to **pedal** (not **paddle**) a bicycle.

pedant ['pedənt] *n* **1** a person who makes a great show of his knowledge. **2** a person who attaches too much importance to minor details. **pe'dantic** [-'dan-] *adj.* **pe'dantically** *adv.* **'pedantry** *n.*

peddle ['pedl] *v* to go from place to place or house to house selling (small objects): *Gypsies often peddle* (*goods*) *from door to door.* **'pedlar,** (*also, esp Amer*) **'peddler** *n* a person who peddles: *I bought it from a pedlar.*

pedestal ['pedistl] *n* the foot or base of a column, statue *etc*: *The statue fell off its pedestal.*

pedestrian [pi'destriən] *n* a person who travels on foot: *Three pedestrians were hit by the car.* – *adj* ordinary; rather boring or unexciting: *a pedestrian account.*

pediatrics *etc see* **paediatrics.**

pedigree ['pedigriː] *n* **1** a list of the ancestors from whom a person or animal is descended: *a dog's pedigree.* **2** distinguished descent or ancestry: *a man of pedigree.* – *adj* (of an animal) pure-bred; from a long line of ancestors of the same breed: *a herd of pedigree cattle.*

pedlar see **peddle**.

peek [pi:k] v to look, esp quickly and in secret: He opened the door slightly and peeked out; Cover your eyes and don't peek. – n a quick look: Take a peek through the window.

peel [pi:l] v **1** to take off the skin or outer covering of (a fruit or vegetable): She peeled the potatoes. **2** to take off or come off in small pieces: The paint is beginning to peel (off). – n the skin of certain fruits, esp oranges, lemons etc.
'**peeler** n a tool etc that peels (something): a potato-peeler.
'**peelings** n pl the strips or pieces of skin peeled off an apple, potato etc: potato peelings.

peep[1] [pi:p] v **1** to look through a narrow opening or from behind something: She peeped through the window. **2** to look quickly and in secret: He peeped at the answers at the back of the book. – n a quick look (usu in secret): She took a peep at the visitor.
'**peep-hole** n a hole (in a door etc) through which one can look.

peep[2] [pi:p] v to make a high pitched sound: The car horns were peeping. – n such a sound: the peep of a car horn.

peer[1] [piə] n **1** a nobleman (in Britain, one from the rank of baron upwards). **2** a person's equal in rank, merit or age: The child was disliked by his peers; (also adj) He is more advanced than the rest of his peer group.
'**peerage** [-ridʒ] n **1** a peer's title or status: He was granted a peerage. **2** (often with pl verb when considered as a number of separate individuals) all noblemen as a group: The peerage has/have many responsibilities.
'**peeress** n **1** the wife or widow of a peer. **2** a woman who is a peer in her own right.
'**peerless** adj without equal; better than all others: Sir Galahad was a peerless knight.

peer[2] [piə] v to look with difficulty: He peered at the small writing.

peevish ['pi:viʃ] adj easily made angry; irritable; frequently complaining: a peevish old man. '**peevishly** adv. '**peevishness** n.
peeved adj angry; annoyed: She was peeved about it.

peg [peg] n **1** a usu short, not very thick, piece of wood, metal etc used to fasten or mark something: There were four pegs stuck in the ground. **2** a hook on a wall or door for hanging clothes etc on: Hang your clothes on the pegs in the cupboard. **3** (also '**clothes-peg**) a wooden or plastic clip for holding clothes etc to a rope while drying. – v – pt, ptp **pegged** – to fasten with a peg: She pegged the clothes on the washing-line.
take (someone) down a peg (or two) to make

(a proud person) more humble: We must find some way of taking her down a peg or two.

pelican ['pelikən] n a kind of large water-bird with a large beak with a pouch for carrying fish.

pellet ['pelit] n a little ball or similarly-shaped object: He bought a box of lead pellets for his gun.

pell-mell [pel'mel] adv quickly and in disorder or great confusion: The children rushed in pell-mell.

pelmet ['pelmit] n a strip of cloth, wood etc hiding a curtain rail.

pelt [pelt] v **1** to throw (things) at: The children pelted each other with snowballs. **2** to run very fast: He pelted down the road. **3** (of rain; sometimes also of hailstones) to fall very heavily: You can't leave now – it's pelting (down).
at full pelt (running) as fast as possible: They set off down the road at full pelt.

pelvis ['pelvis] n the framework of bone around the body below the waist. '**pelvic** adj.

pen[1] [pen] n a small enclosure, usu for animals: a sheep-pen.

pen[2] [pen] n an instrument for writing in ink: My pen needs a new nib.
'**pen-friend**, '**pen-pal** ns a usu young person (usu living abroad) with whom another (usu young) person regularly exchanges letters: My daughter has pen-friends in India and Spain.
'**pen-knife** n a pocket-knife with blades which fold into the handle.
'**pen-name** n a name used by a writer instead of his own name: Samuel Clemens used the pen-name of Mark Twain.
pen-pal see **pen-friend** above.

penalize, **-ise** ['pi:nəlaiz] v **1** to punish (someone) for doing something wrong (eg breaking a rule in a game), eg by the loss of points etc or by the giving of some advantage to an opponent: The child was penalized for her untidy handwriting. **2** to punish (some wrong action etc) in this way: Any attempt at cheating will be heavily penalized.

penalty ['penlti] – pl '**penalties** – n **1** a punishment for doing wrong, breaking a contract etc: They did wrong and they will have to pay the penalty; The death penalty has been abolished in this country. **2** in sport etc, a disadvantage etc that must be suffered for breaking the rules etc: The referee awarded the team a penalty; (also adj) a penalty kick (=in football, a chance to kick the ball towards the goal from a spot in front of the goal without being tackled by members of the other team).

penance ['penəns] n punishment that a person suffers willingly to show that he is sorry for something wrong he has done: *He did penance for his sins.*

pence *see* penny.

pencil ['pensl] *n* a long, thin instrument (*usu* of wood) containing a thin stick of graphite or some similar solid substance for writing or drawing: *This pencil needs sharpening/to be sharpened; He wrote in pencil;* (*also adj*) *a pencil sharpener.* – *v* – *pt, ptp* 'pencilled, (*Amer*) 'penciled – to write or draw with a pencil: *He pencilled an outline of the house.*

pendant ['pendənt] *n* **1** an ornament hung from a necklace: *a pendant hanging from a silver chain.* **2** the ornament and the necklace together: *She fastened a gold pendant round her neck.*

pendulum ['pendjuləm, (*Amer*) -dʒu-] *n* a swinging weight, *eg* that which operates the mechanism of a clock: *The little girl watched the pendulum swing back and forwards;* (*also adj*) *a pendulum clock.*

penetrate ['penitreit] *v* to move, go or make a way into, past, or through (something): *The bullet penetrated his shoulder; Their minds could not penetrate the mystery.*
'penetrating *adj* **1** (of a voice, sound *etc*) loud and clear; easily heard: *a penetrating voice.* **2** (of a glance, stare *etc*) hard and searching, as if trying, or able, to see into a person's mind: *a penetrating glance.* 'penetratingly *adv.*
,pene'tration *n.*

penguin ['peŋgwin] *n* a large sea-bird which is found in Antarctic regions and which cannot fly.

penicillin [peni'silin] *n* a kind of antibiotic medicine which kills many harmful bacteria: *The doctor gave her penicillin;* (*also adj*) *penicillin injections.*

peninsula [pə'ninsjulə] *n* a piece of land that is almost surrounded by water: *the Malay peninsula.*
pe'ninsular *adj* of or like a peninsula.

penis ['pi:nis] *n* the male sexual organ in humans and many animals.

pennant ['penənt], (*also* **pennon** ['penən]) *n* a small flag, *usu* in the shape of a long narrow triangle: *The boy had fastened a brightly-coloured pennant to the front of his bike.*

penny ['peni] – *pls* **pence** [pens], 'pennies – *n* **1** in British currency, the hundredth part of £1: *It costs seventy-five pence; Oranges, 12p each.* **2** in certain countries, a coin of low value. **3** the value of such a coin.
'penniless *adj* very poor; with little or no money: *a penniless old man.*

pension ['penʃən] *n* a sum of money paid regularly to a widow, a person who has retired from work, a soldier who has been seriously injured in a war *etc*: *He lives on his pension; a retirement pension.*
'pensioner *n* a person who receives a pension,

esp (**old age pensioner**) one who receives a retirement pension.
pension off to allow to retire, or to dismiss, with a pension: *They pensioned him off when they found a younger man for the job.*

pensive ['pensiv] *adj* thinking deeply (about something): *a pensive mood.* 'pensively *adv.* 'pensiveness *n.*

*****pentagon** ['pentəgən, (*Amer*) -gon] *n* a 5-sided geometrical figure. pen'tagonal [-'ta-] *adj.*

pentathlon [pen'taθlən] *n* a competition in the Olympic games *etc* which consists of contests in swimming, cross-country riding and running, fencing and pistol-shooting.

penthouse ['penthaus] *n* a (*usu* luxurious) flat at the top of a building: *That apartment building has a beautiful penthouse;* (*also adj*) *a penthouse flat.*

people ['pi:pl] *n pl* **1** persons: *There were three people in the room.* **2** men and women in general: *People often say such things.* **3** (*n sing*) a nation or race: *all the peoples of this world.*
the people the ordinary people of a country as opposed to the aristocracy *etc*: *government for the people by the people.*

people is usually plural: *The people waiting at the airport were impatient.*
people is singular, and has the plural **peoples**, when it means a nation: *a defeated people; the peoples of eastern Europe.*

pep [pep] *n* an informal word for energy: *full of pep.*
'pep-talk *n* a talk intended to arouse enthusiasm, or to make people work harder, better *etc*: *The director gave all the staff a pep-talk.*

pepper ['pepə] *n* **1** the dried, powdered berries of a certain plant, used for seasoning food: *white/black pepper; This soup has too much pepper in it.* **2** the plant bearing these berries: *a pepper plant.* **3** any of several red, yellow, or green, hollow seed-containing fruits used as food: *red peppers stuffed with rice.* **4** any of the plants which bear these. – *v* **1** to put pepper in or on (some food): *You don't have to pepper the soup.* **2** (*with* **with**) to throw, fire *etc* many, *usu* small, objects at (someone): *He peppered them with bullets.*
'peppery *adj* **1** (of food) containing a lot of pepper: *The soup is too peppery.* **2** easily made angry: *a peppery old man.*
'peppercorn *n* the berry of the pepper plant.
'pepper-mill *n* a small container in which peppercorns are ground into a powder.
'peppermint *n* **1** a flavouring taken from a type of plant and used in sweets *etc.* **2** (*sometimes abbreviated* **mint**) a sweet flavoured with peppermint: *The little boy had a bag of peppermints.*

per [pə:] *prep* **1** out of: *We have less than one mistake per page.* **2** for each: *The dinner will cost $15 per person.* **3** in each: *six times per week.*

per cent [pə'sent] (*often written* % *with figures*) (of numbers, amounts *etc*) stated as a fraction of one hundred: *Twenty-five per cent of one hundred and twenty is thirty; 25% of the people did not reply to our letters.*

perceive [pə'siːv] *v* to be or become aware of (something); to understand; to realize: *She perceived that he was tired.*

percentage [pə'sentidʒ] *n* **1** an amount, number or rate given as a fraction of one hundred: *We've expressed all these figures as percentages.* **2** a part or proportion of something: *A large percentage of the population can't read or write.*

perception [pə'sepʃən] *n* the ability to see, understand *etc* clearly: *a man of great perception.*

per'ceptive [-tiv] *adj* able to see, understand *etc* clearly: *a very perceptive man.* **per'ceptively** *adv.* **per'ceptiveness** *n.*

perch [pə:tʃ] *n* **1** a branch *etc* on which a bird sits or stands: *The pigeon would not fly down from its perch.* **2** any high seat or position: *He looked down from his perch on the roof.* – *v* **1** (of birds) to go to (a perch); to sit or stand on (a perch): *The bird flew up and perched on the highest branch of the tree.* **2** to put, or be, in a high seat or position: *He perched the child on his shoulder; They perched on the fence.*

percussion [pə'kʌʃən] *n* **1** (in an orchestra, the group of people who play) musical instruments in which the sound is produced by striking them *eg* drums, cymbals *etc*: *He plays (the) percussion in the orchestra; (also adj) a percussion instrument.* **2** the striking of one hard object against another: *A gun is fired by means of percussion.*

per'cussionist *n* a person who plays percussion instruments in an orchestra *etc.*

perennial [pə'reniəl] *n, adj* (a plant) which lasts for more than two years: *Daffodils are perennial plants; They are perennials.*

perfect ['pə:fikt] *adj* **1** without fault or flaw; excellent: *a perfect day for a holiday; a perfect rose.* **2** exact: *a perfect copy.* **3** very great; complete: *a perfect stranger.* – [pə'fekt] *v* to make perfect: *He went to France to perfect his French.*

per'fection [-ʃən] *n* the state of being perfect: *Absolute perfection in a dictionary is rare.*

per'fectionist [-ʃə-] *n* a person who is only satisfied if what he is doing is perfect: *She's a perfectionist – her work is perfect in every detail.*

'perfectly *adv* **1** without mistakes or flaws: *She performed the dance perfectly.* **2** very; completely: *He was perfectly happy.*

perforate ['pə:fəreit] *v* to make a hole or holes in, *esp* a line of small holes in paper, so that it may be torn easily: *Sheets of postage stamps are perforated.* **'perforated** *adj.*

,perfo'ration *n* **1** a small hole, or a number or line of small holes, made in a sheet of paper *etc*: *The purpose of the perforation(s) is to make the paper easier to tear.* **2** the act of perforating or being perforated.

perform [pə'fo:m] *v* **1** to do, *esp* with care or as a duty: *The doctor performed the operation.* **2** to act (in the theatre *etc*) or do anything musical, theatrical *etc* to entertain an audience: *The company will perform a Greek play; She performed on the violin.*

per'formance *n* **1** the doing of something: *He is very conscientious in the performance of his duties.* **2** the way in which something or someone performs: *His performance in the exams was not very good.* **3** something done on stage *etc*: *The company gave a performance of 'Othello'; His last three performances have not been very good.*

per'former *n* a person who performs, *esp* theatrically or musically.

perfume ['pə:fjuːm] *n* **1** a sweet smell or fragrance: *the perfume of roses.* **2** a liquid, cream *etc* which has a sweet smell when put on the skin, hair, clothes *etc*: *She loves French perfume(s).* – [pə'fjuːm] *v* **1** to put perfume on or in: *She perfumed her hair.* **2** to give a sweet smell to: *Flowers perfumed the air.*

per'fumery [-'fjuː-] – *pl* **per'fumeries** – *n* a shop where perfume is sold or a factory where it is made.

perhaps [pə'haps] *adv* possibly: *Perhaps it will rain.*

peril ['peril] *n* great danger: *You are in great peril; The explorers knew they would face many perils.*

'perilous *adj* very dangerous: *a perilous journey.* **'perilousness** *n.*

'perilously *adv* dangerously: *He came perilously close to death.*

perimeter [pə'rimitə] *n* the outside edge of any area: *the perimeter of the city; the perimeter of a circle.*

period ['piəriəd] *n* **1** any length of time: *a period of three days; a period of waiting.* **2** a stage in the Earth's development, an artist's development, in history *etc*: *the Pleistocene period; the modern period.* **3** the punctuation mark (.), put at the end of a sentence; a full stop. – *adj* (of furniture, costumes *etc*) of or from the same or appropriate time in history; antique or very old: *period costumes; His house is full of period furniture* (= antique furniture).

,peri'odic [-'o-] *adj* **1** happening, done *etc* occasionally: *He suffers from periodic fits of depression.* **2** (*also* **,peri'odical**) happening, done *etc* at regular intervals: *periodical reports.*

peri'odically *adv*: *We see each other periodically.*

peri'odical [-'o-] *n* a magazine which is issued regularly (every week, month *etc*). – *adj see* **periodic.**

periphery [pə'rifəri] *n* (*usu in sing with* **the**) the edge (of something): *The shops are on the periphery of the housing estate.* **pe'ripheral** *adj.*

periscope ['periskoup] *n* a tube containing mirrors, through which a person can look in order to see things which cannot be seen from the position the person is in, *esp* one used in submarines when under water to allow a person to see what is happening on the surface of the sea.

perish ['periʃ] *v* to die, *esp* in war, accident *etc*: *Many people perished in the earthquake.* **'perishable** *adj* (*esp* of food) likely to go bad quickly: *Butter is perishable.*

periwinkle ['periwiŋkl] *n* **1** a blue-flowered trailing plant. **2** a pink-flowered tropical herb.

perk [pə:k]: **perk up** to recover one's energy or cheerfulness: *I gave her a cup of tea and she soon perked up.* **perky** *adj* lively; cheerful: *You're in a perky mood.* **'perkily** *adv.* **'perkiness** *n.*

perm [pə:m] *n* a permanent wave in a person's hair: *She's had a perm.* – *v* to give a permanent wave to (hair): *She's had her hair permed.*

permanent ['pə:mənənt] *adj* lasting; not temporary: *After many years of travelling, they made a permanent home in England.* **'permanently** *adv.* **'permanence** *n.*

permanent wave *n* (*usu abbrev* **perm** [pə:m]) a wave or curl put into a person's hair by a special process and *usu* lasting for several months.

permeate ['pə:mieit] *v* (of a liquid, gas *etc*) to pass or spread into or through: *The water had permeated (through/into) the soil.*

permit [pə'mit] – *pt, ptp* **per'mitted** – *v* **1** to agree to (another person's action); to allow or let (someone do something): *Permit me to answer your question; Smoking is not permitted.* **2** to make possible: *My aunt's legacy permitted me to go to America.* – ['pə:mit] *n* a written order allowing a person to do something: *We have a permit to export our product.*

permission [pə'miʃən] *n* a written, spoken *etc* agreement that someone may do something: *She gave me permission to leave.*

permutation [pə:mju'teiʃən] *n* a particular order in which things are arranged: *We can write down these numbers in various permutations.*

perpendicular [pə:pən'dikjulə] *adj* standing,

rising *etc* straight upwards; vertical: *a perpendicular cliff.* **perpen'dicularly** *adv.*

perpetual [pə'petʃuəl] *adj* lasting for ever or for a long time; occurring repeatedly over a long time: *He lives in perpetual fear of being discovered; perpetual noise.* **per'petually** *adv.*

perplex [pə'pleks] *v* to puzzle or confuse (someone); to make (someone) unable to understand: *She was perplexed by his questions.* **per'plexed** *adj.* **per'plexedly** [-'pleksid-] *adv.*

per'plexity *n*: *She stood there in perplexity.*

persecute ['pə:sikju:t] *v* to make (someone) suffer, *esp* because of their opinions or beliefs: *They were persecuted for their religion.* **perse'cution** *n.* **'persecutor** *n.*

persevere [pə:si'viə] *v* to continue to (try to) do something in spite of difficulties: *He persevered in his task.* **perse'verance** *n.*

persist [pə'sist] *v* to keep doing, thinking *etc* in spite of opposition or difficulty; to continue asking, persuading *etc*: *It will not be easy but you will succeed if you persist; He didn't want to tell her, but she persisted (in asking).* **per'sistent** *adj*: *She was persistent in her demands/denials; persistent questions.* **per'sistently** *adv.* **per'sistence** *n.*

person ['pə:sn] – *pl* **people** ['pi:pl], **'persons** – *n* **1** a human being: *There's a person outside who wants to speak to you.* **2** a person's body: *He never carried money on his person* (=with him; in his pockets *etc*).

'personal *adj* **1** one's own: *This is his personal opinion; The matter will have my personal attention.* **2** private: *This is a personal matter between him and me.* **3** in person: *The Prime Minister will make a personal appearance.* **4** (making remarks which are) insulting, *esp* about a person's appearance *etc*: *personal remarks; Don't be personal!*

perso'nality – *pl* **perso'nalities** – *n* **1** a person's characteristics (of the mind, the emotions *etc*) as a whole: *a likeable/forceful* (=strong) *personality.* **2** strong, distinctive (*usu* attractive) character: *She is not beautiful but she has a lot of personality.* **3** a well-known person: *a television personality*; (*also adj*) *a personality cult* (=very great, *usu* too great, admiration for a person, *usu* a political leader).

'personally *adv* **1** in one's own opinion: *Personally, I prefer the other.* **2** doing something oneself, not having or letting someone else do it on one's behalf: *He thanked me personally.*

personal pronoun a pronoun which refers to the first, second or third persons: *I am going; He hit her. She saw you.*

in person personally; one's self, not represented by someone else: *The Queen was there in person; I'd like to thank him in person.*

personnel [pə:sə'nel] *n* the people employed in

a firm, factory, shop *etc*; the staff: *Our personnel are very highly trained*; (*also adj*) *a personnel manager*.

perspective [pə'spektiv] *n* **1** the way of drawing solid objects, natural scenes *etc* on a flat surface, so that they appear to have the correct shape, distance from each other *etc*: *Early medieval paintings lacked perspective.* **2** a picture or view of something: *I would like a clearer perspective of the situation.*

in/out of perspective 1 (of an object in a painting, photograph *etc*) having, or not having, the correct size, shape, distance *etc* in relation to the rest of the picture: *These houses don't seem to be in perspective in your drawing.* **2** with, or without, a correct or sensible understanding of something's true importance: *Try to get these problems in(to) perspective; Keep things in perspective.*

perspire [pə'spaiə] *v* to lose moisture through the skin when hot; to sweat: *He was perspiring in the heat.*

,perspi'ration [pə:spi-] *n* the moisture lost when perspiring: *The perspiration was running down his face.*

persuade [pə'sweid] *v* **1** to make (someone) (not) do something, by arguing with him or advising him: *We persuaded him (not) to go.* **2** to make (someone) certain (that something is the case); to convince: *We eventually persuaded him that we were serious.*

per'suasion [-ʒən] *n* the act of persuading: *He gave in to our persuasion and did what we wanted him to do.*

per'suasive [-siv] *adj* able to persuade: *He is a persuasive speaker; His arguments are persuasive.* **per'suasively** *adv.* **per'suasiveness** *n.*

perturb [pə'tə:b] *v* to make (someone) worried or anxious: *His threats didn't perturb her in the least.*

perverse [pə'və:s] *adj* **1** continuing to do, think *etc* something which one knows, or which one has been told, is wrong or unreasonable: *a perverse child.* **2** deliberately wrong; unreasonable: *perverse behaviour.* **per'versely** *adv.* **per'verseness, per'versity** *ns.*

pervert [pə'və:t] *v* **1** to change (something) from what is normal or right: *to pervert the course of justice.* **2** to lead (someone) to crime or to evil or immoral (*esp* sexually immoral) acts: *The man was accused of trying to pervert children.* – ['pə:və:t] *n* a person who does perverted (*esp* sexually immoral) acts.

per'version [-ʃən] *n* **1** (the) act of perverting: *a perversion of justice.* **2** a perverted act: *He is capable of any perversion.* **per'verted** *adj.*

peseta [pə'seitə] *n* the standard unit of currency in Spain.

peso ['peisou] – *pl* **'pesos** – *n* the standard unit

of currency in many South and Central American countries and in the Philippines.

pessimism ['pesimizəm] *n* the state of mind of a person who always expects bad things to happen.

'pessimist *n* a person who thinks in this way: *He is such a pessimist that he always expects the worst.* **,pessi'mistic** *adj.* **,pessi'mistically** *adv.*

pest [pest] *n* **1** a creature that is harmful or destructive, *eg* a mosquito, a rat *etc.* **2** a troublesome person or thing: *He is always annoying me – he is an absolute pest!*

'pesticide [-tisaid] *n* a substance that kills animal and insect pests.

pester ['pestə] *v* to annoy (someone) frequently or continually: *He pestered me with questions; She pestered him to help her.*

pestilence ['pestiləns] *n* any type of deadly epidemic disease, *esp* bubonic plague.

pestle ['pesl] *n* a tool like a small club, used for pounding things to powder, *esp* in a mortar: *He ground the nutmeg to a powder with a mortar and pestle.*

pet [pet] *n* **1** a tame animal *etc*, *usu* kept in the home: *She keeps a rabbit as a pet*; (*also adj*) *a pet rabbit/goldfish.* **2** (*esp* of children) a delightful or lovely person (used also as a term of affection): *Isn't that baby a pet?*; *Would you like some ice-cream, pet?* – *adj* favourite; greatest: *What is your pet ambition/hate?* – *v* – *pt, ptp* **'petted** – to stroke or caress (an animal) in a loving way: *The old lady sat by the fire petting her dog.*

pet name a particular name used to express affection: *His pet name for her was 'Kitten'.*

petal ['petl] *n* one of the *usu* brightly coloured leaf-like parts of a flower: *This rose has yellow petals edged with pink.*

peter ['pi:tə]: **peter out** to come gradually to an end: *As the river dried up our water-supply petered out; Their enthusiasm gradually petered out.*

petite [pə'ti:t] *adj* (of women and girls) small and neat: *That girl is very petite.*

petition [pə'tiʃən] *n* a formal request made to someone in authority and *usu* signed by a large number of people. – *v* to make such a request: *They petitioned the government for the release of the prisoners.* **pe'titioner** *n.*

petrify ['petrifai] *v* to make (someone) very frightened; to terrify: *The thought of having to make a speech petrified him.*

petro- [petrou] of or related to petrol, as in **petrochemical**.

petrochemical [petrə'kemikəl] *n* any chemical obtained from petroleum or natural gas: *the petrochemical industry.*

petrol ['petrəl] *n* (*Amer* **gas** *or* **gasoline**) a liquid got from petroleum, used as fuel for motor cars *etc*: *I'll stop at the next garage* *and buy more petrol*; (*also adj*) *a petrol engine*.

petroleum [pə'trouliəm] *n* oil in its raw, unrefined form, which is found in natural wells below the earth's surface and from which petrol, paraffin *etc* are obtained.

petroleum jelly a soft substance got from petroleum, used *eg* in ointments.

petrol pump (*Amer* **gasoline pump**) an apparatus at a petrol station which pumps petrol into cars *etc*, and which measures the amount of petrol it pumps.

petrol station (*esp Amer* **filling station** or informally **gas station**) a garage where petrol is sold.

petticoat ['petikout] *n* an underskirt: *a lace-trimmed petticoat*.

petty ['peti] *adj* **1** of very little importance; trivial: *petty details*. **2** deliberately nasty for a foolish or trivial reason: *petty behaviour*. **'pettily** *adv*. **'pettiness** *n*.

petty cash money used for small, everyday expenses in an office *etc*.

pew [pju:] *n* a seat or bench in a church.

pewter ['pju:tə] *n, adj* (of) a metal made by mixing tin and lead: *That mug is* (*made of*) *pewter*; *a pewter mug*.

phantom ['fantəm] *n* a ghost: *The castle is said to be haunted by a phantom*.

pharmacy ['fa:məsi] – *pl* **'pharmacies** – *n* **1** the preparation of medicines: *He is studying pharmacy*. **2** a shop *etc* where medicines are sold or given out: *the hospital pharmacy*.
,pharma'ceutical [-'sju:tikəl] *adj*.
'pharmacist *n* (*Amer* **'druggist**) a person who prepares and sells medicines; a chemist.

phase [feiz] *n* **1** a stage in the development of something: *We are entering a new phase in the war*. **2** one in a series of regular changes in the shape or appearance of something (*esp* the moon or a planet): *the phases of the moon*.

pheasant ['feznt] – *pls* **'pheasants, 'pheasant** – *n* **1** a type of long-tailed bird, the male of which has brightly-coloured feathers and certain types of which are often shot for sport: *a brace of pheasant*(*s*); *two pheasants*. **2** (the flesh of) the bird as food: *We had roast pheasant for dinner*.

phenomenon [fə'nomənən, (*Amer*) -non] – *pl* **phe'nomena** [-nə] – *n* a natural fact or event that is seen or happens regularly or frequently: *Magnetic attraction is an interesting phenomenon*.
phe'nomenal *adj* very unusual; remarkable: *a phenomenal amount of money*. **phe'nomenally** *adv*.

phew [fju:] *interj* a word or sound used to express disgust, tiredness, relief *etc*: *Phew! It's hot today!*

philanthropy [fi'lanθrəpi] *n* love for mankind, *usu* as shown by money given to, or work

done for, other people: *He shows his philanthropy by helping people who have been in prison*.
philanthropic [filən'θropik] *adj* giving money or other help *etc* to others: *a philanthropic person*; *a philanthropic act*.
phi'lanthropist *n* a philanthropic person.

philately [fi'latəli] *n* the study and collecting of postage-stamps. **,phila'telic** [-'te-] *adj*. **phi-'latelist** *n*.

philosophy [fi'losəfi] – *pl* **phi'losophies** – *n* **1** the search for knowledge and truth, *esp* about the nature of man and his behaviour and beliefs: *moral philosophy*. **2** a particular system of philosophical theories: *I have a very simple philosophy* (=attitude to life) – *enjoy life!*

phi'losopher *n* a person who studies philosophy, *esp* one who develops a particular set of theories: *Rousseau was a famous philosopher*.

,philo'sophical, ,philo'sophic [-'so-] *adjs* **1** of philosophy: *a philosophical discussion*; *philosophical works*. **2** (of a person) calm, not easily upset or worried: *He's had a lot of bad luck, but he's philosophical about it*. **,philo'sophically** *adv*.

phi'losophize, -ise *v* to think about or discuss the nature of man, the purpose of life *etc*: *He spends all his time philosophizing and never does any work*.

phlegm [flem] *n* thick, slimy liquid brought up from the throat by coughing.
phlegmatic [fleg'matik] *adj* calm; not easily excited: *She's very phlegmatic – nothing would ever make her panic*.

phobia ['foubiə] *n* an intense fear or hatred of something: *She has a phobia about birds*.

phoenix ['fi:niks] *n* a mythological bird that burns itself and is born again from its own ashes.

phone [foun] *n* a telephone: *We were talking on the phone*. – *v* to telephone (a person, message or place): *I'll phone you this evening*.
phone up (try to) speak to (someone) by means of the telephone: *I'll phone (him) up and ask about it*.

phonetic [fə'netik] *adj* relating to the sounds of (a) language: *He's making a phonetic study of the speech of the deaf*.
pho'netics *n sing* the study of the sounds of language. – *n sing, n pl* (a system of) symbols used to show the pronunciation of words.

phon(e)y ['founi] *adj* not genuine; fake; false: *a phoney French accent*. – *n* a person who is not what he pretends to be: *He's not a real doctor – he's a phoney*.

phonics ['founiks or 'foniks] *n pl* the science of sound, or of spoken sounds.

photo ['foutou] – *pl* **'photos** – *n* a photograph.

photocopy ['foutəkopi] – *pl* '**photocopies** – *n* a copy of a document *etc* made by a machine which photographs it: *I'll get some photocopies made of this letter*. – *v* to make a copy in this way: *Will you photocopy this letter for me?*
'**photocopier** *n* a machine that makes photocopies.

photograph ['foutəgrɑːf] *n* (*abbrev* **photo** ['foutou]) a picture taken by a camera, using the action of light on film or plates covered with certain chemicals: *I took a lot of photographs during my holiday*. – *v* to take a photograph or photographs of (a person, thing *etc*): *He spends all his time photographing old buildings*.
photographer [fə'togrəfə] *n*: *He is a professional photographer*.
,**photo'graphic** [-'gra-] *adj* of photographs or photography: *a photographic record of his journey*.
photography [fə'togrəfi] *n* the act of taking photographs: *He's very keen on photography*.

Photostat® ['foutəstat] *n* (a copy made by) a type of camera for producing copies of documents *etc*.

phrase [freiz] *n* **1** a small group of words (*usu* without a finite verb) which forms part of an actual or implied sentence: *He arrived after dinner*. **2** a small group of musical notes which follow each other to make a definite individual section of a melody: *the opening phrase of the overture*. – *v* to express (something) in words: *I phrased my explanations in simple language*.
phraseology [freizi'olədʒi] *n* the manner of putting words and phrases together to express oneself: *His phraseology shows that he is a foreigner*.
'**phrasing** *n* **1** phraseology. **2** the act of putting musical phrases together either in composing or playing.
'**phrase-book** *n* a book (*eg* for tourists) which contains and translates useful words and phrases in a foreign language.
phrasal verb a phrase consisting of a verb and adverb or preposition, which together function as a verb: *'Leave out', 'go without', 'go away'*, are phrasal verbs.

physical ['fizikəl] *adj* **1** of the body: *Playing football is one form of physical exercise*. **2** of things that can be seen or felt: *the physical world*. **3** of the laws of nature: *It's a physical impossibility for a man to fly like a bird*. **4** relating to the natural features of the surface of the Earth: *physical geography*. **5** relating to physics: *physical chemistry*.
'**physically** *adv*.

physician [fi'ziʃən] *n* a doctor who specializes in medical rather than surgical treatment of

patients: *My doctor sent me to a physician at the hospital*.

physics ['fiziks] *n sing* the study of natural phenomena such as heat, light, sound, electricity, magnetism *etc* but not *usu* chemistry or biology: *Physics is his main subject at university*.
'**physicist** [-sist] *n* a person who studies, or is an expert in, physics.

physiotherapy [fiziə'θerəpi] *n* the treatment of disease by physical exercise, massage *etc*, not drugs. ,**physio'therapist** *n*.

physique [fi'ziːk] *n* the structure of a person's body: *He has a poor/powerful physique*.

piano [pi'anou] – *pl* **pi'anos** – *n* a large musical instrument played by pressing keys which make hammers strike stretched wires: *She plays the piano very well*; (*also adj*) *piano music*.
pianist ['piənist] *n* a person who plays the piano.
pianoforte [pianou'foːti] *n* a piano.
grand piano a large piano in which the wires are stretched horizontally.

piccolo ['pikəlou] – *pl* '**piccolos** – *n* a kind of small, high-pitched flute: *He plays the piccolo*.

pick¹ [pik] *v* **1** to choose or select: *Pick the one you like best*. **2** to take (flowers from a plant, fruit from a tree *etc*), *usu* by hand: *The little girl sat on the grass and picked flowers*. **3** to lift (someone or something): *He picked up the child*. **4** to unlock (a lock) with a tool other than a key: *When she found that she had lost her key, she picked the lock with a hair-pin*. – *n* **1** whatever or whichever a person wants or chooses: *Take your pick of these prizes*. **2** the best one(s) from or the best part of something: *These grapes are the pick of the bunch*.
'**pickpocket** *n* a person who steals from people's pockets: *He kept his wallet in his hand because he knew there would be pickpockets in the crowd*.
*'**pick-up** *n* **1** a type of small lorry or van. **2** the part of a record-player that holds the stylus.
pick and choose to select or choose very carefully: *When I'm buying apples, I like to pick and choose (the ones I want)*.
pick at to eat very little of (something): *He was not very hungry, and just picked at the food on his plate*.
pick someone's brains to ask (a person) questions in order to get ideas, information *etc* from him which one can use oneself: *You might be able to help me with this problem – can I come and pick your brains for a minute!*
pick holes in to criticize or find faults in (an argument, theory *etc*): *He sounded very*

convincing, but I'm sure one could pick holes in what he said.

pick off to shoot (*esp* people in a group) one by one: *He picked off the enemy soldiers.*

pick on 1 to choose (someone) to do a *usu* difficult or unpleasant job: *Why do they always pick on me to do the washing-up?* 2 to speak to or treat (a person) angrily or critically: *Don't pick on me – it wasn't my fault.*

pick out 1 to choose or select: *She picked out one dress that she particularly liked.* 2 to see or recognize (a person, thing *etc*): *He must be among those people getting off the train, but I can't pick him out.* 3 to play (a piece of music), *esp* slowly and with difficulty, *esp* by ear, without music in front of one: *I don't really play the piano, but I can pick out a tune on one with one finger.*

pick someone's pocket to steal something from a person's pocket: *My wallet has gone – someone has picked my pocket!*

pick a quarrel/fight with (someone) to start a quarrel, argument or fight with (someone) on purpose: *He was angry because I beat him in the race, and he tried to pick a fight with me afterwards.*

pick up 1 to learn gradually, without formal teaching: *I never studied Italian – I just picked it up when I was in Italy.* 2 to let (someone) into a car, train *etc* in order to take him somewhere: *I picked him up at the station and drove him home.* 3 to get (something) by chance: *I picked up a bargain at the shops today.* 4 to right (oneself) after a fall *etc*; to stand up: *He fell over and picked himself up again.* 5 to collect (something) from somewhere: *I ordered some meat from the butcher – I'll pick it up on my way home tonight.* 6 (of radio, radar *etc*) to receive signals: *We picked up a foreign broadcast last night.* 7 to find; to catch: *We lost his trail but picked it up again later; The police picked up the criminal.*

pick up speed to go faster; to accelerate: *The car picked up speed as it ran down the hill.*

pick one's way to walk carefully (around or between something one wishes to avoid touching *etc*): *She picked her way between the puddles.*

pick² [pik] *n* (*also* (*Brit*) **'pickaxe**, (*Amer*) **'pickax** – *pl* **'pickaxes**) a tool with a heavy metal head pointed at one or both ends, used for breaking hard surfaces *eg* walls, roads, rocks *etc*.

pickaback ['pikəbak], **piggyback** ['pigibak] *adv* (of a child) carried on the back: *He carried the boy pickaback.* – *n* a ride on someone's back: *Give me a pickaback, Daddy.*

pickax(e) *see* **pick².**

picket ['pikit] *n* 1 (any one of) a number of people employed at a factory *etc* who are on strike and who try to persuade workers not to go to work there, not to deliver goods there *etc*: *The men set up a picket to stop lorries getting into the factory*; (*also adj*) *a picket line.* 2 a soldier or a small group of soldiers on special duty, *usu* to guard against a sudden attack by the enemy: *The commander placed pickets at various points round the camp*; (*also adj*) *picket duty.* – *v* 1 to place a group of soldiers, strikers *etc* somewhere as a picket: *The strikers' leaders decided to picket the factory*; *The commander picketed the camp.* 2 to act as a picket (at): *In this country, strikers have the legal right to picket*; *The soldiers picketed the camp.*

pickle ['pikl] *n* 1 a vegetable or vegetables preserved in vinegar, salt water *etc*: *Do you want some pickle(s) on your salad?* 2 trouble; an unpleasant situation: *She got herself into a real pickle.* – *v* to preserve in vinegar, salt water *etc*: *I think I will pickle these cucumbers.*

picnic ['piknik] *n* a very informal meal eaten in the open air, *usu* as part of a trip, outing *etc*: *We'll go to the seaside and take a picnic*; *Let's go for a picnic!*; (*also adj*) *a picnic lunch.* – *v* – *pt, ptp* **'picnicked** – to have a picnic: *We picnicked on the beach.*

pictorial [pik'to:riəl] *adj* 1 having many pictures: *a pictorial magazine.* 2 consisting of a picture or pictures: *a pictorial map.* **pic'torially** *adv*.

picture ['piktʃə] *n* 1 a painting or drawing: *This is a picture of my mother.* 2 a photograph: *I took a lot of pictures when I was on holiday.* 3 a cinema film: *There's a good picture on at the cinema tonight.* 4 (*with* **the**) a symbol or perfect example (of something): *She looked the picture of health/happiness.* 5 (*with* **a**) a beautiful sight: *She looked a picture in her new dress.* 6 a clear description: *He gave me a good picture of what was happening.* – *v* to imagine: *I can picture the scene.*

put (someone)/be in the picture to give or have all the necessary information (about something): *He put me in the picture about what had happened.*

the pictures the cinema: *We went to the pictures last night, but it wasn't a very good film.*

picturesque [piktʃə'resk] *adj* (of places) pretty and interesting: *a picturesque village.* **,pictu'resquely** *adv.* **,pictu'resqueness** *n*.

pidgin ['pidʒən] *n* any of a number of languages which consist of a mixture of English, French, Portuguese *etc* and some non-European (*esp* African) language: *Beach-la-mar is a pidgin spoken in parts of* *the southern Pacific Ocean*; (*also adj*) *pidgin English*.

pie [pai] *n* food baked in a covering of pastry: *a steak/apple pie*.

pie in the sky something good promised for the future but which one is not certain or likely to get: *He says he will get a well-paid job but it's just pie in the sky*.

piece [pi:s] *n* **1** a part of anything: *a piece of cake*; *He examined it carefully piece by piece* (=each piece separately). **2** a single thing or example of something: *a piece of paper*; *a piece of news*. **3** a composition in music, writing (an article, short story *etc*), drama, sculpture *etc*: *He wrote a piece on social reform in the local newspaper*. **4** a coin of a particular value: *a five-pence piece*. **5** in chess, draughts and other games, a small shape made of wood, metal, plastic *etc* that is moved according to the rules of the game. **.piece'meal** *adv* a little bit at a time; not as a whole: *He did the work piecemeal*. – *adj* done *etc* in this way: *He has a rather piecemeal way of working*.

go (all) to pieces (of a person) to collapse physically or nervously: *She went to pieces when her husband died*.

in pieces 1 with its various parts not joined together: *The bed is delivered in pieces and the customer has to put it together himself*. **2** broken: *The vase was lying in pieces on the floor*.

piece together to put (the pieces of something) together: *They tried to piece together the fragments of the broken vase*.

to pieces into separate, *usu* small pieces, or into the various parts from which (something) is made: *It was so old, it fell to pieces when I touched it*.

pier [piə] *n* a platform of stone, wood *etc* stretching from the shore into the sea, a lake *etc*, used as a landing-place for boats or as a place of entertainment: *The passengers stepped down on to the pier*.

pierce [piəs] *v* **1** (of pointed objects) to go into or through (something): *The arrow pierced his arm*; *A sudden light pierced the darkness*. **2** to make a hole in or through (something) with a pointed object: *Pierce the lid before removing it from the jar*. **'piercing** *adj* **1** loud; shrill: *a piercing scream*. **2** (of cold weather, winds *etc*) sharp; intense: *a piercing wind*; *piercing cold*. **3** looking intently or sharply as though able to see through things: *piercing eyes*; *a piercing glance*. **'piercingly** *adv*. **'piercingness** *n*.

piety *see* **pious**.

pig [pig] *n* **1** a kind of farm animal whose flesh is eaten as pork, ham and bacon: *He keeps pigs*. **2** an offensive word for an unpleasant, greedy or dirty person: *You pig!*

'piggy – *pl* **'piggies** – *n* a child's word for a (little) pig. – *adj* like a pig's: *piggy eyes*.

'piglet [-lit] *n* a baby pig.

piggyback *see* **pickaback**.

.pig'headed *adj* stubborn: *a pigheaded idiot*. **.pig'headedness** *n*.

'pigskin *n*, *adj* (of) a kind of leather made from the skin of a pig: *Her purse was (made of) pigskin*.

'pigsty – *pl* **'pigsties**, **'pigstyes** – *n* **1** a building in which pigs are kept. **2** a dirty, untidy place: *This room is a pigsty!*

pigswill *see* **swill**.

'pigtail *n* a plait *usu* worn at the back of the head: *She wears her hair in pigtails*.

pigs might fly said of something very unlikely to happen: *'We might have fine weather for our holidays.' 'Yes, and pigs might fly!'*

pigeon ['pidʒən] *n* any of several kinds of bird of the dove family.

'pigeon-hole *n* a small compartment for letters, papers *etc* in a desk *etc* or *eg* hung on the wall of an office, staffroom *etc*: *He has separate pigeon-holes for bills, for receipts, for letters from friends and so on*.

.pigeon-'toed *adj* (of a person or his manner of walking) with toes turned inwards: *a pigeon-toed person/walk*.

piglet *see* **pig**.

pigment ['pigmənt] *n* **1** any substance used for colouring, making paint *etc*: *People used to make paint and dyes from natural pigments*. **2** a substance in plants or animals that gives colour to the skin, leaves *etc*: *Some people have darker pigment in their skin than others*. **.pigmen'tation** *n* colouring (of skin *etc*): *Some illnesses cause a loss of pigmentation*.

pigmy *see* **pygmy**.

pike [paik] – *pl* **pike** – *n* a large fierce freshwater fish.

pile[1] [pail] *n* **1** a (large) number of things lying on top of each other in a tidy or untidy heap; a (large) quantity of something lying in a heap: *There was a neat pile of books in the corner of the room*; *There was pile of rubbish at the bottom of the garden*. **2** a large quantity, *esp* of money: *He must have piles of money to own a car like that*. – *v* to make a pile of (something); to put (something) in a pile: *He piled the boxes on the table*.

'pile-up *n* an accident or crash involving *usu* several vehicles: *There has been a serious pile-up on the motorway, involving three cars and a lorry*.

pile up to make or become a pile; to accumulate: *He piled up the earth at the end of the garden*; *The rubbish piled up in the kitchen*.

pile[2] [pail] *n* a large pillar or stake driven into

the ground as a foundation for a building, bridge *etc*: *The entire city of Venice is built on piles.*

'**pile-driver** *n* a machine for driving piles into the ground.

pile[3] [pail] *n* the thick soft surface of carpets and some kinds of cloth *eg* velvet: *The rug has a deep/thick pile.*

pilfer ['pilfə] *v* to steal (small things): *He pilfered enough pieces of wood from the factory to make a chair.* '**pilferage, 'pilferer** *ns*.

pilgrim ['pilgrim] *n* a person who travels to a holy place: *Every year thousands of pilgrims visit Jerusalem.*

'**pilgrimage** [-midʒ] *n* a journey to a holy place: *She went on a pilgrimage to Lourdes.*

pill [pil] *n* a small ball or tablet of medicine, to be swallowed: *She took a pill; sleeping-pills.*

pillar ['pilə] *n* an upright post used in building as a support or decoration: *The hall was surrounded by stone pillars.*

'**pillarbox** *n* a box found in public places, into which letters are posted to be collected by a postman.

pillion ['piljən] *n* a passenger seat on a motorcycle: *He drove the motorbike and she sat on the pillion*; (*also adj*) *a pillion passenger/seat.*

pillow ['pilou] *n* a kind of cushion for the head, *esp* on a bed. – *v* to rest (one's head): *He pillowed his head on her breast.*

'**pillowcase/'pillowslip** *ns* a cover for a pillow: *They bought linen sheets and pillowcases.*

pilot ['pailət] *n* **1** a person who flies an aeroplane: *The pilot and crew were all killed in the air crash.* **2** a person who directs a ship in and out of a harbour, river, or coastal waters. – *adj* experimental: *a pilot scheme* (= one done on a small scale, *eg* to solve certain problems before a larger, more expensive project is started). – *v* to guide as a pilot: *He piloted the ship/plane.*

'**pilot-light** *n* a small gas light *eg* on a gas cooker, which burns continuously and is used to light the main gas jets when they are turned on.

pimple ['pimpl] *n* a small round swelling on the skin: *He had a pimple on his nose.*

'**pimpled/'pimply** *adjs* having pimples: *a pimpled/pimply face.*

pin [pin] *n* **1** a short, thin, pointed piece of metal used *eg* to hold pieces of fabric, paper *etc* together, *esp* when making clothes: *The papers are fastened together by a pin.* **2** a similar but more ornamental object: *a hatpin.* – *v* – *pt, ptp* **pinned** – **1** to fasten with a pin: *She pinned the material together.* **2** to hold by pressing against something: *The fallen tree pinned him to the ground.*

'**pincushion** *n* a small cushion or similar

object into which pins are pushed for keeping.

'**pinhole** *n* a hole made by a pin: *A pinhole camera does not need a lens.*

'**pinpoint** *v* to place or show very exactly: *He pinpointed the position on the map.*

'**pin-up** *n* **1** a picture of an attractive girl (or man), often pinned on a wall: *He has dozens of pin-ups in his room*; (*also adj*) *a pin-up girl.* **2** the girl (or man): *She's the favourite pin-up of the soldiers.*

pin down to make (someone) give a definite answer, statement, opinion or promise: *I can't pin him down to a definite date for his arrival.*

pins and needles a tingling feeling in one's hands, arms, feet or legs: *I've got pins and needles in my arm.*

pinafore ['pinəfoː] *n* **1** a kind of apron covering the clothes above and below the waist: *The children wore pinafores at nursery school.* **2** (*also* **pinafore dress**: *Amer* '**jumper**) a kind of dress with no sleeves, designed to be worn over a blouse, sweater *etc.*

pincers ['pinsəz] *n pl* **1** a tool for gripping things tightly: *He used (a pair of) pincers.* **2** the claws of lobsters, crabs *etc.*

pinch [pintʃ] *v* **1** to squeeze or press tightly (flesh), *esp* between the thumb and forefinger: *He pinched her arm.* **2** to hurt by being too small or tight: *My new shoes are pinching (me).* **3** to steal: *Who pinched my bicycle?* – *n* **1** an act of pinching; a squeeze or nip: *He gave her a pinch on the cheek.* **2** a very small amount; what can be held between the thumb and forefinger: *a pinch of salt.*

pinched *adj* (of a person's face) looking cold, pale or thin because of cold, poverty *etc*: *Her face was pinched with cold.*

feel the pinch to be in difficulty because of lack of money.

***pine**[1] [pain] *n* **1** any of several kinds of evergreen trees with cones ('**pine-cones**) and needlelike leaves ('**pine-needles**). **2** its wood: *The table is made of pine*; (*also adj*) *a pine table.*

pine[2] [pain] *v* **1** (*often with* **away**) to lose strength, become weak (with pain, grief *etc*): *Since his death she has been pining (away).* **2** (*usu with* **for**) to want (something) very much; to long (for someone or something, or to do something): *He knew that his wife was pining for home.*

pineapple ['painapl] *n* a type of large tropical fruit shaped like a large pine-cone, or the plant which produces it.

ping [piŋ] *n* a sharp, ringing sound such as that of a glass being lightly struck, or a stretched wire, thread *etc* being pulled and released: *His knife struck the wine-glass*

with a loud ping. – *v* to make such a sound:
The glass pinged.

ping-pong ['piŋpoŋ] *n* **1** the game of table
tennis: *Do you play ping-pong?*. **2** (®) in
the US, the equipment used in table tennis.

pink [piŋk] *n, adj* **1** (of) (any shade of) a
colour between red and white: *a dress of
pink satin.* **2** (of) the colour of healthy
skin: *pink cheeks; Her cheeks are pink with
health.* **'pinkness** *n*.

'pinkish *adj* fairly pink; close to pink: *The
flowers of this plant are pinkish in colour.*

pinnacle ['pinəkl] *n* **1** a tall thin spire built on
the roof of a church, castle *etc*. **2** a high
pointed rock or mountain: *It was a dangerous pinnacle to climb.* **3** a high point (of
achievement, success *etc*): *He has reached
the pinnacle of his career.*

pint [paint] *n* a unit for measuring liquids,
one-eighth of a gallon (in Britain, 0·57 litre;
in the US, 0·47 litre): *a pint of milk/beer.*

pioneer [paiə'niə] *n* **1** a person who goes to a
new, often uninhabited or uncivilized (part
of a) country to live and work there: *The
American pioneers; (also adj) a pioneer family.* **2** a person who is the first to study some
new subject, or use or develop a new technique *etc*: *Lister was one of the pioneers of
modern medicine.* – *v* to be the first to do or
make: *Who pioneered the use of vaccine for
preventing polio?*

pious ['paiəs] *adj* having or showing strong
religious feelings, reverence for or devotion
to God *etc*: *a pious woman/attitude.* **'piously**
adv. **piety** ['paiəti] *n*.

pip¹ [pip] *n* a seed of a fruit: *an orange/apple
pip.*

pip² [pip] *n* a short sharp sound on radio, a
telephone *etc*, used *eg* to show the exact
time: *He put his watch right by the pips.*

pipe [paip] *n* **1** a tube, *usu* made of metal,
earthenware *etc*, through which water, gas
etc can flow: *a water pipe; a drainpipe.* **2** a
small tube with a bowl at one end, in which
tobacco is smoked: *He smokes a pipe; (also
adj) pipe tobacco.* **3** a musical instrument
consisting of a hollow wooden, metal *etc*
tube through which the player blows or
causes air to be blown in order to make a
sound: *He played a tune on a bamboo pipe;
an organ pipe.* – *v* **1** to convey gas, water *etc*
by a pipe: *Water is piped to the town from
the reservoir.* **2** to play (music) on a pipe or
pipes: *He piped a tune.* **3** to speak in a high
voice, make a high-pitched sound: *'Hallo,'
the little girl piped.*

'piper *n* a person who plays a pipe or pipes,
esp the bagpipes.

pipes *n pl* **1** bagpipes or some similar instrument: *He plays the pipes.* **2** a set of musical
pipes joined together to form a single instrument: *the pipes of Pan.*

'piping *n* **1** the act of playing a musical pipe
or pipes. **2** (the act or process of conveying
water, gas *etc* by means of) a length of pipe
or number of pipes: *lead piping; Piping the
oil ashore will not be easy.* – *adj* (of a sound)
high-pitched: *a piping voice.*

pipe dream an idea which can only be
imagined, and which would be impossible
to carry out: *For most people a journey
round the world is only a pipe dream.*

'pipeline *n* a long line of pipes used for
conveying oil, gas, water *etc*: *an oil pipeline
across the desert.*

piping hot very hot: *piping hot soup.*

piquant ['pi:kənt] *adj* sharp in taste; appetizing: *a piquant sauce; a piquant (=exciting
or interesting) situation.* **'piquantly** *adv.*
'piquancy *n*.

pique [pi:k] *n* anger caused by one's pride
being hurt: *She walked out of the room in a
fit of pique.*

pirate ['paiərət] *n* **1** a person who attacks and
robs ships at sea: *Their ship was attacked by
pirates; (also adj) a pirate ship.* **2** a person
who does something without legal right, *eg*
publishes someone else's work as his own
or broadcasts without a licence: *a pirate
radio-station.* – *v* to publish, broadcast *etc*
without the legal right to do so: *The dictionary was pirated and sold abroad.*

'piracy *n* the act(s) of a pirate: *He was
accused of piracy on the high seas; Publishing that book under his own name was
piracy.*

pirouette [piru'et] *n* a dancer's quick turning
movement: *The ballerina did/danced a pirouette.* – *v* to do one or a series of these
movements: *She pirouetted across the stage.*

pistachio [pi'sta:ʃiou] – *pl* **pis'tachios** – *n* a
greenish nut used as flavouring for food.

pistol ['pistl] *n* a small gun, held in one hand
when fired: *He shot himself with a pistol.*

piston ['pistən] *n* (in engines, pumps *etc*) a
round piece *usu* of metal that fits inside a
cylinder and moves up and down or
backwards and forwards inside it.

pit¹ [pit] *n* **1** a large hole in the ground: *The
campers dug a pit for their rubbish.* **2** a place
from which minerals are dug, *esp* a coalmine: *a chalk-pit; He works at/down the pit.*
3 a place beside a motor race track for
repairing and refuelling racing cars: *The
leading car has gone into the pit(s).* – *v* – *pt,
ptp* **'pitted** – (*with* **against**) to set (a person
or thing) against another in a fight, competition *etc*: *He was pitted against a much
stronger man.*

'pitfall *n* a possible danger: *She has managed to avoid most of the pitfalls of life.*

pit² [pit] *n* the hard stone of a peach, cherry
etc. – *v* – *pt, ptp* **'pitted** – to remove the
stone from (a peach, cherry *etc*).

pitch[1] [pitʃ] v **1** to set up (a tent or camp): *They pitched their tent in the field.* **2** to throw: *He pitched the stone into the river.* **3** to (cause to) fall heavily: *He pitched forward.* **4** (of a ship) to rise and fall violently: *The boat pitched up and down on the rough sea.* **5** to set (a note or tune) at a particular level: *He pitched the tune too high for my voice.* – n **1** the field or ground for certain games: *a cricket-pitch; a football pitch.* **2** the degree of highness or lowness of a musical note, voice *etc.* **3** an extreme point or intensity: *His anger reached such a pitch that he hit her.* **4** the part of a street *etc* where a street-seller or entertainer works: *He has a pitch on the High Street.* **5** the act of pitching or throwing or the distance something is pitched: *That was a long pitch.* **6** (of a ship) the act of pitching.

-pitched of a (certain) musical pitch: *a high-pitched/low-pitched voice.*

'pitcher n a person who pitches *esp* (in baseball) the player who throws the ball.

pitched battle a battle between armies that have been prepared and arranged for fighting beforehand: *They fought a pitched battle.*

'pitchfork n a large long-handled fork for lifting and moving hay.

pitch[2] [pitʃ] n a thick black substance obtained from tar: *as black as pitch.*

‚pitch-'black, ‚pitch-'dark adjs as black, or dark, as pitch; completely black or dark: *Outside the house it was pitch-black; It's a pitch-dark night.*

pitcher[1] see **pitch**[1].

pitcher[2] ['pitʃə] n a large jug: *a pitcher of water.*

piteous see **pity**.

pith [piθ] n **1** the white substance between the peel of an orange, lemon *etc* and the fruit itself. **2** the soft substance in the centre of the stems of plants. **3** the most important part of anything: *the pith of the argument.*

pitiable, pitiful, pitiless see **pity**.

pitter-patter ['pitə'patə] n a light, tapping sound: *the pitter-patter of rain on a window.* – v to make such a sound. – adv while making this sound: *The mouse ran pitter-patter across the floor.*

pity ['piti] n **1** a feeling of sorrow for the troubles and sufferings of others: *He felt a great pity for her.* **2** a cause of sorrow or regret: *What a pity (that) she can't come.* – v to feel pity for (someone): *She pitied him; She is to be pitied.*

piteous ['pitiəs] adj pitiful: *a piteous cry/sight.* **'piteously** adv. **'piteousness** n.

'pitiable adj pitiful: *He was in a pitiable condition; He made a pitiable attempt.* **'pitiably** adv.

'pitiful adj **1** very sad; causing pity: *a pitiful*

sight. **2** very poor, bad *etc*; causing contempt: *a pitiful attempt; a pitiful amount of money.* **'pitifully** adv. **'pitifulness** n.

'pitiless adj without pity: *pitiless cruelty.* **'pitilessly** adv. **'pitilessness** n.

'pityingly adv in a way which shows that one feels pity for someone: *He looked at her pityingly.*

have pity on to feel pity for (someone because of something): *Have pity on the old man.*

take pity on to act kindly, or relent, towards (someone), from a feeling of pity: *He took pity on the hungry children and gave them food.*

pivot ['pivət] n the pin or centre on which anything balances and turns. – v – pt, ptp **'pivoted** – (with on) to turn (on): *The door pivoted on a central hinge.*

pixy (pl **'pixies**), **pixie** ['piksi] n a kind of fairy.

pizza ['pi:tsə] n a flat piece of dough spread with tomato, cheese *etc* and baked.

placard ['plaka:d] n a notice printed on *eg* wood or cardboard and carried, hung *etc*, in a public place: *The protesters were carrying placards denouncing the government's policy.*

placate [plə'keit, (Amer) 'pleikeit] v to stop (an angry person) feeling angry: *He placated her with an apology.*

place [pleis] n **1** a particular spot or area: *a quiet place in the country; I spent my holiday in various different places.* **2** an empty space: *There's a place for your books on this shelf.* **3** an area or building with a particular purpose: *a market-place.* **4** a seat (in a theatre, train, at a table *etc*): *He went to his place and sat down.* **5** a position in an order, series, queue *etc*: *She got the first place in the competition; I lost my place in the queue.* **6** a person's position or level of importance in society *etc*: *You must keep your secretary in her place.* **7** a point in the text of a book *etc*: *The wind was blowing the pages of my book and I kept losing my place.* **8** duty or right: *It's not my place to tell him he's wrong.* **9** a job or position in a team, organization *etc*: *He's got a place in the team; He's hoping for a place on the staff.* **10** house; home: *Come over to my place.* **11** (often abbrev **Pl.** when written) a word used in the names of certain roads, streets or squares. **12** a number or one of a series of numbers following a decimal point: *Make the answer correct to four decimal places.* – v **1** to put: *He placed it on the table; He was placed in command of the army.* **2** to remember who a person is: *I know I've seen her before, but I can't quite place her.*

'place-name n the name of a town, hill, valley *etc.*

go places to be successful, *esp* in one's career: *That young man is sure to go places.*

in the first, second *etc* **place** expressions used to show steps in an argument, explanation *etc*: *He decided not to buy the house, because in the first place it was too expensive, and in the second place it was too far from his office.*

in place in the proper position; tidy: *He left everything in place.*

in place of instead of: *We advise discussion in place of argument; John couldn't go, so I went in his place.*

out of place 1 not suitable (to the occasion *etc*): *His clothes are quite out of place at a formal dinner.* **2** not in the proper position; untidy: *Although he had had to run most of the way, he arrived with not a hair out of place.*

put oneself in someone else's place to imagine what it would be like to be someone else: *If you put yourself in his place, you can understand why he is so careful.*

put (someone) in his place to remind (someone), often in a rude or angry way, of his lower social position, or lack of importance, experience *etc*.

take place to happen: *What took place after that?*

take the place of to be used instead of, or to be a substitute for: *I don't think television will ever take the place of books.*

placid ['plasid] *adj* calm and not easily disturbed or upset: *a placid child.* **'placidly** *adv.* **'placidness** *n.*

plague [pleig] *n* **1** *esp* formerly, an extremely infectious and deadly disease, *esp* one carried by fleas from rats. **2** a large and annoying quantity: *a plague of flies.* – *v* to annoy or pester continually or frequently: *The child was plaguing her with questions.*

plaice [pleis] – *pl* **plaice** – *n* a type of flat fish.

plain [plein] *adj* **1** simple or ordinary; without ornament or decoration: *plain living; good, plain food.* **2** easy to understand; clear: *His words were quite plain.* **3** absolutely open or honest, with no attempt to be tactful: *I'll be quite plain with you; plain speaking.* **4** obvious: *It's plain (to see) you haven't been practising your music.* **5** not pretty: *a rather plain girl.* – *n* **1** a large flat level piece of land: *the plains of central Canada.* **2** a kind of knitting stitch. **'plainly** *adv.* **'plainness** *n.*

plain chocolate dark chocolate not containing milk.

plain clothes ordinary clothes, not a uniform: *Detectives usually wear plain clothes;* (*also adj*) *a plain-clothes job.*

plain sailing progress without difficulty.

plain-'spoken *adj* speaking plainly, not trying to be tactful.

plaintiff ['pleintif] *n* a person who starts a legal case against another.

plaintive ['pleintiv] *adj* sounding sad or sorrowful: *a plaintive cry.* **'plaintively** *adv.* **'plaintiveness** *n.*

plait [plat] *n* **1** a length of hair arranged by dividing it into sections and passing these over one another in turn: *She wore her hair in a long plait.* **2** a similar arrangement of any material: *a plait of straw.* – *v* to arrange in this way: *She plaited three strips of leather to make a belt; She plaited her hair.*

plan [plan] *n* **1** an idea of how to do something; a method of doing something: *If everyone follows this plan, we will succeed; I have worked out a plan for making a lot of money.* **2** an intention or arrangement: *My plan is to rob a bank and leave the country quickly; What are your plans for tomorrow?* **3** a drawing, diagram *etc* showing a building, town *etc* as if seen from above: *These are the plans of/for our new house; a street-plan.* – *v* – *pt, ptp* **planned** – **1** (*sometimes with on*) to intend (to do something): *We are planning on going to Italy this year; We were planning to go last year but we hadn't enough money; They are planning a trip to Italy.* **2** to decide how something is to be done; to arrange (something): *We are planning a party; We'll have to plan very carefully if we are to succeed.* **3** to design (a building, town *etc*): *This is the architect who planned the building.*

'planner *n* a person who plans (*esp* buildings *etc*): *a town-planner.*

'planning *n* the act of planning: *town-planning.*

go according to plan to happen as arranged or intended: *The journey went according to plan.*

plan ahead to plan something a long time before it will happen *etc*.

plane¹ [plein] *n* **1** an aeroplane. **2** a level or standard: *Man is on a higher plane (of development) than the apes.* **3** in geometry, a flat surface. – *v* to move smoothly over the surface (of water *etc*).

*plane² [plein] *n* a carpenter's tool for making a level or smooth surface. – *v* to make (a surface) level, smooth or lower by using a plane.

plane³ [plein] *n* a type of tree with broad leaves.

planet ['planit] *n* any of the bodies (*eg* the Earth) which move round the Sun or round another star: *Mars and Jupiter are planets, but the Moon is not.* **'planetary** *adj*.

plank [plaŋk] *n* a long, flat piece of wood: *The floor was made of planks.*

plankton ['plaŋktən] *n* very tiny living creatures floating in seas, lakes *etc*.

planner *see* **plan.**

* see illustration on p. 566

plant [pla:nt] *n* **1** anything growing from the ground, having a stem, a root and leaves: *flowering/tropical plants*. **2** industrial machinery: *engineering plant*. **3** a factory. – *v* **1** to put (something) into the ground so that it will grow: *We have planted vegetables in the garden*. **2** to make (a garden *etc*); to cause (a garden *etc*) to have (plants *etc*) growing in it: *The garden was planted with shrubs*; *We're going to plant an orchard*. **3** to place heavily or firmly: *He planted himself between her and the door*. **4** to put in someone's possession, *esp* as false evidence: *He claimed that the police had planted the weapon on his brother*.

plan'tation [plan-] *n* **1** a place that has been planted with trees. **2** a piece of land or estate for growing certain crops, *esp* cotton, sugar, rubber, tea and tobacco: *He owned a rubber plantation in Malaysia*.

'planter *n* the owner of a plantation for growing tea, rubber *etc*: *a tea-planter*.

plantation, planter *see* **plant**.

plaque [pla:k] *n* **1** a plate of metal *etc* fixed to a wall *etc* as a memorial: *His name was inscribed on a brass plaque*. **2** a china *etc* ornament for fixing on the wall. **3** a deposit of saliva and bacteria which forms on the teeth.

plasma ['plazmə] *n* the liquid part of blood and certain other fluids produced by the body.

plaster ['pla:stə] *n* **1** (*also adj*) (of) a substance put on walls, ceilings *etc* which dries to form a hard smooth surface: *He mixed up some plaster to repair the wall*; *a plaster ceiling*. **2** (*also adj*) (*also* **plaster of Paris**) (of) a similar quick-drying substance used for supporting broken limbs, making models *etc*: *She's got her arm in plaster*; *a plaster model*. **3** (*also* **'sticking-plaster**) (a piece of) sticky tape (sometimes with a dressing) used to cover a wound *etc*: *You should put a plaster on that cut*. – *v* **1** to plaster on: *They plastered the walls*. **2** to spread or apply rather too thickly: *She'd look nicer if she didn't plaster so much make-up on her face*.

'plasterer *n* a person whose job is to put plaster on walls, ceilings *etc*.

plastic ['plastik] *n, adj* (of) any of many chemically manufactured substances that can be moulded when still soft: *This cup is made of plastic*; *a plastic cup*. – *adj* easily made into different shapes.

plastic surgery surgery to repair or replace damaged skin, or to improve the appearance *usu* of the face (*n* **plastic surgeon**).

Plasticine® ['plastisi:n] *n* a coloured substance like clay used for modelling *esp* by children.

plate [pleit] *n* **1** a shallow dish for holding food *etc*: *china plates*. **2** a sheet of metal *etc*: *The ship was built of steel plates*. **3** articles made of, or plated with, *usu* gold or silver: *a collection of gold plate*. **4** a flat piece of metal inscribed with *eg* a name, for fixing to a door, or with a design *etc*, for use in printing. **5** an illustration in a book, *usu* on glossy paper: *The book has ten full-colour plates*. **6** (*also* **dental plate**) a piece of plastic that fits in the mouth with false teeth attached to it. **7** a sheet of glass *etc* coated with a sensitive film, used in photography.

'plated *adj* covered with a thin layer of a different metal: *gold-plated dishes*.

'plateful *n* the complete contents of a plate: *a plateful of potatoes*; *two platefuls of chips*.

'plating *n* a thin covering of metal: *silver-plating*.

plate glass a kind of glass made in thick sheets for windows, mirrors *etc*.

plateau ['platou, (*Amer*) pla'tou] – *pls* **'plateaus, 'plateaux** [-z] – *n* an area of high flat land; a mountain with a wide, flat top.

platform ['platfo:m] *n* **1** a raised part of a floor *eg* in a hall, for speakers, entertainers *etc*: *The orchestra arranged themselves on the platform*. **2** the raised area between or beside the lines in a railway station: *They waited on the platform for their train to arrive*; *The London train will leave from platform 6*.

plating *see* **plate**.

platinum ['platinəm] *n, adj* (of) an element, a heavy, valuable grey metal, often used in making jewellery: *a platinum ring*.

platoon [plə'tu:n] *n* a section of a company of soldiers.

platter ['platə] *n* a kind of large, flat plate: *a wooden platter*.

plausible ['plo:zəbl] *adj* **1** seeming reasonable or convincing: *a plausible excuse*. **2** clever at talking persuasively but not to be trusted: *a plausible fellow*.

play [plei] *v* **1** to amuse oneself: *The child is playing in the garden*; *He is playing with his toys*; *The little girl wants to play with her friends*. **2** to take part in (games *etc*): *He plays football*; *He is playing in goal*; *Here's a pack of cards – who wants to play (with me)?*; *I'm playing golf with him this evening*. **3** to act in a play *etc*; to act (a character): *She's playing Lady Macbeth*; *The company is playing in London this week*. **4** (of a play *etc*) to be performed: *'Oklahoma' is playing at the local theatre*. **5** to (be able to) perform on (a musical instrument): *She plays the piano*; *Who was playing the piano this morning?*; *He plays (the oboe) in an orchestra*. **6** (*usu with* **on**) to carry out or do (a trick): *He played a trick on me*. **7** (*usu with* **at**) to compete against (someone) in a game *etc*: *I'll play you at tennis*. **8** (of light) to pass with a flickering movement: *The fire-light played across the ceiling.* **9** to direct (over or towards something): *The firemen played their hoses over the burning house.* **10** to put down or produce (a playing-card) as part of a card game: *He played the seven of hearts.* – *n* **1** recreation; amusement: *A person must have time for both work and play.* **2** an acted story; a drama: *Shakespeare wrote many great plays.* **3** the playing of a game: *At the start of today's play, England was leading India by fifteen runs.* **4** freedom of movement (*eg* in part of a machine). '**player** *n*.

'**playable** *adj* (*neg* **un-**) (of a ground, pitch *etc*) not good enough for a game to be played on it: *Because of the rain the referee decided the ground was not playable.*

'**playful** *adj* **1** happy; full of the desire to play: *a playful kitten.* **2** joking; not serious: *a playful remark.* '**playfully** *adv.* '**playfulness** *n*.

'**playboy** *n* a rich man who spends his time and money on pleasure.

'**playground** *n* an area in which children can play in a park, outside a school *etc*.

'**playing-card** *n* one of a pack of cards used in card games.

'**playing-field** *n* a field which is specially prepared and used for sport.

'**playmate** *n* a childhood friend.

'**playschool** *n* an informal nursery school.

'**plaything** *n* a toy.

'**playtime** *n* a set time for children to play (at school *etc*): *The children go outside at playtime.*

'**playwright** *n* a person who writes plays: *He is a famous playwright.*

at play playing: *children at play.*

bring/come into play to (cause to) be used or exercised: *The job allowed him to bring all his talents into play.*

child's play something that is very easy: *Of course you can do it – it's child's play!*

in play, out of play (of a ball) according to the rules of the game, (not) in a position where it can be hit, kicked *etc*.

play at 1 to pretend to be *etc*: *The children were playing at cowboys and Indians.* **2** used when asking angrily what someone is doing: *What does he think he's playing at* (=doing)?

play back to play (music, speech *etc*) on a record or tape after it has just been recorded (*n* '**play-back**).

play down to try to make (something) appear less important: *He played down the fact that he had failed the exam.*

play fair to act honestly and fairly.

play for time to delay an action, decision *etc* in the hope that conditions will improve.

play havoc with to cause a lot of damage to:

The storm played havoc with the farmer's crops.

play into someone's hands to do exactly what an opponent or enemy wants one to do.

play off (in games) to play a final deciding game after a draw (*n* '**play-off**).

play off against to set (one person) against (another) in order to gain an advantage: *He played his father off against his mother to get more pocket money.*

play on to make use of (someone's feelings, fears *etc*): *He played on my sympathy until I lent him $10.*

play a, no part in (not) to be one of the people who are doing (something): *He played no part in the robbery.*

play safe to take no risks.

play the game to act fairly and honestly.

play up to be troublesome or disobedient: *The children are playing up today.*

plea [pli:] *n* **1** a prisoner's answer to a charge: *He made a plea of* (*not*) *guilty.* **2** an urgent request: *The hospital sent out a plea for blood-donors.*

plead [pli:d] – *pts, ptps* '**pleaded,** (*Amer also*) **pled** – *v* **1** (of a prisoner) to answer a charge, saying whether one is guilty or not: *'How does the prisoner plead?' 'He pleads guilty.'* **2** to present a case in court: *My lawyer will plead my case*; *My lawyer will plead for me.* **3** (*often with* **with**) to make an urgent request: *He pleaded with me not to go*; *He pleaded to be allowed to go.*

pleasant ['pleznt] *adj* giving pleasure; agreeable: *a pleasant day/person.* '**pleasantly** *adv.* '**pleasantness** *n*.

please [pli:z] **1** to do what is wanted by (a person); to give pleasure or satisfaction to: *You can't please everyone all the time*; *It pleases me to read poetry.* **2** to choose, want, like: *He does as he pleases.* – *adv* a word added to an order or request in order to be polite: *Please open the window*; *Close the door, please*; *Will you please come with me?*

pleased *adj* happy; satisfied: *Aren't you pleased about moving house?*; *She was pleased with the dress.*

'**pleasing** *adj* giving pleasure; attractive: *a pleasing view.* '**pleasingly** *adv.*

if you please please: *Come this way, if you please.*

please yourself do what you choose: *I don't think you should go; but please yourself.*

pleasure ['pleʒə] *n* something that gives one enjoyment; joy or delight: *the pleasures of country life*; *I get a lot of pleasure from listening to music.*

'**pleasurable** *adj* giving pleasure; agreeable: *a pleasurable pastime.* '**pleasurably** *adv.*

'pleasure-boat/'pleasure-craft ns a boat used for pleasure.
   take pleasure in to get enjoyment from: He takes great pleasure in annoying me.

pleat [pli:t] n a fold sewn or pressed into cloth etc: a skirt with pleats. – v to make pleats in. 'pleated adj: a pleated skirt.

plectrum ['plektrəm] n a small piece of plastic etc for plucking the strings of a guitar.

pled see plead.

pledge [pledʒ] n 1 a promise: He gave me his pledge. 2 something given by a person who is borrowing money etc to the person he has borrowed it from, to be kept until the money etc is returned: He borrowed $20 and left his watch as a pledge. 3 a sign or token: They exchanged rings as a pledge of their love. – v 1 to promise: He pledged his support. 2 to give to someone when borrowing money etc: to pledge one's watch.

plenty ['plenti] pron 1 a sufficient amount; enough: I don't need any more books – I've got plenty; We've got plenty of time to get there. 2 a large amount: He's got plenty of money. – adj: That's plenty, thank you! 'plenteous [-tiəs] adj plentiful.
'plentiful adj existing in large amounts: a plentiful supply.

pliable ['plaiəbl] adj easily bent: pliable wire. ,plia'bility n.

*pliers ['plaiəz] n pl a kind of tool used for gripping, bending or cutting wire etc: He used a pair of pliers to pull the nail out; Where are my pliers?

plight[2] [plait] n a (bad) situation or state: She was in a terrible plight, as she had lost all her money.

plod [plod] – pt, ptp 'plodded – v 1 to walk heavily and slowly: The elderly man plodded down the street. 2 to work slowly but thoroughly: They plodded on with the work.

plonk [ploŋk] v to place or put noisily and rather clumsily: He plonked his books on the table; She plonked herself down in front of the fire.

plop [plop] n the sound of a small object falling into water etc: The raindrop fell into her teacup with a plop. – v – pt, ptp plopped – to fall with this sound: A stone plopped into the pool.

plot [plot] n 1 a plan, esp for doing something evil; a conspiracy: a plot to assassinate the President. 2 the story of a play, novel etc: The play has a very complicated plot. 3 a small piece of land eg for use as a gardening area or for building a house on. – v – pt, ptp 'plotted – 1 to plan to bring about (something evil): They were plotting the death of the king. 2 to make a plan, map, graph etc of: The navigator plotted the course of the ship.

plough, (Amer) plow [plau] n a type of farm tool pulled through the top layer of the soil to turn it over. – v 1 to turn over (the earth) with such a tool: The farmer was ploughing (in) a field. 2 to travel with difficulty, force a way etc: The ship ploughed through the rough sea; I've all this work to plough through. 3 to crash: The lorry ploughed into the back of a bus.

ploy [ploi] n 1 a plan; a manoeuvre: She uses various ploys for getting her own way. 2 a piece of business; a little task: The children were off on some ploy of their own.

pluck [plʌk] v 1 to pull: She plucked a grey hair from her head; He plucked at my sleeve. 2 to pull the feathers off (a chicken etc) before cooking it. 3 to pick (flowers etc). 4 to pull hairs out of (eyebrows) in order to improve their shape. 5 to pull and let go (the strings of a musical instrument). – n courage: He showed a lot of pluck.
'plucky adj courageous: a plucky young fellow. 'pluckily adv. 'pluckiness n.
pluck up (the) courage, energy etc to gather up one's courage etc (to do something): She plucked up (the) courage to ask a question.

plug [plʌg] n 1 a device for putting into a mains socket in order to allow an electric current to flow through the appliance to which it is attached by cable: She changed the plug on the electric kettle. 2 an object shaped for fitting into the hole in a bath or sink to prevent the water from running away, or a piece of material for blocking any hole. – v – pt, ptp plugged – to block (a hole) by putting a plug in it: He plugged the hole in the window with a piece of newspaper.
plug in to connect up (an electrical apparatus) by inserting its plug into a socket: Could you plug in the electric kettle?

plum [plʌm] n a type of fruit, usu dark-red or purple, with a stone in the centre.
plum cake/pudding (a) cake or pudding containing raisins, currants etc.

plumage ['plu:midʒ] n the feathers of a bird or birds: The peacock has (a) brilliant plumage.

plumber ['plʌmə] n a person who fits and mends domestic water, gas and sewage pipes: Send for a plumber – we have a leaking pipe.
'plumbing n 1 the system of pipes in a building etc: We shall have to have the plumbing repaired. 2 the fitting and repairing etc of pipes.

plume [plu:m] n a large decorative feather: She wore a plume in her hat.

plummet ['plʌmit] – pt, ptp 'plummeted – v (of a heavy weight) to fall or drop swiftly: The rock plummeted to the bottom of the cliff.

plump[1] ['plʌmp] adj pleasantly fat and

rounded; well filled out: *plump cheeks*.
plumply *adv*. **'plumpness** *n*.

plump up to shake (pillows *etc*) to restore their shape.

plump² [plʌmp]: **plump for** to choose or decide on: *She finally plumped for a house in the country*.

plunder ['plʌndə] to rob or steal from (a place): *The soldiers plundered and looted (the city)*. – *n* the things stolen: *They ran off with their plunder*. **'plunderer** *n*.

plunge [plʌndʒ] *v* **1** to throw oneself down (into deep water *etc*); to dive: *He plunged into the river*. **2** to push (something) violently or suddenly into: *He plunged a knife into the meat*. – *n* an act of plunging; a dive: *He took a plunge into the pool*.

'plunger *n* an instrument for clearing blocked pipes *etc* by suction.

take the plunge to (decide to) start doing something new or difficult.

plural ['pluərəl] *n, adj* (in) the form of a word which expresses more than one: *'Mice' is the plural of 'mouse'; a plural noun/verb; Is the verb in the singular or the plural?*

plus [plʌs] *prep* used to show addition: *Two plus three equals five* $(2+3=5)$. – *n* (*also* **plus sign**) a sign (+) used to show addition or positive quality. – *adj* positive or more than zero: *a plus quantity; The temperature was plus fifteen degrees*.

plutonium [plu:'touniəm] *n* a radioactive element used in many nuclear processes.

ply¹ [plai] *v* **1** an old word for to work at: *He plies his trade as weaver*. **2** to use (a tool *etc*) vigorously. **3** to keep supplying: *They plied their guests with drink*.

ply² [plai] *n* a thickness, layer or strand, as in *three-ply/two-ply wool*.

'plywood *n, adj* (of) a material made up of thin layers of wood glued together: *a plywood box*.

pneumatic [nju'matik] *adj* **1** filled with air: *pneumatic tyres*. **2** worked by air: *a pneumatic pump/drill*. **pneu'matically** *adv*.

pneumonia [nju'mouniə] *n* an illness in which the lungs become inflamed.

poach¹ [poutʃ] *v* to cook (*eg* an egg without its shell, a fish *etc*) in boiling liquid, *esp* water or milk.

poached *adj*: *a poached egg*.

poach² [poutʃ] *v* to hunt (game) or catch (fish) illegally on someone else's land. **poacher** *n*.

pocket ['pokit] *n* **1** a small bag sewn into or on to clothes, for carrying things in: *He stood with his hands in his pockets; a coat-pocket; (also adj) a pocket-handkerchief, a pocket-knife*. **2** a small bag attached to the corners and sides of a billiard-table *etc* to catch the balls. **3** a small isolated area or group: *a pocket of warm air*. **4** (a person's)

income or amount of money available for spending: *a range of prices to suit every pocket*. – *v* **1** to put in a pocket: *He pocketed his wallet; He pocketed the red ball*. **2** to steal: *Be careful he doesn't pocket the silver*.

'pocketful *n* the amount contained by a pocket: *a pocketful of coins*.

'pocket-book *n* a wallet for holding papers.

'pocket-money *n* money for personal use, *esp* a child's regular allowance: *He gets $2 a week pocket-money*.

'pocket-size(d) *adj* small enough to carry in one's pocket: *a pocket-size(d) dictionary*.

pockmark ['pokma:k] *n* a scar or small dent in the skin caused by smallpox *etc*. **'pockmarked** *adj*.

pod [pod] *n* the long seed-case of the pea, bean *etc*.

podgy ['podʒi], **pudgy** ['pʌdʒi] *adjs* plump; fat. **'podginess, 'pudginess** *ns*.

podium ['poudiəm] *n* a platform on which a lecturer, musical conductor *etc* stands.

poem ['pouim] *n* a piece of writing arranged in lines which *usu* have a regular rhythm and often rhyme.

poet ['pouit] – *fem* **'poet, 'poetess** – *n* a person who writes poems.

poetic [pou'etik] *adj* of, like, or suitable for, a poem: *a poetic expression*. **po'etically** *adv*.

'poetry *n* **1** poems in general: *He writes poetry*. **2** the art of composing poems: *Poetry comes naturally to some people*.

point [point] *n* **1** the sharp end of anything: *the point of a pin; a sword point; at gunpoint* (= threatened by a gun). **2** a piece of land that projects into the sea *etc*: *The ship came round Lizard Point*. **3** a small round dot or mark (·): *a decimal point; five point three six* (= 5·36); *In punctuation, a point is another name for a full stop*. **4** an exact place or spot: *When we reached this point of the journey we stopped to rest*. **5** an exact moment: *Her husband walked in at that point*. **6** a place on a scale *esp* of temperature: *the boiling-point of water*. **7** a division on a compass *eg* north, south-west *etc*. **8** a mark in scoring a competition, game, test *etc*: *He has won by five points to two*. **9** a particular matter for consideration or action: *The first point we must decide is, where to meet; That's a good point; You've missed the point; That's the whole point; We're wandering away from the point*. **10** (a) purpose or advantage: *There's no point (in) asking me – I don't know*. **11** a personal characteristic or quality: *We all have our good points and our bad ones*. **12** an electrical socket in a wall *etc* into which a plug can be put: *Is there only one electrical point in this room?* – *v* **1** to aim in a particular direction: *He pointed the gun at her*. **2** to call attention to something *esp* by stretching the index finger in its direction: *He pointed (his finger) at the door*; *He pointed to a sign.* **3** to fill worn places in (a stone or brick wall *etc*) with mortar.

'**pointed** *adj* having a sharp end: *a pointed nose*; *pointed shoes.*

'**pointer** *n* **1** a long stick used to indicate places on a large map *etc.* **2** an indicator on a dial: *The pointer is on/at zero.* **3** a hint; a suggestion: *Give me some pointers on how to do it.*

'**pointless** *adj* having no meaning or purpose: *a pointless journey.* '**pointlessly** *adv.*

points *n pl* **1** a movable section of rails which allow a train to cross over other lines or pass from one line to another: *The points had to be changed before the train could continue.* **2** the solid tips in the toes of ballet shoes: *She can dance on her points.*

be on the point of to be about to (do something): *I was on the point of going out when the telephone rang.*

come to the point 1 (*also* **get to the point**) to reach the most important consideration in a conversation *etc*: *He talked and talked but never came to the point.* **2** (*only with* **it** *as subject*) to arrive at the moment when something must be done: *He always promises to help, but when it comes to the point he's never there.*

make a point of to be especially careful to (do something): *I'll make a point of asking her today.*

make one's point to state one's opinion persuasively.

point out to indicate or draw attention to: *He pointed out his house to her*; *I pointed out that we needed more money.*

point one's toes to stretch the foot out, shaping the toes into a point, when dancing *etc.*

point-blank [point'blaŋk] *adj, adv* **1** (in shooting) very close: *He fired at her at point-blank range.* **2** abrupt(ly); without warning or explanation: *He asked her point-blank how old she was.*

poise [poiz] *v* to balance: *He poised himself on the diving-board.* – *n* **1** balance and control in bodily movement: *Good poise is important for a dancer.* **2** dignity and self-confidence: *He lost his poise for a moment.*

poised *adj* **1** staying in a state of balance and stillness: *The car was poised on the edge of the cliff.* **2** having the body in a state of tension and readiness to act: *The animal was poised ready to leap.*

poison ['poizn] *n* any substance which causes death or illness when taken into the body: *She killed herself by taking poison*; (*also adj*) *poison gas.* – *v* **1** to kill or harm with

poison: *He poisoned his wife.* **2** to put poison into (food *etc*): *He poisoned her coffee.* '**poisoner** *n.*

'**poisonous** *adj* containing or using poison: *That fruit is poisonous*; *a poisonous snake.* '**poisonously** *adv.*

poison-pen letter an anonymous letter saying wicked things about a person *etc.*

poke [pouk] **1** to push something into; to prod: *He poked a stick into the hole*; *He poked her in the ribs with his elbow.* **2** to make (a hole) by doing this: *She poked a hole in the sand with her finger.* **3** to (cause to) protrude or project: *She poked her head in at the window*; *His foot was poking out of the blankets.* – *n* an act of poking; a prod or nudge: *He gave me a poke in the arm.*

'**poker** *n* a (*usu* metal) rod for stirring up a fire.

'**poky, pokey** *adjs* (of a room *etc*) small, with not enough space.

poke about/around to look or search for something among other things.

poke fun at to laugh at unkindly: *The children often poked fun at him because of his stammer.*

poke one's nose into to interfere with other people's business: *He is always poking his nose into my affairs.*

poker[1] ['poukə] *n* a kind of card game *usu* played for money.

poker[2], **poky** *see* **poke**.

polar *see* **pole**[1].

pole[1] [poul] *n* **1** the north or south end of the Earth's axis: *the North/South Pole.* **2** the points in the heavens opposite the Earth's North and South Poles, around which stars seem to turn. **3** either of the opposite ends of a magnet: *The opposite poles of magnets attract each other.* **4** either of the opposite terminals of an electric battery: *the positive/negative pole.*

'**polar** *adj* of the earth's North or South Pole or the region around it: *the polar ice-cap*; *the polar region.*

polar bear a type of bear found near the North Pole.

be poles apart to be as different or as far apart as possible.

pole[2] [poul] *n* a long, thin, rounded piece of wood, metal *etc*: *a telegraph pole*; *a tent pole.*

'**pole-vault** *n* (in athletics *etc*) a type of jump made with the help of a pole.

polecat ['poulkat] *n* **1** a kind of large weasel. **2** (*Amer*) a skunk.

police [pə'li:s] *n pl* the men and women whose job is to prevent crime, keep order, see that laws are obeyed *etc*: *Call the police!*; *The police are investigating the matter*; (*also adj*) *the police force, a police officer.* – *v* to supply (a place) with police: *We cannot police the whole area.*

police dog a dog trained to work with policemen (in tracking criminals, finding drugs *etc*).

po'liceman, po'licewoman *ns* a member of the police.

police station the office or headquarters of a local police force: *The lost dog was taken to the police station.*

policy¹ ['poləsi] – *pl* **'policies** – *n* a planned or agreed course of action *usu* based on particular principles: *the government's policies on education.*

policy² ['poləsi] – *pl* **'policies** – *n* a (written) agreement with an insurance company: *an insurance policy.*

polio ['pouliou] (short for **poliomyelitis** [poulioumaiə'laitis]) *n* a disease of the spinal cord often causing paralysis.

polish ['poliʃ] *v* **1** to make smooth and shiny by rubbing: *She polished her shoes.* **2** (*esp* with **up**) to improve: *Polish up your English!* – *n* **1** smoothness and shininess: *There's a wonderful polish on this old wood.* **2** a kind of liquid, or other substance used to make something shiny: *furniture polish*; *silver polish.* **'polished** *adj* (*neg* **un-**).

polish off to finish: *She polished off the last of the ice-cream.*

polite [pə'lait] *adj* having or showing good manners; courteous: *a polite child*; *a polite apology.* **po'litely** *adv.* **po'liteness** *n.*

politics ['politiks] *n sing or pl* the science or business of, or ideas about, or affairs concerning, government.

po'litical *adj* of, or concerning, politics: *for political reasons*; *political studies.* **po'litically** *adv.*

,poli'tician [,-'tiʃən] *n* a person whose job is in politics; a member of parliament.

political asylum protection given by a government to a foreigner who has left his own country for political reasons.

political prisoner a person who has been imprisoned for political reasons and not for any crime.

polka ['polkə, (*Amer*) 'poulkə] *n* (a piece of music for) a type of quick, lively dance.

poll [poul] *n* **1** an election: *They organized a poll to elect a president.* **2** the number of votes: *There has been a heavy poll* (= a large number of votes). **3** (*also* **opinion poll**) a test of public opinion by asking people questions. – *v* to receive a number of votes: *He polled fifty per cent of the votes.*

'polling-booth *n* a small place or stall where one can mark one's voting-paper.

'polling-station *n* a place where one goes to vote.

go to the polls to have an election.

pollen ['polən] *n* the powder inside a flower

which fertilizes other flowers: *Bees carry pollen from flower to flower.*

pollinate ['poləneit] *v* to make (a plant) fertile by carrying pollen to it from another flower: *Insects pollinate the flowers.* **,polli-'nation** *n.*

pollute [pə'luːt] *v* to make dirty: *Chemicals are polluting the air.* **pol'lution** [-ʃən] *n.*

polo ['poulou] *n* a game like hockey, played on horseback.

'polo-neck *n* (a garment *esp* a sweater with) a high, close-fitting part around the neck: *He was wearing a polo-neck*; (*also adj*) *a polo-neck sweater.*

poltergeist ['poltəgaist, (*Amer*) 'poul-] *n* a kind of ghost that moves furniture *etc.*

polygon ['poligən, (*Amer*) -gon] *n* a two-dimensional figure with many angles and sides. **po'lygonal** [-'li-] *adj.*

polytechnic [poli'teknik] *n* a school or college in which technical subjects, *eg* engineering and building, are taught.

polythene ['poliθiːn] *n, adj* (of) any of several types of plastic that can be moulded when hot: *It's made of polythene*; *a polythene bag.*

***pomegranate** ['pomigranət] *n* a type of fruit with a thick skin and many seeds.

***pomelo** ['poməlou] – *pl* **'pomelos** – *n* a large tropical citrus fruit similar to a grapefruit.

pomp [pomp] *n* solemn stateliness and magnificence, *eg* at a ceremonial occasion: *The Queen arrived with great pomp and ceremony.*

'pompous *adj* too grand in manner or speech: *The headmaster is inclined to be a bit pompous.* **'pompously** *adv.* **'pompousness, pom'posity** [-'po-] *ns.*

pomposity *see* **pomp.**

poncho ['pontʃou] – *pl* **'ponchos** – *n* a garment made of, or like, a blanket, with a hole for the head.

pond [pond] *n* a small lake or pool: *the village pond.*

ponder ['pondə] *v* to consider carefully: *He pondered (on) the suggestion.*

pong pong [poŋ poŋ] a tropical tree with white scented flowers and round fruits with a fibrous husk.

pontiff ['pontif] *n* (in the Roman Catholic church) a bishop, *esp* the Pope.

pontoon [pon'tuːn] *n* one of the flat-bottomed boats used to support a temporary roadway (a **pontoon bridge**) across a river *etc.*

pony ['pouni] – *pl* **'ponies** – a small horse: *The child was riding a brown pony.*

'pony-tail *n* (a kind of hairstyle with the) hair tied in a bunch at the back of the head.

poodle ['puːdl] *n* a breed of dog whose curly hair is often clipped in a decorative way.

pool¹ [puːl] *n* **1** a small area of still water: *The rain left pools in the road.* **2** a similar area of any liquid: *a pool of blood/oil.* **3** a deep part of a stream or river: *He was fishing (in) a pool near the river-bank.* **4** a swimming-pool: *They spent the day at the pool.*

pool² [pu:l] *n* a stock or supply: *We put our money into a general pool.* – *v* to put together for general use: *We pooled our money and bought a caravan that we could all use.*

(football) pools *n pl* organized gambling on the results of football matches.

poor [puə] *adj* **1** having little money or property: *She is too poor to buy clothes for the children; the poor nations of the world.* **2** not good; of bad quality: *His work is very poor; a poor effort.* **3** deserving pity: *Poor fellow!* **'poorness** *n.*

'poorly *adv* not well; badly: *a poorly written essay.* – *adj* ill: *He is very poorly.*

pop¹ [pop] *n* **1** a sharp, quick, explosive noise, such as that made by a cork as it comes out of a bottle: *The paper bag burst with a loud pop.* **2** fizzy drink: *a bottle of pop.* – *v* – *pt, ptp* **popped** – **1** to (cause to) make a pop: *He popped the balloon; My balloon has popped.* **2** to spring upwards or outwards: *His eyes nearly popped out of his head in amazement.* **3** to go quickly and briefly somewhere: *He popped out to buy a newspaper.* **4** put quickly: *He popped the letter into his pocket.*

'popcorn *n* a kind of maize that bursts open when it is heated, and is eaten either sweetened or salted.

'pop-gun *n* a toy gun that fires pellets by means of compressed air.

pop up to appear: *I never know where he'll pop up next.*

pop² [pop] *adj* (short for **popular**) **1** (of music) written, played *etc* in a modern style. **2** of, or related to, pop music: *a pop group; a pop singer; a pop records.*

pope [poup] *n* (*often with cap*) the bishop of Rome, head of the Roman Catholic church: *A new Pope has been elected.*

poppy ['popi] – *pl* **'poppies** – *n* a type of plant with large, *usu* red flowers.

populace ['popjuləs] *n* the people (of a country *etc*).

popular ['popjulə] *adj* **1** liked by most people: *a popular holiday resort;' a popular person; She is very popular with children.* **2** believed by most people: *a popular theory.* **3** of the people in general: *popular rejoicing.* **4** easily read, understood *etc* by most people: *a popular history of Britain.* **'popularly** *adv* amongst, or by, most people: *He was popularly believed to have magical powers.*

'popu'larity [-'la-] *n* the state of being well liked.

'popularize, -ise *v* to make popular or

widely known: *She did much to popularize women's sport.*

populate ['popjuleit] *v* (*usu in passive*) to fill with people: *That part of the world used to be populated by wandering tribes.*

,popu'lation *n* the people living in a particular country, area *etc*: *the population of London is 8 million; a rapid increase in population.*

'populous *adj* full of people: *a populous area.*

population is singular: *The population of the city increases in the summer.*

porcelain ['po:səlin] *n, adj* (of) a kind of fine china: *That dish is made of porcelain; a porcelain figure.*

porch [po:tʃ] *n* **1** a covered entrance to a building: *They waited in the porch until it stopped raining.* **2** a veranda.

*****porcupine** ['po:kjupain] *n* a kind of gnawing animal covered with long prickles (called quills), and larger than a hedgehog.

pore¹ [po:] *n* a tiny hole, *esp* of a sweat gland in the skin.

'porous *adj* allowing liquid to pass through: *porous clay.*

pore² [po:] **pore over** to study with great attention: *He pored over his books.*

pork [po:k] *n* the flesh of a pig used as food.

pornography [po:'nogrəfi] *n* literature, pictures, films *etc* that are indecent in a sexual way. **pornographic** [po:nə'grafik] *adj.*

porous *see* pore¹.

porpoise ['po:pəs] *n* a type of blunt-nosed sea animal of the dolphin family.

porridge ['poridʒ] *n* a food made from oatmeal boiled in water or milk.

port¹ [po:t] *n* **1** (*usu without* **a** *or* **the**) a harbour: *The ship came into port; We reached port next morning.* **2** a town with a harbour: *the port of Hull.*

port² [po:t] *n* the left side of a ship or aircraft: *The helmsman steered the ship to port;* (*also adj*) *the port wing.*

port³ [po:t] a strong, dark-red, sweet wine *orig* from Portugal.

portable ['po:təbl] *adj* able to be carried, or moved easily from place to place: *a portable radio.*

portent ['po:tent] *n* something *usu* strange and remarkable that warns of some future happening: *strange signs and portents.*

porter ['po:tə] *n* **1** a person whose job is to carry luggage in a railway station *etc*: *The old lady could not find a porter to carry her suitcase from the train.* **2** a person whose job is to carry things *eg* in rough country where there is no other form of transport: *He set off into the jungle with three porters.* **3** a doorman or attendant in a hotel *etc*: *a hospital porter.*

* see illustration on p. 17

portfolio [po:t'fouliou] – *pl* **port'folios** – *n* **1** a case for carrying papers, drawings *etc*. **2** the post or job of a government minister.

porthole ['po:thoul] *n* a small, *usu* round, window in a ship.

portico ['po:tikou] – *pl* **'portico(e)s** – *n* a row of pillars supporting a roof, *usu* forming a porch to a building.

portion ['po:ʃən] *n* **1** a part: *Read this portion of the book.* **2** a share: *Her portion of the money amounted to $200.* **3** an amount of food *usu* for one person: *a portion of salad.*
   portion out to divide into portions or shares: *The money was portioned out between the three children.*

portrait ['po:trət] *n* **1** a drawing, painting, photograph *etc* of a person: *She had her portrait painted by a famous artist.* **2** a written description of a person, place *etc*: *a book called 'A portrait of London'.*

portray [po:'trei] *v* **1** to make a portrait of: *In this painting, the king is portrayed sitting on his throne.* **2** to act the part of: *the actor who portrays Hamlet.*
   portrayal [po:'treiəl] *n* the act of portraying.

pose¹ [pouz] *n* **1** a position or attitude of the body: *a relaxed pose.* **2** a false manner or way of behaving assumed in order to impress others; a pretence: *His indignation was only a pose.* – *v* **1** to position oneself *eg* for a photograph to be taken: *She posed in the doorway.* **2** (*with* **as**) to pretend to be: *He posed as a doctor.*

pose² [pouz] *v* to set or offer (a question or problem) for answering or solving: *He posed a difficult question; This poses a problem.*

posh [poʃ] *adj* of a superior type or class: *a posh family; posh clothes.*

position [ə'ziʃən] *n* **1** a way of standing, sitting *etc*: *He lay in an uncomfortable position.* **2** a place or situation: *The house is in a beautiful position.* **3** a job; a post: *He has a good position with a local bank.* **4** a point of view: *Let me explain my position on employment.* – *v* to put or place: *He positioned the lamp in the middle of the table.*
   be in, out of position to be (not) in the right place: *Is everything in position for the photograph?*

positive ['pozətiv] *adj* **1** meaning or saying 'yes': *a positive answer; They tested the water for the bacteria and the result was positive* (= the bacteria were present). **2** definite; leaving no doubt: *positive proof.* **3** certain or sure: *I'm positive he's right.* **4** complete or absolute: *His work is a positive disgrace.* **5** optimistic and prepared to make plans for the future: *Take a more positive attitude to life.* **6** not showing any comparison; not comparative or super-

lative. **7** (of a number *etc*) greater than zero. **8** having fewer electrons than normal: *In an electrical circuit, electrons flow to the positive terminal.* – *n* **1** a photographic print, made from a negative, in which light and dark are as normal. **2** (an adjective or adverb of) the positive (not comparative or superlative) degree. **'positiveness** *n*.

'positively *adv* **1** in a positive way: *He stated positively that he was innocent.* **2** absolutely; completely: *He is positively the nastiest person I know.*

possess [pə'zes] *v* to own or have: *How much money does he possess?*
   pos'session [-ʃən] *n* **1** something which is owned by a person, country *etc*: *She lost all her possessions in the fire.* **2** the state of possessing.
   pos'sessive [-siv] *adj* **1** showing that someone or something possesses an object *etc*: *'Yours', 'mine', 'his', 'hers', 'theirs' are possessive pronouns; 'your', 'my', 'his', 'their' are possessive adjectives.* **2** acting as though things and people are one's personal possessions: *a possessive mother.* **pos'sessively** *adv*. **pos'sessiveness** *n*.
   pos'sessor *n*: *He is the proud possessor of a new car.*

possible ['posəbl] *adj* **1** able to happen or be done: *It's possible that the train will be delayed; We'll come as soon as possible; I'll do everything possible; She did the only possible thing in the circumstances.* **2** satisfactory; acceptable: *I've thought of a possible solution to the problem.*
   ,possi'bility – *pl* **possi'bilities** – *n* something that is possible; the state of being possible; (a) likelihood: *There isn't much possibility of that happening; There's a possibility of war; The plan has possibilities* (= looks as if it may be a good one).
   'possibly *adv* **1** perhaps: *'Will you have time to do it?' 'Possibly.'* **2** in a way or manner that is possible: *I'll come as fast as I possibly can; I can't possibly eat any more; Could you possibly lend me your pen?*

post¹ [poust] *n* a long piece of wood, metal *etc*, *usu* fixed upright in the ground: *The notice was nailed to a post; a gate-post; the winning-post.*
   be first past the post to win.
   keep (somebody) posted to give regular information to (a person).

post² [poust] *n* (the system of collecting, transporting and delivering) letters, parcels *etc*: *I sent the book by post; Has the post arrived yet?; Is there any post for me?* – *v* to send (a letter *etc*) by post: *He posted the parcel yesterday.*
   'postage [-tidʒ] *n* (the money paid for) the sending of a letter *etc* by post: *The postage was $1·20.*

'postal adj of, or concerning, the system of sending letters etc: the postal service.

postage stamp a small printed label fixed to a letter, parcel etc to show that postage has been paid.

postal order a printed document bought at a post office, which can be exchanged at another post office for the amount of money paid for it.

postbox ['pousbɒks] n (also **'letterbox**, **'mailbox, pillar box**) a box into which letters etc are put to be collected (and sent to their destination).

postcard ['pouska:d] n a card on which a message may be sent by post, often with a picture on one side (a **picture postcard**): She sent me a postcard of the Taj Mahal when she was in India.

postcode ['pouskoud] n (Amer **zip code**) a set of letters and numbers added to the address on a letter to make delivery easier.

,post-'free adj, adv without charge for sending by post: You can send it post-free.

,post(-)'haste adv very quickly: He travelled post(-)haste to London.

postman ['pousmən] n (Amer **'mailman**) a person whose job is to (collect and) deliver letters etc: Has the postman been this morning yet?

postmark ['pousma:k] n a mark put on a letter at a post office, showing the date and place of posting, and cancelling the postage stamp: The postmark read 'Beirut'.

postmaster ['pousma:stə] – fem **postmistress** ['pousmistris] – n the manager of a post office.

post office an office for receiving and dispatching letters, parcels etc: Where is the nearest post office?

post³ [poust] n **1** a job: He has a post in the government; a teaching post. **2** a place of duty: The soldier remained at his post. **3** a settlement, camp etc esp in a distant or unpopulated area: a trading-post. – v to send somewhere on duty: He was posted abroad.

post⁴ [poust]: **the first/last post** in the army, the morning/evening bugle-call.

postage, postal, postbox, postcard, postcode see **post²**.

poster ['poustə] n a large notice or advertisement for sticking on a wall etc: Have you seen the posters advertising the circus?

posterity [po'steriti] n people coming after; future generations: The treasures must be kept for posterity.

post-free see **post²**.

post-graduate [pous'gradjuət, (Amer) -dʒuət] adj (of studies etc) done etc after a (first) university degree. – n a student doing post-graduate studies.

post(-)haste see **post²**.

posthumous ['postjuməs] adj **1** happening, coming etc to a person after his death: the posthumous publication of his book. **2** (of a child) born after its father has died. **'posthumously** adv.

postman, postmark, postmaster, postmistress see **post²**.

post mortem, postmortem [pous'mo:təm] n a medical examination of a dead body in order to find out the cause of death.

post-natal [pous'neitl] adj concerned with, or happening, in the period after birth.

post office see **post²**.

postpone [pəs'poun] v to cancel until a future time: The football match has been postponed (till tomorrow). **post'ponement** n.

postscript ['pousskript] n (often abbrev **P.S.**) a part added to a letter after the writer has signed it.

posture ['postʃə] n **1** the way in which a person places or holds his body when standing, sitting, walking etc: Good posture is important for a dancer. **2** a position or pose: He knelt in an uncomfortable posture.

postwar [poust'wo:] adj of, or belonging to, the time after a war: postwar depression.

posy ['pouzi] – pl **'posies** – n a small bunch of flowers: a posy of primroses.

pot [pot] n any one of many kinds of deep container used in cooking, for holding food, liquids etc or for growing plants: a cooking-pot; a plant-pot; a jam-pot; The waiter brought her a pot of tea. – v – pt, ptp **'potted** – to plant in a pot.

'potted adj **1** (of food) pressed into a pot or jar in order to preserve it: potted meat. **2** contained in a pot: a potted plant. **3** brief; summarized: a potted history of Britain.

'pothole n **1** a hole or cave made in rock by the action of swirling water. **2** a hole worn in a road-surface.

'pot-shot n an easy or casual shot that doesn't need careful aim: He took a pot-shot at a bird on the fence.

take pot luck to take whatever happens to be available, eg as an unexpected guest at a meal-time.

potassium [pə'tasiəm] n a silvery-white element.

potato [pə'teitou] – pl **po'tatoes** – n **1** a type of plant with round underground stems (called **tubers**) which are used as a vegetable. **2** the tuber or tubers: She bought 2 kilos of potatoes.

potato crisp (usu **crisp**: Amer **potato chip**: usu in pl) a thin, crisp, fried slice of potato: a packet of (potato) crisps.

potent ['poutənt] adj powerful; strong: a potent drink. **'potency** n.

potential [pə'tenʃəl] adj possible; that may develop into the thing mentioned: That hole in the road is a potential danger. – n the

pothole

2396

practicable

possibility, or likelihood, of successful development (in a particular way): *The land has great farming potential*; *He shows potential as a teacher.* **po'tentially** *adv.*

pothole *etc see* **pot.**

potion ['pouʃən] *n* a drink containing *eg* medicine or poison, or having a magic effect: *a love-potion.*

potter[1] ['potə] *n* a person who makes plates, cups, vases *etc* out of clay and fires them in an oven (called a **kiln**).
  '**pottery** *n* **1** articles made by fired clay: *He is learning how to make pottery.* **2** (*pl* '**potteries**) a place where articles of fired clay are made: *He is working in the pottery.* **3** the art of making such articles: *He is learning pottery.*

potter[2] ['potə] *v* to wander about doing small jobs or doing nothing important: *I spent the afternoon pottering (about).*

potty ['poti] *adj* mad; crazy: *He must be potty to do that!*

pouch [pautʃ] *n* **1** a small bag: *a tobacco-pouch.* **2** something bag-like: *This animal stores its food in two pouches under its chin.* **3** the pocket of skin in which the young of certain kinds of animal, *eg* the kangaroo, are reared.

pouffe, pouf [pu:f] *n* a large firm kind of cushion used as a seat.

poulterer *see* **poultry.**

poultry ['poultri] *n* farmyard birds, *eg* hens, ducks, geese, turkeys: *They keep poultry.*
  '**poulterer** *n* a person who sells poultry (and game) as food: *We ordered a turkey from the poulterer.*

pounce [pauns] *v* to jump suddenly, in order to seize or attack: *The cat waited beside the bird-cage, ready to pounce.* – *n* an act of pouncing; a sudden attack: *The cat made a pounce at the bird.*
  pounce on to leap upon (*eg* one's prey) in order to attack or grab it: *The tiger pounced on its victim.*

pound[1] [paund] *n* **1** (*also* **pound sterling**: *usu abbrev* **£** *when written with a number*) the standard unit of British currency, 100 (new) pence. **2** (*usu abbrev* **lb(s)** *when written with a number*) a measure of weight (0·454 kilograms).

pound[2] [paund] *n* an enclosure or pen into which stray animals are put: *a dog-pound.*

pound[3] [paund] *v* **1** to hit or strike heavily; to thump: *He pounded at the door*; *The children were pounding on the piano.* **2** to walk or run heavily: *He pounded down the road.* **3** to break up (a substance) into powder or liquid: *She pounded the dried herbs.*

pour [po:] *v* **1** to (cause to) flow in a stream: *She poured the milk into a bowl*; *Water poured down the wall*; *People were pouring*

out of the factory. **2** (*only with* **it** *as subject*) to rain heavily: *It was pouring this morning.*

pout [paut] *v* (of a sulky child *etc*) to push the lips out as a sign of displeasure. – *n* this expression of the face.

poverty ['povəti] *n* the condition of being poor: *They lived in extreme poverty*; *the poverty of the soil.*

powder ['paudə] *n* **1** any substance in the form of fine particles: *soap powder*; *milk-powder.* **2** a special kind of substance in this form, used as a cosmetic *etc*: *face-powder*; *talcum powder.* **3** formerly, gun-powder: *powder and shot.* – *v* to put powder on (one's face or body): *She powdered her nose.*
  '**powdered** *adj* in the form of fine particles of dust: *powdered chocolate.*
  '**powdery** *adj* like powder: *powdery soil.*
  powder puff a piece of very soft material used to apply face-powder *etc.*

power ['pauə] *n* **1** (an) ability: *A witch has magic power*; *A cat has the power of seeing in the dark*; *He no longer has the power to walk.* **2** strength, force or energy: *muscle power*; *water-power*; (*also adj*) *a power tool* (= a tool operated by electricity *etc*, not by hand). **3** authority or control: *political groups fighting for power*; *How much power does the Queen have?*; *I have him in my power at last.* **4** a right belonging to *eg* a person in authority: *The police have the power of arrest.* **5** a person with great authority or influence: *He is quite a power in the town.* **6** a strong and influential country: *the Western powers.* **7** the result obtained by multiplying a number by itself a given number of times: $2 \times 2 \times 2$ or 2^3 is the third power of 2, or 2 to the power of 3.
  '**powered** *adj* supplied with mechanical power: *The machine is powered by electricity*; *an electrically-powered machine.*
  '**powerful** *adj* having great strength, influence *etc*: *a powerful engine*; *He's powerful in local politics.* '**powerfully** *adv.* '**powerfulness** *n.*
  '**powerless** *adj* having no power: *The king was powerless to prevent the execution.* '**powerlessness** *n.*
  power cut, failure a break in the electricity supply: *We had a power cut last night.*
  ,**power-'driven** *adj* worked by electricity or other mechanical means, not by hand.
  power point a socket on a wall *etc* into which an electric plug can be fitted.
  power station a building where electricity is produced.
  be in power (of a political party) to be the governing party.

practicable ['praktikəbl] *adj* able to be used or done: *a practicable plan.* '**practicably** *adv.* '**practicableness, ,practica'bility** *ns.*

practical ['praktikəl] *adj* **1** concerned with the doing of something: *practical difficulties*; *His knowledge is practical rather than theoretical.* **2** (of a thing, idea *etc*) useful; effective: *You must try to find a practical answer to the problem.* **3** (*neg* **un-**) (of a person) able to do or deal with things well or efficiently: *He can look after himself – he's a very practical child.* ,practi'cality ['ka-] *n.*

'**practically** *adv* **1** almost: *The room was practically full.* **2** in a practical way: *Practically, it's more difficult than you think.*

practical joke a *usu* irritating joke consisting of an action done to someone, rather than a story told: *He nailed my chair to the floor as a practical joke.*

practice ['praktis] *n* **1** the actual doing of something, as opposed to the theory or idea: *In theory the plan should work, but in practice there are a lot of difficulties.* **2** the usual way(s) of doing things; (a) habit or custom: *It was his usual practice to rise at 6.00 a.m.* **3** the repeated performance or exercise of something in order to learn to do it well: *She has musical talent, but she needs a lot of practice*; *Have a quick practice before you start.* **4** a doctor's or lawyer's business: *He has a practice in Southampton.*

be in/out of practice (not) having had a lot of practice recently: *I haven't played the piano for months – I'm very out of practice.*

make a practice of to do (something) habitually: *He makes a practice of arriving late at parties.*

put into practice to do, as opposed to planning *etc*: *He never gets the chance to put his ideas into practice.*

practice is a noun: **practice** (not **practise**) makes perfect.

practise ['praktis] *v* **1** to do exercises to improve one's performance in a particular skill *etc*: *She practises the piano every day*; *You must practise more if you want to enter the competition.* **2** to make (something) a habit: *to practise self-control.* **3** to do or follow (a profession, *usu* medicine or law): *He practises (law) in London.*

'**practised** *adj* skilled through much practice: *a practised performer.*

practise is a verb: to **practise** (not **practice**) the guitar.

practitioner *see* **general practitioner**.

prahu ['praːhuː] *n* a swift Malay sailing boat.

prairie ['preəri] *n* (*often in pl*) in N America, an area of flat, treeless, grass-covered land.

praise [preiz] *v* **1** to express admiration or approval of; to commend: *He praised her singing.* **2** to glorify (God) by singing hymns *etc*: *Praise the Lord!* – *n* the expression of approval or honour: *He has received a lot of praise for his musical skill.*

'**praiseworthy** *adj* deserving praise: *a praiseworthy attempt.*

pram [pram] *n* (*Amer* **baby buggy/carriage**) a kind of small carriage on wheels for carrying a baby, pushed by its mother *etc*.

prance [praːns] *v* (*eg* of horses) to dance or jump about.

prank [praŋk] *n* a trick; a practical joke.

prattle ['pratl] *v* to talk or chatter about unimportant things or like a child. – *n* childish talk; chatter.

prawn [proːn] *n* a type of edible shellfish like the shrimp.

pray [prei] *v* **1** to speak reverently to God or a god in order to express thanks, make a request *etc*: *Let us pray*; *She prayed to God to help her.* **2** to hope earnestly: *Everybody is praying for rain.*

'**prayer** *n* (an) act of praying: *a book of prayer*; *The child said his prayers*; *My prayers have been answered* (= I've got what I desired).

pray is a verb: to **pray** (not **prey**) for peace.

preach [priːtʃ] *v* **1** to give a talk (called a sermon), *usu* during a religious service, about religious or moral matters: *The vicar preached (a sermon) on/about pride.* **2** to speak to someone as though giving a sermon: *Don't preach at me!* **3** to advise: *He preaches caution.* '**preacher** *n.*

prearranged [priːəˈreindʒd] *adj* arranged or agreed previously: *At a prearranged signal, they all rose to their feet.*

precarious [priˈkeəriəs] *adj* insecure; risky or dangerous. **pre'cariously** *adv.* **pre'cariousness** *n.*

precaution [priˈkoːʃən] *n* care taken to avoid accidents, disease *etc*: *They took every precaution to ensure that their journey would be safe and enjoyable.* **pre'cautionary** *adj.*

precede [priˈsiːd] *v* to go, happen *etc* before: *She preceded him into the room.*

precedence ['presidəns] *n* (the right of) going before in order of importance *etc*: *This matter is urgent and should be given precedence over others at the moment.*

,**precedent** ['presidənt] *n* a past action, *esp* a legal decision, which may act as a guide or rule in the future.

pre'ceding *adj*: *on the preceding page.*

precinct ['priːsiŋkt] *n* **1** (*often in pl*) the space surrounding a building *etc* (originally within walls or boundaries): *the cathedral precincts.* **2** (*esp Amer*) an administrative district: *a police precinct.*

pedestrian/shopping precinct an area of shops where no cars are allowed.

precious ['preʃəs] *adj* of great value: *precious jewels.*

precious metal a valuable metal such as gold, silver or platinum.

precious stone a jewel; a gem: *diamonds, emeralds and other precious stones.*

precious few/little very few/little: *I've precious little money left.*

precipice ['presipis] *n* a steep cliff.

precipitous [pri'sipitəs] *adj* very steep.

precipitate [pri'sipiteit] *n* the substance that settles at the bottom of a liquid.

precipitous *see* precipice.

précis ['preisi:, *(Amer also)* prei'si:] – *pl* **'précis** [-z] – *n* a summary of a piece of writing.

precise [pri'sais] *adj* **1** exact: *Give me his precise words; precise instructions; a precise translation.* **2** careful to be accurate and exact in manner, speech *etc*: *He is always very precise.* **pre'ciseness** *n.*

pre'cisely *adv* **1** exactly: *at midday precisely; Precisely what do you mean?; He spoke very precisely.* **2** used to express complete agreement: *'So you think we should wait until tomorrow?' 'Precisely.'*

pre'cision [-'siʒən] *n* exactness; accuracy: *He spoke with great precision; (also adj) precision tools* (= tools used for obtaining very accurate results).

predator ['predətə] *n* a bird, *eg* a hawk, or animal, *eg* a lion, that attacks and kills others for food.

'predatory *adj* living by attacking and feeding on others: *a predatory animal.*

predecessor ['pri:disesə, *(Amer)* 'pre-] *n* **1** someone who has had a particular job or position before: *He was my predecessor as manager.* **2** an ancestor: *My predecessors came from Scotland.*

predicament [pri'dikəmənt] *n* an unfortunate or difficult situation.

predicate ['predikət] *n* what is said about the subject of a sentence: *We live in London; The president of the republic died.*

predict [pri'dikt] *v* to say in advance; to foretell: *He predicted a change in the weather.*

pre'dictable *adj (neg un-)* able to be foretold: *His anger was predictable.*

pre'diction [-ʃən] *n: I'm making no predictions about the result of the race.*

predominate [pri'domineit] *v* to be the stronger or greater in amount, size, number *etc*: *In this part of the country industry predominates (over agriculture).*

pre'dominant *adj* stronger, more numerous, more noticeable *etc*: *The English language is predominant in America.* **pre'dominantly** *adv.* **pre'dominance** *n.*

preen [pri:n] *v* **1** (of birds) to arrange (the feathers): *The sea-gulls were preening themselves/their feathers.* **2** used unkindly, meaning to attend to one's appearance: *The woman was preening herself in front of the mirror.*

prefabricated [pri:'fabrikeitid] *adj* (of a building *etc*) made of parts manufactured in advance and ready to be put together: *prefabricated bungalows.*

preface ['prefəs] *n* an introduction to a book *etc*: *The preface explained how to use the dictionary.*

prefect ['pri:fekt] *n* **1** one of a number of senior pupils having special powers in a school *etc*. **2** in some countries, an administrative official.

prefer [pri'fə:] – *pt, ptp* **pre'ferred** – *v* to like better: *Which do you prefer – tea or coffee?; I prefer reading to watching television; She would prefer to come with you rather than stay here.*

'preferable ['pre-] *adj* more desirable: *Is it preferable to write or make a telephone call?* **'preferably** *adv.*

'preference ['pre-] *n* (a) choice of, or (a) liking for, one thing rather than another: *He likes most music but he has a preference for classical music.*

> I **prefer** apples **to** (not **than**) oranges.
> **preferable**, adjective, is spelt with **-r-**.
> **preference**, noun, is spelt with **-r-**.
> **preferred** and **preferring** are spelt with **-rr-**.

prefix ['pri:fiks] *n* a syllable or syllables put at the beginning of another word to change its meaning: *dislike; unemployed; remake; ineffective.*

pregnant ['pregnənt] *adj* carrying unborn young in the womb. **'pregnancy** (*pl* **'pregnancies**) *n.*

prehistoric [pri:i'storik] *adj* of, or belonging to, the time before recorded history: *a prehistoric monster.*

prejudge [pri:'dʒʌdʒ] *v* to make a decision about something before hearing all the facts.

prejudice ['predʒədis] *n* (an) opinion or feeling for or *esp* against something, formed unfairly or unreasonably *ie* without proper knowledge: *The jury must listen to his statement without prejudice; Is racial prejudice* (= dislike of people because of their race) *increasing in this country? – v* **1** to cause to feel prejudice for or against something. **2** to harm or endanger (a person's position, prospects *etc*) in some way: *Your terrible handwriting will prejudice your chances of passing the exam.*

'prejudiced *adj* having or showing prejudice: *a prejudiced attitude to people of other races; Don't be so prejudiced.*

preliminary [pri'liminəri] *adj* coming before, and preparing for, something: *The chair-*

man made a few preliminary remarks before introducing the speaker.

prelude ['prelju:d] *n* **1** an event *etc* that goes before, and acts as an introduction to, something. **2** a piece of music played as an introduction to the main piece.

premature [premə'tʃuə, (*Amer*) pri:-] *adj* happening *etc* before the right or expected time: *a premature birth*; *The baby was three weeks premature.* ,**prema'turely** *adv.*

premeditated [pri'mediteitid] *adj* thought out in advance; planned: *premeditated murder.*

premier ['premiə, (*Amer*) 'pri:-] *adj* first or leading: *Italy's premier industrialist. – n* a prime minister: *the French premier.*

première ['premiеə, (*Amer*) pri'miər] *n* the first performance of a play, film *etc.*

premises ['premisiz] *n pl* (a part of) a building and the area of ground belonging to it: *These premises are used by the local football team.*

premonition [premə'niʃən] *n* a feeling that something (*esp* something unpleasant) is going to happen.

preoccupy [pri'okjupai] *v* to engage or occupy (a person's mind *etc*) or the attention of (someone) completely: *His mind was pre-occupied with plans for his holiday.* **pre,occu'pation** *n.*

prepaid *see* **prepay.**

prepare [pri'peə] *v* to make or get ready: *Have you prepared your speech for Thursday?*; *My mother prepared a meal*; *He prepared to go out*; *Prepare yourself for a shock.* **preparation** [prepə'reiʃən] *n* **1** the act of preparing: *You can't pass an exam without preparation.* **2** something done to prepare: *She was making hasty preparations for her departure.*
preparatory [-'parə-] *adj* acting as an introduction or in order to prepare for something: *Political leaders have agreed to meet for preparatory talks about an end to the war.*
pre'pared *adj* (*neg* **un-**) made ready.
preparatory school [-'parə-] a private school which educates children in preparation for a senior school (*abbrev* **prep school** [prep-]).
be prepared (of a person) to be ready (for something, to do something *etc*): *We must be prepared for a disappointment; I'm not prepared (=willing) to lend him more money; The motto of the Scouts is 'Be Prepared!'.*

prepay [pri:'pei] – *pt, ptp* ,**pre'paid** – *v* to pay in advance. ,**pre'payment** *n.*

preposition [prepə'ziʃən] *n* a word put before a noun or pronoun to show how it is related to another word: *through the window*; *in the garden*; *written by me.* ,**prepo'sitional** *adj.*

preposterous [pri'postərəs] *adj* very foolish; ridiculous. **pre'posterously** *adv.*

prerequisite [pri:'rekwizit] *n, adj* (something that is) necessary for something else to be done or happen: *An interest in children is (a) prerequisite for a teacher.*

prerogative [prə'rogətiv] *n* a special right or privilege belonging to a person because of his rank, position *etc.*

prescribe [prə'skraib] *v* to advise or order (the use of): *My doctor prescribed some pills for my cold*; *Here is a list of books prescribed by the examiners for the exam.*
pre'scription [-'skrip-] **1** a doctor's (*usu* written) instructions for the preparing and taking of a medicine: *He gave me a pre-scription to give to the chemist.* **2** the act of prescribing.

presence ['prezns] *n* **1** the state, or fact, of being present: *The committee requests your presence at Thursday's meeting.* **2** a striking, impressive manner or appearance: *The headmistress certainly has presence.*
in the presence of while (someone) is present: *This document must be signed in the presence of a witness*; *Don't talk about it in my mother's presence.*
presence of mind calmness and the ability to act sensibly (in an emergency *etc*): *He showed great presence of mind in the face of danger.*

present¹ ['preznt] *adj* **1** being here, or at the place, occasion *etc* mentioned: *My father was present on that occasion*; *Who else was present at the wedding?*; *Now that the whole class is present, we can begin the lesson.* **2** existing now: *the present moment*; *the present prime minister.* **3** (of the tense of a verb) indicating action now: *In the sentence 'She wants a chocolate', the verb is in the present tense.*
'**presently** *adv* **1** soon: *He will be here presently.* **2** (*esp Amer*) at the present time: *The manager is presently on holiday.*
the present the time now: *Forget the past – think more of the present and the future!*
at present at the present time: *He's away from home at present.*
for the present as far as the present time is concerned: *You've done enough work for the present.*

present² [pri'zent] *v* **1** to give, *esp* formally or ceremonially: *The child presented a bunch of flowers to the Queen*; *He was presented with a gold watch when he retired.* **2** to introduce: *My I present my wife (to you)?* **3** to arrange the production of (a play, film *etc*): *The Elizabethan Theatre Company present 'Hamlet', by William Shakespeare.* **4** to offer (ideas *etc*) for consideration, or (a problem *etc*) for solving: *She presents (=expresses) her ideas very clearly*; *The* *situation presents a problem.* **5** to bring (oneself); to appear: *He presented himself at the dinner table half an hour late.* **pre-'senter** *n.*

pre'sentable *adj* suitable to be seen, introduced *etc*: *You don't look very presentable in those clothes.*

,presen'tation [pre-] *n* **1** the act of presenting: *the presentation of the prizes; the presentation of a new play; (also adj) a presentation ceremony; a presentation gold watch.* **2** the manner in which written work *etc* is presented or set out: *Try to improve the presentation of your work.* **3** a performance, or set of repeated performances, of a play, opera *etc*: *This is the best presentation of 'Macbeth' that I've ever seen.*

present³ ['preznt] *n* a gift: *a wedding present; birthday presents.*

presently *see* **present¹**.

preserve [pri'zɔːv] *v* **1** to keep safe from harm: *(May) Heaven preserve us from danger!* **2** to keep in existence: *They have managed to preserve many old documents.* **3** to treat (food), *eg* by cooking it with sugar, so that it will not go bad: *What is the best method of preserving raspberries? – n* **1** an activity, kind of work *etc* in which only certain people are allowed to take part. **2** a place where game animals, birds *etc* are protected: *a game preserve.* **3** jam: *blackberry jam and other preserves.*

,preser'vation [pre-] *n* the action of preserving or the state or process of being preserved.

pre'servative [-vətiv] *n* something that preserves, *esp* that prevents food *etc* from going bad: *a chemical preservative.*

preside [pri'zaid] *v* to be the chairman of a meeting *etc*: *The prime minister presided at/over the meeting.*

presidency ['prezidənsi] – *pl* **'presidencies** – *n* **1** the rank or office of a president: *His ambition is the presidency.* **2** the period of time for which somebody is president: *during the presidency of Dwight D. Eisenhower.*

president ['prezidənt] *n* **1** the leading member of a club, association *etc*: *She was elected president of the Music Society.* **2** the leader of a republic: *the President of the United States.*

presidential [prezi'denʃəl] *adj*: *a presidential election.*

press [pres] *v* **1** to use a pushing motion (against): *Press the bell twice!; The children pressed close to their mother.* **2** to squeeze; to flatten: *The grapes are pressed to extract the juice.* **3** *v* to urge or hurry: *He pressed her to enter the competition.* **4** to insist on: *The printers are pressing their claim for higher pay.* **5** to iron: *Your trousers need to be pressed. – n* **1** an act of pressing: *He gave*

her hand a press; *You had better give your shirt a press.* **2** *(also* **'printing-press)** a printing machine. **3** newspapers in general: *It was reported in the press; (also adj) a press photographer.* **4** the people who work on newspapers and magazines; journalists: *The press is/are always interested in the private lives of famous people.* **5** a device or machine for pressing: *a wine-press; a flower-press.*

'pressing *adj* urgent: *a pressing invitation.*

press conference a meeting in which information is given to journalists.

'press-cutting *n* an article cut out of a newspaper or magazine.

be hard pressed to be in difficulties: *He's hard pressed financially.*

be pressed for to be short of: *I must hurry – I'm pressed for time.*

press for to try to get; to keep demanding: *The miners are pressing for higher wages.*

press forward/on to continue (in spite of difficulties): *She pressed on with her work.*

pressure ['preʃə] *n* **1** (the amount of force exerted by) the action of pressing: *to apply pressure to a cut to stop bleeding; A barometer measures atmospheric pressure.* **2** (a) strain or stress: *The pressures of her work are sometimes too much for her.* **3** strong persuasion; compulsion or force: *He agreed under pressure.*

'pressurize, -ise *v* **1** to fit (an aeroplane *etc*) with a device that keeps air pressure normal: *The cabins have all been pressurized.* **2** to force: *He was pressurized into giving up his job.*

pressure cooker a type of saucepan in which food is cooked quickly by steam kept under great pressure.

prestige [pre'stiːʒ] *n* reputation or influence due to success, rank *etc*.

presume [prə'zjuːm] *v* **1** to believe that something is true without proof; to take for granted: *When I found the room empty, I presumed that you had gone home; 'Has he gone?' 'I presume so.'* **2** to be bold enough (to act without the right, knowledge *etc* to do so): *I wouldn't presume to advise someone as clever as you.*

pre'sumably *adv* I presume: *She's not in her office – presumably she went home early.*

pre'sumption [-'zʌmp-] *n* **1** something presumed: *She married again, on the presumption that her first husband was dead.* **2** unsuitable boldness, *eg* in one's behaviour towards another person.

pre'sumptuous [-'zʌmptjuəs, *(Amer)* -'zʌmptʃuəs] *adj* impolitely bold. **pre'sumptuousness** *n*.

pretend [pri'tend] *v* **1** to make believe that something is true, in play: *Let's pretend that this room is a cave!; Pretend to be a lion!;*

He wasn't really angry – he was only pre-tending. **2** to try to make it appear (that something is true), in order to deceive: *He pretended that he had a headache; She was only pretending to be asleep; I pretended not to understand.*

pre'tence, (*Amer*) **pre'tense** [-s] *n* (an) act of pretending: *Under the pretence of friendship, he persuaded her to get into his car.*

false pretences acts or behaviour intended to deceive: *He got the money under false pretences.*

pretext ['pri:tekst] *n* a reason given in order to hide the real reason; an excuse.

pretty ['priti] *adj* **1** (not *usu* of boys and men) pleasing or attractive: *a pretty girl/tune/picture/dress.* **2** used jokingly: *This is a pretty mess!* – *adv* rather: *That's pretty good; He's pretty old now.* **'prettily** *adv.* **'prettiness** *n.*

pretty much the same, alike *etc* more or less the same, alike *etc.*

pretty well nearly: *I've pretty well finished.*

prevail [pri'veil] *v* **1** (*with* **over** *or* **against**) to win or succeed: *With God's help we shall prevail over sin and wickedness; Truth must prevail in the end.* **2** to be most usual or common: *This mistaken belief still prevails in some parts of the country.*

pre'vailing *adj* **1** most frequent: *The prevailing winds are from the west.* **2** common or widespread at the present time: *the prevailing mood of discontent among young people.*

prevalent ['prevələnt] *adj* common; widespread: *Lung diseases used to be prevalent among miners.* **prevalence** ['prevələns] *n.*

prevail on, upon to persuade: *Can I prevail on you to stay for supper?*

prevent [pri'vent] *v* to stop (someone doing something or something happening): *He prevented me from going.*

pre'vention [-ʃən] *n* the act of preventing: *a society for the prevention of road accidents.* **pre'ventive** [-tiv] *adj* that helps to prevent illness *etc*: *preventive medicine.*

preview ['pri:vju:] *n* a viewing of a performance, exhibition *etc* before it is open to the public.

previous ['pri:viəs] *adj* earlier in time or order: *on a previous occasion; the previous owner of the house.* **'previously** *adv.*

previous to before: *They told their families about their engagement previous to publishing it in the newspaper.*

prey [prei] – *pl* **prey** – *n* a bird or animal, birds or animals, that is/are hunted by other birds or animals for food: *The lion tore at its prey.*

beast/bird of prey an animal, *eg* the lion, or a bird, *eg* the eagle, that kills and eats others.

prey on, upon to attack as prey: *Hawks prey upon smaller birds.*

prey is a noun or a verb: a bird of prey (not pray); to prey on (not pray on) smaller creatures.

price [prais] *n* **1** the amount of money for which a thing is or can be bought or sold; the cost: *The price of the book was $10.* **2** what one must give up or suffer in order to gain something: *Loss of freedom is often the price of success.* – *v* **1** to mark a price on: *I haven't priced these articles yet.* **2** to find out the price of: *He went into the furniture shop to price the beds.*

'priceless *adj* **1** too valuable to have a price: *priceless jewels.* **2** very funny: *a priceless story.*

'pricey *adj* expensive.

at a price at a high price: *We can get dinner at this hotel – at a price.*

beyond/without price very precious: *Good health is beyond price.*

prick [prik] *v* to pierce slightly or stick a sharp point into: *She pricked her finger on a pin; He pricked a hole in the paper.* – *n* **1** (a pain caused by) an act of pricking: *You'll just feel a slight prick in your arm.* **2** a tiny hole made by a sharp point: *a pin-prick.*

prick (up) one's ears (of an animal) to raise the ears in excitement, attention *etc*: *The dog pricked up its ears at the sound of the doorbell.*

prickle ['prikl] *n* **1** a sharp point growing on a plant or animal: *A hedgehog is covered with prickles.* **2** a feeling of being pricked: *a prickle of fear.*

'prickly *adj* **1** covered with prickles: *Holly is a prickly plant.* **2** pricking; stinging: *a prickly rash.* **'prickliness** *n.*

pride [praid] *n* **1** a feeling of pleasure and satisfaction at one's achievements, possessions, family *etc*: *She looked with pride at her handsome sons.* **2** personal dignity: *His pride was hurt by her criticism.* **3** a group (of lions or of peacocks): *a pride of lions.*

be the pride and joy of to be the object of the pride of: *He was his parents' pride and joy.*

the pride of the finest thing in (a certain group *etc*): *The pride of our collection is this painting.*

pride of place the most important place: *They gave pride of place at the exhibition to a Chinese vase.*

pride oneself on to take pride in, or feel satisfaction with (something one has done, achieved *etc*): *He prides himself on his driving skill.*

take pride in to feel pride about: *You should take more pride in* (=care more for) *your appearance.*

priest [pri:st] *n* **1** (in the Christian Church, *esp* the Roman Catholic, Orthodox and Anglican churches) a clergyman. **2** (*fem* **'priestess**) (in non-Christian religions) an official who performs sacrifices *etc* to the god(s).
'priesthood *n* **1** priests in general: *the Anglican priesthood.* **2** the office or position of a priest: *He was called to the priesthood.*

prig [prig] *n* a person who is too satisfied with his/her own behaviour, beliefs *etc*. **'priggish** *adj*. **'priggishly** *adv*. **'priggishness** *n*.

prim [prim] *adj* (of a person, behaviour *etc*) too formal and correct: *a prim manner*; *a prim old lady.* **'primly** *adv*. **'primness** *n*.

prima ['pri:mə]: **prima ballerina** the leading female dancer in a ballet company.
prima donna [-'donə] a leading female opera singer.

primary *see* prime¹.

primate¹ ['praimeit] *n* an archbishop.

primate² ['praimət] *n* a member of the highest order of mammals, *ie* man, monkeys, apes, lemurs.

prime¹ [praim] *adj* **1** first or most important: *the prime minister*; *a matter of prime importance.* **2** best: *in prime condition.* – *n* the best part (of a person's *etc* life, *usu* early middle age): *He is in his prime*; *the prime of life.*
'primary *adj* **1** first or most important: *his primary concern.* **2** of the first level or stage: *a primary school.*
'primarily [(*Amer*) prai'me-] *adv* chiefly; in the first place: *I wrote the play primarily as a protest, and only secondarily as entertainment.*
primary colours (of pigments, but not of light) those colours from which all others can be made, *ie* red, blue and yellow.
prime minister the chief minister of a government.
prime number a number that can only be divided without a remainder by itself and 1, *eg* 3, 5, 7, 31.

prime² [praim] *v* to prepare (something) by putting something into or on it: *He primed* (=put gunpowder into) *his gun*; *You must prime* (=treat with primer) *the wood before you paint it.*
'primer *n* **1** a book that gives basic information about a subject. **2** a substance put on a surface to prime it before painting.

primitive ['primətiv] *adj* **1** belonging to the earliest times: *primitive stone tools.* **2** simple or rough: *He made a primitive boat out of some pieces of wood.*

primrose ['primrouz] *n* **1** a kind of pale yellow spring flower common in woods and hedges. **2** (*also adj*) (of) its colour: *primrose walls.*

prince [prins] *n* **1** a male member of a royal family, *esp* the son of a king or queen:

Prince Charles. **2** the ruler of some states or countries: *Prince Rainier of Monaco.*
'princely *adj* **1** of a prince: *princely duties.* **2** magnificent; splendid: *a princely gift.*

princess [prin'ses, (*Amer*) 'prinsəs] *n* **1** the wife or widow of a prince. **2** a woman of the same rank as a prince in her own right: *Princess Anne.*

princi'pality [-'pa-] – *pl* **,princi'palities** – *n* a state or country ruled by a prince.

principal ['prinsəpəl] *adj* most important: *Shipbuilding was one of Britain's principal industries.* – *n* **1** the head of a school, college or university. **2** a leading actor, singer or dancer in a theatrical production. **3** the amount of money in a bank *etc* on which interest is paid.
'principally *adv* mostly; chiefly: *I am principally concerned with teaching English.*

principality *see* prince.

principle ['prinsəpəl] *n* **1** a general truth, rule or law: *the principle of gravity.* **2** the theory by which a machine *etc* works: *the principle of the jet engine.*
'principles *n pl* one's own personal rules or standards of behaviour: *It is against my principles to borrow money.*
in principle in general, as opposed to in detail.
on principle because of one's principles: *I never borrow money, on principle.*

print [print] *n* **1** a mark made by pressure: *a footprint*; *a fingerprint.* **2** printed lettering: *I can't read the print in this book.* **3** a photograph made from a negative: *I entered three prints for the photographic competition.* **4** a printed reproduction of a painting or drawing. – *v* **1** to mark (letters *etc*) on paper (by using a printing press *etc*): *The invitations will be printed on white paper.* **2** to publish (a book, article *etc*) in printed form: *His new novel will be printed next month.* **3** to produce (a photographic image) on paper: *He develops and prints his own photographs.* **4** to mark designs on (cloth *etc*): *When the cloth has been woven, it is dyed and printed.* **5** to write, using capital letters: *Please print your name and address.*
'printer *n* a person who prints books, newspapers *etc*.
'printing *n* the work of a printer.
'printing-press *n* (*also* **press**) a machine for printing.
'print-out *n* the printed information given by a computer.
in/out of print (of books) available/unavail-

able to be bought from the publisher: *That book has been out of print for years.*

prior[1] ['praiə] *adj* **1** already arranged for the same time: *a prior engagement.* **2** more important: *She gave up her job as she felt her family had a prior claim on her attention.* **pri'ority** [-'o-] **1** the right to be or go first: *An ambulance must have priority over other traffic.* **2** (*pl* **pri'orities**) something that must be considered or done first: *Our* (*first*) *priority is to feed the hungry.*
prior to before: *Prior to working in America, he had travelled in Europe.*

prior[2] ['praiə] – *fem* **'prioress** – *n* the head of a priory.
'priory – *pl* **'priories** – *n* a building in which a community of monks or nuns live.

prise, (*esp Amer*) **prize** [praiz] *v* to use force to dislodge (something) from its position: *He prised open the lid with a knife.*

prism ['prizm] *n* **1** a solid figure whose sides are parallel and whose two ends are the same in shape and size. **2** a glass object of this shape, *usu* with triangular ends, which breaks up a beam of white light into the colours of the rainbow. **pris'matic** [-'ma-] *adj.*

prison ['prizn] *n* a building in which criminals are kept; a jail: *He was sent to prison; He is in prison.*
'prisoner *n* anyone who has been captured and is held against his will as a criminal, in a war *etc*: *The prisoners escaped from jail.*
prisoner of war – *pl* **prisoners of war** – a member of the armed forces captured in a war.
take, keep, hold prisoner to (capture and) confine (a person) against his will: *Many soldiers were killed and the rest taken prisoner; She was kept prisoner in a locked room.*

private ['praivət] *adj* **1** of, for, or belonging to, one person or group, not to the general public: *The headmaster lives in a private apartment in the school; in my private* (= *personal*) *opinion; This information is to be kept strictly private; You shouldn't listen to private conversations.* **2** having no public or official position or rank: *It is your duty as a private citizen to report this matter to the police.* – *n* in the army, an ordinary soldier, not an officer.
privacy ['privəsi, (*Amer*) 'prai-] *n* the state of being away from other people's sight or interest: *in the privacy of your own home.*
'privately *adv.*
private enterprise the management and financing of industry *etc* by individual persons or companies and not by the state.
private means money that does not come from one's work but from investment, inheritance *etc.*

in private with no-one else listening or watching; not in public: *May I speak to you in private?*

privation [prai'veiʃən] *n* poverty; hardship.

privilege ['privəlidʒ] *n* (a) favour or right available, or granted, to only one person, or to a small number of people: *Senior students are usually allowed certain privileges.*
'privileged *adj.*

privy ['privi]: **privy council** a group of statesmen appointed as advisers to a king or queen.

prize[1] [praiz] *n* **1** a reward for good work *etc*: *He was awarded a lot of prizes at school.* **2** something won in a competition *etc*: *I've won first prize!*; (*also adj*) *a prize* (= having won, or worthy of, a prize) *bull.* – *v* to value highly: *He prized my friendship above everything else.*

prize[2] see **prise**.

pro[1] [prou] short for **professional**.

pro[2] [prou]: **pros and cons** [prouzən'konz] the arguments for and against: *Let's hear all the pros and cons before we make a decision.*

pro- [prou] in favour of: **pro-British**.

probable ['probəbl] *adj* that may be expected to happen or be true; likely: *the probable result; Such an event is possible but not probable.*
'probably *adv*: *I'll probably telephone you this evening.*
proba'bility – *pl* **proba'bilities** – *n* **1** the state or fact of being probable; likelihood: *There isn't much probability of that happening.* **2** an event, result *etc* that is probable: *Let's consider the probabilities.*
in all probability most probably; most likely.

probation [prə'beiʃən, (*Amer*) prou-] *n* **1** the system allowing people who have broken the law to go free on condition that they commit no more crimes and report regularly to a social worker. **2** (in certain jobs) a period of time during which a person is carefully watched to see that he is capable of the job. **pro'bationary** *adj.*
be/put on probation to (cause to) undergo a period of probation.

probe [proub] *n* **1** a long thin instrument used by doctors to examine a wound *etc*. **2** an investigation: *a police probe into illegal activities.* – *v* **1** to investigate: *He probed into her private life.* **2** to examine (as if) with a probe: *The doctor probed the wound; He probed about in the hole with a stick.*

problem ['probləm] *n* **1** a difficulty; a matter about which it is difficult to decide what to do: *Life is full of problems*; (*also adj*) *a problem child.* **2** a question to be answered or solved: *mathematical problems.* **,proble'matic(al)** [-'ma-] *adj.*

proboscis [prə'bosis] *n* a nose, or mouth-part in certain animals, insects *etc*.

procedure [prə'si:dʒə] *n* the order or method of doing something: *They followed the usual procedure(s)*. **pro'cedural** *adj*.

proceed [prə'si:d] *v* 1 to go on; to continue: *They proceeded along the road*; *They proceeded with their work*. 2 to follow a course of action: *I want to make a cupboard, but I don't know how to proceed*. 3 to begin (to do something): *They proceeded to ask a lot of questions*. 4 to result: *Fear often proceeds from ignorance*. 5 to take legal action (against): *The police decided not to proceed against her*.

pro'ceedings *n pl* 1 the things said and done at a meeting of a society *etc*. 2 a legal action: *We shall start proceedings against him if the bill is not paid*.

proceeds ['prousi:dz] *n pl* money or profit made (from a sale *etc*): *They gave the proceeds of the sale to charity*.

process ['prouses, (*Amer*) 'pro-] *n* ‧ 1 a method or way of manufacturing things: *We are using a new process to make glass*. 2 a series of events that produce change or development: *The process of growing up can be difficult for a child*; *the digestive processes*. 3 a course of action undertaken: *Carrying him down the mountain was a slow process*. – *v* to deal with (something) by the appropriate process: *Have your photographs been processed?*; *The information is being processed by computer*.

'processed *adj* (of food) treated in a special way: *processed cheese/peas*.

in the process of in the course of: *He is in the process of changing jobs*; *These goods were damaged in the process of manufacture*.

procession [prə'seʃən] *n* a line of people, vehicles *etc* moving forward in order, *esp* for a ceremonial purpose: *The procession moved slowly through the streets*.

proclaim [prə'kleim, (*Amer*) prou-] *v* to announce or state publicly: *He was proclaimed the winner*.

procla'mation [proklə-] *n* 1 an official, *usu* ceremonial, announcement made to the public: *a royal proclamation*. 2 the act of proclaiming.

procrastinate [prə'krastineit] *v* to delay or put off doing something: *Stop procrastinating and do it now!*

procure [prə'kjuə] *v* to get or obtain: *He managed to procure a car*.

prod [prod] – *pt, ptp* **'prodded** – *v* 1 to push with something pointed; to poke: *He prodded her arm with his finger*. 2 to urge or encourage: *He prodded her into action*. – *n* an act of prodding: *She gave him a prod*.

prodigal ['prodigəl] *adj* spending (money *etc*) too extravagantly; wasteful. **'prodigally** *adv*. **prodi'gality** [-'ga-] *n*.

prodigy ['prodidʒi] – *pl* **'prodigies** – *n* something strange and wonderful: *A very clever child is sometimes called a child prodigy*; *prodigies of nature*.

produce [prə'dju:s] *v* 1 to bring out: *She produced a letter from her pocket*. 2 to give birth to: *A cow produces one or two calves a year*. 3 to cause: *His joke produced a shriek of laughter from the children*. 4 to make or manufacture: *The factory produces furniture*. 5 to give or yield: *The country produces enough food for the population*. 6 to arrange and prepare (a theatre performance, film, television programme *etc*): *The play was produced by Henry Dobson*. – ['prodju:s] *n* something that is produced, *esp* crops, eggs, milk *etc* from farms: *agricultural/farm produce*.

pro'ducer *n* a person who produces a play, film, *etc*, but is *usu* not responsible for instructing the actors.

product ['prodəkt] *n* 1 a result: *The plan was the product of hours of thought*. 2 something manufactured: *The firm manufactures metal products*. 3 the result of multiplying one number by another: *The product of 9 and 2 is 18*.

pro'duction [-'dʌkʃən] *n* 1 the act or process of producing something: *car-production*; *The production of the film cost a million dollars*. 2 the amount produced, *esp* of manufactured goods: *The new methods increased production*. 3 a particular performance, or set of repeated performances, of a play *etc*: *I prefer this production of 'Hamlet' to the one I saw two years ago*.

pro'ductive [-'dʌktiv] *adj* (*neg* **un-**) producing a lot; fruitful: *productive land*; *Our discussion was not very productive*.

productivity [prodək'tivəti] *n* the rate or efficiency of work *esp* in industrial production.

profess [prə'fes] *v* 1 to state or declare openly. 2 to claim or pretend: *He professed to be an expert*.

pro'fession [-ʃən] *n* 1 an occupation or job that needs special knowledge, *eg* medicine, law, teaching, engineering *etc*. 2 the people who have such an occupation: *the legal profession*. 3 an open statement or declaration.

pro'fessional [-ʃə-] *adj* (*neg* **un-**) 1 of a profession: *professional skill*. 2 of a very high standard: *a very professional performance*. 3 earning money by performing, or giving instruction, in a sport or other activity that is a pastime for other people; not amateur: *a professional musician/golfer*. – *n* (*abbrev* **pro** [prou]) a person who is professional: *a golf professional/pro*.

pro'fessionally adv.

professor [prə'fesə] n (often abbrev **Prof.** when written) **1** a university teacher who is the head of a department: He is a professor of English at Leeds; Professor Jones. **2** (Amer) a university teacher. **,profes'sorial** [profə'so:-] adj.
pro'fessorship n the post of a professor.

proficient [prə'fiʃənt] adj skilled; expert. **pro'ficiently** adv. **pro'ficiency** n.

profile ['proufail] n the view of a face, head etc from the side; a side view: She has a beautiful profile.

profit ['profit] n **1** money which is gained in business etc, eg from selling something for more than one paid for it: I made a profit of $8 000 on my house; He sold it at a huge profit. **2** advantage; benefit: A great deal of profit can be had from travelling abroad. – v – pt, ptp **'profited** – (with **from** or **by**) to gain profit(s) from: The business profited from its exports; He profited by his opponent's mistakes.
'profitable adj (neg **un-**) giving profit: The deal was quite profitable; a profitable experience. **'profitably** adv.

profound [prə'faund] adj **1** deep: profound sleep. **2** showing great knowledge or understanding: a profound remark. **pro'foundly** adv. **pro'fundity** [-'fʌn-] n.

profuse [prə'fju:s] adj (too) plentiful; excessive: profuse thanks. **pro'fusely** adv.
pro'fusion [-ʒən] n (sometimes with **a**) (too) great abundance: a profusion of flowers.

programme, (Amer) **program** ['prougram] n **1** (a booklet or paper giving the details of) the planned events in an entertainment etc: According to the programme, the show begins at 8.00. **2** a plan or scheme: a programme of reforms. **3** (Brit and Amer usu **'program**) a set of data, instructions etc put into a computer.
'program v – prp **'programming** (Amer also **'programing**): pt, ptp **'programmed** (Amer also **'programed**) – to give information, instructions etc to (a machine, esp a computer, so that it can do a particular job).
'programmer n a person who prepares a program for a computer.

progress ['prougres, (Amer) 'pro-] n **1** movement forward; advance: the progress of civilization. **2** improvement: The students are making (good) progress. – [prə'gres] v **1** to go forward: We had progressed only a few miles when the car broke down. **2** to improve: Your French is progressing.
pro'gressive [-siv] adj **1** developing and advancing by stages: a progressive illness. **2** using, or favouring, new methods: progressive education; The new headmaster is very progressive. **pro'gressively** adv. **pro'gressiveness** n.

in progress happening; taking place: There is a meeting in progress.

prohibit [prə'hibit] v to forbid: Smoking is prohibited.
prohibition [proui'biʃən] n **1** the act of prohibiting: We demand the prohibition by the government of the sale of this drug. **2** a rule, law etc forbidding something: The headmaster issued a prohibition against bringing knives into school.

project ['prodʒekt] n **1** a plan or scheme: a building project. **2** a piece of study or research: I am doing a project on Italian art. – [prə'dʒekt] v **1** to throw outwards, forwards or upwards: The missile was projected into space. **2** to stick out: A sharp rock projected from the sea. **3** to plan or propose.
pro'jectile [-tail, (Amer) -tl] n something that is thrown, usu as a weapon.
pro'jection [-ʃən] n.
pro'jector n a machine for projecting films on to a screen.

prologue ['proulog] n an introduction, esp to a play.

prolong [prə'loŋ] v to make longer: Please do not prolong the discussion unnecessarily.
prolongation [prouloŋ'geiʃən] n.
pro'longed adj very long: prolonged discussions.

prom [prom] see **promenade**.

promenade [promə'na:d, (Amer) -'neid] n (abbrev **prom** [prom]) a level road for the public to walk along, usu beside the sea: They went for a walk along the promenade.

prominent ['prominənt] adj **1** standing out; projecting: prominent front teeth. **2** easily seen: The tower is a prominent landmark. **3** famous: a prominent politician. **'prominently** adv. **'prominence** n.

promise ['promis] v **1** to say, or give one's word (that one will, or will not, do something etc): I promise (that) I won't be late; I promise not to be late; I won't be late, I promise (you)! **2** to say or give one's assurance that one will give: He promised me a new dress. **3** to show signs of future events or developments: This situation promises well for the future. – n **1** something promised: He made a promise; I'll go with you – that's a promise! **2** a sign of future success: She shows great promise in her work.
'promising adj showing promise; likely to be good: She's a promising pianist; Her work is promising.

promontory ['proməntəri] – pl **'promontories** – n a piece of land that projects from the coastline.

promote [prə'mout] v **1** to raise (to a higher rank or position): He was promoted to head teacher. **2** to encourage, organize, or help the progress of: He worked hard to promote *peace/this scheme.* **3** to encourage the buying of; to advertise: *We are promoting a new brand of soap-powder.* **pro'moter** *n.*

pro'motion [-ʃən] *n* **1** the raising of a person to a higher rank or position: *He has just been given (a) promotion.* **2** encouragement (of a cause, charity *etc*): *the promotion of world peace.* **3** the activity of advertising a product *etc*: *He is against the promotion of cigarettes.*

prompt¹ [prompt] *adj* acting, or happening, without delay or punctually: *a prompt reply; I'm surprised that she's late. She's usually so prompt.*

'promptly *adv* **1** immediately: *He promptly accepted my offer.* **2** punctually: *They arrived promptly.*

'promptness *n.*

at one/two *etc* **o'clock prompt** punctually at one/two *etc* o'clock.

prompt² [prompt] *v* **1** to persuade to do something: *What prompted you to say that?* **2** to remind (*esp* an actor) of the words that he is to say: *Several actors forgot their words and had to be prompted.* **'prompter** *n.*

prone [proun] *adj* **1** lying flat, *esp* face downwards. **2** *(with* **to**) inclined to; likely to experience *etc*: *He is prone to illness.*

prong [proŋ] *n* a spike of a fork.

pronged *adj*: *a pronged instrument; a two-pronged fork.*

pronoun ['prounaun] *n* a word used instead of a noun (or a phrase containing a noun): *'He', 'it', 'who', and 'anything' are pronouns.*

pronounce [prə'nauns] *v* **1** to speak (words or sounds, *esp* in a certain way): *He pronounced my name wrongly; The 'b' in 'lamb' and the 'k' in 'knob' are not pronounced.* **2** to announce officially or formally: *He pronounced judgement on the prisoner.*

pro'nounceable *adj* (*neg* **un-**) able to be pronounced.

pro'nounced *adj* noticeable; definite: *He walks with a pronounced limp.*

pro'nouncement *n* an announcement.

pro,nunci'ation [-nʌnsi-] *n* the act, or a way, of saying a word *etc*: *She had difficulty with the pronunciation of his name.*

proof [pruːf] *n* **1** (a piece of) evidence, information *etc* that shows definitely that something is true: *We still have no proof that he is innocent.* **2** a first copy of a printed sheet, that can be corrected before the final printing: *She was correcting the proofs of her novel.* **3** in photography, the first print from a negative.

-proof able to withstand or avoid something: *waterproof covering.*

prop¹ [prop] *n* a support: *The ceiling was held up with wooden props.* – *v* – *pt, ptp* **propped** – to lean (something) against something else: *He propped his bicycle against the wall.*

prop up to support (something) in an up-

right position, or stop it from falling: *We had to prop up the roof; He propped himself up against the wall.*

prop² *see* **property.**

propaganda [propə'gandə] *n* the activity of spreading particular ideas, opinions *etc* according to an organized plan, *eg* by a government; the ideas *etc* spread in this way: *political propaganda.*

propagate ['propəgeit] *v* **1** to spread (news *etc*). **2** to (make plants) produce seeds. **,propa'gation** *n.*

propel [prə'pel] – *pt, ptp* **pro'pelled** – *v* to drive forward, *esp* mechanically: *The boat is propelled by a diesel engine.*

pro'peller *n* a device, consisting of revolving blades, used to drive a ship or an aircraft.

pro'pulsion [-'pʌlʃən] *n* the process of propelling or being propelled: *jet-propulsion.*

pro,pelling-'pencil *n* a pencil consisting of a metal or plastic case containing a lead that is pushed forward by a screwing mechanism.

proper ['propə] *adj* **1** right, correct, or suitable: *That isn't the proper way to clean the windows; You should have done your schoolwork at the proper time – it's too late to start now.* **2** complete or thorough: *Have you made a proper search?* **3** respectable or well-mannered: *Such behaviour isn't quite proper.*

'properly *adv* **1** correctly or rightly: *She can't pronounce his name properly.* **2** completely or thoroughly: *I didn't have time to read the book properly.*

proper noun/name a noun or name which names a particular person, thing or place (beginning with a capital letter): *'John' and 'New York' are proper nouns.*

property ['propəti] – *pl* **'properties** – *n* **1** something that a person owns: *These books are my property.* **2** land or buildings that a person owns: *He has property in Scotland.* **3** a quality (*usu* of a substance): *Hardness is a property of diamonds.* **4** (*usu abbrev* **prop** [prop]) a small piece of furniture or an article used by an actor in a play.

prophecy ['profəsi] – *pl* **'prophecies** – *n* **1** the power of foretelling the future. **2** something that is foretold: *He made many prophecies about the future.*

'prophesy [-sai] *v* to foretell: *He prophesied (that there would be) another war.*

'prophet [-fit] – *fem* **'prophetess** – *n* **1** a person who (believes that he) is able to foretell the future. **2** a person who tells people what God wants, intends *etc*: *the prophet Isaiah.* **pro'phetic** [-'fe-] *adj.* **pro'phetically** *adv.*

prophecy is a noun: *Her prophecy (not prophesy) came true.*
prophesy is a verb: *to prophesy (not prophecy) the future.*

pro'portion [prə'po:ʃən] n 1 a part (of a total amount): *Only a small proportion of the class passed the exam.* 2 the (correct) quantity, size, number *etc* (of one thing compared with that of another): *For this dish, the butter and flour should be in the proportion of three to four* (= *eg* 300 grammes of butter with every 400 grammes of flour). **pro'portional** *adj.* **pro'portionally** *adv.*

pro'portionate [-nət] *adj* being in correct proportion: *Are her wages really proportionate to the amount of work she does?* **pro'portionately** *adv.*

be, get *etc* **in proportion (to)** to (cause to) have a correct relationship (to each other or something else): *In drawing a person, it is difficult to get all the parts of the body in proportion.*

be, get *etc* **out of (all) proportion (to)** to (cause to) have an incorrect relationship (to each other or something else): *An elephant's tail seems out of (all) proportion to the rest of its body.*

in proportion to in relation to; in comparison with: *You spend far too much time on that work in proportion to its importance.*

propose [prə'pouz] *v* 1 to offer for consideration; to suggest: *I proposed my friend for the job*; *Who proposed this scheme?* 2 to intend: *He proposes to build a new house.* 3 to make an offer of marriage: *He proposed (to me) last night and I accepted him.* **pro'posal** *n* 1 something proposed or suggested; a plan: *proposals for peace.* 2 an offer of marriage: *She received three proposals.* 3 the act of proposing.

proposition [propə'ziʃən] *n* 1 a proposal or suggestion. 2 a thing or situation that must be done or dealt with: *a difficult proposition.*

proprietor [prə'praiətə] – *fem* **pro'prietress** – *n* an owner, *esp* of a shop, hotel *etc.*

propriety [prə'praiəti] *n* correctness of behaviour; decency; rightness.

propulsion *see* **propel.**

prose [prouz] *n* writing that is not in verse; ordinary written or spoken language.

prosecute ['prosikju:t] *v* to bring a legal action against: *He was prosecuted for theft.* **prose'cution** *n* 1 (an) act of prosecuting or process of being prosecuted: *He faces prosecution for drunken driving*; *There are numerous prosecutions for this offence every year.* 2 the person/people bringing a legal action, including the lawyer(s) representing them: *First the prosecution stated its case, then the defence.*

prospect ['prospekt] *n* 1 an outlook for the future; a view of what one may expect to happen: *He didn't like the prospect of going abroad*; *a job with good prospects.* 2 a view or scene: *a fine prospect.* – [prə'spekt,

(*Amer*) 'prospekt] *v* to make a search (for gold *etc*): *He is prospecting for gold.*

prospector [prə'spektə, (*Amer*) 'prospektər] *n* a person who prospects for gold *etc.*

prospectus [prə'spektəs] *n* a booklet giving information about a school, organization *etc.*

prosper ['prospə] *v* to do well; to succeed: *His business is prospering.*

pro'sperity [-'spe-] *n* success; wealth: *We wish you happiness and prosperity.*

'prosperous *adj* successful, *esp* in business: *a prosperous businessman.* **'prosperously** *adv.*

prostitute ['prostitju:t] *n* a person who has sexual intercourse for payment. **,prosti'tution** *n.*

prostrate ['prostreit] *adj* 1 lying flat, *esp* face downwards. 2 completely exhausted or overwhelmed: *prostrate with grief.* – [prə-'streit] *v* 1 to throw (oneself) flat on the floor, *esp* in respect or reverence: *They prostrated themselves before the emperor.* 2 to exhaust or overwhelm: *prostrated by the long journey.* **pro'stration** *n.*

protect [prə'tekt] *v* to guard or defend from danger; to keep safe: *She protected the children from every danger*; *Which type of helmet protects the head best?*; *He wore a fur jacket to protect himself against the cold.* **pro'tected** *adj* (of certain animals or birds) protected by law from being shot *etc.* **pro'tection** [-ʃən] *n* 1 the act of protecting or state of being protected: *He ran to his mother for protection*; *This type of lock gives extra protection against burglary.* 2 something that protects: *The trees were a good protection against the wind.* **pro'tective** [-tiv] *adj* giving, or intended to give, protection: *protective clothing/glasses.* **pro'tector** *n.*

protein ['prouti:n] *n* any of a large number of substances present in milk, eggs, meat *etc*, which are necessary as part of the food of human beings and animals.

protest [prə'test] *v* 1 to express a strong objection: *They are protesting against the new law.* 2 to state or declare definitely, *esp* in denying something: *She protested that she was innocent.* – ['proutest] *n* a strong statement or demonstration of objection or disapproval: *He made no protest*; (*also adj*) *a protest march.* **pro'tester** *n.*

Protestant ['protəstənt] *n, adj* (a member) of any of the Christian churches that separated from the Roman Catholic church at or after the Reformation. **'Protestantism** *n.*

proton ['prouton] *n* a particle with a positive electrical charge, forming part of the nucleus of an atom.

protoplasm ['proutəplazəm] *n* the half-liquid substance that is found in all living cells.

prototype ['proutətaip] *n* the first or original model from which others are copied.

protractor [prə'traktə, (*Amer*) prou-] *n* an instrument for drawing and measuring angles.

protrude [prə'truːd, (*Amer*) prou-] *v* to stick out; to project: *His teeth protrude.*

proud [praud] *adj* 1 feeling pleasure or satisfaction at one's achievements, possessions, connections *etc*: *He was proud of his new house*; *She was proud of her son's achievements*; *He was proud to play football for the school.* 2 having a (too) high opinion of oneself; arrogant: *She was too proud to talk to us.* 3 wishing to be independent: *She was too proud to accept help.* 4 splendid or impressive: *The assembled fleet was a proud sight.* 'proudly *adv*.

do (someone) proud to give (a person) good treatment or entertainment: *We always do them proud when they come to dinner.*

prove [pruːv] *v* 1 to show to be true or correct: *This fact proves his guilt*; *He was proved guilty*; *Can you prove your theory?* 2 to turn out, or be found, to be: *His suspicions proved (to be) correct*; *This tool proved very useful.* 'proven *adj* (*esp* in law) proved.

proverb ['provəːb] *n* a well-known saying that gives good advice or expresses a supposed truth: *Two common proverbs are 'Many hands make light work' and 'Don't count your chickens before they're hatched!'* pro'verbial *adj*. pro'verbially *adv*.

provide [prə'vaid] *v* 1 to give or supply: *He provided the wine for the meal*; *He provided them with a bed for the night.* 2 (with **for**) to have enough money to supply what is necessary: *He is unable to provide for his family.*

pro'vided, pro'viding *conjs* if; on condition (that): *We can buy it provided/providing (that) we have enough money.*

province ['provins] *n* a division of a country, empire *etc*: *Britain was once a Roman province.* pro'vincial [-'vinʃəl] *adj*.

provision [prə'viʒən] *n* 1 the act of providing: *The government are responsible for the provision of education for all children.* 2 an agreed arrangement. 3 a rule or condition. – *v* to supply (*esp* an army) with food.

pro'visional *adj* temporary; appointed, arranged *etc* only for the present time: *a provisional government.* pro'visionally *adv*.

pro'visions *n pl* (a supply of) food: *The campers got their provisions at the village shop.*

make provision for to provide what is necessary for: *You should make provision for your old age.*

provoke [prə'vouk] *v* 1 to make angry or irritated: *Are you trying to provoke me?* 2 to cause: *His words provoked laughter.* 3 to cause (a person *etc*) to react in an angry way: *He was provoked into hitting her.*

provocation [provə'keiʃən] *n* the act of provoking or state of being provoked.

pro'vocative [-'vokətiv] *adj* likely to rouse feeling, *esp* anger or sexual interest: *provocative remarks*; *a provocative dress.* pro'vocatively *adv*.

prow [prau] *n* the front part of a ship; the bow.

prowess ['prauis] *n* skill or ability: *athletic prowess.*

prowl [praul] *v* to move about stealthily in order to steal, attack, catch *etc*: *Tigers were prowling in the jungle.* 'prowler *n*.

be on the prowl to be prowling: *Pickpockets are always on the prowl.*

proximity [prok'siməti] *n* nearness: *Their house is in close proximity to ours.*

prudent ['pruːdənt] *adj* wise and careful: *a prudent person/attitude.* 'prudently *adv*. 'prudence *n* wisdom and caution.

prune[1] [pruːn] *v* to trim (a tree *etc*) by cutting off unnecessary twigs and branches: *He pruned the roses.*

prune[2] [pruːn] *n* a dried plum.

pry [prai] *v* to try to find out about something that is secret, *esp* other people's affairs: *He is always prying into my business.*

psalm [saːm] *n* a sacred song, *esp* one from the Book of Psalms in the Bible.

pseudonym ['sjuːdənim] *n* a false name used by an author: *He wrote under a pseudonym.*

psychiatry [sai'kaiətri, (*Amer also*) si-] *n* the treatment of mental illness. **psychiatric** [saiki'atrik] *adj*. psy'chiatrist *n* a doctor who treats mental illness.

psychic(al) ['saikik(əl)] *adjs* concerned with the mind, *esp* with supernatural influences and forces that act on the mind and senses.

psychoanalyse, (*Amer*) **psychoanalyze** [saikou'anəlaiz] *v* to treat (a person suffering from mental illness) by discussing events in his/her past life which may have caused it. ,psychoa'nalysis [-'naləsis] *n*. ,psycho'analyst [-list] *n* a person who gives this treatment.

psychology [sai'kolədʒi] *n* the study or science of the human mind. ,psycho'logical [-'lo-] *adj* of the mind, or of psychology. ,psycho'logically *adv*. psy'chologist *n* a person whose work is to study the human mind.

pub [pʌb] *see* **public house** under **public**.

puberty ['pjuːbəti] *n* the time when a child's body becomes sexually mature.

public ['pʌblik] *adj* of, for, or concerning, the people (of a community or nation) in general: *a public library*; *a public meeting*; *Public opinion turned against him*; *The public announcements are on the back page of the newspaper*; *This information should be made* *public and not kept secret any longer.* '**publicly** *adv.*

pu'**blicity** [-'blisə-] *n* **1** advertising: *There is a lot of publicity about the dangers of smoking.* **2** the state of being widely known: *Film stars usually like publicity.*

'**publicize, -ise** [-saiz] *v* to make widely known; to advertise: *We are publicizing a new product.*

public holiday a day on which all (or most) shops, offices and factories are closed for a holiday.

public house (*usu abbrev* **pub** [pʌb]) a house where alcoholic drinks are sold to the public.

public relations the attitude, understanding *etc* between a firm, government *etc* and the public.

public spirit a desire to do things for the good of the community. ,**public-'spirited** *adj.*

public transport the bus, tram and train services provided by a state or community for the public.

in public in front of other people, not in private: *They are always quarrelling in public.*

the public people in general: *This swimming pool is open to the public every day.*

public opinion poll a way of finding out public opinion by questioning a certain number of people.

the public is singular: *The public is entitled to know the facts.*

publication [pʌbliˈkeiʃən] *n* **1** the act of publishing or announcing publicly: *the publication of a new novel; the publication of the facts.* **2** something that has been published *eg* a book or magazine: *recent publications.*

publish ['pʌbliʃ] *v* **1** to prepare, print and produce for sale (a book *etc*): *His new novel is being published this month.* **2** to make known: *They published their engagement.*

'**publisher** *n* a person who publishes books *etc.*

'**publishing** *n* the business of a publisher.

pudding ['pudiŋ] *n* **1** any of several types of soft sweet foods made with eggs, flour, milk *etc*: *sponge pudding; rice pudding.* **2** the sweet course of a meal; dessert: *What's for pudding?*

puddle ['pʌdl] *n* a small, *usu* dirty, pool (of water): *It had been raining, and there were puddles in the road.*

pudgy *see* **podgy.**

puff [pʌf] *n* **1** a small blast of air, wind *etc*; a gust: *A puff of wind moved the branches.* **2** any of various kinds of soft, round, light or hollow objects: *a powder puff*; (*also adj*) *puff sleeves.* – *v* **1** to blow in small blasts: *Stop puffing cigarette smoke into my face!; He puffed at his pipe.* **2** to breathe quickly,

after running *etc*: *He was puffing as he climbed the stairs.*

puffed *adj* short of breath; breathing quickly: *I'm puffed after running so fast!*

'**puffy** *adj* swollen, *esp* unhealthily: *a puffy face/ankle.*

puff pastry a light, flaky type of pastry.

puff out to cause to swell or expand: *The bird puffed out its feathers; He puffed out his cheeks.*

puff up to swell: *Her eye (was all) puffed up after the wasp stung her.*

pull [pul] *v* **1** to (try to) move something *esp* towards oneself *usu* by using force: *He pulled the chair towards the fire; She pulled at the door but couldn't open it; He kept pulling the girls' hair for fun; Help me to pull my boots off; This railway engine can pull twelve carriages.* **2** (*with* **at** *or* **on**) in *eg* smoking, to suck at: *He pulled at his cigarette.* **3** to row: *He pulled towards the shore.* **4** (of a driver or vehicle) to steer or move in a certain direction: *The car pulled in at the garage; I pulled into the side of the road; The train pulled out of the station; The motorbike pulled out to overtake; He pulled off the road.* – *n* **1** an act of pulling: *I felt a pull at my sleeve; He took a pull at his beer/pipe.* **2** a pulling or attracting force: *magnetic pull; the pull (=attraction) of the sea.* **3** influence: *He thinks he has some pull with the headmaster.*

pull apart/to pieces to tear or destroy completely by pulling.

pull down to destroy or demolish (buildings).

pull a face/faces (at) to make strange expressions with the face *eg* to show disgust, or to amuse: *The children were pulling faces at each other; He pulled a face when he smelt the fish.*

pull a gun *etc* **on** to produce and aim a gun *etc* at (a person).

pull off to succeed in doing: *He's finally pulled it off!*

pull on to put on (a piece of clothing) hastily: *She pulled on a sweater.*

pull oneself together to control oneself; to regain one's self-control: *At first she was terrified, then she pulled herself together.*

pull through to (help to) survive an illness *etc*: *He is very ill, but he'll pull through; The expert medical treatment pulled him through.*

pull up (of a driver or vehicle) to stop: *He pulled up at the traffic lights.*

pull one's weight to take one's fair share of work, duty *etc.*

pull someone's leg *see* **leg.**

pulley ['puli] *n* a wheel over which a rope *etc* can pass in order to lift heavy objects.

pullover ['puləuvə] *n* a knitted garment for the top part of the body; a sweater.

pulp [pʌlp] n **1** the soft, fleshy part of a fruit. **2** a soft mass of other matter, eg of wood etc from which paper is made: wood-pulp. – v to make into pulp: The fruit was pulped and bottled.
'**pulpy** adj of or like pulp.

pulpit ['pulpit] n a raised box or platform in a church, where the priest or minister stands, esp to preach the sermon.

pulse [pʌls] n the regular beating of the heart, which can be checked by feeling the pumping action of the artery in the wrist: The doctor felt/took her pulse. – v to throb.
pulsate [pʌl'seit, (Amer) 'pʌlseit] v to beat or throb. **pulsation** [pʌl'seiʃən] n.

pulverize, -ise ['pʌlvəraiz] v to make or crush into dust or powder. ,**pulveri'zation, -s-** n.

puma ['pjuːmə] n (also **cougar** ['kuːgə]) a type of wild animal like a large cat, found in America.

pump [pʌmp] n **1** a machine for making water etc rise from under the ground: Every village used to have a pump from which everyone drew their water. **2** a machine or device for forcing liquid or gas into, or out of, something: a bicycle pump (for forcing air into the tyres). – v **1** to raise or force with a pump: Oil is being pumped out of the ground. **2** to get information from by asking questions: He tried to pump me about the exam.
pump up to inflate (tyres etc) with a pump.

pumpkin ['pʌmpkin] n a kind of large, round, thick-skinned yellow fruit, eaten as food.

pun [pʌn] n a type of joke in which words are used that have a similar sound, but a different meaning: One example of a pun would be 'A pun is a punishable offence'. – v – pt, ptp **punned** – to make a pun.

punch[1] [pʌntʃ] n a kind of drink made of spirits or wine, water and sugar etc.

punch[2] [pʌntʃ] v to hit with the fist: He punched him on the nose. – n **1** a blow with the fist: He gave him a punch. **2** the quality of liveliness in speech, writing etc.
'**punch-drunk** adj (of a boxer) dizzy from being continually hit.
'**punch-up** n a fight (using fists).

punch[3] [pʌntʃ] n a tool or device for making holes in leather, paper etc. – v to make holes in with such a tool.

punctual ['pʌŋktʃuəl] adj arriving etc on time; not late: Please be punctual for your appointment; She's a very punctual person. ,**punctu'ality** [-'a-] n.
'**punctually** adv on time: He arrived punctually.

punctuate ['pʌŋktʃueit] v to divide up sentences etc by commas, full stops, colons etc.
†**punctuation** n **1** the act of punctuating. **2** the use of punctuation marks.
punctuation mark any of the symbols used

for punctuating, eg comma, full stop, question mark etc.

puncture ['pʌŋktʃə] v to make or get a small hole in: Some glass on the road punctured my new tyre. – n a hole in a tyre: My car has had two punctures this week.

pungent ['pʌndʒənt] adj (of a taste or smell) sharp and strong. '**pungently** adv.

punish ['pʌniʃ] v **1** to cause to suffer for a crime or fault: He was punished for stealing the money. **2** to give punishment for: The teacher punishes disobedience.
'**punishable** adj (of offences etc) able or likely to be punished by law: Driving without a licence is a punishable offence.
'**punishment** n **1** the act of punishing or process of being punished. **2** suffering, or a penalty, imposed for a crime, fault etc: He was sent to prison for two years as (a) punishment.
punitive ['pjuːnətiv] adj giving punishment.

puny ['pjuːni] adj small and weak: a puny child. '**punily** adv. '**puniness** n.

pup [pʌp] n **1** (also **puppy** ['pʌpi] – pl '**puppies**) a young dog: a sheepdog pup(py). **2** the young of certain other animals: a seal pup.

pupa ['pjuːpə] – pl '**pupae** [-piː] – n the form that an insect takes when it is changing from a larva (eg a caterpillar) to its perfect form (eg a butterfly); a chrysalis.

pupil[1] ['pjuːpl] n a person who is being taught by a teacher or tutor: The school has 2000 pupils.

pupil[2] ['pjuːpl] n the round opening in the middle of the eye through which the light passes.

puppet ['pʌpit] n a doll that can be moved eg by wires, or by putting the hand inside the body.
'**puppetry** n the art of making puppets and producing puppet shows.
'**puppet-show** n a play etc performed by puppets.

puppy see pup.

purchase ['pəːtʃəs] v to buy: I purchased a new house. – n **1** anything that has been bought: She carried her purchases home in a bag. **2** the act of buying: The purchase of a car should never be a hasty matter.
'**purchaser** n a buyer.

pure ['pjuə] adj **1** not mixed with anything esp dirty or less valuable: pure gold. **2** clean, esp morally: pure thoughts. **3** complete; absolute: a pure accident. **4** (of sounds) clear; keeping in tune: She sang in a high pure tone. '**purely** adv. '**pureness, 'purity** ns.
'**purify** [-fai] v to make pure: What is the best way to purify the air? ,**purifi'cation** [-fi-] n.
,**pure-'blooded** adj of unmixed race: a pure-blooded Englishman.

,**pure-'bred** *adj* (of animals) of unmixed breed; thoroughbred: *a pure-bred Arab horse*.

pure and simple (*used after a noun*) nothing but: *It was an accident pure and simple*.

purge [pə:dʒ] *v* **1** to make (something) clean by clearing it of everything that is bad, not wanted *etc*. **2** to rid (a political party *etc*) of disloyal members. – *n* an act of purging.

purgative ['pə:gətiv] *n*, *adj* (a medicine) which clears waste matter out of the body.

purification, purify *see* pure.

puritan ['pjuəritən] *n* **1** a person who is strict and disapproves of many kinds of enjoyment. **2** formerly, in England and America, a member of a religious group wanting to make church worship *etc* simpler and plainer. ,**puri'tanical** [-'ta-] *adj*.

purity *see* pure.

purl [pə:l] *n* a kind of knitting stitch.

purple ['pə:pl] *n*, *adj* (of) a dark colour made by mixing blue and red.

purpose ['pə:pəs] *n* **1** the reason for doing something; the aim to which an action *etc* is directed: *What is the purpose of your visit?* **2** the use or function of an object: *The purpose of this lever is to stop the machine in an emergency*. **3** determination: *a man of purpose*.

'**purposeful** *adj* having a definite purpose: *with a purposeful look on his face*. '**purposefully** *adv*.

'**purposeless** *adj* having no purpose: *purposeless destruction*.

'**purposely** *adv* intentionally: *He did it purposely to attract my attention*.

on purpose intentionally: *Did you break the cup on purpose?*

serve a purpose to be useful in some way.

to no purpose with no useful results.

purr [pə:] *v* to make the low, murmuring sound of a cat when it is pleased. – *n* such a sound.

purse [pə:s] *n* **1** a small bag for carrying money: *I looked in my purse for some change*. **2** (*Amer*) a handbag. – *v* to close (the lips) tightly: *She pursed her lips in anger*.

'**purser** *n* the officer in charge of a ship's money, supplies *etc*.

pursue [pə'sju:] *v* **1** to follow *esp* in order to catch or capture; to chase: *They pursued the thief through the town*. **2** to occupy oneself with (studies, enquiries *etc*); to continue: *He is pursuing his studies at the University*. **pur'suer** *n*.

pursuit [pə'sju:t] *n* **1** the act of pursuing: *The thief ran down the street with a policeman in* (*hot*) *pursuit*. **2** an occupation or hobby: *holiday pursuits*.

pus [pʌs] *n* a thick, yellowish liquid that forms in infected wounds *etc*.

push [puʃ] *v* **1** to press against something, in order to (try to) move it further away: *He pushed the door open*; *She pushed him away*; *He pushed against the door with his soldier*; *The queue can't move any faster, so stop pushing!*; *I had a good view of the race till someone pushed in front of me*. **2** to try to make (someone) do something; to urge on, *esp* foolishly: *She pushed him into applying for the job*. **3** to sell (drugs) illegally. – *n* **1** a movement of pressure against something; a thrust: *She gave him a push*. **2** energy and determination: *He has enough push to do well in his job*.

'**push-bike** *n* a bicycle that does not have a motor.

'**push-chair** *n*, *esp* in U.K., a small wheeled chair for a child, pushed by its mother *etc*.

be pushed for to be short of; not to have enough of: *I'm a bit pushed for time*.

push around to treat roughly: *He pushes his younger brother around*.

push off to go away: *I wish you'd push off!*

push on to go on; to continue: *Push on with your work*.

push over to cause to fall; to knock down: *He pushed me over*.

puss [pus], **pussy** ['pusi] (*pl* '**pussies**) *n* a cat.

'**pussyfoot** *v* to behave in a wary or timid way.

put [put] – *prp* '**putting**: *pt*, *ptp* **put** – *v* **1** to place in a certain position or situation: *He put the plate in the cupboard*; *Did you put any sugar in my coffee?*; *He put his arm round her*; *I'm putting a new lock on the door*; *You're putting too much strain on that rope*; *When did the Russians first put a man into space?*; *You've put me in a bad temper*; *Can you put* (=translate) *this sentence into French?* **2** to submit or present (a proposal, question *etc*): *I put several questions to him*; *She put her ideas before the committee*. **3** to express in words: *He put his refusal very politely*; *Children sometimes have such a funny way of putting things!* **4** to write down: *I'm trying to write a letter to her, but I don't know what to put*. **5** to sail in a particular direction: *We put out to sea*; *The ship put into harbour for repairs*.

'**put-on** *adj* pretended; not genuine: *a put-on foreign accent*; *Her accent sounded put-on*.

a put-up job something done to give a false appearance, in order to cheat or trick someone.

put about to spread (news *etc*).

put across/over to convey or communicate (ideas *etc*) to others: *He's very good at putting his ideas across*.

put aside **1** to abandon (work *etc*) temporarily: *She put aside her needlework*. **2** to save or preserve for the future: *He tries to put aside a little money each month*.

put away to return to its proper place, *esp* out of sight: *She put her clothes away in the drawer.*

put back to return to its proper place: *Did you put my keys back?*

put by to save or preserve for the future: *I have put by some money for emergencies.*

put down 1 to lower: *The teacher asked the pupil to put his hand down.* **2** to place on the floor or other surface, out of one's hands: *Put that knife down immediately!* **3** to subdue (a rebellion *etc*). **4** to kill (an animal) painlessly when it is old or very ill.

put down for to write the name of (someone) on a list *etc* for a particular purpose: *You have been put down for the one hundred metres' race.*

put one's feet up to take a rest.

put forth (of plants *etc*) to produce (leaves, shoots *etc*).

put in 1 to insert or install: *We're having a new shower put in.* **2** to do (a certain amount of work *etc*): *He put in an hour's training today.*

put in for to apply for, or claim: *Are you putting in for that job?*

put off 1 to switch off (a light *etc*): *Please put the light off!* **2** to delay; to postpone: *He put off leaving/his departure till Thursday.* **3** to cancel an arranged meeting *etc* with (a person): *I had to put the Browns off because I had 'flu.* **4** to cause (a person) to feel disgust or dislike (for): *The cheese looked nice but the smell put me off; The conversation about illness put me off my dinner.*

put on 1 to switch on (a light *etc*): *Put the light on!* **2** to dress oneself in: *Which shoes are you going to put on?* **3** to add or increase: *The car put on speed; I've put on weight.* **4** to present or produce (a play *etc*): *They're putting on 'Hamlet' next week.* **5** to provide (*eg* transport): *They always put on extra buses between 8.00 and 9.00 a.m.* **6** to make a false show of; to pretend: *She said she felt ill, but she was just putting it on.* **7** to bet (money) on: *I've put a pound on that horse to win.*

put out 1 to extend (a hand *etc*): *He put out his hand to steady her.* **2** (of plants *etc*) to produce (shoots, leaves *etc*). **3** to extinguish (a fire, light *etc*): *The fire brigade soon put out the fire.* **4** to issue, give out: *They put out a distress call.* **5** to cause bother or trouble to: *Don't put yourself out for my sake!* **6** to annoy: *I was put out by his decision.*

put through 1 to arrange (a deal, agreement *etc*). **2** to connect by telephone: *I'm trying to put you through (to London).*

put together to construct: *The vase broke, but I managed to put it together again.*

put up 1 to raise (a hand *etc*). **2** to build; to erect: *They're putting up some new houses.* **3** to fix on a wall *etc*: *He put the poster up.* **4** to increase (a price *etc*): *They're putting up the fees again.* **5** to offer or show (resistance *etc*): *He's putting up a brave fight.* **6** to provide (money) for a purpose: *He promised to put up the money for the scheme.* **7** to provide a bed *etc* for (a person) in one's home: *Can you put us up next Thursday night?*

put up to to persuade (a person) to do something: *Who put you up to writing that letter?*

put up with to bear patiently: *I cannot put up with all this noise.*

The job of the fire brigade is to **put out** (not **put off**) fires.

putrefy ['pju:trəfai] *v* to make or go bad or rotten: *The meat putrefied in the heat.*

putrid ['pju:trid] *adj* (smelling) rotten: *putrid fish.*

putt [pʌt] *v* (in golf) to send a ball gently forward when aiming for the hole.

'**putter** *n* a golf-club used for putting.

putty ['pʌti] *n* a type of paste made from ground chalk and oil, used to fix glass in windows *etc*.

puzzle ['pʌzl] *v* **1** to perplex, baffle or bewilder: *The question puzzled them; What puzzles me is how he got here so soon.* **2** to think long and carefully about a problem *etc*: *I puzzled over the sum for hours.* – *n* **1** a problem that causes a lot of thought: *Her behaviour was a puzzle to him.* **2** a kind of game or toy to test one's thinking, knowledge or skill: *a jig-saw puzzle; a crossword puzzle.*

'**puzzling** *adj* difficult to understand: *a puzzling remark.*

puzzle out to solve (a problem *etc*).

pygmy, pigmy ['pigmi] – *pl* '**pygmies, 'pigmies** – *n* a member of an African race of very small people.

pyjamas, (*Amer*) **pajamas** [pə'dʒa:məz] *n pl* a suit for sleeping, consisting of trousers and a jacket: *two pairs of pyjamas.*

pylon ['pailən, (*Amer*) -lon] *n* **1** a tall steel tower for supporting electric power cables. **2** a guiding mark at an airfield.

***pyramid** ['pirəmid] *n* **1** a solid shape *usu* with a square or triangular base, and sloping triangular sides meeting in a point. **2** an ancient tomb built in this shape in Egypt.

pyre ['paiə] *n* a pile of wood on which a dead body is ceremonially burned: *a funeral pyre.*

pyrotechnics [pairə'tekniks] *n pl* (a display of) fireworks.

python ['paiθən] *n* a type of large nonpoisonous snake that twists around its prey and crushes it.

* see illustration on p. 476

Qq

quack [kwak] *n* the cry of a duck. – *v* to make such a sound: *The ducks quacked noisily as they swam across the pond.*

quad *see* **quadrangle, quadruplet**.

quadrangle ['kwodraŋgl] *n* (*abbrev* **quad** [kwod]) a four-sided open space surrounded by buildings, *esp* in a school, college *etc*.

quadrilateral [kwodri'latərəl] *n* a two-dimensional figure with four straight sides.

quadruped ['kwodruped] *n* a four-footed animal: *An elephant is a quadruped.*

quadruple [kwo'dru:pl] *adj* **1** four times as much or as many. **2** made up of four parts *etc*. – *v* to make or become four times as great.

quadruplet [kwo'dru:plit] *n* (*abbrev* **quad** [kwod]) one of four children born at the same time to one mother.

quadruplicate [kwo'dru:plikət]: **in quadruplicate** in four identical copies: *Please fill out this form in quadruplicate.*

quail [kweil] *v* to draw back in fear; to shudder: *The little boy quailed at the teacher's angry voice.*

quaint [kweint] *adj* pleasantly odd or strange, *esp* because of being old-fashioned: *quaint customs.* '**quaintly** *adv.* '**quaintness** *n*.

quake [kweik] *v* **1** (of people) to shake or tremble, *esp* with fear. **2** (of the ground) to shake: *The ground quaked under their feet.* – *n* an earthquake.

qualify ['kwolifai] *v* **1** to cause to be or to become able or suitable for: *A degree in English does not qualify you to teach English*; *She is too young to qualify for a place in the team.* **2** (*with* **as**) to show that one is suitable for a profession or job *etc, esp* by passing a test or examination: *I hope to qualify as a doctor.* **3** (*with* **for**) to allow, or be allowed, to take part in a competition *etc, usu* by reaching a satisfactory standard in an earlier test or competition: *She failed to qualify for the long jump.* **4** (of an adjective) to describe, or add to the meaning of: *In 'red books', the adjective 'red' qualifies the noun 'books'.*

,**qualifi'cation** [-fi-] **1** (the act of gaining) a skill, achievement *etc* (*eg* an examination pass) that makes (a person) able or suitable to do a job *etc*: *What qualifications do you need for this job?* **2** something that gives a person the right to do something. **3** a limitation to something one has said or written: *I think this is an excellent piece of work – with certain qualifications.*

'**qualified** *adj* (*neg* **un-**) having the necessary qualification(s) to do (something): *a qualified engineer.*

'**qualifying** *adj* in which players, teams *etc* attempt to qualify for a competition *etc*: *Our team was beaten in the qualifying round.*

quality ['kwoləti] – *pl* '**qualities** – *n* **1** the extent to which something has features which are good or bad, *esp* features which are good: *We produce several different qualities of paper*; *In this firm, we look for quality rather than quantity*; (*also adj*) *quality goods.* **2** some (*usu* good) feature which makes a person or thing special or noticeable: *Kindness is a human quality which everyone admires.*

qualm [kwa:m] *n* a feeling of uncertainty about whether one is doing right: *She had no qualms about reporting her husband's crime to the police.*

quandary ['kwondəri] – *pl* '**quandaries** – *n* a state of uncertainty; a situation in which it is difficult to decide what to do.

quantity ['kwontəti] *n* the size, weight, number *etc* of something, *esp* a large size *etc*: *What quantity of paper do you need?*; *I buy these goods in quantity*; *a small quantity of cement*; *large quantities of tinned food.*

quantity surveyor a person who is responsible for estimating the quantities of building materials needed for constructing something, and their probable cost.

an unknown quantity a person or thing whose characteristics, abilities *etc* cannot be predicted.

quarantine ['kworənti:n] *n* **1** the keeping away from other people or animals of people or animals that might be carrying an infectious disease: *My dog was in quarantine for six months.* **2** the period in or for which this is done: *The quarantine for a dog entering Britain from abroad is six months.* – *v* to put (a person or animal) in quarantine.

quarrel ['kworəl] *n* an angry disagreement or argument: *I've had a quarrel with my girlfriend.* – *v* – *pt, ptp* '**quarrelled**, (*Amer*) '**quarreled** – to have an angry argument (with someone): *I've quarrelled with my girl-friend*; *My girl-friend and I have quarrelled.*

'**quarrelsome** *adj* inclined to quarrel: *quarrelsome children.* '**quarrelsomeness** *n*.

quarry[1] ['kwori] – *pl* '**quarries** – *n* a place, *usu* a very large hole in the ground, from which stone is got for building *etc*. – *v* to dig (stone) in a quarry.

quarry[2] ['kwori] – *pl* '**quarries** – *n* **1** a hunted animal or bird. **2** someone or something that is hunted, chased or eagerly looked for.

quarter ['kwo:tə] *n* **1** one of four equal parts of something which together form the whole (amount) of the thing: *There are four* *of us, so we'll cut the cake into quarters; It's (a) quarter past/(Amer) after four; In the first quarter of the year his firm made a profit; The shop is about a quarter of a mile away; an hour and a quarter; two and a quarter hours.* **2** in the US and Canada, (a coin worth) twenty-five cents, the fourth part of a dollar. **3** a district or part of a town *esp* where a particular group of people live: *He lives in the Polish quarter of the town.* **4** a direction: *People were coming at me from all quarters.* **5** mercy shown to an enemy. **6** the leg of a *usu* large animal, or a joint of meat which includes a leg: *a quarter of beef; a bull's hindquarters.* **7** the shape of the moon at the end of the first and third weeks of its cycle; the first or fourth week of the cycle itself. **8** one of four equal periods of play in some games. **9** a period of study at a college *etc usu* 10 to 12 weeks in length. – *v* **1** to cut into four equal parts: *We'll quarter the cake and then we'll all have an equal share.* **2** to divide by four: *If we each do the work at the same time, we could quarter the time it would take to finish the job.* **3** to give (*esp* a soldier) somewhere to stay: *The soldiers were quartered all over the town.*

'**quarterly** *adj* happening, published *etc* once every three months: *a quarterly journal; quarterly payments.* – *adv* once every three months: *We pay our electricity bill quarterly.* – *pl* '**quarterlies** – *n* a magazine *etc* which is published once every three months.

'**quarters** *n pl* a place to stay *esp* for soldiers.
'**quarter-deck** *n* the part of the upper deck of a ship between the stern and the mast nearest it.
,**quarter-'final** *n* (*often in pl*) the third-last round in a competition. ,**quarter-'finalist** *n*.
'**quartermaster** *n* an officer whose job is to provide soldiers with food, transport, a place to live *etc*.

at close quarters close to; close together: *The soldiers were fighting with the enemy at close quarters.*

quartet [kwoː'tet] *n* **1** a group of four singers or people playing musical instruments. **2** a piece of music written for such a group: *a Mozart quartet.*
quartz [kwoːts] *n, adj* (of) a kind of hard substance found in rocks, often in the form of crystals.
quaver ['kweivə] (*esp* of a sound or a person's voice) to shake or tremble: *The old man's voice quavered.* – *n* **1** a shaking or trembling: *There was a quaver in her voice.* **2** a note equal to half a crotchet in length.
quay [kiː] *n* a solid, *usu* stone, landing-place, where boats are loaded and unloaded: *The boat is moored at the quay.*

'**quayside** *n* the side or edge of a quay: *The boat was tied up at the quayside.*
queasy ['kwiːzi] *adj* feeling as if one is about to be sick: *The motion of the boat made her feel queasy.*
queen [kwiːn] *n* **1** a woman who rules a country, who inherits her position by right of birth: *the Queen of England; Queen Elizabeth II.* **2** the wife of a king: *The king and his queen were both present.* **3** a woman who is in some way important, excellent or special: *a beauty queen; a movie queen.* **4** a playing-card with a picture of a queen on it: *I have two aces and a queen.* **5** an important chess-piece: *a bishop, a king and a queen.* **6** the egg-laying female of certain kinds of insect (*esp* bees, ants and wasps).
'**queenly** *adj* of, like or suitable for, a queen.
queen mother the mother of the reigning king or queen, who was herself once a queen.
queer [kwiə] *adj* **1** odd, strange or unusual: *queer behaviour; queer noises in the middle of the night.* **2** sick; unwell: *I do feel a bit queer – perhaps I ate too many oysters.*
'**queerly** *adv*. '**queerness** *n*.
quell [kwel] *v* **1** to put an end to (a rebellion *etc*) by force. **2** to put an end to, or take away (a person's fears *etc*).
quench [kwentʃ] *v* **1** to drink enough to take away (one's thirst): *I had a glass of lemonade to quench my thirst.* **2** to put out (a fire): *The firemen were unable to quench the fire.*
query ['kwiəri] – *pl* '**queries** – *n* **1** a question: *In answer to your query about hotel reservations I am sorry to tell you that we have no vacancies.* **2** a question mark: *You have omitted the query.* – *v* **1** to question (a statement *etc*): *I think the waiter has added up the bill wrongly – you should query it.* **2** to ask: *'What time does the train leave?' she queried.*
quest [kwest] *n* a search: *the quest for gold; the quest for truth.*
†**question** ['kwestʃən] *n* **1** something which is said, written *etc* which asks for an answer from someone: *The question is, do we really need a computer?* **2** a problem or matter for discussion: *There is the question of how much to pay him.* **3** a single problem in a test or examination: *We had to answer four questions in three hours.* **4** criticism; doubt; discussion: *He is, without question, the best man for the job.* **5** a suggestion or possibility: *There is no question of our dismissing him.* – *v* **1** to ask (a person) questions: *I'll question him about what he was doing last night.* **2** to regard as doubtful: *He questioned her right to use the money.*
'**questionable** *adj* **1** doubtful; uncertain. **2** probably not true, honest, respectable: *questionable behaviour.* '**questionably** *adv*. '**questionableness** *n*.

† see notes on question-tags in Grammatical Notes on pp. 627–632

question mark a mark (?) used in writing to indicate a question.

'question-master *n* a person who asks the questions in *eg* a quiz.

,**question'naire** [-'neə] *n* a written list of questions to be answered by a large number of people to provide information for a survey or report.

in question being talked about: *The matter in question can be left till next week.*

out of the question not to be thought of as possible; not to be done: *It is quite out of the question for you to go out tonight.*

queue [kju:] *n* a line of people waiting for something or to do something: *a queue for the bus. – v* to stand in a queue: *We had to queue to get into the cinema; We had to queue for the cinema.*

queue up to form, or stand in, a queue: *We queued up for tickets.*

quick [kwik] *adj* **1** done, said, finished *etc* in a short time: *a quick trip into town.* **2** moving, or able to move, with speed: *He's a very quick walker; I made a grab at the dog, but it was too quick for me.* **3** doing something, able to do something, or done, without delay; prompt; lively: *He is always quick to help; a quick answer; He's very quick at arithmetic. – adv* quickly: *quick-frozen food.*

'quickly *adv.*

'quicken *v* to make or become quicker: *He quickened his pace.*

'quickness *n.*

'quicklime *n* lime which has not been mixed with water.

'quicksands *n pl* (an area of) loose, wet sand that sucks in anyone or anything that stands on it.

'quicksilver *n* mercury.

,**quick-'tempered** *adj* easily made angry.

,**quick-'witted** *adj* thinking very quickly: *a quick-witted policeman.* ,**quick-'wittedly** *adv.* ,**quick-'wittedness** *n.*

quiet ['kwaiət] *adj* **1** not making very much, or any, noise; without very much, or any, noise: *Tell the children to be quiet; It's very quiet out in the country; a quiet person.* **2** free from worry, excitement *etc*: *I live a very quiet life.* **3** without much movement or activity; not busy: *We'll have a quiet afternoon watching television.* **4** (of colours) not bright. – *n* a state, atmosphere, period of time *etc* which is quiet: *In the quiet of the night; All I want is peace and quiet. – v* (*esp Amer*: often with **down**) to quieten.

'quieten *v* **1** (*often with* **down**) to make or become quiet: *I expect you to quieten down when I come into the classroom.* **2** to remove or lessen (a person's fears, doubts *etc*).

'quietly *adv.*

'quietness *n.*

keep quiet about to say nothing about; to

keep secret: *I'd like you to keep quiet about the child's father being in prison.*

on the quiet secretly; without letting anyone find out: *He went out of the office to enjoy a cigarette on the quiet.*

quiet is an adjective: *She has a quiet voice*; *Keep quiet.*
quite is an adverb: *This book is quite good.*

quill [kwil] *n* **1** a large feather, *esp* the feather of a goose, made into a pen. **2** one of the sharp spines of certain animals (*eg* the porcupine).

quilt [kwilt] *n* a bedcover filled with down, feathers *etc.*

'quilted *adj* made of two layers of material (often decoratively) stitched together with padding between them: *a quilted jacket.*

quin [kwin] *see* **quintuplet**.

quince [kwins] *n* a fruit with a sharp taste, used in making jam *etc.*

quinine ['kwini:n, (*Amer*) 'kwainain] *n* a bitter-tasting drug got from the bark of a type of tree, used as a medicine, *esp* for malaria.

quintet [kwin'tet] *n* **1** a group of five singers or people playing musical instruments. **2** a piece of music written for such a group.

quintuplet [kwin'tju:plit] *n* (*abbrev* **quin** [kwin]) one of five children born to one mother at the same time.

quip [kwip] *n* a quick, witty remark: *He is very good at making clever quips. – v – pt, ptp* **quipped** – *v* to make a quip or quips.

quirk [kwə:k] *n* a strange or unusual feature of a person's behaviour *etc.*

quit [kwit] – *pts, ptps* **'quitted, quit** – *v* **1** to leave, stop, or resign from *etc*: *I'm going to quit teaching; They have been ordered to quit the house by next week.*

be quit of to be rid of: *I am glad to be quit of that job.*

quite [kwait] *adv* **1** completely; entirely: *This is quite impossible.* **2** fairly; rather; to a certain extent: *It's quite warm today; He's quite a good artist; I quite like the idea. – interj* exactly; indeed; I agree: *'I think he is being unfair to her.' 'Quite.'*

see also quiet.

quiver[1] ['kwivə] *v* to tremble or shake: *The leaves quivered in the breeze. – n* a quivering sound, movement *etc.*

quiver[2] ['kwivə] *n* a long, narrow case for carrying arrows in.

quiz [kwiz] – *pl* **'quizzes** – *n* a game or competition in which knowledge is tested by asking questions: *a television quiz; a general-knowledge quiz.*

'quiz-master *n* a question-master.

quoits [koits, (*Amer*) kwoits] *n sing* a game in

which rings of metal, rope *etc*, called **quoits**, are thrown on to one or more small rods or hooks.

quorum ['kwo:rəm] *n* the smallest number of members necessary at a meeting before any business can be done.

quota ['kwoutə] *n* the part, share or amount allotted to each member of a group *etc*.

quote [kwout] *v* **1** to repeat the exact words of a person as they were said or written: *to quote Shakespeare/Shakespeare's words/*

from Shakespeare, 'Is this a dagger which I see before me?' **2** to name (a price). **3** to mention or state in support of an argument: *to quote an example.*

quo'tation *n* **1** a person's exact words, as repeated by someone else: *a quotation from Shakespeare.* **2** a price mentioned (for a job *etc*). **3** the act of quoting.

quotation marks marks (" " or ' ') used to show that a person's words are being repeated exactly: *He said 'I'm going out.'*

Rr

rabbi ['rabai] *n* a Jewish priest or teacher of the law.

rabbit ['rabit] *n* a type of small long-eared burrowing animal, found living wild in fields or sometimes kept as a pet.

rabble ['rabl] *n* a noisy, disorderly crowd.

rabies ['reibi:z] *n* a disease that causes madness (and *usu* death) in dogs and other animals (including humans).

raccoon, racoon [rə'ku:n, (*Amer*) ra-] *n* a type of small, furry, N American animal, with a striped, bushy tail.

race¹ [reis] *n* a competition to find who or which is the fastest: *a horse race.* – *v* **1** to (cause to) run in a race: *I'm racing my horse on Saturday*; *The horse is racing against five others.* **2** to have a competition with (someone) to find out who is the fastest: *I'll race you to that tree.* **3** to go *etc* quickly: *He raced along the road on his bike.*

'**racer** *n* a car, bicycle *etc* built for competitive racing.

'**racecourse** *n* (a place with) a course over which horse races are run.

'**racehorse** *n* a horse bred and used for racing.

'**racetrack** *n* (a place with) a course over which races are run by cars, dogs, athletes *etc*.

'**racing-car** *n* a car specially designed and built for racing.

a race against time a desperate attempt to do something before a certain time.

the races a meeting for horse-racing.

race² [reis] *n* **1** any one section of mankind, having a particular set of characteristics which make it different from other sections: *the Negro race*; *the white races*; (*also adj*) *race relations.* **2** the fact of belonging to any of these various sections: *the problem of race.* **3** a group of people who share the same culture, language *etc*; *the Anglo-Saxon race.*

racial ['reiʃəl] *adj* of, or having to do with, race or a particular race: *racial characteristics*; *racial discrimination/hatred.*

'**racialism** ['reiʃə-], '**racism** *ns* **1** the belief that some races of men are better than others. **2** prejudice against someone on the grounds of his race.

'**racialist** ['reiʃə-], '**racist** *ns, adjs*: *racist attitudes.*

the human race mankind.

of mixed race having ancestors (*esp* parents) from two or more different human races.

rack¹ [rak] *n* a frame or shelf in or on which objects (*eg* letters, plates, luggage *etc*) are put until they are wanted or needed: *Put these tools back in the rack*; *Put your bag in the luggage-rack.*

rack² [rak]: **rack one's brains** to think desperately hard.

rack³ [rak]: **go to rack and ruin** to get into a state of neglect and decay.

racket¹, **racquet** ['rakit] *n* a wooden or metal frame strung with catgut or nylon, used in tennis and certain other games: *tennis-racket/squash-racket/badminton racket.*

racket² ['rakit] *n* **1** a great deal of noise: *What a racket the children are making!* **2** a dishonest way of making money: *the drug racket.*

racoon *see* **raccoon**.

racquet *see* **racket**¹.

racy ['reisi] *adj* lively: *a racy style of writing.* '**racily** *adv*. '**raciness** *n*.

radar ['reida:] *n* a method of showing the direction and distance of an object by means of radio waves which bounce off the object and return to their source.

radiant ['reidiənt] *adj* **1** showing great joy: *a radiant smile.* **2** sending out rays of heat, light *etc* or carried, sent *etc* in the form of, or by means of, rays of heat, light *etc*. '**radiantly** *adv*.

'radiance n: *the radiance of her smile.*

radiate ['reidieit] v 1 to send out rays of (light, heat *etc*): *A fire radiates heat.* 2 to go out or be sent out in rays, or in many directions from a central point: *Heat radiates from a fire*; *All the roads radiate from the centre of the town.*

,radi'ation n rays of light, heat *etc* or of any radioactive substance.

'radiator n 1 a type of apparatus for heating a room. 2 an apparatus in a car which, with a fan, cools the engine.

radical ['radikəl] adj 1 relating to the basic nature of something: *radical faults in the design.* 2 thorough; complete: *radical changes.* 3 wanting or involving great or extreme political, social or economic changes. – n a person who wants radical political changes.

'radically adv.

radio ['reidiou] – pl 'radios – n (an apparatus for) the sending and receiving of human speech, music *etc*: *a pocket radio*; *The concert is being broadcast on radio*; *I heard about it on the radio*; (*also adj*) *a radio programme, radio waves.* – v – *3rd pers sing prt* 'radios : *pt, ptp* 'radioed – to send (a message) by radio: *When someone on the island is ill, we have to radio (to) the mainland for a doctor*; *An urgent message was radioed to us this evening.*

radioactive [reidiou'aktiv] adj 1 (of some substances, *eg* uranium) giving off rays which can be dangerous, but which can also be used in *eg* medicine: *radioactive metals.* 2 containing radioactive substances: *radioactive waste/dust.* ,radioac'tivity n.

radiograph ['reidiəgra:f] n a photograph taken by means of X-rays or other rays.

,radi'ographer [-'o-] n a person who makes such photographs. radi'ography [-'o-] n.

radiology [reidi'olədʒi] n 1 the branch of medicine involving the use of radioactive substances and radiation in the diagnosis (and treatment) of diseases. 2 the scientific study of (the use of) radioactive substances and radiation. ,radi'ologist n.

radiotherapy [reidiou'θerəpi] n the treatment of disease by X-rays and other forms of radiation.

*radish ['radiʃ] n a plant with a red-skinned white root used as food.

radium ['reidiəm] n a radioactive metallic element, used in treating certain diseases.

radius ['reidiəs] n 1 (pl 'radiuses) the area within a given distance from a central point: *They searched within a radius of one mile from the school.* 2 (pl 'radii [-diai]) a straight line from the centre of a circle to its circumference.

raffia ['rafiə] n (strips of) fibre from the leaves of a type of palm tree, used for making mats, baskets *etc.*

raffle ['rafl] n a way of raising money by selling numbered tickets, one or more of which win a prize: *I won this doll in a raffle*; (*also adj*) *raffle tickets.* – v to give as the prize in a raffle: *They raffled a bottle of whisky to raise money for cancer research.*

raft [ra:ft] n a number of logs, planks *etc* fastened together and used as a boat.

rafter ['ra:ftə] n a beam supporting the roof of a house.

rag [rag] n a piece of old, torn or worn cloth: *I'll polish my bike with this old rag.*

'ragged ['ragid] adj 1 dressed in old, worn or torn clothing: *a ragged beggar.* 2 torn: *ragged clothes.* 3 rough or uneven; not straight or smooth: *a ragged edge.* 'raggedly adv. 'raggedness n.

rags n pl old, worn or torn clothes: *The beggar was dressed in rags.*

ragamuffin ['ragəmʌfin] n a ragged, dirty person, *esp* a child.

rage [reidʒ] n 1 (a fit of) violent anger: *He flew into a rage*; *He shouted with rage.* 2 violence; great force: *the rage of the sea.* – v 1 to act or shout in great anger: *He raged at his secretary.* 2 (of wind, storms *etc*) to be violent; to blow with great force: *The storm raged all night.* 3 (of battles, arguments *etc*) to be carried on with great violence: *The battle raged for two whole days.* 4 (of diseases *etc*) to spread quickly and affect many people: *Fever was raging through the town.*

'raging adj violent; extreme: *raging toothache*; *a raging storm.*

(all) the rage very much in fashion.

raid [reid] n a sudden, short and *usu* unexpected attack: *The enemy made a raid on the docks*; *The police carried out a raid on the gambling den.* – v 1 to make a raid on: *The police raided the gambling club.* 2 to take things from: *I'm hungry – let's raid the fridge.*

'raider n: *The raiders burned down all the houses.*

rail [reil] n 1 a (*usu* horizontal) bar of metal, wood *etc* used in fences *etc*, or for hanging things on: *Don't lean over the rail*; *a curtain-rail*; *a towel-rail.* 2 (*usu in pl*) a long bar of steel which forms the track on which trains *etc* run. – v (*usu with* in *or* off) to surround with a rail or rails: *We'll rail that bit of ground off to stop people walking on it.*

'railing n (*usu in pl*) a fence or barrier of (*usu* vertical) metal or wooden bars: *They've put railings up all round the park.*

'railroad n (*Amer*) a railway.

'railway, (*Amer*) 'railroad n 1 a track with (*usu* more than one set of) two (or sometimes three) parallel steel rails on which trains run: *They're building a new railway*; (*also adj*) *a railway station.* **2** (*sometimes in pl*) the whole organization which is concerned with the running of trains, the building of tracks *etc*: *He has a job on the railway*; *The railways are very badly run in some countries.*

by rail by or on the railway: *goods sent by rail.*

rain [rein] *n* **1** water falling from the clouds in liquid drops: *We've had a lot of rain today*; *walking in the rain*; *We had flooding because of last week's heavy rains.* **2** a great number of things falling like rain: *a rain of arrows.* – *v* **1** (*only with* **it** *as subject*) to cause rain to fall: *I think it will rain today.* **2** to (cause to) fall like rain: *Arrows rained down on the soldiers.*

'**rainy** *adj* having (many) showers of rain: *a rainy day*; *the rainy season*; *rainy weather.* '**raininess** *n.*

'**rainbow** *n* the coloured arch sometimes seen in the sky opposite the sun when rain is falling.

'**raincoat** *n* a waterproof coat worn to keep out the rain.

'**raindrop** *n* a single drop of rain.

'**rainfall** *n* the amount of rain that falls in a certain place in a certain time: *We haven't had much rainfall this year*; *the annual rainfall.*

'**rain-gauge** *n* an instrument for measuring rainfall.

'**rain-tree** *n* a tropical tree of the mimosa family, whose pods are eaten by cattle.

keep, save *etc* **for a rainy day** to keep (*esp* money) until one needs it or in case one may need it.

rain cats and dogs to rain very hard.

the rains (in tropical countries) the rainy season.

raise [reiz] *v* **1** to move or lift to a high(er) position: *Raise your right hand*; *Raise the flag.* **2** to make higher: *If you paint your flat, that will raise the value of it considerably*; *We'll raise that wall about 20 centimetres.* **3** to grow (crops) or breed (animals) for food: *We don't raise pigs on this farm.* **4** to rear, bring up (a child): *She has raised a large family.* **5** to state (a question, objection *etc* which one wishes to have discussed): *Has anyone in the audience any points they would like to raise?* **6** to collect; to gather: *We'll try to raise money*; *The revolutionaries managed to raise a small army.* **7** to cause: *His remarks raised a laugh.* **8** to cause to rise or appear: *The car raised a cloud of dust.* **9** to build (a monument *etc*): *They've raised a statue of Robert Burns/in memory of Robert Burns.* **10** to give (a shout *etc*). **11** to make contact with by radio: *I can't raise the mainland.* – *n* an

increase in wages or salary: *I'm going to ask the boss for a raise.*

raise someone's hopes to make someone more hopeful than he was.

raise hell/Cain/the roof *etc* to make a great deal of noise.

raise someone's spirits to make someone less unhappy.

raisin ['reizən] *n* a dried grape: *She put raisins and sultanas in the cake.*

rajah ['ra:dʒə] *n* an Indian king or prince.

rake [reik] *n* **1** a tool which consists of a *usu* metal bar with teeth at the end of a long handle, used for smoothing earth, gathering *eg* leaves together *etc*. **2** any similar tool: *a croupier's rake in a casino.* **3** the act of raking: *to give the soil a rake.* – *v* **1** to smooth or gather with a rake: *I'll rake these grass-cuttings up later.* **2** (*often with* **out**) to remove the ashes from (a fire) with a poker *etc*. **3** to fire guns at (a target) from one end of it to the other: *The soldiers raked the entire village with machine-gun fire.*

rake through to make a thorough search: *I'm raking through these boxes of old clothes.*

rake up to find out and tell or remind people about (something, *usu* something unpleasant that would be better forgotten).

rally ['rali] *v* **1** to come or bring together again: *The general tried to rally his troops after the defeat*; *The troops rallied round the general.* **2** to come or bring together for a joint action or effort: *The supporters rallied to save the club from collapse*; *The politician asked his supporters to rally to the cause.* **3** to (cause to) recover health or strength: *She rallied from her illness.* – *n* – *pl* '**rallies** – **1** a *usu* large gathering of people for some purpose: *a Scouts' rally.* **2** a meeting (*usu* of cars or motorcycles) for a competition, race *etc*. **3** an improvement in health after an illness. **4** (in tennis *etc*) a (*usu* long) series of shots before the point is won or lost.

rally round to come together for a joint action or effort, *esp* of support: *When John's business was in difficulty, his friends all rallied round* (*to help*) *him.*

ram [ram] *n* **1** a male sheep. **2** something heavy, *esp* a part of a machine, used for ramming. – *v* – *pt, ptp* **rammed** – **1** (of ships, cars *etc*) to run into, and cause damage to: *The destroyer rammed the submarine*; *His car rammed into/against the car in front of it.* **2** to push down, into, on to *etc* with great force: *We rammed the fence-posts into the ground.*

ramble ['rambl] *v* **1** to go for a long walk or walks, *usu* in the countryside, for pleasure. **2** to speak in an aimless or confused way. – *n* a long walk, *usu* in the countryside, taken for pleasure.

'**rambler** n 1 a climbing plant (usu a rose).
2 a person who goes walking in the country
for pleasure.

'**rambling** adj 1 aimless and confused; not
keeping to the topic: a long, rambling
speech. 2 built (as if) without any plan,
stretching in various directions: a rambling
old house. 3 (of plants, usu roses) climbing.
ramble on to talk for a long time in an
aimless or confused way.

rambutan ['rambutan] n a sweet, juicy red or
yellow fruit with one seed and a hairy rind.

ramp [ramp] n a sloping surface between
places, objects etc which are at different
levels: The car drove up the ramp from the
quay to the ship.

rampage [ram'peidʒ] v to rush about angrily,
violently or in excitement: The elephants
rampaged through the jungle.
be/go on the rampage ['rampeidʒ] to rush
about angrily, violently or in excitement,
often causing great destruction.

rampant ['rampant] adj very common and
uncontrolled: Vandalism is rampant in the
town.

rampart ['rampɑːt] n (often in pl) a mound or
wall for defence: The defenders were drawn
up on the ramparts.

ramshackle ['ramʃakl] adj badly made; likely
to fall to pieces: a ramshackle car.

ran see run.

ranch [rɑːntʃ] n a farm, esp one in N America
for rearing cattle or horses.

rancid ['ransid] adj (of food, esp butter)
tasting or smelling bad.

rand [rand] – pl **rand(s)** – n the standard unit
of S African currency.

random ['randəm] adj done etc without any
particular plan or system; irregular: The
opinion poll was based on a random sample
of adults. '**randomly** adv.
at random without any particular plan or
system: The police were stopping cars at
random and checking their brakes; Choose a
number at random.

rang see **ring**².

range [reindʒ] n 1 a selection or variety: a
wide range of books for sale; He has a very
wide range of interests. 2 the distance over
which an object can be sent or thrown,
sound can be heard etc: What is the range of
this missile?; We are within range of/beyond
the range of/out of range of their guns. 3 the
amount between certain limits: I'm hoping
for a salary within the range $10 000 to
$14 000; the range of a person's voice be-
tween his highest and lowest notes. 4 a row
or series: a mountain range. 5 in the US,
land, usu without fences, on which cattle
can graze. 6 a place where a person can
practise shooting etc; a rifle-range. 7 a large
kitchen stove with a flat top. – v 1 to put in

a row or rows: The two armies were ranged
on opposite sides of the valley. 2 to vary
between certain limits: Weather conditions
here range between bad and dreadful/from
bad to dreadful. 3 to go, move, extend etc:
His talk ranged over a number of topics.

'**ranger** n 1 a person who looks after a
forest or park. 2 (Amer) a soldier who is a
member of a specially trained force; a
commando.

rank¹ [raŋk] n 1 a line or row (esp of soldiers
or taxis): The officer ordered the front rank
to fire. 2 (in the army, navy etc) a person's
position of importance: He was promoted to
the rank of sergeant/colonel. 3 a social class:
the lower social ranks. – v to have, or give, a
place in a group, according to importance:
I would rank him among our greatest
writers; Apes rank above dogs in intelligence.
the rank and file 1 ordinary people. 2 ordinary soldiers, not officers.

rank² [raŋk] adj 1 complete; absolute: rank
stupidity; The race was won by a rank
outsider. 2 unpleasantly stale and strong: a
rank smell of tobacco. '**rankness** n.

ransack ['ransak, (Amer) ran'sak] v 1 to
search thoroughly in: She ransacked the
whole house for her keys. 2 loot, plunder:
The army ransacked the conquered city.

ransom ['ransəm] n 1 a sum of money etc
paid for the freeing of a prisoner: They paid
a ransom of $40 000; (also adj) They paid
$40 000 in ransom money. – v 1 to pay
money etc to free (someone). 2 to keep (a
person) as a prisoner until a sum of money
etc is paid for his release.
hold to ransom to keep (a person) as a
prisoner until a sum of money etc is paid
for his release.

rant [rant] v to talk angrily: He's still ranting
(and raving) about the damage to his car.

rap [rap] n a quick, brief knock or tap: He
heard a rap on the door. – v – pt, ptp **rapped**
– to hit or knock quickly and briefly: The
teacher rapped the child's fingers with a
ruler; He rapped on the table and called for
silence.
rap out to say quickly: He rapped out his
orders.

rapacious [rə'peiʃəs] adj greedy (esp for
money); eager to seize as much as possible.
ra'paciously adv. **ra'paciousness, ra'pacity**
[-'pasə-] ns.

rape [reip] n 1 the crime of having sexual
intercourse with a woman against her will.
2 the act of causing great damage, destruction etc to land etc. – v 1 to force (a
woman) to have sexual intercourse against
her will. 2 to cause great damage, destruction etc to (countryside etc).
'**rapist** n a man who rapes a woman.

rapid ['rapid] adj quick; fast: He made some

rapid calculations; *He looked feverish and had a rapid pulse.* '**rapidly** *adv.* **ra'pidity,** '**rapidness** *ns.*

'**rapids** *n pl* a place in a river where the water flows quickly, often having dangerous rocks in mid-stream.

rapier ['reipiə] *n* a type of long thin sword.

rapist *see* **rape.**

rapt [rapt] *adj* fascinated (*usu* in admiration): *He listened to the speaker with rapt attention.*

rapture ['raptʃə] *n* great delight.

'**rapturous** *adj* showing great delight: *They gave him a rapturous welcome.* '**rapturously** *adv.*

in raptures greatly delighted: *She was in raptures about her beautiful new car.*

rare ['reə] *adj* **1** not done, found, seen *etc* very often; uncommon: *a rare flower*; *a rare occurrence.* **2** (of meat) only slightly cooked: *I like my steak rare.* '**rareness** *n.*

'**rarely** *adv* not often: *I rarely go to bed before midnight.*

'**rarity** *n* **1** the state of being uncommon. **2** (*pl* '**rarities**) something which is uncommon: *This stamp is quite a rarity.*

raring ['reəriŋ]: **raring to go** very keen to begin, go *etc.*

rascal ['ra:skəl] *n* a cheeky or naughty person, *esp* a child: *a cheeky little rascal.* '**rascally** *adj.*

rase *see* **raze.**

rash[1] [raʃ] *adj* acting, or done, with little caution or thought: *a rash person/action/statement*; *It was rash of you to leave your present job without first finding another.* '**rashly** *adv.* '**rashness** *n.*

rash[2] [raʃ] *n* a large number of red spots on the skin: *That child has a rash – is it measles?*

rasher ['raʃə] *n* a thin slice (of bacon or ham).

raspberry ['ra:zbəri] – *pl* '**raspberries** – *n* a type of edible red berry.

rasping ['ra:spiŋ] *adj* (of a sound, voice *etc*) harsh, rough and unpleasant.

rat [rat] *n* **1** a small animal with a long tail, like a mouse but larger: *The rats have eaten holes in those bags of flour.* **2** an offensive word for an unpleasant and untrustworthy person. – *v* – *pt, ptp* '**ratted** – **1** to break an agreement, promise *etc.* **2** to betray one's friends, colleagues *etc*: *The police know we're here. Someone must have ratted.*

rat race the fierce, unending competition for success *etc.*

smell a rat to have a feeling that something is not as it should be; to have suspicions.

rate [reit] *n* **1** the number of occasions within a given period of time when something happens or is done: *a high (monthly) accident rate in a factory.* **2** the number or

amount of something (in relation to something else); a ratio: *There was a failure rate of one pupil in ten in the exam.* **3** the speed with which something happens or is done: *He works at a tremendous rate*; *the rate of increase/expansion.* **4** the level (of pay), cost *etc* (of or for something): *What is the rate of pay for this job?* **5** (*usu* in *pl*) a tax, *esp*, in UK, paid by house-owners *etc* to help with the running of their town *etc.* – *v* to estimate or be estimated, with regard to worth, merit, value *etc*: *I don't rate this book very highly*; *He doesn't rate very highly as a dramatist in my estimation.*

'**rating 1** (*usu* in *pl*) the position of importance, popularity *etc* (of a person, thing *etc*): *This television programme has had some very bad ratings recently.* **2** an ordinary sailor, as opposed to an officer.

at this, at that rate if this or if that is the case; if this or if that continues: *He says that he isn't sure whether we'll be allowed to finish, but at that rate we might as well not start.*

rate of exchange the relative values of the currencies of two or more countries: *I want to change some dollars into francs – what is the rate of exchange?*

rather ['ra:ðə] *adv* **1** to a certain extent; slightly; a little: *He's rather nice*; *That's a rather silly question/rather a silly question*; *I've eaten rather more than I should have.* **2** more willingly; preferably: *I'd rather do it now than later*; *Can we do it now rather than tomorrow?*; *I'd rather not do it at all*; *I would/had rather you didn't do that*; *Wouldn't you rather have this one?*; *I'd resign rather than do that.* **3** more exactly; more correctly: *He agreed, or rather he didn't disagree*; *One could say he was foolish rather than wicked.*

ratify ['ratifai] *v* to approve and agree to formally and officially, *esp* in writing. ,**rati-fi'cation** *n.*

rating *see* **rate.**

ratio ['reiʃiou] – *pl* '**ratios** – *n* the amount or proportion of one thing compared to another: *There is a ratio of two girls to one boy in this class.*

ration ['raʃən] *n* a measured amount of food *etc* allowed during a particular period of time: *The soldiers were each given a ration of food for the day.* – *v* to allow only a certain amount of (food *etc*) to a person or animal during a particular period of time: *During the oil shortage, petrol was rationed.* '**rations** *n pl* the amount of food allowed to a soldier *etc.*

ration out to give or allow a ration of (food *etc*), *eg* to a number of people.

rational ['raʃənl] *adj* **1** able to think, reason and judge *etc*: *Man is a rational animal.*

2 sensible; reasonable; logical; not (over-) influenced by emotions *etc*: *There must be a rational explanation for those strange noises.* **'rationally** *adv.* **,ration'ality** *n.*

rattle [ratl] *v* 1 to (cause to) make a series of short, sharp noises by knocking together: *The cups rattled as he carried the tray in*; *The strong wind rattled the windows.* 2 to move quickly: *The car was rattling along at top speed.* 3 to upset and confuse (a person): *Don't let him rattle you – he likes annoying people.* – *n* 1 a series of short, sharp noises: *the rattle of cups.* 2 a child's toy, or a wooden instrument, which makes a noise of this sort: *The baby waved its rattle.* 3 the bony rings of a rattlesnake's tail.
'rattling *adj* fast; lively: *The car travelled at a rattling pace.*
'rattlesnake *n* a type of poisonous American snake with bony rings in its tail which rattle.
rattle off to say quickly and *usu* without any feeling or expression: *The boy rattled off the poem.*
rattle through to say or do (something) quickly: *The teacher rattled through his explanation so quickly that no-one could understand him.*

raucous ['rɔːkəs] *adj* hoarse or harsh (and *usu* loud); *a raucous voice.* **'raucously** *adv.* **'raucousness** *n.*

ravage ['ravidʒ] *v* (of enemies, invaders *etc*) to cause great damage or destruction in, or to plunder (a town, country *etc*).

rave [reiv] *v* 1 to talk wildly because, or as if, one is mad. 2 to talk very enthusiastically: *He's been raving about this new record he's heard.*
'raving: **raving mad** so mad as to be raving.

raven ['reivən] *n* a large black bird of the crow family.

ravenous ['ravənəs] *adj* very hungry. **'ravenously** *adv.* **'ravenousness** *n.*

ravine [rə'viːn] *n* a deep narrow valley.

ravioli [ravi'ouli] *n* small envelopes of pasta containing minced meat.

ravishing ['raviʃiŋ] *adj* extremely delightful; very lovely: *She looks ravishing tonight.* **'ravishingly** *adv.*

raw [rɔː] *adj* 1 not cooked: *raw onions/meat.* 2 not prepared or refined; in the natural state: *raw cotton*; *What raw materials are used to make plastic?* 3 with the skin rubbed and sore: *My heel is raw because my shoe doesn't fit properly.* 4 untrained; inexperienced: *raw recruits.* **'rawness** *n.*
a raw deal unfair treatment.

ray [rei] *n* 1 a narrow beam (of light, heat *etc*): *the sun's rays*; *X-rays*; *heat-rays*; *a ray of light.* 2 a slight amount (of hope *etc*).

rayon ['reion] *n, adj* (of) a type of artificial silk: *a rayon scarf.*

raze, (*rare*) **rase** [reiz] *v* to destroy completely, *esp* by fire: *to raze a city to the ground.*

razor ['reizə] *n* an instrument for shaving, having a sharp cutting edge, blade (a **razor=blade**), or electrically-powered revolving cutters.
,razor-'sharp *adj* as sharp as a razor.

reach [riːtʃ] *v* 1 to arrive at (a place, age *etc*): *We'll never reach London before dark*; *Money is not important when you reach my age*; *The noise reached our ears*; *Has the total reached a thousand dollars yet?*; *Have they reached an agreement yet?* 2 to (be able to) touch or get hold of (something): *My keys have fallen down this hole and I can't reach them.* 3 to stretch out one's hand in order to touch or get hold of something: *He reached (across the table) for another cake*; *She reached out and took the book*; *He reached across/over and slapped her.* 4 to make contact with; to communicate with: *If anything happens you can always reach me by phone.* 5 to stretch or extend: *My property reaches from here to the river.* – *n* 1 the distance that can be travelled easily: *My house is within (easy) reach (of London).* 2 the distance one can stretch one's arm: *I keep medicines on the top shelf, out of the children's reach*; *My keys are down that hole, just out of reach (of my fingers)*; *The boxer has a very long reach.* 3 (*usu in pl*) a straight part of a river, canal *etc*: *the lower reaches of the Thames.*

react [ri'akt] *v* 1 to behave in a certain way as a result of something: *How did he react when you called him a fool?*; *He reacted angrily to the criticism*; *Hydrogen reacts with oxygen to form water.* 2 (*with* **against**) to behave or act in a certain way in order to show rejection of: *Young people tend to react against their parents.* 3 (*with* **to**) to be affected, *usu* badly, by (a drug *etc*): *I react very badly to penicillin.*
re'action [-ʃən] *n* 1 the act of reacting: *What was his reaction to your remarks?*; *I get a bad reaction from penicillin*; *I'd like to ask you for your reactions to these suggestions.* 2 a change of opinions, feelings *etc* (*usu* against someone or something): *The new government was popular at first, but then a reaction began.* 3 a process of change which occurs when two or more substances are put together: (*a*) *nuclear reaction*; *a chemical reaction between iron and acid.*
re'actor *n* (*also* **nuclear reactor**) an apparatus in which nuclear energy is produced which can be used as a source of power, *eg* when converted into electricity.

read [riːd] – *pt, ptp* **read** [red] – *v* 1 to look at and understand (printed or written words or other signs): *Have you read this letter?*; *Can your little girl read yet?*; *Can anyone here read Chinese?*; *to read music*; *I can read* (= understand without being told) *her thoughts/mind.* **2** to learn by reading: *I read in the paper today that the government is going to cut taxes again.* **3** to read aloud, *usu* to someone else: *I read my daughter a story before she goes to bed*; *I read to her before she goes to bed.* **4** to pass one's time by reading books *etc* for pleasure *etc*: *I don't have much time to read these days.* **5** to study (a subject) at a university *etc*. **6** to look at or be able to see (something) and get information from it: *I can't read the clock without my glasses*; *The nurse read the thermometer.* **7** to be written or worded; to say: *His letter reads as follows: 'Dear Sir, …'* **8** (of a piece of writing *etc*) to make a (good, bad *etc*) impression: *This report reads well.* **9** (of dials, instruments *etc*) to show a particular figure, measurement *etc*: *The thermometer reads −5° C.* **10** to (cause a word, phrase *etc* to) be replaced by another, *eg* in a document or manuscript: *There is one error on this page. For 'two yards', read 'two metres'*; *'Two yards long' should read 'two metres long'.* − *n* the act, or a period, of reading: *I like a good read before I go to sleep.*

'readable *adj* (*neg* **un-**) **1** easy or pleasant to read: *I don't usually enjoy poetry but I find these poems very readable.* **2** able to be read: *Your handwriting is scarcely readable.* **'readableness**, **,reada'bility** *ns*.

'reader *n* **1** a person who reads books, magazines *etc*: *He's a keen reader.* **2** a person who reads a particular newspaper, magazine *etc*: *The editor asked readers to write to him with their opinions.* **3** a reading-book, *esp* for children or for learners of a foreign language: *a Latin reader.*

'readership *n* the (number of) people who read a newspaper, magazine *etc*.

'reading *n* **1** the act of reading. **2** the reading of something aloud as a (public) entertainment: *a poetry reading.* **3** the ability to read: *The boy is good at reading.* **4** the figure, measurement *etc* on a dial, instrument *etc*: *The reading on the thermometer was −5° C.*

reading- **1** for the purpose of reading: *reading-glasses*; *a reading-room in a library.* **2** for learning to read: *a reading-book.*

'read-out − *pl* **'read-outs** − *n* data produced by a computer, *eg* on magnetic or paper tape.

read between the lines to look for or find information (*eg* in a letter) which is not actually stated.

read off to read from a dial, instrument *etc*: *The engineer read off the temperatures one by one.*

read on to continue to read; to read further: *He paused for a few moments, and then read on.*

read out to read aloud: *Read out the answers to the questions.*

read over/through to read from beginning to end: *I'll read through your manuscript, and let you know if I find any mistakes.*

readdress [riːə'dres] *v* to change the address on (a letter *etc*): *This letter is for the person who used to live here − I'll readdress it and send it to him.*

readily, readiness *see* **ready.**

reading *see* **read.**

readjust [riːə'dʒʌst] (*with* **to**) to get used again to (something one has not experienced for a time): *Some soldiers find it hard to readjust to civilian life when they leave the army.* **,rea'djustment** *n*.

ready ['redi] *adj* **1** (*neg* **un-**) prepared; able to be used *etc* immediately or when needed; able to do (something) immediately or when necessary: *I've packed our cases, so we're ready to leave*; *Is tea ready yet?*; *Your coat has been cleaned and is ready* (*to be collected*). **2** (*neg* **un-**) willing: *I'm always ready to help.* **3** quick: *You're too ready to find faults in other people*; *He always has a ready answer.* **4** likely, about (to do something): *My head feels as if it's ready to burst.* **'readiness** *n*.

'readily *adv* **1** willingly: *I'd readily help you.* **2** without difficulty: *I can readily answer all your questions.*

ready cash ready money.

,ready-'made *adj* (*esp* of clothes) made in standard sizes, and for sale to anyone who wishes to buy, rather than being made for one particular person: *a ready-made suit.*

ready money coins and banknotes: *I want to be paid in ready money, not by cheque.*

,ready-to-'wear *adj* (of clothes) ready-made.

in readiness ready: *I want everything in readiness for his arrival.*

real [riəl] *adj* **1** which actually exists: *There's a real monster in that cave.* **2** not imitation; genuine: *real leather*; *Is that diamond real?* **3** actual: *He may own the factory, but it's his manager who is the real boss.* **4** great: *a real surprise/problem.* − *adv* (*esp Amer*) very; really: *a real nice house.*

'realist *n* a person who sees, or claims to see, life as it is, without being affected by emotion *etc*. **'realism** *n*.

,rea'listic *adj* (*neg* **un-**) **1** showing things as they really are: *a realistic painting.* **2** taking a sensible, practical view of life: *I'd like to think we'd sell five of these a day, but it would be more realistic to say two.* **,rea'listically** *adv*.

reality [ri'aləti] *n* **1** that which is real and not imaginary: *It was a relief to get back to* *reality after hearing the ghost story.* **2** the state of being real. **3** (*often in pl* – **re'alities**) a fact: *Death and sorrow are two of the grim realities of human existence.*

'really *adv* **1** in fact: *He looks a fool but he is really very clever.* **2** very: *That's a really nice hat! – interj* an expression of surprise, protest, doubt *etc*: *'I'm going to be the next manager.' 'Oh really?'*; *Really! You mustn't be so rude!*

real estate (the buying and selling of) land and houses.

for real (*esp Amer*) genuine; true: *He says he's got a new bike, but I don't know if that's for real.*

in reality really; actually: *He pretends to be busy, but in reality he has very little to do.*

realism, reality *etc see* **real.**

realize, -ise ['riəlaiz] *v* **1** to know; to understand: *I realize that I can't have everything I want*; *I realized my mistake.* **2** to make real; to make (something) come true: *He realized his ambition to become an astronaut*; *My worst fears were realized.* **3** to make (money) by selling something: *He realized $60 000 on the sale of his apartment.*

,reali'zation, -s- *n* the act of realizing: *the realization of his mistake/hopes.*

really *see* **real.**

realm [relm] *n* **1** a kingdom. **2** an area of activity, interest *etc*: *She's well-known in the realm of sport.*

ream [ri:m] *n* a measure for paper, equal to 480 sheets.

reap [ri:p] *v* to cut and gather (corn *etc*): *The farmer is reaping the wheat.*

'reaper *n* a person or machine that reaps.

reappear [ri:ə'piə] *v* to appear again: *The boy disappeared behind the wall, and reappeared a few yards away.* **,reap'pearance** *n.*

rear[1] [riə] *n* **1** the back part of something: *There is a second bathroom at the rear of the house*; *The enemy attacked the army in the rear.* **2** the buttocks; bottom: *The horse kicked him in his rear. – adj* positioned behind: *the rear wheels of the car.*

,rear-'admiral *n* in the navy, (a person of) the rank above commodore.

'rearguard *n sing or n pl* (the group of) soldiers who protect the rear of an army (*eg* when it is retreating).

rear[2] [riə] *v* **1** to feed and care for (a family, animals *etc* while they grow up): *She has reared six children*; *He rears cattle.* **2** (*esp* of a horse) to rise up on the hind legs: *The horse reared in fright as the car passed.* **3** to raise (the head *etc*): *The snake reared its head.*

rear up 1 (*esp* of horses) to rear. **2** of problems *etc*) to appear.

rearm [ri:'a:m] *v* to give or get weapons again,

esp weapons of a new type. **re'armament** [-məmənt] *n.*

rearrange [ri:ə'reindʒ] *v* to change the position of; to arrange differently: *We'll rearrange the chairs.* **,rear'rangement** *n.*

reason ['ri:zn] *n* **1** something which makes something happen, describes why it happened, should happen or is going to happen *etc*: *What is the reason for this noise?*; *What is your reason for going to London?*; *The reason (why) I am going is that I want to.* **2** the power of the mind to think, form opinions and judgements *etc*: *Only man has reason – animals have not. – v* **1** to (be able to) think, form opinions and judgements *etc*: *Man alone has the ability to reason.* **2** to argue; to work out after some thought: *She reasoned that if he had caught the 6.30 p.m. train, he would not be home before 8.00.*

'reasonable *adj* **1** sensible: *a reasonable suggestion.* **2** willing to listen to argument; acting with good sense: *You will find him very reasonable.* **3** fair; correct; which one should or could accept: *Is $10 a reasonable price for this book?* **4** satisfactory; as much as one might expect or want: *There was a reasonable number of people at the meeting.* **'reasonableness** *n.*

'reasonably *adv*: *He behaved very reasonably*; *The car is reasonably priced*; *The meeting was reasonably well attended.*

'reasoning *n* the act or process of reaching a decision, conclusion *etc*: *I don't understand his reasoning at all.*

have reason to (believe, think *etc*) to feel justified in (believing *etc*): *I have (good) reason to think that he is lying.*

it stands to reason it is obvious or logical: *If you go to bed so late it stands to reason that you will be tired next morning.*

listen to reason to allow oneself to be persuaded to do something more sensible than what one was going to do; to pay attention to common sense.

lose one's reason to become insane.

reason with to argue with (a person) in order to persuade him to be more sensible: *We tried to reason with the worried mother but she went out alone in the storm to look for the child.*

see reason to (be persuaded to) be more sensible than one is or has been.

within reason within the limits of good sense: *I'll do anything/go anywhere within reason.*

reassemble [ri:ə'sembl] *v* **1** to put (things) together after taking them apart: *The mechanic took the engine to pieces, then reassembled it.* **2** to come together again: *The tourists went off sight-seeing, then reassembled for their evening meal.*

reassure [riə'ʃuə] *v* to take away the doubts or

fears of: *The woman was worried about the dangers of taking aspirins, but her doctor reassured her.*

,reas'surance *n* **1** the process of reassuring or being reassured. **2** something said *etc* that makes a person feel reassured: *She wants reassurance; Despite his reassurances, I'm still not happy.*

,reas'suring *adj*: *the doctor's reassuring remarks.* **,reas'suringly** *adv.*

rebate ['ri:beit] *n* a part of a payment, tax *etc* which is given back to the person paying it.

rebel ['rebl] *n* **1** a person who opposes or fights against people in authority, eg a government: *The rebels killed many soldiers;* (*also adj*) *rebel troops.* **2** a person who does not accept the rules of normal behaviour *etc*: *My son is a bit of a rebel.* – [rə'bel] *v* – *pt, ptp* **re'belled** – to fight (against people in authority): *The people rebelled against the dictator; Teenagers often rebel against their parents' way of life.*

rebellion [rə'beljən] *n* **1** an open or armed fight against a government *etc.* **2** a refusal to obey orders or to accept rules *etc.*

rebellious [rə'beljəs] *v* rebelling or likely to rebel: *rebellious troops/children.* **re'belliously** *adv.* **re'belliousness** *n.*

rebound [ri'baund] *v* to bounce back: *The ball rebounded off the wall.*

on the rebound ['ri:baund] as (something) bounces back: *He caught the ball on the rebound.*

rebuff [ri'bʌf] *n* an unkind or unfriendly refusal or rejection. – *v* to reject or refuse in an unkind of unfriendly way: *He rebuffed all the attempts of his friends to help him.*

rebuke [rə'bju:k] *v* to speak severely to (a person), because he has done wrong: *The boy was rebuked by his teacher for cheating.* – *n* (stern) words spoken to a person, because he has done wrong.

recall [ri'ko:l] *v* **1** to order (a person *etc*) to return: *He had been recalled to his former post.* **2** to remember: *I don't recall when I last saw him.* – *n* **1** an order to return: *the recall of soldiers to duty.* **2** ['ri:ko:l] the ability to remember and repeat what one has seen, heard *etc*: *He has total recall.*

recapitulate [ri:kə'pitjuleit] *v* (*abbrev* **recap** ['ri:kap] – *pt, ptp* **'recapped**) to go over again (the chief points of a statement, argument *etc*). **'reca,pitu'lation** (*abbrev* **'recap**) *n.*

recapture [ri'kaptʃə] *v* **1** to capture again: *The soldiers recaptured the city; The prisoners were recaptured.* **2** to convey (the feeling of something from the past): *to recapture the atmosphere of medieval London.* – *n* the process of recapturing or being recaptured.

recede [ri'si:d] *v* **1** to go or move back: *When*

the rain stopped, the floods receded; His hair is receding from his forehead.* **2** to become distant: *The coast receded behind us as we sailed away.*

receipt [rə'si:t] *n* **1** the act of receiving or being received: *Please sign this form to acknowledge receipt of the money.* **2** a written note saying that money *etc* has been received: *I paid the bill and he gave me a receipt.*

receive [rə'si:v] *v* **1** to get or be given: *He received a letter; They received a good education.* **2** to have a formal meeting with: *The Pope received the Queen in the Vatican.* **3** to allow to join something: *He was received into the group.* **5** to greet, react to, in some way: *The news was received in silence; The townspeople received the heroes with great cheers.* **6** to accept (stolen goods) *esp* with the intention of reselling (them).

re'ceiver *n* **1** the part of a telephone which is held to one's ear. **2** an apparatus for receiving radio or television signals. **3** a person who receives stolen goods. **4** a person who is appointed to take control of the business of someone who has gone bankrupt. **5** a stereo amplifier with a built-in radio.

receive is spelt with -ei-.

recent ['ri:snt] *adj* happening, done *etc* not long ago: *Things have changed in recent weeks; recent events.*

'recently *adv*: *He came to see me recently.*

receptacle [rə'septəkl] *n* a container of some kind: *A dustbin is a receptacle for rubbish.*

reception [rə'sepʃən] *n* **1** the act of receiving or being received: *His speech got a good reception.* **2** a formal party or social gathering to welcome guests: *a wedding reception.* **3** the quality of radio or television signals: *Radio reception is poor in this area.* **4** the part of a hotel, hospital *etc* where visitors enter and are attended to.

re'ceptionist *n* a person who is employed (eg in a hotel, office *etc*) to answer the telephone, attend to guests, clients *etc.*

receptive [rə'septiv] *adj* (of people, their minds *etc*) quick to understand and accept new ideas *etc.*

recess [ri'ses, 'ri:ses] *n* **1** a part of a room set back from the main part; an alcove: *We can put the dining-table in that recess.* **2** the time during which Parliament or the law-courts do not work: *Parliament is in recess.* **3** (*Amer*) a short period of free time between school classes.

recession [rə'seʃən] *n* a temporary fall in a country's or the world's business activities.

recipe ['resəpi] *n* a set of instructions on how to prepare and cook something: *a recipe for curry;* (*also adj*) *a recipe book.*

recipient [rə'sipiənt] *n* a person who receives something: *the recipient of a letter.*

recite [rə'sait] *v* to repeat aloud from memory: *to recite a poem.*

re'cital *n* **1** a public performance (of music or songs) *usu* by one person or a small number of people: *a recital of Schubert's songs.* **2** the act of reciting.

,reci'tation [resi-] *n* **1** a poem *etc* which is recited: *a recitation from Shakespeare.* **2** the act of reciting.

reckless ['rekləs] *adj* very careless; acting or done without any thought of the consequences: *a reckless driver; reckless driving.* **'recklessly** *adv.* **'recklessness** *n.*

reckon ['rekən] *v* **1** to consider: *He is reckoned (to be/as/as being) the best pianist in Britain.* **2** (*esp Amer*) to think; to have decided; to intend: *Do you reckon we'll succeed?; Is he reckoning on coming?*

'reckoning *n* **1** calculation; counting: *By my reckoning, we must be about eight kilometres from the town.* **2** the settling of debts, *etc.*

day of reckoning the time when one has to pay for, or be punished for, one's mistakes, crimes *etc.*

reckon on to depend on or expect: *I was reckoning on meeting him tonight.*

reckon up to count or calculate: *to reckon up the total cost.*

reckon with to be prepared for; to take into consideration: *I didn't reckon with all these problems; He's a man to be reckoned with* (= a powerful man).

reclaim [ri'kleim] *v* **1** to ask for (something one owns which has been lost, stolen *etc* and found by someone else): *A wallet has been found and can be reclaimed at the manager's office.* **2** to make (wasteland) fit for use; to get back (land) from under the sea *etc* by draining *etc.* **,recla'mation** [rə-klə-] *n.*

recline [rə'klain] *v* to lean or lie on one's back or side: *The invalid was reclining on the sofa.*

reclining chair an armchair with a back which can be made to slope backwards.

recluse [rə'klu:s] *n* a person who lives alone and avoids other people.

recognize, -ise ['rekəgnaiz] *v* **1** to see, hear *etc* (a person, thing *etc*) and know who or what that person, thing *etc* is, because one has seen or heard him, it *etc* before: *I recognized his voice/handwriting; I recognized him by his voice.* **2** to admit, acknowledge: *Everyone recognized his skill.* **3** to be willing to have political relations with: *Many countries were unwilling to recognize the new republic.* **4** to accept as valid, well-qualified *etc*: *I don't recognize the authority of this court.* **,recog'nizable, -s-** *adj* (*neg* **un-**). **,recog'nizably, -s-** *adv.*

,recog'nition [-'niʃən] *n* the act or state of

recognizing or being recognized: *They gave the boy a medal in recognition of his courage; I said hello to him but he showed no recognition.*

recoil [rə'koil] *v* **1** to move back or away, *usu* quickly, in horror or fear: *He recoiled at/from the sight of the murdered child.* **2** (of guns when fired) to jump back. – ['ri:koil] *n* the act of recoiling.

recollect [rekə'lekt] *v* to remember: *I don't recollect having seen him before.*

,recol'lection [-ʃən] *n* **1** the act or power of recollecting. **2** something that is remembered: *My book is called 'Recollections of Childhood'.*

recommend [rekə'mend] *v* **1** to advise: *The doctor recommended a long holiday.* **2** to suggest as being particularly good, particularly suitable *etc*: *He recommended her (to me) for the job.*

,recommen'dation *n* **1** the act of recommending: *I gave her the job on his recommendation.* **2** something recommended: *The recommendations of the committee.*

recompense ['rekəmpens] *n* money *etc* given to someone in return for his trouble, inconvenience or effort. – *v* to give (someone) money *etc* in return for effort, inconvenience *etc*: *The nobleman recompensed his followers for their loyalty.*

reconcile ['rekənsail] *v* **1** to cause (people) to become friendly again, *eg* after they have quarrelled: *Why won't you be reconciled (with him)?* **2** to bring (two or more different aims, points of view *etc*) into agreement: *The unions want high wages and the bosses want high profits – it's almost impossible to reconcile these two aims.* **3** to (make someone) accept (a situation, fact *etc*) patiently: *Her mother didn't want the marriage to take place but she is reconciled to it now.*

'recon,cili'ation [-sili-] *n*: *There has been a reconciliation between her and her husband; an act of reconciliation.*

recondition [ri:kən'diʃən] *v* to put in good condition again by cleaning, repairing *etc.* **,recon'ditioned** *adj*: *a reconditioned television set.*

reconnaissance [rə'konəsəns] *n* (the act of making) a study (of land, enemy troops *etc*) to obtain information, *eg* before a battle.

reconnoitre, (*Amer*) **reconnoiter** [rekə'noitə] *v* to make a reconnaissance of (land, enemy troops *etc*).

reconsider [ri:kən'sidə] *v* to think about again and possibly change one's opinion, decision *etc*: *Please reconsider your decision to leave the firm.* **'recon,side'ration** *n.*

reconstitute [ri:'konstitju:t] *v* to put or change (something) back to its original form *eg* by adding liquid: *to reconstitute dried milk.* re,consti'tution *n*.

reconstruct [riːkən'strʌkt] *v* to create a complete description or idea, on the basis of certain known facts: *Let us try to reconstruct the crime.* ,recon'struction [-ʃən] *n*.

record ['rekoːd, -kəd, (*Amer*) -kərd] *n* 1 a written report of facts, events *etc*: *historical records*; *I wish to keep a record of everything that is said at this meeting.* 2 a round flat piece of (*usu* black) plastic on which music *etc* is recorded: *a record of Beethoven's Sixth Symphony.* 3 (in races, games, or almost any activity) the best performance so far; something which has never yet been beaten: *He holds the record for the 1000 metres*; *The record for the high jump was broken/beaten this afternoon*; *He claimed to have eaten fifty sausages in a minute and asked if this was a record*; (*also adj*) *a record score.* 4 the collected facts from the past of a person, institution *etc*: *This school has a very poor record of success in exams*; *He has a criminal record.* – [rə'koːd] *v* 1 to write a description of (an event, facts *etc*) so that they can be read in the future: *The decisions will be recorded in the minutes of the meeting.* 2 to put (the sound of music, speech *etc*) on a record or tape so that it can be listened to in the future: *I've recorded the whole concert*; *Don't make any noise when I'm recording.* 3 (of a dial, instrument *etc*) to show (a figure *etc*) as a reading: *The thermometer recorded 30° C yesterday.* 4 to give or show, *esp* in writing: *to record one's vote in an election.*

re'corder *n* 1 a type of musical wind instrument, made of wood, plastic *etc.* 2 an instrument for recording on to tape.

re'cording *n* something recorded on tape, a record *etc*: *This is a recording of Beethoven's Fifth Symphony.*

'record-player *n* an electrical instrument which reproduces the sounds recorded on records.

in record time very quickly.

off the record (of information, statements *etc*) not intended to be repeated or made public: *The Prime Minister admitted off the record that the country was going through a serious crisis.*

on record recorded: *This is the coldest winter on record.*

recount [ri'kaunt] *v* to tell (a story *etc*) in detail: *He recounted his adventures.*

re-count [riː'kaunt] *v* to count again. – ['riːkaunt] *n* a second count: *a re-count of votes.*

recover [rə'kʌvə] *v* 1 to become well again; to return to good health *etc*: *He is recovering from a serious illness*; *The country is recovering from an economic crisis.* 2 to get

back: *The police have recovered the stolen jewels*; *He will recover the cost of the repairs through the insurance.* 3 to get control of (one's actions, emotions *etc*) again: *The actor almost fell over but quickly recovered (his balance).*

re'covery *n* (an) act or process of recovering: *The patient made a remarkable recovery after his illness*; *the recovery of stolen property.*

re-cover [riː'kʌvə] *v* to put a new cover on: *This chair needs to be re-covered.*

re-create [riːkri'eit] *v* to describe or show realistically: *In the film, they had tried to recreate the horrors of the war.* ,re-cre'ation *n*.

recreation [rekri'eiʃən] *n* (a) pleasant activity which one enjoys doing in one's spare time (*eg* a sport, hobby): *I have little time for recreation*; *amusements and recreations.* ,recre'ational *adj*.

recreation ground a piece of land for playing sports, games *etc* on.

recruit [rə'kruːt] *n* 1 a person who has (just) joined the army, air force *etc.* 2 a person who has (just) joined a society, group *etc*: *Our party needs new recruits before the next election.* – *v* to cause to join the army, a society *etc*: *We must recruit more troops*; *Can't you recruit more members to the music society?* re'cruitment *n*.

*****rectangle** ['rektaŋgl] *n* a two-dimensional, four-sided figure with opposite sides equal and all its angles right angles. rec'tangular [-gjulə] *adj*.

rectify ['rektifai] *v* to put right or correct (a mistake *etc*): *We shall rectify the error as soon as possible.* ,recti'fiable *adj*. ,rectifi'cation [-fi-] *n*.

rectum ['rektəm] *n* the lower part of the alimentary canal, through which waste substances pass from the intestines.

recumbent [rə'kʌmbənt] *adj* lying down.

recuperate [rə'kjuːpəreit] *v* to recover, *eg* after an illness. re,cupe'ration *n*.

recur [ri'kəː] – *pt, ptp* re'curred – *v* to happen again; to come back again: *This problem keeps recurring.*

re'currence [-'kʌ-, (*Amer*) -'kəː-] *n*: *He has had several recurrences of his illness.*

re'current [-'kʌ-, (*Amer*) -'kəː-] *adj* happening often or regularly: *a recurrent nightmare.*

recycle [riː'saikl] *v* to put (a used substance) through a particular process so that it is fit to use again.

red [red] *n, adj* 1 (of) the colour of blood: *a red car/dress/cheeks*; *Her eyes were red with crying.* 2 (of hair or fur) (of) a colour which varies between a golden brown and a deep reddish-brown. 3 (a) communist: *Red*

China; *A lot of his university friends are Reds.*

'redden *v* **1** to make or become red or redder: *to redden the lips with lipstick.* **2** to blush: *She reddened as she realized her mistake.*

'reddish *adj* slightly red: *reddish hair.*

'redness *n.*

red herring 1 something that leads people away from the main point in a discussion. **2** a false clue or line of enquiry.

,red-'hot *adj* (of metal *etc*) so hot that it is glowing red: *red-hot steel*; *This iron is red-hot.*

Red Indian a N American Indian. – *adj* of a Red Indian or Red Indians: *Red Indian carvings.*

red-letter day a day which will always be remembered because of something especially good that happened on it.

red tape annoying and unnecessary rules and regulations.

be in the red to be in debt.

catch red-handed to find (a person) in the act of doing wrong: *The police caught the thief red-handed.*

the Red Army the army of the USSR.

see red to become angry: *When he started criticizing my work, I really saw red.*

redeem [rəˈdiːm] *v* **1** to buy back (something that has been pawned): *I'm going to redeem my gold watch.* **2** to set (a person) free by paying a ransom; (of Jesus Christ) to free (a person) from sin. **3** to compensate for or cancel out the faults of: *His willingness to work redeemed him in her eyes.*

Re'deemer *n* (*often with* **the**) Jesus Christ.

redemption [rəˈdempʃən] *n*: *the redemption of man by Christ.*

redeeming feature a good quality that somewhat makes up for the bad qualities in a person or thing.

redirect [riːdiˈrekt] *v* to put a new address on, and post (a letter *etc*).

re-do [riːˈduː] – *pt* **re-did** [riːˈdid]: *ptp* **re-done** [riːˈdʌn] – *v* to do again: *Your homework will have to be re-done.*

redouble [riˈdʌbl] *v* to make twice as great: *He redoubled his efforts.*

redoubtable [rəˈdautəbl] *adj* (of a person) brave; bold.

redress [rəˈdres] *v* to set right or compensate for: *The company offered the man a large sum of money to redress the harm that their product had done to him.* – *n* (money *etc* which is paid as) compensation for some wrong that has been done.

reduce [rəˈdjuːs] *v* **1** to make less, smaller *etc*: *The shop reduced its prices*; *The train reduced speed.* **2** to lose weight by dieting: *I must reduce to get into that dress.* **3** to drive, or put, into a particular (bad) state: *The*

bombs reduced the city to ruins; *She was so angry, she was almost reduced to tears*; *During the famine, many people were reduced to eating grass and leaves.* **re'ducible** *adj.*

re'duction [-ˈdʌk-] *n*: *The government promised a reduction in prices later*; *price reductions.*

reed [riːd] *n* **1** a kind of tall, stiff grass growing on wet or marshy ground: *reeds along a river-bank.* **2** a thin piece of cane or metal in certain wind instruments (*eg* the oboe, clarinet) which vibrates and makes a sound when the instrument is played.

reef [riːf] *n* a line of rocks *etc* just above or below the surface of the sea: *The ship got stuck on a reef.*

reek [riːk] *n* a strong, *usu* unpleasant smell. – *v* to smell strongly (of something).

reel [riːl] *n* **1** a round wheel-shaped or cylindrical object of wood, metal *etc* on which thread, film, fishing-lines *etc* can be wound: *a reel of sewing-cotton*; *He changed the reel in the projector.* **2** (the music for) a type of lively Scottish, Irish or American dance: *The fiddler played a reel*; *to dance a reel.* – *v* **1** to stagger; to sway; to move in an unsteady way: *The drunk man reeled along the road*; *My brain was reeling with all the information that he gave me.*

reel in to pull (*eg* a fish out of the water) by winding the line to which it is attached on to a reel.

reel off to say or repeat quickly and easily, without pausing: *He reeled off the list of names.*

re-elect [riːiˈlekt] *v* to elect again: *They have re-elected him to Parliament.* **,re-e'lection** [-ʃən] *n.*

re-enter [riːˈentə] *v* to enter again: *The spaceship will re-enter the Earth's atmosphere tomorrow.*

,re-'entry *n*: *The spaceship's re-entry will take place tomorrow afternoon at two o'clock.*

refer [rəˈfəː] – *pt*, *ptp* **re'ferred** – *v* (*with* **to**) **1** to talk or write (about something); to mention: *He doesn't like anyone referring to his wooden leg*; *I referred to your theories in my last book.* **2** to relate to, concern, or apply to: *My remarks refer to your last letter.* **3** to send or pass on to someone else for discussion, information, a decision *etc*: *The case was referred to a higher law-court*; *I'll refer you to the managing director.* **4** to look for information (in something): *If I'm not sure how to spell a word, I refer to a dictionary.*

referee [refəˈriː] *n* **1** a person who controls boxing, football *etc* matches, makes sure that the rules are not broken *etc*: *The referee sent two of the players off the field.*

2 a person who is willing to provide a note about one's character, ability *etc, eg* when one applies for new job. – *v* – *pt, ptp* ˌrefeˈreed – to act as a referee for a match: *I've been asked to referee (a football match) on Saturday.*

reference [ˈrefərəns] *n* **1** (an) act of referring (to something); a mention (of something): *He made several references to her latest book; With reference to your request for information, I regret to inform you that I am unable to help you.* **2** a note about one's character, ability *etc, eg* when one applies for a new job: *Our new secretary had excellent references from her previous employers.* **3** an indication in a book, report *etc*, showing where one got one's information or where further information can be found.

reference book a book which is not usually read from beginning to end but which is consulted occasionally for information, *eg* a dictionary or encyclopaedia.

reference library a library of books to be looked at for information but not borrowed.

> reference, noun, is spelt with **-r-**.
> referred and referring are spelt with **-rr-**.

referendum [refəˈrendəm] – *pls* ˌrefeˈrendums, ˌrefeˈrenda [-də] – *n* a general vote made by the people of a country *etc* for or against a particular government proposal *etc*.

refill [ˈriːfil] *n* the amount (*usu* in a container) of some material needed to fill up some object which becomes empty through use: *I must go and buy some refills for my pen.* – [riːˈfil] *v* to fill up again: *He refilled his pipe.*

refine [rəˈfain] *v* **1** to make (a substance *eg* sugar) pure by taking out dirt,, waste substances *etc*: *Oil is refined before it is used.* **2** to improve: *We have refined our techniques considerably since the work began.*

reˈfined *adj* (*neg* **un-**) **1** very polite; well-mannered; elegant. **2** having been refined: *refined sugar.*

reˈfinement *n* **1** good manners, good taste, polite speech *etc*. **2** (an) improvement: *to make refinements.*

reˈfinery – *pl* **reˈfineries** – *n* a place where sugar or oil *etc* is refined: *an oil refinery.*

refit [riːˈfit] – *pt, ptp* ˌreˈfitted – *v* to repair or fit new parts to (a ship): *They are refitting the liner.*

reflect [rəˈflekt] *v* **1** to send back (light, heat *etc*): *The white sand reflected the sun's heat.* **2** (of a mirror *etc*) to give an image of: *She was reflected in the mirror/water.* **3** to think carefully: *Give him a minute to reflect (on what he should do).*

reˈflecting *adj* able to reflect (light *etc*): *a reflecting surface.*

reflection, reflexion [rəˈflekʃən]: *She looked at her reflection in the water; After reflection I felt I had made the wrong decision; The book is called 'Reflections of a Politician'.*

reˈflective [-tiv] *adj* **1** thoughtful: *a reflective mood.* **2** reflecting: *Reflective number-plates.* **reˈflectively** *adv*.

reˈflector *n* something, *esp* of glass or metal, that reflects light, heat *etc*.

reflex [ˈriːfleks] *n, adj* (an action which is) automatic or not intended: *The doctor tapped the patient's knee in order to test his reflexes; a reflex action.*

reflexion *see* **reflect**.

reflexive [rəˈfleksiv] *adj* **1** (of a pronoun) showing that the object of a verb is the same person or thing as the subject: *In 'He cut himself', 'himself' is a reflexive pronoun.* **2** (of a verb) used with a reflexive pronoun: *In 'control yourself!', 'control' is a reflexive verb.*

reform [rəˈfoːm] *v* **1** to improve or remove faults from: *The criminal's wife stated that she had made great efforts to reform her husband.* **2** to give up bad habits, improve one's behaviour *etc*: *He admitted that he had been a criminal, but said that he intended to reform.* – *n* **1** the act of improving: *the reform of our political system.* **2** an improvement: *He intends to make several reforms in the prison system.* ˌreforˈmation [refə-] *n*.

reˈformed *adj* (*neg* **un-**) improved, *esp* in behaviour.

reˈformer *n* a person who wishes to bring about improvements: *one of the reformers of our political system.*

refrain¹ [rəˈfrein] *n* a line of words or music repeated regularly in a song, *esp* at the end of or after each verse; a chorus.

refrain² [rəˈfrein] *v* (with **from**) not to do; to avoid: *You are asked to refrain from smoking/from (drinking) alcohol.*

refresh [rəˈfreʃ] *v* to give new strength and energy to; to make (a person *etc*) feel less hot, tired *etc, eg* after or during a period of hard work: *This glass of cool lemonade will refresh you.*

reˈfreshing *adj* **1** giving new strength and energy; having a cooling and relaxing effect: *a refreshing drink of cold water.* **2** particularly pleasing because different from normal: *It is refreshing to hear a politician speak so honestly.* **reˈfreshingly** *adv*.

reˈfreshments *n pl* food and drink served *eg* at a meeting: *Light refreshments are available in the other room.*

refresh someone's memory to remind (someone) of the facts and details of something.

refrigerator [rəˈfridʒəreitə] *n* (*also* **fridge** [fridʒ]: *Amer also* **'icebox**) a machine which keeps food cold and so prevents it from going bad: *Milk should be kept in the refrigerator*.

re'frigerate *v* to keep (food) cold to prevent it from going bad: *Meat should be refrigerated*. **re,frige'ration** *n*.

refuel [ri:'fjuəl] – *pt, ptp* **re'fuelled**, (*Amer also*) **re'fueled** – *v* to supply (an aeroplane *etc*) with more fuel: *The plane has to be refuelled every thousand miles*; *The plane stopped to refuel*.

refuge ['refju:dʒ] *n* (a place which gives) shelter or protection from danger, trouble *etc*: *The escaped prisoner sought refuge in the church*.

,**refu'gee** *n* a person who seeks shelter *esp* in another country, from war, disaster, or persecution: *Refugees were pouring across the frontier*; (*also adj*) *a refugee camp*.

refund [ri'fʌnd] *v* to pay back: *When the concert was cancelled, the people who had bought tickets had their money refunded*. – ['ri:fʌnd] *n* the paying back of money: *They demanded a refund*.

refuse[1] [rə'fju:z] *v* **1** not to do what one has been asked, told or is expected to do: *He refused to help me*; *She refused to believe what I said*; *When I asked him to leave, he refused*. **2** not to accept: *He refused my offer of help*; *They refused our invitation*; *She refused the money*. **3** not to give (permission *etc*): *I was refused admittance to the meeting*.

re'fusal *n*: *I was surprised at his refusal to help me*; *When we sent out the wedding invitations, we had several refusals*.

refuse[2] ['refju:s] *n* rubbish; waste material from *eg* a kitchen.

refuse collector, refuse collection vehicle, a person who collects, a vehicle for collecting, rubbish.

refute [rə'fju:t] *v* to prove that (a person, statement *etc*) is wrong: *You can easily refute his argument*. **re'futable** *adj*. ,**refu'tation** [refju-] *n*.

regain [ri'gein] *v* **1** to get back again: *The champion was beaten in January but regained the title in March*. **2** to get back to (a place): *The swimmer was swept out to sea, but managed to regain the shore*.

regal ['ri:gəl] *adj* of, like, or suitable for, a king or queen: *She has a regal appearance*; *regal robes*. **regally** *adv*.

regalia [rə'geiliə] *n sing or n pl* **1** objects (*eg* the crown and sceptre) which are a sign of royalty, used *eg* at a coronation. **2** any ornaments, ceremonial clothes *etc* which are worn as a sign of a person's importance or authority.

regard [rə'ga:d] *v* **1** (*with* **as**) to consider to be: *I regard his conduct as totally unacceptable*. **2** to think of as being very good, important *etc*; to respect: *He is very highly* regarded by his friends. **3** to think of (with a particular emotion or feeling): *I regard him with horror*; *He regards his wife's behaviour with amusement*. **4** to look at: *He regarded me over the top of his glasses*. **5** to pay attention to (advice *etc*). – *n* **1** thought; attention: *He ran into the burning house without regard for his safety*. **2** sympathy; care; consideration: *He shows no regard for other people*. **3** good opinion; respect: *I hold him in high regard*.

re'garding *prep* about; concerning: *Have you any suggestions regarding this project?*

re'gardless *adj, adv* not thinking or caring about costs, problems, dangers *etc*: *There may be difficulties but I shall carry on regardless (of the consequences)*.

re'gards *n pl* greetings; good wishes: *Give my regards to your mother*; *He sent her his regards*.

as regards as far as (something) is concerned: *As regards the meeting tomorrow, I hope as many people will attend as possible*.

with regard to about; concerning: *I have no complaints with regard to his work*.

with regards is sometimes used in ending a letter.
with regard to means 'about'.

regatta [rə'gatə] *n* a meeting for yacht or (*usu* small) boat races.

regent ['ri:dʒent] *n* a person who governs in place of a king or queen: *The prince was only two years old when the king died, so his uncle was appointed regent*.

régime, regime [rei'ʒi:m] *n* a (system of) government: *a Communist régime*.

regiment ['redʒimənt] *n* a body of soldiers commanded by a colonel. – [-ment] *v* to organize or control (people) very strictly: *Children in schools are no longer regimented as they used to be*. ,**regimen'tation** *n*. ,**regi'mental** [-'men-] *adj* of a regiment.

region ['ri:dʒən] *n* a part of a country, the world *etc*; *Do you know this region well?*; *in tropical regions*.

'**regional** *adj*: *regional variations in speech*. '**regionally** *adv*.

in the region of about; around; near: *The cost of the new building will be somewhere in the region of $200 000*.

register ['redʒistə] *n* (a book containing) a written list, record *etc*: *a school attendance register*; *a register of births, marriages and deaths*. – *v* **1** to write or cause to be written in a register: *to register the birth of a baby*. **2** to write one's name, or have one's name written, in a register *etc*: *They arrived on Friday and registered at the Hilton Hotel*. **3** to insure (a parcel, letter *etc*) against loss in the post. **4** (of an instrument, dial *etc*) to

show (a figure, amount *etc*): *The thermometer registered 25°C.*
'registered *adj*: *a registered letter.*
,regi'strar [-'stra:] *n* **1** a person whose duty it is to keep a register (*esp* of births, marriages and deaths). **2** in the UK *etc* one of the grades of hospital doctors.
'registry – *pl* **'registries** – *n* an office or place where registers are kept.
register office/registry office an office where records of births, marriages *etc* are kept and where marriages may be performed.
registration number (*also* **licence number**) the letters and numbers which a car, bus *etc* has on a plate at the front and rear.
regret [rə'gret] – *pt, ptp* **re'gretted** – *v* to be sorry about: *I regret my foolish behaviour; I regret that I missed the concert; I regret missing the concert; I regret to inform you that your application for the job was unsuccessful.* – *n* a feeling of sorrow, or of having done something wrong: *I have no regrets/I feel no regret about what I did; It was with deep regret that I heard the news of his death.*
re'gretful *adj* feeling regret.
re'gretfully *adv* with regret: *Regretfully, we have had to turn down your offer.*
re'grettable *adj*: *a regrettable mistake.*
re'grettably *adv.*

regrettable is spelt with two ts.

regular ['regjulə] *adj* **1** usual: *Saturday is his regular day for shopping; That isn't our regular postman, is it?* **2** (*Amer*) normal: *He's too handicapped to attend a regular school.* **3** occurring, acting *etc* with equal amounts of space, time *etc* between: *They placed guards at regular intervals round the camp; Is his pulse regular?* **4** involving doing the same things at the same time each day *etc*: *a man of regular habits.* **5** frequent: *He's a regular visitor; He's one of our regular customers.* **6** permanent; lasting: *He's looking for a regular job.* **7** (of a noun, verb *etc*) following one of the usual grammatical patterns of the language: *'Walk' is a regular verb, but 'go' is an irregular verb.* **8** the same on both or all sides or parts; neat; symmetrical: *a girl with regular features; A square is a regular figure.* **9** of ordinary sizes *etc*: *I don't want the large size of packet – just give me the regular one.* **10** (of a soldier) employed full-time, professional; (of an army) composed of regular soldiers. – *n* **1** a soldier in the regular army. **2** a regular customer (*eg* at a bar).
,regu'larity [-'la-] *n.*
'regularly *adv* **1** at regular times, places *etc*: *His heart was beating regularly.* **2** frequently: *He comes here regularly.*
'regulate [-leit] *v* **1** to control: *We must*

regulate our spending; Traffic lights are used to regulate traffic.* **2** to adjust (a piece of machinery *etc*) so that it works at a certain rate *etc*: *Can you regulate this watch so that it keeps time accurately?*
,regu'lation *n* **1** a rule or instruction: *There are certain regulations laid down as to how this job should be done, and these must be obeyed;* (*also adj*) *Please use envelopes of the regulation size.* **2** the act of regulating: *the regulation of a piece of machinery.*
'regulator [-lei-] *n* a thing that regulates (a piece of machinery *etc*).
rehabilitate [ri:ə'biliteit] *v* to bring (a criminal or someone who has been ill) back to a normal life, normal standards of behaviour *etc* by treatment or training.
'reha,bili'tation *n.*
rehearse [rə'hə:s] *v* to practise (a play, piece of music *etc*) before performing it in front of an audience: *You must rehearse the scene again.*
re'hearsal *n* **1** the act of rehearsing. **2** a performance done for practice: *I want the whole cast at tonight's rehearsal.*
dress rehearsal a final rehearsal (of a play, opera *etc*) in which the actors or singers wear their costumes *etc.*
rehouse [ri:'hauz] *v* to provide with a new or different house: *After the fire, the family had to be rehoused.*
reign [rein] *n* the time during which a king or queen rules: *in the reign of Queen Victoria.* – *v* **1** to rule, as a king or queen: *The king reigned (over his people) for forty years.* **2** to be present or exist: *Silence reigned at last.*
rein [rein] *n* **1** (*usu in pl*) one of two straps attached to a bridle for guiding a horse. **2** (*in pl*) straps fitted round a toddler so that he can be prevented from straying in the street *etc.*
rein in to stop or restrain (a horse *etc*) by pulling on its reins.
reincarnation [ri:inka:'neiʃən] *n* the rebirth of the soul in another body after death.
reindeer ['reindiə] – *pl* **'reindeer** – *n* a kind of large deer found in Northern Europe, Asia and America.
reinforce [ri:in'fo:s] *v* to make stronger: *I've reinforced the elbows of this jacket with leather patches; Extra troops will be sent to reinforce the army.*
,rein'forcement *n* **1** the act of reinforcing. **2** (*in pl*) men added to an army *etc* in order to strengthen it: *As the enemy attacks increased, the general called for reinforcements.*
reject [rə'dʒekt] *v* to refuse to accept: *She rejected his offer of help; He asked her to marry him, but she rejected him.* – ['ri:dʒekt] *n* something that is rejected because it is faulty *etc.*

re'jection [-ʃən] n (an) act of rejecting.

rejoice [rə'dʒɔis] v to feel or show great happiness: They rejoiced at the victory.

re'joicing n the act of feeling or showing great joy; celebrations: There was great rejoicing at the news of the victory; The rejoicings over the birth of the baby lasted well into the night.

rejoinder [rə'dʒɔində] n an answer.

relapse [rə'laps] v to return to a former bad or undesirable state (eg ill health, bad habits). – n a return to a former bad or undesirable state, esp ill health.

relate [rə'leit] v 1 to tell (a story etc): He related all that had happened to him. 2 (with to) to be about, concerned or connected with: Have you any information relating to the effect of penicillin on mice? 3 (with to) to behave towards: He finds it difficult to relate normally to his mother.

re'lated adj belonging to the same family (as): I'm related to the Prime Minister; The Prime Minister and I are related. 2 connected: other related topics.

re'lation n 1 a person who belongs to the same family as oneself either by birth or because of marriage: uncles, aunts, cousins and other relations. 2 a relationship (between facts, events etc). 3 (in pl) contact and communications between people, countries etc: to establish friendly relations.

re'lationship n 1 the friendship, contact, communications etc which exist between people: He finds it very difficult to form lasting relationships. 2 the fact that, or the way in which, facts, events etc are connected: Is there any relationship between crime and poverty? 3 the state of being related by birth or because of marriage.

relative ['relətiv] n a member of one's family; a relation: All his relatives attended the funeral. – adj 1 compared with something else, or with each other, or with a situation in the past etc: the relative speeds of a car and a train; She used to be rich but now lives in relative poverty. 2 (of a pronoun, adjective or clause) referring back to something previously mentioned: the girl who sang the song; the girl who sang the song.

relatively ['relətivli] adv when compared to someone or something else: He seems relatively happy now; This is a fairly unimportant problem, relatively speaking.

relax [rə'laks] v 1 to make or become less tight or tense or less worried etc; to rest completely: The doctor gave him a drug to make him relax; Relax your shoulders; He relaxed his grip for a second and the rope was dragged out of his hand. 2 to make or become less strict or severe: The rules were relaxed because of the Queen's visit.

relax'ation [ri:laks-] n: I play golf for relaxation; Golf is one of my favourite relaxations.

relay [ri'lei] – pt, ptp re'layed – v to receive and pass on (news, a message, a television programme etc). – n ['ri:lei] (the sending out of) a radio, television etc signal or programme which has been received (from another place).

relay race a race between teams of runners, swimmers etc, in which the members of the team run, swim etc one after another, each covering one part of the total distance to be run, swum etc.

in relays in groups which perform some job, task etc one after another, one group starting when another group stops: During the flood, firemen and policemen worked in relays to rescue people who were trapped.

release [rə'li:s] v 1 to set free; to allow to leave: He was released from prison yesterday; I am willing to release him from his promise to me. 2 to stop holding etc; to allow to move, fall etc: He released (his hold on) the rope. 3 to move (a catch, brake etc) which prevents something else from moving, operating etc: He released the handbrake and drove off. 4 to allow (news etc) to be made known publicly: The list of winners has just been released. 5 to offer (a film, record etc) to the general public: Their latest record will be released next week. – n 1 the act of releasing or being released: After his release, the prisoner returned to his home town; the release of a new film; (also adj) the release catch. 2 something that is released: This record is their latest release; The Government issued a press release (= a statement giving information about something, sent or given to newspapers, reporters etc).

relent [rə'lent] v to become less severe or unkind; to agree after refusing at first: At first she wouldn't let them go to the cinema, but in the end she relented.

re'lentless adj without pity; not allowing anything to keep one from what one is doing or trying to do: The police fight a relentless battle against crime. re'lentlessly adv. re'lentlessness n.

relevant ['reləvənt] adj connected with or saying something important about what is being spoken about or discussed: I don't think his remarks are relevant (to our discussion); Any relevant information should be given to the police. 'relevance n.

reliable, reliance etc see rely.

relic ['relik] n 1 something left from a past time: relics of an ancient civilization. 2 something connected with, esp the bones of, a dead person (esp a saint).

relief [rə'li:f] n 1 a lessening or stopping of pain, worry, boredom etc: When one has a *headache, an aspirin brings relief; He gave a sigh of relief; It was a great relief to find nothing had been stolen.* **2** help (*eg* food) given to people in need of it: *famine relief; (also adj) A relief fund has been set up to send supplies to the refugees.* **3** a person who takes over some job or task from another person, *usu* after a given period of time: *The bus-driver was waiting for his relief; (also adj) a relief driver.* **4** the act of freeing a town *etc* from siege: *the relief of Mafeking.* **5** a way of carving *etc* in which the design is raised above the level of its background: *a carving in relief.*

re'lieve [-v] *v* **1** to lessen or stop (pain, worry *etc*): *The doctor gave him some drugs to relieve the pain; to relieve the hardship of the refugees.* **2** to take over a job or task from: *You guard the door first, and I'll relieve you in two hours.* **3** to dismiss (a person) from his job or position: *He was relieved of his post/duties.* **4** to take (something heavy, difficult *etc*) from someone: *May I relieve you of that heavy case?; The new gardener relieved the old man of the burden of cutting the grass.* **5** to come to the help of (a town *etc* which is under siege or attack).

re'lieved *adj* no longer anxious or worried: *I was relieved to hear you had arrived safely.*

religion [rə'lidʒən] *n* **1** a belief in, or the worship of, a god or gods. **2** a particular system of belief or worship: *Christianity and Islam are two different religions.*

re'ligious *adj* **1** of religion: *religious education; a religious leader/instructor.* **2** following the rules, forms of worship *etc* of a religion: *a religious man.* **re'ligiously** *adv.* **re'ligiousness** *n.*

relinquish [rə'liŋkwiʃ] *v* to give up: *The dictator was forced to relinquish control of the country.*

relish ['reliʃ] *v* to enjoy greatly: *He relishes his food; I relished the thought of telling my husband about my promotion.* – *n* **1** pleasure; enjoyment: *He ate the food with great relish; I have no relish for such a boring task.* **2** a strong flavour, or a sauce *etc* for adding flavour.

reluctant [rə'lʌktənt] *adj* unwilling: *He was reluctant to accept the medal for his bravery.* **re'luctantly** *adv.*

re'luctance *n: I don't understand his reluctance to go.*

rely [rə'lai]: **rely on 1** to depend on or need: *The people on the island relied on the supplies that were brought from the mainland; I am relying on you to help me.* **2** to trust (someone) to do something; to be certain that (something will happen): *Can he rely on him to keep a secret?; He can be relied on; That is what will probably happen, but we can't rely on it.*

re'liable [-'lai-] *adj* (*neg* **un-**) able to be trusted: *Is he reliable?; Is this information reliable?* **re,lia'bility** *n.*

re'liably [-'lai-] *adv* from a reliable source; by a reliable person: *I am reliably informed that the Prime Minister is going to resign.*

re'liance [-'lai-] *n: a country's reliance on aid from other countries; a child's reliance on its mother.* **re'liant** *adj.*

remain [rə'mein] *v* **1** to be left: *Only two tins of soup remain; Very little remained of the cinema after the fire; A great many things still remain to be done.* **2** to stay; not to leave: *I shall remain here.* **3** to continue to be: *The problem remains unsolved.*

re'mainder [-də] *n* the amount or number that is left when the rest has gone, been taken away *etc: I've corrected most of the essays – the remainder will get done tomorrow.*

re'mains *n pl* **1** what is left after part has been taken away, eaten, destroyed *etc: the remains of a meal.* **2** a dead body: *to dispose of someone's remains.*

remand rə'ma:nd] *v* to send (a person who has been accused of a crime) back to prison until more evidence can be collected.

remark [rə'ma:k] *n* a comment; something said: *The chairman made a few remarks, then introduced the speaker.* – *v* to say; to comment: 'She's a good-looking girl,' he remarked; He remarked that she was good-looking; He remarked on her good looks.*

re'markable *adj* unusual; worth mentioning; extraordinary: *What a remarkable coincidence!; He really is a remarkable man; It is quite remarkable how alike the two children are.*

re'markably *adv: Their replies were remarkably similar.*

remedy ['remədi] – *pl* **'remedies** – *n* a cure for an illness or something bad: *I know a good remedy for toothache.* – *v* to put right: *These mistakes can be remedied.*

remedial [rə'mi:diəl] *adj* able to, or intended to, put right or to correct or cure: *She does remedial work with the less clever children; remedial exercises.*

remember [ri'membə] *v* **1** to keep in the mind, or to bring back into the mind after forgetting for a time: *I remember you – we met three years ago; I remember watching the first men landing on the moon; Remember to telephone me tonight; I don't remember where I hid it.* **2** to reward or make a present to: *He remembered her in his will.* **3** to pass (a person's) good wishes (to someone): *Remember me to your parents.*

re'membrance *n* the act of remembering or reminding: *a statue erected in remembrance of the dead.*

remind [rə'maind] *v* **1** to tell (someone) that

there is something he or she ought to do, remember *etc*: *Remind me to post that letter*; *She reminded me of my promise.* **2** to make (someone) remember or think of (a person, thing *etc*): *She reminds me of her sister*; *This reminds me of my schooldays.*

re'**minder** *n* something said, done, written, noticed *etc* that reminds one to do something: *Leave the bill on the table as a reminder that I still have to pay it.*

remit [rə'mit] – *pt, ptp* re'**mitted** – *v* to send (money) *usu* in payment for something.

re'**mission** [-ʃən] *n* **1** a lessening in the severity of an illness *etc*. **2** a shortening of a person's prison sentence. **3** the act of remitting.

re'**mittance** *n* (the sending of) money in payment for something.

remnant ['remnənt] *n* a small piece or amount or a small number left over from a larger piece, amount or number: *The shop is selling remnants of cloth at half price*; *the remnant of the army.*

remorse [rə'mo:s] *n* regret about something wrong or bad which one has done.

re'**morseful** *adj* feeling remorse. re'**morsefully** *adv*.

re'**morseless** *adj* cruel; without pity: *a remorseless tyrant.* re'**morselessly** *adv*.

remote [rə'mout] *adj* **1** far away in time or place; far from any (other) village, town *etc*: *a remote village in New South Wales*; *a farmhouse remote from civilization.* **2** distantly related: *a remote cousin.* **3** very small or slight: *a remote chance of success*; *He hasn't the remotest idea what is going on.* re'**motely** *adv*. re'**moteness** *n*.

re**mote control** the control of *eg* a switch or other device from a distance, by means of radio waves *etc*: *The model plane is operated by remote control.*

remove [rə'mu:v] *v* **1** to take away : *Will someone please remove all this rubbish!*; *He removed all the evidence of his crimes*; *I can't remove this stain from my shirt*; *He has been removed from his post as minister of education.* **2** to take off (a piece of clothing): *Please remove your hat.* **3** to move to a new house *etc*: *He has removed to London.* re'**movable** *adj*.

re'**moval** *n* the act of removing or the state of being removed, *esp* the moving of furniture *etc* to a new home: *After his removal from power, the dictator was sent into exile*; *Our removal is to take place on Monday*; *(also adj) a removal van.*

re'**mover** *n* a person or thing that removes: *a stain remover*; *a firm of furniture removers.*

remunerate [rə'mju:nəreit] *v* to pay (someone) for something he has done. re,**mune'ration** *n*.

re'**munerative** [-rətiv] *adj* bringing a good profit.

render ['rendə] *v* **1** to cause to become: *His remarks rendered me speechless.* **2** to give or produce (a service, a bill, thanks *etc*). **3** to perform (music *etc*).

rendezvous ['rondivu:] – *pl* '**rendezvous** [-vu:] – *n* **1** an agreement to meet someone somewhere: *They had made a rendezvous to meet at midnight.* **2** the place where such a meeting is to be: *The park was the lovers' usual rendezvous.* **3** the meeting itself: *The rendezvous took place at midnight.* **4** a place where a certain group of people meet or go regularly: *This pub is the rendezvous for the local artists and poets.*

renew [rə'nju:] *v* **1** to begin, do, produce *etc* again: *He renewed his efforts*; *We must renew our attack on drug abuse.* **2** to cause (*eg* a licence) to continue for another or longer period of time: *My television licence has to be renewed in October.* **3** to make new or fresh or as if new again: *The panels on the doors have all been renewed.* re'**newable** *adj*. re'**newal** *n*.

renounce [ri'nauns] *v* **1** to give up (a title, claim, intention *etc*) *esp* formally or publicly: *He renounced his claim to the throne.* **2** to say *esp* formally or publicly that one will no longer have anything to do with (something): *I have renounced alcohol.* re**nunciation** [rinʌnsi'eiʃən] *n*.

renovate ['renəveit] *v* to make as good as new again: *to renovate an old building.* '**renovator** *n*. ,**reno'vation** *n*.

renown [rə'naun] *n* fame.

re'**nowned** *adj* famous: *He is renowned for his paintings*; *a renowned actress.*

rent[1] [rent] *n* money paid, *usu* regularly, for the use of a house, shop, land *etc* which belongs to someone else: *The rent for this flat is $50 a week.* – *v* to pay or receive rent for the use of a house, shop, land *etc*: *We rent this flat from Mr Smith*; *Mr Smith rents this flat to us.*

'**rental** *n* **1** money paid as rent. **2** the act of renting.

,**rent-**'**free** *adv* without payment of rent: *He lives there rent-free.* – *adj* for which rent does not need to be paid: *a rent-free flat.*

rent out to allow people to use (a house *etc* which one owns) in exchange for money.

see also let.

rent[2] [rent] an old word for a tear (in clothes *etc*).

renunciation *see* **renounce**.

reorganize, -ise [ri:'o:gənaiz] *v* to organize differently; to put in a different order: *We'll have to reorganize our filing system.* re-,**organi'zation**, **-s-** *n*.

rep *see* **representative**.

repaid *see* **repay**.

repair [ri'peə] *v* **1** to mend; to make (something) that is damaged or has broken down work again; to restore to good condition: *to repair a broken lock/torn jacket*. **2** to put right or make up for: *Nothing can repair the harm done by your foolish remarks.* – *n* **1** (*often in pl*) the act of repairing something damaged or broken down: *I put my car into the garage for repairs*; *The bridge is under repair*. **2** a condition or state: *The road is in bad repair*; *The house is in a good state of repair*.

re'pairable *adj* (*neg* **un-**) able to be mended.

reparable ['repərəbl] *adj* able to be put right.

,repa'ration [repə-] *n* **1** the act of making up for something wrong that has been done. **2** money paid for this purpose.

re'pairman [-man] *n* a man who repairs televisions *etc*.

repay [ri'pei] – *pt, ptp* **repaid** [ri'peid] – *v* to pay back: *When are you going to repay the money you borrowed?*; *I must find a way of repaying his kindness/repaying him for his kindness*. **re'payment** *n*.

repeal [rə'pi:l] *v* to make (a law *etc*) no longer valid. – *n* the act of repealing a law *etc*.

repeat [rə'pi:t] *v* **1** to say or do again: *Would you repeat those instructions, please?* **2** to say (something one has heard) to someone else, sometimes when one ought not to: *Please do not repeat what I've just told you.* **3** to say (something) one has learned by heart: *to repeat a poem.* – *n* something which is repeated: *I'm tired of seeing all these repeats on television*; (*also adj*) *a repeat performance*.

re'peated *adj* said, done *etc* many times: *In spite of repeated warnings, he went on smoking.*

re'peatedly *adv* many times: *I've asked him for it repeatedly.*

repetition [repə'tiʃən] *n* (an) act of repeating.

repetitive [rə'petətiv] *adj* doing, saying, the same thing too often: *His speeches are very repetitive*; *My job is a bit repetitive*. **re'petitively** *adv*. **re'petitiveness** *n*.

repeat oneself to repeat what one has already said: *Listen carefully because I don't want to have to repeat myself.*

to repeat (not repeat again) the lessons.

repel [rə'pel] – *pt, ptp* **re'pelled** – *v* **1** to resist or fight (an enemy) successfully : *to repel invaders.* **2** to cause a feeling of dislike or disgust: *She was repelled by his dirty appearance.* **3** to force to move away: *Oil repels water.*

repent [rə'pent] **1** (*esp* in religion) to be sorry

for one's past sins. **2** (with **of**) to wish that one had not done, made *etc*: *He repented of his generosity*. **re'pentance** *n*.

re'pentant *adj* (*neg* **un-**): *a repentant sinner.*

repetition, repetitive *see* **repeat**.

replace [rə'pleis] *v* **1** to put, use *etc* (a person, thing *etc*), or to be put, used *etc*, in place of another: *I must replace that broken lock*; *He replaced the cup he broke with a new one*; *Cars have replaced horses as the normal means of transport*. **2** to put (something) back where it was: *Please replace the books on the shelves*. **re'placeable** *adj*.

re'placement *n*: *I must find a replacement for my secretary – she's leaving next week.*

replay [ri:'plei] *v* to play (a football match *etc*) again (*eg* because neither team won): *The match ended in a draw – it will have to be replayed.* – ['ri:plei] *n* a replayed football match *etc*.

replenish [rə'pleniʃ] *v* to fill up again; to fill up (one's supply of something) again: *We must replenish our stock of coal.* **re'plenishment** *n*.

replica ['replikə] *n* an exact copy, *esp* of a work of art.

reply [rə'plai] *v* to answer: '*I don't know,*' *he replied*; *Should I reply to his letter?*; *She replied that she had never seen the man before*; *She replied by shrugging her shoulders*. – *n* – *pl* **re'plies** – **1** an answer: '*I don't know,*' *was his reply*; *I'll write a reply to his letter*. **2** the act of answering: *What did he say in reply (to your question)?*

to reply to a letter (not reply a letter).

report [rə'po:t] *n* **1** a statement or description of what has been said, seen, done *etc*: *a child's school report*; *a police report on the accident*. **2** rumour; general talk: *According to report, the manager is going to resign*. **3** a loud noise, *esp* of a gun being fired. – *v* **1** to give a statement or description of what has been said, seen, done *etc*: *A serious accident has just been reported*; *He reported on the results of the conference*; *Our spies report that troops are being moved to the border*; *His speech was reported in the newspaper*. **2** to make a complaint about; to give information about the misbehaviour *etc* of: *The boy was reported to the headmaster for being rude to a teacher*. **3** to tell someone in authority about: *He reported the theft to the police*. **4** to go (to a place or a person) and announce that one is there, ready for work *etc*: *The boys were ordered to report to the police-station every Saturday afternoon*; *Report to me when you return*; *How many policemen reported for duty?*

re'porter *n* a person who writes articles and reports for a newspaper: *Reporters and photographers rushed to the scene of the fire.*

reported speech indirect speech.

report back to come again and report (to someone); to send a report (to someone): *He was asked to study the matter in detail and report back to the committee.*

epose [rə'pouz] *n* rest; calm; peacefulness.

eprehensible [repri'hensəbl] *adj* deserving blame: *a reprehensible act.* ,repre'hensibly *adv.*

epresent [reprə'zent] *v* 1 to speak or act on behalf of: *You have been chosen to represent our association at the conference.* 2 to be a sign, symbol, picture *etc* of: *In this play, the man in black represents Death and the young girl Life.* 3 to be a good example of; to show or illustrate: *What he said represents the feelings of many people.*
,represen'tation *n* 1 the act of representing or the state of being represented. 2 a person or thing that represents: *These primitive statues are intended as representations of gods and goddesses.* 3 (*often in pl*) a strong appeal, demand or protest.
,repre'sentative [-tətiv] *adj* being a good example (of something); typical: *We need opinions from a representative sample of people; Is this poem representative of his work?* 2 carried on by elected people: *representative government.* – *n* 1 (*also* rep [rep]) a person who represents a business; a travelling salesman: *Our representative will call on you this afternoon.* 2 a person who represents a person or group of people: *A Member of Parliament is the representative of the people in his constituency.*

epress [rə'pres] *v* to keep (an impulse, a desire to do something *etc*) under control: *He repressed a desire to hit the man.* re'pression [-ʃən] *n.*
re'pressive [-siv] *adj* severe; harsh. re'pressiveness *n.*

eprieve [rə'priːv] *v* to pardon (a criminal) or delay his punishment: *The murderer was sentenced to death, but later reprieved.* – *n* the act of pardoning a criminal or delaying his punishment; the order to do this.

eprimand [repri'maːnd, (*Amer also*) 'reprimand] *v* (*esp* of a person in authority) to speak or write angrily or severely to (someone) because he has done wrong; to rebuke: *The soldier was severely reprimanded for being drunk.* – *n* ['reprimaːnd] *n* angry or severe words; a rebuke: *He was given a severe reprimand.*

eprint [riː'print] *v* to print more copies of (a book *etc*): *We are reprinting his new novel already.* – ['riːprint] *n* a copy of a book *etc* made by reprinting the original without any changes.

eprisal [rə'praizəl] *n* something bad done to someone in return for something bad he has done to one; an act of revenge.

reproach [rə'proutʃ] *v* to rebuke or blame but *usu* with a feeling of sadness and disappointment rather than anger: *She reproached me for not telling her about my money troubles; There is no need to reproach yourself – you did the best you could.* – *n* (an) act of reproaching: *a look of reproach; He didn't deserve that reproach from you.*
re'proachful *adj* showing or expressing reproach: *a reproachful look; reproachful words.* re'proachfully *adv.*

reproduce [riːprə'djuːs] 1 *v* to make or produce a copy of; to make or produce again: *Good as the film is, it fails to reproduce the atmosphere of the book; A record-player reproduces the sound which has been recorded on a record.* 2 (of humans, animals and plants) to produce (young, seeds *etc*): *How do fish reproduce?*
,repro'duction [-'dʌk-] *n* 1 the act or process of reproducing: *He is studying reproduction in rabbits.* 2 a copy (of a work of art *etc*): *These paintings are all reproductions.*
,repro'ductive [-'dʌktiv] *adj* of or for reproduction: *the reproductive organs of a rabbit.*

reproof [rə'pruːf] *n* (an) act of rebuking or reproaching: *a glance of stern reproof; He has received several reproofs for bad behaviour.*

reprove [rə'pruːv] *v* to tell (a person) that he has done wrong: *The teacher reproved the boys for coming late to school.*
re'proving *adj: a reproving look.* re'provingly *adv.*

reptile ['reptail] *n* any of the group of cold-blooded animals to which snakes, lizards, crocodiles *etc* belong. rep'tilian [-'ti-] *adj.*

republic [rə'pʌblik] *n* (a country with) a form of government in which there is no king or queen, the power of government, law-making *etc* being given to one or more elected representatives (*eg* a president, members of a parliament *etc*): *The United States is a republic – the United Kingdom is not.*
re'publican *adj* 1 of a republic: *a republican form of government.* 2 (*also n*) (a person) who supports a republican form of government: *He is not a monarchist – he is a republican; my republican friends.*

repulse [rə'pʌls] *v* 1 to repel (an enemy). 2 to refuse to accept *eg* help from, or be friendly to. – *n* (an) act of repulsing.
re'pulsion [rə'pʌlʃən] *n* disgust.
re'pulsive [rə'pʌlsiv] *adj* horrible; disgusting. re'pulsively *adv.* re'pulsiveness *n.*

reputation [repju'teiʃən] *n* the opinion which people in general have about a person *etc*, a persons's abilities *etc*: *That firm has a good/bad reputation; He has made a reputation for himself as an expert in computers;*

He has the reputation of being difficult to please; *The scandal damaged his reputation.*
'reputable *adj* respectable; well thought of: *Is that a reputable firm?*
reputed [ri'pju:tid] *adj* generally reported and believed: *He is reputed to be very wealthy.*
live up to one's reputation to behave or do as people expect one to.

request [ri'kwest] *n* 1 the act of asking for something: *I did that at his request*; *After frequent requests, he eventually agreed to sing.* 2 something asked for: *The next record I will play is a request.* – *v* to ask (for) something; *People using this library are requested not to talk*; *Many people have requested this next song.*
by request when or because one is asked to: *I'm singing this next song by request.*
on request when requested: *Buses only stop here on request.*

requiem ['rekwiem] *n* (a piece of music written for) a mass for the souls of the dead.

require [rə'kwaiə] *v* 1 to need: *Is there anything else you require?* 2 to ask, force or order to do something: *You are required by law to send your children to school*; *I will do everything that is required of me.*
re'quirement *n* something that is needed, asked for, ordered *etc*: *It is a legal requirement that all cars have brakes which work*; *Our firm will be able to supply all your requirements.*

rescue ['reskju:] *v* to get or take out of a dangerous situation, captivity *etc*: *The lifeboat was sent out to rescue the sailors from the sinking ship.* – *n* (an) act of rescuing or state of being rescued: *The lifeboat crew performed four rescues last week*; *After his rescue, the climber was taken to hospital*; *They came quickly to our rescue.* **'rescuer** *n.*

research [ri'sə:tʃ, (*esp Amer*) 'ri:sə:(r)tʃ] *n* a close and careful study to find out (new) facts or information: *He is engaged in cancer research*; *His researches resulted in some amazing discoveries*; (*also adj*) *a research student.* – [ri'sə:(r)tʃ] *v* to carry out such a study: *He's researching (into) Thai poetry.*
re'searcher [ri'sə:tʃə, (*Amer also*) 'ri:sə:rtʃər] *n.*

resemble [rə'zembl] *v* to be like or look like: *He doesn't resemble either of his parents.*
re'semblance *n*: *I can see some resemblance(s) between him and his father.*

resent [ri'zent] *v* to feel annoyed about (something) because one thinks it is unfair, insulting *etc*: *I resent his interference in my affairs.*
re'sentful *adj* having or showing such a feeling of annoyance: *She feels resentful that her sister married before she did.* **re'sentfully** *adv.* **re'sentfulness** *n.*

re'sentment *n*: *He has a feeling of resentment against the police after the way he was treated by them.*

reserve [rə'zə:v] *v* 1 to ask for or order to be kept for the use of a particular person, often oneself: *The restaurant is busy on Saturdays, so I'll phone up today and reserve a table.* 2 to keep for the use of a particular person or group of people, or for a particular use: *These seats are reserved for the committee members.* – *n* 1 something which is kept for later use or for use when needed: *The farmer kept a reserve of food in case he was cut off by floods.* 2 a piece of land used for a special purpose *eg* for the protection of animals: *a wild-life reserve*; *a nature reserve.* 3 the habit of not saying very much, not showing what one is feeling, thinking *etc*; shyness. 4 (*often in pl*) soldiers, sailors *etc* who do not belong to the regular full-time army, navy *etc* but who are called into action when needed *eg* during a war.
,reser'vation [rezə-] *n* 1 the act of reserving: *the reservation of a room.* 2 something (*eg* a table in a restaurant) which has been reserved: *Have you a reservation, Sir?* 3 a doubt. 4 a piece of land set aside for a particular purpose: *an Indian reservation in the United States.*
re'served *adj* not saying very much; not showing what one is feeling, thinking *etc*: *a reserved manner.*
have, keep *etc* **in reserve** to have or keep (something) in case or until it is needed: *If you go to America please keep some money in reserve for your fare home.*

reservoir ['rezəvwa:] *n* a place, *usu* a man-made lake, where water for drinking *etc* is stored.

resident ['rezidənt] *n* a person who lives or has his home in a particular place: *a resident of Edinburgh.* – *adj* 1 living or having one's home in a place: *He is now resident abroad.* 2 living, having to live, or requiring a person to live, in the place where he works: *a resident caretaker.*
reside [rə'zaid] *v* to live or have one's home in a place: *He now resides abroad.*
'residence *n* 1 a person's home, *esp* the grand house of someone important. 2 the act of living in a place, or the time of this: *during his residence in Spain.*
'residency – *pl* **'residencies** – *n* the home of the governor *etc* in a colony *etc.*
,resi'dential [-'denʃəl] *adj* 1 (of an area of a town *etc*) containing houses rather than offices, shops *etc*: *This district is mainly residential*; *a residential neighbourhood/area.* 2 requiring a person to live in the place where he works: *a residential post.* 3 of, concerned with, living in a place.

in residence (*esp* of someone important) staying in a place, sometimes to perform some official duties: *The Queen is in residence here this week.*

take up residence to go and live (in a place, building *etc*): *He has taken up residence in France.*

residue ['rezidju:] *n* what remains or is left over. **residual** [rə'zidjuəl, (*Amer*) -dʒu-] *adj.*

resign [rə'zain] *v* **1** to leave a job *etc*: *If he criticizes my work again I'll resign; He resigned (from) his post.* **2** (*with* **to**) to make (oneself) accept (a situation, fact *etc*) with patience and calmness: *He has resigned himself to the possibility that he may never walk again.*

resignation [rezig'neiʃən] *n* **1** the act of resigning. **2** a letter *etc* stating that one is resigning: *You will receive my resignation tomorrow.* **3** (the state of having or showing) patient, calm acceptance (of a situation, fact *etc*): *He accepted his fate with resignation.*

re'signed *adj* (*often with* **to**) having or showing patient, calm acceptance (of a fact, situation *etc*): *He is resigned to his fate.*

resin ['rezin] *n* a sticky substance produced by certain trees (*eg* firs, pines) and some other plants. **'resinous** *adj.*

resist [rə'zist] *v* **1** to fight against, *usu* successfully: *The soldiers resisted the enemy attack; He tried to resist arrest; It's hard to resist temptation.* **2** to be able to stop oneself doing, taking *etc* (something): *I couldn't resist kicking him when he bent down; I just can't resist strawberries.* **3** to be unaffected or undamaged by: *a metal that resists rust/acids.*

re'sistance *n* **1** the act of resisting: *The army offered strong resistance to the enemy;* (*also adj*) *a resistance force.* **2** the ability or power to be unaffected or undamaged by something: *resistance to disease.* **3** the force that one object, substance *etc* exerts against the movement of another object *etc.*

re'sistant *adj*: *This breed of cattle is resistant to disease; heat-resistant table-mats.*

resolution [rezə'lu:ʃən] *n* **1** a firm decision (to do something): *He made a resolution to get up early.* **2** an opinion or decision formally expressed by a group of people, *eg* at a public meeting: *The meeting passed a resolution in favour of allowing women to join the society.* **3** resoluteness. **4** the act of resolving (a problem *etc*).

'resolute [-lu:t] *adj* doing what one has decided to do, in spite of opposition, criticism *etc*: *a resolute attitude.* **'resolutely** *adv.* **'resoluteness** *n.*

resolve [rə'zolv] *v* **1** to make a firm decision (to do something): *I've resolved to stop smoking.* **2** to pass (a resolution): *It was resolved that women should be allowed to join the society.* **3** to take away (a doubt, fear *etc*) or produce an answer to (a problem, difficulty *etc*). – *n* **1** determination to do what one has decided to do: *He showed great resolve.* **2** a firm decision: *It is his resolve to become a director of this firm.*

resolved [rə'zolvd] *adj* determined: *I am resolved to go and nothing will stop me.*

resonant ['rezənənt] *adj* (of sounds) loud; echoing; easily heard. **'resonance** *n.*

resort [rə'zo:t] *v* (*with* **to**) to begin to use, do *etc* as a way of solving a problem *etc* when other methods have failed: *He couldn't persuade people to do what he wanted, so he resorted to threats of violence.* – *n* a place visited by many people (*esp* for holidays): *Brighton is a popular (holiday) resort.*

as a last resort when all other methods *etc* have failed: *If we can't get the money in any other way, I suppose we could, as a last resort, sell the car.*

resound [rə'zaund] *v* to sound loudly or for a long time: *The audience's cheers resounded through the hall.*

re'sounding *adj* **1** loud: *resounding cheers.* **2** very great; complete: *a resounding victory/success.* **re'soundingly** *adv.*

resource [rə'zo:s] *n* **1** (*usu in pl*) something that gives help, support *etc* when needed; a supply; a means: *We have used up all our resources; We haven't the resources at this school for teaching handicapped children.* **2** (*usu in pl*) the wealth of a country, or the supply of materials *etc* which bring this wealth: *This country is rich in natural resources.* **3** the ability to find ways of solving difficulties: *He is full of resource.*

re'sourceful *adj* good at finding ways of solving difficulties, problems *etc.* **re'sourcefully** *adv.* **re'sourcefulness** *n.*

respect [rə'spekt] *n* **1** admiration; good opinion: *He is held in great respect by everyone; He has no respect for politicians.* **2** consideration; thoughtfulness; willingness to obey *etc*: *He shows no respect for his parents.* **3** a particular detail, feature *etc*: *These two poems are similar in some respects.* – *v* **1** to show or feel admiration for: *I respect you for what you did.* **2** to show consideration for, a willingness to obey *etc*: *One should respect other people's feelings/property.*

re'spectable *adj* **1** having a good reputation or character: *a respectable family.* **2** correct; acceptable: *respectable behaviour.* **3** (of clothes) good enough or suitable to wear: *You can't go out in those torn trousers – they're not respectable.* **4** large, good *etc* enough; fairly large, good *etc*: *Four goals is*

a respectable score. **re'spectably** *adv.*
re,specta'bility *n.*
re'spectful *adj* having or showing respect.
re'spectfully *adv.* **re'spectfulness** *n.*
re'specting *prep* about; concerning: *Respecting your salary, we shall come to a decision later.*
re'spective [-tiv] *adj* belonging to *etc* each person or thing mentioned: *Peter and George went to their respective homes.*
re'spectively [-tiv-] *adv* referring to each person or thing mentioned, in the order in which they are mentioned: *Peter, James and John were first, second and third, respectively.*
re'spects *n pl* greetings: *He sends his respects to you.*
pay one's respects (to someone) to visit (a person) as a sign of respect to him.
with respect to about; concerning: *With respect to your request, we regret that we are unable to assist you in this matter.*
respire [rə'spaiə] *v* to breathe.
respiration [respə'reiʃən] *n* breathing.
respirator ['respəreitə] *n* **1** a sort of mask worn to purify the air breathed in *eg* by firemen. **2** a piece of apparatus used to help very ill or injured people to breathe.
respiratory ['respərətəri] *adj* related to breathing: *respiratory diseases.*
respite ['respait, (*Amer*) -pit] *n* a pause or rest.
resplendent [rə'splendənt] *adj* very bright or splendid in appearance. **re'splendently** *adv.* **re'splendence** *n.*
respond [rə'spond] *v* (*with* **to**) **1** to answer with words, a reaction, gesture *etc*: *He didn't respond to my question; I smiled at her, but she didn't respond.* **2** to show a good reaction *eg* to some course of treatment: *His illness did not respond to treatment by drugs.* **3** (of vehicles *etc*) to be guided easily by controls: *The pilot said the plane did not respond to the controls.*
re'sponse [-s] *n* **1** a reply or reaction: *Our letters have never met with any response; My suggestions met with little response.* **2** (*usu in pl*) in church services, a part spoken by the congregation rather than the priest.
re,sponsi'bility [-sə-] – *pl* **re,sponsi'bilities** – *n* **1** something which a person has to look after, do *etc*: *He takes his responsibilities very seriously.* **2** the state of having important duties: *a position of responsibility.* **3** the state of being responsible: *his responsibility for the accident.*
re'sponsible [-səbl] *adj* **1** having a duty to see that something is done *etc*: *We'll make one person responsible for buying the food for the trip.* **2** (of a job *etc*) having many duties *eg* the making of important decisions: *The job of manager is a very respon-*sible post. **3** (*with* **for**) being the cause of something: *Who is responsible for the stain on the carpet?* **4** (of a person) able to be trusted; sensible: *We need a responsible person for this job.* **5** (*with* **for**) able to control, and fully aware of (one's actions): *The lawyer said that at the time of the murder, his client was not responsible for his actions.*
re'sponsibly [-sə-] *adv* in a trustworthy or serious way: *Do try to behave responsibly.*
re'sponsive [-siv] *adj* (*neg* **un-**): *a responsive, kindly girl; a responsive smile; The disease is responsive to treatment.* **re'sponsively** *adv.* **re'sponsiveness** *n.*
rest[1] [rest] *n* **1** a (*usu* short) period of not working *etc* after, or between periods of, effort; (a period of) freedom from worries *etc*: *Digging the garden is hard work – let's stop for a rest; Let's have/take a rest; I need a rest from all these problems – I'm going to take a week's holiday.* **2** sleep: *He needs a good night's rest.* **3** something which holds or supports: *a book-rest; a headrest on a car seat.* **4** a state of not moving: *The machine is at rest.* – *v* **1** to (allow to) stop working *etc* in order to get new strength or energy: *We've been walking for four hours – let's stop and rest; Stop reading for a minute and rest your eyes; Let's rest our legs.* **2** to sleep; to lie or sit quietly in order to get new strength or energy, or because one is tired: *Mother is resting at the moment.* **3** to (make or allow to) lean, lie, sit, remain *etc* on or against something: *Her head rested on his shoulder; He rested his hand on her arm; Her gaze rested on the jewels.* **4** to relax, be calm *etc*: *I will never rest until I know the murderer has been caught.* **5** to (allow to) depend on: *Our hopes now rest on him, since all else has failed.* **6** (*with* **with**) (of a duty *etc*) to belong to: *The choice rests with you.*
'restful *adj* **1** bringing rest: *a restful holiday.* **2** (of colours, music *etc*) causing a person to feel calm and relaxed: *Some people find blue a restful colour; After a hard day's work, I like to listen to some restful music.* **3** relaxed: at rest: *The patient seems more restful now.* **'restfully** *adv.* **'restfulness** *n.*
'restless *adj* **1** always moving; showing signs of worry, boredom, impatience *etc*: *a restless child; He's been doing the same job for years now and he's beginning to get restless.* **2** during which a person does not sleep: *a restless night.* **'restlessly** *adv.* **'restlessness** *n.*
'rest-room *n* (*Amer*) a toilet in a theatre, factory *etc.*
at rest free from pain, worry *etc.*
come to rest to stop moving: *The ball came to rest under a tree.*
lay to rest to bury (someone) in a grave.

let the matter rest to stop discussing *etc* a matter.

rest assured to be certain: *You may rest assured that we will take your views into consideration.*

set someone's mind at rest to take away a person's worries about something.

rest² [rest]: **the rest 1** what is left when part of something is taken away, finished *etc*: *the rest of the meal.* **2** all the other people, things *etc*: *Jack went home, but the rest of us went to the cinema.*

restaurant ['restront, (*Amer*) -tərənt] *n* a place where meals may be bought and eaten.

'restaurant-car *n* a carriage on a train in which meals are served to travellers.

restitution [resti'tju:ʃən] *n* the act of giving back to a person *etc* what has been taken away, or the giving of money *etc* to pay for damage, loss or injury.

restive ['restiv] *adj* beginning to show displeasure, impatience, boredom *etc eg* at delay, discipline *etc*; restless. **'restively** *adv*. **'restiveness** *n*.

restore [rə'stɔ:] *v* **1** to repair (a building, a painting, a piece of furniture *etc*) so that it looks as it used to or ought to. **2** to bring back to a normal or healthy state: *The patient was soon restored to health.* **3** to bring or give back: *to restore law and order; The police restored the stolen cars to their owners.* **4** to bring or put (a person) back to a position, rank *etc* he once had: *He was asked to resign but was later restored to his former job as manager.* **,resto'ration** [restə-] *n*: *The building was closed for restoration(s).*

re'storer *n* a person or thing that restores: *a furniture-restorer.*

restrain [rə'strein] *v* to prevent from doing something; to control: *He was so angry he could hardly restrain himself; He had to be restrained from hitting the man; He restrained his anger with difficulty.*

re'strained *adj* controlling, or able to control, one's feelings.

restrict [rə'strikt] *v* **1** to keep within certain limits: *I try to restrict myself/my smoking to five cigarettes a day; Use of the car-park is restricted to senior staff.* **2** to make less than usual, desirable *etc*: *He feels this new law will restrict his freedom.*

re'stricted *adj* **1** limited; narrow, small: *a restricted space.* **2** to which entry has been restricted to certain people: *The battlefield was a restricted zone.* **3** in which certain restrictions (*eg* a speed limit) apply: *a restricted area.*

re'striction [-ʃən] *n* **1** a rule *etc* that limits or controls: *Even in a free democracy a person's behaviour must be subject to certain*

restrictions. **2** the act of restricting: *restriction of freedom.*

re'strictive [-tiv] *adj* restricting or intended to restrict.

result [rə'zʌlt] *n* **1** anything which is due to something already done: *His deafness is the result of a car accident; He went deaf as a result of an accident; He tried a new method, with excellent results; He tried again, but without result.* **2** the answer to a sum *etc*: *Add all these figures and tell me the result.* **3** the final score: *What was the result of Saturday's match?* **4** (*often in pl*) the list of people who have been successful in a competition, of subjects a person has passed or failed in an examination *etc*: *He had very good exam results; The results will be published next week.* – *v* **1** (*often with* **from**) to be caused (by something): *We will pay for any damage which results (from our experiments).* **2** (*with* **in**) to cause or have as a result: *The match resulted in a draw.*

resume [rə'zju:m] *v* to begin again after stopping: *After tea, the meeting resumed; We'll resume the meeting after tea.* **resumption** [rə'zʌmpʃən] *n*.

resurrection [rezə'rekʃən] *n* the process of being brought to life again after death.

resuscitate [rə'sʌsəteit] *v* to bring (a person) back to consciousness. **re,susci'tation** *n*.

retail ['ri:teil] *v* to sell (goods) (*usu* in small quantities) to the person who is going to use them (rather than to someone who is going to sell them to someone else). – *adj* relating to the sale of goods in this way: *a retail price.*

'retailer *n* a person who sells goods retail; a shopkeeper.

retain [rə'tein] *v* **1** to continue to have, use, remember *etc*; to keep in one's possession, memory *etc*: *He finds it difficult to retain information; These dishes don't retain heat very well.* **2** to hold (something) back or keep (something) in its place: *This wall was built to retain the water from the river in order to prevent flooding.*

retake [ri:'teik] – *pt* ,**re'took** [-'tuk]: *ptp* ,**re'taken** – *v* **1** to capture again: *The soldiers retook the fort.* **2** to film (part of a film *etc*) again. – ['ri:teik] *n* the filming of part of a film again: *the fourth retake.*

retaliate [rə'talieit] *v* to do something unpleasant to a person in return for something unpleasant he has done to one: *If you insult him, he will retaliate.* **re,tali'ation** *n*.

retard [rə'ta:d] *v* to make slower or later: *The country's economic progress was retarded by strikes; The baby's development was retarded by an accident he had shortly after birth.* **,retar'dation** [ri:ta:-] *n*.

re'tarded *adj*: *a mentally retarded child.*

retention [rə'tenʃən] *n* the act of retaining: *the retention of information.*

re'tentive [-tiv] *adj* able to retain: *a retentive memory.*

retina ['retinə] the part of the back of the eye that receives the image of what is seen.

retinue ['retinju:] *n* the servants, officials *etc* who accompany a person of importance.

retire [rə'taiə] *v* **1** stop working permanently, *usu* because of age: *He retired at the age of sixty-five.* **2** to leave; to withdraw: *When he doesn't want to talk to anyone, he retires to his room and locks the door; We retired to bed at midnight; The troops were forced to retire to a safer position.*

re'tired *adj* having stopped working: *My father is retired now; a retired professor.*

re'tirement *n* **1** the act of retiring from work: *It is not long till his retirement.* **2** a person's life after retiring from work: *He's enjoying his retirement.*

re'tiring *adj* shy: *a very quiet, retiring person.*

retook see **retake.**

retort [rə'tо:t] *v* to make a quick and clever or angry reply: *'You're too old', she said. 'You're not so young yourself,' he retorted.* – *n* such a reply.

retrace [ri'treis] *v* to go back along (a path *etc*) one has just come along: *She lost her keys somewhere on the way to the station, and had to retrace her steps/journey until she found them.*

retract [rə'trakt] *v* to pull, or be pulled, into the body *etc*: *A cat can retract its claws; A cat's claws can retract.* **re'traction** [-ʃən] *n.*

re'tractable *adj* able to be pulled up or in: *An aeroplane has retractable wheels.*

retreat [rə'tri:t] *v* **1** to move back or away from a battle (*usu* because the enemy is winning): *After a hard struggle, they were finally forced to retreat.* **2** to withdraw; to take oneself away: *He retreated to the peace of his own room.* – *n* **1** the act of retreating (from a battle, danger *etc*): *After the retreat, the soldiers rallied once more.* **2** a signal to retreat: *The bugler sounded the retreat.* **3** (a place to which a person can go for) a period of rest, religious meditation *etc*: *He has gone to a retreat to pray.*

retribution [retri'bju:ʃən] *n* punishment, *esp* deserved.

retrieve [rə'tri:v] *v* **1** to get back (something which was lost *etc*): *My hat blew away, but I managed to retrieve it; Our team retrieved its lead in the second half.* **2** (of *usu* trained dogs) to search for and bring back (birds or animals that have been shot by a hunter). **re'trieval** *n.*

re'triever *n* a breed of dog trained to find and bring back birds and animals that have been shot.

return [rə'tə:n] *v* **1** to come or go back: *He returns home tomorrow; He returned to London from Paris yesterday; The pain has returned.* **2** to give, send, put *etc* (something) back where it came from: *He returned the book to its shelf; Don't forget to return the books you borrowed.* **3** *I'll return to this topic in a minute.* **4** to do (something) which has been done to oneself: *She hit him and he returned the blow; He said how nice it was to see her again, and she returned the compliment.* **5** (of voters) to elect (someone) to Parliament. **6** (of a jury) to give (a verdict): *The jury returned a verdict of not guilty.* **7** (in tennis *etc*) to hit (a ball) back to one's opponent: *She returned his serve.* – *n* **1** the act of returning: *On our return, we found the house had been burgled; (also adj) a return journey.* **2** *esp* in UK, a round-trip ticket, a return ticket: *Do you want a single or a return?*

re'turnable *adj* that can be or that must be returned.

return match a second match played between the same (teams of) players: *We played the first match on our football pitch – the return match will be on theirs.*

return ticket a round-trip ticket, allowing a person to travel to a place and back again to where he started.

by return (of post) by the very next post: *Please send me your reply by return (of post).*

in return (for) as an exchange (for something): *We'll send them whisky and they'll send us vodka in return: They'll send us vodka in return for whisky.*

many happy returns (of the day) an expression of good wishes said to a person on his birthday: *He visited his mother on her birthday to wish her many happy returns.*

to return (not return back) someone's book.

reunion [ri:ju:njən] *n* **1** a meeting of people who have not met for some time: *We attended a reunion of former pupils of our school.* **2** the act of reuniting or state of being reunited.

reunite [ri:ju'nait] *v* to bring or come together after being separated: *The family was finally reunited after the war; The children were reunited with their parents.*

rev [rev] – *pt, ptp* **revved** – (*often* **rev up**) *v* to increase the speed of revolution of (a car engine *etc*): *He revved the engine (up); He was revving up in the yard.*

revs *n pl* revolutions (of a car engine *etc*): *thirty revs a second.*

reveal [rə'vi:l] *v* **1** to make known: *All their secrets have been revealed.* **2** to show; to allow to be seen: *He scraped away the top layer of paint from the picture, revealing an earlier painting underneath.*

re'vealing *adj* allowing or causing something to be known or seen: *a revealing statement.*

reveille [ri'vali, (*Amer*) 'revəli] *n* a bugle call at daybreak to waken soldiers.

revel ['revl] – *pt, ptp* 'revelled, (*Amer*) 'reveled — *v* (*with* in) to take great delight in something: *He revels in danger.* – *n* (*usu in pl*) noisy, lively enjoyment: *midnight revels.* 'reveller *n.*

'revelry – *pl* 'revelries – *n* (*often in pl*) noisy, lively enjoyment: *midnight revelries.*

revelation [revə'leiʃən] *n* 1 the act of revealing secrets, information *etc*: *the revelation of the true facts.* 2 something made known: *amazing revelations.*

revelry *see* revel.

revenge [rə'vendʒ] *n* 1 harm done to another person in return for harm which he has done (to oneself or to someone else): *The man told the manager he would get/have his revenge/take revenge on the company for dismissing him; His revenge was to burn down the factory.* 2 the desire to do such harm: *The man said he had burned down the factory out of revenge/in revenge for being dismissed.* – *v* (*with* on) to get (one's) revenge: *He revenged himself on his enemies; I'll soon be revenged on you all.*

revenue ['revinju:] *n* money which comes to a person *etc* from any source or sources (*eg* property, shares), *esp* the money which comes to a government from taxes *etc*.

revere [rə'viə] *v* to feel or show great respect for: *The students revere the professor.*

reverence ['revərəns] *n* great respect: *He was held in reverence by those who worked for him.*

Reverend ['revərənd] *n* (*usu abbrev* Rev. *when written*) a title given to a clergyman: (*the*) *Rev. John Brown.*

reverent ['revərənt] *adj* showing great respect: *A reverent silence followed the professor's lecture.* 'reverently *adv.*

reverie ['revəri] *n* 1 a state of pleasant dreamy thought: *He was lost in reverie.* 2 (*usu in pl*) a day-dream: *pleasant reveries.*

reverse [rə'və:s] *v* 1 to move backwards or in the opposite direction to normal: *He reversed (the car) into the garage; He reversed the film through the projector.* 2 to put into the opposite position, state, order *etc*: *This jacket can be reversed (=worn inside out).* 3 to change (a decision, policy *etc*) to the exact opposite: *The man was found guilty, but the judges in the appeal court reversed the decision.* – *n* 1 (*also adj*) (the) opposite: *'Are you hungry?' 'Quite the reverse – I've eaten far too much!'; I take the reverse point*

of view. 2 a defeat; a piece of bad luck. 3 (a mechanism *eg* one of the gears of a car *etc* which makes something move in) a backwards direction or a direction opposite to normal: *He put the car into reverse;* (*also adj*) *a reverse gear.* 4 (*also adj*) (of) the back of a coin, medal *etc*: *the reverse (side) of a coin.*

re'versal *n*: *a reversal of his previous decision.*

re'versed *adj* in the opposite state, position, order *etc*: *Once he worked for me. Now our positions are reversed and I work for him.*

re'versible *adj* 1 able to be reversed. 2 (of clothes) able to be worn with either side out: *Is that raincoat reversible?*

reverse the charges to make a telephone call (a reverse-charge call) which is paid for by the person who receives it instead of by the caller.

reversion *see* revert.

revert [rə'və:t] *v* to come or go back (to a previous state, point in a discussion *etc*). re'version [-ʃən, (*Amer*) -ʒən] *n.*

review [rə'vju:] *n* 1 a written report on a book, play *etc* giving the writer's opinion of it. 2 an inspection of troops *etc*. – *v* 1 to make or have a review of: *The book was reviewed in yesterday's paper; The Queen reviewed the troops.* 2 to reconsider: *We'll review the situation at the end of the month.*

re'viewer *n* a person who reviews books *etc*: *Who was the reviewer of the biography of Churchill?*

revise [rə'vaiz] *v* 1 to correct faults and make improvements in (a book *etc*): *This dictionary has been completely revised.* 2 to study one's previous work, notes *etc* in preparation for an examination *etc*: *You'd better start revising (your Latin) for your exam.* 3 to change (one's opinion *etc*). revision [rə'viʒən] *n.*

revive [rə'vaiv] *v* 1 to come, or bring, back to consciousness, strength, health *etc*: *They attempted to revive the woman who had fainted; She soon revived; The flowers revived in water; to revive someone's hopes.* 2 to come or bring back to use *etc*: *This old custom has recently (been) revived.*

re'vival *n* 1 the act of reviving or state of being revived: *the revival of the invalid/of our hopes.* 2 (a time of) new or increased interest in something: *a religious revival.* 3 (the act of producing) an old and almost forgotten play, show *etc*.

revoke [rə'vouk] *v* to change (a decision); to make (a law *etc*) no longer valid. revocation [revə'keiʃən] *n.*

revolt [rə'voult] *v* 1 to rebel (against a government *etc*): *The army revolted against the dictator.* 2 to disgust: *His habits revolt me.*

– n 1 the act of rebelling: *The peasants rose in revolt.* 2 a rebellion.

re'volted *adj* having a feeling of disgust: *I felt quite revolted at the sight.*

re'volting *adj* causing a feeling of disgust: *revolting food.*

revolution [revə'luːʃən] *n* 1 (the act of making) a successful, violent attempt to change or remove a government *etc*: *the American Revolution.* 2 a complete change in ideas, methods *etc*: *There's been a complete revolution in the way things are done in this office.* 3 a complete circle or turn round a central point, axis *etc* (*eg* as made by a record turning on a record-player, or the Earth moving on its axis or round the Sun.

,**revo'lutionary** *adj* 1 involving or causing great changes in ideas, methods *etc*: *a revolutionary new process for making paper.* 2 of a revolution against a government *etc*: *revolutionary activities.* – n – *pl* **revo'lutionaries** – a person who takes part in, or is in favour of, (a) revolution.

,**revo'lutionize, -ise** *v* to cause great changes in (ideas, methods *etc*): *This new machinery will revolutionize the paper-making industry.*

revolve [rə'vɔlv] *v* to move, roll or turn (in a complete circle) around a central point, axis *etc*: *A wheel revolves on its axle*; *This disc can be revolved*; *The Moon revolves (a)round the Earth*; *The Earth revolves about the Sun and also revolves on its axis.*

re'volver *n* a type of pistol: *She shot him with a revolver.*

re'volving *adj*: *revolving doors.*

reward [rə'wɔːd] *n* 1 something given in return for or got from work done, good behaviour *etc*: *He was given a gold watch as a reward for his services to the firm*; *Apart from the salary, teaching children has its own particular rewards.* 2 a sum of money offered for finding a criminal, lost or stolen property *etc*: *A reward of $100 has been offered to the person who finds the diamond brooch.* – v to give a reward to someone for something: *He was rewarded for his services*; *His services were rewarded.*

re'warding *adj* (*neg* **un-**) giving pleasure, satisfaction *etc*: *a rewarding job.*

reword [riː'wɔːd] *v* to say or write with different words: *to reword a sentence.*

rewrite [riː'rait] – *pt* **rewrote** [ri'rout]: *ptp* **re'written** [ri'ritn] – *v* to write again.

rhapsody ['rapsədi] – *pl* **'rhapsodies** – *n* an expression of strong feeling or excitement in *eg* music or speech.

rheumatism ['ruːmətizəm] *n* a disease which causes stiffness and pain in one's joints. **rheu'matic** [-'ma-] *adj*.

rhino ['rainou] – *pl* **'rhinos** – short for **rhinoceros.**

*****rhinoceros** [rai'nosərəs] – *pls* **rhi'noceroses,**

rhi'noceros – *n* a type of large thick-skinned animal with one or two horns on its nose.

*****rhombus** ['rombəs] *n* an equilateral parallelogram, other than a square.

rhyme [raim] *n* 1 a short poem: *a book of rhymes for children.* 2 a word which is like another in its final sound(s): *Beef and leaf are rhymes.* 3 verse or poetry using such words at the ends of the lines: *To amuse his colleagues he wrote his report in rhyme.* – v (of words) to be rhymes: *Beef rhymes with leaf*; *Beef and leaf rhyme.*

rhythm ['riðəm] *n* 1 a regular, repeated pattern of sounds, stresses or beats in music, poetry *etc*: *Just listen to the rhythm of those drums*; *complicated rhythms.* 2 a regular, repeated pattern of movements: *The rowers lost their rhythm.* 3 an ability to sing, move *etc* with rhythm: *That girl has got rhythm.* **'rhythmic, 'rhythmical** *adjs* of or with rhythm: *rhythmic movement*; *The dancing was very rhythmical.* **'rhythmically** *adv*.

rib [rib] *n* 1 any one of the bones which curve round and forward from the backbone, enclosing the heart and lungs. 2 one of the curved pieces of wood which are joined to the keel to form the framework of a boat. 3 a vertical raised strip in *eg* knitted material, or the pattern formed by a row of these. 4 any of a number of things similar in shape, use *etc* to a rib, *eg* one of the supports for the fabric of an aeroplane wing or of an umbrella.

ribbed *adj* having ribs: *a ribbed pattern.*

'ribbing *n* a pattern or arrangement of ribs.

ribbon ['ribən] *n* a long narrow strip of material used in decorating clothes, tying hair *etc*: *a blue ribbon*; *four metres of red ribbon.*

rice [rais] *n* a plant, grown in well-watered ground in tropical countries, whose seeds are used as food.

rich [ritʃ] *adj* 1 wealthy; having a lot of money, possessions *etc*: *a rich man/country.* 2 (*with* **in**) having a lot (of something): *This part of the country is rich in coal.* 3 valuable: *a rich reward*; *rich materials.* 4 containing a lot of fat, eggs, spices *etc*: *a rich sauce.* 5 (of clothes, material *etc*) very beautiful and expensive. **'richly** *adv*. **'richness** *n*.

'riches *n pl* wealth.

rickety ['rikəti] *adj* not well built; unsteady; likely to fall over or collapse: *a rickety table.*

rickshaw ['rikʃɔː] *n* in Japan *etc*, a small two-wheeled carriage pulled by a man.

ricochet ['rikəʃei] – *pt, ptp* **'ricocheted** [-ʃeid] – *v* to hit something and bounce away at an angle: *The bullet ricocheted off the wall.*

rid [rid] – *ptp* **'ridding**: *pt, ptp* **rid** – *v* (*with* **of**); to free (someone *etc*) from: *We must try to rid the town of rats.*

* see illustrations on pp. 17, 476

be rid of, get rid of to have removed, to remove; to free oneself from: *I thought I'd never get rid of these weeds*; *I'm rid of my debts at last.*

good riddance ['rɪdəns] I am happy to have got rid of it, him *etc*: *I've thrown out all those old books, and good riddance (to the lot of them)!*

ridden *see* **ride.**

riddle[1] ['rɪdl] *n* a puzzle *usu* in the form of a question, which describes an object, person *etc* in a mysterious or misleading way: *Can you guess the answer to this riddle?*; *The answer to the riddle 'What flies for ever, and never rests?' is 'The wind'.*

riddle[2] ['rɪdl] *v* to make (something) full of holes: *They riddled the car with bullets.*

ride [raɪd] – *pt* **rode** [roʊd] : *ptp* **ridden** ['rɪdn] – *v* 1 to travel or be carried (in a car, train *etc* or on a bicycle, horse *etc*): *He rides to work every day on an old bicycle*; *The horsemen rode past.* 2 to (be able to) ride on and control (a horse, bicycle *etc*): *Can you ride a bicycle?* 3 to take part in (in a horse-race *etc*): *He's riding in the first race.* 4 to go out regularly on horseback (*eg* as a hobby): *My daughter rides every Saturday morning.* – *n* 1 a journey on horseback, on a bicycle *etc*: *He likes to go for a long ride on a Sunday afternoon.* 2 a *usu* short period of riding on or in something: *Can I have a ride on your bike?*

'rider *n.*

'riding-school *n* a place where people are taught to ride horses.

ridge [rɪdʒ] *n* 1 a long narrow piece of ground *etc* raised above the level of the ground *etc* on either side of it. 2 a long narrow row of hills. 3 anything like a ridge in shape: *A ridge of high pressure is a long narrow area of high pressure as shown on a weather map.* 4 the top edge of something where two sloping surfaces meet, *eg* on a roof.

ridiculous [rə'dɪkjʊləs] *adj* very silly; deserving to be laughed at: *That's a ridiculous suggestion*; *You look ridiculous in that hat!*

ri'diculously *adv.* **ri'diculousness** *n.*

ridicule ['rɪdɪkjuːl] *v* to laugh at; to mock: *They ridiculed him because he was wearing one brown shoe and one black shoe.* – *n* laughter at someone or something; mockery: *Despite the ridicule of his neighbours he continued to build a spaceship in his garden.*

rife [raɪf] *adj* (*esp* of bad or dangerous things) very widespread: *After the failure of the harvest, disease and starvation were rife.*

rifle ['raɪfl] *n* a gun with a long barrel, fired from the shoulder: *The soldiers are being taught to shoot with rifles.* – *v* 1 to search (through something): *The thief rifled through the drawers.* 2 to steal: *The document had been rifled.*

'rifle-range *n* a place for rifle practice.

rift [rɪft] *n* 1 a split or crack. 2 a disagreement between friends.

rig [rɪg] – *pt, ptp* **rigged** – *v* to fit (a ship) with ropes and sails. – *n* 1 an oil-rig. 2 any special equipment, tools *etc* for some purpose. 3 the arrangement of sails *etc* of a sailing-ship.

'rigging *n* the ropes *etc* which control a ship's masts and sails.

rig out to dress: *She was rigged out in rather odd clothes* (*n* **'rig-out**: *She was wearing a strange rig-out*).

rig up to build *usu* quickly with whatever material is available: *They rigged up a rough shelter with branches and mud.*

right [raɪt] *adj* 1 on or related to the side of the body which in most people has the more skilful hand, or to the side of a person or thing which is toward the east when that person or thing is facing north (opposite to **left**): *When I'm writing, I hold my pen in my right hand.* 2 correct: *Put that book back in the right place*; *Is that the right answer to the question?* 3 morally correct; good: *It's not right to let thieves keep what they have stolen.* 4 suitable; appropriate: *He's not the right man for this job*; *When would be the right time to ask him?* – *n* 1 something a person is, or ought to be, allowed to have, do *etc*: *Everyone has the right to a fair trial*; *You must fight for your rights*; *You have no right to say that.* 2 that which is correct or good: *Who's in the right in this argument?* 3 the right side, part or direction: *Turn to the right*; *Take the second road on the right.* 4 in politics, the people, group, party or parties holding the more traditional beliefs *etc.* –, *adv* 1 exactly: *He was standing right here.* 2 immediately: *I'll go right after lunch*; *I'll come right down.* 3 close: *He was standing right beside me.* 4 completely; all the way: *The bullet went right through his arm.* 5 to the right: *Turn right.* 6 correctly: *Have I done that right?*; *I don't think this sum is going to turn out right.* – *v* 1 to bring back to the correct, *usu* upright, position: *The boat tipped over, but righted itself again.* 2 to put an end to and make up for something wrong that has been done: *He's like a medieval knight, going about the country looking for wrongs to right.* – *interj* I understand; I'll do what you say *etc*: *'I want you to type some letters for me.' 'Right, I'll do them now.'*

righteous ['raɪtʃəs] *adj* 1 (of anger *etc*) justifiable: *righteous indignation.* 2 living a good moral life: *a righteous man.* 3 good; morally right: *a righteous action.*

'righteously *adv.* **'righteousness** *n.*

'rightful *adj* proper; correct; that ought to

be or has a right to be something: *He is the rightful king of this country.*

'rightfully *adv*: *It rightfully belongs to me, although she has it at the moment.*

'rightly *adv* **1** justly, justifiably; it is right, good or just that (something is the case): *He was punished for his stupidity and rightly: Rightly or wrongly she refused to speak to him.* **2** correctly; accurately: *They rightly assumed that he would refuse to help.*

'rightness *n* the state of being good or morally correct: *They believe in the rightness of their cause.*

righto, right-oh [rait'ou] *interj* right: *Right-oh! I'll come now.*

rights *n pl* the legal right given in return for a sum of money to produce *eg* a film from a book: *He has sold the film rights of his new book to an American company.*

right angle an angle of ninety degrees, like any of the four angles in a square.

'right-angled *adj* having a right angle: *a right-angled triangle.*

'right-hand *adj* **1** at the right; to the right of something else: *the top right-hand drawer of my desk.* **2** towards the right: *a right-hand bend in the road.*

,right-'handed *adj* (of people) using the right hand more easily than the left, *eg* for writing: *The majority of people are right-handed.*

by right(s) rightfully: *By rights, I ought to be in charge of this department.*

get, keep on the right side of to make (someone) feel, or continue to feel, friendly or kind towards oneself: *If you want a pay rise, you'd better get on the right side of the boss.*

get right to understand, do, say *etc* (something) correctly: *Did I get the answer right?*

go right to happen as expected, wanted or intended; to be successful or without problems: *Nothing ever goes right for him.*

not in one's right mind, not (quite) right in the head (slightly) mad: *He can't be in his right mind – making incredible suggestions like that!*

put right 1 to repair; to remove faults *etc* in (something): *There is something wrong with this kettle – can you put it right?* **2** to put an end to or change (something that is wrong): *You've made a mistake in that sum – you'd better put it right.* **3** to put (a watch, clock *etc*) to the correct time. **4** to correct (someone who has made a mistake): *I thought the meeting was at 2.30, but he put me right.* **5** to make healthy again: *That medicine will soon put you right.*

put/set to rights to put back into the correct order, state *etc*: *The room was in a dreadful mess, and it took us the whole day to set it to rights.*

right away immediately; at once.

right-hand man a person's most trusted and useful assistant.

right now immediately.

right of way 1 the right of the public to use a path that goes across private property. **2** (,right-of-'way – *pl* ,rights-of-'way) a road or path over private land, along which the public have a right to walk. **3** the right of one car *etc* to move first *eg* when crossing a cross-roads, or going round a roundabout: *It was your fault that our cars crashed – I had right of way.*

serve right to be the punishment deserved by: *If you fall and hurt yourself, it'll serve you right for climbing up there when I told you not to.*

rigid ['ridʒid] *adj* **1** completely stiff; not able to be bent (easily): *An iron bar is rigid.* **2** very strict, and not likely to change: *rigid rules; rigid discipline; rigid views on education; a stern, rigid headmaster.* **'rigidly** *adv*. **'rigidness, ri'gidity** *ns*.

rigour, (*Amer*) **rigor** ['rigə] *n* **1** strictness; harshness. **2** (*also* **'rigours** *n pl*) (of weather *etc*) the state of being very bad or unpleasant, or the hardship caused by this: *the rigour(s) of life in the Arctic Circle.*

'rigorous *adj* **1** strict: *a rigorous training.* **2** harsh; unpleasant: *a rigorous climate.* **'rigorously** *adv*. **'rigorousness** *n*.

rim [rim] *n* an edge or border: *the rim of a wheel; the rim of a cup.*

'rimless *adj* without a rim: *rimless spectacles.*

rimmed *adj*: *horn-rimmed spectacles; Her eyes were red-rimmed from crying.*

rind [raind] *n* a thick, hard outer layer or covering, *esp* the outer surface of cheese or bacon, or the peel of fruit: *bacon-rind; lemon-rind.*

ring¹ [riŋ] *n* **1** a small circle *eg* of gold or silver, sometimes having a jewel set in it, worn on the finger: *a wedding ring; She wears a diamond ring.* **2** a circle of metal, wood *etc* for any of various purposes: *a scarf-ring; a key-ring; The trap-door had a ring attached for lifting it.* **3** anything which is like a circle in shape: *The children formed a ring round their teacher; The hot teapot left a ring on the polished table.* **4** an enclosed space for boxing matches, circus performances *etc*: *the circus-ring; The crowd cheered as the boxer entered the ring.* **5** a small group of people formed for business or criminal purposes: *a drugs ring.* – *v* – *pt, ptp* **ringed** – *v* **1** to form a ring round. **2** to put, draw *etc* a ring round (something): *He has ringed all your errors.* **3** to put a ring on the leg of (a bird) as a means of identifying it.

'ringlet [-lit] *n* a long curl of hair.

'**ringleader** *n* the leader of a group of people who are doing something wrong: *The teacher punished the ring-leader.*

'**ringmaster** *n* a person who is in charge of performances in a circus ring.

ring² [riŋ] – *pt* **rang** [raŋ]: *ptp* **rung** [rʌŋ] – *v* **1** to (cause to) sound: *The doorbell rang; He rang the doorbell; The telephone rang.* **2** (*often with* **up**) to telephone (someone): *I'll ring you (up) tonight.* **3** (*often with* **for**) to ring a bell (*eg* in a hotel) to tell someone to come, to bring something *etc*: *She rang for the maid.* **4** (of certain objects) to make a high sound like a bell: *The glass rang as she hit it with a metal spoon.* **5** to be filled with sound: *The hall rang with the sound of laughter.* **6** (*often with* **out**) to make a loud, clear sound: *His voice rang through the house; A shot rang out.* – *n* **1** the act or sound of ringing: *the ring of a telephone.* **2** a telephone call: *I'll give you a ring.* **3** a suggestion, impression or feeling: *His story has a ring of truth about it.*

ring a bell to have been seen, heard *etc* before, but not remembered in detail: *His name rings a bell, but I don't remember where I've heard it before.*

ring back to telephone (someone who has telephoned): *If he is busy at the moment, he can ring me back; He'll ring back tomorrow.*

ring off to end a telephone call.

ring true to sound true: *His story does not ring true.*

rink [riŋk] *n* **1** (*usu* '**ice-rink**) (a building containing) an area of ice, for ice-skating, ice hockey *etc*. **2** (a building containing) a smooth floor for roller-skating.

rinse [rins] *v* (*often with* **out**) **1** to wash (clothes *etc*) in clean water to remove soap *etc*: *After washing the towels, rinse them (out).* **2** to clean (a cup, one's mouth *etc*) by filling with clean water *etc* and then emptying the water out: *The dentist asked me to rinse my mouth out.* – *n* **1** the act of rinsing: *Give the cup a rinse.* **2** a liquid used for changing the colour of hair: *a blue rinse.*

riot ['raiət] *n* a noisy disturbance created by a *usu* large group of people: *The protest march developed into a riot.* – *v* to form or take part in a riot: *The protesters were rioting in the street.* '**rioter** *n*.

'**riotous** *adj* **1** starting, or likely to start, a riot: *a riotous crowd.* **2** very active, noisy and cheerful: *a riotous party.* '**riotously** *adv*. '**riotousness** *n*.

run riot to behave wildly; to go out of control.

rip [rip] – *pt*, *ptp* **ripped** – *v* **1** to make or get a hole or tear in by pulling, tearing *etc*: *He ripped his shirt on a branch; His shirt ripped.* **2** to pull (off, up *etc*) by breaking or tearing: *The roof of the car was ripped off in the* crash; *to rip up floorboards; He ripped open the envelope.* – *n* a tear or hole: *a rip in my shirt.*

ripe [raip] *adj* (*neg* **un-**) (of fruit, grain *etc*) ready to be gathered in or eaten: *ripe apples/corn.* '**ripeness** *n*.

'**ripen** *v* to make or become ripe or riper: *The sun ripened the corn; The corn ripened in the sun.*

ripe (old) age a very old age: *He lived to the ripe (old) age of ninety-five.*

ripple ['ripl] *n* a little wave or movement on the surface of water *etc*: *He threw the stone into the pond, and watched the ripples spread across the water.* – *v* to (cause to) have ripples: *The grass rippled in the wind; The wind rippled the grass.*

rise [raiz] – *pt* **rose** [rouz]: *ptp* **risen** ['rizn] – *v* **1** to become greater, larger, higher *etc*; to increase: *Food prices are still rising; His temperature rose; If the river rises much more, there will be a flood; Her voice rose to a scream; Bread rises when it is baked; His spirits rose at the good news.* **2** to move upwards: *Smoke was rising from the chimney; The birds rose into the air; The curtain rose to reveal an empty stage.* **3** to get up from bed: *He rises every morning at six o'clock.* **4** to stand up: *The children all rose when the headmaster came in.* **5** (of the sun *etc*) to appear above the horizon: *The sun rises in the east and sets in the west.* **6** to slope upwards: *Hills rose in the distance; The ground rises at this point.* **7** to rebel: *The people rose (up) in revolt against the dictator.* **8** to move to a higher rank, a more important position *etc*: *He rose to the rank of colonel.* **9** (of a river) to begin or appear: *The Rhône rises in the Alps.* **10** (of wind) to begin; to become stronger: *Don't go out in the boat – the wind has risen.* **11** to be built: *Office blocks are rising all over the town.* **12** to come back to life: *Jesus has risen.* – *n* **1** (the) act of rising: *He had a rapid rise to fame; a rise in prices.* **2** an increase in salary or wages: *She asked her boss for a rise.* **3** a slope or hill: *The house is just beyond the next rise.* **4** the beginning and early development of something: *the rise of the Roman Empire.*

'**rising** *n* **1** the act or rising: *the rising of the sun.* **2** a rebellion: *The king executed those who took part in the rising.* – *adj*: *the rising sun; rising prices; the rising generation; a rising young politician.*

early, late riser a person who gets out of bed early or late in the day.

give rise to to cause: *This plan has given rise to various problems.*

rise to the occasion to be able to do what is required in an emergency *etc*: *He had never* *had to make a speech before, but he rose to the occasion magnificently.*

risk [risk] *n* (a person, thing *etc* which causes or could cause) danger or possible loss or injury: *He thinks we shouldn't go ahead with the plan because of the risks involved/because of the risk of failure.* – *v* **1** to expose to danger; to lay open to the possibility of loss: *He would risk his life for his friend; He risked all his money on betting on that horse.* **2** to take the chance of (something bad happening): *He was willing to risk death to save his friend; I'd better leave early as I don't want to risk being late for the play.*

'**risky** *adv* possibly causing or bringing loss, injury *etc*: *Motor-racing is a risky business.*
at (a person's) own risk with the person agreeing to accept any loss, damage *etc* involved: *Cars may be parked here at their owner's risk.*
at risk in danger; likely to suffer loss, injury *etc*: *Heart disease can be avoided if people at risk take medical advice.*
at the risk of with the possibility of (loss, injury, trouble *etc*): *He saved the little girl at the risk of his own life; At the risk of offending you, I must tell you that I disapprove of your behaviour.*
run/take the risk (of) to do something which involves a risk: *I took the risk of buying that jumper for you – I hope it fits; He didn't want to run the risk of losing his money.*
take risks/take a risk to do something which might cause loss, injury *etc*: *One cannot be successful in business unless one is willing to take risks.*

rite [rait] *n* a solemn ceremony, *esp* a religious one: *marriage rites.*

ritual ['ritʃuəl] *n* (a particular set of) traditional or fixed actions *etc* used in a religious *etc* ceremony: *Christian rituals; the ritual of the Roman Catholic church.* – *adj* forming (part of) a ritual or ceremony: *a ritual dance/sacrifice.*

rival ['raivəl] *n* a person *etc* who tries to compete with another; a person who wants the same thing as someone else: *For students of English, this dictionary is without a rival; The two brothers are rivals for the girl next door – they both want to marry her;* (*also adj*) *rival companies; rival teams.* – *v* – *pt, ptp* '**rivalled**, (*Amer*) '**rivaled** – to (try to) be as good as someone or something else: *He rivals his brother as a chess-player; Nothing rivals football for excitement and entertainment.*
'**rivalry** – *pl* '**rivalries** – *n* the state of or an instance of being rivals: *the rivalry/rivalries between business companies.*

river ['rivə] *n* a large stream of water flowing across country: *The Thames is a river; the*

river Thames; the Hudson River; (*also adj*) *a river animal.*
'**river-bed** *n* the ground over which a river runs.
'**riverside** *n* the ground along or near the side of a river: *He has a bungalow on the riverside.*

rivet ['rivit] *n* a sort of metal nail; a bolt for fastening plates of metal together *eg* when building the sides of a ship. – *v* – *pt, ptp* '**riveted** – **1** to fasten with rivets: *They riveted the sheets of metal together.* **2** to fix firmly: *He stood riveted to the spot with fear; His eyes were riveted on the television.* '**riveter** *n*.

road [roud] *n* **1** a strip of ground *usu* with a hard level surface for people, vehicles *etc* to travel on: *This road takes you past the school;* (*also adj*) *road safety.* **2** (*often abbrev* **Rd** *when written*) used in the names of roads or streets: *His address is 24 School Road.* **3** a route; the correct road(s) to follow in order to arrive somewhere: *We'd better look at the map because I'm not sure of the road.* **4** a way that leads to something: *the road to peace; He's on the road to ruin.*
'**roadblock** *n* a barrier put across a road (*eg* by the police) in order to stop or slow down traffic: *to set up a roadblock.*
'**road map** a map showing the roads of (part of) a country.
'**roadside** *n* the ground beside a road: *flowers growing by the roadside;* (*also adj*) *a roadside café.*
'**roadway** *n* the part of a road on which cars *etc* travel: *Don't walk on the roadway.*
'**roadworks** *n pl* the building or repairing of a road: *The traffic was held up by the roadworks.*
by road in a lorry, car *etc*: *We'll send the furniture by road rather than by rail; We came by road.*

roam [roum] *v* to walk about without any fixed plan or purpose; to wander: *He roamed from town to town; He roamed (over) the hills.* '**roamer** *n*.

roar [ro:] *v* **1** to give a loud deep cry; to say loudly; to shout: *The lions roared; The sergeant roared (out) his commands.* **2** to laugh loudly: *The audience roared (with laughter) at the man's jokes.* **3** to make a loud deep sound: *The cannons/thunder roared.* **4** to make a loud deep sound while moving: *He roared past on his motorbike.* – *n* **1** a loud deep cry: *a roar of pain/laughter; the lion's roars.* **2** a loud, deep sound: *the roar of traffic.*
do a roaring trade to have a very successful business; to sell a lot of something: *She's doing a roaring trade in/selling home-made cakes.*

roast [roust] *v* **1** to cook or be cooked in an oven, or over or in front of a fire *etc*: *to roast* *a chicken over the fire*; *The beef was roasting in the oven.* **2** to heat (coffee-beans) before grinding. – *adj* roasted: *roast beef/chestnuts.* – *n* meat that has been roasted or is for roasting: *She bought a roast*; *a delicious roast.*

'roasting *adj* very hot: *It's roasting outside.*

rob [rob] – *pt, ptp* **robbed** – *v* **1** to steal from (a person, place *etc*): *He robbed a bank/an old lady*; *I've been robbed!* **2** (*with* **of**) to take (something) away from; to deprive of: *An accident robbed him of his sight at the age of 21.*

'robber *n*: *The bank robbers got away with nearly $50 000.*

'robbery – *pl* **'robberies** – *n* the act of robbing: *Robbery is a serious crime*; *He was charged with four robberies.*

to rob a bank or a person;
to steal a watch, pencil, money *etc*.

robe [roub] *n* **1** (*often in pl*) a long, loose piece of clothing: *Many Arabs still wear robes*; *a baby's christening-robe.* **2** (*usu in pl*) a long, loose piece of clothing worn as a sign of a person's rank *eg* on official occasions: *a judge's robes.* **3** (*esp Amer*) a loose garment worn casually; a dressing-gown: *She wore a robe over her nightdress*; *a bath-robe*; *a beach-robe.*

robed *adj* wearing robes: *judges robed in black.*

robin ['robin] *n* **1** a small European bird with a red breast. **2** an American thrush with an orange-red breast.

robot ['roubot] *n* a machine which behaves, works, and often looks like a human being.

robust [rə'bʌst] *adj* strong; healthy: *a robust child.* **ro'bustly** *adv.* **ro'bustness** *n.*

rock¹ [rok] *n* **1** (a large lump or mass of) the solid parts of the surface of the Earth: *The ship struck a rock and sank*; *the rocks on the seashore*; *He built his house on solid rock.* **2** a large stone: *The climber was killed by a falling rock.* **3** a type of hard sweet made in sticks: *a stick of Edinburgh rock.*

'rockery – *pl* **'rockeries** – *n* a heap of rocks in a garden with earth between them in which small plants are grown.

'rocky *adj*: *a rocky coastline.* **'rockiness** *n.*

,rock-'bottom *n, adj* (at) the lowest level possible: *Prices have reached rock-bottom*; *rock-bottom prices.*

'rock-garden *n* a rockery.

'rock-plant *n* any plant which grows among rocks *eg* on mountains, often also grown in rockeries.

on the rocks in a state of ruin or of great financial difficulty: *Their marriage is on the rocks*; *The firm is on the rocks.*

rock² [rok] *v* **1** to (cause to) swing gently backwards and forwards or from side to side: *The mother rocked the cradle*; *This cradle rocks.* **2** to swing (a baby) gently in one's arms to comfort it or make it sleep. **3** to shake or move violently: *The earthquake rocked the building.*

'rocker *n* **1** one of *usu* two curved supports on which a cradle, rocking-chair *etc* rocks. **2** a rocking-chair.

'rocky *adj* which rocks or shakes; unsteady; unsafe. **'rockiness** *n.*

'rocking-chair *n* a chair which rocks backwards and forwards on rockers.

'rocking-horse *n* a toy horse which rocks backwards and forwards on rockers.

off one's rocker mad; crazy.

rock³ [rok] *n* (*also* **rock music**) music or songs with a strong, heavy beat and *usu* a simple melody: *She likes rock*; (*also adj*) *a rock band.*

,rock'n''roll *n* (*also* ,**rock-and-'roll**) a simpler, earlier form of rock music.

rocket ['rokit] *n* **1** a tube containing materials which, when set on fire, give off a jet of gas which drives the tube forward, *usu* up into the air, used *eg* as a firework, for signalling, or for launching a spacecraft. **2*** a spacecraft launched in this way: *The Americans have sent a rocket to Mars.* – *v* – *pt, ptp* **'rocketed** – to rise or increase very quickly: *Bread prices have rocketed.*

rocky *see* **rock¹**, **rock².**

rod [rod] *n* a long thin stick or piece of wood, metal *etc*: *an iron rod*; *a fishing-rod*; *a measuring-rod.*

rode *see* **ride.**

rodent ['roudənt] *n* any of a number of types of animal with large front teeth for gnawing, *eg* squirrels, beavers, rats *etc.*

rodeo ['roudiou] – *pl* **'rodeos** – *n esp* in the US, a show or contest of riding, lassoing *etc.*

roe¹ [rou] *n* the eggs of fish: *cod roe.*

roe² [rou]: **'roe deer** – *pls* **'roe deer, 'roe deers** – *n* a small deer found in Europe and Asia.

rogue [roug] *n* **1** a dishonest person: *I wouldn't buy a car from a rogue like him.* **2** a mischievous person, *esp* a child: *She's a little rogue sometimes.*

rôle, role [roul] *n* **1** a part played by an actor or actress in a play *etc*: *He is playing the rôle of King Lear.* **2** the actions or functions of a person in some activity: *He played the rôle of peacemaker in the dispute.*

roll¹ [roul] *n* **1** anything flat (*eg* a piece of paper, a carpet) rolled into the shape of a tube, wound round a tube *etc*: *a roll of kitchen foil*; *a toilet-roll.* **2** a small piece of baked bread dough, used *eg* for sandwiches: *a cheese roll.* **3** an act of rolling: *Our dog loves a roll on the grass.* **4** a ship's action of rocking from side to side: *She said that the roll of the ship made her feel ill.* **5** a long low sound: *the roll of thunder.* **6** a thick mass of

* see illustration on p. 504·

flesh: *I'd like to get rid of these rolls of fat round my waist.* **7** a series of quick beats (on a drum). – *v* **1** to move by turning over like a wheel or ball: *The coin/pencil rolled under the table*; *He rolled the ball towards the puppy*; *The ball rolled away.* **2** to move on wheels, rollers *etc*: *The children rolled the cart up the hill, then let it roll back down again.* **3** to form (a piece of paper, a carpet) into the shape of a tube by winding: *to roll the carpet back.* **4** (of a person or animal in a lying position) to turn over: *The doctor rolled the patient (over) on to his side*; *The dog rolled on to its back.* **5** to shape (clay *etc*) into a ball or cylinder by turning it about between the hands: *He rolled the clay into a ball.* **6** to cover with something by rolling: *When the little girl's dress caught fire, they rolled her in a blanket.* **7** to make (something) flat or flatter by rolling something heavy over it: *to roll a lawn*; *to roll pastry (out).* **8** (of a ship) to rock from side to side while travelling forwards: *The storm made the ship roll.* **9** to make a series of low sounds: *The thunder rolled*; *The drums rolled.* **10** to move (one's eyes) round in a circle to express fear, surprise *etc.* **11** to travel in a car *etc*: *We were rolling along merrily when a tyre burst.* **12** (of waves, rivers *etc*) to move gently and steadily: *The waves rolled in to the shore.* **13** (of time) to pass: *Months rolled by.*

'roller *n* **1** any of a number of tube-shaped objects, or machines fitted with one or more such objects, for flattening, crushing, printing *etc*: *a garden roller*; *a road-roller.* **2** a small tube-shaped object on which hair is wound to curl it. **3** a small solid wheel or cylinder on which something can be rolled along. **4** a long large wave on the sea.

'rolling *adj* (of a landscape) having low hills and shallow valleys, without steep slopes.

'roller-skate *n* a skate with wheels instead of a blade: *a pair of roller-skates.* – *v* to move on roller-skates: *You shouldn't roller-skate on the pavement.*

'rolling-pin *n* a *usu* wooden roller for flattening out dough.

roll in *v* to come in or be got in large numbers or amounts: *I'd like to own a chain store and watch the money rolling in.*

roll up 1 to form into a roll: *to roll up the carpet*; *He rolled up his sleeves.* **2** to arrive: *John rolled up ten minutes late.* **3** (*esp* shouted to a crowd at a fair *etc*) to come near: *Roll up! Roll up! Come and see the bearded lady!*

roll² *n* a list of names, *eg* of pupils in a school *etc*: *There are nine hundred pupils on the roll.*

'roll-call *n* an act of calling names from a list, to find out if anyone is missing *eg* in a prison or school class.

Roman ['rəumən] *adj* **1** connected with Rome,

esp ancient Rome: *Roman coins.* **2** (*no cap*) (of printing) in ordinary upright letters like these. – *n* a person belonging to Rome, *esp* to ancient Rome.

Roman alphabet the alphabet in which Western European languages such as English are written.

Roman Catholic (*also* **Catholic**) (a member) of the Christian church which recognizes the Pope as its head.

Roman Catholicism (*also* **Catholicism**) the beliefs, government *etc* of the Roman Catholic Church.

Roman numerals I, II, III *etc*, as opposed to the Arabic numerals 1, 2, 3 *etc.*

romance [rə'mans] *n* **1** the relationship, actions *etc* of people who are in love: *It was a beautiful romance, but it didn't last.* **2** a story about such a relationship *etc, esp* one in which the people, events, *etc* are more exciting *etc* than in normal life: *She writes romances.* **3** this kind of excitement: *She felt her life was lacking in romance.*

ro'mantic [-tik] *adj* **1** (*neg* **un-**) (of a story) about people who are in love: *a romantic novel.* **2** causing or feeling love, *esp* the beautiful love described in a romance: *Her husband is very romantic – he brings her flowers every day*; *romantic music.* **3** too concerned with love and excitement: *Her head is full of romantic notions.* **ro'mantically** *adv.*

romp [romp] *v* **1** to play in a lively way, *esp* by running about, jumping *etc*: *The children and their dog were romping about on the grass.* **2** to progress quickly and easily: *Some people find these problems difficult but he just romps through them.* – *n* the act of romping: *The children had a romp in the grass.*

roof [ru:f] *n* the top covering of a building *etc*: *a flat roof*; *a tiled roof*; *the roof of a car.* – *v* to cover with a roof: *They'll finish roofing the house next week.*

go through the roof/hit the roof to become very angry.

roof of the mouth the upper part of the mouth.

rook [ruk] *n* **1** a kind of crow. **2** (*usu* **'castle**) a chess-piece.

room [ru:m] (*in cmpds* rum, (*Amer*) ru:m)] *n* **1** one part of a house or building, *usu* used for a particular purpose: *This house has six rooms*; *a bedroom*; *a dining-room.* **2** the space or area in which a person, thing *etc* is or could be put *etc*: *The bed takes up a lot of room*; *There's no room for you in our car*; *We'll move the bookcase to make room for the television.* **3** a need or possibility (for something): *There is room for improvement in his work.*

-roomed: *a four-roomed house.*

rooms *n pl* a set of rented rooms for living in.
'roomy *adj* having plenty of room: *roomy cupboards.*

'room-mate *n* a person who shares a room with another person *eg* in a hostel for students *etc.*

roost [ru:st] *n* a branch *etc* on which a bird rests at night. – *v* (of birds) to sit or sleep on a roost.

'rooster *n* (*esp Amer*) a farmyard cock.

rule the roost to be the person in a group, family *etc* whose orders, wishes *etc* are obeyed.

root[1] [ru:t] *n* **1** the part of a plant that grows under the ground and draws food and water from the soil: *Trees often have deep roots*; *Carrots and turnips are edible roots.* **2** the base of something growing in the body: *the roots of one's hair/teeth.* **3** cause; origin: *Love of money is the root of all evil*; *We must get at the root of the trouble.* **4** (in *pl*) family origins: *Our roots are in Scotland.* – *v* to (make something) grow roots: *These plants aren't rooting very well*; *He rooted the plants in compost.*

root beer a kind of non-alcoholic drink made from the roots of certain plants.

root crop plants with roots that are grown for food: *The farm has three fields of root crops.*

root out 1 to pull up or tear out by the roots: *The gardener began to root out the weeds.* **2** to get rid of completely: *We must do our best to root out poverty.*

take root to grow firmly; to become established: *The plants soon took root.*

root[2] [ru:t] *v* **1** to poke about in the ground: *The pigs were rooting about for food.* **2** to search by turning things over *etc*: *She rooted about in the cupboard.*

rope [roup] *n* (a) thick cord, made by twisting together lengths of hemp, nylon *etc*: *He tied it with a (piece of) rope*; *a skipping rope.* – *v* **1** to tie or fasten with a rope: *He roped the suitcase to the roof of the car.* **2** to catch with a rope; to lasso: *to rope a calf.*

,rope-'ladder *n* a ladder made of rope.

rope in to include; to persuade to join in: *We roped him in to help.*

rope off to put a rope round or across (a place) in order to prevent people going in: *The end of the room was roped off for the most important guests.*

rosary ['rouzəri] – *pl* **'rosaries** – *n* (a string of beads representing) a group of prayers, used by Roman Catholics.

rose[1] [rouz] *n* **1** a kind of brightly-coloured, *usu* sweet-scented flower, *usu* with sharp thorns. **2** (*also adj*) (of) a pink colour: *Her dress was pale rose.*

rosette [rə'zet, (*Amer*) rou-] *n* a badge or

decoration in the shape of a rose, made of coloured ribbon *etc.*

'rosy *adj* **1** rose-coloured; pink: *rosy cheeks.* **2** bright; hopeful: *His future looks rosy.*
'rosily *adv.* **'rosiness** *n.*

'rosewood *n, adj* (of) a dark wood used for making furniture: *a rosewood cabinet.*

look at/see through rose-coloured spectacles/glasses to take an over-optimistic view of.

rose[2] *see* **rise.**

rosette *see* **rose**[1].

rosin ['rozin] *n* the hardened resin of some trees, used on the bows of stringed musical instruments.

roster ['rostə] *n* a list showing the work, duties *etc* that people are to do: *a duty roster.*

rostrum ['rostrəm] *n* a platform on which a public speaker stands.

rosy *see* **rose**[1].

rot [rot] – *pt, ptp* **'rotted** – *v* to make or become bad or decayed: *The fruit is rotting on the ground*; *Water rots wood.* – *n* **1** decay: *The floorboards are affected by rot.* **2** nonsense: *Don't talk rot!*

'rotten *adj* **1** (of meat, fruit *etc*) having gone bad; decayed: *rotten vegetables.* **2** bad; mean: *What rotten luck!*; *It was a rotten thing to do.* **'rottenness** *n.*

'rotter *n* a mean, bad person: *an absolute rotter.*

rota ['routə] *n* a list showing duties that are to be done in turn, and the names of the people who are to do them.

rotary ['routəri] *adj* turning like a wheel: *a rotary movement.*

rotate [rə'teit, (*Amer*) 'routeit] *v* to turn like a wheel: *He rotated the handle*; *The earth rotates.* **ro'tation** *n.*

rotor ['routə] *n* the rotating part of an engine, *esp* the blades of a helicopter.

rotten, rotter *see* **rot.**

rouble ['ru:bl] *n* the standard unit of Russian currency.

rough [rʌf] *adj* **1** not smooth: *Her skin felt rough.* **2** uneven: *a rough path.* **3** harsh; unpleasant: *a rough voice*; *She's had a rough time since her husband died.* **4** noisy and violent: *rough behaviour.* **5** stormy: *The sea was rough*; *rough weather.* **6** not complete or exact; approximate: *a rough drawing*; *a rough idea/estimate.* – *n* **1** a violent bully: *a gang of roughs.* **2** uneven or uncultivated ground on a golf course: *I lost my ball in the rough.*

'roughly *adv.* **'roughness** *n.*

'roughage [-fidʒ] *n* substances in food, *eg* bran or fibre, which help digestion.

'roughen *v* to make or become rough: *The sea roughened as the wind rose.*

rough diamond a person of fine character but rough manners.

,rough-and-'ready *adj* **1** not carefully made

or finished, but good enough: *a rough-and-ready meal.* **2** (of people) friendly enough but without politeness *etc.*

,rough-and-'tumble *n* friendly fighting between children *etc.*

rough out to draw or explain roughly: *I roughed out a diagram; He roughed out his plan.*

roulette [ru'let] *n* a game of chance, played with a ball on a revolving wheel.

round [raund] *adj* **1** shaped like a circle or globe: *a round hole; a round stone; This plate isn't quite round.* **2** rather fat; plump: *a round face.* – *adv* **1** in the opposite direction: *He turned round.* **2** in a circle: *They all stood round and listened; A wheel goes round; All (the) year round.* **3** from one person to another: *They passed the letter round; The news went round.* **4** from place to place: *We drove round for a while.* **5** in circumference: *The tree measured two metres round.* **6** to a particular place, *usu* a person's home: *Are you coming round (to our house) tonight?* – *prep* **1** on all sides of: *There was a wall round the garden; He looked round the room.* **2** passing all sides of (and returning to the starting-place): *They ran round the tree.* **3** changing direction at: *He came round the corner.* **4** in or to all parts of: *The news spread all round the town.* – *n* **1** a complete circuit: *a round of drinks* (= one for everyone present); *a round of golf.* **2** a regular journey one takes to do one's work: *a postman's round.* **3** a burst of cheering, shooting *etc*: *They gave him a round of applause; The soldier fired several rounds.* **4** a single bullet, shell *etc*: *five hundred rounds of ammunition.* **5** a stage in a competition *etc*: *The winners of the first round will go through to the next.* **6** a type of song sung by several singers singing the same tune starting in succession. – *v* to go round: *The car rounded the corner.*

'rounded *adj* curved; like part of the line forming a circle: *a rounded arch.*

'roundly *adv* plainly; rudely: *He rebuked her roundly.*

'roundness *n.*

rounds *n pl* a doctor's visits to his patients: *The doctor is (out) on his rounds.*

'all-round *adj* complete: *It was an all-round success.*

,all-'rounder *n* a person who has a talent for several different kinds of work, sport *etc*, or who can play in any position in a game.

'roundabout *n* **1** a revolving machine on which one can ride for pleasure; a merry-go-round. **2** a circular piece of ground where several roads meet, and round which traffic must travel. – *adj* not direct: *a roundabout route.*

round figures/numbers the nearest conveni-

ent or easily remembered numbers: *Tell me the cost in round figures (ie* $20 *rather than* $19.87).

,round-'shouldered *adj* with stooping shoulders.

round trip 1 (*Amer*) a journey to a place and back again (**round-trip ticket** a ticket for such a journey). **2** a trip to several places and back, taking a circular route.

all round surrounding: *There were people all round him.*

round about 1 surrounding: *She sat with her children round about her.* **2** near: *There are not many houses round about.* **3** approximately: *There must have been round about a thousand people there.*

round off 1 to make something smooth *etc*: *He rounded off the sharp corners with a file.* **2** to complete successfully: *He rounded off his career by becoming president.*

round on to turn to face (a person) suddenly, *esp* angrily.

round up to collect together: *The farmer rounded up the sheep* (*n* **'round-up**).

rouse [rauz] *v* **1** to awaken: *I'll rouse you at 6 o'clock.* **2** to stir or excite: *Her interest was roused by what he said.*

'rousing *adj* stirring; exciting: *a rousing speech.*

rout [raut] *v* to defeat (an army *etc*) completely. – *n* a complete defeat.

route [ru:t] *n* a way of getting somewhere; a road: *Our route took us through the mountains.* – *v* to arrange a route for: *Heavy traffic was routed round the outside of the town.*

route march a long march for soldiers in training.

routine [ru:'ti:n] *n* a regular, fixed way of doing things: *one's daily routine; One needs some routine.* – *adj* regular; ordinary: *routine work.*

rove [rouv] *v* to wander; to roam: *He roved (through) the streets.* **'rover** *n.*

'roving *adj*: *a roving band of robbers.*

row¹ [rou] *n* a line: *two rows of houses; They were sitting in a row; They sat in the front row in the theatre.*

row² [rou] *v* **1** to move (a boat) through the water using oars: *He rowed (the dinghy) up the river.* **2** to transport by rowing: *He rowed them across the lake.* – *n* a trip in a rowing-boat: *They went for a row on the river.*

'rower *n* a person who rows; an oarsman.

'rowing-boat, 'row-boat *ns* a boat which is moved by oars.

row³ [rau] *n* **1** a noisy quarrel: *They had a terrible row; a family row.* **2** a continuous loud noise: *They heard a row in the street.*

rowdy ['raudi] *adj* noisy and rough: *rowdy children.* **'rowdily** *adv.* **'rowdiness** *n.*

royal ['rɔiəl] *adj* 1 of, concerning *etc* a king, queen *etc*: the *royal family*; *His Royal Highness Prince Charles*. 2 magnificent: *a royal feast*. **'royally** *adv*.

'royalist *n* a person who supports a king or queen: *The republicans fought the royalists*.

'royalty – *pl* **'royalties** – *n* 1 a payment made to a writer, recording artist *etc* for every book, record *etc* sold. 2 the state of being royal, or royal people in general: *The commands of royalty must be obeyed*.

royal blue (of) a bright, darkish blue: *a royal-blue dress*.

rub [rʌb] – *pt*, *ptp* **rubbed** – *v* to move against the surface of something else, pressing at the same time: *He rubbed his eyes*; *The horse rubbed its head against my shoulder*; *The back of the shoe is rubbing against my heel*. – *n* an act of rubbing: *He gave the teapot a rub with a polishing cloth*.

rub down to dry (a horse) after exercise by rubbing.

rub it in to keep reminding someone of something unpleasant.

rub out to remove (a mark, writing *etc*) with a rubber; to erase.

rub shoulders with to meet or mix with (other people).

rub up to polish: *She rubbed up the silver*.

rub up the wrong way to annoy or irritate (someone).

rubber ['rʌbə] *n* 1 (*also adj*) (of) a strong elastic substance made from the juice of certain plants (*esp* the **rubber tree**), or an artificial substitute for this: *Tyres are made of rubber*; *rubber boots*. 2 (*also* **e'raser**) a piece of rubber used to rub out pencil *etc* marks: *a pencil, a ruler and a rubber*.

'rubbery *adj* like rubber.

rubber band an elastic band.

rubber stamp an instrument with rubber figures, letters *etc* which is used to stamp a name, date *etc* on books or papers.

rubbish ['rʌbiʃ] *n* 1 waste material; things that have been or are to be thrown away: *Our rubbish is taken away twice a week*; (*also adj*) *a rubbish bin/bag*. 2 nonsense: *Don't talk rubbish!*

rubble ['rʌbl] *n* small pieces of stone, brick *etc*.

ruby ['ru:bi] – *pl* **'rubies** – *n* 1 a kind of deep red precious stone: *a ring set with rubies*; (*also adj*) *a ruby necklace*. 2 (*also adj*) (of) its colour: *a ruby dress*.

rucksack ['rʌksak] *n* a type of bag carried on the back by walkers, climbers *etc*.

rudder ['rʌdə] *n* 1 a flat piece of wood, metal *etc* fixed to the back of a boat for steering. 2 a similar piece on an aircraft.

ruddy ['rʌdi] *adj* 1 (of the face) rosy and showing good health: *ruddy cheeks*. 2 red: *The sky was filled with a ruddy glow*.

rude [ru:d] *adj* 1 not polite; showing bad manners: *rude behaviour*. 2 vulgar; indecent: *rude pictures*. **'rudely** *adv*. **'rudeness** *n*.

'rudiments ['ru:dimənts] *n pl* the first simple facts or rules of anything: *to learn the rudiments of cookery*.

rudi'mentary [-'men-] *adj* primitive or undeveloped: *rudimentary tools*.

rueful ['ru:ful] *adj* regretful; sorrowful. **'ruefully** *adv*. **'ruefulness** *n*.

ruffian ['rʌfiən] *n* a violent, brutal person: *He was attacked by a gang of ruffians*.

ruffle ['rʌfl] *v* to make wrinkled or uneven, *esp* hair, feathers *etc*: *The wind ruffled her hair*; *The bird ruffled its feathers in anger*.

rug [rʌg] *n* 1 a mat for the floor; a small carpet. 2 (*also* **'travelling-rug**) a thick *usu* patterned blanket for keeping one warm when travelling.

***Rugby, rugby** ['rʌgbi] *n* (*also* **Rugby/rugby football**: *abbrev* **rugger** ['rʌgə]) a kind of football using an oval ball which can be carried.

rugged ['rʌgid] *adj* 1 rocky; uneven: *rugged mountains*. 2 strong; tough: *a rugged character*; *He had rugged good looks*; *He is tall and rugged*. **'ruggedly** *adv*. **'ruggedness** *n*.

rugger ['rʌgə] *see* **Rugby/rugby**.

ruin ['ru:in] *n* 1 a broken, collapsed or decayed state: *the ruin of a city*. 2 a cause of collapse, decay *etc*: *Drink was his ruin*. 3 financial disaster; complete loss of money: *The company is facing ruin*. – *v* 1 to cause ruin to: *The scandal ruined his career*. 2 to spoil; to treat too indulgently: *You are ruining that child!* **,rui'nation** *n*.

'ruined *adj* 1 collapsed; decayed: *ruined houses*. 2 completely spoiled: *My dress is ruined!*

'ruins *n pl* collapsed and decayed buildings: *the ruins of the castle*.

in ruins in a ruined state: *The town lay in ruins*.

rule [ru:l] *n* 1 government: *under foreign rule*. 2 a regulation or order: *school rules*. 3 what usually happens or is done; a general principle: *He is an exception to the rule that fat people are usually happy*. 4 a general standard that guides one's actions: *I make it a rule never to be late for appointments*. 5 a marked strip of wood, metal *etc* for measuring: *He measured the windows with a rule*. – *v* 1 to govern: *The king ruled (the people) wisely*. 2 to decide officially: *The judge ruled that the witness should be heard*. 3 to draw (a straight line): *He ruled a line across the page*.

ruled *adj* having straight lines drawn across: *ruled paper*.

'ruler *n* 1 a person who governs: *the ruler of the state*. 2 a long narrow piece of wood, plastic *etc* for drawing straight lines: *I can't draw straight lines without a ruler*.

* see illustration on p. 206

'ruling *adj* governing: *the ruling party.* – *n* an official decision: *The judge gave his ruling.*

as a rule usually: *I don't go out in the evening as a rule.*

rule off to draw a line in order to separate: *He ruled off the rest of the page.*

rule out to leave out; not to consider: *We mustn't rule out the possibility of bad weather.*

rum [rʌm] *n* a type of alcoholic drink, a spirit made from sugar cane: *a bottle of rum.*

rumba ['rʌmbə] *n* (a piece of music for) a South American dance.

rumble ['rʌmbl] *v* to make a low grumbling sound: *Thunder rumbled in the distance.* – *n* this kind of sound: *the rumble of thunder.*

rummage ['rʌmidʒ] *v* to search by turning things out or over: *He rummaged in the drawer for a clean shirt.* – *n* a thorough search.

rumour, (*Amer*) **rumor** ['ruːmə] *n* 1 a piece of news or a story passed from person to person, which may not be true: *I heard a rumour that you had got a new job.* 2 general talk or gossip: *Don't listen to rumour.*

rump [rʌmp] *n* the hind part of an animal's body.

rumpus ['rʌmpəs] *n* a noisy disturbance; an uproar.

run [rʌn] *n* –*prp* '**running**: *pt* **ran** [ran]: *ptp* **run** – *v* 1 (of a person or animal) to move quickly, faster than walking: *He ran down the road.* 2 to move smoothly: *Trains run on rails.* 3 (of water *etc*) to flow: *Rivers run to the sea*; *The tap is running.* 4 (of a machine *etc*) to work or operate: *The engine is running*; *He ran the motor to see if it was working.* 5 to organize or manage: *He runs the business very efficiently.* 6 to race: *Is your horse running this afternoon?* 7 (of buses, trains *etc*) to travel regularly: *The buses run every half hour*; *The train is running late.* 8 to last or continue; to go on: *The play ran for six weeks.* 9 to own and use, *esp* of cars: *He runs a Rolls Royce.* 10 (of colour) to spread: *When I washed my new dress the colour ran.* 11 to drive (someone); to give (someone) a lift: *He ran me to the station.* 12 to move (something): *She ran her fingers through his hair*; *He ran his eyes over the letter.* 13 (in certain phrases) to be or become: *The river ran dry*; *My blood ran cold* (= I was afraid). – *n* 1 the act of running: *He went for a run before breakfast.* 2 a trip or drive: *We went for a run in the country.* 3 a length of time (for which something continues): *He's had a run of bad luck.* 4 a ladder (in a stocking *etc*): *I've got a run in my tights.* 5 the free use (of a place): *He gave me the run of his house.* 6 in cricket, a batsman's act of running from one end of the wicket to the other, representing a single score: *He scored/made 50 runs*

for his team. 7 an enclosure or pen: *a chicken-run.*

'**runner** *n* 1 a person who runs: *There are five runners in this race.* 2 the long narrow part on which a sledge *etc* moves: *He polished the runners of the sledge.* 3 a long stem of a plant which puts down roots.

'**running** *adj* 1 of or for running: *running shoes.* 2 continuous: *a running commentary on the football match.* – *adv* one after another; continuously: *We travelled for four days running.*

'**runny** *adj* liquid; watery: *Do you like your egg yolk firm or runny?*; *The baby has a runny nose.*

'**runaway** *n* a person, animal *etc* that runs away: *The police caught the two runaways*; (*also adj*) *a runaway horse.*

,**run-'down** *adj* tired or exhausted because one has worked too hard: *He feels run-down.*

,**runner-'up** *n* a person, thing *etc* that is second in a race or competition: *My friend won the prize and I was the runner-up.*

'**runway** *n* a wide path from which aircraft take off and on which they land: *The plane landed on the runway.*

in, out of the running having (no) chance of success: *She's in the running for the job of director.*

on the run escaping; running away: *He's on the run from the police.*

run across to meet: *I ran across an old friend.*

run after to chase: *The dog ran after a cat.*

run aground (of a ship) to become stuck on rocks *etc.*

run along to go away: *Run along now, children!*

run away 1 to escape: *He ran away from school.* 2 (*with* **with**) to steal: *He ran away with all her money.* 3 (*with* **with**) to go too fast *etc* to be controlled by: *The horse ran away with him.*

run down 1 (of a clock, battery *etc*) to finish working: *My watch has run down – it needs rewinding.* 2 (of a vehicle or driver) to knock down: *I was run down by a bus.* 3 to speak badly of: *He is always running me down.*

run for to stand for election for: *He is running for president.*

run for it to try to escape: *Quick – run for it!*

run in to get (a new engine *etc*) working properly.

run into 1 to meet: *I ran into her in the street.* 2 to crash into or collide with: *The car ran into a lamp-post.*

run its course to develop or happen in the usual way: *The fever ran its course.*

run off 1 to print or copy: *I want 500 copies run off at once.* 2 (*with* **with**) to steal or take away: *He ran off with my wife.*

run out 1 (of a supply) to come to an end: *The food has run out.* 2 (*with* **of**) to have no more: *We've run out of money.* **3** in cricket, to put (a batsman) out by getting the ball to the end of the wicket before he reaches it when he is making a run.

run over 1 (of a vehicle or driver) to knock down or drive over: *Don't let the dog out of the garden or he'll get run over.* **2** to repeat for practice: *Let's run over the plan again.*

run a temperature to have a fever.

run through to look at, deal with *etc*, one after another: *He ran through their instructions.*

run to to have enough money for: *We can't run to a new car this year.*

run up 1 to hoist (a flag). **2** to make quickly or roughly: *I can run up a dress in a couple of hours.* **3** to collect up, accumulate (debts): *He ran up an enormous bill.*

run wild to go out of control: *They let their children run wild; The garden was running wild.*

rung[1] [rʌŋ] *n* a step on a ladder: *a missing rung.*

rung[2] *see* **ring**.

runny *see* **run**.

runway *see* **run**.

rupee [ru'pi:] *n* the standard unit of currency in India, Pakistan and Sri Lanka *etc*.

rupture ['rʌptʃə] *n* a tearing or breaking. – *v* to break or tear.

rural ['ruərəl] *adj* of the countryside: *a rural area.*

ruse [ru:z] *n* a clever trick or plan.

rush[1] [rʌʃ] *v* to (make someone or something) hurry or go quickly: *He rushed into the room; She rushed him to the doctor.* – *n* **1** a sudden quick movement: *They made a rush for the door.* **2** a hurry: *I'm in a dreadful rush.*

rush hour a period when there is a lot of traffic on the roads, *usu* when people are going to or leaving work.

rush[2] [rʌʃ] *n* a tall grass-like plant growing in or near water: *They hid their boat in the rushes.*

rust [rʌst] *n* the reddish-brown substance which forms on iron and steel, caused by air and moisture: *The car was covered with rust.* – *v* to (cause to) become covered with rust: *The rain has rusted the gate; There's a lot of old metal rusting in the garden.*

'rustproof *adj* that will not (allow) rust: *rustproof paint.*

'rusty *adj* **1** covered with rust: *a rusty old bicycle.* **2** not as good as it was because of lack of practice: *My French is rusty.* **'rustily** *adv.* **'rustiness** *n.*

rustic ['rʌstik] *adj* **1** of the countryside: *rustic life.* **2** roughly made: *a rustic fence.*

rustle ['rʌsl] *v* **1** to (make something) make a soft, whispering sound: *The wind rustled in the trees; She rustled her papers.* **2** (*Amer*) to steal (cattle *etc*).

'rustler *n* (*Amer*) a person who steals cattle *etc*.

rustle up to get or make quickly: *He rustled up a meal.*

rut [rʌt] *n* a deep track made by a wheel *etc* in soft ground: *The road was full of ruts.*

'rutted *adj* having ruts: *a deeply-rutted path.*

in a rut having a fixed, monotonous way of life: *I felt that I was in a rut, so I changed my job.*

ruthless ['ru:θlis] *adj* without pity: *a ruthless attack; a ruthless tyrant.* **'ruthlessly** *adv.* **'ruthlessness** *n.*

rye [rai] *n* a kind of cereal.

rye bread a kind of bread made with flour made from rye.

Ss

Sabbath ['sabəθ] *n* (*usu with* **the**) a day of the week regularly set aside for religious services and rest – among the Jews, Saturday; among most Christians, Sunday.

saber *see* **sabre**.

sable ['seibl] *n* **1** a kind of small animal found in Arctic regions, valued for its glossy fur. **2** its fur: *Artists' brushes are sometimes made of sable*; (*also adj*) *a sable coat.*

sabotage ['sabəta:ʒ] *n* the deliberate destruction in secret of machinery, bridges, equipment *etc*, by *eg* enemies in wartime, dissatisfied workers *etc*. – *v* to destroy, damage or cause to fail by sabotage.

,sabo'teur [-'tə:] *n* a person who sabotages: *The soldiers shot the three saboteurs.*

sabre, (*Amer*) **saber** ['seibə] *n* a type of curved sword, used by cavalry.

saccharin(e) ['sakərin] *n* a very sweet substance used instead of sugar.

sachet ['saʃei, (*Amer*) sa'ʃei] *n* a (small) sealed packet containing a product in liquid or powder form: *a sachet of shampoo.*

sack[1] [sak] *n* a large bag of coarse cloth, strong paper or plastic: *The potatoes were put into sacks.*

'sacking *n* a type of coarse cloth for making sacks.

'sackcloth *n* a type of coarse cloth formerly worn as a sign of mourning or of sorrow for sin.

sack[2] [sak] *v* to dismiss (a person) from his

job: *One of the workmen was sacked for drunkenness.*

get the sack to be sacked: *I'll get the sack if I arrive at the office late!*

sacrament ['sakrəmənt] *n* in the Christian church, a ceremony regarded as especially sacred, *eg* marriage, or baptism. ,**sacra'mental** [-'men-] *adj.*

sacred ['seikrid] *adj* **1** of God or a god; (that must be respected because) connected with religion or with God or a god: *Temples, mosques, churches and synagogues are all sacred buildings.* **2** (of a duty *etc*) which must be done *etc eg* because of respect for someone: *He considered it a sacred duty to fulfil his dead father's wishes.* '**sacredness** *n.*

nothing is sacred (to him, them *etc*) he, they *etc* have no respect for anything.

sacrifice ['sakrifais] *n* **1** the act of offering something (*eg* an animal that is specially killed) to a god: *A lamb was offered in sacrifice.* **2** the thing that is offered in this way. **3** something of value given away or up in order to gain something more important or to benefit another person: *His parents made sacrifices to pay for his education.* – *v* **1** to offer as a sacrifice: *He sacrificed a sheep in the temple.* **2** to give away *etc* for the sake of something or someone else: *He sacrificed his life trying to save the children from the burning house.* ,**sacri'ficial** [-'fiʃəl] *adj: sacrificial victims.* ,**sacri'ficially** *adv.*

sad [sad] *adj* unhappy or causing unhappiness: *She's sad because her son is ill; a sad face.* '**sadness** *n.*

'**sadden** *v* to make or become sad: *She was saddened by her son's ingratitude.*

'**sadly** *adv: He stared sadly at the ruins of his house.*

saddle ['sadl] *n* a seat for a rider: *The bicycle saddle is too high.* – *v* (*neg* **un-**) to put a saddle on: *He saddled his horse and rode away.*

safari [sə'fɑːri] *n* an expedition or tour, *esp* in Africa, for hunting or observing animals: *A safari was organized to the lion reserve; We often went out on safari.*

safari park a large area of land reserved for wild animals, in which they can move freely and be seen by the public who *usu* drive through the park in cars.

safe¹ [seif] *adj* **1** (*neg* **un-**) protected, or free (from danger *etc*): *The children are safe from danger in the garden.* **2** providing good protection: *You should keep your money in a safe place.* **3** unharmed: *The missing child has been found safe and well.* **4** not likely to cause harm: *These pills are not safe for children.* **5** (of a person) reliable: *a safe driver; He's a very fast driver but he's safe enough.* '**safeness** *n.*

'**safely** *adv* without harm or risk: *He got home safely.*

'**safety** *n* the state of being safe: *I worry about the children's safety on these busy roads; a place of safety;* (*also adj*) **safety goggles; safety helmet.**

'**safeguard** *n* anything that gives security or protection: *a safeguard against burglary.* – *v* to protect: *Put a good lock on your door to safeguard your property.*

'**safety-belt** *n* a fixed belt in a car or aircraft used to keep a passenger from being thrown out of the seat in an accident, crash *etc.*

safety lamp a type of lamp used in mines that does not set fire to any inflammable gases there.

'**safety-pin** *n* a pin that has a cover over its point when it is closed.

safety valve a valve *eg* on a pressure cooker that opens if the pressure of the steam in it becomes too great.

be on the safe side to avoid risk or danger: *I'll lock the door just to be on the safe side.*

safe and sound unharmed: *He returned safe and sound.*

safe² [seif] *n* a heavy metal chest or box in which money *etc* can be locked away safely: *There is a small safe hidden behind that picture on the wall.*

saffron ['safrən] *n* **1** a yellow colouring and flavouring substance used in cooking: *We added some saffron to the rice.* **2** an orange-yellow colour. – Also *adj: Many Buddhist monks wear saffron robes.*

sag [sag] – *pt, ptp* **sagged** – *v* **1** to bend, hang down, *esp* in the middle: *There were so many books on the shelf that it sagged.*

saga ['sɑːɡə] *n* a long, detailed story: *I expect he told you the saga of his troubles.*

sagacious [sə'geiʃəs] *adj* showing intelligence, wisdom and good judgement: *The old priest was learned and sagacious.* **sa'gaciously** *adv.* **sagacity** [sə'gasəti] *n.*

sage¹ [seidʒ] *n* a plant whose leaves are used as flavouring in cooking.

sage² [seidʒ] *n* a wise man: *the sages of past centuries.* – *adj* wise: *sage advice.* '**sagely** *adv.*

sago ['seiɡou] *n* a starchy substance obtained from inside the trunk of certain palm trees. – Also *adj: sago pudding.*

said [sed] *v see* **say.**

sail [seil] *n* **1** a sheet of strong cloth spread to catch the wind, by which a ship is driven forward. **2** a journey in a ship: *a sail in his yacht; a week's sail to the island.* **3** an arm of a windmill. – *v* **1** (of a ship) to be moved by sails: *The yacht sailed away.* **2** to steer or navigate a ship or boat: *He sailed (the boat) to the island.* **3** to go in a ship or boat (with or without sails): *I've never sailed through the Mediterranean.* **4** to begin a voyage:

The ship sails today; *My aunt sailed today.*
5 to travel on (the sea *etc*) in a ship: *He sailed the North Sea.* **6** to move steadily and easily: *Clouds sailed across the sky*; *He sailed through his exams*; *She sailed into the room.*
'**sailing** *n* the activity or sport of navigating a ship or boat that has sails: *Sailing is one of his hobbies.*
sailing- having a sail or sails: *sailing-boat.*
'**sailor** *n* a member of a ship's crew whose job is helping to sail a ship.
in full sail with all the sails spread: *The ship was in full sail.*

saint [seint, (*before a name*) snt] *n* **1** (*often abbrev* St, *esp when used in the names of places, plants etc*) a title given *esp* by the Roman Catholic and Orthodox churches to a very good or holy person after his death: *Saint Matthew*; *St John's Road.* **2** a very good, kind person: *You really are a saint to put up with her.*
'**saintly** *adj*: *He led a saintly life*; *a saintly expression.* '**saintliness** *n*.

sake [seik]: **for the sake of 1** in order to benefit: *He bought a house in the country for the sake of his wife's health.* **2** because of a desire for: *For the sake of peace, he said he agreed with her.*

salad ['saləd] *n* (a dish of) mixed raw vegetables.
fruit salad a mixture of chopped fruits *usu* eaten as a dessert.
salad cream a type of mayonnaise *usu* sold in bottles.
salad dressing a sauce for putting on salad, *usu* consisting of oil and vinegar and sometimes spices.

salary ['saləri] – *pl* '**salaries** – *n* a fixed, regular *usu* monthly payment for work: *Secretarial salaries in London are quite high.*

sale [seil] *n* **1** the act of giving something to someone in exchange for money: *the sale of a house*; *Sales of cars have increased.* **2** in a shop *etc*, an offer of goods at lowered prices for a short time: *I bought my dress in a sale.* **3** an event at which goods are sold: *an auction sale*; *a book sale.*
'**saleroom** *n* a room or building where public auctions are held: *His furniture was taken to the saleroom.*
'**salesman** ['seilz-] – *pl* '**salesmen** – *fem* '**saleswoman** (*pl* '**saleswomen**), '**salesgirl** – *n* a person who sells, or shows, goods to customers in a shop *etc*.
'**salesmanship** ['seilz-] *n* the art of persuading people to buy things.
for sale intended to be sold: *Have you any pictures for sale?*
sale of work an event at which articles *usu* made by members of an association are sold to raise money: *a sale of work at the church.*

salient ['seiliənt] *adj* main; chief; most noticeable: *What were the salient points of his speech?*

saliva [sə'laivə] *n* the liquid that forms in the mouth to help digestion.
salivate ['saliveit] *v* to produce saliva, *esp* in large amounts.

sallow ['salou] *adj* (of a complexion) pale or yellowish, not pink. '**sallowness** *n*.

salmon ['samən] – *pl* '**salmon** – *n* a type of large fish with orange-pink flesh.

salon ['salon, (*Amer*) sə'lon] *n* a name sometimes given to a place where hairdressing *etc* is done: *a beauty-salon*; *My hairdresser has opened a new salon.*

saloon [sə'lu:n] *n* **1** a large public room on a ship: *the dining-saloon.* **2** (*Amer* **se'dan**) a motor car with enclosed seating space for driver and at least three passengers. **3** a place where alcoholic drinks are sold: *The police searched in all the saloons for the thief.*

salt [so:lt] *n* **1** (*also* **common salt**) sodium chloride, a white substance frequently used for seasoning: *The soup needs more salt.* **2** any other substance formed, like common salt, from a metal and an acid. **3** a sailor, *esp* an experienced one: *an old salt.* – *adj* containing, tasting of, preserved in salt: *salt water*; *salt pork.* – *v* to put salt on or in: *Have you salted the potatoes?*
'**salted** *adj* (*neg* **un-**) containing or preserved with salt: *salted butter*; *salted beef.*
'**saltness** *n*.
'**salty** *adj* containing or tasting of salt: *Tears are salty water.* '**saltiness** *n*.
take (something) with a grain/pinch of salt to receive (a statement, news *etc*) with a slight feeling of disbelief: *I took his story with a pinch of salt.*

salute [sə'lu:t] *v* **1** (*esp* in the forces) to raise the (*usu* right) hand to the forehead to show respect: *They saluted their commanding officer.* **2** to honour by firing *eg* large guns: *They saluted the Queen by firing one hundred guns.* – *n* an act of saluting: *The officer gave a salute*; *a 21-gun salute.*

salvage ['salvidʒ] *v* **1** to save from loss or destruction in a fire, shipwreck *etc*: *He salvaged his books from the burning house.* – *n* **1** the act of salvaging. **2** property *etc* which has been salvaged: *Was there any salvage from the wreck?*

salvation [sal'veiʃən] *n* **1** in religion, the freeing of a person from sin or the saving of his soul. **2** the cause, means, or act of saving: *This delay was the salvation of the army.*

same [seim] *adj* (*usu with* **the**) **1** alike; very similar: *The houses in this road are all the same*; *You have the same eyes as your* *brother* (*has*). **2** not different: *My friend and I are the same age*; *He went to the same school as me.* **3** unchanged: *My opinion is the same as it always was.* – *pron* (*usu with* **the**) the same thing: *He sat down and we all did the same.* – *adv* (*usu with* **the**) in the same way: *I don't feel the same about you as I did.*

all/just the same nevertheless: *I'm sure I locked the door, but, all the same, I think I'll go and check.*

at the same time 1 together. **2** nevertheless: *Mountain-climbing is fun, but at the same time we must not forget the danger.*

be all the same to to be a matter of no importance to: *I'll leave now, if it's all the same to you.*

same here I think, feel *etc* the same: *'This job bores me.' 'Same here.'*

samfoo ['samfu:] *n* a Chinese woman's costume consisting of a short, close-fitting jacket and long trousers.

sampan ['sampan] *n* a small flat-bottomed Chinese boat.

sample ['sa:mpl] *n* a part taken from something to show the quality of the whole: *samples of the artist's work*; (*also adj*) *a sample tube of ointment.* – *v* to test a sample of: *He sampled my cake.*

samsu ['samsu:] *n* a Chinese alcoholic drink made from rice or millet.

sanatorium [sanə'to:riəm] – *pls* ,**sana'toriums**, ,**sana'toria** [-riə] – *n* **1** (*Amer also* ,**sani'tarium**) a hospital, *esp* for people with certain diseases of the lungs or for people who are recovering from an illness. **2** a place in a school, college *etc* for those who are ill.

sanctify ['saŋktifai] *v* to make sacred, holy or free from sin. ,**sanctifi'cation** [-fi-] *n.*

sanction ['saŋkʃən] *n* permission or approval: *The soldier's action did not have the sanction of his commanding officer.* – *v* to permit or agree to: *We cannot sanction the use of force.*

sanctuary ['saŋktʃuəri] – *pl* '**sanctuaries** – *n* **1** a holy or sacred place: *the sanctuary of the god Apollo.* **2** a place of safety from *eg* arrest: *In earlier times a criminal could use a church as a sanctuary.* **3** an area of land in which the killing of wild animals *etc* - is forbidden: *a bird sanctuary.*

sand [sand] *n* **1** a large amount of tiny particles of crushed rocks, shells *etc,* found on beaches *etc.* **2** an area of sand, *esp* on a beach: *We lay on the sand.* – *v* to smooth with *eg* sand-paper: *The floor should be sanded before you varnish it.*
'**sandy** *adj* **1** filled or covered with sand: *a sandy beach.* **2** (of hair) yellowish-red in colour: *She has fair skin and sandy hair.*

sandbank ['sanbaŋk] *n* a bank of sand formed by tides and currents.

sandcastle ['sanka:sl] *n* a pile of sand, sometimes made to look like a castle, built *esp* by children on beaches.

sandpaper ['sanpeipə] *n* a type of paper with sand glued to it, used for smoothing and polishing. – *v* to make smooth with sandpaper.

sandshoes ['sanʃu:z] *n pl* soft light shoes, often with rubber soles.

sandstone ['sanstoun] *n* a soft type of rock made of layers of sand pressed together.

sand-storm ['sansto:m] *n* a storm of wind, carrying with it clouds of sand: *We were caught in a sandstorm in the desert.*

sandal ['sandl] *n* a type of light shoe, the sole of which is held on to the foot by straps: *a pair of sandals.*

sandwich ['sanwidʒ, (*Amer*) -witʃ] *n* **1** slices of bread *etc* with food between: *cheese sandwiches.* – *v* to place or press between two objects *etc*: *His car was sandwiched between two lorries.*

sane [sein] *adj* **1** not mad: *in a perfectly sane state of mind.* **2** sensible: *a very sane person.* '**sanely** *adv.*
'**sanity** ['sa-] *n* the state or quality of being sane: *I am concerned about her sanity.*

sang *see* **sing.**

sanitarium [sani'teəriəm] – *pls* ,**sani'tariums**, ,**sani'taria** – *n* (*Amer*) a sanatorium.

sanitary ['sanitəri] *adj* **1** of or concerning conditions or arrangements that encourage good health. **2** free from dirt and germs: *The conditions in that camp are not sanitary.*
,**sani'tation** *n* the arrangements for protecting health, *esp* drainage.

sanity *see* **sane.**

sank *see* **sink.**

sap[1] [sap] *n* the liquid in trees, plants *etc*: *The sap flowed out when he broke the stem of the flower.*

sap[2] [sap] – *pt, ptp* **sapped** – *v* to weaken or destroy (a person's strength, confidence, courage *etc*): *The disease slowly sapped his strength.*

sapling ['sapliŋ] *n* a young tree.

sapphire ['safaiə] *n* a kind of dark-blue precious stone: *a gold brooch set with a sapphire*; (*also adj*) *a sapphire ring.*

sarcasm ['sa:kazəm] *n* (the use of) unpleasant remarks intended to hurt a person's feelings.
sar'castic [-'kas-] *adj* containing, or using, sarcasm: *a sarcastic person.* **sar'castically** *adv.*

sardine [sa:'di:n] *n* a young pilchard, often packed in oil in small tins.

sari ['sa:ri:] *n* a garment worn by Hindu women, a long cloth wrapped round the waist and passed over the shoulder.

sarong [sə'roŋ], in Singapore and Malaysia **sarung** n a kind of skirt worn by Malay men and women.

sash[1] [saʃ] n a broad band of cloth worn round the waist, or over one shoulder: *a white dress with a red sash at the waist.*

sash[2] [saʃ] n a frame fitted with glass, forming part of a window: *the lower sash.*

sat see **sit**.

Satan ['seitən] n the Devil; the spirit of evil. **satanic** [sə'tanik, (*Amer*) sei-] adj.

satay ['satei] n small pieces of flavoured meat, skewered and roasted or broiled on a spit.

satchel ['satʃəl] n small bag for schoolbooks etc.

satellite ['satəlait] n **1** a smaller body that revolves around a planet: *The Moon is a satellite of the Earth.* **2*** a man-made object fired into space to travel round *usu* the Earth: *a weather satellite.* **3** a state *etc* controlled by a more powerful neighbouring state: *Russia and her satellites.*

satin ['satin] n a closely woven type of silk with a shiny surface: *The baby's skin was as smooth as satin*; (*also adj*) *a satin dress.*

satire ['sataiə] n (a piece of) writing *etc* that makes someone look foolish: *a satire on university life.*
sa'tirical [-'ti-] adj **1** of satire: *satirical writing.* **2** mocking: *in a satirical mood.*
'satirist [-'ti-] a person who writes or performs satire(s).
'satirize, -ise [-'ti-] v to make look foolish by using satire.

satisfy ['satisfai] v **1** to give (a person) enough of what is wanted or needed to take away hunger, curiosity *etc*: *The apple didn't satisfy my hunger; I told him enough to satisfy his curiosity.* **2** to please: *She is very difficult to satisfy.*
,satis'faction [-'fakʃən] n **1** the act of satisfying or state of being satisfied: *the satisfaction of desires.* **2** pleasure or contentment: *Your success gives me great satisfaction.*
,satis'factory [-'faktəri] adj (*neg* un-) giving satisfaction; good enough to satisfy: *Your work is not satisfactory; The condition of the sick man is satisfactory.* **,satis'factorily** [-'faktə-] adv.
'satisfied adj (*sometimes with* with) pleased: *I'm satisfied with his progress; a satisfied customer.*
'satisfying adj pleasing: *The story had a satisfying ending.*

saturate ['satʃəreit] v **1** to make very wet: *Saturate the earth round the plants.* **2** to fill completely: *The market has been saturated with paintings like that.* **satu'ration** n.

Saturday ['satədei] n the seventh day of the week, the day following Friday: *I'll see you on Saturday*; (*also adj*) *on Saturday morning.*

sauce [so:s] n a *usu* thick liquid that is poured over other food in order to add moisture and flavour: *tomato sauce; an expert at making sauces.*
'saucy adj slightly rude: *a saucy remark.*
'saucily adv. **'sauciness** n.
'saucepan [-pən, (*Amer*) -pan] n a deep pan *usu* with a long handle for boiling or stewing food.

saucer ['so:sə] n a small shallow dish for placing under a cup: *Could you bring me another cup and saucer?*

saucy see **sauce**.

sauna ['so:nə] n (a building or room equipped for) a Finnish form of steam bath: *They have a sauna in their house; They had a refreshing sauna.*

saunter ['so:ntə] v (*often with* along, off, past *etc*) to walk or stroll about without much purpose or hurry: *I was working in the garden when he sauntered by.* – n a walk or stroll.

sausage ['sosidʒ] n (a section of) minced meat seasoned and pushed into a tube of animal gut or a similar material: *We had sausages for breakfast; garlic sausage.*
,sausage-'roll n a piece of sausage meat cooked in a roll of pastry: *They had sausage-rolls at the children's party.*

savage ['savidʒ] adj **1** uncivilized: *savage tribes.* **2** fierce and cruel: *The elephant can be quite savage; bitter and savage remarks.* – v to attack: *He was savaged by wild animals.* – n **1** a person in an uncivilized state: *tribes of savages.* **2** a person who behaves in a cruel, uncivilized way: *I hope the police catch the savages who attacked the old lady.*
'savagely adv. **'savageness, 'savagery** ns.

savanna(h) [sə'vanə] n a grassy plain with few trees: *the savanna(h)s of Central America.*

save[1] [seiv] v **1** to rescue or bring out of danger: *He saved his friend from drowning; The house was burnt but he saved the pictures.* **2** to keep (money *etc*) for future use: *He's saving (his money) to buy a bicycle; They're saving for a house.* **3** to prevent the using or wasting of (money, time, energy *etc*): *Frozen foods save a lot of trouble; I'll telephone and that will save me writing a letter.* **4** in football *etc*, to prevent the opposing team from scoring a goal: *The goalkeeper saved six goals.* **5** to free from the power of sin and evil. – n (in football *etc*) an act of preventing the opposing team from scoring a goal.
'saver n a person or thing that saves, avoids waste *etc*: *The telephone is a great time-saver.*
'saving n a way of saving money *etc* or the

amount saved in this way: *It's a great saving to be able to make one's own clothes.*

'savings *n pl* money saved up: *He keeps his savings in the bank.*

saviour, (*Amer*) **savior** ['seivjə] *n* **1** (*usu with cap*) a person or god who saves people from sin, hell *etc*. **2** a person who rescues a person *etc* from danger *etc*: *He was the saviour of his country.*

saving grace a good quality that makes up for a fault: *His speeches are boring but they have the saving grace of being short.*

savings account an account in a bank or post office on which interest is paid.

savings bank a bank that receives small savings and gives interest.

save up to save: *He's been saving up for a new bike.*

save² [seiv] *prep, conj* except: *All save him had gone; We have no news save that the ship reached port safely.*

savour, (*Amer*) **savor** ['seivə] *v* to eat, drink *usu* slowly in order to appreciate taste or quality: *He savoured the delicious soup.*

'savoury *adj* having a *usu* salty or sharp, but not sweet, taste or smell: *a savoury omelette.* – *n* something savoury served with *eg* alcoholic drinks.

savour of to have a suggestion or give an impression of (*usu* something bad): *Their action savours of rebellion.*

saw¹ *see* see.

saw² [so:] *n* a tool for cutting, having a toothed edge: *He used a saw to cut through the branch.* – *v* – *pt* **sawed**: *ptps* **sawn, sawed** – to cut with a saw: *He sawed the log in two.*

'sawdust *n* a dust of tiny fragments of wood, made by sawing.

'sawmill *n* a place in which wood is mechanically sawn. – Also *adj*: *a sawmill worker.*

saxophone ['saksəfoun] *n* a type of musical instrument with a curved metal tube, played by blowing. **saxophonist** [sak'sofənist] *n*.

say [sei] – *3rd pers sing prt* **says** [sez] – *pt, ptp* **said** [sed] – *v* **1** to speak or utter: *What did you say?; She said 'Yes'.* **2** to tell, state or declare: *She said how she had enjoyed meeting me; She is said to be very beautiful.* **3** to repeat: *The child says her prayers every night.* **4** to guess or estimate: *I can't say when he'll return.* – *n* the right or opportunity to state one's opinion: *I haven't had my say yet; We have no say in the decision.*

'saying *n* something often said, *esp* a proverb *etc*.

have (something, nothing *etc*) **to say for oneself** to be able/unable to explain one's actions *etc*: *Your work is very careless – what have you to say for yourself?*

I wouldn't say no to I would like: *I wouldn't say no to an ice-cream.*

(**let's**) **say** roughly; approximately; about: *You'll arrive there in, (let's) say, three hours.*

that is to say in other words; I mean: *He was here last Thursday, that's to say the 4th of June.*

scab [skab] *n* **1** a crust formed over a sore or wound. **2** any of several diseases of animals or plants. **3** a workman who refuses to join a strike. **'scabby** *adj*.

scabbard ['skabəd] *n* a case in which the blade of a sword is kept.

scaffold ['skafəld] *n* a raised platform *esp* for use formerly when putting a criminal *etc* to death.

'scaffolding *n* an erection of metal poles and wooden planks used by men at work on (the outside of) a building.

scald [sko:ld] *v* **1** to hurt with hot liquid or steam: *He scalded his hand with boiling water.* **2** in cooking, to heat (*eg* milk) to just below boiling-point. – *n* a hurt caused by hot liquid or steam.

'scalding *adj* (of a liquid) hot enough to scald.

scale¹ [skeil] *n* **1** a set of regularly spaced marks made on something (*eg* a thermometer or a ruler) for use as a measure; a system of numbers, measurement *etc*: *This thermometer has two scales marked on it, one in Fahrenheit and one in Centigrade.* **2** a series or system of items of increasing or decreasing size, value *etc*: *a wage/salary scale.* **3** in music, a group of notes going up or down in order: *The boy practised his scales on the piano.* **4** the size of measurements on a map *etc* compared with the real size of the country *etc* shown by it: *In a map drawn to the scale 1 : 50 000, one centimetre represents half a kilometre.* **5** the size of an activity: *These guns are being manufactured on a large scale.*

scale² [skeil] *v* to climb (a ladder, cliff *etc*): *The prisoner scaled the prison walls and escaped.*

scale³ [skeil] *n* any of the small thin plates or flakes that cover the skin of fishes, reptiles *etc*: *A herring's scales are silver in colour.* **'scaly** *adj* (of fish *etc*) covered with scales.

scales [skeilz] *n pl* a *usu* small weighing-machine: *kitchen scales; a set of scales.*

scallop, *also* **scollop** ['skoləp] *n* an edible shellfish that has a pair of hinged, fan-shaped shells.

'scalloped *adj* (of the edge of a garment *etc*) cut into curves and notches: *The collar of the blouse has a scalloped edge.*

scalp [skalp] *n* **1** the skin of the part of the head usually covered by hair: *Rub the shampoo well into your scalp.* **2** the skin and hair of the top of the head: *Some North American Indians used to cut the scalps from* *their prisoners.* − *v* to cut the scalp from: *The Indians killed and scalped him.*

scalpel ['skalpəl] *n* a small knife with a thin blade, used in surgical operations.

scaly *see* scale³.

scamper ['skampə] *v* to run quickly and lightly: *The mouse scampered away when it saw me.*

scan [skan] − *pt, ptp* **scanned** − *v* **1** to examine carefully: *He scanned the horizon for any sign of a ship.* **2** to look at quickly but not in detail: *She scanned the newspaper for news of the murder.* **3** to pass radar beams *etc* over: *The area was scanned for signs of enemy aircraft.* **4** to fit into a particular rhythm or metre: *The second line of that verse doesn't scan properly.*

'**scanner** *n* a machine *etc* that scans.

scandal ['skandl] *n* **1** something that is considered shocking or disgraceful: *The price of such food is a scandal.* **2** an outburst of public indignation caused by something shocking or disgraceful: *Her love affair caused a great scandal amongst the neighbours; They kept the matter secret, in order to avoid a scandal.* **3** gossip: *all the latest scandal.*

'**scandalize, -ise** *v* to shock or horrify: *Their behaviour used to scandalize the neighbours.*

'**scandalous** *adj* **1** shocking or disgraceful. **2** (of stories *etc*) containing scandal.

'**scandalously** *adv* in a disgraceful way.

scant [skant] *adj* hardly enough; not very much: *scant attention; scant experience.*

'**scanty** *adj* small in size; hardly enough: *scanty clothing.* '**scantiness** *n.*

'**scantily** *adv: scantily dressed.*

scapegoat ['skeipgout] *n* a person who is blamed or punished for the mistakes of others: *The manager of the football team was made a scapegoat for the team's failure, and was forced to resign.*

scar [ska:] *n* the mark that is left by a wound or sore: *a scar on the arm where the dog bit him.* − *v* − *pt, ptp* **scarred** − to mark with a scar: *He recovered from the accident but his face was badly scarred.*

scarce [skeəs] *adj* not many or enough in number: *Paintings by this artist are very scarce; Food is scarce because of the drought.*

'**scarcely** *adv* **1** only just; not quite: *Speak louder please − I can scarcely hear you; scarcely enough money to live on.* **2** used to suggest that something is unreasonable: *You can scarcely expect me to work when I'm ill.*

'**scarcity** *n* (a) lack or shortage: *a scarcity of work/jobs; times of scarcity.*

scare [skeə] *v* **1** to startle or frighten: *You'll scare the baby if you shout; His warning scared her into obeying him.* − *n* **1** a feeling

of fear or alarm: *The noise gave me a scare.* **2** a feeling of fear or panic among a large number of people: *a smallpox scare.*

scared *adj* frightened: *I'm scared of spiders; a scared little girl.*

'**scarecrow** *n* a figure set up *eg* in a field, to scare away birds and stop them eating the seeds *etc.*

'**scaremonger** *n* a person who spreads alarming rumours.

scare away/off to make go away or stay away because of fear: *The birds were scared away by the dog.*

scarf [ska:f] − *pls* **scarves** [ska:vz], **scarfs** − *n* a long strip of material to wear round one's neck.

scarlet ['ska:lit] *n, adj* (of) a bright red colour: *scarlet poppies; She blushed scarlet.*

scarlet fever an infectious fever *usu* with a sore throat and red rash.

scathing ['skeiðiŋ] *adj* cruel, bitter, or hurtful: *scathing comments; He was very scathing about her book.* '**scathingly** *adv.*

scatter ['skatə] *v* **1** to (make) go or rush in different directions: *The sudden noise scattered the birds; The crowds scattered when the bomb exploded.* **2** to throw loosely in different directions: *The load from the overturned lorry was scattered over the road.*

'**scattered** *adj* occasional; not close together: *Scattered showers are forecast for this morning; The few houses in the valley are very scattered.*

'**scattering** *n* a small amount scattered here and there: *a scattering of sugar.*

'**scatterbrain** *n* a forgetful or unreliable person. '**scatterbrained** *adj.*

scavenge ['skavindʒ] *v* to search for useful or usable objects, food *etc* amongst rubbish *etc.* '**scavenger** *n.*

scene [si:n] *n* **1** the place where something real or imaginary happens: *A murderer sometimes revisits the scene of his crime; The scene of this opera is laid/set in Switzerland.* **2** an incident *etc* which is seen or remembered: *He recalled scenes from his childhood.* **3** a show of anger: *I was very angry but I didn't want to make a scene.* **4** a view of a landscape *etc: The sheep grazing on the hillside made a peaceful scene.* **5** one part or division of a play *etc: The hero died in the first scene of the third act of the play.* **6** the setting or background for a play *etc: Scene-changing must be done quickly.* **7** a particular area of activity: *the academic/business scene.*

'**scenery** *n* **1** the painted background for a play *etc* on a stage: *The scenery looked rather shabby.* **2** the general appearance of a landscape *etc: beautiful scenery.*

'**scenic** *adj* **1** of scenery, real or theatrical:

clever scenic effects in the film. **2** having beautiful scenery: *a scenic highway.*

behind the scenes out of sight of the audience or public.

come on the scene to arrive: *We were enjoying ourselves till she came on the scene.*

scenery is never used in the plural.

scent [sent] *v* **1** to discover by the sense of smell: *The dog scented a cat.* **2** to suspect: *As soon as he came into the room I scented trouble.* **3** to cause to smell pleasantly: *The roses scented the air.* – *n* **1** a (*usu* pleasant) smell: *This rose has a delightful scent.* **2** a trail consisting of the smell which has been left and may be followed: *The dogs picked up the man's scent and then lost it again.* **3** a liquid with a pleasant smell; perfume.
'scented *adj* (*neg* **un-**) sweet-smelling: *scented soap.*
put/throw (someone) off the scent to give (a person) wrong information so that he will not find the person, thing *etc* he is looking for: *She told the police a lie in order to throw them off the scent.*

scepter *see* **sceptre.**

sceptic (*Amer also* **skeptic**) ['skeptik] *n* a person who is unwilling to believe: *Most people now accept this theory, but there are a few sceptics.*
'sceptical *adj* (*often with* **about**) unwilling to believe: *They say apples clean your teeth, but I'm sceptical about that myself.*
'sceptically *adv.*
'scepticism ['-sizəm] *n* a doubting or questioning attitude: *I regard his theories with scepticism.*

sceptre, (*Amer*) **scepter** ['septə] *n* the ornamental rod carried by a monarch on ceremonial occasions as a sign of power.

schedule ['ʃedjuːl, (*Amer*) 'sked-] *n* a statement of details, *esp* of timing of activities, or of things to be done: *a work schedule for next month.* – *v* to plan the time of (an event *etc*): *The meeting is scheduled for 9.00 a.m. tomorrow.*

scheme [skiːm] *n* **1** a plan or arrangement; a way of doing something: *a colour scheme for the room*; *There are various schemes for improving the roads.* **2** a (*usu* secret) dishonest plan: *His schemes to steal the money were discovered.* – *v* to make (*esp* dishonest) schemes: *He was punished for scheming against the President*; *They have all been scheming for my dismissal.*
'schemer *n*: *He's a dangerous schemer.*
'scheming *adj* having or making (*usu* secret) dishonest plans: *a scheming woman.*

schizophrenia [skitsə'friːniə] *n* a form of insanity in which the patient becomes severely withdrawn from reality, has delusions *etc.* **schizo'phrenic** [-'fre-] *adj.*

scholar ['skolə] *n* **1** a person of great knowledge and learning: *a fine classical scholar.* **2** a person who has been awarded a scholarship: *As a scholar, you will not have to pay college fees.*
'scholarly *adj* **1** having or showing knowledge: *a scholarly person*; *a scholarly book.*
'scholarliness *n.*
'scholarship *n* **1** knowledge and learning: *a man of great scholarship.* **2** money awarded to a good student to enable him to go on with further studies: *She was awarded a travel scholarship.*

school¹ [skuːl] *n* **1** a place for teaching *esp* children: *She goes to the school*; *He's not at university – he's still at school*; (*Amer*) *He's still in school.* **2** the pupils of a school: *The behaviour of this school in public is sometimes not very good.* **3** a series of meetings or a place for instruction *etc*: *She runs a sewing school*; *a driving school.* **4** a department of a university or college dealing with a particular subject: *the School of Mathematics.* **5** (*Amer*) a university or college. **6** a group of people with the same ideas *etc*: *There are two schools of thought about the treatment of this disease.* – *v* to train through practice: *We must school ourselves to be patient.*
'schoolbag *n* a bag for carrying books *etc* to and from school: *She had a schoolbag on her back.*
'schoolboy, 'schoolgirl *ns* a boy or girl who goes to school.
'schoolchild – *pl* **'schoolchildren** – *n* a child who goes to school.
'school-day *n* a day on which children go to school: *On a school-day I get up at seven o'clock.*
'schooldays *n pl* the time of a person's life during which he goes to school.
'schoolfellow *n* a person who is or was taught at the same school, *esp* in the same class: *I met an old schoolfellow of yours.*
'school-leaver *n* a school-pupil who is about to leave, or has just left, school *eg* because he has finished his course of education there.
'schoolmaster – *fem* **'schoolmistress** – *n* a person who teaches in school.
'schoolmate *n* a schoolfellow, *esp* a friend.
'school-teacher *n* a person who teaches in a school.

school² [skuːl] *n* a group of certain kinds of fish, whales or other water animals swimming about: *a school of porpoises.*

schooner ['skuːnə] *n* a type of fast sailing-ship with two or more masts.

science ['saiəns] *n* **1** knowledge gained by observation and experiment. **2** a branch of such knowledge *eg* biology, chemistry, physics *etc.* **3** these sciences considered as a whole: *My daughter prefers science to lan-guages.*

,**scien'tific** [-'ti-] *adj* **1** of science: *scientific discoveries.* **2** (*neg* **un-**) following the rules of science: *scientific methods.* ,**scien'tifically** [-'ti-] *adv.*

'**scientist** *n* a person who studies one or more branches of science.

science fiction stories dealing with future times on Earth or in space.

scissors ['sizəz] *n pl* a type of cutting instru-ment with two blades: *a pair of scissors.*

scoff [skof] *v* (*sometimes with* **at**) to express scorn: *She scoffed at my poem.*

scold [skould] *v* to criticize or blame loudly and angrily: *She scolded the child for com-ing home so late.*

'**scolding** *n* a stern or angry rebuke: *I got a scolding for doing careless work.*

scollop *see* **scallop**.

scoop [sku:p] *n* **1** any of several types of spoon-like tool, used for lifting, serving *etc*: *a grain scoop; an ice-cream scoop.* **2** a piece of news *etc* that one newspaper gets and prints before the others: *The reporter was sure that he had a scoop for his paper.* – *v* to move with, or as if with, a scoop: *He scooped the crumbs together with his fingers.*

scoot [sku:t] *v* (*often with* **along, away, past** *etc*) to move (away) fast: *He scooted down the road.*

'**scooter** *n* **1*** a type of small motor-bicycle. **2** a child's two-wheeled toy vehicle pro-pelled by the foot.

scope [skoup] *n* **1** (*often with* **for**) the oppor-tunity or chance to do, use or develop: *There's no scope for originality in this job.* **2** the area or extent of an activity *etc*: *Few things are beyond the scope of a child's imagination.*

scorch [sko:tʃ] *v* to burn slightly: *She scorched her dress with the iron; That material scorches easily.* – *n* a mark made *eg* on cloth by scorching: *scorch-marks.*

'**scorching** *adj* very hot.

score [sko:] – *pls* **scores**, (after a number or a word signifying a quantity) **score** – *n* **1** the number of points, goals *etc* gained in a game, competition *etc*: *The cricket score is 59 for 3.* **2** a written piece of music showing all the parts for instruments and voices: *the score of an opera.* **3** a set or group of twenty: *There was barely a score of people there.* – *v* **1** to gain (goals *etc*) in a game *etc*: *He scored two goals before half-time.* **2** (*sometimes with* **off** *or* **out**) to remove (*eg* a name) from *eg* a list by putting a line through it: *Please could you score my name off (the list)?; Is that word meant to be scored out?* **3** to keep score: *Will you score for us, please?*

'**scorer** *n* **1** a person who scores points,

goals *etc*: *Our team scored two goals – Smith and Brown were the scorers.* **2** a per-son who writes down the score during *eg* a cricket match.

'**score-board** *n* a *usu* large board on which the score is shown at a cricket match, a quiz-programme *etc*.

on that score for that reason: *He's perfectly healthy, so you don't need to worry on that score.*

scores (of) very many: *She received scores of letters about her radio programme.*

settle old scores to get revenge for past wrongs: *I have some old scores to settle with you.*

scorn [sko:n] *n* contempt or disgust: *He looked at my drawing with scorn.* – *v* to show contempt for; to despise: *They scorned my suggestion.*

'**scornful** *adj* **1** feeling or showing scorn: *a scornful expression/remark.* **2** making scornful remarks: *He was rather scornful about your book.* '**scornfully** *adv.* '**scornful-ness** *n*.

scorpion ['sko:piən] *n* an animal of the same class as spiders that has a tail with a sting.

scotch [skotʃ] *v* to put an end to (a rumour, plan *etc*): *They scotched his attempt to become the chairman.*

Scotch tape® [skotʃ teip] (*Amer*) a kind of (transparent) adhesive tape: *He mended the torn page with Scotch tape.*

scot-free [skot'fri:]: **escape/get off/go scot= free** to be or remain unhurt or unpunished: *The car was badly damaged in the accident, but the driver escaped scot-free.*

scoundrel ['skaundrəl] *n* a very wicked per-son: *She knew he was a scoundrel even before she married him.*

scour[1] ['skauə] *v* to clean by hard rubbing.

scour[2] ['skauə] *v* to make a thorough search of: *They scoured the woods for the child.*

scourge [skə:dʒ] *n* a cause of great suffering to many people: *Vaccination has freed us from the scourge of smallpox.*

scout [skaut] *n* **1** a person, aircraft *etc* sent out to bring in information, spy *etc*: *The scouts reported that there were Indians nearby.* **2** (*with cap*: *formerly* **Boy Scout**) a member of the Scout Movement, an organi-zation of boys formed to develop alertness and strong character. – *v* to act as a scout or spy: *A party was sent ahead to scout.*

scowl [skaul] *v* to wrinkle the brow in dis-pleasure: *He scowled furiously (at her).* – *n* an angry expression on the face.

Scrabble® ['skrabl] *n* a kind of word-building game.

scrabble ['skrabl] *v* (*usu with* **about** *or* **around**) to make scratching noises or movements: *He was scrabbling about looking for the money he had dropped.*

* see illustration on p. 595

scraggy ['skragi] *adj* unattractively thin: *a scraggy neck*. **'scragginess** *n*.

scramble ['skrambl] *v* **1** to crawl or climb quickly, using arms and legs: *They scrambled up the slope*; *He scrambled over the rocks*. **2** to move hastily: *He scrambled to his feet*. **3** (*with* **for**) to rush, or struggle with others, to get: *The boys scrambled for the ball*. **4** to distort (a telephone message *etc*) so that it can only be received and understood with a special receiver. – *n* (*sometimes with* **for**) an act of scrambling; a rush or struggle: *There was a scramble for the best bargains*.

scrambled egg(s) beaten eggs cooked with milk and butter until thick.

scrap[1] [skrap] *n* **1** a small piece or fragment: *a scrap of paper*. **2** (*usu in pl*) a piece of food left over after a meal: *They gave the scraps to the dog*. **3** waste articles that are only valuable for the material they contain: *The old car was sold as scrap*; (*also adj*) *scrap metal*. **4** a picture *etc* for sticking into a scrapbook. – *v* – *pt, ptp* **scrapped** – to discard: *They scrapped the old television set*; *She decided to scrap the whole plan*.

'scrappy *adj* made up of bits and pieces: *a scrappy meal*. **'scrappily** *adv*. **'scrappiness** *n*.

'scrapbook *n* a book with blank pages on which to stick pictures *etc*: *The actor kept a scrapbook of newspaper cuttings about his career*.

scrap heap a heap of waste material, unwanted objects *etc*.

scrap[2] [skrap] *n* a fight: *He tore his jacket in a scrap with another boy*. – *v* – *pt, ptp* **scrapped** – to fight: *The dogs were scrapping over a bone*.

scrape [skreip] *v* **1** to rub against something sharp or rough, *usu* causing damage: *He drove too close to the wall and scraped his car*. **2** to clean, clear or remove by rubbing with something sharp: *He scraped his boots clean*; *He scraped the paint off the door*. **3** to make a harsh noise by rubbing: *Stop scraping your feet!* **4** to move along something while just touching it: *The boat scraped against the landing-stage*. **5** to make by scraping: *The dog scraped a hole in the sand*. – *n* **1** an act or sound of scraping. **2** a mark or slight wound made by scraping: *a scrape on the knee*. **3** a situation that may lead to punishment: *The child is always getting into scrapes*.

'scraper *n* a tool or instrument for scraping, *esp* one for scraping paint and wallpaper off walls *etc*.

scrape the bottom of the barrel to (be obliged to) use the least useful, efficient, person or thing available: *We're short of players for the game but including John*

would really be scraping the bottom of the barrel.

scrape through to only just avoid failing: *He scraped through his exams*.

scrape together/up to manage (with difficulty) to find (enough): *I'll try to scrape a team together for tomorrow's game*.

scrappy see **scrap**[1].

scratch [skratʃ] *v* **1** to mark or hurt by drawing a sharp point across: *The cat scratched my hand*; *How did you scratch your leg?*; *I scratched myself on a rose bush*. **2** to rub to relieve itching: *You should try not to scratch insect bites*. **3** to make by scratching: *He scratched his name on the rock with a sharp stone*. **4** to remove by scratching: *She threatened to scratch his eyes out*. **5** to withdraw from a game, race *etc*: *That horse has been scratched*. – *n* **1** a mark, injury or sound made by scratching: *covered in scratches*; *a scratch at the door*. **2** a slight wound: *I hurt myself, but it's only a scratch*. **3** in certain races or competitions, the starting point for people with no handicap or advantage.

'scratchy *adj*. **'scratchiness** *n*.

scratch the surface to deal too slightly with a subject: *We started to discuss the matter, but only had time to scratch the surface*.

start from scratch to start (an activity *etc*) from nothing, from the very beginning, or without preparation: *He now has a very successful business but he started from scratch*.

scrawl [skroːl] *v* to write untidily or hastily: *I scrawled a hasty note to her*. – *n* untidy or bad handwriting: *I hope you can read this scrawl*.

scrawny ['skroːni] *adj* thin, bony and wrinkled: *a scrawny neck*. **'scrawniness** *n*.

scream [skriːm] *v* to cry or shout in a loud shrill voice because of fear or pain or with laughter; to make a shrill noise: *He was screaming in agony*; *'Look out!' she screamed*; *We screamed with laughter*. – *n* **1** a loud, shrill cry or noise. **2** a cause of laughter: *She's an absolute scream*.

screech [skriːtʃ] *v* to make a harsh, shrill cry, shout or noise: *She screeched (abuse) at him*; *The car screeched to a halt*. – *n* a loud, shrill cry or noise: *screeches of laughter*; *a screech of brakes*.

screed [skriːd] *n* a long report, letter *etc*: *He wrote screeds about the conference*.

screen [skriːn] *n* **1** a flat, movable, often folding, covered framework for preventing a person *etc* from being seen, for decoration, or for protection from heat, cold *etc*: *Screens were put round the patient's bed*; *a tapestry fire-screen*. **2** anything that so protects *etc* a person *etc*: *He hid behind the screen of bushes*; *a smokescreen*. **3** the sur-

face on which films or television pictures appear: *cinema/television/radar screen.* – *v* **1** to hide, protect or shelter: *The tall grass screened him from view.* **2** to make or show a cinema film. **3** to test for loyalty, reliability *etc.* **4** to test for a disease: *Women should be regularly screened for cancer.*
'screenplay *n* the script of a film.
the screen cinema or television films: *You can see him on the screen quite often*; (*also adj*) *screen actors.*

screw [skru:] *n* **1** a type of nail that is driven into something by a firm twisting action: *I need four strong screws for fixing the cupboard to the wall.* **2** an action of twisting a screw *etc*: *He tightened it by giving it another screw.* – *v* **1** to fix, or be fixed, with a screw or screws: *He screwed the handle to the door*; *The handle screws on with these screws.* **2** to fix or remove, or be fixed or removed, with a twisting movement: *Make sure that the hook is fully screwed in*; *He screwed off the lid.*
****'screwdriver** *n* a kind of tool for turning screws.
have a screw loose (of a person) to be a bit mad.
put the screws on to use force or pressure in dealing with a person: *If he won't give us the money, we'll have to put the screws on (him).*
screw up 1 to twist or wrinkle (the face or features): *The baby screwed up its face and began to cry.* **2** to crumple: *She screwed up the letter.*
screw up one's courage to make oneself brave enough to do something: *He screwed up his courage to ask her to marry him.*

scribble ['skribl] *v* **1** to write quickly or carelessly: *He scribbled a message.* **2** to make meaningless marks with a pencil *etc*: *That child has scribbled all over the wall.* – *n* **1** untidy, careless handwriting. **2** a mark *etc* made by scribbling. **'scribbler** *n*.

scrimp [skrimp]: **scrimp and save** to be mean or very careful with money: *She scrimps and saves for her sons' education.*

script [skript] *n* the text of a play, talk *etc*: *Have the actors all got their scripts?*
'scriptwriter *n* a person who writes the texts for radio or television programmes.

scripture ['skriptʃə] *n* **1** the sacred writings of a religion: *Buddhist and Hindu scriptures.* **2** the Bible. **'scriptural** *adj*.

scroll [skroul] *n* a roll of paper or parchment with writing on it.

scrounge [skraundʒ] *v* to get by begging from someone else: *May I scrounge some coffee?* **'scrounger** *n*.

scrub [skrʌb] – *pt, ptp* **scrubbed** – *v* **1** to rub hard in order to clean: *She's scrubbing the floor.* **2** to remove by scrubbing: *She scrubbed the mess off the carpet.* **3** to cancel:

We planned to go but had to scrub the idea. – *n* an act of scrubbing.
'scrubbing-brush *n* a brush with short stiff bristles for scrubbing.

scruff [skrʌf]: **the scruff of the neck** the back of the neck by which an animal can be grasped or lifted: *She picked up the cat by the scruff of the neck.*

scruffy ['skrʌfi] *adj* dirty and untidy: *a scruffy person*; *Their house is a bit scruffy.*

scrum [skrʌm] *n* in rugby football, a struggle for the ball by the rival forwards hunched tightly round it.

scrupulous ['skru:pjuləs] *adj* careful in attending to detail, doing nothing wrong, dishonest *etc*: *He is scrupulous in his handling of the accounts*; *scrupulous attention to instructions.* **'scrupulously** *adv*. **'scrupulousness** *n*.

scrutiny ['skru:təni] *n* careful, detailed examination or inspection: *Famous people live their lives under continuous public scrutiny.*
'scrutinize, -ise *v* to examine carefully: *He scrutinized the coin with a magnifying-glass.*

scuffle ['skʌfl] *n* a confused fight *usu* between a few people using their fists, feet *etc*: *The two men quarrelled and there was a scuffle.*

scull [skʌl] *n* a short, light oar. – *v* to move a boat with a pair of these or with an oar worked at the stern of the boat.

scullery ['skʌləri] – *pl* **'sculleries** – *n* a room for rough kitchen work such as cleaning pots, pans *etc.*

sculptor ['skʌlptə] – *fem* **'sculptress** – *n* an artist who carves or models in stone, clay, wood *etc.*
'sculpture [-tʃə] *n* **1** the art of modelling or carving figures, shapes *etc*: *He went to art school to study painting and sculpture.* **2** work done by a sculptor: *These statues are all examples of ancient Greek sculpture.*

scum [skʌm] *n* **1** dirty foam that forms on the surface of a liquid: *The pond was covered with (a) scum.* **2** bad, worthless people: *People of that sort are the scum of the earth.*

scurf [skə:f] *n* dandruff: *Some shampoos help to get rid of scurf.* **'scurfy** *adj*.

scurrilous ['skʌriləs, (*Amer*) 'skə:-] *adj* insulting or abusive: *a scurrilous poem.* **'scurrilously** *adv*. **'scurrilousness** *n*.

scurry ['skʌri, (*Amer*) 'skə:ri] *v* (*usu with* **away, off** *etc*) to run with short, quick steps: *It began to rain and we scurried home.* – *n* an act or a noise of hurrying: *a scurry of feet.*

scuttle[1] ['skʌtl] *v* to hurry with short, quick steps.

scuttle[2] ['skʌtl] *v* (of a ship's crew) to make a hole in (the ship) in order to sink it: *The sailors scuttled the ship to prevent it falling into enemy hands.*

scythe [saið] *n* a tool with a long, curved blade

---

* see illustration on p. 566

for cutting tall grass *etc*. – *v* to cut (grass *etc*) with a scythe.

sea [si:] *n* **1** (*often with* the) the mass of salt water covering most of the Earth's surface: *I enjoy swimming in the sea*; *over land and sea*; *The sea is very deep here*; (*also adj*) *A whale is a type of large sea animal*. **2** a particular area of sea: *the Baltic Sea*; *These fish are found in tropical seas*. **3** a particular state of the sea: *mountainous seas*.

'seaward(s) *adv* towards the sea; away from the land: *The yacht left the harbour and sailed seawards*.

'seaboard *n* the seacoast: *the eastern seaboard of the United States*.

sea breeze a breeze blowing from the sea towards the land.

'seafaring *adj* of work or travel on ships: *a seafaring man*.

'seafood *n* fish, *esp* shellfish. – *Also adj*: *seafood restaurants*.

'seafront *n* a promenade or part of a town with its buildings facing the sea.

'sea-going *adj* designed and equipped for travelling on the sea: *a sea-going yacht*.

'seagull *n* a gull.

sea level the level of the surface of the sea used as a base from which the height of land can be measured: *three hundred metres above sea level*.

'sea-lion *n* a type of large seal.

'seaman – *pl* **'seamen** – *n* a sailor, *esp* a member of a ship's crew who is not an officer.

'seaport *n* a port on the coast.

'seashell *n* the (empty) shell of a sea creature.

'seashore *n* the land close to the sea.

'seasick *adj* ill because of the motion of a ship at sea: *Were you seasick on the voyage?* **'seasickness** *n*.

'seaside *n* (*usu with* the) a place beside the sea: *We like to go to the seaside in the summer*.

'seaweed *n* plants growing in the sea: *The beach was covered with seaweed*.

'seaworthy *adj* (*neg* un-) (of a ship) suitably built and in good enough condition to sail at sea. **'seaworthiness** *n*.

at sea 1 on a ship and away from land: *He has been at sea for four months*. **2** puzzled or bewildered: *Can I help you? You seem all at sea*.

go to sea to become a sailor: *He wants to go to sea*.

put to sea to leave the land or a port: *They planned to put to sea the next day*.

seal[1] [si:l] *n* **1** a piece of wax or other material bearing a design, attached to a document to show that it is genuine and legal. **2** a piece of wax *etc* used to seal a parcel *etc*. **3** (something that makes) a complete closure or covering: *Paint and varnish act as protective seals for woodwork*. – *v* **1** to mark with a seal: *The document was signed and sealed*. **2** (*neg* un-) to close completely: *He licked and sealed the envelope*; *All the air is removed from a can of food before it is sealed*. **3** to settle or decide: *This mistake sealed his fate*.

'sealing-wax *n* a type of wax for sealing letters *etc*.

seal of approval official approval: *Doctors have now given this new drug their seal of approval*.

seal off to prevent all approach to, or exit from, (an area): *The police have sealed off the area where the murdered girl was found*.

set one's seal to to give one's authority or agreement to: *He set his seal to the proposals for reforms*.

seal[2] [si:l] *n* any of several types of sea animal, some furry, living partly on land.

'sealskin *n*, *adj* (of) the fur of the furry type of seal: *sealskin boots*; *made of sealskin*.

seam [si:m] *n* **1** the line formed by the sewing together of two pieces of cloth *etc*. **2** the line where two things meet or join: *Water was coming in through the seams of the boat*. **3** a thin line or layer of coal *etc* in the earth: *a coal seam*. – *v* to sew a seam in: *I've pinned the skirt together but I haven't seamed it yet*.

'seamstress ['sem-] *n* a woman who earns her living by sewing.

the seamy side (of life) the roughest, most unpleasant side or aspect of human life.

seaman *see* sea.

search [sə:tʃ] *v* **1** (*often with* for) to look for something by careful examination: *Have you searched through your pockets thoroughly?*; *I've been searching for that book for weeks*. **2** (of the police *etc*) to examine, looking for *eg* stolen goods: *He was taken to the police station, searched and questioned*. – *n* an act of searching: *His search did not take long*. **'searcher** *n*.

'searching *adj* trying to find out the truth by careful examination: *He gave me a searching look*. **'searchingly** *adv*.

'searchlight *n* a strong light with a beam that can be turned in any direction, used *eg* to see enemy aeroplanes in the sky.

search party a group of people looking for a missing person: *When the climbers failed to return, a search party was sent out*.

search warrant a warrant giving legal permission to the police to search a house *etc*.

in search of searching for: *We went in search of a restaurant*.

season ['si:zn] *n* **1** one of the main divisions of the year according to the regular variation of the weather, length of day *etc*: *The four seasons are spring, summer, autumn and* winter; *The monsoon brings the rainy season.* 2 the usual, proper or suitable time for something: *the football season.* – *v* 1 to add salt, pepper, mustard *etc* to: *She seasoned the meat with plenty of pepper.* 2 to let (wood) be affected by rain, sun *etc* until it is ready for use.

'seasonable *adj* (*neg* **un-**) (of weather) of the kind that is to be expected for a particular time of year.

'seasonal *adj* done at a particular season only: *seasonal work as a waitress; seasonal sports.*

'seasoned *adj* experienced: *seasoned political campaigners.*

'seasoning *n* something used to season food: *Salt and pepper are used as seasonings.*

season ticket a ticket (*usu* for travel) that can be used repeatedly during a certain period: *a three-month season ticket.*

in season (of food) available, ready for eating: *That fruit is not in season just now.*

out of season not in season.

seat [si:t] *n* 1 something for sitting on: *Are there enough seats for everyone?* 2 the part of a chair *etc* on which the body sits: *This chair-seat is broken.* 3 (the part of a garment covering) the buttocks: *I've got a sore seat after all that horse riding; a hole in the seat of his trousers.* 4 a place in which a person has a right to sit: *two seats for the play; a seat in Parliament; a seat on the board of the company.* 5 a place that is the centre of some activity *etc*: *Universities are seats of learning.* – *v* 1 to cause to sit down: *I seated him in the armchair.* 2 to have seats for: *Our table seats eight.*

-seater having seats for: *The bus is a thirty-seater.*

'seating *n* the supply or arrangement of seats: *She arranged the seating for the lecture.*

seat belt in a car, aeroplane *etc*, a safety-belt which will hold a person in his seat in an accident *etc*.

take a seat to sit down: *Please take a seat!*

secluded [si'klu:did] *adj* not able to be seen, talked to *etc* by other people; far away from other people *etc*: *a secluded cottage.*

se'clusion [-ʒən] *n* the state of being secluded; privacy: *She wept in the seclusion of her own room.*

second¹ ['sekənd] *adj* 1 next after, or following, the first in time, place *etc*: *February is the second month of the year; She finished the race in second place.* 2 additional or extra: *a second house in the country.* 3 lesser in importance, quality *etc*: *She's a member of the school's second swimming team.* – *adv* next after the first: *He came second in the race.* – *n* 1 a second person, thing *etc*: *You're the second to arrive.* 2 a person who

supports and helps a person who is fighting in a boxing match *etc*. – *v* to agree with (something said by a previous speaker), *esp* to do so formally: *He proposed the motion and I seconded it.*

'secondary *adj* 1 coming after, and at a more advanced level than, primary: *secondary education.* 2 lesser in importance: *a matter of secondary importance.* – *n* – *pl* **'secondaries** – a secondary school.

'seconder *n* a person who seconds.

'secondly *adv* in the second place: *I have two reasons for not buying the house – firstly, it's too big, and secondly it's too far from town.*

secondary colours colours got by mixing primary colours: *Orange and purple are secondary colours.*

,second-'best *n, adj* next after the best; not the best: *She wore her second-best hat; I want your best work – your second-best is not good enough.*

,second-'class *adj* 1 of or in the class next after or below the first; not of the very best quality: *a second-class restaurant; He gained a second-class honours degree in French.* 2 (for) travelling in a part of a train *etc* that is not as comfortable or luxurious as some other part: *a second-class passenger; His ticket is second-class;* (*also adv*) *I'll be travelling second-class.*

,second-'hand *adj* previously used by someone else: *second-hand clothes.*

second lieutenant a person of the rank below lieutenant: *Second Lieutenant Jones.*

,second-'rate *adj* inferior: *The play was pretty second-rate.*

second thoughts a change of opinion, decision *etc*: *I'm having second thoughts about selling the piano.*

at second hand through or from another person: *I heard the news at second hand.*

come off second best to be the loser in a struggle: *That cat always comes off second best in a fight.*

every second week, month *etc* (on or during) alternate weeks, months *etc*: *He comes in every second day.*

second to none better than every other of the same type: *As a portrait painter, he is second to none.*

second² ['sekənd] *n* 1 the sixtieth part of a minute: *He ran the race in three minutes and forty-two seconds.* 2 a short time: *I'll be there in a second.*

secret ['si:krit] *adj* hidden from, unknown to, or not told to, other people: *a secret agreement; He kept his illness secret from everybody.* – *n* 1 something which is, or must be kept, secret: *The date of their marriage is a secret; industrial secrets.* 2 a hidden explanation: *I wish I knew the secret of her success.*

'secrecy n the state of being or the act of keeping secret.

'secretive [-tiv] adj inclined to conceal one's activities, thoughts etc: secretive behaviour. **'secretively** adv. **'secretiveness** n.

'secretly adv in such a way that others do not know, see etc: He secretly copied the numbers down in his notebook.

secret agent a spy.

secret police a police force whose activities are kept secret and which is concerned mostly with political crimes.

in secret secretly: This must all be done in secret.

keep a secret not to tell (something secret) to anyone else: You can't trust her to keep a secret.

secretary ['sekrətəri] – pl **'secretaries** – n 1 a person employed to write letters, keep records and make business arrangements etc for another person: He dictated a letter to his secretary. 2 a (sometimes unpaid) person who deals with the official business of an organization etc: The secretary read out the minutes of the society's last meeting. **,secre'tarial** [-'teə-] adj of a secretary or his/her duties: trained in secretarial work; at secretarial college.

secrete [si'kri:t] v 1 (of a gland or similar organ of the body) to separate (a fluid) from the blood, store it, and give it out: The liver secretes bile. 2 to hide: He secreted the money under his mattress. **se'cretion** [-ʃən] n 1 the process of secreting a fluid. 2 a substance produced by this process: Saliva and urine are secretions.

sect [sekt] n a group of people within a larger, esp religious, group, having views different from those of the rest of the group. **sec'tarian** adj 1 concerned with, esp the narrow interests of, a sect or sects: sectarian loyalties. 2 caused by membership of a sect: a sectarian murder. – n a member of a sect.

section ['sekʃən] n 1 a part or division: He divided the orange into sections; There' is disagreement in one section of the community; the accounts section of the business. 2 a view of the inside of anything when, or as if, it is cut right through or across: a section of the stem of a flower. **'sectional** adj.

sector ['sektə] n a section of a circle whose sides are a part of the circumference and two straight lines drawn from the centre to the circumference.

secular ['sekjulə] adj not spiritual or religious: secular art/music.

secure [si'kjuə] adj 1 (often with against or from) safe; free from danger, loss etc: Is your house secure against burglary?; He went on holiday, secure in the knowledge that he had done well in the exam. 2 firm, fastened, or fixed: Is that door secure?

3 definite; not likely to be lost: She has had a secure offer of a job; He has a secure job. – v 1 (with against or from (something bad)) to guarantee or make safe: Keep your jewellery in the bank to secure it against theft. 2 to fasten or make firm: He secured the boat with a rope. **se'curely** adv.

se'curity n the state of being, or making safe, secure, free from danger etc: the security of a happy home; This alarm system will give the factory some security; There has to be tight security at a prison; (also adj) the security forces; a security guard.

security risk a person considered not safe to be given a job involving knowledge of secrets because he might give secret information to an enemy etc.

sedan [si'dan] n (Amer) a covered car for four or more people.

sedate¹ [si'deit] adj calm, serious and dignified: a sedate, middle-aged woman. **se'dately** adv. **se'dateness** n.

sedate² [si'deit] v to give a sedative: The doctor sedated her with some pills.

sedative ['sedətiv] n, adj (a medicine, drug etc) having a soothing or calming effect: This medicine will have a sedative effect.

sedentary ['sedntəri] adj (of a job, way of living etc) requiring or involving much sitting and little exercise: a sedentary job in a tax office.

sediment ['sedimənt] n the material that settles at the bottom of a liquid: Her feet sank into the sediment on the river bed.

seduce [si'dju:s] v to persuade or attract into doing, thinking etc (something, esp something foolish or wrong): She was seduced by the attractions of the big city. **se'duction** [-'dʌk-] n something that tempts or attracts: the seductions of life in the big city.

seductive [si'dʌktiv] adj tempting, attractive or charming: a seductive melody.

see¹ [si:] – pt **saw** [so:]; ptp **seen** – v 1 to have the power of sight: After six years of blindness, he found he could see. 2 to be aware of by means of the eye: I can see her in the garden. 3 to look at: Did you see that play on television? 4 to have a picture in the mind: I see many difficulties ahead. 5 to understand: She didn't see the point of the joke. 6 to investigate: Leave this here and I'll see what I can do for you. 7 to meet: I'll see you at the usual time. 8 to accompany: I'll see you home.

see about to attend to, or deal with: I'll see about this tomorrow.

seeing that since; considering that: Seeing that he's ill, he's unlikely to come.

see off to accompany (a person starting on a journey) to the airport, railway station etc from which he is to leave: *He saw me off at the station.*

see through 1 to give support to (a person, plan *etc*) until the end is reached: *I'd like to see the job through.* **2** not to be deceived by (a person, trick *etc*): *We soon saw through him and his little plan.*

see to to attend to or deal with: *I must see to the baby.*

I, we *etc* will see I, we *etc* shall wait and consider the matter later: '*May I have a new bicycle?' 'We'll see.'*

see[2] [si:] *n* the district over which a bishop or archbishop has authority.

seed [si:d] *n* **1** the (part of) the fruit of a tree, plant *etc* from which a new plant may be grown: *sunflower seeds; grass seed.* **2** the beginning from which anything grows: *There was already a seed of doubt in her mind.* **3** (in a sporting competition *etc*) a seeded player. – *v* **1** (of a plant) to produce seed: *A plant seeds after it has flowered.* **2** in golf, tennis *etc*, to arrange (good players) in a competition so that they do not compete against each other till the later rounds.

'seeded *adj* having been seeded: *a seeded player.*

'seedling [-liŋ] *n* a young plant just grown from a seed: *Don't walk on the lettuce seedlings!*

'seedbed *n* ground prepared for growing seeds.

seek [si:k] – *pt, ptp* **sought** [so:t] – *v* **1** (sometimes with **for**) to try to find, get or achieve: *He is seeking (for) an answer; You should seek your lawyer's advice; She's seeking fame in the world of television.* **2** to try: *These men are seeking to destroy the government.*

sought after wanted; asked for: *This book is much sought after; a much sought-after book.*

seem [si:m] *v* to have the appearance or give the impression of being or doing: *A thin person always seems (to be) taller than he really is; She seems kind; He seemed to hesitate for a minute.*

'seeming *adj* existing in appearance, though not *usu* in reality: *her seeming indifference.*

'seemingly *adv* apparently; according to report: *Seemingly, her mother is very ill.*

'seemly *adj* (*neg* **un-**) (of behaviour *etc*) suitable, proper or decent: *seemly conduct.*

seen *see* **see**[1].

seep [si:p] *v* (of liquids) to flow slowly *eg* through a very small opening: *Blood seeped out through the bandage round his head; All his confidence seeped away.*

seer [siə] *n* a prophet.

seesaw ['si:so:] *n* a long flat piece of wood, metal *etc*, balanced on a central support so that one end of it goes up as the other goes

down: *The boy fell off the seesaw in the park.* – *v* to move up and down like a seesaw: *The boat seesawed on the crest of the wave.*

seething ['si:ðiŋ] *adj* **1** (sometimes with **with**) very crowded: *a seething mass of people; The beach is seething with people.* **2** (*usu* with **with**) very excited or agitated: *seething with excitement/anger.* **3** very angry: *He was seething when he left the meeting.*

segment ['segmənt] *n* **1** a part or section: *He divided the orange into segments.* **2** a part of *eg* a circle cut off by a straight line.

segmented [seg'mentid, (*Amer*) 'segmentid] *adj* divided into segments: *An insect has a segmented body.*

segregate ['segrigeit] *v* to separate from others; to keep (people, groups *etc*) apart from each other: *At the swimming-pool, the sexes are segregated.* **,segre'gation** [-ʃən] *n.*

seismic ['saizmik] *adj* of earthquakes: *seismic disturbances.*

seis'mology [-'molədʒi] *n* the science or study of earthquakes. **,seismo'logical** [-'lo-] *adj.* **seis'mologist** *n.*

seize [si:z] *v* **1** to take or grasp suddenly, *esp* by force: *She seized the gun from him; He seized her by the arm; He seized the opportunity of leaving.* **2** to take, *esp* by force or by law: *The police seized the stolen property.*

'seizure [-ʒə] *n* the act of seizing: *seizure of property.*

seize on to accept with enthusiasm: *I suggested a cycling holiday, and he seized on the idea.*

seize up (of machinery *etc*) to get stuck and stop working: *The car seized up yesterday.*

seize is spelt with -ei- (not -ie-).

seldom ['seldəm] *adv* rarely; not often: *I've seldom experienced such rudeness.*

select [sə'lekt] *v* to choose or pick from among a number: *She selected a blue dress from the wardrobe; You have been selected to represent us on the committee.* – *adj* **1** picked or chosen carefully: *A select group of friends was invited.* **2** intended only for carefully chosen (*usu* rich or upper-class) people: *That school is very select.*

se'lection [-ʃən] *n* **1** the act or process of selecting or being selected: *a selection of boys for the choir;* (*also adj*) *a selection committee.* **2** a collection or group of things that have been selected: *a selection of verses/fruit.*

se'lective [-tiv] *adj* having the power of choice and using it, *esp* carefully: *She is very selective about clothes.*

sel'lectively *adv.* **se'lectiveness** *n.*

se'lector *n* a person who chooses, *esp* athletes, a team *etc*: *The selectors have* announced the cricket team to meet Australia.

self [self] – *pl* **selves** [selvz] – *n* **1** a person's own body and personality. **2** one's own personal interests or advantage: *He always thinks first of self.*
'selfish *adj* (*neg* **un-**) thinking of one's own pleasure or good and not considering other people: *a selfish person/attitude.* **'selfishly** *adv.* **'selfishness** *n.*
'selfless *adj* utterly unselfish: *As a soldier, he showed selfless devotion to duty.* **'selflessly** *adv.* **'selflessness** *n.*

self- [self] **1** showing that the person or thing acting is acting upon himself or itself, as in **self-respect. 2** showing that the thing is acting automatically, as in **self-closing doors. 3** by oneself, as in **self-made. 4** in, within *etc* oneself or itself, as in **self-centred.**

self-addressed [selfə'drest] *adj* addressed to oneself: *a stamped, self-addressed envelope.*

self-assurance [selfə'ʃuərəns] *n* self-confidence. **,self-as'sured** *adj.*

self-centred [self'sentəd] *adj* interested only in one's own affairs; selfish: *She's too self-centred to take any interest in my troubles.*

self-closing [self'klouziŋ] *adj* which close automatically: *self-closing doors.*

self-coloured, (*Amer*) **self-colored** [self'kʌləd] *adj* of one colour all over: *a self-coloured carpet.*

self-confidence [self'konfidəns] *n* belief or trust in one's own powers: *You need plenty of self-confidence to be a good airline pilot.* **,self-'confident** *adj.* **,self-'confidently** *adv.*

self-conscious [self'konʃəs] *adj* too easily becoming shy or embarrassed when in the presence of others: *She'll never be a good teacher – she's too self-conscious.* **'self=consciously** *adv.* **,self-'consciousness** *n.*

self-control [selfkən'troul] *n* control of oneself, one's emotions and impulses: *He behaved with admirable self-control although he was very angry.*

self-defence, (*Amer*) **self-defense** [selfdi'fens] *n* defence of one's own body, property *etc* against attack: *He killed his attacker in self-defence.*

self-employed [selfim'ploid] *adj* working for oneself and not employed by someone else: *a self-employed dressmaker.*

self-esteem [selfi'sti:m] *n* a person's respect for himself: *My self-esteem suffered when I failed the exam.*

self-evident [self'evidənt] *adj* clear enough to need no proof: *It is self-evident that we need food to stay alive.*

self-explanatory [selfik'splanətəri] *adj* needing no explanation: *I think the pictures in the instruction manual are self-explanatory.*

self-government [self'gʌvəmənt] *n* government by the people of the country without outside control.

self-important [selfim'po:tənt] *adj* having too high an opinion of one's own importance: *a self-important little man.* **,self-im'portance** *n.*

self-indulgent [selfin'dʌldʒənt] *adj* too ready to satisfy one's own desires: *self-indulgent habits/behaviour.* **,self-in'dulgence** *n.*

self-inflicted [selfin'fliktid] *adj* (of wounds *etc*) done to oneself: *The doctors proved that the man's injuries were self-inflicted.*

self-interest [self'intrəst] *n* consideration only for one's own aims and advantages: *He acted out of self-interest.*

selfish, selfless *see* **self.**

self-made [self'meid] *adj* owing wealth or important position to one's efforts, not to advantages given by birth, education *etc*: *a self-made man.*

self-portrait [self'po:trit] *n* a person's portrait or description of himself: *Rembrandt painted several self-portraits; The man described is a self-portrait of the author.*

self-possessed [selfpə'zest] *adj* calm, and able to act confidently in an emergency: *a calm, self-possessed person.* **,self-pos'session** [-'ʃən] *n.*

self-preservation ['selfprezə'veiʃən] *n* the natural inclination towards the protection of oneself from harm, danger *etc*: *Self-preservation is our strongest instinct.*

self-raising [self'reiziŋ] *adj* (of flour) already containing an ingredient to make cakes *etc* rise.

self-respect [selfri'spekt] *n* respect for oneself and concern for one's reputation: *Well-known personalities should have more self-respect than to take part in television advertising.* **,self-re'specting** *adj.*

self-sacrifice [self'sakrifais] *n* the act of sacrificing one's own desires *etc* in order to help others: *With great self-sacrifice, she gave up the holiday to care for her sick aunt.*

self-satisfied [self'satisfaid] *adj* too easily pleased with oneself and one's achievements: *'Our house is the cleanest in the row,' she said in her self-satisfied way.* **'self-,satis'faction** [-'fakʃən] *n.*

self-service [self'sə:vis] *n* an arrangement by which customers themselves collect the goods that they want to buy. – *Also adj*: *a self-service restaurant.*

self-sufficient [selfsə'fiʃənt] *adj* not dependent on others for help *etc*: *a self-sufficient community.* **,self-suf'ficiency** *n.*

self-willed [self'wild] *adj* determined to do, or have, what one wants: *a self-willed little brat.*

sell [sel] – *pt, ptp* **sold** [sould] – *v* **1** to give something in exchange for money: *He sold her a car; I've got some books to sell.* **2** to have for sale: *The farmer sells milk and* *eggs.* **3** to be sold: *His book sold well.* **4** to cause to be sold: *Packaging sells a product.*

,sell-out *n* **1** an event, *esp* a concert, for which all the tickets are sold: *His concert was a sell-out.* **2** a betrayal: *The gang realized it was a sell-out and tried to escape.*

be sold on to be enthusiastic about: *I'm sold on the idea of a holiday in Canada.*

be sold out 1 to be no longer available: *The second-hand records are all sold out*; *The concert is sold out.* **2** to have no more available to be bought: *We are sold out of children's socks.*

sell off to sell quickly and cheaply: *They're selling off their old stock.*

sell out 1 (*sometimes with* of) to sell all of something: *We sold out our entire stock.* **2** to be all sold: *The second-hand records sold out within minutes of the sale starting.*

sell up to sell a house, business *etc*: *He has sold up his share of the business.*

Sellotape® ['seləteip] *n* (*also no cap*) a type of transparent adhesive tape, used *eg* for sticking pieces of paper together.

selves *see* **self**.

semaphore ['seməfo:] *n* a system of signalling with flags held in each hand: *He signalled the message to them in semaphore.*

semblance ['sembləns] *n* an appearance or likeness: *I have to coach them into some semblance of a football team by Saturday.*

semi- [semi] **1** half, as in **semicircle**. **2** partly, as in **semi-conscious**.

semibreve ['semibri:v] *n* in music, a note equal in length to two minims.

semicircle ['semisə:kl] *n* a half circle: *The chairs were arranged in a semicircle round the speaker.* **,semi'circular** [-'sə:kju-] *adj*.

semicolon [semi'koulən, (*Amer*) 'semikoulən] *n* the punctuation mark (;) used *esp* to separate parts of a sentence which have more independence than clauses separated by a comma: *He wondered what to do. He couldn't go back; he couldn't borrow money.*

semi-conscious [semi'konʃəs] *adj* partly conscious: *He was semi-conscious when they took him to hospital.* **,semi-'consciousness** *n*.

semi-detached [semidi'tatʃt] *adj* (of a house) joined to another house on one side but separate on the other: *a semi-detached bungalow.*

semi-final [semi'fainl] *n* a match, round *etc* immediately before the final: *She reached the semi-finals of the competition.* **,semi-'finalist** *n* a person, team *etc* competing in a semi-final.

seminary ['seminəri] – *pl* **'seminaries** – *n* a training college for · Roman Catholic priests.

semi-precious [semi'preʃəs] *adj* (of a stone) having some value, but not considered a gem: *garnets and other semi-precious stones.*

semitone ['semitoun] *n* half a tone in the musical scale: *F sharp is a semitone above F natural.*

senate ['senət] *n* **1** a lawmaking body, *esp* the upper house of the parliament in some countries. **2** in ancient Rome, the chief legislative and administrative body.

'senator *n* **1** (*sometimes abbrev* **Sen.** *in titles*) a member of a lawmaking senate: *Senator Smith.* **2** a member of a Roman senate.

send [send] – *pt, ptp* **sent** [sent] – *v* **1** to cause or order to go or be taken: *The teacher sent the disobedient boy to the headmaster*; *She sent me this book.* **2** to move rapidly or with force: *He sent the ball right into the goal.* **3** to cause to go into a certain, *usu* bad, state: *The news sent them into a panic.*

'sender *n* a person who sends *eg* a letter.

send away for to order by post: *I've sent away for some things that I saw in the catalogue.*

send for to ask to come, or order to be delivered: *Her son was sent for*; *I'll send for a taxi.*

send in to offer or submit, *eg* for a competition: *He sent in three drawings for the competition.*

send off to accompany (a person) to the place, or be at the place, where he will start a journey: *A great crowd gathered at the station to send the football team off* (*n* **'send= off**).

send off for to send away for.

send out 1 to distribute *eg* by post: *A notice has been sent out to all employees.* **2** (*eg* of plants) to produce: *This plant has sent out some new shoots.*

send (someone) packing/send (someone) about his business to send (a person) away firmly and without politeness: *He tried to borrow money from me again, but I soon sent him packing.*

senile ['si:nail] *adj* showing the feebleness or childishness of old age: *a senile old woman.* **se'nility** [sə'ni-] *n*.

senior ['si:njə] *n, adj* (a person who is) older in years or higher in rank or authority: *John is senior to me by two years*; *He is two years my senior*; *senior army officers.* – *adj* (*often abbrev* **Snr, Sr** *or* **Sen.** *when written*) used to indicate the father of a person who is alive and who has the same name: *John Jones Senior.* **,seni'ority** [-ni'o-] *n* the state of being senior: *The officers sat at the table in order of seniority.*

senior citizen a person who has passed retirement age.

older than but **senior to**.

sensation [sen'seiʃən] *n* **1** the ability to feel through the sense of touch: *Cold can cause* *a loss of sensation in the fingers and toes.* **2** a feeling: *a sensation of faintness.* **3** a general feeling, or a cause, of excitement or horror: *The murder caused a sensation; His arrest was the sensation of the week.*

sen'sational *adj* **1** causing great excitement or horror: *a sensational piece of news.* **2** very good: *The film was sensational.* **3** intended to create feelings of excitement, horror *etc*: *That magazine is too sensational for me.* **sen'sationally** *adv.*

sense [sens] *n* **1** one of the five powers (hearing, taste, sight, smell, touch) by which a person or animal feels or notices. **2** a feeling: *He has an exaggerated sense of his own importance.* **3** an awareness of (something): *a well-developed musical sense; She has no sense of humour.* **4** good judgement: *You can rely on him – he has plenty of sense.* **5** a meaning (of a word). **6** something which is meaningful: *Can you make sense of his letter? – v* to feel, become aware of, or realize: *He sensed that she disapproved.*

'senseless *adj* **1** stunned or unconscious: *The blow knocked him senseless.* **2** foolish: *What a senseless thing to do!* **'senselessly** *adv.* **'senselessness** *n.*

'senses *n pl (usu with* **my, his, her** *etc)* a person's normal, sane state of mind: *He must have taken leave of his senses; When he came to his senses, he was lying in a hospital bed.*

sixth sense an ability to feel or realize something apparently not by means of any of the five senses: *He couldn't hear or see anyone, but a sixth sense told him that he was being followed.*

sensibility [sensi'biləti] an awareness of, or an ability to create, art, literature *etc* showing very high standards of beauty and good taste: *a writer of great sensibility.*

sensi'bilities *n pl* feelings that can be easily hurt by criticism *etc*: *Do try not to offend her sensibilities.*

sensible ['sensəbl] *adj* **1** wise; having or showing good judgement: *She's a sensible, reliable person; a sensible suggestion.* **2** (of clothes *etc*) practical rather than attractive or fashionable: *She wears flat, sensible shoes.*

'sensibly *adv* in a sensible way: *He sensibly brought a spare pair of shoes.*

sensitive ['sensitiv] *adj* **1** (*usu with* **to**) strongly or easily affected (by something): *sensitive skin; sensitive to light.* **2** (*usu with* **about** *or* **to**) easily hurt or offended: *She is very sensitive to criticism.* **3** having or showing artistic good taste: *a sensitive writer; a sensitive performance.* **'sensitively** *adv.* **'sensitiveness, ,sensi'tivity** *ns.*

sensual ['sensjuəl] *adj* **1** of the senses and the body rather than the mind: *sensual*

pleasures. **2** having or showing a fondness for bodily pleasures: *a sensual person.* **'sensually** *adv.* **'sensu'ality** [-'a-] *n.*

sensuous ['sensjuəs] *adj* affecting the senses pleasantly: *Her sculptures have a sensuous quality.* **'sensuously** *adv.*

sent *see* **send.**

sentence ['sentəns] *n* **1** a number of words forming a complete statement: *'I want it', and 'Give it to me!' are sentences.* **2** a punishment imposed by a lawcourt: *a sentence of three years' imprisonment; He is under sentence of death. – v (usu with* **to**) to condemn to a particular punishment: *He was sentenced to life imprisonment.*

sentiment ['sentimənt] *n* tender feeling or emotion: *a song full of patriotic sentiment.* **,senti'mental** [-'men-] *adj* **1** (*sometimes with* **about**) having, showing or causing much tender feeling: *a sentimental person; a sentimental film about a little boy and a donkey.* **2** of the emotions or feelings: *The ring has sentimental value, as my husband gave it to me.* **,senti'mentally** *adv.* **,sentimen'tality** [-'ta-] *n.*

sentinel ['sentinl] *n* a sentry.

sentry ['sentri] – *pl* **'sentries** – *n* a soldier or other person on guard to stop anyone who has no right to enter, pass *etc*: *The entrance was guarded by two sentries.*

'sentry-box *n* a small shelter for a sentry.

separate ['sepəreit] *v* **1** (*sometimes with* **into** *or* **from**) to place, take, keep or force apart: *He separated the money into two piles; A policeman tried to separate the men who were fighting.* **2** to go in different directions: *We all walked along together and separated at the cross-roads.* **3** (of a husband and wife) to start living apart from each other by choice. *– [-rət] adj* **1** divided; not joined: *He sawed the wood into four separate pieces; The garage is separate from the house.* **2** different or distinct: *This happened on two separate occasions; I like to keep my job and my home life separate.* **'separateness** *n.*

'separable *adj* that can be separated.

'separately [-rət-] *adv* in a separate way; not together.

'separates [-rəts] *n pl* garments (*eg* jerseys, skirts, trousers, blouses, shirts) that can be worn together in varying combinations.

,sepa'ration *n* **1** the act of separating or the state or period of being separated: *They were together again after a separation of three years.* **2** a (legal) arrangement by which a husband and wife remain married but live separately.

'separatist [-rə-] *n* a person who urges separation from an established political state, church *etc.* **'separatism.**

separate off to make or keep (a part or parts) separate.

separate out to make or keep separate or distinct.

separate up (*often with* **into**) to divide: *The house has been separated up into different flats.*

separate is spelt with **-ar-** (not **-er-**).

September [səp'tembə] *n* the ninth month of the year, the month following August.

septic ['septik] *adj* (of a wound *etc*) full of or caused by germs that are poisoning the blood: *a septic finger; septic poisoning.*

septic tank a tank in which sewage is partially purified by the action of bacteria.

septuagenarian [septjuədʒi'neəriən, (*Amer*) -tʃuə-] *n* a person from seventy to seventy-nine years old.

sequel ['si:kwəl] *n* (*sometimes with* **to**) 1 a result or consequence: *an unpleasant sequel to an incident.* 2 a story that is a continuation of an earlier story: *a sequel to a story about a boy called Matthew.*

sequence ['si:kwəns] *n* a series of events *etc* following one another in a particular order: *He described the sequence of events leading to his dismissal from the firm; a sequence of numbers; a dance sequence.*

serenade [serə'neid] *n* a piece of music played or sung in the open air at night. – *v* to entertain with a serenade: *The girl stood on her balcony and was serenaded by her lover.*

serene [sə'ri:n] *adj* happy and peaceful: *a calm and serene person.* **se'renely** *adv.* **se'reneness**, **se'renity** [-'re-] *ns.*

sergeant ['sa:dʒənt] *n* (*often abbrev* **Sgt**) 1 in the British army or air force, the rank above corporal: *Sergeant Brown.* 2 (a police officer of) the rank next above constable or patrolman.

sergeant-'major *n* (*often abbrev* **Sgt-Maj.**) in the British army, the highest rank of non-commissioned officer: *Sergeant-Major Brown.*

serial *see* **series**.

series ['siəri:z] – *pl* **'series** – *n* a number of *usu* similar things done, produced *etc* one after another: *a series of brilliant scientific discoveries; Are you watching the television series on Britain's castles?; a series of school textbooks.*

'serial [-riəl] *adj* 1 of or in a series: *serial numbers on banknotes.* 2 (of a story *etc*) published or broadcast in parts. – *n* a serial story, play *etc.*

'serialize, -ise [-riə-] *v* to publish or broadcast as a serial. **,seriali'zation, -s-** *n.*

serious ['siəriəs] *adj* 1 grave or solemn: *a quiet, serious boy; You're looking very serious.* 2 (*often with* **about**) in earnest; sincere: *Is he serious about wanting to be a doctor?* 3 intended to make people think: *He reads very serious books.* 4 causing worry; dan-

gerous: *a serious head injury; The situation is becoming serious.* **'seriousness** *n.*

'seriously *adv* in a serious way; to a serious extent: *Is he seriously thinking of being an actor?; She is seriously ill.*

take (someone or something) seriously 1 to regard (a person or his statement *etc*) as in earnest: *You mustn't take his jokes/promises seriously.* 2 to regard (a matter) as a subject for concern or serious thought: *He refuses to take anything seriously.*

sermon ['sə:mən] *n* a serious talk, *esp* one given in church based on or discussing a passage in the Bible: *The text for this morning's sermon is taken from the fifth chapter of Exodus.*

serpent ['sə:pənt] *n* a snake.

serrated [sə'reitid, (*Amer*) 'sereitid] *adj* notched, as the edge of a saw is: *A breadknife is often serrated.*

serum ['siərəm] *n* a watery fluid which is given as an injection to fight, or give immunity from, a disease: *Diphtheria vaccine is a serum.*

servant ['sə:vənt] *n* 1 a person who is hired to work for another, *esp* in helping to run a house. 2 a person employed by the government, or in the administration of a country *etc*: *a public servant; civil servants.*

serve [sə:v] *v* 1 to work for a person *etc eg* as a servant: *He served his master for forty years.* 2 to distribute food *etc* or supply goods: *She served the soup to the guests; Which shop assistant served you (with these goods)?* 3 to be suitable for a purpose: *This upturned bucket will serve as a seat.* 4 to perform duties, *eg* as a member of the armed forces: *He served (his country) as a soldier for twenty years; I served on the committee for five years.* 5 to undergo (a prison sentence): *He served (a sentence of) six years for armed robbery.* 6 in tennis and similar games, to start the play by throwing up the ball *etc* and hitting it: *He served the ball into the net; Is it your turn to serve? – n* the act of serving (a ball).

'server *n* 1 (*usu in pl*) a utensil used in serving food: *salad servers.* 2 a person who serves (a ball).

'serving *n* a portion of food served: *I had two servings of pie.*

it serves you *etc* **right** you *etc* deserve your misfortune *etc*: *He has done no work so it will serve him right if he fails his exam.*

serve an apprenticeship to spend a (fixed) period of time as an apprentice.

serve out to distribute to each of a number of people: *She served out the pudding.*

serve up to start serving (a meal).

service ['sə:vis] *n* 1 the process of serving customers in a hotel, shop *etc*: *You get very slow service in that shop; (also adj) a service* charge on a hotel bill. **2** the act of doing something to help: *He was rewarded for his service to refugees.* **3** the condition or work of a servant: *In the last century, many young women went into service; She had been in service as a kitchen maid; He has given faithful service to the church for many years.* **4** a check made of all parts of *eg* a car, machine *etc* to ensure that it is in a good condition: *Bring your car in for a service.* **5** a regular public supply of something *eg* transport: *a good train service into the city.* **6** a regular meeting for worship, or a religious ceremony (in church): *He attends a church service every Sunday; the marriage service.* **7** in tennis and similar games, the act or manner of serving the ball: *He has a strong service.* **8** a department of public or government work: *the Civil Service.* **9** (*often in pl*) one of the three fighting forces, the army, navy or air force. **10** employment in one of these: *military service.* – *v* to check (a car, machine *etc*) thoroughly to ensure that it works properly.

'serviceable *adj* (*neg* **un-**) **1** useful; capable of being used: *This tractor is so old it is barely serviceable now.* **2** hard-wearing: *He walks to school every day, so he must have serviceable shoes.*

'serviceman – *fem* **'servicewoman** – *n* a person in one of the armed services.

service station a petrol station with facilities for servicing cars *etc*.

serviette [sə:vi'et] *n* a table napkin: *a paper serviette.*

servile ['sə:vail] *adj* excessively obedient or respectful: *servile obedience/flattery.* **'servilely** *adv.* **ser'vility** [-'vi-] *n*.

servitude ['sə:vitju:d] *n* the state of being a slave: *Their lives were spent in servitude.*

session ['sefən] *n* **1** a meeting, or period for meetings, of a court, council, parliament *etc*: *The judge will give his summing up at tomorrow's court session.* **2** a period of time spent on a particular activity: *a filming session.* **3** a university or school year or one part of this: *the summer session.*

set [set] – *prp* **'setting**: *pt, ptp* **set** – *v* **1** to put or place: *She set the tray down on the table.* **2** to put plates, knives, forks *etc* on (a table) for a meal: *Please would you set the table for me?* **3** to settle or arrange (a date, limit, price *etc*): *It's difficult to set a price on a book when you don't know its value.* **4** to give a person (a task *etc*) to do: *The witch set the prince three tasks; The teacher set a test for her pupils; He should set the others a good example.* **5** to cause to start doing something: *His behaviour set people talking.* **6** (of the sun *etc*) to disappear below the horizon: *It gets cooler when the sun sets.* **7** to become firm or solid: *Has the concrete*

set? **8** to adjust (*eg* a clock or its alarm) so that it is ready to perform its function: *He set the alarm for 7.00 a.m.* **9** to arrange (hair) in waves or curls. **10** to fix in the surface of something, *eg* jewels in a ring. **11** to put (broken bones) into the correct position for healing: *They set his broken arm.* – *adj* **1** fixed or arranged previously: *There is a set procedure for doing this.* **2** (*often with* **on**) ready, intending or determined (to do something): *He is set on going.* **3** deliberate: *He had the set intention of hurting her.* **4** stiff; fixed: *He had a set smile on his face.* **5** not changing or developing: *set ideas.* **6** (*with* **with**) having something set in it: *a gold ring set with diamonds.* – *n* **1** a group of things used or belonging together: *a set of carving tools; a complete set of (the novels of) Jane Austen.* **2** an apparatus for receiving radio or television signals: *a television/radio set.* **3** a group of people: *the musical set.* **4** the process of setting hair: *a shampoo and set.* **5** scenery for a play or film: *There was a very impressive set in the final act.* **6** a group of six or more games in tennis: *She won the first set and lost the next two.*

'setting *n* **1** a background: *This castle is the perfect setting for a murder.* **2** an arrangement of jewels in *eg* a ring. **3** music composed for a poem *etc*: *settings of folk songs.*

'setback *n* a delay in progress.

set phrase a phrase which always occurs in one form, and which cannot be changed: *'Of no fixed abode' is a set phrase.*

'set-square *n* a triangular instrument with one right angle, used in geometrical drawing *etc*.

'setting-lotion *n* a lotion that is used in setting the hair.

'set-up *n* an arrangement: *There are several families living together in that house – it's a funny set-up.*

all set (*often with* **to**) ready or prepared (to do something); just on the point of (doing something): *We were all set to leave when the phone rang.*

set about to begin: *She set about planning her holiday; How will you set about this task?*

set (someone) against (someone) to cause (a person) to dislike (another person): *She set the children against their father.*

set aside to keep for a special use or purpose: *He set aside some cash for use at the weekend.*

set back to delay the progress of: *His illness set him back a bit at school.*

set down (of a bus *etc*) to stop and let (passengers) out: *The bus set us down outside the post-office.*

set in to begin or become established: *Boredom soon set in among the children.*

set off 1 (*sometimes with* **on**) to start a journey: *We set off to go to the beach.* **2** to cause to start doing something: *She had almost stopped crying, but his harsh words set her off again.* **3** to explode or ignite: *You should let your father set off all the fireworks.*

set (something or someone) on (someone) to cause (*eg* dogs) to attack (a person): *He set his dogs on me.*

set out 1 to start a journey: *He set out to explore the countryside.* **2** to intend: *I didn't set out to prove him wrong.*

set to to start to do something (vigorously): *They set to, and finished the work the same day.*

set up 1 to establish: *When was the organization set up?* **2** to arrange or construct: *He set up the apparatus for the experiment.*

set up camp to erect tents *etc*: *They set up camp in a field.*

set up house to establish one's own home: *He'll soon be earning enough to set up house on his own.*

set up shop to start a shop.

set upon (*also* **set on**) to attack: *He set upon me in the dark.*

set(t) [set] *n* a block of stone used in street paving.

settee [se'ti:] *n* a sofa.

setter ['setə] *n* a type of large dog.

settle ['setl] *v* **1** to place in a position of rest or comfort: *I settled myself in the armchair.* **2** to come to rest: *Dust had settled on the books.* **3** to soothe: *I gave him a pill to settle his nerves.* **4** to go and live: *Many Scots settled in New Zealand.* **5** to reach a decision or agreement: *Have you settled with the builders when they are to start work?*; *The dispute between management and employees is still not settled.* **6** to pay (a bill).

'settlement *n* **1** an agreement: *The two sides have at last reached a settlement.* **2** a small community: *a farming settlement.*

'settler *n* a person who settles in a country that is being newly populated: *They were among the early settlers on the east coast of America.*

settle down 1 to (cause to) become quiet, calm and peaceful: *He waited for the audience to settle down before he spoke*; *She settled the baby down at last.* **2** to make oneself comfortable: *She settled (herself) down in the back of the car and went to sleep.* **3** to begin to concentrate on something, *eg* work: *He settled down to (do) his schoolwork.*

settle in to become used to and comfortable in new surroundings.

settle on to agree about or decide.

settle up to pay (a bill): *He asked the waiter for the bill, and settled up.*

seven ['sevn] *n* **1** the number or figure 7. **2** the age of 7. – *adj* **1** 7 in number. **2** aged 7.

seven- having seven (of something): *a seven-sided figure.*

'seventh *n* **1** one of seven equal parts. **2** (*also adj*) (the) last of seven (people, things *etc*); (the) next after the sixth.

'seven-year-old *n* a person or animal that is seven years old. – *adj* (of a person, animal or thing) that is seven years old.

seventeen [sevn'ti:n] *n* **1** the number or figure 17. **2** the age of 17. – *adj* **1** 17 in number. **2** aged 17.

seventeen- having seventeen: *a seventeen-page report.*

,seven'teenth *n* **1** one of seventeen equal parts. **2** (*also adj*) (the) last of seventeen (people, things *etc*); (the) next after the sixteenth.

,seven'teen-year-old *n* a person or animal that is seventeen years old. – *adj* (of a person, animal or thing) that is seventeen years old.

seventy ['sevnti] *n* **1** the number or figure 70. **2** the age of 70. – *adj* **1** 70 in number. **2** aged 70.

seventy- having seventy: *a seventy-year -lease.*

'seventies *n pl* **1** the period of time between a person's seventieth and eightieth birthdays. **2** the range of temperatures between seventy and eighty degrees. **3** the period of time between the seventieth and eightieth years of a century.

'seventieth *n* **1** one of seventy equal parts. **2** (*also adj*) (the) last of seventy (people, things *etc*); (the) next after the sixty-ninth.

'seventy-year-old *n* a person or animal that is seventy years old. – *adj* (of a person, animal or thing) that is seventy years old.

sever ['sevə] *v* **1** to put an end to: *He severed relations with his family.* **2** to cut or break off: *His arm was severed in the accident.* **'severance** *n*.

several ['sevrəl] *adj* more than one or two, but not a great many: *Several weeks passed before he got a reply to his letter.* – *pron* some or a few: *Several of them are ill*; *Of the eggs, several were broken.*

severe [sə'viə] *adj* **1** (of something unpleasant) serious; extreme: *severe shortages of food*; *a severe illness*; *Our team suffered a severe defeat.* **2** strict or harsh: *a severe mother*; *severe criticism.* **3** (of style in dress *etc*) very plain: *a severe hairstyle.* **se'verely** *adv*.

se'verity [-'ve-] *n*: *the severity of the punishment*; *the severity of her dress.*

sew [sou] – *pt* **sewed**; *ptp* **sewn** – *v* to make, stitch or attach with thread, using a needle:

She sewed the pieces together; *Have you sewn my button on yet?*
'**sewer** *n*: *She's a good sewer.*
'**sewing** *n* **1** the activity of sewing: *I was taught sewing at school.* **2** work to be sewn: *She picked up a pile of sewing.*
'**sewing-machine** *n* a machine for sewing.
sew up to fasten completely or mend by sewing.
sewn up completely settled or arranged: *The contract is all sewn up.*

to **sew** (not **sow**) a button on.

sewer[1] ['sjuə] *n* an underground pipe or channel for carrying away water *etc* from drains.
'**sewage** [-idʒ] *n* waste matter (carried away in sewers).
sewage farm a place where sewage is treated and disposed of.
sewer[2] *see* **sew**.

sex [seks] *n* **1** either of the two classes (male and female) into which human beings and animals are divided according to the part they play in producing children or young: *Jeans are worn by people of both sexes*; *What sex is the puppy?* **2** the fact of belonging to either of these two groups: *discrimination on the grounds of sex*; (*also adj*) *sex discrimination.*
'**sexist** *adj* showing contempt for the other sex: *a very sexist remark.*
'**sexless** *adj* neither male nor female.
sexual ['sekʃuəl] *adj* concerned with the production of young or children: *the sexual organs.* '**sexually** *adv.*
'**sexy** *adj* having sex appeal.
sex appeal the quality of being attractive to people of the other sex: *That actress has sex appeal.*
sexual intercourse the sexual activity between a man and woman that is necessary for the producing of children.
sexagenerian [seksədʒi'neəriən] *n* a person from sixty to sixty-nine years old.
sextet [seks'tet] *n* **1** a group of six singers or musicians. **2** a piece of music composed for such a group.
sexton ['sekstən] *n* a person who looks after a church and often is responsible for bellringing *etc.*
shabby ['ʃabi] *adj* **1** looking old and worn: *shabby curtains*; *shabby clothes.* **2** wearing old or dirty clothes: *a shabby old man*; *He used to be so smart but he looks shabby now.* **3** (of behaviour) unworthy or mean: *That was a shabby thing to do.* '**shabbily** *adv.* '**shabbiness** *n.*
shack [ʃak] *n* a roughly-built hut: *a wooden shack.*
shackles ['ʃaklz] *n pl* a pair of iron rings joined by a chain that are put on a

prisoner's wrists, ankles' *etc*, to limit movement: *His captors put shackles on him.*
'**shackle** *v* to put shackles on.

shade [ʃeid] *n* **1** slight darkness caused by the blocking of some light: *I prefer to sit in the shade rather than the sun.* **2** the dark parts of a picture: *light and shade in a portrait.* **3** something that screens or shelters from light or heat: *a large sunshade*; *a shade for a light.* **4** a variety of a colour; a slight difference: *a pretty shade of green*; *shades of meaning.* **5** a slight amount: *The weather is a shade better today.* – *v* **1** (*sometimes with* **from**) to shelter from light or heat: *He put up his hand to shade his eyes.* **2** to make darker: *You should shade the foreground of that drawing.* **3** (*with* **into**) to change very gradually *eg* from one colour to another.
'**shaded** *adj* (of parts of a picture) made darker.
shades *n pl* (*esp Amer*) sunglasses.
'**shading** *n* (in a picture *etc*) the marking that shows the darker parts.
'**shady** *adj* **1** sheltered or giving shelter from heat or light: *a shady tree*; *a shady corner of the garden.* **2** dishonest: *a shady business.* '**shadiness** *n.*
put in the shade to cause to seem unimportant: *She is so beautiful that she puts her sister in the shade.*

shadow ['ʃadou] *n* **1** (a patch of) shade on the ground *etc* caused by an object blocking the light: *We are in the shadow of that building.* **2** (*in pl with* **the**) darkness or partial darkness caused by lack of (direct) light: *The child was afraid that wild animals were lurking in the shadows at the corner of his bedroom.* **3** a dark patch or area: *You look tired* – *there are shadows under your eyes.* **4** a very slight amount: *There's not a shadow of doubt that he stole the money.* – *v* **1** to hide or darken with shadow: *A broad hat shadowed her face.* **2** to follow closely, *esp* as a detective, spy *etc*: *We shadowed him for a week.*
'**shadowy** *adj* **1** full of shadows: *shadowy corners.* **2** dark and indistinct: *A shadowy figure went past.* '**shadowiness** *n.*
shaft [ʃa:ft] *n* **1** the long straight part or handle of a tool, weapon *etc*: *the shaft of a golf-club.* **2** one of two poles on a cart *etc* to which a horse *etc* is harnessed: *The horse stood patiently between the shafts.* **3** a revolving bar transmitting motion in an engine: *the driving-shaft.* **4** a long, narrow space, made for *eg* a lift in a building: *a liftshaft*; *a mineshaft.* **5** a ray of light: *a shaft of sunlight.*
shaggy ['ʃagi] *adj* (covered with hair, fur *etc* that is) rough and untidy in appearance: *The dog had a shaggy coat*; *a shaggy dog.* '**shagginess** *n.*

hake [ʃeik] – *pt* **shook** [ʃuk]: *ptp* **shaken** – *v*
1 to (cause to) tremble or move with jerks:
The explosion shook the building; *We were
shaking with laughter*; *Her voice shook as
she told me the sad news*. **2** to shock, disturb
or weaken: *He was shaken by the accident*;
My confidence in him has been shaken. – *n*
1 an act of shaking: *He gave the bottle a
shake*. **2** drink made by shaking the ingredients together vigorously: *a chocolate milkshake*.

'shaking *n* an act of shaking or state of
being shaken, shocked *etc*: *They got a
shaking in the crash*.

'shaky *adj* **1** weak or trembling with age,
illness *etc*: *a shaky voice*; *shaky handwriting*.
2 unsteady or likely to collapse: *a shaky
chair*. **3** (*sometimes with* at) not very good,
accurate *etc*: *He's a bit shaky at arithmetic*;
My arithmetic has always been very shaky;
*I'd be grateful if you would correct my rather
shaky spelling*. **'shakily** *adv*. **'shakiness** *n*.

'shake-up *n* a disturbance or reorganization.

shake one's fist at to hold up one's fist as
though threatening to punch: *He shook his
fist at me when I drove into the back of his
car*.

shake one's head to move one's head round
to left and right to mean 'No': *'Are you
coming?' I asked. She shook her head*.

shake off to rid oneself of: *He soon shook off
the illness*.

shake up to disturb or rouse (people) so as
to make them more energetic.

hale [ʃeil] *n* a type of rock from which oil is
sometimes obtained.

hall [ʃəl, ʃal] – *short forms* **I'll**, **we'll**: *neg
short form* **shan't** [ʃɑ:nt] – *v* **1** used to form
future tenses of other verbs when the subject is **I** or **we**: *We shall be leaving tomorrow*; *I shall have arrived by this time tomorrow*. **2** used to show the speaker's intention: *I shan't be late tonight*. **3** used in
questions, the answer to which requires a
decision: *Shall I tell him, or shan't I?*; *Shall
we go now?* **4** used as a form of command:
You shall go if I say you must.

hallow [ʃalou] *adj* **1** not deep: *shallow
water*; *a shallow pit*. **2** not able to think
seriously or feel deeply: *a rather shallow
personality*. **'shallowness** *n*.

'shallows *n pl* a place where the water is
shallow: *There are dangerous rocks and
shallows near the island*.

ham [ʃam] *n* something that is pretended, not
genuine: *The whole trial was a sham*. – *adj*
pretended, artificial or false: *a sham fight*;
Are those diamonds real or sham? – *v* – *pt,
ptp* **shammed** – to pretend (to be in some
state): *He shammed sleep/anger*; *He
shammed dead*; *I think she's only shamming*.

shamble ['ʃambl] *v* to walk slowly and

awkwardly, (as if) not lifting one's feet
properly off the ground: *The old man sham-
bled wearily along the street*.

shambles ['ʃamblz] *n sing* a confused mess;
(something in) a state of disorder: *His room
was a shambles*; *We're in a bit of a shambles
at the moment*.

shame [ʃeim] *n* **1** (*often with* at) an unpleasant
feeling caused by awareness of guilt, fault,
foolishness or failure: *I was full of shame at
my rudeness*; *He felt no shame at his behaviour*. **2** dishonour or disgrace: *The news
that he had accepted bribes brought shame
on his whole family*. **3** (*with* a) a cause of
disgrace or a matter for blame: *It's a shame
to treat a child so cruelly*. **4** (*with* a) a pity:
What a shame that he didn't get the job! – *v*
1 (*often with* into) to force or persuade to
do something by making ashamed: *He was
shamed into paying his share*. **2** to cause to
have a feeling of shame: *His cowardice
shamed his parents*.

'shameful *adj* disgraceful: *shameful behaviour*. **'shamefully** *adv*. **'shamefulness** *n*.

'shameless *adj* **1** without shame; blatant: *a
shameless liar*; *shameless deception*. **2** not
modest: *a shameless woman*. **'shamelessly**
adv. **'shamelessness** *n*.

'shamefaced *adj* showing shame or embarrassment: *He was very shamefaced about his
mistake*.

put to shame to make feel ashamed of
something or to make seem to be of poor
quality by showing greater excellence: *Your
beautiful drawing puts me/mine to shame*.

to my, his *etc* **shame** it is a cause of shame to
me, him *etc* that: *To my shame, my daughter
always beats me at chess*.

shampoo [ʃam'pu:] – *pl* **shampoos** – *n* **1** a
soapy liquid or other substance for washing
the hair and scalp or for cleaning carpets,
upholstery *etc*: *a special shampoo for greasy
hair*; *carpet shampoo*. **2** an act of washing
etc with shampoo: *I had a shampoo and set
at the hairdresser's*. – *v* – *pt, ptp* **sham'pooed**
– to wash or clean with shampoo: *She
shampoos her hair every day*; *We shampooed
the rugs yesterday*.

shandy ['ʃandi] – *pl* **'shandies** – *n* a mixture of
beer and lemonade or ginger beer.

shank [ʃaŋk] *n* **1** the leg, *esp* the part between
the knee and foot. **2** the long straight part
of *eg* a nail or screw.

shan't *see* **shall**.

shanty ['ʃanti] – *pl* **'shanties** – *n* a roughly-
built hut or shack.

***shape** [ʃeip] *n* **1** the external form or outline
of anything: *People are all (of) different
shapes and sizes*; *The house is built in the
shape of a letter L*. **2** an indistinct form: *I
saw a large shape in front of me in the
darkness*. **3** condition or state: *You're in

Shapes

Key

1 Circle
2 Square
3 Triangle
4 Rectangle
5 Pentagon
6 Diamond
7 Hexagon
8 Rhombus
9 Octagon
10 Oval
11 Cube
12 Sphere
13 Cone
14 Pyramid
15 Cylinder

better physical shape than I am. – v 1 to make into a certain shape, to form or model: *She shaped the dough into three separate loaves.* 2 to influence the nature of strongly: *This event shaped his whole life.* 3 (*sometimes with* up) to develop: *The team is shaping (up) well.*

shaped *adj* having a certain shape: *A rugby ball is egg-shaped.*

'**shapeless** *adj* lacking shape: *She wears a shapeless, baggy coat.* '**shapelessness** *n*.

'**shapely** *adj* well-formed and having an attractive shape: *She has long, shapely legs.* '**shapeliness** *n*.

in any shape (or form) at all: *I don't accept bribes in any shape or form.*

out of shape not in the proper shape: *I sat on my hat and it's rather out of shape.*

take shape to develop into a definite form: *My garden is gradually taking shape.*

share [ʃeə] *n* 1 one of the parts of something that is divided among several people *etc*: *We all had a share of the cake; We each paid our share of the bill.* 2 the part played by a person in something done *etc* by several people *etc*: *I had no share in the decision.* 3 a fixed sum of money invested in a business company by a '**shareholder**. – v 1 (*usu with* **among, between, with**) to divide among a number of people: *We shared the money between us.* 2 to have, use *etc* (something that another person has or uses); to allow someone to use(something one has or owns): *The students share a sitting-room; The little boy hated sharing his toys.* 3 (*sometimes with* in) to have a share of with someone else: *He wouldn't let her share the cost of the taxi.*

shark [ʃɑːk] *n* a type of large, fierce, flesh-eating fish.

sharp [ʃɑːp] *adj* 1 having a thin edge that can cut or a point that can pierce: *a sharp knife.* 2 (of pictures, outlines *etc*) clear and distinct: *the sharp outline of the mountain.* 3 (of changes in direction) sudden and quick: *a sharp left turn.* 4 (of pain *etc*) keen, acute or intense: *He gets a sharp pain after eating.* 5 (*often with* with) severe: *Don't be so sharp with the child!; She got a sharp reproach from me.* 6 alert: *Dogs have sharp ears.* 7 shrill and sudden: *a sharp cry.* 8 of a musical note, raised a semitone; too high in pitch: *F sharp; That last note was sharp.* – adv 1 punctually: *Come at six (o'clock) sharp.* 2 with an abrupt change of direction: *Turn sharp left here.* 3 at too high a pitch: *You're singing sharp.* – n 1 a sharp note: *sharps and flats.* 2 a sign (#) to show that a note is to be raised a semitone.

'**sharpen** *v* to make or grow sharp: *He sharpened his pencil.*

'**sharpener** *n* an instrument for sharpening: *a pencil-sharpener.*

'**sharply** *adv* in a sharp manner: *a sharply-pointed piece of glass; The road turned sharply to the left; He rebuked her sharply.* '**sharpness** *n*.

sharp practice dishonesty or cheating.

,**sharp-'witted** *adj* intelligent and alert: *a sharp-witted boy.*

look sharp to be quick or to hurry: *Bring me the books and look sharp (about it)!*

shatter [ʃatə] *v* 1 to break in small pieces, *usu* suddenly or forcefully: *The stone shattered the window; The window shattered.* 2 to upset greatly: *She was shattered by the news of his death.* '**shattered** *adj*.

shave [ʃeiv] *v* 1 to cut away (hair) from (*usu* oneself) with a razor: *He only shaves once a week.* 2 (*sometimes with* off) to scrape or cut away (the surface of wood *etc*): *The joiner shaved a thin strip off the edge of the door.* 3 to touch lightly in passing: *The car shaved the wall.* – n (the result of) an act of shaving.

'**shaven** *adj* shaved: *He was dark and clean-shaven.*

'**shavings** *n pl* very thin strips *esp* of wood: *The glasses were packed in wood shavings.*

shawl [ʃɔːl] *n* a piece of fabric used as a covering for the shoulders *etc*.

she [ʃiː] *pron* (used only as the subject of a verb) 1 a female person or animal already spoken about: *When the girl saw us, she asked the time.* 2 any female person: *She who runs the fastest will be the winner.* – n a female person or animal: *Is a cow a he or a she?*

she- female: *a she-wolf.*

sheaf [ʃiːf] – *pl* **sheaves** [ʃiːvz] – *n* a bundle *usu* tied or held together: *a sheaf of corn/notes.*

shear [ʃiə] – *pt* **sheared**; *ptps* **sheared, shorn** [ʃɔːn] – *v* 1 to clip or cut wool from (a sheep). 2 (*pt* **shorn**: *often with* off) to cut (hair) off: *All her curls have been shorn off.* 3 (*pt* **shorn**: *esp with* of) to cut hair from (someone): *He has been shorn (of all his curls).* 4 to cut or (cause to) break: *A piece of the steel girder sheared off.*

shears *n pl* a cutting-tool with two blades, like a large pair of scissors: *a pair of shears.*

sheath [ʃiːθ] – *pl* **sheaths** [ʃiːðs, ʃiːðz] – *n* 1 a case for a sword or blade. 2 a long close-fitting covering: *The rocket is encased in a metal sheath.*

sheathe [ʃiːð] *v* to put into a sheath: *He sheathed his sword.*

sheaves *see* sheaf.

shed[1] [ʃed] *n* a *usu* small building for working in, or for storage: *a wooden shed; a garden shed.*

shed[2] [ʃed] – *prp* '**shedding**; *pt, ptp* **shed** – *v* 1 to send out (light *etc*): *The torch shed a* *bright light on the path ahead.* **2** to cast off (clothing, skin, leaves *etc*): *Many trees shed their leaves in autumn.* **3** to produce (tears, blood): *I don't think many tears were shed when she left.*

shed light on to make clearer: *This letter sheds light on the reasons for his departure.*

she'd *see* **have, would.**

sheen [ʃiːn] *n* shine or glossiness.

sheep [ʃiːp] – *pl* **sheep** – *n* a kind of animal related to the goat, whose flesh is used as food and from whose wool clothing is made: *a flock of sheep.*
'**sheepish** *adj* embarrassed: *a sheepish expression.* '**sheepishly** *adv.*
'**sheepdog** *n* a dog (of a kind often) trained to work with sheep.

sheer[1] [ʃɪə] *adj* **1** absolute: *Her singing was a sheer delight; It all happened by sheer chance.* **2** very steep: *a sheer drop to the sea.* **3** (of cloth) very thin: *sheer silk.* – *adv* vertically: *The land rises sheer out of the sea.*

sheer[2] [ʃɪə]: **sheer off/away** to turn aside or swerve: *The speed-boat sheered off course.*

sheet [ʃiːt] *n* **1** a broad piece of cloth *eg* for a bed: *She put clean sheets on all the beds.* **2** a large, thin, *usu* flat, piece: *a sheet of paper/glass.*
,**sheet-'lightning** *n* the kind of lightning which appears in broad flashes.

sheik(h) [ʃeik, (*Amer*) ʃiːk] *n* an Arab chief.
'**sheik(h)dom** *n* a state ruled by a sheik(h).

shelf [ʃelf] – *pl* **shelves** [ʃelvz] – *n* a board for laying things on: *There are shelves on the kitchen walls.*
shelve [ʃelv] *v* **1** to put aside, *usu* for consideration, completion *etc* later: *The project has been shelved for the moment.* **2** to put up shelves in. **3** (of land) to slope gradually: *The land shelves towards the sea.*
on the shelf (of an unmarried woman) no longer likely to attract a man enough for him to want to marry her.

shell [ʃel] *n* **1** the hard outer covering of a shellfish, egg, nut *etc*: *an eggshell; A tortoise can pull its head and legs under its shell.* **2** an outer covering or framework: *After the fire, all that was left was the burned-out shell of the building.* **3** a metal case filled with explosives and fired from a gun *etc*: *A shell exploded right beside him.* – *v* **1** to remove from its shell or pod: *You have to shell peas before eating them.* **2** to fire explosive shells at: *The army shelled the enemy mercilessly.*
'**shellfish** – *pl* '**shellfish** – *n* any of several kinds of sea animal covered with a shell (*eg* oyster, crab).
come out of one's shell to become more confident and less shy.
shell out to pay out (money): *I had to shell out twenty dollars.*

she'll *see* **will.**

shelter [ʃeltə] *n* **1** protection against wind, rain, enemies *etc*: *We gave the old man shelter for the night.* **2** a building *etc* designed to give such protection: *a bus-shelter.* – *v* **1** to be in, or go into, a place of shelter: *He sheltered from the storm.* **2** to give protection: *That line of trees shelters my garden.*
'**sheltered** *adj* protected from harm and unpleasantness of all kinds: *a sheltered existence.*

shelve, shelves *see* **shelf.**

shepherd [ʃepəd] – *fem* '**shepherdess** – *n* a person who looks after sheep: *The shepherd and his dog gathered in the sheep.* – *v* (*often with* **around, in, out** *etc*) to guide or lead carefully: *He shepherded me through a maze of corridors.*

sheriff [ʃerif] *n* in the US, the chief law officer of a county, concerned with maintaining peace and order.

she's *see* **be, have.**

shield [ʃiːld] *n* **1** a broad piece of metal, wood *etc* carried as a protection against weapons. **2** something or someone that protects: *A thick steel plate acted as a heat shield.* **3** a trophy shaped like a shield won in a sporting competition *etc*: *My son has won the archery shield.* – *v* (*often with* **from**) **1** to protect: *The goggles shielded the motorcyclist's eyes from dust.* **2** to prevent from being seen clearly: *That group of trees shields the house from the road.*

shift [ʃift] *v* **1** to change (the) position or direction (of): *We spent the whole evening shifting furniture around; The wind shifted to the west overnight.* **2** to transfer: *She shifted the blame on to me.* **3** to get rid of: *This detergent shifts stains.* – *n* **1** a change (of position *etc*): *a shift of emphasis.* **2** a group of people who begin work on a job when another group stop work: *The night shift does the heavy work.* **3** the period during which such a group works: *an eight-hour shift*; (*also adj*) *shift work.*
'**shiftless** *adj* inefficient, lazy, or without a set purpose: *He's rather shiftless – he's had four jobs in six months.* '**shiftlessness** *n.*
'**shifty** *adj* looking cunning and dishonest: *I don't trust him – he has a very shifty look.* '**shiftily** *adv.* '**shiftiness** *n.*

shilling [ʃiliŋ] *n* **1** in Britain until 1971, a coin worth one-twentieth of £1. **2** in certain E African countries, a coin worth 100 cents.

shimmer [ʃimə] *v* to shine with a quivering or unsteady light: *The moonlight shimmered on the lake.*

shin [ʃin] *n* the front part of the leg below the knee: *He kicked him on the shins.* – *v* – *pt, ptp* **shinned** – (*usu with* **up**) to climb by alternate movements of both arms and both legs: *He shinned up the tree.*

ine [ʃain] – *pt, ptp* **shone** [ʃon, (*Amer*) ʃoun] – *v* **1** to (cause to) give out light; to direct such light towards someone or something: *The light shone from the window*; *The policeman shone his torch*; *He shone a torch on the body.* **2** to be bright: *She polished the silver till it shone.* **3** (*pt, ptp* **shined**) to polish: *He tries to make a living by shining shoes.* **4** (*often with* **at**) to be very good (at something): *He shines at games*; *You really shone in yesterday's match.* – *n* **1** brightness; the state of being well polished: *He likes a good shine on his shoes*; *a ray of sunshine.* **2** an act of polishing: *I'll just give my shoes a shine.*

'shining *adj* very bright and clear; producing or reflecting light; polished: *a shining star*; *The windows were clean and shining.*

'shiny *adj* glossy; reflecting light; polished: *a shiny cover on a book*; *a shiny nose*; *shiny shoes.* **'shininess** *n*.

hingle ['ʃiŋgl] *n* coarse gravel: *There's too much shingle and not enough sand on this beach.*

hingles ['ʃiŋglz] *n sing* a kind of infectious disease causing a rash of painful blisters.

hiny *see* **shine**.

hip [ʃip] *n* **1** a large boat: *The ship sank and all the passengers and crew were drowned.* **2** any of certain types of transport that fly: *a spaceship.* – *v* – *pt, ptp* **shipped** – to send or transport by ship: *The books were shipped to Australia.*

'shipment *n* **1** a load of goods sent by sea: *a shipment of wine from Portugal.* **2** the sending of goods by sea.

'shipper *n* a person who arranges for goods to be shipped: *a firm of shippers.*

'shipping *n* ships taken as a whole: *The harbour was full of shipping.*

'shipbuilder *n* a person whose business is the construction of ships: *a firm of shipbuilders.* **'shipbuilding** *n*.

,**ship'shape** *adj* in good order: *She left everything shipshape in her room when she left.*

'shipwreck *n* **1** the accidental sinking or destruction of a ship: *There were many shipwrecks on the rocky coast.* **2** a wrecked ship: *an old shipwreck on the shore.* – *v*: *We were shipwrecked off the coast of Africa.*

'shipyard *n* a place where ships are built or repaired.

ship water (of a boat) to let water in over the side: *The boat shipped water and nearly capsized.*

hirk [ʃəːk] *v* to avoid doing, accepting responsibility for *etc* (something one ought to): *She shirked telling him the bad news that night.* **'shirker** *n*.

hirt [ʃəːt] *n* a kind of garment worn on the upper part of the body: *a casual shirt*; *a short-sleeved shirt*; *She wore black jeans and a white shirt.*

in one's shirt-sleeves without a jacket or coat: *I work better in my shirt-sleeves.*

shirty ['ʃəːti] *adj* angry; bad-tempered: *He was a bit shirty with her when she arrived late.*

shit [ʃit] *n* an impolite or offensive word for the solid waste material that is passed out of the body. – *v* – *prp* **'shitting**: *pts, ptps* **shit, shat** – to pass waste matter from the body.

shiver ['ʃivə] *v* to quiver or tremble (with cold, fear *etc*). – *n* an act of shivering.

'shivery *adj* inclined to shiver: *The mention of ghosts gave her a shivery feeling.*

the shivers a feeling of horror: *The thought of working for him gives me the shivers.*

shoal¹ [ʃoul] *n* a great number of fish swimming together in one place: *The fishing-boats were searching for large shoals of fish.*

shoal² [ʃoul] *n* a shallow place in the sea *etc*; a sandbank: *The boat grounded on a shoal.*

shock¹ [ʃok] *n* **1** a severe emotional disturbance: *The news gave us all a shock.* **2** (*often* **electric shock**) the effect on the body of an electric current: *He got a slight shock when he touched the live wire.* **3** a sudden blow coming with great force: *the shock of an earthquake.* **4** a medical condition caused by a severe mental or physical shock: *He was suffering from shock after the crash.* – *v* to give a shock to; to upset or horrify: *Everyone was shocked by his death*; *The amount of violence shown on television shocks me.*

'shocker *n* a very unpleasant person or thing: *This headache is a real shocker.*

'shocking *adj* **1** causing horror or dismay: *shocking news.* **2** very bad: *a shocking cold.*

'shockingly *adv* **1** very: *shockingly expensive.* **2** very badly: *It was shockingly made.*

'shock-absorber *n* a device (in a motor car *etc*) for reducing the effect of bumps.

shock² [ʃok] *n* a bushy mass (of hair) on a person's head.

shod *see* **shoe**.

shoddy ['ʃodi] *adj* **1** of poor material or quality: *shoddy furniture.* **2** mean and contemptible: *a shoddy trick.* **'shoddily** *adv*. **'shoddiness** *n*.

shoe [ʃuː] *n* **1** an outer covering for the foot: *a new pair of shoes.* **2** (*also* **'horseshoe**) a curved piece of iron nailed to the hoof of a horse. – *v* – *prp* **'shoeing**: *pts, ptps* **shod** [ʃod], **shoed** – to put a shoe or shoes on (a horse *etc*).

shod [ʃod] *adj* with a shoe or shoes on.

'shoelace, (*Amer*) **'shoestring** *n* a kind of string or cord for fastening a shoe.

'shoemaker *n* a person who makes, repairs, or sells shoes.

on a **shoestring** with or using very little money: *He has to live on a shoestring.*

shone *see* **shine.**

shoo [ʃuː] *interj* an exclamation used when chasing a person, animal *etc* away. – *v* to chase away: *She shooed the pigeons away.*

shook *see* **shake.**

shoot [ʃuːt] – *pt, ptp* **shot** [ʃot] – *v* 1 (*often with* **at**) to send or fire (bullets, arrows *etc*) from a gun, bow *etc*: *The enemy were shooting at us; He shot an arrow through the air.* 2 to hit or kill with a bullet, arrow *etc*: *He went out to shoot pigeons; He was sentenced to be shot at dawn.* 3 to direct swiftly and suddenly: *She shot them an angry glance.* 4 to move swiftly: *He shot out of the room; The pain shot up his leg; The force of the explosion shot him across the room.* 5 to take (*usu* moving) photographs (for a film): *That film was shot in Spain; We will start shooting next week.* 6 to kick or hit at a goal in order to try to score. 7 to kill (game birds *etc*) for sport. – *n* a new growth on a plant: *The deer were eating the young shoots on the trees.*

shooting-star *see* **meteor.**

shoot down to hit (a plane) with *eg* a shell and cause it to crash.

shoot rapids to pass through rapids (in a canoe).

shoot up to grow or increase rapidly: *Prices have shot up.*

shop [ʃop] *n* 1 a place where goods are sold: *a baker's shop.* 2 a workshop, or a place where any kind of industry is carried on: *a machine-shop.* – *v* – *pt, ptp* **shopped** – (*often* **go shopping**) to visit shops for the purpose of buying: *We shop on Saturdays; She goes shopping once a week.*

'shopper *n* 1 a person who is shopping: *The street was full of shoppers.* 2 a large bag used when shopping.

'shopping *n* 1 the activity of buying goods in shops: *Have you a lot of shopping to do?*; (*also adj*) *a shopping-list.* 2 the goods bought: *He helped her carry her shopping home*; (*also adj*) *a shopping-basket/bag.*

shop assistant (*Amer* **'salesclerk, clerk**) a person employed in a shop to serve customers.

shop floor the workers in a factory or workshop, as opposed to the management.

'shopkeeper *n* a person who runs a shop of his own.

'shoplifter *n* a person who steals goods from a shop. **'shoplifting** *n.*

shopping centre a place, often a very large building, where there is a large number of different shops.

shop around to compare prices, quality of goods *etc* at several shops before buying anything.

shore [ʃoː] *n* land bordering on the sea or on any large area of water: *a walk along the shore; When the ship reached Gibraltar the passengers were allowed on shore.*

shorn *see* **shear.**

short [ʃoːt] *adj* 1 not long: *You look nice with your hair short; Do you think my dress is too short?* 2 not tall; smaller than usual: *a short man.* 3 not lasting long; brief: *a short film; in a very short time; I've a very short memory for details.* 4 not as much as it should be: *When I checked my change, I found it was 20 cents short.* 5 (with **of**) not having enough (money *etc*): *Most of us are short of money these days.* 6 (of pastry) made so that it is crisp and crumbles easily. – *adv* 1 suddenly; abruptly: *He stopped short when he saw me.* 2 not as far as intended: *The shot fell short.* **'shortness** *n.*

'shortage [-tidʒ] *n* a lack; the state of not having enough: *a shortage of water.*

'shorten *v* to make or become shorter: *The dress is too long – we'll have to shorten it.*

'shortening *n* (*esp Amer*) the fat used for making pastry.

'shortly *adv* soon: *He will be here shortly; Shortly after that, the police arrived.*

shorts *n pl* short trousers for men or women.

'shortbread *n* a kind of crisp, crumbling biscuit.

short-'change *v* to cheat (a buyer) by giving him too little change.

short circuit the missing out by an electric current of a part of an electrical circuit (*v* **short-'circuit**).

'shortcoming *n* a fault.

'shortcut *n* a quicker way between two places: *I'm in a hurry – I'll take a shortcut across the field.*

'shorthand *n* a method of writing rapidly, using strokes, dots *etc* to represent sounds.

short-'handed *adj* having fewer workers than are necessary or usual.

'short-list *n* a list of candidates selected from the total number of applicants for a job *etc.* – *v* to put on a short-list: *We've short-listed three of the twenty applicants.*

short-'lived [-'livd, (*Amer*) -'laivd] *adj* living or lasting only for a short time: *short-lived insects; short-lived enthusiasm.*

short-'range *adj* 1 not reaching a long distance: *short-range missiles.* 2 not covering a long time: *a short-range weather forecast.*

short-'sighted *adj* seeing clearly only things that are near: *I don't recognize people at a distance because I'm short-sighted.* **short-'sightedly** *adv.* **short-'sightedness** *n.*

short-'tempered *adj* easily made angry: *My husband is very short-tempered in the mornings.*

short-'term *adj* 1 concerned only with the

near future: *short-term plans.* **2** lasting only a short time: *a short-term loan.*

by a short head by a very small amount: *to win by a short head.*

for short as an abbreviation: *His name is Victor, but we call him Vic for short.*

go short to cause oneself not to have enough of something: *Save this carton for tomorrow, or else we'll go short (of milk).*

in short in a few words.

in short supply not available in sufficient quantity: *Fresh vegetables are in short supply.*

make short work of to dispose of very quickly: *The children made short work of the ice-cream.*

run short 1 (of a supply) to become insufficient: *Our money is running short.* **2** (with **of**) not to have enough: *We're running short of money.*

short and sweet: *His reply was short and sweet: 'Get out!' he shouted.*

short for an abbreviation of: *'Phone' is short for 'telephone'; What is 'Ltd.' short for?*

short of not as far as or as much as: *Our total came to just short of $1000; We stopped five miles short of London.*

shot[1] [ʃot] *n* **1** a single act of shooting: *He fired one shot.* **2** the sound of a gun being fired: *He heard a shot.* **3** a throw, hit, turn *etc* in a game or competition: *It's your shot; Can I have a shot?; He played some good shots in that tennis match; Good shot!* **4** an attempt: *I don't know if I can do that, but I'll have a shot (at it).* **5** something which is shot or fired, *esp* small lead bullets used in cartridges: *lead shot.* **6** a photograph, *esp* a scene in a film. **7** an injection: *The doctor gave me a shot.* **8** a marksman: *He's a good shot.*

'shotgun *n* a type of rifle that fires shot: *a double-barrelled shotgun.*

like a shot very quickly; eagerly: *He accepted my invitation like a shot.*

a shot in the dark a guess based on little or no information: *The detective admitted that his decision to check the factory had just been a shot in the dark.*

shot[2] *see* **shoot.**

should [ʃud] – *neg short form* **shouldn't** [ˈʃudnt] – *v* **1** *pt of* **shall**: *I thought I should never see you again.* **2** used to state that something ought to happen, be done *etc*: *You should hold your knife in your right hand; You shouldn't have said that.* **3** used to state that something is likely to happen *etc*: *If you leave now, you should arrive there by six o'clock.* **4** used after certain expressions of sorrow, surprise *etc*: *I'm surprised you should think that.* **5** used after **if** to state a condition: *If anything should happen*

to me, I want you to remember everything I have told you today. **6** (with **I** or **we**) used to state that a person wishes something was possible: *I should love to go to France (if only I had enough money).* **7** used to refer to an event *etc* which is rather surprising: *I was just about to get on the bus when who should come along but John, the very person I was going to visit.*

shoulder [ˈʃouldə] *n* **1** the part of the body between the neck and the upper arm: *He was carrying the child on his shoulders.* **2** anything that resembles a shoulder: *the shoulder of the hill.* **3** the part of a garment that covers the shoulder: *the shoulder of a coat.* **4** the upper part of the foreleg of an animal. – *v* **1** to lift on to the shoulder: *He shouldered his pack and set off on his walk.* **2** to bear the full weight of: *He must shoulder his responsibilities.* **3** to make (one's way) by pushing with the shoulder: *He shouldered his way through the crowd.*

'shoulder-blade *n* the broad flat bone of the back of the shoulder.

put one's shoulder to the wheel to begin to work very hard.

shoulder to shoulder close together; side by side: *We'll fight shoulder to shoulder.*

shouldn't *see* **should.**

shout [ʃaut] *n* **1** a loud cry or call: *He heard a shout.* **2** a loud burst (of laughter, cheering *etc*): *A shout went up from the crowd when he scored a goal.* – *v* to say very loudly: *He shouted the message across the river; I'm not deaf – there's no need to shout; Calm down and stop shouting at each other.*

shove [ʃʌv] *v* to thrust; to push: *I shoved the papers into a drawer; I'm sorry I bumped into you – somebody shoved me; Stop shoving!; He shoved (his way) through the crowd.* – *n* a push: *He gave the table a shove.*

shovel [ˈʃʌvl] *n* a tool like a spade, with a short handle, used for scooping up and moving coal, gravel *etc*. – *v* – *pt, ptp* **'shovelled,** (*Amer*) **'shoveled** – to move (as if) with a shovel, *esp* in large quantities: *He shovelled snow from the path; Don't shovel your food into your mouth!*

'shovelful *n* the amount that can be held, carried *etc* on a shovel: *a shovelful of coal.*

show [ʃou] – *pt* **showed**: *ptps* **showed, shown** – *v* **1** to allow or cause to be seen: *Show me your new dress; Please show your membership card when you come to the club; His work is showing signs of improvement.* **2** to be able to be seen: *The tear in your dress hardly shows; a faint light showing through the curtains.* **3** to offer or display, or to be offered or displayed, for the public to look at: *Which picture is showing at the cinema?; They are showing a new film; His paintings are being shown at the art gallery.* **4** to point out or point to: *He showed me the road to take*; *Show me the man you saw yesterday.* **5** (*often with* (**a**)**round**) to guide or conduct: *Please show this lady to the door*; *They showed him* (*a*)*round* (*the factory*). **6** to demonstrate to: *Will you show me how to do it?*; *He showed me a clever trick.* **7** to prove: *That just shows/goes to show how stupid he is.* **8** to give or offer (someone) kindness *etc*: *He showed him no mercy.* – *n* **1** an entertainment, public exhibition, performance *etc*: *a horse-show*; *a flower show*; *the new show at the theatre*; *a TV show.* **2** a display or act of showing: *a show of strength.* **3** an act of pretending to be, do *etc* (something): *He made a show of working, but he wasn't really concentrating.* **4** appearance, impression: *They just did it for show, in order to make themselves seem more important than they are.* **5** an effort or attempt: *He put up a good show in the chess competition.*

'**showy** *adj* giving an impression of value by a bright and striking outward appearance: *His clothes are too showy for my liking.* '**showiness** *n.*

'**show-business** *n* the entertainment industry, *esp* the branch of the theatre concerned with variety shows, comedy *etc.*

'**showcase** *n* a glass case for displaying objects in a museum, shop *etc.*

'**showdown** *n* an open, decisive quarrel *etc* ending a period of rivalry *etc.*

'**showground** *n* an area where displays *etc* are held.

'**show-jumping** *n* a competitive sport in which horses and their riders have to jump a series of artificial fences, walls *etc.*

'**showman** *n* a person who owns or manages an entertainment, a stall at a fair *etc.*

'**showroom** *n* a room where objects for sale *etc* are displayed for people to see: *a car showroom.*

give the show away to make known a secret, trick *etc.*

good show! that's good!

on show being displayed in an exhibition, showroom *etc*: *There are over five hundred paintings on show here.*

show off 1 to show or display for admiration: *He showed off his new car by taking it to work.* **2** to try to impress others with one's possessions, ability *etc*: *She is just showing off – she wants everyone to know how well she speaks French* (*n* '**show-off** a person who does this).

show up 1 to make obvious: *This light shows up the places where I've mended this coat.* **2** to reveal the faults of: *Mary was so neat that she really showed me up.* **3** to stand out clearly: *The scratches showed up on the*

photograph. **4** to appear or arrive: *I waited for her, but she never showed up.*

shower ['ʃauə] *n* **1** a short fall (of rain): *I got caught in a shower on my way here.* **2** anything resembling such a fall of rain: *a shower of sparks*; *a shower of bullets.* **3** a bath in which water is sprayed down on the bather from above: *I'm just going to have/ take a shower.* **4** the equipment used for such a bath: *We're having a shower fitted in the bathroom.* – *v* **1** to pour down in large quantities (on): *They showered confetti on the bride.* **2** to bathe in a shower: *He showered and dressed.*

'**showery** *adj* raining from time to time: *showery weather.*

'**showerproof** *adj* (of material, a coat *etc*) which will not be soaked by a light shower of rain.

shown *etc see* **show**.

shrank *see* **shrink**.

shrapnel ['ʃrapnəl] *n* small pieces of metal from an explosive shell, bomb *etc*: *His leg was torn open by shrapnel.*

shred [ʃred] *n* a long, narrow strip (*esp* very small) torn or cut off: *The lion tore his coat to shreds*; *a tiny shred of material.* – *v* – *pt*, *ptp* '**shredded** – to cut or tear into shreds: *to shred paper.*

shrew [ʃruː] *n* a type of small mouse-like animal with a long, pointed nose.

shrewd [ʃruːd] *adj* showing good judgement; wise: *a shrewd man*; *a shrewd choice.* '**shrewdly** *adv.* '**shrewdness** *n.*

shriek [ʃriːk] *v* to give out, or say with, a high scream or laugh: *She shrieked whenever she saw a spider*; *shrieking with laughter.* – *n* such a scream or laugh: *She gave a shriek as she felt someone grab her arm*; *shrieks of laughter.*

shrill [ʃril] *adj* high-pitched and piercing: *the shrill cry of a child.* '**shrilly** *adv.* '**shrillness** *n.*

shrimp [ʃrimp] *n* **1** a kind of small long-tailed shellfish. **2** an unkind word for a small person.

shrine [ʃrain] *n* **1** a holy or sacred place: *Many people visited the shrine where the saint lay buried.* **2** a *usu* highly-decorated case for holding holy objects.

shrink [ʃriŋk] – *pt* **shrank** [ʃraŋk]: *ptp* **shrunk** [ʃrʌŋk] *v* **1** to (cause material, clothes *etc* to) become smaller: *My jersey shrank in the wash*; *Do they shrink the material before they make it up into clothes?* **2** to move back in fear, disgust *etc* (from): *She shrank (back) from the man.* **3** to wish to avoid something unpleasant: *I shrank from telling him the terrible news.*

'**shrinkage** [-kidʒ] *n* the act of shrinking, or the amount by which something shrinks.

shrunken ['ʃrʌŋk(ən)] *adj* having been made or become smaller.

shrivel ['ʃrivl] – *pt*, *ptp* 'shrivelled, (*Amer*) 'shriveled – *v* to make or become dried up, wrinkled and withered: *The flowers shrivelled in the heat.*

shrivel up to shrivel: *The flowers shrivelled up; The heat shrivelled up the flowers.*

shroud [ʃraud] *n* 1 a cloth wrapped around a dead body. 2 something that covers: *a shroud of mist.* – *v* to cover or hide: *The incident was shrouded in mystery.*

shrub [ʃrʌb] *n* a small bush or woody plant: *He has planted bushes and shrubs in his garden.*

'shrubbery – *pl* 'shrubberies – *n* a part of a garden where shrubs are grown.

shrug [ʃrʌg] – *pt*, *ptp* shrugged – *v* to show doubt, lack of interest *etc* by raising (the shoulders): *When I asked him if he knew what had happened, he just shrugged (his shoulders).* – *n* an act of shrugging: *She gave a shrug of disbelief.*

shrug off to dismiss, get rid of or treat as unimportant: *She shrugged off all criticism.*

shrunk, shrunken *see* shrink.

shudder ['ʃʌdə] *v* to tremble from fear, disgust, cold *etc*. – *n* an act of trembling in this way: *a shudder of horror.*

shuffle ['ʃʌfl] *v* 1 to move (one's feet) along the ground *etc* without lifting them: *Do stop shuffling (your feet)!; The old man shuffled along the street.* 2 to mix (playing-cards *etc*): *It's your turn to shuffle (the cards).* – *n* an act of shuffling: *He gave the cards a shuffle.*

shun [ʃʌn] – *pt*, *ptp* shunned – *v* to avoid or keep away from.

shut [ʃʌt] – *prp* 'shutting: *pt*, *ptp* shut – *v* 1 to move (a door, window, lid *etc*) so that it covers or fills an opening; to move (a drawer, book *etc*) so that it is no longer open: *Shut that door, please!; Shut your eyes and don't look.* 2 to become closed: *The window shut with a bang.* 3 to close and *usu* lock (a building *etc*) *eg* at the end of the day or when people no longer work there: *The shops all shut at half past five; There's a rumour that the factory is going to be shut.* 4 to keep in or out of some place or keep away from someone by shutting something: *The dog was shut inside the house.* – *adj* closed.

shut down (of a factory *etc*) to close or be closed, for a time or permanently: *There is a rumour going round that the factory is going to (be) shut down (n 'shut-down).*

shut off 1 to stop an engine working, a liquid flowing *etc*: *I'll need to shut the gas off before I repair the fire.* 2 to keep away (from); to make separate (from): *He shut himself off from the rest of the world.*

shut up 1 to (cause to) stop speaking: *Tell them to shut up!; That'll shut him up!* 2 to close and lock: *It's time to shut up the shop.*

shutter ['ʃʌtə] *n* 1 one of *usu* two *usu* wooden covers over a window: *He closed the shutters.* 2 the moving cover over the lens of a camera, which opens when a photograph is taken: *When the shutter opens, light is allowed into the camera and reacts with the film.*

'shuttered *adj*: *shuttered windows.*

shuttle ['ʃʌtl] *n* 1 in weaving, a piece of equipment for carrying the thread backwards and forwards across the other threads. 2 a piece of machinery for making loops in the lower thread in a sewing-machine. 3 an air, train or other transport service *etc* which operates constantly backwards and forwards between two places: *an airline shuttle between London and Edinburgh; space shuttle (= a craft travelling between space stations).*

'shuttlecock *n* a rounded cork *etc*, with feathers *etc* fixed in it, used in the game of badminton.

shy [ʃai] – *compar* 'shyer *or* 'shier: *superl* 'shyest *or* 'shiest – *adj* 1 lacking confidence in the presence of others, *esp* strangers; not wanting to attract attention: *She is too shy to go to parties.* 2 drawing back from (an action, person *etc*): *She is shy of strangers.* 3 (of a wild animal) easily frightened; timid: *Deer are very shy animals.* – *v* (of a horse) to jump or turn suddenly aside in fear: *The horse shied at the strangers.*

'shyly *adv*. 'shyness *n*.

sick [sik] *adj* 1 vomiting or inclined to vomit: *He has been sick several times today; I feel sick; She's inclined to be seasick/airsick/carsick.* 2 (*esp Amer*) ill: *He is a sick man; The doctor told me that my husband is very sick and may not live very long.* 3 very tired (of); wishing to have no more (of): *I'm sick of doing this; I'm sick and tired of hearing about it!* 4 affected by strong, unhappy or unpleasant feelings: *I was really sick at making that bad mistake.* 5 in bad taste: *a sick joke.* – *n* vomit: *The bedclothes were covered with sick.*

'sicken *v* 1 to become sick. 2 to disgust: *The very thought sickens me.*

'sickening *adj* causing sickness, disgust or weariness; very unpleasant or annoying: *There was a sickening crunch; The weather is really sickening!* 'sickeningly *adv*.

'sickly *adj* 1 tending to be often ill: *a sickly child.* 2 suggesting sickness; pale; feeble: *She looks sickly.*

'sickness *n* the state of being sick or ill: *There seems to be a lot of sickness in the town; seasickness.*

'sick-leave *n* time taken off from work *etc* because of sickness: *He has been on sick-leave for the last three days.*

make (someone) sick to make (someone) feel very annoyed, upset *etc*: *It makes me sick to see him waste money like that.*
the sick ill people: *He visits the sick.*
worried sick very worried: *I'm worried sick about it.*

see also ill.

sickle ['sikl] *n* a tool with a curved blade for cutting grain *etc*.
side [said] *n* **1** (the ground beside) an edge, border or boundary line: *He walked round the side of the field; He lives on the same side of the street as me.* **2** a surface of something: *A cube has six sides.* **3** one of the two of such surfaces which are not the top, bottom, front, or back: *There is a label on the side of the box.* **4** either surface of a piece of paper, cloth *etc*: *Don't waste paper – write on both sides!* **5** the right or left part of the body: *I've got a pain in my side.* **6** a part or division of a town *etc*: *He lives on the north side of the town.* **7** a slope (of a hill): *a mountain-side.* **8** a point of view; an aspect: *We must look at all sides of the problem.* **9** a party, team *etc* which is opposing another: *Whose side are you on?*; *Which side is winning?* – *adj* additional, but less important: *a side issue.*
-side (the ground *etc* beside) the edge of something: *He walked along the dockside/ quayside*; *a roadside café.*
-sided having (a certain number or type of) sides: *a four-sided figure.*
'**sidelong** *adj, adv* from or to the side; not directly: *a sidelong glance*; *He glanced sidelong.*
'**sideways** *adj, adv* to or towards one side: *He moved sideways*; *a sideways movement.*
'**sideburns** *n pl* the *usu* short hair grown on the side of a man's face in front of the ears.
side effect an additional (often bad) effect of a drug *etc*: *These pills have unpleasant side effects.*
'**sidelight** *n* a light fixed to the side, or at the side of the front or back, of a car, boat *etc*: *He switched his sidelights on when it began to get dark.*
'**sideline** *n* **1** a business *etc* carried on outside one's regular job or activity: *He runs a mail-order business as a sideline.* **2** the line marking one of the long edges of a football pitch *etc*.
'**sidelines** *n pl* the position or point of view of a person not actually taking part in a sport, argument *etc*: *He threw in the occasional suggestion from the sidelines.*
side road a small, minor road.
'**sidestep** – *pt, ptp* '**sidestepped** – *v* **1** to step to one side: *He sidestepped as his attacker tried to grab him.* **2** to avoid: *to sidestep a problem.*

'**side-street** *n* a small, minor street: *The man ran down a side-street and disappeared.*
'**sidetrack** *v* to turn (a person) aside from what he was about to do: *I intended to write letters this evening, but was sidetracked into going to the pictures instead.*
'**sidewalk** *n* (*Amer*) a pavement or footpath.
from all sides from every direction: *People were running towards him from all sides.*
on all sides all around: *With enemies on all sides, we were trapped.*
side by side beside one another; close together: *They walked along the street side by side.*
side with to give support to in an argument *etc*: *Don't side with him against us!*
take sides to choose to support a particular opinion, group *etc* against another: *Everybody in the office took sides in the dispute.*
sidle ['saidl] *v* to go or move in a manner intended not to attract attention or as if one is shy or uncertain: *He sidled out of the room.*
siege [si:dʒ] *n* an attempt to capture a fort or town by keeping it surrounded by an armed force until it surrenders: *The town is under siege.*

siege is spelt with -ie- (not -ei-).

sieve [siv] *n* a container with a bottom full of very small holes, used to separate liquids from solids or small, fine pieces from larger ones *etc*: *He poured the soup through a sieve to remove all the lumps.* – *v* to pass (something) through a sieve.
sift [sift] *v* **1** to separate by passing through a sieve *etc*: *Sift the flour before making the cake.* **2** to examine closely: *He sifted the evidence carefully.*
sigh [sai] *v* **1** to take a long, deep-sounding breath showing tiredness, sadness, longing *etc*: *She sighed with exasperation.* **2** to say, or express, with sighs: *'I've still got several hours' work to do,' he sighed.* – *n* an act of sighing.
heave a sigh to sigh: *She heaved a sigh of relief when she found her purse.*
sight [sait] *n* **1** the act or power of seeing: *The blind man had lost his sight in the war.* **2** the area within which things can be seen by someone: *The boat was within sight of land*; *The end of our troubles is in sight.* **3** something worth seeing: *She took her visitors to see the sights of London.* **4** a view or glimpse. **5** something seen that is unusual, ridiculous, shocking *etc*: *She's quite a sight in that hat.* **6** (on a gun *etc*) an apparatus to guide the eye in taking aim: *Where is the sight on a rifle?* – *v* **1** to get a view of; to see suddenly: *We sighted the coast as dawn broke.* **2** to look at (something) through the

sight of a gun: *He sighted his prey and pulled the trigger.*

'sight-seeing *n* visiting the chief buildings, places of interest *etc* of an area: *They spent a lot of their holiday sight-seeing in London;* (*also adj*) *a sight-seeing tour.* **'sight-seer** *n.*

catch sight of to get a brief view of; to begin to see: *He caught sight of her as she came round the corner.*

lose sight of to stop being able to see: *She lost sight of him in the crowd.*

sign [sain] *n* **1** a mark used to mean something; a symbol: *+ is the sign for addition.* **2** a notice set up to give information (a shopkeeper's name, the direction of a town *etc*) to the public: *road-sign.* **3** a movement (*eg* a nod, wave of the hand) used to mean or represent something: *He made a sign to me to keep still.* **4** a piece of evidence suggesting that something is present or about to come: *There were no signs of life at the house and he was afraid they were away; Clouds are often a sign of rain.* – *v* **1** to write one's name (on): *Sign at the bottom, please.* **2** to write (one's name) on a letter, document *etc*: *He signed his name on the document.* **3** to make a movement of the head, hand *etc* in order to show one's meaning: *She signed to me to say nothing.*

'signboard *n* a board with a notice: *In the garden was a signboard which read 'House for Sale'.*

'signpost *n* a post with a sign on it, showing the direction and distance of places: *We saw a signpost which told us we were 80 kilometres from London.*

sign in/out to record one's arrival or departure by writing one's name: *He signed in at the hotel when he arrived.*

sign up 1 to join an organization or make an agreement to do something *etc* by writing one's name. **2** to engage for work by making a legal contract.

signal [ˈsignəl] *n* **1** a sign (*eg* a movement of the hand, a light, a sound), *esp* one arranged beforehand, giving a command, warning or other message: *He gave the signal to advance.* **2** a machine *etc* used for this purpose: *a railway signal.* **3** the wave, sound received or sent out by a radio set *etc.* – *v* – *pt, ptp* **'signalled,** (*Amer*) **'signaled** – **1** to make signals (to): *The policeman signalled the driver to stop.* **2** to send (a message *etc*) by means of signals.

'signalman *n* **1** a person who operates railway signals. **2** a person who sends signals in general: *He is a signalman in the army.*

signature [ˈsignətʃə] *n* **1** a signed name: *That is his signature on the cheque.* **2** an act of signing one's name: *Signature of this document means that you agree with us.*

signify [ˈsignifai] *v* **1** to be a sign of; to mean:

His frown signified disapproval. **2** to show; to make known by a sign, gesture *etc*: *He signified his approval with a nod.*

significance [sigˈnifikəns] *n* meaning or importance: *a matter of great significance.*

significant [sigˈnifikənt] *adj* having a lot of meaning or importance: *There was no significant change in the patient's condition.*

significantly [sigˈnifikəntli] *adv* **1** in a significant manner: *He patted his pocket significantly.* **2** to an important degree: *Sales-levels are significantly lower than last year, which is very disappointing.*

silence [ˈsailəns] *n* **1** (a period of) absence of sound or of speech: *A sudden silence followed his remark.* **2** failure to mention, tell something *etc*: *Your silence on this subject is disturbing.* – *v* to cause to be silent: *The arrival of the teacher silenced the class.* – *interj* be silent!

'silencer *n* a piece of equipment fitted to a gun, or (*Amer* **'muffler**) in an engine, for making noise less.

'silent [-t] *adj* **1** free from noise: *The house was empty and silent.* **2** not speaking: *He was silent on that subject.* **3** not making any noise: *This lift is quite silent.* **'silently** *adv.*

in silence without saying anything: *The children listened in silence to the story.*

silhouette [siluˈet] *n* **1** an outline drawing of a person: *A silhouette in a silver frame hung on the wall.* **2** a dark image, *esp* a shadow, seen against the light.

silk [silk] *n* **1** very fine, soft threads made by silkworms. **2** thread, cloth *etc* made from this: *The dress was made of silk;* (*also adj*) *a silk dress.*

'silky *adj* soft, fine and rather shiny like silk. **'silkiness** *n.*

'silkworm *n* the caterpillar of certain moths, which makes silk.

sill [sil] *n* a ledge of wood, stone *etc* at the foot of an opening, such as a window or a door: *The windows of the old house were loose, and the sills were crumbling.*

silly [ˈsili] *adj* foolish; not sensible: *Don't be so silly!; silly children.* **'silliness** *n.*

silt [silt] *n* fine sand and mud left behind by flowing water.

silt up to (cause to) become blocked by mud *etc*: *The harbour had gradually silted up, so that large boats could no longer use it.*

silver [ˈsilvə] *n* **1** an element, a precious grey metal which is used in making jewellery, ornaments *etc*: *The tray was made of solid silver.* **2** anything made of, or looking like, silver *esp* knives, forks, spoons *etc*: *Burglars broke into the house and stole all our silver.* – *adj* **1** made of, of the colour of, or looking like, silver: *a silver brooch; silver stars/paint.* **2** (of a wedding anniversary, jubilee *etc*) twenty-fifth: *We celebrated our silver wedding (anniversary) last month.*

'silvery *adj* like silver, *esp* in colour.

silver foil/paper a common type of wrapping material, made of metal and having a silvery appearance: *Chocolate bars are sold wrapped in silver paper.*

similar ['similə] *adj* (*often with* **to**) alike in many (often most) ways: *My house is similar to yours; Our jobs are similar.* **simi'larity** [-'la-] (*pl* **simi'larities**) *n*.

'similarly *adv* in the same, or a similar, way.

simile ['siməli] *n* a form of expression using 'like' or 'as', in which one thing is compared to another which it only resembles in one or a small number of ways: *'Her hair was like silk' is a simile.*

simmer ['simə] *v* to (cause to) cook gently at or just below boiling point: *The stew simmered on the stove; Simmer the ingredients in water for five minutes.*

simmer down to calm down.

simple ['simpl] *adj* **1** not difficult; easy: *a simple task.* **2** not complicated or involved: *The matter is not as simple as you think.* **3** not fancy or unusual; plain: *a simple dress/design; He leads a very simple life.* **4** pure; mere: *the simple truth.* **5** trusting and easily cheated: *She is too simple to see through his lies.* **6** weak in the mind; not very intelligent: *I'm afraid he's a bit simple, but he's good with animals.*

'simpleton [-tən] *n* a foolish person.

simplicity [sim'plisəti] *n* the state of being simple: *The beauty of this idea is its simplicity; He answered with a child's simplicity.*

simplifi'cation *n* **1** the process of making simpler. **2** something made simpler; a simpler form: *The Americans have made some simplifications in English spelling.*

'simplified *adj* made less difficult or complicated: *simplified language/tasks.*

'simplify [-plifai] *v* to make simpler: *Can you simplify your language a little?*

'simply *adv* **1** only: *I do it simply for the money.* **2** absolutely: *simply beautiful.* **3** in a simple manner: *She was always very simply dressed.*

simple-'minded *adj* of low intelligence; stupid. **simple-'mindedness** *n*.

simulate ['simjuleit] *v* to cause (something) to appear to be real *etc*: *This machine simulates the take-off and landing of an aircraft.*

'simulated *adj* artificial; having the appearance of: *simulated leather; a simulated accident.*

simu'lation *n* **1** (an act of) simulating. **2** something made to resemble something else.

simultaneous [siməl'teiniəs, (*Amer*) sai-] *adj* happening, or done, at exactly the same time: *He fell, and there was a simultaneous gasp from the crowd.* **simul'taneously** *adv*.

sin [sin] *n* wickedness, or a wicked act, *esp* one that breaks a religious law: *It is a sin to envy the possessions of other people; Lying and cheating are both sins.* – *v* – *pt, ptp* **sinned** – to do wrong; to commit a sin, *esp* in the religious sense: *Forgive me, Father, for I have sinned.* **'sinner** *n*.

'sinful *adj* wicked. **'sinfully** *adv*. **'sinfulness** *n*.

since *conj* **1** (*often with* **ever**) from a certain time onwards: *I have been at home (ever) since I returned from Italy.* **2** at a time after: *Since he agreed to come, he has become ill.* **3** because: *Since you are going, I will go too.* – *adv* **1** (*usu with* **ever**) from that time onwards: *We fought and I have avoided him ever since.* **2** at a later time: *We have since become friends.* – *prep* **1** from the time of (something in the past) until the present time: *She has been very unhappy ever since her quarrel with her boyfriend.* **2** at a time between (something in the past) and the present time: *I've changed my address since last year.* **3** from the time of (the invention, discovery *etc* of): *the greatest invention since the wheel.*

sincere [sin'siə] *adj* **1** true; genuine: *a sincere desire; sincere friends.* **2** not trying to pretend or deceive: *a sincere person.*

sin'cerely *adv*: *I sincerely hope that you will succeed.*

sin'cerity [-'se-] *n* the state of being sincere: *The sincerity of his comments was obvious to all.*

sinful *see* **sin**.

sing [siŋ] – *pt* **sang** [saŋ]: *ptp* **sung** [sʌŋ] – *v* to make (musical sounds) with one's voice: *He sings very well; She sang a Scottish song; I could hear the birds singing in the trees.*

'singer *n* a person who sings, *eg* as a profession: *Are you a good singer?; He's a trained singer.*

'singing *n* the art or activity of making musical sounds with one's voice: *Do you do much singing nowadays?; (also adj) a singing lesson/teacher.*

sing out to shout or call out: *Sing out when you're ready to go.*

singe [sindʒ] – *prp* **'singeing**: *pt, ptp* **singed** – *v* to (cause to) burn on the surface; to scorch: *She singed her dress by pressing it with too hot an iron.*

single ['siŋgl] *adj* **1** one only: *The spider hung on a single thread.* **2** for one person only: *a single bed/mattress.* **3** unmarried: *a single person.* **4** for or in one direction only: *a single ticket/journey/fare.* – *n* **1** a gramophone record with only one tune or song on each side: *This group have just brought out a new single.* **2** a one-way ticket. **'singleness** *n*.

'**singles** n pl **1** (also n sing) in tennis etc, a match or matches with only one player on each side: *The men's singles are being played this week*; (also adj) *a singles match.* **2** (esp Amer) unmarried (usu young) people: *a bar for singles*; (also adj) *a singles holiday/club.*

'**singly** adv one by one; separately: *They came all together, but they left singly.*

,**single-'breasted** adj (of a coat, jacket etc) having only one row of buttons: *a single-breasted tweed suit.*

,**single-'decker** n, adj (a bus etc) having only one deck or level: *a single-decker (bus).*

,**single-'handed** adj, adv working etc by oneself, without help: *He runs the restaurant single-handed; single-handed efforts.*

single out to choose or pick out for special treatment: *He was singled out to receive special thanks for his help.*

singular ['singjulə] n **1** (also adj) (in) the form of a word which expresses only one: *'Foot' is the singular of 'feet'*; *a singular noun/verb*; *The noun 'foot' is singular.* **2** the state of being singular: *Is this noun in the singular or the plural?*

sinister ['sinistə] adj suggesting, or warning of, evil: *sinister happenings*; *His disappearance is extremely sinister.*

sink [siŋk] – pt **sank** [saŋk]: ptp **sunk** [sʌŋk] – v **1** to (cause to) go down below the surface of water etc: *The torpedo sank the battleship immediately*; *The ship sank in deep water.* **2** to go down or become lower (slowly): *The sun sank slowly behind the hills*; *Her voice sank to a whisper.* **3** to (cause to) go deeply (into something): *The ink sank into the paper*; *He sank his teeth into an apple.* **4** (of one's spirits etc) to become depressed or less hopeful: *My heart sinks when I think of the difficulties ahead.* **5** to invest (money): *He sank all his savings in the business.* – n a kind of basin with a drain and a water supply connected to it: *He washed the dishes in the sink.*

'**sunken** adj **1** sunk under water: *a sunken ship.* **2** below the level of the surrounding area: *a sunken garden.*

be sunk to be defeated, in a hopeless position etc: *If he finds out that we've been disobeying him, we're sunk.*

sink in 1 to be fully understood: *The news took a long time to sink in.* **2** to be absorbed: *The surface water on the paths will soon sink in.*

sinner see sin.

sinus ['sainəs] n (usu in pl) an air-filled hollow in the bones of the skull, connected with the nose: *His sinuses frequently become blocked in the winter*; (also adj) *He suffers from sinus trouble.*

sip [sip] – pt, ptp **sipped** – v to drink in very small mouthfuls. – n a very small mouthful: *She took a sip of the medicine.*

siphon ['saifən] n **1** a bent pipe or tube through which liquid can be drawn off from one container to another at a lower level: *He used a siphon to get some petrol out of the car's tank.* **2** (also '**soda-siphon**) a glass bottle with such a tube, used for soda water. – v (with **off, into** etc) to draw (off) through a siphon: *They siphoned the petrol into a can.*

sir [sə:] n **1** a polite form of address (spoken or written) to a man: *Excuse me, sir!*; *He started his letter 'Dear Sirs, ...'.* **2** in the UK, the title of a knight or baronet: *Sir Francis Drake.*

siren ['saiərən] n a kind of instrument that gives out a loud hooting noise as a (warning) signal: *a factory siren.*

sirloin ['sə:loin] n a joint of beef cut from the upper part of the back.

sisal ['saisəl] n, adj (of) a type of fibre from a kind of Central American plant, used in making ropes etc.

sister ['sistə] n **1** the title given to a female child to describe her relationship to the other children of her parents: *She's my sister*; *my father's sister.* **2** a type of senior nurse: *She's a sister on Ward 5.* **3** a female member of a religious group. **4** a female fellow member of any group: *We must fight for equal opportunities, sisters!* – adj closely similar in design, function etc: *sister ships.*

'**sister-in-law** – pl '**sisters-in-law** – n **1** the sister of one's husband or wife. **2** the wife of one's brother.

sit [sit] – prp **sitting**: pt, ptp **sat** [sat] – v **1** to (cause to) rest on the buttocks; to (cause to) be seated: *He likes sitting on the floor*; *They sat me in the chair and started asking questions.* **2** to lie or rest; to have a certain position: *The parcel is sitting on the table.* **3** (with **on**) to be an official member of (a board, committee etc): *He sat on several committees.* **4** (of birds) to perch: *An owl was sitting in the tree by the window.* **5** to undergo (an examination). **6** to take up a position, or act as a model, in order to have one's picture painted or one's photograph taken: *She is sitting for a portrait/photograph.* **7** (of a committee, parliament etc) to be in session: *Parliament sits from now until Christmas.*

'**sitter** n **1** a person who poses for a portrait etc. **2** a baby-sitter.

'**sitting** n a period of continuous action, meeting etc: *I read the whole book at one sitting*; *The committee were prepared for a lengthy sitting.*

'**sit-in** n an occupation of a building etc by protesters: *The students staged a sit-in.*

'sitting-room *n* a room used mainly for sitting in.

sitting target, sitting duck someone or something that is in an obvious position to be attacked: *If they're reducing staff, he's a sitting target.*

sit back to rest and take no part in an activity: *He just sat back and let it all happen.*

sit down to (cause to) take a seat, take a sitting position: *Let's sit down over here; He sat the child down on the floor.*

sit out 1 to remain seated during a dance: *Let's sit (this one) out.* **2** to remain inactive and wait until the end of: *They'll try to sit out the crisis.*

sit tight to keep the same position or be unwilling to move or act: *The best thing to do is to sit tight and see if things improve.*

sit up 1 to rise to a sitting position: *Can the patient sit up?* **2** to remain awake, not going to bed: *I sat up until 3 a.m. waiting for you!*

site [sait] *n* a place where a building, town *etc* is, was, or is to be, built: *He's got a job on a building-site; The site for the new factory has not been decided.*

situation [sitju'eiʃən] *n* **1** circumstances; a state of affairs: *an awkward situation.* **2** the place where anything stands or lies: *The house has a beautiful situation beside a lake.* **3** a job: *the situations-vacant columns of the newspaper.*

'situated *adj* to be found; placed: *The new school is situated on the north side of town.*

six [siks] *n* **1** the number or figure 6. **2** the age of 6. – *adj* **1** 6 in number. **2** aged 6.

six- having six (of something): *a six-cylinder engine.*

sixth *n* **1** one of six equal parts. **2** (*also adj*) (the) last of six (people, things *etc*); (the) next after the fifth.

'six-year-old *n* a person or animal that is six years old. – *adj* (of a person, animal or thing) that is six years old.

at sixes and sevens in confusion; completely disorganized: *On the day before the wedding, the whole house was at sixes and sevens.*

sixteen [siks'ti:n] *n* **1** the number or figure 16. **2** the age of 16. – *adj* **1** 16 in number. **2** aged 16.

sixteen- having sixteen (of something): *a sixteen-page booklet.*

six'teenth *n* **1** one of sixteen equal parts. **2** (*also adj*) (the) last of sixteen (people, things *etc*); (the) next after the fifteenth.

six'teen-year-old *n* a person or animal that is sixteen years old. – *adj* (of a person, animal or thing) that is sixteen years old.

sixty ['siksti] *n* **1** the number or figure 60. **2** the age of 60. – *adj* **1** 60 in number. **2** aged 60.

'sixties *n pl* **1** the period of time between one's sixtieth and seventieth birthdays. **2** the range of temperatures between sixty and seventy degrees. **3** the period of time between the sixtieth and seventieth years of a century.

'sixtieth *n* **1** one of sixty equal parts. **2** (*also adj*) (the) last of sixty (people, things *etc*); (the) next after the fifty-ninth.

sixty- having sixty (of something): *a sixty-page supplement.*

'sixty-year-old *n* a person or animal that is sixty years old. – *adj* (of a person, animal or thing) that is sixty years old.

size [saiz] *n* **1** largeness: *an area the size of a football pitch; The size of the problem alarmed us.* **2** one of a number of classes in which shoes, dresses *etc* are grouped according to measurements: *I take size 5 in shoes.*

'sizeable *adj* fairly large: *His income is quite sizeable, now that he has been promoted.*

size up to form an opinion about a person, situation *etc*: *He sized up the situation and acted immediately.*

skate¹ [skeit] *n* **1** a boot with a steel blade fixed to it for moving on ice *etc*: *I can move very fast across the ice on skates.* **2** a roller-skate. – *v* **1** to move on skates: *She skates beautifully.* **2** to move over, along *etc* by skating. **'skater** *n*.

'skating-rink *n* an area of ice set aside or designed for skating on.

skate² [skeit] – *pls* **skate, skates** – *n* **1** a kind of large, flat fish. **2** its flesh, used as food.

skeleton ['skelitn] *n* **1** the bony framework of an animal or person: *The archaeologists dug up the skeleton of a dinosaur.* **2** any framework or outline: *the steel skeleton of a building.*

skeleton key a key which can open many different locks.

skeptic *see* **sceptic**.

sketch [sketʃ] *n* **1** a rough plan, drawing or painting: *He made several sketches before starting the portrait.* **2** a short (written or spoken) account without many details: *The book began with a sketch of the author's life.* **3** a short play, dramatic scene *etc*: *a comic sketch.* – *v* **1** to draw, describe, or plan without completing the details. **2** to make rough drawings, paintings *etc*: *She sketches as a hobby.*

'sketchy *adj* **1** incompletely done or carried out: *a sketchy search.* **2** slight or incomplete: *a sketchy knowledge of French.* **'sketchily** *adv*. **'sketchiness** *n*.

'sketch-book *n* a book for drawing sketches in.

skew [skju:] *adj* not straight or symmetrical. – *v* to make or be distorted, not straight.

skewer ['skjuə] *n* a long pin of wood or metal

for keeping meat together while roasting: *Put the cubes of meat on a skewer.*

ski [ski:] *n* one of a pair of long narrow strips of wood *etc* that are attached to the feet for gliding over snow, water *etc.* – *v* – *prp* **'skiing**; *pt, ptp* **skied** [ski:d] – to travel on or use skis *esp* as a leisure activity: *He broke his leg when he was skiing.*

ski- of or for the activity of skiing: *ski-suits*; *ski-jump.*

'skier *n*: *The slope was crowded with skiers.*
'skiing *n*: *Skiing is her favourite sport*; (*also adj*) *a skiing holiday.*

skid [skid] – *pt, ptp* **'skidded** – *v* to slide accidentally sideways: *His back wheel skidded and he fell off his bike.* – *n* **1** an accidental slide sideways. **2** a wedge *etc* put under a wheel to check it on a steep place.

skill [skil] *n* **1** cleverness at doing something, resulting either from practice or from natural ability: *This job requires a lot of skill.* **2** a job or activity that requires training and practice; an art or craft: *the basic skills of reading and writing.*
'skilful *adj* having, or showing, skill: *a skilful surgeon*; *It was very skilful of you to repair my bicycle.* **'skilfully** *adv.* **'skilfulness** *n.*
skilled *adj* **1** (*neg* **un-**) (of a person *etc*) having skill, *esp* skill gained by training: *a skilled craftsman*; *She is skilled at all types of dressmaking.* **2** (of a job *etc*) requiring skill: *a skilled trade.*

skilful is spelt with **-l-** (not **-ll-**).

skim [skim] – *pt, ptp* **skimmed** – *v* **1** to remove (floating matter, *eg* cream) from the surface of (a liquid): *Skim the fat off the gravy.* **2** to move lightly and quickly over (a surface): *The skier skimmed across the snow.* **3** to read (something) quickly, missing out parts: *She skimmed (through) the book.*
skim milk milk from which the cream has been skimmed.

skimp [skimp] *v* **1** (*with* **on**) to take, spend, use, give *etc* too little or only just enough: *She skimped on meals in order to send her son to college.* **2** to do (a job) imperfectly: *He's inclined to skimp his work.*
'skimpy *adj* too small; inadequate: *a skimpy dress.* **'skimpily** *adv.* **'skimpiness** *n.*

skin [skin] *n* **1** the natural outer covering of an animal or person: *She couldn't stand the feel of wool against her skin*; *A snake can shed its skin.* **2** a thin outer layer, as on a fruit: *a banana-skin*; *onion-skins.* **3** a (thin) film or layer that forms on a liquid: *Boiled milk often has a skin on it.* – *v* – *pt, ptp* **skinned** – to remove the skin from: *He skinned and cooked the rabbit.*
'skin-diving *n* diving and swimming under

water with simple equipment (a mask, flippers *etc*).
'skin-'tight *adj* fitting as tightly as one's skin: *skin-tight jeans*; *Her new sweater is skin-tight.*
by the skin of one's teeth very narrowly; only just: *We escaped by the skin of our teeth.*

skinny ['skini] *adj* very thin: *Most fat girls long to be skinny.* **'skinniness** *n.*

skip [skip] – *pt, ptp* **skipped** – *v* **1** to go along with a hop on each foot in turn: *The little girl skipped up the path.* **2** to jump over a rope that is being turned under the feet and over the head (as a children's game). **3** to miss out (a meal, part of a book *etc*): *I skipped lunch and went shopping instead*; *Skip chapter two.* – *n* a hop on one foot in skipping.

skipper ['skipə] *n* the captain of a ship, aeroplane or team. – *v* to act as skipper of: *Who skippered the team?*

skirt [skə:t] *n* **1** a garment, worn by women, that hangs from the waist: *Was she wearing trousers or a skirt?* **2** the lower part of a dress, coat *etc*: *a dress with a flared skirt.*

skittle ['skitl] *n* a bottle-shaped, *usu* wooden object used as a target for knocking over in the game of skittles.
'skittles *n sing* a game in which the players try to knock down a number of skittles with a ball: *a game of skittles*; *Do you play skittles?*; (*also adj*) *a skittles match.*

skulk [skʌlk] *v* to wait about or keep oneself hidden (often for a bad purpose): *Someone was skulking in the bushes.*

skull [skʌl] *n* the bony case that encloses the brain: *He's fractured his skull.*

skunk [skʌŋk] *n* a small North American animal which defends itself by squirting out an unpleasant-smelling liquid.

sky [skai] – *pl* **skies** (*often with* **the**) – *n* the part of space above the earth, in which the sun, moon *etc* can be seen; the heavens: *The sky was blue and cloudless*; *We had grey skies and rain throughout our holiday*; *The skies were grey all week.*
,sky-'blue *adj, n* (of) the light blue colour of cloudless sky: *She wore a sky-blue dress.*
'sky-diving *n* the sport of jumping from aircraft and waiting for some time before opening one's parachute. **'sky-diver** *n.*
,sky-'high *adv, adj* very high: *The car was blown sky-high by the explosion*; *sky-high prices.*
'skylight *n* a window in a roof or ceiling: *The attic had only a small skylight and was very dark.*
'skyline *n* the outline of buildings, hills *etc* seen against the sky: *the New York skyline*; *I could see something moving on the skyline.*

'skyscraper n a high building of very many storeys, *esp* in the US.

the sky's the limit there is no upper limit *eg* to the amount of money that may be spent: *Choose any present you like – the sky's the limit!*

slab [slab] n a thick slice or thick flat piece of anything: *concrete slabs; a slab of cake.*

slack [slak] adj 1 loose; not firmly stretched: *Leave the rope slack.* 2 not firmly in position: *He tightened a few slack screws.* 3 not strict; careless: *He is very slack about getting things done.* 4 in industry *etc*, not busy; inactive: *Business has been rather slack lately.*

'slacken v (*sometimes with* off *or* up) 1 to make or become looser: *She felt his grip on her arm slacken.* 2 to make or become less busy, less active or less fast: *The doctor told him to slacken up if he wanted to avoid a heart-attack.*

'slackly adv. 'slackness n.

slacks n pl trousers, *usu* loose-fitting, worn informally by men or women: *a pair of slacks.*

slain see slay.

slam [slam] – *pt, ptp* slammed – v 1 to shut with violence *usu* making a loud noise: *The door suddenly slammed (shut); He slammed the door in my face.* 2 to strike against something violently *esp* with a loud noise: *The car slammed into the wall.* – n (the noise made by) an act of closing violently and noisily: *The door closed with a slam.*

slander ['slɑːndə] n (the act of making) an untrue spoken, not written, statement about a person with the intention of damaging that person's reputation: *That story about her is nothing but a wicked slander!* – v to make such statements about (a person *etc*).

slang [slaŋ] n words and phrases (often in use for only a short time) used very informally, *eg* words used mainly by, and typical of, a particular group: *army slang; teenage slang; 'A stiff' is slang for 'a corpse'.* – v to speak rudely and angrily to or about (someone); to abuse: *I got furious when he started slanging my mother.*

slant [slɑːnt] v to be, lie *etc* at an angle, away from a vertical or horizontal position or line; to slope: *The house is very old and all the floors and ceilings slant a little.* – n a sloping line or direction: *The roof has a steep slant.*

'slanting adj: *He has backward-slanting writing; slanting eyes.*

slap [slap] n a blow with the palm of the hand or anything flat: *The child got a slap from his mother for being rude.* – v – *pt, ptp* slapped – to give a slap to: *He slapped my face.*

slash [slaʃ] v 1 to make long cuts in (cloth *etc*): *He slashed his victim's face with a razor.* 2 (*with* at) to strike out violently at (something): *He slashed at the bush angrily with a stick.* 3 to reduce greatly: *A notice in the shop window read 'Prices slashed!'* – n 1 a long cut or slit. 2 a sweeping blow.

slat [slat] n a thin strip of wood, metal *etc.*

'slatted adj having, or made with, slats: *a slatted door.*

slate[1] [sleit] n 1 (a piece of) a type of easily split rock of a dull blue-grey colour, used for roofing *etc*: *Slates fell off the roof in the wind;* (*also adj*) *a slate roof.* 2 a small writing-board made of this, used by school-children.

slate[2] [sleit] v to say harsh things to or about: *The new play was slated by the critics.*

slaughter ['slɔːtə] n 1 the killing of people or animals in large numbers, cruelly and *usu* unnecessarily: *Many people protested at the annual slaughter of seals.* 2 the killing of animals for food: *Methods of slaughter must be humane.* – v 1 to kill (animals) for food: *Thousands of cattle are slaughtered here every year.* 2 to kill in a cruel manner, *esp* in large numbers. 3 to criticize unmercifully or defeat very thoroughly: *Our team absolutely slaughtered the other side.*

'slaughter-house n a place where animals are killed in order to be sold for food; an abattoir.

slave [sleiv] n 1 a person who works for a master to whom he belongs: *In the nineteenth century many Africans were sold as slaves in the United States.* 2 a person who works very hard for someone else: *He has a slave who types his letters and organizes his life for him.* – v to work very hard, often for another person: *I've been slaving away for you all day while you sit and watch television.*

'slavery n 1 the state of being a slave. 2 the system of ownership of slaves. 3 very hard and badly-paid work: *Her job is sheer slavery.*

slay [slei] – *pt* slew [sluː]: *ptp* slain [slein] – v to kill: *Cain slew his brother Abel.*

sleazy ['sliːzi] adj dirty and neglected: *This area is rather sleazy.*

sledge [sledʒ] n (*also, esp Amer,* sled [sled]) a vehicle, *usu* with runners, made for sliding upon snow. – v to ride on a sledge: *The children were sledging all afternoon.*

sledge-hammer ['sledʒhamə] n a large heavy hammer.

sleek [sliːk] adj 1 (of hair, an animal's fur *etc*) smooth, soft and glossy: *The dog has a lovely sleek coat.* 2 well fed and cared for: *a sleek Siamese cat lay by the fire.* 'sleekly adv. 'sleekness n.

sleep [sliːp] – *pt, ptp* slept [slept] – v to rest

with the eyes closed and in a state of natural unconsciousness: *Goodnight – sleep well!*; *I can't sleep – my mind is too active.* – *n* (a) rest in a state of natural unconsciousness: *It is bad for you to have too little sleep, since it makes you tired*; *I had only four hours' sleep last night.*

'sleeper *n* 1 a person who sleeps: *Nothing occurred to disturb the sleepers.* 2 a berth or compartment for sleeping, on a railway train: *I'd like to book a sleeper on the London train.*

'sleepless *adj* without sleep: *He spent a sleepless night worrying about the situation.*

'sleepy *adj* 1 inclined to sleep; drowsy: *I feel very sleepy after that long walk.* 2 not (seeming to be) alert: *She always has a sleepy expression.* 3 (of places *etc*) very quiet; lacking entertainment and excitement: *a sleepy town.* **'sleepily** *adv*. **'sleepiness** *n*.

'sleeping-bag *n* a kind of large warm bag for sleeping in, used by campers *etc*.

'sleeping-pill/'sleeping-tablet *ns* a kind of pill that can be taken to make one sleep: *She tried to commit suicide by swallowing an overdose of sleeping-pills.*

'sleepwalk *v* to walk about while asleep: *She was sleepwalking again last night.* **'sleepwalker** *n*.

put to sleep 1 to cause (a person or animal) to become unconscious by means of an anaesthetic; to anaesthetize: *The doctor will give you an injection to put you to sleep.* 2 to kill (an animal) painlessly, *usu* by the injection of a drug: *As she was so old and ill my cat had to be put to sleep.*

sleep like a log/top to sleep very well and soundly.

sleep off to recover from (something) by sleeping: *She's in bed sleeping off the effects of the party.*

sleep on to put off making a decision about (something) overnight: *I'll sleep on it and let you know tomorrow.*

sleet [sliːt] *n* rain mixed with snow or hail: *That isn't snow – it's just sleet.* – *v* to hail or snow, with a mixture of rain: *It seems to be sleeting outside.*

sleeve [sliːv] *n* 1 the part of a garment that covers the arm: *He tore the sleeve of his jacket*; *a dress with long/short sleeves.* 2 (*also* **'record-sleeve**) a stiff envelope for a gramophone record. 3 something, *eg* a tubular part in a piece of machinery, that covers as a sleeve of a garment does the arm.

-sleeved having (a certain kind of) sleeve(s): *a long-sleeved dress.*

'sleeveless *adj* without sleeves: *a sleeveless dress.*

have/keep (something) up one's sleeve to

keep (a plan *etc*) secret for possible use at a later time: *I'm keeping this idea up my sleeve for the time being.*

sleigh [slei] *n* a *usu* large sledge pulled by a horse *etc*.

slender ['slendə] *adj* 1 thin, slim or narrow. 2 slight or small: *His chances of winning are extremely slender.*

slept *see* sleep.

slew[1] [sluː] *v* to (cause to) turn or swing in a certain direction: *The car skidded and slewed across the road.*

slew[2] *see* slay.

slice [slais] *n* 1 a thin broad piece (of something): *How many slices of meat would you like?* 2 a part or share: *Who got the largest slice of the profits?* – 1 *v* to cut into slices: *He sliced the sausage/cucumber.* 2 to cut (as) with a sharp blade or knife: *The blade slipped and sliced off the tip of his forefinger.* 3 in golf *etc*, to hit (a ball) in such a way that it curves away to the right (or in the case of a left-handed player, to the left).

sliced *adj* (*neg* **un-**) cut into slices: *a sliced loaf.*

slick[1] [slik] *adj* clever *esp* in a sly or dishonest way; smart: *That was a very slick move!* **'slickly** *adv*. **'slickness** *n*.

slick[2] [slik] *n* (*also* **'oil-slick**) a broad band of oil floating on the surface of the sea *etc*: *An oil-slick is threatening the coast.*

slide [slaid] – *pt, ptp* **slid** [slid] – *v* 1 to (cause to) move or pass along smoothly: *He slid the drawer open*; *Children must not slide in the school corridors.* 2 to move quietly or secretly: *I slid hurriedly past the window*; *He slid the book quickly out of sight under his pillow.* – *n* 1 an act of sliding. 2 a slippery track, or apparatus with a smooth sloping surface, on which people or things can slide: *The children were taking turns on the slide in the playground.* 3 a small transparent photograph for projecting on to a screen *etc*: *The lecture was illustrated with slides.* 4 a glass plate on which objects are placed to be examined under a microscope. 5 (*also* **'hair-slide**) a (decorative) hinged fastening for the hair.

'slide-rule *n* an instrument for calculating, like a ruler in shape and having a central section that slides up and down between the outer sections.

sliding door a type of door that slides across an opening rather than swinging on a hinge.

slight [slait] *adj* 1 small; not great; not serious or severe: *a slight breeze*; *We have a slight problem.* 2 (of a person) slim and delicate-looking: *It seemed too heavy a load for such a slight woman.*

'slightest *adj* (*often in negative sentences, questions etc*) least possible; any at all: *I* *haven't the slightest idea where he is*; *The slightest difficulty seems to upset her.*

'**slighting** *adj* insulting; disrespectful: *He made rather a slighting remark about her parents.* '**slightingly** *adv.*

'**slightly** *adv* **1** to a small extent: *I'm still slightly worried about it.* **2** slenderly: *slightly built.*

in the slightest (*in negative sentences, questions etc*) at all: *You haven't upset me in the slightest*; *That doesn't worry me in the slightest.*

slily *see* **sly.**

slim [slim] *adj* **1** not thick or fat; thin: *She has a slim, graceful figure*; *Taking exercise is one way of keeping slim.* **2** not good; slight: *There's still a slim chance that we'll find the child alive.* – *v* – *pt, ptp* **slimmed** – to use means (such as eating less) in order to become slimmer: *I mustn't eat cakes – I'm trying to slim.*

'**slimming** the process or practice of trying to become slimmer: *Slimming should be done carefully.* '**slimness** *n.*

slime [slaim] *n* thin, slippery mud or other matter that is soft, sticky and half-liquid: *There was a layer of slime at the bottom of the pond.*

'**slimy** *adj* covered with, consisting of, or like, slime: *a slimy mess on the floor.* '**sliminess** *n.*

sling [sliŋ] *n* **1** a type of bandage hanging from the neck or shoulders to support an injured arm: *He had his broken arm in a sling.* **2** a band of cloth *etc* worn over the shoulder for supporting a rifle *etc* on the back. **3** a looped arrangement of ropes, chains *etc* for supporting, hoisting, carrying and lowering heavy objects. – *v* – *pt, ptp* **slung** [slʌŋ] – **1** to throw violently: *The boy slung a stone at the dog.* **2** to support, hang or swing by means of a strap, sling *etc*: *He had a camera and binoculars slung round his neck.*

'**slingshot** *n* (*Amer*) a catapult.

slink [sliŋk] – *pt, ptp* **slunk** [slʌŋk] – *v* to move as if wanting to avoid attention: *He slunk into the kitchen and stole a cake.*

slip[1] [slip] – *pt, ptp* **slipped** – *v* **1** to slide accidentally and lose one's balance or footing: *I slipped and fell on the path.* **2** to slide, or drop, out of the right position or out of control: *The plate slipped out of my grasp.* **3** to drop in standard: *I'm sorry about my mistake – I must be slipping!* **4** to move quietly *esp* without being noticed: *She slipped out of the room.* **5** to escape from: *The dog had slipped its lead and disappeared.* **6** to put or pass (something) with a quick, light movement: *She slipped the letter back in its envelope.* – *n* **1** an act of slipping: *Her sprained ankle was a result of a slip on the*

path. **2** a *usu* small mistake: *Everyone makes the occasional slip.* **3** a kind of undergarment worn under a dress; a petticoat. **4** (*also* '**slipway**) a sloping platform next to water used for building and launching ships. **5** in cricket, the position of a fielder standing behind and to the (right) side of the batsman: *He was caught at first slip/in the slips*; (*also adj*) a *slip fielder.*

'**slipper** *n* a loose, soft kind of shoe for wearing indoors.

'**slippery** *adj* **1** so smooth as to cause slipping: *The path is slippery – watch out!* **2** not trustworthy: *He's rather a slippery character.* '**slipperiness** *n.*

slip road a road for joining or leaving a motorway.

'**slipshod** *adj* (of work *etc*) untidy; careless: *The teacher told him his work was slipshod.*

give (someone) the slip to escape from or avoid (someone) in a secretive manner: *The crooks gave the policemen the slip.*

let slip 1 to miss (an opportunity *etc*): *I let the chance slip, unfortunately.* **2** to say (something) unintentionally: *She let slip some remark about my daughter.*

slip into to put on (clothes) quickly: *She slipped into her nightdress.*

slip off 1 to take (clothes) off quickly: *Slip off your shoe.* **2** to move away noiselessly or hurriedly: *We'll slip off when no-one's looking.*

slip on to put on (clothes) quickly.

slip up to make a mistake; to fail to do something: *They certainly slipped up badly over the new appointment* (*n* '**slip-up**).

slip[2] [slip] *n* a strip or narrow piece of paper: *She wrote down his telephone number on a slip of paper.*

slipper, slippery *see* **slip**[1].

slit [slit] – *prp* '**slitting**: *pt, ptp* **slit** – *v* to make a long cut in: *She slit the envelope open with a knife.* – *n* a long cut; a narrow opening: *a slit in the material.*

slither ['sliðə] *v* to slide or slip while trying to walk (*eg* on mud): *The dog was slithering about on the mud.*

slog [slog] – *pt, ptp* **slogged** – *v* **1** to hit hard (*usu* without aiming carefully): *She slogged him with her handbag.* **2** to make one's way with difficulty: *We slogged on up the hill.* **3** to work very hard: *She has been slogging all week at the shop.* – *n* **1** (a period of) hard work: *months of hard slog.* **2** a hard blow: *He gave the ball a slog.*

slogan ['slougən] *n* an easily-remembered and frequently repeated phrase which is used in advertising *etc.*

slop [slop] – *pt, ptp* **slopped** – *v* to (cause liquid to) splash, spill, or move around violently in a container: *The water was slopping about in the bucket.*

'sloppy *adj* **1** semi-liquid; tending to slop: *sloppy food.* **2** careless and untidy; messy: *His work is sloppy.* **3** very sentimental: *That film is rather sloppy.* **'sloppily** *adv.* **'sloppiness** *n.*

slope [sloup] *n* **1** a position or direction that is neither level nor upright; an upward or downward slant: *The floor is on a slight slope.* **2** a surface with one end higher than the other: *The house stands on a gentle slope.* – *v* to be in a position which is neither level nor upright: *The field slopes towards the road.*
'sloping *adj*: *a sloping roof.*

slot [slot] *n* **1** a small narrow opening, *esp* one to receive coins: *I put the correct money in the slot, but the machine didn't start.* **2** a (*usu* regular) position (in *eg* the schedule of television/radio programmes): *The early-evening comedy slot.* – *v* – *pt, ptp* **'slotted** – (*with* **in** *or* **into**) to fit (something) into a small space: *He slotted the last piece of the puzzle into place; I managed to slot in my tea-break between two jobs.*
slot machine a machine, *esp* one containing cigarettes, sweets *etc* for sale, worked by putting a coin in a slot.

slouch [slautʃ] *v* to sit, move or walk with shoulders rounded and head hanging: *He slouched sulkily out of the room; He was slouching in an armchair.*

slow [slou] *adj* **1** not fast; not moving quickly; taking a long time: *a slow train; The service at that restaurant is very slow; He was very slow to offer help.* **2** (of a clock *etc*) showing a time earlier than the actual time; behind in time: *My watch is five minutes slow.* **3** not clever; not quick at learning: *He's particularly slow at arithmetic.* – *v* to make, or become slower: *The car slowed to take the corner.*
'slowly *adv*: *He slowly opened his eyes; He drove home slowly.* **'slowness** *n.*
slow motion movement which is slower than normal or actual movement *esp* as a special effect in films: *Let's watch it, in slow motion.*
slow down/up to make or become slower: *The police were warning drivers to slow down; The fog was slowing up the traffic.*

sludge [slʌdʒ] *n* soft, slimy mud, grease or other matter which settles at the bottom of a liquid: *The river-bed is covered with thick sludge.*

slug¹ [slʌg] *n* a kind of animal like a snail.
'sluggish *adj* moving slowly; not active or alert: *a sluggish river; I always feel rather sluggish in the mornings.* **'sluggishly** *adv.* **'sluggishness** *n.*

slug² [slʌg] *n* a piece of metal, *esp* an irregularly shaped lump used as a bullet. – *v* – *pt, ptp* **slugged** – to strike (a person) heavily *usu* causing unconsciousness: *The man had* been slugged on the back of the neck with a heavy object.

sluice [sluːs] *n* **1** (*often* **'sluice-gate**) a sliding gate for controlling a flow of water in an artificial channel: *We shall have to open the sluice.* **2** the channel or the water which flows through it.

slum [slʌm] *n* a group of houses, blocks of flats, street *etc* where the conditions are dirty and overcrowded and the building(s) *usu* in a bad state: *That new block of flats is rapidly turning into a slum; a slum dwelling.*
the slums the area(s) of a town *etc* where there are slums: *As a social worker, she does a lot of work in the slums.*

slumber ['slʌmbə] *v* to sleep. – *n* sleep: *She was in a deep slumber; I didn't want to disturb your slumbers.*

slump [slʌmp] *v* **1** to fall or sink suddenly and heavily: *He slumped wearily into a chair.* **2** (of prices, stocks, trade *etc*) to become less; to lose value suddenly: *Business has slumped.* – *n* **1** a sudden fall in value, trade *etc*: *a slump in prices.* **2** a time of very bad economic conditions, with serious unemployment *etc*; a depression: *There was a serious slump in the 1930s.*

slung *see* **sling.**

slunk *see* **slink.**

slush [slʌʃ] *n* **1** melting snow: *The streets are covered with slush.* **2** (something said or written showing) weak sentimentality: *I think most romantic novels are just slush!* **'slushy** *adj.* **'slushiness** *n.*

sly [slai] *adj* **1** cunning or deceitful: *He sometimes behaves in rather a sly manner.* **2** playfully mischievous: *He made a sly reference to my foolish mistake.* **'slyly, 'slily** *advs.* **'slyness** *n.*

smack¹ [smak] *v* to strike smartly and loudly; to slap: *She smacked the child's hand/bottom.* – *n* (the sound of) a blow of this kind; a slap: *He could hear the smack of the waves against the side of the ship.* – *adv* directly and with force: *He ran smack into the door.*
a smack on the cheek a quick, loud kiss on the cheek: *He gave her a quick smack on the cheek.*

smack² [smak] *v* (*with* **of**) to have a suggestion of: *The whole affair smacks of prejudice.* – *n*: *There's a smack of corruption about this affair.*

small [smoːl] *adj* **1** little in size, degree, importance *etc*; not large or great: *She was accompanied by a small boy of about six; There's only a small amount of sugar left; She cut the meat up small for the baby.* **2** not doing something on a large scale: *He's a small businessman.* **3** little; not much: *You have small reason to be satisfied with yourself.* **4** (of the letters of the alphabet) not capital: *The teacher showed the children how to write a capital G and a small g.*

small ads advertisements in the personal columns of a newspaper.

small arms weapons small and light enough to be carried by a man: *They found a hoard of rifles and other small arms belonging to the rebels.*

small change coins of small value: *a pocketful of small change.*

small hours the hours immediately after midnight: *He woke up in the small hours.*

'smallpox *n* a type of serious infectious disease in which there is a severe rash of large, pus-filled spots that *usu* leave scars.

small screen television, not the cinema: *This play is intended for the small screen.*

'small-time *adj* (of a thief *etc*) not working on a large scale: *a small-time crook/thief.*

feel/look small to feel or look foolish or insignificant: *He criticized her in front of her colleagues and made her feel very small.*

smart [smɑːt] *adj* **1** neat and well-dressed; fashionable: *You're looking very smart today*; *a smart suit.* **2** clever and quick in thought and action: *We need a smart boy to help in the shop*; *I don't trust some of those smart salesmen.* **3** brisk; sharp: *She gave him a smart slap on the cheek.* – *v* **1** (of part of the body) to be affected by a sharp stinging feeling: *The thick smoke made his eyes smart.* **2** to feel annoyed, resentful *etc* after being insulted *etc*: *He is still smarting from your remarks.* – *n* the stinging feeling left by a blow or the resentful feeling left by an insult: *He could still feel the smart of her slap/insult.*

'smarten (*often with* **up**) *v* to make or become smarter: *He has smartened up a lot in appearance lately.*

'smartly *adv*: *The soldiers stood smartly to attention*; *She is always smartly dressed.*

'smartness *n.*

smash [smaʃ] *v* **1** (*sometimes with* **up**) to (cause to) break in pieces or be ruined: *The plate dropped on the floor and smashed into little pieces*; *This unexpected news had smashed all his hopes*; *He had an accident and smashed up his car.* **2** to strike with great force; to crash: *The car smashed into a lamp-post.* – *n* **1** (the sound of) a breakage; a crash: *A plate fell to the ground with a smash*; *There has been a bad car smash.* **2** a strong blow: *He gave his opponent a smash on the jaw.* **3** in tennis *etc*, a hard downward shot.

'smashing *adj* marvellous; splendid: *What a smashing idea!*; *a smashing new bike.*

smash hit a song, show *etc* that is a great success: *This play was a smash hit in New York.*

smear [smiə] *v* **1** to spread (something sticky

or oily) over a surface: *The little boy smeared jam on the chair.* **2** to make or become blurred; to smudge: *He brushed against the newly painted notice and smeared the lettering.* **3** to try to discredit (a person *etc*) by slandering him: *He has been spreading false stories in an attempt to smear us.* – *n* **1** a mark made by smearing. **2** a piece of slander.

smell [smel] *n* **1** the sense or power of being aware of things through one's nose: *My sister never had a good sense of smell.* **2** the quality that is noticed by using this power: *a pleasant smell*; *There's a strong smell of gas.* **3** an act of using this power: *Have a smell of this!* – *v* – *pts, ptps* **smelled, smelt** [smelt] – **1** to notice by using one's nose: *I smell gas*; *I thought I smelt (something) burning.* **2** to give off a smell: *The roses smelt beautiful*; *Her hands smelt of fish.* **3** to examine by using the sense of smell: *Let me smell those flowers.*

-smelling having a (particular kind of) smell: *a nasty-smelling liquid*; *sweet-smelling roses.*

'smelly *adj* having a bad smell: *smelly fish.*

'smelliness *n.*

smell out to find (as if) by smelling: *We buried the dog's bone, but he smelt it out again.*

smelt¹ [smelt] *v* to melt (ore) in order to separate metal from waste.

smelt² *see* **smell**.

smile [smail] *v* to show pleasure, amusement *etc* by turning up the corners of the mouth: *He smiled warmly at her as he shook hands*; *They all smiled politely at the joke*; *He asked her what she was smiling at.* – *n* an act of smiling, or the resulting facial expression: *'How do you do?' he said with a smile*; *the happy smiles of the children.*

'smiling *adj*: *a happy, smiling face.*

be all smiles to be, or look, very happy: *He was all smiles when he heard the good news.*

smirk [sməːk] *v* to smile in a self-satisfied or foolish manner: *He sat there smirking after the teacher had praised him.* – *n* a smile of this sort.

smith [smiθ] *n* **1** a blacksmith. **2** a person whose job is to work with a particular metal, or make a particular type of article: *a goldsmith*; *a silversmith*; *a gunsmith.*

smock [smok] *n* a loose, shirt-like garment.

smog [smog] *n* fog mixed with smoke and fumes from factories, houses, vehicles *etc*: *Some big cities have a problem with smog.*

smoke [smouk] *n* **1** the cloudlike gases and particles of soot given off by something which is burning: *Smoke was coming out of the chimney*; *He puffed cigarette smoke into my face.* **2** an act of smoking (a cigarette *etc*): *I came outside for a smoke.* – *v* **1** to

give off smoke. **2** to draw in and puff out the smoke from (a cigarette *etc*): *I don't smoke, but he smokes cigars.* **3** to dry, cure, preserve (ham, fish *etc*) by hanging it in smoke.
smoked *adj* treated with smoke: *smoked cheese.*
'**smokeless** *adj* **1** allowing no smoke: *Our part of the town is a smokeless zone.* **2** burning without smoke: *smokeless fuel.*
'**smoker** *n* a person who smokes cigarettes *etc*: *When did you become a smoker?*; *He's a pipe-smoker.*
'**smoking** *n* the habit of smoking cigarettes *etc*: *He has given up cigarette-smoking at last*; *Smoking can damage your health.*
'**smoky** *adj* **1** filled with, or giving out (too much) smoke: *The atmosphere in the room was thick and smoky.* **2** like smoke in appearance *etc*. '**smokiness** *n*.
smoke detector a device in a building which sounds a fire alarm when smoke passes through it.
'**smokescreen** *n* **1** a cloud of smoke used to conceal the movements of troops *etc*. **2** something intended to conceal one's activities *etc*.
go up in smoke 1 to be completely destroyed by fire: *The whole house went up in smoke.* **2** to vanish very quickly leaving nothing behind: *All his plans have gone up in smoke.*
smolder *see* **smoulder**.
smooth [smuːð] *adj* **1** having an even surface; not rough: *Her skin is as smooth as satin.* **2** without lumps: *Mix the ingredients to a smooth paste.* **3** (of movement) without breaks, stops or jolts: *Did you have a smooth flight from New York?* **4** without problems or difficulties: *a smooth journey*; *His progress towards promotion was smooth and rapid.* **5** (too) agreeable and pleasant in manner *etc*: *I don't trust those smooth salesmen.* – *v* **1** (*often with* **down, out** *etc*) to make (something) smooth or flat: *She tried to smooth the creases out.* **2** (*with* **into** *or* **over**): to rub (a liquid substance *etc*) gently over (a surface): *Smooth the moisturizing cream into/over your face and neck.*
'**smoothen** *v* to make smooth.
'**smoothly** *adv*: *The plane landed smoothly*; *The meeting went very smoothly.*
'**smoothness** *n*.
smother ['smʌðə] *v* **1** to kill or die from lack of air, caused *esp* by a thick covering over the mouth and nose; to suffocate: *He smothered his victim by holding a pillow over her face.* **2** to prevent (a fire) from burning by covering it thickly: *He threw sand on the fire to smother it.* **3** to cover (too) thickly; to overwhelm: *When he got home his children smothered him with kisses.*
smoulder, (*Amer*) **smolder** ['smouldə] *v* to

burn slowly or without flame: *A piece of coal had fallen out of the fire and the hearth-rug was smouldering.*
smudge [smʌdʒ] *n* a smear or a blurred mark: *There's a smudge of ink on your nose.* – *v* to make or become blurred or smeared.
'**smudgy** *adj*. '**smudginess** *n*.
smug [smʌg] *adj* well satisfied, or too obviously pleased, with oneself: *I don't like that smug little man.* '**smugly** *adv*. '**smugness** *n*.
smuggle ['smʌgl] *v* **1** to bring (goods) into, or send them out from, a country illegally, or without paying duty: *He was caught smuggling (several thousand cigarettes through the Customs).* **2** to send or take secretly: *I smuggled some food out of the kitchen.*
'**smuggler** *n* a person who smuggles.
'**smuggling** *n*: *the laws against smuggling*; *drug-smuggling.*
smut [smʌt] *n* vulgar or indecent talk *etc*: *There is too much smut on television nowadays!*
'**smutty** *adj* (of a conversation, film *etc*) indecent; vulgar: *He could not be prevented from telling smutty stories.* '**smuttiness** *n*.
snack [snak] *n* a light, hasty meal: *I usually have only a snack at lunchtime*; (*also adj*) *We had a snack lunch in the pub.*
snag [snag] *n* **1** a difficulty or drawback: *We did not realize at first how many snags there were in our plan.* **2** a place on a garment where a thread has been torn or pulled out of place.
snail [sneil] *n* a kind of soft-bodied small crawling animal with a coiled shell: *Snails leave a silvery trail as they move along.*
at a snail's pace very slowly: *The old man walked along at a snail's pace.*
snake [sneik] *n* any of a group of legless reptiles with long bodies that move along on the ground with a twisting movement, many of which have a poisonous bite: *He was bitten by a snake and nearly died.* – *v* to move like a snake: *He snaked his way through the narrow tunnel.*
'**snake-bite** *n* the wound resulting from the bite of a snake: *What is the best treatment for (a) snake-bite?*
'**snake-charmer** *n* a person who can handle snakes and make them perform rhythmical movements.
snap [snap] – *pt, ptp* **snapped** – *v* **1** (*with* **at**) to make a biting movement, to try to grasp with the teeth: *The dog snapped at his ankles.* **2** to break with a sudden sharp noise: *He snapped the stick in half*; *The handle of the cup snapped off.* **3** to (cause to) make a sudden sharp noise, in moving *etc*: *The lid snapped shut.* **4** to speak in a sharp *esp* angry way: *'Mind your own business!' he snapped.* **5** to take a photograph of: *He*

snapped the children playing in the garden. – *n* **1** (the noise of) an act of snapping: *There was a loud snap as his pencil broke.* **2** a photograph; a snapshot: *He wanted to show us his holiday snaps.* **3** a kind of simple card game: *They were playing snap.* – *adj* done, made *etc* quickly: *a snap decision.*

'snappy *adj* **1** irritable; inclined to snap: *He is always rather snappy on a Monday morning.* **2** quick; prompt: *You'll have to be snappy if you're catching that bus!* **3** smart: *He's certainly a snappy dresser.* **'snappily** *adv.* **'snappiness** *n.*

'snapshot *n* a photograph taken quickly and without a lot of equipment: *That's a good snapshot of the children playing in the garden.*

snap one's fingers to make a sharp noise by moving the thumb quickly across the top joint of the middle finger, as an informal gesture *eg* to attract someone's attention, mark the rhythm in music *etc*.

snap up to grab eagerly: *I saw this bargain in the shop and snapped it up straight away.*

snare [snɛə] *n* a trap for catching an animal. – *v* to catch with a snare: *He snared a couple of rabbits.*

snarl [snɑːl] *v* (of a dog *etc*) to growl angrily, showing the teeth: *The dog snarled at the burglar.* – *n* an angry sound of this kind.

snatch [snatʃ] *v* **1** to (try to) seize or grab suddenly: *The monkey snatched the biscuit out of my hand.* **2** to take quickly, when one has time or the opportunity: *She managed to snatch an hour's sleep.* – *n* **1** an attempt to seize: *The thief made a snatch at her handbag.* **2** a short piece or extract *eg* from music, conversation *etc*: *a snatch of conversation.*

sneak [sniːk] *v* **1** to go quietly and secretly, *esp* for a dishonest purpose: *He must have sneaked into my room when no-one was looking and stolen the money.* **2** to take secretly: *He sneaked the letter out of her drawer.* – *n* a mean, deceitful person, *esp* a telltale.

'sneakers *n pl* soft shoes with soles made of rubber, rope *etc*: *He was wearing blue jeans and sneakers.*

'sneaking *adj* (of a feeling) slight but not easy to suppress: *She knew he was wicked but she had a sneaking admiration for his courage.*

'sneaky *adj*: *It was a bit sneaky of him to tell the teacher about me.* **'sneakiness** *n.*

sneer [snɪə] *v* **1** to raise the top lip at one side in a kind of smile that expresses scorn: *What are you sneering for?* **2** (*with* **at**) to show contempt for (something) by such an expression or by scornful words *etc*: *He sneered at our attempts to improve the situation.* **3** to say with contempt: *'You haven't a*

chance of getting that job,' he sneered. – *n* a scornful expression, words *etc* that express contempt.

sneeze [sniːz] *v* to. blow out air suddenly, violently and involuntarily through the nose: *The pepper made him sneeze.* – *n* an act of sneezing.

snide [snaid] *adj* sneering or critical in a sly, not open, manner: *He made a snide remark about her relationship with the boss.*

sniff [snif] *v* **1** to draw in air through the nose with a slight noise. **2** to do this in an attempt to smell something: *The dog sniffed me all over; He sniffed suddenly, wondering if he could smell smoke.* – *n* an act of sniffing.

sniff out to discover or detect (by using the sense of smell): *The police used dogs to sniff out the explosives.*

snigger ['snigə] *v* to laugh quietly in an unpleasant manner *eg* at someone else's misfortune: *When he fell off his chair we all sniggered.* – *n* an act of sniggering.

snip [snip] – *pt, ptp* **snipped** – *v* to cut sharply, *esp* with a single quick action, with scissors *etc*: *I snipped off two inches of thread.* – *n* **1** a cut with scissors: *With a snip of her scissors she cut a hole in the cloth.* **2** a small piece cut off: *The floor was covered in snips of paper.* **3** a bargain: *It's a snip at $3!*

'snippet [-pit] *n* a little piece, *esp* of information, gossip *etc*: *a snippet of news.*

snipe [snaip] **snipe at** to shoot at (someone) from a hidden position: *The rebels were sniping at the government troops.*

'sniper *n*: *The soldier was shot by a sniper.*

snippet *see* **snip**.

snob [snob] *n* a person who admires people of high rank or social class, and despises those in a lower class *etc* than himself: *Being a snob, he was always trying to get to know members of the royal family.*

'snobbery *n* behaviour, talk *etc* that is typical of a snob: *She couldn't bear her mother's snobbery.*

'snobbish *adj*: *She always had a snobbish desire to live in an area of expensive housing.* **'snobbishly** *adv.* **'snobbishness** *n.*

snoop [snuːp] *v* (*often with* **around** *or* **into**) to make secretive investigations into things that do not concern oneself: *She's always snooping into other people's business.*

snooze [snuːz] *v* to doze or sleep lightly: *His grandfather was snoozing in his armchair.* – *n* a short period of light sleep.

snore [snoː] *v* to make a noise like a snort while sleeping, when one is breathing in: *He was obviously asleep because he was snoring loudly.* – *n* an act of snoring.

snorkel ['snoːkəl] *n* a tube with the end(s) above water for allowing an underwater swimmer to breathe or a submarine to take in air.

snort [snoːt] *v* **1** (*usu* of animals) to force air noisily through the nostrils, breathing either in or out: *The horses snorted impatiently.* **2** (of people) to make a similar noise, showing disapproval, anger, contempt, amusement *etc*: *She snorted at the very suggestion that she was tired.* – *n* an act of snorting: *a snort of impatience*; *She gave a snort of laughter.*

snout [snaut] *n* the projecting mouth and nose part of certain animals, *esp* of a pig.

snow [snou] *n* frozen water vapour that falls to the ground in soft white flakes: *We woke up to find snow on the ground*; *We were caught in a heavy snow-shower*; *About 15 centimetres of snow had fallen overnight.* – *v* to shower down in, or like, flakes of snow: *It's snowing heavily.*

'**snowy** *adj* **1** full of, or producing a lot of, snow: *The weather has been very snowy recently.* **2** white like snow: *the old man's snowy (white) hair.*

'**snowball** *n* a ball of snow pressed hard together, *esp* made by children for throwing, as a game.

'**snow-capped** *adj* (of mountains *etc*) having tops which are covered with snow: *snow-capped peaks.*

'**snowdrift** *n* a bank of snow blown together by the wind: *There were deep snowdrifts at the side of the road.*

'**snowfall** *n* **1** a fall or shower of snow that settles on the ground: *There was a heavy snowfall last night.* **2** the amount of snow that falls in a certain place: *The snowfall last year was much higher than average.*

'**snowflake** *n* one of the soft, light flakes composed of groups of crystals, in which snow falls: *A few large snowflakes began to fall from the sky.*

'**snowstorm** *n* a heavy fall of snow *esp* accompanied by a strong wind.

,**snow-'white** *adj* white like snow.

snub [snʌb] – *pt*, *ptp* **snubbed** – *v* to treat, or speak to, in a cold, scornful way; to insult: *He snubbed me by not replying to my question.* – *n* an act of snubbing; an insult. – *adj* (of the nose) short and slightly turned up at the end: *a snub nose.*

snuff[1] [snʌf] *n* powdered tobacco for sniffing up into the nose: *He took a pinch of snuff.*

snuff[2] [snʌf] *v* to snip off the burnt part of the wick of (a candle or lamp).

snuff out 1 to extinguish the flame of (a candle *etc*): *He snuffed out the candle by squeezing the wick between his thumb and forefinger.* **2** to (cause to) come to a sudden end: *Opposition was quickly snuffed out.*

snuffle ['snʌfl] *v* to make sniffing noises, or breathe noisily: *He's snuffling because he has a cold.*

snug [snʌg] *adj* **1** warm, comfortable; sheltered from the cold: *The house is small but snug.* **2** (of clothes *etc*) fitting closely: *This jacket is a nice snug fit.*

'**snuggle** *v* to curl one's body up *esp* closely against another person, for warmth *etc*: *She snuggled up to her mother and went to sleep.*

'**snugly** *adv* **1** tightly and neatly: *The gun fitted snugly into my pocket.* **2** comfortably or warmly: *The girl had a scarf wrapped snugly round her neck.*

'**snugness** *n*.

so [sou] *adv* **1** (used in several types of sentence to express degree) to this extent, or to such an extent: *'The snake was about so long,' he said, holding his hands about a metre apart*; *Don't get so worried!*; *She was so pleased with his progress in school that she bought him a new bicycle*; *They couldn't all get into the room, there were so many of them*; *He departed without so much as* (= without even) *a goodbye*; *You've been so* (= very) *kind to me!*; *Thank you so much!* **2** (used to express manner) in this/that way: *As you hope to be treated by others, so you must treat them*; *He likes everything to be (arranged) just so* (= in one particular and precise way); *It so happens that I have to go to an important meeting tonight.* **3** (used in place of a word, phrase *etc* previously used, or something previously stated) as already indicated: *'Are you really leaving your job?' 'Yes, I've already told you/said so'*; *'Is she arriving tomorrow?' 'Yes, I hope so'*; *If you haven't read the notice, please do so now*; *'Is that so* (= true)?' *'Yes, it's really so'*; *'Was your father angry?' 'Yes, even more so than I was expecting.* – *in fact, so much so that he refused to speak to me all day!* **4** in the same way; also: *'I hope we'll meet again.' 'So do I.'*; *She has a lot of money and so has her husband.* **5** (used to express agreement or confirmation) indeed: *'You said you were going shopping today.' 'So I did, but I've changed my mind.'*; *'You'll need this book tomorrow, won't you?' 'So I will.'* – *conj* (and) therefore: *John had a bad cold, so I took him to the doctor*; *'So you think you'd like this job, then?' 'Yes.'*; *And so they got married and lived happily ever after.*

,**so-'called** *adj* wrongly described or named in such a way: *Your so-called friends have gone without you!*

,**so-'so** *adj* neither very good nor very bad: *His health is so-so.*

and so on/forth and more of the same kind of thing: *He reminded me of what I owed him and so on.*

or so *see* **or**.

so as to in order to: *He sat at the front so as to be able to hear.*

so far, so good all is well up to this point: *So far, so good – we've checked the equipment, and everything's ready.*

so that 1 with the purpose that; in order that: *I'll wash this dress so that you can wear it.* **2** with the result that: *He got up very late, so that he missed the bus and was late for work.*

so to say/speak if one may use such an expression; in a way; it could be said: *The dog is, so to speak, a member of this family.*

soak [souk] *v* **1** to (let) stand in a liquid: *She soaked the clothes overnight in soapy water.* **2** to make very wet: *That shower has completely soaked my clothes.* **3** (*with* **in, into, through** *etc*) (of a liquid) to penetrate: *The blood from his wound has soaked right through the bandage.*

soaked *adj* (*often with* **through**): *She got soaked (through) in that shower.*

-soaked: *rain-soaked/blood-soaked clothing.*

'soaking *adj* very wet: *She took off her soaking garments.*

soaking wet soaking; very wet: *I've washed my hair and it's still soaking wet.*

soak up to draw in or suck up; to absorb: *You'd better soak that spilt coffee up with a cloth.*

soap [soup] *n* a mixture containing oils or fats and other substances, *esp* formed into small regularly-shaped pieces and used in washing: *He found a bar of soap and began to wash his hands.* – *v* to rub with soap: *She soaped the baby all over.*

'soapy *adj* **1** covered with, or full of, soap: *soapy water.* **2** like soap: *This chocolate has a soapy taste.* **'soapiness** *n*.

soap opera a radio or television serial broadcast weekly, daily *etc, esp* one that continues from year to year, that concerns the daily life, troubles *etc* of the characters in it.

soar [so:] *v* to fly high: *Seagulls soared above the cliffs; Prices have soared recently.*

sob [sob] – *pt, ptp* **sobbed** – *v* **1** to weep noisily: *I could hear her sobbing in her bedroom.* **2** to say, while weeping: *'I can't find my mother,' sobbed the child.* – *n* the loud gasp for breath made when one is weeping *etc*.

sober ['soubə] *adj* **1** not drunk: *He was still sober when he left.* **2** serious in mind: *a sober mood.* **3** (of colour) not bright: *She wore a sober (grey) dress.* **4** moderate; not overdone or too emotional: *His account of the accident was factual and sober.*

'sobering *adj*: *a sobering experience/thought.*

'soberly *adv*.

'soberness *n* the quality which a thing,

person *etc* has when sober: *soberness of mind.*

sober up to make or become (more) sober.

so-called *see* **so**.

soccer ['sokə] *n* football played according to certain rules.

sociable ['souʃəbl] *adj* (*neg* **un-**) fond of the company of others; friendly: *He's a cheerful, sociable man.* **'sociably** *adv*.

social ['souʃəl] *adj* **1** concerning or belonging to the way of life and welfare of people in a community: *social problems.* **2** concerning the system by which such a community is organized: *social class.* **3** living in communities: *Ants are social insects.* **4** concerning the gathering together of people for the purposes of recreation or amusement: *a social club; His reasons for calling were purely social.*

'socialism *n* the belief or theory that a country's wealth (its land, mines, industries, railways *etc*) should belong to the people as a whole, not to private owners.

'socialist *n* a person who believes in and/or practises socialism. – *adj* of or concerning socialism: *socialist policies/governments.*

'socialize, -ise *v* to mix socially (*eg* with guests at a party *etc*).

'socially *adv* in a social way: *I've seen him at various conferences, but we've never met socially.*

social work work which deals with the care of people in a community, *esp* of the poor, under-privileged *etc* (*n* **social worker**).

society [sə'saiəti] – *pl* **so'cieties** – *n* mankind considered as a whole: *He was a danger to society.* **2** a particular group or part of mankind considered as a whole: *middle-class society; modern western societies.* **3** an association or club: *a model railway society.* **4** the class of people who are wealthy, fashionable or of high rank in any area: *high society.* **5** company or companionship: *I enjoy the society of young people.*

sock [sok] *n* **1** a (*usu* wool, cotton or nylon) covering for the foot and ankle, sometimes reaching to the knee, worn inside a shoe, boot *etc*: *I need a new pair of socks.*

socket ['sokit] *n* a specially-made or specially-shaped hole or set of holes into which something is fitted: *We'll need to have a new electric socket fitted into the wall for the television plug.*

soda ['soudə] *n* **1** the name given to several substances formed with sodium, *esp* one (washing soda or **sodium carbonate**) in the form of crystals, used for washing, or one (baking soda or **sodium bicarbonate**) used in baking. **2** soda-water: *whisky and soda.* **3** (*Amer*) a drink made with flavoured soda-water and *usu* ice-cream.

'soda-water *n* water through which the gas

carbon dioxide has been passed, making it fizzy.

odium ['sodiəm] *n* an element from which many substances are formed, including common salt (**sodium chloride**).

sodium bicarbonate/carbonate *see* soda.

ofa ['soufə] *n* a kind of long seat, stuffed and with a back and arms: *We were sitting on the sofa.*

oft [soft] *adj* **1** not hard or firm; easily changing shape when pressed: *a soft cushion.* **2** pleasantly smooth to the touch: *The dog has a soft, silky coat.* **3** not loud: *a soft voice.* **4** (of colour) not bright or harsh: *a soft pink.* **5** not strict (enough): *You are too soft with him.* **6** (of a drink) not alcoholic: *At the party they were serving soft drinks as well as wine and spirits.* **7** childishly weak, timid or silly: *Don't be so soft – the dog won't hurt you.* '**softly** *adv.* '**softness** *n.*

soften ['sofn] *v* to make or become soft or softer, less strong or less painful: *The thick walls softened the noise of the explosion.*

,**soft-'boiled** *adj* (of eggs) slightly boiled, so that the yolk is still soft: *She likes her eggs soft-boiled.*

,**soft-'hearted** *adj* kind-hearted and generous: *He had been given some money by a soft-hearted aunt.*

,**soft-'spoken** *adj* having a gentle voice or manner: *She was a soft-spoken woman with a shy smile.*

'**software** *n* computer programs, as opposed to the machines themselves ('**hardware**).

'**softwood** *n, adj* (of) the wood of a cone-bearing tree *eg* a pine: *softwood furniture.*

have a soft spot for to have a weakness for (someone or something) because of great affection: *He's always had a soft spot for his youngest son.*

oggy ['sogi] *adj* very wet and soft: *In the centre of the puddle was a piece of soggy cardboard.* '**sogginess** *n.*

oil[1] [soil] *n* the upper layer of the earth, in which plants grow: *to plant seeds in the soil*; *a handful of soil.*

oil[2] [soil] *v* to dirty or stain: *Don't soil your dress with these dusty books!*

olar ['soulə] *adj* having to do with, powered by, or influenced by, the sun: *the solar year*; *a solar heating system.*

,**solar-'powered** *adj.*

solar system the Sun or any star and the planets which move round it.

old *see* sell.

older ['souldə, (*Amer*) 'sodər] *n* melted metal or alloy used to join one piece of metal to another. – *v* to join (two or more pieces of metal) with solder: *He soldered the broken wire back on to the transistor*; *I'd like to learn how to solder.*

'**soldering-iron** *n* a type of tool for providing the heat needed when soldering.

soldier ['souldʒə] *n* a member (*usu* male) of an army, often one who is not an officer: *The boy wants to be a soldier when he grows up.*

soldier on to keep going despite difficulties *etc*: *There have been several power-cuts in the office, but we are trying to soldier on (despite them).*

sole[1] [soul] *n* **1** the underside of the foot, the part on which one stands and walks. **2** the flat surface of a boot or shoe that covers this part of the foot.

sole[2] [soul] – *pls* **sole, soles** – *n* **1** a type of small, flat fish: *They were fishing for sole*; *three soles.* **2** its flesh as food: *We had sole for supper.*

sole[3] [soul] *adj* **1** only; single: *my sole purpose/reason.* **2** not shared; belonging to one person or group only: *the sole rights to a book.*

'**solely** *adv* only: *She is solely responsible for the crisis.*

solemn ['soləm] *adj* **1** serious and earnest: *a solemn question*; *He looked very solemn as he announced the bad news.* **2** stately; having formal dignity: *a solemn procession.* '**solemnly** *adv.* '**solemnness** *n.*

solemnity [sə'lemnəti] *n* the state of being solemn: *the solemnity of the occasion.*

solicit [sə'lisit] *v* to ask (for): *People working for charities are permitted to solicit (money from) the public.*

so'licitor *n* a lawyer who prepares legal documents and briefs, gives legal advice, and (in the lower courts only) speaks on behalf of his clients.

solid ['solid] *adj* **1** not easily changing shape; not in the form of liquid or gas: *Water becomes solid when it freezes*; *solid substances.* **2** not hollow: *The tyres of the earliest cars were solid.* **3** firm and strongly made (and therefore sound and reliable): *That's a solid piece of furniture*; *His argument is based on good solid facts/reasoning.* **4** completely made of one substance: *This bracelet is made of solid gold*; *We dug till we reached solid rock.* **5** without breaks, gaps or flaws: *The policemen formed themselves into a solid line*; *They are solid in their determination to strike.* **6** having height, breadth and width: *A cube is a solid figure.* **7** consecutive; without a pause: *I've been working for six solid hours.* – *adv* without interruption; continuously: *She was working for six hours solid.* – *n* **1** a substance that is solid: *Butter is a solid but milk is a liquid.* **2** a shape that has length, breadth and height.

,**soli'darity** [-'darə-] *n* the uniting of the interests, feelings or actions (of a group): *We must try to preserve our solidarity.*

so'lidify [-difai] *v* to make or become solid.
so,lidifi'cation [-difi-] *n*. **so'lidity, 'solidness** *ns*.

'solidly *adv* **1** firmly; strongly: *solidly-built houses*. **2** continuously: *I worked solidly from 8.30 a.m. till lunchtime*. **3** unanimously: *We're solidly in agreement with your suggestions*.

solid fuel a fuel, such as coal, that is solid rather than an oil or gas.

solitary ['solitəri] *adj* **1** alone; without companions: *a solitary traveller*. **2** living or being alone, by habit or preference: *She was a solitary person*. **3** single: *not a solitary example*.

'solitude [-tjuːd] *n* the state of being alone: *He likes solitude*; *He lives in solitude*.

solitary confinement imprisonment in a cell by oneself: *He was sentenced to six months' solitary confinement*.

solo ['soulou] – *pl* **'solos** – *n* something (*eg* a musical piece for one voice or instrument, a dance or other entertainment) in which only one person takes part: *a cello/soprano solo*. – *adj* in which only one takes part: *a solo flight in an aeroplane*.

'soloist *n* a person who plays, sings *etc* a solo.

solstice ['solstis] *n* the time of year when there is the greatest length of daylight (**summer solstice**) or the shortest (**winter solstice**).

soluble ['soljubl] *adj* **1** able to be dissolved or made liquid: *This dye is soluble in water*. **2** (of a problem, difficulty *etc*) able to be solved.

solution [sə'luːʃən] *n* **1** an answer to a problem, difficulty or puzzle: *the solution to a crossword*. **2** the act of finding such an answer. **3** a liquid with something dissolved in it: *a solution of salt and water*.

solve [solv] *v* **1** to discover the answer to (a problem *etc*): *The mathematics teacher gave the children some problems to solve*. **2** to clear up or explain (a mystery, crime *etc*): *That crime has never been solved*.

solvent ['solvənt] *adj* having enough money to be able to pay all one's debts. – *n* a substance, *eg* petrol, that dissolves grease *etc*.

sombre, (*Amer usu*) **somber** ['sombə] *adj* **1** dark (and gloomy): *Black is a sombre colour*. **2** grave; serious: *He was in a sombre mood*.

some [sʌm] *pron, adj* **1** an indefinite amount or number (of): *I can see some people walking across the field*; *You'll need some money if you're going shopping*; *Some of the ink was spilt on the desk*. **2** (said with emphasis) a certain, or small, amount or number (of): *'Has she any experience of the work?' 'Yes, she has some.'*; *Some people like the idea and some don't*. **3** (said with emphasis) at least one/a few/a bit (of): *Surely there are some people who agree with me?*; *I don't need much rest from work, but I must have some*. **4** certain: *He's quite kind in some ways*. – *adj* **1** a large, considerable or impressive (amount or number of): *I spent some time trying to convince her*; *I'll have some problem sorting out these papers!* **2** an unidentified or unnamed (thing, person *etc*): *She was hunting for some book that she's lost*. **3** (used with numbers) about; at a rough estimate: *There were some thirty people at the reception*. – *adv* (*Amer*) somewhat; to a certain extent: *I think we've progressed some*.

'somebody *pron* someone.

'someday, *adv* (also **some day**) at an unknown time in the future: *We'll manage it someday*.

'somehow *adv* in some way not known for certain: *I'll get there somehow*.

'someone *pron* **1** an unknown or unnamed person: *There's someone at the door – would you answer it?*; *We all of us know someone who needs help*. **2** a person of importance: *He thinks he is someone*.

'something *pron* **1** a thing not known or not stated: *Would you like something to eat?*; *I've got something to tell you*. **2** a thing of importance: *There's something in what you say*.

'sometime *adv* at an unknown time in the future or the past: *We'll go there sometime next week*; *They went sometime last month*.

'sometimes *adv* occasionally: *He sometimes goes to America*; *He goes to America sometimes*; *Sometimes he seems very forgetful*.

'somewhat *adv* rather; a little: *He is somewhat sad*; *The news puzzled me somewhat*.

'somewhere *adv* (*Amer* **'someplace**) (in or to) some place not known or not named: *They live somewhere in London*; *I won't be at home tonight – I'm going somewhere for dinner*.

mean something to have meaning; to be significant: *Do all these figures mean something?*

or something used when the speaker is uncertain or being vague: *Her name is Mary or Margaret or something*.

something like 1 about: *We have something like five hundred people working here*. **2** rather like: *A zebra is something like a horse with stripes*.

something tells me I have reason to believe; I suspect: *Something tells me she's lying*.

somersault ['sʌməsoːlt] *n* a leap or roll in which a person turns with his feet going over his head. – *v* to make such a leap or roll.

son [sʌn] *n* a male child (when spoken of in relation to his parents): *He is the son of the manager*.

'son-in-law – *pl* **'sons-in-law** – *n* a daughter's husband.

ong [soŋ] *n* **1** something (to be) sung: *He wrote this song for his wife to sing.* **2** singing: *He burst into song.* **3** the sound(s) made by a bird: *birdsong.*

'songbird *n* any of the types of bird which have a pleasant song.

'songwriter *n* a person who writes songs (*usu* pop songs) for a living.

ongkok ['soŋkok] *n* a kind of round felt cap, usually black, with a flat top and no brim, worn by Muslim men in Malaysia and Indonesia.

onic ['sonik] *adj* of, or using, sound waves.
sonic boom a sudden loud noise heard when an aircraft which is travelling faster than the speed of sound passes overhead.

onnet ['sonit] *n* a type of poem with fourteen lines; *Milton's/Shakespeare's sonnets.*

oon [su:n] *adv* **1** in a short time from now or from the time mentioned: *They'll be here sooner than you think*; *I hope he arrives soon.* **2** early: *It's too soon to tell.* **3** willingly: *I would sooner stand than sit.*

as soon as (not later than the moment) when: *You may have a biscuit as soon as we get home.*

no sooner ... than when ... immediately: *No sooner had we set off than we realized we'd left the dog behind.*

sooner or later eventually: *He'll come home sooner or later, I suppose.*

the sooner the better as quickly as possible: *'When shall I tell him?' 'The sooner the better!'*

oot [sut] *n* the black powder left after the burning of coal *etc.*

'sooty *adj* **1** covered with soot. **2** of the colour of soot. **'sootiness** *n.*

oothe [su:ð] *v* **1** to calm, comfort or quieten (a person, his feelings *etc*): *She was so upset that it took half an hour to soothe her.* **2** to ease (pain *etc*): *The medicine soothed the child's toothache.* **'soothing** *adj*. **'soothingly** *adv.*

ooty *see* soot.

ophisticated [sə'fistikeitid] *adj* (*neg* **un-**) **1** (of a person) having a great deal of experience and worldly wisdom, knowledge of how to dress elegantly *etc*: *a sophisticated young man*; *She has become very sophisticated since she went to live in London.* **2** suitable for, or typical of, sophisticated people: *The joke was too sophisticated for the child to understand*; *sophisticated clothes/hairstyles.* **3** (of machines, processes *etc*) highly-developed, elaborate and produced with a high degree of skill and knowledge: *sophisticated photographic techniques.* **so,phisti'cation** *n.*

oprano [sə'pra:nou] – *pl* **so'pranos** – *n* (a

singer having) a singing voice of the highest pitch for a woman.

sorcery ['so:səri] *n* **1** the use of power gained from evil spirits. **2** witchcraft or magic in general.
'sorcerer – *fem* **'sorceress** – *n* a person who practises sorcery.

sordid ['so:did] *adj* **1** (of a place *etc*) dirty, mean and poor: *a very sordid neighbourhood.* **2** (of a person's behaviour *etc*) showing low standards or ideals *etc*; not very pleasant or admirable: *The whole affair was rather sordid.* **'sordidly** *adv*. **'sordidness** *n.*

sore [so:] *adj* **1** painful: *My leg is very sore; I have a sore leg.* **2** suffering pain: *I am still a bit sore after my operation.* **3** (*Amer*) irritated, annoyed or offended: *He is still sore about what happened.* – *n* a painful, injured or diseased spot on the skin: *His hands were covered with horrible sores.*
'sorely *adv* badly; acutely.
'soreness *n.*

sorrow ['sorou] *n* (something which causes) pain of mind or grief: *He felt great sorrow when she died.*
'sorrowful *adj* showing or feeling sorrow: *sorrowful people*; *a sorrowful expression.* **'sorrowfully** *adv*. **'sorrowfulness** *n.*

sorry ['sori] *adj* **1** used when apologizing or expressing regret: *I'm sorry (that) I forgot to return your book; Did I give you a fright? I'm sorry.* **2** apologetic or full of regret: *I think he's really sorry for his bad behaviour; I'm sure you were sorry to hear about his death.* **3** unsatisfactory; poor; wretched: *a sorry state of affairs.* – *interj* **1** used when apologizing: *Did I tread on your toe? Sorry!* **2** (used when asking a person to repeat what he has said) I beg your pardon?: *Sorry (, what did you say)?*
be/feel sorry for to pity: *I'm/I feel really sorry for that poor woman.*

sort [so:t] *n* a class, type or kind: *I like all sorts of books; She was wearing a sort of crown.* – *v* to separate into classes or groups, putting each item in its place: *She sorted the buttons into large ones and small ones.*
'sorter *n* a person or machine that separates and arranges, *esp* letters, postcards *etc.*
of a sort/of sorts of a (*usu* poor) kind: *She threw together a meal of sorts but we were still hungry afterwards.*
out of sorts 1 slightly unwell: *I felt a bit out of sorts after last night's heavy meal.* **2** not in good spirits or temper: *He's been a little out of sorts since they told him to stay at home.*
sort of rather; in a way; to a certain extent: *He was sort of peculiar!; I feel sort of worried about him.*
sort out 1 to separate (one lot or type of)

things from a general mixture: *I'll try to sort out some books that he might like.* **2** to correct, improve, solve *etc*: *You must sort out your business affairs.* **3** to attend to, *usu* by punishing or reprimanding: *I'll soon sort you out, you evil little man!*

sortie ['sɔːti] *n* **1** a sudden raid or attacking mission. **2** a short trip or expedition.

SOS [esou'es] *n* a call for help or rescue, often in code and *usu* from a distance: *Send an SOS to the mainland to tell them that we are sinking!*

soufflé ['suːflei, (*Amer*) suː'flei] *n* a kind of frothy cooked dish, made with whisked whites of egg: *I made a cheese soufflé.*

sought *see* **seek.**

soul [soul] *n* **1** the spirit; the non-physical part of a person, which is often thought to continue in existence after he or she dies: *People often discuss whether animals and plants have souls.* **2** a person: *She's a wonderful old soul.* **3** (of an enterprise *etc*) the organizer or leader: *He is the soul of the whole movement.* **4** soul music.

'**soulful** *adj* full of (*usu* sad, wistful *etc*) feeling: *a soulful expression.* '**soulfully** *adv.*

'**soulless** *adj* **1** (of a person) without fine feeling or nobleness. **2** (of life, a task *etc*) dull or very unimportant.

'**soul-destroying** *adj* (of a task *etc*) very dull, boring, repetitive *etc*.

soul music (*also* **soul**) a type of music, descended from American Negro gospel songs, which has great emotion.

sound[1] [saund] *adj* **1** strong or in good condition: *The foundations of the house are not very sound*; *He's 87, but he's still sound in mind and body.* **2** (of sleep) deep: *She's a very sound sleeper.* **3** full; thorough: *a sound basic training.* **4** accurate; free from mistakes: *a sound piece of work.* **5** having or showing good judgement or good sense: *His advice is always very sound.* '**soundly** *adv.* '**soundness** *n.*

sound asleep sleeping deeply: *The baby is sound asleep.*

sound[2] *n* **1** the impressions transmitted to the brain by the sense of hearing: *a barrage of sound*; (*also adj*) *sound waves.* **2** something that is, or can be, heard: *The sounds were coming from the garage.* **3** the impression created in the mind by a piece of news, a description *etc*: *I didn't like the sound of her hairstyle at all!* – *v* **1** to (cause something to) make a sound: *Sound the bell!*; *The bell sounded.* **2** to signal (something) by making a sound: *Sound the alarm!* **3** (of something heard or read) to make a particular impression; to seem; to appear: *Your singing sounded very good*; *That sounds like a train.* **4** to pronounce: *In the word 'pneumonia', the letter p is not sounded!* **5** to examine by

tapping and listening carefully: *She sounded the patient's chest.*

'**soundless** *adj.* '**soundlessly** *adv.*

sound effects sounds other than dialogue or music, used in films, radio *etc*.

'**soundproof** *adj* not allowing sound to pass in, out, or through: *The walls are soundproof.* – *v* to make (walls, a room *etc*) soundproof.

'**sound-track** *n* (a recording of) the music from a film: *I've just bought the sound-track of that new film.*

sound[3] [saund] *v* to measure the depth of (water *etc*).

'**sounding** *n* **1** (a) measurement of depth of water *etc*. **2** a depth measured. **3** (an) act of trying to find out views *etc*.

sound out to try to find out someone's thoughts and plans *etc*: *Will you sound out your father on this?*

soup [suːp] *n* a liquid food made from meat, vegetables *etc*: *She made some chicken soup.*

in the soup in serious trouble: *If she's found out about it, we're all in the soup!*

sour ['sauə] *adj* **1** having a taste or smell similar in nature to that of lemon juice or vinegar: *Unripe apples are/taste very sour.* **2** having a similar taste as a stage in going bad: *sour milk.* **3** (of a person, his character *etc*) discontented, bad-tempered or disagreeable: *She was looking very sour this morning.* – *v* to make or become sour. '**sourly** *adv.* '**sourness** *n.*

source [sɔːs] *n* **1** the place, person, circumstance, thing *etc* from which anything begins or comes: *They have discovered the source of the trouble.* **2** the spring from which a river flows: *the source of the Nile.*

*****soursop** ['sauəsop] *n* (a tropical tree bearing) a large spiny fruit with a sharp-tasting pulp.

south [sauθ] *n* **1** the direction to the right of a person facing the rising sun, or any part of the earth lying in that direction: *He stood facing towards the south*; *She lives in the south of France.* **2** one of the four main points of the compass. – *adj* **1** in the south: *She works on the south coast.* **2** from the direction of the south: *a south wind.* – *adv* towards the south: *This window faces south.*

southerly ['sʌðəli] *adj* **1** (of a wind *etc*) coming from the south: *a southerly wind.* **2** looking, lying *etc* towards the south: *in a southerly direction.*

southern ['sʌðən] *adj* of the south: *Your speech sounds southern to me*; *Australia is in the southern hemisphere.*

southerner ['sʌðənə] *n* a person who lives, or was born, in a southern region or country.

southernmost ['sʌðənmoust] *adj* being furthest south: *the southernmost point on the mainland.*

'**southward** *adj* towards the south: *in a southward direction.*

'**southward(s)** *adv* towards the south: *We are moving southwards.*

'**southbound** *adj* travelling southwards: *southbound traffic.*

,**south-'east**/,**south-'west** *ns* the direction midway between south and east or south and west, or any part of the earth lying in that direction. – *adjs* 1 in the south-east or south-west: *the south-east coast.* 2 from the direction of the south-east or south-west: *a south-east or south-west.* – *advs* towards the south-east or south-west: *The gateway faces south-west.*

,**south-'easterly**/,**south-'westerly** *adjs* 1 (of a wind *etc*) coming from the south-east or south-west: *a south-easterly wind.* 2 looking, lying *etc* towards the south-east or south-west: *a south-westerly direction.*

,**south-'eastern**/,**south-'western** *adjs* of the south-east or south-west: *a south-western dialect.*

the South Pole the southern end of the imaginary line through the earth, round which it turns.

souvenir [suːvəˈniə, (*Amer*) ˈsuːvəniər] *n* something (bought, kept or given) which reminds one of a place, person or occasion: *a souvenir of one's holiday.*

sovereign [ˈsovrin] *n* a king or queen. – *adj* (of a country) self-governing: *a sovereign state.*

soviet [ˈsouviət] *adj* (*often with cap*) of the USSR. – *n* (*Amer*) one of the people, *esp* one of the leaders, of the USSR.

sow[1] [sou] – *pt* **sowed** – *v* 1 to scatter over, or put in, the ground: *I sowed lettuce in this part of the garden.* 2 to plant seed over: *This field has been sown with wheat.*

to sow (not sew) seed.

sow[2] [sau] *n* a female pig.

soya bean [ˈsoiəbiːn], **soybean** [ˈsoibiːn] *n* a type of bean, processed and used as a substitute for meat *etc*.

soy(a) sauce a sauce made from soya beans, used in Chinese *etc* cooking.

space [speis] *n* 1 a gap; an empty or uncovered place: *I couldn't find a space for my car.* 2 room; the absence of objects; the area available for use: *Have you enough space to turn round?*; *Is there space for one more?* 3 (*often* **outer space**) the region outside the Earth's atmosphere, in which all stars and other planets *etc* are situated: *travellers through space.* – *v* (*also* **space out**) to set (things) apart from one another: *He spaced the rows of potatoes half a metre apart.*

'**spacing** *n* the amount of distance left be-

tween objects, words *etc* when they are set or laid out.

spacious [ˈspeiʃəs] *adj* providing or having plenty of room: *Their dining-room is very spacious.* '**spaciously** *adv.* '**spaciousness** *n.*

'**space-age** *adj* extremely up-to-date and advanced: *space-age technology.*

'**spacecraft** *n* a vehicle *etc*, manned or unmanned, for travelling in space.

'**spaceship** *n* a spacecraft, *esp* a manned one.

'**spacesuit** *n* a suit designed to be worn by a '**spaceman**.

spade[1] [speid] *n* a tool with a broad blade and a handle, used for digging.

spade[2] [speid] *n* one of the playing-cards of the suit spades.

spades *n pl* (sometimes treated as *n sing*) one of the four card suits: *the ten of spades.*

spaghetti [spəˈgeti] *n* an Italian food consisting of long strands of pasta.

span [span] *n* 1 the length between the supports of a bridge or arch: *The first span of the bridge is one hundred metres long.* 2 the full time for which anything lasts: *Seventy or eighty years is the normal span of a man's life.* – *v* – *pt, ptp* **spanned** – to stretch across: *A bridge spans the river.*

spaniel [ˈspanjəl] *n* a breed of dog with large ears which hang down.

spank [spaŋk] *v* to strike or slap with the flat of the hand, *esp* on the buttocks, *usu* as a punishment: *The child was spanked for his disobedience.* – *n* a slap of this kind.

spanner [ˈspanə] *n* a type of tool used for tightening or loosening nuts, bolts *etc*.

throw a spanner in the works to frustrate or ruin (a plan, system *etc*).

spar[1] [spaː] *n* a strong, thick pole of wood or metal, *esp* one used as a ship's mast *etc*.

spar[2] [spaː] – *pt, ptp* **sparred** – *v* 1 to box, *usu* for practice only. 2 (*usu with* **with**) to have an argument, *usu* a friendly one.

'**sparring-partner** *n* 1 a person with whom a boxer practises. 2 a person with whom one enjoys a lively argument.

spare [speə] *v* 1 to manage without: *No-one can be spared from this office.* 2 to afford or set aside for a purpose: *I can't spare the time for a holiday.* 3 to treat with mercy; to avoid injuring *etc*: *'Spare us!' they begged.* 4 to avoid causing grief, trouble *etc* to (a person): *Break the news gently in order to spare her as much as possible.* 5 to avoid using, spending *etc*: *He spared no expense in his desire to help us.* 6 to avoid troubling (a person with something); to save (a person trouble *etc*): *I answered the letter myself in order to spare you the bother.* – *adj* 1 extra; not actually being used: *We haven't a spare (bed)room for guests in our house.* 2 (of time *etc*) free for leisure *etc*: *What do you do in your spare time?* – *n* 1 a spare part (for a

Space

Key
1 Astronaut or Spaceman in Spacesuit
2 Spacecraft
3 Rocket
4 Satellite in Orbit

car etc): They sell spares at that garage.
2 an extra wheel etc, kept for emergencies.
'sparing adj careful or economical.
'sparingly adv.
spare part a part for a machine etc, used to
replace an identical part if it breaks etc.
spare rib a rib of pork with only a small
amount of meat left on it.
(and) to spare in greater supply or quantity
than is needed; extra: I'll go to an exhibition
if I have time to spare; I have enough food
and to spare.

spark [spɑːk] n 1 a tiny red-hot piece thrown
off by something burning, or when two very
hard (eg metal) surfaces are struck together: Sparks were being thrown into the
air from the burning building. 2 an electric
current jumping across a gap: a spark from
a faulty light-socket. 3 a trace (eg of life,
humour): a spark of enthusiasm. – v 1 to
give off sparks. 2 (often with off) to start (a
row, disagreement etc): Their action
sparked off a major row.

sparkle ['spɑːkl] n 1 an effect like that made
by little sparks: There was a sudden sparkle
as her diamond ring caught the light. 2 liveliness or brightness: She has lots of sparkle. –
v 1 to glitter, as if throwing off tiny sparks:
The snow sparkled in the sunlight. 2 to be
lively or witty: She really sparkled at that
party.
'sparkling adj 1 (of wines) giving off
bubbles of gas. 2 lively: sparkling humour/
wit.

sparrow ['sparou] n a common type of small
brown bird related to the finch family.

sparse [spɑːs] adj thinly scattered: sparse vegetation. 'sparsely adv. 'sparseness n.

spasm ['spazəm] n a sudden uncontrollable
jerking of the muscles: A spasm of pain
twisted his face for a moment.

spastic ['spastik] n, adj (a person) suffering
from brain damage that causes extreme
muscle spasms and/or muscular paralysis:
Their youngest child is (a) spastic.

spat see spit.

spatula ['spatjulə, (Amer) -tʃu-] n a kind of
tool with a broad blunt blade: Spread the
icing on the cake with a spatula.

spawn [spɔːn] n the eggs of fish, frogs etc: In
the spring, the pond is full of frog-spawn. – v
(of frogs, fish etc) to produce spawn.

speak [spiːk] – pt spoke [spouk]: ptp 'spoken
['spoukən] – v 1 to say (words) or talk: He
can't speak; He spoke a few words to us.
2 (often with to or (Amer) with) to talk or
converse: Can I speak to/with you for a
moment?; We spoke for hours about it. 3 to
(be able to) talk in (a language): She speaks
Russian. 4 to tell or make known (one's
thoughts, the truth etc): I always speak my
mind. 5 to make a speech, address an audi-

ence: The Prime Minister spoke on unemployment.
'speaker n 1 a person who is or was speaking. 2 (sometimes ˌloud'speaker) the device
in a radio, record-player etc which converts
the electrical impulses into audible sounds:
Our record-player needs a new speaker.
'speaking adj 1 involving speech: a speaking
part in a play. 2 used in speech: a pleasant
speaking voice.
'spoken adj produced by speaking: the
spoken word.
-spoken speaking in a particular way: plain-
spoken; smooth-spoken.
generally speaking in general: Generally
speaking, men are stronger than women.
speak for itself/themselves to have an obvious meaning; not to need explaining: The
facts speak for themselves.
speak out to say boldly what one thinks: I
feel the time has come to speak out.
speak up to speak (more) loudly: Speak up!
We can't hear you!
to speak of worth mentioning: He has no
talent to speak of.

spear [spiə] n a type of long-handled weapon,
usu with an iron or steel point on the end:
He was armed with a spear and a round
shield. – v to pierce or kill with a spear: He
went out in a boat and speared some fish.
'spearhead n the leading part of an attacking force. – v to lead (a movement, an
attack etc).

special ['speʃəl] adj 1 out of the ordinary;
unusual or exceptional: a special occasion;
a special friend. 2 appointed, arranged, designed etc for a particular purpose: a special messenger; a special tool for drilling
holes. – n something which is special:
There's a special (=a special train) due
through here at 5.20.
'specialist n a person who makes a very
deep study of one branch of a subject or
field: Dr Brown is a heart specialist.
speciality [speʃi'aləti], (Amer) specialty
['speʃəlti] – pls speci'alities, 'specialties – n
1 a special product for which one is well-
known: Brown bread is this baker's speciality. 2 a special activity, or subject about
which one has special knowledge: His speciality is physics.
'specialize, -ise v (usu with in) go give one's
attention (to), work (in), or study (a particular job, subject etc): He specializes in
fixing computers. ˌspeciali'zation, -s- n.
'specialized, -s- adj (of knowledge, skills
etc) of the accurate detailed kind obtained
by specializing.
'specially adv 1 with one particular purpose: I picked these flowers specially for
you; a splendid cake, specially made for the

occasion. **2** particularly; exceptionally: *He's a nice child, but not specially clever.*

species ['spiːʃiːz] – *pl* **species** – *n* **1** a group (of animals *etc*) whose members are so similar or closely related as to be able to breed together: *There are several species of zebra.* **2** a kind or sort.

specify ['spesifai] *v* **1** to name as wanted or demanded. **2** to make particular or definite mention of: *He specified three types of mistake which had occurred.*

specific [spə'sifik] *adj* **1** giving all the details clearly: *specific instructions.* **2** particular; exactly stated or described: *Each of the bodily organs has its own specific function.*

spe'cifically *adv*: *I specifically told you not to do that*; *This dictionary is intended specifically for learners of English.*

specimen ['spesimin] *n* something used as a sample (of a group or kind of something, *esp* an object to be studied or to be put in a collection): *We looked at specimens of different types of rock under the microscope.*

speck [spek] *n* **1** a small spot or stain: *a speck of ink.* **2** a tiny piece (*eg* of dust).

speckle ['spekl] *n* a little spot on a different-coloured background: *The eggs were pale blue with dark green speckles.*

'speckled *adj* marked with speckles.

specs [speks] short for **spectacles**.

spectacle ['spektəkl] *n* a sight, *esp* one that is very impressive or wonderful: *The royal wedding was a great spectacle.*

spec'tacular [-'takju-] *adj* (*neg* **un-**) **1** making a great show or display: *a spectacular performance.* **2** impressive; dramatic: *a spectacular recovery.* **spec'tacularly** *adv*.

spectacles ['spektəklz] *n pl* glasses which a person wears to help his eyesight: *a pair of spectacles.*

spectator [spek'teitə, (*Amer*) 'spekteitər] *n* a person who watches (an event): *Fifty thousand spectators came to the match.*

spec'tate *v* to be a spectator (at an event).

spectre, (*Amer usu*) **specter** ['spektə] *n* a ghost.

spectrum ['spektrəm] – *pls* **'spectrums**, **'spectra** [-trə] – *n* **1** the visible spectrum. **2** the full range (of something): *The actress's voice was capable of expressing the whole spectrum of emotion.* **3** the entire range of radiation of different wavelengths, part of which (the **visible spectrum**) is normally visible to the naked eye. **4** a similar range of frequencies of sound (the **sound spectrum**).

speculate ['spekjuleit] *v* to make guesses: *He's only speculating – he doesn't know*; *There's no point in speculating about what's going to happen.*

,specu'lation *n* **1** a guess: *Your speculations were all quite close to the truth.* **2** the act of

speculating: *There was great speculation as to what was happening.*

sped *see* **speed**.

speech [spiːtʃ] *n* **1** (the act of) saying words, or the ability to say words: *Speech is one method of communication between people.* **2** the words said: *His speech is full of colloquialisms.* **3** manner or way of speaking: *His speech is very slow.* **4** a formal talk given to a meeting *etc*: *parliamentary speeches.*

'speechless *adj* unable to speak, often because of surprise, shock *etc*: *He looked at her in speechless amazement.* **'speechlessly** *adv*. **'speechlessness** *n*.

speed [spiːd] *n* **1** rate of moving: *a slow speed*; *The car was travelling at high speed.* **2** quickness of moving. – *v* **1** (*pts, ptps* **sped** [sped] **'speeded**) to (cause to) move or progress quickly; to hurry: *The car sped/ speeded along the motorway.* **2** (*pt, ptp* **'speeded**) to drive very fast in a car *etc*, faster than is allowed by law: *The policeman said that I had been speeding.*

'speeding *n* driving at (an illegally) high speed: *He was fined for speeding.*

'speedy *adj* done, carried out *etc* quickly: *a speedy answer.* **'speedily** *adv*. **'speediness** *n*.

speedometer [spiː'domitə] *n* an instrument on a car *etc* showing how fast one is travelling.

speed up – *pt, ptp* **'speeded** – **1** to increase speed: *The car speeded up as it left the town.* **2** to quicken the rate of: *We are trying to speed up production.*

spell[1] [spel] – *pt, ptp* **spelt** [-t], **spelled** – *v* **1** to name or give in order the letters of (a word): *I asked him to spell his name for me.* **2** (of letters) to form (a word): *C-a-t spells 'cat'.* **3** to (be able to) spell words correctly: *I can't spell!* **4** to mean or amount to: *This spells disaster.*

'spelling *n*: *Her spelling is terrible*; (*also adj*) *The teacher gave the children a spelling lesson/test.*

spell[2] [spel] *n* **1** a set or words which, when spoken, is supposed to have magical power: *The witch recited a spell and turned herself into a swan.* **2** a strong influence: *He was completely under her spell.*

spell[3] [spel] *n* **1** a turn (at work): *Shortly afterwards I did another spell at the machine.* **2** a period of time during which something lasts: *a spell of bad health.* **3** a short time: *We stayed in the country for a spell and then came home.*

spelt *see* **spell[1]**.

spend [spend] – *pt, ptp* **spent** [-t] – *v* **1** to use up or pay out (money): *He spends more than he earns.* **2** to pass (time): *I spent a week in Spain this summer.*

spent [spent] *adj* **1** used: *a spent match.*

2 exhausted: *By the time we had done half of the job we were all spent.*

'spendthrift *n* a person who spends his money freely and carelessly.

perm [spɔːm] *pl* **sperms, sperm** – *n* **1** the fluid in a male animal *etc* that fertilizes the female egg. **2** one of the fertilizing cells in this fluid.

*sphere [sfiə] *n* a solid object with a surface on which all points are an equal distance from the centre, like *eg* most types of ball. **spherical** ['sferikəl] *adj* completely round, like not flat, but spherical: *It is now known that the world is not flat, but spherical; a spherical object.*

pice [spais] *n* **1** a *usu* strong-smelling, sharp-tasting vegetable substance used to flavour food (*eg* pepper or nutmeg): *We added cinnamon and other spices.* **2** anything that adds liveliness or interest: *Her arrival added spice to the party.* – *v* to flavour with spice: *The curry had been heavily spiced.*
spiced *adj* containing spice(s): *The dish was heavily spiced.*
'spicy *adj* tasting or smelling of spices: *a spicy cake; He complained that the sausages were too spicy for him.* **'spiciness** *n*.

pider ['spaidə] *n* a kind of small creature with eight legs and no wings, which spins a web.

pike [spaik] *n* **1** a hard, thin, pointed object (of wood, metal *etc*): *The fence had long spikes on top.* **2** a pointed piece of metal attached to the sole of a shoe *etc* to prevent slipping. **spiked** *adj*.
'spiky *adj* having spikes, or points similar to spikes: *the spiky coat of a hedgehog.* **'spikiness** *n*.

pill [spil] – *pt, ptp* **spilt** [-t], **spilled** – *v* to (cause something to) fall or run out (*usu* accidentally): *He spilt milk on the floor; Vegetables spilled out of the burst bag.*
spill the beans to give away a secret: *By Monday it was evident that someone had spilled the beans to the newspapers.*

pin [spin] – *prp* **'spinning**: *pt, ptp* **spun** [spʌn] – *v* **1** to (cause to) go round and round rapidly: *She spun round in surprise; He spun the revolving door round and round.* **2** to form threads from (wool, cotton *etc*) by drawing out and twisting: *The old woman was spinning (wool) in the corner of the room.* – *n* **1** a whirling or turning motion: *The patch of mud sent the car into a spin.* **2** a ride, *esp* on wheels: *After lunch we went for a spin in my new car.*
'spinner *n* a person or thing that spins.
spin-'drier *n* a machine which dries clothes by spinning them round and round and forcing the water out of them.
spin out to cause to last a long or longer time: *He spun out his speech for an extra five minutes.*

pinach ['spinidʒ, -nitʃ] *n* **1** a kind of plant whose young leaves are eaten as a vegetable: *He grows spinach in his garden.* **2** the leaves as food: *We had steak and spinach for dinner.*

spinal *see* **spine**.

spindle ['spindl] *n* a thin pin on which something turns: *I can't turn on the radio any more, because the spindle of the control knob has broken.*

spine [spain] *n* **1** the line of linked bones running down the back of humans and many animals; the backbone: *She damaged her spine when she fell.* **2** something like a backbone in shape or function: *the spine of a book.* **3** a thin, stiff, pointed part growing on an animal or a plant.
'spinal *adj* of or concerned with the backbone: *a spinal injury.*
'spineless *adj* **1** of an animal, having no spine; invertebrate. **2** of a person, having a weak character; easily dominated.
'spiny *adj* full of, or covered with, spines: *a spiny cactus.*
spinal cord a cord of nerve cells running up through the backbone.

spinner *see* **spin**.

spinster ['spinstə] *n* a woman who is not married.

spiny *see* **spine**.

spiral ['spaiərəl] *adj* **1** coiled round like a spring, with each coil the same size as the one below: *a spiral staircase.* **2** winding round and round, *usu* tapering to a point: *a spiral shell.* – *n* **1** an increase or decrease, or rise or fall, becoming more and more rapid (*eg* in prices). **2** a spiral line or object: *A spiral of smoke rose from the chimney.* – *v* – *pt, ptp* **'spiralled,** (*Amer*) **'spiraled** – to go or move in a spiral, *esp* to increase more and more rapidly: *Prices have spiralled in the last six months.*
'spirally *adv*.

spire ['spaiə] *n* a tall, pointed tower, *esp* one built on the roof of a church.

spirit ['spirit] *n* **1** a principle or emotion which makes someone act: *The spirit of kindness seems to be lacking in the world nowadays.* **2** a person's mind, will, personality *etc* thought of as distinct from the body, or as remaining alive *eg* as a ghost when the body dies: *Our great leader may be dead, but his spirit still lives on;* (*also adj*) *the spirit world; Evil spirits have taken possession of him.* **3** liveliness; courage: *He acted with spirit.*
'spirited *adj* full of courage or liveliness: *a spirited attack/description.* **'spiritedly** *adv*.
'spirits *n pl* **1** a person's mood: *He's in good/high/low spirits* (=He's happy/very cheerful/depressed); *This news may raise his spirits.* **2** strong alcoholic drink, *eg* whisky, gin, vodka *etc*.

---

* see illustration on p. 476

'spiritual [tʃul] *adj* of one's spirit or soul, or of one's religious beliefs. 'spiritually *adv*.

*spirit level a tool consisting of a bar containing a glass tube of liquid, for testing whether a surface is level.

spit[1] [spit] *n* (*also* spittle ['spitl]) the liquid that forms in the mouth. – *v* – *prp* 'spitting; *pt, ptp* spat [spat] – 1 to throw out (spit) from the mouth: *He spat in the gutter as an indication of contempt.* 2 to send (out) with force: *The fire spat* (*out*) *sparks*.

spit[2] [spit] *n* a type of sharp-pointed metal bar on which meat is roasted.

spite [spait] *n* ill-will or desire to hurt or offend: *She neglected to give him the message out of spite.* – *v* to annoy, offend or frustrate, because of spite: *He only did that to spite me!*
'spiteful *adj*: *a spiteful remark/person*; *You're being very spiteful.* 'spitefully *adv*. 'spitefulness *n*.
in spite of 1 taking no notice of: *He went in spite of his father's orders.* 2 although something has or had happened, is or was a fact *etc*: *In spite of all the rain that had fallen, the ground was still pretty dry.*

spittle *see* spit[1].

splash [splaʃ] *v* 1 to make wet with drops of liquid, mud *etc, esp* suddenly and accidentally: *A passing car splashed my coat* (*with water*). 2 to (cause to) fly about in drops: *Water splashed everywhere.* 3 to fall or move with splashes: *The children were splashing in the sea.* 4 to display *etc* in a place, manner *etc* that will be noticed: *Posters advertising the concert were splashed all over the wall.* – *n* 1 a scattering of drops of liquid or the noise made by this: *He fell in with a loud splash.* 2 a mark made by splashing: *There was a splash of mud on her dress.* 3 a bright patch: *a splash of colour.*

spleen [spli:n] *n* an organ of the body, close to the stomach, which causes changes in the blood.

splendid ['splendid] *adj* 1 brilliant, magnificent, very rich and grand *etc*: *He looked splendid in his robes.* 2 very good or fine: *a splendid piece of work.* 'splendidly *adv*. 'splendour [-də], 'splendidness *ns*.

splint [splint] *n* a piece of wood *etc* used to keep a broken arm or leg in a fixed position while it heals.
'splinter *n* a small sharp broken piece of wood *etc*: *The rough plank gave her a splinter in her finger.* – *v* to split into splinters: *The door splintered under the heavy blow.*

split [split] – *prp* 'splitting; *pt, ptp* split – *v* 1 to cut or (cause to) break lengthwise: *to split firewood*; *The skirt split all the way down the back seam.* 2 to divide or (cause to) disagree: *The dispute split the workers*

into two opposing groups. – *n* a crack or break: *There was a split in one of the sides of the box.*
,split-'level *adj* built, made *etc* on two levels: *a split-level dining room/cooker.*
split second a fraction of a second.
splitting headache a very bad headache: *Turn down the radio – I've a splitting headache.*
the splits the gymnastic exercise of sitting down on the floor with one leg straight forward and the other straight back: *to do the splits.*

spoil [spoil] – *pts, ptps* spoiled, spoilt [-t] – *v* 1 to damage or ruin; to make bad or useless: *If you touch that drawing you'll spoil it.* 2 to give (a child *etc*) too much of what he wants and possibly make his character, behaviour *etc* worse by doing so: *They spoil that child dreadfully and she's becoming unbearable!*
spoils *n pl* profits or rewards: *the spoils of war*; *the spoils of success.*
spoilt *adj*: *He's a very spoilt child!*
'spoilsport *n* a person who spoils, or refuses to join in, the fun of others.

spoke[1] [spouk] *n* one of the ribs or bars from the centre to the rim of the wheel of a bicycle, cart *etc*.

spoke[2], spoken *see* speak.

spokesman ['spouksmən] – *fem* 'spokeswoman – *n* a person who speaks on behalf of a group of others: *Who is the spokesman for your party?*

sponge [spʌndʒ] *n* 1 a type of sea animal, or its soft skeleton, which has many holes and is able to suck up and hold water. 2 a piece of such a skeleton or a substitute, used for washing the body *etc*. 3 a sponge pudding or cake: *We had jam sponge for dessert.* 4 an act of wiping *etc* with a sponge: *Give the table a quick sponge over, will you?* – *v* 1 to wipe or clean with a sponge: *She sponged the child's face.* 2 to get a living, money *etc* (from someone else): *He's been sponging off/on us for years.*
'sponger *n* a person who lives by sponging on others.
'spongy *adj* soft and springy or holding water like a sponge: *spongy ground.* 'spongily *adv*. 'sponginess *n*.
sponge cake, sponge pudding (a) very light cake or pudding made from flour, eggs and sugar *etc*.

sponsor ['sponsə] *v* 1 to take on the financial responsibility for (a person, project *etc*), often as a form of advertising or for charity: *The firm sponsors several golf tournaments.* 2 to promise (a person) that one will pay a certain sum of money to a charity *etc* if that person completes a set task (*eg a* walk, swim *etc*). – *n* a person, firm *etc* that acts in this way.

'sponsorship *n* (the money given as) the act of sponsoring.

pontaneous [spən'teiniəs] *adj* **1** said, done *etc* of one's own free will without pressure from others: *His offer was quite spontaneous.* **2** natural; not forced: *spontaneous behaviour.* **spon'taneously** *adv.* **spon'taneousness, spontaneity** [spontə'neiəti, -'ni:əti] *ns.*

pook [spu:k] *n* a ghost.

'spooky *adj* eerie and suggesting the presence of ghosts: *It's very spooky walking through the graveyard at night.* **'spookiness** *n.*

pool [spu:l] *n* **1** a type of cylindrical holder: *How can I wind this film back on to its spool?* **2** the amount of thread, film *etc* held by such a holder: *She used three spools of thread in one week.*

poon [spu:n] *n* **1** an instrument shaped like a shallow bowl with a handle for lifting food (*esp* soup or pudding) to the mouth, or for stirring tea, coffee *etc*: *a teaspoon/soup-spoon.* **2** a spoonful. – *v* to lift or scoop up with a spoon: *She spooned food into the baby's mouth.*

'spoonful *n* the amount held by a spoon: *three spoonfuls of sugar.*

'spoon-feed – *pt, ptp* **'spoon-fed** – *v* **1** to feed with a spoon. **2** to teach or treat (a person) in a way that does not allow him to think or act for himself.

pore [spɔ:] *n* a tiny seedlike cell from which ferns and other types of non-flowering plant grow.

port [spɔ:t] *n* **1** games or competitions involving physical activity: *She's very keen on sport of all kinds.* **2** a particular game or amusement of this kind: *Hunting, shooting and fishing are not sports I enjoy.* **3** a good-natured and obliging person: *He's a good sport to agree to do that for us!* **4** fun; amusement: *I only did it for sport.* – *v* to wear, *esp* in public: *He was sporting a pink tie.*

'sporting *adj* **1** of, or concerned with, sports: *the sporting world.* **2** (*neg* **un-**) showing fairness and kindness or generosity, *esp* if unexpected: *a sporting gesture.*

sports *adj* (*Amer also* **sport**) designed, or suitable, for sport: *a sports centre; sports equipment.*

sports car a small, fast car with only two seats.

sports jacket a type of jacket for men, designed for casual wear.

'sportsman ['spɔ:ts-] – *fem* **'sportswoman** – *n* **1** a person who takes part in sports: *He is a very keen sportsman.* **2** a person who shows a spirit of fairness and generosity in sport: *He's a real sportsman who doesn't seem to care if he wins or loses.*

'sportswear *n* clothing designed for playing sports in.

a sporting chance a reasonably good chance.

spot [spot] *n* **1** a small mark or stain (made by mud, paint *etc*): *She was trying to remove a spot of grease from her skirt.* **2** a small, round mark of a different colour from its background: *His tie was blue with white spots.* **3** a pimple or red mark on the skin caused by an illness *etc*: *She had measles and was covered in spots.* **4** a place or small area, *esp* the exact place (where something happened *etc*): *There was a large number of detectives gathered at the spot where the body had been found.* **5** a small amount: *Can I borrow a spot of sugar?* – *v* – *pt, ptp* **'spotted** – **1** to catch sight of: *She spotted him eventually at the very back of the crowd.* **2** to recognize or pick out: *No-one watching the play was able to spot the murderer.*

'spotless *adj* very clean: *a spotless kitchen.* **'spotlessly** *adv.* **'spotlessness** *n.*

'spotted *adj* marked or covered with spots: *Her dress was spotted with grease; a spotted tie.*

'spotty *adj* (of people) covered with spots: *a spotty face/young man.* **'spottiness** *n.*

spot check an inspection made without warning, *esp* on items chosen at random from a group: *We only found out about the flaw during a spot check on goods leaving the factory.*

'spotlight *n* (a lamp for projecting) a circle of light that is thrown on to a small area. – *v* – *pt, ptp* **'spotlit, 'spotlighted** – **1** to light with a spotlight: *The stage was spotlit.* **2** to show up clearly or draw attention to: *The incident spotlighted the difficulties with which we were faced.*

in a spot in trouble: *His failure to return the papers on time put her in a spot.*

on the spot 1 at once: *She liked it so much that she bought it on the spot;* (*also adj*) *an on-the-spot decision.* **2** in the exact place referred to; in the place where one is needed: *It was a good thing you were on the spot when he had his heart attack;* (*also adj*) *our on-the-spot reporter.* **3** (*esp with* **put**) in a dangerous, difficult or embarrassing position: *The interviewer's questions really put the Prime Minister on the spot.*

spot on very accurate or exactly on the target: *His description of Mary was spot on!*

spouse [spaus] *n* a husband or wife.

spout [spaut] *v* **1** to throw out or be thrown out in a jet: *Water spouted from the hole in the tank.* **2** to talk or say (something) loudly and dramatically: *He started to spout poetry, of all things!* – *n* **1** the part of a kettle, teapot, jug, water-pipe *etc* through which the liquid it contains is poured out. **2** a jet or strong flow (of water *etc*).

sprain [sprein] v to twist (a joint, esp the ankle or wrist) in such a way as to tear or stretch the ligaments: *She sprained her ankle yesterday.* – n a twisting of a joint in this way.

sprang see **spring**.

sprawl [spro:l] v **1** to sit, lie or fall with the arms and legs spread out widely and carelessly: *Several tired-looking people were sprawling in armchairs.* **2** (of a town etc) to spread out in an untidy and irregular way. – n **1** an act of sprawling: *He was lying in a careless sprawl on the sofa.* **2** an untidy and irregular area (of houses etc): *She lost her way in the grimy sprawl of the big city.*
'sprawling adj: *the huge, sprawling city of Los Angeles.*

spray [sprei] n **1** a fine mist of small flying drops (of water etc) such as that given out by a waterfall: *The perfume came out of the bottle in a fine spray.* **2** a device with many small holes, or other instrument, for producing a fine mist of liquid: *She used a spray to rinse her hair.* **3** a liquid for spraying: *He bought a can of fly-spray.* – v **1** to (cause liquid to) come out in a mist or in fine jets: *The water sprayed all over everyone.* **2** to cover with a mist or with fine jets of liquid: *He sprayed the roses to kill pests.*

spread [spred] – pt, ptp **spread** – v **1** to (cause to) go (often more widely or more thinly) over a surface: *She spread honey thickly on her toast.* **2** to cover (a surface with something): *She spread the bread with jam.* **3** to (cause to) reach a wider area, affect a larger number of people etc: *The news spread through the village very quickly.* **4** to distribute over a wide area, period of time etc: *The exams were spread over a period of ten days.* **5** to open out: *He spread the map on the table.* – n **1** the process of reaching a wider area, affecting more people etc: *the spread of information/television; the spread of crime among schoolchildren.* **2** something to be spread on bread etc: *Have some chicken spread.* **3** the space or time covered (by something) or the extent of spreading: *a spread of several miles.*

spread out 1 to extend or stretch out: *The fields spread out in front of him.* **2** to distribute over a wide area or period of time: *She spread the leaflets out on the table.* **3** to scatter and go in different directions, in order to cover a wider area: *They spread out and began to search the entire area.*

sprig [sprig] n a small piece of a plant; a twig.

spring [spriŋ] – pt **sprang** [spraŋ]: ptp **sprung** [sprʌŋ] – v **1** to jump, leap or move swiftly (usu upwards): *She sprang into the boat.* **2** to arise or result from: *His bravery springs from his love of adventure.* **3** to (cause a trap to) close violently: *The trap*

must have sprung when the hare stepped in it. – n **1** a coil of wire or other similar device which can be compressed or squeezed down but returns to its original shape when released: *a watch-spring; the springs in a chair.* **2** the season of the year when plants begin to grow, February or March to April or May in cooler northern regions: *Spring is my favourite season.* **3** a leap or sudden movement: *The lion made a sudden spring on its prey.* **4** the ability to stretch and spring back again: *There's not a lot of spring in this old trampoline.* **5** a small stream flowing out from the ground.
'springy adj **1** able to spring back into its former shape: *The grass is very springy.* **2** having spring: *These floorboards are springy.* **'springiness** n.
sprung [sprʌŋ] adj having springs: *a sprung mattress.*
'springboard n **1** a springy type of diving-board. **2** a board on which gymnasts jump before vaulting.
spring cleaning thorough cleaning of a house etc esp in spring.
'springtime n the season of spring.
spring up to develop or appear suddenly: *New buildings are springing up everywhere.*

sprinkle ['spriŋkl] v to scatter something over something else in small drops or bits: *He sprinkled salt over his food; He sprinkled the roses with water.*
'sprinkler n an apparatus for sprinkling eg water over a lawn.
'sprinkling n a small amount or a few: *There were mostly women at the meeting but there was a sprinkling of men.*

sprint [sprint] n **1** a run or running race performed at high speed over a short distance: *Who won the 100 metres sprint?* **2** the pace of this: *He ran up the road at a sprint.* – v to run at full speed esp (in) a race: *He sprinted (for) the last few hundred metres.*
'sprinter n a person who is good at sprinting.

sprite [sprait] n an elf or fairy: *a water-sprite.*

sprout [spraut] v **1** to (cause to) develop leaves, shoots etc: *The trees are sprouting new leaves.* **2** (of animals, birds etc) to develop eg horns, produce eg feathers: *The young birds are sprouting their first feathers.* – n a new shoot or bud: *bean sprouts.*
sprout up (of plants or children) to grow: *That fruit bush has sprouted up fast; At the age of fourteen he really began to sprout up.*

spruce [spru:s] adj neat and smart: *You're looking very spruce today.*
spruce up to make oneself or somebody else smarter: *I'll go and spruce up before going out.*

sprung see **spring**.

spry [sprai] *adj* lively or active: *a spry old gentleman*. 'spryly *adv*. 'spryness *n*.

spun *see* spin.

spur [spə:] *n* 1 a small instrument with a sharp point or points that a rider wears on his heels and digs into the horse's sides to make it go faster. 2 anything that urges a person to make greater efforts: *He was driven on by the spur of ambition*.

on the spur of the moment suddenly; without previous planning: *We decided to go to Paris on the spur of the moment*.

spur on to urge a horse to go faster, using spurs, or a person to make greater efforts: *He spurred his horse on*; *The thought of the prize spurred her on*.

spurt [spə:t] *v* (of a liquid) to spout or gush: *Blood spurted from the wound*. – *n* a sudden gush or burst: *a spurt of blood/energy*.

put a spurt on/put on a spurt to run or go faster *eg* towards the end of a race: *He put a sudden spurt on and passed the other competitors*.

spy [spai] *n* a secret agent or person employed to gather information secretly *esp* about the military affairs of other countries: *She was arrested as a spy*; *industrial spies*. – *v* 1 to be a spy: *He had been spying for the Russians for many years*. 2 to see or notice: *She spied a human figure on the mountainside*.

'spyhole *n* a peep-hole.

spy on to watch (a person *etc*) secretly: *The police had been spying on the gang for several months*.

squabble ['skwobl] *v* to quarrel noisily, *usu* about something unimportant: *The children are always squabbling over the toys*. – *n* a noisy quarrel.

squad [skwod] *n* 1 a small group of soldiers drilled or working together: *The men were divided into squads to perform different duties*. 2 a group of people, *esp* a working-party: *a squad of workmen*.

squadron ['skwodrən] *n* a division of a regiment, a section of a fleet, or a group of aeroplanes.

squalid ['skwolid] *adj* very dirty or filthy: *The houses are squalid and overcrowded*.

'squalor [-lə] *n*: *They lived in squalor*.

squall [skwo:l] *n* a sudden violent wind, *eg* bringing rain: *The ship was struck by a squall*.

squalor *see* squalid.

squander ['skwondə] *v* to waste: *He squandered all his money on gambling*.

*square [skweə] *n* 1 a four-sided two-dimensional figure with all sides equal in length and all angles right angles. 2 something in the shape of this. 3 an open place in a town, with the buildings round it. 4 the resulting number when a number is multiplied by itself: *3 × 3, or 3² = 9, so 9 is the square of 3*. – *adj* 1 having the shape of a square or right angle: *I need a square piece of paper*; *He has a short, square body/a square chin*. 2 (of business dealings, scores in games *etc*) level, even, fairly balanced *etc*: *If I pay you an extra $5 shall we be (all) square?*; *Their scores are (all) square (=equal)*. 3 measuring a particular amount on all four sides: *This piece of wood is two metres square*. 4 old-fashioned: *square ideas about clothes*. – *adv* 1 at right angles, or in a square shape: *The carpet is not cut square with the corner*. 2 firmly and directly: *She hit him square on the point of the chin*. – *v* 1 to give a square shape to or make square. 2 to settle, pay *etc* (an account, debt *etc*): *I must square my account with you*. 3 to (cause to) fit or agree: *His story doesn't square with the facts*. 4 to multiply a number by itself: *Two squared is four*.

squared *adj* 1 marked or ruled with squares: *squared paper*. 2 having been squared.

'squarely *adv* directly and firmly: *He stood squarely in front of me*; *She looked squarely at me*.

square centimetre, metre *etc* (*often abbrev* cm^2, m^2 *etc when written*) an area equal to a square in which each side is one centimetre, metre *etc*: *If the door is 3 metres high and 1½ metres wide, its area is 4½ square metres*.

square root the number which, multiplied by itself, gives the number that is being considered: *The square root of 16 is 4 ($\sqrt{16}=4$)*.

fair and square directly: *He hit him fair and square on the nose*.

go back to square one to start all over again.

a square deal a fair bargain; fair treatment.

squash [skwoʃ] *v* 1 to press, squeeze or crush: *He tried to squash too many clothes into his case*; *The tomatoes got squashed (flat) at the bottom of the shopping-bag*. 2 to defeat (a rebellion *etc*). – *n* 1 a state of being squashed or crowded: *There was a great squash in the doorway*. 2 (a particular flavour of) a drink containing the juice of crushed fruit: *Have some orange squash!* 3* (*also* **squash rackets**) a type of game played in a walled court with rackets and a rubber ball.

'squashy *adj* soft or easily squashed: *The rain makes the fruit very squashy*.

squat [skwot] – *pt, ptp* 'squatted – *v* to sit down on the heels or in a crouching position: *The beggar squatted all day in the market place*. – *adj* short and fat; dumpy: *a squat little man*; *an ugly, squat building*.

squawk [skwo:k] *n* a loud harsh cry made *eg* by an excited or angry bird: *The hen gave a squawk when she saw the fox.* – *v* to make a sound of this sort.

squeak [skwi:k] *n* a shrill cry or sound: *the squeaks of the mice/puppies.* – *v* to make a shrill cry or sound: *The door-hinge is squeaking.*
'**squeaky** *adj* making squeaks: *squeaky shoes.* '**squeakily** *adv.* '**squeakiness** *n.*

squeal [skwi:l] *n* a long, shrill cry: *The children welcomed him with squeals of delight.* – *v* to give a cry of this sort: *The puppy squealed with pain.*

squeeze [skwi:z] *v* **1** to press (something) together or from all sides tightly: *He squeezed her hand affectionately*; *He squeezed the clay into a ball.* **2** to force (eg oneself) eg into or through a narrow space: *The dog squeezed himself/his body into the hole*; *We were all squeezed into the back seat of the car.* **3** to force something, eg liquid, out of something by pressing: *She squeezed the oranges (into a jug)*; *We might be able to squeeze some more money/information out of him.* – *n* **1** an act of squeezing: *He gave his sister an affectionate squeeze.* **2** a condition of being squeezed: *We all got into the car, but it was a squeeze.* **3** a few drops produced by squeezing. **4** a time of financial restriction: *an economic squeeze.*
'**squeezer** *n* an instrument for squeezing: *a lemon squeezer.*
squeeze up to move closer together: *Could you all squeeze up on the bench and make room for me?*

squelch [skweltʃ] *n* the sucking sound made by movement in a thick, sticky substance eg mud. – *v* to make squelches: *He squelched across the marsh.*

squid [skwid] – *pls* **squid, squids** – *n* a type of sea creature with ten tentacles.

squint [skwint] *v* **1** to have the physical defect of having the eyes turning towards or away from each other or to cause the eyes to do this: *The child squints*; *You squint when you look down at your nose.* **2** (*with* **at, up at, through** *etc*) to look with half-shut or narrowed eyes: *He squinted through the telescope.* – *n* **1** a squinting position of the eyes: *an eye-operation to correct her squint.* **2** a glance or look at something: *Let me have a squint at that photograph.* – *adj, adv* (placed *etc*) crookedly or not straight: *Your hat is squint.*

squirm [skwə:m] *v* **1** to twist the body or wriggle: *He lay squirming on the ground with pain.* **2** to be very embarrassed or ashamed: *I squirmed when I thought of how rude I'd been.*

squirrel ['skwirəl, (*Amer*) 'skwə:rəl] *n* a type of animal of the rodent family, *usu* either reddish-brown or grey, with a large bushy tail.

squirt [skwə:t] *v* to (make a liquid *etc*) shoot out in a narrow jet: *The elephant squirted water over itself*; *Water squirted from the hose.*

stab [stab] – *pt, ptp* **stabbed** – *v* to wound or pierce with a pointed instrument or weapon: *He stabbed him (through the heart/in the chest) with a dagger.* – *n* an act of stabbing or a piercing blow.
'**stabbing** *adj* (of pain *etc*) very acute as though caused by a stab: *He complained of a stabbing pain just before he collapsed.*
stab (someone) in the back to act treacherously towards (someone).

stable[1] ['steibl] *adj* (*neg* **un-**) **1** firm and steady or well-balanced: *This chair isn't very stable.* **2** firmly established and likely to last: *a stable government.* **3** (of a person or his character) unlikely to become unreasonably upset or hysterical: *She's the only stable person in the whole family.* **4** (of a substance) not easily decomposed.
stability [stə'bi-] *n* the quality of being stable.
'**stabilize, -ise** [-bi-] *v* to make (more) stable: *He put a wedge of paper under the table to stabilize it.* ,**stabili'zation, -s-** *n.*

stable[2] ['steibl] *n* **1** a building in which horses are kept. **2** (*in pl*) a horse-keeping establishment: *He runs the riding stables.*

stack [stak] *n* **1** a large, *usu* neatly shaped, pile eg of hay, straw, wood *etc*: *a haystack.* **2** a set of shelves for books eg in a library. – *v* to arrange in a large, *usu* neat, pile: *Stack the books up against the wall.*

stadium ['steidiəm] – *pls* '**stadiums, 'stadia** [-diə] – *n* a large sports-ground or race-course *usu* with seats for spectators: *The athletics competitions were held in the new Olympic stadium.*

staff[1] [sta:f] *n or n pl* a group of people employed in running a business, school *etc*: *The school has a large teaching staff*; *The staff are annoyed about the changes.* – *v* to supply with staff: *Most of our offices are staffed by volunteers.*
'**staffroom** *n* a sitting-room for the staff of eg a school: *A meeting will be held in the staffroom.*

staff[2] [sta:f], **stave** [steiv] – *pl* **staves** – *n* a set of lines and spaces on which music is written or printed.

stag [stag] *n* a male deer, *esp* a red deer.

stage[1] [steidʒ] *n* a raised platform *esp* for performing or acting on, eg in a theatre. – *v* **1** to prepare and produce (a play *etc*) in a theatre *etc*: *This play was first staged in 1928.* **2** to organize (an event *etc*): *The protesters are planning to stage a demonstration.*
'**staging** *n* **1** wooden planks *etc* forming a platform. **2** the way in which a play *etc* is

presented on a stage: *The staging was good, but the acting poor.*

stage direction an order to an actor playing a part to do this or that: *a stage direction to enter from the left.*

stage fright the nervousness felt by an actor *etc* when in front of an audience, *esp* for the first time: *The young actress was suffering from stage fright and could not utter a word.*

'stagehand *n* a workman employed to help with scenery *etc*.

stage manager a person who is in charge of scenery and equipment for plays *etc*.

stage[2] [steidʒ] *n* **1** a period or step in the development of something: *The plan is in its early stages*; *At this stage, we don't know how many survivors there are.* **2** part of a journey: *The first stage of our journey will be the flight to Singapore.* **3** a section of a bus route. **4** a section of a rocket.

stagger ['stagə] *v* **1** to sway, move or walk unsteadily: *The drunk man staggered along the road.* **2** to astonish: *I was staggered to hear he had died.* **3** to arrange (people's hours of work, holidays *etc*) so that they do not begin and end at the same times.

'staggering *adj* causing unsteadiness, shock or astonishment: *a staggering blow on the side of the head*; *That piece of news is staggering.*

staging *see* **stage**[1].

stagnant ['stagnənt] *adj* **1** (of water) standing still rather than flowing and therefore *usu* dirty: *a stagnant pool.* **2** dull or inactive: *Our economy is stagnant.*

stagnate [stag'neit, (*Amer*) 'stagneit] *v* **1** (of water) to be or become stagnant. **2** to become dull and inactive. **stag'nation** *n*.

stain [stein] *v* **1** to leave a (permanent) dirty mark or coloured patch on *eg* a fabric: *The coffee I spilt has stained my trousers.* **2** to become marked in this way: *Silk stains easily.* **3** *v* to dye or colour (*eg* wood): *The wooden chairs had been stained brown.* – *n* a dirty mark on a fabric *etc* that is difficult or impossible to remove: *His overall was covered with paint-stains*; *There is not the slightest stain upon her reputation.*

stainless steel (of) a metal alloy composed of steel and chromium that does not rust: *a sink made of stainless steel*; *stainless steel knives/cutlery.*

stair [steə] *n* (any one of) a number of steps, *usu* inside a building, going from one floor to another: *He fell down the stairs.*

'staircase, 'stairway *ns* a series or flight of stairs: *A dark and narrow staircase led up to the top floor.*

stake[1] [steik] *n* a strong stick or post, *esp* a pointed one used as a support or as part of a fence.

stake[2] [steik] *n* a sum of money risked in betting: *He and his friends enjoy playing cards for high stakes.* – *v* to bet or risk (money or something of value): *I'm going to stake $5 on that horse.*

at stake 1 to be won or lost: *A great deal of money is at stake.* **2** in great danger: *The peace of the country/Our children's future is at stake.*

stalactite ['staləktait, (*Amer*) stə'laktait] *n* a spike of limestone hanging from the roof of a cave *etc* formed by the dripping of water containing lime.

stalagmite ['staləgmait, (*Amer*) stə'lagmait] *n* a spike of limestone rising from the floor of a cave, formed by water dripping from the roof.

stale [steil] *adj* **1** (of food *etc*) not fresh and therefore dry and tasteless: *stale bread.* **2** no longer interesting: *His ideas are stale and dull.* **3** no longer able to work *etc* well because of too much study *etc*: *If she practises the piano for more than two hours a day, she will grow stale.*

stalemate ['steilmeit] *n* **1** a position in chess in which a player cannot move without putting his king in danger. **2** in any contest, dispute *etc*, a position in which neither side can win: *The recent discussions ended in stalemate.*

stalk[1] [stoːk] *n* the stem of a plant or of a leaf, flower or fruit: *If the stalk is damaged, the plant may die.*

stalk[2] [stoːk] *v* **1** to walk stiffly and proudly, *eg* in anger: *He stalked out of the room in disgust.* **2** to move menacingly through a place: *Disease and famine stalk (through) the country.* **3** in hunting, to move gradually as close as possible to game, *eg* deer, trying to remain hidden: *Have you ever stalked deer/been deer-stalking?*

'stalker *n* a person who stalks game.

stall[1] [stoːl] *n* **1** a compartment in a cowshed *etc*: *cattle stalls.* **2** a small shop or a counter or table on which goods are displayed for sale: *He bought a newspaper at the bookstall on the station*; *traders' stalls.*

stalls *n pl* (*often with* **the**) in a theatre, the seats on the ground floor: *I always sit in the stalls.*

stall[2] [stoːl] *v* **1** (of a car *etc* or its engine) to stop suddenly through lack of power, braking too quickly *etc*: *The car stalled when I was halfway up the hill.* **2** (of an aircraft) to lose speed while flying and so go out of control: *The plane stalled just after take-off and crashed on to the runway.* **3** to cause (a car *etc*, or aircraft) to do this: *Use the brake gently or you'll stall the engine.* – *n* a dangerous loss of flying speed in an aircraft, causing it to drop: *The plane went into a stall.*

stall[3] [stɔ:l] *v* to avoid making a definite decision in order to give oneself more time.

stallion ['staljən] *n* a fully-grown male horse.

stamen ['steimən] *n* one of the thread-like spikes in a flower that bear the pollen.

stamina ['staminə] *n* strength or power to endure fatigue *etc*: *Long-distance runners require plenty of stamina.*

stammer ['stamə] *n* the speech defect of being unable to produce easily certain sounds: *'You m-m-must m-m-meet m-m-my m-m-mother' is an example of a stammer*; *That child has a bad stammer.* – *v* to speak with a stammer or in a similar way because of *eg* fright, nervousness *etc*: *He stammered an apology.*

'stammerer *n* a person who has a stammer.

stamp [stamp] *v* **1** to bring (the foot) down with force (on the ground): *He stamped his foot with rage*; *She stamped on the insect.* **2** to print or mark on to: *He stamped the date at the top of his letter*; *The oranges were all stamped with the exporter's name.* **3** to stick a postage stamp on (a letter *etc*): *I've addressed the envelope but haven't stamped it.* – *n* **1** an act of stamping the foot: *'Give it to me!' she shouted with a stamp of her foot.* **2** the instrument used to stamp a design *etc* on a surface: *He marked the date on the bill with a rubber date-stamp.* **3** a postage stamp: *He stuck the stamps on the parcel*; *He collects foreign stamps.* **4** a design *etc* made by stamping: *All the goods bore the manufacturer's stamp.*

stamp out 1 to put out or extinguish (a fire) by stamping on it: *She stamped out the remains of the fire.* **2** to crush (a rebellion *etc*).

stampede [stam'pi:d] *n* a sudden wild rush of wild animals *etc*: *a stampede of buffaloes*; *The school bell rang for lunch and there was a stampede for the door.* – *v* to (cause to) rush in a stampede: *The noise stampeded the elephants/made the elephants stampede.*

stance [sta:ns] *n* a person's position or manner of standing, *eg* in playing golf, cricket *etc*.

stand [stand] – *pt, ptp* **stood** [stud] – *v* **1** to be in an upright position, not sitting or lying: *His leg was so painful that he could hardly stand*; *After the storm, few trees were left standing.* **2** (*often with* **up**) to rise to the feet: *He pushed back his chair and stood up*; *Some people like to stand* (**up**) *when the National Anthem is played.* **3** to remain motionless: *The train stood for an hour outside Newcastle.* **4** to remain unchanged: *This law still stands.* **5** to be in or have a particular place: *There is now a factory where our house once stood.* **6** to be in a particular state, condition or situation: *As matters stand, we can do nothing to help*;

How do you stand financially? **7** to accept or offer oneself for a particular position *etc*: *He is standing as Parliamentary candidate for our district.* **8** to put in a particular position, *esp* upright: *He picked up the fallen chair and stood it beside the table.* **9** to undergo or endure: *He will stand (his) trial for murder*; *I can't stand her rudeness any longer.* **10** to pay for (a meal *etc*) for (a person): *Let me stand you a drink!* – *n* **1** a position or place in which to stand ready to fight *etc*, or an act of fighting *etc*: *The guard took up his stand at the gate*; *I shall make a stand for what I believe is right.* **2** an object, *esp* a piece of furniture, for holding or supporting something: *a coat-stand*; *The sculpture had been removed from its stand for cleaning.* **3** a stall where goods are displayed for sale or advertisement. **4** a large structure beside a football pitch, race course *etc* with rows of seats for spectators: *The stand was crowded.* **5** (*Amer*) a witness box in a law court.

'standing *adj* permanent: *The general's standing orders must be obeyed.* – *n* **1** time of lasting: *an agreement of long standing.* **2** rank or reputation: *a diplomat of high standing.*

'stand-by – *pl* **'stand-bys** – *n* **1** readiness for action: *Two fire-engines went directly to the fire, and a third was on stand-by* (= ready to go if ordered). **2** something that can be used in an emergency *etc*: *Fruit is a good stand-by when children get hungry between meals.* – *adj* (of an airline passenger or ticket) costing or paying less than the usual fare, as the passenger does not book a seat for a particular flight, but waits for the first available seat. – *adv* travelling in this way: *It costs a lot less to travel stand-by.*

'stand-in *n* a person who takes someone else's job *etc* for a temporary period, *esp* in making films.

'standing-room *n* space for standing only, not sitting: *There was standing-room only on the bus.*

make someone's hair stand on end to frighten someone very greatly: *The horrible scream made his hair stand on end.*

stand aside to move to one side or withdraw out of someone's way: *He stood aside to let me past.*

stand back to move backwards or away: *A crowd gathered round the injured man, but a policeman ordered everyone to stand back.*

stand by 1 to watch something happening without doing anything: *I couldn't just stand by while he was hitting the child.* **2** to be ready to act: *The police are standing by in case of trouble.* **3** to support; to stay loyal to: *She stood by him throughout his trial.*

stand down to withdraw *eg* from a contest.

stand fast/firm to refuse to yield.

stand for 1 to be a candidate for election to: *He stood for Parliament.* **2** to be an abbreviation for: *HQ stands for Headquarters.* **3** to represent: *I like to think that our school stands for all that is best in education.* **4** to tolerate: *I won't stand for this sort of behaviour.*

stand in to take another person's place, job etc for a time: *The leading actor was ill and another actor stood in for him.*

stand on one's own (two) feet to manage one's own affairs without help.

stand out 1 to be noticeable: *She stood out as one of the prettiest girls in the school.* **2** to go on resisting or to refuse to yield: *The garrison stood out (against the besieging army) as long as possible.*

stand over to supervise closely: *I have to stand over him to make him do his schoolwork.*

stand up for to support or defend: *She stood up for him when the others bullied him.*

stand up to to show resistance to: *He stood up to the bigger boys who tried to bully him; These chairs have stood up to very hard use.*

standard ['standəd] *n* **1** something used as a basis of measurement: *The kilogram is the international standard of weight.* **2** a basis for judging quality, or a level of excellence aimed at, required or achieved: *You can't judge an amateur artist's work by the same standards as you would judge that of a trained artist; high standards of behaviour; His performance did not reach the required standard.* **3** a flag or carved figure etc fixed to a pole and carried eg at the front of an army going into battle. – *adj* (accepted as) normal or usual; *The Post Office likes the public to use a standard size of envelope.*

'standardize, -ise *v* to make or keep (eg products) of one size, shape etc for the sake of convenience etc. ,**standardi'zation, -s-** *n*.

'standard-bearer *n* a person who carries a standard or banner.

be up to/below standard to (fail to) achieve the required standard: *Her work is well up to standard.*

standard of living the level of comfort and welfare achieved in any particular society.

standpoint ['standpoint] *n* a point of view: *From my standpoint, 3.00 p.m. would be a suitable time.*

standstill ['standstil]: **be at, come to, reach a standstill** to remain without moving; to stop, halt etc: *The traffic was at a standstill.*

stank *see* **stink.**

staple¹ ['steipl] *n* **1** a chief product of trade or industry. **2** a chief or main item (of diet etc).

staple² ['steipl] *n* **1** a U-shaped type of nail. **2** a U-shaped piece of wire that is driven through sheets of paper etc to fasten them together. – *v* to fasten or attach (paper etc) with staples.

'stapler *n* an instrument for stapling papers etc.

star [sta:] *n* **1** the fixed bodies in the sky, which are really distant suns: *The Sun is a star, and the Earth is one of its planets.* **2** any of the bodies in the sky appearing as points of light: *The sky was full of stars.* **3** an object, shape or figure with a number of pointed rays, usu five or six, often used as a means of marking quality etc: *The teacher stuck a gold star on the child's neat exercise book; a four-star hotel.* **4** a leading actor or actress or other well-known performer eg in sport etc: *a film/television star; a football star;* (*also adj*) *She has had many star rôles in films.* – *v* – *pt, ptp* **starred** – to play a leading rôle in a play, film etc: *She has starred in two recent films.* **3** (of a film etc) to have (a certain actor etc) as its leading performer: *The film starred Elvis Presley.*

'stardom *n* the state of being a famous performer: *to achieve stardom.*

'starry *adj* full of or shining like stars: *a starry night; starry eyes.*

'starfish *n* a type of small sea creature with five points as arms.

*****'starfruit** *n* a juicy, yellow, oblong, tropical fruit, which, when cut across, is star-shaped.

'starlight *n* the light from the stars.

'starlit *adj* bright with stars: *a starlit night.*

see stars to see flashes of light as a result of a hard blow on the head.

thank one's lucky stars to be grateful for one's good luck.

starboard ['sta:bəd] *n* the right side of a ship or aircraft, from the point of view of a person looking towards the bow or front.

starch [sta:tʃ] *n* **1** a white food substance found esp in flour, potatoes etc: *Bread contains starch.* **2** a powder prepared from this, used for stiffening clothes. – *v* to stiffen (clothes) with starch.

'starchy *adj* like or containing starch: *cake, biscuits and other starchy foods.* **'starchiness** *n*.

stardom *see* **star.**

stare [steə] *v* (*often with* at) to look at with a fixed gaze: *They stared at her clothes in amazement; Don't stare – it's rude!* – *n* a staring look: *a bold stare.*

stare in the face to be easy to see or obvious: *The answer to the problem was staring me in the face.*

starfish *see* **star.**

stark [sta:k] *adj* bare, harsh or simple in a severe way: *a stark, rocky landscape.*

stark crazy/mad completely mad.

stark naked (of a person) completely naked.

* see illustration on p. 201

starling ['sta:liŋ] n a type of small bird with glossy dark feathers.

starry see star.

start[1] [sta:] v **1** to leave or begin a journey: *We shall have to start at 5.30 a.m. in order to get to the boat in time.* **2** to begin: *He starts working at six o'clock every morning; She started to cry; She starts her new job next week; Haven't you started (on) your meal yet?; What time does the play start?* **3** to (cause an engine etc to) begin to work: *I can't start the car; The car won't start; The clock stopped but I started it again.* **4** to cause something to begin or begin happening etc: *One of the students decided to start a college magazine.* – n **1** the beginning of an activity, journey, race etc: *I told him at the start that his idea would not succeed; The runners lined up at the start; He stayed in the lead after a good start; I shall have to make a start on that work.* **2** in a race etc, the advantage of beginning before or further forward than others, or the amount of time, distance etc gained through this: *The youngest child in the race got a start of five metres; The driver of the stolen car already had twenty minutes' start before the police began the pursuit.*

'**starter** n **1** a person, horse etc that actually runs etc in a race. **2** a person who gives the signal for the race to start. **3** a device in a car etc for starting the engine.

'**starting-point** n the point from which something begins.

for a start (used in argument etc) in the first place, or as the first point in an argument: *You can't have a new bicycle because for a start we can't afford one.*

get off to a good, bad start to start well or badly in a race, business etc.

start off 1 to begin a journey: *It's time we started off.* **2** to cause or allow something to begin, someone to start doing something etc: *The money lent to him by his father started him off as a bookseller.*

start out to begin a journey; to start off: *We shall have to start out at dawn.*

start up to (cause to) begin or begin working etc: *The machine suddenly started up; He has started up a new boys' club.*

to start with 1 at the beginning: *He was very nervous to start with.* **2** as the first point (in an argument etc): *There are many reasons why he shouldn't get the job. To start with, he isn't qualified.*

start[2] [sta:t] v to jump or jerk suddenly because of fright, surprise etc: *The sudden noise made me start.* – n **1** a sudden movement of the body: *He gave a start of surprise.* **2** a shock: *What a start the news gave me!*

startle ['sta:tl] v to give a shock or surprise to: *The sound startled me.*

starve [sta:v] v **1** to (cause to) die, or suffer greatly, from hunger: *In the drought, many people and animals starved (to death); They were accused of starving their prisoners.* **2** to be very hungry: *Can't we have supper now? I'm starving.*

star'vation n a starving state: *They died of starvation.*

state[1] [steit] n **1** the condition in which a thing or person is: *the bad state of the roads; The room was in an untidy state; He inquired about her state of health; What a state you're in!; He was not in a fit state to take the class.* **2** a country considered as a political community, or, as in the United States, one division of a federation: *The Prime Minister visits the Queen once a week to discuss affairs of state; The care of the sick and elderly is considered partly the responsibility of the state; (also adj) The railways are under state control; state-controlled/owned industries.* **3** ceremonial dignity and spendour: *The Queen, wearing her robes of state, drove in a horse-drawn coach to Westminster; (also adj) state occasions/banquets.*

'**stately** adj noble, dignified and impressive in appearance or manner: *She is tall and stately; a stately house.* '**stateliness** n.

'**statesman** ['steits-] n a person who plays an important part in the government of a state.

'**statesmanlike** ['steits-] adj showing the qualities of a good statesman.

'**statesmanship** ['steits-] n skill in directing the affairs of a state.

get into a state to become very upset or anxious.

lie in state (of a corpse) to be laid in a place of honour for the public to see, before burial.

state[2] [steit] v to say or announce clearly, carefully and definitely: *You have not yet stated your intentions.*

'**statement** n **1** the act of stating. **2** something that is stated: *The prime minister will make a statement tomorrow on the crisis.* **3** a written statement of how much money a person has, owes etc: *I'll look at my bank statement to see how much money is in my account.*

static ['statik] adj still; not moving. – n atmospheric disturbances causing poor reception of radio or television programmes.

static (electricity) electricity that accumulates on the surface of objects (eg hair, nylon garments etc).

station ['steiʃən] n **1** a place with a ticket office, waiting rooms etc, where trains, buses or coaches stop to allow passengers

to get on or off: *a bus station*; *She arrived at the station in good time for her train.* **2** a local headquarters or centre of work of some kind: *How many fire-engines are kept at the fire station?*; *a radio station*; *Where is the police station?*; *military/naval stations.* **3** a post or position (*eg* of a guard or other person on duty): *The watchman remained at his station all night.* – *v* to put (a person, oneself, troops *etc* in a place or position to perform some duty): *He stationed himself at the corner of the road to keep watch*; *The regiment is stationed abroad.*
'**stationary** *adj* standing still, not moving: *a stationary vehicle.*
stationer ['steiʃənə] *n* **1** a person who sells stationery.
'**stationery** *n* paper, envelopes, pens and other articles used in writing *etc*.
statistics [stə'tistiks] *n pl* figures giving information about something: *There were 900 deaths and 20 000 injuries on the roads last year, but the statistics for the previous year were worse.* – *n sing* the study of such figures. **sta'tistical** *adj*. **sta'tistically** *adv*.
statistician [stati'stiʃən] *n* a person who is an expert in statistics.
statue ['statju:] *n* a sculptured figure of a person, animal *etc* in bronze, stone, wood *etc*: *A statue of Nelson stands at the top of Nelson's Column*; *The children stood as still as statues.*
stature ['statʃə] *n* **1** height of body: *a man of gigantic stature.* **2** importance or reputation: *a musician of stature.*
status ['steitəs, (*Amer also*) 'sta-] *n* **1** the position of a person with regard to his legal rights *etc*: *If she marries a foreigner, will her status as a British citizen be affected?* **2** a person's social rank.
status symbol a possession that indicates one's social importance: *a car, a private swimming-pool and other status symbols.*
statute ['statju:t] *n* a written law of a country.
staunch [sto:ntʃ] *adj* firm, trusty: *a staunch friend.* '**staunchly** *adv*. '**staunchness** *n*.
stave [steiv] *n* in music, a staff.
stay [stei] *v* **1** to remain (in a place) for a time, *eg* while travelling, or as a guest *etc*: *We stayed three nights at that hotel/with a friend/in Paris*; *Aunt Mary is coming to stay (for a fortnight)*; *Would you like to stay for supper?*; *Stay and watch that television programme.* **2** to remain (in a particular position, place, state or condition): *The doctor told her to stay in bed*; *He never stays long in any job*; *Stay away from the office till your cold is better*; *Why won't these socks stay up?*; *Stay where you are – don't move!*; *In 1900, people didn't realize that motor cars were here to stay.* – *n* a period of staying (in

a place *etc*): *We had an overnight stay/a two days' stay in London.*
stay behind to remain in a place after others have left it: *They all left the office at five o'clock, but he stayed behind to finish some work.*
stay in to remain in one's house *etc* and not go out of doors: *I'm staying in tonight to watch television.*
stay out to remain out of doors and not return to one's house *etc*: *The children mustn't stay out after 9 p.m.*
stay put to remain where placed: *Once a child can crawl, he won't stay put for long.*
stay up not to go to bed: *The children wanted to stay up and watch television.*
steadfast ['stedfa:st] *adj* firm; unchanging: *a steadfast friend.* '**steadfastly** *adv*. '**steadfastness** *n*.
steady ['stedi] *adj* **1** (*neg* **un-**) firmly fixed, balanced or controlled: *The table isn't steady*; *You need a steady hand to be a surgeon.* **2** regular or even: *a steady temperature*; *He was walking at a steady pace.* **3** unchanging or constant: *steady faith.* **4** (of a person) sensible and hardworking in habits *etc*: *a steady young man.* – *v* to make or become steady: *He stumbled but managed to steady himself*; *His heart-beat gradually steadied.*
'**steadily** *adv*: *His work is improving steadily.* '**steadiness** *n*.
steady (on)! *interj* don't be so angry, upset *etc!*: *Steady on! Stop shouting!*
steak [steik] *n* a slice of meat (*usu* beef) or fish (often cod) for *eg* frying or stewing: *a piece of steak*; *two cod steaks.*
steal [sti:l] – *pt* **stole** [stoul]: *ptp* **stolen** ['stoulən] – *v* **1** to take (another person's property), *esp* secretly, without permission or legal right: *Thieves broke into the house and stole money and jewellery*; *He was expelled from the school because he had been stealing (money).* **2** to obtain or take (*eg* a look, a nap *etc*) quickly or secretly: *He stole a glance at her.* **3** to move quietly: *He stole quietly into the room.*
stealth [stelθ] *n* a secret manner of acting: *If I can't get what I want openly, I get it by stealth.*
'**stealthy** *adj* acting, or done, with stealth: *stealthy footsteps.* '**stealthily** *adv*. '**stealthiness** *n*.
steam [sti:m] *n* **1** a gas or vapour that rises from hot or boiling water or other liquid: *Steam rose from the plate of soup/the wet earth in the hot sun*; *a cloud of steam*; (*also adj*) *A sauna is a type of steam bath.* **2** power or energy obtained from this: *The machinery is driven by steam*; *Diesel fuel has replaced steam on the railways*; (*also adj*) *steam power, steam engines.* – *v* **1** to give

out steam: *A kettle was steaming on the stove.* **2** (of a ship, train *etc*) to move by means of steam: *The ship steamed across the bay.* **3** to cook by steam: *The pudding should be steamed for four hours.*

steam-: *steam-driven/steam-powered machinery.*

'**steamer** *n* a steamboat or steamship.

'**steamy** *adj* of, or full of, steam: *the steamy atmosphere of the laundry.* '**steaminess** *n*.

'**steamboat,** '**steamship** *ns* a ship driven by steam.

steam engine a moving engine for pulling a train, or a fixed engine, driven by steam.

steam roller a type of vehicle driven by steam, with wide and heavy wheels for flattening the surface of newly-made roads *etc*.

full steam ahead at the greatest speed possible.

get steamed up to get very upset or angry.

get up steam to build up energy ready for effort.

let off steam 1 to release steam into the air. **2** to release or get rid of excess energy, emotion *etc*: *The children were letting off steam by running about in the playground.*

run out of steam to lose energy, or become exhausted.

steam up to (cause to) become covered with steam: *The windows steamed up/became steamed up.*

under one's own steam by one's own efforts, without help from others: *John gave me a lift in his car, but Mary arrived under her own steam.*

steed [sti:d] *n* an old word for a horse for riding.

steel [sti:l] *n, adj* (of) a very hard alloy of iron and carbon, used for making tools *etc*: *tools of the finest steel; steel knives/chisels; He had a grip of steel* (= a very strong grip). – *v* to harden and strengthen (oneself, one's nerves *etc*) in preparation for doing, or resisting, something: *He steeled himself to meet the attack/to tell his wife the truth.*

'**steely** *adj* hard, cold, strong or bright like steel. '**steeliness** *n*.

steel wool a pad, ball *etc* of steel shavings used for scouring (pans *etc*) and polishing.

'**steelworks** *n pl or n sing* a factory where steel is made.

steep[1] [sti:p] *adj* **1** (of *eg* a hill, stairs *etc*) rising with a sudden rather than a gradual slope: *The hill was too steep for me to cycle up; a steep path; a steep climb.* **2** (of a price asked or demand made) unreasonable or too great: *He wants rather a steep price for his house, doesn't he?; That's a bit steep!* '**steepness** *n*.

'**steeply** *adv* in a steep or sudden way; *The path/prices rose steeply.*

steep[2] [sti:p] to soak thoroughly.

steeple ['sti:pl] *n* a high tower of a church *etc*, *usu* having a spire.

'**steeplechase** *n* a race on horseback or on foot across open country, over hedges *etc*, or over a course on which obstacles (*eg* fences, hedges *etc*) have been made.

steer[1] [stiə] *n* a young ox raised to produce beef.

steer[2] [stiə] *v* to guide or control the course of (*eg* a ship, car *etc*): *He steered the car through the narrow streets; I steered out of the harbour; She managed to steer the conversation towards the subject of her birthday.*

'**steering** *n* the equipment or apparatus for steering a ship or car *etc*: *The steering is faulty.*

'**steering-wheel** *n* the wheel in a car for steering it, fixed to the '**steering-column,** or the wheel on a ship that is turned to control the rudder.

steer clear of to avoid: *I want to steer clear of trouble if possible.*

stellar ['stelə] *adj* of stars: *stellar clusters.*

stem[1] [stem] *n* **1** the part of a plant that grows upward from the root, or the part from which a leaf, flower or fruit grows; a stalk: *Poppies have long, hairy, twisting stems.* **2** the narrow part of various objects, *eg* of a wine-glass between the bowl and the base: *the stem of a wine-glass/of a tobacco-pipe.* **3** the upright piece of wood or metal at the bow of a ship: *As the ship struck the rock, she shook from stem to stern.* – *v* – *pt, ptp* **stemmed** – (*with* **from**) to be caused by: *Hate sometimes stems from envy.*

-stemmed: *a thick-stemmed plant; He smoked a short-stemmed pipe.*

stem[2] [stem] – *pt, ptp* **stemmed** – *v* to stop (a flow, *eg* of blood).

stench [stentʃ] *n* a strong, bad smell: *the stench of stale tobacco smoke.*

stencil ['stensl] *n* **1** a thin piece of metal or card in which a design *etc* has been cut which can be reproduced on another surface, *eg* paper, by printing or inking over the metal *etc*. **2** a piece of waxed paper into which words have been cut by a typewriter, to be reproduced by a similar process. – *v* – *pt, ptp* '**stencilled** – to produce (a design, pattern *etc*) by using a stencil.

step [step] *n* **1** one movement of the foot in walking, running, dancing *etc*: *He took a step forward; walking with hurried steps.* **2** the distance covered by this: *He moved a step or two nearer; The restaurant is only a step* (= a short distance) *away.* **3** the sound made by someone walking *etc*: *I heard (foot)steps.* **4** a particular movement with the feet, *eg* in dancing: *The dance has some complicated steps.* **5** a flat surface, or one flat surface in a series, *eg* on a stair or stepladder, on which to place the feet or foot in moving up or down: *A flight of steps led down to the cellar*; *Mind the step!*; *She was sitting on the doorstep.* **7** a stage in progress, development *etc*: *Mankind made a big step forward with the invention of the wheel*; *His present job is a step up from his previous one.* **8** an action or move (towards accomplishing an aim *etc*): *That would be a foolish/sensible step to take*; *I shall take steps to prevent this happening again.* – *v* – *pt, ptp* **stepped** – to make a step, or to walk: *He opened the door and stepped out*; *She stepped briskly along the road.*

steps *n pl* a stepladder: *May I borrow your steps?*

'stepladder *n* a ladder with a hinged support at the back and flat steps, not rungs.

'stepping-stones *n pl* large stones placed in a shallow stream *etc*, on which a person can step when crossing.

in, out of step (of two or more people walking together) with, without the same foot going forward at the same time: *to march in step*; *Keep in step!*; *He got out of step.*

step aside to move to one side: *He stepped aside to let me pass.*

step by step gradually: *He improved step by step.*

step in to intervene: *The children began to quarrel, and I thought it was time I stepped in.*

step out to walk with a long(er) and (more) energetic stride.

step up to increase: *The firm must step up production.*

watch one's step to be careful, *esp* over one's own behaviour.

step- [step] showing a relationship not by blood but by another marriage.

'step-father, 'step-mother *ns* the husband, who is not the person's father, of a person's own mother, or the wife, who is not the person's mother, of a person's own father.

'step-sister, 'step-brother *ns* a daughter or son of a person's step-father or step-mother.

'step-son, 'step-daughter, 'step-child *ns* a son or daughter from another marriage of a person's wife or husband.

steppe [step] *n* a dry, grassy plain, as in the south-east of Europe and in Asia.

stereo ['steriou] *adj* short for **stereophonic** or **stereoscopic**: *a stereo recording.* – *n* **1** stereophonic equipment, *esp* a record-player: *Have you got (a) stereo?* **2** stereophonic sound or stereoscopic vision: *recorded/filmed in stereo.*

stereophonic [steriə'fonik] *adj* **1** (of recorded or broadcast sound) giving the effect of coming from different directions, and *usu*

requiring two loudspeakers placed apart from each other. **2** (of equipment, apparatus *etc*) intended for recording or playing such sound.

stereoscopic [steriə'skopik] *adj* (of films, pictures *etc*) filmed, shown *etc* by an apparatus taking or showing two photographs at different angles, so that a three-dimensional image is produced.

sterile ['sterail] *adj* **1** (of soil, plants, humans and other animals) unable to produce crops, seeds, children or young. **2** free from germs: *A surgeon's equipment must be absolutely sterile.* **ste'rility** [-'ri-] *n*.

'sterilize, -ise [-ri-] *v* **1** to make (a woman *etc*) sterile. **2** to kill germs in (*eg* milk) or on (*eg* surgical instruments) by boiling. **,sterili'zation, -s-** *n*.

sterling ['stə:liŋ] *n* British money, *esp* in international trading *etc*. – *adj* **1** (of silver) of a certain standard of purity. **2** (of a person or his qualities *etc*) worthy and admirable.

stern[1] [stə:n] *adj* harsh, severe or strict: *The teacher looked rather stern*; *stern discipline.* **'sternly** *adv*. **'sternness** *n*.

stern[2] [stə:n] *n* the back part of a ship.

stethoscope ['steθəskoup] *n* an instrument by which a doctor can listen to the beats of the heart, *etc*.

stevedore ['sti:vədo:] *n* a person who loads and unloads ships; a docker.

stew [stju:] *v* to cook (meat, fruit *etc*) by slowly boiling and simmering: *She stewed apples*; *The meat was stewing in the pan.* – *n* (a dish of) stewed meat *etc*: *I've made some beef stew.*

steward ['stjuəd] – *fem* **'stewardess** – *n* **1** a passenger's attendant on ship or aeroplane: *an air stewardess.* **2** a person who helps to arrange, and is an official at, races, entertainments *etc*. **3** a person who supervises the supply of food and stores in a club, on a ship *etc*. **4** a person who manages an estate or farm for another person.

stick[1] [stik] – *pt, ptp* **stuck** [stʌk] – *v* **1** to push (something sharp or pointed) into or through something: *She stuck a pin through the papers to hold them together*; *Stop sticking your elbow into me!* **2** (of something pointed) to be pushed into or through something: *Two arrows were sticking in his back.* **3** to fasten or be fastened (by glue, gum *etc*): *He licked the flap of the envelope and stuck it down*; *These labels don't stick very well*; *He stuck (the broken pieces of) the vase together again*; *His brothers used to call him Bonzo and the name has stuck.* **4** to (cause to) become fixed and unable to move or progress: *The car stuck in the mud*; *The cupboard door has stuck*; *I'll help you with your arithmetic if you're stuck.*

'sticker *n* an adhesive label or sign bearing

eg a design, political message *etc*, for sticking *eg* on a car's window *etc*: *The car sticker read 'Blood donors needed'.*

'**sticky** *adj* **1** able, or likely, to stick or adhere to other surfaces: *He mended the torn book with sticky tape; sticky sweets.* **2** (of a situation or person) difficult; awkward. '**stickily** *adv.* '**stickiness** *n.*

sticking-plaster *see* **plaster.**

'**stick-in-the-mud** *n* a person who never does anything new.

come to a sticky end to have an unpleasant fate or death.

stick at to persevere with (work *etc*): *He must learn to stick at his job.*

stick by to support or be loyal to (a person): *His friends stuck by him when he was in trouble.*

stick it out to endure a situation for as long as necessary.

stick out 1 to (cause to) project; *His front teeth stick out; He stuck out his tongue.* **2** to be noticeable: *She has red hair that sticks out in a crowd.*

stick one's neck out to take a risk.

stick to/with not to abandon: *We've decided to stick to our previous plan; If you stick to me, I'll stick to you.*

stick together 1 to (cause to) be fastened together: *We'll stick the pieces together; The rice is sticking together.* **2** (of friends *etc*) to remain loyal to each other: *They've stuck together all these years.*

stick up for to speak in defence of (a person *etc*): *When my father is angry with me, my mother always sticks up for me.*

stick² [stik] *n* **1** a branch or twig from a tree: *They were sent to find sticks for firewood.* **2** a long thin piece of wood *etc* shaped for a special purpose: *She always walks with a stick nowadays; a walking-stick/hockey-stick; a drumstick; candlesticks.* **3** a long piece: *a stick of rhubarb.*

get (hold of) the wrong end of the stick to misunderstand a situation, something said *etc.*

sticky *see* **stick**¹.

stiff [stif] *adj* **1** rigid or firm, and not easily bent, folded *etc*: *He has walked with a stiff leg since he injured his knee; stiff cardboard.* **2** moving, or moved, with difficulty, pain *etc*: *I can't turn the key – the lock is stiff; I woke up with a stiff neck; I felt stiff the day after the climb.* **3** (of a cooking mixture *etc*) thick, and not flowing: *a stiff dough.* **4** difficult to do: *a stiff examination.* **5** strong: *a stiff breeze.* **6** (of a person or his manner *etc*) formal and unfriendly: *I received a stiff note from the bank manager.* '**stiffly** *adv.* '**stiffness** *n.*

'**stiffen** *v* to make or become stiff(er): *You*

can stiffen cotton with starch; He stiffened when he heard the unexpected sound.

'**stiffening** *n* material used to stiffen something: *The collar has some stiffening in it.*

bore, scare stiff to bore or frighten very much.

stifle ['staifl] *v* **1** to prevent, or be prevented, from breathing (easily) *eg* because of bad air, an obstruction over the mouth and nose *etc*; to suffocate: *He was stifled to death when smoke filled his bedroom; I'm stifling in this heat!* **2** to extinguish or put out (flames). **3** to suppress (a yawn, a laugh *etc*).

'**stifling** *adj* very hot, stuffy *etc*: *stifling heat; It's stifling in here.*

stile [stail] *n* a step, or set of steps, for climbing over a wall or fence.

still¹ [stil] *adj* **1** without movement or noise: *The city seems very still in the early morning; Please stand/sit/keep/hold still while I brush your hair!; still* (=calm) *water/weather.* **2** (of drinks) not fizzy: *still orange juice.* – *n* a photograph selected from a cinema film: *The magazine contained some stills from the new film.* '**stillness** *n.*

'**stillborn** *adj* dead when born: *a stillborn baby.*

still² [stil] *adv* **1** up to and including the present time, or the time mentioned previously: *Are you still working for the same firm?; By Saturday he had still not/still hadn't replied to my letter.* **2** nevertheless; in spite of that: *Although the doctor told him to rest, he still went on working; This picture is not valuable – still, I like it.* **3** even: *He seemed very ill in the afternoon and in the evening looked still worse.*

stilts [stilts] *n pl* **1** a pair of poles with supports for the feet, on which a person may stand and so walk raised off the ground. **2** tall poles fixed under a house *etc* to support it *eg* if it is built on a steep hillside.

stimulant ['stimjulənt] *n* something, *eg* a medicine, drink *etc* that makes one more alert: *tea, coffee and other stimulants.*

stimulate ['stimjuleit] *v* to rouse or make more alert, active *etc*: *After listening to the violin concerto, he felt stimulated to practise the violin again.* ,**stimu'lation** *n.*

'**stimulating** *adj* rousing; very interesting: *a stimulating discussion.*

stimulus ['stimjuləs] – *pl* '**stimuli** [-li:] – *n* **1** something that causes a reaction in a living thing: *Light is the stimulus that causes a flower to open.* **2** something that rouses or encourages a person *etc* to action or greater effort: *Many people think that children need the stimulus of competition to make them work better in school.*

sting [stiŋ] *n* **1** a part of some plants, insects *etc, eg* nettles and wasps, that can prick and inject an irritating or poisonous fluid into the wound. **2** an act of piercing with this part: *Some spiders give a poisonous sting.* **3** the wound, swelling, or pain caused by this: *You can soothe a wasp sting by putting vinegar on it.* – *v* – *pt, ptp* **stung** [stʌŋ] – **1** to wound or hurt by means of a sting: *The child was badly stung by nettles*; *Do those insects sting?* **2** (of a wound, or a part of the body) to smart or be painful: *The salt water made his eyes sting.*

stingy ['stindʒi] *adj* mean or ungenerous: *My father's very stingy with his money*; *stingy portions of food.* '**stingily** *adv.* '**stinginess** *n.*

stink [stiŋk] – *pt* **stank** [staŋk]: *ptp* **stunk** [stʌŋk] – *v* to have a very bad smell: *That fish stinks*; *The house stinks of cats.* – *n* a very bad smell: *What a stink!*

stir [stəː] – *pt, ptp* **stirred** – *v* **1** to cause (a liquid *etc*) to be mixed *esp* by the constant circular movement of a spoon *etc*, in order to mix it: *He put sugar and milk into his tea and stirred it*; *She stirred the sugar into the mixture.* **2** to move, either slightly or vigorously: *The breeze stirred her hair*; *He stirred in his sleep*; *Come on – stir yourselves!* **3** to arouse or touch (a person or his feelings): *He was stirred by her story.* – *n* a fuss or disturbance: *The news caused a stir.*
'**stirring** *adj* exciting: *a stirring tale.*
stir up to cause (trouble *etc*): *He was trying to stir up trouble at the factory.*

stirrups ['stirəps, (*Amer*) 'stəː-] *n pl* a pair of metal loops hanging on straps from a horse's saddle, to support a rider's feet.

stitch [stitʃ] *n* **1** a loop made in thread, wool *etc* by a needle in sewing or knitting: *She sewed the hem with small, neat stitches*; *Bother! I've dropped a stitch.* **2** a type of stitch forming a particular pattern in sewing, knitting *etc*: *The cloth was edged in blanket stitch*; *The jersey was knitted in stocking stitch.* **3** a sharp pain in a person's side caused by *eg* running: *I've got a stitch.* – *v* to sew or put stitches into: *She stitched the two pieces together*; *I stitched the button on.*
'**stitching** *n* stitches: *The stitching is very untidy.*
in stitches laughing a lot: *His stories kept us in stitches.*
stitch up to close by stitching: *The doctor stitched up the wound.*

stock [stok] *n* **1** (*often in pl*) a store of goods in a shop, warehouse *etc*: *Buy while stocks last!*; *The tools you require are in/out of stock* (=available/not available). **2** a supply of something: *We bought a large stock of food for the camping trip.* **3** farm animals: *He would like to purchase more* (*live*)*stock.* **4** (*often in pl*) money lent to the government or to a business company at a

fixed interest: *government stock*; *He has $20 000 in stocks and shares.* **5** liquid obtained by boiling meat, bones *etc* and used for making soup *etc*. **6** the handle of a whip, rifle *etc*. – *adj* common; usual: *stock sizes of shoes.* – *v* **1** to keep a supply of for sale: *Does this shop stock writing-paper?* **2** to supply (a shop, farm *etc*) with goods, animals *etc*: *He cannot afford to stock his farm.*

stocks *n pl* **1** the wooden framework upon which a ship is supported when being built, repaired *etc*. **2** formerly a wooden frame in which a criminal was fastened as a punishment.

'**stockbroker** *n* a person who buys and sells stocks and shares for others.

stock exchange a place where stocks and shares are bought and sold.

stock market a stock exchange, or the dealings on that.

,**stock-'still** *adj, adv* motionless: *He stood absolutely stock-still.*

'**stock-taking** *n* a regular check of the goods in a shop, warehouse *etc*.

stock up to accumulate a supply of (something): *The boys were stocking up on/with chocolate and lemonade for their walk.*

take stock to form an opinion (about a situation *etc*): *Before you decide, give yourself time to take stock (of the situation).*

stockade [sto'keid] *n* a fence of strong posts put up round an area for defence.

stockbroker *see* **stock.**

stocking ['stokiŋ] *n* one of a pair of close-fitting coverings for the legs and feet, reaching to or above the knee: *Most women prefer tights to stockings nowadays.*

stocky ['stoki] *adj* (of a person *etc*) short, often rather stout and *usu* strong: *a stocky little boy.* '**stockily** *adv.* '**stockiness** *n.*

stodge [stodʒ] *n* heavy, solid food.
'**stodgy** *adj* (of meals *etc*) consisting of stodge: *stodgy food.* **2** (of people, books *etc*) dull; not lively. '**stodginess** *n.*

stoke [stouk] *v* to put coal or other fuel on (a fire) *eg* in the furnace of a boiler *etc*: *The men stoked the furnaces.* '**stoker** *n.*
stoke up to stoke: *Have they stoked up (the fires)?*

stole, stolen *see* **steal.**

stolid ['stolid] *adj* (of a person *etc*) not easily excited and rather dull. **sto'lidity, 'stolidness** *ns.* '**stolidly** *adv.*

stomach ['stʌmək] *n* **1** the bag-like organ in the body into which food passes when swallowed, and where most of it is digested. **2** the part of the body between the chest and thighs; the belly: *a pain in the stomach.*
'**stomach-ache** *n* a pain in the belly.

stomp [stomp] *v* to stamp or tread heavily.

stone [stoun] *n* **1** (*also adj*) (of) the material

of which rocks are composed: *limestone*;
sandstone; *a stone house*; *stone walls*; *In
early times, men made tools out of stone*. **2** a
piece of this, of any shape or size: *He threw
a stone at the dog*. **3** a piece of this shaped
for a special purpose: *a tombstone*; *paving-
stones*; *a grindstone*. **4** a gem or jewel: *She
lost the stone out of her ring*; *diamonds,
rubies and other stones*. **5** the hard shell
containing the nut or seed in some fruits *eg*
peaches and cherries: *a cherry-stone*. **6** a
measure of weight still used in Britain,
equal to 6·35 kilogrammes: *She weighs 9½
stone*. **7** a piece of hard material that forms
in the kidney, bladder *etc* and causes pain.
− *v* **1** to throw stones at, *esp* as a ritual
punishment: *Saint Stephen was stoned to
death*. **2** to remove the stones from (fruit):
She washed and stoned the cherries.
'**stony** *adj* **1** full of, or covered with, stones:
stony soil; *a stony path/beach*; *It's very
stony around here*. **2** (of a person's expression *etc*) like stone in coldness, hardness
etc: *He gave me a stony stare*. '**stonily** *adv*.
'**stoniness** *n*.
,**stone-'cold**, ,**stone-'dead**, ,**stone-'deaf** *adjs*
completely cold, dead, or deaf: *He's almost
stone-deaf*; *Your soup is stone-cold*.
'**stoneware** *n, adj* (of) a hard type of pottery
made of clay containing pieces of stone: *a
stoneware jug*.
'**stonework** *n* construction done in stone, *esp*
the stone parts of a building.
leave no stone unturned to try every possible
means: *The police left no stone unturned to
(try to) find the child*.
a stone's throw a very short distance: *They
live only a stone's throw away from here*.
stood *see* **stand**.
stooge [stu:dʒ] *n* **1** a comedian's assistant who
is made the object of all his jokes. **2** a person
who is used by another to do humble or
unpleasant jobs.
stool [stu:l] *n* a seat without a back: *a piano-
stool*; *a kitchen stool*.
fall between two stools to lose both of two
possibilities by hesitating between them or
trying for both.
stoop [stu:p] *v* **1** to bend the body forward
and downward: *The doorway was so low
that he had to stoop (his head) to go through
it*; *She stooped down to talk to the child*. **2** to
lower one's (moral) standards by doing
something: *Surely he wouldn't stoop to
cheating!* − *n* a stooping position of the
body, shoulder *etc*: *Many people develop a
stoop as they grow older*.
stooped *adj*: *stooped shoulders*; *He is
stooped with age*.
stop [stop] − *pt ptp* **stopped** − *v* **1** to (make
something) cease moving, or come to rest, a
halt *etc*: *He stopped the car and got out*;

This train does not stop at Birmingham; *He
stopped to look at the map*; *He signalled with
his hand to stop the bus*. **2** to prevent from
doing something: *We must stop him (from)
going*; *I was going to say something rude but
stopped myself just in time*. **3** to discontinue
or cease *eg* doing something: *That woman
just can't stop talking*; *The rain has stopped*;
It has stopped raining. **4** to block or close:
*He stopped his ears with his hands when she
started to shout at him*. **5** to close (a hole, *eg*
on a flute) or press down (a string on a
violin *etc*) in order to play a particular note.
6 to stay: *Will you be stopping long at the
hotel?* − *n* **1** an act of stopping or state of
being stopped: *We made only two stops on
our journey*; *Work came to a stop for the
day*. **2** a place for *eg* a bus to stop: *a bus
stop*. **3** in punctuation, a full stop: *Put a
stop at the end of the sentence*. **4** a device on
a flute *etc* for covering the holes in order to
vary the pitch, or knobs for bringing certain
pipes into use on an organ. **5** a device, *eg* a
wedge *etc*, for stopping the movement of
something, or for keeping it in a fixed
position: *a door-stop*.
'**stoppage** [-pidʒ] *n* (an) act of stopping or
state or process of being stopped: *The
building was at last completed after many
delays and stoppages*.
'**stopper** *n* an object, *eg* a cork, that is put
into the neck of a bottle, jar, hole *etc* to
close it.
'**stopping** *n* a filling in a tooth: *One of my
stoppings has come out*.
'**stopcock** *n* a tap and valve for controlling
flow of liquid through a pipe.
'**stopgap** *n* a person or thing that fills a gap
in an emergency: *He was made headmaster
as a stopgap till a new man could be appointed*; (*also adj*) *stopgap arrangements*.
'**stopwatch** *n* a watch with a hand that can
be stopped and started, used in timing a
race *etc*.
put a stop to to prevent from continuing:
We must put a stop to this waste.
stop at nothing to be willing to do anything,
however dishonest *etc*, in order to get something: *He'll stop at nothing to get what he
wants*.
stop dead to stop completely: *I stopped dead
when I saw him*.
stop off to make a halt on a journey *etc*: *We
stopped off at Edinburgh to see the castle*.
stop over to make a stay of a night or more:
We're planning to stop over in Amsterdam (*n
'**stop-over**).
stop up to block: *Some rubbish got into the
drain and stopped it up*.
storage *see* **store**.
store [sto:] *n* **1** a supply of *eg* goods from
which things are taken when required: *They

took a store of dried and canned food on the expedition; *The quartermaster is the officer in charge of stores.* **2** a (large) collected amount or quantity: *He has a store of interesting facts in his head.* **3** a place where a supply of goods *etc* is kept; a storehouse or storeroom: *It's in the store(s).* **4** a shop: *The post office here is also the village store*; *a department store.* – *v* **1** to put into a place for keeping: *We stored our furniture in the attic while the tenants used our house.* **2** to stock (a place *etc*) with goods *etc*: *The museum is stored with interesting exhibits.*

'storage [-ridʒ] *n* the act of storing or state of being stored: *We've put our furniture into storage at a warehouse*; *The meat will have to be kept in cold storage* (= stored under refrigeration).

'storehouse, 'storeroom *ns* a place or room where goods *etc* are stored: *There is a storeroom behind the shop.*

in store 1 kept or reserved for future use: *I keep plenty of tinned food in store for emergencies.* **2** coming in the future: *There's trouble in store for her!*

set (great) store by to value highly (*eg* a person's approval *etc*).

store up to collect and keep (for future need): *I don't know why she stores up all those old magazines.*

storey (*pl* **'storeys**), **story** (*pl* **'stories**) ['stɔːri] *n* one of the floors or levels in a building: *an apartment block of seventeen storeys.*

-storeyed, -storied: *A two-storied house is one with a ground floor and one floor above it.*

stork [stɔːk] *n* a type of wading bird with long beak, neck and legs.

storm [stɔːm] *n* **1** a violent disturbance in the air causing wind, rain, thunder *etc*: *a rainstorm*; *a thunderstorm*; *a storm at sea*; *The roof was damaged by the storm.* **2** a violent outbreak of feeling *etc*: *A storm of anger greeted his speech*; *a storm of applause.* – *v* **1** to shout very loudly and angrily: *He stormed at her.* **2** to move or stride in an angry manner: *He stormed out of the room.* **3** (of soldiers *etc*) to attack with great force, and capture (a building *etc*): *They stormed the castle.*

'stormy *adj* **1** having a lot of strong wind, heavy rain *etc*: *a stormy day*; *stormy weather*; *a stormy voyage.* **2** full of anger or uncontrolled feeling: *in a stormy mood*; *a stormy discussion.* **'stormily** *adv.* **'storminess** *n.*

a storm in a teacup a fuss made over an unimportant matter.

take by storm to capture by means of a sudden violent attack: *The invaders took the city by storm.*

story[1] ['stɔːri] – *pl* **'stories** – *n* **1** an account of

an event, or series of events, real or imaginary: *the story of the disaster*; *the story of his life*; *He went to the police with his story*; *What sort of stories do boys aged 10 like?*; *adventure/murder/love stories*; *a story-book*; *He's a good story-teller.* **2** (used *esp* to children) a lie: *Don't tell stories!*

the story goes people say: *He has been in jail or so the story goes.*

a tall story an obviously untrue story; a lie.

story[2] *see* **storey**.

stout[1] [staut] *adj* **1** strong or thick: *a stout stick.* **2** brave and resolute: *stout resistance*; *stout opposition.* **3** fat: *He's getting stout.* **,stout-'hearted** *adj* brave.

stout[2] [staut] *adj* **1** a dark, strong type of beer.

stove[1] [stouv] *n* an apparatus using coal, gas, electricity or other fuel, used for cooking, or for heating a room: *a gas/electric (cooking) stove*; *Put the saucepan on the stove.*

stow [stou] *v* to pack neatly and *esp* out of sight: *The sailor stowed his belongings in his locker.*

'stowaway *n* a person who stows away: *They found a stowaway on the ship.*

stow away 1 to hide oneself on a ship, aircraft *etc* before its departure, in order to travel on it without paying the fare: *He stowed away on a cargo ship for New York.* **2** to put or pack in a (secret) place until required: *My jewellery is safely stowed away in the bank.*

straggle ['straɡl] *v* **1** to grow or spread untidily: *His beard straggled over his chest.* **2** to walk too slowly to remain with a body of *eg* marching soldiers, walkers *etc.*

'straggler *n* a person who walks too slowly during a march *etc* and gets left behind: *A car was sent to pick up the stragglers.*

'straggly *adj* straggling untidily: *straggly hair.* **'straggliness** *n.*

straight [streit] *adj* **1** not bent or curved: *a straight line*; *straight* (= not curly) *hair*; *That line is not straight.* **2** (of a person, his behaviour *etc*) honest, frank and direct: *Give me a straight answer!* **3** properly or levelly positioned: *Your tie isn't straight.* **4** correct and tidy: *I'll never get this house straight!*; *Now let's get the facts straight!* **5** (of drinks) not mixed: *a straight gin.* **6** (of a face, expression *etc*) not smiling or laughing: *You should keep a straight face while you tell a joke.* **7** (of an actor) playing normal characters, or (of a play) of the ordinary type – not a musical or variety show. – *adv* **1** in a straight, not curved, line; directly: *His route went straight across the desert*; *She can't steer straight*; *Keep straight on.* **2** immediately, without any delay: *He went straight home after the meeting.* **3** honestly or fairly: *You're not playing*

(= behaving) *straight*. – *n* the straight part of something, *eg* of a racecourse: *He's in the final straight*.

'**straighten** *v* to make or become straight: *He straightened his tie*; *The road curved and then straightened*.

'**straightness** *n*.

straight'forward *adj* **1** without difficulties or complications; simple: *a straightforward task*. **2** (of a person, his manner *etc*) frank and honest: *a nice straightforward boy*. **straight'forwardly** *adv*. **straight'forwardness** *n*.

straight talking frank discussion.

go straight (of a former criminal) to lead an honest life.

straight away immediately: *Do it straight away!*

straighten out/up: *Their house is where the lane straightens out*; *He was bending over his work, but straightened up when he saw me*; *She straightened the room up*; *He's trying to straighten out the facts*.

a straight fight an election contest involving only two candidates.

straight off straight away.

strain[1] [strein] *v* **1** to exert oneself or a part of the body to the greatest possible extent: *He strained his ears to hear the whisper*; *They strained at the door, trying to pull it open*; *He strained to reach the rope*. **2** to injure (a muscle *etc*) through too much use, exertion *etc*: *He has strained a muscle in his leg*; *You'll strain your eyes by reading in such a poor light*. **3** to force or stretch (too far): *The constant interruptions were straining his patience*. **4** to put (*eg* a mixture) through a sieve *etc* in order to separate solid matter from liquid: *She strained the coffee*. – *n* **1** force exerted; *Can nylon ropes take more strain than the old kind of rope?* **2** (something, *eg* too much work *etc*, that causes) a state of anxiety and fatigue: *The strain of nursing her dying husband was too much for her*; *to suffer from strain*. **3** (an) injury *esp* to a muscle caused by too much exertion: *muscular strain*. **4** too great a demand: *These constant delays are a strain on our patience*.

strained *adj* (of a person's manner, behaviour *etc*) not natural, easy or relaxed: *a strained smile*.

'**strainer** *n* a sieve or other utensil for separating solids from liquids: *a coffee-/tea-strainer*.

strain off to remove (liquid) from *eg* vegetables by using a sieve *etc*: *When the potatoes were cooked, she strained off the water*.

strain[2] [strein] *n* **1** a kind or breed (of animals, plants *etc*): *a new strain of cattle*. **2** a tendency in a person's character: *I'm sure there's a strain of madness in her*. **3** (*often in*

pl) (the sound of) a tune: *I heard the strains of a hymn coming from the church*.

strait [streit] *n* **1** (*often in pl*) a narrow strip of sea between two pieces of land: *the straits of Gibraltar*; *the Bering Strait*. **2** (*in pl*) difficulty; (financial) need.

'**strait-jacket** *n* a type of jacket with long sleeves tied behind to hold back the arms of *eg* a violent and insane person.

,**strait-'laced** *adj* strict and severe in attitude and behaviour.

strand[1] [strand]: **be stranded 1** (of a ship) to go aground: *The ship was stranded on the rocks*. **2** (*also* **be left stranded**) to be left helpless without *eg* money or friends: *He was left stranded in Yugoslavia without his money or his passport*.

strand[2] [strand] *n* a thin thread, *eg* one of those twisted together to form rope, string, knitting-wool *etc*, or a long thin lock of hair: *She pushed the strands of hair back from her face*.

strange [streindʒ] *adj* **1** not known, seen *etc* before; unfamiliar or foreign: *What would you do if you found a strange man in your house?*; *Whenever you're in a strange country, you should take the opportunity of learning the language*. **2** unusual, odd or queer: *She had a strange look on her face*; *a strange noise*. '**strangely** *adv*. '**strangeness** *n*.

'**stranger** *n* **1** a person who is unknown to oneself: *I've met her once before, so she's not a complete stranger* (*to me*). **2** a visitor: *I can't tell you where the post office is – I'm a stranger here myself*.

strange to say/tell/relate surprisingly: *Strange to say, he did pass his exam after all*.

strangely enough it is strange (that): *He lives next door, but strangely enough I rarely see him*.

strangle ['straŋgl] *v* to kill by gripping or squeezing the neck tightly, *eg* by tightening a cord *etc* round it: *He strangled her with a nylon stocking*; *This top button is nearly strangling me!* ,**strangu'lation** [-gju-] *n*.

strap [strap] *n* **1** a narrow strip of leather, cloth, or other material, *eg* with a buckle for fastening something (*eg* a suitcase, wristwatch *etc*) or by which to hold, hang or support something (*eg* a camera, rucksack *etc*): *I need a new watch-strap*; *luggage straps*. **2** a short round strip of leather *etc*, hanging from the roof of a train, by which a standing passenger can support himself. – *v* – *pt, ptp* **strapped** – **1** to beat (*eg* a schoolchild) on the hand with a leather strap: *He was strapped for being rude to the teacher*. **2** to fasten with a strap *etc*: *The two pieces of luggage were strapped together*; *He strapped on his new watch*.

'strapping *adj* large and strong: *a big strapping girl.*

strap in to confine with a strap, *eg* by a safety-belt in a car: *I won't start this car till you've strapped yourself in.*

strap up to fasten or bind with a strap, bandage *etc*: *His injured knee was washed and neatly strapped up.*

stratagem ['stratədʒəm] *n* a trick or plan.

strategy ['stratədʒi] – *pl* **'strategies** – *n* **1** the art of planning a campaign or large military operation: *military strategy.* **2** the art of, or a scheme for, managing an affair cleverly. **stra'tegic** [-'ti:-] *adj.* **stra'tegically** *adv.*

'strategist *n* a person who is an expert in strategy.

straw [strɔ:] *n* **1** (*also adj*) (of) the cut stalks of corn *etc*, having many uses, *eg* as bedding for cattle *etc*, making mats and other goods *etc*: *The cows need fresh straw*; *a straw hat.* **2** a single stalk of corn: *There's a straw in your hair*; *Their offer isn't worth a straw!* **3** a paper or plastic tube through which to suck a drink into the mouth: *He was sipping orange juice through a straw.*

the last straw an additional and intolerable circumstance in a disagreeable situation: *The hotel was expensive, the food poor, and the bad weather was the last straw.*

strawberry ['strɔ:bəri] – *pl* **'strawberries** – *n* a type of small juicy red fruit.

stray [strei] *v* to wander, *esp* from the right path, place *etc*: *The shepherd went to search for some sheep that had strayed*; *to stray from the point.* – *n* a cat, dog *etc* that has strayed and has no home. – *adj* **1** wandering or lost: *stray cats and dogs.* **2** occasional, or not part of a general group or tendency: *The sky was clear except for one or two stray clouds.*

streak [stri:k] *n* **1** a long, irregular mark or stripe: *There was a streak of blood on her cheek*; *a streak of lightning.* **2** a trace of some quality in a person's character *etc*: *She has a streak of selfishness.* – *v* **1** to mark with streaks: *Her dark hair was streaked with grey*; *The child's face was streaked with tears.* **2** to move very fast: *The runner streaked round the racetrack.*

'streaky *adj* marked with streaks.

stream [stri:m] *n* **1** a small river or brook: *He managed to jump across the stream.* **2** a flow of *eg* water, air *etc*: *A stream of water was pouring down the gutter*; *A stream of people was coming out of the cinema*; *He got into the wrong stream of traffic and uttered a stream of curses.* **3** the current of a river *etc*: *He was swimming against the stream.* **4** in schools, one of the classes into which children of the same age are divided according to ability. – *v* **1** to flow: *Tears streamed down her face*; *Workers streamed out of the* *factory gates*; *Her hair streamed out in the wind.* **2** to divide schoolchildren into classes according to ability: *Many people disapprove of streaming* (*children*) *in schools.*

'streamer *n* a long narrow banner, or narrow paper ribbon: *The aeroplane dragged a streamer that read 'Come to the Festival'*; *The classroom was decorated with balloons and streamers.*

'streamlined *adj* **1** (of a plane, car, ship *etc*) shaped so as to move faster and more efficiently: *the newest, most streamlined aircraft.* **2** efficient and economical: *streamlined business methods.*

street [stri:t] *n* **1** a road with houses, shops *etc* on one or both sides, in a town or village: *the main shopping street*; *I met her in the street.* **2** (*abbrev* **St** *when written*) used in the names of certain roads: *Her address is 4 Shakespeare St.*

'streetcar *n* (*esp Amer*) a tramcar.

street directory a booklet giving an index and plans of a city's streets.

strength, strengthen *see* **strong**.

strenuous ['strenjuəs] *adj* energetic; requiring effort or energy: *a strenuous climb*; *a strenuous effort.* **'strenuously** *adv.*

stress [stres] *n* **1** the worry experienced by a person in particular circumstances, or the state of anxiety caused by this: *the stresses of modern life*; *Her headaches may be caused by stress.* **2** force exerted by (parts of) bodies on each other: *Bridge-designers have to know about stress.* **3** force or emphasis placed, in speaking, on particular syllables or words: *In the word 'widow' we put stress on the first syllable.* – *v* to emphasize (a syllable *etc*, or a fact *etc*): *Should you stress the last syllable in 'violin'?*; *He stressed the necessity of being punctual.*

lay/put stress on to emphasize (a fact *etc*): *He laid stress on this point.*

stretch [stretʃ] *v* **1** to make or become longer or wider *esp* by pulling or by being pulled: *She stretched the piece of elastic to its fullest extent*; *His scarf was so long that it could stretch right across the room*; *This material stretches*; *The dog yawned and stretched* (*itself*); *He stretched* (*his arm/hand*) *up as far as he could, but still could not reach the shelf*; *Ask someone to pass you the jam instead of stretching across the table for it.* **2** (of land *etc*) to extend: *The plain stretched ahead of them for miles.* – *n* **1** an act of stretching or state of being stretched: *He got out of bed and had a good stretch.* **2** a continuous extent, of *eg* a type of country, or of time: *a pretty stretch of country*; *a stretch of bad road*; *a stretch of twenty years.*

'stretcher *n* a light folding bed with handles for carrying the sick or wounded: *The* *injured man was carried to the ambulance on a stretcher.*

'stretchy *adj* (of materials *etc*) able to stretch: *a stretchy bathing-costume.*

at a stretch continuously: *He can't work for more than three hours at a stretch.*

be at full stretch to be using all one's powers, energy *etc* to the limit in doing something.

stretch one's legs to go for a walk for the sake of exercise: *I need to stretch my legs.*

stretch out in moving the body, to straighten or extend: *She stretched out a hand for the child to hold*; *He stretched (himself) out on the bed.*

strew [stru:] – *pt* **strewed**; *ptp* **strewn** – *v* to scatter: *Rubbish was strewn about on the ground*; *The ground was strewn with rubbish.*

stricken ['strikən] *adj* deeply affected, overwhelmed or afflicted: *In his youth he was stricken with a crippling disease*; *grief-stricken parents*; *panic-stricken crowds.*

strict [strikt] *adj* **1** severe, stern, and compelling obedience: *This class needs a strict teacher*; *His parents were very strict with him*; *The school rules are too strict*; *strict orders.* **2** exact or precise: *If the strict truth were known, he was drunk, not ill.* **'strictness** *n.* **'strictly** *adv.*

strictly speaking if we must be completely accurate, act according to rules *etc*: *Strictly speaking, he should be punished for this.*

stride [straid] – *pt* **strode** [stroud]: *ptp* **stridden** ['stridn] – *v* to walk with long steps: *He strode along the path*; *He strode off in anger.* – *n* a long step: *He walked with long strides.*

make great strides to progress well: *He's making great strides in his piano-playing.*

take in one's stride to accept or cope with (a matter) successfully without worrying about it: *She takes difficulties in her stride.*

strife [straif] *n* conflict, fighting or quarrelling: *a country torn by strife*; *industrial strife* (=disagreement between employers and workers).

strike [straik] – *pt* **struck** [strʌk]: *ptps* **struck, stricken** ['strikən] – *v* **1** to hit, knock or give a blow to: *He struck me in the face with his fist*; *Why did you strike him?*; *The stone struck me a blow on the side of the head*; *His head struck the table as he fell*; *The tower of the church was struck by lightning.* **2** to attack: *The enemy troops struck at dawn*; *We must prevent the disease striking again.* **3** to produce (sparks or a flame) by rubbing: *He struck a match/light*; *He struck sparks from the stone with his knife.* **4** (of workers) to stop work as a protest, or in order to force employers to give better pay: *The men decided to strike for higher wages.* **5** to discover or find:

After months of prospecting they finally struck gold/oil; *If we walk in this direction we may strike the right path.* **6** to (make something) sound: *He struck a note on the piano/violin*; *The clock struck twelve.* **7** to impress, or give a particular impression to (a person): *I was struck by the resemblance between the two men*; *How does the plan strike you?*; *It/The thought struck me that she had come to borrow money.* **8** to mint or manufacture (a coin, medal *etc*). **9** to go in a certain direction: *He left the path and struck (off) across the fields.* **10** to lower or take down (tents, flags *etc*). – *n* **1** an act of striking: *a miners' strike.* **2** a discovery of oil, gold *etc*: *He made a lucky strike.*

'striker *n* **1** a worker who strikes. **2** in football, a forward player.

'striking *adj* noticeable or impressive: *She is tall and striking*; *She wears striking clothes.* **'strikingly** *adv.*

be (out) on strike (of workers) to be striking: *The electricity workers are (out) on strike.*

call a strike (of a trade union leader *etc*) to ask workers to strike.

come out on strike (of workers) to strike.

come, be within striking distance of to come very close to.

strike at to attempt to strike, or aim a blow at (a person *etc*): *He struck at the dog with his stick.*

strike an attitude/pose to place oneself in a particular *usu* rather showy pose.

strike a balance to reach a satisfactory middle level of compromise between two undesirable extremes.

strike a bargain/agreement to make a bargain; to reach an agreement.

strike down to hit or knock (a person) down: *He was struck down by a car/a terrible disease.*

strike dumb to amaze: *I was struck dumb at the news.*

strike fear/terror *etc* **into** to fill (a person) with fear *etc*: *The sound struck terror into them.*

strike home (of a blow, insult *etc*) to reach the place where it will hurt most.

strike it rich to make a lot of money.

strike lucky to have good luck in a particular matter.

strike out 1 to erase or cross out (a word *etc*): *He read the essay and struck out a word here and there.* **2** to start fighting: *He's a man who strikes out with his fists whenever he's angry.*

strike up 1 to begin to play a tune *etc*: *The band struck up (with) 'The Red Flag'.* **2** to begin (a friendship, conversation *etc*): *He struck up an acquaintance with a girl on the train.*

string [striŋ] n 1 (a piece of) long narrow cord made of threads twisted together, or tape, for tying, fastening etc: a piece of string to tie a parcel; a ball of string; a puppet's strings; apron-strings. 2 a fibre etc, eg on a vegetable. 3 a piece of wire, gut etc on a musical instrument, eg a violin: His A-string broke; (also adj) He plays the viola in a string orchestra. 4 a series or group of things threaded on a cord etc: a string of beads. – v – pt, ptp strung [straŋ] – 1 to put (beads etc) on a string etc: The pearls were sent to a jeweller to be strung. 2 to put a string or strings on (eg a bow or stringed instrument): The archer strung his bow and aimed an arrow at the target. 3 to remove strings from (vegetables etc). 4 to tie and hang with string etc: The farmer strung up the dead crows on the fence.

strings n pl (in an orchestra, the group of people who play) stringed instruments, ie violins, violas, 'cellos and double basses: The conductor said the strings were too loud.
'stringy adj (esp of meat or vegetables) having a lot of tough fibres. **'stringiness** n.
string bean the long, edible green or yellow pod of certain beans.
stringed instruments musical instruments that have strings eg violins, guitars etc.
have (someone) on a string to have (a person) under one's control.
pull strings to use one's influence or that of others to gain an advantage.
pull the strings to be the person who is really, though usu not apparently, controlling the actions of others.
string out to stretch into a long line: The runners were strung out along the course.
strung up very nervous.

stringent ['strindʒənt] adj (of rules etc) very strict, or strongly enforced: There should be much more stringent laws against the dropping of rubbish in the streets. **'stringently** adv.
'stringency n 1 the quality of being strict. 2 scarcity of money for lending etc: in times of stringency; (also adj) The government are demanding stringency measures.

stringy see string.

strip [strip] – pt, ptp stripped – v 1 to remove the covering from something: He stripped the old varnish off the wall; He stripped the branch (of its bark) with his knife. 2 to undress: She stripped the child (naked) and put him in the bath; He stripped and dived into the water; They were told to strip to the waist. 3 to remove the contents of (a house etc): The house/room was stripped bare/stripped of its furnishings; They stripped the house of all its furnishings. 4 to deprive (a person) of something: The officer was stripped of his rank for misconduct. – n 1 a

long narrow piece of (eg cloth, ground etc): a strip of paper. 2 a strip cartoon. 3 a footballer's shirt, shorts, socks etc: The team has a red and white strip.
strip cartoon a row of drawings, eg in a newspaper or comic paper, telling a story.
'strip-lighting n lighting by long tubes rather than bulbs.
,strip-'tease n the act, by a woman, of removing her clothes one by one as a theatrical entertainment. – adj: a strip-tease show.
strip off to remove clothes or a covering from a thing or person: He stripped (his clothes) off and had a shower; The doctor stripped his bandage off.

stripe [straip] n 1 a band of colour etc: The wallpaper was grey with broad green stripes; A zebra has black and white stripes. 2 a (usu V-shaped) badge worn on an army uniform to show rank.
striped adj having stripes: a striped shirt; blue-and-white-striped curtains.
'stripy adj covered with stripes: A tiger has a stripy coat.

stripling ['stripliŋ] n a boy or youth not yet fully grown.

strive [straiv] – pt strove [strouv]: ptp striven ['strivn] – v to try very hard or struggle: He always strives to please his teacher.

strode see stride.

stroke¹ [strouk] n 1 an act of hitting, or the blow given: He felled the tree with one stroke of the axe; the stroke of a whip. 2 a sudden occurrence of something: a stroke of lightning; an unfortunate stroke of fate; What a stroke of luck to find that money! 3 the sound made by a clock striking the hour: She arrived on the stroke of (= punctually at) ten. 4 a movement or mark made in one direction by a pen, pencil, paintbrush etc: short, even pencil strokes. 5 a single pull of an oar in rowing, or a hit with the bat in playing cricket. 6 a movement of the arms and legs in swimming, or a particular method of swimming: He swam with slow, strong strokes; Can you do breast-stroke/backstroke? 7 an effort or action: I haven't done a stroke (of work) all day. 8 a sudden attack of illness which damages the brain, causing paralysis, loss of feeling in the body etc.
at a stroke with a single effort: We can't solve all these problems at a stroke.

stroke² [strouk] v to rub (eg a furry animal) gently and repeatedly in one direction, esp as a sign of affection: He stroked the cat/her hair; The dog loves being stroked. – n an act of stroking: He gave the dog a stroke.

stroll [stroul] v to walk or wander without hurry: He strolled along the street. – n an act of strolling: *I went for a stroll round the town.*

strong [stroŋ] *adj* **1** firm, sound, or powerful, and therefore not easily broken, destroyed, attacked, defeated, resisted, or affected by weariness, illness *etc*: *strong furniture*; *a strong castle*; *a strong wind*; *She's a strong swimmer*; *He has a very strong will/personality*; *He has never been very strong* (=healthy); *He is not strong enough to lift that heavy table.* **2** very noticeable; very intense: *a strong colour*; *a strong smell*; *I took a strong dislike to him.* **3** containing a large amount of the flavouring ingredient: *strong tea.* **4** (of a group, force *etc*) numbering a particular amount: *An army 20 000 strong was advancing towards the town.* **'strongly** *adv*.

strength [streŋθ] *n* **1** the quality of being strong: *He got his strength back slowly after his illness*; *I hadn't the strength to resist him.* **2** the number of people *etc* in a force, organization *etc*, considered as an indication of its power or effectiveness: *The force is below strength.*

strengthen ['streŋθən] *v* to make or become strong or stronger: *He did exercises to strengthen his muscles*; *The wind strengthened.*

'strongbox *n* a safe or box for valuables.
strong drink alcoholic liquors.
'stronghold *n* a fort, fortress or castle *etc*.
strong language swearing or abuse.
,strong-'minded *adj* having determination.
strong point a quality, skill *etc* in which a person excels: *Arithmetic isn't one of my strong points.*
strongroom *n* a room specially constructed for keeping valuable articles, with thick walls and a heavy steel door *etc*.
on the strength of relying on: *On the strength of this offer of money, we plan to start building soon.*

strove *see* **strive.**
struck *see* **strike.**

structure ['strʌktʃə] *n* **1** the way in which something is arranged or organized: *A flower has quite a complicated structure*; *the structure of a human body.* **2** a building, or something that is built or constructed: *The Eiffel Tower is one of the most famous structures in the world.* **'structural** *adj* of structure: *You must get permission before making structural alterations to your house.* **'structurally** *adv*.

struggle ['strʌgl] *v* **1** to twist violently when trying to free oneself: *The child struggled in his arms.* **2** to make great efforts or try hard: *All his life he has been struggling with illness/against injustice.* **3** to move with difficulty: *He struggled out of the hole.* – *n*

an act of struggling, or a fight: *The struggle for independence was long and hard.*
struggle along to have only just enough money to live.

strum [strʌm] – *pt*, *ptp* **strummed** – *v* to play *esp* noisily and unskilfully on a piano or stringed instrument: *to strum a tune.*

strung *see* **string.**

strut [strʌt] – *pt*, *ptp* **'strutted** – *v* to walk in a stiff, proud way: *The cock strutted about the farmyard*; *The man was strutting along looking very pleased with himself.*

stub [stʌb] *n* **1** a stump or short remaining end of *eg* a cigarette, pencil *etc*: *The ashtray contained seven cigarette stubs.* **2** the counterfoil or retained section of a cheque *etc*. – *v* – *pt*, *ptp* **stubbed** – to hurt (*esp* a toe) by striking it against something hard: *She stubbed her toe(s) against the bedpost.*
'stubby *adj* being a stub, or short and thick like a stub: *a stubby tail*; *stubby fingers.*
stub out to extinguish (a cigarette or cigar) by pressing it against a hard surface.

stubborn ['stʌbən] *adj* obstinate, or unwilling to yield, obey *etc*: *He's as stubborn as a donkey.*

stubby *see* **stub.**
stuck *see* **stick[1].**

stud[1] [stʌd] *n* a collection of horses and mares kept for breeding.

stud[2] [stʌd] *n* **1** a knob, or nail with a large head, put into the surface of something as a protection or decoration *etc*: *metal studs on the soles of football boots*; *a belt decorated with studs.* **2** a type of button with two heads for fastening a collar: *a collar stud.* – *v* – *pt*, *ptp* **'studded** – to cover with studs: *The sky was studded with stars.*

student ['stjuːdənt] *n* **1** an undergraduate or graduate studying for a degree at a university *etc*: *university students*; *a medical student*; (*also adj*) *She is a student nurse/teacher.* **2** (*esp Amer*) a boy or girl at school. **3** a person studying a particular thing: *a student of politics.*

studio ['stjuːdiou] – *pl* **'studios** – *n* **1** the workroom of an artist or photographer. **2** (*often pl*) a place in which cinema films are made: *This film was made at Ramrod Studios.* **3** a room from which radio or television programmes are broadcast: *a television studio.*

studious ['stjuːdiəs] *adj* spending much time in careful studying: *a studious girl.* **'studiously** *adv*. **'studiousness** *n*.

study ['stʌdi] *v* **1** to give time and attention to gaining knowledge of a subject: *What subject is he studying?*; *He is studying French*; *He is studying for a degree in mathematics*; *She's studying to be a teacher.* **2** to look at or examine carefully: *He studied the railway timetable*; *Give yourself time to study the* *problem in detail.* – *n* **1** the act of devoting time and attention to gaining knowledge: *He spends all his evenings in study*; *She has made a study of the habits of bees.* **2** a musical or artistic composition: *a book of studies for the piano*; *The picture was entitled 'A Study in Grey'.* **3** a room in a house *etc*, in which to study, read, write *etc*: *The headmaster wants to speak to the senior pupils in his study.*

stuff[1] [stʌf] *n* **1** material or substance: *What is that black oily stuff on the beach?*; *The doctor gave me some good stuff for removing warts*; *Show them what stuff you're made of!* (= how brave, strong *etc* you are). **2** (unimportant) matter, things, objects *etc*: *We'll have to get rid of all this stuff when we move house.* **3** an old word for cloth.
know one's stuff to be skilful and knowledgeable in one's chosen subject.
that's the stuff! that's just what is wanted!

stuff[2] [stʌf] *v* **1** to pack or fill tightly, often hurriedly or untidily: *His drawer was stuffed with papers*; *She stuffed the fridge with food*; *The children have been stuffing themselves with ice-cream.* **2** to fill (eg a turkey, chicken *etc*) with stuffing before cooking. **3** to fill the skin of (a dead animal or bird) to preserve the appearance it had when alive: *They stuffed the golden eagle.*
'stuffing *n* **1** material used for stuffing eg toy animals: *The teddy-bear had lost its stuffing.* **2** a mixture containing eg breadcrumbs, spices, sausage-meat *etc*, used for stuffing chickens *etc*.
stuff up to block: *He stuffed the hole up with some newspaper*; *I've got a cold and my nose is stuffed up.*

stuffy ['stʌfi] *adj* **1** (of a room *etc*) too warm, and lacking fresh air: *Why do you sit in this stuffy room all day?* **2** formal and dull: *Must we visit those stuffy people?* **'stuffily** *adv*. **'stuffiness** *n*.

stumble ['stʌmbl] *v* **1** to strike the foot against something and lose one's balance, or nearly fall: *He stumbled over the edge of the carpet.* **2** to walk unsteadily: *He stumbled along the track in the dark.* **3** to make mistakes, or hesitate in speaking, reading aloud *etc*: *He stumbles over his words when speaking in public.*
'stumbling-block *n* a difficulty that prevents progress.
stumble across/on to find by chance: *I stumbled across this book today in a shop.*

stump [stʌmp] *n* **1** the part of a tree left in the ground after the trunk has been cut down: *He sat on a (tree-) stump and ate his sandwiches.* **2** the part of a limb, tooth, pencil *etc* remaining after the main part has been cut or broken off, worn away *etc*. **3** in cricket, one of the three upright sticks

forming the wicket. – *v* **1** to walk with heavy, stamping steps: *He stumped angrily out of the room.* **2** to puzzle or baffle completely: *I'm stumped!* **3** in cricket, to get (a batsman who is not in his crease) out by hitting his stumps with the ball.
'stumpy *adj* being a stump; short and thick like a stump: *The cat had a stumpy tail.*
stump up to pay (a sum of money), often unwillingly: *We all stumped up $2 for his present.*

stun [stʌn] – *pt, ptp* **stunned** – *v* **1** to make unconscious or knock senseless eg by a blow on the head: *The blow stunned him.* **2** to shock or astonish: *He was stunned by the news of her death.*
'stunning *adj* marvellous: *a stunning dress.*

stung *see* **sting**.

stunk *see* **stink**.

stunt[1] [stʌnt] *v* to prevent or check the full growth or development of: *It is thought that smoking by a pregnant mother may stunt the baby's growth.*
'stunted *adj* not well grown: *a stunted tree.*

stunt[2] [stʌnt] *n* something (daring or spectacular) done to attract attention *etc*: *One of his stunts was to cross the Niagara Falls blindfold on a tightrope.*
'stuntman [-man] *n* a person who takes the place of an actor in film sequences involving eg athletic skill and danger.

stupefy ['stju:pifai] *v* to bewilder, confuse or amaze. **,stupe'faction** [-'fakʃən] *n*.

stupendous [stju'pendəs] *adj* astonishing or tremendous.

stupid ['stju:pid] *adj* **1** foolish; slow at understanding: *a stupid mistake*; *He isn't as stupid as he looks.* **2** in a bewildered or dazed state: *He was (feeling) stupid from lack of sleep.* **'stupidly** *adv*. **stu'pidity** *n*.

stupor ['stju:pə] *n* a half-conscious, dazed or bewildered condition caused by eg alcohol, drugs, shock *etc*: *He was in a drunken stupor.*

sturdy ['stə:di] *adj* **1** strong and healthy: *He is small but sturdy.* **2** firm and well-made: *sturdy furniture.* **'sturdily** *adv*. **'sturdiness** *n*.

stutter ['stʌtə] *v* to stammer: *He stutters sometimes when he's excited*; *'I've s-s-seen a gh-gh-ghost,' he stuttered.* – *n* a stammer: *He has a stutter.*
'stutterer *n* a person who has a stammer.

sty[1] [stai] *n* a pigsty.

sty[2], **stye** [stai] – *pls* **sties**, **styes** – *n* a small inflamed swelling on the eyelid.

style [stail] *n* **1** a manner or way of doing something, eg writing, speaking, painting, building *etc*: *different styles of architecture*; *What kind of style are you going to have your hair cut in?*; *a new hairstyle.* **2** a fashion in clothes *etc*: *the latest Paris styles*; *I don't like the new style of shoe.* **3** elegance in

dress, behaviour *etc*: *She certainly has style.*
– *v* **1** to arrange (hair) in a certain way: *I'm
going to have my hair cut and styled.* **2** to
design in a certain style: *These chairs/
clothes are styled for comfort.*
'**stylish** *adj* elegant or fashionable: *stylish
clothes/furniture.* '**stylishly** *adv.* '**stylishness** *n.*
'**stylist** *n* a person who arranges or designs a
style *esp* in hairdressing: *a hair-stylist.*
in style in a luxurious, elegant way without
worrying about the expense: *The bride arrived at the church in style, in a horse-drawn
carriage.*
stylus ['stailəs] *n* a gramophone needle.
Styrofoam® ['stairəfoum] *n* plastic foam used
for insulation *etc.*
suave [swa:v] *adj* (of a man or his manner)
pleasant, elegant, polite and agreeable.
'**suavely** *adv.* '**suaveness**, '**suavity** *ns.*
sub [sʌb] *n* short for several words *eg* **submarine**, **subscription** *etc*: *He's the commander of a sub; Several people still haven't
paid their subs.*
subcommittee [sʌbkə'miti] *n* a committee having powers given to it by a larger committee.
subconscious [sʌb'konʃəs] *adj*, *n* (of) those
activities of the mind of which we are not
aware: *I suspect that his generosity arose
from a subconscious desire for praise; We
can't control the activities of the subconscious.* **sub'consciously** *adv.*
subcontinent [sʌb'kontinənt] *n* a mass of land
almost the size of a continent, forming part
of a larger mass of land: *the Indian Subcontinent* (= India, Pakistan and Bangladesh).
subcontractor [sʌbkən'traktə, *(Amer)*
sʌb'kontraktər] *n* a person who undertakes
work for a contractor and is therefore not
directly employed by the person who wants
such work done: *The building contractor
has employed several subcontractors to build
the block of flats.*
subdivide [sʌbdi'vaid] *v* to divide into smaller
parts or divisions: *Each class of children is
subdivided into groups according to reading
ability.* ˌ**subdi'vision** [-'viʒən] *n.*
subdue [səb'dju:] *v* to conquer, overcome or
bring under control: *After months of fighting the rebels were subdued.*
sub'dued *adj* quiet; not bright or lively:
subdued voices; He seems subdued today.
subject ['sʌbdʒikt] *adj* (of countries *etc*) not
independent, but dominated by another
power: *subject nations.* – *n* **1** a person who
is under the rule of a monarch or a member
of a country that has a monarchy *etc*: *We
are loyal subjects of the Queen; He is a
British subject.* **2** someone or something
that is talked about, written about *etc*: *We
discussed the price of food and similar sub-

jects; What was the subject of the debate?*;
*The teacher tried to think of a good subject
for their essay; I've said all I can on that
subject.* **3** a branch of study or learning in
school, university *etc*: *He is taking exams in
seven subjects; Mathematics is his best subject.* **4** a thing, person or circumstance suitable for, or requiring, a particular kind of
treatment, reaction *etc*: *I don't think her
behaviour is a subject for laughter.* **5** in
English, the word(s) representing the person or thing that *usu* does the action shown
by the verb, and with which the verb
agrees: *The cat sat on the mat; He hit her
because she broke his toy; He was hit by the
ball.* – [səb'dʒekt] *v* **1** to bring (a person,
country *etc*) under control: *They have subjected all the neighbouring states (to their
rule).* **2** to cause to suffer, or submit (to
something): *He was subjected to cruel treatment; These tyres are subjected to various
tests before leaving the factory.* **subjection**
[səb'dʒekʃən] *n.*
subjective [səb'dʒektiv] *adj* (of a person's
attitude *etc*) arising from, or influenced by,
his own thoughts and feelings only; not
objective or impartial: *You must try not to
be too subjective if you are on a jury in a
court of law.* **sub'jectively** *adv.*
subject matter the subject discussed in an
essay, book *etc.*
change the subject to start talking about
something different: *I mentioned the money
to her, but she changed the subject.*
subject to 1 liable or likely to suffer from or
be affected by: *He is subject to colds; The
programme is subject to alteration.* **2** depending on: *These plans will be put into
practice next week, subject to your approval.*
sublime [sə'blaim] *adj* of overwhelming greatness, grandeur, beauty *etc.* **su'blimely** *adv.*
su'blimity [-'bli-] *n.*
submarine [sʌbmə'ri:n] *n* (*abbrev* **sub**) a ship
that can travel under the surface of the sea.
– *adj* existing, or intended for use *etc*, under
the surface of the sea: *submarine vegetation.*
submerge [səb'mə:dʒ] *v* to cover with, or sink
under, water or other liquid: *I watched the
submarine submerging.*
sub'merged *adj* sunk beneath the surface:
*Submerged rocks are a great danger to
shipping.*
sub'mergence, **sub'mersion** [-ʃən, *(Amer)*
-ʒən] *ns.*
submission, submissive *see* **submit.**
submit [səb'mit] – *pt*, *ptp* **sub'mitted** – *v* **1** to
yield to control or to a particular kind of
treatment by another person *etc*: *I refuse to
submit to his control; The rebels were ordered to submit.* **2** to offer (a plan, suggestion, proposal, entry *etc*): *Competitors for

the painting competition must submit their entries by Friday.

su'bmission [-ʃən] *n* 1 the act of submitting. 2 humbleness or obedience.

sub'missive [-siv] *adj* obedient and humble. sub'missively *adv.* sub'missiveness *n.*

subnormal ['sʌb'nɔːməl] *adj* below the normal level or standard: *subnormal temperatures.*

subordinate [sə'bɔːdinət] *adj* lower in rank, power, importance *etc*: *A colonel is subordinate to a brigadier.* – *n* a person who is subordinate: *to give orders to one's subordinates.*

subordinate clause a clause introduced in a sentence by a conjunction, *etc*, and acting as a noun, adjective or adverb: *I don't know who she is; The book that's on the table is mine; She's crying because you were unkind.*

subscribe [səb'skraib] *v* 1 to give money, with other people, to a charity or other cause: *He subscribes to a lot of charities; We each subscribed $1 towards the present.* 2 (with to) to promise to receive and pay for a series of issues of (a magazine *etc*): *I've been subscribing to that magazine for four years.*

sub'scriber *n* a person who subscribes to a charity or a magazine *etc.*

subscription [səb'skripʃən] *n* 1 the act of subscribing. 2 a sum of money that is subscribed *eg* for receiving a magazine, for a membership of a club *etc.*

subsequent ['sʌbsikwənt] *adj* following or coming after: *His misbehaviour and subsequent dismissal from the firm were reported in the newspaper.*

'subsequently *adv* afterwards: *He escaped from prison but was subsequently recaptured.* subsequent to after: *The child became ill subsequent to receiving an injection against measles.*

subside [səb'said] *v* 1 (of land, streets, buildings *etc*) to sink lower: *When a building starts to subside, cracks usually appear in the walls.* 2 (of floods) to become lower and withdraw: *Gradually the water subsided.* 3 (of a storm, noise or other disturbance) to become quieter: *They stayed anchored in harbour till the wind subsided.*

subsidiary [səb'sidjəri] *adj* 1 adding to, or making a contribution towards, something larger, more important *etc*: *questions that are subsidiary to the main one.* 2 (of a firm, company *etc*) controlled by another, larger firm. – *n* – *pl* sub'sidiaries – something that is subsidiary: *this firm and its subsidiaries.*

subsidy ['sʌbsidi] – *pl* 'subsidies – *n* (a sum of) money paid by a government *etc* to an industry *etc* that needs help, or to farmers *etc* to keep the price of their products low.

'subsidize, -ise *v* to give a subsidy to: *Some industries are subsidized by the government.*

subsoil ['sʌbsɔil] *n* the layer of earth beneath the surface soil.

substance ['sʌbstəns] *n* 1 a material: *Rubber is a tough, stretchy substance obtained from the juice of certain plants.* 2 as a scientific term, an element, compound or mixture.

substandard [sʌb'standəd] *adj* below the (officially) approved standard: *substandard working conditions.*

substantial [səb'stanʃəl] *adj* 1 solid or strong: *a nice substantial table.* 2 large: *a substantial sum of money; That meal was quite substantial.* subs'tantially *adv.*

substantiate [səb'stanʃieit] *v* to give the facts that are able to prove or support (a claim, theory *etc*): *He cannot substantiate his claim/accusation.*

substitute ['sʌbstitjuːt] *v* to put in, or to take, the place of someone or something else: *I substituted your name for mine on the list.* – *n* a person or thing used or acting instead of another: *Guesswork is no substitute for investigation; She is not well enough to play in the tennis match, so we must find a substitute;* (*also adj*) *I was substitute headmaster for a term.*

,substi'tution *n* the act of substituting, or process of being substituted.

subterranean [sʌbtə'reiniən] *adj* lying, situated or constructed underground: *subterranean passages.*

subtitle ['sʌbtaitl] *n* 1 a second or explanatory title to a book. 2 on a cinema film *etc*, a translation of foreign speech appearing at the bottom of the screen: *I found it difficult to read the subtitles.*

subtle ['sʌtl] *adj* 1 faint or delicate in quality, and therefore difficult to describe or explain: *There is a subtle difference between 'unnecessary' and 'not necessary'; a subtle flavour.* 2 clever or cunning: *He has a subtle mind.* subtlety ['sʌtlti] *n.* 'subtly *adv.*

subtract [səb'trakt] *v* to take one number or quantity from another: *If you subtract 5 from 8, 3 is left; In their first year at school, most children learn to add and subtract.* sub'traction [-ʃən] *n.*

subtropical [sʌb'tropikəl] *adj* (belonging to those areas) close to the tropical zone: *a subtropical climate.*

suburb ['sʌbəːb] *n* (often in *pl*) an area of houses on the outskirts of a city, town *etc*: *Edgbaston is a suburb of Birmingham; They decided to move out to the suburbs.* su'burban *adj* of suburbs: *suburban housing.* su'burbia [-biə] *n* the suburbs.

subvert [səb'vəːt] *v* to overthrow or ruin completely (*eg* a person's morals, loyalty, arguments, a government). sub'version [-ʃən, (*Amer*) -ʒən] *n.*

sub'versive [-siv] *adj* likely to destroy or overthrow (government, discipline in a school *etc*): *That boy is a subversive influence in this class.*

subway ['sʌbwei] *n* **1** an underground passage *eg* for pedestrians, under a busy road: *Cross by the subway.* **2** an underground railway in a city: *Go by subway.*

succeed [sək'siːd] *v* **1** to manage to do what one is trying to do; to achieve one's aim or purpose: *He succeeded in persuading her to do it; He's happy to have succeeded in his chosen career; She tried three times to pass her driving-test, and at last succeeded; Our new teaching methods seem to be succeeding.* **2** to follow next in order, and take the place of someone or something else: *He succeeded his father as manager of the firm/as king; The cold summer was succeeded by a stormy autumn; If the duke has no children, who will succeed to* (=inherit) *his property?*

success [sək'ses] *n* **1** (the prosperity gained by) the achievement of an aim or purpose: *He has achieved great success as an actor/in his career.* **2** a person or thing that succeeds or prospers: *She's a great success as a teacher.*

suc'cessful [-'ses-] *adj* (*neg* **un-**) having success: *Were you successful in finding a new house?; The successful applicant for this job will be required to start work next month; a successful career.* **suc'cessfully** *adv.*

succession [sək'seʃən] *n* **1** the right of succeeding to a throne as king, to a title *etc*: *The Princess is fifth in* (*order of*) *succession* (*to the throne*). **2** a number of things following after one another: *a succession of bad harvests.* **3** the act or process of following and taking the place of someone or something else: *his succession to the throne.* **successive** [sək'sesiv] *adj* following one after the other: *He won three successive matches.* **suc'cessively** [-'sesiv-] *adv.*

suc'cessor [-'se-] *n* a person who follows, and take the place of another: *Who will be appointed as the manager's successor?*

in succession one after another: *five wet days in succession.*

succulent ['sʌkjulənt] *adj* **1** (of fruit or other food *eg* meat) juicy and delicious: *a succulent peach.* **2** (of plants) having thick stems and leaves that are full of moisture. – *n* a plant of this type: *A cactus is a type of succulent.*
'succulence *n.*

succumb [sə'kʌm] *v* to yield: *She succumbed to temptation and ate the chocolate.*

such [sʌtʃ] *adj* **1** of the same kind as that already mentioned or being mentioned: *Animals that gnaw, such as mice, rats, rabbits and weasels are called rodents; He came from Bradford or some such place; She* asked to see Mr Johnson but was told there was no such person there; I've seen several such buildings; I've never done such a thing before; doctors, dentists and such people.* **2** of the great degree already mentioned or being mentioned: *If you had telephoned her, she wouldn't have got into such a state of anxiety; She never used to get such bad headaches* (*as she does now*). **3** of the great degree, or the kind, to have a particular result: *He shut the window with such force that the glass broke; She's such a good teacher that the headmaster asked her not to leave; Their problems are such as to make it impossible for them to live together any more.* **4** used for emphasis: *This is such a shock! They have been such good friends to me! – pron* such a person or thing, or such persons or things: *I have only a few photographs, but can show you such as I have; This isn't a good book as such* (=as a book) *but it has interesting pictures.*

'suchlike *adj, pron* (things) of the same kind: *I don't like books about love, romance and suchlike* (*things*).

'such-and-such *adj, pron* used to refer to some unnamed person or thing: *Let's suppose that you go into such-and-such a shop and ask for such-and-such.*

such as it is though it scarcely deserves the name: *You can borrow our lawn mower, such as it is.*

suck [sʌk] *v* **1** to draw liquid *etc* into the mouth: *As soon as they are born, young animals learn to suck* (*milk from their mothers*); *She sucked up the lemonade through a straw.* **2** to hold something between the lips or inside the mouth, as though drawing liquid from it: *I told him to take the sweet out of his mouth, but he just went on sucking; He sucked the end of his pencil.* **3** to pull or draw in a particular direction with a sucking or similar action: *The vacuum cleaner sucked up all the dirt from the carpet; A plant sucks up moisture from the soil. – n* an act of sucking: *I gave him a suck of my lollipop.*

'sucker *n* **1** a person or thing that sucks: *Are these insects bloodsuckers?* **2** an organ on an animal, *eg* an octopus, by which it sticks to objects. **3** a curved pad or disc (of rubber *etc*) that can be pressed on to a surface and stick there. **4** a side shoot coming from the root of a plant.

suckle ['sʌkl] *v* (of a woman or female animal) to give milk from the breasts or teats to (a baby or young).

suction ['sʌkʃən] *n* **1** the action of sucking. **2** the process of creating a vacuum by reducing air pressure on the surface of a liquid so that it can be drawn up into a tube etc, or between two surfaces; eg a rubber disc and a wall, so that they stick together.

sudden ['sʌdn] adj happening etc quickly and unexpectedly: a sudden attack; His decision to get married is rather sudden!; a sudden bend in the road. **'suddenness** n.

'suddenly adv: He suddenly woke up; Suddenly he realized that she had a gun.

all of a sudden suddenly or unexpectedly: All of a sudden the lights went out.

suds [sʌdz] n pl soapsuds.

sue [suː] v 1 to start a law case against. 2 (with **for**: esp in law) to ask for (eg divorce).

suede, suède [sweid] n, adj (of) leather from a sheep or lamb etc with a soft, rough surface: suede shoes.

suffer ['sʌfə] v 1 to undergo, endure or bear pain, misery etc: He suffered terrible pain from his injuries; The crash killed him instantly – he didn't suffer at all; I'll make you suffer for this insolence. 2 to undergo or experience: The army suffered enormous losses. 3 to be neglected: I like to see you enjoying yourself, but you mustn't let your work suffer. 4 (with **from**) to have or to have often (a particular illness etc): She suffers from stomach-aches.

'suffering n (a feeling of) pain or misery: The shortage of food caused widespread suffering; She keeps complaining about her sufferings.

suffice [sə'fais] v to be enough for a purpose or person: Will $10 suffice (you) till Monday?

sufficient adj enough: We haven't sufficient food to feed all these people; Will $10 be sufficient for your needs? **suf'ficiency** n. **suf'ficiently** adv.

suffice it to say I need only say.

suffix ['sʌfiks] n a small part added to the end of a word that changes the meaning: goodness; quickly; advisable; misty; yellowish.

suffocate ['sʌfəkeit] v to kill, die, cause distress to or feel distress, through lack of air or the prevention of free breathing: A baby may suffocate if it sleeps with a pillow; The smoke was suffocating him; May I open the window? I'm suffocating. **,suffo'cation** n.

suffrage ['sʌfridʒ] n 1 the right to vote. 2 voting.

sugar ['ʃugə] n the sweet substance that is obtained from sugar-cane, or from the juice of certain other plants, and used in cooking and for sweetening tea, coffee etc: Do you take sugar in your coffee? – v to sweeten, cover or sprinkle with sugar.

'sugary adj 1 tasting of sugar, or containing a lot of sugar: sugary foods. 2 too sweet or sentimental: a sugary story. **'sugariness** n.

'sugar-cane n a type of tall grass from whose juice sugar is obtained.

,sugar-'coated adj covered with icing: sugar-coated biscuits.

sugar lump a small cube of sugar used for sweetening tea etc.

sugar tongs an instrument for lifting sugar lumps: a pair of sugar tongs.

suggest [sə'dʒest, (Amer also) səg-] v 1 to put (an idea etc) before another person etc for consideration; to propose: He suggested a different plan; I suggest doing it a different way; She suggested to me one or two suitable people for the committee; I suggest that we have lunch now. 2 to put (an idea etc) into a person's mind; to hint: Are you suggesting that I'm too old for the job?; An explanation suddenly suggested itself to me.

sug'gestion [-tʃən] n 1 the act of suggesting. 2 something that is suggested; a proposal or idea: Has anyone any other suggestions to make?; What a clever suggestion! 3 a slight trace or sign: There was a suggestion of boredom in his tone.

suicide ['suːisaid] n 1 the/an act of killing oneself deliberately: She committed suicide; an increasing number of suicides. 2 a person who kills himself deliberately.

,sui'cidal adj 1 inclined to suicide: She sometimes feels suicidal. 2 extremely dangerous, or likely to lead to death or disaster: He was driving at a suicidal speed. **,sui'cidally** adv.

suit [suːt] n 1 a set of clothes usu all of the same cloth etc, made to be worn together, eg a jacket, trousers (and waistcoat) for a man, or a jacket and skirt or trousers for a woman. 2 a piece of clothing for a particular purpose: a bathing-suit/diving-suit. 3 a case in a law court: He won/lost his suit. 4 an old word for a formal request, eg a proposal of marriage to a lady. 5 one of the four sets of playing-cards – spades, hearts, diamonds, clubs. – v 1 to satisfy the needs of, or be convenient for: The arrangements did not suit us; The climate suits me very well. 2 (of clothes, styles, fashions etc) to be right or appropriate for: Long hair suits her; That dress doen't suit her. 3 to adjust or make appropriate or suitable: He suited his speech to his audience.

'suited adj (neg **un-**) fitted, or appropriate (to or for): I don't think he's suited to/for this work.

'suitor n an old word for a man who tries to gain the love of a woman.

'suitcase n a case with flat sides for clothes etc, used by a person when travelling: He hastily packed his (clothes in his) suitcase.

follow suit to do just as someone else has done: He went to bed and I followed suit.

suit oneself to do what one wants to do.

suitable ['su:təbl] *adj* (*neg* **un-**) **1** right or appropriate for a purpose or occasion: *I haven't any suitable shoes for the wedding*; *Those shoes are not suitable for walking in the country*; *Many people applied for the job but not one of them was suitable.* **2** convenient: *We must find a suitable day for our meeting.* **,suita'bility, 'suitableness** *ns*.
'**suitably** *adv*: *You're not suitably dressed*.

suite [swiːt] *n* a number of things forming a set: *a suite of furniture*; *He has composed a suite of music for the film*.

sulfur *see* **sulphur**.

sulk [sʌlk] *v* to show anger or resentment by being silent: *He's sulking because his mother won't let him have an ice-cream.*
'**sulky** *adj* sulking, or tending to sulk: *in a sulky mood*; *a sulky girl.* '**sulkily** *adv*. '**sulkiness** *n*.

sullen ['sʌlən] *adj* silent and bad-tempered: *a sullen young man*; *a sullen expression.* '**sullenly** *adv*. '**sullenness** *n*.

sulphur, (*Amer*) **sulfur** ['sʌlfə] *n* a light yellow non-metallic element found in the earth, which burns with a blue flame giving off a choking smell and is used in matches, gunpowder *etc*.
'**sulphate** [-feit] *n* any of several substances containing sulphur, oxygen and some other element.

sultan ['sʌltən] *n* a ruler in certain Muslim countries.
sultana[1] [-'taːnə] *n* the mother, wife, sister or daughter of a sultan.
sultana[2] [səl'taːnə] *n* a type of small, seedless raisin.

sultry ['sʌltri] *adj* **1** (of weather) hot but cloudy, and likely to become stormy. **2** (of a person, *esp* a woman) passionate.
'**sultriness** *n*.

sum [sʌm] *n* **1** the amount or total made by two or more things or numbers added together: *The sum of 12, 24, 7 and 11 is 54.* **2** a quantity of money: *It will cost an enormous sum to repair the swimming pool.* **3** a problem in arithmetic: *My children are better at sums than I am.*
sum total the complete or final total: *The sum total of the damage cannot be calculated.*
sum up – *pt, ptp* **summed** – *v* to give the main or important points of: *He summed up the various proposals.*

summary ['sʌməri] – *pl* '**summaries** – *n* a shortened form of a statement, story *etc* giving only the main points: *A summary of his speech was printed in the newspaper.*
'**summarize, -ise** *v* to make a summary of: *He summarized the arguments.*

summer ['sʌmə] *n* the warmest season of the year, May or June till August in cooler northern regions: *I went to Italy last summer*; (*also adj*) *summer holidays*.
'**summery** *adj* like, or appropriate for, summer: *summery weather*; *summery clothes*.
'**summertime** *n* the season of summer.

summit ['sʌmit] *n* the highest point: *They reached the summit of the mountain at midday*; *At the age of thirty he was at the summit of his powers as a composer.* – *adj* (of a conference *etc*) at the highest level of international negotiation, at which heads of state meet for discussion.

summon ['sʌmən] *v* to order to come or appear: *He was summoned to appear in court*; *The head teacher summoned her to his room*; *A meeting was summoned.*

sump [sʌmp] *n* the part of a motor-engine that contains the oil.

sumptuous ['sʌmptʃuəs] *adj* expensive and splendid: *They live in sumptuous surroundings.*

sun [sʌn] *n* **1** the round body in the sky that gives light and heat to the earth: *The Sun is nearly 150 million kilometres away from the Earth.* **2** any of the fixed stars: *Do other suns have planets revolving round them?* **3** light and heat from the sun; sunshine: *We sat in the sun*; *In Britain they don't get enough sun*; *The sun has faded the curtains.* – *v* – *pt, ptp* **sunned** – to expose (oneself) to the sun's rays: *He's sunning himself in the garden.*
'**sunless** *adj* without sun, or lacking sunlight: *a sunless room.*
'**sunny** *adj* **1** filled with sunshine: *sunny weather.* **2** cheerful and happy: *The child has a sunny nature.* '**sunniness** *n*.
'**sunbathe** *v* to lie or sit in the sun, *esp* wearing few clothes, in order to get a suntan.
'**sunbeam** *n* a ray of the sun.
'**sunburn** *n* the brown or red colour of the skin caused by exposure to the sun's rays.
'**sunburned, 'sunburnt** *adjs*: *sunburnt faces.*
'**sundial** *n* a device, *usu* in a garden, for telling time from the shadow of a rod or plate on its surface cast by the sun.
'**sunflower** *n* a type of large yellow flower with petals like rays of the sun, from whose seeds we get oil.
'**sunglasses** *n pl* glasses of dark-coloured glass or plastic to protect the eyes in bright sunlight.
'**sunlight** *n* the light of the sun: *The cat was sitting in a patch of sunlight.*
'**sunlit** *adj* lighted up by the sun: *a sunlit room.*
'**sunrise** *n* the rising of the sun in the morning, or the time of this.
'**sunset** *n* the setting of the sun, or the time of this; *the red glow of the sunset.*

'sunshade n a type of umbrella for sheltering a person from the sun; a parasol.

'sunshine n 1 the light of the sun: *The children were playing in the sunshine.* 2 cheerfulness or happiness.

'sunstroke n a serious illness caused by being in very hot sunshine for too long.

'suntan n a brown colour of the skin caused by exposure to the sun: *I'm trying to get a suntan.*

catch the sun to become sunburnt.

under the sun in the whole world: *I'm sure that he must have visited every country under the sun.*

sundae ['sʌndei] n a portion of ice-cream served with fruit, syrup *etc*: *a fruit sundae.*

Sunday ['sʌndi] n the first day of the week, the day following Saturday, kept for rest and worship among Christians.

Sunday best/clothes the smart garments that a person wears for special occasions.

Sunday school a school attended by children on Sundays for religious instruction.

a month of Sundays a very long time.

sundial *see* sun.

sunflower *see* sun.

sung *see* sing.

sunglasses *see* sun.

sunk, sunken *see* sink.

sunlight ... suntan *see* sun.

super[1] ['su:pə] adj a slang word for extremely good, nice *etc*: *a super new dress.*

super[2] *see* superintendent *under* superintend.

superb [su'pə:b] adj magnificent or excellent: *a superb view/meal.* su'perbly adv.

superficial [su:pə'fiʃəl] adj 1 on, or affecting, the surface only: *The wound is only superficial.* 2 not thorough: *He has only a superficial knowledge of the subject.* ,super,fici'ality [-ʃi'a-] n. ,super'ficially adv.

superfluous [su:pə'fluəs] adj extra; beyond what is needed or wanted.

superhuman [su:pə'hju:mən] adj divine, or beyond what is human: *superhuman powers; a man of superhuman strength.*

superintend [su:pərin'tend] v to supervise: *An adult should be present to superintend the children's activities.*

,superin'tendence n: *He placed his estate under the superintendence of a manager.*

,superin'tendent n 1 a person who superintends something, or is in charge of an institution, building *etc*: *the superintendent of a hospital.* 2 (*abbrev* super; *often abbrev* Supt *when written*) a police officer of the rank above chief inspector.

superior [su'piəriə] adj 1 (*often with* to) higher in rank, better, or greater, than: *Is a captain superior to a commander in the navy?*; *With his superior strength he managed to overwhelm his opponent.* 2 high, or above the average, in quality: *superior workmanship.* 3 (of a person or his attitude) contemptuous or disdainful: *a superior smile.* – n a person who is better than, or higher in rank than, another or others: *The servant was dismissed for being rude to her superiors.* su,peri'ority [-'o-] n.

superlative [su'pə:lətiv] adj (of an adjective or adverb) of the highest degree of comparison: *'Biggest' is a superlative adjective.* – n (an adjective or adverb of) the superlative degree: *'Best' and 'worst' are the superlatives of 'good' and 'bad'*; *She is the prettiest girl in the room*; *We'll go by different roads to see who will arrive (the) soonest/most quickly.*

superman ['su:pəman] n an imagined man of the future with amazing powers: *a race of supermen.*

supermarket ['su:pəma:kit] n a large, self-service store selling food and other goods.

supernatural [su:pə'natʃərəl] adj (of *eg* matters concerning ghosts *etc*) beyond what is natural or physically possible: *supernatural happenings; a creature of supernatural strength.*

supersonic [su:pə'sonik] adj faster than the speed of sound: *These planes travel at supersonic speeds.*

superstition [su:pə'stiʃən] n 1 (the state of fear and ignorance resulting from) the belief in magic, witchcraft and other things that cannot be explained by reason. 2 an example of this type of belief: *There is an old superstition that those who marry in May will have bad luck.*

,super'stitious adj: *superstitious beliefs; She has always been very superstitious.* ,super'stitiously adv.

supervise ['su:pəvaiz] v to direct, control or be in charge of (work, workers *etc*): *She supervises the typists.*

,super'vision [-'viʒən] n the act or work of supervising or state of being supervised: *The firm's accounts are under the personal supervision of the manager*; *These children should have more supervision.*

'supervisor n a person who supervises.

supper ['sʌpə] n a meal taken at the end of the day: *Would you like some supper?*; *She has invited me to supper.*

'supper-time n the time in the evening when people eat supper: *I'll be back at supper-time.*

supple ['sʌpl] adj (of the body *etc*) bending easily: *Take exercise if you want to keep supple; supple dancers.* 'suppleness n.

supplement ['sʌpləmənt] n an addition made to supply something lacking, or to correct errors *etc*: *A supplement to the dictionary is to be published next year.* – [-ment] v to make, or be, an addition to: *He does an evening job to supplement his wages.*

,supple'mentary [-'men-] *adj* added to supply what is lacking; additional.

supply [sə'plai] *v* to give or provide: *Who is supplying the rebels with guns and ammunition?*; *Extra paper will be supplied by the teacher if it is needed*; *The town is supplied with water from a reservoir in the hills*; *The shop was unable to supply what she wanted.* – *n* **1** the act or process of supplying. **2** (*often in pl*) an amount or quantity that is supplied; a stock or store: *She left a supply of food for her husband when she went away for a few days*; *Who will be responsible for the expedition's supplies?*; *Fresh supplies will be arriving soon.*

be in short supply (of goods *etc*) to be scarce: *Bread is in short supply.*

support [sə'po:t] *v* **1** to bear the weight of, or hold upright, in place *etc*: *That chair won't support him/his weight*; *He limped home, supported by a friend on either side of him.* **2** to give help, or approval to: *He has always supported our cause*; *His family supported him in his decision.* **3** to provide evidence for the truth of: *New discoveries have been made that support his theory*; *The second witness supported the statement of the first one.* **4** to supply with the means of living: *He has a wife and four children to support.* – *n* **1** the act of supporting or state of being supported: *That type of shoe doesn't give the foot much support*; *The plan was cancelled because of lack of support*; *Her job is the family's only means of support*; *I would like to say a word or two in support of his proposal.* **2** something that supports: *One of the supports of the bridge collapsed.*

sup'porter *n* a person who helps or supports (a person, cause, team *etc*): *a crowd of football supporters.*

sup'porting *adj* (of an actor, rôle *etc*) secondary to the leading actor, rôle *etc*: *He has had many supporting rôles*; *a supporting cast.*

suppose [sə'pouz] *v* **1** to think probable; to believe or guess: *Who do you suppose telephoned today?*; *'I suppose you'll be going to the meeting?' 'Yes, I suppose so/No, I don't suppose so.'*; *Do you suppose she'll win?*; *'Surely her statement can't be correct?' 'No, I suppose not.'* **2** to accept as true for the sake of argument; to consider as a possibility: *(Let's) suppose we each had $100 to spend*; *Suppose the train's late – what shall we do?* **3** used to make a suggestion or give an order in a polite way: *Suppose we have lunch now!*; *Suppose you make us a cup of tea!*

sup'posing if: *Supposing she doesn't come, what shall we do?*

be supposed to (be/do *etc*) **1** to have the reputation of (being *etc*): *He's supposed to be the best doctor in the town.* **2** to be expected or obliged to (do something *etc*): *You're supposed to make your own bed every morning.*

suppress [sə'pres] *v* **1** to defeat or put a stop to (*eg* a rebellion). **2** to keep back or stifle: *She suppressed a laugh.* **3** to prevent from being published, known *etc*: *to suppress information.* **sup'pression** [-ʃən] *n.*

supreme [su'pri:m] *adj* **1** the highest, greatest, or most powerful: *the supreme ruler.* **2** the greatest possible: *an act of supreme courage.* **su'premely** *adv.*

supremacy [su'preməsi] *n* the state of being the greatest or most powerful: *How did Rome maintain her supremacy over the rest of the world for so long?*

surcharge ['sə:tʃa:dʒ] *n* an extra amount of money charged: *We paid for our holiday abroad in advance but we had to pay a surcharge because of the devaluation of the pound.*

sure [ʃuə] **1** (*neg* **un-**) having no doubt; certain: *I'm sure that I gave him the book*; *I'm not sure where she lives/what her address is*; *'There's a bus at two o'clock.' 'Are you quite sure?'*; *I thought the idea was good, but now I'm not so sure*; *I'll help you – you can be sure of that!* **2** unlikely to fail (to do or get something): *He's sure to win*; *You're sure of a good dinner if you stay at that hotel.* **3** reliable or trustworthy: *a sure way to cure hiccups*; *a safe, sure method*; *a sure aim with a rifle.* – *adv* (*esp Amer*) certainly; of course: *Sure I'll help you!*; *'Would you like to come?' 'Sure!'*

'surely *adv* **1** used in questions, exclamations *etc* to indicate what the speaker considers probable: *Surely she's finished her work by now!*; *You don't believe what she said, surely?* **2** without doubt, hesitation, mistake or failure: *Slowly but surely we're achieving our aim.* **3** (in answers) certainly; of course: *'May I come with you?' 'Surely!'* **'sureness** *n.*

,sure-'footed *adj* not likely to slip or stumble: *Goats are sure-footed animals.*

as sure as used in various phrases that mean 'without fail' or 'without doubt': *As sure as fate/anything/eggs are eggs, he'll be late again.*

be sure don't fail to: *Be sure to switch off the television.*

be/feel sure of oneself to be confident.

for sure definitely or certainly: *We don't know for sure that he's dead.*

make sure to act so that, or check that, something is certain or sure: *Arrive early at the cinema to make sure of (getting) a seat!*; *I think he's coming today but I'll telephone to make sure (of that/that he is).*

sure enough in fact, as was expected: *I thought she'd be angry, and sure enough she was.*

surf [səːf] *n* the foam made as waves break on rocks or on the shore: *The children were playing in the white surf.*

'surfing *n* (*also* **'surf-riding**) the sport of riding on a surfboard.

'surfboard *n* a board on which a bather rides towards shore on the surf.

surface ['səːfis] *n* **1** the outside part (of anything): *Two-thirds of the earth's surface is covered with water*; *This road has a very uneven surface.* **2** the outward appearance of, or first impression made by, a person or thing: *On the surface he seems cold and unfriendly, but he's really a kind person.* – *v* **1** to put a surface on (a road *etc*): *The road has been damaged by frost and will have to be surfaced again.* **2** (of a submarine, diver *etc*) to come to the surface.

surface mail mail sent by ship, train *etc* and not by aeroplane.

surge [səːdʒ] *v* (of *eg* water or waves) to move forward with great force: *The waves surged over the rocks.* – *n* a surging movement, or a sudden rush: *The stone hit his head and he felt a surge of pain; a sudden surge of anger.*

surgeon ['səːdʒən] *n* **1** a doctor who treats injuries or diseases by operations in which the body sometimes has to be cut open, *eg* to remove a diseased part. **2** a doctor in the army or navy.

surgery ['səːdʒəri] – *pl* **'surgeries** – **1** the practice or art of a surgeon: *to specialize in surgery.* **2** a doctor's or dentist's room in which he examines patients.

surgical ['səːdʒikəl] *adj* of, or by means of, surgery: *surgical instruments; He is in need of surgical treatment.* **'surgically** *adv.*

surly ['səːli] *adj* bad-tempered or rude. **'surliness** *n.*

surmount [səˈmaunt] *v* to overcome or deal with (problems, obstacles *etc*) successfully: *He surmounted these obstacles without trouble.*

surname ['səːneim] *n* a person's family name: *The common way of addressing people is by their surnames, preceded by Mr, Mrs, Miss, Dr etc; Smith is a common British surname.*

surpass [səˈpaːs] *v* to be, or do, better, or more than.

surplus ['səːpləs] *n* the amount left over when what is required has been used *etc*: *Canada produces a surplus of raw materials*; (*also adj*) *surplus stocks; The country had a trade surplus* (= exported more than it imported) *last month.*

surprise [səˈpraiz] *n* (the feeling caused by) something sudden or unexpected: *His statement caused some surprise; Your letter was a pleasant surprise; There were some nasty*

surprises waiting for her when she returned; He stared at her in surprise; To my surprise the door was unlocked; (*also adj*) *He paid them a surprise visit.* – *v* **1** to cause to feel surprise: *The news surprised me.* **2** to lead, by means of surprise, into doing something: *Her sudden question surprised him into betraying himself.* **3** to find, come upon, or attack, without warning: *They surprised the enemy from the rear.*

sur'prised *adj* showing or feeling surprise: *his surprised face; I'm surprised (that) he's not here; You behaved badly – I'm surprised at you!; I wouldn't be surprised if he won.*

sur'prising *adj* likely to cause surprise: *surprising news; It is not surprising that he resigned.*

sur'prisingly *adv: Surprisingly, he did win.*

take by surprise 1 to catch unawares: *The news took me by surprise.* **2** to capture (a fort *etc*) by a sudden, unexpected attack.

surrender [səˈrendə] *v* **1** to yield: *The general refused to surrender to the enemy; We shall never surrender!* **2** to give up or abandon: *He surrendered his claim to the throne; You must surrender your old passport when applying for a new one.* – *n* (an) act of surrendering: *The garrison was forced into surrender.*

surround [səˈraund] *v* **1** to be, or come, all round: *Britain is surrounded by sea; Enemy troops surrounded the town; Mystery surrounds his death.* **2** to enclose: *He surrounded the castle with a high wall.*

sur'rounding *adj* lying or being all round: *the village and its surrounding scenery.*

sur'roundings *n pl* **1** the scenery *etc* that is round a place: *a pleasant hotel in delightful surroundings.* **2** the conditions *etc* in which a person, animal *etc* lives: *He was happy to be at home again in his usual surroundings.*

survey [səˈvei] *v* **1** to look at, or view, in a general way: *He surveyed his neat garden with satisfaction.* **2** to examine carefully or in detail. **3** to measure, and estimate the position, shape *etc* of (a piece of land *etc*): *They have started to survey the piece of land that the new motorway will pass through.* **4** to make a formal or official inspection of (a house *etc* that is being offered for sale). – ['səːvei] *n* **1** a look or examination; a report: *After a brief survey of the damage he telephoned the police; He has written a survey of crime in big cities.* **2** a careful measurement of land *etc.*

sur'veyor *n* a person whose job is to survey buildings or land.

survive [səˈvaiv] *v* **1** to remain alive in spite of (a disaster *etc*): *Few birds managed to survive the bad winter; He didn't survive long after the accident.* **2** to live longer than: *He died in 1940 but his wife survived him by* *another twenty years*; *He is survived by his wife and two sons.*

sur'vival *n* the state of surviving: *the problem of survival in sub-zero temperatures*; (*also adj*) *survival equipment.*

sur'viving *adj* remaining alive: *She has no surviving relatives.*

sur'vivor *n* a person who survives a disaster *etc*: *There were no survivors of the air crash.*

suspect [sə'spekt] *v* **1** to think (a person *etc*) guilty: *Whom do you suspect (of the crime)?*; *I suspect him of killing the girl.* **2** to distrust: *I suspected her motives/air of honesty.* **3** to think probable: *I suspect that she's trying to hide her true feelings*; *I began to suspect a plot.* – ['sʌspekt] *n* a person who is thought guilty: *There are three possible suspects in this murder case.* – *adj* not trustworthy: *I think his statement is suspect.*

suspicion [sə'spiʃən] *n* **1** the process of suspecting or being suspected; the/a feeling causing a person to suspect: *They looked at each other with suspicion*; *I have a suspicion that she is not telling the truth.* **2** a slight quantity or trace: *There was a suspicion of triumph in his tone.*

suspicious [sə'spiʃəs] *adj* **1** having or showing suspicion: *I'm always suspicious of men like him*; *a suspicious glance.* **2** causing or arousing suspicion: *suspicious circumstances.* **suspiciously** [sə'spiʃəsli] *adv.* **su'spiciousness** *n.*

suspend [sə'spend] *v* **1** to hang: *The meat was suspended from a hook.* **2** to keep from falling or sinking: *Particles of dust are suspended in the air.* **3** to stop or discontinue temporarily: *All business will be suspended until after the funeral.* **4** to prevent (a person) temporarily from continuing his (professional) activities or having his usual privileges: *Two footballers were suspended after yesterday's match.*

su'spenders *n pl* **1** a pair, or set, of elastic straps for holding up socks or stockings. **2** (*Amer*) braces for holding up trousers.

su'spense [-s] *n* a state of uncertainty and anxiety: *We waited in suspense for the result of the competition.*

su'spension [-ʃən] *n* **1** the act of suspending. **2** in a motor vehicle *etc*, the system of springs *etc* supporting the frame on the axles. **3** a liquid with solid particles that do not sink.

suspension bridge a type of bridge that has its roadway suspended from cables supported by towers.

suspicion, suspicious *etc see* **suspect.**

sustain [sə'stein] *v* **1** to bear (the weight of): *The branches could hardly sustain the weight of the fruit.* **2** to give help or strength to:

The thought of seeing her again sustained him throughout his ordeal.

swag [swag] *n* **1** stolen goods. **2** in Australia, a tramp's bundle.

swagger ['swagə] *v* to walk as though very pleased with oneself: *I saw him swaggering along the street in his new suit.* – *n* a swaggering way of walking.

swallow[1] ['swolou] *v* **1** to allow to pass down the throat to the stomach: *Try to swallow the pill*; *His throat was so painful that he could hardly swallow.* **2** to accept (*eg* a lie or insult) without question or protest: *You'll never get her to swallow that story!* – *n* an act of swallowing.

swallow one's pride to behave humbly *eg* by making an apology.

swallow up to cause to disappear completely: *She was swallowed up in the crowd.*

swallow[2] ['swolou] *n* a type of insect-eating bird with long wings and a divided tail.

swam *see* **swim.**

swamp [swomp] *n* (an area of) wet, marshy ground: *These trees grow best in swamp(s).* – *v* to cover or fill with water: *A great wave swamped the deck.*

'swampy *adj* (of land) covered with swamp; marshy. **'swampiness** *n.*

swan [swon] *n* a large, *usu* white, water-bird of the duck family, with a long graceful neck.

swan song the last work or performance of *eg* a poet, musician *etc* before his death or retirement.

swap *see* **swop.**

swarm [swo:m] *n* **1** a great number (of insects or other small creatures) moving together: *a swarm of ants.* **2** (*often in pl*) a great number or crowd: *swarms of people.* – *v* **1** (of bees) to follow a queen bee in a swarm. **2** to move in great numbers: *The children swarmed out of the school.* **3** to be full of moving crowds: *The Tower of London was swarming with tourists.*

swastika ['swostikə] *n* a cross with the ends bent at right angles, adopted as the badge of the Nazi party in Germany before the Second World War.

swat [swot] – *pt, ptp* **'swatted** – *v* to crush (a fly *etc*) by slapping it with something flat: *He swatted the fly with a folded newspaper.* – *n* an act of swatting: *He gave the wasp a swat.*

sway [swei] *v* **1** to (cause to) move from side to side or up and down with a swinging or rocking action: *The branches swayed gently in the breeze.* **2** to influence the opinion *etc* of: *She's too easily swayed by her feelings.* – *n* **1** the motion of swaying: *the sway of the ship's deck.* **2** power, rule or control: *the countries under the sway of Russia.*

swear [sweə] – *pt* **swore** [swo:]; *ptp* **sworn** [swo:n] – *v* **1** to state, declare, or promise solemnly with an oath, or very definitely and positively: *The witness must swear to tell the truth*; *He swore an oath of loyalty*; *Swear never to reveal the secret*; *I could have sworn* (=I'm sure) *she was here a minute ago*. **2** to use the name of God and other sacred words, or obscene words, for emphasis or abuse; to curse: *Don't swear in front of the children!*

sworn [swɔːn] *adj* **1** (of friends, enemies *etc*) (determined, as if) having taken an oath always to remain so: *They are sworn enemies*. **2** (of evidence, statements *etc*) given by a person who has sworn to tell the truth: *The prisoner made a sworn statement*.

'**swear-word** *n* a word used in cursing: '*Damn' is a mild swear-word*.

swear by **1** to appeal to (*eg* God) as a witness of one's words: *I swear by Heaven that I'm innocent*. **2** to put complete trust in (a remedy *etc*): *She swears by aspirin for all the children's illnesses*.

swear in to introduce (a person) into a post or office formally, by making him swear an oath: *The new Governor is being sworn in next week*.

swear to to make a solemn statement, with an oath, in support of: *I'll swear to the truth of what he said*; *I think he was here this morning, but I wouldn't like to swear to it*.

sweat [swet] *n* the moisture given out through the skin: *He was dripping with sweat after running so far in the heat*. – *v* **1** to give out sweat: *Vigorous exercise makes you sweat*. **2** to work hard: *I was sweating (away) at my work from morning till night*.

'**sweater** *n* any kind of knitted pullover or jersey.

'**sweaty** *adj* wet or stained with, or smelling of, sweat: *sweaty clothes/bodies*. '**sweatiness** *n*.

a cold sweat (coldness and dampness of the skin when a person is in) a state of shock, fear *etc*.

sweep [swiːp] – *pt, ptp* **swept** [swept] – *v* **1** to clean (a room *etc*) using a brush or broom: *The room has been swept clean*. **2** to move as though with a brush: *She swept the crumbs off the table with her hand*; *The wave swept him overboard*; *Don't get swept away by* (=become over-enthusiastic about) *the idea!*; *She swept aside my objections*. **3** to move quickly over: *The disease/craze is sweeping the country*. **4** to move swiftly or in a proud manner: *High winds sweep across the desert*; *She swept into my room without knocking on the door*. – *n* **1** an act of sweeping, or process of being swept, with a brush *etc*: *She gave the room a sweep*. **2** a sweeping movement: *He indicated the damage with a sweep of his hand*. **3** a person who cleans chimneys. **4** a sweepstake.

'**sweeper** *n* a person or thing that sweeps: *a road-sweeper*; *May I borrow your carpet-sweeper?*

'**sweeping** *adj* **1** that sweeps: *a sweeping gesture*. **2** (of changes *etc*) very great: *a sweeping victory*; *sweeping reforms*.

'**sweeping-brush** *n* a type of brush with a long handle that is used for sweeping floors *etc*.

at one/a sweep by one action, at one time: *He sacked half of his employees at one sweep*.

sweep (someone) off his feet to affect (a person) with strong emotion or enthusiasm.

sweep out to sweep (a room *etc*) thoroughly; to clean by sweeping: *to sweep the classroom out*.

sweep the board to be very successful; to win all the prizes.

sweep under the carpet to avoid facing, or dealing with (an unpleasant situation *etc*) by pretending it does not exist.

sweep up to gather together or remove (dirt *etc*) by sweeping: *She swept up the crumbs/mess*.

sweepstake ['swiːpsteik] *n* a system of gambling *eg* on a horse-race, in which the person who holds a ticket for the winning horse gets all the money staked by the other ticketholders.

sweet [swiːt] *adj* **1** tasting like sugar; not sour, salty or bitter: *as sweet as honey*; *Children eat too many sweet foods*. **2** tasting fresh and pleasant: *young, sweet vegetables*. **3** (of smells) pleasant or fragrant: *the sweet smell of flowers*. **4** (of sounds) agreeable or delightful to hear: *the sweet song of the nightingale*. **5** attractive or charming: *What a sweet little baby!*; *a sweet face/smile*; *You look sweet in that dress*. **6** kindly and agreeable: *She's a sweet girl*; *The child has a sweet nature*. – *n* **1** (*Amer* '**candy**) a small piece of sweet food *eg* chocolate, toffee *etc*: *a packet of sweets*; *Have a sweet*. **2** (a dish or course of) sweet food near or at the end of a meal; (a) pudding or dessert: *The waiter served the sweet*. **3** dear; darling: *Hallo, my sweet!*

'**sweeten** *v* to make or become sweet or sweeter: *Did you sweeten* (=put sugar in) *my tea?*

'**sweetener** *n* something that sweetens, *eg* a substance used for sweetening food: *Saccharin is an artificial sweetener, often used instead of sugar*.

'**sweetly** *adv* in an attractive, charming, agreeable or kindly manner: *She sang/smiled very sweetly*.

'**sweetness** *n*.

'**sweetheart** *n* **1** a boyfriend or girlfriend. **2** used as an endearment for any beloved person, *eg* a child: *Goodbye, sweetheart!*

*sweet potato (the edible tuber of) a tropical twining plant.

sweet-'smelling *adj*: *sweet-smelling flowers.*

sweet-'tempered *adj* kind and friendly.

swell [swel] – *pt* **swelled**: *ptp* **swollen** ['swəulən] – *v* to make or become larger, greater or thicker: *The insect-bite made her finger swell*; *The continual rain had swollen the river*; *I invited her to join us on the excursion in order to swell the numbers.* – *n* a rolling condition of the sea, *usu* after a storm: *The sea looked fairly calm but there was a heavy swell.* – *adj* (*esp Amer*) used as a term of approval: *a swell idea*; *That's swell!*

'swelling *n* a swollen area, *esp* on the body as a result of injury, disease *etc*: *She had a swelling on her arm where the wasp had stung her.*

swollen ['swəulən] *adj* increased in size, thickness *etc*, through swelling: *a swollen river*; *He had a swollen ankle after falling down the stairs.*

,swollen-'headed *adj* too pleased with oneself; conceited: *He's very swollen-headed about his success.*

swell out to (cause to) bulge: *The sails swelled out in the wind.*

swell up (of a part of the body) to swell: *The toothache made her face swell up.*

swelter ['sweltə] *v* (of a person *etc*) to be uncomfortably hot: *I'm sweltering in this heat!*

swept *see* **sweep**.

swerve [swəːv] *v* to turn away (from a line or course), *esp* quickly: *The car driver swerved to avoid the dog*; *She never swerved from her purpose.* – *n* an act of swerving: *The sudden swerve rocked the passengers in their seats.*

swift[1] [swift] *adj* fast or quick: *a swift horse*; *Our methods are swift and efficient*; *a swift-footed animal.* **'swiftly** *adv*. **'swiftness** *n*.

swift[2] [swift] *n* a type of bird rather like a swallow.

swig [swig] – *pt, ptp* **swigged** – *v* to drink: *He's in the bar swigging beer.* – *n* a long gulp: *He took a swig from the bottle.*

swill [swil] *v* to (cause to) flow around: *Water was swilling around in the bottom of the boat.* – *n* **1** a rinse: *He brushed his teeth and then gave his mouth a swill.* **2** (*also* **'pigswill**) semi-liquid food given to pigs.

swill out to rinse: *She swilled her mouth out with fresh water.*

swim [swim] – *prp* **'swimming**: *pt* **swam** [swæm]: *ptp* **swum** [swʌm] – *v* **1** to move through water using arms and legs or fins, tails *etc*: *The children aren't allowed to go sailing until they've learnt to swim*; *I'm going/I've been swimming*; *He swam into the cave*; *They watched the fish swimming about in the aquarium.* **2** to cross (a river *etc*),

compete in (a race), cover (a distance *etc*) by swimming: *He swam three lengths of the swimming-pool*; *She can't swim a stroke* (= at all). **3** to seem to be moving round and round, as a result of dizziness *etc*: *His head was swimming*; *Everything began to swim before his eyes.* – *n* an act of swimming: *We went for a swim in the lake.*

'swimmer *n* a person who swims or who can swim: *He's a strong swimmer.*

'swimming *adj* covered with, or floating in, a liquid: *meat swimming in/with grease.*

'swimming-bath, **'swimming-pool** *ns* an indoor or outdoor pool for swimming in.

'swimming-trunks *n pl* short pants worn by boys and men for swimming.

'swimsuit, **'swimming-costume** *ns* a (woman's) garment worn for swimming.

swindle ['swindl] *v* to cheat: *That shopkeeper has swindled me!*; *He swindled me out of $4.* – *n* an act or example of swindling; a fraud: *an insurance swindle*; *Our new car's a swindle – it's falling to pieces.*

'swindler *n* a person who swindles.

swine [swain] *n* **1** (*pl* **swine**) an old word for a pig. **2** (*pl* **swines**) an offensive word for a person who behaves in a cruel or disgusting way towards others.

swing [swiŋ] – *pt, ptp* **swung** [swʌŋ] – *v* **1** to (cause to) move or sway in a curve (from side to side or forwards and backwards) from a fixed point: *You swing your arms when you walk*; *The children were swinging on a rope hanging from a tree*; *The door swung open*; *He swung the load on to his shoulder.* **2** to walk with a stride: *He swung along the road.* **3** to turn suddenly: *He swung round and stared at them*; *He is hoping to swing the voters in his favour.* – *n* **1** an act, period, or manner, of swinging: *He was having a swing on the rope*; *Most golfers would like to improve their swing.* **2** a swinging movement: *the swing of the dancers' skirts.* **3** a strong dancing rhythm: *The music should be played with a swing.* **4** a change in public opinion *etc*: *a swing away from the government.* **5** a seat for swinging, hung on ropes or chains from a supporting frame *etc*.

'swinging *adj* fashionable and exciting: *the swinging city of London.*

swing bridge a type of bridge that swings open to let ships pass.

swing door a door that swings open in both directions.

be in full swing to be going ahead, or continuing, busily or vigorously: *The work was in full swing.*

get into the swing (of things) to begin to fit into a routine *etc*.

go with a swing (of an organized event *etc*) to proceed or go easily and successfully.

swipe [swaip] *v* to hit hard: *She swiped the tennis ball over the net*; *He swiped at the wasp but didn't hit it.* – *n* a hard hit: *She gave the child a swipe.*

swirl [swɔːl] *v* to (cause to) move quickly, with a whirling or circling motion: *The leaves were swirled along the ground by the wind.* – *n* a whirling or circling motion or shape: *The dancers came on stage in a swirl of colour.*

swish [swiʃ] *v* to (cause to) move with a hissing or rustling sound: *He swished the stick about in the air.* – *n* an act, or the sound, of swishing: *The horse cantered away with a swish of its tail.*

switch [switʃ] *n* 1 a small lever, handle or other device *eg* for putting or turning an electric current on or off: *The switch is down when the power is on and up when it's off*; *He couldn't find the light-switch.* 2 an act of turning or changing: *After several switches of direction they found themselves on the right road.* 3 a thin stick. – *v* to change, turn: *He switched the lever to the 'off' position*; *Let's switch over to another programme*; *Having considered that problem, they switched their attention to other matters.*

'switchboard *n* a board with many switches for controlling electric currents *etc*, or for making connections by telephone, *eg* within a large office *etc*.

switch on/off to put or turn on/off (an electric current/light *etc*): *He switched on the light*; *Switch off the electricity before going on holiday.*

swivel ['swivl] *n* a type of joint between two parts of an object (*eg* between a chair and its base) that enables one part to turn without the other. – *v* – *pt*, *ptp* **'swivelled** – to move round (as though) on a swivel: *He swivelled his chair round to face the desk.*

swollen *see* **swell**.

swoon [swuːn] *v* (an old word for) to faint. – *n* a fainting fit.

swoop [swuːp] *v* to rush or fly downwards: *The owl swooped down on its prey.* – *n* an act of swooping.

at one fell swoop all at the same time; in a single movement or action.

swop, swap [swop] – *pt*, *ptp* **swopped, swapped** – *v* to exchange one thing for another: *He swopped his ball with another boy for a pistol*; *They swopped books with each other.* – *n* an exchange: *a fair swop.*

sword [soːd] *n* a weapon with a long blade that is sharp on one or both edges: *He drew his sword (from its sheath) and killed the man.*

'sword-play *n* the activity of fencing.

'swordsman ['soːdz-] *n* a man who can fight or fence with a sword.

'swordtail *n* a tropical fish of fresh water, the male having a long sword-shaped tail.

cross swords to quarrel or disagree: *I try not to cross swords with my boss.*

swore, sworn *see* **swear**.

swot [swot] – *pt*, *ptp* **'swotted** – *v* to study hard, *esp* by memorizing *eg* for an examination. – *n* an unkind word for a person who studies hard.

swum *see* **swim**.

swung *see* **swing**.

syllable ['siləbl] *n* a word or part of a word *usu* containing a vowel sound: *'Cheese' has one syllable, 'but-ter' two and 'mar-ga-rine' three.* **syllabic** [-'la-] *adj*.

syllabus ['siləbəs] *n* a programme or list, *eg* of a course of lectures, or of courses of study.

symbol ['simbəl] *n* a thing that is regarded as representing or standing for another: *The dove is the symbol of peace.*

sym'bolic [-'bo-] *adj*: *In the Christian religion, bread and wine are symbolic of Christ's body and blood.* **sym'bolically** *adv*.

'symbolize, -ise *v* to be a symbol of or represent by a symbol: *A ring symbolizes everlasting love.* **'symbolism** *n*.

symmetry ['simitri] *n* the state in which two parts, on either side of a dividing line, are equal in size, shape and position.

sym'metrical [-'me-] *adj* having symmetry: *The two sides of a person's face are never completely symmetrical.* **sym'metrically** *adv*.

sympathy ['simpəθi] *n* 1 a feeling of pity or sorrow for a person in trouble: *When her husband died, she received many letters of sympathy.* 2 the state or feeling of being in agreement with, or of being able to understand, the attitude or feelings of another person: *I have no sympathy with such a stupid attitude*; *Are you in sympathy with the strikers?*

sympa'thetic [-'θetik] *adj* (*neg* **un-**) showing or feeling sympathy: *She was very sympathetic when I failed my exam*; *a sympathetic smile.* **sympa'thetically** *adv*.

'sympathize, -ise *v* to show or feel sympathy to: *I find it difficult to sympathize with him when he complains so much.*

symphony ['simfəni] – *pl* **'symphonies** – *n* a *usu* long piece of music for an orchestra of many different instruments, in three or four movements or parts. **sym'phonic** [-'fo-] *adj*.

symptom ['simptəm] *n* something that a person suffers from that indicates a particular disease: *abdominal pain is a symptom of appendicitis.* **sympto'matic** [-'matik] *adj*.

synagogue ['sinəgog] *n* (the building used by) a gathering of Jews meeting together for worship.

synchronize, -ise ['siŋkrənaiz] *v* to (cause to) happen at the same time, go at the same speed *etc*, as something else: *In the film, the* *movements of the actors' lips did not synchronize with the sounds of their words; to synchronize watches.* ,synchroni'zation, -s- n.

syndicate ['sindikət] n 1 a council or number of persons who join together to manage a piece of business. 2 a group of newspapers under the same management.

syntax ['sintaks] n (the rules for) the correct arrangement of words in a sentence.

synthesis ['sinθəsis] – pl 'syntheses [-si:z] – n (something produced through) the process of combining separate parts, eg chemical elements or substances, into a whole: *Plastic is produced by synthesis; His recent book is a synthesis of several of his earlier ideas.* 'synthesize, -ise v to make (eg a drug) by synthesis: *Some hormones can be synthesized.*

synthetic [sin'θetik] n, adj (a substance) produced artificially by a chemical process: *nylon and other synthetic materials/synthetics.*

syphon see **siphon**.

syringe [si'rindʒ] n an instrument for sucking up and squirting out liquids, sometimes having a needle for giving injections. – v to clean or wash eg ears using a syringe.

syrup ['sirəp, (Amer) 'sə:-] n 1 water or the juice of fruits boiled with sugar and made thick and sticky. 2 a purified form of treacle.

'**syrupy** adj of, or like, syrup.

system ['sistəm] n 1 an arrangement of many parts that work together: *a railway system; the solar system; the digestive system.* 2 a person's body: *Take a walk every day – it's good for the system!* 3 a way of organizing something according to certain ideas, principles etc: *a system of government/education.* 4 a plan or method: *What is your system for washing the dishes?* 5 the quality of being efficient and methodical: *Your work lacks system.* ,syste'matic [-'matik] adj. ,syste'matically adv.

Tt

T [ti:]: '**T-shirt** (also '**tee shirt**) n a light shirt of knitted cotton etc with short sleeves.

ta [ta:] interj (used esp by or to young children) thank you: *The baby says 'please' and 'ta'.*

tab [tab] n 1 a small flat piece of some material attached to, or part of, something larger, which stands up so that it can be seen, held, pulled etc: *You open the packet by pulling the tab.* 2 a strip of material attached to a piece of clothing by which it can be hung up: *Hang your jacket up by the tab.* 3 a piece of material with a person's name or some other mark on it, attached to a piece of clothing so that its owner can be identified.

tabby ['tabi] – pl 'tabbies – n (also 'tabby-cat) a usu grey or brown cat with darker stripes, esp a female one.

table ['teibl] n 1 a piece of furniture consisting of a flat, horizontal surface on legs used eg to put food on at meals, or for some games: *Put all the plates on the table.* 2 a statement of facts or figures arranged in columns etc: *The results of the experiments can be seen in table 5.* 3 the people sitting at a table: *The whole table heard what he said.* '**tablecloth** n a cloth for covering a table, usu for a meal: *an embroidered tablecloth.*

table linen tablecloths, napkins etc: *They gave us table linen as a wedding present.*

'**tablespoon** n 1 a large spoon, used eg for serving food. 2 a tablespoonful: *Add a tablespoon of sugar.*

'**tablespoonful** n the amount that will fill a tablespoon: *two tablespoonfuls of jam.*

*'table tennis a game played on a table with small bats and a light ball.

lay/set the table to put a tablecloth, plates, knives, forks etc on a table for a meal: *The meal is ready – will you lay the table?*

tablet ['tablit] n 1 a pill: *Take these tablets for your headache; a sleeping-tablet* (= a tablet to make one sleep). 2 a flat piece or bar (of soap etc): *I bought a tablet of soap.* 3 a piece of usu stone with a flat surface on which words are engraved etc: *They put up a marble tablet in memory of his father.*

taboo, tabu [tə'bu:] – pls ta'boos, ta'bus – n, adj (something) forbidden for religious reasons or because it is against social custom: *Alcohol is (a) taboo in Muslim societies.*

tack [tak] n 1 a short nail with a broad flat head: *a carpet-tack.* 2 in sewing, a large, temporary stitch used to hold material together while it is being sewn together properly. 3 in sailing, a movement diagonally against the wind: *We sailed on an easterly tack.* 4 a direction or course: *After they moved, their lives took a different tack.* – v 1 (with **down, on** etc) to fasten (with tacks): *I tacked the carpet down; She tacked the material together.* 2 (of sailing-boats) to move diagonally (backwards and forwards)

* see illustration on p. 206

against the wind: *The boat tacked into harbour.*

tackle ['takl] *n* **1** an act of tackling: *a rugby tackle.* **2** equipment, *esp* for fishing: *fishing tackle.* **3** ropes, pulleys *etc* for lifting heavy weights: *lifting tackle.* **4** in sailing, the ropes, rigging *etc* of a boat. – *v* **1** to try to grasp or seize (someone): *The policeman tackled the thief.* **2** to deal with or try to solve (a problem); to ask (someone) about a problem: *He tackled the problem; She tackled the teacher about her child's work.* **3** in football, hockey *etc*, to (try to) take the ball *etc* from (a player in the other team): *He tackled his opponent.*

tact [takt] *n* care and skill in one's behaviour to people, in order to avoid hurting or offending them: *He showed tact in dealing with difficult customers.*
'tactful *adj* showing tact: *a tactful person; tactful behaviour.* **'tactfully** *adv.* **'tactfulness** *n.*
tactless *adj* without tact: *a tactless person/remark.* **'tactlessly** *adv.* **'tactlessness** *n.*

tactics ['taktiks] *n pl* (*sometimes in sing*) the art of arranging troops, warships *etc* during a battle, order to win or gain an advantage over one's opponents: *They planned their tactics for the election/game/meeting.*
'tactical *adj* of or concerned with tactics or successful planning: *a tactical advantage.*
'tactically *adv.*
tac'tician [-'tiʃən] *n* a person who is good at tactics or successful planning.

tadpole ['tadpoul] *n* a young frog or toad in its first stage of development.

tag [tag] *n* **1** a label: *a price-tag; a name-tag.* **2** a saying or quotation that is often repeated: *a well-known Latin tag.* **3** something small that is added on or attached: *a question-tag such as 'isn't it?'* – *v* – *pt, ptp* **tagged** – to put a tag or label on something: *All the clothes have been tagged.*
tag along (*often with* **behind** *or* **with**) to follow or go (with someone), often when one is not wanted: *We never get away from him – everywhere we go, he insists on tagging along (with us)!*
tag on **1** (*usu with* **at** *or* **to**) to attach (something) to something: *These comments weren't part of his speech – he just tagged them on at the end.* **2** to follow (someone) closely: *The child always tags on to his elder brother.*

tail [teil] *n* **1** the part of an animal, bird or fish that sticks out behind the rest of its body: *The dog wagged its tail; A fish swims by moving its tail.* **2** anything which has a similar function or position: *the tail of an aeroplane/comet.* – *v* to follow closely: *The detectives tailed the thief to the station.*

-tailed having a (certain size, type *etc* of) tail: *a black-tailed duck; a long-tailed dog.*
tails *n, adv* (on) the side of a coin that does not have the head of the sovereign *etc* on it: *He tossed the coin and it came down tails.* – *interj* a call showing that a person has chosen that side of the coin when tossing a coin to make a decision *etc.*
,tail-'end *n* the very end or last part: *the tail-end of the procession.*
'tail-light *n* the (*usu* red) light on the back of a car, train, *etc*: *He followed the tail-lights of the bus.*
tail wind a wind coming from behind: *We sailed home with a tail wind.*
tail off **1** to become fewer, smaller or weaker (at the end): *His interest tailed off towards the end of the film.* **2** (*also* **tail away**) (of voices *etc*) to become quieter or silent: *His voice tailed away into silence.*

tailor ['teilə] *n* a person who cuts and makes suits, overcoats *etc*: *He has his clothes made by a London tailor.* – *v* **1** to make and fit (suits, coats *etc*): *He has his suits tailored in London.* **2** to make (something) fit the circumstances; to adapt: *He tailored his way of living to his income.*
,tailor-'made *adj* **1** (*esp* of women's clothes) made by a tailor to fit a person exactly. **2** very well suited or adapted for some purpose: *His new job seems tailor-made for him.*

taint [teint] *v* **1** to spoil (something) by touching it or bringing it into contact with something bad or rotten: *The meat has been tainted.* **2** to affect (someone or something) with something evil or immoral; to corrupt: *He has been tainted by his contact with criminals.* – *n* a mark or trace of something bad, rotten or evil: *the taint of decay.*
'tainted *adj* spoiled or corrupted: *tainted food; The nation is tainted with evil and corruption.*

take [teik] – *pt* **took** [tuk]; *ptp* **taken** – *v* **1** (*often with* **down, out** *etc*) to reach out for and grasp, hold, lift, pull *etc*: *He took my hand; He took the book down from the shelf; He opened the drawer and took out a gun; I've had a tooth taken out.* **2** (*often with* **away, in, off, out** *etc*) to carry, conduct or lead to another place: *I took the books (back) to the library; He's taking me with him; Take her into my office; The police took him away; I took the dog out for a walk; He took her out for dinner.* **3** to do or perform some action: *I think I'll take a walk; Will you take a look?; to take a bath.* **4** to get, receive, buy, rent *etc*: *I'm taking French lessons; I'll take three kilos of strawberries; We took a house in London.* **5** (*sometimes with* **back**) to agree to have; to accept; *He took my advice; They refused to take respon-*

sibility; *I won't take that* (*insult*) *from you!*; *I'm afraid we can't take back goods bought in a sale*. **6** to need or require: *How long does it take you to go home?*; *It takes time to do a difficult job like this*. **7** to travel by (bus etc): *I'm taking the next train to London*; *I took a taxi*. **8** to have enough space for: *The car takes five people*. **9** to make a note, record etc: *He took a photograph of the castle*; *The nurse took the patient's temperature*. **10** to remove, use, occupy etc with or without permission: *Someone's taken my coat*; *He took all my money*. **11** to consider (as an example): *Take John for example*. **12** to capture or win: *He took the first prize*. **13** (*often with* **away, from, off**) to make less or smaller by a certain amount: *Take* (*away*) *four from ten, and that leaves six*. **14** to suppose or think (that something is the case): *Do you take me for an idiot?* **15** to eat or drink: *Take these pills*. **16** to conduct, lead or run; to be in charge or control of: *Will you take the class/lecture/meeting this evening?* **17** to consider or react or behave to (something) in a certain way: *He took the news calmly*. **18** to feel: *He took pleasure/pride/a delight/an interest in his work*. **19** to go down or go into (a road): *Take the second road on the left*. – *n* **1** the amount of money taken in a day; takings: *What was the take today?* **2** the filming of a single scene in a cinema film: *After five takes, the director was satisfied*.

taker *n* a person who takes (something) *esp* one who accepts an offer or takes a bet: *I offered my friends my car, but there were no takers*.

takings *n pl* the amount of money taken at a concert, in a shop etc: *the day's takings*.

'take-away *n* (*Amer* **'carry-out** *or* **'take-out**) **1** food prepared and bought in a restaurant but taken away and eaten somewhere else eg at home: *I'll go and buy a take-away*; (*also adj*) *a take-away meal*. **2** a restaurant where such food is prepared and bought.

be taken up with to be busy or occupied with: *He's very taken up with his new job*.

be taken with/by to find pleasing or attractive: *He was very taken with the village*.

take after to be like (someone, *esp* a parent or relation) in appearance or character: *She takes after her father*.

take back 1 to make (someone) remember or think about (something): *Meeting my old friends took me back to my childhood*. **2** to admit that what one has said is not true: *Take back what you said about my sister!*

take down to make a note or record of: *He took down her name and address*.

take an examination/test to have one's knowledge or ability tested formally, often in writing.

take (someone) for to believe (mistakenly) that (someone) is (someone or something else): *I took you for your brother*.

take in 1 to include: *Literature takes in drama, poetry and the novel*. **2** to give (someone) shelter: *He had nowhere to go, so I took him in*. **3** to understand and remember: *I didn't take in what he said*. **4** to make (clothes) smaller: *I lost a lot of weight, so I had to take all my clothes in*. **5** to deceive or cheat: *He took me in with his story*.

take it from me (that) you can believe me when I say (that): *Take it from me – it's true*.

take it into one's head (to) to decide (to): *She took it into her head to go to Spain*.

take off 1 to remove (clothes etc): *He took off his coat*. **2** (of an aircraft) to leave the ground: *The plane took off for Rome* (*n* **'take-off**). **3** not to work during (a period of time): *I'm taking tomorrow morning off*. **4** to imitate someone (often unkindly): *He used to take off his teacher to make his friends laugh* (*n* **'take-off**).

take on 1 to agree to do (work etc); to undertake: *He took on the job*. **2** to employ: *They are taking on five hundred more men at the factory*. **3** (*with* **at**) to challenge (someone) to a game etc: *I'll take you on at tennis*. **4** to get; to assume: *His writing took on a completely new meaning*. **5** to allow (passengers) to get on or in: *The bus only stops here to take on passengers*. **6** to be upset: *Don't take on so!*

take it out on to be angry with or unpleasant to because one is angry, disappointed etc oneself: *You're upset, but there's no need to take it out on me!*

take over 1 to take control (of): *He has taken the business over* (*n* **'take-over**). **2** (*often with* **from**) to do (something) after someone else stops doing it: *He retired last year, and I took over* (*his job*) *from him*.

'take to 1 to find acceptable or pleasing: *I soon took to her children/idea*. **2** to begin to do (something) regularly: *He took to smoking a pipe*.

take up 1 to use or occupy (space, time etc): *I won't take up much of your time*. **2** to begin doing, playing etc: *He has taken up the violin/teaching*. **3** to shorten (clothes): *My skirts were too long, so I had them taken up*. **4** to lift or raise; to pick up: *He took up the book*.

take (something) upon oneself to take responsibility for: *I took it upon myself to make sure she arrived safely*.

take (something) up with (someone) to discuss (*esp* a complaint): *Take the matter up with your MP*.

see also **bring**.

talc [talk] *n* **1** a kind of soft mineral that feels like soap. **2** talcum.

    talcum ['talkəm] *n* (*also* **talcum powder**: *often abbrev* **talc**) a kind of fine, *usu* perfumed, powder made from talc, used on the body.

tale [teil] *n* **1** a story: *He told me the tale of his travels.* **2** an untrue story; a lie: *He told me he had a lot of money, but that was just a tale.*

talent ['talənt] *n* a special ability or cleverness; a skill: *a talent for drawing.*

    'talented *adj* (*neg* **un-**) naturally clever or skilful; having or showing great ability: *a talented pianist.*

talk [to:k] *v* **1** to speak; to have a conversation or discussion: *We talked about it for hours*; *My parrot can talk* (=imitate human speech). **2** to gossip: *You can't stay here – people will talk!* **3** to talk about: *They spent the whole time talking philosophy.* – *n* **1** (*sometimes in pl*) a conversation or discussion: *We had a long talk about it*; *The Prime Ministers met for talks on their countries' economic problems.* **2** a lecture: *The doctor gave us a talk on family health.* **3** gossip: *Her behaviour causes a lot of talk among the neighbours.* **4** useless discussion; statements of things a person says he will do but which will never actually be done: *There's too much talk and not enough action.*

    talkative ['to:kətiv] *adj* talking a lot: *a talkative person.*

    'talking-point *n* something to talk about; a subject, *esp* an interesting one: *Football is the main talking-point in my family.*

    talk back (*often with* **to**) to answer rudely: *Don't talk back to me!*

    talk big to talk as if one is very important; to boast: *He's always talking big about his job.*

    talk down to to speak to (someone) as if he/she is much less important, clever *etc*: *Children dislike being talked down to.*

    talk (someone) into/out of (doing) to persuade (someone) (not) to do (something): *He talked me into changing my job.*

    talk over to discuss: *We talked over the whole idea.*

    talk round 1 to persuade: *I managed to talk her round.* **2** to talk about (something) for a long time without reaching the most important point: *We talked round the question for hours.*

    talk sense/nonsense to say sensible, or ridiculous, things: *Don't talk nonsense*; *I do wish you would talk sense.*

    talk shop to talk about one's work: *We agreed not to talk shop at the party.*

tall [to:l] *adj* **1** (of people and thin or narrow objects such as buildings or trees) higher than normal: *a tall man/tree.* **2** (of people) having a particular height: *John is only four feet tall.* **'tallness** *n*.

    a tall order something very difficult to do: *Finding somewhere for fifty children to stay tonight is rather a tall order.*

    a tall story a story which is hard to believe: *He is always telling tall stories.*

> **tall** is used *esp* of people, and of other (narrow) upright objects: *a tall girl, tree, building.*
> **high** is used of objects that are a long way off the ground, or reach a great height: *a high shelf, diving-board, mountain, wall.*

tally ['tali] – *pl* **'tallies** – *n* an account: *He kept a tally of all the work he did.* – *v* (*often with* **with**) to agree or match: *Their stories tally*; *His story tallies with mine.*

talon ['talən] *n* the claw of a bird of prey.

'tamarind ['tamərind] *n* a tropical fruit, a brown pod with a juicy, spicy pulp used in medicines, drinks *etc*.

tambourine [tambə'ri:n] *n* a shallow, one-sided drum with tinkling metal discs in the rim, held in the hand and shaken or beaten.

tame [teim] *adj* **1** (of animals) used to living with people; not wild or dangerous: *He kept a tame bear as a pet.* **2** dull; not exciting: *My job is very tame.* – *v* to make tame: *It is impossible to tame some animals.* **'tamely** *adv*. **'tameness** *n*.

    'tameable *adj* (*neg* **un-**) able to be tamed.

tamper ['tampə] *v* to interfere or meddle *usu* in such a way as to damage, break, alter *etc*: *Don't tamper with the engine.*

tampon ['tampon] *n* a piece of cottonwool *etc* inserted in a wound *etc* to absorb blood.

tan [tan] – *pt*, *ptp* **tanned** – *v* **1** to make an animal's skin into leather (by treating it with certain substances). **2** to (cause a person's skin to) become brown in the sun: *She was tanned by the sun.* – *n, adj* (of) a light brown colour: *tan shoes.* – *n* suntanned skin: *He came back from holiday with a tan.*

    tanned *adj* sunburnt: *a tanned face.*

    'tanner *n* a person who tans leather.

    'tannery – *pl* **'tanneries** – *n* a place where leather is tanned.

tandem ['tandəm] *n* a long bicycle with two seats and two sets of pedals, one behind the other. – *adv* (*usu* of two people on a tandem) one behind the other: *They rode tandem.*

tang [taŋ] *n* a strong or sharp taste, flavour or smell: *The air had a salty tang.*

tangent ['tandʒənt] *n* a line that touches a curve but does not cut it.

    go off at a tangent to go off suddenly in another direction or on a different line of thought, action *etc*: *It is difficult to have a* *sensible conversation with her, as she keeps going off at a tangent.*

tangerine [tandʒə'ri:n] *n* a type of small orange that has a sweet taste and is easily peeled.

tangible ['tandʒəbl] *adj* **1** real or definite: *tangible evidence.* '**tangibly** *adv.* '**tangibility** *n.*

tangle ['taŋgl] *n* an untidy, confused or knotted state: *The child's hair was in a tangle.* – *v* to make or become tangled: *Don't tangle my wool when I'm knitting.*
'**tangled** *adj* in a tangle: *tangled hair/branches; Her hair is always tangled.*
tangle with to become involved in a quarrel or struggle with (a person *etc*): *I tangled with him over politics.*

tango ['taŋgou] – *pl* '**tangos** – *n* (music for) a type of South American dance. – *v* – *3rd pers sing prt* '**tangos**: *pt, ptp* '**tangoed** – to perform this dance.

tank [taŋk] *n* **1** a large container for liquids or gas: *a hot-water/cold-water tank.* **2** a heavy steel-covered vehicle armed with guns.
'**tanker** *n* **1*** a ship or large lorry for carrying oil. **2** an aircraft used to transport fuel *etc.*

tankard ['taŋkəd] *n* a large drinking-mug of metal, glass *etc*: *a beer tankard.*

tantalize, -ise ['tantəlaiz] *v* to tease or torment (a person *etc*) by making him want something he cannot have and by keeping it just beyond his reach: *The expensive clothes in the shop-window tantalized her.*
'**tantalizing, -s-** *adj*: *tantalizing smells in the kitchen.*

tantrum ['tantrəm] *n* a fit of extreme rage, with *eg* shouting and stamping: *That child is always throwing tantrums.*

tap[1] [tap] *n* a quick touch or light knock or blow: *I heard a tap at the door.* – *v* – *pt, ptp* **tapped** – (*often with* **at, on** *or* **with**) to give a light knock (on or with something): *He tapped at/on the window.*
'**tap-dancing** *n* a type of dancing performed with special shoes that make a tapping noise. '**tap-dancer** *n.*

tap[2] [tap] *n* (*Amer* '**faucet**) any of several types of device (*usu* with a handle and valve that can be shut or opened) for controlling the flow of liquid or gas from a pipe, barrel *etc*: *Turn the tap off/on.* – *v* – *pt, ptp* **tapped** – **1** to start using (a source, supply *etc*): *The country has many rich resources that have not been tapped.* **2** to attach a device to (someone's telephone wires) in order to be able to listen to his telephone conversations: *My phone was being tapped.*

tape [teip] *n* **1** (a piece of) a narrow strip or band of cloth used for tying *etc*: *bundles of letters tied with tape.* **2** a piece of this or something similar, *eg* a string, stretched above the finishing line on a race track: *The*

two runners reached the tape together. **3** a narrow strip of paper, plastic, metal *etc* used for sticking materials together, recording sounds *etc*: *adhesive tape; insulating tape; I recorded the concert on tape.* **4** a tape-measure. – *v* **1** to fasten or seal with tape. **2** to record (the sound of something) on tape: *He taped the concert.*
'**tape-measure,** '**measuring-tape** *ns* a length of *eg* plastic, cloth or metal tape, marked with centimetres, metres *etc* for measuring.
'**tape-recorder** *n* a machine which records sounds on magnetic tape and reproduces them when required. '**tape-record** *v.* '**tape-recording** *n.*

taper ['teipə] *n* a long, thin type of candle. – *v* (*sometimes with* **off**) to make or become narrower or slimmer at one end: *The leaves taper (off) to a point.*
'**tapered,** '**tapering** *adjs* becoming narrower or slimmer at one end: *tapering fingers.*

tapestry ['tapəstri] – *pl* '**tapestries** – *n* (a piece of) cloth into which a picture or design has been sewn or woven, hung on a wall for decoration or used to cover *eg* the seats of chairs: *Four large tapestries hung on the walls.*

***tapioca** [tapi'oukə] *n* a type of food obtained from the underground part of the cassava plant.

tar [ta:] *n* any of several kinds of thick, black, sticky material obtained from wood, coal *etc* and used *eg* in roadmaking. – *v* – *pt, ptp* **tarred** – to cover with tar: *The road has just been tarred.*
'**tarry** *adj* of or like tar; covered with tar.

target ['ta:git] *n* **1** a marked board or other object aimed at in shooting practice, competitions *etc* with a rifle, bow and arrow *etc*: *His shots hit the target every time.* **2** any object at which shots, bombs *etc* are directed: *Their target was the royal palace.* **3** a person, thing *etc* against which unfriendly comment or behaviour is directed: *the target of criticism.*

tariff ['tarif] *n* **1** a list of prices or charges *eg* in a hotel: *A copy of the tariff is placed in each bedroom.* **2** (a list of) taxes to be paid on imported or exported goods: *the customs tariff.*

tarmac ['ta:mak] *n* the surface of a road, runway at an airport *etc*: *The plane was waiting on the tarmac.*
tarmacadam [ta:mə'kadəm] *n* a mixture of small stones and tar used for road surfaces *etc.*

tarnish ['ta:niʃ] *v* to (cause a metal to) become dull and stained: *Silver tarnishes easily.* – *n* a dull, stained appearance on a metal surface. '**tarnished** *adj.*

tarpaulin [ta:'pɔ:lin] *n* (a sheet of) a kind of

strong waterproof material: *He covered his car with a (sheet of) tarpaulin.*

arry *see* **tar**.

art¹ [ta:t] *adj* sharp or sour in taste: *These apples taste rather tart.* **'tartly** *adv.* **'tartness** *n.*

art² [ta:t] *n* a pie containing *eg* fruit or jam: *an apple tart.*

artan ['ta:tən] *n* **1** (woollen or other cloth woven with) a pattern of different coloured lines and broader stripes, crossing each other at right angles, *originally* used by clans of the Scottish Highlands. **2** any one pattern of this sort, *usu* associated with a particular clan *etc*: *the Cameron tartan.*

ask [ta:sk] *n* a piece of *esp* hard work; a duty that must be done: *household tasks.*

task force a force selected from the armed services for a special task.

assel ['tasəl] *n* a decoration, consisting of a hanging bunch of threads tied firmly at one end and loose at the other end, put *eg* on a cushion, a hat, a shawl *etc*. **'tasselled** *adj* decorated with tassels: *a tasselled hat.*

aste [teist] *v* **1** to be aware of, or recognize, the flavour of something: *I can taste ginger in this cake.* **2** to test or find out the flavour or quality of (food *etc*) by eating or drinking a little of it: *Please taste this and tell me if it is too sweet.* **3** to have a particular flavour or other quality that is noticed through the act of tasting: *This milk tastes sour; The sauce tastes of garlic.* **4** to eat (food) *esp* with enjoyment: *I haven't tasted such a beautiful curry for ages.* **5** to experience: *He tasted the delights of country life.* – *n* **1** one of the five senses, the sense by which we are aware of flavour: *one's sense of taste; bitter to the taste.* **2** the quality or flavour of anything that is known through this sense: *This wine has an unusual taste.* **3** an act of tasting or a small quantity of food *etc* for tasting: *Do have a taste of this cake!* **4** a liking or preference: *a taste for music; a queer taste in books; expensive tastes.* **5** the ability to judge what is suitable in behaviour, dress *etc* or what is fine and beautiful: *She shows good taste in clothes; a man of taste; That joke was in good/bad taste.* **'tasteful** *adj* showing good judgement or taste: *a tasteful flower arrangement.* **'tastefully** *adv.* **'tastefulness** *n.* **'tasteless** *adj* **1** lacking flavour: *tasteless food.* **2** showing a lack of good taste or judgement: *tasteless behaviour*; **'tastelessly** *adv.* **'tastelessness** *n.* **-tasting** having a (particular kind of) taste: *a sweet-tasting liquid.* **'tasty** *adj* having a good, *esp* savoury, flavour: *tasty food.* **'tastiness** *n.*

ta-ta [ta'ta:] (often used to or by young children) good-bye: *Say ta-ta to Gran.*

tatters ['tatəz] *n pl* torn and ragged pieces: *tatters of clothing.* **'tattered** *adj* ragged or torn: *a tattered cloak/book.* **in tatters** in a torn and ragged condition: *His clothes were in tatters.*

tattoo [tə'tu:, (Amer) ta-] – *3rd pers sing prt* **tat'toos**: *pt, ptp* **tat'tooed** – *v* to make coloured patterns or pictures on part of a person's body by pricking the skin and putting in dyes: *The design was tattooed on his arm.* – *n* – *pl* **tat'toos** – a design tattooed on the skin: *His arms were covered with tattoos.* **tat'tooed** *adj.*

tatty ['tati] *adj* shabby and untidy: *tatty clothes.*

taught *see* **teach**.

taunt [to:nt] *v* to tease, or say unpleasant things to (a person) in a cruel way: *The children at school taunted him for being dirty.* – *n* cruel, unpleasant remarks: *He did not seem to notice their taunts.* **'taunting** *adj.* **'tauntingly** *adv.*

taut [to:t] *adj* pulled tight: *Keep the string taut while you tie a knot in it.* **'tauten** *v* to make or become taut: *The ropes were tautened.*

tawny ['to:ni] *adj* (*usu* of animals' fur *etc*) yellowish-brown.

tax [taks] *n* **1** money, *eg* a percentage of a person's income or of the price of goods *etc* taken by the government to help pay for the running of the state: *income tax; a tax on tobacco.* **2** a strain or burden: *The continual noise was a tax on her nerves.* – *v* **1** to make (a person) pay (a) tax; to put a tax on (goods *etc*): *He is taxed on his income; Alcohol is taxed.* **2** to put a strain on: *Don't tax your strength!* **'taxable** *adj* liable to be taxed: *taxable income/goods.* **tax'ation** *n* the act or system of taxing. **'taxing** *adj* mentally or physically difficult: *a taxing job.* **tax-'free** *adj, adv* without payment of tax: *tax-free income.* **'taxpayer** *n* a citizen who pays taxes.

taxi ['taksi] – *pls* **'taxis, 'taxies** – *n* (*also* **'taxi=cab**: (Amer) **cab**) a car, *usu* fitted with a taximeter, that can be hired with its driver, *esp* for short journeys: *I took a taxi from the hotel to the station.* – *v* – *3rd pers sing prt* **'taxies, 'taxis**: *prps* **'taxiing, 'taxying**: *pt, ptp* **'taxied** – (of an aeroplane) to move slowly along the ground before beginning to run forward for take-off: *The plane taxied along the runway.* **'taximeter** *n* (*usu abbrev* **meter**) an instrument *usu* fitted to taxis to show the fare owed for the distance travelled.

taxi rank a place where taxis stand until hired: *There is a taxi rank at the railway station.*

taxidermy ['taksidə:mi] *n* the art of preparing and stuffing the skins of animals *etc*. '**taxidermist** *n*.

tea [ti:] *n* **1** a type of plant grown in Asia, *esp* India, Ceylon and China, or its dried and prepared leaves: *I bought half a kilo of tea.* **2** a drink made by adding boiling water to these: *Have a cup of tea!* **3** a cup *etc* of tea: *Two teas, please!* **4** a small meal in the afternoon (**afternoon tea**) or a larger one in the early evening, at which tea is often drunk: *She invited him to tea.*

'**tea-bag** a small bag or sachet of thin paper containing tea, on to which boiling water is poured in a pot or cup.

'**teacup** *n* a cup, *usu* of medium size, in which tea is served.

'**tea-party** – *pl* '**tea-parties** – *n* an afternoon party at which tea is *usu* served: *She has been invided to a tea-party.*

'**teapot** *n* a pot with a spout used for making and pouring tea.

'**tearoom** *n* a restaurant where tea, coffee, cakes *etc* are served.

'**tea-set**, '**tea-service** *ns* a set of cups, saucers and plates, sometimes with a teapot and milk-jug.

'**teaspoon** *n* **1** a small spoon for use with a teacup: *I need a teaspoon to stir my tea.* **2** a teaspoonful: *a teaspoon of salt.*

'**teaspoonful** *n* an amount that fills a teaspoon: *two teaspoonfuls of salt.*

'**tea-time** *n* the time in the late afternoon or early evening at which people take tea: *He said he would be back at tea-time.*

'**tea-towel** *n* a cloth for drying dishes after they have been washed *eg* after a meal.

teach [ti:tʃ] – *pt, ptp* **taught** [tɔ:t] – *v* to give knowledge, skill or wisdom to a person; to instruct or train (a person): *She teaches English/the piano; Experience has taught him nothing.*

'**teacher** *n* a person who teaches, *esp* in a school.

teaching *n* **1** the work of teacher: *Teaching is a satisfying job; (also adj) the teaching staff of a school.* **2** guidance or instruction: *She followed her mother's teaching.* **3** something that is taught: *one of the teachings of Christ.*

teak [ti:k] *n* **1** a type of tree that grows in India, Malaysia, Burma *etc*. **2** its very hard wood: *The table is (made of) teak; (also adj) teak furniture.*

team [ti:m] *n* **1** a group of people forming a side in a game: *a football team.* **2** a group of people working together: *A team of doctors.* **3** two or more animals working together *eg*

pulling a cart, plough *etc*: *a team of horses/oxen.*

team spirit willingness of each member of a team or group to work together with loyalty and enthusiasm.

'**team-work** *n* cooperation between those who are working together on a task *etc*.

team up to join with another person in order to do something together: *They teamed up with another family to rent a house for the holidays.*

tear[1] [tiə] *n* a drop of liquid coming from the eye, as a result of emotion (*esp* sadness) or because something (*eg* smoke) has irritated it: *tears of joy/laughter/rage.*

'**tearful** *adj* **1** inclined to cry or weep; with much crying or weeping: *She was very tearful; a tearful farewell.* **2** covered with tears: *tearful faces.* '**tearfully** *adv*. '**tearfulness** *n*.

tear gas a kind of gas causing blinding tears, used against *eg* rioters.

'**tear-stained** *adj* marked with tears: *a tear-stained face.*

in tears crying or weeping: *She was in tears over the broken doll.*

tear[2] [teə] – *pt* **tore** [tɔ:n]: *ptp* **torn** [tɔ:] – *v* **1** (*sometimes with* **off** *etc*) to make a split or hole in (something), intentionally or unintentionally, with a sudden or violent pulling action, or to remove (something) from its position by such an action or movement: *He tore the photograph into pieces; You've torn a hole in your jacket; I tore the picture out of a magazine.* **2** to become torn: *Newspapers tear easily.* **3** to rush: *He tore along the road.* – *n* a hole or split made by tearing: *There's a tear in my dress.*

be torn between (one thing and another) to have a very difficult choice to make between (two things): *He was torn between obedience to his parents and loyalty to his friends.*

tear (oneself) away to leave a place, activity *etc* unwillingly: *I couldn't tear myself away from the television.*

tear one's hair to be in despair with impatience and frustration: *Their inefficiency makes me tear my hair.*

tear up 1 to remove from a fixed position by violence; *The wind tore up several trees.* **2** to tear into pieces: *She tore up the letter.*

tease [ti:z] *v* **1** to annoy or irritate on purpose: *He's teasing the cat.* **2** to annoy or laugh at (a person) playfully: *His schoolfriends tease him about his size.* – *n* a person who enjoys teasing others: *He's a tease!*

'**teaser** *n* **1** a puzzle or difficult problem: *This question is rather a teaser.* **2** a person who teases.

'**teasingly** *adv* in a teasing manner.

teat [ti:t] *n* the part of a female animal's

breast or udder through which milk passes to the young; the nipple.

technical ['teknikəl] *adj* **1** having, or relating to, a particular science or skill, *esp* of a mechanical or industrial kind: *a technical college*; *technical skill*; *technical drawing*. **2** (having many terms) relating to a particular art or science: *'Myopia' is a technical term for 'short-sightedness'.* **3** according to strict laws or rules: *a technical defeat*.
,**techni'cality** [-'ka-] – *pl* ,**techni'calities** – *n* **1** a technical detail or technical term: *Their instructions were full of technicalities.* **2** a (trivial) detail or problem, *eg* caused by (too) strict obedience to laws, rules *etc*: *I'm not going to be put off by mere technicalities.*
'**technically** *adv* **1** in a technical way; *He described the machine in simple terms, then more technically.* **2** as far as skill and technique are concerned: *The pianist gave a very good performance technically, although she seemed to lack feeling for the music.* **3** according to strict obedience to laws or rules: *Technically, you aren't allowed to do that, but I don't suppose anyone will object.*
tech'nician [-'niʃən] *n* a person who has been trained to do something which involves some skill, *eg* with a piece of machinery: *One of our technicians will repair the machine.*

technique [tek'niːk] *n* the way in which a (*usu* skilled) process is, or should be, carried out: *They admired the pianist's faultless technique.*

technology [tek'nolədʒi] – *pl* **tech'nologies** – *n* (the study of) science applied to practical, (*esp* industrial) purposes: *a college of science and technology*. ,**techno'logical** [-'lo-] *adj*. **tech'nologist** *n*.

teddy ['tedi] – *pl* '**teddies** – *n* (*also* **teddy bear**) a child's stuffed toy bear.

tedious ['tiːdiəs] *adj* boring and continuing for a long time: *a tedious speech/speaker*. '**tediously** *adv*. '**tediousness** *n*. '**tedium** *n* boredom; tediousness: *the tedium of a long journey*.

teem [tiːm] *v* **1** (*with* **with**) to be full of: *The pond was teeming with fish*. **2** to rain heavily: *The rain was teeming down.*

teens [tiːnz] *n pl* **1** the years of a person's life between the ages of thirteen and nineteen: *She's in her teens*. **2** the numbers from thirteen to nineteen.
'**teenage** [-eidʒ] *adj* of, or suitable for, people in their teens: *teenage children/clothes/behaviour*.
'**teenager** [-eidʒə] *n* a person in his or her teens.

teeny ['tiːni] *adj* (*also* **teeny-weeny** [tiːni'wiːni]) an informal or child's word for tiny: *There's a teeny little insect crawling up your neck.*

tee shirt *see* **T-shirt** *under* **T**.
teeth, teethe, teething *see* **tooth**.
teetotal [tiː'toutl] *adj* never taking alcoholic drink: *The whole family is teetotal*.
tee'totaller, (*Amer*) **tee'totaler** *n* a person who is teetotal.
telecast ['telikaːst] *n* a television broadcast. – *v* to broadcast on television.
telecommunications ['telikəmjuːni'keiʃənz] *n pl* the science of sending messages, information *etc* by telephone, telegraph, radio, television *etc*.
telegram ['teligram] *n* a message sent by telegraph: *He received a telegram saying that his mother had died.*
telegraph ['teligraːf] *n* **1** a system of sending messages using either wires and electricity or radio: *Send it by telegraph*. **2** an instrument for this: *Send the message on the telegraph.* – *v* **1** to send by telegraph: *He telegraphed the time of his arrival.* **2** to inform by telegraph: *He telegraphed us to say when he would arrive.*
te'legrapher [-'le-], **te'legraphist** [-'le-] *ns* a person who operates a telegraph.
te'legraphy [-'le-] *n* the process, science or skill of sending messages by telegraph. ,**tele'graphic** [-'gra-] *adj*.
telegraph pole a high, wooden pole which supports telegraph wires.
telepathy [tə'lepəθi] *n* the communication of ideas, thoughts *etc* directly from one person's mind to another person's mind without the use of hearing, sight *etc*: *He knew just what I was thinking – it must have been telepathy*.
telepathic [teli'paθik] *adj*. **tele'pathically** *adv*.
te'lepathist *n* a person who studies or practises telepathy.
telephone ['telifoun] *n* (*often abbrev* **phone** [foun]) an instrument for speaking to someone from a distance, using either an electric current which passes along a wire or radio waves: *He spoke to me by telephone/on the telephone*; (*also adj*) *a telephone number/operator*. – (*often abbrev* **phone** [foun]) *v* **1** to (try to) speak to (someone) by means of the telephone: *I'll telephone you tomorrow*. **2** to send (a message) or ask for (something) by means of the telephone: *I'll telephone for a taxi*. **3** to reach or make contact with (another place) by means of the telephone: *Can one telephone England from Australia?*
te'lephonist [-'le-] *n* a person who operates a telephone switchboard in a telephone exchange.
telephone booth, telephone box (*also* '**call-box**) a small room or compartment containing a telephone for public use.
telephone directory a book containing a list

of the names, addresses and telephone numbers of all the people with telephones in a particular area: *Look them up in the telephone directory.*

telephone exchange a central control through which telephone calls are directed.

telephoto [teli'foutou]: **telephoto lens** a photographic lens used for taking photographs from a long distance away.

teleprinter ['teliprintə] *n* telegraph system or instrument by which messages are sent out at one place, and received and printed at another.

telescope ['teliskoup] *n* a kind of tube containing lenses through which distant objects appear closer: *He looked at the ship through his telescope.* – *v* to push or be pushed together so that one part slides inside another, like the parts of a closing telescope: *The crash telescoped the railway coaches.*

,tele'scopic [-'sko-] *adj* 1 of, like, or containing, a telescope: *a telescopic sight on a rifle.* 2 made in parts which can slide inside each other: *a telescopic radio aerial.*

television ['teliviʒən] (*often abbrev* TV [ti:'vi:]) *n* 1 the sending of pictures from a distance, and the reproduction of them on a screen: *We saw it on television.* 2 (*also* **television set**) an apparatus with a screen for receiving these pictures.

'tele**vise** [-vaiz] *v* to send a picture of by television: *The football match was televised.*

tell [tel] – *pt, ptp* **told** [tould] *v* 1 to inform or give information to (a person) about (something): *He told the whole story to John; He told John about it.* 2 to order or command; to suggest or warn: *I told him to go away.* 3 to say or express in words: *to tell lies/the truth/a story.* 4 to distinguish; to see (a difference); to know or decide: *Can you tell the difference between them?; I can't tell one from the other; You can tell if the meat is cooked by/from the colour.* 5 to give away a secret: *You mustn't tell or we'll get into trouble.* 6 to be effective; to be seen to give (good) results: *Good teaching will always tell.*

'tell**er** *n* a person who tells (stories): *a storyteller.*

'tell**ing** *adj* having a great effect: *a telling argument.* 'tell**ingly** *adv.*

'tell**tale** *adj* giving information (often which a person would not wish to be known): *the telltale signs of guilt.*

I told you so I told or warned you that this would happen, had happened *etc*, and I was right: *'I told you so, but you wouldn't believe me.'*

tell off to scold: *The teacher used to tell me off for not doing my homework* (*n* ,tell**ing='off**: *He gave me a good telling-off*).

tell on 1 to have a bad effect on: *Smoking began to tell on his health.* 2 to give information about (a person, *usu* if they are doing something wrong): *I'm late for work – don't tell on me!*

tell tales to give away secret or private information about the (*usu* wrong) actions of others: *You must never tell tales.*

tell the time to (be able to) know what time it is by looking at a clock *etc* or by any other means: *He can tell the time from the position of the sun; Could you tell me the time, please?*

there's no telling it is impossible to know: *There's no telling what he'll do!*

you never can tell it is possible: *It might rain – you never can tell.*

temper ['tempə] *n* 1 a state of mind; a mood or humour: *He's in a bad temper.* 2 a tendency to become (unpleasant when) angry: *He has a terrible temper.* 3 a state of anger: *She's in a temper.* – *v* 1 to bring metal to the right degree of hardness by heating and cooling: *The steel must be carefully tempered.* 2 to soften or make less severe: *One must try to temper justice with mercy.*

-tempered having a (certain) state of mind: *good-tempered; mean-tempered; sweet-tempered.*

keep one's temper not to lose one's temper: *He was very annoyed but he kept his temper.*

lose one's temper to show anger: *He lost his temper and shouted at me.*

temperament ['tempərəmənt] *n* a person's natural way of thinking, behaving *etc*: *She has a sweet/nervous temperament.*

,tempera'mental [-'men-] *adj* emotional; excitable; showing quick changes of mood. ,tempera'mentally [-'men-] *adv* 1 by or according to one's temperament: *She is temperamentally unsuited to this job.* 2 excitably: *She behaved very temperamentally yesterday.*

temperate ['tempərət] *adj* (of climate) neither too hot nor too cold.

temperature ['temprətʃə] *n* 1 the amount or degree of cold or heat: *The food must be kept at a low temperature.* 2 a level of body heat that is higher than normal: *She had a temperature and wasn't feeling well.*

take someone's temperature to measure a person's body heat, using a thermometer.

tempest ['tempist] *n* a violent storm, with very strong winds: *A tempest arose and they were drowned at sea.*

tempestuous [tem'pestjuəs] *adj* 1 (of a person, behaviour *etc*) violently emotional; passionate: *a tempestuous argument/relationship.* 2 very stormy; of or like a tempest: *tempestuous winds.*

tem'pestuously *adv.* tem'pestuousness *n.*

temple¹ ['templ] *n* a building in which people worship, *usu* as part of a non-Christian religion: *a Greek/Hindu temple.*

temple² ['templ] *n* either of the flat parts of the head at the side of the forehead: *The stone hit him on the temple.*

tempo ['tempou] – *pls* 'tempos, (*music*) 'tempi [-pi:] – *n* the speed at which a piece of music should be or is played.

temporary ['tempərəri] *adj* lasting, acting, used *etc* for a (short) time only: *a temporary job; He made a temporary repair.* 'temporarily *adv.* 'temporariness *n.*

tempt [tempt] *v* to (try to) persuade or attract to do something; to make (someone) want to do (something): *The sunshine tempted them* (*to go*) *out.*
  temp'tation *n* **1** the act of tempting: *the temptation of Christ* (*by the Devil*). **2** something that tempts: *He was surrounded by temptations.*
  'tempter – *fem* 'temptress – *n* a person who tempts.
  'tempting *adj* attractive: *That cake looks tempting.* 'temptingly *adv.*
  be tempted (to do something) to think that it would be pleasant, interesting *etc* to do (something): *I'm tempted to go to the party.*

ten [ten] *n* **1** the number or figure 10. **2** the age of 10. – *adj* **1** 10 in number. **2** aged 10.
  ten- having ten (of something): *a ten-pound fine.*
  tenth *n* **1** one of ten equal parts. **2** (*also adj*) the last of ten (people, things *etc*); the next after the ninth.
  ten-pin bowling *n* a game in which a ball is rolled at ten skittles in order to knock down as many as possible.
  'ten-year-old *n* a person or animal that is ten years old. – *adj* (of a person, animal or thing) that is ten years old.

tenant ['tenənt] *n* a person who pays rent to another for the use of a house, building, land *etc*: *That man is a tenant of the estate*; (*also adj*) *tenant farmers.*
  'tenanted *adj* (*neg* un-) occupied; lived in: *a tenanted house.*

tend¹ [tend] *v* to take care of; to look after: *A shepherd tends his sheep.*
  'tender *n* **1** a person who looks after something: *a bartender.* **2** a small boat which carries stores or passengers to and from a larger boat.

tend² [tend] *v* **1** to be likely (to do something); to do (something) frequently: *Plants tend to die in hot weather; He tends to get angry.* **2** to move, lean or slope in a certain direction: *This bicycle tends to*(*wards*) *the left.*
  'tendency – *pl* 'tendencies – *n* likelihood; inclination: *He has a tendency to forget things.*

tender¹ ['tendə] *adj* **1** soft; not hard or tough: *The meat is tender.* **2** sore; painful when touched: *His injured leg is still tender.* **3** loving; gentle: *She had a tender heart.* 'tenderness *n.*
  'tenderly *adv* in a loving and gentle manner: *He kissed her tenderly.*
  ,tender-'hearted *adj* kind and sympathetic; easily made to feel pity. ,tender-'heartedness *n.*

tender² *see* tend¹.

tendon ['tendən] *n* a strong cord joining a muscle to a bone *etc*: *He has damaged a tendon in his leg.*

*** tennis** ['tenis] *n* (*also* lawn tennis) a game for two or four players who use rackets to hit a ball to each other over a net stretched across a tennis-court: *Let's play* (*a game of*) *tennis;* (*also adj*) *a tennis match.*
  'tennis-court *n* a specially-marked area on which tennis is played.
  'tennis-racket *n* a racket with which one plays tennis.

tenor ['tenə] *n* (a man with) a singing voice of the highest normal pitch for an adult male.

tense¹ [tens] *n* a form of a verb that shows the time of its action in relation to the time of speaking: *a verb in the past/future/present tense.*

tense² [tens] *adj* **1** strained; nervous: *The crowd was tense with excitement; a tense situation.* **2** tight; tightly stretched. – *v* to make or become tense: *He tensed his muscles.* 'tensely *adv.* 'tenseness *n.*
  'tension [-ʃən] *n* **1** the state of being stretched, or the degree to which something is stretched: *the tension of the rope.* **2** mental strain; anxiety: *She is suffering from nervous tension; the tensions of modern life.*

tent [tent] *n* a movable shelter made of canvas or other material, supported by poles or a frame and fastened to the ground with ropes and pegs: *When we go on holiday, we usually sleep in a tent.*

tentacle ['tentəkl] *n* a long, thin, flexible arm-like or horn-like part of an animal, used to feel, grasp *etc*: *An octopus has eight tentacles.*

tenterhooks ['tentəhuks]: be on tenterhooks to be uncertain and anxious about what is going to happen: *He was on tenterhooks about the result of the exam.*

tenth *see* ten.

tepid ['tepid] *adj* **1** slightly or only just warm; lukewarm: *tepid water.* **2** not very enthusiastic: *a tepid welcome.* 'tepidly *adv.* 'tepidness, te'pidity *ns.*

term [tə:m] *n* **1** a (*usu* limited) period of time: *a term of imprisonment; a term of office.* **2** a division of a school or university year: *the autumn term.* **3** a word or expression: *Myopia is a medical term for short-sightedness.*

* see illustration on p. 206

terms *n pl* **1** the rules or conditions of an agreement or bargain: *They had a meeting to arrange terms for an agreement.* **2** fixed charges (for work, service *etc*): *The firms sent us a list of their terms.* **3** a relationship between people: *They are on bad/friendly terms.* – *v* to name or call: *That kind of painting is termed 'abstract'.*

come to terms 1 to reach an agreement or understanding: *They came to terms with the enemy.* **2** to find a way of living with or tolerating (some personal trouble or difficulty): *He managed to come to terms with his illness.*

in terms of using as a means of expression, a means of assessing value *etc*: *He thought of everything in terms of money.*

terminate ['tə:mineit] *v* to bring or come to an end or limit: *She terminated the conversation.* **termi'nation** *n*.

terminal ['tə:minəl] *n* **1** a building containing the arrival and departure areas for passengers at an airport or one in the centre of a city or town where passengers can buy tickets for air travel *etc* and can be transported by bus *etc* to an airport: *an air terminal.* **2** a *usu* large station at either end of a railway line, or one for long-distance buses: *a bus terminal.* **3** in an electric circuit, a point of connection to a battery *etc*: *the positive/negative terminal.* **4** a device linked to a computer by which the computer can be operated. – *adj* (of an illness *etc*) in the final stage before death: *This ward is for patients with terminal cancer.* **'terminally** *adv*.

terminology [tə:mi'nolədʒi] – *pl* **termi'nologies** – *n* the special words or phrases used in a particular art, science *etc*: *legal terminology*; *Every science has its own terminology.* **,termino'logical** *adj*.

terminus ['tə:minəs] *n* an end, *esp* of a railway or bus route: *I get off at the bus terminus.*

termite ['tə:mait] *n* a pale-coloured wood-eating kind of insect, like an ant.

terrace ['terəs] *n* **1** (one of a number of) raised level banks of earth *etc*, like large steps, on the side of a hill *etc*: *Vines are grown on terraces on the hillside.* **2** a row of houses connected to each other. – *v* to make into a terrace or terraces: *The hillside has been terraced to make new vineyards.*

terrible ['terəbl] *adj* **1** very bad: *a terrible singer*; *That music is terrible!* **2** causing great pain, suffering, hardship *etc*: *War is terrible*; *It was a terrible disaster.* **3** causing great fear or horror: *The noise of the guns was terrible.*

'terribly *adv* **1** very: *She is terribly clever.* **2** in a terrible way: *Does your leg hurt terribly?*

terrier ['teriə] *n* any of several breeds of small dog: *a fox-terrier.*

terrify ['terifai] *v* to make very frightened: *She was terrified by his appearance.*

terrific [tə'rifik] *adj* **1** marvellous; wonderful: *a terrific party.* **2** very great, powerful *etc*: *He gave the ball a terrific kick.*

terrifically [tə'rifikəli] *adv* very (much): *She enjoyed herself terrifically.*

'terrified *adj*: *The terrified little girl screamed.*

'terrifying *adj*.

territory ['teritəri] – *pl* **'territories** – *n* **1** a stretch of land; a region: *They explored the territory around the North Pole.* **2** the land under the control of a ruler or state: *British territory.* **3** an area of interest, knowledge *etc*: *Ancient history is outside my territory.* **,terri'torial** [-'to:-] *adj* of or belonging to (*esp* national) territory: *territorial rights/claims.*

territorial waters the sea close to a country, considered to belong to it.

terror ['terə] *n* **1** very great fear: *She screamed with/in terror*; *She has a terror of spiders.* **2** something which makes one very afraid: *The terrors of war.* **3** a troublesome person, *esp* a child: *That child is a real terror!*

'terrorism *n* the actions or methods of terrorists: *international terrorism.*

'terrorist *n* a person who tries to frighten people or governments into doing what he/she wants by using or threatening violence: *The plane was hijacked by terrorists*; (*also adj*) *terrorist activities.*

'terrorize, -ise *v* to make very frightened by using or threatening violence: *A lion escaped from the zoo and terrorized the whole town.* **,terrori'zation, -s-** *n*.

'terror-stricken *adj* feeling very great fear: *The children were terror-stricken.*

tertiary ['tə:ʃəri] *adj* of or at a third level, degree, stage *etc*: *Tertiary education follows secondary education.*

test [test] *n* **1** a set of questions or exercises intended to find out a person's ability, knowledge *etc*; a short examination: *an arithmetic/driving test.* **2** something done to find out whether a thing is good, strong, efficient *etc*: *a blood test.* **3** an event, situation *etc* that shows how good or bad something is: *a test of his courage.* **4** a way to find out if something exists or is present: *a test for radioactivity.* **5** a test match. – *v* to carry out a test or tests on (someone or something): *The students were tested on their French*; *They tested the new aircraft.*

test match in cricket, (one of) a series of matches between teams from two countries.

test pilot a pilot who tests new aircraft.

'test-tube *n* a glass tube closed at one end, used in chemical tests or experiments.

testament ['testəmənt] *n* a written statement *esp* of what one wants to be done with one's personal property after one dies: *This is his last will and testament.*

Old Testament, New Testament the two main parts of the Bible.

testicle ['testikl] *n* (*usu in pl*) one of the two glands in the male body in which sperm is produced.

testify ['testifai] *v* **1** to give evidence, *esp* in a law court: *He agreed to testify on behalf of/against the accused man.* **2** to show or give evidence of; to state that (something) is so: *I will testify to her kindness.*

testimony ['testiməni] – *pl* **'testimonies** – *n* the statement(s) made by a person or people who testify in a law-court; evidence: *The jury listened to his testimony.*

testi'monial ['mouniəl] *n* a (written) statement saying what one knows about a person's character, abilities *etc*: *When applying for a job, one usually needs a testimonial from one's last employer.*

tetanus ['tetənəs] *n* a type of serious disease, caused by an infected wound *etc*, in which certain muscles (*esp* of the jaw) become stiff.

tether ['teðə] *n* a rope or chain for tying an animal to a post *etc*: *He put a tether on his horse.* – *v* to tie with a tether: *He tethered the goat to the post.*

text [tekst] *n* **1** in a book, the written or printed words, as opposed to the illustrations, notes *etc*: *First the text was printed, then the drawings added.* **2** a passage from the Bible about which a sermon is preached: *He preached on a text from St John's gospel.*

'textbook *n* a book used in teaching, giving the main facts about a subject: *a history textbook.*

textile ['tekstail] *n* a cloth or fabric made by weaving: *woollen textiles*; (*also adj*) *the textile industry.*

texture ['tekstjuə] *n* **1** the way something feels when touched, eaten *etc*: *the texture of wood, stone, skin etc.* **2** the way that a piece of cloth looks or feels, caused by the way in which it is woven: *the loose texture of this material.*

than [ðən, ðan] *conj, prep* a word used in comparisons: *It is easier than I thought*; *I sing better than he does*; *He sings better than me.*

thank [θaŋk] *v* to express appreciation or gratitude to (someone) for a favour, service, gift *etc*: *He thanked me for the present*; *She thanked him for inviting her.*

'thankful *adj* grateful; relieved and happy: *He was thankful that the journey was over*; *a thankful sigh.* **'thankfully** *adv.* **'thankfulness** *n.*

'thankless *adj* for which no-one is grateful: *Collecting taxes is a thankless task.* **'thanklessly** *adv.* **'thanklessness** *n.*

thanks *n pl* expression(s) of gratitude: *I really didn't expect any thanks for helping them.* – *interj* thank you: *Thanks (very much) for your present*; *Thanks a lot!*; *No, thanks*; *Yes, thanks.*

'thanksgiving *n* the act of giving thanks, *esp* to God, *eg* in a church service: *a service of thanksgiving.*

Thanks'giving *n* (*also* **Thanksgiving Day**) in the US, a special day (the fourth Thursday in November) for giving thanks to God.

thanks to because of: *Thanks to the bad weather, our journey was very uncomfortable.*

thank you I thank you: *Thank you (very much) for your present*; *No, thank you.*

that [ðat] – *pl* **those** [ðouz] – *adj* used to indicate a person, thing *etc* spoken of before, not close to the speaker, already known to the speaker and listener *etc*: *Don't take this book – take that one*; *At that time, I was living in Italy*; *When are you going to return those books?* – *pron* used to indicate a thing *etc*, or (*in pl* or with the verb **be**) person or people, spoken of before, not close to the speaker, already known to the speaker and listener *etc*: *What is that you've got in your hand?*; *Who is that?*; *That is the Prime Minister*; *Those present at the concert included the composer and his wife.* – [ðət, ðat] *relative pron* used to refer to a person, thing *etc* mentioned in a preceding clause in order to distinguish it from others: *Where is the parcel that arrived this morning?*; *Who is the man (that) you were talking to?* – [ðət, ðat] *conj* **1** (often omitted) used to report what has been said *etc* or to introduce other clauses giving facts, reasons, results *etc*: *I know (that) you didn't do it*; *I was surprised (that) he had gone.* **2** used to introduce expressions of sorrow, wishes *etc*: *That I should be accused of murder!*; *Oh, that I were with her now!* – [ðat] *adv* so; to such an extent: *I didn't realize she was that ill.*

like that in that way: *Don't hold it like that – you'll break it!*

that's that an expression used to show that a decision has been made, that something has been completed, made impossible *etc*: *He has said that we can't do it, so that's that.*

thatch [θatʃ] *n* straw, rushes *etc* used as a roofing material for houses. – *v* to cover the roof of (a house) with thatch.

thatched *adj* covered with thatch: *thatched cottages.*

that'd ['ðatəd], **that'll** ['ðatl], **that's** [ðats] short for **that had/that would, that will, that is.**

thaw [θɔ:] v **1** (of ice, snow etc) to melt, or make or become liquid: *The snow thawed quickly.* **2** (of frozen food etc) to make or become unfrozen: *Frozen food must be thawed before cooking.* – n (the time of) the melting of ice and snow at the end of winter, or the change of weather that causes this: *The thaw has come early this year.*

the [ðə, ði] adj (The form [ðə] is used before words beginning with a consonant eg *the house* [ðə haus] or consonant sound eg *the union* [ðə 'ju:njən]; the form [ði] is used before words beginning with a vowel eg *the apple* [ði 'apl] or vowel sound eg *the honour* [ði 'onə]). **1** used to refer to a person, thing etc mentioned previously, described in a following phrase, or already known: *Where is the book I put on the table?; Who was the man you were talking to?; My mug is the tall blue one; Switch the light off!* **2** used with a singular noun or an adjective to refer to all members of a group etc or to a general type of object, group of objects etc: *The horse is a beautiful animal; I spoke to him on the telephone; He plays the piano/violin very well.* **3** used to refer to unique objects etc, esp in titles and names: *the Duke of Edinburgh; the Atlantic (Ocean).* **4** used after a preposition with words referring to a unit of quantity, time etc: *In this job we are paid by the hour.* **5** used with superlative adjectives and adverbs to denote a person, thing etc which is or shows more of something than any other: *He is the kindest man I know; We like him (the) best of all.* **6** (often with **all**) used with comparative adjectives to show that a person, thing etc is better, worse etc: *He has had a week's holiday and looks (all) the better for it.*
the..., the... (with comparative adjs or advs) used to show the connection or relationship between two actions, states, processes etc: *The harder you work, the more you earn.*

theatre, (Amer) **theater** ['θiətə] n **1** a place where plays, operas etc are publicly performed. **2** plays in general; any theatre: *Are you going to the theatre tonight?* **3** (also **'operating-theatre**) a room in a hospital where surgical operations are performed: *Take the patient to the theatre; (also adj) a theatre nurse.*
the'atrical [-'a-] adj **1** of theatres or acting: *a theatrical performance/career.* **2** (behaving) as if in a play; over-dramatic: *theatrical behaviour.* **the'atrically** adv.
the,atri'cality [θiatri'ka-] n.
the'atricals [-'a-] n pl dramatic performances: *He's very interested in amateur theatricals.*
the theatre 1 the profession of actors: *He's in the theatre.* **2** drama: *His special interest is the theatre.*

thee [ði:] pron an old word for 'you' used only when addressing one person, esp God (usu **Thee**), as the object of a verb: *We thank Thee for Thy goodness.*

theft [θeft] n (an act of) stealing: *He was jailed for theft.*

their [ðeə] adj **1** belonging to them: *This is their car; Take a note of their names and addresses.* **2** used instead of **his, his or her** etc where a person of unknown sex or people of both sexes are referred to: *Everyone should buy their own ticket.*
theirs [ðeəz] pron a person, thing etc belonging to them: *The child is theirs; a friend of theirs* (= one of their friends).

them [ðəm, ðem] pron (used as the object of verb or preposition) **1** people, animals, things etc already spoken about, being pointed out etc: *Let's invite them to dinner; What will you do with them?* **2** used instead of **him, him or her** etc where a person of unknown sex or people of both sexes are referred to: *If anyone touches that, I'll hit them.*
them'selves pron **1** used as the object of a verb or preposition when people, animals etc are the object of actions they perform: *They hurt themselves; They looked at themselves in the mirror.* **2** used to emphasize **they, them** or the names of people, animals etc: *They themselves did nothing wrong.* **3** without help etc: *They decided to do it themselves.*

theme [θi:m] n **1** the subject of a discussion, essay etc: *The theme for tonight's talk is education.* **2** in a piece of music, the main melody, which may be repeated often.

then [ðen] adv **1** at that time in the past or future: *I was at school then; If you're coming next week, I'll see you then.* **2** used with prepositions to mean that time in the past or future: *John should be here by then; I'll need you before then; I have been ill since then; Until then; Goodbye till then!* **3** after that: *I had a drink, (and) then I went home.* **4** in that case: *He might not give us the money and then what would we do?* **5** often used esp at the end of sentences in which an explanation, opinion etc is asked for, or which show surprise etc: *What do you think of that, then?* **6** also; in addition: *I have two brothers, and then I have a cousin in America.* – conj in that case; as a result: *If you're tired, than you must rest.* – adj at that time (in the past): *the then Prime Minister.*

theology [θi'olədʒi] n the study of God and religious belief. **,theo'logical** [-'lo-] adj. **theo'logically** [-'lo-] adv. **,theo'logian** [-'loudʒiən] n a person who studies, or is an expert in, theology.

theorem ['θiərəm] n esp in mathematics, something that has been or must be proved to be true by careful reasoning: *a geometri-cal theorem.*

theory ['θiəri] – *pl* '**theories** – *n* **1** an idea or explanation which has not yet been proved to be correct: *There are many theories about the origin of life*; *In theory, I agree with you, but it would not work in practice.* **2** the main principles and ideas in an art, science *etc* as opposed to the practice of actually doing it: *A musician has to study both the theory and practice of music.* ,**theo'retical** [-'reti-] *adj.* ,**theo'retically** [-'reti-] *adv.*

'**theorize, -ise** *v* to make theories: *He did not know what had happened, so he could only theorize about it.* '**theorist** *n.*

therapy ['θerəpi] *n* the (methods of) treat-ment of disease, disorders of the body *etc*: *speech therapy*; *physiotherapy.* '**therapist** *n.*

therapeutic [θerə'pjuːtik] *adj* of or concern-ing the healing and curing of disease: *thera-peutic treatment/exercises.*

there [ðeə, ðə] *adv* **1** (at, in, or to) that place: *He lives there*; *Don't go there.* **2** used to introduce sentences in which a state, fact *etc* is being announced: *There has been an accident at the factory*; *There seems to be something wrong*; *I don't want there to be any mistakes in this.* **3** at that time; at that point in a speech, argument *etc*: *There I cannot agree with you*; *Don't stop there – tell me what happened next!* **4** (with the subject of the sentence following the verb except when it is a pronoun) used at the beginning of a sentence, *usu* with **be** or **go**, to draw attention to, or point out, someone or something: *There she goes now! There it is!* **5** (*placed immediately after noun*) used for emphasis or to point out someone or something: *That book there is the one you need.* – *interj* **1** used to calm or comfort: *There, now. Things aren't as bad as they seem.* **2** used when a person has been shown to be correct, when something bad hap-pens, or when something has been com-pleted: *There! I told you he would do it!*; *There! That's that job done*; *There! I said you would hurt yourself!*

,**therea'bout(s)** *adv* approximately in that place, of that number, at that time *etc*: *a hundred or thereabouts*; *at three o'clock or thereabouts.*

therefore ['ðeəfɔː] *adv* for that reason: *He worked hard, and therefore he was able to save money.*

there's [ðeəz] short for **there is.**

thermal ['θəːməl] *adj* of heat: *thermal springs* (= natural springs of warm or hot water); *thermal units.*

thermometer [θə'mɒmitə] *n* an instrument (*usu* a thin, glass tube with *eg* mercury in it) used for measuring temperature, *esp* body temperature: *The nurse took his temper-ature with a thermometer.*

Thermos (flask)® ['θəːməs(flaːsk)] *n* a type of vacuum-flask: *He had some tea in a Ther-mos (flask).*

thermostat ['θəːməstat] *n* an apparatus which automatically controls the temperature of a room, of water in a boiler *etc* by switching a heater or heating system on or off.

,**thermo'static** *adj* using a thermostat: *thermostatic control.* ,**thermo'statically** *adv.*

thesaurus [θi,sɔːrəs] *n* a book which gives information (*eg* a dictionary or encyclo-pedia) *esp* one which lists words according to their meanings.

these *see* **this.**

thesis ['θiːsis] – *pl* '**theses** [-siːz] – *n* a long written essay, report *etc*, often done for a university degree: *a doctoral thesis*; *He is writing a thesis on the works of John Milton.*

they [ðei] *pron* used only as the subject of a verb) **1** persons, animals or things already spoken about, being pointed out *etc*: *They are in the garden.* **2** used instead of **he, he or she** *etc* when the person's sex is unknown or when people of both sexes are being re-ferred to: *If anyone does that, they are to be severely punished.*

they'd *see* **have, would.**

they'll *see* **will.**

they're *see* **be.**

they've *see* **have.**

thick [θik] *adj* **1** having a relatively large distance between opposite sides; not thin: *a thick book*; *thick walls*; *thick glass.* **2** having a certain distance between opposite sides: *It's two inches thick*; *a two-inch-thick pane of glass.* **3** (of liquids, mixtures *etc*) con-taining solid matter; not flowing (easily) when poured: *thick soup.* **4** made of many single units placed very close together; dense: *a thick forest*; *thick hair.* **5** difficult to see through: *thick fog.* **6** full of, covered with *etc*: *The room was thick with dust*; *The air was thick with smoke.* **7** stupid: *Don't be so thick!* – *n* the thickest, most crowded or active part: *in the thick of the forest*; *in the thick of the fight.*

'**thickly** *adv.* '**thickness** *n.*

'**thicken** *v* to make or become thick or thicker: *We'll add some flour to thicken the soup*; *The fog thickened and we could no longer see the road.*

,**thick-'skinned** *adj* not easily hurt by criti-cism or insults: *You won't upset her – she's very thick-skinned.*

thick and fast frequently and in large num-bers: *The bullets/insults were flying thick and fast.*

through thick and thin whatever happens; in spite of all difficulties: *They were friends through thick and thin.*

thicket ['θikit] *n* a group of trees or bushes growing closely together: *He hid in a thicket.*

thief [θiːv] – *pl* **thieves** [θiːvs] – *n* a person who steals: *The thief got away with all my money.*

thieve [θiːf] *v* to steal: *He is always thieving my pencils.*

thigh [θai] *n* the part of the leg between the knee and hip.

thimble ['θimbl] *n* a kind of metal or plastic cap to protect the finger and push the needle when sewing.

thin [θin] *adj* **1** having a short distance between opposite sides: *thin paper*; *The walls of these houses are too thin.* **2** (of people or animals) not fat: *She looks thin since her illness.* **3** (of liquids, mixtures *etc*) not containing any solid matter; rather lacking in taste; (tasting as if) containing a lot of water or too much water: *thin soup.* **4** not set closely together; not dense or crowded: *His hair is getting rather thin.* **5** not convincing or believable: *a thin excuse.* – *v* – *pt, ptp* **thinned** – to make or become thin or thinner: *The crowd thinned after the parade was over.*

'thinly *adv.* **'thinness** *n.*

thin air nowhere: *He disappeared into thin air.*

thin-'skinned *adj* sensitive; easily hurt or upset: *Be careful what you say – she's very thin-skinned.*

thin out to make or become less dense or crowded: *The trees thinned out near the river.*

thine *see* **thy**.

thing [θiŋ] *n* **1** an object; something that is not living: *What do you use that thing for?* **2** a person, *esp* a person one likes: *She's a nice old thing.* **3** any fact, quality, idea *etc* that one can think of or refer to: *Music is a wonderful thing*; *I hope I haven't done the wrong thing*; *That was a stupid thing to do.*

things *n pl* things, *esp* clothes, that belong to someone: *Take all your wet things off.*

first thing (**in the morning** *etc*) early in the morning just after getting up, starting work *etc*: *I'll do it first thing (in the morning).*

last thing (**at night** *etc*) late at night, just before stopping work, going to bed *etc*: *She always has a cup of tea last thing at night.*

the thing is ... the important fact or question is; the problem is: *The thing is, is he going to help us?*

think [θiŋk] – *pt, ptp* **thought** [θɔːt] – *v* **1** (*often with* **about**) to have or form ideas in one's mind: *Can babies think?*; *I was thinking about my mother.* **2** to have or form opinions in one's mind; to believe: *He thinks (that) the world is flat*; *What do you think of his poem?*; *What do you think about*

his suggestion?; *He thought me very stupid.* **3** to intend or plan (to do something), *usu* without making a final decision: *I must think what to do*; *I was thinking of/about going to London next week.* **4** to imagine or expect: *I never thought to see you again*; *Little did he think that I would be there as well.* – *n* the act of thinking: *Go and have a think about it.*

'thinker *n* a person who thinks, *esp* deeply and constructively: *He's one the world's great thinkers.*

-thought-out planned: *a well-thought-out campaign.*

think better of 1 to think again and decide not to; to reconsider: *He was going to ask for more money, but he thought better of it.* **2** to think that (someone) could not be so bad *etc*: *I thought better of you than to suppose you would do that.*

think highly, well, badly *etc* **of** to have a good, or bad, opinion of: *She thought highly of him and his poetry.*

think little of/not think much of to have a very low opinion of: *He didn't think much of what I had done*; *He thought little of my work.*

think of 1 to remember to do (something); to keep in one's mind; to consider: *You always think of everything!*; *Have you thought of the cost involved?* **2** to remember: *I couldn't think of her name when I met her at the party.* **3** (*with* **would, should, not, never** *etc*) to be willing to do (something): *I would never think of being rude to her*; *He couldn't think of leaving her.*

think out to plan; to work out in the mind: *He thought out the whole operation.*

think over to think carefully about; to consider all aspects of (an action, decision *etc*): *He thought it over, and decided not to go.*

think twice (*often with* **about**) to hesitate before doing (something); to decide not to do (something one was intending to do): *I would think twice about going, if I were you.*

think up to invent; to devise: *He thought up a new process.*

think the world of to be very fond of: *He thinks the world of his wife.*

third [θəːd] *n* **1** one of three equal parts. **2** (*also adj*) the last of three (people, things *etc*); the next after the second. – *adv* in the third position: *John came first in the race, and I came third.*

'thirdly *adv* in the third place: *Firstly, I haven't enough money*; *secondly, I'm too old*; *and thirdly it's raining.*

third-'class *adj, adv* of or in the class next after or below the second.

third degree a severe method of questioning

people, sometimes using torture *etc*: *The police gave him the third degree.*

third party a third person who is not directly involved in an action, contract *etc*: *Was there a third party present when you and she agreed to the sale?*

,third-'rate *adj* of very bad quality: *a third-rate performance.*

the Third World the developing countries, those not part of or aligned with the two main powers: *the needs of the Third World.*

thirst [θəːst] *n* **1** a feeling of dryness (in the mouth) caused by a lack of water or moisture: *I have a terrible thirst.* **2** a strong and eager desire for something: *thirst for knowledge.* – *v* to have a great desire for: *He's thirsting for revenge.*

'thirsty *adj* **1** suffering from thirst: *I'm so thirsty – I must have a drink.* **2** causing a thirst: *Digging the garden is thirsty work.* **'thirstily** *adv*. **'thirstiness** *n*.

thirteen [θəːˈtiːn] *n* **1** the number or figure 13. **2** the age of 13. – *adj* **1** 13 in number. **2** aged 13.

thirteen- having thirteen (of something): *a thirteen-year campaign.*

,thir'teenth *n* **1** one of thirteen equal parts. **2** (*also adj*) the last of thirteen (people, things *etc*); the next after the twelfth.

,thir'teen-year-old *n* a person or animal that is thirteen years old. – *adj* (of a person, animal or thing) that is thirteen years old.

thirty [ˈθəːti] *n* **1** the number or figure 30. **2** the age of 30. – *adj* **1** 30 in number. **2** aged 30.

'thirties *n pl* **1** the period of time between one's thirtieth and fortieth birthdays. **2** the range of temperatures between thirty and forty degrees. **3** the period of time between the thirtieth and fortieth years of a century. **'thirtieth** *n* **1** one of thirty equal parts. **2** (*also adj*) the last of thirty (people, things *etc*); the next after the twenty-ninth.

thirty- having thirty (of something): *a thirty-pound fine.*

'thirty-year-old *n* a person or animal that is thirty years old. – *adj* (of a person, animal or thing) that is thirty years old.

this [ðis] – *pl* **these** [ðiːz] – *adj* **1** used to indicate a person, thing *etc* nearby or close in time: *This book is better than that (one); I prefer these trousers.* **2** used in stories to indicate a person, thing *etc* that one is describing or about to describe: *Then this man arrived.* – *pron* used for a thing *etc* or a person nearby or close in time: *Read this – you'll like it; This is my friend John Smith.* – *adv* so; to this degree: *I didn't think it would be this easy.*

like this in this way: *It would be quicker if you did it like this.*

tho' [ðou] short for **though**.

thorn [θɔːn] *n* a hard, sharp point sticking out from the stem of certain plants: *She pricked her finger on a thorn.*

'thorny *adj* **1** full of or covered with thorns: *a thorny branch.* **2** difficult, causing trouble *etc*: *a thorny problem.*

thorough [ˈθʌrə, (*Amer*) ˈθəːrou] *adj* **1** (of a person) very careful; attending to every detail: *a thorough worker.* **2** (of a task *etc*) done with a suitably high level of care, attention to detail *etc*: *His work is very thorough.* **3** complete; absolute: *a thorough waste of time.*

'thoroughly *adv* **1** with great care, attending to every detail: *She doesn't do her job very thoroughly.* **2** completely: *He's thoroughly stupid/bored.*

'thoroughness *n* care; attention to detail.

'thoroughfare [-feə] *n* **1** a public road or street: *Don't park your car on a busy thoroughfare.* **2** (the right of) passage through: *A sign on the gate said 'No Thoroughfare'.*

those see **that**.

thou [ðau] *pron* an old word for 'you' used only when addressing one person, *esp.* God (*usu* Thou), as the subject of a verb: *Thou, O God …; thou villain!*

though [ðou] *conj* (*rare abbrev* **tho'**) despite the fact that; although: *He went out, (even) though it was raining.* – *adv* however: *I wish I hadn't done it, though.*

as though as if: *You sound as though you've caught a cold.*

thought [θɔːt] *v* see **think**. – *n* **1** something that one thinks; an idea: *I had a sudden thought.* **2** the act of thinking; consideration: *After a great deal of thought we decided to emigrate to America.* **3** general opinion: *scientific thought.*

'thoughtful *adj* (appearing to be) thinking deeply: *You look thoughtful; a thoughtful mood.* **2** thinking of other people; consideration: *It was very thoughtful of you to do that.* **'thoughtfully** *adv*. **'thoughtfulness** *n*.

'thoughtless *adj* not thinking about other people; showing no thought, care or consideration; inconsiderate: *thoughtless words.* **'thoughtlessly** *adv*. **'thoughtlessness** *n*.

thousand [ˈθauzənd] – *pls* **'thousand, 'thousands** *n* **1** the number 1000: *one thousand; two thousand; several thousand.* **2** the figure 1000. **3** a thousand pounds or dollars: *This cost us several thousand(s).* – *adj* 1000 in number: *a few thousand people; I have a couple of thousand pounds.*

thousand- having a thousand (of something): *a thousand-mile journey.*

'thousandth *n* **1** one of a thousand equal parts. **2** (*also adj*) the last of a thousand (people, things *etc*) or (the person, thing *etc*) in an equivalent position.

thousands of 1 several thousand: *He's got thousands of pounds in the bank.* **2** lots of: *I've read thousands of books.*

thrash [θraʃ] *v* **1** to strike with blows: *The child was soundly thrashed.* **2** to move about violently: *The wounded animal thrashed about/around on the ground.* **3** to defeat easily, by a large margin: *Our team was thrashed eighteen-nil.*

'thrashing *n* a physical beating: *He needs a good thrashing!*

thread [θred] *n* **1** a thin strand of cotton, wool, silk *etc, esp* when used for sewing: *a needle and some thread.* **2** the spiral ridge around a screw: *This screw has a worn thread.* **3** the connection between the various events or details (in a story, account *etc*): *I've lost the thread of what he's saying.* – *v* **1** to pass a thread through: *I cannot thread this needle; The child was threading beads.* **2** to make (one's way) through: *She threaded her way through the crowd.*

'threadbare *adj* (of material) worn thin; shabby: *a threadbare jacket.*

threat [θret] *n* **1** a warning that one is going to hurt or punish someone: *He will certainly carry out his threat to harm you.* **2** a sign of something dangerous or unpleasant which may be, or is, about to happen: *a threat of rain.* **3** a source of danger: *His presence is a threat to our plan/success.*

'threaten *v* to make or be a threat (to): *She threatened to kill herself; He threatened me with violence/with a gun; A storm is threatening.*

three [θri:] *n* **1** the number or figure 3. **2** the age of 3. – *adj* **1** 3 in number. **2** aged 3.

three- having three (of something): *a three-page letter.*

,three-di'mensional *adj* (*abbrev* **3-D**) having three dimensions, *ie* height, width and depth.

three-'quarter *adj* not quite full-length: *a three-quarter (-length) coat.*

'three-year-old *n* a person or animal that is three years old. – *adj* (of a person, animal or thing) that is three years old.

thresh [θreʃ] *v* to beat (the stalks of corn) in order to extract the grain.

threshold ['θreʃould] *n* **1** (a piece of wood or stone under) a doorway forming the entrance to a house *etc*: *He paused on the threshold and then entered.* **2** beginning: *She is on the threshold of a brilliant career.*

threw *see* **throw.**

thrift [θrift] *n* careful spending of money, or using of food or other resources, so that one can save or have some left in reserve; economy: *She is noted for her thrift but her husband is very extravagant.*

'thrifty *adj* showing thrift: *a thrifty housewife.* **'thriftily** *adv.* **'thriftiness** *n.*

thrill [θril] *v* to (cause someone to) feel excitement: *She was thrilled at/by the invitation.* – *n* **1** an excited feeling: *a thrill of pleasure/expectation.* **2** something which causes this feeling: *Meeting the Queen was a great thrill.*

'thriller *n* an exciting novel or play, *usu* about crime, detectives *etc*: *I always take a thriller to read on the train.*

'thrilling *adj* exciting.

thrive [θraiv] *v* to grow strong and healthy: *Children thrive on milk; The business is thriving.*

'thriving *adj* successful: *a thriving industry.*

thro' [θru:] short for **through.**

throat [θrout] *n* **1** the back part of the mouth connecting the openings of the stomach, lungs and nose: *She has a sore throat.* **2** the front part of the neck: *She wore a silver brooch at her throat.*

-throated having a (certain type of) throat: *a red-throated bird.*

'throaty *adj* (of a voice) coming from far back in the throat; deep and hoarse. **'throatily** *adv.* **'throatiness** *n.*

throb [θrob] – *pt, ptp* **throbbed** – *v* **1** (of the heart) to beat: *Her heart throbbed with excitement.* **2** to beat regularly like the heart: *The engine was throbbing gently.* **3** to beat regularly with pain; to be very painful: *His head is throbbing (with pain).* – *n* a regular beat: *the throb of the engine/her heart/her sore finger.*

throne [θroun] *n* **1** the ceremonial chair of a king, queen *etc*, pope or bishop. **2** the king or queen: *He swore allegiance to the throne.*

throng [θroŋ] *n* a crowd: *Throngs of people gathered to see the queen.* – *v* to crowd or fill: *People thronged the streets to see the president.*

throttle ['θrotl] *n* (in engines, the lever attached to) the valve controlling the flow of steam, petrol *etc*: *The car went faster as he opened the throttle.* – *v* to choke (someone) by gripping the throat: *This scarf is throttling me!*

through [θru:] *prep* **1** into from one direction and out of in the other: *The water flows through a pipe.* **2** from side to side or end to end of: *He walked (right) through the town.* **3** from the beginning to the end of: *She read through the magazine.* **4** because of: *He lost his job through his own stupidity.* **5** by way of: *He got the job through a friend.* **6** (*Amer*) from ... to (inclusive): *I go to work Monday through Friday.* – *adv* into and out of; from one side or end to the other; from beginning to end: *He went straight/right through.* – *adj* **1** (of a bus or train) that goes all the way to one's destination, so that one doesn't have to change (buses or trains): *There isn't a through train*

– *you'll have to change.* **2** finished: *Are you through yet?*

through'out *prep* **1** in all parts of: *They searched throughout the house.* **2** from start to finish of: *She complained throughout the journey.* – *adv* in every part: *The house was furnished throughout.*

all through 1 from beginning to end of: *The baby cried all through the night.* **2** in every part of: *Road conditions are bad all through the country.*

soaked, wet through very wet: *His coat was wet through.*

through and through completely: *He was a gentleman through and through.*

through with finished with: *Are you through with the newspaper yet?*

throw [θrou] – *pt* **threw** [θruː]: *ptp* **thrown** – *v* **1** to send through the air with force; to hurl or fling: *He threw the ball to her/threw her the ball.* **2** (of a horse) to make its rider fall off: *My horse threw me.* **3** to puzzle or confuse: *He was completely thrown by her question.* **4** (in wrestling, judo *etc*) to wrestle (one's opponent) to the ground. – *n* an act of throwing: *That was a good throw!*

throw away 1 to get rid of: *He always throws away his old clothes.* **2** to lose through lack of care, concern *etc*: *Don't throw your chance of promotion away by being careless.*

throw doubt on to suggest or hint that (something) is not true: *The latest scientific discoveries throw doubt on the original theory.*

throw in to include or add as a gift or as part of a bargain: *When I bought his car he threw in the radio and a box of tools.*

throw light on to help to solve or give information on (a mystery, puzzle, problem *etc*): *Can anyone throw any light on the problem?*

throw oneself into to begin (doing something) with great energy: *She threw herself into her work with enthusiasm.*

throw off 1 to get rid of: *She finally managed to throw off her cold; They were following us but we threw them off.* **2** to take off very quickly: *He threw off his coat and sat down.*

throw open to open suddenly and wide: *He threw open the door and walked in.*

throw out to get rid of by throwing or by force: *He was thrown out of the meeting; The committee threw out the proposal.*

throw a party to hold, organize *etc* a party: *They threw a party for her birthday.*

throw up 1 a slang expression for to vomit: *She had too much to eat, and threw up on the way home.* **2** to give up or abandon: *He threw up his job.* **3** to build hurriedly: *They threw up a temporary building.*

throw one's voice to make one's voice appear to come from somewhere else, *eg* the mouth of a ventriloquist's dummy.

thrust [θrʌst] – *pt, ptp* **thrust** – *v* to push suddenly and violently: *He thrust his spade into the ground; She thrust forward through the crowd.* – *n* **1** a sudden violent forward movement: *The army made a sudden thrust through Africa.* **2** a force pushing forward: *the thrust of the engines.*

thrust/on upon to bring (something or someone) forcibly to someone's notice, into someone's company *etc*: *He thrust $100 on me; She is always thrusting herself on other people; Fame was thrust upon him.*

thud [θʌd] *n* a dull sound like that of something heavy falling to the ground: *He dropped the book with a thud.* – *v* – *pt, ptp* **'thudded** – to move or fall with such a sound: *The tree thudded to the ground.*

thug [θʌg] *n* a violent, brutal person: *Where are the young thugs who robbed the old man?*

thumb [θʌm] *n* **1** the short thick finger of the hand, set at a different angle from the other four. **2** the part of a glove covering this finger. – *v* (*often with* **through**) to turn over (the pages of a book) with the thumb or fingers: *She was thumbing through the dictionary.*

'thumb-nail *n* the nail on the thumb.

'thumbprint *n* a mark made by pressing the thumb on to a surface, sometimes used as means of identification.

,thumbs-'up *n* a sign expressing a wish for good luck, success *etc*: *He gave me the thumbs-up.*

'thumbtack *n* (*Amer*) a drawing-pin: *She hung the picture on the wall with thumbtacks.*

under someone's thumb controlled or greatly influenced by someone: *She is completely under her husband's thumb.*

thump [θʌmp] *n* (the sound of) a heavy blow or hit: *They heard a thump on the door; He gave him a thump on the head.* – *v* to hit, move or fall with, or make, a dull heavy noise.

thunder ['θʌndə] *n* **1** the deep rumbling sound heard in the sky after a flash of lightning: *a clap/peal of thunder; a thunderstorm.* **2** a loud rumbling: *the thunder of horses' hooves.* – *v* **1** to sound, rumble *etc*: *It thundered all night.* **2** to make a noise like thunder: *The tanks thundered over the bridge.*

'thundering *adj* very great: *a thundering idiot.*

'thunderous *adj* like thunder: *a thunderous noise.* **'thunderously** *adv.*

'thundery *adj* warning of, or likely to have or bring, thunder: *thundery clouds/weather*:

'thunderbolt *n* **1** a flash of lightning immediately followed by thunder. **2** a sudden great surprise: *Her arrival was a complete thunderbolt.*

Thursday ['θəːzdi] *n* the fifth day of the week, the day following Wednesday: *She came on Thursday*; (*also adj*) *Thursday evening.*

thus [ðʌs] *adv* (referring to something mentioned immediately before or after) in this or that way or manner: *He spoke thus; Thus, he was able to finish the work quickly.*

thwart [θwoːt] *v* **1** to stop or hinder (someone) from doing something: *He doesn't like to be thwarted.* **2** to prevent (something being done by someone): *All his attempts to become rich were thwarted.*

thy [ðai] *adj* an old word for 'your' used only when addressing one person, *esp* God: *thy father.*

thine [ðain] *pron* an old word for 'yours' used only when addressing one person, *esp* God: *Thine is the glory.* – *adj* the form of **thy** used before a vowel or vowel sound: *Thine anger is great; thine honour.*

thy'self *pron* an old word for 'yourself': *Look at thyself.*

thyself *see* **thy.**

tiara [ti'aːrə] *n* a jewelled ornament for the head, similar to a crown.

tibia ['tibiə] *n* the larger of the two bones between the knee and ankle: *a broken tibia.*

tic [tik] *n* a nervous, involuntary movement or twitch of a muscle, *esp* of the face: *She has a nervous tic below her left eye.*

tick[1] [tik] *n* **1** a regular sound, *esp* that of a watch, clock *etc.* **2** a moment: *Wait a tick!* – *v* to make a sound like this: *Your watch ticks very loudly!*

tick[2] [tik] *n* a mark (✓) used to show that something is correct, has been noted *etc.* – *v* (*often with* **off**) to put this mark beside an item or name on a list *etc*: *She ticked everything off on the list.*

tick (someone) off, give (someone) a ticking= off to scold someone: *The teacher gave me a ticking-off for being late.*

tick over to run quietly and smoothly at a gentle pace: *The car's engine is ticking over.*

tick[3] [tik] *n* a type of small, blood-sucking insect: *Our dog has ticks.*

ticket ['tikit] *n* **1** a piece of card or paper which gives the holder a certain right, *eg* of travel, entering a theatre *etc*: *a bus-ticket; a cinema-ticket.* **2** a notice advising of a minor motoring offence: *a parking-ticket.* **3** a card or label stating the price *etc* of something.

tickle ['tikl] *v* **1** to touch (sensitive parts of someone's skin) lightly, often making the person laugh: *He tickled me/my feet with a feather.* **2** (of a part of the body) to feel as if it is being touched in this way: *My nose tickles.* **3** to amuse: *The funny story tickled him.* – *n* **1** an act or feeling of tickling. **2** a

feeling of irritation in the throat (making one cough).

'ticklish *adj* **1** easily made to laugh when tickled: *Are you ticklish?* **2** not easy to manage; difficult: *a ticklish problem/ situation.*

be tickled pink to be very pleased.

tidal *see* **tide.**

tidbit *see* **titbit.**

tide [taid] *n* the regular, twice-a-day ebbing and flowing movement of the sea: *It's high/ low tide; The tide is coming in/going out.*

'tidal *adj* of or affected by tides: *tidal currents; a tidal river.*

tidal wave an enormous wave in the sea, caused by an earthquake *etc.*

tidings ['taidiŋz] *n pl* news: *They brought tidings of a great victory.*

tidy ['taidi] *adj* **1** (*neg* **un-**) in good order; neat: *a tidy room/person; Her hair never looks tidy.* **2** fairly big: *a tidy sum of money.* – *v* (*sometimes with* **up, away** *etc*) to put in good order; to make neat: *He tidied* (*away*) *his papers; She was tidying the room* (*up*) *when her mother arrived.*

'tidily *adv.* **'tidiness** *n.*

tie [tai] – *prp* **'tying**: *pt, ptp* **tied** – *v* **1** (*often with* **to, on** *etc*) to fasten with a string, rope *etc*: *He tied the horse to a tree; The parcel was tied with string; I don't like this job – I hate being tied to a desk.* **2** to fasten by knotting; to make a knot in: *He tied his shoelaces.* **3** to be joined by a knot *etc*: *The belt of this dress ties at the front.* **4** to score the same number of points *etc* (in a game, competition *etc*): *Three people tied for first place.* – *n* **1** a strip of material worn tied round the neck under the collar of a shirt: *He wore a shirt and tie.* **2** something that joins: *the ties of friendship.* **3** an equal score or result (in a game, competition *etc*); a draw. **4** a game or match to be played.

be tied up 1 to be busy; to be involved (with): *I can't discuss this matter just now – I'm tied up with other things.* **2** (*with* **with**) to be connected with.

tie (someone) down to limit someone's freedom *etc*: *Her work tied her down.*

tie in/up to be linked or joined (logically): *This doesn't tie in* (*with what he said before*).

tier [tiə] *n* a row of seats: *They sat in the front/first tier.*

tiff [tif] *n* a slight quarrel: *She's had a tiff with her boy-friend.*

tiger ['taigə] – *fem* **'tigress** – *n* a large wild animal of the cat family, with a striped coat.

tight [tait] *adj* **1** fitting very or too closely: *I couldn't open the box because the lid was too tight; My trousers are too tight.* **2** stretched to a great extent; not loose: *He made sure that the ropes were tight.* **3** (of control *etc*) strict and very careful: *She keeps (a) tight control over on her emotions.* **4** not allowing much time: *We hope to finish this next week but the schedule's a bit tight.* – *adv* (*also* **'tightly**) closely; with no extra room or space: *The bags were packed tight/tightly packed.*

-tight sealed so as to keep (something) in or out, as in **airtight, watertight.**

'tighten *v* to make or become tight or tighter.

'tightness *n.*

tights *n pl* a close-fitting (*usu* nylon or woollen) garment covering the feet, legs and body to the waist: *She bought three pairs of tights.*

tight-'fisted *adj* mean and ungenerous with money: *a tight-fisted employer.*

'tightrope *n* a tightly-stretched rope or wire on which acrobats balance.

a tight corner/spot a difficult position or situation: *His refusal to help put her in a tight corner/spot.*

tighten one's belt to make sacrifices and reduce one's standard of living: *If the economy gets worse, we shall just have to tighten our belts.*

tigress *see* **tiger.**

tile [tail] *n* **1** a piece of baked clay used in covering roofs, walls, floors *etc*: *Some of the tiles were blown off the roof during the storm.* **2** a similar piece of plastic material used for covering floors *etc*. – *v* to cover with tiles: *We had to have the roof tiled.*

tiled *adj* covered with tiles.

till¹ [til] *prep, conj* to the time of or when: *I'll wait till six o'clock; Go on till you reach the station.*

till² [til] *n* (in a shop *etc*) a container or drawer in which money is put and registered.

tiller ['tilə] *n* the handle or lever used to turn the rudder of a boat.

tilt [tilt] *v* to go or put (something) into a sloping or slanting position: *He tilted his chair backwards; The lamp tilted and fell.* – *n* a slant; a slanting position: *The table is at a slight tilt.*

(at) full tilt at full speed: *He rushed down the street at full tilt.*

timber ['timbə] *n* **1** wood, *esp* for building: *This house is built of timber.* **2** trees suitable for this: *a hundred acres of good timber.* **3** a wooden beam used in the building of a house, ship *etc*.

time [taim] *n* **1** the hour of the day: *What time is it?; Can your child tell the time yet?* **2** the passage of days, years, events *etc*: *time and space; Time will tell.* **3** a point at which, or period during which, something happens: *at the time of his wedding; break-fast-time.* **4** the quantity of minutes, hours,

days *etc*, eg spent in, or available for, a particular activity *etc*: *This won't take much time to do; I enjoyed the time I spent in Paris; At the end of the exam, the supervisor called 'Your time is up!'* **5** a suitable moment or period: *Now is the time to ask him.* **6** one of a number occasions: *He's been to France four times.* **7** a period characterized by a particular quality in a person's life, experience *etc*: *He went through an unhappy time when she died; We had some good times together.* **8** the speed at which a piece of music should be played; tempo: *in slow time.* – *v* **1** to measure the time taken by (a happening, event *etc*) or by (a person, in doing something): *He timed the journey.* **2** to choose a particular time for: *You timed your arrival beautifully!*

'timeless *adj* **1** not belonging to, or typical of, any particular time: *timeless works of art.* **2** never-ending: *the timeless beauty of Venice.* **'timelessly** *adv.* **'timelessness** *n.*

'timely *adj* coming at the right moment: *Your arrival was most timely.* **'timeliness** *n.*

'timer *n* **1** a person who, or a device which, measures the time taken by anything. **2** a clock-like device which sets something off or switches something on or off at a given time.

times *n pl* **1** a period; an era: *We live in difficult times.* **2** in mathematics, used to mean multiplied by: *Four times two is eight.*

'timing *n* **1** the measuring of the amount of time taken. **2** the regulating of speech or actions to achieve the best effect: *All comedians should have a good sense of timing.*

time bomb a bomb that has been set to explode at a particular time.

time limit a fixed length of time during which something must be done and finished: *The examination has a time limit of three hours.*

'timetable *n* a list of the times of trains, school classes *etc.*

all in good time soon enough.

all the time continually.

at times occasionally; sometimes.

be behind time to be late.

for the time being meanwhile: *I am staying at home for the time being.*

from time to time occasionally; sometimes: *From time to time he brings me a present.*

in good time early enough; before a set time (for an appointment *etc*): *We arrived in good time for the concert.*

in time 1 early enough: *He arrived in time for dinner; Are we in time to catch the train?* **2** (*with* **with**) at the same speed or rhythm: *They marched in time with the music.*

no time (at all) a very short time indeed: *The journey took no time (at all).*

one, two *etc* **at a time** singly, or in groups of two etc: *They came into the room three at a time.*

on time at the right time: *The train left on time.*

save, waste time to avoid spending time; to spend time unnecessarily: *Take my car instead of walking, if you want to save time; We mustn't waste time discussing unimportant matters.*

take one's time to do something as slowly as one wishes.

time and (time) again again and again; repeatedly: *I asked her time and (time) again not to do that.*

timid ['timid] *adj* easily frightened; nervous; shy: *A mouse is a timid creature.* **'timidly** *adv.* **ti'midity, 'timidness** *ns*.

tin [tin] *n* **1** an element, a silvery white metal: *Is that box made of tin or steel?* **2** (*also* **can**) a container, *usu* for food, made of **'tin-plate**, thin sheets of iron covered with tin or other metal: *a tin of fruit; a biscuit-tin.* – *adj* made of tin or tin-plate: *a tin plate.*

tinned *adj* (of food) sealed in a tin for preservation *etc*: *tinned foods.*

'tinfoil *n* tin or other metal in the form of very thin sheets, used for wrapping *etc*: *I'm going to bake the ham in tinfoil.*

'tin-opener *n* (*Amer* **'can-opener**) any of several types of tool or device for opening tins of food.

tinge [tindʒ] *n* a trace, or slight amount, of a colour: *Her hair had a tinge of red.*

tingle ['tiŋgl] *v* to feel a prickling sensation: *The cold wind made my face tingle; My fingers were tingling with cold.* – *n* this feeling.

tinker ['tiŋkə] *n* a person who travels around like a gypsy, mending kettles, pans *etc*. – *v* (*often with* **about** *or* **around**) to fiddle, or work in an unskilled way, with machinery *etc*: *He enjoys tinkering around (with car engines).*

tinkle ['tiŋkl] *v* to (cause to) make a sound of, or like, the ringing of small bells: *The doorbell tinkled.* – *n* this sound: *I heard the tinkle of breaking glass.*

tinsel ['tinsəl] *n* a sparkling, glittering substance used for decoration: *The Christmas tree was decorated with tinsel.* **'tinselly** *adj.*

tint [tint] *n* a variety, or shade, of a colour. – *v* to colour slightly: *She had her hair tinted red.*

tiny ['taini] *adj* very small: *a tiny insect.*

tip[1] [tip] *n* the small or thin end, point or top of something: *the tips of my fingers.* – *v* – *pt, ptp* **tipped** – to put, or form, a tip on: *The spear was tipped with an iron point.*

tipped *adj* having a tip of a particular kind: *filter-tipped cigarettes; a white-tipped tail.*

,tip-'top *adj* excellent: *The horse is in tip-top condition.*

be on the tip of one's tongue to be almost, but *usu* not, spoken or said: *Her name is on the tip of my tongue* (= I can't quite remember it); *It was on the tip of my tongue to tell him* (= I almost told him).

tip[2] [tip] – *pt, ptp* **tipped** – *v* **1** to (make something) slant: *The boat tipped to one side.* **2** to empty (something) from a container, or remove (something) from a surface, with this kind of motion: *He tipped the water out of the bucket.* **3** to dump (rubbish): *People have been tipping their rubbish in this field.* – *n* a place where rubbish is thrown: *a refuse/rubbish tip.*

tip over to knock or fall over; to overturn: *He tipped the lamp over; She put the jug on the end of the table and it tipped over.*

tip[3] [tip] *n* a gift of money given to a waiter *etc*, for personal service: *I gave him a generous tip.* – *v* – *pt, ptp* **tipped** – to give such a gift to.

tip[4] [tip] *n* a piece of useful information; a hint: *He gave me some good tips on/about gardening.*

tip off to give information or a hint to; to warn: *He tipped me off about her arrival* (*n* **'tip-off**).

tipsy ['tipsi] *adj* slightly drunk. **'tipsily** *adv.* **'tipsiness** *n*.

tiptoe ['tiptou] *v* to walk on the toes, *usu* in order to be quiet: *He tiptoed past her bedroom door.*

walk, stand *etc* **on tiptoe(s)** to walk, stand *etc* on the toes: *He stood on tiptoe(s) to reach the shelf.*

tire[1] *see* **tyre.**

tire[2] ['taiə] *v* to make, or become, physically or mentally in want of rest, because of lack of strength, patience, interest *etc*; to weary: *Walking tired her; She tires easily.*

tired *adj* **1** wearied; exhausted: *She was too tired to continue; a tired child.* **2** (*with* **of**) no longer interested in; bored with: *I'm tired of (answering) stupid questions!* **'tiredness** *n*.

'tireless *adj* never becoming weary or exhausted; never resting: *a tireless worker; tireless energy/enthusiasm.* **'tirelessly** *adv.* **'tirelessness** *n*.

'tiresome *adj* troublesome; annoying. **'tiresomely** *adv.* **'tiresomeness** *n*.

'tiring *adj* causing (physical) tiredness: *I've had a tiring day; The journey was very tiring.*

tire out to tire or exhaust completely: *The hard work tired her out.*

tissue ['tiʃuː] *n* **1** (one of the kinds of) substance of which the organs of the body are made: *nervous tissue; the tissues of the body.* **2** (a piece of) thin soft paper used for wiping the nose *etc*: *He bought a box of tissues for his cold.*

tissue paper very thin paper, used for packing, wrapping *etc*.

tit [tit]: **tit for tat** [tat] blow for blow; repayment of injury with injury: *He tore my dress, so I spilt ink on his suit. That's tit for tat.*

tbit ('titbit), **tidbit** ['tidbit] *n* a tasty little piece of food: *He gave the dog a titbit.*

tle ['taitl] *n* **1** the name of a book, play, painting, piece of music *etc*: *The title of the painting is 'A Winter Evening'.* **2** a word put before a person's name to show rank, honour, occupation *etc*: <u>Sir</u> John; <u>Lord</u> Henry; <u>Captain</u> Smith; <u>Professor</u> Brown; <u>Dr (Doctor)</u> Peter Jones.

'titled *adj* having a title that shows noble rank: *a titled lady.*

title deed a document that proves legal ownership: *I have the title deeds of the house.*

title page the page at the beginning of a book on which are the title, the author's name *etc*.

title rôle the rôle or part in a play of the character named in the title: *He's playing the title rôle in 'Hamlet'.*

tter ['titə] *v* to giggle: *He tittered nervously.* – *n* a giggle.

NT [ti:en'ti:] *n* a type of explosive material: *The bridge was blown up with TNT.*

) [tə,tu] *prep* **1** towards; in the direction of: *I cycled to the station; The book fell to the floor; I went to the concert/lecture/play.* **2** as far as: *His story is a lie from beginning to end.* **3** until: *Did you stay to the end of the concert?* **4** sometimes used to introduce the indirect object of a verb: *He sent it to us; You're the only person I can talk to.* **5** used in expressing various relations: *Listen to me!; Did you reply to his letter?; Where's the key to this door?; He sang to (the accompaniment of) his guitar.* **6** into a particular state or condition: *She tore the letter to pieces.* **7** used in expressing comparison or proportion: *He's junior to me; Your skill is superior to mine; We won the match by 5 goals to 2.* **8** showing the purpose or result of an action *etc*: *He came quickly to my assistance; To my horror, he took a gun out of his pocket.* **9** [tə] used before an infinitive *eg* after various verbs and adjectives, or in other constructions: *I want to go!; He asked me to come; He worked hard to (= in order to) earn a lot of money; These buildings were designed to (= so as to) resist earthquakes; She opened her eyes to find him standing beside her; I arrived too late to see him.* **10** used instead of a complete infinitive: *He asked her to stay but she didn't want to.* – [tu:] *adv* **1** into a closed or almost closed position: *He pulled/pushed the door to.* **2** used in phrasal verbs and compounds:

He came to (= regained consciousness); *They set to* (= They began).

to and fro [tu:ən'frou] backwards and forwards: *they ran to and fro in the street.*

toad [toud] *n* a kind of reptile, like a large frog.

'toadstool *n* any of several kinds of mushroom-like fungi, often poisonous.

toast[1] [toust] *v* to make (bread *etc*) brown in front of direct heat: *We toasted slices of bread for tea.* – *n* bread that has been toasted: *He always has two pieces of toast for breakfast.*

'toasted *adj* heated by direct heat, *eg* under a grill: *toasted cheese; Do you like your bread toasted?*

'toaster *n* an electric machine for toasting bread.

'toastrack *n* a small stand in which slices of toast can be served: *Put the toastrack on the table.*

toast[2] [toust] *v* to drink ceremonially in honour of, or to wish success to (someone or something): *We toasted the bride and bridegroom/the new ship.* – *n* **1** an act of toasting: *Let's drink a toast to our friends!* **2** the wish conveyed, or the person *etc* honoured, by such an act.

tobacco [tə'bakou] – *pl* **tobaccos** – *n* (a type of plant that has) leaves that are dried and used for smoking in pipes, cigarettes, cigars *etc*, or as snuff: *Tobacco is bad for your health.*

to'bacconist [-nist] *n* a person who sells tobacco, cigarettes *etc*.

toboggan [tə'bogən] *n* a kind of light sledge. – *v* to go on a toboggan: *We went tobogganing.*

today [tə'dei] *n*, *adv* **1** (on) this day: *Today is Friday; Here is today's newspaper; I'm working today.* **2** (at) the present time: *Life is easier today than a hundred years ago.*

toddle ['todl] *v* (*esp* of a very young child) to walk unsteadily: *The child is toddling.*

'toddler *n* a very young child (who has just begun to be able to walk).

toddy ['todi] *n* a drink made of spirits, sugar, hot water *etc*.

toe [tou] *n* **1** one of the five finger-like end parts of the foot: *These tight shoes hurt my toes.* **2** the front part of a shoe, sock *etc*: *There's a hole in the toe of my sock.*

'toenail *n* the nail that grows on one's toes: *He was cutting his toenails.*

toe the line to act according to the rules.

toffee ['tofi] *n* (a piece of) a kind of sticky sweet made of sugar and butter: *Have a (piece of) toffee.*

toga ['tougə] *n* the loose outer garment worn by a citizen of ancient Rome.

together [tə'geðə] *adv* **1** with someone or something else; in company: *They travelled* *together.* **2** at the same time: *They all arrived together.* **3** so as to be joined or united: *He nailed/fitted/stuck the pieces of wood together.* **4** by action with one or more other people: *Together we persuaded him.*

to'getherness *n* the state of being close together: *Their evenings round the fire gave them a feeling of togetherness.*

together with in company with: in addition to: *My knowledge, together with his money, should be very useful.*

toil [toil] *v* **1** to work hard and long: *He toiled all day in the fields.* **2** to move with great difficulty: *He toiled along the road with all his luggage.* – *n* hard work: *He slept well after his hours of toil.*

toilet ['toilit] *n* (a room containing) a receptacle for the body's waste matter, *usu* with a supply of water for washing this away; a lavatory: *Do you want to go to the toilet?*; *Where is the ladies' toilet?*; (*also adj*) *a toilet seat.*

'toilet-paper *n* paper for use in a toilet.

'toilet-roll *n* a roll of toilet-paper.

'toilet-water *n* a type of perfumed liquid for the skin.

token ['toukən] *n* **1** a mark or sign: *Wear this ring, as a token of our friendship.* **2** a card or piece of metal, plastic *etc*, for use instead of money: *The shopkeeper will exchange these tokens for goods to the value of $10.*

told *see* **tell.**

tolerate ['toləreit] *v* to bear or endure; to put up with: *I couldn't tolerate his rudeness.*

'tolerable *adj* **1** able to be borne or endured: *The heat was barely tolerable.* **2** quite good: *The food was tolerable.*

'tolerance *n* **1** the ability to be fair and understanding to people whose ways, opinions *etc* are different from one's own: *We should always try to show tolerance to other people.* **2** the ability to resist the effects of *eg* a drug: *If you take a drug regularly, your body gradually acquires a tolerance of it.*

'tolerant *adj* showing tolerance: *He's very tolerant towards his neighbours.* **'tolerantly** *adv.*

,tole'ration *n* **1** the act of tolerating: *His toleration of her behaviour amazed me.* **2** tolerance, *esp* in religious matters: *The government passed a law of religious toleration.*

toll[1] [toul] *v* to ring (a bell) slowly: *The church bell tolled solemnly.*

toll[2] [toul] *n* **1** a tax charged for crossing a bridge, driving on certain roads *etc*: *All cars pay a toll of $1*; (*also adj*) *a toll bridge.* **2** an amount of loss or damage suffered, *eg* as a result of disaster: *Every year there is a heavy toll of human lives on the roads.*

tomato [tə'ma:tou, (*Amer*) -'mei-] – *pl*

to'matoes – *n* **1** a type of fleshy, juicy fruit, *usu* red, used in salads, sauces *etc*: *We had a salad of lettuce, tomatoes and cucumbers*; (*also adj*) *tomato sauce.* **2** the plant which bears these.

tomb [tu:m] *n* a hole or vault in the ground in which a dead body is put; a grave: *He was buried in the family tomb.*

'tombstone *n* an ornamental stone placed over a grave on which the dead person's name *etc* is engraved.

tomboy ['tomboi] *n* a girl who likes rough games and activities: *She's a real tomboy!*

tomcat ['tomkat] *n* a male cat.

tomorrow [tə'morou] *n, adv* **1** (on) the day after today: *Tomorrow is Saturday*; *The news will be announced tomorrow.* **2** (in) the future: *tomorrow's world.*

tom-tom ['tomtom] *n* a kind of drum *usu* beaten with the hands.

ton [tʌn] *n* **1** a unit of weight, 2240 lb, (*Amer*) 2000 lb; a **metric ton** (*also* **tonne** [tʌn]) is 2204·6 lb (1000 kilogrammes): *It weighs a ton and a half*; *a three-ton weight.* **2** a unit of space in a ship (100 cubic feet).

'tonnage [-nidʒ] *n* the space available on a ship, measured in tons.

tons *n pl* a lot: *I've got tons of letters to write.*

tonal *see* **tone.**

tone [toun] *n* **1** (the quality of) a sound, *esp* a voice: *He spoke in a low/angry/gentle tone*; *He told me about it in tones of disapproval*; *That singer/violin/piano has very good tone.* **2** a shade of colour: *various tones of green.* **3** firmness of body or muscle: *Your muscles lack tone – you need exercise.* **4** in music, one of the larger intervals in an octave *eg* between C and D. – *v* to fit in well; to blend: *The brown sofa tones (in) well with the walls.*

'tonal *adj* of musical tones.

'toneless *adj* without tone; with no variation in sound, *etc*: *She spoke in a toneless voice.* **'tonelessly** *adv.*

tone down to make or become softer, less harsh *etc*: *He toned down some of his criticisms.*

tongs [toŋz] *n pl* an instrument for holding and lifting objects: *sugar-tongs*; *a pair of tongs.*

tongue [tʌŋ] *n* **1** the fleshy organ inside the mouth, used in tasting, swallowing, speaking *etc*: *The doctor looked at her tongue.* **2** the tongue of an animal used as food. **3** something with the same shape as a tongue: *a tongue of flame.* **4** a language: *English is his mother-tongue/native tongue*; *a foreign tongue.*

tonic ['tonik] *n* **1** (a) medicine that gives strength or energy: *The doctor prescribed a (bottle of) tonic.* **2** (*also* **'tonic-water**) water containing quinine, often drunk with gin etc: *I'd like a gin and tonic.*

onight [tə'nait] *n, adv* (on) the night of this present day: *Here is tonight's weather forecast; I'm going home early tonight.*

onnage, tonne see **ton**.

onsil ['tonsil] *n* either of two lumps of tissue at the back of the throat: *He had to have his tonsils (taken) out.*

,tonsil'litis [tonsi'laitis] *n* painful inflammation of the tonsils: *She had/was suffering from tonsillitis.*

oo [tu:] *adv* **1** to a greater extent, or more, than is required, desirable or suitable: *He's too fat for his clothes; I'm not feeling too well.* **2** in addition; also; as well: *My husband likes cycling, and I do, too.*

ook see **take**.

*tool [tu:l] *n* an instrument for doing work, *esp* by hand: *hammers, saws and other tools; the tools of his trade; Advertising is a powerful tool.*

oot [tu:t] *n* a quick blast of a trumpet, motor-horn *etc*. – *v* to blow or sound a horn *etc*: *He tooted (on) the horn.*

ooth [tu:θ] – *pl* **teeth** [ti:θ] – *n* **1** any of the hard, bone-like objects that grow in the mouth and are used for biting and chewing: *He has had a tooth out at the dentist's.* **2** something that looks or acts like a tooth: *the teeth of a comb/saw.*

teethe [ti:ð] *v* (of a baby) to grow one's first teeth: *He cries a lot because he's teething.*

toothed *adj* having teeth: *a toothed wheel.*

'toothless *adj* without teeth: *a toothless old woman.*

'toothy *adj* showing a lot of teeth: *a toothy grin.*

'toothache *n* a pain in a tooth: *He has/is suffering from toothache.*

'toothbrush *n* a brush for cleaning the teeth.

'toothpaste *n* a kind of paste used to clean the teeth: *a tube of toothpaste.*

'toothpick *n* a small piece of wood, plastic *etc* for picking out food *etc* from between the teeth.

be, get *etc* **long in the tooth** (of a person or animal) to be, become *etc*, old: *I'm getting a bit long in the tooth to climb mountains.*

a fine-tooth comb a comb with the teeth set close together, for removing lice, dirt *etc* from hair *etc*.

a sweet tooth a liking for sweet food: *My friend has a sweet tooth.*

tooth and nail fiercely and with all one's strength: *They fought tooth and nail.*

op¹ [top] *n* **1** the highest part of anything: *the top of the hill; the top of her head; The book is on the top shelf.* **2** the position of the cleverest in a class *etc*: *He's at the top of the class.* **3** the upper surface: *the table-top.* **4** a lid: *I've lost the top to this jar; a bottle-top.*

5 a (woman's) garment for the upper half of the body; a blouse, sweater *etc*: *I bought a new skirt and top.* – *adj* having gained the most marks, points *etc, eg* in a school class: *He's top (of the class) again.* – *v* – *pt, ptp* **topped** – **1** to cover on the top: *She topped the cake with cream.* **2** to rise above; to surpass: *Our exports have topped $100 000.* **3** to remove the top of.

'topless *adj* **1** having no top. **2** very high.

'topping *n* something that forms a covering on top of something, *esp* food: *a tart with a topping of cream.*

top hat (*abbrev* **topper** ['topə]) a man's tall hat, worn as formal dress.

,top-'heavy *adj* having the upper part too heavy for the lower: *That pile of books is top-heavy – it'll fall over!*

,top-'secret *adj* very secret.

at the top of one's voice very loudly: *They were shouting at the top(s) of their voices.*

be/feel *etc* **on top of the world** to feel very well and happy: *She's on top of the world – she's just got engaged to be married.*

from top to bottom completely: *They've painted the house from top to bottom.*

the top of the ladder/tree the highest point in one's profession.

top up to fill (a cup *etc* that has been partly emptied) to the top: *Let me top up your glass/drink.*

top² [top] *n* a kind of toy that spins.

sleep like a top to sleep very well; *The child slept like a top after a day on the beach.*

topaz ['toupaz] *n* a kind of precious stone, of various colours.

topi, topee ['toupi, (*Amer*) tou'pi:] *n* a helmet-like hat worn in hot countries as protection against the sun.

topic ['topik] *n* something spoken or written about; a subject: *They discussed the weather and other topics.*

'topical *adj* of interest at the present time.

'topically *adv*.

topless see **top¹**.

topper short for **top hat**.

topping see **top¹**.

topple ['topl] *v* to (make something) fall: *He toppled the pile of books; The child toppled over.*

topsyturv(e)y [topsi'tə:vi] *adj, adv* upside down; in confusion: *Everything was turned topsyturvy.*

torch [to:tʃ] *n* **1** (*Amer* **'flashlight**) a small portable light worked by an electric battery: *He shone his torch into her face.* **2** a piece of wood *etc* set on fire and carried as a light.

tore see **tear²**.

torment ['to:ment] *n* **1** (a) very great pain, suffering, worry *etc*: *He was in torment.* **2** something that causes this. – [to:'ment] *v*

---

* see illustration overleaf

Tools

Key

1 File	**4** Hammer	**7** Pliers	**10** Electric drill
2 Chisel	**5** Hacksaw	**8** Spanner	**11** Hand drill
3 Screwdriver	**6** Mallet	**9** Spirit level	**12** Plane

to cause pain, suffering, worry *etc* to: *She was tormented with worry/toothache.*

tor'mentor [-'men-] *n* a person who torments.

rn *see* **tear**².

rnado [to:'neidou] – *pl* **tor'nadoes** – *n* a violent whirlwind that can cause great damage: *The village was destroyed by a tornado.*

rpedo [to:'pi:dou] – *pl* **tor'pedoes** – *n* an underwater missile fired at ships: *an enemy torpedo* – *v* – *3rd pers sing prt* **torpedoes** : *pt, ptp* **tor'pedoed** – to attack, damage or destroy with torpedoes: *The ship was torpedoed.*

rrent ['torənt] *n* a rushing stream: *The rain fell in torrents*; *She attacked him with a torrent of abuse.*

torrential [tə'renʃəl] *adj* of, or like, a torrent: *torrential rain*; *The rain was torrential.*

rrid ['torid] *adj* **1** very hot: *the torrid zone* (= the area of the world on either side of the equator). **2** passionate: *a torrid love affair.*

rso ['to:sou] – *pl* **'torsos** – *n* the body, excluding the head and limbs: *He had a strong torso.*

rtoise ['to:təs] *n* a kind of four-footed, slow-moving reptile covered with a hard shell.

rture ['to:tʃə] *v* to treat (someone) cruelly or painfully, or in order to make him/her confess something, give information *etc*: *He tortured his prisoners*; *She was tortured by rheumatism/jealousy.* – *n* **1** the act or practice of torturing: *The king would not permit torture.* **2** (something causing) great suffering: *the torture of waiting to be executed.*

ss [tos] *v* **1** to throw into or through the air: *She tossed the ball up into the air.* **2** (*often with* **about**) to throw oneself restlessly from side to side: *She tossed about all night, unable to sleep.* **3** (of a ship) to be thrown about: *The boat tossed wildly in the rough sea.* **4** to throw (a coin) into the air and decide a matter according to (a correct guess about) which side falls uppermost: *They tossed a coin to decide which of them should go first.* – *n* an act of tossing.

toss up to toss a coin to decide a matter: *We tossed up (to decide) whether to go to the play or the ballet.*

win/lose the toss to guess rightly or wrongly which side of the coin will fall uppermost: *He won the toss so he started the game of cards first.*

t¹ [tot] *n* **1** a small child: *a tiny tot.* **2** a small amount of alcoholic drink: *a tot of whisky.*

t² [tot] – *pt, ptp* **'totted: tot up** to add up: *He totted up the figures on the bill.*

tal ['toutəl] *adj* whole; complete: *What is the total cost of the holiday?*; *The car was a*

total wreck. – *n* the whole amount, *ie* of various sums added together: *The total came to/was $10.* – *v* – *pt, ptp* **'totalled** – to add up or amount to: *The doctor's fees totalled $20.*

'totally *adv* completely: *I was totally unaware of his presence.*

total up to add up: *He totalled up (the amount he had sold) at the end of the week.*

totem ['toutəm] *n* (an image of) an animal or plant used as the badge or sign of a tribe, among North American Indians *etc.*

totem pole a large wooden pole on which totems are carved and painted.

totter ['totə] *v* to move unsteadily as if about to fall: *The building tottered and collapsed*; *He tottered down the road.*

touch [tatʃ] *v* **1** to be in, come into, or make, contact with something else: *Their shoulders touched*; *He touched the water with his foot.* **2** to feel (lightly) with the hand: *He touched her cheek.* **3** to affect the feelings of; to make (someone) feel pity, sympathy *etc*: *I was touched by her generosity.* **4** to be concerned with; to have anything to do with: *I wouldn't touch a job like that.* – *n* **1** an act or sensation of touching: *I felt a touch on my shoulder.* **2** (*often with* **the**) one of the five senses, the sense by which we feel things: *the sense of touch*; *The stone felt cold to the touch.* **3** a mark or stroke *etc* to improve the appearance of something: *The painting still needs a few finishing touches.* **4** skill or style: *He hasn't lost his touch as a writer.* **5** (in football) the ground outside the edges of the pitch (which are marked out with **'touchlines**): *He kicked the ball into touch.*

'touching *adj* moving; causing emotion: *a touching story.*

'touchingly *adv* in a moving way, so as to cause emotion: *Her face was touchingly childlike.*

'touchy *adj* easily annoyed or offended: *You're very touchy today*; *in rather a touchy mood.* **'touchily** *adv.* **'touchiness** *n.*

in touch (with) in communication (with): *I have kept in touch with my school-friends.*

lose touch (with) to stop communicating (with): *I used to see him quite often but we have lost touch.*

out of touch (with) 1 not in communication (with). **2** not sympathetic or understanding (towards): *Older people sometimes seem out of touch with the modern world.*

a touch a small quantity or degree: *The soup needs a touch of salt*; *a touch of imagination.*

touch down 1 (of aircraft) to land: *The plane should touch down at 2 o'clock.* **2** in rugby football, to put the ball on the ground behind the opposite team's goal line (*n* **'touch-down**).

touch off to make (something) explode: *a spark touched off the gunpowder; His remark touched off an argument.*

touch up to improve *eg* paintwork, a photograph *etc* by small touches: *The photograph had been touched up.*

touch wood (*used as an interjection*) to touch something made of wood superstitiously, in order to avoid bad luck: *None of the children has ever had a serious illness, touch wood!*

tough [tʌf] *adj* **1** strong; not easily broken, worn out *etc*: *Plastic is a tough material.* **2** (of food *etc*) difficult to chew. **3** (of people) strong; able to bear hardship, illness *etc*: *She must be tough to have survived such a serious illness.* **4** rough and violent: *It's a tough neighbourhood.* **5** difficult to deal with or overcome: *a tough problem; The competition was really tough.* – *n* a rough, violent person; a bully.
'**toughness** *n*.
'**toughen** *v* to make or become tough.
tough luck bad luck: *That was tough luck.*
get tough with (someone) to deal forcefully with or refuse to yield to (a person): *When he started to argue, I got tough with him.*

toupee ['tuːpei, (*Amer*) tuː'pei] *n* a small wig.

tour [tuə] *n* **1** a journey to several places and back: *They went on a tour of Italy.* **2** a visit around a particular place: *He took us on a tour of the house and gardens.* **3** an official period of time of work *usu* abroad: *He did a tour of duty in Fiji.* – *v* to go on a tour (around): *to tour Europe.*
'**tourism** *n* the industry dealing with tourists *ie* hotels, catering *etc*: *Tourism is an important part of our economy.*
'**tourist** *n* a person who travels for pleasure: *London is usually full of tourists;* (*also adj*) *the tourist industry.*

tournament ['tuənəmənt] *n* a competition in which many players compete in many separate games: *I'm playing in the next tennis tournament.*

tourniquet ['tuənikei, (*Amer*) -kit] *n* a bandage, or other device, tied very tightly round an injured arm or leg to prevent too much blood being lost.

tout [taut] *v* to go about in search of buyers, jobs, support, votes *etc*: *The taxi-driver drove around touting for custom.*

tow [tou] *v* to pull (a ship, barge, car, trailer *etc*) by a rope, chain or cable: *The tugboat towed the ship out of the harbour; The car broke down and had to be towed to the garage.* – *n* (an) act of towing or process of being towed: *Give us a tow!*
'**towline/'tow-rope** *ns* a rope *etc* used in towing.

towards, toward [tə'woːd(z), (*Amer*) toːrd(z)] *prep* **1** (moving, facing *etc*) in the direction of: *He walked toward the door; She turned towards him.* **2** in relation to: *What are your feelings towards him?* **3** as a contribution or help to: *Here's $3 towards the cost of the journey.* **4** (of time) near: *Towards night-time, the weather worsened.*

towel ['tauəl] *n* a piece of any of several types of absorbent cloth or paper for drying oneself, dishes *etc* after washing *etc*: *After her swim she dried herself with a towel; a roll of paper kitchen towels.* – *v* – *pt, ptp* '**towelled,** (*Amer*) '**toweled** – to rub with a towel.
'**towelling** *n* a kind of rough cloth from which towels *etc* are made.

tower ['tauə] *n* a tall, narrow (part of a) building, *esp* (of) a castle: *the Tower of London; a church-tower.* – *v* to rise high: *She is so small that he towers above her.*
'**towering** *adj* **1** very high: *towering cliffs.* **2** (of rage, fury *etc*) very violent or angry: *He was in a towering rage.*
'**tower-block** *n* a very high block of flats, offices *etc*: *They live in a tower-block.*

towline *see* tow.

town [taun] *n* **1** a group of houses, shops, schools *etc*, that is bigger than a village but smaller than a city: *I'm going into town to buy a dress; He's in town doing some shopping.* **2** the people who live in such a group of houses *etc*: *The whole town turned out to greet the heroes.* **3** towns in general as opposed to the countryside: *Do you live in the country or the town?*
town centre the main shopping and business area of a town: *You can get a bus from the town centre.*
town hall the building in which the official business of a town is done.
'**townsfolk, 'townspeople** *n pl* the people living in a town.
go to town to do something very thoroughly or with great enthusiasm or expense: *He really went to town on (preparing) the meal.*

toxic ['toksik] *adj* poisonous: *toxic substances.*

toy [toi] *n* an object made for a child to play with: *He got lots of toys for Christmas; a toy soldier.* – *v* (*with* with) to play with in an idle way: *He wasn't hungry and sat toying with his food.*

trace [treis] *n* **1** a mark or sign left by something: *There were traces of egg on the plate; There's still no trace of the missing child.* **2** a small amount: *Traces of poison were found in the cup.* – *v* **1** to follow or discover by means of clues, evidence *etc*: *The police have traced him to London; The source of the infection has not yet been traced.* **2** to make a copy of (a picture *etc*) by putting transparent paper over it and drawing the outline *etc*: *I traced the map.*

'tracing n a copy made by tracing: *I made a tracing of the diagram.*

trace elements elements that are needed in small quantities for the growing and developing of animal and plant life.

'tracing-paper n thin transparent paper used for tracing.

track [trak] n 1 a mark left, *esp* a footprint *etc*: *They followed the lion's tracks.* 2 a path or rough road: *a mountain track.* 3 (*also* 'racetrack) a course on which runners, cyclists *etc* race: *a running track;* (*also adj*) *the 100 metres sprint and other track events.* 4 a railway line. – v to follow (*eg* an animal) by the marks, footprints *etc* that it has left: *They tracked the wolf to its lair.*

'track-suit n a warm suit worn by athletes *etc* when exercising, or before and after performing.

in one's tracks where one stands or is: *He stopped dead in his tracks.*

keep/lose track of (not) to keep oneself informed about (the progress or whereabouts of): *I've lost track of what is happening.*

make tracks (for) to depart, or set off (towards): *We ought to be making tracks (for home).*

track down to pursue or search for (someone or something) until it is caught or found: *I managed to track down an old copy of the book.*

tract [trakt] n 1 a piece of land. 2 a system formed by connected parts of the body: *the digestive tract.* 3 a short essay or booklet.

'tractor ['traktə] n a motor vehicle for pulling *esp* agricultural machinery: *I can drive a tractor.*

trade [treid] n 1 the buying and selling of goods: *Japan does a lot of trade with Britain.* 2 (a) business, occupation, or job: *He's in the jewellery trade.* – v 1 (*often with* in *or* with) to buy and sell: *They made a lot of money by trading; They trade in fruit and vegetables.* 2 to exchange: *I traded my watch for a bicycle.*

'trader n a person who trades.

'trademark, 'tradename ns an officially registered mark or name belonging to a particular company, and not to be used by anyone else, that is put on all goods made by the company.

'tradesman ['treidz-] n 1 a shopkeeper. 2 a workman in a skilled job: *My husband cannot mend the television-set. – I'll have to send for a tradesman.*

trade(s) union a group of workers of the same trade who join together to bargain with employers for fair wages, better working conditions *etc*.

trade(s) unionist a member of a trade(s) union. (n trade(s) unionism).

trade wind a wind that blows towards the equator (from the north-east and south-east).

trade in to give (something) as part-payment for something else: *We decided to trade in our old car and get a new one (n* 'trade-in).

tradition [trə'diʃən] n 1 (the process of passing on from generation to generation) customs, beliefs, stories *etc*: *These songs have been preserved by tradition.* 2 a custom, belief, story *etc* that is passed on. tra'ditional adj. tra'ditionally adv.

traffic ['trafik] n 1 vehicles, aircraft, ships *etc* moving about: *There's a lot of traffic on the roads/on the river.* 2 trade, *esp* illegal or dishonest: *the drug traffic.* – v – pt, ptp 'trafficked – to deal or trade in, *esp* illegally or dishonestly: *They were trafficking in smuggled goods.*

'trafficker n a *usu* illegal or dishonest dealer: *a trafficker in drugs.*

traffic island a small pavement in the middle of a road, for pedestrians to stand on on their way across.

traffic jam a situation in which large numbers of road vehicles are prevented from proceeding freely.

traffic lights lights of changing colours for controlling traffic at road crossings *etc*: *Turn left at the traffic lights.*

traffic warden see warden.

tragedy ['tradʒədi] – pl 'tragedies – n 1 (a) drama about unfortunate events with a sad outcome: *'Hamlet' is one of Shakespeare's tragedies.* 2 an unfortunate or sad event: *His early death was a great tragedy for his family.*

'tragic adj 1 sad; unfortunate: *I heard of the tragic death of her son.* 2 of tragedy or tragedies: *a tragic hero.*

trail [treil] v 1 to drag, or be dragged, along loosely: *Garments were trailing from the suitcase.* 2 to walk slowly and *usu* wearily: *He trailed down the road.* 3 to follow the track of: *The herd of reindeer was being trailed by a pack of wolves.* – n 1 a track (of an animal): *The trail was easy for the hunters to follow.* 2 a path through a forest or other wild area: *a mountain trail.* 3 a line, or series of marks, left by something as it passes: *There was a trail of blood across the floor.*

'trailer n 1 a vehicle pulled behind a motor car: *We carry our luggage in a trailer.* 2 (*Amer*) a caravan. 3 a short film advertising a complete film.

train¹ [trein] n 1 a railway engine with its carriages and/or trucks: *I caught the train to London.* 2 a part of a long dress or robe that trails behind the wearer: *The bride wore a dress with a train.* 3 a connected series: *Then began a train of events which ended in disaster.* **4** a line of animals carrying people or baggage: *a mule train; a baggage train.*

train² [trein] *v* **1** to prepare, be prepared, or prepare oneself, through instruction, practice, exercise *etc*, for a sport, job, profession *etc*: *I was trained as a teacher; The racehorse was trained by my uncle.* **2** to point or aim (a gun, telescope *etc*) in a particular direction: *He trained the gun on/at the soldiers.* **3** to make (a tree, plant *etc*) grow in a particular direction.

trained *adj* (*neg* **un-**) having had teaching: *She's a trained nurse; a well-trained dog.*

,**trai'nee** *n* a person who is being trained: *He's a trainee with an industrial firm; (also adj) a trainee teacher.*

'**trainer** *n* **1** a person who prepares people or animals for sport, a race *etc*. **2** an aircraft used for training pilots.

'**training** *n* **1** preparation for a sport: *He has gone into training for the race.* **2** the process of learning (the practical side of) a job: *It takes many years of training to be a doctor.*

trait [treit] *n* a particular quality of a person's character: *Patience is one of his good traits.*

traitor ['treitə] *n* a person who changes to the enemy's side or gives away information to the enemy: *He was a traitor to his country.*

tram [tram] *n* (*also* '**tramcar**: *Amer* '**streetcar**) a long car running on rails and *usu* driven by electric power, for carrying passengers *esp* along the streets of a town.

'**tramway** *n* a system of tracks for trams.

tramp [tramp] *v* **1** to walk with heavy footsteps: *He tramped up the stairs.* **2** to walk *usu* for a long distance: *She loves tramping over the hills.* – *n* **1** a person with no fixed home or job, who travels around on foot and *usu* lives by begging: *He gave his old coat to a tramp.* **2** a long walk. **3** the sound of heavy footsteps. **4** (*also* **tramp steamer**) a small cargo-boat with no fixed route.

trample ['trampl] *v* to tread heavily (on): *The horses trampled the grass (underfoot).*

trampoline ['trampəli:n] *n* a horizontal framework across which a piece of canvas *etc* is stretched, attached by springs, for gymnasts *etc* to jump on: *Children love jumping on trampolines.*

tramway *see* **tram**.

trance [tra:ns] *n* a sleep-like or half-concious state: *The hypnotist put her into a trance.*

tranquil [ˈtraŋkwil] *adj* quiet; peaceful: *Life in the country is not always tranquil.* '**tranquilly** *adv.* **tran'quillity** *n.*

'**tranquillizer, -s-** *n* a drug *esp* a pill to calm the nerves or cause sleep: *He took a tranquillizer.*

trans- [trans, tranz] across or through.

transact [tran'sakt] *v* to do or carry out (business).

tran'saction [-ʃən] *n* **1** a particular piece of business; a business deal. **2** the act of transacting: *The transaction of the deal took several days.*

transatlantic [tranzət'lantik] *adj* crossing the Atlantic ocean: *transatlantic flights/telephone calls.*

transcontinental ['tranzkonti'nentl] *adj* crossing a continent: *a transcontinental railway.*

transfer [trans'fə:] – *pt, ptp* **trans'ferred** – *v* **1** to remove to another place: *He transferred the letter from his briefcase to his pocket.* **2** to (cause to) move to another place, job, vehicle *etc*: *I'm transferring/ They're transferring me to the Bangkok office.* **3** to give to another person, *esp* legally: *I intend to transfer the property to my son.* – *n* ['transfə:] **1** the act of transferring: *The manager arranged for his transfer to another football club.* **2** a design, picture *etc* that can be transferred from one surface to another, *eg* from paper to material as a guide for embroidery.

trans'ferable *adj* that can be transferred from one place or person to another: *This ticket is not transferable* (= may not be used except by the person to whom it is issued).

transform [trans'fo:m] *v* to change the appearance or nature of completely: *He transformed the old kitchen into a beautiful sitting-room; His marriage has transformed him.*

,**transfor'mation** *n* **1** the act of transforming or process of being transformed: *the transformation of water into ice.* **2** a change: *The event caused a transformation in her character.*

trans'former *n* an apparatus for changing electrical energy from one voltage to another.

transfuse [trans'fju:z] *v* to transfer (the blood of one person) into the veins of another.

trans'fusion [-ʒən] *n* **1** a quantity of blood transferred from one person to another: *She was given a blood transfusion.* **2** the act or process of transferring blood from one person to another.

transistor [tran'sistə] *n* **1** a small electronic device that controls the flow of an electric current. **2** (*also* **transistor radio**) a portable radio that uses these: *She took her transistor everywhere with her.*

transit ['transit] *n* the carrying or movement of goods, passengers *etc* from place to place: *The goods have been lost in transit.*

transition [tran'ziʃən] *n* (a) change from one place, state, subject *etc* to another: *The transition from child to adult can be difficult.*

tran'sitional *adj* of or concerning transition: *a transitional stage/period.*

transitive ['transitiv] *adj* (of a verb) having an object: *He hit the ball; Open the door!*

translate [trans'leit] *v* to put (something said or written) into another language: *He translated the book from French into English.*

trans'lation *n* **1** the act of translating: *The translation of poetry is difficult.* **2** a version of a book, something said *etc*, in another language: *He gave me an Italian translation of the Bible.*

trans'lator *n* a person who translates.

translucent [trans'lu:snt] *adj* allowing light to pass through, but not transparent: *translucent silk.* **trans'lucence, trans'lucency** *ns.*

transmit [tranz'mit] – *pt, ptp* **trans'mitted** – *v* **1** to pass on: *He transmitted the message; Insects can transmit disease.* **2** to send out (radio or television signals, programmes *etc*): *The programme will be transmitted at 5.00 p.m.*

trans'mission [-ʃən] *n* **1** the act of transmitting: *the transmission of disease/radio signals.* **2** a radio or television broadcast.

trans'mitter *n* an apparatus for transmitting, or a person who transmits: *a radio transmitter.*

transparent [trans'parənt, -'peə-] *adj* able to be seen through: *The box has a transparent lid.* **trans'parently** *adv.*

trans'parency [-'pa-] – *pl* **trans'parencies** – *n* **1** the state of being transparent: *the transparency of the water.* **2** a photograph printed on transparent material, a slide: *I took some transparencies of the cathedral.*

transplant [trans'pla:nt] *v* **1** to remove (an organ of the body) and put it into another person or animal: *Doctors are able to transplant kidneys.* **2** to remove (skin) and put it on another part of the body. **3** to plant in another place: *We transplanted the rosebush (into the back garden).* – ['transpla:nt] *n* **1** an operation in which an organ or skin is transplanted: *He had to have a kidney transplant.* **2** an organ, skin, or a plant that is transplanted: *The transplant was rejected by the surrounding tissue.*

transport [trans'po:t] *v* to carry (goods, passengers *etc*) from one place to another: *The goods were transported by air; A bus transported us from the airport to the city.* – ['transpo:t] *n* the process of transporting or being transported: *road transport; My husband is using my car, so I have no (means of) transport.*

trans'portable *adj* able to be transported.

transpor'tation *n* transport.

trans'porter *n* someone or something that transports, *esp* a heavy vehicle for carrying large goods.

trap [trap] *n* **1** a device for catching animals: *He set a trap to catch the bear; a mousetrap.* **2** a plan or trick for taking a person by surprise: *She led him into a trap; He fell straight into the trap.* – *v* – *pt, ptp* **trapped** – to catch in a trap or by a trick: *He lives by trapping animals and selling their fur; She trapped him into admitting that he liked her.*

'trapper *n* a person who traps animals and sells their fur.

'trap-door *n* a small door, or opening, in a floor or ceiling: *A trap-door in the ceiling led to the attic.*

trapeze [trə'pi:z, (*Amer*) tra-] *n* a horizontal bar hung on two ropes, on which gymnasts or acrobats perform: *They performed on the trapeze*; (*also adj*) *a trapeze artist.*

trapper *see* **trap.**

trappings ['trapiŋz] *n pl* clothes or ornaments suitable for a particular occasion or person: *all the trappings of royalty.*

trash [traʃ] *n* rubbish: *Throw it away! It's just trash.*

'trashy *adj* worthless: *trashy jewellery/ novels/music.*

'trashcan *n* (*Amer*) a dustbin.

travel ['travl] – *pt, ptp* **'travelled,** (*Amer*) **'traveled** – *v* **1** to go from place to place; to journey: *I travelled to Scotland by train; He has to travel a long way to school.* **2** to move: *Light travels in a straight line.* **3** to visit places, *esp* foreign countries: *He has travelled a great deal.* – *n* the act of travelling: *Travel to and from work can be very tiring.*

'traveller *n* a person who travels: *a weary traveller.*

'travelogue, (*Amer*) **'travelog** *n* a film, article, talk *etc* about travels.

'travels *n pl* the visiting of foreign countries *etc*: *She's off on her travels again.*

travel agency, travel bureau a place where one can arrange journeys, book tickets *etc*: *We went to the travel agency to book our holidays.*

travel agent a person in charge of, or working in, a travel agency.

traveller's palm a palm of the banana family, with a row of large leaves at the crown.

trawl [tro:l] *n* a wide-mouthed, bag-shaped net used to catch sea fish. – *v* to fish with a trawl.

'trawler *n* a fishing-boat used in trawling.

tray [trei] *n* a flat piece of wood, metal *etc* with a low edge, for carrying dishes *etc*: *She brought in the tea on a tray; a tea-tray.*

treacherous ['tretʃərəs] *adj* **1** betraying or likely to betray: *a treacherous person/act.* **2** dangerous: *The roads are treacherous in winter.* **'treacherously** *adv.* **'treacherousness** *n.*

'treachery *n* (an act of) betraying someone;

disloyalty: *His treachery led to the capture and imprisonment of his friend.*

tread [tred] – *pt* **trod** [trod]; *ptp* **trodden** ['trodn] – *v* **1** to place one's feet on: *He threw his cigarette on the ground and trod on it.* **2** to walk on, along, over *etc*: *He trod the streets looking for a job.* **3** to crush by putting one's feet on: *We watched them treading the grapes.* – *n* **1** a way of walking or putting one's feet: *I heard his heavy tread.* **2** the grooved and patterned surface of a tyre: *The tread has been worn away.* **3** the horizontal part of a step or stair on which the foot is placed.

tread water to keep oneself afloat in an upright position by moving the legs (and arms).

treason ['tri:zn] *n* (*also* **high treason**) disloyalty to, or betrayal of, one's own country: *They were convicted of (high) treason.*

treasure ['treʒə] *n* **1** a store of money, gold, jewels *etc*: *The miser kept a secret hoard of treasure*; (*also adj*) *a treasure chest.* **2** something very valuable: *Our babysitter is a real treasure!* – *v* **1** to value; to think of as very valuable: *I treasure the hours I spend in the country.* **2** to keep (something) carefully because one values it: *I treasure the book you gave me.*

'treasured *adj* regarded as precious; valued: *The photograph of her son is her most treasured possession.*

'treasurer *n* the person in a club, society *etc*, who looks after the money.

treat [tri:t] *v* **1** to deal with, or behave towards (a thing or person), in a certain manner: *The soldiers treated me very well*; *The police are treating his death as a case of murder.* **2** to try to cure (a person or disease, injury *etc*): *They treated her for a broken leg.* **3** to put (something) through a process: *The woodwork has been treated with a new chemical.* **4** to buy (a meal, present *etc*) for (someone): *I'll treat you to lunch*; *She treated herself to a new hat.* **5** to write or speak about; to discuss. – *n* something that gives pleasure, *eg* an arranged outing, or some special food: *He took them to the theatre as a treat.*

'treatment *n* (an) act or manner of treating: *This chair seems to have received rough treatment*; *This patient/disease requires urgent treatment.*

treaty ['tri:ti] – *pl* **'treaties** – *n* a formal agreement between states or governments: *They signed a peace treaty.*

treble ['trebl] *n, adj* (something that is) three times as much, many *etc* as something else, or as the normal: *He earns treble what I do.* – *v* to make, or become, three times as much: *He trebled his earnings*; *His income has trebled.* **'trebly** *adv.*

tree [tri:] *n* the largest kind of plant, with a thick, firm, wooden stem and branches: *We have three apple trees growing in our garden.*

'treetop *n* the top of a tree: *the birds in the treetops.*

'tree-trunk *n* the trunk of a tree.

trek [trek] – *pt, ptp* **trekked** – *v* to make a long, hard journey. – *n* a long, hard journey: *a trek through the mountains*; *a trek round the supermarket.*

tremble ['trembl] *v* to shake *eg* with cold, fear, weakness *etc*: *She trembled with cold*; *His hands trembled as he lit a cigarette.* – *n* a shudder; a tremor: *a tremble of fear*; *The walls gave a sudden tremble as the lorry passed by.*

tremendous [trə'mendəs] *adj* very large; very great: *That required a tremendous effort*; *The response to our appeal was tremendous.* **tre'mendously** *adv* very: *It's tremendously interesting*; *He's tremendously strong.*

tremor ['tremə] *n* a shaking or quivering: *Earth tremors* (=slight earthquakes) *were felt in Sicily yesterday.*

trench [trentʃ] *n* a long narrow ditch dug in the ground, *esp* as a protection for soldiers against gunfire: *The soldiers returned to the trenches.*

trend [trend] *n* a general direction or tendency: *She follows all the latest trends in fashion*; *an upward trend in share prices.* **'trendy** *adj* following the latest fashions: *trendy people/clothes*; *Her mother tries to be trendy.*

trespass ['trespəs] *v* to enter illegally: *You are trespassing (on my land).* – *n* the act of trespassing. **'trespasser** *n* a person who trespasses.

trestle ['tresl] *n* a wooden support with legs: *The platform was on trestles*; (*also adj*) *a trestle table.*

trial ['traiəl] *n* **1** an act of testing or trying; a test: *Give the new car a trial*; *The disaster was a trial of his courage.* **2** a legal process by which a person is judged in a court of law: *Their trial will be held next week.* **3** a (source of) trouble or anxiety: *My son is a great trial (to me).*

trial run a rehearsal, first test *etc* of anything, *eg* a play, car, piece of machinery *etc*.

on trial 1 the subject of a legal action in court: *She's on trial for murder.* **2** undergoing tests or examination: *We've had a new television installed, but it's only on trial.*

trial and error the trying of various methods, alternatives *etc* until the right one happens to appear or be found: *They didn't know how to put in a central-heating system, but they managed it by trial and error.*

*triangle ['traiaŋgl] *n* **1** a two-dimensional figure with three sides and three angles. **2** a musical instrument consisting of a triangu-

* see illustration on p. 476

Trees

Key

1 Casuarina
2 Oil Palm
3 Pine
4 Lime
5 Flame of the Forest

lar metal bar that is struck with a small hammer.

tri'angular [-gju-] *adj* in the shape of a triangle: *a triangular road-sign*; *It is triangular in shape.*

tribe [traib] *n* **1** a race of people, or a family, who are all descended from the same ancestor: *the tribes of Israel.* **2** a group of families, *esp* of a primitive or wandering people, ruled by a chief: *the desert tribes of Africa.* **'tribal** *adj* of a tribe or tribes: *tribal lands/customs*; *the tribal system.*

'tribesman ['traibz-] *n* a man who belongs to a tribe: *an African tribesman.*

tribunal [trai'bju:nl] *n* a group of people appointed to give judgement, *esp* on official decisions: *The case was dealt with by a tribunal.*

tributary ['tribjutəri] – *pl* **'tributaries** – *n* a stream flowing into a river: *The River Thames has many tributaries*; (*also adj*) *tributary streams.*

tribute ['tribju:t] *n* (an) expression of praise, thanks *etc*: *This statue has been erected as a tribute to a great man*; *We must pay tribute to his great courage.*

be a tribute to to be the (praiseworthy) result of: *The success of the scheme is a tribute to his hard work.*

trick [trik] *n* **1** something which is done, said *etc* in order to cheat or deceive someone, and sometimes to frighten them or make them appear stupid: *The message was just a trick to get her to leave the room.* **2** a clever or skilful action (to amuse *etc*): *The magician performed some clever tricks.* – *adj* intended to deceive or give a certain illusion: *trick photography.*

'trickery *n* the act of deceiving or cheating: *She could not stand his trickery.*

'trickster *n* a cheat.

'tricky *adj* difficult: *a tricky problem/job*; *a tricky person to deal with.* **'trickily** *adv.* **'trickiness** *n.*

do the trick to do or be what is necessary: *I need a piece of paper. This old envelope will do the trick!*

play a trick/tricks on to do something which is amusing to oneself because it deceives or frightens (someone else), or makes them appear stupid: *He played a trick on her by jumping out from behind a wall as she passed.*

a trick of the trade one of the ways of being successful in a job *etc*: *Remembering the customers' names is one of the tricks of the trade.*

trickle ['trikl] *v* to flow in small amounts: *Blood was trickling down her face.* – *n* a small amount: *a trickle of water*; *At first there was only a trickle of people but soon a crowd arrived.*

tricky *see* **trick.**

tricycle ['traisikl] *n* a kind of cycle with three wheels.

trier, tries *see* **try.**

trifle ['traifl] *n* **1** anything of very little value: *$100 is a trifle when one is very rich.* **2** (a dish of) a sweet pudding made of spongecake, fruit, cream *etc*: *I'm making a trifle for dessert.*

'trifling *adj* unimportant: *a trifling amount of money.*

trigger ['trigə] *n* **1** a small lever on a gun, which is pulled to make the gun fire: *He aimed the rifle at her but did not pull the trigger.* **2** anything which starts a series of actions or reactions. – *v* (*often with* **off**) to start (a series of events): *The attack triggered (off) a full-scale war.*

trim [trim] – *pt, ptp* **trimmed** – *v* **1** to cut the edges or ends of (something) in order to make it shorter and/or neat: *He's trimming the hedge*; *She had her hair trimmed.* **2** to decorate (a dress, hat *etc, usu* round the edges): *She trimmed the sleeves with lace.* **3** to arrange (the sails of a boat *etc*) suitably for the weather conditions. – *n* a haircut: *She went to the hairdresser's for a trim.* – *adj* neat and tidy: *a trim appearance.* **'trimly** *adv.* **'trimness** *n.*

'trimming *n* **1** something added as a decoration: *lace trimming.* **2** (*usu in pl*) a piece cut off; an end or edge.

in (good) trim in good condition: *Her figure's in good trim after all those exercises.*

trinket ['triŋkit] *n* a small (*usu* cheap) ornament or piece of jewellery: *That shop sells postcards and trinkets.*

trio ['tri:ou] – *pl* **'trios** – *n* **1** a group of three (people or things). **2** (a piece of music for) three players: *A trio was playing in the hotel lounge*; *a trio by Mozart.*

trip [trip] – *pt, ptp* **tripped** – *v* **1** (*often with* **up** *or* **over**) to (cause to) catch one's foot and stumble or fall: *She tripped and fell*; *She tripped over the carpet.* **2** to walk with short, light steps: *She tripped happily along the road.* – *n* a journey or tour: *She went on/took a trip to Paris.*

triple ['tripl] *adj* **1** three times (as big, much *etc* as usual): *He received triple wages for all his extra work*; *a triple whisky.* **2** made up of three (parts *etc*): *a triple agreement.* – *v* to make or become three times as much, big *etc*; to treble: *He tripled his income*; *His income tripled in ten years.* – *n* three times the (usual) amount: *If you work the bank holiday, you will be paid triple.*

'triplet [-lit] *n* one of three children or animals born to the same mother at the same time: *She's just had triplets.*

triplicate ['triplikət]: **in triplicate** on three

separate copies (of the same form *etc*): *Fill in the form in triplicate.*

tripod ['traipod] *n* a stand with three legs, *esp* for a camera.

trishaw ['traiʃɔ:] *n* a small, light vehicle with three wheels for carrying people or goods, pedalled by the operator.

trite [trait] *adj* (of a remark, saying *etc*) already said in exactly the same way so often that it no longer has any worth, effectiveness *etc*: *His poetry is full of trite descriptions of nature.* '**tritely** *adv*. '**triteness** *n*.

triumph ['traiʌmf] *n* **1** a great victory or success: *The battle ended in a triumph for the Romans.* **2** a state of happiness, celebration, pride *etc* after a success: *They went home in triumph.* – *v* to win a victory: *The Romans triumphed (over their enemies).* **tri'umphal** *adj* having to do with (a) triumph: *a triumphal battle.* **tri'umphant** *adj* (glad and excited because of) having won a victory, achieved something difficult *etc*: *He gave a triumphant shout.* **tri'umphantly** *adv*.

trivia ['triviə] *n pl* unimportant matters or details: *I haven't time to worry about such trivia.* '**trivial** *adj* **1** of very little importance: *trivial details.* **2** (*esp* of people) only interested in unimportant things; not at all serious: *She's a very trivial person.* '**trivially** *adv*. **tri'viality** [-'a-] *n* **1** the state of being trivial. **2** (*pl* **tri'vialities**) something which is trivial: *He is always worrying about some triviality or other.*

trod, trodden *see* **tread**.

troll [troul] *n* an imaginary creature of human-like form, very ugly and evil-tempered.

trolley ['troli] *n* **1** a type of small cart for carrying things *etc*: *She quickly filled the trolley with groceries.* **2** (*also* '**tea-trolley**, (*Amer*) '**teacart**) a small cart, *usu* consisting of two or three trays fixed on a frame, used for serving tea, food *etc*: *She brought the tea in on a trolley.* '**trolley-bus** *n* a bus which is driven by power from an overhead wire to which it is connected.

trombone [trom'boun] *n* a type of brass musical wind instrument, on which the pitch of notes is altered by sliding a tube in and out: *He plays the trombone; He played a tune on his trombone.* **trom'bonist** *n* a person who plays the trombone.

troop [tru:p] *n* **1** a group of ordinary soldiers. **2** a crowd or collection (of people or animals): *A troop of visitors arrived.* – *v* to go in a group: *They all trooped into his office.* '**trooper** *n* an ordinary soldier.

troops *n pl* soldiers.

trophy ['troufi] – *pl* '**trophies**. – *n* **1** a prize for winning in a sport *etc*: *He won a silver trophy for shooting.* **2** something which is kept in memory of a victory, success *etc*.

tropic ['tropik] *n* either of two imaginary circles running round the earth at about 23 degrees north (**Tropic of Cancer**) or south (**Tropic of Capricorn**) of the equator. '**tropics** *n pl* the hot regions between or (*loosely*) near these lines: *The ship is heading for the tropics.* '**tropical** *adj* **1** of the tropics; *The climate there is tropical.* **2** growing *etc* in hot countries: *tropical plants.* '**tropically** *adv*.

trot [trot] – *pt, ptp* '**trotted** – *v* (of a horse) to move with fairly fast, bouncy steps, faster than a walk but slower than a canter or gallop: *The horse trotted down the road; The child trotted along beside his mother.* – *n* the pace at which a horse or rider *etc* moves when trotting: *They rode at a trot.* '**trotter** *n* a pig's foot.

trouble ['trʌbl] *n* **1** (something which causes) worry, difficulty, work, anxiety *etc*: *He never talks about his troubles; We've had a lot of trouble with our children; I had a lot of trouble finding the book you wanted.* **2** disturbances; rebellion, fighting *etc*: *It occurred during the time of the troubles in Cyprus.* **3** illness or weakness (in a particular part of the body): *He has heart trouble.* – *v* **1** to cause worry, anger or sadness to: *She was troubled by the news of her sister's illness.* **2** used as part of a very polite and formal request: *May I trouble you to close the window?* **3** to make any effort: *He didn't even trouble to tell me what had happened.* '**troubled** *adj* (*neg* **un-**) **1** worried or anxious: *He is obviously a troubled man.* **2** disturbed and not peaceful: *troubled sleep.* '**troublesome** *adj* causing worry or difficulty: *troublesome children/tasks.* '**troublemaker** *n* a person who continually (and *usu* deliberately) causes worry, difficulty or disturbance to other people: *Beware of her – she is a real troublemaker.*

trough [trof] *n* **1** a long, low, open container for animals' food or water: *a drinking-trough for the cattle.* **2** a low part between two waves (in the sea *etc*): *The boat went down into a trough.* **3** an area of low pressure in the atmosphere, *usu* causing rain.

trounce [trauns] *v* to beat or defeat completely: *Our football team was trounced.*

troupe [tru:p] *n* a performing group (of actors, dancers *etc*): *a circus troupe.* '**trouper** *n* **1** a member of a group of this kind. **2** a hard-working colleague.

trousers ['trauzəz] *n pl* an outer garment for the lower part of the body, covering each leg separately: *He wore (a pair of) black* *trousers*; *She was dressed in trousers and a sweater.*

trouser- of trousers: *a trouser-button*; *That dog has torn my trouser-leg.*

trout [traut] – *pl* **trout** – *n* **1** a type of freshwater fish of the salmon family: *He caught five trout.* **2** its flesh, used as food: *Have some more trout!*

trowel ['trauǝl] *n* **1** a tool like a small shovel, used in gardening: *He filled the flowerpot with earth, using a trowel.* **2** a tool with a flat blade, for spreading mortar, plaster *etc.*

truant ['truǝnt] *n* someone who stays away from school *etc* without permission: *The truants were caught and sent back to school.* **'truancy** *n*: *Truancy is a great problem in some schools.*

play truant to be a truant and stay away from school *etc*: *He was always playing truant (from school).*

truce [truːs] *n* a (*usu* temporary) rest from fighting, agreed to by both sides.

truck [trʌk] *n* **1** a railway vehicle for carrying goods. **2** (*esp Amer*) a lorry: *He drives a truck*; (*also adj*) *a truck-driver.*

trudge [trʌdʒ] *v* to walk with slow, tired steps: *He trudged wearily up the hill.* – *n* such a walk or way of walking.

true [truː] *adj* **1** (*neg* un-) telling of something that really happened; not invented; agreeing with fact; not wrong: *That is a true statement*; *Is it true that you did not steal the ring?* **2** (*neg* un-) accurate: *They don't have a true idea of its importance.* **3** (*neg* un-) faithful; loyal: *He has been a true friend.* **4** properly so called: *A spider is not a true insect.* **'trueness** *n*.

'truly *adv* **1** really: *I truly believe that this decision is the right one.* **2** in a true manner: *He loved her truly.*

trump [trʌmp] *n* in some card games, any card of a suit which has been declared to rank higher than the other suits: *This time, hearts are trumps*; (*also adj*) *a trump card.* – *v* to defeat (an ordinary card) by playing a card from the trump suit: *He trumped (my king) with a heart.*

trumpet ['trʌmpit] *n* **1** a brass musical wind instrument with a high, clear tone: *He plays the trumpet*; *He played a tune on his trumpet.* **2** the cry of an elephant: *The elephant gave a loud trumpet.* – *v* to make a noise like a trumpet.

'trumpeter *n* a person who plays the trumpet.

blow one's own trumpet to boast, praise oneself greatly *etc.*

truncheon ['trʌntʃǝn] *n* a short heavy stick, carried *esp* by British policemen.

trundle ['trʌndl] *v* to (cause to) roll slowly and heavily along on wheels: *He trundled*

the wheelbarrow down the garden; *The huge lorry trundled along the road.*

trunk [trʌŋk] *n* **1** the main stem (of a tree): *The trunk of this tree is five metres thick.* **2** a large box or chest for packing or keeping clothes *etc* in: *He packed his trunk and sent it to Canada by sea.* **3** an elephant's long nose: *The elephant sucked up water into its trunk.* **4** the body (not including the head, arms and legs) of a person (and certain animals): *He had a powerful trunk, but thin arms.* **5** (*Amer*) a boot (of a car): *Put your baggage in the trunk.*

trunks *n pl* short trousers or pants worn by boys or men, *esp* the type used for swimming: *swimming-trunks*; *He wore only a pair of bathing-trunks.*

truss [trʌs] *v* to tie or bind tightly: *She trussed the chicken and put it in the oven*; *The burglars trussed up the guards.*

trust [trʌst] *v* **1** to have confidence or faith; to believe: *She trusted (in) him.* **2** to give (something to someone), believing that it will be used well and responsibly: *I can't trust him with my car*; *I can't trust my car to him.* **3** to hope or be confident (that): *I trust (that) you had/will have a good journey.* – *n* **1** belief or confidence in the power, reality, truth, goodness *etc* of a person or thing: *The firm has a great deal of trust in your ability*; *trust in God.* **2** charge or care; responsibility: *The child was placed in my trust.* **3** a task *etc* given to a person by someone who believes that they will do it, look after it *etc* well: *He holds a position of trust in the firm.* **4** arrangement(s) by which something (*eg* money) is given to a person to use in a particular way, or to keep until a particular time: *The money was to be held in trust for his children*; (*also adj*) *a trust fund.* **5** a group of business firms working together: *The companies formed a trust.*

,trus'tee *n* a person who keeps and takes care of something (*esp* money or property) for someone else.

'trustworthy *adj* (*neg* un-) worthy of trust: *Is your friend trustworthy?* **'trustworthiness** *n*.

'trusty *adj* able to be trusted or depended on: *a trusty sword*; *a trusty friend.* **'trustily** *adv*. **'trustiness** *n*.

truth [truːθ] – *pl* **truths** [truːðz, truːθs] – *n* **1** trueness; the state of being true: *I am certain of the truth of his story*; *'What is truth?' asked the philosopher.* **2** the true facts: *I don't know, and that's the truth!*; *Tell the truth about it.*

'truthful *adj* (*neg* un-) **1** (of a person) telling the truth: *She's a truthful child.* **2** true: *a truthful account of what happened.* **'truthfully** *adv*. **'truthfulness** *n*.

tell the truth to confess or make a true statement.

to tell the truth really; actually: *To tell the truth I forgot it was your birthday last week.*

try [trai] *v* **1** to attempt or make an effort (to do, get *etc*): *He tried to answer the questions*; *Let's try and climb that tree!* **2** to test; to make an experiment (with) in order to find out whether something will be successful, satisfactory *etc*: *She tried washing her hair with a new shampoo*; *Have you tried the local beer?* **3** to judge (someone or their case) in a court of law: *The prisoners were tried for murder.* **4** to test the limits of; to strain: *You are trying my patience.* – *n* – *pl* **tries** – **1** an attempt or effort: *Have a try (at the exam).* *I'm sure you will pass.* **2** in rugby football, an act of putting the ball on the ground behind the opponents' goal-line: *Our team scored three tries.*

'trier *n* a person who keeps on trying, who does not give up: *He's not very good, but he's a trier.*

'trying *adj* **1** difficult; causing strain or anxiety: *Having to stay such a long time in hospital must be very trying.* **2** (of people) stretching one's patience to the limit; annoying: *She's a very trying woman!*

try on to put on (clothes *etc*) to see if they fit: *She tried on a new hat.*

try out to test (something) by using it: *We are trying out new teaching methods.*

tsar, czar, tzar [za:] *n* (the status of) any of the former emperors of Russia: *He was crowned tsar*; *Tsar Nicholas.*

T-shirt *see* T.

tub [tʌb] *n* **1** a round (*usu* wooden) container for keeping water, washing clothes *etc*: *a huge tub of water.* **2** a bath: *He was sitting in the tub.* **3** a small round container for ice-cream *etc*.

'tubby *adj* rather fat: plump: *She was rather tubby as a child but she is very slim now.*

tuba ['tju:bə] *n* a large brass musical wind instrument giving a low-pitched range of notes: *He plays the tuba.*

tubby *see* **tub**.

tube [tju:b] *n* **1** a long, low cylinder-shaped object through which liquid can pass; a pipe: *The water flowed through a rubber tube*; *a glass tube.* **2** an organ of this kind in animals or plants. **3** an underground railway (*esp* in London): *I go to work on the tube/by tube*; (*also adj*) *a tube train/station.* **4** a container for a semi-liquid substance which is got out by squeezing: *I must buy a tube of toothpaste.*

'tubing *n* (material for) a length or system of tubes: *two metres of tubing.*

'tubular [-bjulə] *adj* **1** made of, or consisting of tubes: *tubular steel.* **2** shaped like a tube: *The container is tubular in shape.*

tuber ['tju:bə] *n* a swelling on the stem or root of a plant, in which food is stored: *Potatoes are the tubers of the potato plant.*

tuberculosis [tjubə:kju'lousis] *n* (*often abbrev* **TB** [ti:'bi:]) an infectious disease *usu* affecting the lungs: *He suffers from/has tuberculosis.*

tubing, tubular *see* **tube**.

tuck [tʌk] *n* **1** a fold sewn into a piece of material: *Her dress had tucks in the sleeves.* **2** sweets, cakes *etc*: *Schoolboys used to spend their money on tuck*; (*also adj*) *a tuck shop.* – *v* to push, stuff *etc*: *He tucked his shirt into his trousers.*

tuck in **1** to gather bedclothes *etc* closely round: *I said goodnight and tucked him in.* **2** to eat greedily or with enjoyment: *They sat down to breakfast and started to tuck in straight away.*

Tuesday ['tju:zdi] *n* the third day of the week, the day following Monday: *He came on Tuesday*; (*also adj*) *Tuesday evening.*

tuft [tʌft] *n* a small bunch or clump (of grass, hair, feathers *etc*): *She sat down on a tuft of grass.*

'tufted *adj* having or growing in tufts: *a tufted carpet*; *tufted grass.*

tug [tʌg] – *pt, ptp* **tugged** – *v* to pull (something) sharply and strongly: *He tugged (at) the door but it wouldn't open.* – *n* **1** a strong, sharp pull: *He gave the rope a tug.* **2** a tug-boat.

'tug-boat *n* a small boat with a very powerful engine, for towing larger ships.

,tug-of-'war *n* a competition in which two people or teams pull at opposite ends of a rope, trying to pull their opponents over a centre line.

tuition [tju'iʃən] *n* teaching, *esp* private: *He gives music tuition/tuition in music.*

tulip ['tju:lip] *n* a kind of plant with brightly-coloured cup-shaped flowers, grown from a bulb.

tumble ['tʌmbl] *v* to (cause to) fall, *esp* in a helpless or confused way: *She tumbled down the stairs*; *The box suddenly tumbled off the top of the wardrobe.* – *n* a fall: *She took a tumble on the stairs.*

'tumbler *n* **1** a large drinking glass: *a tumbler of whisky.* **2** a tumblerful.

'tumblerful *n* the amount contained by a tumbler: *two tumblerfuls of water.*

,tumble-'drier *n* a machine for drying clothes by tumbling them around and blowing hot air into them.

tummy ['tʌmi] – *pl* **'tummies** – *n* a (*esp* child's) word for stomach: *She has a pain in her tummy*; (*also adj*) *a tummy-ache.*

tumour, (*Amer*) **tumor** ['tju:mə] *n* an abnormal (dangerous) mass of tissue growing on or in the body: *a brain tumour*; *The surgeon removed a tumour from her bladder.*

tumult ['tjuːmʌlt] *n* a great noise (*usu* made by a crowd): *He could hear a great tumult in the street.*

tu'multuous [-tʃuəs] *adj* with great noise or confusion: *The crowd gave him a tumultuous welcome*; *tumultuous applause.* **tu'multuously** *adv.*

tuna(-fish) ['tʃuːnə(fiʃ), (*Amer*) 'tuːnə(-)] – *pls* **'tuna, 'tuna-fish, 'tunas** – (*also* **tunny(-fish)** ['tʌni(fiʃ)] – *pls* **'tunnies, 'tunny, 'tunny-fish**) – *n* **1** a kind of large seafish of the mackerel family. **2** its flesh, used as food.

tune [tjuːn] *n* musical notes put together in a particular (melodic and pleasing) order; a melody: *He played a tune on the violin.* – *v* **1** to adjust (a musical instrument, or its strings *etc*) to the correct pitch: *The orchestra tuned their instruments.* **2** to adjust a radio so that it receives a particular station: *The radio was tuned to a German station.* **3** to adjust (an engine *etc*) so that it runs well.

'tuneful *adj* having a good, clear, pleasant *etc* tune: *That song is very tuneful.* **'tunefully** *adv.* **'tunefulness** *n.*

'tuneless *adj* without a good *etc* tune; unmusical: *The child was singing in a tuneless voice.* **'tunelessly** *adv.* **'tunelessness** *n.*

'tuner *n* **1** (*also* **pi'ano-tuner**) a person whose profession is tuning pianos. **2** the dial on a radio *etc* used to tune in to the different stations. **3** a radio which is part of a stereo system.

change one's tune to change one's attitude, opinions *etc.*

in tune 1 (of a musical instrument) having been adjusted so as to give the correct pitches: *Is the violin in tune with the piano?* **2** (of a person's singing voice) at the same pitch as that of other voices or instruments: *Someone in the choir isn't (singing) in tune.*

out of tune not in tune.

tune in to tune a radio (to a particular station or programme): *We usually tune (the radio) in to the news.*

tune up (of an orchestra *etc*) to tune instruments.

tunic ['tjuːnik] *n* **1** a soldier's or policeman's jacket. **2** a loose garment worn *esp* in ancient Greece and Rome. **3** a similar type of modern garment.

tunnel ['tʌnl] *n* a (*usu* man-made) underground passage, *esp* one cut through a hill or under a river: *The road goes through a tunnel under the river.* – *v* – *pt, ptp* **'tunnelled,** (*Amer*) **'tunneled** – to make a tunnel: *They escaped from prison by tunnelling under the walls.*

tunny(-fish) *see* **tuna(-fish).**

turban ['təːbən] *n* a long piece of cloth worn wound round the head, *esp* by men belonging to certain of the races and religions of Asia.

turbine ['təːbain] *n* a type of motor, operated by the action of water, steam, gas *etc*: *a steam turbine.*

turbo- [təːbou] having a turbine engine: *a turbojet (aircraft).*

turbulent ['təːbjulənt] *adj* violently disturbed or confused: *The seas are turbulent*; *the turbulent years of war.* **'turbulently** *adv.* **'turbulence** *n.*

turf [təːf] – *pl* **turfs** [-fs], **turves** [-vz] – *n* **1** rough grass and the earth it grows out of: *He walked across the springy turf.* **2** (a *usu* square piece of) grass and earth: *We laid turf in our garden to make a lawn.* – *v* **1** to cover with turf(s): *We are going to turf that part of the garden.* **2** to throw: *We turfed him out of the house.*

turkey ['təːki] *n* **1** a kind of large farmyard bird. **2** its flesh used as food, eaten *esp* at Christmas or (in the US) Thanksgiving: *We had turkey for dinner.*

turmoil ['təːmoil] *n* a state of wild confused movement or disorder: *The crowd/His mind was in (a) turmoil.*

turn [təːn] *v* **1** to (make something) move or go round; to revolve: *The wheels turned*; *He turned the handle.* **2** to face or go in another direction: *He turned and walked away*; *She turned towards him.* **3** to change direction: *The road turned to the left.* **4** to direct; to aim or point: *He turned his attention to his work.* **5** to go round: *They turned the corner.* **6** to (cause something to) become or change to: *You can't turn lead into gold*; *At what temperature does water turn into ice?* **7** to (cause to) change colour to: *Her hair turned white*; *The shock turned his hair white.* – *n* **1** an act of turning: *He gave the handle a turn.* **2** a winding or coil: *There are eighty turns of wire on this aerial.* **3** (*also* **'turning**) a point where one can change direction, *eg* where one road joins another: *Take the third turn(ing) on/to the left.* **4** one's chance or duty (to do, have *etc* something shared by several people): *It's your turn to choose a record*; *You'll have to wait your turn in the bathroom.* **5** one of a series of short circus or variety acts, or the person or persons who perform it: *The show opened with a comedy turn.*

'turning-point *n* a place where a turn is made: *the turning-point in the race*; *a turning-point in his life.*

'turnover *n* **1** the total value of sales in a business during a certain time: *The firm had a turnover of \$100 000 last year.* **2** the rate at which money or workers pass through a business.

'turnstile *n* a revolving gate which allows only one person to pass at a time, *usu* after payment of entrance fees *etc*: *There is a turnstile at the entrance to the football ground.*

'**turntable** *n* the revolving part of a record-player on which the record rests while it is being played: *He put another record on the turntable so that people could dance to the music.*

'**turn-up** *n* a piece of material which is folded up at the bottom of a trouser-leg: *Trousers with turn-ups are not fashionable at the moment.*

by turns in turn (*see below*).

do (someone) a good turn to do something helpful for someone: *He did me several good turns.*

in turn, by turns one after another, in regular order: *They answered the teacher's questions in turn.*

out of turn out of the correct order.

take a turn for the better, worse (of things or people) to become better or worse: *His fortunes have taken a turn for the better; Her health has taken a turn for the worse.*

take turns (of two or more people) to do something one after the other, not at the same time: *They took turns to look after the baby.*

turn a blind eye to pretend not to see or notice (something): *Because he works so hard, his boss turns a blind eye when he comes in late.*

turn against to become dissatisfied with or hostile to (people or things that one previously liked *etc*): *He turned against his friends.*

turn away to move or send away: *He turned away in disgust; The police turned away the crowds.*

turn back to (cause to) go back in the opposite direction: *He got tired and turned back; The travellers were turned back at the frontier.*

turn down 1 to say 'no' to; to refuse: *He turned down her offer/request.* **2** to reduce (the level of light, noise *etc*) produced by (something): *Please turn down (the volume on) the radio – it's far too loud!*

turn in to hand over (a person or thing) to people in authority: *They turned the escaped prisoner in to the police.*

turn loose to set free: *He turned the horse loose in the field.*

turn off 1 to cause (water, electricity *etc*) to stop flowing: *I've turned off the water/the electricity.* **2** to turn (a tap, switch *etc*) so that something stops: *I turned off the tap.* **3** to cause (something) to stop working by switching it off: *He turned off the light/the oven.*

turn on 1 to make water, electric current *etc* flow: *He turned on the water/the gas.* **2** to

turn (a tap, switch *etc*) so that something works: *I turned on the tap.* **3** to cause (something) to work by switching it on: *He turned on the radio.* **4** to attack: *The dog turned on him.*

turn out 1 to send away; to make (someone) leave. **2** to make or produce: *The factory turns out ten finished articles an hour.* **3** to empty or clear: *I turned out the cupboard.* **4** (of a crowd) to come out; to get together for a (public) meeting, celebration *etc*: *A large crowd turned out to see the procession.* **5** to turn off: *Turn out the light!* **6** to happen or prove to be: *He turned out to be right; It turned out that he was right.*

turn over to give (something) up (to): *He turned the money over to the police.*

turn up 1 to appear or arrive: *He turned up at our house.* **2** to be found: *Don't worry – it'll turn up again.* **3** to increase (the level of noise, light *etc*) produced by (something): *Turn up (the volume on) the radio.*

turnip [tə:nip] *n* **1** a type of plant with a large round root: *a field of turnips.* **2** the root used as food: *Would you like some turnip?*

turnstile, turntable *see* **turn.**

turpentine [tə:pəntain] *n* a type of oil used for thinning certain kinds of paint, cleaning paint-brushes *etc*.

turquoise ['tə:kwoiz] *n* **1** a kind of greenish-blue precious stone: *The ring was set with a turquoise.* **2** (*also adj*) (of) its colour: (*a*) *pale turquoise (dress).*

turtle *n* a kind of large tortoise, *esp* one living in water.

'**turtle-neck** *n* (a garment, *esp* a sweater, with) a high round neck: *He was wearing a turtle-neck;* (*also adj*) *a turtle-neck sweater.*

turtle soup made from the flesh of a type of turtle.

turves *see* **turf.**

tusk [tʌsk] *n* one of a pair of large curved teeth which project from the mouth of certain animals *eg* the elephant, walrus, wild boar *etc*.

tut(-tut) (*sometimes* [tʌt('tʌt)]) *interj* used in writing to represent the sound used to express disapproval, mild annoyance *etc*.

tutelage ['tju:təlij] *n* **1** guardianship. **2** tuition, instruction.

tutor ['tju:tə] *n* **1** a teacher of a group of students in a college or university. **2** a privately-employed teacher: *His parents employed a tutor to teach him Greek.* **3** a book which teaches a subject, *esp* music: *I bought a violin tutor.* – *v* to teach: *He tutored the child in mathematics.*

tu'torial [-'to:-] *adj* of or concerning a tutor. – *n* a lesson by a tutor at a college or university: *We have lectures and tutorials in history.*

tutu ['tu:tu:] *n* a female ballet dancer's short stiff skirt.

twang [twaŋ] *n* a sound of or like a tightly-stretched string breaking or being plucked: *The string broke with a sharp twang.* – *v* to make a twang: *He twanged his guitar; The wire twanged.*

tweak [twi:k] *v* to pull with a sudden jerk. – *n* a sudden sharp pull: *He gave her nose a playful tweak.*

tweezers ['twi:zəz] *n pl* a tool for gripping or pulling hairs, small objects *etc*: *She used a pair of tweezers to pluck her eyebrows.*

twelve [twelv] *n* 1 the number or figure 12. 2 the age of 12. – *adj* 1 12 in number. 2 aged 12.
twelve- having twelve (of something): *a twelve-week delay.*
'twelfth [-fθ] *n* 1 one of twelve equal parts. 2 (*also adj*) (the) last of twelve (people, things *etc*); (the) next after the eleventh.
'twelve-year-old *n* a person or animal who is twelve years old. – *adj* (of a person, animal or thing) that is twelve years old.

twenty ['twenti] *n* 1 the number or figure 20. 2 the age of 20. – *adj* 1 20 in number. 2 aged 20.
'twenties *n pl* 1 the period of time between one's twentieth and thirtieth birthdays. 2 the range of temperatures between twenty and thirty degrees. 3 the period of time between the twentieth and thirtieth years of a century.
'twentieth *n* 1 one of twenty equal parts. 2 (*also adj*) (the) last of twenty (people, things *etc*); (the) next after the nineteenth.
twenty- having twenty (of something).
'twenty-year-old *n* a person who is twenty years old. – *adj* (of a person or thing) twenty years old.

twice [twais] *adv* 1 two times: *I've been to London twice.* 2 two times the amount of: *She has twice his courage.* 3 two times as good *etc* as: *He is twice the man you are.*
think twice about (doing) something to be very careful about considering (doing) something: *I wouldn't think twice about sacking him.*

twiddle ['twidl] *v* to twist (something) round and round: *He twiddled the knob on the radio.*

twig [twig] *n* a small branch of a tree: *The ground was covered with broken twigs.*

twilight ['twailait] *n* 1 (the time of) the dim light just before the sun rises or just after it sets. 2 the time when the full strength or power of something is decreasing: *in the twilight of his life.*

twin [twin] *n* 1 one of two children or animals born of the same mother at the same time: *She gave birth to twins; (also adj) They have twin daughters.* 2 one of two similar or identical things: *Her dress is the exact twin of mine.*

twine [twain] *n* a strong kind of string made of twisted threads: *He tied the parcel with twine.* – *v* (*neg* **un-**) to twist: *The ivy twined round the tree.*

twinge [twindʒ] *n* a sudden sharp pain: *He felt a twinge (of pain) in his neck; a twinge of regret.*

twinkle ['twiŋkl] *v* 1 to shine with a small, slightly unsteady light: *The stars twinkled in the sky.* 2 (of eyes) to shine in this way *usu* to express amusement: *His eyes twinkled mischievously.* – *n* 1 an expression of amusement (in one's eyes). 2 the act of twinkling.

twirl [twə:l] *v* to (cause to) turn round (and round); to spin: *She twirled her hair round her finger.* – *n* an act of twirling.

twist [twist] *v* 1 to turn round (and round): *He twisted the knob; The road twisted through the mountains.* 2 to wind around or together: *He twisted the pieces of string (together) to make a rope.* 3 to force out of the correct shape or position: *The heat of the fire twisted the metal; He twisted her arm painfully.* – *n* 1 the act of twisting. 2 a twisted piece of something: *He added a twist of lemon to her drink.* 3 a turn, coil *etc*: *There's a twist in the rope.* 4 a change in direction (of a story *etc*): *The story had a strange twist at the end.*
'twisted *adj* bent out of shape: *a twisted branch; a twisted report.*
'twister *n* a dishonest or deceiving person.

twit [twit] *n* a fool or idiot: *Stupid twit!*

twitch [twitʃ] *v* 1 to (cause to) move jerkily: *His hands were twitching.* 2 to give a little pull or jerk to (something): *He twitched her sleeve.* – *n* a twitching movement.

twitter ['twitə] *n* a light, repeated chirping sound, *esp* made by (small) birds: *He could hear the twitter of sparrows.* – *v* to make such a noise.

two [tu:] *n* 1 the number or figure 2. 2 the age of 2. – *adj* 1 2 in number. 2 aged 2.
two- having two (of something): *a two-door car.*
,two-'faced *adj* deceitful: *a two-faced person.*
,two-'handed *adj, adv* (to be used, played *etc*) with two hands: *a two-handed stroke.*
twosome *n* two people; a couple: *They usually travel in a twosome.*
,two-'way *adj* able to act, operate, be used *etc* in two ways or directions: *two-way traffic; a two-way radio.*
'two-year-old *n* a person or animal that is two years old. – *adj* (of a person, animal or thing) that is two years old.
in two (broken) in two pieces: *The magazine was torn in two.*

tycoon [tai'ku:n] *n* a rich and powerful businessman: *an oil tycoon.*

tying *see* **tie.**

type[1] [taip] *n* a kind, sort; variety: *What type of house would you prefer to live in?; They are marketing a new type of washing powder.*

type[2] [taip] *n* **1** (a particular variety of) metal blocks with letters, numbers *etc* used in printing: *Can we have the headline printed in a different type?* **2** printed letters, words *etc*: *I can't read the type – it's too small.* – *v* to write (something) using a typewriter: *Can you type?; I'm typing a letter.*
'**typing, typewriting** *n* writing produced by a typewriter: *fifty pages of typing.*
'**typist** *n* a person whose job is to type: *She works as a typist; She is a typist in a publishing firm.*
'**typewriter** *n* a machine with keys for printing letters on a piece of paper: *a portable/an electric typewriter.*

typhoid (fever) ['taifoid] *n* a dangerous type of infectious disease, caused by germs in food or drinking water: *He died of typhoid (fever).*

typhoon [tai'fu:n] *n* a violent sea-storm occurring in the East: *They were caught in a typhoon in the China seas.*

typhus ['taifəs] *n* a dangerous type of infectious disease, spread by lice: *She is suffering from typhus.*

typical ['tipikəl] *adj* (*neg* **un-**) having or showing the usual characteristics (of): *He is a typical Englishman; They're typical civil servants.* '**typically** *adv.*

typify ['tipifai] *v* to be a very good example of: *Vandalism at football matches typifies the modern disregard for law and order.*

typing, typist *see* **type**[2].

tyrant ['tairənt] *n* a cruel and unjust ruler: *The people suffered under foreign tyrants.*
tyrannical [ti'ranikəl], **tyrannous** ['tirənəs] *adjs* of or like a tyrant: *a tyrannical ruler; His actions were tyrannous.* **ty'rannically,** '**tyrannously** *advs.*
tyrannize, -ise ['ti-] *v* to rule or treat (a person or people) cruelly and unjustly: *He tyrannizes his family.*
'**tyranny** ['ti-] *n* an action, or the method of ruling, of a tyrant: *People will always resist tyranny.*

tyre, (*Amer*) **tire** ['taiə] *n* a thick, rubber, *usu* air-filled strip around the edge of the wheel of a car, bicycle *etc*: *The tyres of this car don't have enough air in them.*

tzar *see* **tsar.**

Uu

u [ju:]: '**U-turn** *n* a turn, in the shape of the letter U, made by a motorist *etc* in order to reverse his direction.

udder ['ʌdə] *n* the bag-like part of a cow, goat *etc*, with teats that supply milk for their young or for humans: *The cow has a diseased udder.*

ugh! [ə:(x), ʌ(x)] *interj* expressing disgust: *Ugh! The cat has been sick!*

ugly ['ʌgli] *adj* **1** unpleasant to look at: *She is rather an ugly young woman.* **2** unpleasant, nasty or dangerous: *ugly black clouds; The crowd was in an ugly mood.* '**ugliness** *n.*

ulcer ['ʌlsə] *n* a kind of sore that does not heal easily, on the skin or inside the body: *a mouth/stomach ulcer.*

ultimate ['ʌltimət] *adj* last or final.
'**ultimately** *adv* in the end: *We hope ultimately to be able to buy a house of our own.*

ultimatum [ʌlti'meitəm] – *pl* ,**ulti'matums** – *n* a final demand made by one person, nation *etc* to another, with a threat to stop peaceful discussion and declare war *etc* if the demand is ignored: *An ultimatum has been issued to him to withdraw his troops from our territory.*

ultra- [ʌltrə] **1** beyond, as in **ultraviolet.**

2 very or excessively: *He's ultra-cautious when he drives a car.*

ultrasonic [ʌltrə'sonik] *adj* (of sound waves *etc*) beyond the range of human hearing: *ultrasonic vibrations.*

ultraviolet [ʌltrə'vaiəlit] *adj* (of light) consisting of rays from the invisible part of the spectrum beyond the purple, that have an effect on the skin, *eg* causing suntan.

umbrella [ʌm'brelə] *n* an apparatus for protecting a person from the rain, made of a folding covered framework attached to a stick with a handle: *Take an umbrella – it's going to rain.*

umpire ['ʌmpaiə] *n* in cricket, tennis *etc*, a person who supervises a game, makes sure that it is played according to the rules, and decides doubtful points: *Tennis players usually have to accept the umpire's decision.* – *v* to act as umpire: *Have you umpired a tennis match before?*

unable [ʌn'eibl] *adj* without enough strength, power, skill, opportunity, information *etc* to be able (to do something): *I am unable to get out of bed; I shall be unable to meet you for lunch today.*

unaccountable [ʌnəˈkauntəbl] *adj* that cannot be explained: *his unaccountable absence.*

unac'countably *adv* in a way that cannot be explained: *He was unaccountably late/ill.*

unadulterated [ʌnəˈdʌltəreitid] *adj* pure, or not mixed with anything else: *a feeling of unadulterated hatred.*

unaffected [ʌnəˈfektid] *adj* 1 of (a person, his feelings *etc*) not moved or affected: *The child seemed unaffected by his father's death.* 2 (of an arrangement *etc*) not altered: *It has been raining heavily, but this evening's football arrangements are unaffected.*

unafraid [ʌnəˈfreid] *adj* not afraid.

unanimous [juˈnaniməs] *adj* having, or showing, complete agreement: *The whole school was unanimous in its approval of the headmaster's plan.* **u'nanimously** *adv*.

una'nimity [juːnə-] *n* complete agreement: *Unanimity among politicians is rare.*

unarmed [ʌnˈaːmd] *adj* without weapons or other means of defence: *The gangster shot an unarmed policeman*; *Judo is a type of unarmed fighting.*

unashamedly [ʌnəˈʃeimidli] *adv* showing no shame or embarrassment: *She was weeping unashamedly.*

unattached [ʌnəˈtatʃt] *adj* not married or engaged to be married: *A woman sometimes gives up hope of marriage if she is still unattached at the age of thirty.*

unattended [ʌnəˈtendid] *adj* not under the care or supervision of anybody: *It is dangerous to leave small children unattended in the house.*

unauthorized, -s- [ʌnˈoːθəraizd] *adj* not having the permission of the people in authority: *unauthorized use of the firm's equipment.*

unaware [ʌnəˈweə] *adj* not aware or not knowing: *I was unaware of the man's presence.*

take (someone) unawares to surprise or startle (someone): *He came into the room so quietly that he took me unawares.*

unbalanced [ʌnˈbalənst] *adj* 1 without the proper amount of attention being given to everything: *If we don't hear both sides of the argument, we'll get an unbalanced view of the situation.* 2 disordered in the mind; not quite sane: *The murderer was completely unbalanced.*

unbar [ʌnˈbaː] – *pt, ptp* **un'barred** – *v* to open (a door, gate, entrance *etc*) by moving the bars that are keeping it closed: *He unlocked and unbarred the door.*

unbearable [ʌnˈbeərəbl] *adj* too painful, unpleasant *etc* to bear or to tolerate: *I am suffering from unbearable toothache.*

un'bearably *adv*: *unbearably painful*; *unbearably rude.*

unbelievable [ʌnbiˈliːvəbl] *adj* too bad, good *etc* to be believed in: *unbelievable rudeness*;

Her good luck is unbelievable! **unbe'lievably** *adv*.

unbolt [ʌnˈboult] *v* to open the bolt of (*eg* a door): *The shop-keeper unbolted the door and let the customers enter.*

unborn [ʌnˈboːn] *adj* (of a baby) still in the mother's womb: *When she was involved in a car accident the doctor was worried in case her unborn baby had been injured.*

unbuckle [ʌnˈbʌkl] *v* to undo the buckle or buckles of: *He unbuckled his belt.*

unbutton [ʌnˈbʌtn] *v* to unfasten the buttons of: *She unbuttoned her coat.*

uncalled-for [ʌnˈkoːldfoː] *adj* (of actions, remarks *etc*) unnecessary and *usu* rude: *Some of his comments are a bit uncalled-for.*

uncanny [ʌnˈkani] *adj* strange or mysterious: *She looks so like her sister that it's quite uncanny.* **un'cannily** *adv*.

unceasing [ʌnˈsiːsiŋ] *adj* never stopping: *his unceasing efforts to help the sick and wounded.* **un'ceasingly** *adv*.

uncertain [ʌnˈsəːtn] *adj* 1 (of a person) not sure; not definitely knowing: *I'm uncertain of my future plans*; *The government is uncertain what is the best thing to do.* 2 not definitely known or settled: *My plans are still uncertain*; *The uncertain weather delayed our departure.* **un'certainly** *adv*.

uncivil [ʌnˈsivl] *adj* rude: *He apologized for being uncivil to her.* **un'civilly** *adv*.

uncle [ˈʌŋkl] *n* the brother of a person's father or mother, or the husband of an aunt: *He's my uncle*; *Hallo, Uncle Jim!*

unclean [ʌnˈkliːn] *adj* (*eg* of food) not pure: *The Jews are not allowed to eat pork, as pigs are considered unclean.*

uncoil [ʌnˈkoil] *v* to straighten from a coiled position: *The snake uncoiled (itself).*

uncomfortable [ʌnˈkʌmfətəbl] *adj* 1 not relaxed: *He looked uncomfortable when she mentioned marriage.* 2 producing a bad physical feeling: *That's a very uncomfortable chair.* **un'comfortably** *adv*.

uncommon [ʌnˈkomən] *adj* rare; unusual: *This type of animal is becoming very uncommon.*

un'commonly *adv* very; unusually: *an uncommonly clever person.*

uncompromising [ʌnˈkomprəmaiziŋ] *adj* keeping firmly to a particular attitude, policy *etc*: *You should not adopt such an uncompromising attitude.*

unconcern [ʌnkənˈsəːn] *n* lack of interest or anxiety: *He received the news of his failure with apparent unconcern.* **uncon'cerned** *adj*. **'uncon,cernedly** [-nid-] *adv*.

unconditional [ʌnkənˈdiʃənl] *adj* complete and absolute, and not dependent on certain terms or conditions: *The victorious side demanded unconditional surrender.* **,uncon'ditionally** *adv*.

unconfirmed [ʌnkən'fəːmd] *adj* not yet shown or proved to be true: *There are unconfirmed reports of another earthquake in China.*

unconscious [ʌn'konʃəs] *adj* **1** senseless or stunned, *eg* because of an accident: *She was unconscious for three days after the crash.* **2** not aware: *He was unconscious of having said anything rude.* **3** unintentional: *Her prejudice is quite unconscious.* – *n* the deepest level of the mind, the processes of which are revealed only through *eg* psychoanalysis: *the secrets of the unconscious.*
un'consciously *adv* unintentionally, or without being aware: *She unconsciously addressed me by the wrong name.* **un'consciousness** *n*.

uncover [ʌn'kʌvə] *v* to remove the cover from: *His criminal activities were finally uncovered.*

uncurl [ʌn'kəːl] *v* to straighten from a curled position: *The hedgehog slowly uncurled (itself).*

uncut [ʌn'kʌt] *adj* **1** (of a book, film *etc*) not shortened. **2** (of a diamond *etc*) not yet cut into shape for using in jewellery *etc*.

undaunted [ʌn'doːntid] *adj* fearless; not discouraged: *He was undaunted by his failure.*

undecided [ʌndi'saidid] *adj* **1** (of a person) unable to make a decision about something. **2** (of a matter) not settled: *The date of the meeting is still undecided.*

under ['ʌndə] *prep* **1** in or to a position lower than, or covered by: *Your pencil is under the chair; Strange plants grow under the sea.* **2** less than, or lower in rank than: *Children under five should not cross the street alone; You can do the job in under an hour.* **3** subject to the authority of: *As a foreman, he has about fifty workers under him.* **4** used to express various states: *The fort was under attack; The business improved uder the new management; The matter is under consideration/discussion.* – *adv* in or to a lower position, rank *etc*: *The swimmer surfaced and went under again; children aged seven and under.*
under- **1** beneath, as in **underline**. **2** too little, as in **underpay**. **3** lower in rank: *the under-manager.* **4** less in age than: *a nursery for under-fives* (= children aged four and under).

undercarriage ['ʌndəkaridʒ] *n* the landing-gear of an aircraft: *The pilot had some difficulty in lowering the undercarriage.*

underclothes ['ʌndəklouðz, (Amer) -klouz] *n pl* underwear: *Have you packed my underclothes?*
'underclothing *n* underclothes.

undercover ['ʌndə'kʌvə] *adj* working or done in secret: *He is an undercover agent for the Americans.*

undercut [ʌndə'kʌt] – *pt, ptp* ,**under'cut** – *v* to

sell goods *etc* at a lower price than (a competitor): *Japanese car-exporters are able to undercut British motor manufacturers.*

underdog ['ʌndədog] *n* a weak person who is dominated by someone else, or who is the loser in a struggle: *He always likes to help the underdog.*

underestimate [ʌndər'estimeit] *v* to estimate (a person, a thing *etc*) at less than his or its real amount, value, strength *etc*: *Never underestimate your opponent!*

underfed [ʌndə'fed] *adj* not given enough to eat: *That child looks underfed.*

underfoot [ʌndə'fut] *adj* on the ground under the feet of anyone walking: *It is not actually raining just now but it is very wet underfoot.*

undergarment ['ʌndəgaːmənt] *n* an article of clothing worn under the outer clothes.

undergo [ʌndə'gou] – *pt* ,**under'went** [-'went]; *ptp* ,**under'gone** [-'gon] – *v* **1** to experience or endure: *They underwent terrible hardships.* **2** to go through (a process): *The car is undergoing tests/repairs; She has been undergoing medical treatment.*

undergraduate [ʌndə'gradjuət] *n* a student who is studying for his first degree.

underground [ʌndə'graund] *adj* below the surface of the ground: *underground railways; underground streams.* – *adv* **1** (to a position) under the surface of the ground: *Rabbits live underground.* **2** into hiding: *He will go underground if the police start looking for him.* – ['ʌndəgraund] *n* (*Amer* **subway**) an underground railway: *She hates travelling by/on the underground.*

undergrowth ['ʌndəgrouθ] *n* low bushes or large plants growing among trees: *She tripped over in the thick undergrowth.*

underline [ʌndə'lain] *v* **1** to draw a line under: *He wrote down the title of his essay and underlined it.* **2** to emphasize or stress: *In his speech he underlined several points.*

undermine [ʌndə'main] *v* **1** to make (*eg* a building) insecure by digging away or destroying the base or foundations: *The road was being undermined by a stream.* **2** to weaken (*eg* a person's health or authority): *Constant hard work had undermined his health.*

underneath [ʌndə'niːθ] *prep, adv* at or to a lower position (than); beneath: *She was standing underneath the light; Have you looked underneath the bed?* – *n* the part or side beneath: *Have you ever seen the underneath of a bus?*

undernourished [ʌndə'nʌriʃt, (Amer) -'nəː-] *adj* suffering from lack of food or nourishment.

underpaid *see* **underpay**.

underpants ['ʌndəpants] *n pl* a short under-

* see illustration on p. 595

garment worn (*usu* by men) over the buttocks: *a clean pair of underpants.*

underpay [ʌndə'pei] – *pt, ptp* ,under'paid – *v* to pay (a person) too little: *They claim that they are underpaid and overworked.*

underrate [ʌndə'reit] *v* to underestimate.

undersell [ʌndə'sel] – *pt, ptp* ,under'sold [-'sould] – *v* to sell goods at a lower price than (a competitor).

underside ['ʌndəsaid] *n* the lower surface; the part or side lying beneath.

undersold *see* undersell.

understand [ʌndə'stand] – *pt, ptp* ,under'stood [-'stud] – *v* 1 to see or know the meaning of (something): *I can't understand his absence; Speak slowly to foreigners so that they'll understand you.* 2 to know (*eg* a person) thoroughly: *She understands children/dogs.* 3 to learn or realize (something), *eg* from information received: *At first I didn't understand how ill she was; I understood that you were planning to leave today.*

,under'standable *adj* that can be understood: *His anger is quite understandable.*

,under'standing *adj* (of a person) good at knowing how other people feel; sympathetic: *an understanding person; Try to be more understanding!* – *n* 1 the power of thinking clearly: *a man of great understanding.* 2 the ability to sympathize with another person's feelings: *His kindness and understanding were a great comfort to her.* 3 a (state of) informal agreement: *The two men have come to/reached an understanding after their disagreement.*

make (oneself) understood to make one's meaning or intentions clear: *He tried speaking German to them, but couldn't make himself understood.*

understate [ʌndə'steit] *v* to state less than the truth about (something): *She has understated her difficulties.*

,under'statement *n*: *It's an understatement to say he's foolish – he's quite mad.*

understood *see* understand.

understudy ['ʌndəstʌdi] *v* to study (a part in a play, opera *etc*) so as to be able to take the place of (another actor, singer *etc*). – *n* – *pl* 'understudies – a person who understudies: *He was ill, so his understudy had to take the part.*

undertake [ʌndə'teik] – *pt* ,under'took [-'tuk], *ptp* ,under'taken – *v* 1 to accept (a duty, task, responsibility *etc*): *He undertook the job willingly.* 2 to promise (*eg* to do something): *He has undertaken to appear at the police court tomorrow.*

'undertaker [-teikə] *n* a person who organizes funerals.

,under'taking *n* 1 a task or piece of work: *I didn't realize what a large undertaking this job would be.* 2 a promise: *He made an undertaking that he would pay the money back.*

undertook *see* undertake.

underwear ['ʌndəweə] *n* clothes worn under the outer clothes: *She washed her skirt, blouse and underwear.*

underwent *see* undergo.

underworld ['ʌndəwə:ld] *n* the part of the population that gets its living from crime *etc*: *A member of the underworld told the police where the murderer was hiding.*

undesirable [ʌndi'zairəbl] *adj* 1 not wanted: *These pills can have some undesirable effects.* 2 unpleasant or objectionable: *his undesirable friends; undesirable behaviour/habits.*

undid *see* undo.

undivided [ʌndi'vaidid] *adj* (of attention *etc*) not distracted; wholly concentrated: *Please give the matter your undivided attention.*

undo [ʌn'du:] – *pt* un'did [-'did]; *ptp* un'done [-'dʌn] – *v* 1 to unfasten or untie: *Could you undo the knot in this string?* 2 to reverse, or destroy, the effect of: *The evil that he did can never be undone.*

un'doing *n* (the cause of) ruin or disaster: *Gambling was his undoing.*

un'done [-'dʌn] *adj* (of work, a task *etc*) not done, or not finished: *I don't like going to bed leaving jobs/work undone.*

undoubted [ʌn'dautid] *adj* not doubted or denied: *the undoubted excellence of the work.*

un'doubtedly *adv* definitely: *'Is he mistaken?' 'Undoubtedly!'*

undress [ʌn'dres] *v* 1 to take the clothes off (a person): *She undressed the child; Undress yourself and get into bed.* 2 to undress oneself: *I undressed and went to bed.*

undue [ʌn'dju:] *adj* too great; more than is necessary: *You show undue caution in distrusting him.*

un'duly *adv*: *You were unduly severe with the child.*

unearth [ʌn'ə:θ] *v* to discover (something) or remove it from a place where it is put away or hidden: *During his studies, he unearthed several new facts about the history of the place.*

unearthly [ʌn'ə:θli] *adj* 1 supernatural, mysterious or frightening: *an unearthly sight.* 2 outrageous or unreasonable: *He telephoned at the unearthly* (= very early) *hour of 6.30 a.m.*

uneasy [ʌn'i:zi] *adj* (of a person or a situation *etc*) troubled, anxious or unsettled: *When her son did not return, she grew uneasy.*

un'ease *n* uneasiness.

un'easily *adv* in an uneasy or embarrassed way: *He glanced uneasily at her.*

un'easiness *n* the state of being uneasy: *I could not understand her apparent uneasiness.*

unemployed [ʌnim'ploid] *adj* not having, or not able to find, work: *He has been unemployed for three months.* – *n pl* people who are unemployed: *The numbers of (the) unemployed are still increasing.*

,unem'ployment *n* **1** the state of being unemployed: *If the factory is closed, many men will face unemployment.* **2** the numbers of people without work: *Unemployment has reached record figures this year.*

unending [ʌn'endiŋ] *adj* never finishing: *their unending struggle for survival.*

unequal [ʌn'iːkwəl] *adj* not equal in quantity, quality *etc*: *They got unequal shares of/an unequal share in the money.* **un'equally** *adv.*

unerring [ʌn'əːriŋ] *adj* (always) accurate: *He threw the spear with unerring aim.* **un'erringly** *adv.*

uneven [ʌn'iːvn] *adj* **1** not even: *The road surface here is very uneven.* **2** (of work *etc*) not all of the same quality: *His work is very uneven.* **un'evenness** *n.*

un'evenly *adv* in an uneven or unequal way: *The teams are unevenly matched.*

unexpected [ʌnik'spektid] *adj* not expected, *eg* because sudden: *his unexpected death*; *His promotion was quite unexpected.*

unfailing [ʌn'feiliŋ] *adj* constant: *Her unfailing courage inspired us all.*

un'failingly *adv* constantly: *He is unfailingly polite.*

unfair [ʌn'feə] *adj* not fair or just: *He has received unfair treatment.* **un'fairly** *adv.* **un'fairness** *n.*

unfaithful [ʌn'feiθful] *adj* not loyal and true.

unfamiliar [ʌnfə'miljə] *adj* **1** not well-known: *He felt nervous about walking along unfamiliar streets.* **2** not knowing about: *I am unfamiliar with the plays of Shakespeare.* **unfa'miliarly** *adv.* **unfamili'arity** *n.*

unfasten [ʌn'faːsn] *v* to undo (something that is fastened): *He unfastened (the buttons of) his jacket.*

unfit [ʌn'fit] *adj* **1** not good enough; not in a suitable state: *He has been ill and is quite unfit to travel.* **2** (of a person, dog, horse *etc*) not as strong and healthy as is possible: *You become unfit if you don't take regular exercise.* **un'fitness** *n.*

unflagging [ʌn'flagiŋ] *adj* not tiring or losing vigour: *her unflagging energy.*

unflappable [ʌn'flapəbl] *adj* able to remain calm in a crisis.

unflinching [ʌn'flintʃiŋ] *adj* not yielding *etc* because of pain, danger, difficulty *etc*: *his unflinching courage/determination.* **un'flinchingly** *adv.*

unfold [ʌn'fould] *v* **1** to open and spread out (a map *etc*): *He sat down and unfolded his newspaper.* **2** to (cause to) be revealed or become known: *She gradually unfolded her plan to them.*

unforgettable [ʌnfə'getəbl] *adj* never able to be forgotten: *The experience was unforgettable.* **,unfor'gettably** *adv.*

unfortunate [ʌn'foːtʃənət] *adj* **1** unlucky: *He has been very unfortunate.* **2** regrettable: *He has an unfortunate habit of giggling all the time.*

un'fortunately *adv*: *I'd like to help but unfortunately I can't.*

unfounded [ʌn'faundid] *adj* not based on facts or reality: *The rumours are completely unfounded.*

ungainly [ʌn'geinli] *adj* awkward, clumsy or ungraceful: *She is rather large and ungainly.* **un'gainliness** *n.*

ungracious [ʌn'greiʃəs] *adj* rude; impolite: *It was rather ungracious of you to refuse his invitation.* **un'graciously** *adv.*

ungrateful [ʌn'greitful] *adj* not showing thanks for kindness: *It will look very ungrateful if you don't write and thank him.*

unguarded [ʌn'gaːdid] *adj* **1** without protection: *The castle gate was never left unguarded.* **2** careless: *an unguarded remark.*

unhappy [ʌn'hapi] *adj* **1** sad or miserable: *He had an unhappy childhood.* **2** regrettable: *He has an unhappy knack of always saying the wrong thing.* **un'happiness** *n.*

un'happily *adv* **1** in a sad or miserable way: *He stared unhappily at her angry face.* **2** unfortunately: *Unhappily, I shan't be able to see you tomorrow.*

unhealthy [ʌn'helθi] *adj* **1** not healthy: *He is fat and unhealthy – he doesn't take enough exercise.* **2** dangerous: *The situation was getting unhealthy.* **un'healthily** *adv.* **un'healthiness** *n.*

unholy [ʌn'houli] *adj* **1** disrespectful or irreverent: *shrieks of unholy laughter.* **2** outrageous or unreasonable: *an unholy din.*

unhook [ʌn'huk] *v* to take or release (something) from a hook: *He unhooked the picture from the wall.*

unicorn ['juːnikoːn] *n* in mythology, an animal like a horse, but with one straight horn on the forehead.

unidentified [ʌnai'dentifaid] *adj* not identified: *an unidentified victim.*

unidentified flying object (*often abbrev* **UFO** [juːef'ou, 'juːfoul]) an object from outer space, *eg* a flying saucer.

unification *see* **unify.**

uniform ['juːnifoːm] *adj* the same always or everywhere; not changing or varying: *The sky was a uniform grey.* – *n* (a set of) clothes worn by *eg* soldiers, children at a particular school *etc*: *Full uniform must be worn*; *The new uniforms will arrive tomorrow.*

'uniformed *adj* (*eg* of police) wearing a uniform, not plain clothes.

,uni'formity *n* the condition of being uniform: *The houses in the street had no uniformity of appearance.*

'uniformly *adv* in a uniform way: *The essays were uniformly dull.*

unify ['ju:nifai] *v* to combine into a single whole: *The country consisted of several small states and was unified only recently.* ,unifi'cation [-fi-] *n.*

uninhibited [ʌnin'hibitid] *adj* expressing feelings *etc* freely and without embarrassment: *uninhibited people/behaviour.*

unintelligible [ʌnin'teligəbl] *adj* not able to be understood: *unintelligible writing/words.*

uninterested [ʌn'intristid] *adj* not having or showing any interest: *I told him the news but he seemed uninterested.*

uninterrupted [ʌnintə'rʌptid] *adj* 1 continuing without pause: *four hours of uninterrupted rain.* 2 (of a view) not blocked by anything: *We have an uninterrupted view of the sea.*

uninvited [ʌnin'vaitid] *adj* 1 without an invitation: *uninvited guests.* 2 not required or encouraged: *his uninvited interference.*

union ['ju:njən] *n* 1 the act of uniting or process of being united: *Union between the two countries would be impossible.* 2 the state of being united, *eg* in marriage, friendship *etc*: *Their marriage was a perfect union.* 3 states, countries *etc* forming a single political group: *The Union of Soviet Socialist Republics.* 4 a club or association: *trade unions.*

Union Jack (*usu with* the) the national flag of the United Kingdom.

unique [ju:'ni:k] *adj* being the only one of its kind, or having no equal: *His style is unique.*

unisex ['ju:niseks] *adj* (of clothes *etc*) in a style that can be worn by both men and women: *unisex clothes; a unisex hairstyle.*

unison ['ju:nisn] *n* 1 an identical musical note, or series of notes, produced by several voices singing, or instruments playing, together: *They sang in unison.* 2 agreement: *They acted in unison.*

unit ['ju:nit] *n* 1 a single thing, individual *etc* within a group: *The building is divided into twelve different apartments or living units.* 2 an amount or quantity that is used as a standard in a system of measuring or coinage: *The dollar is the standard unit of currency in America.* 3 the smallest whole number, 1, or any number between 1 and 9: *In the number 23, 2 is a ten, and 3 is a unit.*

unite [ju'nait] *v* 1 to join together, or to make or become one: *England and Scotland were united under one parliament in 1707; He was united with his friends again.* 2 to act together: *Let us unite against the common enemy.*

u'nited *adj* 1 joined into a political whole:

the United States of America. 2 joined together by love, friendship *etc*: *They're a very united pair/family.* 3 made as a result of several people *etc* working together for a common purpose: *Let us make a united effort to make our business successful.*

unity ['ju:nəti] – *pl* 'unities – *n* 1 the state of being united or in agreement: *When will men learn to live in unity with each other?* 2 singleness, or the state of being one complete whole: *Unity of design in his pictures is this artist's main aim.* 3 something arranged to form a single complete whole: *This play is not a unity, but a series of unconnected scenes.*

universe ['ju:nivə:s] *n* everything – earth, planets, sun, stars *etc* – that exists anywhere: *Somewhere in the universe there must be another world like ours.*

,uni'versal *adj* affecting, including *etc* the whole of the world or all or most people: *English may become a universal language that everyone can learn and use.* ,uni'versally *adv.* ,univer'sality [-'sa-] *n.*

university [ju:ni'və:səti] – *pl* uni'versities – *n* (the buildings or colleges of) a centre of advanced education and research, that has the power to grant degrees: *He'll have four years at university after he leaves school;* (*also adj*) *a university student.*

unjust [ʌn'dʒʌst] *adj* not just; unfair: *Your suspicions are unjust.*

unkind [ʌn'kaind] *adj* cruel or harsh: *You were very unkind to her.*

unknowingly [ʌn'nouiŋli] *adv* without being aware: *She had unknowingly given the patient the wrong medicine.*

un'known *adj* 1 not known: *her unknown helper.* 2 not famous; not well-known: *That actor was almost unknown before he played that part.*

unless [ən'les] *conj* 1 if not: *Don't come unless I telephone.* 2 except when: *The directors have a meeting every Friday, unless there is nothing to discuss.*

unlike [ʌn'laik] *adj* 1 different (from): *I never saw twins who were so unlike (each other); Unlike poles of a magnet attract each other.* 2 not typical or characteristic of: *It is unlike Mary to be so silly.*

unlikely [ʌn'laikli] *adj* not likely or probable: *an unlikely explanation for his absence; She's unlikely to arrive before 7.00 p.m.; It is unlikely that she will come.*

unload [ʌn'loud] *v* to remove (cargo) from (*eg* a ship, vehicle *etc*): *The men were unloading the ship.*

unlock [ʌn'lok] *v* to open (something locked): *Unlock this door, please!*

unlucky [ʌn'lʌki] *adj* not lucky or fortunate: *I am unlucky – I never win at cards.*

un'luckily adv unfortunately: *Unluckily he has hurt his hand and cannot play the piano.*

unmanned [ʌnˈmand] adj (of eg an aircraft or spacecraft) automatically controlled and therefore without a crew: *unmanned flights to Mars.*

unmistakable [ʌnmiˈsteikəbl] adj very clear; impossible to mistake: *His meaning was unmistakable.*

unmoved [ʌnˈmuːvd] adj not affected or moved in feelings, determination etc: *He was unmoved by her tears.*

unnatural [ʌnˈnatʃərəl] adj strange or queer: *an unnatural silence.* **un'naturally** adv.

unnecessary [ʌnˈnesəsəri] adj 1 not necessary: *It is unnecessary to waken him yet.* 2 that might have been avoided: *Your mistake caused a lot of unnecessary work in the office.*

un,neces'sarily adv: *He was unnecessarily rude.*

unobtrusive [ʌnəbˈtruːsiv] adj not too obvious or noticeable: *She is quiet and unobtrusive.* **,unob'trusively** adv: *unobtrusively dressed.*

unoccupied [ʌnˈɔkjupaid] adj 1 empty or vacant: *The room/seat was unoccupied.* 2 not busy: *I paint in my unoccupied hours/when I'm otherwise unoccupied.*

unpack [ʌnˈpak] v 1 to take out (things that are packed): *He unpacked his clothes.* 2 to take (clothes etc) out of (a case etc): *Have you unpacked (your case)?*

unpick [ʌnˈpik] v to take out stitches from (something sewn or knitted): *She unpicked the seam of the dress.*

unpleasant [ʌnˈpleznt] adj disagreeable: *an unpleasant task/smell.* **un'pleasantly** adv.

unplug [ʌnˈplʌg] – pt, ptp **un'plugged** – v 1 to take the plug out of. 2 to disconnect from the electricity supply: *He unplugged the television.*

unpopular [ʌnˈpɔpjulə] adj generally disliked: *an unpopular person/law; He was unpopular at school.* **un,popu'larity** [-ˈla-] n.

unpractical [ʌnˈpraktikəl] adj (of a person) not good at practical tasks: *She's so unpractical that she can't even change an electric plug.*

unprecedented [ʌnˈpresidentid] adj never known to have happened before: *Such an action by a prime minister is unprecedented.*

unprofessional [ʌnprəˈfeʃənl] adj 1 (of a person's conduct) not according to the (usu moral) standards required in his profession: *The doctor was dismissed from his post for unprofessional conduct.* 2 (of a piece of work etc) not done with the skill of a trained person: *This repair looks a bit unprofessional.*

unqualified [ʌnˈkwɔlifaid] adj 1 not having the necessary qualifications (eg for a job): *unqualified teachers/nurses; He is unqual-*ified for the job. 2 complete; without limits: *He deserves our unqualified praise.*

unquestionable [ʌnˈkwestʃənəbl] adj that cannot be doubted; completely certain: *unquestionable proof.*

un'questionably adv certainly: *Unquestionably, he deserves to be punished.*

un'questioning adj (done etc) without any disagreement or protest: *unquestioning obedience/belief.*

unravel [ʌnˈravəl] – pt **un'ravelled**, (Amer) **un'raveled** – v 1 to take (eg string, thread etc) out of its tangled condition; to disentangle: *She could not unravel the tangled thread.* 2 (esp of a knitted fabric) to undo or become undone: *My knitting (got) unravelled when it fell off the needles.* 3 to solve (a problem, mystery etc): *Is there no-one who can unravel this mystery?*

unreal [ʌnˈriəl] adj not existing in fact: *He lives in an unreal world imagined by himself.* **,unre'ality** [ʌnriˈa-] n.

unreasonable [ʌnˈriːzənəbl] adj 1 not guided by good sense or reason: *It is unreasonable to expect children to work so hard.* 2 excessive, or too great: *That butcher charges unreasonable prices.*

unreserved [ʌnriˈzɔːvd] adj 1 (of a seat etc) not reserved: *These seats are unreserved.* 2 complete: *The committee gave his suggestion unreserved approval.* 3 frank: *She had a cheerful, unreserved nature.*

,unre'servedly [-vid-] adv 1 completely: *utterly: We are unreservedly delighted/relieved about the result.* 2 frankly: *She spoke unreservedly.*

unrest [ʌnˈrest] n a state of trouble or discontent, esp among a group of people: *political unrest.*

unrivalled, (Amer) **unrivaled** [ʌnˈraivəld] adj having no equal or rival: *She is unrivalled as a Shakespearian actress.*

unroll [ʌnˈroul] v to open from a rolled position: *He unrolled the mattress.*

unruly [ʌnˈruːli] adj uncontrollable or disorderly: *unruly teenagers/behaviour.* **un'ruliness** n.

unsavoury [ʌnˈseivəri] adj very unpleasant or disgusting: *I have heard some unsavoury stories about that man.*

unscramble [ʌnˈskrambl] v to decode (a message) or make clear the words of (a telephone message).

unscrew [ʌnˈskruː] v to remove or loosen (something) by taking out screws, or with a twisting or screwing action: *He unscrewed the cupboard door; Can you unscrew this lid?*

unscrupulous [ʌnˈskruːpjuləs] adj having no conscience or scruples; wicked: *He is an unscrupulous rogue.*

unsettle [ʌnˈsetl] v to disturb or upset: *Will a change of schools unsettle the child?*

un'settled *adj* **1** (of weather) changeable. **2** anxious or restless: *in an unsettled mood.*

unsightly [ʌn'saitli] *adj* ugly: *Those new buildings are very unsightly.*

unspeakable [ʌn'spiːkəbl] *adj* that cannot be expressed in words, *esp* because too bad to describe: *his unspeakable cruelty/rudeness.* **un'speakably** *adv*: *The house is unspeakably filthy.*

unstop [ʌn'stop] – *pt, ptp* **un'stopped** – *v* to remove a blockage from (*eg* a drain): *The plumber has unstopped the pipe.*

unstrap [ʌn'strap] – *pt, ptp* **un'strapped** – *v* to unfasten the strap of: *She unstrapped her suitcase.*

unstuck [ʌn'stʌk]: **come unstuck 1** to stop sticking: *The label has come unstuck.* **2** to fail: *Our plans have come unstuck.*

unsuspected [ʌnsə'spektid] *adj* not imagined or known to exist: *He had unsuspected talents.* ,**unsu'specting** *adj* not aware of (coming) danger: *He stole all her money and she was completely unsuspecting.*

untangle [ʌn'taŋgl] *v* to take (*eg* string, thread *etc*) out of its tangled condition; to disentangle: *She tried to untangle her hair.*

unthinkable [ʌn'θiŋkəbl] *adj* too outrageous to be considered: *It would be unthinkable to ask him to do that.* **un'thinking** *adj* showing lack of thought or consideration: *His unthinking words had hurt her deeply.*

untidy [ʌn'taidi] *adj* disordered; in a mess: *His room is always very untidy; an untidy person.*

untie [ʌn'tai] *v* to loosen or unfasten: *He untied the string from the parcel.*

until [ən'til] *prep, conj* to the time of or when: *He was here until one o'clock; I won't know until I get a letter from him.*

until is spelt with one l.

untiring [ʌn'taiəriŋ] *adj* (of a person or his efforts *etc*) never stopping or ceasing because of weariness: *his untiring efforts/energy.* **un'tiringly** *adv.*

unto ['ʌntu] *prep* an old word for 'to'.

untrue [ʌn'truː] *adj* not true; false: *The statement is untrue.* **un'truth** [-θ] *n* a lie or false statement: *His autobiography contains many untruths.*

untwist [ʌn'twist] *v* to straighten from a twisted position: *He untwisted the wire.*

unusual [ʌn'juːʒuəl] *adj* not usual; rare; uncommon: *It is unusual for him to arrive late; He has an unusual job.* **un'usually** *adv*: *She is unusually cheerful today.*

unutterable [ʌn'ʌtərəbl] *adj* **1** (of a feeling) too strong to be expressed: *To his unutterable horror, the ground began to shake.* **2** too bad to describe: *What unutterable rudeness!*

unveil [ʌn'veil] *v* **1** to remove a veil (from *eg* a face): *After the marriage ceremony, the bride unveils (her face).* **2** to uncover (a new statue *etc*) ceremonially: *The prime minister was asked to unveil the plaque on the wall of the new college.*

unwary [ʌn'weəri] *adj* not cautious: *If you are unwary he will cheat you.* **un'warily** *adv.* **un'wariness** *n.*

unwelcome [ʌn'welkəm] *adj* received unwillingly or with disappointment: *unwelcome news/guests; I felt that we were unwelcome.*

unwell [ʌn'wel] *adj* not in good health: *He felt unwell this morning.*

unwieldy [ʌn'wiːldi] *adj* large and awkward to carry or manage: *A piano is an unwieldy thing to move.* **un'wieldiness** *n.*

unwilling [ʌn'wiliŋ] *adj* not willing; reluctant: *He's unwilling to accept the money.* **un'willingness** *n.* **un'willingly** *adv*: *He did agree to go, but rather unwillingly.*

unwind [ʌn'waind] – *pt, ptp* **un'wound** [-'waund] – *v* **1** to take or come out of a coiled or wound position: *He unwound the bandage from his ankle.* **2** to relax after a period of tension: *Give me a chance to unwind!*

unwise [ʌn'waiz] *adj* not wise; foolish: *an unwise suggestion; It was rather unwise of you to agree to do that.* **un'wisely** *adv.*

unworthy [ʌn'wəːði] *adj* **1** shameful or disgraceful: *That was an unworthy act/thought.* **2** not deserving: *Such a remark is unworthy of notice; He's unworthy to have the same name as his father.* **3** less good than should be expected from (*eg* a person): *Such bad behaviour is unworthy of him.* **un'worthily** *adv.* **un'worthiness** *n.*

unwound *see* **unwind.**

unwrap [ʌn'rap] – *pt, ptp* **un'wrapped** – *v* to open (something wrapped or folded): *He unwrapped the gift.*

unzip [ʌn'zip] – *pt, ptp* **un'zipped** – *v* to undo the zip of: *Will you unzip this dress please?*

up [ʌp] *adv, adj* **1** to, or at, a higher or better position: *Is the elevator going up?; The office is up on the top floor; She looked up at him; The price of coffee is up again.* **2** erect: *Sit/Stand up; He got up from his chair.* **3** out of bed: *What time do you get up?; I'll be up all night finishing this work.* **4** to the place or person mentioned or understood: *A taxi drove up and she got in; He came up (to me) and shook hands.* **5** into the presence, or consideration, of a person, group of people *etc*: *He brought up the subject during the conversation.* **6** to an increased degree *eg* of loudness, speed *etc*: *Please turn the radio up a little!; Speak up! I can't hear* *you; Hurry up!* **7** used to indicate completeness; throughly or finally: *You'll end up in hospital if you don't drive more carefully; He locked up the house; Help me wash up the dishes!; I've used up the whole supply of paper; He tore up the letter.* – *prep* **1** to or at a higher level on: *He climbed up the tree.* **2** (at a place) along: *They walked up the street; Their house is up the road.* **3** towards the source of (a river): *When do the salmon start swimming up the river?* – *v* – *pt, ptp* **upped** – to increase (a price *etc*): *They upped the price that they wanted for their house.*

'upward *adj* going up or directed up: *They took the upward path; an upward glance.*

'upward(s) *adv* (facing) towards a higher place or level: *He was lying on the floor face upwards; The path led upwards.*

,up-and-'coming *adj* (of *eg* a person starting a career) progressing well: *an up-and-coming young doctor.*

,up'hill *adv* up a slope: *We travelled uphill for several hours.* – *adj* **1** sloping upwards; ascending: *an uphill road/journey.* **2** difficult: *This will be an uphill struggle.*

,up'stairs *adv* on or to an upper floor: *His room is upstairs; She went upstairs to her bedroom.* – *n* – *pl* **up'stairs** – the upper floor(s): *The ground floor needs painting, but the upstairs is nice;* (*also adj*) *an upstairs sitting-room.*

up'stream *adv* towards the upper part or source of a stream, river *etc*: *Salmon swim upstream to lay their eggs.*

be up and about to be out of bed: *I've been up and about for hours; Is she up and about again after her accident?*

be up to 1 to be busy or occupied with (an activity *etc*): *What is he up to now?* **2** to be capable of: *He isn't quite up to the job.* **3** to reach the standard of: *This work isn't up to your best.* **4** to be the duty or privilege of: *It's up to you to decide; The final choice is up to him.*

up to as far, or as much, as: *He counted up to 100; Up to now, the work has been easy.*

upbringing ['ʌpbriŋiŋ] *n* (an example of) the process of bringing up a child: *He had a stern upbringing.*

update [ʌp'deit] *v* to make (something) suitable for the present time by adapting it to recent ideas *etc*: *Dictionaries constantly need to be updated.*

upheaval [ʌp'hi:vəl] *n* a great change or disturbance: *Moving house causes a great upheaval.*

upheld *see* **uphold**.

uphold [ʌp'hould] – *pt, ptp* **up'held** [-'held] – *v* **1** to support (a person's action): *His family upholds* (*him in*) *his present action.* **2** to confirm (*eg* a claim, legal judgement,

etc): *The decision of the judge was upheld by the court.* **3** to maintain (*eg* a custom): *The old traditions are still upheld in this village.*

upholster [ʌp'houlstə] *v* to fit (seats) with springs, stuffing, covers *etc*: *He upholstered the chair.*

up'holstered *adj*: *upholstered chairs.*

up'holsterer *n* a person who makes, repairs or sells upholstered furniture.

up'holstery *n* **1** the business or process of upholstering. **2** the springs, coverings *etc* of *eg* a chair: *luxurious upholstery.*

upkeep ['ʌpki:p] *n* (the cost of) the process of keeping *eg* a house, car *etc* in a good condition: *She can no longer afford the upkeep of this house.*

upon [ə'pon] *prep* on: *He sat upon the floor; Please place it upon the table; Upon arrival, they went in search of a hotel.*

upon my word! an exclamation indicating surprise *etc*.

upper ['ʌpə] *adj* higher in position, rank *etc*: *the upper floors of the building; He has a scar on his upper lip.* – *n* (*usu in pl*) the part of a shoe above the sole: *There's a crack in the upper.*

'uppermost *adj* highest: *in the uppermost room of the castle.* – *adv* in the highest place or position: *Thoughts of him were uppermost in her mind.*

upper class (of) the highest rank of society; (of) the aristocracy: *The upper classes can no longer afford to have many servants; He speaks with an upper-class accent.*

get/have the upper hand (of/over someone) to have or win an advantage over: *Our team managed to get the upper hand in the end.*

uppercut ['ʌpəkʌt] *n* in boxing *etc*, a blow aimed upwards, *eg* to the chin.

upright ['ʌprait] *adj* **1** (*also adv*) standing straight up; erect or vertical: *He placed the books upright in the bookcase; She stood upright; a row of upright posts.* **2** (of a person) just and honest: *an upright, honourable man.* – *n* an upright post *etc* supporting a construction: *When building the fence, place the uprights two metres apart.*

uprising ['ʌpraiziŋ] *n* a rebellion or revolt: *The Hungarian uprising was quickly suppressed.*

uproar ['ʌpro:] *n* **1** (an outbreak of) noise, shouting *etc*: *The whole town was in (an) uproar after the football team's victory.*

up'roarious *adj* very noisy, *esp* with much laughter: *The team were given an uproarious welcome.* **up'roariously** *adv*.

uproot [ʌp'ru:t] *v* to pull (a plant *etc*) out of the earth with the roots: *I uprooted the weeds and burnt them.*

upset [ʌp'set] – *pt, ptp* **up'set** – *v* **1** to overturn: *He upset a glass of wine over the table.*

2 to disturb or put out of order: *His illness has upset all our arrangements.* **3** to distress: *His friend's death upset him very much.* – *adj* disturbed or distressed: *Is he very upset about failing his exam?* – ['ʌpset] *n* a disturbance: *He has a stomach upset*; *I couldn't bear the upset of moving house again.*

upshot ['ʌpʃot]: **the upshot** the result or end (of a matter): *What was the final upshot of that affair?*

upside down [ʌpsai'daun] **1** with the top part underneath: *The plate was lying upside down on the floor.* **2** into confusion: *The burglars turned the house upside down.*

upstart ['ʌpstɑːt] *n* a person who has risen quickly to wealth or power but seems to lack dignity or ability: *I shall leave the firm if that little upstart becomes manager.*

uptake ['ʌpteik]: **quick, slow on the uptake** quick or slow to understand: *She's inexperienced, but very quick on the uptake.*

uranium [ju'reiniəm] *n* a radioactive element.

urban ['ɔːbən] *adj* of, consisting of, or living in, a city or town: *He dislikes urban life*; *urban traffic.*

urchin ['əːtʃin] *n* a mischievous, *usu* dirty or ragged, child, *esp* a boy: *He was chased by a crowd of urchins.*

urge [əːdʒ] *v* **1** to try to persuade or request earnestly (someone to do something): *He urged her to drive carefully*; *'Come with me,' he urged.* **2** to try to convince a person of (*eg* the importance of, or necessity for, some action): *He urged (on them) the necessity for speed.* – *n* a strong impulse or desire: *I felt an urge to hit him.*

urge on to drive or try to persuade (a person *etc*) to go on or forwards: *He urged himself on in spite of his weariness.*

urgent ['əːdʒənt] *adj* needing immediate attention: *There is an urgent message for the doctor.* **'urgently** *adv.*

'urgency *n* need for immediate action, speed *etc*: *This is a matter of great urgency.*

urine ['juːrin] *n* the waste fluid passed out of the body of animals from the bladder.

'urinary *adj*: *a urinary infection.*

'urinate ['juərineit] *v* to pass urine from the bladder.

urn [əːn] *n* **1** a tall vase or other container, *esp* for holding the ashes of a dead person: *a stone-age burial urn.* **2** a large metal container with a tap, in which tea or coffee is made *eg* in a canteen *etc*: *a tea-urn.*

us [ʌs] *pron* (used as the object of a verb or preposition) the speaker or writer plus one or more other people: *She gave us a present*; *A plane flew over us.*

use¹ [juːz] *v* **1** to employ (something) for a purpose: *What did you use to open the can?*; *Use your common sense!* **2** to consume: *We're using far too much electricity.*

'usable *adj* that can be used: *Are any of these clothes usable?*

used *adj* **1** employed or put to a purpose: *This road is not used any more.* **2** not new: *used cars.*

'user *n* a person who uses something: *road-users*; *electricity users.*

used to (something) ['juːstu] accustomed to: *She isn't used to such hard work.*

used to ['juːstu] – *neg short forms* **usedn't to, usen't to** ['juːsntu] – (I, he *etc*) was in the habit of (doing something); (I, he *etc*) was (usually) in a particular position, state *etc*: *I used to swim every day*; *She used not to be so forgetful*; *They used to play golf, didn't they?*; *Didn't you use(d) to live near me?*; *There used to be a butcher's shop there, didn't there?*

use² [juːs] *n* **1** the act of using or state of being used: *The use of force to persuade workers to join a strike cannot be justified*; *This telephone number is for use in emergencies.* **2** the/a purpose for which something may be used: *This little knife has plenty of uses*; *I have no further use for these clothes.* **3** (often in questions or with negatives) value or advantage: *Is this coat (of) any use to you?*; *It's no use offering to help when it's too late.* **4** the power of using: *She lost the use of her right arm as a result of the accident.* **5** permission, or the right, to use: *They let us have the use of their car while they were away.*

'useful *adj* helpful or serving a purpose well: *a useful tool/dictionary*; *She made herself useful by doing the washing for her mother.*

'usefulness *n.*

'usefully *adv* in a useful way: *He spent the day usefully in repairing the car.*

'useless *adj* having no use or no effect: *Why don't you throw away those useless things?*; *We can't do it – it's useless to try.*

be in use, out of use to be used or not used: *How long has the gymnasium been in use/out of use?*

come in useful to become useful: *My French came in useful on holiday.*

have no use for to despise: *I have no use for such silliness/silly people.*

it's no use it's impossible or useless: *He tried in vain to do it, then said 'It's no use.'*

make (good) use of, put to (good) use: *He makes use of his training*; *He puts his training to good use in that job.*

use(d)n't *see* **use¹**.

usher ['ʌʃə] – *fem* **,ushe'rette** [-'ret] – *n* a person who shows people to their seats in a theatre *etc*. – *v* to lead, escort: *The waiter ushered him to a table.*

usual ['juːʒuəl] *adj* done, happening *etc* most often; customary: *Are you going home by the usual route?*; *There are more people here* *than usual*; *Such behaviour is quite usual with children of that age*; *As usual, he was late.*

'usually *adv* on most occasions: *We are usually at home in the evenings*; *Usually we finish work at 5 o'clock.*

usurp [ju'zə:p] *v* to take (another person's power, position *etc*) without the right to do so: *The king's uncle tried to usurp the throne*; *I shall not allow him to usurp my authority.* **u'surper** *n.*

utensil [ju'tensl] *n* an instrument or vessel used in everyday life: *pots and pans and other kitchen utensils.*

uterus ['ju:tərəs] *n.* the womb.

utility [ju'tiləti] – *pl* **u'tilities** – *n* **1** usefulness: *Some kitchen gadgets have only a limited utility.* **2** a useful public service, *eg* the supply of water, gas, electricity *etc.*

u.tili'tarian *adj* useful rather than ornamental: *Our plates and glasses are utilitarian rather than beautiful.*

utilize, -ise ['ju:tilaiz] *v* to find a useful purpose for (something): *The extra money is being utilized to buy books for the school library.* **utili'zation, -s-** *n.*

utmost ['ʌtmoust] *adj* **1** most distant: *the utmost ends of the earth.* **2** greatest possible: *Take the utmost care!*

do one's utmost to make the greatest possible effort: *She has done her utmost to help him.*

Utopia [ju:'toupiə] *n* an imaginary country that has a perfect social and political system.

U'topian *adj* (of *eg* plans for benefiting mankind) desirable, but idealistic and impossible: *Utopian schemes.*

utter¹ ['ʌtə] *adj* complete or total: *There was utter silence*; *utter darkness.*

'utterly *adv* completely or totally: *She was utterly unaware of her danger.*

utter² ['ʌtə] *v* to produce (sounds, *eg* cries, words *etc*) with the mouth: *She uttered a sigh of relief*; *She didn't utter a single word of encouragement.*

Vv

v *see* **versus.**

V- [vi:] shaped like a V: *a V-neck(ed) pullover.*

vac [vak] short for **vacation**: *the summer vac.*

vacant ['veikənt] *adj* **1** empty or unoccupied: *a vacant chair*; *Are there any rooms vacant in this hotel?* **2** showing no thought, intelligence or interest: *a vacant stare.*

'vacancy – *pl* **'vacancies** – *n* **1** an unoccupied post: *We have a vacancy for a typist.* **2** the condition of being vacant; emptiness: *The vacancy of his expression made me doubt if he was listening.*

'vacantly *adv* absent-mindedly; without concentration: *He stared vacantly out of the window.*

vacation [və'keiʃən, (*Amer*) vei-] *n* a holiday: *a summer vacation.* – *v* (*Amer*) to take a holiday: *He vacationed in Paris last year.*

on vacation not working; having a holiday: *She has gone to Italy on vacation.*

vaccine ['vaksi:n] *n* a substance made from the germs that cause a particular disease, *esp* smallpox, and given to a person or animal to prevent him from catching that disease.

'vaccinate [-ksi-] *v* to protect (a person *etc*) against a disease by putting vaccine into his blood: *Has your child been vaccinated against smallpox?*

vacci'nation [-ksi-] *n* (an) act of vaccinating or process of being vaccinated: *I'm to have a vaccination tomorrow*; *Vaccination was introduced in the eighteenth century.*

vacuum ['vakjum] *n* **1** a space from which (almost) all air or other gas has been removed. **2** short for **vacuum cleaner.** – *v* to clean (something) using a vacuum cleaner: *She vacuumed the carpet.*

vacuum cleaner a machine that cleans carpets *etc* by sucking dust *etc* into itself.

('vacuum-)flask *n* a container with double walls that have a vacuum between them to keep the contents from losing or gaining heat: *a (vacuum-)flask of hot coffee.*

vagabond ['vagəbond] *n* an old word for a person having no settled home, or roving from place to place, *esp* in an idle or disreputable manner: *rogues and vagabonds.*

vagrant ['veigrənt] *n* a person who has no fixed home; a tramp.

'vagrancy *n* the state of being a vagrant: *Vagrancy is a crime in some countries.*

vague [veig] *adj* **1** not clear, distinct or definite: *Through the fog we saw the vague outline of a ship*; *She has only a vague idea of how this machine works.* **2** (of people) imprecise, or impractical and forgetful: *He is always very vague when making arrangements.* **'vagueness** *n.*

'vaguely *adv* **1** in a vague manner: *I remem-*

ber him very vaguely. **2** slightly: *She felt vaguely irritated; I feel vaguely uneasy.*

vain [vein] *adj* **1** having too much pride in one's appearance, achievements *etc*; conceited: *She's very vain about her good looks.* **2** unsuccessful: *He made a vain attempt to reach the drowning woman.* **3** empty; meaningless: *vain threats; vain promises.*

'vainly *adv* unsuccessfully: *He searched vainly for the treasure.*

vanity ['vanəti] *n* **1** excessive admiration of oneself; conceit: *Vanity is her chief fault.* **2** worthlessness or pointlessness: *the vanity of human ambition.*

in vain with no success: *He tried in vain to open the locked door.*

vale [veil] *n* a valley.

valentine ['valəntain] *n* a sweetheart chosen, or a card, love letter *etc* sent, on St. Valentine's Day, February 14: *Will you be my valentine?; He sent her a valentine; (also adj)* a valentine card.

valet ['valit, 'valei] *n* a manservant who looks after his master's clothes *etc*: *His valet laid out his evening suit.*

valiant ['valiənt] *adj* (of a person, his actions *etc*) brave, courageous or heroic: *valiant deeds; He was valiant in battle.* **'valiantly** *adv.*

valid ['valid] *adj* **1** (of reasons, arguments *etc*) true; reasonable or acceptable: *That is not a valid excuse.* **2** legally effective; having legal force: *He has a valid passport.* **'validly** *adv.*

valise [və'li:z, *(Amer)* -s] *n (Amer)* a type of soft bag in which clothes and personal items are carried when travelling.

valley ['vali] *n* a stretch of flat, low land between hills or mountains, *usu* drained by a river and its tributaries: *a beautiful green valley between the mountains.*

valour ['valə] *n* courage or bravery, *esp* in battle: *He displayed his valour on the battlefield.*

value ['valju:] *n* **1** worth, importance or usefulness: *His special knowledge was of great value during the war; She sets little value on wealth.* **2** price: *What is the value of that stamp?* **3** purchasing power: *Are those coins of any value?* **4** fairness of exchange for one's money *etc*): *You get good value for money at this supermarket!* **5** the length of a musical note. – *v* **1** to suggest a suitable price for: *This painting has been valued at $50 000.* **2** to regard as good or important: *He values your advice very highly.*

'valuable *adj* having high value: *a valuable painting.*

'valuables *n pl* things of special value: *She keeps her jewellery and other valuables in a locked drawer.*

'valued *adj* regarded as valuable or precious: *What is your most valued possession?*

'valueless *adj* having no value; worthless: *The necklace is completely valueless.*

'values *n pl* standards or principles: *People have very different moral values.*

valve [valv] *n* **1** a device for allowing a liquid or gas to pass through an opening in one direction only. **2** a structure with the same effect in an animal body: *Valves in the heart control the flow of blood in the human body.* **3** a type of electronic component found in many, *esp* older, types of television, radio *etc.*

vampire ['vampiə] *n* a dead person who is imagined to rise from the grave at night and suck the blood of sleeping people.

*****van** [van] *n* a vehicle for carrying goods on roads or railways: *He drives a van; (also adj)* a van-driver; a vanload of waste paper.

vandal ['vandəl] *n* a person who purposely and pointlessly damages or destroys public buildings or other property: *Vandals have damaged this telephone kiosk.*

'vandalism *n* the behaviour of a vandal: *All the telephones are out of order owing to vandalism.*

'vandalize, -ise *v*: *The lift in our block of flats has been vandalized.*

vanguard ['vanga:d] *n* **1** the part of an army going in front of the main body. **2** the leaders in any movement: *We're in the vanguard of the movement for reform!*

vanilla [və'nilə] *n* a flavouring obtained from a tropical orchid, and used in ice-cream and other foods: *vanilla ice-cream.*

vanish ['vaniʃ] *v* to become no longer visible, *esp* suddenly: *The ship vanished over the horizon; Our hopes suddenly vanished.*

vanity *see* **vain**.

vanquish ['vaŋkwiʃ] *v* to defeat or conquer: *You must vanquish your fears.*

vapour, *(Amer)* **vapor** ['veipə] *n* **1** the gas-like form into which a substance can be changed by heating: *water vapour.* **2** mist, fumes or smoke in the air: *Near the marshes the air was filled with a strange-smelling vapour.*

'vaporize, -ise *v* to (cause to) change into a gas-like state.

variable, variation *see* **vary**.

variegated ['veərigeitid] *adj* (of leaves *etc*) varied in colour.

variety [və'raiəti] – *pl* **va'rieties** – *n* **1** the quality of being of many different kinds or of being varied: *There's a great deal of variety in this job.* **2** a mixed collection or range: *The children got a variety of toys on their birthdays.* **3** a sort or kind: *They grow fourteen different varieties of rose.* **4** a type of mixed theatrical entertainment including dances, songs, short sketches *etc*: *I much prefer operas to variety; (also adj)* a variety show.

various ['veəriəs] *adj* **1** different; varied: *His*

reasons for leaving were many and various.
2 several: *Various people have told me about you.* **'variously** *adv.*

varnish ['vɑːnɪʃ] *n* **1** a *usu* clear sticky liquid which gives protection and a glossy surface to wood, paint *etc.* **2** the glossy surface given by this liquid: *Be careful or you'll take the varnish off the table! – v* to cover with varnish: *Don't sit on that chair – I've just varnished it.*

vary ['veəri] *v* to make, be or become different: *These apples vary in size from small to medium.*
'variable *adj* **1** that may be varied: *The machine works at a variable speed.* **2** (of *eg* winds, weather *etc*) liable or likely to change: *British weather is very variable. – n* something that varies, *eg* in quantity, value, effect *etc*: *Have you taken all the variables into account in your calculations?* **'variably** *adv.* **,varia'bility** – *pl* **varia'bilities** – *n.*
,vari'ation *n* **1** the extent to which a thing changes: *In the desert there are great variations in temperature.* **2** one of a series of musical elaborations made on a basic theme or melody: *Brahms' variations on Haydn's 'St Anthony's Chorale'.*
'varied *adj*: *He has had a very varied career.*

vase [vɑːz, (*Amer*) veis] *n* a type of jar or jug used mainly as an ornament or for holding cut flowers: *a vase of flowers.*

vast [vɑːst] *adj* of very great size or amount: *He inherited a vast fortune.* **'vastness** *n.*

vat [vat] *n* a large vessel or tank, *esp* one for holding fermenting spirits.

vaudeville ['vɔːdəvil] *n* the type of theatre show in which there is a variety of short acts: music-hall: *There are very few theatres now where vaudeville is performed.*

vault¹ [vɔːlt] *n* **1** (a room, *esp* a cellar, with) an arched roof or ceiling: *the castle vaults.* **2** an underground room, *esp* for storing valuables: *The thieves broke into the bank vaults.* **3** a burial chamber, often for all the members of a family: *He was buried in the family vault.*
'vaulted *adj* **1** (of a roof or ceiling) arched. **2** (of a building *etc*) having an arched roof or ceiling.

vault² [vɔːlt] *n* a leap aided by the hands or by a pole: *With a vault he was over the fence and away. – v* to leap (over): *He vaulted (over) the fence.*

veal [viːl] *n* the flesh of a calf, used as food: *We had veal for dinner.*

veer [viə] *v* to change direction suddenly: *The car veered across the road to avoid hitting a small boy.*

*vegetable ['vedʒtəbl] *n* **1** a plant or part of a plant, other than a fruit, used as food: *We grow potatoes, beans and other vegetables;* (*also adj*) *vegetable oils.* **2** a plant: *Grass is*

a vegetable, gold is a mineral and a human being is an animal.
,vege'tarian [vedʒi-] *n* a person who does not eat meat of any kind: *Has he always been a vegetarian?;* (*also adj*) *This is a vegetarian dish.* **,vege'tarianism** *n.*
vegetate ['vedʒiteit] *v* to live an idle, boring and pointless life: *I would like to get a job – I don't want to vegetate.*
,vege'tation [vedʒi-] *n* plants in general; plants of a particular region or type: *tropical vegetation.*

*vehicle ['viːəkl] *n* any means of transport on land, *esp* on wheels, *eg* a car, bus, bicycle *etc.*

veil [veil] *n* a piece of thin cloth worn over the face or head to hide, cover, or protect it: *Some women wear veils for religious reasons, to prevent strangers from seeing their faces; a veil of mist over the mountains; a veil of secrecy. – v* to cover with a veil.
veiled *adj* **1** wearing, or covered by, a veil: *a veiled lady; The bride was veiled.* **2** (only slightly) disguised: *a veiled threat.*

vein [vein] *n* **1** any of the tubes that carry the blood back to the heart. **2** a similar-looking line on a leaf.

velocity [və'losəti] *n* speed, *esp* in a given direction.

velvet ['velvit] *n, adj* (of) a type of cloth made from silk *etc* with a soft, thick surface: *Her dress was made of velvet; a velvet jacket.* **'velvety** *adj.*

vendetta [ven'detə] *n* a fierce, often violent, long-lasting dispute: *There has been a bitter vendetta between the two families for many years.*

venerate ['venəreit] *v* to respect; to honour greatly: *In some countries, old people are venerated more than in others.*
'venerable *adj* worthy of great respect because of age or for special goodness: *a venerable old man.*
,vene'ration *n*: *His pupils regarded him with veneration.*

Venetian [və'niːʃən]: **Venetian blind** a window blind made of thin, movable, horizontal strips of wood, metal or plastic: *We have put up Venetian blinds to stop our neighbours looking in our front windows.*

vengeance ['vendʒəns] *n* harm done in return for injury received; revenge.

venison ['venisn] *n* the flesh of deer, used as food: *We had roast venison for dinner;* (*also adj*) *venison stew.*

venom ['venəm] *n* **1** the poison produced by some snakes, scorpions *etc*, transmitted by biting or stinging: *the venom of a cobra.* **2** great ill-feeling, anger *etc*: *He spoke with venom.*
'venomous *adj* **1** (of snakes *etc*) poisonous: *venomous reptiles.* **2** (of people, their words*

Vegetables

Key

1 Radish	6 Yam
2 Bittergourd	7 Brinjal
3 Lady's Finger	8 Sweet Potato
4 French Beans	9 Tapioca
5 Cabbage	10 Watercress

Vehicles

Key

1	Lorry	**3**	Coach	**5**	Tanker	**7**	Van	**9**	Scooter	**11**	Bicycle
2	Double-decker	**4**	Pick-up	**6**	Hovercraft	**8**	Container ship	**10**	Motorcycle	**12**	Underground Railway
						13	Barge				

etc) full of ill-feeling: *a venomous speech.*
'venomously *adv.*

vent [vent] *n* a hole to allow air, smoke *etc* to pass out or in: *an air-vent.* – *v* to give expression or an outlet to (an emotion *etc*): *He was angry with himself and vented his rage on his son by beating him violently.*
give vent to to express (an emotion *etc*) freely: *He gave vent to his anger in a furious letter to the newspaper.*

ventilate ['ventileit] *v* to allow fresh air to enter (*eg* a room).
,venti'lation *n* the act or means of ventilating or the state of being ventilated: *There was no window in the room, and no other* (*means of*) *ventilation.*
'ventilator *n* a device for ventilating a room *etc.*

ventriloquist [ven'trilǝkwist] *n* a professional entertainer who can speak so that his voice seems to come from some other person or place, *esp* from a dummy which he controls.
ven'triloquism *n.*

venture ['ventʃǝ] *n* an undertaking or scheme that involves some risk: *his latest business venture.* – *v* **1** to dare to go: *Every day the child ventured further into the forest.* **2** to dare (to do (something), *esp* to say (something)): *He ventured to kiss her hand; I ventured* (*to remark*) *that her skirt was too short.* **3** to risk: *He decided to venture all his money on the scheme.*

veranda(h) [vǝ'randǝ] *n* (*Amer* **porch**) a kind of covered balcony, with a roof extending beyond the main building supported by light pillars.

†**verb** [vǝ:b] *n* the word or phrase that gives the action, or asserts something, in a sentence, clause *etc: I saw him; He ran away from me; I have a feeling; What is this?*
'verbal *adj* **1** of, or concerning, verbs: *verbal endings such as '-fy', '-ize'.* **2** consisting of, or concerning, spoken words: *a verbal warning/agreement.*
'verbally *adv* in or by speech, not writing: *I replied to the invitation verbally.*

verdict ['vǝ:dikt] *n* **1** the decision of a jury at the end of a trial: *The jury brought in a verdict of guilty.* **2** an opinion or decision reached after consideration: *The competitors are still waiting for the verdict of the judges.*

verge [vǝ:dʒ] *n* the (grass) edging of a garden bed, a road *etc: It's illegal to drive on the grass verge.* – *v* to be on the border (of): *She is verging on insanity.*

verify ['verifai] *v* to confirm the truth or correctness of (something): *Can you verify her statement?* **'verifiable** *adj.* **,verifi'cation** [-fi-] *n.*

vermilion [vǝ'miljǝn] *n, adj* (of) a bright red colour.

vermin ['vǝ:min] *n* undesirable or troublesome pests such as fleas, rats, or mice: *Farmers are always having trouble with various types of vermin; It is vermin such as these men that are trying to destroy society.*

vernacular [vǝ'nakjulǝ] *adj* colloquial or informally conversational: *vernacular speech, language.* – *n* the common informal language of a country *etc* as opposed to its formal or literary language: *They spoke to each other in the vernacular of the region.*

versatile ['vǝ:sǝtail] *adj* **1** (of people *etc*) able to turn easily and successfully from one task, activity or occupation to another: *a versatile entertainer; He will easily get another job* – *he is so versatile.* **2** (of a material *etc*) capable of being used for many purposes: *a versatile tool.* **,versa'tility** [-'ti-] *n.*

verse [vǝ:s] *n* **1** a number of lines of poetry, grouped together and forming a separate unit within the poem, song, hymn *etc: This song has three verses.* **2** a short section in a chapter of the Bible. **3** poetry, as opposed to prose: *He expressed his ideas in verse.*

version ['vǝ:ʃǝn, (*Amer*) -ʒǝn] *n* an account from one point of view: *The boy gave his version of what had occurred.*

versus ['vǝ:sǝs] *prep* (*often abbrev* **v** *or* **vs** *when written*) against: *the England v Wales rugby match.*

vertebra ['vǝ:tibrǝ] – *pl* **'vertebrae** [-bri:] – *n* any of the bones of the spine: *She has a broken vertebra.*
'vertebrate [-brǝt] *n, adj* (an animal) having a backbone: *Insects are not vertebrates.*

vertical ['vǝ:tikǝl] *adj* standing straight up at right angles to the earth's surface, or to a horizontal plane or line; upright: *The hillside looked almost vertical.* **'vertically** *adv.*

vertigo ['vǝ:tigou] *n* dizziness, *esp* as brought on by fear of heights: *Keep her back from the edge of the cliff* – *she suffers from vertigo.*

very ['veri] *adv* to a great degree: *He's very clever; You came very quickly; I'm not feeling very well.* **2** absolutely; in the highest degree: *The very first thing you must do is ring the police; She has a car of her very own.* – *adj* **1** exactly or precisely the thing, person *etc* mentioned: *You're the very man I want to see; At that very minute the door opened.* **2** extreme: *at the very end of the day; at the very top of the tree.* **3** used for emphasis in other ways: *The very suggestion of a sea voyage makes her feel seasick.*
very well used to express (reluctant) agreement to a request *etc: 'Please be home before midnight.' 'Very well.'*

vessel ['vesl] *n* **1** a container, *usu* for liquid: *a plastic vessel containing acid.* **2** a ship: *a 10000-ton grain-carrying vessel.*

† see Grammatical Notes on pp. 627–632

vest [vest] *n* **1** a kind of sleeveless shirt worn under a shirt, blouse *etc*: *He was dressed only in (a) vest and underpants.* **2** (*esp Amer*) a waistcoat: *jacket, vest and trousers*; (*also adj*) *a vest pocket.*

vet¹ *see* **veterinary.**

vet² [vet] – *pt, ptp* **'vetted** – *v* to investigate carefully (and pass as satisfactory): *Every member of staff has been vetted by our security department before he starts work here.*

veteran ['vetərən] *n, adj* **1** a person who is (old and) experienced as a soldier *etc* or in some other occupation: *a veteran footballer/entertainer.* **2** (*Amer*) a person who has been in the army *etc*: *war veterans.*

veterinary [vetə'rinəri] *adj* of, or concerning, the treatment of diseases in animals: *veterinary medicine*; *veterinary care.*

veterinary surgeon (*Amer* **veterinarian** [vetəri'neəriən] *n*) (*both often abbrev* **vet** [vet]) a doctor for animals.

veto ['vi:tou] – *3rd pers sing prt* **'vetoes:** *pt, ptp* **'vetoed** – *v* to forbid, or refuse to consent to: *They vetoed your suggestion.* – *n* – *pl* **'vetoes** – (*also* **power of veto**) the power or right to refuse or forbid: *the chairman's (power of) veto.*

vex [veks] *v* to annoy or distress (a person): *There were no other problems to vex us.*

vex'ation *n* **1** the state of being vexed. **2** a cause of annoyance or trouble: *minor worries and vexations.*

via ['vaiə] *prep* by way of: *We went to America via Japan*; *The news reached me via my aunt.*

viaduct ['vaiədʌkt] *n* a *usu* long bridge carrying a road or railway over a valley *etc.*

vibrate [vai'breit, (*Amer*) 'vaibreit] *v* to (cause to) shake, tremble, or move rapidly back and forth: *Every sound that we hear is making part of our ear vibrate*; *The engine has stopped vibrating.*

vi'bration [(*Brit and Amer*) -'brei-] *n* (an) act of vibrating: *This building is badly affected by the vibration of all the heavy traffic that passes.*

vicar ['vikə] *n* a clergyman of the Church of England.

'vicarage [-ridʒ] *n* the house of a vicar.

vice¹, (*Amer usu*) **vise** [vais] *n* a kind of strong tool for holding an object firmly, *usu* between two metal jaws: *The carpenter held the piece of wood in a vice*; *He has a grip like a vice.*

vice² [vais] *n* **1** a serious moral fault: *Continual lying is a vice.* **2** a bad habit: *Smoking is not one of my vices.*

vice- [vais] second in rank and acting as deputy for: *the Vice-President*; *the vice-chairman.*

vice versa [vaisi'və:sə] (of two things or people) the other way round: *Dogs often chase cats but not usually vice versa.*

vicinity [vi'sinəti] *n* a neighbourhood or local area: *Are there any cinemas in the/this vicinity?*

vicious ['viʃəs] *adj* evil; cruel; likely to attack or cause harm: *Keep back from that dog – it's vicious.* **'viciously** *adv.* **'viciousness** *n.*

victim ['viktim] *n* a person who receives illtreatment, injury *etc*: *a murder victim*; *Food is being sent to the victims of the disaster.*

victor ['viktə] *n* the person who wins a battle or other contest.

vic'torious [-'to:-] *adj* successful or winning: *the victorious army*; *Which team was victorious?* **vic'toriously** *adv.*

'victory – *pl* **'victories** – *n* (a) defeat of an enemy or rival: *Our team has had two defeats and eight victories*; *At last they experienced the joy of victory.*

Victorian [vik'to:riən] *adj* **1** of the reign of Queen Victoria (1837–1901): *Victorian writers*; *Victorian households/furniture.* **2** (of an attitude towards morals *etc*) strict and conservative: *a Victorian attitude to life.* – *n* a person living in Queen Victoria's reign: *The Victorians were great engineers and industrialists.*

video ['vidiou] – *pl* **'videos** – *n* **1** the recording or broadcasting (by means of a **video recorder**) of television pictures and sound. **2** a videotape. **3** a video recorder. – *v* to record on a video recorder or videotape: *He videoed the television programme on volcanoes.*

'videotape ['vidiouteip] *n* recording tape carrying pictures and sound.

vie [vai] – *prp* **'vying** ['vaiiŋ]: *pt, ptp* **vied** – *v* to compete with: *The two parents vied with each other in their attempts to gain the children's love.*

view [vju:] *n* **1** (an outlook on to, or picture of) a scene: *Your house has a fine view of the hills*; *He painted a view of the harbour.* **2** an opinion: *Tell me your view/views on the subject.* **3** an act of seeing or inspecting: *We were given a private view of the exhibition before it was opened to the public.* – *v* to look at, or regard (something): *She viewed the scene with astonishment.*

'viewer *n* **1** a person who watches television: *This programme has five million viewers.* **2** a device with a magnifying lens, and often with a light, used in viewing transparencies.

'viewpoint *n* a point of view: *I am looking at the matter from a different viewpoint.*

in view of taking into consideration; because of: *In view of the committee's criticisms of him, he felt he had to resign.*

on view being shown or exhibited: *There's a marvellous collection of prints on view at the gallery.*

point of view a way or manner of looking at a subject, matter *etc*: *You must consider everyone's point of view before deciding.*

vigilance ['vidʒiləns] *n* watchfulness or readiness for danger: *He watched her with the vigilance of a hawk.* **'vigilant** *adj.*

vigour, (*Amer*) **vigor** ['vigə] *n* strength and energy: *He began his new job with enthusiasm and vigour.*

'vigorous *adj*: *a vigorous dance.* **'vigorously** *adv.*

The adjective is always spelt **vigorous**.

vile [vail] *adj* horrible; wicked; disgusting: *That was a vile thing to say!*; *The food tasted vile.* **'vilely** *adv.* **'vileness** *n.*

villa ['vilə] *n* a type of detached or semi-detached (*usu* luxury) house, *usu* in the country or suburbs, or used for holidays at the seaside: *They have a villa at the seaside.*

village ['vilidʒ] *n* **1** a group of houses *etc* which is smaller than a town: *They live in a little village*; (*also adj*) *a village school.* **2** the people who live in such a group of houses: *The whole village turned out to see the celebrations.*

'villager *n* a person who lives in a village.

villain ['vilən] *n* a person who is wicked or of very bad character: *the villain of the play/story.* **'villainous** *adj.*

'villainy – *pl* **'villainies** – *n* (an instance of) wickedness: *His villainy was well known.*

vine [vain] *n* **1** a type of climbing plant which bears grapes. **2** any climbing or trailing plant.

'vineyard ['vin-] *n* an area which is planted with grape vines: *We spent the summer touring the French vineyards.*

vinegar ['vinigə] *n* a sour liquid made from wine, beer *etc*, used in seasoning or preparing food: *Mix some oil and vinegar as a dressing for the salad.*

vintage ['vintidʒ] *n* (a wine from) the grape-harvest of a certain (particularly good) year: *What vintage is this wine?*; *a vintage year* (=a year in which good wine was produced); *vintage port* (=port from a vintage year).

viola [vi'oulə] *n* a type of musical instrument very similar to, but slightly larger than, the violin: *She plays the viola in the school orchestra.*

violent ['vaiələnt] *adj* **1** having, using, or showing, great force: *There was a violent storm at sea*; *a violent earthquake*; *He has a violent temper.* **2** caused by force: *a violent death.* **'violently** *adv.*

'violence *n* great roughness and force, often causing severe physical injury or damage: *I was amazed at the violence of his temper*; *She was terrified by the violence of the storm.*

violet ['vaiəlit] *n* **1** a kind of small bluish-purple flower. **2** (*also adj*) (of) a bluish-purple colour.

violin [vaiə'lin] *n* a type of musical instrument with four strings, played with a bow: *She played the violin in the school orchestra*; *Can you play that on the violin?*

,vio'linist *n* a violin player: *She is a leading violinist.*

violoncello [vaiələn'tʃelou] *n* full form of **cello.**

,violon'cellist *n* full form of **cellist.**

viper ['vaipə] *n* an adder.

virgin ['vɜːdʒin] *n* a person, *esp* a woman, who has had no sexual intercourse: *She was still a virgin when she married.*

'virginal *adj* of a virgin: *Her face had a virginal look.*

vir'ginity *n* the state of being a virgin.

virtually ['vɜːtʃuəli] *adv* more or less, though not strictly speaking; in effect: *He was virtually penniless.*

virtue ['vɜːtʃuː] *n* **1** a good moral quality: *Honesty is a virtue.* **2** a good quality: *The house is small, but it has the virtue of being easy to clean.* **3** goodness of character *etc*: *She is a person of great virtue.*

'virtuous *adj* morally good: *She is a virtuous young woman.* **'virtuously** *adv.* **'virtuousness** *n.*

virtuoso [vɜːtʃu'ousou] – *pls* **,virtu'osos, virtu'osi** – *n* a person who knows a great deal about *eg* music, painting, *esp* a skilled performer: *He's a virtuoso on the violin*; (*also adj*) *a virtuoso pianist/performance.*

,virtu'osity [-'o-] *n* great skill in one of the fine arts: *I am impressed by the virtuosity of that musician.*

virus ['vaiərəs] *n* any of various types of germs that are a cause of disease. – *adj*: *He is suffering from a virus infection.*

visa ['viːzə] *n* a mark or stamp put on a passport by the authorities of a country to show that the bearer may travel to, or in, that country: *I have applied for a visa for the United States.*

viscount *n* a nobleman next in rank below an earl.

'viscountess *n* **1** the wife or widow of a viscount. **2** a woman of the same rank as a viscount.

vise *see* **vice**[1].

visible ['vizəbl] *adj* able to be seen: *The house is visible through the trees*; *The scar on her face is scarcely visible now.* **'visibly** *adv.*

,visi'bility *n* the range of distance over which things may be (clearly) seen: *Visibility is poor today*; *Visibility in the fog was down to twenty yards in places.*

vision ['viʒən] *n* **1** something seen in the imagination or in a dream: *God appeared to him in a vision.* **2** the ability to see or plan into the future: *Politicians should be men of vision.* **3** the ability to see or the sense of sight: *He is slowly losing his vision.*

visit ['vizit] *v* **1** to go to see (a person or place): *We visited my parents at the weekend; They visited the ruins at Pompeii while they were on holiday.* **2** to stay in (a place) or with (a person) for a time: *Many birds visit (Britain) only during the summer months.* – *n* an act of going to see someone or something for pleasure, socially, professionally *etc*, or going to stay for a time: *We went on a visit to my aunt's; the children's visit to the museum.*
'visitor *n* a person who visits, socially or professionally: *I'm expecting visitors from America; We're having visitors next week.*

visual ['viʒuəl] *adj* of sight or the process of seeing: *strange visual effects.* **'visually** *adv*.

vital ['vaitl] *adj* **1** essential; of the greatest importance: *Speed is vital to the success of our plan; It is vital that we arrive at the hospital soon.* **2** lively and energetic: *a vital person/personality.*
,vi'tality [-'ta-] *n* liveliness and energy: *a girl of tremendous vitality.*

vitamin ['vitəmin, (*Amer*) 'vai-] *n* any of a group of substances necessary for healthy life, different ones occurring in different natural things such as raw fruit, dairy products, fish, meat *etc*: *A healthy diet is full of vitamins; Vitamin C is found in fruit and vegetables; (also adj) vitamin pills.*

vivacious [vi'veiʃəs] *adj* lively and bright: *She is vivacious and attractive.* **vi'vaciously** *adv.* **vi'vaciousness** *n*.

vivid ['vivid] *adj* **1** (of colours *etc*) brilliant; very bright: *The door was painted a vivid yellow; The trees were vivid in their autumn colours.* **2** clear; striking: *I have many vivid memories of that holiday; a vivid image/description.* **3** (of the imagination) active; lively: *She has a vivid imagination.* **'vividly** *adv.* **'vividness** *n*.

vixen ['viksn] *n* a female fox: *The vixen was followed by her cubs.*

vocabulary [və'kabjuləri] – *pl* **vo'cabularies** – *n* **1** words in general: *This book contains some difficult vocabulary.* **2** (the stock of) words known and used *eg* by one person, or within a particular trade or profession: *He has a vocabulary of about 20000 words; the specialized vocabulary of nuclear physics.* **3** a list of words in alphabetical order with meanings *eg* added as a supplement to a book dealing with a particular subject: *This edition of Shakespeare's plays has a good vocabulary at the back.*

vocal ['voukəl] *adj* **1** of, or concerning, the voice: *vocal music.* **2** (of a person) talkative; keen to make one's opinions heard by other people: *He's always very vocal at meetings.* **vo'cally** *adv*.
'vocalist *n* a singer: *a female vocalist.*
vocal cords folds of membrane in the larynx that produce the sounds used in speech, singing *etc* when vibrated.

vocation [və'keiʃən, (*Amer*) vou-] *n* **1** a feeling of having been called (by God), or born *etc*, to do a particular type of work: *He had a sense of vocation about his work as a doctor.* **2** the work done, profession entered *etc* (as a result of such a feeling): *Nursing is her vocation; Many people regard teaching as a vocation.*

vodka ['vodkə] *n* an alcoholic spirit made from rye or sometimes from potatoes, originating in Russia.

vogue [voug] *n* a fashion: *Short hair is the vogue.*
in vogue fashionable: *The French style of dress is in vogue just now.*

voice [vois] *n* **1** the sounds from the mouth made in speaking or singing: *He has a very deep voice; He spoke in a quiet/loud/angry/kind voice.* **2** the voice regarded as the means of expressing opinion: *The voice of the people should not be ignored; the voice of reason/conscience.* – *v* **1** to express (feelings *etc*): *He voiced the discontent of the whole group.* **2** to produce the sound of (*esp* a consonant) with a vibration of the vocal cords as well as with the breath: *'Th' should be voiced in 'this' but not in 'think'.*
voiced *adj* (*neg* **un-**).
'voiceless *adj*.
be in good voice to have one's voice in good condition for singing or speaking: *The choir was in good voice tonight.*
lose one's voice to be unable to speak *eg* because of having a cold, sore throat *etc*: *When I had 'flu I lost my voice for three days.*
raise one's voice to speak more loudly than normal *esp* in anger: *I don't want to have to raise my voice to you again.*

void [void] *adj* **1** not valid or binding: *The treaty has been declared void.* **2** (*with* **of**) lacking entirely: *a statement void of meaning.* – *n* a huge empty space, *esp* (*with* **the**) outer space: *The rocket shot up into the void; Her death left a void in her husband's life.*

volcano [vol'keinou] – *pl* **vol'canoes** – *n* a hill or mountain with an opening through which molten rock, ashes *etc* periodically erupt, or have erupted in the past, from inside the earth: *The village was destroyed when the volcano erupted.*

vol'canic [-'ka-] *adj* of, like, or produced by, a volcano: *volcanic rock.*

volley ['voli] *n* **1** in tennis, the hitting of a ball before it bounces. **2** a burst of firing *etc*: *a volley of shots*; *a volley of questions/curses.* – *v* **1** to hit (a ball *etc*) before it bounces: *He volleyed the ball back to his opponent.* **2** to fire a rapid burst of (bullets, questions *etc*).

'volleyball** *n* a game in which a ball is volleyed over a high net, using the hands.

volt [voult] *n* (*often abbrev* **V**) the unit used in measuring the force driving electricity through a circuit, or the strength of an electric current.
'voltage [-tidʒ] *n* (a) force measured in volts: *Low voltage reduces the current, making the lights burn dimly.*

volume ['voljum] *n* **1** a book: *This library contains over a million volumes.* **2** one of a series of connected books: *Where is volume fifteen of the encyclopedia?* **3** the amount of space occupied by something, expressed in cubic measurement: *What is the volume of the petrol tank?* **4** amount: *A large volume of work remains to be done.* **5** level of sound *eg* on a radio, television *etc*: *Turn up the volume on the radio.*

voluntary ['voləntəri] *adj* **1** done, given *etc* by choice, not by accident or because of being forced: *Their action was completely voluntary – nobody asked them to do that.* **2** run, financed *etc* by such actions, contributions *etc*: *He does a lot of work for a voluntary organization.* **voluntarily** ['voləntərəli, volən'terəli] *adv.*

volunteer [volən'tiə] *v* **1** to offer oneself for a particular task, of one's own free will: *He volunteered to act as messenger*; *She volunteered for the dangerous job.* **2** to offer (*eg* an opinion, information *etc*): *Two or three people volunteered suggestions.* – *n* a person who offers to do, or does, something (*esp* who joins the army) of his own free will: *If we can get enough volunteers we shall not force people to join the Army.*

vomit ['vomit] *v* to throw out (the contents of the stomach or other matter) through the mouth; to be sick: *Whenever the ship started to move she felt like vomiting.* – *n* food *etc* ejected from the stomach.

voodoo ['vu:du:] *n* a type of witchcraft originally practised by certain Negro races in the West Indies.

vote [vout] *n* (the right to show) one's wish or opinion, *eg* in a ballot or by raising a hand *etc*, *esp* at an election or in a debate: *In Britain, the vote was given to women over twenty-one in 1928*; *Nowadays everyone over eighteen has a vote*; *A vote was taken to decide the matter.* – *v* **1** to cast or record one's vote: *She voted for the Conservative candidate*; *I always vote Labour*; *I shall vote against the restoration of capital punishment.* **2** to allow, by a vote, the provision of (something) *eg* to someone, for a purpose *etc*: *They were voted $5000 to help them in their research.*
'voter *n* a person who votes or has the right to vote.

vote of confidence a vote taken to establish whether the government or other authority still has the majority's support for its policies.

vote of thanks an invitation, *usu* in the form of a short speech, to an audience *etc* to show gratitude to a speaker *etc* by applauding *etc*: *Mrs Smith proposed a vote of thanks to the organizers of the concert.*

vouch [vautʃ] *v* **1** to say that one is sure that something is fact or truth: *Will you vouch for the truth of the statement?* **2** to guarantee the honesty *etc* of (a person): *My friends will vouch for me.*
'voucher *n* a piece of paper which confirms that a sum of money has been, or will be, paid: *a sales voucher.*

vow [vau] *n* a solemn promise, *esp* one made to God: *The monks have made/taken a vow of silence*; *marriage vows.* – *v* **1** to make a solemn promise (that): *He vowed that he would die rather than surrender.* **2** to threaten: *He vowed revenge on all his enemies.*

vowel ['vauəl] *n* **1** in English and many other languages, the letters *a, e, i, o, u.* **2** (*also* **vowel sound**) any of the sounds represented by these five letters or by *y*, or by combination of these with each other and/or *w.*

voyage ['voiidʒ] *n* a *usu* long journey, *esp* by sea: *The voyage to America used to take many weeks.* – *v* to make such a journey: *They voyaged for many months.*
'voyager *n* an old word for a person making a voyage, or who has made several voyages.

vs *see* **versus**.

vulgar ['vʌlgə] *adj* **1** not generally socially acceptable, decent or polite; ill-mannered: *Such behaviour is regarded as vulgar.* **2** of the common or ordinary people: *the vulgar tongue/language.* **'vulgarly** *adv.*
vul'garity [-'ga-] – *pl* **vul'garities** – *n* (an example of) bad manners, bad taste *etc*, in *eg* speech, behaviour *etc*: *the vulgarity of his language.*

vulnerable ['vʌlnərəbl] *adj* unprotected against attack; liable to be hurt or damaged: *Small animals are often vulnerable to attack.* **,vulnera'bility** *n.*

vulture ['vʌltʃə] *n* a type of large bird of prey feeding chiefly on dead bodies.

vying *see* **vie**.

* see illustration on p. 206

Ww

addle ['wodl] v to take short steps and move from side to side in walking (as a duck does): *The ducks waddled across the road*; *The fat old lady waddled down the street.* – *n* a clumsy, rocking way of walking.

ade [weid] v **1** to go or walk (through water, mud *etc*) with some difficulty: *He waded across the river towards me*; *I've finally managed to wade through that boring book I had to read.* **2** to cross (a river *etc*) by wading: *We'll wade the stream at its shallowest point.*

'wader *n* any of several types of bird that wade in search of food.

afer ['weifə] *n* **1** a type of very thin biscuit, often eaten with ice-cream.

,wafer-'thin *adj* extremely thin.

ag [wag] – *pt, ptp* **wagged** – v (*esp* of a dog's tail) to (cause to) move to and fro, *esp* from side to side: *The dog wagged its tail with pleasure.* – *n* a single wagging movement: *The dog's tail gave a feeble wag.*

age[1] [weidʒ] v to carry on or engage in (*esp* a war): *The North waged war on/against the South.*

age[2] [weidʒ] *n* (*also* **'wages** *n pl*) a regular, *usu* weekly rather than monthly, payment for the work that one does: *He spends all his wages on books*; *What is his weekly wage?*

'wage-packet *n* **1** the packet in which wages are paid: *The cashier puts the workmen's money in wage-packets.* **2** wages: *Because of heavier taxation, my wage-packet has been getting smaller.*

ager ['weidʒə] *n* a bet: *We made a wager that he would win.* – *v* to bet (something) on the chance of something happening: *I'll wager (ten dollars) that I can jump further than you.*

aggle ['wagl] v to (cause to) move from side to side: *She waggled her hips as she walked down the street*; *His beard waggled as he ate.* – *n* such a movement.

agon, waggon ['wagən] *n* **1** a type of four-wheeled vehicle for carrying heavy loads: *a hay wagon.* **2** an open railway carriage for goods: *a goods wagon.*

aif [weif] *n* a stray, uncared-for child: *a poor little waif.*

ail [weil] v to utter sorrowful or complaining cries: *The child is wailing over its broken toy.* – *n* a long cry: *wails of grief*; *I heard the wail of a police siren.*

aist [weist] *n* **1** (the measurement round) the narrow part of the human body between the ribs and hips: *She has a very small waist.* **2** the narrow middle part of something similar, *eg* a violin, guitar *etc.*

3 the part of an article of clothing which goes round one's waist: *Can you take in the waist of these trousers?*

'waisted *adj* shaped to fit round the waist: *a waisted jacket.*

waistband ['weisband] *n* the part of a pair of trousers, skirt *etc* which goes round the waist: *The waistband of this skirt is too tight.*

waistcoat ['weiskout] *n* (*Amer* **vest**) a short, usu sleeveless jacket worn immediately under the outer jacket: *a three-piece suit consists of trousers, jacket and waistcoat.*

wait [weit] v **1** (*with* **for**) to remain or stay (in the same place or without doing anything): *Wait (for) two minutes (here) while I go inside*; *I'm waiting for John (to arrive).* **2** (*with* **for**) to expect: *I was just waiting for that pile of dishes to fall!* **3** (*with* **on**) to serve dishes, drinks *etc* (at table): *This servant will wait on your guests*; *He waits at table.* – *n* an act of waiting; a delay: *There was a long wait before they could get on the train.*

'waiter – *fem* **'waitress** – *n* a person who serves people with food *etc* at table: *She is a waitress in a café*; *Which waiter served you in the restaurant?*

'waiting-list *n* a list of the names of people who are waiting for something: *She is on the waiting-list for medical treatment.*

'waiting-room *n* a room in which people may wait (*eg* at a station, doctor's surgery *etc*).

waive [weiv] **1** to give up or not insist upon (*eg* a claim or right): *He waived his claim to all the land north of the river.* **2** not to demand or enforce (a fine, penalty *etc*): *The judge waived the sentence and let him go free.*

wake[1] [weik] – *pt* **woke** [wouk], (*rare*) **waked**: *ptp* **woken** ['woukən], (*rare*) **waked** – *v* to bring or come back to consciousness after being asleep: *He woke to find that it was raining*; *Go and wake the others, will you?*

'wakeful *adj* **1** not asleep; not able to sleep: *a wakeful child.* **2** (of a night) in which one gets little sleep: *We spent a wakeful night worrying about her.*

'wakefully *adv.* **'wakefulness** *n.*

'waken *v* to wake: *What time are you going to waken him?*; *I wakened early.*

wake up 1 to wake: *Wake up! You're late*; *The baby woke up in the middle of the night.* **2** to become aware of: *It is time you woke up to the fact that you are not working hard enough.*

wake[2] [weik] *n* a strip of smooth-looking or foamy water left behind a ship.

in the wake of immediately behind or after: *Our tiny boat was caught in the wake of the huge ship.*

walk [wo:k] *v* **1** (of people or animals) to (cause to) move on foot at a pace slower than running, never having both or all the feet off the ground at once: *He walked across the room and sat down*; *How long will it take to walk to the station?*; *She walks her dog in the park every morning.* **2** to travel on foot for pleasure: *We're going walking in the hills for our holidays.* **3** to move on foot along: *It's dangerous to walk the streets of New York alone after dark.* – *n* **1** (the distance covered during) an outing or journey on foot: *She wants to go for/to take a walk*; *It's a long walk to the station.* **2** a way or manner of walking: *I recognised her walk.* **3** a route for walking: *There are many pleasant walks in this area.*

'**walker** *n* a person who goes walking for pleasure: *We met a party of walkers as we were going home.*

,**walkie-'talkie** *n* a portable two-way radio: *The soldiers spoke to each other on the walkie-talkie.*

'**walking-stick** *n* a stick used (*esp* as an aid to balance) when walking: *The old lady has been using a walking-stick since she hurt her leg.*

'**walkover** *n* an easy victory: *It was a walkover! We won 8–nil.*

'**walkway** *n* a path *etc* for pedestrians only.

walk all over (someone) to pay no respect to (a person's) rights, feelings *etc*: *He'll walk all over you if you let him.*

walk off with 1 to win easily: *He walked off with all the prizes at the school sports.* **2** to steal: *The thieves have walked off with my best silver and china.*

walk of life a way of earning one's living; an occupation or profession: *People from all walks of life went to the minister's funeral.*

walk on air to feel extremely happy *etc*: *She's walking on air since he asked her to marry him.*

wall [wo:l] *n* **1** something built of stone, brick, plaster, wood *etc* and used to separate off or enclose something: *There's a wall at the bottom of the garden*: *The Great Wall of China*; *a garden wall.* **2** any of the sides of a building or room: *One wall of the room is yellow – the rest are white.* – *v* (*often with* **in**) to enclose (something) with a wall: *We've walled in the playground to prevent the children getting out.*

walled *adj*: *a walled city.*

-walled having (a certain type or number of) wall(s): *a high-walled garden.*

'**wallpaper** *n* paper used to decorate interior walls of houses *etc*: *My wife wants to put wallpaper on the walls but I would rather paint them.* – *v* to put such paper on: *I have wallpapered the front room.*

,**wall-to-'wall** *adj* (of a carpet *etc*) covering the entire floor of a room *etc*.

have one's back to the wall to be in a desperate situation: *The army in the south have their backs to the wall, and are fighting a losing battle.*

up the wall crazy: *This business is sending driving me up the wall!*

wallet ['wolit] *n* **1** a small (*usu* folding) case made of soft leather, plastic *etc*, carried in the pocket and used for holding (*esp* paper money, personal papers *etc*: *He has lost all his money – his wallet has been stolen.* **2** a similar case containing other things: *a plastic wallet containing a set of small tools.*

wallop ['woləp] *v* to strike (something or someone) hard: *He walloped the desk with his fist*; *I'll wallop you if you do that again!* – *n* a heavy or powerful blow: *He gave John a wallop right on the chin.*

wallow ['wolou] *v* to roll about with enjoyment: *This hippopotamus wallowed in the mud.* – *n* an act of wallowing.

walnut ['wo:lnʌt] *n* **1** a type of tree whose wood is used for making furniture *etc*. **2** the nut produced by this tree. **3** (*also adj*) (of) the wood of the tree: *a walnut table.*

walrus ['wo:lrəs] – *pls* '**walruses**, '**walrus** – *n* a type of large sea animal with huge tusks, related to the seal.

waltz [wo:lts] *n* (a piece of music for) a type of slow ballroom dance performed by couples: *The band is playing a waltz*; (*also adj*) *waltz music.* – *v* **1** to dance a waltz (with): *Can you waltz?*; *He waltzed his partner round the room.* **2** to move cheerfully or with confidence: *He waltzed into the room and told us that he was getting married the next day.*

wan [won] *adj* pale and sickly-looking: *She still looks wan after her illness.* '**wanly** *adv*. '**wanness** *n*.

wand [wond] *n* a long slender rod *eg* used as the symbol of magic power by conjurors, fairies *etc*: *In the story, the fairy waved her magic wand and the frog became a prince.*

wander ['wondə] *v* **1** to go, move, walk *etc* (about, in or on) from place to place with no definite destination in mind: *I'd like to spend a holiday wandering through France*; *The mother wandered the streets looking for her child.* **2** to go astray or move away from the proper place or home: *His mind wanders*; *My attention was wandering.* – *n* an act of wandering: *He's gone for a wander round the shops.* '**wanderer** *n*.

'**wanderlust** *n* the wish to travel: *He's always travelling – his wanderlust will never be satisfied.*

wane [wein] *v* (of the moon) to appear to become smaller as less of it is visible.

on the wane becoming less: *His power is on the wane.*

angle ['waŋgl] *v* to obtain or achieve (something) by trickery: *He got us seats for the concert – I don't know how he wangled it.*

ant [wont] *v* **1** to be interested in having or doing, or to wish to have or do (something); to desire: *Do you want a cigarette?*; *She wants to know where he is*; *She wants to go home.* **2** to need: *This wall wants a coat of paint.* **3** to lack: *This house wants none of the usual modern features but I do not like it*; *The people will want* (= be poor) *no longer. – n* **1** something desired: *The child has a long list of wants.* **2** poverty: *They have lived in want for many years.* **3** a lack: *There's no want of opportunities these days.*

'wanted *adj* **1** being searched for by the police because of having committed a criminal act: *He is a wanted man*; *He is wanted for murder.* **2** (*neg* **un-**) (of people) needed; cared for: *Old people must be made to feel wanted.*

want for to lack: *She wants for nothing.*

anton ['wontən] *adj* **1** without reason; motiveless: *wanton cruelty*; *the wanton destruction of property.* **2** (of a person) immoral: *wanton young women.*

'wantonly *adv.* **'wantonness** *n.*

ar [wo:] *n* (an) armed struggle, *esp* between nations: *Their leader has declared war on Britain*; *The larger army will win the war*; *the horrors of war*; (*also adj*) *He is guilty of war crimes. – v – pt, ptp* **warred** – to fight: *The two countries have been warring constantly for generations.*

'warlike *adj* (*neg* **un-**) fond of, or likely to begin, war: *a warlike nation.*

'warrior ['wo-] *n* a soldier or skilled fighting man, *esp* in primitive societies: *The chief of the tribe called his warriors together*; (*also adj*) *a warrior prince.*

war correspondent a newspaper reporter who writes articles on a war *esp* from the scene of fighting.

'war-cry – *pl* **'war-cries** – *n* a shout used in battle as an encouragement to the soldiers: *'For king and country' was the war-cry of the troops as they faced the enemy.*

'war-dance *n* a dance performed by the people of some primitive societies before going to war.

'warfare *n* fighting, as in a war: *He refused to fight, because he has religious objections to warfare.*

'warhead *n* the explosive section of a missile, torpedo *etc*: *nuclear warheads.*

'warhorse *n* a horse used in battle.

'warlord *n* a very powerful military leader.

'warmonger *n* a person who encourages war(s), often for personal reasons.

'warpaint *n* paint applied to the face *etc* by

the people of some primitive societies before going into battle.

'warship *n* a ship used in war or defence.

'wartime *n* the time during which a country, a people *etc* is at war: *There is a great deal of hardship and misery in wartime*; (*also adj*) *a wartime economy.*

war of nerves a war, contest *etc* in which each side tries to win by making the other nervous, *eg* by bluff, rather than by actually fighting: *That game of chess was a war of nerves.*

warble ['wo:bl] *v* to sing in a trembling voice, as some birds do: *The bird was warbling (his song) on a high branch. – n* an act, or the sound, of warbling: *the warble of a bird in summer.*

'warbler *n* any of several kinds of small singing bird.

ward [wo:d] *n* **1** a room with a bed or beds for patients in a hospital *etc*: *He is in a surgical ward of the local hospital.* **2** a person who is under the legal control and care of someone who is not his or her parent or (a **ward of court**) of a court: *She was made a ward of court so that she could not marry until she was eighteen.*

'warder *n* a person who guards prisoners in a jail: *He shot a warder and escaped from jail.*

warden ['wo:dn] *n* **1** the person in charge of an old people's home, a student residence *etc*: *The warden has reported that two students are missing from the hostel.* **2** (*also* **traffic warden**) a person who controls parking and the flow of traffic in an area: *If the (traffic) warden finds your car parked there you will be fined.* **3** a person who has been appointed to look after the civil population in case of *eg* air raids (an **air-raid warden**). **4** (*also* **game warden**) a person who guards a game reserve.

wardrobe ['wo:droub] *n* **1** a cupboard in which clothes may be hung: *Hang your suit in the wardrobe.* **2** a stock of clothing: *She bought a complete new wardrobe in Paris.*

-ward(s) [wəd(z)] in a (certain) direction, as in **backward(s)**, **homeward(s)**.

-ware [weə] manufactured articles (made of a particular material): *silverware/glassware.*

wares *n pl* articles for sale: *a tradesman selling his wares.*

warehouse *n* a building in which goods are stored: *a furniture warehouse.*

warm [wo:m] *adj* **1** moderately, or comfortably, hot: *Are you warm enough, or shall I close the window?*; *a warm summer's day.* **2** (of clothes) protecting the wearer from the cold: *a warm jumper.* **3** welcoming, friendly, enthusiastic *etc*: *a warm welcome*; *a warm smile.* **4** tending to make one hot: *This is warm work!* **5** (of colours, *esp* the pale ones) enriched by a certain quantity of red or pink, or (of red *etc*) rich and bright: *a warm red*; *I don't want white walls – I want something warmer.* – *v* **1** to make moderately hot: *He warmed his hands in front of the fire.* **2** to become friendly (towards) or enthusiastic (about): *She warmed to his charm.* – *n* an act of warming: *Give your hands a warm in front of the fire.*

'**warmly** *adv.* **warmness** *n.*

'**warmth** [-θ] *n* the state of being warm: *the warmth of the fire*; *The actor was delighted by the warmth of the applause*; *The warmth of her smile made me feel welcome.*

,**warm-'blooded** *adj* **1** having a blood temperature greater than that of the surrounding atmosphere: *warm-blooded animals such as man.* **2** enthusiastic; passionate: *When I was young and warm-blooded, I was passionate about many things that don't interest me now.*

,**warm'hearted** *adj* kind and affectionate: *a warmhearted old lady*; *a warmhearted action.* ,**warm'heartedness** *n.*

warm up to make or become warm: *The room will soon warm up*; *Have a cup of coffee to warm you up.*

warn [wo:n] *v* **1** to tell (a person) in advance (about a danger *etc*): *Black clouds warned us of the approaching storm*; *They warned her that she would be ill if she didn't rest.* **2** to advise (someone against doing something): *I was warned about/against speeding by the policeman*; *They warned him not to be late.*

'**warning** *n* **1** an event, or something said or done, that warns: *He gave her a warning against driving too fast*; *His heart attack will be a warning to him not to work so hard.* **2** advance notice or advance signs: *The earthquake came without warning.* – *adj* giving a warning: *She received a warning message.*

'**warningly** *adv*: *She looked warningly at the naughty boy.*

warp[1] [wo:p] *v* **1** to make or become twisted out of shape: *The door has been warped by all the rain we've had lately.* **2** to cause to think or act in an abnormal way: *His experiences had warped his judgement/mind.* – *n* the shape into which something is twisted by warping: *The rain has given this wood a permanent warp.* **warped** *adj.*

warp[2] [wo:p] *n* (*usu* with **the**) the set of threads lying lengthwise in a loom during weaving (the other being the **weft** [weft]).

warrant ['worənt] *v* **1** to justify: *A slight cold does not warrant your staying off work.* **2** an old word to state confidently or (be willing to) bet that: *I'll warrant he's gone riding*

instead of doing his work. – *n* something that gives authority, *esp* a legal document giving the police the authority for searching someone's house, arresting someone *etc*: *The police have a warrant for his arrest.*

warren ['worən] *n* a place where many rabbits have their burrows.

warrior *see* **war.**

wart [wo:t] *n* a small hard growth on the skin: *He has warts on his fingers.*

wary ['weəri] *adj* cautious or on one's guard (about or concerning): *a wary animal*; *Be wary of lending money to him.* '**warily** *adv* '**wariness** *n.*

was *see* **be.**

wash [woʃ] *v* **1** to clean (a thing or person, *esp* oneself) with (soap and) water or other liquid: *How often do you wash your hair?*; *You wash (the dishes) and I'll dry*; *We can wash in the stream.* **2** to be able to be washed without being damaged: *This fabric doesn't wash very well.* **3** to flow (against over *etc*): *The waves washed (against) the ship.* **4** to sweep (away *etc*) by means of water: *The floods have washed away hundreds of houses.* – *n* **1** an act of washing: *He's just gone to have a wash.* **2** things to be washed or being washed: *Your sweater is in the wash.* **3** the flowing or lapping (of waves *etc*): *the wash of waves against the rocks.* **4** a liquid with which something is washed: *a mouthwash.* **5** a thin coat (of water-colour paint *etc*), *esp* in a painting: *The background of the picture was a pale blue wash.* **6** the waves caused by a moving boat *etc*: *The rowing-boat was tossing about in the wash from the ship's propellers.*

'**washable** *adj* able to be washed without being damaged: *Is this dress washable?*

'**washer** *n* **1** a person or thing (*eg* a machine) that washes: *They've just bought an automatic dish-washer.* **2** a flat ring of rubber, metal *etc* to keep nuts or joints tight: *Our tap needs a new washer.*

'**washing** **1** *n* (an) act of cleaning by water: *I don't mind washing, but I hate ironing.* **2** clothes washed or to be washed: *I'll hang the washing out to dry.*

,**washed-'out** *adj* **1** completely lacking in energy *etc*: *I feel quite washed-out today.* **2** (of garments *etc*) pale, having lost colour as a result of washing: *She wore a pair of old, washed-out jeans.*

'**washerwoman, washerman** *ns* a person who is paid to wash clothes.

'**wash-(hand) basin** a basin in which to wash one's face and hands: *We are having a new washhand basin installed in the bathroom.*

'**washing-machine** *n* an electric machine for washing clothes: *She has an automatic washing-machine.*

'**washing-powder** n a powdered detergent used when washing clothes.

,**washing-'up** n dishes etc cleaned or to be cleaned after a meal etc: I'll help you with the washing-up.

'**washout** n (an idea, project, person etc which is) a complete failure: She was a complete washout as a secretary.

'**washroom** n a lavatory.

wash up 1 to wash dishes etc after a meal: I'll help you wash up; We've washed the plates up. **2** (Amer) to wash one's hands and face. **3** to bring up on to the shore: The ship was washed up on the rocks; A lot of rubbish has been washed up on the beach.

asn't see be.

asp [wosp] n a type of winged insect having a sting and a slender waist.

'**waspish** adj (of a person) unpleasant in manner, temper etc: a nasty, waspish young woman. '**waspishly** adv. '**waspishness** n.

aste [weist] v to fail to use (something) fully or in the correct or most useful way: You're wasting my time with all these stupid questions. – n **1** material which is or has been made useless: industrial waste from the factories; (also adj) waste material. **2** (the) act of wasting: That was a waste of an opportunity. **3** a huge stretch of unused or infertile land, or of water, desert, ice etc: the Arctic wastes.

'**wastage** [-tidʒ] n loss by wasting; the amount wasted: Of the total amount, roughly 20% was wastage.

'**wasteful** adj involving or causing waste: Throwing away that bread is wasteful. '**wastefully** adv. '**wastefulness** n.

waste paper paper which is thrown away as not being useful: Offices usually have a great deal of waste paper.

wastepaper basket ['weispeipə] a basket or other (small) container for waste paper: Put those old letters in the wastepaper basket.

waste pipe ['weispaip] a pipe to carry off waste material, or water from a sink etc: The kitchen waste pipe is blocked.

waste away to decay; to lose weight, strength and health etc: He is wasting away because he has a terrible disease.

atch [wotʃ] n **1** a small instrument for telling the time by, worn on the wrist or carried in the pocket of a waistcoat etc: He wears a gold watch; a wrist-watch. **2** a period of standing guard during the night: I'll take the watch from two o'clock till six. **3** in the navy etc, a group of officers and men who are on duty at a given time: The night watch come(s) on duty soon. – v **1** to look at (someone or something): He was watching her carefully; He is watching television. **2** to keep a lookout (for): They've gone to watch

for the ship coming in; Could you watch for the postman? **3** to be careful of (someone or something): Watch (that) you don't fall off!; Watch him! He's dangerous. **4** to guard or take care of: Watch the prisoner and make sure he doesn't escape; Please watch the baby while I go shopping. **5** to wait for (a chance, opportunity etc): Watch your chance, and then run. '**watcher** n.

'**watchful** adj alert and cautious: watchful eyes; If you are watchful you will not be robbed. '**watchfully** adv. '**watchfulness** n.

'**watchdog** n a dog which guards someone's property etc: We leave a watchdog in our office at night to scare away thieves.

'**watchmaker** n a person who makes and repairs watches, clocks etc.

'**watchman** n (often ,**night-'watchman**) a man employed to guard a building etc against thieves, esp at night: The bank-robbers shot the (night-) watchman.

'**watchtower** n an old word for a tower on which a lookout is posted.

'**watchword** n a motto or slogan used by members of a group of people who think (or act) alike: Let freedom be our watchword!

keep watch to be on guard: He kept watch while the other soldiers slept.

watch one's step to be careful what one does or says: He's in a bad mood, so watch your step and don't say anything wrong!

watch out (with **for**) to be careful (of): Watch out for the cars!; Watch out! The police are coming!

watch over to guard or take care of: The mother bird is watching over her young.

water ['wo:tə] n a colourless, transparent liquid compound of hydrogen and oxygen, having no taste or smell, which turns to steam when boiled and to ice when frozen: She drank two glasses of water; 'Are you going swimming in the sea?' 'No, the water's too cold'; Each bedroom in the hotel is supplied with hot and cold running water; (also adj) The plumber had to turn off the water supply in order to repair the pipe; transport by land and water. – v **1** to supply with water: He watered the plants. **2** (of the mouth) to produce saliva: His mouth watered at the sight of all the food. **3** (of the eyes) to fill with tears: The dense smoke made his eyes water.

'**waters** n pl a body of water such as the sea, a river etc: the stormy waters of the bay.

'**watery** adj **1** like water; diluted: a watery fluid. **2** (of eyes) full of fluid eg because of illness, cold winds etc. **3** (of a colour) pale: eyes of a watery blue. '**wateriness** n.

water boatman a water insect with oarlike back legs that propel it through the water.

'**waterborne** *adj* carried or transmitted by water: *Typhoid is a waterborne disease.*

'**water-closet** *n* (*abbrev* **WC** [dʌblju'si:]) a lavatory.

'**water-colour** *n* a type of paint which is thinned with water instead of with oil.

*'**watercress** *n* a herb which grows in water and is often used in salads.

'**waterfall** *n* a natural fall of water from a height such as a rock or a cliff.

'**waterfowl** *n or n pl* a bird or birds which live on or beside water.

'**waterfront** *n* that part of a town *etc* which faces the sea or a lake: *He lives on the waterfront.*

'**waterhole** *n* a spring or other place where water can be found in a desert or other dry country: *The elephant drank from the waterhole.*

water hyacinth a floating water plant with violet or blue flowers.

'**watering-can** *n* a container used when watering plants.

water level the level of the surface of a mass of water: *The water level in the reservoir is sinking/rising.*

'**waterlily** – *pl* '**waterlilies** – *n* a water plant with broad flat floating leaves.

'**waterlogged** *adj* (of ground) soaked in water.

water main a large underground pipe carrying a public water supply.

*'**water-melon** a type of melon with green skin and red flesh.

water moss fern a tiny floating water plant with hairy boat-shaped leaves.

'**waterproof** *adj* not allowing water to soak through: *waterproof material.* – *n* a coat made of waterproof material: *She was wearing a waterproof.* – *v* to make (material) waterproof.

'**watershed** *n* an area of high land from which rivers flow in different directions into different basins.

'**water-skiing** *n* the sport of skiing on water, towed by a motor-boat. '**water-ski** *v*.

water stick-insect a long thin-legged water insect with a breathing-tube that it raises above the water.

'**watertight** *adj* made in such a way that water cannot pass through.

water vapour water in the form of a gas, produced by evaporation.

'**waterway** *n* a channel, *eg* a canal or river, along which ships can sail.

'**waterwheel** *n* a wheel moved by water to work machinery *etc*.

'**waterworks** *n pl or n sing* a place in which water is purified and stored before distribution to an area.

hold water to be convincing: *His explanation won't hold water.*

in(to) deep water in(to) trouble or danger: *I got into deep water during that argument.*

water down to dilute: *This milk has been watered down.*

watt [wot] *n* (*abbrev* **W** *when written*) a unit of power, *esp* of heat or light.

wave [weiv] *n* 1 a moving ridge, larger than a ripple, moving on the surface of water: *rolling waves; a boat tossing on the waves.* 2 a vibration travelling *eg* through the air: *radio waves; sound waves; light waves.* 3 a curve or curves in the hair: *Are those waves natural?* 4 a (*usu* temporary) rise or increase: *the recent crime wave; a wave of violence; The pain came in waves.* 5 an act of waving: *She recognized me, and gave me a wave.* – *v* 1 to move backwards and forwards or flutter: *The flags waved gently in the breeze.* 2 to (cause hair to) curve first one way then the other: *She's had her hair waved; Her hair waves naturally.* 3 to make a gesture (of greeting *etc*) with (*eg* the hand): *She waved to me across the street; Everyone was waving handkerchiefs in farewell; They waved goodbye.*

'**wavy** *adj* (of hair) full of waves: *Her hair is wavy but her sister's hair is straight.* '**waviness** *n*.

'**wave(band)** *n* a range of wavelengths on which *eg* radio signals are broadcast.

'**wavelength** *n* the distance from any given point on one (radio *etc*) wave to the corresponding point on the next.

wave aside to dismiss (a suggestion *etc*) without paying much attention to it.

waver ['weivə] *v* to be unsteady or uncertain: *He wavered between accepting and refusing.*

wax[1] [waks] *n* 1 the sticky, fatty substance of which bees make their cells; beeswax. 2 the sticky, yellowish substance formed in the ears. 3 a manufactured, fatty substance used in polishing, to give a good shine: *furniture wax.* 4 (*also adj*) (*also* '**candle-wax**) (of) a substance made from paraffin, used in making candles, models *etc*, that melts when heated: *a wax model.* 5 sealing-wax. – *v* to smear, polish or rub with wax.

waxed *adj* having a coating of wax: *waxed paper.*

'**waxen**, '**waxy** *adjs*.

'**waxwork** *n* a wax model (*usu* of a well-known person).

'**waxworks** *n pl* an exhibition of such models.

wax[2] [waks] *v* 1 (of the moon) to appear to grow in size as more of it becomes visible. 2 an old word for to grow or increase.

way [wei] *n* 1 an opening or passageway: *This is the way in/out; There's no way through.* 2 a route, direction *etc*: *Which way shall we go?; Which is the way to Princes Street?; His house is on the way from here to the* school; *Will you be able to find your/the way to my house?*; *Your house is on my way home*; *The errand took me out of my way*; *a motorway*; *a railway*. **3** used in the names of roads: *His address is 21 Melville Way.* **4** a distance: *It's a long way to the school*; *The nearest shops are only a short way away.* **5** a method or manner: *What is the easiest way to write a book?*; *I know a good way of doing it*; *He's got a funny way of talking*; *This is the quickest way to chop onions.* **6** an aspect or side of something: *In some ways this job is quite difficult*; *In a way I feel sorry for him.* **7** a characteristic of behaviour; a habit: *He has some rather unpleasant ways.* **8** used with many verbs to give the idea of progressing or moving: *He pushed his way through the crowd*; *They soon ate their way through the food.* – *adv* (*esp Amer*) by a long distance or time; far: *The winner finished the race way ahead of the other competitors*; *It's way past your bedtime.*

'**wayfarer** *n* a traveller, *esp* on foot.

'**wayside** *n* the side of a road, path *etc*: *We can stop by the wayside and have a picnic*; (*also adj*) *a wayside inn.*

be/get on one's way to start or continue a walk, journey *etc*: *Well, thanks for the cup of tea, but I must be on my way now.*

by the way incidentally, in passing, while I remember *etc*: *By the way, did you know he was getting married?*

fall by the wayside (of projects, ideas *etc*) to be abandoned; to fail.

get/have one's own way to do, get *etc* what one wants: *You can't always have your own way.*

get into/out of the way of (doing) something to become accustomed to (not) doing; to get into/out of the habit of doing: *They got into the way of waking up late when they were on holiday.*

go out of one's way to do more than is really necessary: *He went out of his way to help us.*

have a way with to be good at dealing with or managing: *She has a way with children.*

have it one's own way to get one's own way: *Oh, have it your own way – I'm tired of arguing.*

in a bad way unwell; in poor condition: *The patient is in a bad way.*

in, out of the/someone's way (not) blocking someone's progress, or occupying space that is needed by someone: *Don't leave your bicycle where it will get in the way of pedestrians*; *Will I be in the/your way if I work at this table?*; *'Get out of my way!' he said rudely.*

lose one's way to stop knowing where one is, or in which direction one ought to be going: *I lost my way through the city.*

make one's way 1 to go: *They made their*

way towards the centre of the town. **2** to get on in the world.

make way (for) to stand aside and leave room (for): *The crowd parted to make way for the ambulance.*

under way moving, in progress *etc*: *Her plans are under way.*

way of life a manner of spending one's life: *I enjoy farming – it's a pleasant way of life.*

ways and means methods, *esp* of providing money.

waylay [wei'lei] – *pt, ptp* **way'laid** – *v* to ambush: *He was waylaid by a crowd of angry demonstrators.*

wayward ['weiwəd] *adj* (of a child *etc*) self-willed and rebellious.

WC *see* **water-closet** *under* **water**.

we [wi:] *pron* (used only as the subject of a verb) the word used by a speaker or writer in mentioning himself or herself together with other people: *We are going home tomorrow.*

weak [wi:k] *adj* **1** lacking in physical strength: *Her illness has made her very weak.* **2** not strong in character: *I'm very weak when it comes to giving up cigarettes.* **3** (of a liquid) diluted; not strong: *weak tea.* **4** (of an explanation *etc*) not convincing. **5** (of a joke) not particularly funny. '**weakly** *adv*.

'**weaken** *v* to (cause to) become weak, *esp* in physical strength or character: *The patient has weakened*; *The strain of the last few days has weakened him.*

'**weakling** [-liŋ] *n* a weak person, animal, or plant: *She married a weakling.*

'**weakness** *n* **1** the state of being weak. **2** something weak or faulty; a defect: *weaknesses of character*; *Smoking is one of my weaknesses.*

have a weakness for to have a liking for: *She has a weakness for chocolate biscuits.*

wealth [welθ] *n* **1** riches: *He is a man of great wealth.* **2** a great quantity (of): *a wealth of information.*

'**wealthy** *adj* having much money and/or many possessions; rich: *She is a wealthy young widow.*

wean [wi:n] *v* to cause (a child or young animal) to become used to food other than the mother's milk: *The baby has been weaned (on to solid foods).*

weapon ['wepən] *n* any instrument or means which is used for one's own defence or for attacking others: *Rifles, arrows, atom bombs and tanks are all weapons*; *The police are looking for the murder weapon*; *Surprise is our best weapon.*

wear [weə] – *pt* **wore** [wo:]: *ptp* **worn** [wo:n] – *v* **1** to be dressed in or carry on (a part of) the body: *She wore a white dress*; *Does she usually wear spectacles?* **2** to arrange (one's hair) in a particular way: *She wears her hair* *in a pony-tail.* **3** to have or show (a particular expression): *She wore an angry expression.* **4** to (cause to) become thinner *etc* because of use, rubbing *etc*: *This carpet has worn in several places*; *This sweater is wearing thin at the elbows.* **5** to make (a bare patch, a hole *etc*) by rubbing, use *etc*: *I've worn a hole in the elbow of my jacket.* **6** to stand up to use: *This material doesn't wear very well.* – *n* **1** use as clothes *etc*: *I use this suit for everyday wear*; *Those shoes won't stand much wear.* **2** articles for use as clothes: *casual wear*; *sportswear*; *leisurewear.* **3** (*sometimes* **wear and tear**) damage due to use: *The hall carpet is showing signs of wear.* **4** ability to withstand use: *There's plenty of wear left in it yet.*

'**wearable** *adj* (*neg* **un-**) fit to be worn: *My only wearable coat is at the cleaners.*

'**wearer** *n*: *a dress that makes the wearer feel elegant.*

'**wearing** *adj* exhausting: *I've had rather a wearing day.*

worn [woːn] *adj* damaged as a result of use: *a badly-worn carpet.*

wear away to make or become damaged, thinner, smoother *etc* through use, rubbing *etc*: *The steps have (been) worn away in places.*

wear off to become less: *The pain is wearing off.*

wear out to (cause to) become unfit for further use: *My socks have worn out*; *I've worn out my socks.*

worn out 1 so damaged by use as to be unfit for further use: *These shoes are worn out*; *a worn-out sweater.* **2** very tired: *His wife is worn out after looking after the children.*

weary ['wiəri] *adj* tired; with strength or patience exhausted: *a weary sigh*; *He looks weary*; *I am weary of his jokes.* – *v* to (cause to) become tired: *The patient wearies easily*; *Don't weary the patient.*

'**wearily** *adv.* '**weariness** *n.*

'**wearisome** *adj* causing weariness: *a wearisome journey.* '**wearisomely** *adv.*

weasel ['wiːzl] *n* a type of small flesh-eating animal with a long slender body.

weather ['weðə] *n* conditions in the atmosphere, *esp* as regards heat or cold, wind, rain, snow *etc*: *The weather is too hot for me*; *stormy weather*; (*also adj*) *a weather chart/report, the weather forecast.* – *v* **1** to affect or be affected by exposure to the air, resulting in drying, change of colour, shape *etc*: *The wind and sea have weathered the rocks quite smooth.* **2** to survive safely: *The ship weathered the storm although she was badly damaged.*

'**weatherbeaten** *adj* showing effects of exposure to the weather: *a weatherbeaten face.*

'**weathercock**, '**weathervane** *ns* a piece of

metal (often in the form of a farmyard cock), placed on top of a building, which turns to show the direction of the wind.

under the weather in poor health: *I'm feeling under the weather this week.*

weather refers to climate: *fine weather.* **whether** is a conjunction: *Do you know whether he is coming?*

weave [wiːv] – *pt* **wove** [wouv]; *ptp* **woven** ['wouvən] – *v* **1** to make by crossing strands in a pattern: *to weave cloth.* **2** to tell (an interesting story). **3** (*pt, ptp* **weaved**) to move backwards and forwards or from side to side: *The cyclist weaved in and out of the traffic.* '**weaver** *n.*

web [web] *n* **1** a type of trap for flies *etc* made of fine silk threads, spun by a spider *etc*: *a spider's web.* **2** the skin between the toes of a waterfowl.

'**webbed** *adj* (of ducks' *etc* feet) joined between the toes by a web.

'**webbing** *n* a tough woven fabric used in making belts, straps, upholstery *etc.*

'**web-'footed**, '**web-'toed** *adj* having webbed feet.

wed [wed] – *pts, ptps* '**wedded**, **wed** – *v* to marry.

'**wedding** *n* a marriage ceremony: *The wedding will take place on Saturday*; (*also adj*) *wedding-cake*; *her wedding-day*; *a wedding ring.*

we'd *see* **have, would.**

wedge [wedʒ] *n* **1** a piece of wood or metal thick at one end and sloping to a thin edge at the other, used in splitting wood *etc* or in fixing something tightly in place: *She used a wedge under the door to prevent it swinging shut.* **2** something similar in shape: *a wedge of cheese.* – *v* to fix or become fixed by, or as if by, a wedge or wedges: *He is so fat that he got wedged in the doorway.*

wedlock ['wedlok] *n* the state of being married.

Wednesday ['wenzdi] *n* the fourth day of the week, the day following Tuesday.

weed [wiːd] *n* any wild plant, *esp* when growing among cultivated plants or where it is not wanted: *The garden is full of weeds.* – to remove weeds (from): *to weed the garden.*

'**weedkiller** *n* a chemical *etc* used to kill weeds.

weed out to remove (things which are unwanted) from a group or collection.

week [wiːk] *n* **1** any sequence of seven days, *esp* from Sunday to Saturday: *It's three weeks since I saw her.* **2** the five days from Monday to Friday inclusive: *He can't go during the week, but he'll go on Saturday or Sunday.* **3** the amount of time spent work ing during a period of seven days: *He works a forty-eight-hour week*.

'**weekly** *adj* happening, published *etc* once a week: *a weekly magazine*. – *adv* once a week: *The newspaper is published weekly*. – *n* – *pl* '**weeklies** – a publication coming out once a week: *Is this newspaper a weekly or a daily?*

'**weekday** *n* any day except a Saturday or Sunday: *Our office is open only on weekdays*; (*also adj*) *weekday flights*.

,**week'end** *n* the period from the end of one working week until the beginning of the next (*ie* Saturday and Sunday, or Friday evening to Sunday evening): *We spent a weekend in Paris*; (*also adj*) *a weekend trip*.

a week last Friday *etc* the Friday *etc* before last: *She died a week last Tuesday*.

a week today, tomorrow, (on/next) Friday *etc* a week from today, tomorrow, Friday *etc*: *I'm going away a week tomorrow*; *Could we meet a week (on/next) Monday?*

eep [wi:p] – *pt, ptp* **wept** [wept] – *v* to shed tears: *She wept when she heard the terrible news*; *They wept tears of happiness*.

eft *see* **warp**².

eigh [wei] *v* **1** to find the heaviness of (something) by placing it on a scale: *He weighed himself on the bathroom scales*; *You must have your luggage weighed at the airport*. **2** to be equal to in heaviness: *This parcel weighs one kilo*; *How much/What does this box weigh?* **3** to be a heavy burden to: *She was weighed down with two large suitcases*.

weight [weit] *n* **1** the amount which a person or thing weighs: *He's put on a lot of weight* (=got much fatter) *over the years*. **2** a piece of metal *etc* of a standard weight: *seven-pound weight*. **3** burden; load: *You have taken a weight off my mind*. **4** importance: *Her opinion carries a lot of weight*. – *v* **1** to attach, or add, a weight or weights to: *The plane is weighted at the nose so that it balances correctly in flight*. **2** to hold down by attaching weights: *They weighted the balloon to prevent it from flying away*.

'**weightless** *adj* not affected by the earth's gravity pull: *The astronauts became weightless on going into orbit round the earth*. '**weightlessness** *n*.

'**weighty** *adj* **1** important: *a weighty reason*. **2** heavy. '**weightily** *adv*. '**weightiness** *n*.

'**weighing-machine** *n* a (public) machine for weighing people, loads *etc*: *I weighed myself on the weighing-machine at the railway station*.

weigh anchor to lift a ship's anchor in preparation for sailing.

weigh in to find one's weight before a fight, after a horse-race *etc* (*n* '**weigh-in**).

weigh out to measure out by weighing: *He weighed out six kilos of sand*.

weigh up to calculate, estimate; to consider: *He weighed up his chances of success*.

weir [wiə] *n* a dam across a river, with a drop on one side.

weird [wiəd] *adj* odd or very strange: *a weird story*; *She wears weird clothes*. '**weirdly** *adv*. '**weirdness** *n*.

welcome ['welkəm] *adj* received with gladness and happiness: *She will make you welcome*; *He is a welcome visitor at our house*; *The extra money was very welcome*; *The holiday made a welcome change*. – *n* reception; hospitality: *We were given a warm welcome*. – *v* to receive or greet with pleasure and gladness: *We were welcomed by our hosts*; *She will welcome the chance to see you again*. – *interj* used to express gladness at someone's arrival: *Welcome to Britain!* '**welcoming** *adj*: *a welcoming smile*.

be welcome to to be gladly given permission to (have, do or accept something): *You're welcome to stay as long as you wish*.

you're welcome! (*esp Amer*) that's quite all right, no thanks are necessary: *'Thanks!' 'You're welcome!'*

weld [weld] *v* to join (pieces of metal) by pressure, often using heat, electricity *etc*. – *n* a joint made by welding. '**welder** *n*.

welfare ['welfeə] *n* mental and physical health; living conditions: *Who is looking after the child's welfare?*

welfare state a country which runs insurance schemes for its inhabitants, supplying them with free medical care, pensions *etc*.

well¹ [wel] *n* **1** a lined shaft made in the earth from which to obtain water, oil, natural gas *etc*. **2** the space round which a staircase winds: *He fell down the stair-well*. – *v* (of water from the earth or of tears) to flow freely: *Tears welled up in her eyes*.

well² [wel] – *compar* **better** ['betə]: *superl* **best** [best] – **1** *adj* healthy: *I don't feel very/at all well*; *She doesn't look very well*; *She's been ill but she's quite well now*. **2** in a satisfactory state or condition: *All is well now*. – *adv* **1** in a good, correct, successful, suitable *etc* way: *He's done well to become a millionaire at thirty*; *She plays the piano well*; *Mother and baby are both doing well*; *How well did he do in the exam?* **2** with good reason; with justice: *You may well look ashamed – that was a cruel thing to do*; *You can't very well refuse to go*. **3** with approval or praise: *He speaks well of you*. **4** used (*with eg* **damn, jolly** *etc*) for emphasis: *You can jolly well do it yourself!* **5** thoroughly: *Examine the car well before you buy it*. **6** to a great or considerable extent: *He is well over fifty*. – *interj* **1** used to express surprise *etc*: *Well! I'd never have believed it!* **2** used when re-starting a conversation, starting an explanation *etc*: *Do you remember John Watson? Well, he's become a teacher.*

well- 1 in a good, satisfactory *etc* way *etc*, as in **well-behaved**. 2 very much, as in **well=known**.

,well-be'haved *adj* behaving correctly: *well-behaved children.*

,well-'being *n* welfare: *She is always very concerned about her mother's well-being.*

,well-'bred *adj* (of a person) having good manners.

,well-'built *adj* muscular; having a strong, handsome figure.

,well-'earned *adj* thoroughly deserved: *a well-earned rest.*

,well-'educated *adj* educated to a good standard.

,well-'fed *adj* correctly and sufficiently fed.

,well-'groomed *adj* of smart, tidy appearance.

,well-in'formed *adj* having or showing a thorough knowledge: *a well-informed person/essay.*

,well-'known *adj* familiar or famous: *a well-known TV personality.*

,well-'made *adj*: *a well-made table.*

,well-'mannered *adj* polite.

,well-'off *adj* 1 rich: *He is very well-off*; *a well-off young lady.* 2 fortunate: *You do not know when you are well off.*

,well-'read [-'red] *adj* having read many books *etc*; intelligent.

,well-'spoken *adj* (of a person) speaking with a pleasing voice, in a grammatically correct way *etc*.

,well-to-'do *adj* having enough money to live comfortably.

,well-wisher *n* a person who wishes one success *etc*.

as well in addition; too: *If you will go, I'll go as well.*

as well as in addition to: *She works in a restaurant in the evenings as well as doing a full-time job during the day.*

be just as well to be fortunate; to be no cause for regret: *It's just as well (that) you didn't go – the meeting was cancelled.*

be as well to to be advisable or sensible: *It would be as well to go by train – the roads are flooded.*

very well fine, okay: *Have you finished? Very well, you may go now.*

well done! used in congratulating a person: *I hear you won the competition. Well done!*

well enough fairly, but not particularly, well.

well up in knowing a great deal about: *He's very well up in financial matters.*

we'll *see* **will, shall**.

wellingtons ['welịŋtənz] *n pl* rubber boots loosely covering the calves of the legs.

went *see* **go**.

wept *see* **weep**.

were, we're, weren't *see* **be**.

west [west] *n* 1 the direction in which the sun sets or any part of the earth lying in that direction: *They travelled towards the west*; *The wind is blowing from the west*; *in the west of Britain.* 2 (*often with cap*: *also* **W**) one of the four main points of the compass. – *adj* 1 in the west: *She's in the west wing of the hospital.* 2 from the direction of the west: *a west wind.* – *adv* towards the west: *The cliffs face west.*

'westerly *adj* 1 (of a wind, breeze *etc*) coming from the west: *a westerly wind.* 2 looking, lying *etc* towards the west: *moving in a westerly direction.*

'western *adj* of the west or the West: *Western customs/clothes.* – *n* a film or novel about the Wild West: *Most westerns are about cowboys and Red Indians.*

'westernmost *adj* furthest west: *the westernmost point.*

'westward *adj* towards the west: *in a westward direction.*

'westward(s) *adv* towards the west: *We journeyed westwards for two weeks.*

the West Europe and North and South America.

the Wild West the western United States, before the establishment of law and order.

wet [wet] *adj* 1 containing, soaked in, or covered with, water or another liquid: *We got soaking wet when it began to rain*; *His shirt was wet through with sweat*; *wet hair*; *The car skidded on the wet road.* 2 rainy: *a wet day*; *wet weather*; *It was wet yesterday.* – *v* – *prt* **'wetting**: *pts, ptps* **wet, 'wetted** – to make wet: *She wet her hair and put shampoo on it*; *The baby has wet himself/his nappy/the bed.* – *n* 1 moisture: *a patch of wet.* 2 rain: *Don't go out in the wet.*

'wetness *n*.

wet blanket a depressing companion.

'wet-nurse *n* a woman employed to breast-feed someone else's baby.

'wetsuit *n* a rubber suit for wearing in cold conditions when diving *etc*.

wet through soaked to the skin.

we've *see* **have**.

whack [wak] *v* to strike smartly, making a loud sound: *His father whacked him for misbehaving.* – *n* a blow: *His father gave him a whack across the ear.*

whale [weil] *n* a type of very large mammal that lives in the sea.

'whalebone *n, adj* (of) a light bendable substance got from the upper jaw of certain whales.

whale oil oil obtained from the fatty parts of a whale.

have a whale of a time to enjoy oneself very much.

wharf [wo:f] – pls **wharfs, wharves** [wo:vz] – n a platform alongside which ships are moored for loading and unloading.

what [wot] pron, adj **1** used in questions etc when asking someone to point out, state etc one or more persons, things etc: What street is this?; What's your name/address/ telephone number?; What time is it?; What (kind of) bird is that?; What is he reading?; What did you say?; What is this cake made of?; 'What do you want to be when you grow up?' 'A doctor.'; Tell me what you mean; I asked him what clothes I should wear. **2** (also adv) used in exclamations of surprise, anger etc: What clothes she wears!; What a fool he is!; What naughty children they are!; What a silly book this is!; What (on earth/in the world/ever) is happening? – relative pron **1** the thing(s) that: Did you find what you wanted?; These tools are just what I need for this job; What that child needs is a good spanking! **2** (also relative adj) any (things or amount) that; whatever: I'll lend you what clothes you need; Please lend me what you can.

what'ever relative adj, relative pron any (thing(s) or amount) that: I'll lend you whatever (books) you need. – adj, pron no matter what: You have to go on, whatever (trouble) you meet; Whatever (else) you do, don't say that! – adj whatsoever; at all: I had nothing whatever to do with that. – pron (also **what ever**) used in questions or exclamations to express surprise etc: Whatever will he say when he hears this?

'whatnot n such things: He told me all about publishing and whatnot.

'what's-his, -her, -its etc **-name** n used in referring vaguely to a person or thing: Where does what's-his-name live?

,whatso'ever [-sou-] adj at all: That's nothing whatsoever to do with me.

know what's what to be able to tell what is important.

what about? 1 used in asking whether the listener would like (to do) something: What about a glass of milk?; What about going to the cinema? **2** used in asking for news or advice: What about your new book?; What about the other problem?

what ... for 1 why(?): What did he do that for? **2** for what purpose(?): What is this switch for?

what have you and similar things; and so on: clothes, books and what have you.

what if? what will or would happen if...?: What if he comes back?

what...like? used when asking for information about someone or something: 'What does it look like?' 'It's small and square.'; 'What's her mother like?' 'Oh, she's quite nice.'; We may go – it depends (on) what the weather's like.

what of it? used in replying, to suggest that what has been done, said etc is not important: 'You've offended him.' 'What of it?'

what with because of: What with taking no exercise and being too fat, he had a heart attack.

what'll ['wotl], **what's** [wots] short for **what shall/what will, what is/what has**.

wheat [wi:t] n a type of grain from which flour, much used in making bread, cakes etc, is obtained.

'wheaten adj made of wheat: a wheaten loaf.

wheel [wi:l] n **1** a circular frame or disc turning on a rod or axle, on which vehicles etc move along the ground: A bicycle has two wheels, a tricycle three, and most cars four; a cartwheel. **2** any of several things similar in shape and action: a potter's wheel; He was found drunk at the wheel (= steering-wheel) of his car. – v **1** to cause to move on wheels: He wheeled his bicycle along the path. **2** to (cause to) turn quickly: He wheeled round and slapped me. **3** (of birds) to fly in circles.

wheeled adj: a wheeled vehicle.

-wheeled: a four-wheeled vehicle.

'wheelbarrow n a small carrier with one wheel at the front, and two legs and two handles at the back: He used a wheelbarrow to move the manure to the back garden.

'wheelchair n a chair with wheels, used for moving from place to place by invalids or those who cannot walk.

'wheelhouse n the shelter in which a ship's steering-wheel is placed.

'wheelwright n a craftsman who makes wheels.

wheeze [,wi:z] v to breathe with a hissing sound and with difficulty. – n such a sound.

'wheezy adj. **'wheezily** adv. **'wheeziness** n.

when [wen] adv at what time(?): When did you arrive?; When will you see her again?; I asked him when the incident had occurred; Tell me when to jump. – [wən, wen] conj **1** (at or during) the time at which: It happened when I was abroad; When you see her, give her this message; When I've finished, I'll telephone you. **2** in spite of the fact that; considering that: Why do you walk when you have a car?

whence [wens] adv from what place or circumstance (?); from where (?).

when'ever adv, conj **1** at any time that: Come and see me whenever you want to. **2** at every time that: I go to the theatre whenever I get the chance.

where [weə] adv (to or in) which place (?): Where are you going (to)?; Do you know where we are?; Where does he get his ideas from?; We asked where to find a good restaurant. – relative pron ((to or in) the place) to or in which: *It's nice going on holiday to a place where you've been before*; *This is the town where I was born*; *It's still where it was*; *I can't see him from where I am.*

wherea'bouts *adv* near or in what place(?): *Whereabouts is it?*; *I don't know whereabouts it is.*

'whereabouts *n sing or n pl* the place where a person or thing is: *I don't know his whereabouts.*

where'as *conj* when in fact; but on the other hand: *He thought I was lying, whereas I was telling the truth.*

where'by *relative pron* by which.

whereu'pon *conj* at or after which time, event *etc*: *He insulted her, whereupon she slapped him.*

wher'ever *relative pron* **1** no matter where: *I'll follow you wherever you may go*; *Wherever he is he will be thinking of you.* **2** (to or in) any place that: *Go wherever he tells you to go.* – *adv* (*also* **where ever**) used in questions or exclamations to express surprise *etc*: *Wherever did she get that hat?*

where's short for **where is, where has**.

whet [wet] – *pt, ptp* **'whetted** – *v* **1** to sharpen (a tool) by rubbing it on a grindstone or whetstone. **2** to make (one's appetite) keen.

'whetstone *n* a stone for sharpening the blades of knives *etc*.

whether ['weðə] *conj* if: *I don't know whether it's possible.*

whether…or introducing alternatives: *He can't decide whether to go or not/whether or not to go*; *Whether you like the idea or not, I'm going ahead with it*; *Decide whether you're going or staying.*

see also **weather**.

whey [wei] *n* the watery part of milk separated from the curd (the thick part), *esp* in making cheese.

which [witʃ] *adj, pron* used in questions *etc* when asking someone to point out, state *etc* one or more persons, things *etc* from a particular known group: *Which (colour) do you like best?*; *Which route will you travel by?*; *At which station should I change trains?*; *Which of the two girls do you like better?*; *Tell me which books you would like*; *Let me know which train you'll be arriving on*; *I can't decide which to choose.* – *relative pron* (used to refer to a thing or things mentioned previously to distinguish it or them from others: able to be replaced by **that** except after a preposition: able to be omitted except after a preposition or when the subject of a clause) (the) one(s) that: *This is the book which/that was on the table*; *This is the book (which/that) you wanted*; *A scalpel is a type of knife which/that is used by*

surgeons; *The chair (which/that) you are sitting on is broken*; *The documents for which they were searching have been recovered.* – *relative adj, relative pron* used, after a comma, to introduce a further comment on something: *My new car, which I paid several thousand pounds for, is not running well*; *He said he could speak Russian, which was untrue*; *My father may have to go into hospital, in which case he won't be going on holiday.*

which'ever *relative adj, relative pron* **1** any (one(s)) that: *I'll take whichever (books) you don't want*; *The prize will go to whichever of them writes the best essay.* **2** no matter which (one(s)): *Whichever way I turned, I couldn't escape.*

which is which(?) which is one and which is the other (?): *Mary and Susan are twins and I can't tell which is which.*

whiff [wif] *n* a sudden puff (of air, smoke, smell *etc*): *a whiff of petrol*; *a whiff of cigar smoke.*

while [wail] *conj* (*also* **whilst** [wailst]) **1** during the time that: *I saw him while I was out walking.* **2** although: *While I sympathize, I can't really do very much to help.* – *n* a space of time: *It took me quite a while*; *It's a long while since we saw her.*

while away to pass (time) without boredom: *He whiled away the time by reading.*

worth one's while worth one's time and trouble: *It's not worth your while reading this book, because it isn't accurate.*

whim [wim] *n* a sudden desire or change of mind: *I am tired of that child's whims.*

whimper ['wimpə] *v* to cry with a low, shaky or whining voice: *I heard a puppy/a child whimpering.* – *n* a cry of this kind: *The dog gave a little whimper.*

whine [wain] *v* **1** to utter a complaining cry or a cry of suffering: *The dog whines when it's left alone in the house.* **2** to make a similar noise: *I could hear the engine whine.* **3** to complain unnecessarily: *Stop whining about how difficult this job is!* – *n* such a noise: *the whine of an engine.*

'whiningly *adv.*

whinny ['wini] *v* to make the cry of a horse: *The horse whinnied when it saw its master.* – *n* – *pl* **'whinnies** – such a cry.

whip [wip] *n* **1** a long cord or strip of leather attached to a handle, used for punishing people, driving horses *etc*: *He carries a whip but he would never use it on the horse.* **2** in parliament, a member chosen by his party to make sure that no one fails to vote on important questions. – *v* – *pt, ptp* **whipped** – **1** to strike with a whip: *He whipped the horse to make it go faster*; *The criminals were whipped.* **2** to beat (eggs *etc*). **3** to move fast *esp* with a twisting motion like a

whip: *Suddenly he whipped round and saw me; He whipped out a revolver and shot her.*
'whiplash *n* (the action of) the lash or cord of a whip.

whip up 1 to whip: *I'm whipping up eggs for the dessert.* **2** to produce or prepare quickly: *I'll whip up a meal in no time.*

whir(r) [wə:] – *pt, ptp* **whirred** – *v* to make, or move with, a buzzing sound, *esp* as of something turning through the air: *The propellers whirred and we took off.* – *n* such a sound.

whirl [wə:l] *v* to move rapidly (round, away *etc*): *She whirled round when I called her name; The wind whirled my hat away before I could grab it.* – *n* **1** an excited confusion: *a whirl of activity; My head's in a whirl – I can't believe it's all happening!* **2** a rapid turn.
'whirlpool *n* a circular current in a river or sea, caused by opposing tides, winds or currents.
'whirlwind *n* a violent circular current of wind with a whirling motion.

whirr *see* **whir(r).**

whisk [wisk] *v* **1** to sweep, or cause to move, rapidly: *He whisked the dirty dishes off the table; He whisked her off to the doctor.* **2** to beat (eggs *etc*) with a fork or whisk. – *n* **1** a rapid, sweeping motion. **2** a kitchen tool made of wire *etc*, for beating eggs, cream *etc*.

whisker ['wiskə] *n* **1** *in pl* a man's moustache, beard and/or sideburns. **2** (*usu in pl*) one of the long hairs between the nose and the mouth of a cat *etc*. **'whiskered, 'whiskery** *adjs*.

miss *etc* **by a whisker** to manage only barely to miss *etc*.

whisky, (*Irish and Amer*) **whiskey** ['wiski] *n* a type of alcoholic drink made from grain.

whisper ['wispə] *v* **1** to speak or say very softly: *You'll have to whisper or he'll hear you; 'Don't tell him,' she whispered.* **2** (of trees *etc*) to make a soft sound in the wind: *The leaves whispered in the breeze.* – *n* a very quiet sound, *esp* something said: *They spoke in whispers.*
'whisperer *n*.

whistle ['wisl] *v* **1** to make a shrill, often musical, sound by forcing one's breath between the lips or teeth: *Can you whistle?; He whistled to attract my attention; He whistled a happy tune.* **2** to make such a sound with a device designed for this: *The electric kettle's whistling; The referee whistled for half-time.* **3** to make a shrill sound in passing through the air: *The bullet whistled past his head.* **4** (of the wind) to blow with a shrill sound. – *n* **1** the sound made by whistling: *He gave a loud whistle to his friend across the road.* **2** a musical pipe

designed to make a whistling noise. **3** an instrument used by policemen, referees *etc* to make a whistling noise: *The referee blew his whistle at the end of the game.*

white [wait] *adj* **1** of the colour of the paper on which these words are printed: *The bride wore a white dress.* **2** having light-coloured skin, through being of European *etc* descent: *the first white man to explore Africa.* **3** abnormally pale, because of fear, illness *etc*: *He went white with shock.* **4** with milk in it: *A white coffee, please.* – *n* **1** the colour of the paper on which these words are printed: *White and black are opposites.* **2** a white-skinned person: *racial trouble between blacks and whites.* **3** (*also* **'egg-white**) the clear fluid in an egg, surrounding the yolk: *This recipe tells you to separate the yolks from the whites.* **4** (of an eye) the white part surrounding the pupil and iris: *The whites of her eyes are bloodshot.*
'whiten *v* to make or become white or whiter: *She used a little bleach to whiten the sheets.*
'whiteness *n*.
'whitening *n* a substance used to make certain things (*eg* tennis shoes) white again.
'whitish *adj* fairly white; close to white.
,white-'collar *adj* (of workers, jobs *etc*) not manual; (working) in an office *etc*.
white elephant a useless, unwanted possession.
,white-'hot *adj* (of metals) so hot that they have turned white: *a white-hot poker.*
white lie a not very serious lie: *I'd rather tell my mother a white lie than tell her the truth and upset her.*
'whitewash *n* a mixture of *usu* lime and water, used for whitening walls. – *v* to cover with whitewash. **'whitewashed** *adj*.
white wine *see* **wine.**

whither ['wiðə] *relative pron, adv* to which place(?).

whittle ['witl] *v* to cut or shape (*eg* a stick) with a knife.

whizz [wiz] *v* to fly through the air with a hissing sound: *The arrow whizzed past his shoulder.*

who [hu:] *pron* (used as the subject of a verb) what person(s)(?): *Who is that woman in the green hat?; Who did that?; Who won?; Do you know who all these people are?* – *relative pron* **1** (used to refer to a person or people mentioned previously to distinguish him or them from others: used as the subject of a verb: *usu* replaceable by **that**) (the) one(s) that: *The man who/that telephoned was a friend of yours; A doctor is a person who looks after people's health.* **2** used, after a comma, to introduce a further comment on a person or people: *His* *mother, who by that time was tired out, gave him a smack.*

who'ever *relative pron* any person or people that: *Whoever gets the job will have a lot of work to do.* – *pron* **1** no matter who: *Whoever rings, tell him/them I'm out.* **2** (also **who ever**) used in questions to express surprise etc: *Whoever said that?*

whom [hu:m] *pron* (used as the object of a verb or preposition, but in everyday speech sometimes replaced by **who**) what person(s)(?): *Whom/who do you want to see?; Whom/who did you give it to?; To whom shall I speak?* – *relative pron* (used as the object of a verb or preposition but in everyday speech sometimes replaced by **who**) **1** (used to refer to a person or people mentioned previously, to distinguish him or them from others: able to be omitted or replaced by **that** except when following a preposition) (the) one(s) that: *The man (whom/that) you mentioned is here; Today I met some friends (whom/that) I hadn't seen for ages; This is the man to whom I gave it; This is the man (whom/who/that) I gave it to.* **2** used, after a comma, to introduce a further comment on a person or people: *My father, whom I'd like you to meet one day, is interested in your work.*

know who's who to know which people are important.

who'd short for **who would, who should, who had**.

whole [houl] *adj* **1** including everything and/or everyone; complete: *The whole staff collected the money for your present; a whole pineapple.* **2** not broken; in one piece: *She swallowed the biscuit whole.* – *n* **1** a single unit: *The different parts were joined to form a whole.* **2** the entire thing: *We spent the whole of one week sunbathing on the beach.* **'wholeness** *n*.

'wholly *adv* completely or altogether: *I am not wholly certain yet.*

,whole'hearted *adj* sincere and enthusiastic: *wholehearted support.*

'wholemeal *n* flour made from the entire wheat grain or seed: *wholemeal flour/bread.*

on the whole taking everything into consideration: *Our trip was successful on the whole.*

wholesale ['houlseil] *adj* **1** (also *adv*) buying and selling goods on a large scale, *usu* from a manufacturer and to a retailer: *a wholesale business; He buys the materials wholesale.* **2** on a large scale: *the wholesale slaughter of innocent people.*

'wholesaler *n* a person who buys and sells goods wholesale.

wholesome ['houlsəm] *adj* healthy: causing good health: *wholesome food; wholesome*

exercise. **'wholesomely** *adv*. **'wholesomeness** *n*.

who'll short for **who shall, who will**.

whom *see* **who**.

whoop [wu:p, (*Amer also*) hu:p] *n* **1** a loud cry of delight, triumph etc: *a whoop of joy.* **2** the noisy sound made when breathing in after prolonged coughing. – *v* to give a loud cry of delight, triumph etc.

'whooping-cough, 'hooping-cough ['hu:-] *n* an infectious disease with violent bouts of coughing followed by a whoop.

who's short for **who is, who has**.

whose [hu:z] *adj, pron* belonging to which person(?): *Whose is this jacket?; Whose (jacket) is this?; Whose car did you come back in?; In whose house did this incident happen?; Tell me whose (pens) these are.* – *relative adj, relative pron* of whom or which (the): *Show me the boy whose father is a policeman; What is the name of the man whose this book is?*

why [wai] *adv* for which reason (?): *'Why did you hit the child?'; 'He hit the child.' 'Why?'; Why haven't you finished?; 'I haven't finished.' 'Why not?'; 'Let's go to the cinema.' 'Why not?'* (=Let's!); *Tell me why you came here.* – *relative pron* for which: *Give me one good reason why I should help you!*

wick [wik] *n* the twisted threads of cotton etc in a candle, lamp etc, which draw up the oil or wax into the flame.

wicked ['wikid] *adj* evil; sinful: *He is a wicked man; That was a wicked thing to do.* **'wickedly** *adv*. **'wickedness** *n*.

wicker ['wikə] *adj* (of eg a chair or basket) made of twigs, rushes etc woven together. **'wickerwork** *n* articles made in this way.

wicket ['wikit] *n* (in cricket) **1** a set of three upright wooden rods at which the bowler aims the ball. **2** the ground between two sets of these rods: *The wicket has dried out well.* **3** the ending of a batsman's period of batting: *They scored fifty runs for (the loss of) one wicket.*

'wicket-keeper *n* (in cricket) the fielder who stands immediately behind the wicket.

wide [waid] *adj* **1** great in extent, *esp* from side to side: *wide streets; Her eyes were wide with surprise.* **2** being a certain distance from one side to the other: *This material is three metres wide; How wide is it?* **3** great or large: *He won by a wide margin.* **4** covering a large and varied range of subjects etc: *a wide experience of teaching.* – *adv* with a great distance from top to bottom or side to side: *He opened his eyes wide.* **'widely** *adv*.

'widen *v* to make, or become, wide or wider: *They have widened the road; The lane widens here.*

'wideness *n*.

width [widθ] *n* **1** size from side to side: *What is the width of this material?; This fabric comes in three different widths.* **2** the state of being wide.

,wide-'ranging *adj* (of interests *etc*) covering a large number of subjects *etc*.

'widespread *adj* spread over a large area or among many people: *widespread hunger and disease.*

give a wide berth (to) to keep well away from: *I give people with colds a wide berth/give a wide berth to people with colds.*

wide apart a great (or greater than average) distance away from one another: *He held his hands wide apart.*

wide awake fully awake.

wide open fully open: *The door was wide open; Her eyes are wide open but she seems to be asleep.*

idow ['widou] *n* a woman whose husband is dead: *My brother's widow has married again.* – *v* to cause to become a widow or widower: *She/He was widowed in 1943.*

'widower *n* a man whose wife is dead.

idth *see* **wide**.

ield [wi:ld] *v* **1** to use: *He can certainly wield an axe.* **2** to have and use: *to wield authority.*

ife [waif] – *pl* **wives** [waivz] – *n* the woman to whom one is married: *Come and meet my wife; He is looking for a wife.*

old wives' tale a superstitious and misleading story.

ig [wig] *n* an artificial covering of hair for the head: *Does she wear a wig?*

iggle ['wigl] *v* to waggle or wriggle: *She wiggled her hips.*

'wiggly *adj* not straight; going up and down, from side to side *etc*: *a wiggly line.*

igwam ['wigwam, (*Amer*) -wa:m] *n* a North American Indian tent made of skins *etc*.

ild [waild] *adj* **1** (of animals) not tamed: *wolves and other wild animals.* **2** (of land) not cultivated. **3** uncivilized or lawless; savage: *wild tribes.* **4** very stormy; violent: *a wild night at sea; a wild rage.* **5** mad, crazy, insane *etc*: *wild with hunger; wild with anxiety.* **6** rash: *a wild hope.* **7** not accurate or reliable: *a wild guess.* **8** very angry. **'wildly** *adv*. **'wildness** *n*.

'wildfire: spread like wildfire (of *eg* news) to spread extremely fast.

'wildfowl *n pl* wild birds, *esp* water birds such as ducks, geese *etc*.

,wild-'goose chase an attempt to catch or find something one cannot possibly obtain.

'wildlife *n* wild animals, birds, insects *etc* collectively: *to protect wildlife.*

in the wild (of an animal) in its natural surroundings: *Young animals have to learn to look after themselves in the wild.*

the wilds the uncultivated areas (of a coun-

try *etc*): *They're living out in the wilds of Australia somewhere.*

the Wild West *see* **west**.

wilderness ['wildanas] *n* (a) desert or wild area of a country *etc*.

wilful *see* **will**.

will [wil] *n* **1** the mental power by which one controls one's thought, actions and decisions: *Do you believe in freedom of the will?* **2** (control over) one's desire(s) or wish(es); determination: *It was done against her will; He has no will of his own – he always does what the others want; Children often have strong wills; He has lost the will to live.* **3** (a legal paper having written on it) a formal statement about what is to be done with one's belongings, body *etc* after one's death: *Have you made a will yet?* – *v* – *short forms* **I'll** [ail], **you'll** [ju:l], **he'll** [hi:l], **she'll** [ʃi:l], **it'll** ['itl], **we'll** [wi:l], **they'll** [ðeil]: *neg short form* **won't** [wount] – **1** used to form future tenses of other verbs: *We'll go at six o'clock tonight; Will you be here again next week?; Things will never be the same again; I will have finished the work by tomorrow evening.* **2** used in requests or commands: *Will you come into my office for a moment, please?; Will you please stop talking!* **3** used to show willingness: *I'll do that for you if you like; I won't do it!* **4** used to state that something happens regularly, is quite normal *etc*: *Accidents will happen.*

'wilful *adj* **1** obstinate. **2** intentional: *wilful damage to property.* **'wilfully** *adv*. **'wilfulness** *n*.

-willed: *weak-willed/strong-willed people.*

'willing *adj* ready to agree (to do something): *a willing helper; She's willing to help in any way she can.* **'willingly** *adv*. **'willingness** *n*.

'willpower *n* the determination to do something: *I don't have the willpower to stop smoking.*

at will as, or when, one chooses.

with a will eagerly and energetically: *They set about (doing) their tasks with a will.*

willow ['wilou] *n* a type of tree with long, slender branches.

wilt [wilt] *v* (of flowers) to droop: *The plants are wilting because they haven't been watered.*

'wily ['waili] *adj* crafty, cunning, sly *etc*: *a wily old fox; He is too wily for the police to catch him.* **'wiliness** *n*.

win [win] – *prp* **'winning**: *pt, ptp* **won** [wʌn] – *v* **1** to obtain (a victory) in a contest; to succeed in coming first in (a contest), *usu* by one's own efforts: *He won a fine victory in the election; Who won the war/match?; He won the bet; He won (the race) in a fast time/by a clear five metres.* **2** to obtain (a prize) in a competition *etc*, *usu* by luck: *to*

win first prize; *I won $5 in the crossword competition.* **3** to obtain by one's own efforts: *He won her respect over a number of years.* – *n* a victory or success: *She's had two wins in four races.*
'winner *n.*
'winning *adj* **1** victorious or successful: *the winning candidate.* **2** attractive or charming: *a winning smile.*
'winning-post *n* in horse-racing, a post marking the place where a race finishes.
win over to succeed in gaining the support and sympathy of: *At first he refused to help us but we finally won him over.*
win the day to gain a victory; to be successful.
win through to succeed in getting (to a place, the next stage *etc*): *It will be a struggle, but we'll win through in the end.*
wince [wins] *v* to start or jump with pain: *He winced as the dentist touched his broken tooth.*
winch [wintʃ] *n* a type of powerful machine for hoisting or hauling heavy loads. – *v* to hoist (up) or haul (in) using a winch.
wind¹ [wind] *n* **1** (an) outdoor current of air: *The wind is strong today; There wasn't much wind yesterday; Cold winds blow across the desert.* **2** breath: *Climbing these stairs takes all the wind out of me.* **3** air or gas in the stomach or intestines: *His stomach pains were due to wind.* – *v* to cause to be out of breath: *The heavy blow winded him.* – *adj* (of a musical instrument) operated or played using air pressure, *esp* a person's breath.
'windy *adj*: *a windy hill-top; a windy day; It's windy today.* **'windiness** *n.*
'windfall *n* **1** an apple *etc* blown from a tree. **2** any unexpected gain or success.
'windmill *n* a machine with sails that work by wind power, for grinding corn or pumping water.
'windpipe *n* the passage for air between mouth and lungs.
'windscreen *n* (*Amer* **'windshield**) a transparent (*usu* glass) screen above the dashboard of a car.
'windsock *n* a device for indicating the direction and speed of wind on an airfield.
'windswept *adj* exposed to the wind and showing the effects of it: *windswept hair; a windswept landscape.*
get the wind up to become nervous or anxious: *She got the wind up when she realized how close we were to the edge.*
get wind of to get a hint of or hear indirectly about.
get one's second wind to recover one's natural breathing after breathlessness.
in the wind about to happen: *A change of policy is in the wind.*

like the wind very quickly: *The horse galloped away like the wind.*
wind² [waind] – *pt, ptp* **wound** [waund] – *v* **1** to wrap round in coils: *He wound the rope around his waist and began to climb.* **2** to make into a ball or coil: *to wind wool.* **3** (of a road *etc*) to twist and turn: *The road winds up the mountain.* **4** to tighten the spring of (a clock, watch *etc*) by turning a knob, handle *etc*: *I forgot to wind my watch.*
'winder *n* a lever or instrument for winding, on a clock or other mechanism.
'winding *adj* full of bends *etc*: *a winding road.*
wind up 1 to turn, twist or coil; to make into a ball or coil: *My ball of wool has unravelled – could you wind it up again?* **2** to wind a clock, watch *etc*: *She wound up the clock.* **3** to end: *I think it's time to wind the meeting up.*
be/get wound up to be, or get, in a very excited or anxious state.
window ['windou] *n* an opening in the wall of a building *etc* which is fitted with a frame of wood, metal *etc* containing glass or similar material, that can be seen through and *usu* opened: *I saw her through the window; Open/Close the window; goods displayed in a shop-window.*
'window-box *n* a box on a window-ledge, in which plants may be grown.
'window-dressing *n* the arranging of goods in a shop window. **'window-dresser** *n.*
'window-frame *n* the wooden or metal frame of a window.
'window-ledge *n* a ledge at the bottom of a window (*usu* on the outside).
'window-pane *n* one of the sheets of glass in a window.
'window-shopping *n* looking at things in shop windows, but not actually buying anything.
'window-sill *n* a ledge at the bottom of a window (inside or outside).
windpipe *etc see* **wind**¹.
wine [wain] *n* a type of alcoholic drink made from the fermented juice of grapes or other fruit: *two bottles of wine; a wide range of inexpensive wines.*
wing [wiŋ] *n* **1** one of the arm-like limbs of a bird or bat, which it *usu* uses in flying, or one of the similar limbs of an insect: *The eagle spread his wings and flew away; The bird cannot fly as it has an injured wing; These butterflies have red and brown wings.* **2** a similar structure jutting out from the side of an aeroplane: *the wings of a jet.* **3** a section built out to the side of a (*usu* large) house: *the west wing of the hospital.* **4** any of the corner sections of a motor vehicle: *The rear left wing of the car was damaged in the accident.* **5** a section of a political party

or of politics in general: *the Left/Right wing*. **6** one side of a football *etc* field: *He made a great run down the left wing*. **7** in rugby and hockey, a player who plays mainly down one side of the field. **8** in the air force, a group of three squadrons of aircraft.

winged *adj* having wings: *a winged creature*. **-winged**: *a four-winged insect*.

'**winger** *n* in football *etc*, a player who plays mainly down one side of the field.

'**wingless** *adj*.

wings *n pl* the sides of a theatre stage: *She waited in the wings*.

wing commander in the air force, the rank above squadron leader.

'**wingspan** *n* the distance from the tip of one wing to the tip of the other when outstretched (of birds, aeroplanes *etc*).

on the wing flying, *esp* away: *The wild geese are on the wing*.

take under one's wing to take (someone) under one's protection.

wink [wiŋk] *v* **1** to shut and open an eye quickly in friendly greeting, or to show that something is a secret *etc*: *He winks at all the girls who pass*; *Her father winked at her and said 'Don't tell your mother about her present.'* **2** (of *eg* lights) to flicker and twinkle. – *n* an act of winking: *'Don't tell anyone I'm here', he said with a wink*.

forty winks a short sleep: *Father often has forty winks in his armchair after lunch*.

winning *etc see* **win**.

winnow ['winou] *v* to separate the chaff from (the grain) by wind.

winter ['wintə] *n* the coldest season of the year, November or December till January or February in cooler northern regions: *We often have snow in winter*; (*also adj*) *winter evenings*.

'**wintry** *adj* like winter in being very cold: *a wintry day*; *wintry weather*. '**wintriness** *n*.

winter sports sports played in the open air on snow and ice, *eg* skiing, tobogganing *etc*.

'**wintertime** *n* the season of winter.

wipe [waip] *v* **1** to clean or dry by rubbing with a cloth, paper *etc*: *Would you wipe the table for me?* **2** to remove by rubbing with a cloth, paper *etc*: *The child wiped her tears away with her handkerchief*; *Wipe that writing off (the blackboard)*; *Please wipe up that spilt milk*. – *n* an act of cleaning by rubbing: *Give the table a wipe*.

'**wiper** *n* (*also* **windscreen wiper**) a moving arm for clearing rain *etc* from a vehicle's windscreen.

wipe out 1 to clean the inside of (a bowl *etc*) with a cloth *etc*. **2** to remove; to get rid of: *You must try to wipe out the memory of these terrible events*. **3** to destroy com-

pletely: *They wiped out the whole regiment in one battle*.

wire ['waiə] *n* **1** (*also adj*) (of) metal drawn out into a long strand, as thick as string or as thin as thread: *We need some wire to connect the battery to the rest of the circuit*; *a wire fence*. **2** a single strand of this: *There must be a loose wire in my radio somewhere*. **3** the metal cable used in telegraphy: *The message came over the wire this morning*. **4** a telegram: *Send me a wire if I'm needed urgently*. – *v* **1** to fasten, connect *etc* with wire: *The house has been wired (up), but the electricity hasn't been connected yet*. **2** to send a telegram to: *Wire me if anything important happens*. **3** to send (a message) by telegram: *You can wire the details to my brother in New York*.

'**wireless** *n* an older word for (a) radio.

'**wiring** *n* the (system of) wires used in connecting up a circuit *etc*.

high wire a high tightrope: *acrobats on the high wire*.

,**wire-'netting** *n* a material with wide mesh woven of wire, used in fencing *etc*.

wiry ['waiəri] *adj* (of a person, his body *etc*) slim but strong.

wise [waiz] *adj* **1** having gained a great deal of knowledge from books or experience or both and able to use it well. **2** sensible: *You would be wise to do as he suggests*; *a wise decision*. '**wisely** *adv*.

wisdom ['wizdəm] *n*: *Wisdom comes with experience*.

wisdom tooth ['wizdəm-] any one of the four back teeth cut after childhood, *usu* about the age of twenty.

'**wisecrack** *n* a joke.

wise guy a person who (shows that he) thinks that he is smart, knows everything *etc*.

be wise to to be fully aware of: *He thinks I'm going to give him some money, but I'm wise to his plan*.

none the wiser not knowing any more than before: *He tried to explain the rules to me, but I'm none the wiser*.

put (someone) wise to tell, inform (someone) of the real facts.

-wise [waiz] **1** in respect of or as regards: *This new idea may prove to be difficult costwise*. **2** in a (particular) way: *The stripes run crosswise*.

wish [wiʃ] *v* **1** to have and/or express a desire: *There's no point in wishing for a miracle*; *Touch the magic stone and wish*; *He wished that she would go away*; *I wish that I had never met him*. **2** to require (to do or have something): *Do you wish to sit down, sir?*; *We wish to book some seats for the theatre*; *I'll cancel the arrangement if you wish*. **3** to say that one hopes for (something for

someone): *I wish you the very best of luck.* –
n **1** a desire or longing, or the thing desired:
*It's always been my wish to go to South
America some day.* **2** an expression of desire: *The fairy granted him three wishes; Did
you make a wish?* **3** (*usu in pl*) an expression
of hope for success *etc* for someone: *He
sends you his best wishes.*
'wishing-well *n* a well which is supposed to
have the power of granting any wish made
when one is beside it.
wisp [wisp] *n* thin strand: *a wisp of hair; a
wisp of smoke.*
'wispy *adj: wispy hair.*
wistful ['wistful] *adj* thoughtful and rather
sad, (as if) longing for something with little
hope: *The dog looked into the butcher's
window with a wistful expression on his face.*
'wistfully *adv.* **'wistfulness** *n.*
wit [wit] *n* **1** humour; the ability to express
oneself in an amusing way: *His plays are
full of wit; I admire his wit.* **2** a person who
expresses himself in a humorous way, tells
jokes *etc*: *He's a great wit.* **3** common
sense, inventiveness *etc*: *He did not have the
wit to defend himself.*
'witless *adj* crazy, stupid *etc.*
-witted having understanding or intelligence
of a certain kind: *quick-/sharp-witted.*
'witty *adj* clever and amusing: *a witty person; witty remarks.* **'wittily** *adv.* **'wittiness** *n.*
at one's wits' end utterly confused and
desperate.
keep one's wits about one to be cautious,
alert and watchful.
live by one's wits to live by cunning rather
than by hard work.
(frighten/scare) out of one's wits (to
frighten) (almost) to the point of madness:
*The sight of the gun in his hand scared me
out of my wits.*
witch [witʃ] *n* a woman who is supposed to
have powers of magic, *usu* through working
with the devil.
'witchcraft *n* magic practised by a witch *etc.*
'witch-doctor *n* in some African tribes, a
person whose profession is to cure illness
and keep away evil magical influences.
with [wiδ] *prep* **1** in the company of; beside;
among; including: *I was walking with my
father; Do they enjoy playing with each
other?; He used to play football with the
Arsenal team; Put this book with the others.*
2 by means of; using: *Mend it with this
glue; Cut it with a knife.* **3** used in expressing the idea of filling, covering *etc*: *Fill this
jug with milk; He was covered with mud.*
4 used in describing conflict: *They quarrelled with each other; He fought with my
brother.* **5** used in descriptions of things: *a
man with a limp; a girl with long hair; a stick
with a handle; Treat this book with care.*

6 as the result of: *He is shaking with fear.*
7 in the care of: *Leave your case with the
porter.* **8** in relation to; in the case of;
concerning: *Be careful with that!; What's
wrong with you?; What shall I do with these
books?* **9** used in expressing a wish: *Down
with fascism!; Up with Manchester United!*
withdraw [wiδ'droː] – *pt* **with'drew** [-'druː]:
ptp **with'drawn** – *v* **1** to (cause to) move
back or away: *The army withdrew from its
position; He withdrew his troops; They withdrew from the competition.* **2** to take back
(something one has said): *She withdrew her
remarks, and apologized; He later withdrew
the charges he'd made against her.* **3** to
remove (money from a bank account *etc*): *I
withdrew all my savings and went abroad.*
with'drawal *n.*
with'drawn *adj* (of a person) not responsive
or friendly.
wither ['wiδə] *v* (of plants *etc*) to (cause to)
fade, dry up, or decay: *The plants withered
because they had no water; The sun has
withered my plants.*
withhold [wiδ'hould] – *pt, ptp* **with'held**
[-'held] – *v* to refuse to give: *to withhold
permission.*
within [wi'δin] *prep* inside (the limits of):
*She'll be here within an hour; I could hear
sounds from within the building; His actions
were within the law* (= not illegal). – *adv*
inside: *Car for sale. Apply within.*
without [wi'δaut] *prep* **1** in the absence of;
not having: *They went without you; I could
not live without him; We cannot survive
without water.* **2** not: *He drove away without saying goodbye; You can't walk along
this street without meeting someone you
know.*
withstand [wiδ'stand] – *pt, ptp* **with'stood**
[-'stud] – *v* to oppose or resist (successfully): *They withstood the siege for eight
months.*
witness ['witnəs] *n* **1** a person who has seen or
was present at an event *etc* and so has direct
knowledge of it: *Someone must have seen
the accident but the police can find no witnesses.* **2** a person who gives evidence, *esp*
in a law court. **3** a person who adds his
signature to a document to show that he
considers another signature on the document to be genuine: *You cannot sign your
will without witnesses.* – *v* **1** to see and be
present at: *This lady witnessed an accident
at three o'clock this afternoon.* **2** to sign
one's name to show that one knows that
(something) is genuine: *He witnessed my
signature on the new agreement.*
'witness-box/'witness-stand *n* the stand from
which a witness gives evidence in a court of
law.

bear witness to give evidence: *She will bear witness to his honesty.*

witty *etc see* **wit.**

wives *see* **wife.**

wizard ['wizəd] *n* a man who is said to have magic powers: *a fairy-story about a wizard.*

wobble ['wobl] *v* to rock unsteadily from side to side: *The bicycle wobbled and the child fell off.* – *n* a slight rocking, unsteady movement: *This wheel has a bit of a wobble.* '**wobbly** *adj.* '**wobbliness** *n.*

woe [wou] *n* (a cause of) grief or misery: *He has many woes; He told a tale of woe.* '**woeful** *adj* miserable; unhappy: *a woeful expression.* '**woefully** *adv.* '**woefulness** *n.* '**woebegone** [-bigon] *adj* sad-looking: *a woebegone face.*

woke, woken *see* **wake**[1].

wolf [wulf] – *pl* **wolves** [wulvz] – *n* a type of wild animal of the dog family, *usu* found hunting in packs. – *v* to eat greedily: *He wolfed (down) his breakfast and hurried out.* '**wolf-cub** *n* **1** a young wolf. **2** an old name for a Cub Scout. '**wolf-whistle** *n* a whistle impolitely made by a man to express his admiration of a woman's appearance. **keep the wolf from the door** to keep away hunger or want.

woman ['wumən] – *pl* **women** ['wimin] – *n* **1** an adult human female: *His sisters are both grown women now;* (*also adj*) *a woman doctor; women doctors.* **2** a female domestic daily helper: *We have a woman who comes in to do the cleaning.* **-woman** sometimes used instead of **-man** when the person performing an activity is a woman, as in **chairwoman.** '**womanhood** *n* the state of being a woman: *She will reach womanhood in a few years' time.* '**womankind, womenkind** ['wimin-] *ns* women generally. '**womanly** *adj* (showing qualities) natural or suitable to a woman: *a womanly figure; womanly charm.* '**womanliness** *n.* '**womenfolk** ['wimin-] *n pl* female people, *esp* female relatives.

womb [wu:m] *n* the part of the body of a female mammal in which the young are developed and kept until birth.

won *see* **win.**

wonder ['wʌndə] *n* **1** the state of mind produced by something unexpected or extraordinary: *He was full of wonder at the amazing sight.* **2** something strange, unexpected or extraordinary: *the Seven Wonders of the World; You work late so often that it's a wonder you don't take a bed to the office!* **3** the quality of being strange or unexpected: *The wonder of the discovery is that it was only made ten years ago.* – *v* **1** to be

surprised: *Caroline is very fond of John – I shouldn't wonder if she married him.* **2** to feel curiosity or doubt: *Have you ever wondered about his reasons for wanting this money?* **3** to feel a desire to know: *I wonder what the news is.* '**wonderful** *adj* arousing wonder; extraordinary, *esp* in excellence: *a wonderful opportunity; a wonderful present; She's a wonderful person.* '**wonderfully** *adv.* '**wonderingly** *adv* with great curiosity and amazement: *The children gazed wonderingly at the puppets.* '**wonderland** [-land] *n* a land or place full of wonderful things. '**wondrous** ['wʌndrəs] *adj* wonderful. **no wonder** it isn't surprising: *No wonder you couldn't open the door – it was locked!*

won't *see* **will.**

woo [wu:] – *3rd pers sing prt* **woos:** *pt, ptp* **wooed** – *v* (of a man) to seek as a wife: *He wooed the daughter of the king.* '**wooer** *n.*

wood [wud] *n* **1** (*also adj*) (of) the material of which the trunk and branches of trees are composed: *My desk is (made of) wood; She gathered some wood for the fire; I like the smell of a wood fire.* **2** (*often in pl*) a group of growing trees: *They went for a walk in the woods.* **3** a golf-club whose head is made of wood. '**wooded** *adj* (of land) covered with trees: *a wooded hillside.* '**wooden** *adj* made of wood: *three wooden chairs.* '**woody** *adj* **1** covered with trees: *woody countryside.* **2** (of a smell *etc*) of or like wood. '**woodcutter** *n* a person whose job is felling trees. '**woodland** *n* land covered with woods: *a stretch of woodland.* '**woodlouse** – *pl* '**woodlice** – *n* a tiny creature with a jointed shell, found under stones *etc.* '**woodpecker** *n* a type of bird which pecks holes in the bark of trees, searching for insects. '**woodwind** [-wind] *n* (in an orchestra, the group of people who play) wind instruments made of wood. '**woodwork** *n* **1** the art of making things from wood; carpentry: *He did woodwork at school.* **2** the wooden part of any structure: *The woodwork in the house is rotting.* '**woodworm** – *pls* '**woodworm, woodworms** – *n* the larva of a certain type of beetle, which bores into wood and destroys it. **out of the wood(s)** out of danger.

wool [wul] *n, adj* (of) the soft hair of sheep and some other animals, often made into yarn *etc* for knitting or into fabric for making clothes *etc*: *I wear wool in winter; knitting-wool; a wool blanket.*

'woollen *adj* made of wool: *a woollen hat.*
'woollens *n pl* clothes (*esp* jumpers *etc*) made of wool: *Woollens should be washed by hand.*
'woolly *adj* 1 made of, or like, wool: *a woolly jumper/rug.* 2 (*also* **,woolly-'headed**) (of a person) vague or hazy: *She's too woolly (-headed) to be in charge of a department.* – *pl* **'woollies** – *n* a knitted garment.
'woolliness *n.*
pull the wool over someone's eyes to deceive someone.

word [wɜːd] *n* 1 the smallest unit of language (whether written, spoken or read). 2 a (brief) conversation: *I'd like a (quick) word with you in my office.* 3 news: *When you get there, send word that you've arrived safely.* 4 a solemn promise: *He gave her his word that it would never happen again.* – *v* to express in written or spoken language: *How are you going to word the letter so that it doesn't seem rude?*
'wording *n* the manner of expressing something, the choice of words *etc.*
by word of mouth by one person telling another in speech, not in writing: *She got the information by word of mouth.*
get a word in edgeways to break into a conversation *etc* and say something.
in a word to sum up briefly: *In a word, I don't like him.*
keep, break one's word to keep or fail to keep one's promise.
take (someone) at his word to believe (someone) without question and act according to his words.
take someone's word for it to assume that what someone says is correct (without checking).
word for word in the exact, original words: *That's precisely what he told me, word for word.*
wore *see* **wear.**

work [wɜːk] *n* 1 effort made in order to achieve or make something: *He has done a lot of work on this project.* 2 employment: *I cannot find work in this town.* 3 a task or tasks; the thing that one is working on: *Please clear your work off the table.* 4 a painting, book, piece of music *etc*: *the works of Van Gogh/Shakespeare/Mozart; This work was composed in 1816.* 5 the product or result of a person's labours: *His work has shown a great improvement lately.* 6 one's place of employment: *He left (his) work at 5.30 p.m.; I don't think I'll go to work tomorrow.* – *v* 1 to (cause to) make efforts in order to achieve or make something: *She works at the factory three days a week; He works his employees very hard; I've been working on/at a new project.* 2 to be employed: *Are you working just now?* 3 to (cause to) operate (in the correct way): *He has no idea how that*

machine works/how to work that machine; *That machine doesn't/won't work, but this one's working.* 4 to be practicable and/or successful: *If my scheme works, we'll be rich!* 5 to make (one's way) slowly and carefully with effort or difficulty: *She worked her way up the rock face.* 6 to get into, or put into, a stated condition or position, slowly and gradually: *The wheel worked loose.* 7 to make by craftsmanship: *The ornaments had been worked in gold.*
-work 1 (the art of making) goods of a particular material: *He learns woodwork at school; This shop sells basketwork.* 2 parts of something, *eg* a building, made of a particular material: *The stonework/woodwork/paintwork needs to be renewed.*
'workable *adj* (of a plan) able to be carried out.
'worker *n* 1 a person who works or who is employed in an office, a factory *etc*: *office-workers; car-workers.* 2 a manual worker rather than an office-worker *etc.* 3 a person who works (hard *etc*): *He's a slow/hard worker.*
works *n sing* or *n pl* a factory *etc*: *The steelworks is/are closed for the holidays.* – *n pl* 1 the mechanism (of a watch, clock *etc*): *The works are all rusted.* 2 deeds, actions *etc*: *She's devoted her life to good works.*
'work-basket, 'work-box *etc ns* a basket, box *etc* for holding thread, needlework *etc.*
'workbook *n* a book of exercises *usu* with spaces for answers.
'workforce *n* the number of workers (available for work) in a particular industry, factory *etc.*
working class the section of society who work with their hands, doing manual labour.
working day, 'work-day *ns* 1 a day on which one goes to work, and is not on holiday. 2 the period of actual labour in a normal day at work: *My working day is eight hours long.*
working hours the times of day between which one is at work: *Normal working hours are 9 a.m. to 5 p.m.*
'working-party, 'work-party *ns* a group of people gathered together (*usu* voluntarily) to perform a particular physical task: *They organized a work-party to clear the canal of weeds.*
working week the five days from Monday to Friday inclusive when people go to work.
'workman *n* a man who does manual work: *the workmen on a building site.*
'workmanlike *adj* 1 suitable to a good workman: *a workmanlike attitude.* 2 well performed: *a workmanlike job.*
'workmanship *n* the skill of a qualified workman; skill in making things.
'workmate *n* one of the people who work in

the same place of employment as oneself: *Her workmates teased her about being the boss's favourite.*

'workout *n* a period of hard physical exercise for the purpose of keeping fit *etc*.

'workshop *n* **1** a room or building, *esp* in a factory *etc* where construction and repairs are carried out. **2** a course of experimental work for a group of people on a particular project.

at work working: *He's writing a novel and he likes to be at work (on it) by eight o'clock every morning.*

get/set to work to start work: *Could you get to work painting that ceiling?; I'll have to set to work on this mending this evening.*

go to work on to begin work on: *We're thinking of going to work on an extension to the house.*

in working order (of a machine *etc*) operating correctly.

out of work having no employment: *He's been out of work for months.*

work of art a painting, sculpture *etc*.

work off to get rid of (something unwanted or unpleasant) by taking physical exercise *etc*: *He worked off his anger by running round the garden six times.*

work out 1 to solve or calculate correctly: *I can't work out how many should be left.* **2** to come to a satisfactory end: *Don't worry – it will all work out (in the end).* **3** to perform physical exercises.

work up 1 to excite or rouse gradually: *She worked herself up into a fury (adj ,worked='up: Don't get so worked-up!)*. **2** to raise or create: *I just can't work up any energy/appetite/enthusiasm today.*

work up to to progress towards and prepare for: *Work up to the difficult exercises gradually.*

work wonders to produce marvellous results: *These pills have worked wonders on my rheumatism.*

world [wəːld] *n* **1** the planet Earth: *every country of the world.* **2** the people who live on the planet Earth: *The whole world is waiting for a cure for cancer.* **3** any planet *etc*: *people from other worlds.* **4** a state of existence: *Many people believe that after death the soul enters the next world; Do concentrate! You seem to be living in another world.* **5** an area of life or activity: *the insect world; the world of the international businessman.* **6** a great deal: *The holiday did him a/the world of good.* **7** the lives and ways of ordinary people: *He's been a monk for so long that he knows nothing of the (outside) world.*

'worldly *adj* of or belonging to this world; not spiritual: *worldly pleasures*. **'worldliness** *n*.

,world'wide *adj, adv* (extending over or found) everywhere in the world: *a worldwide sales network; Their products are sold worldwide.*

the best of both worlds the advantages of both the alternatives in a situation *etc* in which one can normally only expect to have one: *A woman has the best of both worlds when she has a good job and a happy family life.*

for all the world exactly, quite *etc*: *What a mess you're in! You look for all the world as if you'd had an argument with an express train.*

out of this world unbelievably marvellous: *The concert was out of this world.*

what in the world(?) used for emphasis when asking a question: *What in the world have you done to your hair?*

worm [wəːm] *n* a kind of small creeping animal with a ringed body and no backbone; an earth-worm. – *v* **1** to make (one's way) slowly or secretly: *He wormed his way to the front of the crowd.* **2** to get (information *etc*) with difficulty (out of someone): *It took me hours to worm the true story out of him.*

worn *see* **wear**.

worry[1] ['wʌri, (*Amer*) 'wəːri] *v* **1** to (cause to) feel anxious: *His dangerous driving worries me; His mother is worried about his education; There's no need to worry just because he's late.* **2** to annoy; to distract: *Don't worry me just now – I'm busy!* **3** to shake or tear with the teeth *etc* as a dog does its prey *etc*. – *n* (a cause of) anxiety: *That boy is a constant (source of) worry to his mother!; Try to forget your worries.*

'worried *adj* (*neg* **un-**): *a worried look.*

worse [wəːs] *adj* **1** bad to a greater extent: *My exam results were bad but his were much worse (than mine).* **2** not so well: *I feel worse today than I did last week.* **3** more unpleasant: *Waiting for exam results is worse than sitting the exams.* – *adv* not so well: *He behaves worse now than he did as a child.* – *pron* someone or something which is bad to a greater extent than the other (of two people, things *etc*): *the worse of the two alternatives.*

'worsen *v* to (cause to) grow worse: *The situation has worsened.*

none the worse for not in any way harmed by: *The child was lost in the supermarket but fortunately was none the worse for his experience.*

the worse for wear becoming worn out: *These chairs are the worse for wear.*

worship ['wəːʃip] – *pt, ptp* **'worshipped**, (*Amer*) **'worshiped** – *v* **1** to pay great honour to: *to worship God.* **2** to love or admire very greatly: *She worships her older brother.* – *n* the act of worshipping: *A church is a place of worship*; *the worship of God/of money.*

'**worshipper** *n.*

worst [wɔːst] *adj* bad to the greatest extent: *That is the worst book I have ever read.* – *adv* in the worst way or manner: *This group performed worst (of all) in the test.* – *pron* the thing, person *etc* which is bad to the greatest extent: *the worst of the three*; *His behaviour is at its worst when he's with strangers*; *At the worst they can only fine you.*

do one's worst to do the most evil *etc* thing that one can.

get the worst of to be defeated in (a fight *etc*).

if the worst comes to the worst if the worst possible thing happens: *If the worst comes to the worst you can sell your house.*

the worst of it is (that) the most unfortunate *etc* aspect of the situation is (that).

worth [wɔːθ] *n* value: *These books are of little or no worth*; *She sold fifty dollars' worth of tickets.* – *adj* 1 equal in value to: *Each of these stamps is worth a cent.* 2 good enough for: *His suggestion is worth considering*: *The exhibition is well worth a visit.*

'**worthless** *adj* of no value: *worthless old coins.* '**worthlessly** *adv.* '**worthlessness** *n.*

'**worthy** [-ði] *adj* 1 good and deserving: *I willingly give money to a worthy cause.* 2 (*with* **of**) deserving: *She was not worthy of the honour given to her.* 3 (*with* **of**) typical of, suited to, or in keeping with: *a performance worthy of a champion.* 4 of great enough importance *etc*: *She was not thought worthy to be presented to the king.* – *n* – *pl* '**worthies** – a highly respected person.

'**worthily** *adv.* '**worthiness** *n.*

-worthy 1 deserving; fit for: *a blameworthy act.* 2 fit for its appropriate use; *a seaworthy ship.*

worth'while *adj* deserving attention, time and effort *etc*: *a worthwhile cause*; *It isn't worthwhile to ask him – he'll only refuse.*

for all one is worth using all one's efforts, strength *etc*: *He swam for all he was worth towards the shore.*

would [wud] – *short forms* **I'd** [aid], **you'd** [juːd], **he'd** [hiːd], **she'd** [ʃiːd], **it'd** ['itəd], **we'd** [wiːd], **they'd** [ðeid]; *neg short form* **wouldn't** ['wudnt] – *v* 1 *pt of* **will**: *He said he would be leaving at nine o'clock the next morning*; *I asked if he'd come and mend my television set*; *I asked him to do it, but he wouldn't*; *I thought you would have finished by now.* 2 used in speaking of something that will, may or might happen (*eg* if a certain condition is met): *If I asked her to the party, would she come?*; *I would have come to the party if you'd asked me*; *I'd be happy to help you.* 3 used to express a preference, opinion *etc* politely: *I would do it this way*; *It'd be a shame to lose the opportunity*; *I'd prefer to go tomorrow rather than today.* 4 used, said with emphasis, to express annoyance: *I've lost my car-keys – that would happen!*

'**would-be** *adj* trying, hoping, or merely pretending, to be: *a would-be poet.*

would you used to introduce a polite request to someone to do something: (*Please*) *would you close the door?*

wouldn't *see* **would.**

wound[1] *see* **wind**[2].

wound[2] [wuːnd] *n* a physical hurt or injury: *The wound that he had received in the war still gave him pain occasionally*; *He died from a bullet-wound.* – *v* 1 to hurt or injure physically: *He didn't kill the animal – he just wounded it*; *He was wounded in the battle.* 2 to hurt (someone's feelings): *to wound someone's pride.*

'**wounded** *adj* having been injured, *esp* in war *etc*: *the wounded man.* – *n pl* wounded people, *esp* soldiers: *How many wounded are there?*

wove, woven *see* **weave.**

wrangle ['raŋgl] *v* to quarrel or argue angrily. – *n* an angry argument.

wrap [rap] – *pt, ptp* **wrapped** – *v* 1 to roll or fold (round something or someone): *He wrapped his handkerchief round his bleeding finger.* 2 to cover by folding or winding something round: *She wrapped the book (up) in brown paper*; *She wrapped the baby up in a warm shawl.* – *n* a warm covering to put over one's shoulders.

'**wrapper** *n* a paper cover for a sweet, packet of cigarettes *etc*: *a sweet-wrapper.*

'**wrapping** *n* something used to wrap or pack something in: *Christmas wrappings.*

wrapped up in giving all one's attention to: *She's very wrapped up in her work these days.*

wrap up to dress warmly: *You have to wrap up well if you visit England in winter*; *Wrap the child up well.*

wrath [roθ, (*Amer*) raθ] *n* violent anger.

'**wrathful** *adj.*

wreath [riːθ] – *pl* **wreaths** [riːθs, riːðz] – *n* 1 a circular garland of flowers or leaves, placed at a grave, or put on someone's shoulders or head after his/her victory *etc*: *We put a wreath of flowers on her mother's grave.* 2 a drift or curl of smoke, mist *etc*: *wreaths of smoke.*

wreathe [riːð] *v* to cover: *faces wreathed in smiles.*

wreck [rek] *n* 1 a very badly damaged ship: *The divers found a wreck on the sea-bed.* 2 something in a very bad condition: *an old wreck of a car*; *I feel a wreck after cleaning the house.* 3 the destruction of a ship at sea: *The wreck of the Royal George.* – *v* to destroy or damage very badly: *The ship was wrecked on rocks in a storm*; *My son has wrecked my car*; *You have wrecked my plans.*

'wreckage [-kidʒ] *n* the remains of something wrecked: *After the accident, the wreckage (of the cars) was removed from the motorway.*

wren [ren] *n* a type of very small bird.

wrench [rentʃ] *v* **1** to pull with a violent movement: *He wrenched the gun out of my hand.* **2** to sprain: *to wrench one's shoulder.* – *n* **1** a violent pull or twist. **2** a type of strong tool for turning nuts, bolts *etc.*

wrestle ['resl] *v* **1** to struggle physically (with someone), *esp* as a sport. **2** to struggle (with a problem *etc*): *I've been wrestling with the office accounts.*

'wrestler *n* a person who takes part in the sport of wrestling.

wretch [retʃ] *n* **1** a miserable, unhappy creature: *The poor wretch!* **2** a name used in annoyance or anger: *You wretch!*

wretched ['retʃid] *adj* **1** very poor or miserable: *They live in a wretched little house.* **2** used in annoyance: *This wretched machine won't work!* **'wretchedly** *adv.* **'wretchedness** *n.*

wriggle ['rigl] *v* to twist to and fro: *The child kept wriggling in his seat; How are you going to wriggle out of this awkward situation?* – *n* a wriggling movement.

'wriggler *n.*

wring [riŋ] – *pt, ptp* **wrung** [rʌŋ] – *v* **1** to force (water) from (material) by twisting or by pressure: *He wrung the water from his soaking-wet shirt.* **2** to clasp and unclasp (one's hands) in desperation, fear *etc.*

'wringer *n* a machine for forcing water from wet clothes.

wringing wet soaked through: *The clothes are wringing wet; wringing-wet clothes.*

wrinkle ['riŋkl] *n* a small crease on the skin (*usu* on one's face): *Her face is full of wrinkles.* – *v* to (cause to) become full of wrinkles or creases: *The damp had wrinkled the pages.*

'wrinkled *adj* full of wrinkles: *a wrinkled face.*

wrist [rist] *n* the (part of the arm at the) joint between hand and forearm: *I can't play tennis – I've hurt my wrist.*

'wrist-watch, 'wristlet-watch [-lit-] *ns* a watch worn on the wrist.

write [rait] – *pt* **wrote** [rout] *ptp* **written** ['ritn] – *v* **1** to draw (letters or other forms of script) on a surface, *esp* with a pen or pencil on paper: *They wrote their names on a sheet of paper; The child has learned to read and write; Please write in ink.* **2** to compose the text of (a book, poem *etc*): *She wrote a book on prehistoric monsters.* **3** to compose a letter (and send it): *He has written a letter to me about this matter; I'll write you a long letter about my holiday; I wrote to you last week.*

'writer *n* a person who writes, *esp* for a living: *Dickens was a famous English writer; the writer of this letter.*

'writing *n* letters or other forms of script giving the written form of (a) language: *the Chinese form of writing; I can't read your writing.*

'writings *n pl* the collected books, poems, correspondence *etc* of a particular (*usu* famous) person: *the writings of Plato.*

written ['ritn] *adj* in writing: *a written message.*

'writing-paper *n* paper for writing letters *etc* on: *writing-paper and envelopes.*

write down to record in writing: *She wrote down every word he said.*

write out to copy or record in writing: *Write this exercise out in your neatest handwriting.*

writhe [raið] *v* to twist violently to and fro, *esp* in pain or discomfort: *to writhe in agony; She writhed about when I tickled her.*

wrong [roŋ] *adj* **1** having an error or mistake(s); incorrect: *The child gave the wrong answer; We went in the wrong direction.* **2** incorrect in one's answer(s), opinion(s) *etc*; mistaken: *I thought Singapore was south of the Equator, but I was quite wrong.* **3** not good, not morally correct *etc*: *It is wrong to steal.* **4** not suitable: *He's the wrong man for the job.* **5** not right; not normal: *There's something wrong with this engine; What's wrong with that child – why is she crying?* – *adv* incorrectly: *I think I may have spelt her name wrong.* – *n* that which is not morally correct: *He does not know right from wrong.* – *v* to insult or hurt unjustly: *You wrong me by suggesting that I'm lying.*

'wrongful *adj* not lawful or fair: *wrongful dismissal from a job.* **'wrongfully** *adv.* **'wrongfulness** *n.*

'wrongly *adv* **1** incorrectly: *The letter was wrongly addressed.* **2** unjustly: *I have been wrongly treated.*

'wrongdoer *n* a person who does wrong or illegal things: *The wrongdoers must be punished.* **'wrongdoing** *n.*

do (someone) wrong to insult (someone), treat (someone) unfairly *etc.*

do wrong to act incorrectly or unjustly: *You did wrong to punish him.*

go wrong 1 to go astray, badly, away from the intended plan *etc*: *Everything has gone wrong for her in the past few years.* **2** to stop functioning properly: *The machine has gone wrong – I can't get it to stop!* **3** to make a mistake: *Where did I go wrong in that sum?*

in the wrong guilty of an error or injustice: *She is completely blameless. You're the one who's in the wrong!*

wrote *see* **write**.

wrung *see* **wring**.

wry [rai] *adj* slightly mocking: *a wry smile.* **'wryly** *adv.*

Xx

X-rays [eks'reiz] *n pl* rays which can pass through many substances impossible for light to pass through, and which produce a picture of the object through which they have passed.

‚X-'ray *n* (the process of taking) a photograph using X-rays: *I'm going to hospital for an X-ray*; *We'll take an X-ray of your chest*; (*also adj*) *an X-ray photograph*. – *v* to take a photograph of using X-rays: *They X-rayed my arm to see if it was broken.*

Xerox® ['ziəroks] *n* **1** a type of photographic process used for copying documents. **2** a copying-machine using this process. **3** a photocopy (of something) made by such a process. – *v* to photocopy (something) using this process.

Xmas ['krisməs] short for **Christmas**.

xylophone ['zailəfoun] *n* a musical instrument consisting of wooden or metal slats of various lengths, which produce different notes when struck by wooden hammers.

Yy

yacht [jot] *n* a boat or small ship, usually with sails, often with an engine, built and used for racing or cruising: *We spent our holidays on a friend's yacht*; (*also adj*) *a yacht race.*

'yachting *n* the pastime of sailing in a yacht.
'yachtsman ['jots-] *n* a person who sails a yacht: *a keen yachtsman.*
yacht club a club for yacht-owners.

yak [jak] – *pls* **yaks**, **yak** – *n* a type of long-haired ox, found in Tibet.

*yam [jam] *n* any of several kinds of potato-like tropical plants used as food.

yank [jaŋk] *n* a sudden sharp pull; a jerk: *She gave the rope a yank.* – *v* to pull suddenly and sharply: *She yanked the child out of the mud.*

Yank [jaŋk] *n* an impolite word for a person from the United States of America.
Yankee ['jaŋki] *n, adj* a more affectionate word for (an) American.

yap [jap] – *pt, ptp* **yapped** – *v* (of a puppy or small dog) to give a high-pitched bark. – *n* a short, high-pitched bark: *The puppy gave a yap.*

yard¹ [ja:d] *n* (*often abbrev* **yd**) an old unit of length equal to 0·9144 metres.

yard² [ja:d] *n* **1** an area of (enclosed) ground beside a building: *Leave your bicycle in the yard*; *a school-yard*; *a courtyard.* **2** an area of enclosed ground used for a special purpose: *a shipyard*; *a dockyard.*

yarn¹ [ja:n] *n* wool, cotton *etc* spun into thread: *knitting-yarn*; *a length of yarn.*

yarn² [ja:n] *n* an old word for a story or tale: *He told us interesting yarns about his travels.*

yashmak ['jaʃmak] *n* a veil worn by Moslem women, covering the face below the eyes.

yawn [jo:n] *v* to stretch the mouth wide and take a deep breath when tired or bored: *He yawned and fell asleep.* – *n* an act of yawning: *a yawn of boredom.*
'yawning *adj* wide open: *a yawning gap.*

ye [ji:] *pron* an old word for **you**, occurring as the subject of a sentence.

year [jiə] *n* **1** the period of time the earth takes to go once round the sun, about 365 days: *We lived here for five years, from November 1968 to November 1973*; *a two-year delay.* **2** the period from January 1 to December 31, being 365 days, except in a leap year, when it is 366 days: *in the year 1945.*
'yearly *adj* happening *etc* every year: *We pay a yearly visit to my uncle.* – *adv* every year: *The festival is held yearly.*
'year-book *n* a book of information which is updated and published every year: *a students' year-book.*
all (the) year round, long *etc* throughout the whole year: *The weather is so good here that we can swim all (the) year round.*

yearn [jə:n] *v* to feel a great desire; to long: *to yearn for an end to the war.*
'yearning *n* (a) strong desire.

yeast [ji:st] *n* a substance which causes fermentation, used in making beer, bread *etc.*

yell [jel] *n* a loud, shrill cry; a scream: *a yell of pain.* – *v* to make such a noise: *He yelled at her to be careful.*

yellow ['jelou] *adj, n* (of) the colour of gold, the yolk of an egg *etc*: *a yellow dress*; *yellow sands*; *Yellow is my favourite colour.* – *v* to make or become yellow: *It was autumn and the leaves were beginning to yellow.*
'yellowness *n.*

yelp [jelp] v (of a dog *etc*) to give a sharp, sudden cry: *The dog yelped with pain.* – n a sharp, sudden cry: *The dog gave a yelp of pain.*

yen [jen] – *pl* **yen** – n the standard unit of Japanese currency.

yes [jes] *interj* used to express agreement or consent: *Yes, that is true*; *Yes, you may go.*

yesterday ['jestədi] n, adv (on) the day before today: *Yesterday was a tiring day*; *He went home yesterday.*

yet [jet] adv **1** up till now: *He hasn't telephoned yet*; *Have you finished yet?*; *We're not yet ready.* **2** used for emphasis: *He's made yet another mistake/yet more mistakes.* **3** (with a compar adj) even: *a yet more terrible experience.* – conj but; however: *He's pleasant enough, yet I don't like him.*

as yet up to the time referred to, *usu* the present: *I haven't had a book published as yet.*

yew [ju:] n a type of evergreen tree with dark leaves and red berries.

yield [ji:ld] v **1** to give up; to surrender: *He yielded to the other man's arguments*; *He yielded all his possessions to the state.* **2** to give way to force or pressure: *At last the door yielded.* **3** to produce naturally, grow *etc*: *How much milk does that herd of cattle yield?* – n the amount produced by natural means: *the annual yield of wheat.*

yoga ['yougə] n. **1** any of several systems of physical exercises based on a Hindu system of philosophy and meditation. **2** the philosophy (*usu* including the meditation and exercises).

'yogi [-gi] n a person who practises and/or teaches the yoga philosophy.

yog(h)urt, yoghourt ['jogət, (*Amer*) 'jou-] n a type of semi-liquid food made from fermented milk.

yoke [jouk] n **1** a wooden frame placed over the necks of oxen to hold them together when they are pulling a cart *etc*. **2** a frame placed across a person's shoulders, for carrying buckets *etc*. **3** something that weighs people down, or prevents them being free: *the yoke of slavery.* **4** the part of a garment that fits over the shoulders and round the neck: *a black dress with a white yolk.* – v to join with a yoke: *He yoked the oxen to the plough.*

yolk [jouk] n (also **'egg-yolk**) the yellow part of an egg: *The child will only eat the yolk of an egg* – *she won't eat the white.*

you [ju:] *pron* **1** (used as the subject or object of a verb, or as the object of a preposition) the person(s) *etc* spoken or written to: *You look well!*; *I asked you a question*; *Do you all understand?*; *Who came with you?* **2** used with a noun when calling someone something, *esp* something unpleasant: *You idiot!*; *You fools!*

you'd *see* **have, would**.

you'll *see* **will**.

young [jʌŋ] adj in the first part of life, growth, development *etc*; not old: *a young person*; *Young babies sleep a great deal*; *A young cow is called a calf.* – n pl the group of animals or birds produced by parents: *Most animals defend their young.*

'youngster n a young person: *A group of youngsters were playing football.*

the young young people in general.

your [jo:, (*Amer*) juər] adj belonging to you: *your house/car.*

yours [jo:z, (*Amer*) juərz] *pron* something belonging to you: *This book is yours*; *Yours is on that shelf.*

your'self – pl **your'selves** [-'selvz] – *pron* **1** used as the object of a verb or preposition when the person(s) spoken or written to is/are the object(s) of an action he/they perform(s): *Why are you looking at yourselves in the mirror?*; *You can dry yourself with this towel.* **2** used to emphasize **you**: *You yourself can't do it, but you could ask someone else to do it.* **3** without help *etc*: *You can jolly well do it yourself!*

yours (faithfully, sincerely, truly) expressions written before one's signature at the end of a letter.

you're *see* **be**.

youth [ju:θ] – pl **youths** [ju:ðz] – n **1** (the state of being in) the early part of life: *Enjoy your youth!*; *He spent his youth in America.* **2** a boy of fifteen to twenty years old approximately: *He and two other youths were kicking a football about.* **3** young people in general: *Some people say that today's youth has/have no sense of responsibility.*

'youthful adj **1** young: *The boy looked very youthful.* **2** energetic, active, young-looking *etc*: *Exercise will keep you youthful.* **3** of youth: *youthful pleasures.* **'youthfully** adv. **'youthfulness** n.

youth hostel a place for young people, *esp* hikers, on holiday, where cheap and simple accommodation is provided (n **youth hosteller**).

you've *see* **have**.

yo-yo, Yo-yo® ['joujou] n a type of toy, consisting of a pair of discs made of wood, metal *etc* with a groove between them round which a piece of string is tied, the toy being made to run up and down the string: *going up and down like a yo-yo.*

yuan [ju'an] – pl **yu'an** – n the standard unit of currency in the People's Republic of China.

Zz

zeal [zi:l] *n* enthusiasm or keenness.

zealous ['zeləs] *adj* enthusiastic; keen: *He is a zealous supporter of our cause.* **'zealously** *adv*.

zebra ['zi:brə, 'zeb-] – *pl* **'zebras, 'zebra** – *n* a kind of striped animal of the horse family, found wild in Africa: *two zebras; a herd of zebra.*

zebra crossing a place, marked in black and white stripes, where traffic stops for pedestrians to cross a street.

zenith ['zeniθ] *n* the highest point: *The sun reaches its zenith at midday.*

zero ['ziərou] – *pl* **'zeros** – *n* **1** the number or figure 0: *Three plus zero equals three; The figure 100 has two zeros in it.* **2** the point on a scale (*eg* on a thermometer) which is taken as the standard on which measurements may be based: *The temperature was 5 degrees above/below zero.* **3** the exact time fixed for something to happen, *eg* an explosion, the launching of a spacecraft *etc*: *It is now 3 minutes to zero.*

zest [zest] *n* keen enjoyment: *She joined in the games with zest.*

zigzag ['zigzag] *adj* (of a line, road *etc*) having sharp bends or angles from side to side: *a zigzag path through the woods.* – *v* – *pt, ptp* **'zigzagged** – to move in a zigzag manner: *The road zigzagged through the mountains.*

zinc [ziŋk] *n* a bluish-white metallic element.

zip[1] [zip] *n* **1** (*also* **'zipper**) a zip fastener. **2** a whizzing sound: *They heard the zip of a flying bullet.* – *v* – *pt, ptp* **zipped** – **1** to fasten with a zip fastener: *She zipped up her trousers; This dress zips at the back.* **2** to move with a whizzing sound: *A bullet zipped past his head.*

zip fastener (*usu* **zip** *or* **'zipper**) a device for fastening clothes *etc*, in which two rows of metal or nylon teeth are made to fit each other when a sliding tab is pulled along them.

zip[2] [zip]: **zip code** in the US, a postal code, having the form of a five-figure number, placed at the end of an address.

zone [zoun] *n* **1** an area or region, *usu* of a country, town *etc*, *esp* one marked off for a special purpose: *a no-parking zone; a traffic-free zone.* **2** any of the five bands into which the earth's surface is divided according to temperature: *The tropical zone is the area between the Tropic of Capricorn and the Tropic of Cancer.*

zoo [zu:] *n* (short for **zoological garden**) a place where wild animals are kept for the public to see, and for study, breeding *etc*.

zoology [zu'olədʒi] *n* the scientific study of animals. **,zoo'logical** [zuə'lo-] *adj*. **,zoo'logically** [-'lo-] *adv*. **zo'ologist** *n*.

zoom [zu:m] *n* a loud, low-pitched buzzing noise: *the zoom of (an) aircraft.* – *v* to move very quickly with this kind of noise: *The motorbike zoomed past us.*

zoom lens a type of camera lens which can make a distant object appear gradually closer without moving the camera.

zoom in to direct a camera (on to an object *etc*) and use a zoom lens to make it appear to come closer: *Film the whole building first, then zoom in on the door.*

GRAMMATICAL NOTES

Nouns

Singular and Plural Nouns

The following nouns are always in the singular and are used with a singular verb:

> advice baggage clothing dirt dust equipment furniture knowledge
> lightning luggage machinery mud music rust scenery stationery traffic

The following nouns have only a plural form and are used with a plural verb:

> clothes congratulations hackles pants pincers pliers pyjamas riches
> scissors shorts spectacles thanks tights trousers tweezers

The following nouns have the same form in singular and plural:

> cod deer salmon sheep trout aircraft hovercraft spacecraft

Some nouns have a plural form but are used with a singular verb, *eg*:

> billiards bowls checkers draughts
> measles mumps news

Gender

The **masculine gender** denotes the class of persons and animals that are **male**; the **feminine gender** denotes the class of persons and animals that are **female**. Note the following masculine and feminine forms:

masculine	feminine	masculine	feminine
bachelor	spinster	landlord	landlady
boy	girl	man	woman
bridegroom	bride	nephew	niece
brother	sister	sir	madam
comedian	comedienne	son	daughter
father	mother	uncle	aunt
fiancé	fiancée	widower	widow
gentleman	lady	bull	cow
hero	heroine	cock	hen
husband	wife	dog	bitch
king	queen	drake	duck

The feminine form often ends in **-ess**:

masculine	feminine
emperor	empress
god	goddess
heir	heiress
host	hostess
lion	lioness
master	mistress
prince	princess
tiger	tigress

Some names for jobs have masculine and feminine forms, *eg*:

masculine	feminine
actor	actress
conductor	conductress (on a bus *etc*)
manager	manageress
policeman	policewoman
schoolmaster	schoolmistress
salesman	saleswoman
steward	stewardess
waiter	waitress

The **common gender** denotes the class of persons that can be male or female, *eg*:

> adult athlete baby child cousin
> friend guest motorist parent passenger
> person principal pupil tourist worker

Most words for jobs are of common gender:

-er/-or: builder conductor (of an orchestra) director doctor driver editor teacher writer

-ist: artist chemist dentist journalist scientist

-ant/ent: accountant civil servant president shop assistant student travel agent

-ician: musician physician technician

-person: chairperson salesperson

The **neuter gender** denotes the class of things without sex that can be referred to as 'it', *eg* chair, table, book, plant etc; but a baby or animal can also be referred to as 'it'.

Adjectives

Comparison of Adjectives

Adjectives have three degrees of comparison: the **positive** degree, the **comparative** degree and the **superlative** degree.

The **positive** degree is the simple form of the adjective and is used to describe a noun:

John is **tall**.   This table is **high**.   This house is **expensive**.

The **comparative** degree is used to compare two persons or things:

Mr White is **fatter** than Mr Brown.   The ring is **more expensive** than the watch.
The red car is **better** than the blue one.

The **superlative** degree is used to compare three or more persons or things:

Michael is the **most hardworking** pupil in this class.
That dictionary is the **thickest** book on the shelf.
Among the pupils, George has the **most** money in the Post Office Savings Bank.

If the adjective has one syllable, the comparative degree is formed by adding **-er** to it, and the superlative degree by adding **-est**:

Positive	Comparative	Superlative
bright	brighter	brightest
dear	dearer	dearest
warm	warmer	warmest

If the adjective ends in **-e**, then only **-r** is added for the comparative and **-st** for the superlative:

ripe	riper	ripest
pale	paler	palest
true	truer	truest

If the adjective has a single vowel and ends with a single consonant, the consonant is **doubled** before **-er** and **-est**:

red	redder	reddest
big	bigger	biggest
fat	fatter	fattest

If the adjective has two or more syllables the comparative degree is formed by adding **more** in front of it and the superlative degree by adding **most** in front of it:

attractive	more attractive	most attractive
beautiful	more beautiful	most beautiful
careful	more careful	most careful

But the following two-syllable adjectives form their comparative and superlative by adding **-er** and **-est** (or **-r** and **-st**):

clever	cleverer	cleverest
common	commoner	commonest
handsome	handsomer	handsomest
narrow	narrower	narrowest
pleasant	pleasanter	pleasantest
polite	politer	politest
quiet	quieter	quietest
shallow	shallower	shallowest
simple	simpler	simplest
stupid	stupider	stupidest
wicked	wickeder	wickedest

Two-syllable adjectives (and some one-syllable adjectives) ending in **-y** change the **y** to **i** before **-er** and **-est**:

angry	angrier	angriest
busy	busier	busiest
dirty	dirtier	dirtiest
dry	drier	driest

The following adjectives have irregular comparative and superlative forms:

far	farther/further	farthest/furthest
bad	worse	worst
good	better	best
little	less	least
many	more	most
much	more	most
some	more	most

Adverbs

Comparison of Adverbs

Adverbs have three degrees of comparison. They are the **positive, comparative** and **superlative** degrees.

The **positive** degree is the simple form of the adverb:

The monkeys chattered **noisily.** The baby slept **soundly.**
The jewels sparkled **brilliantly.**

The **comparative** degree is used to compare two actions:

I walk **faster** than you.   Mr Black does his work **more carefully** than Mr Green does.
Mary dances **more gracefully** than Anne.

The **superlative** degree is used to compare three or more actions:

Linda can run **fastest** among the girls.   He came **earliest** of all.
She spoke **most politely** to me.

The comparative degree of most adverbs is formed by putting **more** in front of them and the superlative degree by putting **most** in front of them:

Positive	Comparative	Superlative
angrily	more angrily	most angrily
sweetly	more sweetly	most sweetly
warmly	more warmly	most warmly

The comparative degree of adverbs that have one syllable is formed by adding **-er** to the adverb and the superlative degree by adding **-est** to the adverb:

fast	faster	fastest
near	nearer	nearest
soon	sooner	soonest

The following adverbs have irregular comparative and superlative forms:

badly	worse	worst
far	farther/further	farthest/furthest
little	less	least
much	more	most
well	better	best

Punctuation

A **full stop** (.) is used at the end of a statement and often after a command; a **question mark** (?) comes after a question and an **exclamation mark** (!) after an exclamation or interjection, and sometimes after a command:

This is a good essay.   Show it to the headmaster tomorrow.
Would you make a copy for me?   Cheerio!   Don't forget what I said!

Use a **capital letter** at the beginning of a sentence, for names, for the word 'I' and for the months of the year and the days of the week:

Tell Arthur that I can meet him in London at the British Museum on
Saturday 20th April.

A **comma** (,) shows a slight break in a sentence. It is used, for instance:

(a) between two clauses joined by *but* or *or* if the second one has a subject:

I'll come and see you tonight, but I don't want to be out too late.

(b) after a subordinate clause:

When he returned, I made a cup of tea.

(c) around the kind of relative clause that gives additional information (but not around the kind that just identifies a person or thing):

His mother, who was getting angry, gave him a slap. (But no commas in *Those people who would like tickets should write to the secretary.*)

(d) around a descriptive or explanatory phrase referring to a person or thing:

Mr Jones, the headmaster of our school, told me to write to you.

(e) after introductory words, or around words that form a comment:

However, I wasn't late after all. I must leave now, unfortunately. Philip, I'm sorry to say, has been neglecting his homework.

(f) before *please*, after *yes* and *no*, and before or after the name of the person who is being spoken to:

Can you lend me a pencil, please?
Yes, I can.
Don't cry, Mary.

(g) in a list of more than two things and often between adjectives before a noun, where there are two or more:

a pen, a pencil and a rubber
a hot, dusty day (but no commas in *a pretty little girl*, because *little girl* is regarded as a single unit)

A **colon** (:) is used to introduce the answer that the first part of the sentence expects:

There's one thing I'd really like: a new bicycle.
You'll need the following: cardboard, glue and scissors.

A **semicolon** (;) separates parts of a sentence that are equally important and are not linked by *and*, *but*, *or*, etc. Sometimes a semicolon is used to separate items in a list:

One bag of chips is enough; to eat two would be greedy.
I have three ambitions: to visit India and see the Taj Mahal; to fly a plane; to climb a 20 000-foot mountain.

Quotation marks (' ') are used before and after direct speech; a **comma** is usually put before or after the direct speech:

Mary said, 'You're late.'
'You're late,' said Mary.

An **apostrophe** (') is used:

(a) to form possessive nouns; it is placed before the *s* with singular nouns and with plural nouns not ending in *-s*, and after the *s* with plural nouns ending in *-s*:

Anne's book; the children's toys; the twins' bedroom.

(b) in short forms, showing where part of a word has been left out:

I've only two dollars left.
Aren't you going too?

A **hyphen** (-) is used:

(a) in many compound nouns (others are written as one word or as two words without a hyphen):

air-conditioning (but *aircraft* and *air force*).

(b) in compound adjectives placed before the noun:

a six-page essay; a five-year-old child; a well-deserved reward.

(c) sometimes with a prefix:

The votes must be re-counted.